2011-2012

中国及海外会展概览®

Directory of China & Overseas Exhibitions and Meetings

中国及海外会展概览编委会编辑

Edited By Editorial Board of

Directory of China & Overseas Exhibitions and Meetings

经济日报出版社

图书在版编目(CIP)数据

2011～2012中国及海外会展概览 / 张玉敏主编. --
北京 : 经济日报出版社, 2011.3
ISBN 978-7-80257-292-8

Ⅰ. ①2… Ⅱ. ①张… Ⅲ. ①展览会－概况－世界－
2011～2012 Ⅳ. ①G245

中国版本图书馆CIP数据核字（2011）第022775号

Diretory of China & Overseas Exhibitions and Meetings
2011-2012
Editoral Board of DCOEM

书名:**中国及海外会展概览2011-2012**

主　　编:张玉敏
责任编辑:王晓玲
封面设计:金　钥

出版发行:经济日报出版社
社　　址:北京市宣武区白纸坊东街2号
邮政编码:100054
经　　销:全国新a华书店
印　　刷:北京品墨缘彩色印刷有限公司

开　　本:889×1194　1/16
字　　数:1000千字
印　　张:34
印　　次:2011年2月第一版 2011年2月第一次印刷

书　　号:ISBN 978-7-80257-292-8
定　　价:229.00元

2011-2012
中国及海外会展概览®
Directory of China & Overseas Exhibitions and Meetings

中国及海外会展概览编委会编辑
Edited By Editorial Board of
Directory of China & Overseas Exhibitions and Meetings

经济日报出版社

图书在版编目(CIP)数据

2011～2012中国及海外会展概览 / 张玉敏主编. --
北京 : 经济日报出版社, 2011.3
ISBN 978-7-80257-292-8

Ⅰ. ①2… Ⅱ. ①张… Ⅲ. ①展览会一概况一世界一
2011～2012 Ⅳ. ①G245

中国版本图书馆CIP数据核字（2011）第022775号

Diretory of China & Overseas Exhibitions and Meetings
2011-2012
Editoral Board of DCOEM

书名：中国及海外会展概览2011-2012

主　　编：张玉敏
责任编辑：王晓玲
封面设计：金　钥

出版发行：经济日报出版社
社　　址：北京市宣武区白纸坊东街2号
邮政编码：100054
经　　销：全国新a华书店
印　　刷：北京品墨缘彩色印刷有限公司

开　　本：889×1194　1/16
字　　数：1000千字
印　　张：34
印　　次：2011年2月第一版 2011年2月第一次印刷

书　　号：ISBN 978-7-80257-292-8
定　　价：229.00元

特别感谢
给予本书大力支持的机构

With gratitude
to the many of organizations who have contributed to this Directory

泛联展览物流香港有限公司	Agility Fairs & Events Logistics Ltd
中国对外贸易广州展览总公司	China Foreign Trade Guangzhou Exhibition Corporation
中国国际展览中心	China International Exhibition Center
中国国际贸易中心股份有限公司	China World Trade Center Co Ltd
北京爱博西雅展览有限公司	Exposium-SIAL Exhibition Co Ltd
广东现代国际展览中心	Guangdong Modern International Exhibition Center
香港贸易发展局	Hong Kong Trade Development Council
科隆展览中国有限公司	Koelnmesse Co Ltd China
澳门贸易投资促进局	Macao Trade and Investment Promotion Institute
沈阳国际展览中心	Shenyang International Exhibition Center
郑州国际会展中心	Zhengzhou International Convention & Exhibition Centre
奥克坦姆系统科技（苏州）有限公司	OCTANORM® System Technology (Suzhou) Co Ltd
励展博览集团	Reed Exhibitions
全球国际货运有限公司	Schenker China Ltd
上海市国际展览有限公司	Shanghai International Exhibition Co Ltd
上海新国际博览中心有限公司	Shanghai New International Expo Center
显辉国际展览有限公司	Top Repute Co Ltd
澳门威尼斯人®度假村酒店会展及活动中心	The Venetian® Macao - Resort - Hotel
亚洲博闻	UBM Asia
浙江中国小商品城集团股份有限公司	Zhejiang China Commodities City Group Co Ltd

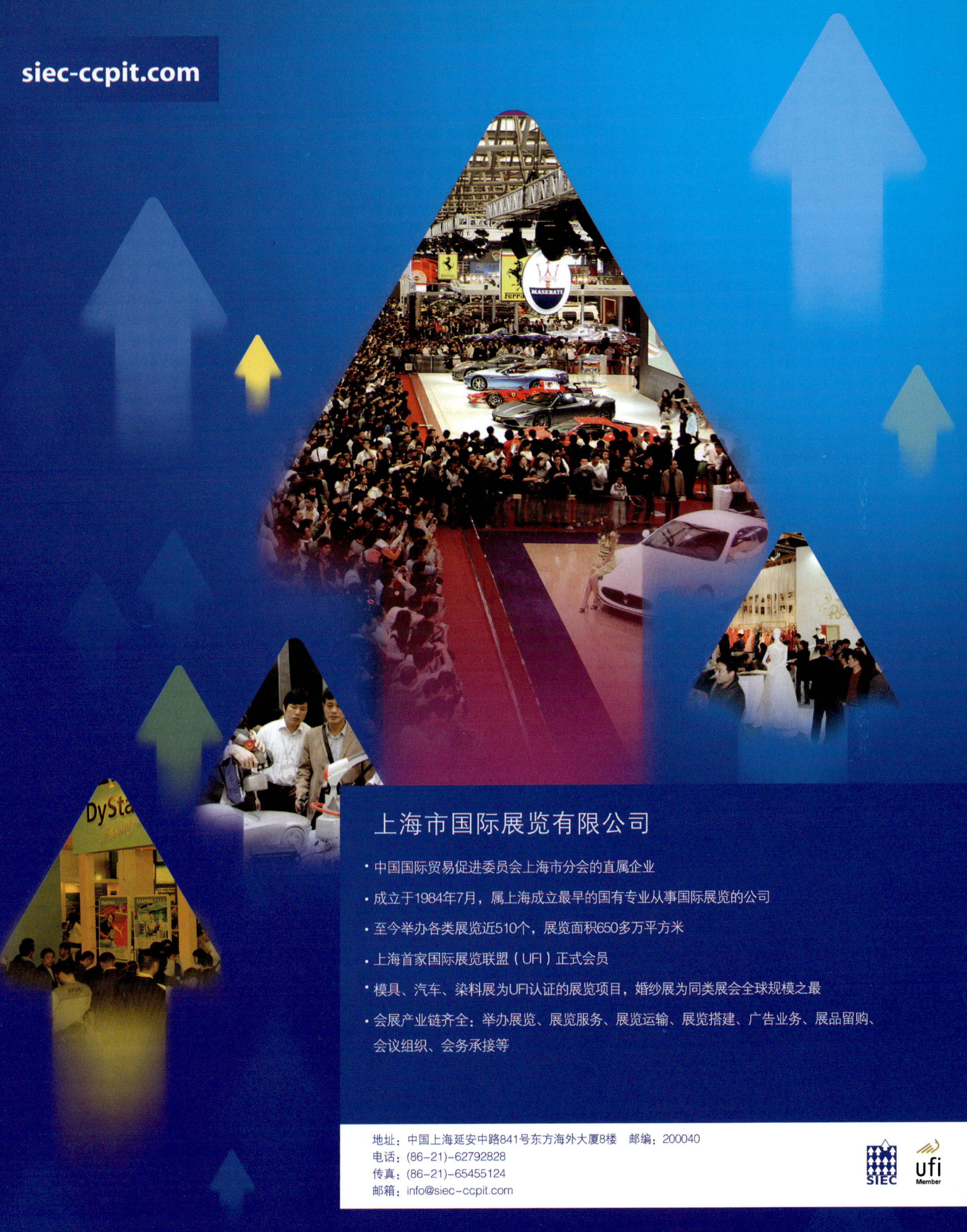

前言 | Preface

随着新年钟声的敲响，中国展览业又进入新的时期。回顾2010展望2011，中国展览业在平静的表面下，依然存在着细微的变化和发展，呈现以下三个特点。

首先，展会大有越专越红火的趋势，大而全的展览正在向专业性更强转化。以北京、上海、广州等地的三大著名建筑装饰建材展为例，均从以往的包罗万象划分为门业展、橱柜展、地板展等诸个专业展的组合。郑州市更结合本地产业优势，2011年将推出首届“女裤展”、“速冻食品”等细分的行业展。全国展览行业呈现越分越专的新趋势。

2011年中国会展业的另一特点是推出新兴的跨界展览。纵观中国展览业的发展，每年都有推陈出新的新型展会诞生。从最近两、三年来文化产业展、动漫展、设计展的相继出现直至新型能源展的遍地生花。随着Internet的广泛应用以及自动识别技术的发展，2011年全国将有至少3项“物联网专业展”诞生以及Call Center等跨界展会的举办。

中国展览业快速向全国经济增长最快的中西部地区发展成为2011年中国会展业的第三大特点。首先，不断有成熟的专业展在中西部开设系列展。另一方面，自2009年开始，每年轮流在全国各地举办的全国性行业展览，有集中选择在成都、郑州、西安等中西部经济的中心城市举办趋势。这一趋势在2011年将得以延续并更加明确。如全国医疗仪器展、医药展、彩盒展等均选择在上述城市之一举办。书中文章《五年磨一剑，郑州会展中心引领郑州会展业步入快车道》更详细的阐述地区会展业风生水起的快速发展势头。

本书将继续隆重推出全国展览排名，在全国综合展12强亮相的同时，本编委会将全国专业贸易展排名增加至80强，囊括更多成熟和著名的展览。这不仅为参展商、买家选择展会提供客观数据和佐证，也以此鞭策排名之上的展会主办者将展会越办越好。

最后，感谢在本书编辑出版过程中给予我们大力帮助的赞助商、展览会议主办方和组织机构。更感谢您选择本书作为了解中国展览会议的工具，并希望您通过本书获得有利信息帮助您在2011年取得更大的成功！

With the bell ringing in the New Year, China exhibition industry marches into its new age. Reviewing 2010 and foreseeing 2011, under its calm disposition, China exhibition industry is brewing a variety of subtle change and development as follows:

Primarily, large and general shows are transforming into subdivisions. For example, the national top three building and decoration exhibitions which held in Beijing, Shanghai and Guangzhou, all of which have subdivided into shows of doors, cabinet, floors, etc. respectively. Taking advantage of its local industry, Zhengzhou will kick off a series of new exhibitions specified as “Woman's Pants Show” and “Frozen Food Exhibition”. All shows are classified into subdivisions.

Another feature of China exhibition industry in 2011 is the renewal of cross-border shows. Throughout development of China exhibitions, each year, innovation results in numerous new types of exhibitions. In the recent two or three years, culture industry, comic and design shows, as well as new energy shows all flourished. Following the wave of internet and auto-ID/RFID technology development, at least 3 “Internet of Things” shows will commence in 2011. “Call Center” show will also emerge.

The third trend in 2011 is that China exhibition industry will receive the fastest development in central and western China. Firstly, mature trade shows held their series in the central and western area of China. Meanwhile, since 2009, those annual series national trade fairs had trended to choose Chengdu, Zhengzhou, Xi'an and other cities for their central or western economic development. This trend will expand in 2011. For instance, interphex china, PharmChina, Chengdu Houseware and Leisure Goods & Gifts Fair all selected the above cities as their new venue locations. An article in this book “Five Years on Sharpening a Sword: Zhengzhou Exhibition and Convention Center Leads Zhengzhou Exhibition and Convention Industry to a Fast Lane” details this stampede towards that exact direction.

Moreover, this book will further highlight and promote national exhibitions ranking. We release China Top 12 General Fairs and an improved Top 80 Trade Shows from the previous Top 70 rank to cover more mature and famous shows. It not only provides exhibitors and purchasers more objective data and evidence for decision making, but also encourages and advises organizers to present greater and better shows.

Last but not least, we would like to express our sincere appreciation to you, our sponsors, exhibition organizers and readers from all over the world for all of your contributions. We thank you for choosing this book to learn about various exhibitions in China. We wish you great benefits from this book in achieving success in the year of the Rabbit, 2011.

欢迎直飞亚洲国际博览馆！

亚洲首屈一指的展览场馆，就在全球最佳机场。

试想，下机即可直达展览场馆，个中方便确实不言而喻！亚洲国际博览馆坐拥优越地理位置，毗邻香港国际机场，全球半数人口均可于五小时内从各地飞抵，配合完善海陆交通，独有的便捷优势，绝非其他场馆所能比拟！

- 傲立中国珠三角核心，繁华汇聚之地，占尽天时地利
- 展览场馆面积达70,000平方米，适合各类活动，拓展营商空间
- 设有10间无柱式地面展馆
- 拥有香港最大型的室内多用途活动场馆
- 拥有香港最大型的室内会议及宴会厅
- 铁路网络连接市中心，车程仅28分钟
- 毗邻多间国际级酒店
- 多个消闲娱乐购物热点近在咫尺

亚洲国际博览馆　中国香港大屿山　香港国际机场

电话 (852) 3606 8888　传真 (852) 3606 8889　电邮 info@asiaworld-expo.com

www.asiaworld-expo.com

亚洲国际博览馆—驻足亚洲　博览全球

目 录

前言

如何使用本书 x
2010年度中国最大综合博览会12强排名 xii
2010年度中国最大专业贸易展80强排名 xvi
推荐参加 xxxvii
2011年全国节庆活动 xxxviii

专题报道 xxiv
巨伞下的会展凝聚力

成功之道 xxxii
位处珠三角地利之宜
亚洲国际博览馆尽享区内经济迅速发展优势

行业聚焦 xxxv
- 沈阳国际展览中心蓄势待发
- FashionNetAsia与Stylesight伙拍出版时尚潮流报告
- 亚洲博闻（泰国）被泰国投资促进委员会委任为2011年BOI Fair的特别顾问
- 第12届中国国际展览和会议展示会在杭州落下帷幕
- 第18届中国国际包装工业展热销喜人
- 终端市场向中西部转移 纸箱设备将上演“西行记”

国内展览会议
分类一 按城市分类-城市索引 1
分类二 按日期分类-日期索引 157
分类三 按行业分类-行业索引 176

香港特区展览会议
会展排期 208
详细介绍 227

澳门特区展览 246

台湾特区展览 247

海外展览会议
国家分类 249
行业分类 315

行业先锋
◆展览会议组织和管理 331
◆展架设计与施工搭建 337
◆展览会议中心 338
◆酒店 340
◆展览运输 340

会展概览

主编
张玉敏

编审
王亚东

编辑
黄继红

撰稿
李文强
罗颖坚
刘佩佩
陈建明

高级客户主任
孙惠兰

翻译
寇明明

编辑助理
孙紫怡
李萌

封面设计
金钥

读者服务和订购信息
北京2930信箱
邮政编码：100053
电话：
010-6340 0061
010-8312 4138
010-8316 7137
传真：
010-8312 7130

读者服务和订购信息：
expoinfo@dcoem.com
dcoem@live.cn
编辑部：
editor@dcoem.com
广告部：
super@dcoem.com

博览世界网
www.dcoem.com

SHANGHAI
NEW INTERNATIONAL
EXPO CENTRE

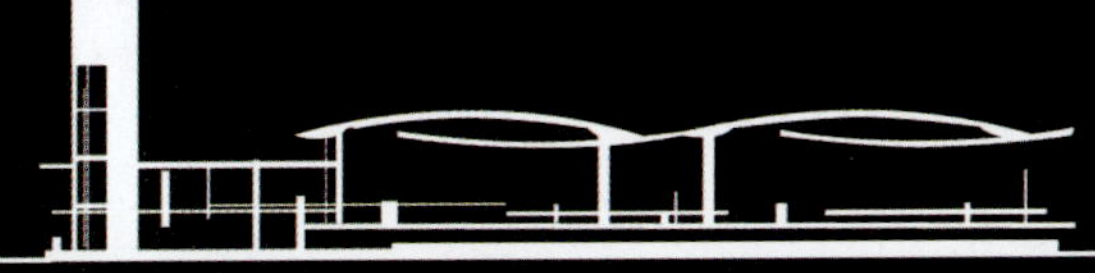

Contents

Preface

How to use this directory x
2010 China's Top 12 General Fairs xii
2010 China's Top 80 Trade Shows xvi
Editor's recommendation xxxvii
China's festivals 2011 xxxviii

Report xxiv
Commitment and Passion for the Zhengzhou Umbrella

Zoom xxxii
AsiaWorld-Expo is uniquely positioned to capitalise on the rapid economic growth of China's Pearl River Delta (PRD) region

Focus xxxv
- FashionNetAsia Partners with Stylesight to Publish Fashion Trends
- AsiaWorlf-Expo wins a high-profile Catering Industry Safety Award
- Agility Opens New Warehouse in Seoul

Exhibitions and Fairs in Mainland China
Register 1
Exhibitions and Fairs by City
Index of Cities 1

Register 2
Exhibitions and Fairs in Chronological Order 157

Register 3
Exhibitions and Fairs by Industry
Index of Industry and Profession Classification 177

Exhibitions and Fairs in Hong Kong, China 208

Exhibitions in Macao, China 246

Ehibitions in Taiwan, China 247

Exhibitions and Fairs Overseas 249

Industry Leaders
Exhibition Management 341
Exhibit Designers and Producers 347
Exhibition and Convention Centers 348
Exhibition Transportation 351

DCOEM

Editor-in-Chief
ZHANG Sarah

Editing Director
WANG Yadong

Editors
HUANG Jihong

Contributors
Li Wenqiang
LAM Josephine
LAW Jennifer
CHEN Kenneth
LAU Fiona

Senior Account Manager
SUN Linda

Translator
KOU Matthew

Editorial Assistant
SUN Ziyi
LI Meng

Art Director
JIN Jessica

Subscription Contact:
P.O.Box 2930 Beijing 100053, China
Telephone
86-10-6340 0061
86-10-8312 4138
Fax
86-10-8312 7130

Reader Service
expoinfo@dcoem.com
Listing
dcoem@live.cn
Editorial Office
editor@dcoem.com
Advertising Office
super@dcoem.com

www.dcoem.com

如何使用本书 | How to Use this Directory

全书国内会展信息有三大分类索引，便于查阅，具体方式如下：

分类一——按城市分类

这是国内会展信息的最主要章节，所有会展的基本信息按照先省区、后城市的汉语拼音顺序排列，城市中的信息再按照举办时间顺序排列。每条会展信息均有一个编号。编号的设置为便于您到后面的时间和行业分类中对应查询。

分类二——按行业分类

会展信息按行业分成78个分类。每个行业中，会展信息按照举办的时间顺序排列。通过编号，您可以在分类一中查到该展会的基本介绍。

分类三——按时间分类

展会在此按举办的时间顺序排列，通过每条信息的唯一编号，您可以在分类一中查到展会的基本介绍。

■ **重要提示**

书中所列的展览和会议信息在编辑出版时，我们已经尽了最大努力核准无误，但个别展会的举办时间或地点等可能因故调整。因此，在决定参加、参观、出席展会之前，请您务必与主办和承办机构联系，获得确认。

★Exhibitions and Fairs in Mainland China

Register 1
Exhibitions and Fairs by City
This is the main chapter and contains basic exhibition and fair information in Mainland China. It is organized alphabetically by provinces, alphabetically by city within each province, and chronologically within each city. To each exhibition there is a cross - reference number which permits quick reference from register 2 and 3.

Register 2
Exhibitions and Fairs by Industry
This chapter lists exhibitions according 78 classifications. The exhibitions within the each branch are listed chronologically. A cross - reference number is provided for quick access to more detailed information in register 1.

Register 3
Exhibitions and Fairs in Chronological Order
Exhibitions are listed in chronological order. A cross - reference number is provided for quick access to more detailed information in register 1.

★How to make phone call to China

1. Country code for China is 86.
2.Taking the phone number of 010-6340 0061 in the book as an example, 010 is the city code of Beijing. If you call from outside China, here is how you should dial: 86 10 6340 0061.
3. Area Code of HongKong is 852.

■arning

We have made best efforts to ensure the accuracy of the listed information at the time of editing. However, before making decision to participate an exhibition or conference, please always contact with the organizer for the very latest confirmation.

2010中国综合博览会12强排名
China Top 12 General Fairs

排名 Rank	展会名称 Exhibition	展出面积 Exhibition Area(m^2)	参展商 Exhibitors	贸易观众 Trade Visiters	承办 Organizer	日期 Date	地点 Venue
1	第108届中国进出口商品交易会（秋季1、II、III期） China Import & Export Fair-Autumn	1,130,000	23,599	200,612	中国对外贸易中心 China Foreign Trade Ctr (Group)	10/15-19 10/23-27 10/31-11/4	中国出口商品交易会展馆 China Import & Export Fair Complex
2	第107届中国进出口商品交易会（春季1、II、III期） China Import & Export Fair-Spring	1,130,000	23,359	203,996	中国对外贸易中心 China Foreign Trade Ctr (Group)	4/15-29 4/23-27 5/1-5	中国出口商品交易会展馆 China Import & Export Fair Complex
3	第12届中国国际高新技术成果交易会 China Hi-Tech Fair	130,000	2,775	525,000	中国国际高新技术成果交易中心 China Hi-Tech Fair Transfer Ctr	11/16-21	深圳会展中心 Shenzhen Convention & Exh Ctr
4	中国国际工业博览会 China Intl Industry Fair	110,000	1,600	100,000	上海世博（集团）有限公司 Shanghai World Expo	11/9-13	上海新国际博览中心 Shanghai New Intl Expo Ctr
5	中国（深圳）国际文化产业博览交易会 China(Shenzhen)Intl Cultural Industries Fair	105,000	1,708	351,000	深圳国际文化产业博览交易会有限公司 Shenzhen Intl Cultural Industry Fair Co Ltd		深圳会展中心 Shenzhen Convention & Exh Ctr
6	中国华东出口商品交易会（20届华交会） East Chian Fair	103,500	3,376	44,000	上海外经贸商务展览有限公司 Intl Trade Promotion Co Ltd	3/1-5	
7	中国哈尔滨国际经济贸易洽谈会（第21届哈洽会） China Harbin Intl Economic and Trade Fair (21st Harbin Trade Fair)	86,000	2,200	120,000	中国哈尔滨经济贸易洽谈会办公室 The administration of China Harbin international econmic and trade fair	6/15-19	哈尔滨国际会展中心 Harbin Intl Conference Exh & Sports Ctr
8	中国昆明进出口商品交易会（第18届昆交会） China Import & Export Fair, Kunming (19th Kunming Fair)	75,000	2,306	50,000	云南省人民政府 The People's Govern ment of Yunnan Province	6/6-10	昆明国际会展中心 Kunming Intl Convention & Exh Ctr
9	中国北京国际文化创意产业博览会 China Beijing Intl Cultural & Creative Industry Expo	65,000	1,370	85,000	北京世界贸易中心 World Trade Center Beijing	11/18-21	中国国际展览中心 China Intl Exh Ctr
10	第13届中国北京国际科技产业博览会 Beijing Intl High-Tech Expo	60,000	2,213	120,000	北京世界贸易中心 World Trade Center Beijing"	5/27-31	中国国际展览中心 China Intl Exhibition Ctr
11	第14届中国国际投资贸易洽谈会 China Intl Fair for Investment and Trade	60,000	2,000	100,000	中国（厦门）国际投资促进中心 MOFCOM	9/8-11	厦门国际会展中心 Xiamen Intl Conference & Exh Ctr
12	中国国际装备制造业博览会 China Intl Equipment Manufacturing Exposition	60,000	800	135,000	沈阳振兴国际展览有限公司 Shenyang Renaissance Intl Exhibitions Co Ltd	9/1-5	沈阳国际会展中心 Shenyang Intl Exhibition Ctr

2010中国专业贸易展80强排名
China Top 80 Trade Shows

排名 Rank	展会名称 Exhibition	展出面积 Exhibition Area(m^2)	参展商 Exhibitors	贸易观众 Trade Visiters	承办 Organizer	日期 Date	地点 Venue
1	中国广州国际家具博览会(春季.两期) China Intl Furniture Fair (Guangzhou)	370,000	1,395	134,85 (观众总数)	中国对外贸易广州展览总公司 China Foreign Trade Guangzhou Exhibition General Corp	3/18-21 3/27-30	中国进出口商品交易会展馆 China Import & Export Fair Complex
2	第16届中国国际家具展览会 Furniture China 2010	300,000	1,925	62,387	上海博华国际展览有限公司 Shanghai CMP Sinoexpo Intl Exhibition Co Ltd	9/7-10	上海新国际博览中心 Shanghai New Intl Expo Ctr
3	国际名家具(东莞)展览会 Intl Famous Furniture Fair (Dongguan)	260,000	915	112,000	东莞名家具俱乐部 Dongguan Famous Furniture Assn	3/16-20	广东现代国际展览中心(广东东莞) Guangdong Modern Intl Exh Ctr(Guangdong-Donguan)
4	中国(广州)国际建筑装饰博览会 China(Guangzhou) Intl Bldg Decoration Fair	250,000	2,157	101,586	中国对外贸易广州展览总公司 China Foreign Trade Guangzhou Exhibition General Corp	7/8-11	中国进出口商品交易会展馆 China Import & Export Fair Complex
5	2010北京国际汽车展览会 Auto China 2010	200,000	2,100	557,624 (观众总数)	中国贸促会汽车行业分会;中国汽车工业国际合作总公司;中国国际展览中心集团公司;中国汽车工程学会 CCPIT AUTO; CNAICO; CIEC; SAE-Chnia	4/25-5/2	中国国际展览中心(新馆) 中国国际展览中心 China Intl Exhibition Ctr (New Venue) /China Intl Exhibition Ctr
6	深圳国际家具展 Shenzhen Intl Furniture Exhibition	200,000	860	133,819	深圳市家具行业协会 Shenzhen Furniture Trade Assn	3/19-22	深圳会展中心 Shenzhen Covention and Exh Ctr
7	长春国际汽车博览会 China Changchun Intl Automobile Fair	166,000	132	509,000	中国长春国际汽车展览组委会 CCPIT Changchun	7/15-24	长春国际会展中心 Changchun Intl Convention & Exh Ctr
8	中国(广州)国际汽车展览会 China (Guangzhou) Intl Automobile Fair	160,000	87	50,000	中国对外贸易广州展览总公司 China Foreign Trade Guangzhou Exhibition General Corp	12/21-27	中国进出口商品交易会展馆 China Import & Export Fair Complex
9	中国国际塑料橡胶工业展览会 Intl Exhibition on Plastics and Rubber Industries	150,000	2,144	96,136	杜塞尔多夫展览(中国)有限公司 Messe Düsseldorf China Ltd.	4/19-22	上海新国际博览中心 Shanghai New Intl Expo Ctr
10	上海国际广告印刷包装纸业展览会 APPPEXPO 2010	150,000	1,268	114,291	上海现代国际展览有限公司(世博集团) Shanghai Modern Intl Exh Co Ltd	7/7-10	上海新国际博览中心 Shanghai New Intl Expo Ctr
11	中国广州国际家具博览会(秋季) China Intl Furniture Fair (Guangzhou)Autumn	150,000	517	33,982 (观众总数)	中国对外贸易广州展览总公司 China Foreign Trade Guangzhou Exhibition General Corp	9/3-6	中国进出口商品交易会展馆 China Import & Export Fair Complex

不断创新价值
www.fairwindow.com

中国对外贸易广州展览总公司

CHINA FOREIGN TRADE GUANGZHOU EXHIBITION GENERAL CORP.

中国对外贸易广州展览总公司（以下简称中贸展）是著名的中国第一展（广交会）、中国第一展馆（广交会展馆）的组织管理者——中国对外贸易中心（集团）的成员企业，下设若干个专业的展览公司，在展览的各个产业领域全面推进发展。中贸展是目前国内最具实力和影响力的国有展览公司之一。

中贸展以专业诚信、以人为本、追求卓越、专注展览、服务全球为核心理念，赢得了业内的好评。中贸展主要业务包括：主办、承办、合作举办各类大型国际博览会；组织出国展览；策划组织大型商业活动。总公司每年自办、合办、承办各类大型国际专业商贸博览会 20 多个，展览题材涉及家居、家纺、办公、木工、户外、建材、地材、卫陶、汽车、印刷、包装、标签、环保、水处理、自动化、玻璃、自行车等多个方面。在过去的十年里，总公司展览业务不断扩展，国内办展和出国参展面积年均增长率分别为 27.3% 和 15.3%， 2010年总展览面积超过1,220,000平方米。同时，总公司每年组团参加世界各地 20 多个国家和地区的知名展会，展览题材涉及消费品、礼品、玩具、动漫、美容用品、办公用品文具、电子、家电、摄影、广告、印刷、包装、食品、能源、鞋、家纺及服装、安保、家具配件、园林、五金、卫浴建材、灯饰等多个类别，出展面积在全国同行业中名列前茅。

中贸展拥有一支专业办展队伍，重视人才建设，建立起一个系统的围绕展览为核心的专业展览服务团队，包括：展览销售队伍、招商推广队伍、展览服务队伍等，建立了一套规范完整的办展信息化系统（包括自助服务、数据库管理）和办公自动化系统，大大提升了服务的效率。

China Foreign Trade Guangzhou Exhibition General Corporation (hereinafter referred to as CFTE) is a member enterprise of China Foreign Trade Center (hereinafter referred to as CFTC)----the management body of China' s No 1 fair (Canton Fair) and China's No 1 fairground (China Import & Export Fair Complex). CFTE comprises several specialized exhibition companies to boost the development of all industries of the exhibition in an all-round way. CFTE is one of the strongest and most influential state-owned exhibition companies in China today.

Based on the core philosophy of specialization & honesty, people-orientation, pursuit of excellence, dedication to exhibition and serving the world, CFTE is well received by the industry. Its main businesses cover: sponsoring, undertaking and co-sponsoring large expos, organizing Chinese enterprises to participate in famous fairs abroad, planning and organizing commercial functions. CFTE sponsors, co-sponsors and undertakes more than 20 large international specialized trade fairs per year. The exhibition themes cover furniture, home textile, office, woodworking, outdoor, building materials, floor materials, sanitary ware, automobile, printing, packaging, label, environmental protection, water treatment, automation, glass and bicycle. In the past 10 years, the company continues to expand exhibition business, and the exhibition area at home and abroad had an average increase of 27.3% and 15.3% respectively per year. The total exhibition area in 2010 was over 1,220,,000 square meters.

CFTE has a professional team specializing in handling exhibitions. It attaches importance to talents growth and establishes a systematic professional exhibition team, including: exhibition sales team, business promotion team and exhibition service team as well as sets up a set of standard & complete exhibition information system (including self-service, database management) and OA system, greatly enhancing service efficiency.

2011年举办展览计划

Exhibition Calendar in 2011

序号	展览会名称	日期	地点
1	第十八届华南国际印刷工业展览会 The 18th South China International Exhibition on Printing Industry 2011中国国际标签印刷技术展览会 The China International Exhibition on Label Printing Industry 2011	2011.3.9 - 11	广交会展馆
2	SIAF GUANGZHOU SPS - Industrial Automation Fair Guangzhou 中国广州国际工业自动化技术及装备展览会	2011.3.9 - 11	广交会展馆
3	第十二届中国(广州)国际给排水、水处理技术与设备展览会 Water, Wastewater & Water Treatment China 2011 2011 中国(广州)国际泵、阀门、管道展览会 Pump, Valve & Pipe China 2011	2011.3.9 - 11	广交会展馆
4	第二十七届中国广州国际家具博览会(民用家具展) The 27th China International Furniture Fair (Guangzhou) --Home Furniture	2011.3.18 - 21	广交会展馆
5	2011中国广州国际户外及休闲展览会 China International Outdoor & Leisure Fair 2011	2011.3.18 - 21	广交会展馆
6	2011(春)中国广州国际家居饰品/用品展览会 Homedecor & Housewares China 2011(March)	2011.3.18 - 21	广交会展馆
7	2011中国(广州)国际家用纺织品及辅料博览会 China (Guangzhou) International Trade Fair for Home Textiles 2011	2011.3.18 - 21	广交会展馆
8	2011中国广州国际家具博览会 （办公环境展） China International Furniture Fair (Guangzhou) --Office Show	2011.3.27 - 30	广交会展馆
9	2011 中国广州国际木工机械、家具配料展览会 China Int'l Woodworking Machinery & Furniture Raw Materials Fair (Guangzhou) interzum guangzhou	2011.3.27 - 30	广交会展馆
10	第十三届中国(广州)国际建筑装饰博览会 The 13th China (Guangzhou) International Building Decoration Fair	2011.7.8 - 11	广交会展馆
11	2011中国(广州)国际地面铺装材料展 China (Guangzhou) Int' l l Floor Covering Fair 2011	2011.7.8 - 11	广交会展馆
12	2011中国(广州)国际卫浴及建筑陶瓷展 China (Guangzhou) Int'l Exhibition for Sanitary Ware and Building Ceramics 2011	2011.7.8 - 11	广交会展馆
13	2011中国（广州）国际厨房设备及配件展 China (Guangzhou) Int'l Kitchen Fair 2011	2011.7.8 - 11	广交会展馆
14	2011中国(广州)国际衣柜展览会 CBD-Wardrobe 2011	2011.7.8 - 11	广交会展馆
15	2011中国(广州)国际门窗展览会 CBD-Windoor 2011	2011.7.8 - 11	广交会展馆
16	第二十八届中国广州国际家具博览会 The 28th China International Furniture Fair (Guangzhou)	2011.9.7 - 10	广交会展馆
17	2011中国广州国际家居饰品、家纺布艺展览会 Homedecor + Hometextiles China 2011	2011.9.7 - 10	广交会展馆
18	第九届中国（广州）国际汽车展览会 The 9th China (Guangzhou) International Automobile Exhibition	2011.11.22 -28	广交会展馆
19	第八届马来西亚中国进出口商品展览会暨投资洽谈会 The 8th China Import & Export Commodities Exhibition (Malaysia)	2011.12.16-19	马来西亚吉隆坡

地 址:广州市海珠区新港东路980号广交会展馆C区16号馆A层 邮编: 510335 电话 Tel: +86-20-89128342 传真Fax: +86-20-89128308 http://www.fairwindow.com
Floor A, Hall 16, Area C, Canton fair Complex, No.980 Xingang Dong Road, Haizhu District,Guangzhou, China 北京办事处电话 Tel: +86-10-65599082 上海办事处电话 Tel: +86-21-63605188

排名 Rank	展会名称 Exhibition	展出面积 Exhibition Area(m^2)	参展商 Exhibitors	贸易观众 Trade Visiters	承办 Organizer	日期 Date	地点 Venue
12	全国糖酒商品交易会(秋季) China Natl Sugar and Alcoholic Commodities Fair - Autumn	130,000	4,000	200,000	中国糖业酒类集团公司 Off. of China Natl Sugar and Alcoholic Commodities Fair	10/10-11	济南国际会展中心 Jinan Intl Convention & Exh Ctr
13	全国糖酒商品交易会(春季) China Natl Sugar and Alcoholic Commodities Fair - Spring	130,000	4,000	180,000	中国糖业酒类集团公司 Off. of China Natl Sugar and Alcoholic Commodities Fair	3/19-22	成都世纪城新国际会展中心 Intl Convention & Expo Ctr Chengdu Century City
14	九月香港珠宝首饰展览会 September Hong Kong Jewellery & Gem Fair	130,000	3,205	44,274 (观众总数)	亚洲博闻 CMP Information	9/14-20	亚洲国际博览馆 香港会议展览中心 Asia World - Expo/ HKCEC
15	广州国际照明展览会 Guangzhou Intl Lighting Exhibition	130,000	2,012	71,801 (观众总数)	广州光亚法兰克福展览有限公司 Guangzhou Guangya Messe Frankfurt Co Ltd	6/9-12	中国进出口商品交易会展馆 China Import & Export Fair Complex
16	中国义乌国际小商品博览会 China Yiwu International Commodities Fair	120,000	2,600	134,393	浙江省对外贸易经济合作厅；义乌市人民政府 Yiwu Municipal People's Government	10/21-25	义乌国际博览中心 Yiwu Intl Exhibition Ctr
17	第17届中国（北京）国际建筑装饰及材料博览会 China Intl Bldg Decorations and Bldg Materials Expo	120,000	1,800	150,000	北京中装华港建筑科技展览有限公司 China B & D Exhibition Co Ltd	3/15-18	中国国际展览中心新馆 China Intl Exhibition Ctr New Venue
18	第十届中国国际机床工具展览会 10th China Intl Machine Tool & Tools Exh	120,000	1,178	60,218	北京国机展览中心；励华展览北京公司 Capital Exhibition Services	6/14-18	中国国际展览中心新馆 China Intl Exh Ctr New Venue
19	成都国际汽车展览会 Chengdu Motor Show 2010	120,000	300	456,850 (观众总数)	成都世纪城新国际会展中心；汉诺威米兰展览会（中国）有限公司 Chengdu Intl Exhibition & Convention Ctr;Hannover Milano Fairs China Ltd	4/27-30	上海新国际博览中心 Shanghai New Intl Expo Ctr
20	大连国际汽车工业展览会 Dalian Intl Automotive Industry Exhibition	120,000		350,000 (观众总数)	中国贸促会大连市分会 Dalian Chamber of Intl Commerce Exhibition Corp	8/18-22	大连星海会展中心/大连世界博览广场 Dalian Xinghai Convention & Exh Ctr/ World Expo Ctr
21	中国国际纺织面料及辅料(秋冬)博览会 China Intl Trade Fair for Apparel Fabrics and Accessories	115,000	2,460	53,948	中国国际贸促会纺织行业分会 CCPIT Textile Industry Sub-Council	10/20-23	上海新国际博览中心 Shanghai New Intl Expo Ctr
22	中国国际家用纺织品及辅料展览会 Intertextile Shanghai Home Textiles	115,000	1,027	38,696	中国贸促会纺织行业分会；法兰克福展览（香港）有限公司 The Sub-Council of Textile Industry, CCPIT; Messe Frankfurt (HK) Ltd	8/24-26	上海新国际博览中心 Shanghai New Intl Expo Ctr

2009亚太地区压铸工业展览会
开幕典礼 2009.9.15-18

排名 Rank	展会名称 Exhibition	展出面积 Exhibition Area(m^2)	参展商 Exhibitors	贸易观众 Trade Visiters	承办 Organizer	日期 Date	地点 Venue
23	中国国际五金展 -《科隆国际五金展》强力推荐 China Intl Hardware Show Powered by Practical World	110,000	2,300	45,000 (观众总数)	科隆国际展览有限公司 Koelnmesse	9/28-30	上海新国际博览中心 Shanghai New Intl Expo Ctr
24	中国国际医疗器械秋季博览会 CMEF Autumn/ICMD-China Intl Medical Equipment Fair	110,000	2,100	54,666	国药励展展览有限责任公司 Reed Sinopharm Exh Co Ltd	10/12-15	沈阳国际展览中心 Shenhang Intl Exh Ctr
25	中国国际医疗器械春季博览会 CMEF Autumn /Icmd-China Intl Medical Equipment Fair	110,000	2,100	66,827 (观众总数)	国药励展展览有限责任公司 Reed Sinopharm Exh Co Ltd	4/18-21	深圳会展中心 Shenzhen Covention and Exh Ctr
26	成都国际家具工业展览会 Intl Furniture Fair Chengdu	110,000	600	110,000 (观众总数)	中国贸促会成都分会 CCPIT Chengdu Sub-Council	7/3-6	成都世纪城新国际会展中心 Intl Convention & Expo Ctr Chengdu Century City
27	中国(深圳)国际玩具及礼品展览会 China (Shenzhen) Intl Toys & Gifts Fair	100,000	2,733	130,023 (观众总数)	励展华博展览（深圳）有限公司 Reed Huabo Exhibitions (Shenzhen) Co	10/21-24	深圳会展中心 Shenzhen Covention and Exh Ctr
28	中国(深圳)国际礼品、工艺品、钟表及家庭用品展览会 Shenzhen Intl Gifts & Crafts, Watches & Houseware Fair	100,000	2,703		励展华博展览（深圳）有限公司 Reed Huabo Exhibitions (Shenzhen) Co	4/25-28	深圳会展中心 Shenzhen Covention and Exh Ctr
29	中国国际自行车展览会 China Intl Bicycle Fair	100,000	1,117	120,022 (观众总数)	上海市国际展览有限公司 Shanghai Intl Exhibition Co Ltd	4/27-30	上海新国际博览中心 Shanghai New Intl Expo Ctr
30	中国国际体育用品博览会(夏季) China Intl Sporting Goods Show Summer	100,000	1,000	50,000	国家体育总局体育器材装备中心 Sports Equipment Administrative Center of China General Administration of Sport	5/20-23	中国国际展览中心新馆 China Intl Exh Ctr New Venue
31	中国广州国际木工机械、家具配料展览会 China Intl Woodworking Machinery & Furniture Raw Materials Fair (Guangzhou)	100,000	997	43,709 (观众总数)	科隆展览有限公司；中国对外贸易广州展览总公司 Koelnmesse Co Ltd; China Foreign Trade Guangzhou Exhibition Corp	3/27-30	中国进出口商品交易会展馆 China Import & Export Fair Complex
32	中国国际服装服饰博览会 China Intl Clothing & Accessories Fair	100,000	900	110,000 (观众总数)	北京时尚博展国际展览有限公司；中国国际贸易中心股份有限公司北京会展分公司 Beijing Fashion-Expo CO Ltd; Beijing Convention & Exh Co-China World Trade Center Co Ltd	3/28-31	中国国际展览中心新馆 China Intl Exh Ctr New Venue
33	广州国际美容美发化妆用品进出口博览会（秋季） Guangzhou Intl Beauty & Cosmedtic Im & Ex Expo (Autumn)	99,000	2,000	310,000 (观众总数)	广东博环美国际展览有限公司 Guangdong Intl Exhibitions Ltd	9/16-18	中国进出口商品交易会展馆 China Import & Export Fair Complex

2011义乌商城展览
品牌展会期待您的光临

Exhibition Schedule of 2011 Yiwu Brand Fairs

2011.4.20-23
第六届中国义乌文化产品交易博览会
The 6th China Yiwu Cultural Products Trade Fair
www.ssofair.com
0579-85415444

2011.4.28-30
第八届中国国际五金电器博览会
The 8th China International Hardware & Electrical Appliances Trade Fair
www.HardwareExpo.cn
0579-85415111

2011.4.28-30
第六届义乌消费品交易会
The 6th Yiwu Sourcing Fair：Consumer Goods
www.yiwusourcingfair.com
0579-85415333

2011.5.26-29
第三届中国国际旅游商品博览会
The 3rd China International Tourism Commodities Fair
www.tourismfair.cn
0579-85415111

YIWU Fair@Dubai

2011.5.31-6.2
中国义乌国际小商品博览会迪拜展
Yiwu Fair @ Dubai
Http://oversea.yiwufair.com
0579-85415012

2011.10.21-25
第十七届中国义乌国际小商品博览会
The 17th China Yiwu International Commodities Fair
www.yiwufair.com
0579-85415888

2011.11.1- 4
第四届中国义乌国际森林产品博览会
The 4th China Yiwu International Forest Products Fair
www.forestryfair.com
0579-85415333

YIWU Fair@India

2011.11.23-25
中国义乌国际小商品博览会印度展
Yiwu Fair @ India
Http://oversea.yiwufair.com
0579-85415012

YIWU H&G 2011

2011.11.24-26
第十二届义乌国际针织及服装机械展
The 12th Yiwu Exhibition On Hosiery，Knitting & Garment Machinery
www.2456.com/yiwu
0579-85415222

排名 Rank	展会名称 Exhibition	展出面积 Exhibition Area(m^2)	参展商 Exhibitors	贸易观众 Trade Visiters	承办 Organizer	日期 Date	地点 Venue
34	中国杨凌农业高新科技成果博览会 China Yangling Agricultural Hi-tech Fair	98,000	1,500	160,000 （观众总数）	陕西省政府 Shaanxi Provincial Government	11/1-5	杨凌农业高新技术产业示范区 Yangling Agricultural Hi-tech Industries Demonstration Zone
35	广东国际汽车展示交易会 Guangdong Intl Auto Exhibition & Trade Fair	96,000	200	206,000 （观众总数）	东莞中汽会展有限公司 China Natl Automobile Con & Exh Dongguan Co Ltd	9/29-10/4	广东现代国际展览中心（广东东莞） Guangdong Modern Intl Exh Ctr(Guangdong-Donguan)
36	中国厦门国际石材展览会 China Xiamen Intl Stone Fair	95,000	1,300	100,000 （观众总数）	中国贸促会厦门分会 CCPIT Xiamen Sub-Council	3/6-9	厦门国际展览中心 Xiamen Intl Conference & Exh Ctr
37	哈尔滨国际车展 Harbin Intl Automoblie Industry Exhibition	95,000	458	250,000 （观众总数）	哈尔滨长城国际展览有限公司 Harbin Great Wall Intl Exhibition Co Ltd	8/2-9	哈尔滨国际会展体育中心 Harbin Intl Conference Exh & Sporter Ctr
38	北京埃森国际焊接与切割展览会 Beijing Essen Welding & Cutting Fair	92,400	973	42,852	中国机械工程学会及其焊接分会 Chinese Mechanical Engineering Society; Welding Institution of CMES	5/27-30	中国国际展览中心新馆 China Intl Exh Ctr New Venue
39	中国国际日用消费品博览会 China Intl Consumer Goods Fair	90,000	5,000	6,023	宁波市对外贸易服务中心有限公司 Ningbo Foreign Trade Service Ctr Co Ltd	6/8-11	宁波国际会展中心 Ningbo Intl Conference & Exh Ctr
40	香港国际珠宝展 Hong Kong Intl Jewellery Show	88,550	2,673	32,007	香港贸易发展局 Hong Kong Trade Development Council	3/5-9	香港会议展览中心 Hong Kong Convention and Exhibition Ctr
41	香港礼品及赠品展 Hong Kong Gifts & Premium Fair	88,143	4,016	48,945	香港贸易发展局 Hong Kong Trade Development Council	4/27-30	香港会议展览中心 Hong Kong Convention and Exhibition Ctr
42	世界制药原料中国展暨世界制药机械、设备与材料中国展 CPHI & ICSE China	85,000	1,719	26,547	上海博华国际展览有限公司 UBM SINOEXPO	6/2-4	上海新国际博览中心 Shanghai New Intl Expo Ctr
43	中国国际专业音响、灯光、乐器及技术展览会 China Intl Exhibition on Pro Audio, Light, Music & Technology	85000	1,150	193,000 （观众总数）	中国演艺设备技术协会 China Entertainment Technology Association	5/20-23	中国国际展览中心 China Intl Exh Ctr
44	中国国际五金博览会 China Intl Hardware Fair	80,800	2,000	27,000	北京金益友联展览有限公司 Beijing Jinyi Youlian Exhibition Co., Ltd.	3/10-12	上海新国际博览中心 Shanghai New Intl Expo Ctr
45	上海国际机床展 13th Shanghai Intl Machine Tool Fair	80,000	1,028	27,712	上海东博展览有限公司 EASTPO Intl Expo Co Ltd	7/15-18	上海新国际博览中心 Shanghai New Intl Expo Ctr

排名 Rank	展会名称 Exhibition	展出面积 Exhibition Area(m^2)	参展商 Exhibitors	贸易观众 Trade Visiters	承办 Organizer	日期 Date	地点 Venue
46	国际制冷、空调、供暖、通风及食品冷冻加工展览会 China Refrigeration	80,000	1,006	40,000（观众总数）	北京贸促会；中国制冷学会 Beijing Intl Exh Ctr	4/7-9	中国国际展览中心新馆 China Intl Exh Ctr New Venue
47	中国国际焙烤展览会 The 13th China International Trade Fair For Bakery & Confectionery	80,000	982	86,000（观众总数）	中国焙烤食品糖制品工业协会；中国贸促会轻工行业分会 China Association of Bakery & Confectionery Industry; CCPIT Sub-Council of Light Industry	5/12-15	上海新国际博览中心 Shanghai New Intl Expo Ctr
48	香港秋季电子产品展 Hong Kong Electronics Fair (Autumn Editrion)	78,300	2,988	57,933	香港贸易发展局 Hong Kong Trade Development Council	10/13-16	香港会议展览中心 Hong Kong Convention and Exhibition Ctr
49	第32届广州国际美容美发化妆用品进出口博览会（春季） Guangzhou Intl Beauty & Cosmedtic Im & Ex Expo (Spring)	77,000	2,000	228,000（观众总数）	广东博环美国际展览有限公司 Guangdong Intl Exhibitions Ltd	3/9-11	中国进出口商品交易会展馆 China Import & Export Fair Complex
50	第11届汽车用品暨改装汽车展览会 11th China Intl Expo for Auto Electronics,Accessories, Tuning & Car Care Products	70,000	2,089	38,000	雅森国际展览有限公司 YASN Intl Exh Co Ltd	11/26-28	哈尔滨国际会展中心 Harbin International Conference Exhibition and Sports Center
51	中国电子展(春季) China Electronics Fair	70,000	1,400	92,357（观众总数）	中国电子器材总公司 Creativity Convention & Exh Co Ltd	4/9-11	深圳会展中心 Shenzhen Convention & Exhibition Ctr
52	中国国际汽车零部件博览会 China Lnternational Auto Parts Expo	70,000	1,385	46,030（观众总数）	北京新京贸国际展览有限公司 Beijing Gold Trade Intl Exh Co Ltd	9/8-10	中国国际展览中心 China Intl Exh Ctr
53	中国(上海)国际乐器展览会 Music China	70,000	1,274	78,047（观众总数）	上海国际展览中心；法兰克福展览（香港） INTEX Shanghai; Messe Frankfurt (SH) Co Ltd	10/12-15	上海新国际博览中心 Shanghai New Intl Expo Ctr
54	广东国际广告展 SIGN CHINA 2010	70,000	1,006	49,674（观众总数）	广州闻信展览服务有限公司 UBM Trust Co Ltd	3/2-5	中国进出口商品交易会展馆 China Import & Export Fair Complex
55	中国(深圳)国际品牌服装服饰交易会 China (Shenzhen) Intl Brand Clothing & Accessories Fair	70,000	800	80,000	深圳市服装行业协会；时尚汇品牌管理有限公司 Shenzhen Garment Industry Assn	7/8-10	深圳会展中心 Shenzhen Convention & Exhibition Ctr
56	2010第九届中国国际门业展览会 The 9th China International Door Industry Exhibition	70,000	628	100,000（观众总数）	北京中装伟佳展览策划有限公司 Beijing Zhongzhuang Weijia Strategy For Exhibition Co Ltd	4/15-18	中国国际展览中心 China Intl Exh Ctr
57	第十七届中国（上海）国际婚纱摄影器材展览会暨国际儿童摄影、主题摄影展览会（秋季） The 17th China (Shanghai) Intl Wedding Photographic Equipment Exh & Intl Children's Photography, Theme Photography Exh (Spring)	70,000	565	150,000（观众总数）	上海国际展览服务公司 Shanghai International Service Corporation	1/20-23	上海国际展览中心 INTEX Shanghai

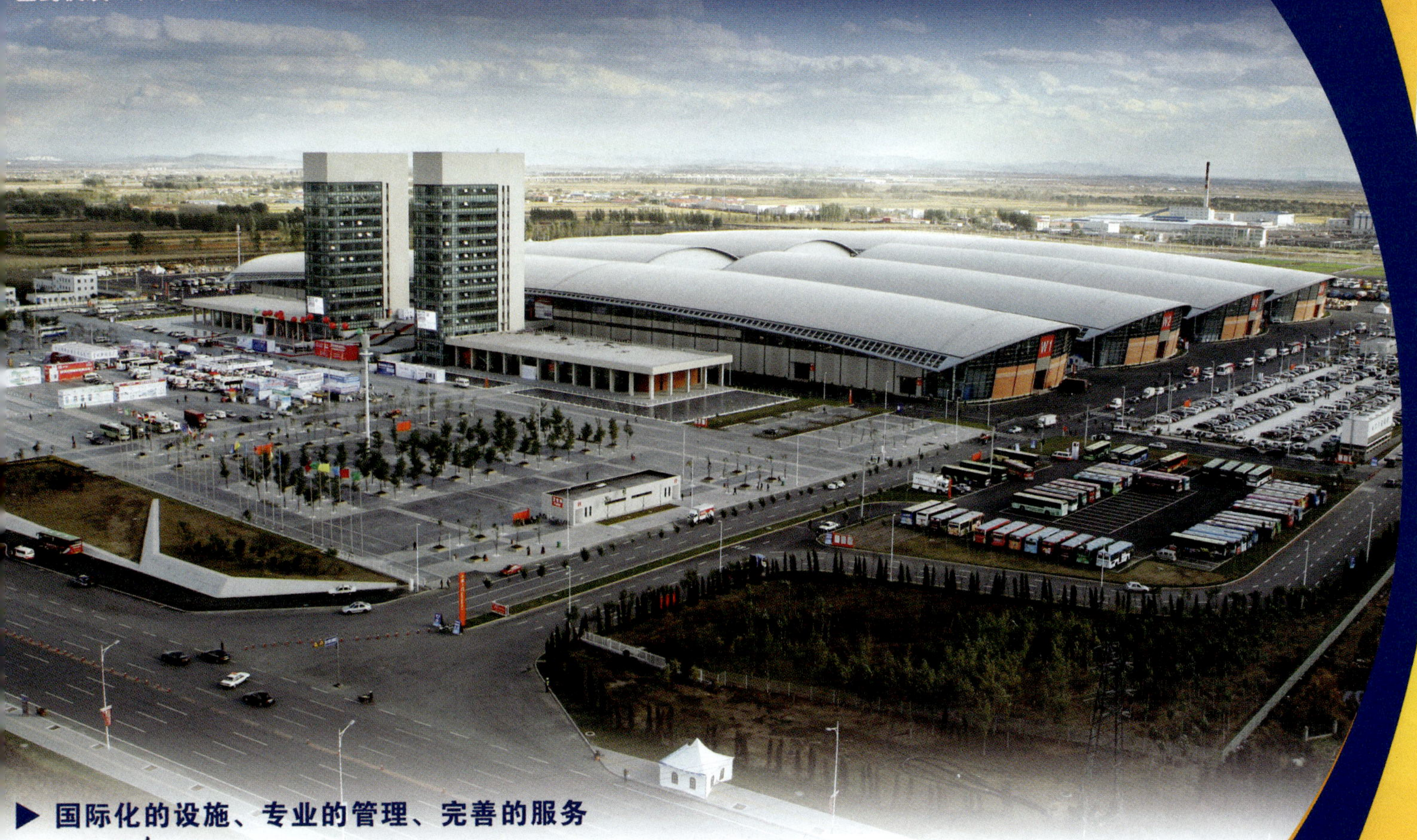

排名 Rank	展会名称 Exhibition	展出面积 Exhibition Area(m^2)	参展商 Exhibitors	贸易观众 Trade Visiters	承办 Organizer	日期 Date	地点 Venue
58	中国北方国际自行车电动车展览会 China North Int'l Bicycle & E-bike Exhibition	70,000	550	30,000	天津市华轮展览有限公司；天津国展中心股份有限公司 Tianjin Hualun Exhibition Co. Ltd.; Tianjin International Exhibition Centre Co.,Ltd.	3/25/-27	天津梅江国际会展中心 天津国际展览中心 Tianjin Meijiang Convention and Exh Ctr/ Tianjin Intl Exh Ctr
59	国际时装及时尚配饰展/中国国际鞋类展/中国国际皮革展 All China Leather Exhibition / China Intl Footware Fair Moda Shanghai	69,000	836	12,967	亚太区皮革展有限公司 中国皮革协会 Asia Pacific Leather Fair Ltd	9/1-3	上海新国际博览中心 Shanghai New Intl Expo Ctr
60	上海国际儿童、婴儿、孕妇产品博览会 Children Baby Maternity Expo	69,000	950	81,539	博闻中国(杭州) CMP (Hangzhou)	7/21-23	上海新国际博览中心 Shanghai New Intl Expo Ctr
61	全国药品交易会(春季) Pharmchina-Spring	65,000	2,000	100,000	国药励展展览有限责任公司 Reed Sinopharm Exh Co Ltd	4/24-26	厦门国际会议展览中心 Xiamen Intl Conference & Exh Ctr
62	全国药品交易会(秋季) Pharmchina-Autumn	65,000	2,000	100,000	国药励展展览有限责任公司 Reed Sinopharm Exh Co Ltd	12/9-11	南昌市国际会展中心 Nanchang Intl Exh Ctr
63	中国(上海)国际石材产品及石材技术装备展 STONETECH	65,000	769	46,962 (观众总数)	北京华港展览有限公司； 中国贸促会建材行业分会 CIEC Exhibition Co Ltd	4/6-9	上海新国际博览中心 Shanghai New Intl Expo Ctr
64	香港春季电子产品展 Hong Kong Electronics Fair (Spring Edition)	60,235	2,305	55,607	香港贸易发展局 HK Trade Development Council	4/13-16	香港会议展览中心 Hong Kong Convention and Exhibition Ctr
65	上海国际酒店用品博览会 Hotelex	60,000	885	43,288	上海博华国际展览有限公司 Shanghai UBM Sinoexpo International Exhibition Co., Ltd	3/29-4/1	上海新国际博览中心 Shanghai New Intl Expo Ctr
66	香港家庭用品展 Hong Kong Houseware Fair	58,255	2,149	38,674	香港贸易发展局 Hong Kong Trade Development Council	4/20-23	香港会议展览中心 Hong Kong Convention and Exhibition Ctr
67	中国国际食品添加剂和配料展览会 Food Ingredients China 2010	58,000	1,058	76,750 (观众总数)	中国食品添加剂和配料协会、中国国际贸易委员会轻工行业分会 China Food Additives & Ingredients Association, CCPIT Sub-Council of Light Industry	3/23-25	上海光大会展中心 上海世贸商城 上海国际展览中心 Shanghai Everbright Convention & Exh Ctr/ ShanghaiMart/ INTEX Shanghai
68	香港玩具展 Hong Kong Toys & Games Fair	57,532	1,915	33,099	香港贸易发展局 HK Trade Development Council	1/11-14	香港会议展览中心 Hong Kong Convention and Exhibition Ctr
69	中国国际旅游交易会 China Intl Travel Mart	57,500		100,000 (观众总数)	中国国家旅游局；云南省人民政府；中国民用航空总局 Natl Tourism Administration	11/18-21	上海新国际博览中心 Shanghai New Intl Expo Ctr

排名 Rank	展会名称 Exhibition	展出面积 Exhibition Area(m^2)	参展商 Exhibitors	贸易观众 Trade Visiters	承办 Organizer	日期 Date	地点 Venue
70	亚太区美容展 Cosmoprof Asia	57,400	1,633	45,100	亚洲博闻 UBM Asia Ltd	11/10-12	香港会议展览中心 Hong Kong Convention and Exhibition Ctr
71	中国国际汽车服务业及汽车文化博览会暨全国汽车保修检测诊断设备(春季)展览会 Auto Maintech	56,000	789	38,232（观众总数）	中国汽车保修行业协会；中国汽车维修行业协会；北京通联国际展览有限公司 Beijing Traders-Link Intl Exhibition Co Ltd	3/18-21	国家会议中心 China Natl Convention Ctr
72	世界制药工业展中国展区（原包装材料、制药设备区） Interphex China Conference & Exhibition	55,000	1,400	30,000	国药励展展览有限责任公司 Reed Sinopharm Exhibitions	11/10-12	苏州国际博览中心 Suzhou Intl Expo Ctr
73	第十五届中国宁波国际住宅产品博览 The 15th China international Exhibition on Housing Industry Productl	55,000	780	50,000	宁波市建设委员会；宁波市城之新展览有限公司 Ningbo Construetion committee; Ningbo Chengzhixin Exh Co .Ltd	10/28-31	宁波国际会议展览中心 Ningbo Intl Conference & Exh Ctr
74	第十八届中国国际建筑装饰展览会 18 TH EXPO BUILD CHINA 2010	51,750	438	29,874	上海博建国际会展有限公司 Shanghai UBM Sinoexpo Intl Exh Co., Ltd.	3/28-4/1	上海新国际博览中心 Shanghai New Intl Expo Ctr
75	第十二届中国国际地面材料及铺装技术展览会 DOMOTEX asia/CHINAFLOOR	51,425	966	41,040	上海万耀企龙展览有限公司/德国汉诺威展览公司 VNU Exhibitions Asia	3/23-25	上海新国际博览中心 Shanghai New Intl Expo Ctr
76	中国电子展览会暨亚洲电子展 China Electronics Fair	50,000	1,500	60,121（观众总数）	中国电子器材总公司 Creativity Convention & Exh Co Ltd	11/9-10	上海新国际博览中心 Shanghai New Intl Expo Ctr
77	中国义乌(国际)森林产品博览会 China Yiwu (Intl) Forest Product Fair	50,000	1,200	112,600（观众总数）	义乌市人民政府 Yiwu Municipal Government	11/1-4	义乌国际博览中心 Yiwu Intl Exh Ctr
78	广州国际鞋类、皮革及工业设备展览会 Intl Exhibition on Shoes & Leather Industry-Guangzhou	50,000	875	36,000（观众总数）	中国对外贸易中心（集团）；显辉国际展览有限公司 China Foreign Trade Center (Group); Top Repute Co Ltd	6/1-3	中国进出口商品交易会展馆 China Import & Export Fair Complex
79	中国国际瓦楞展 SinoCorrugated	50,000	550	23,000（观众总数）	励展博览集团 Reed Exhibitions	4/6-9	上海新国际博览中心 Shanghai New Intl Expo Ctr
80	第19届北京国际广播电影电视设备展览会 Beijing Intl Radio, TV & Film Equipment Exhibition	50,000	453	53,000	中国广播电视国际经济技术合作总公司 China Radio & TV Co. for Intl Techno-Economic Corp	8/23-26	中国国际展览中心 China Intl Exh Ctr

"五年磨一剑"，郑州国际会展中心引领郑州会展业步入快车道
——郑州瞄准中部会展产业带"带头大哥"

文/李文强

"如果在一个城市开一次展览会，就好比有一架飞机在城市上空撒钱。"这句略显夸张的行话，告诉大家一个道理，有着"无烟工业"之称的会展业，能为举办地的经济发展注入相当大的活力。

2005年10月，市政府投资22亿元建成的郑州国际会展中心正式投入运营，郑州会展业步入快速发展时期。岁月荏苒，转眼间五年就过去了。这五年来，郑州国际会展中心为郑州人交上了一份怎样的答卷？郑州会展业又为郑州人撒下了多少"票子"？

一场糖酒会给郑州揽金近10亿元

"几千年前，我也应该是河南人。"郑州国际会展中心总经理温忠东认真地说，就姓氏起源来讲，温是以地名为姓，来源于河南省温县。温忠东是香港人，2009年5月，就任郑州香港会展管理公司郑州国际会展中心的总经理。

回首刚刚过去的2010年，温忠东自豪地说："2010年，会展中心经营管理状况好于开业以来的任何一年。2010年也是近几年中收入最高、盈利最多的一年。"

"做会展业，不能只看场馆的收入，要看这个展会本身给城市带来的效益。"温忠东举例去年的糖酒会，会展直接收入1.15亿元，给郑州带来的效益是9.25亿元。"会展业的产业带动系数为1：9，即展览直接收入如果是1，住宿、餐饮、运输、通讯、旅游、贸易等相关收入将达到9。"

"每年会展业都给郑州带来收益超百亿元"

郑州市会展工作管理办公室主任陈彦表示，五年前，郑州市就提出了发展物流业和会展业。郑州是"流动展的摇篮"，糖酒会、农机会都是从郑州发展壮大，然后走向全国。2005年年底，郑州国际会展中心正式投入运营。从此，郑州市会展业的发展步入了快车道。"当时，郑州市就提出了打造中部会展之都。"陈彦说。经过"十一五"的发展，郑州市作为会展之都的地位已经基本确立了。郑州市会展业综合竞争力大为增强，在中部城市中居首位，在二线城市之中位居前列，仅次于上海、北京等一线城市。这主要表现在 大型流动展会齐聚郑州，自主品牌展会迅速成长，展览队伍发展壮大，既有展营企业办展会，也有媒体办展会，还有商会办展会。

会展业对于城市经济的贡献率是很高的。2006年以来，全市会展业平均每年的直接收入在7亿元左右，每年带动相关产业收入70亿元以上。2010年，郑州市会展业拉动经济社会效益达110亿元左右。2010年，全市共举办展会102个，比去年同期增长21%；全市展览总面积132万平方米，比去年同期增长8%，参会人数220万人次。2010年展览面积是2005年的4倍多，展览数量是2005年的2倍。

高铁时代让郑州的交通优势不再明显

温忠东表示，虽然郑州是"大型巡回展的摇篮"，但是，总体的服务方面，郑州与一线城市还有差距。二线城市中，深圳、南京、济南、西安、成都等，都算是郑州的竞争对手。特别是成都，因为西北、西南的参展商都愿意去成都，并且，四川的旅游业和商业都很发达。

对于目前会展中心的环境，温忠东认为，郑东新区现在只有一个五星级的酒店，酒店总体数量还是偏少。"举办糖酒会，一下子就来了十几万人，对于郑州市的住宿、餐饮、交通都会带来很大的压力。有些客户恨不得开车到开封去住，打出租车也不方便。"他说，虽然，郑东新区这几年，餐厅多了好几倍，但是总体来说，价格普遍偏高。

陈彦认为，随着高铁的四通八达，郑州市的交通优势变得不再那么明显。2003年，郑州市提出开建郑州国际会展中心时，这个6.5万平方米的展览面积，可以排在全国第三位，而现在则滑到了15位。由此可见，会展业的竞争愈来愈激烈。

会展中心业务将走向多元化

"下一步，会展中心还要针对河南省的优势，开发新市场。"温忠东说，将来，会展中心不单是做会展，还要涉足演唱会、表演项目、体育活动等。"过去的业务很单纯，未来将会多元化。不仅要做国内展，还要做国际展。"温忠东指出，毕竟河南艺术中心就在旁边，二者还是要错位竞争，实现互补和双赢。

据介绍，到目前为止，郑州会展中心尚未办过一个国际展。今年，会展中心有可能办两到三个国际展。其中，一个是清真方面的博览会，还有一个是地铁方面的论坛和展览会。"今后，争取每年会展中心都能举办三至五个国际展，这将使郑州市的会展业走在中部其他城市的前列。"

温忠东认为，郑州市地处中原腹地，十省通衢，承东启西，连南贯北。郑州处于居中的位置，是中国铁路、公路、航空的综合性交通信息枢纽，运输成本低，非常适合会展业的发展。"芝加哥、伯明翰、巴黎等城市，在他们的国内，都是处于一个相对居中的位置，方便运输，因此，会展业都很发达。"温忠东说，河南省人口最多，需求大，市场大。"例如，办车展，我们就有宇通、日产等大型汽车企业，具有不可比拟的产业优势。"

立足河南优势办展会

现在郑州市对于会展业的基本思路是"政府推动，市场化运作"。政府推动主要体现在政策引导，郑州市不仅建设了会展中心，而且出台了相关政策，建立了会展业的协调机制。市场化运作就是将政府主导的展会，向市场化运作发展。鼓励民营企业、商会办展会，政府则从具体的会展中退出。

陈彦表示，下一步，政府将会立足于郑州市的产业优势，来办展会，如汽车、服装、速冻食品等。因为郑州女裤占到全国市场的70%，速冻食品占到了70%。

“今年，郑州市初步打算举办女裤展。”据介绍，2010我市举办的较成功的展会，如中国农机产品订货交易会、中国农产品博览会、全国绿化博览会、中国（郑州）国际微型汽车配件博览会、中国国际汽车后市场博览会等，都是与郑州优势产业紧密结合的。另一方面则和市场优势相结合。郑州市商贸、批发市场十分突出。批发市场可以说是永不落幕的展会。“汽车用品展，就是从市场中走出来的展会，第一届就是由市场办的。然而，从市场中走出的展会，就极具生命力。”陈彦说，再一个就是要结合郑州的区位优势来办展会。让国家商协会到郑州来办展，就会将全国的龙头企业带到郑州来。

郑州瞄准中部会展产业带龙头城市

陈彦认为，会展业分作三块，即会议、展览和节庆。今后，仍然要以展为主，兼顾会议和节庆。政府看中的是人流量，希望展会带来更多的客流。他们的衣食住行将会给郑州带来巨大的收益。郑州市将流动展和品牌展并驾并驱。“之所以要办流动展，因为郑州有区位优势，交通便利，又是传统的商贸城。因此，郑州将是流动展的居高地。”

“一个展会能否发展下去，主要看参展商和专业观众。”陈彦说，中国目前已经形成珠江三角洲、长江三角洲、环渤海会展产业带，以郑州为中心的中部会展产业带和以成都为中心的西部会展产业带，正在孕育中。

陈彦介绍说，为科学发展我市会展业，我市聘请商务部国际贸易经济合作研究院制定《郑州会展业发展规划(2010-2020)》。目前《规划》已根据评审会专家意见作出修改，报市政府常务会审定。未来10年，郑州将努力发展成为中部会展产业带的龙头城市。■

Commitment and Passion for the Zhengzhou Umbrella

—— Interview with Mr. Li Qiaosong, Assistant General Manager of Zhengzhou International Convention and Exhibition Centre (ZZICEC)

The Zhengzhou International Convention and Exhibition Centre (ZZICEC) is one of the few venues in China managed by a professional venue management company. A lot of national exhibitions have been hosted at the ZZICEC. Local exhibitions like Zhengzhou National Commodity Fair are growing. A unique landmark of the Zhengzhou skyline that resembles an umbrella, the dignified yet modern ZZICEC has made notable contributions to the development of the exhibition industry of the city. As one of the guardians of the ZZICEC, Mr. Li Qiaosong, the Assistant General Manager of the Centre, is committed to boost the development of Zhengzhou's convention and exhibition industry. During the Zhengzhou National Commodity Fair, Mr. Li was able to grant an interview with us in his busy schedule.

The dual role of service and management

Though it is winter in Nov in North China, the ambience surrounding ZZICEC resembled that of the summer time. The National Agricultural Products Expo and the National Agricultural Machinery Trade Fair had just been held at the end of October, and they were closely followed by the Zhengzhou National Commodity Fair, 2010 China Zhengzhou Industry Transformation Conference, the 8th National Seed Information Exchange & Products Fair, and the 3rd Zhengzhou International Auto Expo. The ZZICEC team can hardly take a break after these events as they have to immediately prepare for other upcoming exhibitions.

People working in the exhibition industry are always “busy and merry”. Since the opening in 2005, ZZICEC has been leading the development of Zhengzhou's exhibition industry and has become the top venue among those in second-tier cities. “Exhibitions bring vitality to the venue, as well as the people who work in this industry,” Mr. Li Qiaosong smiled and explained to us that the prosperous development of Zhengzhou's exhibition industry is inseparable with the local software and hardware environments.

Firstly, governmental support is indispensable. A series of policies aiming at promoting the exhibition industry development of Zhengzhou have been issued by the Zhengzhou Municipal Party Committee and the Municipal Government since 2005. A special fund totaling 1,500 million Yuan has been established to strongly support the fast and sound development of local exhibition industry. Secondly, marketing potential is important. As a major commodity and trade distribution centrewith a population of 200 million, Zhengzhou has devel oped into a mature consumer and logistics base, which greatly facilitates enterprises in either organizing or attending exhibitions at affordable cost. Thirdly, Zhengzhou has geographic advantages. Located in the heart of the Central Plains region,bridging the north and south, connecting east and west, Zhengzhou is a transportation hub of major highways, railways, and airlines. Asia's largest rail marshalling yard is located in Zhengzhou. It is also equipped with advanced telecommunications system. The city is indeed a perfect platform for business exchanges.

All of the elements above endowed Zhengzhou with uniqueadvantages in exhibition development, yet the sustainability of such development doubtlessly depend on the service. Managed by the Hong Kong – Shanghai Venue Management (Zhengzhou) Ltd. (VMZL) – a professional venue management company entrusted by Zhengzhou Convention and Exhibition Co., Ltd (ZCL) (State solely - owned enterprise under subordinate to the Municipal Government) for its international management and professional service ideology, ZZICEC is well recognized in the exhibition industry for its quality and customized service.

Prior to the opening of an event, a lot of detailed preparation works have to be done through the active coordination with related government departments in terms of public security, fire prevention, sanitation and epidemic prevention, city environment, traffic management, etc. A well thought through emergency management plan needs to be carefully prepared before each event to ensure a safe, healthy and orderly exhibition environment for all participants. Such event related services are designed in full consultation with clients. Fake exhibits offered by illegal vendors are strictly controlled in an effort to maintain a fair and harmonious business platform.

"As a venue manager, we should be a good service provider and do our best to help exhibitors and visitors." Mr. Li Qiaosong said cordially. Satisfaction from our exhibitors brings us more clients.

Shift from government-dominated to market-oriented

Sixteen years went by with much experience gained. As the oldest and most influential exhibition of Henan, Zhengzhou National Commodity Fair is not only the extension of the local exhibition industry but also the most representative among national exhibitions. Witnessing ups and downs in its growth, Mr. Li Qiaosong has a very complex feeling about this event. The first Zhengzhou National Commodity Fair was organized by the industry," Mr. Li said, reflecting his strong commitment and passion for the ZZICEC umbrella.Municipal government in 1995 and it went through some an uncertain period around year 2003. It was then reformed in 2006. Zhengzhou National Commodity Fair experienced the "pain" of reform.

From government-dominated to market-oriented operation - it seems to be the natural course for commodity exhibitions. Mr. Li has gone through the pain and joy together with Zhengzhou National Commodity Fair over these years. Having experienced the progression from government-dominated to market-oriented operation, ZCL, as the co-organizer of Zhengzhou National Commodity Fair, has made its best effort in the transformation. Most encouraging results were achieved in 2009 as a record breaking 90% of exhibitors were recruited through promotion in the market. No reform is easy. Mr. Li said, "We relied on the power of media to promote the event and we also provided the best service to attract participants. To be more specific, based on the lessons we learned from the previous events, we selected the relatively mature and experienced promotion agents, and built a specialized promotion team to ensure stable and continuous sales efforts. The results were good as both the exhibition space and the number of exhibitors have increased. We also received good feedback from exhibitors and visitors."

It is important to bring innovative ideas to impress the visitors every time we organize the event. Thus, ASEAN countries were invited to participate in the 16th Zhengzhou National Commodity Fair in order to make the event international. Participation from sister cities and provincial cities were more active than ever before. The city of Lhasa participated in the exhibition for the first time, making it the highlight of this fair.

However, specialization in an exhibition is even more important. "Cultivating specialization during the Zhengzhou National Commodity Fair is our goal." Mr. Li said a show without a specialized theme is not attractive. Fishing Tool Exhibition has been growing well since it came under the banner of the Zhengzhou Commodity Fair in 2009. Some exhibiting companies commented that they could find potential customers by participating in the Zhengzhou National Commodity Fair. The exhibitors were not only able to promote their brands but also broaden the distribution channels for their products, Mr. Li was very pleased, "On hearing the positive feedback from the exhibitors, it means that our efforts are not in vain."

"The reform of the national exhibition can never be accomplished overnight; there is still a long way to go in overcoming many difficulties." Mr. Li said calmly. We will continue to explore the development of this show as well as create new specialties and promotion tools in the direction of professionalism and market-orientation, forging a real platform for business exchange, boosting the prosperity and economic development of Henan and playing an important role in promoting the exchange and cooperation among sister cities.

Interview sidelights:

Zhengzhou National Commodity Fair can be regarded as an attempt by the ZZICEC for self-organized exhibitions. In view of the development status of China's exhibition industry, the self-organized exhibition is indeed an effective way in enhancing a venue's occupancy rate. Apart from that, it helps a venue to develop its own brand event. Mr. Li Qiaosong did not deny the effectiveness of the self-organized event. Will exploring niche markets and creating new exhibitions be ZZICEC's next target? "It is decided by the market demand and development." Mr. Li did not answer directly.

Mr. Li Qiaosong was very serious in responding to each of the reporter's questions about the exhibition business. "Whichever way we take, it is for the benefit of the development of Zhengzhou's exhibition industry," Mr. Li said, reflecting his strong commitment and passion for the ZZICEC umbrella. ■

位处珠三角地利之宜
亚洲国际博览馆尽享区内经济迅速发展优势

文/刘佩佩

近年来，中国内地经济高速发展，世界经济版图重心逐渐由欧美转移面向亚洲，国际贸易的需求亦不断提升。而面对一场席卷全球的金融海啸，中国更被视为带领全球经济走出困局的希望之一。受惠于国家的开放政策及经济发展，香港自然而言成为通往中国及全球的门槛，同时为香港展览业的持续发展打下一支强心针。

诚如早年于亚洲国际博览馆成功举办“国际电信联盟2006世界电信展”后，除温家宝总理高度嘉许外，更明确支持香港继续作为国家的国际展览会议中心及基地。就香港展览业未来的长远发展方向而言，如何配合中央政府的《珠江三角洲地区改革发展规划纲要》及国家《十二·五规划》，融入珠三角经济体系乃一非常重要课题。

港珠澳大桥贯通明日珠三角都会区 博览馆稳踞未来经济发展中心

近年来，香港配合国家的发展策略，一直扮演着双向跳板的角色。一方面协助海外企业走进潜力无限的中国市场，另一方面亦协助内地企业迈向国际商贸舞台。我们可以看到愈来愈多内地企业到港参与各项国际商贸展览和大型会议。而内地来港的展览访客人数亦不断上升，形成香港展览会议业发展的新趋势，联系中国内地及世界市场。据香港展览业最新的调查报告显示，在2009年从内地来港的参展商数目增长达15.7%，接近19,000家；而来自内地的业内展览访客总数则逾21万1千，比前年上升24%。这显示香港依然是中国与世界汇聚之重要平台。

亚洲国际博览馆管理有限公司行政总裁哈永安先生表示：“以上述的国家发展策略为大方向，亚洲国际博览馆经过五年的努力，已成功于亚洲区以至世界各地建立其专业的展览活动场馆品牌和定位，提供一个有效的商贸平台，协助落实国家‘引进来、走出去’的目标。”

2010年是亚洲国际博览馆庆祝成立5周年的日子，过去一直致力开拓新兴的主题展览，以扩大香港展览业的发展空间，并与大型展览主办单位和企业合作，致力发挥国际桥梁的角色。现时，单以商贸展览计，博览馆每年便为香港经济带来约90亿港元进帐。同时，估计提供了相等于约18,000个直接和间接全职职位。

例如去年博览馆成功招揽法国的高美爱博展览集团首次走出欧洲，移师香港举办“亚洲智慧卡工业展”。此项每年于欧洲举行的智能卡展览为全球举足轻重的智能科技展之一，并且是全球业界的标杆。首届“亚洲智慧卡工业展”成功吸引来

自全球超过2,800名优质买家到场参观。主办机构亦已落实将于2011年3月再临亚洲国际博览馆。其亚洲智能卡工业展总监Michael Weatherseed先生表示："亚太地区及中国的电信市场发展迅速，其智能卡科技的增长速度远比全球其他地区快，为行业带来无限商机。亚洲国际博览馆凭借位处中国门槛的策略性地理位置，实为通往区域及内地市场的理想平台。事实上，亚洲国际博览馆为我们提供了一个完美的地点、优质的设施及非常专业的支援团队。"

此外，全球最大规模、专注亚太区商业航空及民用航空市场的单一展览会和论坛—《亚洲国际航空展览会暨论坛》，自2007年起每两年一度在亚洲国际博览馆举行。由于展览会获得中国公营和私营航空业界如中国航空运输协会(CATA)、中国民用机场协会(CCAA)、中国民用航空维修协会(CAMAC)的支持，相信今届展览(2011年3月)定会吸引众多来自全球航空业界的代表出席和参与。

另一项"引进来、走出去"的成功例子乃每年4月及10月定期于亚洲国际博览馆举行的一系列"环球资源采购交易会"。其发展极为迅速，规模更日益壮大。当中的电子产品及零件展便被誉为全球最多中国参展商的电子产品展览之一。数千个参展商中逾75%来自中国内地，证明全球市场对大中华地区生产的优质产品的需求十分殷切。

哈先生续说："展望未来，随着港珠澳大桥跨境基建项目的落成，意味着博览馆今后将稳据珠三角地区的经济枢纽地位，服务这片被誉为未来世界商贸活动的新亮点。预计在港珠澳大桥等跨境基建项目落成后，乘地利之宜，博览馆的服务范围将进一步扩大至覆盖1亿人口版图，继续担当其促进环球商贸交流的重要角色。"■

AsiaWorld-Expo is uniquely positioned to capitalise on the rapid economic growth of China's Pearl River Delta (PRD) region

by/Fiona Lau

In recent years, the centre of the world's economic stage has shifted eastward to the Asian region with the opening up of the China market and its rapid economic growth. International trading of goods and services between China and other countries is poised to expand further, creating many more export and import business opportunities for various industries in the region and the world. As predicted, Mainland China among others is leading the world economy out of the financial tsunami. Hong Kong, strategically located at the heart of Southern China and Asia, is an international city which is not only a very important gateway to China but also a springboard to the globe.

In this regard, Hong Kong continues to live up to the great honour remarked by the Chinese Premier Wen Jiabao after the successful hosting of ITU TELECOM WORLD 2006 that Hong Kong has the full potential to become China's international exhibition and convention hub by welcoming more and more events of global standing, and playing a key role in bringing China and the world together. When considering the long-term development of Hong Kong Exhibition and Convention Industry in view of the "Framework for Development and Reform Planning for Pearl River Delta Region" and "12th Five-Year Plan" announced by the Central Government, the integration into the Pearl River Delta's economy is the key.

Hong Kong-Zhuhai-Macao Bridge links today with the Pearl River Delta Metropolis of tomorrow

With the natural desire to close to where the market is, Hong Kong acts as a two-way springboard for mainland Chinese enterprises to introduce their products and services to the world, as well as the ideal choice for the international business community to access the vibrant and rapidly growing China market. It can be seen in the dramatic growth of mainland Chinese exhibition organisers and exhibitors who are now choosing Hong Kong to showcase their goods and services. A latest exhibition survey reveals that the total number of companies fromMainland China exhibiting in Hong Kong's trade shows rose 15.7% to 19,000 in 2009, and the number of trade visitors from the Mainland reached over 211,000, up 24% when compared to that of 2008.

"In the space of just 5 years, AsiaWorld-Expo has become one of the leading exhibition and convention venues in Asia to provide an international trading platform, as proven by the extraordinary variety of MICE events that it hosted in that time." remarked Mr. Allen Ha, Chief Executive Officer of AsiaWorld-Expo Manage ment Limited.

Year 2010 marked the 5th anniversary of AsiaWorld-Expo. Indeed, in its first year of business alone, AsiaWorld-Expo witnessed a 50% growth in Hong Kong's exhibition industry! This remarkable success is a testament to the world-class quality of AsiaWorld-Expo. In economic terms, the trade fairs at AsiaWorld-Expo contribute an estimated HK$9 billion to the local economy every year with an estimated 18,000 full-time equivalent jobs provided. Already an established venue for high-profile MICE events, AsiaWorld-Expo hasadded a new chapter for Hong Kong's MICE landscape by attracting a wide range of new shows to the territory. For example, Comexposium, a French based organising company, has also chosen AsiaWorld-Expo for the world's foremost smart-technology exhibition and congress, CARTES in Asia in March 2010. The event brought together over 2,800 top executives in the industry from all over the world. As a result of the resounding success of the inaugural events, CARTES in Asia is confirmed to return to AsiaWorld-Expo in March 2011.

"Smart technology is growing faster in Asia Pacific and China than in any other region in the world, which creates extraordinary business opportunities," remarked Mr. Michael Weatherseed, Director of Comexposium's Security Division, which includes the Milipol and Cartes brands. "AsiaWorld-Expo, with its strategic location on the doorstep of China, provides the ideal gateway for accessing this dynamic market. In fact, AsiaWorld-Expo offers a great location, excellent AsiaWorld-Expo in March 2011.

"Smart technology is growing faster in Asia Pacific and China than in any other region in the world, which creates extraordinary business opportunities," remarked Mr. Michael Weatherseed, Director of Comexposium's Security Division, which includes the Milipol and Cartes brands. "AsiaWorld-Expo, with its strategic location on the doorstep of China, provides the ideal gate way for accessing this dynamic market. In fact, AsiaWorld-Expo offers a great location, excellent facilities and a very professional and supportive team."

Another notable event is the Asian Aerospace International Expo and Congress which has been Asia's leading aerospace and aviation event for the last 30 years. Following on from the very successful events at AsiaWorld-Expo in 2007 and 2009, Asian Aerospace set to climb even higher in March 2011, with its unique trio of Right Place, Right People and Right Value factors attracting record levels of interest from the world's leading aerospace companies.The world's aviation community with strong attendance from China by influential trade bodies includingthe China Air Transport Association (CATA), China Civil Airports Association (CCAA) and the Civil Aviation MRO Association of China (CAMAC) all endorsing the event and committed to large scale participation by their members, will once again converge on Hong Kong for the 2011 edition.

In addition, the hugely popular series of China Sourcing Fairs organised by Global Sources during the peak periods of April and October have recorded a significant increase in the number of exhibitors and visitors from the mainland. Its Electronics and Components Fair iseven the world's fastest-growing trade event of its kind with a large number of China suppliers. The Fair featured several thousand exhibiting booths with 80% of them from mainland China suppliers alone. The strong mainland presence is central to the success of the Fairs. This demonstrates the recognition of Hong Kong as the effective platform to source products and services and to tap into the Asia-Pacific regional market.

AsiaWorld-Expo is strategically located at the future economic hub Mr. Allen Ha continued, "Looking ahead, several landmark cross-border in frastructure projects mean that AsiaWorld-Expo is set to become a focal point of the Pearl River Delta region, which itself is forecast to become one of the world's most important economic zones in the coming decades. Projects such as the Hong Kong-Zhuhai-Macao Bridge, which will be adjacent to AsiaWorld-Expo, will give the venue a direct catchment of over 100 million people. AsiaWorld-Expo simply has what it takes to become one of the world's most important MICE venues for many years to come." ■

沈阳国际展览中心蓄势待发

沈阳国际展览中心是辽宁省及沈阳市十大重点工程项目之一，由沈阳市人民政府全额出资建设。

沈阳国际展览中心总占地面积95.96万平方米，计划分两期建设，按国际化展览行业标准建设，一期建筑面积16.6万平方米，每个展厅1.32万平方米，总展览面积10.52万平方米，由八个相互独立的单层、无柱、大跨度展厅组成，可设国际标准展位5000个；坐落于辽宁省沈阳市苏家屯区会展路9号，地处沈阳市未来高铁、地铁四号线的核心地段，周边人文环境优雅，空港、物流辐射能力巨大。是集会议、酒店于一体；展览、洽谈相结合的东北地区服务功能齐全的国际性、现代化、智能化的展览场馆，结束了沈阳市没有现代化大型展览场馆的历史，从而使沈阳具有承接大型会展活动的能力。

依托辽宁省沈阳市独特的地理位置优势，沈阳国际展览中心的建成，对促进东北亚经济圈进行国际间合作与交流发挥了重要的平台作用，正逐步成为国际间日益频繁的经贸往来的重要舞台。

从此，续写了沈阳会展业新的篇章！

FashionNetAsia与Stylesight伙拍出版时尚潮流报告

FashionNewAsia将于Stylesight合作，在其“潮流时尚”栏目定期刊登由Stylesight时尚专家撰写的全球时尚潮流分析及预测报告等。报告内容将集中于FashionNetAsia供应商的产品类别如鞋类、手袋配饰等。

FashionNetAsia属于亚太区皮革展有限公司旗下的B2B网站，供应商及买家可于FashionNetAsia搜罗整个供应链的产品并进行相关交易，从制造物料如皮革、织品及零件，以至制成品如袋子、鞋类、时尚配饰、旅行用具及相关产品都一应俱全。FashionNetAsia于2008年成立，现有超过1,000名供应商在这平台开设了网上陈列室，近60,000名买家会定期浏览网站。

Stylesight 为时尚界的创意设计和产品开发流程提供最新的潮流、设计工具与技术资讯。Stylesight拥有超过200位来自世界各地的专家，深入剖析国际性的T台系列、关键展会及活动，并介绍备受注目的零售商与创新面料的生产商。

从现在开始，FashionNetAsia的登记会员可以免费阅读由Stylesight提供之潮流报告。亚太区皮革展有限公司电子业务经理韩吉宏先生表示：“这次合作将有助时装界的供应商及买家更容易掌握下一季的流行情报，以推出迎合市场的产品。”浏览Stylesight的潮流报告在www.fashionnetasia.com/sc/TrendAndFashion.html。亚太区皮革展有限公司为亚洲博闻（www.ubmasia.com）和 SIC（www.sicgroup.com）的合资企业，专注主办时尚及生活潮流的商贸展览会。Stylesight专门为时尚界创意专家提供潮流资讯、设计工具及技术之领导性资讯平台。2003年由成衣制造业专Frank Bober创办，透过Stylesight的创意平台，令设计及产品开发过程更加有效率、快捷、精准，同时降低成本。Stylesight总部位于纽约，于伦敦、香港、上海等设有分公司。

FashionNetAsia Partners With Stylesight to Publish Fashion Trends

FashionNetAsia will publish Stylesight's reports on global fashion and retail trends. In line with FashionNetAsia's main product categories the reports will focus on footwear, bags and accessories.

FashionNetAsia, an online B2B portal under APLF, serves as the platform for buyers and suppliers to trade products across the fashion supply chain - from materials such as leather, fabrics and components to finished products like bags, shoes, fashion accessories travel ware and more. Established in 2008, there are now over 1,000 sellers operating showrooms at FashionNetAsia and close to 60,000 buyers visiting the site regularly.

Stylesight is the leading provider of trend content, tools and technology for creative professionals in the style and design industries. Stylesight's over 200 experts worldwide analyse global runway collections; delve deep into the most important trade shows and events; profile compelling retailers; and examine innovative textile manufacturers.

Starting from now, registered visitors and members at FashionNetAsia can enjoy Stylesight's reports free-of-charge. "This will help both buyers and sellers in the fashion industry to understand ways of optimising their product ranges for the upcoming season," says Jerome Hainz, Manager eBusiness at APLF.

www.fashionnetasia.com/en/TrendAndFashion.html. APLF, a joint venture between UBM Asia (www.ubmasia.com) and SIC (www.sicgroup.com) organises a number of trade exhibitions which focuses on fashion and lifestyles. Stylesight, headquartered in New York, is the leading online provider of trend content, tools and technology for creative professionals in the style and design industries. Founded in 2003 by apparel manufacturing veteran, Frank Bober, Stylesight targets style professionals involved in the creative design and product development processes.

AsiaWorld-Expo wins a high-profile Catering Industry Safety Award

Award scheme organised by the Labour Department and industry stakeholders to promote excellence in safety and health

AsiaWorld-Expo is proud to receive an award in the Catering Industry Safety Award Scheme (2010/2011) organised by the Labour Department. The venue received the Safety Awareness Award in the Catering Establishment, Restaurants (non-Chinese) category in recognition of its awareness of and adherence to the highest standards of work safety.

This important award scheme plays an important role in enhancing the occupational safety and health awareness of employers, employees and stakeholders in the industry. It also aimsto inculcate a robust occupational safety and health culture in the industry and among the public, and to award catering establishments, supervisors and workers for good performance in work safety and health. to inculcate a robust occupational safety and health culture in the industry and among the public, and to award catering establishments, supervisors and workers for good performance in work safety and health.

"We' re honoured to receive this award," said Mr. H W Lau, Chief Operating Officer, AsiaWorld-Expo ManagementLimited. "Safety is a foremost consideration in every aspect of day-to-day operations at AsiaWorld-Expo. This award not only reflects our commitment to safety, but a lso our dedication to excellence in everything we do."

To qualify for the award, AsiaWorld-Expo underwent a preliminary assessment by Occupational Safety Officers from the Labour Department. During this assessment, the inspection team reviewed the physical condition of AsiaWorld-Expo' s kitchens, including such issues as the overall layout, floor conditions, machinery and equipment, and manual lifting and handling.

After being shortlisted for the award, a final assessment took place by representatives from the Labor Department and the Occupational Safety & Health Council. This secondary team also reviewed the physical conditions of the kitchen, as well as the safety management system in place at AsiaWorld-Expo, such as its safety policy, its safety rules and regulations, its safety training, its emergency preparedness, and its promotion of safe work practices.

亚洲博闻（泰国）被泰国投资促进委员会委任为 2011 年 BOI Fair 的特别顾问

亚洲博闻（泰国）被委任为 2011 年 BOI Fair 的特别顾问，此展会可望成为东南亚历年来举办的最大型商贸展会之一。这已是泰国投资促进委员会第三度举办此展会；而亚洲博闻（泰国）亦是第二度获委员会委任管理展会。上届 BOI Fair 于 2000 年举行，吸引超过 4,500,000 名人士到场参观，亚洲博闻（泰国）于该次展会担当着重要的角色。而这次委任进一步肯定亚洲博闻（泰国）作为泰国首要商贸展会主办商的地位。

亚洲博闻（泰国）于 2011 年 BOI Fair 担当的角色将更为重要，除了分派全职专业团队驻泰国投资促进委员会总办事处，与 BOI 展会协调办公室工作外，亦会安排支援小组专责处理物流及运作事宜。

泰国总理阿披实宣布 2011 年 BOI Fair 的主题为"绿化未来"。这个意义重大的展会将成为重点项目，泰国政府会与私营部门携手合作，以展现泰国工业的雄厚实力与潜质。总理同时表示，有信心该展会不仅能提升泰国的形象，更可增强泰国民众对未来的信心。展会将于 2011 年 11 月 10 至 25 日在蒙堂他尼的 Impact 会展中心举行，并由泰国投资促进委员会主办。

泰国投资促进委员会的秘书长 Atchaka Sibunruang 女士称，展会于 IMPACT 会展中心设有室内及室外展区，总面积约为 24 万平方米。户外展区占地约 16.6 万平方米，毗邻蒙堂他尼湖，并将于八十多个户外展位设置皇家展台，借此展示泰国及其他国家制造商的最新技术与生产机械。

室内展区将分为两个部分。第一部分设于 9 号馆，占地 11,000 平方米，场内包括讲座设备，并设有政府机构、各国大使馆以及商会的展示区。此外亦会同时展出当地工匠的制品。

秘书长表示，室内展区的第二部分将设于 IMPACT 会展中心的 Challenger 1-3，并覆盖约 60,000 平方米。展区主要用作展示和销售不同行业的产品，包括农产品、食品、饮料、电子设备、时尚产品、珠宝，以及家具饰品。此外，展区内更设有"四大区域盛宴"，提供泰国四大区域的特色美食。（文 / 罗颖坚）

Agility Opens New Warehouse in Seoul

Agility, a leading global logistics provider, has opened a new state-of-the-art warehouse near Seoul, South Korea to meet growing demand for logistics services in the fairs and exhibitions sector. The 4,000 square meter facility is located between Seoul city center and the Korean Exhibition Center (KINTEX) with direct access to the national highway network.

"Korea is an important market for Agility. The new warehouse will help us support the dynamic growth in our business in South Korea, focusing on major exhibitions at KINTEX and throughout the country," said Steve Whitting ham, managing director for Korea and Japan.

The 1,300 square meter warehouse has a loading and outside storage area of 2,700 square meters. With more than 2,000 pallet positions, loading dock equipment and 24-hour on-site security the warehouse will also facilitate handling of full containers and cars.

"With many long-term strategic customers, this investment demonstrates our commitment to delivering a broad range of innovative logistics solutions throughout the country," said Nat Wong, president, Agility Fairs & Events.

第十八届中国国际包装工业展销售喜人

海外展团、大牌企业纷纷接力争现

第十八届中国国际包装工业展览会/ 第十五届中国国际啤酒、饮料及液态包装工业展览会(简称："2011中国国际包装/饮料工业展")销售呈现火爆态势，海内外参展商已达到400家，已超越上一届展会规模。展会由中国对外贸易中心(集团)、雅式展览服务有限公司联合举办，2011年3月9-11日在广州中国进出口商品交易会琶洲展馆(A区) 举行。目前，海外展团势头强劲，来自英国加工与包装机械协会(PPMA)、美国包装机械制造协会(PMMI)、中华台北产品包装协会等等将强势登场。来自饮料及包装行业最响亮的王牌企业踊跃报名，众多企业纷纷争抢有利位置。全方位满足食品、医药、日化类等各行业买家的采购需求。

包装饮料界展会黑马　备受买家、媒体追捧

近几年快速发展，中国国际包装/饮料展以准确的市场定位、特色的个性化服务得到各界认可。展会主办方对实力买家的邀请及现场成交的达成非常重视。目前"2011中国国际包装/饮料工业展"与全国多家行业协会和买家机构通力合作，预计40多家终端协会及官方组织将会动员前来参观和采购，分别来自广东、福建、长三角、珠三角、中原等发达地区，买家行业覆盖食品、饮料、糖果、焙烤、桶装水、日化、医药、包装印标等产业领域。

"供优质展商、采对口买家"是2011年展会现场商贸活动的亮点之一，主办方已广邀全国超过200多家企业组织买团进行配对活动，并与海内外100多家媒体携手合作，对展会给予详尽报道和跟踪。

2011 展会精彩亮点 邀您共同参与

本届展会特邀来自食品、饮料、啤酒、医药、日化和包装机械等行业的高端买家及专家，共同演绎高端论坛，围绕主题"包装在食品、饮料、医药和日化上的质量安全管理"，包括食品质量安全与绿色(健康)食品产业发展、饮料行业质量安全与健康饮料产业发展、医药产品质量管理与保健品产业发展、新型包装材料应用、

啤酒低碳酿造技术、设备监理与质量安全及日化行业质量安全与产业技术创新、发展趋势等10多场高端研讨会邀您参加。

热点推荐“包装制品精品展区”— “中国风”包装系列

展会已得到全国精选约 100 家包装精品企业参与，展示以中国古典特色为主题的“中国包装与民间文化精品展示馆”。

第十二届中国国际展览和会议展示会在杭州落下帷幕

第十二届中国国际展览和会议展示会（以下简称：展中展）于 2011 年 1 月 14 日圆满落下帷幕。第十二届展中展作为中国国际贸易促进委员会 (CCPIT)、国际展览业协会 (UFI)、国际展览和活动协会 (IAEE)、独立组展商协会 (SISO)、杭州市人民政府共同主办的“第七届中国会展经济国际合作论坛”(CEFCO 2011) 的重要组成部分，由中国展览馆协会、中国国际展览中心集团公司、杭州市西湖博览会组委会办公室联合承办，于 2011 年 1 月 13－14 日在浙江世贸展览中心顺利举行并取得圆满成功。中国贸促会万季飞会长、王锦珍副会长、杭州市张建庭副市长及参加论坛的与会代表等莅临指导并参观了展览。

第十二届展中展展出面积 10000 余平方米，搭建展台 100 余个（其中特装修展位 28 个，标准展位 43 个，浙江地区展位 37 个），参展企业从国别和地区划分包括中国、德国、韩国、香港、澳门、台湾等国内国际展览公司；从参展企业类型划分，涵盖了国内国际大中型展览展示公司、各大知名展览馆、各大知名展览会以及展览工程公司等。展览会开幕当天即 1 月 13 日，观众人流量达到 3137 人次；14 日，观众人流量达到 1693 人次，不含参加开幕式当天的领导和参观嘉宾。总计达到 7000 余人。

本届展中展在为期 3 个月的招展过程中，招展范围涵盖了北京、天津、上海、广州、重庆、河北省、河南省、湖北省、湖南省、四川省、陕西省、浙江省、黑龙江、吉林省等二十几个省市地区。业务人员按照大黄页索引到的会展企业打电话联系，发出招展函上万件。经过坚持不懈的努力，取得了喜人的招展效果。与去年相比，本届招展在数量上有重大突破，远远多于去年参展数量。大部分参展单位都是首次参与展中展，为本届展会注入了新鲜血液。同时，我们也力邀香港澳门、台湾、德国、韩国等大型展览机构和知名企业参加本届展中展，为本届展会增光添彩。

在本届展中展期间，举办了“绿色展览与中国展装企业可持续发展”、“四季展馆——展览场馆经营新理念交流与对话”、“区域经济合作与会展经济发展”、“两岸会展合作新契机”、“打造国际会展之都——世界城市建设中的北京会展业”、“城市会展特色差异化发展之路”以及“国内一流展览从做大如何走向做强及展会组织者如何更好地为参展商提供服务”等专题讲座和座谈活动，为我们会展人带来了行业内最新理念的交流与对话。

来自台湾中华国际会议展览协会涂建国荣誉理事长、北京市贸促会熊九玲会长、上海国际展览中心有限公司方佩瑛总经理、常州灵通展览用品有限公司章剑副总裁、机械汽车展览联合会张效林秘书长、慕尼黑展览（上海）有限公司毛大奔总经理、香港展览会议业协会张伟雄会长、韩国展览主办机构协会李丙允常任理事等领导和业内嘉宾主持、参加了本届展中展的主题活动。嘉宾与观众积极互动，分别针对绿色展览、四季展馆、区域经济合作与会展经济发展、国内一流展览从做大如何走向做强等行业内普遍关注的热点问题，进行研讨。专家谈观点，碰撞灵感的火花。现场观众分享经验，就所关心的问题与专家进行交流与互动。讲座现场火爆，座无虚席，很多观众站着听讲座。大家普遍反映，本次展中展期间的几场讲座和交流活动，互动效果良好，受到热烈欢迎。

2011 年德国 Euroshop 展

Euroshop 是目前世界上最大的与零售业相关的设施、设备、技术展览活动，是全球最具规模和影响力的行业盛会。2011 年的 Euro Shop，全球的零售行业将会聚集在杜塞尔多夫。这个具有权威性行业的利润亮点三年才有一次机会。这次展会预计将会有 50 多个国家的参展商和来自 93 个国家的观展者，展览总面积将达到 20 万平方米。

2008 年的 Euro Shop 来自中国内地的参展企业有 27 家。预计 2011 年会有更多的中国企业走出国门，参加 此次国际盛会。有关德国 Euroshop 展以及其它相关信息可通过奥克坦姆集团大中华区了解。联系电话 512-6283 3338,4006809758

终端市场向中西部转移 纸箱设备将上演“西行记”

近年来，随着沿海发达地带土地成本、能源成本、劳动力成本和生态环境成本的快速攀升，加上全球金融危机的爆发使国际市场萎缩，扩大内需成为产业发展的根本出路，促使企业不得不思考把生产环节配置到成本更低的区位，而资源富集、人力成本相对低廉的中西部成为首选。

目前，中西部地区经济增长迅速，部分中西部省份在东部增长速度大幅度下滑的同时一致保持高速的增长，如内蒙古一直维持了16%上的增速。而据中国人民大学经济研究所的一项调查研究显示，中西部地区所占 GDP 份额在不断提高，去年提高到 46.16%，今年估计达到 47.1%，并且去年中西部和东北地区的最终消费份额也提高到48.6%,居民消费份额“回升”到48.68%,国家经济重心正在向中西部转移。

为提高中西部经济和社会发展水平，继西部大开发等重大举措之后，“十一五”期间，国家又发布了一系列推动区域均衡发展的政策措施。今年 2 月份，国务院常务会议提出，推动电子信息、轻工、纺织等产业向中西部地区加快转移。9 月，又出台了《国务院中西部地区承接产业转移的指导意见》。《指导意见》指出，中西部地区发挥资源丰富、要素成本低、市场潜力大的优势，积极承接国内外产业转移，不仅有利于加速中西部地区新型工业化和城镇化进程，促进区域协调发展，而且有利于推动东部沿海地区经济转型升级，在全国范围内优化产业分工格局。

市场和政策成为促进产业向中西部转移的两大推手，造就了新一轮产业转移热潮：全球 IT 代工老大富士康科技集团郑州厂区正式投产，芯片巨头英特尔关闭上海工厂并扩建成都生产基地，惠普在重庆设立笔记本电脑出口制造基地，联合利华酝酿湖南新厂，海尔、格力、美的、TCL 等家电企业计划或启动在内地建立新的生产基地……

随着终端市场“西进”浪潮的扩大，在产品包装、运输方面产生了大量的纸箱采购需求，促使作为配套企业的纸箱厂开始紧抓这一重要机遇将市场重点向中西部转移，许多纸箱厂纷纷在中部地区设厂或扩建。可以预见，不久的将来，纸箱厂将伴随着“东企西进”的潮流在中西部地区全面开花。然而面对如此大的市场蛋糕，对于纸箱厂而言想要在市场中占据一席之地，即要满足客户日益提高的生产要求又要取得绝对利润，不得不在成本控制和生产管理、设备革新上下足功夫，以其实现最为高效的生产营运模式。而对供应商而言，意味着中西部地区将需要采购更多的新瓦楞设备和技术，以更好地满足庞大的纸箱生产订单，适应纸箱企业新建、改扩建的要求。

2011 中国国际瓦楞展将成为 2011 年度的瓦楞纸箱行业的最大最专业最高效的商贸合作与交易平台。展会云集全球设备及耗材供应商企业，通过全面展示品种最为丰富、档次最为齐全的纸箱、纸板制造设备及耗材，为纸箱生产企业提供最为理想和高效的一站式考察采购服务平台，促进中国乃至全球纸箱行业的沟通与交流。

2011年全国各地节庆活动

2011 Festivals in China

成都南国冰雪节
2011/01
地点：四川成都
电话：028-8770 6026

Chengdu Southland Ice and Snow Festival
2011/01
Venue: Chengdu, Sichuan
Tel 028-8770 6026

中国长春冰雪旅游节暨净月潭瓦萨国际滑雪节
2011/01/02 - 03/06
地点：吉林长春市
内容：中国长春冰雪旅游节从1998年开始创办，到2010年已成果举办十三届，通过探索与实践，我们将冰雪旅游节产品建设定位在“冰雪结婚、以雪为主，动静结合、以动为主”上。冰雪旅游节将关注民生、惠及市民为宗旨，活动时间涵盖了元旦、春节、元宵节、圣诞节等民众喜闻乐见的节日，活动安排和产品建设上注重体现市民参与。冰雪旅游节现已成为融文化、体育、旅游、经贸、科技等多领域活动为一体的综合性节庆活动，成为向国内外展示长春社会经济发展水平和人民精神面貌的重要窗口。
电话：0431-8588 1979，8588 1978
www.changchun.gov.cn

China Changchun Show Festival
2011/01/02 - 03/06
Venue: Changchun, Jilin
Tel: 0431-8588 1979, 8588 1978
www.changchun.gov.cn

湄州妈祖文化旅游节
2011/01
地点：福建省莆田市湄州妈祖祖庙天后广场
内容：自1994年以来，已成功举办过十一届湄州妈祖文化旅游节，每届节庆都以“日谒妈祖，共享平安”为主题，其深厚的文化内涵，鲜明的地域特色，丰富的活动内容，吸引成千上万的宾朋，特别是台湾妈祖信中国前来参加，在海内外产生了轰动效应。
电话：0594-509 4688
www.mz-mazu.org.cn

Meizhou Matzu Culture Festival
2011/01
Venue: Matzu Temple, Meizhou, Putian, Fujian
Tel: 0594-509 4688
www.mz-mazu.org.cn

第十六届吉林国际雾凇冰雪节
2011/01/04 - 02/28
地点：吉林省吉林市
内容：节庆主题：观赏雾凇奇观•体验滑雪激情•感受温泉文化
打造凇、雪、泉等旅游品牌，把吉林市旅游业培育成为战略性支柱产业，2011年1月4日至2月28日吉林市将举办第十六届中国吉林国际雾凇冰雪节。在此期间将陆续开展冰雪旅游、冰雪文化、冰雪体育、冰雪经贸等八大系列48项活动。本届中国吉林国际雾凇冰雪节由省旅游局、市政府共同主办，其活动主题是：观赏雾凇奇观、体验滑雪激情、感受温泉文化。
电话：0432-216 2200

16th Jilin Intl Rime Snow Festival
2011/01/04-02/28
Venue: Jilin, Jilin
Tel: 0432-216 2200

2011中国洛阳伏牛山滑雪旅游节
2011/01/08 - 03月底
地点：河南洛阳•伏牛山滑雪度假乐园
电话：0371-6590 6029

Luoyang Mountain Funiu Skiing Festival
2011/01/08-2011/03
Venue: Luoyang, Henan
Tel: 027-8751 0686

2011年中国武汉梅花节
2011/01/10
地点：湖北省武汉市东湖梅园
内容：中国武汉梅花节是由武汉东湖风景区管委会举办，以赏梅游园、科普宣传、文化交流等为主要内容的大型文化盛会和园林盛会。
电话：027-8751 0686

Wuhan Plum-Blossom Festival
2011/1/10
Venue: Mei Garden, Donghu Lake, Wuhan, Hubei
Tel: 027-8751 0686

龙庆峡第二十五届冰灯艺术节
2011/01/16 - 02/28
地点：北京延庆龙庆峡
内容：冰灯展示
周期：每年一届
联系人：李科长
电话：010-6919 1020

China Longqingxia Intl Ice and Snow Festival
2011/01/16 - /02/28
Venue: Yanqing, Beijing
Frequency: Annual
Tel: 010-6919 1020

成都青白江第二届草莓采摘节
2011/01
地点：四川省成都市青白江区光明村
主要内容：采果、品果、美食、观光、休闲等。
主办：青白江区区政府
承办：青白江区旅游开发局、姚渡镇
联系人：孙燕
电话：028-8361 1565

2nd Chengdu Qingbaijiao Strawberry Pick-up Festival
2011/01
Venue: Mingguan Village, Qingbaijiang, Chengdu
Organizer: Qingbaijiang District Government, Chengdu, Sichuan
Tel: 028-8361 1565

2011第十三届中国•云南•罗平国际油菜花文化旅游节
2011/01/23 - 04/08
地点：云南省罗平县
节庆主题：东方花园•魅力罗平
电话：0871-634 1912

13th Luoping Rape Flower Culture Festival
2011/01/23-02/17
Venue: Luoping County, Yunnan
Tel: 0871-634 1912

首届中国铜梁龙灯文化旅游节
2011/01/28 - 02/17
地点：重庆铜梁
内容：为打响龙文化旅游品牌，助推经济社会大发展。首届中国铜梁龙灯文化旅游节将于2011年1月28日至2月17日举办。在此期间，将围绕铜梁龙灯文化开展八大系列活动，规模宏大，明星助阵，亮点纷呈。2011年是“十二五”开局之年，成功举办首届中国铜梁龙灯文化旅游节，是丰富群众精神文化生活，转变经济发展方式，做大做强龙灯文化旅游产业，助推铜梁县政治、经济、文化、社会事业和谐进步的重要载体。
电话：023-5416 8609

1st Tongliang Dragon Lantern Festival
2011/01/28-02/17
Venue: Tongliang, Chongqing
Tel: 023-5416 8609

第八届独乐寺庙会
2011/01/31 - 02/08
地点：天津蓟县，以独乐寺为中心，以渔阳古街为线，东到鼓楼广场，西到独乐寺停车场
内容：主题：弘扬民族传统文化，展现蓟州民俗风情；举办开幕式、花会调演、武术表演、戏剧曲艺演出、传统民俗展示等特色活动。
主办：天津市旅游局，蓟县人民政府
承办：县旅游经济委员会，县文化局
联系人：李天胜，蔡习军
电话：022-2914 2907
www.jx-travel.com，www.dulesi.com

Dulesi Temple Fair
2011/1/31-2011/2/8
Venue: Yuyang Ancient City, Ji Country, Tianjin
Frequency: Annual
Tel: 022-2914 2907
www.jx-travel.com
www.dulesi.com

第十一届都匀剑江旅游欢乐节
2011/01/31 - 02/17
地点：贵州都匀市都匀剑江风景区
内容：相约狂欢都匀•体验民俗文化
电话：0854-710 7372

11th Duyun Jian River Travel Festival
2011/01/31 - 02/17
Venue: Duyun, Guizhou
Tel: 0854-710 7372

2011年全国各地节庆活动 2011 Festivals in China

2011第十六届中国南京国际梅花节
2011/02
地点：南京中山陵梅花山景区
内容：中国南京国际梅花节始创于1996年，初名南京梅花节，主会场设在南京市东郊梅花山，1997年起正式定名为中国南京国际梅花节，是南京市人民政府举办的开春第一个国家级大型旅游节庆活动。每年2-3月间，该活动定期举办，并不断推陈出新，影响愈加广泛。
电话：025-8443 1599, 8443 1174

16th Nanjing Plum Blossom Festival
Venue: Meihuashan, Zhongshan Cemetery, Nanjing
Tel: 025-8443 1599, 8443 1174

宁海前童元宵文化旅游节
2011/02/16 - 03/02
地点：浙江省宁海前童古镇
内容：参加民间行会，鸣群锣、抬古亭、放铳花,同时品尝前童特色豆腐宴、特色小吃等。
电话：0574-6522 0880

Ninghai Qiantong Lantern Festival
2011/02/16 - 03/02
Venue: Qiantong Old Town, Ninghai, Zhejiang

中国重庆第十二届垫江牡丹文化节
2011/02/26 - 04/18
地点：重庆垫江县体育场
内容：盛世牡丹•多彩垫江 - 垫江太平牡丹素有"华夏牡丹之源"之称，占地共2万亩，与山石相映衬。不仅其规模大大超过洛阳牡丹，更有山野情趣，与园艺牡丹相比，别有一番韵味。2011年中国重庆第十二届垫江牡丹文化节以"盛世牡丹、多彩垫江"为主题，坚持"政府主导、市场运作、企业承办、全民参与"的总体原则。
电话：023-7468 7733
传真：023-7451 8833

12th Dianjiang Dianjiang Peony Flower Festival
Venue: Dianjiang County, Chongqing
Tel: 023-7468 7733
Fax: 023-7451 8833

成都青白江第四届杏花节
2011/03
地点：四川成都杏花村
内容：文艺演出、赏花、健身、美食、趣味活动等
主办：省旅游局市政府
承办：区旅发局、福洪乡
联系人：孙燕
电话：028-8361 1565

4th Chengdu-Qingbaijiang Apricot Festival
2011/03
Venue: Apricot Village, Chengdu
Organizer: Sichuan Provincial Tourism Bureau; Chengdu Municipal Government
Tel: 028-8361 1565

成都青白江桃花诗会
2011/03
地点：四川成都花园沟、桃花沟
内容：文艺演出、赏花、健身、美食、趣味活动等
主办：杏花村，省旅游局市政府
承办：区旅发局、福洪乡
联系人：孙燕
电话：028-8361 1565

Chengdu Qingbaijiang Peach Poetry
2011/03
Venue: Peach Gully, Qingbaijiang, Chengdu, Sichuan
Organizer: Qingbaijing District Tourism Bureau
Tel: 028-8361 1565

2011中国•成都乡村旅游节
时间：2011/03月上旬
地点：成都青白江
电话：028-8548 3355

C0hengdu Village traveling festival
Venue: Qingbaijiang, Chengdu
Tel: 028-8548 3355

河北石家庄风筝节
时间：2011年3月21—29日
地点：河北石家庄
电话：0311-8870 2005

宁海胡陈桃花节
时间：2011/03月下旬
地点：浙江宁海胡陈乡
内容：赏千亩挑花、桃花诗会、桃树竞标、婚纱摄影
电话：0574-6522 0880

Ninghai Huchen Peach Festival
2011/03
Venue: Huchen Town, Ninghai, Zhejiang
Tel: 0574-6522 0880

宁夏六盘山山花旅游文化节
2011/04
地点：宁夏固原
电话：0954-208 8040

中国兴化岛菜花旅游节
2011/04/02 - 05
地点：江苏
电话：0523-8324 6663

第三届天津渔阳"梨园情"旅游文化节
4月中旬
地点：天津蓟县下营镇团山子梨园
内容：打造春季"蓟北踏青游"旅游品牌，举办开幕式文艺演出，"畅游十里花海"春游活动，"梨花风情"农家游活动，征文、摄影大赛以及八仙山山花节、梨木台杜鹃花节等景区系列专项活动。
主办单位：天津市旅游局，蓟县人民政府
承办单位：蓟县旅游经济委员会
联系人：滕印成
电话：022-2919 1508

3rd Tianjin-Yuyang Liyuan Tourism Festival
2011/04
Venue: TuanShanzi Liyuan, Xiaying Town, Ji County, Tianjin
Organizer: Jixian Tourism Economic Committee
Tel: 022-2919 1508

北京大兴区庞各庄镇梨花节
每年4月
地点：北京大兴庞各庄镇
特色：梨花村赏花、游览万亩梨花庄园航天科普拓展教育基地、游览中国西瓜博物馆，采摘草莓蔬菜、吃农家饭、住农家院、品梨花大餐、逛购瓜乡农产品。
电话：010-8928 8545

Daxing District Panggezhuang Town Pear Festival, Beijing
2011/04
Venue: Panggezhuang Town, Daqing District, Beijing
Date: 2011/04
Tel: 010-8928 8545

安徽砀山梨花节
2011/04
地点：安徽省砀山县
电话：0557-809 5086
网站：www.adangshan.cn

Anhui Dangshan Pear Festival
2011/04
Venue: Dangshan County, Anhui
Tel: 0557-809 5086
www.adangshan.cn

2011年第上海国际茶叶博览会暨第十八届上海国际茶文化节
2011/04/23 - 25
地点：上海国际农展中心
内容：上海国际茶文化节以其独特的形式和风格，连续成功地举办了十六届，成为上海著名的旅游文化品牌和节庆活动。上海茶业•茶乡旅游博览会以"政府主导、市场运作、企业经营、社会参与"的办展模式，以全新的理念，全力打造专业化、国际化、品牌化的展会，以全新的视角，让您感受到茶文化和茶旅游的魅力。
上海茶业•茶乡旅游博览会有利于放大上海国际茶文化节品牌，集聚资源，提升影响，促进发展。展会将展出国内外新茶、精品茶、茶饮料、茶制品及茶科技衍生产品，推荐各地的主题旅游线路、世博旅游线路和景点、景观。同时开展茶艺表演、名茶推荐、旅游推广等活动，集文化旅游与茶业经济于一体，融表演、展示与交流于一炉，办成具有上海特点的茶业•茶乡旅游博览会，同时还将举办"中国名茶"评选活动。
主办：上海国际茶文化节组委会、上海市农业委员会、上海市旅游局、上海市闸北区人民政府、上海市茶叶学会
承办：上海农业展览馆、上海国际茶文化节组委会办公室、上海茶叶公司、上海帝芙特国际茶文化广场
电话：021-3303 0071, 6317 6785
传真：021-6353 5596
邮箱：teaculture@163.com
网址：www.tea-sh.cn

Shanghai International Tea Culture Festival
2011/04/23 - 25
Venue: Shanghai Eastern Art Center
Frequency: Annual
Tel: 021-3303 0071, 6317 6785
Fax: 021-6353 5596
E-mail:teaculture@163.com
www.tea-sh.cn

2011年全国各地节庆活动 2011 Festivals in China

第16届中国周庄国际旅游节开幕式及系列民俗风情活动
2011/04月中下旬
地点：浙江周庄
内容：第16届中国周庄国际旅游节开幕仪式。第三届古镇保护与发展论坛。挑花篮、打连厢、舞龙舞狮、水上划灯等大型民俗活动。
www.zhouzhuang.com

16th Zhouzhuang Tourism Festival
2011/04
Venue: Zhouzhuang, Zhejiang
www.zhouzhuang.com

2011第七届中国国际动漫节
2011/04/28 - 05/03
地点：杭州(萧山)
内容：动情都市•漫优生活
电话：0571-8687 3363

7th China Comics Festival
2011/04/28 - 05/03
Venue: Xianghan, Hangzhou, Zhejiang
Tel: 0571-8687 3363

中国茶都•信阳第十九届国际茶文化节
2011/04/28 - 30
地点：河南信阳市百花会展中心
内容：自1992年以来，信阳已连续成功举办了十八届的“中国茶都•信阳国际茶文化节”，始终坚持以“政府主导，企业参与，市场拉动，专业运作”的发展模式。得到了茶叶行业内广大参展商、专业客商以及社会各界的关心、支持和认可。目前，已逐步展现国际化、专业化的趋势，在同行业中树立了一定的权威地位，也成为国内举办的高层次高规模的茶行业盛会。
电话：0376-660 5835

19th Xinyang Tea Culture Festival
2011/04/28 - 30
Venue: Xinyang Baihua Exhibition Center, Henan
Tel: 0376-660 5835

广西兴安桂林米粉节
2011/04/28 - 05/03
地点：广西桂林
电话：0773-622 2467

Xing'an Rice Noodle Festival
2011/04/28 - 05/03
Venue: Guilin, Guangxi
Tel: 0773-622 2467

第九届中国（宁海）徐霞客开游节
2011/05
地点：浙江省宁海县
内容：第八届中国（宁海）徐霞客开游节届时会有“首届中国百强旅行社宁海高峰论坛”等系列活动，规模宏大，格调高雅。历届凯游节均获全国节庆界高度评价。
电话：0574-6550 0519

9th China(Ninghai) Xu Xiake Tourism Featival
2011/05
Venue: Ninghai, Zhejiang
Tel: 0574-6550 0519

毛家峪高尔夫球练习赛
2011/05
地点：天津毛家峪长寿度假村
内容：组织游客和村民举办高尔夫球健身运动比赛，打造国内首家高尔夫球村。
主办：毛家峪长寿度假村
电话：022-2276 2003

Maojia Valley Golf Tornament
2011/05
Venue: Maojia Valley Resort, Tianjin
Organizer: Maojia Vally Resort
Tel: 022-2276 2003

北京大兴安定桑椹文化节
每年5月下旬
地址：北京大兴安定镇
内容：游园采摘、趣味比赛等活动
电话：010-8023 3242

Beijing Daxing Anding Mulberry Festival
2011/05
Venue: Anding Town, Daxing District, Beijing
Tel: 010-8023 3242

罗江国际龙舟节
2011年（端午节）
地点：江西
电话：0730-525 0456

Luojiang Dragon Boat Festival
Venue: Jiangxi
Tel: 0730-525 0456

第十七届上海电视节
2011/06/07 - 11
地点：上海
内容：上海电视节创办于1986年12月，上海电视节包括白玉兰奖国际电视节目评选及展播、国际电视论坛、国际影视节目交易市场以及国际新媒体与广播影视设备市场。
主办：国家广播电影电视总局，上海市人民政府
承办：上海市文化广播电视管理局，上海文化广播影视管理局，上海文化广播影视集团
电话：021-6253 7115
www.stvf.com

17th Shanghai TV Festival(STVF)
2011/06/07 - 11
Venue: Shanghai
Profile: Established in December 1086, Shanghai TV co-hosted by the State Administration of Radio, Film & TV and the Shanghai Municipal Government, and organized by Shanghai Municipal Administration of Culture, Radio, Film & TV and the Special Events Office of Shanghai Media & Entertainment Group. STVF contains 4 main sections: Magnolia Award International TV Program Competition, International Film and TV Market, New Media and International Broadcasting Equipment Market and International TV Forum.
Tel: 021-6253 7115
www.stvf.com

第十四届上海电影节
2011/06/11 - 19
地点：上海
内容：创办于1993年的上海国际电影节，上海国际电影节是中国唯一经国际电影制片人协会（FIAPH）认证的国际电影节，其主体内容包括：“金爵奖”国际影片评选、“亚洲新人奖”评选、国际电影展映、电影市场和电影论坛。其中，2007年起新设的电影市场，包括电影交易市场和中国电影项目投创两个板块。
主办：中国国家广播电影电视总局，上海市人民政府
承办：上海市文化广播影视剧，上海文化广播影视集团
电话：021-6252 7115
www.siff.com

14th Shanghai International Film Festival(SIFF)
2011/06/11 - 19
Venue: Shanghai
Profile: The Shanghai International Film Festival (SIFF), originated in 1993, is hosted by the State Administration of Radio, Film & Television and Shanghai Municipal Government and organized by Shanghai Municipal Administration of Culture, Radio, Film & TV and SMEG is China' s only A category international film Festival accredited by FIAPH. Its main section are Jin Jue Award. Asian New Talent Award, International Film Panorama, SIFF Mart and Film Forum. The SIFF Mart, initiated in 2007, includes Film Market and China' s Film Pitch & Catch (CFPC)
Tel: 021-6252 7115
www.siff.com

2011年第七届新疆国际旅游节
2011/06/26
地点：新疆克拉玛依
内空：2011年第七届新疆国际旅游节，是在国家和自治区将旅游业列为国民经济支柱性产业的历史背景下，在新疆提出促进旅游业跨越式发展的新形势下举办，国家与自治区人民政府都极为重视，规格高，影响力大。举办新疆国际旅游节，以节造势、以势聚客、以客促发展，对于克拉玛依市打造“世界石油城”、推动社会经济跨越式发展将产生十分深远的影响。
电话：0991-883 3199

Xinjiang Intl Tourism Festival
2011/06/26
Venue: Karamay, Xinjiang
Tel: 0991-883 3199

成都都江堰漂流节
2011/07
地点：四川成都
电话：028-8770 6026

Dujiangyan Drifting Festival
2011/07
Venue: Dujiangyan, Chengdu, Sichuan
Tel: 028-8770 6026

双溪水上狂欢节
2011/07/15
地点：浙江杭州
电话：0571-8850 1938

Shuangxi Water Carnival
2011/07/15
Venue: Hangzhou, Zhejiang
Tel: 0571-8850 1938

2011年全国各地节庆活动 2011 Festivals in China

第二十届青岛国际啤酒节
2011/08/14 - 29
地点：山东青岛
内容：青岛国际啤酒节始创于 1991年，每年在青岛的黄金旅游季节8月的第二个周末开幕，为期16天。 节日由国家有关部委和青岛市人民政府共同主办，是融旅游、文化、体育、经贸于一体的国家级大型节庆活动。 啤酒节的主题口号是“青岛与世界干杯！”。

经过十九届的举办，青岛国际啤酒节已逐渐成为青岛这座美丽海滨 城市的一张亮丽的城市名片，在国内外具有了相当的知名度和影响力。
电话：0532-8889 9019

Qingdao International Beer Festival
2011/08/14 - 29
Venue: Qingdao, Shandong

Qingdao International Beer Festival was initiated in 1991, and opens in the second weekend of August each year for 16 days, which is the golden tourism season in Qingdao. It is hold by the national relevant ministries and commissions and the People's Government of Qingdao Municipality. It is the large national festival combined with tourism, culture, sports, economy and trade. The theme slogan of the Beer Festival is Qingdao Toasts with the World!

After 19 Beer Festivals, Qingdao International Beer Festival has gradually become a bright city name card of Qingdao-the beautiful seaside city, and has well-known reputation and influence in China and the world .

中国石林国际火把节
2011/07 - 2011/08
地点：云南省昆明石林风景区
内容：传统斗牛、摔跤、歌舞、招商引资。
电话：0871-7796 251, 7796 256

Shilin Torch Festival
2011/07 - 2011/08
Venue: Shilin, Yunnan
Tel: 0871-7796 695, 7796 256

北京大兴采育葡萄文化节
每年8月中旬
地址：北京大兴采育镇
内容：特色:观光采摘、吃农家饭、住农家院、品葡萄美酒、观葡萄博物馆等
电话:010-8027 3611

Beijing Daxiang Caiyu Pick-up Grape Festival
2011/08
Venue: Caiyu Town, Daxing District, Beijing
Tel: 010-8027 3611

中国国际钱江观潮节
2011/08
地点：浙江
电话：0573-8728 8406

Qiangtan River Tidal Bore Festival
2011/08
Venue: Zhejiang
Tel: 0415-221 1063

中国鸭绿江国际旅游节
2011/08
地点：辽宁丹东
电话：0415-221 1063

Yalu River Intl Tourism Festival
2011/08
Venue: Dandong, Liaoning

北京大兴庞各庄金秋采摘节
每年9月
地址：北京大兴庞各庄镇
内容观光采摘、参观航天科普教育基地、趣味比赛、文化表演等
电话：010-8928 8545

Daxing Panggezhuang Golden Autumn Pick-up Festival
2011/9
Venue: Panggezhuang Town, Daxing District, Beijing

第六届蓟县“农家乐”厨艺大赛
2011/09
地点：天津蓟县
内容：组织农家院旅游经营户举办厨艺大赛，促进农家餐饮厨艺技能交流，展示我县农家乐旅游发展成果。
主办：蓟县旅游经济委员会
承办：农家院旅游特色村
电话：022-2919 1532

Farmer Happiness Tourism Activities
Whole year long
Venue: Ji County, Tianjin
Tel: 022-2919 1508

中国曲阜国际孔子文化节
2011/09/26 - 30
地点：山东省济宁县曲阜
内容：中国（曲阜）国际孔子文化节是融学术纪念、文化旅游、经科贸于一体的大型国际性节庆活动，自1984年起，每年孔子诞辰（公历9月28日）前后在孔子故里曲阜举行。
电话：0537-3202 805
网址：www.e-kongzi.com

China (Qufu) International Confucius Culture Festival
2011/09/26 - 30
Venue: Qufu, Jining city, Shandong Province, China
Profile: China (Qufu) International Confucius Cultural Festival is a large international celebration integrating commemoration, culture, tourism, economy, science and commerce. It has been held around the birthday of Confucius (28th of September) in his hometown-Qufu since 1984.
Tel: 0537-3202 805
www.e-kongzi.com

成都青白江草地风情节
2011/10
地点：四川成都
内容：文艺演出、民俗文化展示、草地骑马、草地摩托、草地射箭、高尔夫球体验、风情美食等
主办：成都市旅游局、区政府
联系人：孙燕
电话：028-8361 1565

Chengdu Qingbaijiang Grassland Festival
2011/10
Venue: Chengdu, Sichuan
Organizer: Chengdu Municipal Tourism Bureau
Tel: 028-8361 1565

2011年中国云台山国际旅游节
2011/10/23 - 27(拟)
地点：河南焦作
主办：国家旅游局 河南省人民政府
承办：河南省旅游局 焦作市人民政府
电话：0391－770 9001

Yuntai Mountain Intl Tourism Festival
2011/10/23-27
Venue: Jiaozuo, Henan
Organizer: Henan Travel Bureau; Jiaozuo Municipal Government
Tel: 0391-770 9001

中国仙都旅游文化节
2011/10/25 - 27
地点：浙江仙都
电话：0578-312 0301

Xiandu Tourism and Culture Festival
2011/10/25-27
Venue: Jinyun County, Xiandu, Zhejiang

魅力东钱湖幸福休闲节
2011/10/31 - 11/03
地点：浙江宁波
电话：0574－8837 3737

Dongqian Lake Leisure Festival
2011/10/31-11/03
Venue: Ningbo, Zhejiang

中国舟山海洋文化节
2011/10
地点：浙江舟山
电话：0580-203 6333

Zhoushan Sea Culture Festival
2011/10
Venue: Zhoushan, Zhejiang

第四届黄海国际美食文化节
2011/11
地点：江苏盐城
内容：金秋盐城，菊黄蟹肥，稻谷飘香。黄海之滨，鹿踏海缨，茉莉花开，飞鹤传情。

第四届黄海国际美食文化节暨乡绿海蓝杯乡土菜烹饪大奖赛、第二届全国海参烹饪大奖赛，在国家级旅游城市，享有麋鹿之家、丹顶鹤之乡、东方湿都之称的盐城再度登场
电话：0515-8310 0471, 13814341177

4th Yellow Sea Food Festival
2011/11
Venue: Yancheng, Zhejiang
Tel: 0515-8310 0471. 13814341177

中国开渔节
2011/11/14
地点：浙江舟山
电话：0574-6576 7203

China Fishing Opening Festival
2011/11/14
Venue: Zhoushan, Zhejiang

成都火龙节
2011/12
地点：四川成都
电话：028-87706026

Chengdu Fire Dragon Festivel
2011/12
Profile: Lanterns, fireworks, dancing.
Venue: Chengdu, Sichuan

推荐参加下列机构主办的展览和会议

Recommend You the Exhibitions and Conferences Organized by Following Organizers

科隆展览中国有限公司	Koelnmesse Co Ltd China
中国哈尔滨经济贸易洽谈会办公室	Administration Office of China Harbin Fair for Trade and Economic Cooperation
北京中装华港建筑科技展览有限公司	China B&D Exhibition co ltd
中国演艺设备技术协会	China Entertainment Technology Association
中国铸造协会	China Foundry Association
中国对外贸易广州展览总公司	China Foreign Trade Guangzhou Exhibition Corporation
中国昆明进出口商品交易会	China Import & Export Fair, Kunming
中国机械工程学会及焊接分会	Chinese Mechanical Engineering Society;Welding instution of CMES
中国贸促会轻工行业分会	CCPIT Sub-Council of Light Industry
中国国际贸易中心股份有限公司	China World Trade Center Co Ltd
北京爱博西亚展览有限公司	Exposium-SIAL Exhibition Co Ltd
广东省玩具协会	Guangdong Toy Association
香港贸易发展局	Hong Kong Trade Development Council
晋江市展务有限公司	Jinjiang Exhibition Affairs Co Ltd, Fujian
晋江市展务有限公司	Jinjiang Exhibition Affairs Co Ltd, Fujian
澳门贸易投资促进局	Macao Trade and Investment
大韩贸易投资振兴公社	Korea Trade-Investment Promotion Agency
励展博览集团	Reed Exhibitions
励展博览集团国际销售部	Reed Exhibitions International Sales Group
奥克坦姆系统科技（苏州）有限公司	OCTANORM ® System Technology (Suzhou) Co Ltd
上海市国际展览有限公司	Shanghai International Exhibition co ltd
上海里扬展览服务有限公司	Shanghai Neon Exhibition Service Ltd
显辉国际展览有限公司	Top Repute Co Ltd
亚洲博闻	UBM Asia
宁波雅卓展览服务有限公司	Younage Exhibition Co Ltd
浙江中国小商品城集团股份有限公司	Zhejiang China Commodities City Group Co Ltd

国内展览会议
城市索引

北京......2
重庆......24
上海......25
天津......65

安徽-合肥......66
安徽-淮南......67

福建-福州......67
福建-晋江......67
福建-石狮......68
福建-厦门......68

甘肃-兰州......71

广东-东莞......71
广东-佛山......75
广东-广州......75
广东-惠州......95
广东-深圳......96
广东-顺德......102

广西-南宁......102

贵州-贵阳......104
海南-海口......105

河北-唐山......105
黑龙江-哈尔滨......106

河南-漯河......108
河南-洛阳......108
河南-郑州......108

湖北-武汉......111

湖南-长沙......113

内蒙古-包头......114
内蒙古-呼和浩特......114
内蒙古-鄂尔多斯......114

江苏-常州......115
江苏-连云港......116
江苏-南京......116
江苏-苏州......117

江西-南昌......117

吉林-长春......118
辽宁-大连......119
辽宁-沈阳......121

宁夏-银川......127

陕西-西安......128
陕西-杨凌......129

山东-济南......130
山东-临沂......131
山东-青岛......132
山东-烟台......137

山西-太原......139

四川-成都......139

新疆-乌鲁木齐......144

云南-昆明......145

浙江-杭州......147
浙江-宁波......148
浙江-绍兴......150
浙江-台州......150
浙江-温州......151
浙江-义乌......153
浙江-永康......155
浙江-余姚......155

其他......156

Exhibitions and Fairs in Mainland China
Index of Cities

Beijing......2
Chongqing......24
Shanghai......25
Tianjin......65

Anhui-Hefei......66
Anhui-Huainan......67

Fujian-Fuzhou......67
Fujian-Jinjiang......67
Fujian-Shishi......68
Fujian-Xiamen......68

Gansu-Lanzhou......71

Guangdong-Dongguan......71
Guangdong-Foshan......75
Guangdong-Guangzhou......75
Guangdong-Huizhou......95
Guangdong-Shenzhen......96
Guangdong-Shunde......102

Guangxi-Nanning......102

Guizhou-Guiyang......104

Hainan-Haikou......105

Hebei-Tangshan......105

Heilongjiang-Harbin......106

Henan-Luohe......108
Henan-Luoyang......108
Henan-Zhengzhou......108

Hubei-Wuhan......111

Hunan-Changsha......113

Inner Mongolia-Baotou......114
Inner Mongolia-Hohhot......114
Inner Mongolia-Ordos......114

Jiangsu-Changzhou......115
Jiangsu-Lianyungang......116
Jiangsu-Nanjing......116
Jiangsu-Suzhou......117

Jiangxi-Nanchang......117

Jilin-Changchun......118

Liaoning-Dalian......119
Liaoning-Shenyang......121

Ningxia-Yinchuan......127

Shaanxi-Xi'an......128

Shaanxi-Yangling......129

Shandong-Jinan......130
Shandong-Linyi......131
Shandong-Qingdao......132
Shandong-Yantai......137

Shanxi-Taiyuan......139

Sichuan-Chengdu......139

Xinjing-Urumqi......144

Yunnan-Kunming......145

Zhejiang-Hangzhou......147
Zhejiang-Ningbo......148
Zhejiang-Shaoxing......150
Zhejiang-Taizhou......150
Zhejiang-Wenzhou......151
Zhejiang-Yiwu......153
Zhejiang-Yongkang......155
Zhejiang-Yuyao......155

Others......156

北京 Beijing

2011/01/11 - 14
☎ 010-8501 8357
🖷 010-8562 5510
✉ barry@fushionbj.com
www.fur-fair.com

中国国际裘皮革皮制品交易会
地点：国际会议中心，北京
内容：裘皮原料、裘皮服装、鞋帽、配件及饰品、设计与媒体、化工硝染、机械、其他。
始办年份：1976
30 **周期：**每年一届
市场范围：国际性
性质：面向贸易观众
上届规模 2010：展览面积28,000m^2(国外展商8,000m^2)，参展商200家（国外展商30家，来自20个国家）
主办：中国土产畜产进出口总公司
地址：北京市朝阳区朝阳门南大街8号中粮福临门大厦（100020）
联系人：徐洪强

China Fur and Leather Products Fair
Venue: China National Convention Center, Beijing
Profile: Fur Skins, Fur Garments, Shoes and Hats, Accessories and Decorations, Design, Media, Tanning, Machinery, Others.
Established Year: 1976
Frequency: Annual
Market Area: International
Statistics 2010: Exhibition Area 28,000m^2(foreigners 8,000m^2), Exhibitors 200（foreigners 30, came from 20 countries）
Organizer: China National Native Produce and Animal-by Products Imp. & Exp. Corp
Address: COFCO Fortune Plaza, No. 8 Chao Yang Men South Str. Chao Yang District, Beijing
Contact: Barry Xu
www.fur-fair.com

2011/02/17 - 19
☎ 010-5820 3101/02/03
🖷 010-5820 3100
✉ LIJIANG@CHINAFISH.CN
www.chinafishshow.org
www.chinafish.cn

第二十一届中国国际钓鱼用品贸易展览会
地点：中国国际展览中心新馆，北京
内容：为从事渔具产品,渔具设备,原材料,配件以及休闲户外产品的开发,研制,生产及销售的制造商,贸易商及服务商搭建展览会贸易平台。
始办年份：1991
40 首届
周期：每年一届
市场范围：国际性
性质：面向贸易观众
参展费用：标准展位7,920元
上届规模 2010：展览面积35,000m^2(国外展商1,280m^2)，参展商509家（国外展商32家，来自12个国家），专业贸易观众1,852人
主办：北京澳钦润江展览有限公司；中国国际贸易中心股份有限公司
地址：北京市朝阳区建国路93号万达广场5#9层（100022）
联系人：李江

21th International Fishing Trickle Trade Exhibition
Venue: China International Exhibition Center New Venue, Beijing
Profile: WE DEVOTE OUR ATTENTION TO PROVIDE A TRADING PLATFORM FOR THOSE MANUFACTURERS AND TRADERS WHO ENGAGE IN THE DEVELOPMENT, PRODUCTIONS AND SALE OF FISHING TACKLES, OUTDOOR EQUIPMENT, RAW MATERIALS AS WELL AS ACCESSORIES.
Established Year: 1991
Frequency: Annual
Market Area: International
Nature: Trade Only
Participated Fee: Standard Booth RMB 7,920
Statistics 2010: Exhibition Area 35,000m^2(foreigners 1,280m^2), Exhibitors 509（foreigners 32, came from 12 countries）, Trade Visitors 1,852
Organizer: BEIJING ADMIRE EXHIBITION CO LTD; CHINA WORLD TRADE CENTER CO LTD
Address: 9F, BUILDING 5# WANDA PLAZA, NO.93 JIANGUO RD. CHAOYANG DISTRICT, BEIJING CHINA
Contact: LI JIANG

2011/02/25 - 27
☎ 010-5797 0888
🖷 010-5797 0999
www.ciaacexpo.com.cn

第12届汽车用品暨改装汽车展览会
地点：中国国际展览中心新馆，北京
内容：汽车用品展 美容护理用品、汽车内饰、汽车外饰、汽车影音娱乐、车载通讯导航、汽车安全用品、汽车电子电器 节能用
50 品、环保用品、户外用品、汽车轮毂、轮胎、油品、改装车及汽车改装用品
周期：每年两届
市场范围：国际性
入场券价格：50元
参展费用：净地6,800元/展位
上届规模：展览面积70,000m^2，参展商2,000家（来自28个国家）
主办：中国国际商会；北京雅森国际展览有限公司
承办：北京雅森国际展览有限公司
地址：北京市西城区裕民路18号北环中心A座505（100029）
联系人：钟亚楠，胡莹莹
MSN：MSN:zhongyanan@live.cn
QQ：499854194

The 12th China Intl Expo for Auto Electronics, Accessories, Tuning & Car Care products
Venue: China International Exhibition Center New Venue, Beijing
Profile: Car Care, Automotive Interior and Exterior Accessories, Automotive Entertainment, Alarm System, Navigation System, Auto Electronics & Appliances, Car Protection products, ,Auto Environment-friendly Products, Outdoor Equipments, Tires, Tire accessories, Lubricants, Oil additives, Tuning products
Frequency: Biannual
Market Area: International
Cost to Attend: RMB 50:-
Participated Fee: RMB 6,800/booth
Statistics 2010: Exhibition Area 70,000m^2, Exhibitors 2,000（came from 28 countries）
Organizer: YASN International Exhibition Co Ltd
Address: Suite 505, Tower A, North Ring Center, 18 Yumin Rd. Xicheng Dist. Beijing 100029, China

2011/02/27 -
☎ 010-6505 0540, 6505 7688
www.ecwtc.com
60

M.Y.COMIC 游园会
地点：中国国际贸易中心，北京

M.Y.COMIC
Venue: China World Trade Center, Beijing

2011/03/02 - 05
☎ 010-8460 0906, 13522602557
🖷 010-8460 0910

2011北京建材展览会–第十八届中国（北京）国际建筑装饰及材料博览会
地点：中国国际展览中心新馆，北京
70 **内容：**建筑陶瓷及厨房、卫浴设施系列：建筑陶瓷、各类地砖、马赛克、卫生洁具、感应洁具、陶瓷浴缸、淋浴房、整体浴室、

China International Building Decorations and Building Materials Exposition
Venue: China International Exhibition Center New Venue, Beijing
Frequency: Annual
Participated Fee: Standard Booth (3mx3m) USD 250/m^2, Raw Space USD 220/m^2

桑拿游泳设备、龙头、花洒、水箱配件、洗面器、洁身器、烘手器、坐便器、浴室镜、浴室柜、旋转衣架及配套五金、整体厨房、橱柜、壁柜及橱柜板材相关配套产品；厨房家用电器、燃气灶、热水器、抽油烟机等。各类门业五金系列 自动门、车库门、卷帘门、金属门、防盗门、保温门、室内门、复合门、铁艺、仿古铜门、欧式艺术大门等及配套产品及门禁、管状电机；各类建筑装饰五金、门控五金、卫浴配件、幕墙五金、家具五金及各类材质门窗系列。>>墙纸布艺系列 PVC塑料墙纸、草麻墙纸、无纺墙纸、吸音墙纸、胶面墙纸、绒线墙纸、萤光墙纸、玻璃纤维壁布及布基、PVC油墨、印花辊、压花辊及墙纸机械等；各类布艺及地毯 >>玻璃制品系列 玻璃马赛克、装饰艺术玻璃、安全玻璃、防火玻璃、彩色玻璃、钢化玻璃、制镜玻璃、玻璃贴膜、卫浴玻璃、家具玻璃、家居玻璃、石英玻璃、功能玻璃、光电玻璃的专业制造商；装饰类玻璃机械的制造商、玻璃类的相关产品。 石材系列 荒料、板材、异型制品、石雕制品、GRC、砂岩、环境装饰、机械设备及工具。涂料墙衣系列: 各类涂料、墙衣、室内墙体材料。新型建材系列: 天花吊顶系列；智能建筑系列；干混砂浆系列；遮阳系列；阳光房系列；绿色节能建材系列；整体家居: 衣柜、橱柜、推拉门、移门、折叠门、衣帽间厨房/浴室家居、隔断、铝门、型材等。

周期：每年一届

参展费用：标准展台(9m²) :国内企业8,200元，合资企业11,800元，海外企业250美元；净地（36m²起）国内企业850元/m²，合资企业11,800元/m²，海外企业220元/m²

主办：中国建筑装饰协会；中国国际展览中心集团公司

地址：北京市朝阳区北三环东路六号国展中心一号馆四层388室（北京中装华港建筑科技展览有限公司）（100028）

联系人：牛娜

Organizer: China B & D Exhibition Co Ltd
Contact: Ms Niu Na

2011/03/02 - 05
☎ 010-8460 0906, 13522602557
🖷 010-8460 0910

80

中国（北京）国际集成吊顶及天花材料博览会

地点：中国国际展览中心新馆全馆，北京 CIEC

内容：集成吊顶系统：取暖模块、换气模块、照明模块、射灯模块、吊顶模块、音乐模块、其他模块；铝扣板、石膏板、硅酸钙板、矿棉板，ps板、夹板、防火板等系统； 天花集成吊顶的种类大致可分为：石膏吊顶、PVC吊顶、合金吊顶。吊顶天花；吊顶吸音、隔音材料；膨胀珍珠岩吸音板、水泥、纤维复合材料等。集成吊顶的取暖系统、换气系统、照明系统、音乐系统；主龙骨、次龙骨、横撑龙骨、吊杆，龙骨吊件、挂件、浴霸. 连接件等各类吊顶五金配件等。集成环保灶、油烟机、燃气灶、消毒柜、厨房电器、厨房洁具等

周期：每年一届

参展费用：标准展台(9m²) :国内企业8,200元，合资企业11,800元，海外企业250美元；净地（36m²起）国内企业850元/m²，合资企业11,800元/m²，海外企业220元/m²

主办：中国贸促会；中国建筑装饰协会；中国国际展览中心集团公司

地址：北京市朝阳区北三环东路六号国展中心一号馆四层388室（北京中装华港建筑科技展览有限公司）（100028）

联系人：牛娜

Venue: China International Exhibition Center New Venue, Beijing
Frequency: Annual
Participated Fee: Standard Booth (3mx3m) USD 250/m², Raw Space USD 220/m²
Organizer: China B & D Exhibition Co Ltd
Contact: Ms Niu Na

2011/03/02 - 05
☎ 010-8460 0906, 13522602557
🖷 010-8460 0910

90

第十一届中国（北京）国际墙纸布艺展览会

地点：中国国际展览中心新馆，北京 CIEC

内容：墙纸系列:PVC塑料墙纸、草麻墙纸、无纺墙纸、吸音墙纸、胶面墙纸、绒线墙纸、萤光墙纸；玻璃纤维壁布：布艺系列、提花装饰布、印花装饰布、阻燃装饰布、变色装饰布、经编装饰布、色织装饰布、工艺布、静电植绒、手绣、刺绣烂花、剪花、绣花、绉纱、玻璃纱、夹层纱、欧根纱、柯根纱、玻璃纱、雪纱等；家纺设计：窗饰产品系列、百叶帘、卷帘、罗马帘、垂直帘、幕帘、开合帘、木制窗帘、草艺窗帘、电动窗帘、工艺画窗帘、遥控窗帘、PVC窗帘、百叶窗、百折帘、风琴窗帘、水波帘、镂空窗帘、隐形窗帘、遮阳及各种控制系统等。

地毯系列：汽车用地毯、家用地毯、商用地毯、展览用地毯、PVC方块地毯、改性沥青方块地毯、聚铵酯地毯、人造草皮、毛纤及纤维地毯、簇绒地毯、仿丝/丙仑/晴仑/涤仑地毯等；尼龙/纯羊毛/竹地毯等；印花及卷帘地毯机织地毯、手工地毯、针制地毯、机制地毯、皇宫地毯、平针地毯、波斯地毯、手绣地毯、阿克斯明斯特纺织地毯、威尔顿纺织地毯，方块地毯、条毯、挂毯、满铺地毯；墙纸生产及辅料：纸基PVC 油墨、印花辊、压花辊等；窗饰配件系列：窗帘杆、窗帘带、窗帘钩、窗帘轨、窗帘盒、窗帘机、窗帘马达、窗帘夹、窗帘灯、铁环、拉链、按扣、流苏；其它：各类墙饰、墙衣、家居用品

周期：每年一届

参展费用：国内企业：8,200元/9m²，11,000元/12m²，净地850元/m²；合资企业：11,800元/9m²，净地1,280元/m²；海外企业净地220～250美元/m²

主办：中国建筑装饰协会、中国国际展览中心集团公司

地址：北京市朝阳区北三环东路六号国展中心一号馆四层388室（北京中装华港建筑科技展览有限公司）（100028）

联系人：牛娜

11th China (Beijing) Wallpaper Exhibition

Venue: China International Exhibition Center New Venue, Beijing
Frequency: Annual
Participated Fee: Standard Booth (3mx3m) USD 250/m², Raw Space USD 220/m²
Organizer: China B & D Exhibition Co Ltd
Contact: Ms Niu Na

100

2011/03/02 - 05
☎ 010-8460 0906, 13522602557
🖷 010-8460 0910

第十届中国国际橱柜、壁柜、隔断、木业展览会
地点：中国国际展览中心新馆，北京
内容：厨柜、壁柜、隔断：厨柜系列；壁柜系列、衣柜、衣帽间、陈列组合柜、卫浴梳洗组合柜、旋转衣架、鞋帽柜；推拉门、隔断门、折叠门、移门；酒店高隔断、办公间隔断、卫生间隔断、办公位隔断、系统隔断墙木业、玻璃：木制门窗、线条、踢脚、地板等系列环保、木制配套装饰产品；装饰艺术玻璃、幕墙玻璃、安全玻璃、防火玻璃、镀膜玻璃、彩色玻璃、钢化玻璃、制镜玻璃、玻璃家具等；楼梯
参展费用：标准展台($9m^2$) :国内企业8,200元，合资企业11,800元，海外企业250美元；净地（$36m^2$起）国内企业850元/m^2，合资企业11,800元/m^2，海外企业220元/m^2
主办：中国建筑装饰协会；中国国际展览中心集团公司
地址：北京市朝阳区北三环东路六号国展中心一号馆四层388室（北京中装华港建筑科技展览有限公司）（100028）
联系人：牛娜

10th China Cupboard, Closet，Wood Exhibition
Venue: China International Exhibition Center New Venue, Beijing
Participated Fee: Standard Booth (3mx3m) USD 250/m^2, Raw Space USD 220/m^2
Organizer: China B & D Exhibition Co Ltd
Contact: Ms Niu Na

110

2011/03/02 - 05
☎ 010-8460 0906, 13522602557
🖷 010-8460 0910
✉ niuna226@163.com

2011北京玻璃展览会–中国国际建筑装饰艺术玻璃及技术博览会
地点：中国国际展览中心新馆，北京
内容：玻璃系列：建筑玻璃、装饰玻璃、艺术玻璃、移门系列、沙雕系列、吹制系列、玻璃琉璃、车刻彩绘、玻璃贴膜、彩晶立线、玻璃马赛克、制镜玻璃、卫浴玻璃、晶玉玻璃、家具玻璃、功能玻璃专业制造商；装饰类玻璃机械的制造商；玻璃耗材类的相关产品。
参展费用：标准展台($9m^2$) :国内企业8,200元，合资企业11,800元，海外企业250美元；净地（$36m^2$起）国内企业850元/m^2，合资企业11,800元/m^2，海外企业220元/m^2
主办：中国贸促会；中国建筑装饰协会；中国玻璃产业联合商会
承办：北京中装华港建筑科技展览有限公司
地址：北京市朝阳区北三环东路六号国展中心一号馆四层388室（100028）
联系人：牛娜
QQ：1204234541

2011 Beijing Glass Exhibition
Venue: China International Exhibition Center New Venue, Beijing
Participated Fee: Standard Booth (3mx3m) USD 250/m^2, Raw Space USD 220/m^2
Organizer: China B & D Exhibition Co Ltd

120

2011/03/03 - 05
☎ 010-8460 0666/67/68
🖷 010-8460 0669
✉ CIHE-HVAC@163.com
www.cihe-hvac.com

中国(北京)国际供热空调、卫生洁具及城建设备与技术展览会
地点：中国国际展览中心，北京
内容：供热、采暖设备展区，太阳能建筑一体化及新能源展区，燃气技术与设备展区，室内环境、空调、通风设备展区，暖通泵、阀、给排水设备展区，陶瓷卫浴、五金配件及浴室设备展区
参展费用：国内企业：标准展位（$9m^2$）10,800元，室内净地（$36m^2$起）1,100元/m^2；合资企业：标准展位（$9m^2$）11,800元，室内净地（$36m^2$起）1,280元/m^2；外资企业：标准展位（$9m^2$）3,000美元，室内净地（$36m^2$起）300美元/m^2
主办：中国贸促会建设行业分会；中国城镇供热协会；中国建筑金属结构协会采暖散热器委员会；中国城市燃气学会应用专业委员会分户燃气供暖分会；中国建筑金属结构协会地面供暖委员会；中国国际展览中心集团公司
地址：北京市朝阳区北三环东路六号中国国际展览中心一号馆四层380室（100028）

China International Trade Fair for Sanitation, Heating & Air-Conditioning
Venue: China International Exhibition Center, Beijing
Frequency: Annual
Participated Fee: Standard Booth USD 3,000/$9m^2$, Raw Space USD 300/m^2 (min $36m^2$)
Organizer: Beijing B & D Tiger Exhibition Co Ltd

130

2011/03/05 - 08
☎ 010-6505 0540, 6505 7688
www.ecwtc.com

2011北京国际创意礼品及工艺品展览会
地点：中国国际贸易中心，北京

2011 Beijing International Creative Gift & Craftwork Exhibition
Venue: China World Trade Center, Beijing

140

2011/03/09 - 12
☎ 010-8460 0990/91/92/93
🖷 010-8460 0982/89
✉ bjzzwj@126.com
www.door-expo.com

CIDE–2011第十届中国国际门业展览会
地点：中国国际展览中心新馆，北京
内容：门业：包括实木门、装饰工艺门、生态门、钢木门、免漆门、竹木门、防盗门、防火门、复合门、模压门、木塑门、吸塑门、隔断门、橱柜门、折叠门、滑动拉门、保温门、铝塑门、移门、百叶门、镶嵌玻璃木门等；门业辅料：木皮、木塑、高分子材料、密封材料等门业新材料；门业机械：制门机械、门成套生产及加工设备；门禁五金：门控门禁技术、锁具及门窗五金配件；门业化工：门业涂料、油漆化工产品。
始办年份：2002
周期：每年一届
市场范围：国际性
性质：面向贸易观众
入场券价格：凭名片或现场登记观众信息免费入场参观
参展费用：8,800元/展位，净地880元/m^2
上届规模 2010：展览面积70,000m^2，参展商628家，参观人数100,000人
主办：中国林产工业协会
承办：北京中装伟佳展览策划有限公司
地址：北京市朝阳区北三环东路6号中国国际展览中心一号馆4层387室（100028）
联系人：宋斌 吴玉玺
QQ：273978889；873693910

The 10th China International Door Industry Exhibition
Venue: China International Exhibition Center New Venue, Beijing
Profile: Doors: wooden door, decorative door，ectopic door, steel-wood door, paint less door, bamboo door, ant-theft door, fire door, composite door, mould pressing door, wood engraved door, PVC door, partition door, cabinet door, folding door, sliding door, metal door, thermal door, aluminum door, lift door, blind door, copper engraved door, glass embedded wooden door, etc. ; Door auxiliary materials: wood laminate, wood engraving, polymer materials, sealing materials, etc.; Door equipment: door production and processing equipment; Door access technology: Door access door control and door access technologies, lock and door and window hardware supplements; Door chemical industry: Coating and paint products for doors.
Established Year: 2002
Frequency: Annual
Market Area: International
Nature: Trade Only
Cost to Attend: Free to buyers*
Participated Fee: Standard Booth RMB 8,800；Raw Space RMB 880/m^2
Statistics 2010: Exhibition Area 70,000m^2, Exhibitors 628，Visitors 100,000
Organizer: Beijing B & D WSJ United Strategy for Exhibition Co Ltd
Address: Rm.387, 4/F, Hall 1, China International Exhibition Center, No. 6 E. 3rd Ring Rd North, Beijing

2011/03/12 - 13
☎ 010-6505 0540, 6505 7688
www.ecwtc.com
150

第十六届中国国际教育巡回展
地点：中国国际贸易中心，北京

The 16th China International Education Exhibition Tour
Venue: China World Trade Center, Beijing

2011/03/16 - 19
☎ 010-5933 9166
🖷 010-5933 9199
✉ amy.xie@reedhuaqun.com
ada.zhang@reedhuaqun.com
www.giftsbeijing.com
170

第23届北京国际礼品、赠品及家庭用品展览会
地点：中国国际展览中心，北京
内容：成为北方地区最权威、最专业、最具影响力的礼品展览会。包括礼品、玩具、工艺品、赠品、金属摆件、水晶玻璃制品、琉璃制品、陶瓷、广告礼品等；家庭用品、家纺、床上用品、厨房用品、家用小电器等；文具办公用品、精品文具等；纸制品、包装产品、钟表、饰品、时尚配饰、手机饰品、摆件饰品等；旅游用品、户外用品、旅游登山用品、器具、皮具箱包等；美容保健品、保健品、保健器具、美容器具等；收藏品、邮币、古董、微章、纪念品、奥运礼品等；家居饰品、布艺、雕刻工艺品、艺术古典家私、装饰画、字画、花卉、人造植物、艺术灯饰等；媒体、协会及贸易服务等。
参展费用：标准展位（9m^2）1号馆9800元，2～8号馆：单开口8,800元，双开口加500元；特装展位930元/m^2(36m^{2}起租)
性质：面向贸易观众
入场券价格：免费
预计规模：展览总面积40,000m^2, 参展商1,300家
主办：北京励展华群展览有限公司
地址：北京市朝阳区新源南路1-3号平安国际金融中心A座15层01-03，05（100027）
联系人：谢辉

China Beijing Intl Gifts, Premium & Houseware Exhibition
Venue: China International Exhibition Center, Beijing
Profile: The show presents a unique price and made to order sourcing advantage benefiting thousands of buyers arriving from around the region in the peak of the gift sourcing season.
Nature: Trade Only
Cost to Attend: Free
Expectation: Exhibition Area 40,000m^2, Exhibitors 1,300
Organizer: Reed Huaqun Exhibitions
Address: Unit 01-03,05, 15th Floor, Tower A, Ping An International Finance Center, No.1-3, Xinyuan South Road, Chaoyang District, Beijing 100027,China

2011/03/18 - 20
☎ 010-5933 9495
🖷 010-5933 9494
✉ info@reedguanghe.com
www.chinagolfshow.com
180

中国国际高尔夫球博览会
地点：国家会议中心，北京
内容：中国高尔夫球博览会，已经逐步发展成为中国高尔夫产业的第一大行业盛会，获得了中国高尔夫球协会的大力支持，并被认可为这一新兴产业的首选平台。展会观众包括高尔夫专业人士、俱乐部经理、高尔夫球场草坪总监、高尔夫用品分销商/零售商、地产开发商，以及来自中国各地的高尔夫球爱好者。
始办年份：2002
周期：每年两届
市场范围：全国性
上届规模 2010：展览面积19,000m^2, 参展商300家（来自40个国家）
主办：北京励展光合展览有限公司
地址：北京市朝阳区新源南路1-3号平安国际金融中心A座15层01-03,05（100027）

China Golf Show
Venue: China National Convention Center, Beijing
Profile: As vane of the China's golf industry and a bridge between the Chinese and foreign golf industries, the show attract exhibitors and visitors from the industry, and improve the international recognition of the expo. Thus, the expo serves as a professional platform for the exhibitors to expand market and promote brand image.
Established Year: 2002
Frequency: Biannual
Market Area: National
Statistics 2010: Exhibition Area 19,000m^2, Exhibitors 300（came from 40 countries）
Organizer: Reed Guanghe Exhibition Co Ltd
Address: Unit 01-03, 05, 15th Floor, Tower A, Ping An International Finance Center, No.1-3 Xinyuan South Road, Chaoyang District, Beijing 100027, China

2011/03/20 - 23
☎ 010-6505 0540, 6505 7688
www.ecwtc.com
190

2011中国国际婚纱及摄影器材博览会
地点：中国国际贸易中心，北京

China Wedding 2011
Venue: China World Trade Center, Beijing

2011/03/25 - 27
☎ 010-6505 0540, 6505 7688
021-6169 8300
🖷 021-6169 8301
www.ecwtc.com
200

CHINA MED

第23届国际医疗仪器设备展览会
地点：国家会议中心，北京
主办：中国国际贸易中心
地址：北京建国门外大街一号（100004）
主办：杜塞尔多夫展览（上海）有限公司
地址：上海市浦东新区张江高科技园区科苑路88号上海德意志工商中心1号楼307室（201203）

The 23rd International Medical Instruments and Equipment Exhibition
Venue: China National Convention Center, Beijing
Organizer: China World Trade Center
Organizer: Messe Dusseldorf (Shanghai) Co Ltd
Address: Unit 307, Tower 1 German Center for Industry and Trade Shanghai, 88 Keyuan Road, Zhangjiang Hi-Tech Park Pudong, Shanghai 201203, China

2011/03/25 - 27
☎ 010-6505 0540, 6505 7688
www.ecwtc.com
210

2011北京旅居人士服务展览会
地点：中国国际贸易中心，北京

2011 Expat Show
Venue: China World Trade Center, Beijing

2011/03/28 - 31
☎ 010-6505 0546, 8522 9382
🖷 010-6505 3260, 8522 9018
www.chiconline.com.cn
230

中国国际服装服饰博览会
CHINA INT'L CLOTHING
& ACCESSORIES FAIR
chic
3.28–31,2011

第十九届中国国际服装服饰博览会
地点：中国国际展览中心新馆，北京 CIEC
内容：男装,女装,童装,休闲装,羊绒制品,内衣,羽绒服装,皮革/皮草服装,时尚饰品,设计师作品,服装类资源
预计规模：展览面积100,000m^2
主办：中国服装协会；中国国际贸易中心股份有限公司；中国贸促会纺织行业分会
联系人：安毅恒
承办：中国国际贸易中心股份有限公司北京会展分公司
地址：北京建外大街1号国贸展厅2层（100004）
联系人：曾琦

CHIC 2011
The 19th China International Clothing & Accessories Fair
Venue: China International Exhibition Center New Venue, Beijing
Profile: China National Clothing& Accessories Fair (CHIC) covered an area of 100,000 square meters. It comprised 10 specialized zones——Men' s wear, Women' s wear, Casual wear/Sports wear, Kids' wear, Leather/Fur wear, Accessories, Fashion media, Creation design, and Overseas pavilions, drawing over 1,000 excellent brands and more than 100,000 professional visitors from dozens of counties and regions every year.
Established Year: 1993
Frequency: Annual
Market Area: International
Organizer: China National Garment Association; China World Trade Center Co Ltd; The Sub-Council of Textile Industry CCPIT
Organizer: Beijing Convention & Exhibition Company, China World Trade Center Co Ltd
Address: F/2，China World Exhibition Hall，No.1 Jian Wai Ave., Beijing
Contact: Jordan Zeng

2011/03/29 - 30
☎ 0431-8783 5764
🖷 0431-8783 5765
✉ ntcpjg@126.com
www.nongtewang.com
240

第三届全国杂粮产业大会
地点：北京温都水城湖湾西区酒店，北京
内容：杂粮2010年生产情况与行2011年情报告会；杂粮产品及设备展洽订货会；评选推介十大名小米、十大杂粮批发市场及生产十强县、优质品牌杂粮加工产品、金奖产品；全国杂粮联盟2011年会；杂粮加工技术与设备研发座谈会
始办年份：2008
周期：每年一届
市场范围：全国性
性质：面向贸易观众
入场券价格：900元/人
上届规模 2010：展览面积400m^2, 参展商80家，专业贸易观众300人
主办：中国农学会特产分会；全国杂粮联盟；全国杂粮产业专家团；吉林省农特产品加工协会
承办：吉林省农特产品加工协会
地址：长春市西安大路5333号吉林大学军需科技学院104室（130062）

The 3rd National Grain Industry Conference
Venue: Wendu Hot Spring Leisure City, Beijing
Established Year: 2008
Frequency: Annual
Market Area: National
Nature: Trade Only
Cost to Attend: RMB 900/pp
Statistics 2010: Exhibition Area 400m^2, Exhibitors 80, Participants 300
Organizer: Jilin Agricultural Product Processing Assn
Address: 5333 Xi'an Road, Changchun, Jilin 130062

2011/03/29 - 31
☎ 010-8586 1238
🖷 010-8586 1238
250

第十二届中国国际天然气汽车、加气站设备展览会
地点：全国农业展览馆，北京
内容：展会期间有产品展示、贸易洽谈，同期将举办技术交流会，各参展商可以自愿申请，每场技术交流会收费，国内企业为9800元，境外企业为2000美元，时间为2小时
周期：每年一届
市场范围：国际性
性质：面向公众
主办：中国城市燃气学会;中国土木工程学会城市燃气分会;中国天然气汽车专业委员会;北京企发展览服务有限公司
承办：北京企发展览服务有限公司
联系人：王洪国

12th China International Natural Gas Automobile and Gas Station Equipment Exhibition
Venue: National Agricultural Exhibition Center, Beijing
Frequency: Annual
Market Area: International
Nature: Open to Public
Organizer: Beijing Qifa Exhibition Co

2011/03/30 - 01
☎ 010-8522 9463，8522 9488，8522 9440
🖷 010-8522 9296
✉ intertextile.bj@ccpittex.com
www.intertextile.com.cn
260

中国国际纺织面料及辅料（春夏）博览会
地点：中国国际展览中心，北京 CIEC
内容：各类服装面料、辅料、计算机CAD/CAM系统，相关出版物及网络
预计规模：总面积50,000m^2
主办：中国纺织工业协会
承办：中国贸促会纺织行业分会；法兰克福展览（香港）有限公司；中国纺织信息中心
联系人：沈桢，于欣，王壮飞，马一丹，黎明家，吴知真

China International Trade Fair for Apparel Fabrics and Accessories
Venue: China International Exhibition Center, Beijing
Sponsor: China National Textile & Apparel Council
Organizers: The Sub-Council of Textile Industry; CCPIT Messe Frankfurt (HK) Ltd; China Textile Information Center

2011/03/31 - 02
☎ 010-8522 9496, 8522 9148, 8522 9504
🖷 010-8522 9300
✉ yarnexpo@ccpittex.com
www.yarnexpo.com.cn
270

中国国际纺织纱线（春夏）展览会
地点：中国国际贸易中心，北京
内容：各类纺织纤维、纱线及CAD等
预计规模：总面积5,000m^2
主办：中国纺织工业协会
承办：中国贸促会纺织行业分会；法兰克福展览（香港）有限公司；中国棉纺织行业协会；中国毛纺织行业协会；中国化学纤维工业协会；中国麻纺行业协会；中国纺织信息中心
联系人：王小雷，林泽文，林英华

China International Trade Fair for Fibers and Yarns
Venue: China World Trade Center, Beijing
Sponsors: China National Textile & Apparel Council
Organizers: The Sub-Council of Textile Industry, CCPIT; Messe Frankfurt (HK) Ltd; China Cotton Textile Association China Wool Textile Association China Chemical Fiber Association; China Bast & Leaf Fibers Tex

2011/04/07 - 10
☎ 010-6505 0540, 6505 7688
www.ecwtc.com
290

2011年中国北京春季房地产展示交易会
地点：中国国际贸易中心，北京

2011 Springtime Real Estate Trade Fair Beijing China
Venue: China World Trade Center, Beijing

2011/04/08 - 10
☎ 010-58220435
🖷 010-58850839
✉ beijingsbl@126.com

2011北京国际美容美发化妆用品博览会

地点：中国国际展览中心，北京 CIEC

内容：美容产品：皮肤护理、香水、美体、彩妆、水疗、美甲、纹绣、香薰、保健、养生等产品；2.美发产品：洗护染烫产品、
300 发制品、养发育发产品、发用饰品 3.器具产品：美发美容美体设备、用具类、仪器类、沙龙家具、专用工服、织品；整形美容：整形设备、仪器、技术、机构；原料：日化原料、洗涤及个人护理产品；包装材料：包装器械、各类容器、专用箱包、装潢印刷；其它：专业媒体、管理软件、教育培训机构

始办年份：1997

周期：每年两届

市场范围：国际性

性质：面向贸易观众

上届规模 2010：展览面积13,000m^2(国外展商200m^2)，参展商430家（国外展商10家，来自2个国家），参观人数24,234人（专业贸易观众20,000人）

主办：北京世博联展览服务有限公司(SBL)；北京市美发美容行业协会(BHBA)

地址：北京市朝阳区三元桥曙光西里甲1号第三置业B座1006室（100028）

联系人：王龙

QQ：466480157

Chinese International Beauty, Hairdressing & Cosmetics Expo in Beijing 2011

Venue: China International Exhibition Center, Beijing

Profile: Beauty products: skin care, perfume, body care, make-up, SPA, nail care, tattoo, fragrance and health care; Hairdressing products: hair wash, care, color and perm products, hair products, hair-nourishing & growth products, accessories for hair; Appliance products; Plastic-surgery; Materials

Established Year: 1997

Frequency: Biannual

Market Area: International

Nature: Trade Only

Statistics 2010: Exhibition Area 13,000m^2(foreigners 200m^2), Exhibitors 430（foreigners 10, came from 2 countries），Visitors 24,234（trade visitors 20,000）

Organizer: Beijing Shibolian Exhibition Service Co Ltd; Beijing Hairdressing & Beauty Association

Address: Room 1006, Tower B, No.3 Zhiye Building, A- 1, Shuguang Xili, Sanyuanqiao, Beijing

Contact: Wang Long

2011/04/11 - 16
☎ 010-8460 0162, 8460 0163
🖷 010-8460 0739
✉ gaojingjing@ciec.com.cn
www.cimtshow.com

第十二届中国国际机床展览会

地点：中国国际展览中心新馆，北京 CIEC

内容：数字化制造技术及装备包括：各种数控金切机床、数控特种加工机床、数控组合机床及生产线、柔性制造单元及制造
310 系统；数控锻压成形机械、数控系统、滚动功能部件、工业机器人、数控检测仪器、数控切削刀具系统、磨料磨具、涂附磨具、超硬材料及制品、机床附件、数显装置、机床电器；各类产品开发及应用软件、纳米加工技术、高速切削技术、复合加工技术、智能化制造技术、绿色制造技术及专用制造设备等。

始办年份：1989

周期：两年一届

市场范围：国际性

入场券价格：免费

参展费用：国内企业 1,180元/m^2，1080元/m^2；境内合资企业1,850元/m^2，1750元/m^2；境内外资企业 2,450元/m^2，2,150元/m^2

上届规模 2009：展览面积100,000m^2(国外展商40,000m^2)，参展商1,200家（国外展商550家，来自28个国家），参观人数110,000人

主办：中国机床工具工业协会

承办：中国机床工具工业协会；中国国际展览中心集团

地址：北京市朝阳区北三环东路六号中国国际展览中心综合服务楼三层（100028）

联系人：孙荣华，高晶晶

The 12th China International Machine Tool Show

Venue: China International Exhibition Center New Venue, Beijing

Profile: CNC manufacturing technology and equipment, including CNC metal-cutting machine tool, CNC nontraditional processing machinery. CNC modular machine tool and production line, FMC, FMS, CNC system, Metal forming machinery and fabrication equipment. Function components, industrial robots, CNC measuring and testing device, Cutting tool, Abrasive and its product, Material handling equipment, Super-hard material and product, Machinery accessories, Digital display device, Apparatus, Various types Of product development and application software, Nanometer machining technology, High-speed cutting technology. Compound machining technology, Intelligent manufacturing technology, Environment-friendly manufacturing technology and Special-purpose manufacturing equipment etc.

Established Year: 1989

Frequency: Biennial

Market Area: International

Cost to Attend: Free

Participated Fee: RMB 2,450元/m^2, Raw Space RMB 2,150/m^2

Statistics 2009: Exhibition Area 100,000m^2(foreigners 40,000m^2), Exhibitors 1200（foreigners 550, came from 28 countries），Visitors 110,000

Sponsor: China Machine Tool &Tool Builders' Association (CMTBA)

Organizer: China Machine Tool &Tool Builders' Association (CMTBA); China International Exhibition Center Group Corporation (CIEC)

Address: 1/F, General Service Building, CIEC 6 East Beisanhuan Road, Chaoyang District, Beijing, China 100028

Contact: Milton Sun, Christy Gao

2011/04/13 - 15
☎ 010-6336 2354
🖷 010-6343 0660
✉ bj63362354@126.com
www.cnbakery.com

2010年第七届全国（北京）焙烤展览会

地点：全国农业展览馆，北京

内容：食品、糕点（月饼）、面包、蛋糕、饼干、餐饮用原辅材料、装饰品及食品代加工（OEM）；专用油脂、奶油、专用面粉、预拌粉、冷冻面团、淀粉、土豆制品；馅料、果料、果仁、
320 果脯、水果罐头等月饼、糕点辅料；焙烤设备及器具、手艺焙烤配备及器具、焙烤产品与制成品；食品馅料炒锅、夹层锅；（馅料）自动计量包装机械；饼干生产设备、原辅料及包装等；月饼包装、馅料、模具及生产设备；展示柜、储藏与冷藏柜、店面装饰；面粉改良剂、面包改良剂、蛋糕改良剂、方便面改良剂、保鲜剂、酵母、香料、香精、色素、甜味剂等相关食品添加剂；食品（月饼、饼干、冷食、面食、巧克力等）包装机械；饼房、厨房、西餐厅、咖啡厅生产设备、原辅料及用品等；肉松、巧克力制品，糖仔、蜡烛、仿真食品模型等蛋糕装饰材料；咖啡、咖啡制品、咖啡机、咖啡加工设备；金属探测设备

始办年份：2003

周期：每年一届

市场范围：全国性

参展费用：6,200元/9m^2

上届规模 2010：展览面积6,000m^2，专业贸易观众8,000人

主办：中国焙烤食品糖制品工业协会

地址：北京市海淀区北蜂窝2号中盛大厦1305A室（100038）

联系人：侯丽红

MSN：lihong7708@hotmail.com

QQ：754093622

China International Trade Fair for Bakery & Confectionery

Venue: National Agricultural Exhibition Center, Beijing

Profile: Profile: Baking ovens and accessories, baking and pastry-making machinery, refrigeration, fermenting and air conditioning technology, baking agents, raw materials and ingredients, semi-finished and finished products, ice cream manufacturing, pasta making, furnishings and equipment for shops, cafés and patisseries, packaging machinery, equipment and material, decorative items and baking accessories, cleaning and hygiene, laboratory and measuring equipment, computer hardware and software, services.

Established Year: 2003

Frequency: Annual

Market Area: National

Participated Fee: RMB 6,200/9m^2

Statistics 2010: Exhibition Area 6,000m^2, Trade Visitors 8,000

Organizer: China Assn of Bakery & Confectionery Industry

MSN: lihong7708@hotmail.com

www.cnbakery.com

2011/04/13 - 15
☎ 010-6505 0540, 6505 7688
www.ecwtc.com
330

2011中国出境旅游交易会
地点：中国国际贸易中心，北京

China Outbound Travel and Tourism Market 2011
Venue: China World Trade Center, Beijing

2011/04/17 - 19
☎ 010-5919 4402
🖷 010-6591 8986
340

中国国际葡萄酒及烈酒展览会
地点：全国农业展览馆，北京
内容：各种葡萄酒、烈酒及相关产品
始办年份：2009
周期：每年一届
市场范围：国际性
性质：面向公众
主办：中国贸促会农业行业分会
地址：北京市朝阳区麦子店街20号楼805（100125）
联系人：江月朋

China International Wine & Spirits Exhibition
Venue: National Agricultural Exhibition Center, Beijing
Profile: Wine, Spirit and related products
Established Year: 2009
Frequency: Annual
Market Area: International
Nature: Open to Public
Organizer: CCPIT-SSA
Address: Room 805, Building 20, Maizidian Street, Chaoyang District, Beijing
Contact: Linda Jiang

2011/04/20 - 23
☎ 010-8460 0805, 8460 0804
🖷 010-8460 0325
✉ chaitong@ciec.com.cn
wangbingzhe@ciec.com.cn
www.stonetech.org.cn
350

第十八届中国（北京）国际石材产品及石材技术装备展览会
地点：中国国际展览中心，北京 CIEC
内容：荒料、板材、异型制品、石雕制品、墓碑及纪念碑、环境装饰、机械设备及工具、资源利用、环境保护及安全生产，养护、清洁、翻新、抛光、粘胶、着色剂、配件，服务机构、媒体、团体
始办年份：1994
周期：每年一届
市场范围：国际性
性质：面向贸易观众
参展费用：标准展位1100元/m^2，净地1000元/m^2
上届规模 2010：展览面积65,000m^2(国外展商10,000m^2)，参展商769家（国外展商170家，来自30个国家），参观人数46,962人
主办：中展集团北京华港展览有限公司
承办：中展集团北京华港展览有限公司
地址：北京市朝阳区北三环东路6号（100028）
联系人：柴彤 王炳哲

18th China International Stone Processing Machinery, Equipment and Products Exhibition
Venue: China International Exhibition Center, Beijing
Profile: Raw Blocks, Slab, Irregular Crafts, Stone Carvings, Graves and Memorials, Landscaping; Machinery, Plant and Tools; Industrial Safety, Environmental Protection; Maintenance and Accessories
Established Year: 1994
Frequency: Annual
Market Area: International
Nature: Trade Only
Participated Fee: Standard Booth RMB 1,100/m^2, Raw Space RMB 1,000/m^2
Statistics 2010: Exhibition Area 65,000m^2(foreigners 10,000m^2), Exhibitors 769 (foreigners 170, came from 30 countries), Visitors 46,962
Sponsor: CIEC EXHIBITION COMPANY LTD
Organizer: CIEC EXHIBITION COMPANY LTD
Address: 6.East Beisanhuan Road Beijing
Contact: Mr Leo Wang, Mr Kevin Wang

2011/04/20 - 24
☎ 010-6505 0540, 6050 7688
www.ecwtc.com
360

2011中艺博国际画廊博览会
地点：中国国际贸易中心，北京

China International Gallery Exposition 2011
Venue: China World Trade Center, Beijing

2011/04/21 - 24
☎ 010-6859 6577
🖷 010-6853 8552
✉ ccoea@mei.net.cn
www.ccoea.org.cn
370

中国国际照相机械影像器材与技术博览会
地点：国家会议中心，北京
内容：展期为四天。已成为国内外公认的亚洲最具权威的摄影器材博览会，为世界三大国际影像展之一。
始办年份：1998
周期：每年一届
市场范围：国际性
性质：面向公众
上届规模 2010：展览面积15,000m^2，参展商150家（来自20多个国家），参观人数50,000人
主办：中国文化办公设备制造行业协会
地址：北京市西城区月坛南街26号4060室(100825)
联系人：张晋生

CHINA P&E
China International Photograph & Electrical Imaging Machinery and Technology Fair
Venue: China National Convention Center, Beijing
Profile: Digital camera, digital camera-back, camera, lenses, video recorder, printing expansion equipment with other related products; medium and large sized camera of common and economic type for hobby fans, of high grade type for professional persons
Established Year: 1998
Frequency: Annual
Market Area: International
Nature: Open to Public
Statistics 2010: Exhibition Area 15,000m^2, Exhibitors 150 (came from 20 countries), Visitors 50,000
Organizer: China Culture & Office Equipment Association
Address: 26 Yue Yan Nan Jie, Room 4060, Beijing 100825, China
Contact: Zhang Jinsheng

2011/04/25 - 27
☎ 010-8839 5100, 8839 5101
🖷 010-8839 5130
✉ cisile@cisile.com.cn
www.cisile.com.cn
380

第九届中国国际科学仪器及实验室装备展览会
地点：北京展览馆，北京
内容：适应建设创新型国家的需要而打造的专业化、规模化、国际化展示交流平台。展会同期组织了高层次、高水准、针对行业发展热点的现场配套活动，如自主创新奖评选活动、中国科学仪器发展年会、中国科学仪器新技术及应用学术报告会等。2011年该展将展示科学仪器产业新产品与技术。展会将更加重点突出国际化和专业化，同时也将邀请更多的国际参观团到会参观与交流，使CISILE在促进国际科技交流与合作、推动我国科学仪器产业健康快速发展方面发挥更加积极的作用。
始办年份：2003
周期：每年一届
市场范围：国际性
性质：面向公众
上届规模 2010：展览面积25,000m^2，参展商580家（来自39个国家），参观人数20,000人

The 9th China International Scientific Instrument and Laboratory Equipment
Venue: Beijing Exhibition Center, Beijing
Profile: CISILE allocate an area for international exhibitors. And exhibitors will get more promotion opportunities there. CISILE 2010 got fruitful results, capturing the world' s attention. CISILE 2011, the 9th session, with advanced technology in the field of scientific instruments and laboratory equipment will be invited to participate in and visit the exhibition. Meanwhile, the organizers will invite domestic managers and technical personnel and visiting groups to the exhibition for exchanging experiences as well as making procurements this year.
Established Year: 2003
Frequency: Annual
Market Area: International
Nature: Open to Public

主办：中国仪器仪表行业协会/北京朗普展览有限公司
地址：北京市车公庄大街9号院五栋大楼1号楼B2-804室（100044）
联系人：高霞

Statistics 2010: Exhibition Area 25,000m^2, Exhibitors 580（came from 39 countries）, Visitors 20,000
Organizer: China Instrument Manufacturer's Association; Beijing Lamp Exhibition Co Ltd
Address: Room B2-804, Wu Dong Building, No.9 Complex, Chegongzhuang Street, Beijing 100044, China
Contact: Gao Xia

2011/04/26 - 28
☎ 010-6401 6504
Fax 010-6401 6504
✉ cy888@vip.163.com
www.cliexpo.org
390

2011北京酒店用品、厨房设备、清洁用品、咖啡展览会
（第十四届北京酒店设备用品展览会）
地点：中国国际展览中心新馆，北京 CIEC
内容：厨房设备、厨具器具、食品机械、烘烤设备、自助餐设备、各种冷冻冷藏设备、制冰机、中西餐具、陶瓷制品、玻璃器皿、洗碗机、自酿啤酒设备、冷库、活海鲜蓄养装备、冰淇淋机、饮料机、咖啡机。洗地机、抛光机、擦地机、电子打泡箱、吸水机、吹风机、吸尘器、垃圾桶、尘推、地垫、清洁剂、洗涤剂、洗手液、皂液机、干肤器、石材护理设备、空气清新机、洗衣房设备、清洁机械、清洁用品、洗涤机械设备等。卫生洁具、浴缸、浴盆、客户用品、针棉纺织用品、毛毯、毛巾、床上用品、消耗用品、装饰用品、窗帘布、各种标示牌、服务用车。酒店配套家具、酒店超市设备、酒店制冷通暖设备。酒店消防防火设备、电视监控系统、防盗系统、各种门锁、磁卡门锁、保险箱、门类控制系统。酒店电器设备：空中升降台、床头控制板、灯具灯饰。酒店休闲设备
始办年份：1998
周期：每年一届
性质：面向公众
主办：轻工业展览中心
地址：北京市东城区东四六条64号（100007）
联系人：应艳梅
MSN：lengfeier@msn.com
QQ：71229011/925091549

14th Beijing Hospitality Equipment & Supplies Exhibition
Venue: China International Exhibition Center New Venue, Beijing
Established Year: 1998
Frequency: Annual
Nature: Open to Public
Organizer: Exhibition Center of China Light Industry
MSN: lengfeier@msn.com

2011/04/27 - 29
☎ 010-6505 0540, 6505 7688
www.ecwtc.com
400

2011北京国际隧道地下工程、喷涂聚脲、土工材料、工程纤维及建筑化学品展览会
地点：中国国际贸易中心，北京

2011 Beijing International Tunnel Underground Project, Spray Polyurea, Geo-technical Material, Engineering Fiber and Construction Chemicals Exhibition
Venue: China World Trade Center, Beijing

2011/04/29 - 02
☎ 010-6554 7002 / 7003
Fax 010-6554 5213
✉ artfiar_beijing@yahoo.com.cn
www.artbeijing.net
410

艺术北京当代艺术博览会
地点：全国农业展览馆，北京
内容："艺术北京当代艺术博览会"是"艺术北京"这个文化创意品牌的首推项目，自2006年创办艺术北京当代艺术展会至今，艺术北京顺应市场需求，推出了一系列创新举措：于2008年创办艺术北京影像艺术博览会，2009年创立经典艺术博览会，博览会系列品牌的集团效应获得各界广大回响及认同，无论从市场操作还是学术构建都取得了巨大的成功。也给艺术市场带来了新的可能性，信心与激励。
始办年份：2006
周期：每年一届
市场范围：国际性
性质：面向公众
入场券价格：50元
参展费用：68,400元/36m3
上届规模 2010：展览面积17,000m^2(国外展商6,000m^2)，参展商83家（国外展商26家，来自20个国家），参观人数50,000人
主办：北京艾特菲尔文化有限公司
地址：北京朝阳区吉庆里14号佳汇国际中心A座1601（100020）
联系人：范欣

Art Beijing Contemporary Art Fair
Venue: National Agricultural Exhibition Center, Beijing
Profile: Since it was established in 2006, the "Art Beijing Contemporary Art Fair" has served as the primary annual event for the Art Beijing creative culture brand. Over these past four years, Art Beijing has continued to grow, promoting new activities and services to meet the demands of the art collection market. In 2008, it launched the first Art Beijing Photography art fair. The Art Beijing Fine Art Fair was then first organized the following year. The synergy between these fairs and the expanding services Art Beijing offers have had a synergistic relationship, which has been recognized as a huge success by both academic art institutions and the art collection market community. With its exciting events and services, Art Beijing has brought to the art collection market new possibilities, confidence and encouragement.
Established Year: 2006
Frequency: Annual
Market Area: International
Nature: Open to Public
Cost to Attend: RMB 50:-
Participated Fee: RMB 68,400/36m^2
Statistics 2010: Exhibition Area 17,000m^2(foreigners 6,000m^2), Exhibitors 83（foreigners 26, came from 20 countries）, Visitors 50,000
Organizer: Beijing Art Fair Culture Co Ltd
Address: 1601, Jia Hui International Center, No. 14 Jiqingli, Chaoyang District, Beijing
Contact: Fan Xin

2011/05/02 -
☎ 010-6505 0540, 6505 7688
www.ecwtc.com
420

COMIC.G.U动漫交流会
地点：中国国际贸易中心，北京

COMIC.G.U
Venue: China World Trade Center, Beijing

2011/05/07 - 09
☎ 010-6878 4991, 6878 4992
🖷 010-6878 4978
✉ hyq@ccfa.org.cn
ccfahy@126.com
430

2011中国特许展——第13届中国特许加盟展览会
地点：国家会议中心，北京
内容：目前国内特许加盟领域规模大、规范性强、可信度高、影响力广的展览会。中国特许展每年分为"北京站"和"上海站"，2011年将于5月和9月分别在北京和上海举办。中国特许展已经成为中国特许加盟领域的年度盛会，是一个政府支持、社会关注、观众认可的投资平台。 国特许展现已越来越具有国际影响力。每年吸引着美国、德国、韩国、意大利、泰国、马来西亚、新加坡、印尼、香港、台湾等国家和地区的展团或企业参加"北京站"的展览活动，为国内投资者带来加盟国际品牌的投资机会。
始办年份：1999
周期：每年两届
市场范围：国际性
参展费用：标准展位1,600元/m^2，净地1,400元/m^2
上届规模 2010：展览面积4,500m^2，参展商1,665家（国外展商89家，来自9个国家），参观人数22,000人
主办：中国连锁经营协会
承办：北京国际展览中心；北京尚智联协会展咨询有限公司
地址：北京市西城区阜外大街22号外经贸大厦811-815号（100037）
联系人：郝永强、何勇

China Franchise Expo 2011
Venue: China National Convention Center, Beijing
Profile: China Franchise Expo has held successfully for 12 sessions since 1999 and it has expanded very fast. It has developed into the most influential franchise event in China and is considered as the most efficient way to pursue new franchising opportunity. During 3 days exhibition, there will be about 30,000 individual or institutional investors coming to seek the franchise business and exchange new concepts
Established Year: 1999
Frequency: Biennial
Market Area: International
Participated Fee: Standard Booth RMB 1,600/m^2, Raw Space RMB 1,400/m^2
Statistics 2010: Exhibition Area 4,500m^2, Exhibitors 1,665 (foreigners 89, came from 9 countries), Visitors 22,000
Sponsor: China Chain Store & Franchise Association
Organizer: Beijing International Exhibition Center Beijing Shine Co Ltd
Address: Room 811,8th floor, Foreign Economic & Trade Plaza, No 22 Fuchengmenwai Str., Xicheng Dist., Beijing 100037, China
Contact: Evan Hao, John he

2011/05/08 - 10
☎ 010-6505 0540, 6505 7688
440

北京国际减灾应急技术设备博览会
地点：中国国际贸易中心，北京

Disaster Reduction and Emergency Technology Exhibition
Venue: China World Trade Center, Beijing

2011/05/12 - 14
☎ 010-8808 2303
🖷 010-8808 2305
✉ xxd@cbme.cn
www.wallexpochina.com
450

第五届中国国际新型墙体材料技术装备及产品展览会暨中国散装水泥暨预拌混凝土与预拌砂浆技术装备及产品展览会
地点：中国国际展览中心，北京
内容：新型墙体材料及生产设备、建筑保温系统、节能门窗与幕墙 混凝土制品生产技术和设备 混凝土原材料、外加剂、砂浆、混凝土相关工程机械设备、混凝土砌块及生产设备、混凝土施工用建筑模板脚手架及够配件
始办年份：2007
周期：每年一届
市场范围：国际性
性质：面向贸易观众
参展费用：8,800元
上届规模 2010：展览面积6,000m^2(国外展商2,000m^2)，参展商200家（国外展商10家，来自8个国家），参观人数10,000人（专业贸易观众4,000人）
主办：国家建筑材料展贸中心
地址：北京市海淀区三里河路甲11号 中国建材大厦四层406室（100037）
联系人：何徐凌

WALLEXPO CHINA 2011
Venue: China International Exhibition Center, Beijing
Profile: New wall materials products and production facility building heat preservation system energy-saving windows and curtain wall production technology and facility of concrete products
Established Year: 2007
Frequency: Annual
Market Area: International
Nature: Trade Only
Participated Fee: RMB 8,800/booth
Statistics 2010: Exhibition Area 6,000m^2(foreigners 2,000m^2), Exhibitors 200 (foreigners 10, came from 8 countries), Visitors 10,000 (trade visitors 4,000)
Organizer: China National Building Materials Exhibition & Trade Center
Address: China Building Materials Plaza A11# Sanlihe Road, Haidian District Beijing
Contact: He Xuling

2011/05/12 - 14
☎ 010-5152 7160
🖷 010-6218 6579
✉ xum@css.com.cn
www.csia.org.cn
460

2011第十五届中国国际软件博览会
地点：北京展览馆，北京
内容：软件产品、信息服务、系统集成、嵌入式系统、行业应用软件解决方案、动漫游戏、网络应用软件
始办年份：1997
周期：每年一届
市场范围：国际性
性质：面向公众
入场券价格：免费
参展费用：12,000元/标准展位
上届规模 2010：展览面积20,000m^2(国外展商1,000m^2)，参展商600家（国外展商20家，来自10个国家），参观人数80,000人（专业贸易观众2,000人）
主办：工业和信息化部
地址：北京海淀区学院南路55号A401（100081）
联系人：徐萌

INTL SOFT CHINA 2011
Venue: Beijing Exhibition Center, Beijing
Profile: E-government, Network Security & Storage, Mid-ware, Embedded System, SMEs IT, Key Industry Applications, Digital/Mobile/Home Appliance Applications, Education Software, Games/Entertainment Software
Established Year: 1997
Frequency: Annual
Market Area: International
Nature: Open to Public
Cost to Attend: Free
Participated Fee: RMB 12,000/booth*
Statistics 2010: Exhibition Area 20,000m^2(foreigners 1,000m^2), Exhibitors 600 (foreigners 20, came from 10 countries), Visitors 80,000 (trade visitors 2,000) **Organizer**: Ministry of Information Industry the People's Republic of China
Address: No.55 Xueyuan Nan Rold, Haidian District, Beijing, China
Contact: Xu Meng

2011/05/13 - 15
☎ 010-6505 0540, 6505 7688
www.ecwtc.com
480

第13届北京国际玩具及幼教用品展览会暨北京国际婴幼童用品展览会
地点：中国国际贸易中心，北京

2011 Beijing International Toys & Preschool Tools Exhibition, 2011 China International Pregnancy and Baby Show
Venue: China World Trade Center, Beijing

2011/05/18 - 20
☎ 010-6505 0540, 6505 7688
www.ecwtc.com
490

2011中国国际酒店博览会
地点：中国国际贸易中心，北京

Hotel China 2011
Venue: China World Trade Center, Beijing

2011/05/18 - 20
☎ 021-5045 6700转ext 259/280
🖷 021-5045 9355, 2886 2355
✉ fapa@hmf-china.com
maggie.xia@hmf-china.com
edison.li@hmf-china.com
www.fa-pa.com.cn

500

2011国际现代工厂/过程自动化技术与装备展览会
地点：国家会议中心，北京
内容：本展会专注生产及过程自动化、电气系统、工业机器人和工业自动化信息技术及软件四大板块，展会云集众多国内外领先的工厂自动化、过程自动化展商。同期所举办的多项国际专业会议及论坛将力邀行业内专家学者就自动化领域热点问题展开讨论，为该行业未来快速发展建言献策。
周期：每年一届
性质：面向贸易观众
上届规模 2010：参展商121家（来自14个国家），参观人数9,586人
主办：中国机电一体化技术应用协会
承办：汉诺威米兰展览（上海）有限公司
地址：上海市浦东新区银霄路393号百安居浦东商务大厦301室（201204）
联系人：夏薇 女士,李翔 先生

FA/PA 2011
Venue: China National Convention Center, Beijing
Profile: FA/PA 2011 will once again set new standards and put the spotlight on the most innovative and ground-breaking solutions in automation technology. For the second time Hannover Milano Fairs Shanghai Ltd and China Association for Mechatronics Technology & Application combine efforts to raise the Beijing based exhibition fair to another level.
Frequency: Annual
Nature: Trade Only
Statistics 2010: Exhibitors 121（came from 14 countries）, Visitors 9,586
Sponsor: China Association for Mechatronics Technology & Application
Organizer: Hannover Milano Fairs Shanghai Ltd
Address: 301B&Q Office Tower, 393 Yinxiao Road, Pudong, Shanghai, China
Contact: Ms Maggie Xia, Mr Edison Li

2011/05/18 - 21
☎ 010-6806 6669
转ext 8022/8021
🖷 010-6806 6969, 6806 7979
✉ wangpeng@ccpitbj.org
Lj@wtcbj.com
qw@wtcbj.com
www.chitec.cn

510

第十四届中国北京国际科技产业博览会
地点：中国国际展览中心，北京 CIEC
内容：电子信息与现代通讯、生物工程与医药、环境保护产业、新材料与新能源、现代农业与绿色技术、现代工程与先进制造技术
始办年份：1998
周期：每年一届
市场范围：国际性
入场券价格：免费
参展费用：标准展位6,000元/8,300元/16,600元/24,900元/；净地600元/850元/1,660元/2,490元/m^2
上届规模 2010：展览面积60,000m^2(国外展商16,000m^2)，参展商2,112家（国外展商96家，来自12个国家），参观人数205,000人（专业贸易观众120,000人）
主办：科学技术部；商务部；教育部；工业和信息化部；中国贸促会；国家知识产权局；北京市人民政府
承办：北京世界贸易中心
地址：北京市西城区南礼士路19号建邦商务会馆2层（100045）
联系人：王鹏, 刘洁, 齐微

The 14th Beijing International High-Tech Expo
Venue: China International Exhibition Center, Beijing
Profile: Electronics Informatics & Communication, Bio-engineering & Pharmaceuticals, Environmental Protective Industry, New Material & New Energy, Modern Agriculture & Green Technology, Modern Engineering & Manufacturing Technology
Established Year: 1998
Frequency: Annual
Market Area: International
Cost to Attend: Free
Participated Fee: Standard Booth RMB 6,000/8,300/16,600/24,900/ Booth, Raw Space RMB 600/850/1,660/2,490/m^2
Statistics 2010: Exhibition Area 60,000m^2(foreigners 16,000m^2), Exhibitors 2,112（foreigners 96, came from 12 countries）, Visitors 205,000（trade visitors 120,000）
Organizer: Ministry of Science & Technology, China; Ministry of Commerce, China; Ministry of Education, China; Ministry of Industry and Information Technology, China, CCPIT
Address: 2nd Floor Jianbang Business Center, No. 19 Nanlishi Road, Xicheng District, Beijing, China
Contact: Wang Peng, Liu Jie, Qi Wei

2011/05/23 - 26
☎ 010-6505 0540, 6505 7688
www.ecwtc.com

530

2011年中国国际葡萄酒博览会
地点：中国国际贸易中心，北京

Top Wine China 2011
Venue: China World Trade Center, Beijing

2011/05/26 - 29
☎ 010-8402 9994,
6403 3098转ext 201/203
🖷 010-8401 0152
✉ chen@palmexpo.com
www.palmexpo.com

540

第二十届中国国际专业音响·灯光·乐器及技术展览会
地点：灯光音响：中国国际展览中心 CIEC
地点：乐器：全国农业展览馆，北京
内容：1）专业音响器材：话筒、调音系统、扬声器、周边器材、录音系统等；2）专业舞台灯光器材：电脑灯、舞台灯、调光系统、LED视频、电光源产品等；3）舞台机械：升降台、车台、吊杆、防火幕、隔声幕等；4）乐器：键盘乐器、管乐器、弦乐器、打击乐器、电声乐器、电脑作曲器材等；5）专业用摄、录像设备：摄像机、录像机、三维动画系统、监视器等；6）专业类出版刊物：书籍、期刊、报纸、光碟等；7）其他：剧场座椅、剧场隔音材料、卡拉OK点歌器材等。
始办年份：1989
周期：每年一届
市场范围：国际性
入场券价格：20元
上届规模 2010：展览面积85,000m^2(国外展商14,000m^2)，参展商1,150家（国外展商170家，来自20个国家），参观人数193,000人（专业贸易观众30,000人）
主办：中国演艺设备技术协会
地址：北京市东城区安定门东大街28号雍和大厦东楼C座10层（100007）
联系人：陈正纲, 赵清华

20th China International Exhibition on Pro Audio, Light, Music & Technology
Venue: Lighting & Audio：China International Exhibition Center, Beijing
Venue: Music Instrument：National Agricultural Exhibition Center, Beijing
Profile: 1) Professional Sound equipment: Microphone, Tuning system, Peripheral Component Equipment, Sound Recording System, etc: 2) Professional Stage & Light Equipment: Computer Lamp, Stage Lamp, Light control system, LED, Electric Light Source product, etc; 3) Stage machinery: Carrying LT, Turn-table, Boom, Safe Curtain, Sound Insulated Curtain, etc; 4) Musical Instrument: Keyboard instrument, Wind Instrument, Stringed Instrument, Percussion Instrument, Electro-acoustical Instrument, Computer Music composition equipment, etc; 5) Professional video camera & video equipment: Camera, Videotape Recorder, 3D Animation Systems, Monitor , etc; 6) Professional publications: Publication(Book), Periodical, Newspaper, Disc, etc; 7) Others: Theater Chair, Acoustic Celotex Material of Theater, KTV/VOD Equipment, etc.
Established Year: 1989
Frequency: Annual
Market Area: International
Cost to Attend: RMB 20:-
Statistics 2010: Exhibition Area 85,000m^2(foreigners 14,000m^2), Exhibitors 1,150（foreigners 170, came from 20 countries）, Visitors 193,000（trade visitors 30,000）
Organizer: China Entertainment Technology Association
Address: 10 Fl., C, East Building, YongHe Plaza, No.28, An Ding Men Dong Da Jie, Dong Cheng District, Beijing, China
Contact: Chen Zhenggang, Zhao Qinghua

2011/05/28 - 29
☎ 021-34280 006, 3428 0007, 1302 323 8802
🖷 021-3428 5006
✉ Janet198712@126.com
www.chinanewenergy.org
550

2011中国新能源战略与“十二五”新能源发展高峰论坛暨新能源产业十一五成就盘点
地点：人民大会堂，北京
主办：中国新能源行业协会；全国创新委新能源专业委员会；亚洲新能源产业联盟；全国新能源委品牌评价中心
承办：北京创新高科能源科技发展中心
联系人：路瑶

2011 New Energy Strategy Summit
Venue: The Great Hall of the People, Beijing
Organizer: New Energy Branch National Creativity Committee

2011/06/09 - 12
☎ 010-8839 3922
🖷 010-8839 3923
✉ yinhaiyan@ihecc.org
www.sinodent.com.cn
560

第十五届中国国际口腔设备材料展览会暨技术交流会
地点：国家会议中心，北京
内容：口腔器械、设备、材料、保健品
始办年份：1995
周期：每年一届
市场范围：国际性
性质：面向贸易观众
入场券价格：免费
参展费用：18,000～28,000元
上届规模 2010：展览面积28,500m^2(国外展商7,000m^2)，参展商611家（国外展商120家，来自71个国家），参观人数33,000人（专业贸易观众22,000人）
主办：卫生部国际交流与合作中心；中华口腔医学会；北京大学口腔医学院
地址：北京市车公庄大街9号五栋大楼B3座（100044）
联系人：尹海燕

SINO-DENTAL 2010
Venue: China National Convention Center, Beijing
Profile: Dental Equipment, facilities, healthcare products
Established Year: 1995
Frequency: Annual
Market Area: International
Nature: Trade Only
Cost to Attend: Free
Participated Fee: RMB 18,000-28,000
Statistics 2010: Exhibition Area 28,500m^2(foreigners 7,000m^2), Exhibitors 611（foreigners 120, came from 71 countries）, Visitors 33,000（trade visitors 22,000）
Organizer: IHECC, CSA & PUSS
Address: Building B3, Wudongdalou, No.9 Chegongzhuang Street, Beijing
Contact: Yin Haiyan

2011/06/18 - 20
☎ 010-6505 0540, 6505 7688
www.ecwtc.com
580

2011北京国际咖啡博览会
地点：北京国际贸易中心，北京

China International Coffee Industry Exhibition 2011
Venue: China World Trade Center, Beijing

2011/06/22 – 24
☎ 010-6590 7766转ext 736
🖷 010-6590 6139
✉ h.chen@koelnmesse.cn
www.windpowerasia.com
585

亚洲风能大会暨国际风能设备展览会
地点：国家会议中心，北京
内容：风力发电机组生产销售、风电场开发、风力发电机配件、配套服务、咨询辅助
始办年份：2003
周期：每年一届
市场范围：国际性
性质：对专业和贸易观众
入场券价格：专业观众免费
参展费用：国际标准展位260欧元/m^2，国际光地展位235欧元/m^2；国内标准展位9,000元/个，国内光地展位900元/m^2
上届规模 2010：展览面积25,000m^2(国外展商12,000m^2)，参展商400家（国外展商194家，来自22个国家），参观人数5,093人（专业贸易观众6,093人）
主办：中国电力企业联合会；德国科隆国际展览有限公司；中国贸促会北京市分会
承办：科隆展览中国有限公司；中国电力企业联合会电力会展中心；中国国际贸易促进委员会电力行业委员会；中国机械工业企业管理协会，北京国际展览中心
地址：北京市东三环北路8号亮马河大厦2座1018室（100004）
联系人：陈晗

Wind Power Asia
- Asian Wind Energy Exhibition & Conference
Venue: China National Convention Center, Beijing
Profile: Wind Turbine Manufacturers & Dealers, Wind Power Plant Developers & Operators, Accessory Equipment Manufacturers, Construction & Development Services, Studies & Analyses
Established Year: 2003
Frequency: Annual
Market Area: International
Nature: Trade Only
Cost to Attend: Free to Trade Visitors
Participated Fee: Standard Booth EURO 260/m^2, Raw Space EURO 235/m^2
Statistics 2010: Exhibition Area 25,000m^2(foreigners 12,000m^2), Exhibitors 400（foreigners 194, came from 22 countries）, Visitors 5,093（trade visitors 6,093）
Sponsor: CEC
Organizer: Koelnmesse Co Ltd
Address: Unit 1018, Landmark Tower II, No8 Dongsanhuan North Rd., Beijing, China
Contact: Helen Chen

2011/06/22 – 24
☎ 010-6590 7766转ext 736
🖷 010-6590 6139
✉ h.chen@koelnmesse.cn
www.cleanenergyexpochina.com
www.cleanenergyexpochina.cn
586

中国国际清洁能源博览会
地点：国家会议中心，北京
内容：太阳能：光伏技术、光伏电池及其它相关技术、光伏发电系统、光伏项目及系统集成；生物质能：生物质能发电技术与设备、生物质能燃料及相关技术、生物质能气化技术、沼气技术与设备、生物质能压缩技术；能效技术：电动汽车、节能楼宇设计、储能技术；智能电网
始办年份：2009
周期：每年一届
市场范围：国际性
性质：仅对专业和贸易观众
入场价格：专业观众免费
参展费用：国际标准展位260欧元/平米；国际光地展位235欧元/m^2；国内标准展位9,000元/个；国内光地展位900元/m^2
上届规模 2010：展览面积25,000m^2(国外展商12,000m^2)，参展商400家（国外展商194家，来自22个国家），参观人数16,093人（专业贸易观众16,093人）
主办：中国电力企业联合会；德国科隆国际展览有限公司；中国国际贸易促进委员会北京市分会
承办：科隆展览中国有限公司；中国电力企业联合会电力会展中心；中国国际贸易促进委员会电力行业委员会；北京国际展览中心
地址：北京市东三环北路8号亮马河大厦2座1018室
联系人：陈晗

Clean Energy Expo China
Venue: China National Convention Center, Beijing
Profile: Solar Energy: Photovoltaics, Solar Thermal, Solar Technologies; Bio-energy: Biofuels (first to third generation), Technology (gasification, burning, briquette), Waste-to-Energy; Energy Efficiency: Vehicles, Building Design, Energy Conservation, Energy Storage; Hydropower; Geothermal Energy; Hybrid Systems; Consulting & Services
Established Year: 2009
Frequency: Annual
Market Area: International
Nature: Trade Only
Cost to Attend: Free to Trade Visitors
Participated Fee: Standard Booth EURO 260/m^2, Raw Space EURO 235/m^2
Statistics 2010: Exhibition Area 25,000m^2(foreigners 12,000m^2), Exhibitors 400（foreigners 194, came from 22 countries）, Visitors 5,093（trade visitors 6,093）
Sponsor: CEC
Organizer: Koelnmesse Co Ltd
Address: Unit 1018， Landmark Tower II, No8 Dongsanhuan North Rd., Beijing, China
Contact: Helen Chen

2011/06/23 - 26
☎ 010-6505 0540, 6505 7688
www.ecwtc.com
590

2011年中国北京夏季房地产展示交易会
地点：中国国际贸易中心，北京

2011 Summertime Real Estate Trade Fair Beijing China
Venue: China World Trade Center, Beijing

2011/06/28 - 30
☎ 010-8455 6615, 8455 6612
🖷 010-8207 4505
✉ chinahb@reedsinopharm.com
www.chinahb.com
600

China Hair & Beauty

中国国际美发美容博览会
地点：北京
内容：美发美容行业的顶级贸易、学习和交流平台。为期3天的展会将吸引来自多个国家和地区的美发、美容、化妆品领域的生产厂家、行业精英和时尚达人参加。大会同期还将举办秋冬时尚潮流发布秀、论坛等多项活动。
周期：每年一届
主办：国药励展展览有限责任公司
地址：北京市朝阳区新源南路1-3号平安国际金融大厦B座15层（100027）

China Hair & Beauty
Venue: Beijing
Profile: The expo will cover the following parts: exhibition, fashion shows, seminars.
Frequency: Annual
Organizer: Reed Sinopharm Exhibitions

2011/07/01 - 10
☎ 010-6505 0540, 6505 7688
www.ecwtc.com
610

2011年北京欧美超级家具展览会
地点：中国国际贸易中心，北京

2011 Beijing International Luxury Furniture Expo
Venue: China World Trade Center, Beijing

2011/07/06 - 08
☎ 021-5153 5215
🖷 021-5153 5234
✉ Selina.li@reedexpo.com.cn
www.sino-foldingcarton.com
620

SINO FOLDINGCARTON
励华国际彩盒展

2011中国国际彩盒展
地点：中国国际展览中心，北京 CIEC
内容：折叠纸盒类加工设备，硬盒类加工设备，塑（胶）盒类加工设备，纸袋设备，软件类，加工服务类，厂房配套设备类，耗材及配件
上届规模 2010：参观人数16,350人（专业贸易观众1,100人）
主办：励展博览集团
地址：上海市淮海中路775号新华联大厦8楼（201204）
联系人：李凤

SinoFoldingCarton 2011
Venue: China International Exhibition Center, Beijing
Statistics 2010: Visitors 16,350 (trade visitors 1,100)
Organizer: Reed Exhibitions
Address: 8/F., 775 Huaihai Road (M), Shanghai 201204
Contact: Li Feng

2011/07/15 - 18
☎ 010-6505 0540, 6505 7688
www.ecwtc.com
630

2011北京国际珠宝展览会
地点：中国国际贸易中心，北京

The 11th Beijing International Jewelry Fair
Venue: China World Trade Center, Beijing

2011/07/29 - 01
☎ 010-6603 8881
🖷 010-6603 3964
650

中国（北京）玩具动漫教育文化博览会
地点：国家会议中心，北京
内容：旨在传播玩具教育理念、集中品牌推广宣传、打破玩具销售瓶颈，直接与品牌玩具近距离接触，动手动脑中让孩子玩儿得开心，引导家长树立正确的消费观念，激发玩具消费的原动力！以主办方策划的“玩具护照”、“夺宝棋兵”、“中央大舞台展示”等为主线，以参展企业各自精彩的产品体验活动为延伸，涵盖产品独立展示、品牌联合互动、互动式研讨会等不同主题的体验活动，突显企业品牌内涵与产品价值！
始办年份：2010
周期：每年一届
市场范围：国际性
入场券价格：50元
参展费用：16,000元（18m²）
上届规模 2010：展览面积11000m²，参观人数69,000人
主办：中国玩具协会；中国贸促会北京市分会
地址：北京复兴门内大街101号百盛写字楼8009室（100031）

China Toys & Animation Educational Expo
Venue: China National Convention Center, Beijing
Profile: Massive market potential – the population of 16-year-old minus children in China almost amounts to 300 million, with less than USD 15.00 per capita annual consumption of toys, compared to that of the nearly USD 300.00 of industrialized nations and USD 34.00 of the world average. Bottleneck to the market development – the Chinese consumers tend to regard toys as the luxuries for the children mostly as the festival gifts or incentives, instead of the necessities for the children, thus thwarting the sales volume growth.
Established Year: 2010
Frequency: Annual
Market Area: International
Cost to Attend: RMB 50:-
Participated Fee: RMB 16,000(18m²)
Statistics 2010: Exhibition Area 11000m², Visitors 69000
Organizer: China Toy Association, CCPIT Beijing Sub-council (CCPIT Beijing)
Address: No. 101 Fu Xing Men Nei Street Beijing 100031, China

2011/08/10 - 12
☎ 010-6863 0418, 13520561058
🖷 010-8868 0811
✉ sy1768@163.com
660

2011第八届中国(北京)国际铸造展览会
地点：中国国际展览中心，北京 CIEC
内容：经七年倾心打造，举办方立足行业前沿，不断开拓创新，展会规模进一步扩大，展会质量和服务水平得到全面提升，已成为铸造企业不可或缺的商务合作平台。范围包括铸造（特种铸造）设备类；压铸类；铸造、压铸材料类；铸件类；锻造、冲压与辅助设备及锻件类；工业炉类；铸造、锻造、热处理及工业炉行业检测仪器仪表设备、环保技术设备；铸造、锻造的车间通风、降温、冷却及粉尘处理设备；
始办年份：2004
主办：中国设备管理协会；北京机械工程学会；北京机械工程学会铸造分会；北京机械工程学会压力加工分会
承办：北京海闻展览有限公司
地址：北京市石景山区石景山路乙18号院万达广场C座1709（100040）
联系人：施毅

The 8th China (Beijing) International Casting Industry Expo 2011
Venue: China International Exhibition Center, Beijing
Established Year: 2004
Organizer: Beijing Haiwen Exhibition Co Ltd
Contact: Shi Yi

2011/08/10 - 12
☎ 010-6863 0418, 13520561058
🖷 010-8868 0811
✉ sy1768@163.com
670

2011第八届中国(北京)国际冶金工业博览会
地点：中国国际展览中心，北京
内容：联合行业权威机构历经七年倾力打造的国际知名品牌展会，展览会不断走向成熟完善，为促进买卖双方贸易成交发挥了关键作用。参展包括冶金（钢铁及有色金属）：技术及设备，产品、制成品及辅助用品；冶金检测及自动化；用于冶金热加工、机械加工、物料输送、动力传动、冶金轴承、减速机、切断、称重、润滑、液压、除尘、表面处理、起重、电气、工业窑炉、燃烧器、金属圆锯机、倒角机、磨削、抛光设备、冶金锯片、切割、机械设备及各种应用材料；耐火材料；冶金工业环境保护技术和设备
市场范围：全国性
性质：面向贸易观众
参展费用：3x3m：国内企业9,800元，合资企业13,800元，外资企业3,000美元；3x4m：国内企业12,800元，合资企业16,800元，外资企业3,800美元；净地（36m²起）：国内企业1,000元/m²，合资企业1,380元，外资企业300美元/m²
主办：北京金属材料流通协会；北京机械工程学会；中国设备管理协会；中钢协冷弯型钢协会
承办：北京海闻展览有限公司
地址：北京市石景山区石景山路乙18号院万达广场C座1709（100040）
联系人：施毅

The 8th China (Beijing) International Metallurgy Industry Expo 2011
Venue: China International Exhibition Center, Beijing
Market Area: National
Nature: Trade Only
Participated Fee: 3x3mUSD 3,000/booth, 3x4m USD 3,800/booth, Raw Space USD USD 300/m² (min 36m²)
Organizer: Beijing Haiwen Exhibition Co Ltd
Contact: Shi Yi

2011/08/11 - 13
☎ 020-3835 8081, 3837 3263
🖷 020-3835 8082
✉ shipbuildex@126.com
www.shipbuildex.cn
680

2011第三届中国（北京）国际路灯.庭院灯暨户外照明展览会
地点：全国农业展览馆，北京
内容：道路灯系列；庭院及景观灯；LED专题系列；新能源专题系列；城市照明及节能；户外照明系列；户外灯具配件。
始办年份：2009
周期：每年一届
市场范围：国际性
性质：面向贸易观众
入场券价格：免费
参展费用：国内企业：标准展位9800元/个，净地1000元/m²；国际企业：标准展位3,000美元/个，净地300美元/m²
上届规模 2010：展览面积15,000m²(国外展商1,000m²)，参展商153家（国外展商20家，来自6个国家），参观人数16,837人（专业贸易观众5,013人）
主办：中国电子学会
承办：广州汇成展览服务有限公司
地址：广州市中山大道190号骏景花园骏御轩G座18B（510665）
联系人：谭飞荣
MSN：mfjyf021@hotmail.com
QQ：874722692

3rd China Intl Road Lamp, Patio Lamp & Outdoor Lights Exhibition
Venue: National Agricultural Exhibition Center, Beijing
Established Year: 2009
Frequency: Annual
Market Area: International
Nature: Trade Only
Cost to Attend: Free
Participated Fee: USD 3,000/booth, Raw Space USD 300/m²
Statistics 2010: Exhibition Area 15,000m²(foreigners 1,000m²), Exhibitors 153（foreigners 20, came from 6 countries）, Visitors 16,837（trade visitors 5,013）
Sponsor: Chinese Institute Of Electronics
Organizer: Guangzhou Wellexpo Exhibition Service Co Ltd
Address: Room 18B, Building G, JUNYUXUAN, Junjing Garden, 190 Zhongshan Avenue, Guangzhou 510665, Guangdong
Contact: Feirong Tan
MSN: mfjyf021@hotmail.com

2011/08/11 - 14
☎ 010-6505 0540, 6505 7688
www.ecwtc.com
690

2011北京国际创意礼品及工艺品展览会
地点：中国国际贸易中心，北京

2011 Beijing International Creative Gift & Craftwork Exhibition
Venue: China World Trade Center, Beijing

2011/08/17 - 20
☎ 010-5933 9166
🖷 010-5933 9199
✉ amy.xie@reedhuaqun.com
✉ ada.zhang@reedhuaqun.com
www.giftsbeijing.com
700

GIFTS& HOME
礼品|家居·北京

第24届中国北京国际礼品、赠品及家庭用品展览会
地点：中国国际展览中心，北京
内容：中国华北、华东地区的礼品、家居用品旗舰展
市场范围：国际性
性质：面向贸易观众
入场券价格：免费
主办：北京励展华群展览有限公司
地址：北京市朝阳区新源南路1-3号平安国际金融中心A座15层01-03，05（100027）
联系人：谢辉

24th China Beijing Intl Gifts, Premium & Houseware Exhibition
Venue: China International Exhibition Center, Beijing
Profile: The show presents an unique price and made to order sourcing advantage benefiting thousands of buyers arriving from around the region in the peak of the gift sourcing season.
Frequency: Three Times each year
Market Area: International
Nature: Trade Only
Cost to Attend: Free
Organizer: Reed Huaqun Exhibitions
Address: Unit 01-03,05, 15th Floor, Tower A, Ping An International Finance Center, No.1-3, Xinyuan South Road, Chaoyang District, Beijing 100027,China
Contact: Xie Hui

2011/08/18 - 20
☎ 010-8839 3925, 8839 3927
🖷 010-8839 3924
✉ info@chinahospeq.com
www.chinahospeq.com
710

第二十届中国国际医用仪器设备展览会暨技术交流会
地点： 国家会议中心，北京
始办年份： 1991
周期： 每年一届
市场范围： 国际性
性质： 面向贸易观众
上届规模 2010：展览面积22,000m^2
主办： 卫生部国际交流与合作中心
地址： 北京市西城区车公庄大街9号五栋大楼B3座（100044）
联系人： 马冉,南易

CHINA-HOSPEQ 2011
Venue: China National Convention Center, Beijing
Established Year: 1991
Frequency: Annual
Market Area: International
Nature: Trade Only
Statistics 2010: Exhibition Area 22,000m^2
Organizer: International Health Exchange and Cooperation Center

2011/08/18 - 22
☎ 010-6505 0540, 6505 7688
www.ecwtc.com
720

2011北京国际艺术博览会
地点： 中国国际贸易中心，北京

2011 Beijing International Art Exposition
Venue: China World Trade Center, Beijing

2011/08/24 – 27
☎ 010-5205 5116, 5205 5295
🖷 010-5205 5156
✉ liran@birtv.com
qulina@birtv.com
www.birtv.com
725

第二十届北京国际广播电影电视设备展览会
地点： 中国国际展览中心，北京 CIEC
内容： 国内历史最悠久、最具规模、最具权威的专业广播电影电视设备展览会
始办年份： 1987
周期： 每年一届
市场范围： 国际性
入场价格： 专业人士免费
参展费用： 标准展位3,150元/m^2，净地2,750元/m^2
上届规模2010：展览面积50,000m^2(国外展商23,000m^2)，参展商453家（国外展商176家，来自30个国家），参观人数53,000人（专业贸易观众30,000人）
主办： 国家广播电影电视总局
承办： 中国广播电视国际经济技术合作总公司
地址： 北京市朝阳区广渠东路1号（100124）
联系人： 李然，瞿丽娜

Beijing International Radio, TV & Film Equipment Exhibition 2011 (BIRTV2011)
Venue: China International Exhibition Center, Beijing
Profile: The biggest and most-authoritative exhibition of professional Radio, TV & Film equipments in China
Established Year: 1987
Frequency: Annual
Market Area: International
Cost to Attend: Free to Trade Visitors
Participated Fee: Standard Booth RMB 3,150/m^2, Raw Space RMB 2,750/m^2
Statistics 2010: Exhibition Area 50,000m^2(foreigners 23,000m^2), Exhibitors 453（foreigners 176, came from 30 countries）, Visitors 53,000（trade visitors 30,000）
Sponsor: State Administration of Radio, Film and Television (SARFT)
Organizer: China Radio & TV Co. for International Techno-Economic Cooperation
Address: No. 1, Guangqu East Road, Chaoyang District, Beijing 100124, China
Contact: Li Ran, Qu Lina

2011/08/30 - 01
☎ 010-5933 9304
🖷 010-5933 9333
✉ amber.zhang@reedexpo.com.cn
www.cibtm.com
730

cibtm™
www.cibtm.com

中国（北京）国际商务及会奖旅游展览会
地点： 国家会议中心，北京
内容： 中国及亚洲地区会奖行业的五星级展览会。此次展会汇集国内外300多家展商、4000多位专业观众以及300多名专业买家，共同搭建了一个提供最佳商业机会、最佳社交网络、最专业的教育平台。展会还得到中国国家旅游局、北京市人民政府、北京市旅游局（CIBTM 2009联合主办方）、国际专业会议协会ICCA, MPI, SITE以及国际、国内专业媒体的大力支持。
周期： 每年一届
市场范围： 国际性
主办： 励展旅游展览集团
地址： 北京市朝阳区新源南路1-3号平安国际金融中心A座15层01-03,05（100027）

China Incentive, Business Travel & Meetings Exhibition
Venue: China National Convention Center, Beijing
Profile: CIBTM provides the perfect platform from which to influence the local and international meetings and incentives industry. Uniting an elite class of buyers with quality suppliers from China and around the world, attendance at CIBTM promises the ultimate business solution. Exhibitors benefit from the opportunity to meet a range of international and regional buyers with the authority to place real business. The event already has a successful and trusted history behind it, attracting participants from over 28 countries.
Frequency: Annual
Market Area: International
Organizer: Reed Travel Exhibitions
Address: Unit 01-03, 05, 15th Floor, Tower A, Ping An International Finance Center, No.1-3 Xinyuan South Road, Chaoyang District, Beijing 100027, China
Contact: Amber Zhang

2011/08/30 - 02
☎ 010-8280 0630, 8280 0773
🖷 010-8280 0857, 8280 0731
✉ zm@cis.org.cn
lsh@cis.org.cn
zjl@cis.org.cn
zj@cis.org.cn
www.miconex.com.cn
740

第二十二届多国仪器仪表学术会议暨展览会
地点： 中国国际展览中心，北京 CIEC
内容： 中国仪器仪表学会先后与联合国教科文组织、联合国工发组织、美国仪表学会、英国测量与控制学会、日本测量与控制学会共同发起组织了多国仪器仪表学术会议暨展览会到目前为止已经成功地举办了21届。多国仪器仪表展览会是采购人员、终端用户、研发工程师及技术经理行业盛会。作为国内测量控制、仪器仪表及自动化行业的风向标，它已经成为全行业洞察企业动向以及整体市场波动的窗口。展会同期举办多场次学术会议、技术交流会、新品发布会和技术论坛。
始办年份： 1983
周期： 每年一届
市场范围： 国际性
性质： 面向公众
入场券价格： 免费
上届规模 2010：展览面积30,000m^2(国外展商10,000m^2)，参展商593家（国外展商190家，来自22个国家），参观人数18,635人

The 22nd International Conference and Fair for Measurement Instrumentation and Automation
Venue: China International Exhibition Center, Beijing
Profile: Co-sponsored by Instrument Society of America (ISA), Institute of Measurement and Control of U.K (M&C), Society of Instrument and Control Engineers of Japan (SICE),United Nations Educational, Scientific and Cultural Organization (UNESCO) and United Nations Industrial Development Organization (UNIDO), CIS has already held 21 events of Multinational Instrumentation Conference and Exhibition (MICONEX) in succession. Miconex has been the leading show in the field of instrumentation and control in China and an important event in the world.
Established Year: 1983
Frequency: Annual
Market Area: International
Nature: Open to Public
Cost to Attend: Free

主办：中国仪器仪表学会
地址：北京市海淀区知春路6号锦秋国际大厦A座2303（100088）
联系人：周小姐 李小姐 张小姐 张先生

Statistics 2010: Exhibition Area 30,000m^2(foreigners 10,000m^2), Exhibitors 593 (foreigners 190, came from 22 countries), Visitors 18,635
Organizer: China Instrument & Control Society
Address: 23nd Floor, Horizon International Tower, No.6 Zhichun Road, Haidian District, Beijing 100088, China
Contact: Meizhou, Sophie Lee

2011/09 -
☎ 010-6609 4505
✉ hetian112@sina.com

750

第二届北京王府井国际品牌节
地点：王府井，北京
主办：北京市商务委员会；北京市外事办公室；北京市文化局；北京市投资促进局；中国贸促会北京分会
联系人：何天

2nd Beijing Wangfujing Brand Festival
Venue: Wang Fu Jing Street, Beijing
Organizer: CCPIT Beijing

2011/09/08 - 10
☎ 010-6478 7342, 8441 4052
🖷 010-8441 4057, 5804 3750
✉ huoli88@163.com
www.expo-capa.com

760

CIAPE中国国际汽车零部件博览会
地点：中国国际展览中心，北京 CIEC
内容：按照国际化、专业化、市场化原则举办的中国国家级国际汽车零部件博览会，CIAPE作为自主的国家级国际性展示和交易平台，是中外汽车及零部件产业有效沟通的重要桥梁；汽车零部件、汽车改装及用品、汽车材料、通用部件等
始办年份：2007
周期：每年两届
市场范围：国际性
性质：面向贸易观众
参展费用：18,620元/展位，7,830元/展位，1,230元/展位；净地：1,880元/m^2, 1,180元/m^2
上届规模 2010：展览面积70,000m^2(国外展商10,000m^2)，参展商1,385家（国外展商300家，来自106个国家），参观人数46,030人
主办：中华人民共和国商务部
承办：中国通用技术集团
地址：北京市望京西路48号金隅国际大厦G座2705室（100102）
联系人：霍丽
QQ：1355348329

China International Auto Parts Expo
Venue: China International Exhibition Center, Beijing
Profile: In accordance with the international, professional, organized by the China market principles, China International Auto Parts Expo is an independent international exhibition and trade platform for Chinese and foreign automobile and parts industry, an important bridge for effective communication; auto parts, car modification and supplies, automotive materials, components and other common
Established Year: 2007
Frequency: Biannual
Market Area: International
Nature: Trade Only
Participated Fee: RMB 18,620/booth, Raw Space RMB 1,880/m^2
Statistics 2010: Exhibition Area 70,000m^2(foreigners 10,000m^2), Exhibitors 1,385 (foreigners 300, came from 106 countries), Visitors 46,030
Sponsor: Ministry of Commerce, China;
Organizer: China General Technology (Group) Holding, Limited
Address: Room 2705, G Block, 48 Wangjing West Road, Beijing, China

---

2011/09/10 - 11
☎ 0571-8839 3239, 8839 3237, 8839 3235
✉ fashion_baby@163.com
http://party.baby023.com

770

时尚育儿北京嘉年华
地点：中国国际贸易中心，北京
内容：玩具系列、孕妇用品、车床系列、食品保健品、童装系列、早教用品、婴幼儿用品、保险理财、儿童和孕妇摄影。
周期：每年一届
上届规模 2010：展览面积7,300m^2,参观人数60,000人
主办：博闻中国(杭州)
地址：浙江省杭州市拱墅区温州路69号南北商务港2-11F（310015）

Fashion Baby Beijing Carnival
Venue: China World Trade Center, Beijing
Frequency: Annual
Statistics 2010: Exhibition Area 7300m^2, Visitors 60,000
Organizer: UBM China (Hangzhou)
Address: 2-11F South West Business Center, No 69 Wenzhou Road, Gong Shu District, Hangzhou 310015, China

---

2011/09/15 - 18
☎ 010-6505 0540,6505 7688
www.ecwtc.com

790

2011年中国北京秋季房地产展示交易会
地点：中国国际贸易中心，北京

2011 Autumntime Real Estate Trade Fair Beijing China
Venue: China World Trade Center, Beijing

2011/09/19 - 21
☎ 010-8451 1832
🖷 010-8451 1829
✉ phoebe@ejkbeijing.com

800

第十九届中国国际纸浆造纸、林业展览会及会议
地点：中国国际展览中心，北京 CIEC
内容：纸浆造纸机械，废报纸、杂志纸脱墨、漂白浆处理设备,夹网新闻纸机;废箱纸板处理设备；大型双盘磨和高浓盘磨打浆系统；计算机控制低脉动供浆系统；水力式流浆箱及高浓流浆箱；高速机内涂布装置；计算机控制可控中高辊；软压光机和超级软压光机；高速复卷机；高精度、高速同步切纸机；造纸、涂布车间在线检测、纵横向控制QCS、DCS系统；铜版纸、牛皮卡、牛皮箱板、瓦楞原纸、涂布白纸板、白卡;日用纸制品等
始办年份：1987
周期：每年一届
市场范围：国际性
性质：面向贸易观众
上届规模 2010：展览面积6,500m^2(国外展商3,000m^2)，参展商310家（国外展商100家，来自21个国家），专业贸易观众8,000人
主办：Adforum公司；美国克劳斯公司；中国制浆造纸研究院
地址：北京朝阳区新源南路6号京城大厦2005房间（100004）
联系人：丁卉群

China Paper / China Forest 2011
Venue: China International Exhibition Center, Beijing
Profile: Paper Making Section: Bleaching, Chemicals, Coating, Environmental, Paper machines, Pulp quality control, Process controls; Pulp and paper products: Market pulp, Bond paper, Newsprint, Non-woven, Specialty, Corrugating medium, linerboard, corrugated containers, cups, folding boxes, laminations, Paper converting section: Rewind equipment, Winders, Coating machines, Drying equipment, Rolls & rollers
Established Year: 1987
Frequency: Annual
Market Area: International
Nature: Trade Only
Statistics 2010: Exhibition Area 6,500m^2(foreigners 3,000m^2), Exhibitors 310 (foreigners 100, came from 21 countries), Trade Visitors 8,000
Organizer: Adforum AB; E.J.Krause & Associates, Inc; China National Pulp and Paper Research Institute
Address: Room 2005 Capital Mansion, 6 Xinyuan Nan Road, Chaoyang District, Beijing
Contact: Phoebe Ding

2011/09/21 - 25
☎ 010-6505 0540, 6505 7688
www.ecwtc.com
810

首届中国国际名表展
地点：中国国际贸易中心，北京

2011 China International Watch Exhibition
Venue: China World Trade Center, Beijing

2011/09/26 - 28
☎ 010-6505 0540, 6505 7688
www.ecwtc.com
820

第五届中国中部投资贸易博览会
地点：中国国际贸易中心，北京

Expo Central China 2011
Venue: China World Trade Center, Beijing

2011/09/26 - 30
☎ 010-8451 1832
🖷 010-8451 1829
✉ xiaohua@expocommcn.com
830

2011年中国国际信息通信展览会
地点：中国国际展览中心，北京 CIEC
内容：3G，4G, 物联网，传输设备，光缆传输系统、终端，卫星通信设备，公用信息数据网络技术、系统及产品，不停电电源设备、交换系统、蜂窝通讯设备、宽频带网络接口、智能网络平台，大型邮政系统，GSM, CDMA通讯系统,移动通讯设备，ATM，远程会议系统，网站,网上增值服务,互联网络,网络管理等
始办年份：1986
周期：每年一届
市场范围：国际性
上届规模 2010：展览面积22,000m^2(国外展商8,000m^2)，参展商500家（国外展商70家，来自13个国家），参观人数120,000人（专业贸易观众20,000人）
主办：中国人民共和国工业和信息产业部；中国贸促会；中国邮电器材集团公司；中国国际展览中心集团公司
海外组织单位: 美国克劳斯公司
地址：北京市朝阳区新源南路6号京城大厦2005室（100004）
联系人：陈小华

PT / EXPO COMM CHINA 2011
Venue: China International Exhibition Center, Beijing
Profile:3G/4G, Internet of Things, Authoring Tools, Bridges/routers/gateways/multiplexers, Bluetooth Technology, Cabling products & services, CRM, Data communication/storage/management, Fibre optic technology, High speed networking, Internet access hardware/technology, IP technology, Mobile phones/communication/commerce, Wireless communications, Antennas, VSAT, Satellite communications, Power supply
Established Year: 1986
Frequency: Annual
Market Area: International
Statistics 2010: Exhibition Area 22,000m^2(foreigners 8,000m^2), Exhibitors 500（foreigners 70, came from 13 countries）, Visitors 120,000（trade visitors 20,000）
Organizer: Ministry of Industry and Information Technology of PRC; CCPIT; China National Postal and Telecommunications Appliances Corporation; China International Exhibition Center Group Corporation
Overseas **Organizer:** E. J. Krause & Associates Inc
Address: Room 2005 Capital Mansion, 6 Xinyuan Nan Road, Chaoyang District, Beijing, China
Contact: Chen Xiaohua

2011/10/13 - 15
☎ 021-6160 8555转ext 231
🖷 021-5876 9332
✉ susan.wang@china.messefrankfurt.com
www.waterexpo.cn
www.messefrankfurt.com.hk
835

中国水博览会暨中国国际膜与水处理技术装备展览会
地点：国家会议中心，北京
周期：每年一届
主办：法兰克福展览（上海）有限公司
地址：上海浦东新区浦东南路999号上海联合广场32层
联系人：汪静

Water Expo China + Water & Membrane China
Venue: China National Convention Center, Beijing
Frequency: Annual
Organizer: Messe Frankfurt (Shanghai) Ltd

2011/10/14 - 16
☎ 010-8699 7155, 8211 3755
🖷 010-8699 7155
✉ ExpoBeijing@163.com
www.CIBE-CIDF.com
www.JianBoHui.org
840

2011第二届中国国际建筑高科技及城市建设博览会
同期：
2011第二届中国国际供热采暖及暖通空调展览会
2011第三届中国国际路灯及户外照明展览会
2011第二届中国国际轨道交通建设展览会
2011第二届中国国际节能减排和生态建设展览会
地点：中国国际展览中心，北京 CIEC
内容：建筑保温、保温隔热、新型墙体、屋面材料、新型防水、结构材料、绿色建材、住宅部品、智能建筑、建筑遮阳、建筑设备、景观绿化；工程设计、门窗幕墙、卫浴陶瓷、厨房设施、装饰五金、地面材料；暖通管道、电工电器、玻璃制品、化学涂料、家具家纺、时尚家居；供热设备、采暖设备、地暖设备、燃气设备、通风设备、新能源设备；钢结构、木结构、砌体结构、组合结构、房屋技术、混凝土结构；道路照明、户外照明、城市照明、景观照明、LED 照明、新能源照明；建筑设计、城镇规划、商业环境、园林景观、绿色建筑、垃圾处理
始办年份：1999
入场券价格：免费
参展费用：特装展位：境内企业1,350元/m^2，境外企业320美元/m^2；标准展位（9m^2）：境内企业12,800元，境外企业3,000美元
上届规模 2010：展览面积50,000m^2(国外展商3,500m^2)，参展商516家（国外展商69家，来自27个国家），参观人数80,000人（专业贸易观众56,000人）
主办：中国建筑装饰协会；中国建筑业协会；中国建筑学会；中国房地产业协会；中国室内装饰协会；中国美术家协会；中国贸促会建设行业分会；中国国际建博会组织委员会
承办：映德会展（北京）有限公司
地址：北京市海淀区三里河路9号国家住建部（100086）
联系人：王涛，彭博
MSN：ExpoBeijing@msn.com
QQ：8619574

The 2nd China International Building Hi-tech and Urban Construction Expo 2011
Venue: China International Exhibition Center, Beijing
Established Year: 1999
Cost to Attend: Free
Participated Fee: Raw Space USD 320/m^2, Standard Booth USD USD 3,000/booth
Statistics 2010: Exhibition Area 50,000m^2(foreigners 3,500m^2), Exhibitors 516（foreigners 69, came from 27 countries）, Visitors 80,000（trade visitors 56,000）
MSN: ExpoBeijing@msn.com

2011/10/15 - 16
☎ 010-6505 0540, 6505 7688
www.ecwtc.com
850

2011中国国际教育展
地点：中国国际贸易中心，北京

China Education Expo 2011
Venue: China World Trade Center, Beijing

2011/10/18 - 21
☎ 010-5222 0922
🖷 010-5222 0900
✉ info@e-bices.org
www.e-bices.org
870

第十一届中国（北京）国际工程机械、建材机械及矿山机械展览与技术交流会
同期举办：北京国际商用车博览会
地点：北京九华国际会展中心，北京
内容：工程机械、建材机械、矿山机械及商用车
周期：两年一届
市场范围：国际性
入场券价格：免费
上届规模 2009：展览面积150,000m², 参展商800家，专业贸易观众78,600人
主办：中国工程机械工业协会；中工工程机械成套有限公司；中国贸促会机械行业分会
地址：北京市丰台区南四环西路188号总部基地七区16号楼（100070）
主办：中国贸促会机械行业分会
地址：北京市西城区三里河路46号（100823）
联系人：张玉惠, 郭旭萍, 吕春丽
电话：010-6859 4811, 6859 4994, 6859 4910
传真：010-6859 4995
邮箱：zhangyuhui@ccpitmsc.org
www.chinamachine.org.cn

2011 Beijing International Construction Machinery Exhibition & Seminar
Concurrent: 2011 China Intl Commercial Vehicle Exhibition
Venue: Beijing Jiuhua Exhibition Center, Beijing
Profile: Construction Machinery, Building and Building Materials Machinery, Mining Machinery, Commercial and Special Vehicles, Spare Parts and Service Providers
Frequency: Biennial
Market Area: International
Cost to Attend: Free
Statistics 2009: Exhibition Area 150,000m², Exhibitors 880, Trade Visitors 78,600
Organizer: China Construction Machinery Association; China Construction Machinery Co Ltd; CCPIT–Machinery Sub-Council
Address: Building 7-16, No. 188, South 4th West Ring Road, Fengtai District, Beijing, China

---

2011/10/26 - 28
☎ 010-8460 0350
🖷 010-8460 0756
✉ wanghua@ciec.com.cn
www.visionchinashow.net
880

第八届中国国际机器视觉展览会暨机器视觉技术及工业应用研讨会
地点：中国国际展览中心，北京
内容：机器视觉核心部件：智能相机，板卡，软件包，配件；工业镜头，光源，辅助产品 2、机器视觉辅件：图像处理系统：外图像系统；机器视觉集成
始办年份：2004
周期：每年一届
市场范围：国际性
性质：面向贸易观众
入场券价格：免费
参展费用：国际展商：室内净地(18m²起)320美元/m²，标准展位(9m²起)350美元/m²；国内展商 净地(18m²起)1,000元/m²，标准展位(9m²起)12,000元/9m²
上届规模 2010：展览面积3,364m²
主办：中国图象图形学学会；中国国际展览中心
承办：北京华港展览有限公司
地址：北京市朝阳区北三环东路六号中国国际展览中心综合服务楼三层（100028）
联系人：汪小姐

The 8th China International Machine Vision Exhibition and Machine Vision Technology & Application Conference
Venue: China International Exhibition Center, Beijing
Profile: Core Components of Machine Vision Products, Machine Vision Parts
Established Year: 2004
Frequency: Annual
Market Area: International
Nature: Trade Only
Cost to Attend: Free
Participated Fee: Raw Space (18m²) USD 320/m², Standard Booth (min 9m²) USD 350/m²
Statistics 2010: Exhibition Area 3,364m²
Organizer: CIEC Exhibition Co Ltd
Address: 1/F, General Service Building, CIEC 6 East Beisanhuan Road, Chaoyang District, Beijing, China 100028

2011/10/26 - 28
☎ 010-8460 0344, 8460 0329
🖷 010-8460 0325, 8460 0346
✉ fangfang@ciec.com.cn
✉ lishu@ciec.com.cn
www.ilope-expo.com
890

中国光电周
暨第十六届中国国际激光、光电子及LED光显示产品展览会
地点：中国国际展览中心，北京
内容：激光材料、激光器、激光应用及传感器；红外材料、技术及其应用；光电显示及照明；光学元件、仪器、材料。
始办年份：1991
周期：每年一届
市场范围：国际性
入场券价格：免费
参展费用：国际展商3,240美元/展位
上届规模 2010：展览面积15,000m²(国外展商1500m²), 参展商390家（国外展商85家，来自16个国家），参观人数15,904人（专业贸易观众12,786人）
主办：中国贸促会；中国国际展览中心集团；中国光学光电子行业协会
承办：中国光学光电子行业协会；中展集团北京华港展览有限公司
地址：北京市朝阳区北三环东路六号中国国际展览中心综合服务楼三层（100028）
联系人：方芳，李澍

The 16th China International Lasers, Optoelectronics and Photonics Exhibition
Venue: China International Exhibition Center, Beijing
Profile: Lasers, Infrared Sensors and Accessories/Opto-electric Display Material and Equipment/Optical Communications Equipment/Component, Devices and Sub-Systems
Established Year: 1991
Frequency: Annual
Market Area: International
Cost to Attend: Free
Participated Fee: USD 3,240/Booth
Statistics 2010: Exhibition Area 15,000m²(foreigners 1,500m²), Exhibitors 390 (foreigners 85, came from 16 countries), Visitors 15,904 (trade visitors 12,786)
Sponsor: CCPIT (CCPIT) China Optics and Optoelectronics Manufactures Association (COEMA); China International Exhibition Center Group Corporation (CIEC GROUP)
Organizer: China Optics and Optoelectronics Manufactures Association (COEMA); CIEC Exhibition Co Ltd
Address: 1/F, General Service Building, CIEC 6 East Beisanhuan Road, Chaoyang District, Beijing 100028, China
Contact: Ms Fang Fang, Mr Lee Shu

2011/10/28 - 31
☎ 010-6505 0540, 6505 7688
www.ecwtc.com
900

第八届中国国际茶业博览会
地点：中国国际贸易中心，北京

CHINA TEA EXPO 2011
Venue: China World Trade Center, Beijing

2011/11/02 - 04
☎ 010-8471 8060
🖷 010-8471 9746
✉ zhangling@unexpo.com.cn
www.fenestration.com.cn
910

2011第九届中国国际门窗幕墙博览会
地点： 中国国际展览中心新馆，北京 CIEC
内容： 涉及中国门窗幕墙行业、节能降耗产品，形成了博览会的3大节能低碳专区。实木、铝包木、铝木复合等凸显个性和高品质生活要求的产品受到市场的追捧。
周期： 每年一届
市场范围： 国际性
参展费用： 国内企业：标准展位A区7,800元/9m^2，B区7,500元/9m^2；净地A区780元/m^2，B区750元/m^2。海外公司：标准展位280美元/m^2，净地230美元/m^2
上届规模 2010：展览面积35,000m^2(国外展商15,000m^2)，参展商361家，参观人数32,381人
主办： 中国建筑金属结构协会
地址： 北京市朝阳区望京西园北京中德建联国际会展有限公司（100120）
联系人： 张玲

Fenestration China 2011
Venue: China International Exhibition Center New Venue, Beijing
Profile: This exhibition dedicated to windows, doors and curtain wall industry
Frequency: Annual
Market Area: International
Nature: Trade Only
Participated Fee: Standard Booth USD 280/m^2, Raw Space USD 230/m^2
Statistics 2010: Exhibition Area 35,000m^2(foreigners 15,000m^2), Exhibitors 361, Visitors 32,381
Organizer: Beijing International UnionExpo Co., Ltd
Contact: Ms Emily Zhang

2011/11/04 - 06
☎ 010-6505 0540, 6505 7688
www.ecwtc.com
915

2011北京国际钱币博览会
地点： 中国国际贸易中心，北京

Beijing International Coins Exposition 2011
Venue: China World Trade Center, Beijing

2011/11/09-11
☎ 020-8666 0158
🖷 020-8667 7120, 8667 2235
✉ info-china@ubm.com
www.cashmereworldfair.com
920

2011中国国际羊绒交易会（CW）
地点：国家会议中心, 北京
内容：羊绒原料、羊绒纱线、羊绒成衣、化工原料及染料、羊绒机械设备、羊绒检测等。
周期：每年一届
上届规模 2010：展览面积5,000m^2, 150个展位
主办：博闻（广州）展览有限公司；中国食品土畜进出口商会
联系：博闻（广州）展览有限公司
地址：广州市流花路中国大酒店商业大厦1159－1164室（510015）

2011Cashmere World
Venue: China National Convention Center, Beijing
Profile: Variety of cashmere raw materials, cashmere yarns, cashmere garments, process chemicals &dyes, machinery for cashmere ,cashmere testing and others
Frequency: Annual
Statistics 2010: Exhibition Area 5,000m^2, 150 booth
Organizer:UBM China (Guangzhou) Co Ltd; China Chamber of Commerce for Imp and Exp of Foodstuffs, Native Produce & Animal By-Products (CFNA)
Contact:UBM China (Guangzhou) Co Ltd
Address: Rm 1159-1164, China Hotel Office Tower, Liu Hua Rd., Guangzhou China (510015)

2011/11/08 - 09
☎ 010-6505 0540, 6505 7688
www.ecwtc.com
930

中国对外投资合作洽谈会
地点： 中国国际贸易中心，北京

The Second China Overseas Investment Fair
Venue: China World Trade Center, Beijing

2011/11/09 - 11
☎ 010-8776 6833, 021-6437 1178
🖷 010-8776 6835, 021-6437 0982
✉ hotelex@ubmsinoexpo.com
crystal.yang@ubm.com
www.hotelex.cn
940

北京国际酒店用品展览会
地点： 国家会议中心，北京
周期： 每年一届
主办： 上海博华国际展览有限公司
地址： 上海襄阳南路218号现代大厦8楼（200031）

Hotelex Beijing
Venue: China National Convention Center, Beijing
Frequency: Annual
Organizer: Shanghai UBM Sinoexpo

2011/11/09 - 11
☎ 010-6401 6504
🖷 010-6401 6504
✉ cy888@vip.163.com
www.cliexpo.org
950

2011北京国际日化产品原料及设备包装展览会
地点： 国家会议中心，北京
内容： 个人、家居织物清洁护理用品及化妆品原料、表面活性剂及助剂、香精香料、防腐剂、调理剂、添加剂等；个人、家居织物清洁护理用品及化妆品生产设备、仪器仪表及分析检测仪器等；个人、家居、织物清洁护理用品及化妆品包装材料以及机械、设备；口腔清洁护理用品及原材料、包装生产设备等；产品OEM厂商及其他关联产品等；
周期： 每年一届
市场范围： 国际性
性质： 面向公众
主办： 中国洗涤用品工业协会；中国轻工业展览中心
地址： 北京市东城区东四六条64号（100007）
联系人： 应艳梅 MSN：lengfeier@msn.com QQ：71229011

Cosmetics, Personal Care & Detergents Expo
- Ingredients, Equipment and Packaging
Venue: China National Convention Center, Beijing
Frequency: Annual
Market Area: International
Nature: Open to Public
Organizer: Exhibition Center of China Light Industry
MSN: lengfeier@msn.com

2011/11/10 - 13
☎ 010-6806 6669转
ext 8021/8022
🖷 010-6806 6969, 6806 7979
✉ wangpeng@ccpitbj.org
haocheng@ccpitbj.org
Lj@wtcbj.com
qw@wtcbj.com
www.iccie.cn
960

第六届中国北京国际文化创意产业博览会
地点： 中国国际展览中心，北京 CIEC
内容： 文化创意产业、广播电影电视、文物及博物馆相关文化创意产品、青少年文化创意 5、国际文化创意、设计创意、文化旅游景区与旅游商品、画廊及艺术品交易、新闻出版与动漫游戏 10、体育产业、创意礼品与工艺品、城市雕塑作品、涂鸦艺术
始办年份： 2006
周期： 每年一届
市场范围： 国际性
入场券价格： 免费

6th China Beijing International Cultural & Creative Industry Expo
Venue: China International Exhibition Center, Beijing
Profile: Cultural & Creative Industry Comprehensive, Broadcasting, Film and Television, Cultural Relics & Museum Related Creative Products, Youth Students Cultural & Creative Products, International Culture & Creation, Design Creation, Tourist Attraction
Established Year: 2006
Frequency: Annual
Market Area: International
Cost to Attend: Free
Participated Fee: Standard Booth RMB 12,000, Raw Space RMB 1,600/m^2

参展费用： 标准展位(元)6,000/8,000/12,000/16,000，净地(元)600/800/1,200/1,600元/m^2
上届规模 2010：展览面积65,000m^2(国外展商12,500m^2)，参展商1,370家（国外展商115家，来自15个国家），参观人数190,000人（专业贸易观众85,000人）
主办： 文化部；国家广播电影电视总局；中华人民共和国新闻出版总署；北京市人民政府 北京世界贸易中心
地址： 北京市西城区南礼士路19号建邦商务会馆2层（100045）
联系人： 王鹏，张皓成

Statistics 2010: Exhibition Area 65,000m^2(foreigners 12,500m^2), Exhibitors 1,370（foreigners 115, came from 15 countries）, Visitors 190,000（trade visitors 85,000）
Organizer: The Ministry of Culture, China; The State Administration of Radio Film and Television; General Administration of Press and Publications, China; Beijing Municipality; World Trade Center Beijing
Address: 2nd Floor Jianbang Business Center, No. 19 Nanlishi Road, Xicheng District, Beijing, China
Contact: Wang Peng, Zhang Haocheng, Liu Jie, Qi Wei

2011/11/17 - 19
☎ 010-8501 8362
🖷 010-8562 5510
✉ zhangjing1@cofco.com
guoweidong@cofco.com
www.ocex.com.cn
970

中国国际有机食品和绿色食品博览会
地点： 中国国际贸易中心，北京
内容： 有机食品、绿色食品、地方特色食品、进口食品、红酒、茶与咖啡、婴幼儿食品及乳制品、干果、水果、蔬菜、休闲食品、食品机械、食品电子商务、食品保健品
始办年份： 2005
周期： 每年一届
市场范围： 国际性
性质： 面向公众
参展费用： 8,100元/展位
上届规模 2010：展览面积6,000m^2(国外展商120m^2)，参展商86家（国外展商2家，来自2个国家），参观人数10,920人（专业贸易观众134人）
主办： 商务部外贸发展事务局；中粮集团有限公司；中粮集团三利广告展览有限公司
地址： 北京市朝阳门南大街8号中粮福临门大厦11F01（100020）
联系人： 张静，郭伟东

ORGANIC CHINA EXPO BEIJING 2011
Venue: China World Trade Center, Beijing
Established Year: 2005
Frequency: Annual
Market Area: International
Nature: Open to Public
Participated Fee: RMB 8,100
Statistics 2010: Exhibition Area 6000m^2(foreigners 120m^2), Exhibitors 86（foreigners 2, came from 2 countries）, Visitors 10,920（trade visitors 134）
Organizer: Trade Development Bureau Ministry of Commerce COFCO Limited；Sunry Advertising and Exhibition Co Ltd
Address: 11F01, COFCO Fortune Plaza, No.8 Chao Yang Men South St., Chaoyang, Beijing 100020

2011/11/23 - 27
☎ 010-5827 6063, 5827 6062
🖷 010-5827 6064
✉ panmx@Jewelry.org.cn
www.chinajewelryshow.com
1000

2011中国国际珠宝展
地点： 中国国际展览中心，北京 CIEC
内容： 珠宝首饰类：钻石首饰、黄金首饰、翡翠首饰、珍珠首饰、彩色宝石首饰、铂金首饰、白银首饰、玉石首饰、艺术首饰等 宝石及原料类：钻石、翡翠、白玉、珍珠、红蓝宝石、祖母绿、碧玺、水晶、绿松石、海蓝宝石、珊瑚、琥珀、玛瑙、贵金属等 相关产品：玉石、水晶雕件、流行饰品、矿物标本、机械、设备、工具及包装、行业机构、鉴定机构、媒体等
始办年份： 1990
周期： 每年一届
市场范围： 国际性
性质： 面向公众
入场券价格： 免费
参展费用： 标准展位15,000元，净地展位14,000
上届规模 2010：展览面积42,000m^2(国外展商12,000m^2)，参展商961家（国外展商253家，来自22个国家），参观人数65,000人（专业贸易观众15,000人）
主办： 中国珠宝玉石首饰行业协会
承办： 北京中宝协展览有限公司
地址： 北京市东城区北三环东路36号环球贸易中心C座2215（100013）
联系人： 潘沐闲,易晓
MSN：mumuanais@hotmail.com
QQ：1499102596

2011 China International Jewelry Fair
Venue: China International Exhibition Center, Beijing
Profile: Jewelries: Diamond Jewelry; Gold Jewelry; Jade Jewelry; Pearl Jewelry; Gemstone jewelry;Platinum Jewelry;Silver Jewelry; Art Jewelry, and etc. Gems and raw materials: Diamonds; Jade; Pearl; Ruby; Sapphire; Emerald; ;Amethyst; Crystal; Turquoise; Aquamarine; Coral; Amber;Agate;ColorGemstoneSemi-precious stone and etc. Others: Fashion jewelry; Mineral crystal; Lapidary; Jewelry machines, equipments, tools and packages; Testing center; Media
Established Year: 1990
Frequency: Annual
Market Area: International
Nature: Open to Public
Cost to Attend: Free
Participated Fee: Standard Booth 15,000/booth, Raw Space RMB 14,000/booth
Statistics 2010: Exhibition Area 42,000m^2(foreigners 12,000m^2), Exhibitors 961（foreigners 253, came from 22 countries）, Visitors 65,000（trade visitors 15,000）
Sponsor: Gems & Jewelry Trade Association of China
Organizer: Beijing Zhongbaoxie Exhibition Center Co Ltd
Address: Rm2215, Tower C, Global Trade Center, No.36, North Third Ring Road, Dongcheng District, Beijing, China
Contact: Anais Pan, Yi Xiao
MSN: mumuanais@hotmail.com

2011/11/25 - 27
☎ 010-5933 9166
🖷 010-5933 9199
✉ amy.xie@reedhuaqun.com,
ada.zhang@reedhuaqun.com
www.giftsbeijing.com
1020

GIFTS&
HOME
礼品|家居·北京

北京国际礼品、赠品及家用精品（年底）采购订货会
地点： 中国国际贸易中心，北京
内容： 北京年末采购高峰季节的礼品家居展览会
市场范围： 国际性
性质： 面向贸易观众
入场券价格： 免费
主办： 北京励展华群展览有限公司
地址： 北京市朝阳区新源南路1-3号平安国际金融中心A座15层01-03，05（100027）
联系人： 谢辉

The 22nd China International Gifts, Premium & Houseware Exhibition
Venue: China World Trade Center, Beijing
Market Area: International
Nature: Trade Only
Cost to Attend: Free
Organizer: Reed Huaqun Exhibitions
Address: Unit 01-03,05, 15th Floor, Tower A, Ping An International Finance Center, No.1-3, Xinyuan South Road, Chaoyang District, Beijing 100027,China

---

2011/11/30 – 12/02
☎ 010-6856 5634, 8460 0349
🖷 010-8460 0325, 6852 3345
✉ cpfmc-zhlb@263.net
wangxing@ciec.com.cn
www.chinafpma.org
www.foodtechchina.com
1030

第十二届中国国际食品加工和包装机械展览会
地点： 中国国际展览中心，北京 CIEC
内容： 包装和食品加工机械，包括食品加工机械，烹煮设备，食品加工主要机械，其它食品机械，包装印刷机械，包装容器制造机械，包装材料加工机械，药品包装机械
始办年份： 1989
周期： 两年一届（逢单年在北京举办）
市场范围： 国际性
性质： 面向贸易观众

12th China International Food Processing and Packaging Machinery Exhibition
Venue: China International Exhibition Center, Beijing
Profile: Food Processing Machinery, Cooking Machinery, Food Processing General Machinery, Other Food Machinery, Decorating Printing Machinery, Packaging Container Making Machinery, Packaging Materials Processing Machinery, Medicine Packaging Machinery
Established Year: 1989

入场券价格：免费
参展费用：国内展商11,800元/9m²，国际展商3,198美元/展位，325美元/m²
上届规模 2009：展览面积9,000m²(国外展商2,000m²)，参展商315家（国外展商48家，来自14个国家），专业贸易观众18,546人
主办：中国包装和食品机械总公司
地址：北京市德胜门外北沙滩1号82信箱（100083）
联系人：张兆兰
承办：北京华港展览有限公司
地址：北京市朝阳区北三环东路6号中国国际展览中心综合服务楼一层（100028）
联系人：王星

Frequency: Biennial
Market Area: International
Nature: Trade Only
Cost to Attend: Free
Participated Fee: USD 3,198/booth, Raw Space USD 325/m²
Statistics 2009: Exhibition Area 9,000m²(foreigners 2,000m²), Exhibitors 315（foreigners 48, came from 14 countries）, Trade Visitors 18,546
Organizer: China Packaging and Food Machinery Corp
Address: No 1 Beishatan Str., Deshengmenwai, Beijing, China
Contact: Julie Zhang
Organizer: CIEC Exhibition Company Ltd
Address: 1/F, General Service Building, CIEC 6 East Beisanhuan Road, Chaoyang District, Beijing, China
Contact: Nancy Wang

2011/12/09 - 18
☎ 010-6505 0540, 6505 7688
www.ecwtc.com
1040

2011年北京欧美超级家具展览会
地点：中国国际贸易中心，北京

2011 Beijing International Luxury Furniture Expo
Venue: China World Trade Center, Beijing

2012/04 -
☎ 010-8460 0166
🖷 010-8460 0166
✉ zhangjun1415@126.com
zhanghengjie@ciec.com.cn
www.china-autoshow.com
1050

2012（第十二届）北京国际汽车展览会
地点：中国国际展览中心新馆，北京
内容：各种类型的汽车（包括乘用车、商用车及专用车）；各种类型的概念车；各种汽车零部件、总成、模块及系统；各种汽车制造设备，工艺装备；各种检测、测试、实验仪器和设备；计算机开发设计系统及应用技术；汽车工业生产的新工艺、新材料；汽车工业新能源技术与产品；汽车工业环保技术与产品；各种汽车用品、装饰件；各种汽车维修设备
始办年份：1990
周期：两年一届（逢双年在北京举办）
市场范围：国际性
上届规模 2010：展览面积125,000万m²(国外展商70,000m²)，参展商2,100家（国外展商225家，来自18个国家），参观人数780,000人（专业贸易观众80,000人）
主办：中国机械工业联合会；中国机械工业集团公司；中国贸促会；中国汽车工业协会
承办：中国贸促会汽车行业分会；中国汽车工业国际合作总公司；中国国际展览中心集团公司；中国汽车工程学会
地址：北京市朝阳区北三环东路六号中国国际展览中心综合服务楼三层（100028）
联系人：张军，张恒杰

2012 Beijing International Automotive Exhibition
Venue: China International Exhibition Center New Venue, Beijing
Profile: Passenger cars, commercial vehicles and special purpose vehicles; Concept vehicles; Auto parts, assemblies, modules and systems; Vehicle manufacturing and technological process equipments; Vehicle measuring, testing equipment; Vehicle R & D and design techniques and systems and computer application technologies; New technological process and new material in automotive industry; New energy resource technologies and products in automotive industry; Environmental protection technologies and products in automotive industry; Vehicle ornaments and accessories; Vehicle maintenance
Established Year: 1990
Frequency: Biennial
Market Area: International
Statistics 2010: Exhibition Area 125,000m²(foreigners 70,000m²), Exhibitors 2,100（foreigners 225, came from 18 countries）, Visitors 780,000（trade visitors 80,000）
Sponsor: China machinery industry federation (CMIF); China national machinery industry corporation (SINOMACH); CCPIT; China association of automobile manufacturers (CAAM)
Organizer: CCPIT Automotive Sub–Council (CCPIT AUTO); China National Automotive Industry International Corporation (CNAICO); China International Exhibition Center Group Corporation (CIEC); Society of Automotive Engineers of China (SAE–China)
Address: CIEC Exhibition Co Ltd, 1/F, General Service Building, CIEC 6 East Beisanhuan Road, Chaoyang District, Beijing, China 100028
Contact: Zhang Jun, Zhang Hengjie

2012/05 -
☎ 010-8851 4541,
6841 8899转ext 669
🖷 010-6845 8356
✉ wangkunyi@foundry.com.cn
www.expochina.cn
1060

2012中国国际铸造博览会
地点：中国国际展览中心新馆，北京
内容：重机、矿冶、机床、能源、电力铸件、轨道车辆、船舶铸件、石化铸件、航空航天等各类大型铸件；压铸、有色合金及精品铸件、铸管、轧辊等；各种铸造用原辅材料；造型设备、制芯设备、熔炼设备、清理设备、除尘设备、各类检查设备、铸造模具和机械加工设备等各类铸造装备；各用铸造工具等、铸造用环境、劳动保护设备及用品；各科研及生产企业的设计、研究成果、专利和新技术等。
始办年份：1998
周期：两年一届
市场范围：全国性
性质：面向贸易观众
参展费用：标准展位12,000元/9m²，净地1,200元/m²
上届规模 2010：展览面积30,000m²(国外展商6,000 m²)，参展商1,100家（国外展商300家，来自28个国家），参观人数31,000人（专业贸易观众2,000人）
主办：中国铸造协会
地址：北京市海淀区紫竹院路甲32号（100048）
联系人：王坤毅，范琦

2012 China International Foundry Expo (CIFEX)
Venue: China International Exhibition Center New Venue, Beijing
Profile: Castings, Foundry Equipments, Foundry Materials, Foundry Moulds and Patterns, Foundry jigs and fixtures, Foundry Technology, Computer Applications, Business and Trade and Consulting and Services, Technical Publications and Periodicals and networks, other exhibitors.
Established Year: 1998
Frequency: Biannual
Market Area: National
Nature: Trade Only
Participated Fee: Standard Booth RMB 12,000/9m², Raw Space RMB 1,200/m²
Statistics 2010: Exhibition Area 30,000m² (foreigners 6,000 m²), Exhibitors 1,100（foreigners 300, came from 28 countries）, Visitors 31,000（trade visitors 2,000）
Organizer: China Foundry Association
Address: Jia 32 Zizhuyuan Road, Haidian District, Beijing 100048, China
Contact: Wang Kun Yi, Fan Qi

2012/05/09 - 12
☎ 010-6522 0753, 8511 1723
🖷 010-8511 1723
✉ expo@mc-ccpit.com
www.mm-china.com
1070

第十三届中国国际冶金工业展览会
地点：中国国际展览中心新馆，北京
内容：冶金（钢铁及有色金属）：技术及设备，产品、制成品及辅助用品；辅助材料；炭素材料；铁合金；耐火材料及工业陶瓷；用于冶金、热加工、机械加工、耐火材料生产等方面的电动设备、电控及电子检测设备、数据处理技术及仪器仪表；节能减排、环境保护技术及设备；冶金设计与咨询服务；专业技术期刊、杂志、专业网站及其它媒体。

Metallurgy China 2012
Venue: China International Exhibition Center New Venue, Beijing
Profile: Plant and equipment for processing prime and raw material, Plant and equipment for iron making, Plant and equipment for steel making, Plant and equipment for non-ferrous metals production, Plant and equipment for casting and pouring of molten steel, Plant and equipment for casting and pouring of non-ferrous metals, Plant and equipment for shaping of steel, Plant and system for shaping of

始办年份：1988
周期：两年一届
市场范围：国际性
性质：面向贸易观众
入场券价格：免费
上届规模 2010：展览面积9,965m²(国外展商1,736m²)，参展商320家（国外展商69家，来自29个国家），参观人数47,693人
主办：中国钢铁工业协会；中国贸促会冶金行业分会
地址：北京东四西大街46号中国贸促会冶金行业分会（100711）
联系人：马婧 朱晓光

non-ferrous metals; Steel products, products of non ferrous metals, ferroalloy, refractory materials; Electrical engineering and automation measuring and techniques for metallurgical plants and rolling mills; Miscellaneous equipment for metallurgical plants and rolling mills; Environment protection equipment
Established Year: 1988
Frequency: Biennial
Market Area: International
Nature: Trade Only
Cost to Attend: Free
Statistics 2010: Exhibition Area 9,965m²(foreigners 1,736m²), Exhibitors 320（foreigners 69, came from 29 countries）, Visitors 47,693
Organizer: China Iron & Steel Association; Metallurgical Council of CCPIT
Address: 46 Dongsi Xidajie, Dongcheng District, Beijing, China
Contact: Ma Jing, Zhu Xiaoguang

2012/06/12 - 16
☎ 010-5933 9072
🖷 010-5933 9099
✉ edwin.tan@reedexpo.com.cn
http://cimes.reedhuabo.com

1075

第十一届中国国际机床工具展览会

地点：中国国际展览中心新馆，北京
内容：机床，工具与机床附件;自动化控制与动力传动;热加工技术与设备;相关制造技术与设备
始办年份：1992
周期：两年一届
市场范围：国际性
性质：面向贸易观众
上届规模 2010：展览面积136,000m²，参展商1,390家（来自28个国家），参观人数199,762人
主办：中国机床总公司（CNMTC）；励展博览集团
承办：北京国机展览中心(CES)；励华国际展览有限公司
联系人：陈远 鹏先生

The 11th China Intl Machine Tool & Tools Exhibition

Venue: China International Exhibition Center New Venue, Beijing
Profile: CIMES is the largest machine Tool & Tools Exhibition in China & 3rd largest in the world, bringing together buyers from all corners the world with a key focus on 10 major industry group in China, to source new products and services over five trading days.
Established Year: 1992
Frequency: Biennial
Market Area: International
Nature: Trade Only
Statistics 2010: Exhibition Area 136,000m², Exhibitors 1,390（came from 28 countries）, Visitors 199,762
Organizer: Capital Exhibition Services; Reed Huayin

北京其他展览信息
Other Exhibitions in Beijing

举办地点：中国国际展览中心，北京（北京市朝阳区北三环东路28号）
中国国际展览中心新馆，北京（北京市顺义区天竺镇裕翔路88号）

Venue: China International Exhibition Center (Address: 28 Bei Sanhuan Dong Road, Chaoyang District, Beijing, China)
Venue: China International Exhibition Center New Venue
(Address: 88 Yu Xiang Road, Tianzhu Area, Shunyi District, Beijing, China)
咨询电话Tel 010-8046 8251

2011北京图书订货会
2011/01/09-11
中国国际展览中心

DMG年会
2011/01/19
中国国际展览中心

2011年国展首场人才招聘会
2011/02/12-13
中国国际展览中心

人才招聘洽谈会
2011/02/19-20
中国国际展览中心

第12届中国汽车用品暨改装汽车展览会
2011/02/25-27
中国国际展览中心新馆

第十三届国家部委人才联合招聘会
2011/02/26-27
中国国际展览中心

第二十一届中国国际钓鱼用品贸易展览会
2011/02/17-19
中国国际展览中心新馆

中国国际建筑装饰及材料博览会
2011/03/02-05
中国国际展览中心新馆

中国国际供热、通风及空调产品与技术展览会
2011/03/03-05
中国国际展览中心

第十届中国国际门业展览会
2011/03/09-12
中国国际展览中心新馆

第55届全国汽车保修检测诊断设备（春季）展览会
北京国际汽车用品展览会
2011/03/16-19
中国国际展览中心新馆

第二十三届中国国际礼品、赠品及家庭用品展览会
2011/03/16-19
中国国际展览中心

第十一届中国国际石油石化技术装备及管道防爆电气自动化展览会
2011/03/22-24
中国国际展览中心新馆

2011年中国国际广播电视信息网络展览会
2011/03/23-25
中国国际展览中心

中国国际服装服饰博览会
2011/03/28-31
中国国际展览中心新馆

中国国际纺织面料及辅料（春夏）博览会
2011/03/30-04/01
中国国际展览中心

2011年国际照明展览会
2011/04/06-08
中国国际展览中心

2011北京国际烘焙、食品加工和包装机械及包装制品展览会
2011/04/08-10
中国国际展览中心

2011中国国际新能源产业博览会
2011/04/08-10
中国国际展览中心

2011北京国际美容美发化妆用品及养生产品博览会
2011/04/08-10
中国国际展览中心

2011年第十二届中国国际机床展览会
2011/04/11-16
中国国际展览中心新馆

中国国际孕、婴、童用品展览会
2011/04/14-16
中国国际展览中心

中国国际石材产品及石材技术装备展览会
2011/04/20-23
中国国际展览中心

2011北京国际珠宝首饰展览会暨
2011北京国际奢侈品展览会
2011/04/22-25
中国国际展览中心

2011第六届北京国际泳池沐浴SPA展览会
2011/04/26-28
中国国际展览中心

第九届北京国际社会公共安全产品与技术设备展览会
2011/04/26-28
中国国际展览中心

2011北京国际物联网技术设备与应用展览会
2011/04/26-28
中国国际展览中心

2011中国时尚沙发、高端卧室用品暨时尚家居生活展览会
2011/04/27-29
中国国际展览中心

全国名优特产品与外贸商品展
暨中国网络商品交易会
2011/05/07-09
中国国际展览中心

中国国际健康产业博览会暨
北京国际绿色有机食品健康油脂产业展
2011/05/07-09
中国国际展览中心

2011第七届北京国际LED展览会
2011/05/06-08
中国国际展览中心

第五届中国国际新型墙材及装备产品展览会
2011/05/12-14
中国国际展览中心

第十四届中国北京国际科技产业博览会
2011/05/18-22
中国国际展览中心

第二十届中国国际专业音响灯光乐器展览会
2011/05/26-29
中国国际展览中心

第九届中国国际肉类工业展览会
2011/06/01-03
中国国际展览中心

2011第七届中国（北京）国际煤炭装备及矿山设备技术展览会
2011/06/01-03
中国国际展览中心

第十二届中国国际环保展览及会议
2011/06/07-10
中国国际展览中心

北京国际休闲娱乐产业、体育用品展览会
2011/06/09-11
中国国际展览中心

中国国际家居及装饰展览会
2011/06/09-12
中国国际展览中心新馆

第八届北京国际教育博览会
2011/06/17-19
中国国际展览中心

第八届中国（北京）国际钢管工业展览会
2011/06/16-18
中国国际展览中心

第六届中国国际军民两用技术展览会
2011/06/23-25
中国国际展览中心

第五届中国北京电视及网络购物展览会
2011/06/24-26
中国国际展览中心

2011北京国际纯电动车、混合动力暨
清洁能源车及零部件展览会
2011/07/03-05
中国国际展览中心

中国国际彩盒展
2011/07/06-08
中国国际展览中心

2011北京汽车嘉年华
2011/07/22-25
中国国际展览中心

2011第五届中国（北京）红木古典家具、古董艺术品暨传统文化博览会
2011/07/29-08/01
中国国际展览中心

第二届中国（北京）城市交通设施、地铁轨道交通及市政设施展览会
2011/07/29-31
中国国际展览中心
2011中国国际洗染业展览会
2011/08/04-06
中国国际展览中心

2011年北京美化家居展览会
2011/08/05-07
中国国际展览中心

2011北京国际物流叉车、卡车及起重机展览会
2011/08/04-06
中国国际展览中心

2011北京国际制冷、冷冻、冷藏及冷链展览会
2011/08/04-06
中国国际展览中心

2011北京国际五金机电、压缩机、减速机齿轮工业展览会
2011/08/10-12
中国国际展览中心

2011北京国际电子、电池工业展览会
2011/08/10-12
中国国际展览中心

中国（北京）国际金属冶金展
2011/08/10-12
中国国际展览中心

2011中国国际妇幼婴童产业展览会
2011/08/12-14
中国国际展览中心

第二十四届中国国际礼品、赠品及家庭用品展览会
2011/08/17-20
中国国际展览中心

北京国际广播电影电视设备展览会
2011/08/23-27
中国国际展览中心

第二十二届多国仪器仪表展览会
2011/08/30-09/02
中国国际展览中心

北京国际图书博览会
2011/08/31-09/04
中国国际展览中心新馆

中国国际饮用水技术展览会及论坛
2011/09/01-03
中国国际展览中心

2011年中国国际汽车零部件博览会
2011/09/08-10
中国国际展览中心

中国国际眼镜业展览会
2011/09/14-16
中国国际展览中心

中国国际纸浆造纸、林业展览会及会议
2011/09/19-21
中国国际展览中心

第十一届中国国际风能、太阳能、核电工业及智能电网、电力设备展览会
2011/09/19-21
中国国际展览中心

第十二届中国国际给排水、水处理、泵阀管道暨城市环保、脱硫除尘设备展览会
2011/09/19-21
中国国际展览中心

2011年中国国际信息通信展览会
2011/09/26-30
中国国际展览中心

2011中国（北京）国际汽车制造业博览会
2011/10/13-15
中国国际展览中心

第五届中国国际马业马术展览会
2011/10/13-15
中国国际展览中心

2011北京国际美容美发化妆用品及养生产品博览会
2011/10/13-15
中国国际展览中心

中国国际设计艺术博览会
2011/10/14-16
中国国际展览中心

第十四届膜与水处理技术暨装备展览会
2011/10/19-21
中国国际展览中心

2011北京国际风能大会暨展览会
2011/10/19-21
中国国际展览中心新馆

2011北京国际广告技术设备展及LED展览会
2011/10/20-22
中国国际展览中心

第六届中国国际建筑展览会
2011/10/20-22
中国国际展览中心

中国国际玻璃工业新技术展览会暨玻璃艺术及装饰展览会
2011/10/25-27
中国国际展览中心

中国国际光电产业博览会暨中国国际激光，电子及光显产业展览会/中国国际机器视觉展览会暨机器视觉技术及工业应用研讨会
2011/10/26-28
中国国际展览中心

2011年中国国际新能源应用博览会
2011/10/30-11/01
中国国际展览中心

北京国际轨道交通展览会
2011/11/01-04
中国国际展览中心

中国国际门窗幕墙博览会
2011/11/02-04
中国国际展览中心

金属结构协会30周年活动
2011/11/02-04
中国国际展览中心

中国国际贸易服务博览会
2011/11/04-06
中国国际展览中心

2011中国国际福祉博览会
2011/11/04-06
中国国际展览中心

第六届中国北京国际文化创意产业博览会
2011/11/10-13
中国国际展览中心

第十二届中国国际润滑油及调和技术设备展览会
2011/11/16-18
中国国际展览中心

中国国际加油加气站高新技术及设备暨便利店业务博览会
2011/11/16-18
中国国际展览中心

中国国际工业配件及铸锻件展览会
2011/11/16-18
中国国际展览中心

亚洲北京国际纺织品专业处理（洗衣）展览会
2011/11/17-19
中国国际展览中心

2011年中国国际珠宝展览会
2011/11/23-27
中国国际展览中心

中国国际食品加工和包装机械展览会
2011/11/30-12/01
中国国际展览中心

重庆 Chongqing

1100

2011/02/23 - 25
☎ 023-6280 4567, 8907 9843
🖷 023-6280 4567
✉ xinte@hope-tarsus.com
www.cwmee.com

2011中国中西部（重庆）医疗器械展览会
第19届中国重庆国际医疗器械展览会
地点：重庆国际会展中心，重庆
内容：诊断设备：超声诊断设备、X线影像诊断设备、心脑电监护设备、扫描设备、生化检测设备、康复理疗设备、功能检查设备、病理诊断设备、内窥镜检查设备、光学仪器及神经科、骨科、五官科、眼科、骨科等检查诊断设备。治疗设备：内外科手术设备、放射治疗设备、核医学治疗设备、激光设备、理疗设备、低温冷冻治疗设备、透析治疗设备、急救设备、麻醉和止痛设备及病房护理设备等。辅助设备：消毒灭菌设备、制冷设备、供氧设备、空调设备、血库设备、监测系统和软件、分析仪器、数据记录和处理设备、医院管理系统、各种医用车辆；卫生材料及用品：医用搪瓷、玻璃器皿、敷料橡胶用品及一次性消耗品、标准化试剂。口腔设备及用品：口腔放射设备, 口腔内科材料, 口腔外科器械,口腔治疗椅及相关用品材料.
始办年份：1994
周期：每年一届
参展费用：室内特展位6,800元/9m^2；标准展位5,800元/9m^2
主办：重庆市卫生局；重庆市医学会,重庆市医院管理学会
承办：重庆润丰展览有限公司；中英合资好博塔苏斯展览公司成都分公司
联系人：王素梅

China (Chongqing) Medical Equipment Exhibition
Venue: Chongqing International Convention & Exhibition Center, Chongqing
Established Year: 1994
Frequency: Annual
Participated Fee: RMB 6,800/9m^2
Organizer: Hope Exhibition

1110

2011/03/10 - 12
☎ 023-6291 8806
🖷 023-6190 4118
✉ wang9sky@126.com
www.CA8888.com

2011中国重庆第十六届仪器仪表工业控制自动化国际展览会
地点：重庆国际会议展览中心，重庆
内容：动力传动系统、机械驱动系统与控制技术设备；自动化仪器仪表与系统；工业控制计算机、控制系统；机电一体化控制设备、高新技术改造传统产业技术装备；开关、流体自控阀门、液压气动元件；质量控制暨测试、测量仪器仪表及实验室装备；学仪器暨光电、超声波、分析、实验、电子和智能仪器仪表；温度、速度、流量、压力及参数计量、测试仪器仪表；金属与非金属测试器，环境保护、质控及仪器仪表；仪器仪表工艺装备与加工设备；机器人、工业机械手及其配件，机器人视觉；工业组装技术、产品、材料、工具及装备；电子制造系统暨电子零部件及辅助设备。机器人、机械手、视图及零部件；工业连接系统
始办年份：1995
周期：每年一届
主办：重庆市科学技术研究院；重庆市科学技术协会；重庆市自动化与仪器仪表学会；重庆市物流协会
承办：重庆九天展览策划有限公司
地址：重庆市南岸区南坪西路27号福天大厦B-24-2（400060）
联系人：王萍

International Automation& Instrument Exhibition Central & Western China
Venue: Chongqing International Convention & Exhibition Center, Chongqing
Profile: The use of information to promote industrialization, instrumentation, the use of automation technology to promote industrial upgrading
Established Year: 1995
Frequency: Annual
Organizer: Chongqing 9Sky Exhibition Planning Co Ltd
Address: 24-2 room, B building, Futian Mansion, 27 Weat Nanping Road, Chongqing 400060, China

1120

2011/04/14 - 16
☎ 023-8836 0597
🖷 023-8836 0608
✉ 709203593@qq.com
www.goldenexpo.org

2011第二届中国（重庆）国际电子信息产业展览会
地点：重庆国际会议展览中心，重庆
内容：信息通信技术（ICT），消费电子软件及信息服务，物联网应用（RFID、智能卡），云计算，数字生活体验，台湾IT产品
始办年份：2010
周期：每年一届
性质：面向公众
主办：国家工业和信息化部部；重庆市人民政府；中国电子信息产业研究院；重庆市通信管理局；台湾区电机电子工业同业公会
承办：重庆高地会展咨询服务中心
地址：重庆市南岸区江南大道27号江南明珠905室（400060）
联系人：张小姐

2nd China (Chongqing) Electronic Information Industry Exhibition
Venue: Chongqing International Convention & Exhibition Center, Chongqing
Established Year: 2010
Frequency: Annual
Nature: Open to Public
Organizer: Goldenexpo Organization

1130

2011/04/14 - 16
☎ 023-8836 0596
🖷 023-8836 0608
✉ xinlu20@126.com
www.goldenexpo.org

2011中国（重庆）国际物联网技术与应用展览会
地点：重庆国际会议展览中心，重庆
内容：物联网技术应用：RFID（无线射频识别）技术、电子标签生产解决方案、读写器开发最新技术、中间件的精确控制技术、最新非接触的支付技术、短距离通讯技术、传感网技术及物联网技术在工业生产、物流、零售业、防伪、人员、交通、车辆、军事、资产管理、动物、服饰、图书、社会安全、智能城市等领域的全面解决方案和成功应用展示
始办年份：2011

China (Chongqing) Exhibition on Internet of Things
Venue: Chongqing International Convention & Exhibition Center, Chongqing
Established Year: 2011
First Session
Frequency: Annual
Organizer: Goldenexpo Organization

首届
周期：每年一届
主办：重庆市信息化领导小组办公室；重庆市经济和信息化委员会；重庆市通信管理局；台湾区电机电子工业同业公会；重庆高地会展咨询服务中心
地址：重庆市南岸区江南大道27号江南明珠905室（400060）
联系人：张小姐

2011/04/20 - 22
☎ 010-6879 9042/43
023-8638 2821
📠 010-6879 9050
023-8638 2824
✉ liusl@cmes.org
zhangwg@cmes.org
717786606@qq.com
www.cif.com.cn
1160

2011重庆第18届中国国际工业装备展览会
地点：重庆展览中心，重庆
内容：电子信息设备，新能源与电力电工，数控机床与金属加工机械，工业自动化系统、检测设备及各类工业技术，通用机械设备
始办年份：1993
周期：每年一届
市场范围：全国性
上届规模 2010：展览面积5,000m^2(国外展商1,000m^2)，参展商261家（国外展商25家，来自15个国家），参观人数11,210人
主办：中国机械工程学会
联系人：张伟光，刘锁来
承办：重庆博瑞德展览有限公司
地址：重庆市南岸区江南大道19号（400060）
联系人：陈思羽

2011 The 18th China International Industry Fair （CIF）
Venue: Chongqing Exhibition Center, Chongqing
Established Year: 1993
Frequency: Annual
Market Area: National
Statistics 2010: Exhibition Area 5,000m^2(foreigners 1,000m^2), Exhibitors 261（foreigners 25, came from 15 countries）, Visitors 11,210
Organizer: Chinese Mechanical Engineering Society; Chongqing World Exhibition Co Ltd
Contact: Zhang Weiguang, Liu Suolai

上海 Shanghai

2011 -
☎ 010-8522 9440，
8522 9488，8522 9463
📠 010-8522 9296
✉ intertextile.sh@ccpittex.com
www.intertextile.com.cn
1180

中国国际纺织面料及辅料（秋冬）博览会
地点：上海新国际博览中心，上海
内容：各类纺织服装面料、辅料、计算机CAD/CAM系统，相关出版物及网络
主办：中国纺织工业协会
承办：中国贸促会纺织行业分会；法兰克福展览（香港）有限公司；中国纺织信息中心
联系人：王壮飞,于欣,沈桢

China International Trade Fair for Apparel Fabrics and Accessories
Venue: Shanghai New International Expo Center, Shanghai
Sponsor: China National Textile & Apparel Council
Organizers: The Sub-Council of Textile Industry, CCPIT; Messe Frankfurt (HK) Ltd; China Textile Information Center

2011 -
☎ 010-8522 9496, 8522 9148,
8522 9504
📠 010-8522 9300
✉ yarnexpo@ccpittex.com
www.yarnexpo.com.cn
1190

中国国际纺织纱线（秋冬）展览会
地点：上海新国际博览中心，上海
预计规模：展览面积3,000m^2
主办：中国纺织工业协会
承办：中国贸促会纺织行业分会；法兰克福展览（香港）有限公司；中国棉纺织行业协会；中国毛纺织行业协会；中国化学纤维工业协会；中国麻纺行业协会；中国纺织信息中心
联系人：王小雷，林泽文，林英华

China International Trade Fair for Fibres and Yarns
Venue: Shanghai New International Expo Center, Shanghai
Sponsors：China National Textile & Apparel Council
Organizers：The Sub-Council of Textile Industry; CCPIT Messe Frankfurt (HK) Ltd; China Cotton Textile Association; China Wool Textile Association; China Chemical Fiber Association; China Bast & Leaf Fibers Text

2011/01/08 -
☎ 021-6275 5800
📠 021-6275 7210
✉ wanglei@shrc.com.cn
www.shrc.com.cn
1200

上海市高校毕业生就业招聘会
地点：上海国际展览中心，上海
主办：上海市人才服务中心

Shanghai Job Fair for University graduates
Venue: Shanghai International Exhibition Center, Shanghai
Organizer: Shanghai Human Resources Service Center

2011/02/23 - 26
☎ 021-6279 2828, 6247 2387
📠 021-6386 6972
✉ chinawedding@siec-ccpit.com
www.siec-ccpit.com
1210

第十九届中国（上海）国际婚纱摄影器材展览会
地点：上海国际展览中心，上海世贸商城，上海光大会展中心，上海
内容：婚纱礼服、相册相框、影楼摄影背景道具、后期制作、摄背景道具、主题摄影、儿童摄影、彩妆饰品、婚庆用品、影楼培训、婚纱摄影网络和出版物。
周期：每年一届
上届规模 2010：展览面积70,000m^2，参展商565家，参观人数150,000人
主办：中国贸促会上海市分会；中国人像摄影学会；上海市摄影家协会
承办：上海国际展览服务有限公司
地址：上海延安中路841号东方海外大厦25楼2503室

The 19th China (Shanghai) International Wedding Photographic Equipment Exhibition
Venue: Shanghai International Exhibition Center, Shanghai Mart, Shanghai Everbright Convention and Exhibition, Shanghai
Frequency: Annual
Statistics 2010: Exhibition Area 70,000m^2, Exhibitors 565，Visitors 150,000
Sponsor: CCPIT Shanghai Sub-council; China Portrait Photography Society; Shanghai Photographers' Association
Organizer: Shanghai International Exhibition Service Co Ltd
Address: Room 2503, 25/F, OOCL Plaza, 841 YanAn Zhong Rd, Shanghai , China

2011/02/23 - 26
☎ 021-6279 2828
🖷 021-6386 6972
✉ lina@siec-ccpit.com
www.chinaweddingexpo.com.cn
1230

上海国际婚纱摄影器材展览会
暨国际儿童摄影、主题摄影、相册相框展览会
地点：上海国际展览中心、上海世贸商城、上海光大会展中心，上海
内容：婚纱、礼服、相册、相框、彩妆、饰品、婚庆用品、背景、后期制作、冲印彩扩、主题摄影、儿童摄影、影楼培训以及婚纱摄影网络和出版物
始办年份：2002
周期：每年两届
市场范围：国际性
性质：面向贸易观众
主办：中国贸促会上海市分会；中国人像摄影学会；上海市摄影家协会
承办：上海国际展览服务有限公司
地址：上海市延安中路841号8楼（200040）
联系人：张莉娜女士

China Wedding Expo 2011
Venue: Shanghai International Exhibition Center, Shanghai Mart, Shanghai Everbright Convention and Exhibition, Shanghai
Profile: Wedding related products including wedding gowns, formal attires, photo albums & frames, cosmetics, accessories, wedding supplies, backgrounds, post-production photographic products, lighting, developing techniques, printing and enlarging color photos, thematic photography, children's photography, studio-training programs, wedding photography networks and related publications
Established Year: 2002
Frequency: Biannual
Market Area: International
Nature: Trade Only
Sponsor: CCPIT Shanghai Sub-Council; China Portrait Photography Society; Shanghai Photographers' Association
Organizer: Shanghai International Exhibition Service Co Ltd
Address: 8/F, No.841 Yan An Zhong Road, Shanghai, 200040, China
Contact: Ms Zhang Lina

2011/03/01 - 04
☎ 021-6209 5209
🖷 021-6209 5210
✉ tara@chinaallworld.com
www.woodmacchina.net
1240

第十一届中国国际林业、木业机械与供应展览
地点：上海新国际博览中心，上海
内容：国际林业、木业机械与供应、家具生产、装潢与装饰机械及配件、家具、建筑及装潢用木料及木制品
周期：两年一届
市场范围：国际性
性质：面向贸易观众
上届规模 2009：展览面积28,750m^2(国外展商20,000m^2)，参展商406家（国外展商105家，来自26个国家），专业贸易观众13,672人
主办：华汉国际会议展览（上海）有限公司
地址：上海市长宁区仙霞路318-320号2402室（200336）
联系人：蔡祎

WoodMac China 2011
Venue: Shanghai New International Expo Center, Shanghai
Profile: Forestry, Woodworking Machinery and Supplies, Machinery and Accessories for Furniture Production, Upholstery and Hardware, Timber and Wood Products for Furniture & Building Industries
Frequency: Biennial
Market Area: International
Nature: Trade Only
Statistics 2009: Exhibition Area 28,750m^2(foreigners 20,000m^2), Exhibitors 406（foreigners 105, came from 26 countries）, Trade Visitors 13,672
Organizer: China International Exhibitions Ltd
Address: Room 2402, No.320 Xian Xia Road, Shanghai 200336
Contact: Tara Cai

2010/03/01 - 05
☎ 021-6353 9977, 5288 1111
🖷 021-3303 0072
✉ info@ecf.gov.cn
www.ecf.gov.cn
1250

第21届中国华东进出口商品交易会
地点：上海新国际博览中心，上海
内容：服装展区、家用纺织品展区、装饰品展区、日用消费品展区
主办：上海市商务委员会
承办：上海外经贸商务展览有限公司

East China Fair
Venue: Shanghai New International Expo Center, Shanghai
Profile：Fashion/Garments, Home textiles, Art Deco Gifts, Consumer Goods.
Operator: Shanghai International Trade Promotion Co Ltd

2011/03/06 - 08
☎ 021-6275 5800
🖷 021-6275 7210
1260

中国(上海)第十六届国际玩具展暨上海玩具第47届博览会
地点：上海国际展览中心，上海
主办：上海上玩玩具展览有限公司

Toy China 2011 (Spring)
Venue: Shanghai International Exhibition Center, Shanghai
Organizer: Shanghai Toys Industry Import/Export Corporation

2011/03/09 - 11
☎ 021-5499 9745
🖷 021-5499 3541
✉ shfairs-info@yahoo.cn
www.shcnlm.com
1280

2011年第17届上海国际服装纺织品贸易博览会
地点：上海新国际博览中心，上海
内容：服装馆：各类服装，男装、女装、休闲装、童装、牛仔服装等。面料辅料馆：面料：各类丝织、棉织、毛织、麻织、化纤类梭织、针织及涂层面料、各类复合面料及功能性面料 家用纺织品面料 辅料：刺绣、花边、衬里、纽扣、线带、商标、拉链等辅料，各类纤维/纱线
周期：每年一届
入场券价格：免费
参展费用：标准展位12,000～13,800元/9m^2，净地1,200元/m^2（36m^{2}起）
上届规模 2010：展览面积24,000m^2，参观人数30,000人（专业贸易观众24,000人）
主办：上海国际服装文化节组委会
承办：上海纺织技术服务展览中心
地址：上海闵行区莲花南路1108弄58栋701室（201100）
联系人：刘铭
MSN：shlmcn@hotmail.com
QQ：1187 230 500

Shanghai International Clothing & Textile Expo
Venue: Shanghai New International Expo Center, Shanghai
Profile: Silk, Silky aspects, Wool, Cotton, Knitted, Prints, Denim, Linen, Yarns, Fibers, Functional Fabrics, Fabrics Eco Friendly. Interlining, Embroidery/ Lace, zipper, button, ribbon, label. OEM/ODM clothing such as Ladies wear, Menswear, Children and Infants, wear, Sport and Casual Wear, etc.
Frequency: Annual
Cost to Attend: Free
Participated Fee: Standard Booth RMB 12,000～13,800/9m^2, Raw Space RMB 1,200/m^2（min 36m^2）
Statistics 2010: Exhibition Area 24,000m^2, Visitors 30,000（trade visitors 24,000）
Organizer：Shanghai Textile Technology Service & Exhibition Center
Address: Room 701, No 58, 1108 Lane, LianHua South Rd, Minghang Area, Shanghai, China
Contact: Mr Liu Ming
MSN: shlmcn@hotmail.com

2011/03/09 - 11
☎ 010-6335 6966
🖷 010-6335 6950, 6335 6960
✉ jiangxl@hardware-fair.com
www.hardware-fair.com
1290

第十九届中国国际五金博览会
地点：上海新国际博览中心，上海
内容：是中国历史久、底蕴深、影响中国五金三代人的展会。是亚洲规模大、专业化程度高、影响广的国际性展会。参展产品涉及电动工具、手动工具、机械设备、焊接设备、机电产品等。
始办年份：1960
周期：每年两届
市场范围：国际性
入场券价格：免费

The 19th China International Hardware Fair
Venue: Shanghai New International Expo Center, Shanghai
Profile: CIHF is held twice each year, one in Shanghai in March and the other one in major cities in China in September. Now more than 60,000 purchasers home and abroad have visited the fair. Exhibits include hand tools, electric tools, welding machineries, mechanical equipments
Established Year: 1960
Frequency: Biannual

参展费用：标准展位8,000元，净地850元/m²
上届规模 2010：展览面积80,800m²(国外展商6,400m²)，参展商2,000家（国外展商160家，来自6个国家），参观人数30,000人（专业贸易观众27,000人）
主办：中国五金交电化工商业协会；北京金益友联展览有限公司
地址：北京市丰台区菜户营东街58号财富西环名苑901（100054）
联系人：姜小姐

Market Area: International
Cost to Attend: Free
Participated Fee: Standard Booth RMB 8,000, Raw Space RMB 850m²
Statistics 2010: Exhibition Area 80,800m²(foreigners 6,400m²), Exhibitors 2,000（foreigners 160, came from 6 countries）, Visitors 30,000（trade visitors 27,000）
Organizer: China National Hardware, Electric and Chemical Products Commercial Association; Beijing Jinyi Youlian Exhibition Co Ltd
Address: Room 901, Fortune West Plaza, 58 Caihuying, Fengtai District, 100054 Beijing
Contact: Ms Jiang

2011/03/09 - 11
☎ 010-6853 5419, 6853 5399
🖷 010-6853 5408
✉ liufeng@ckcf.cn
www.ckcf.cn
1330

第93届中国针棉织品交易会
第23届中国丝绸交易会
地点：上海新国际博览中心，上海
内容：针织服饰：内衣、家居服、文胸、内裤、袜子、T-恤、运动休闲服、针织面辅料、家纺家居用品、床上用品、巾类产品、夏凉用品、家居布艺、家纺面辅料、丝绸类产品、丝绸家纺、丝绸服饰、丝绸面料
周期：每年一届
市场范围：全国性
性质：面向贸易观众
参展费用：标准展位12,000元，净地1,200元/m²
主办：中国纺织品商业协会
地址：北京市西城区三里河东路5号中商大厦12层（100045）
联系人：刘锋，张军
MSN：feng2659@hotmail.cpm
QQ：313947542

The 93rd China International Trade Fair for Mode
Venue: Shanghai New International Expo Center, Shanghai
Profile: Underwear, loungewear, lingerie, pants, vest hosiery, T-shirt, casual cloth, knitted fabrics and accessories, beddings, towel products, Summer-use products, art cloth, home textiles, fabrics and accessories, sick products
Frequency: Annual
Market Area: National
Nature: Trade Only
Participated Fee: Standard Booth RMB 12,000, Raw Space RMB 1,200/m²
Organizer: China Textile Commerce Association
Address: No.5 Sanlihe East Road, Xicheng District, Beijing, China
Contact: Liu Feng, Zhang Yang
MSN: feng2659@hotmail.cpm

2011/03/10 - 12
☎ 021-6853 2167
🖷 021-6853 2137
✉ lxf214@126.com
1340

20011第二届上海国际教育技术装备及高职教仪器展览会
地点：上海光大会展中心，上海
内容：各种适用于基础教育、职业教育、高等教育的教育技术装备、仪器和材料；IT信息技术设备及软件；电化教学及影音视频设备；远距离教育设备；实验室仪器、设备与材料
始办年份：2007
性质：面向贸易观众
入场券价格：免费
参展费用：标准展位9,800元，净地1,000元/m²
上届规模 2007：展览面积5,000m²，参展商100家（国外展商10家）
主办：中央电化教馆；中国教育技术学会职教专业委员会
地址：上海市桃林路18号B1408室（200135）
联系人：李小凤

2nd Shanghai Intl Educational equipment Exhibition
Venue: Shanghai Everbright Convention & Exhibition Center, Shanghai
Established Year: 2007
Nature: Trade Only
Cost to Attend: Free
Participated Fee: Standard Booth RMB 9,800, Raw Space RMB 1,000/m²
Statistics 2007: Exhibition Area 5,000m², Exhibitors 100（foreigners 10）
Organizer: Shanghai Feng Xiang Biao Exhibition Co Ltd
Address: B1408, 18 Fenglin Road, Shanghai 200135

2011/03/11 - 13
☎ 021-6195 6088
🖷 021-6195 6099
✉ cathy.huang@vnuexhibitions.com.cn
www.petfairasia.com
1360

2011上海宠物大会暨第四届上海宠物医疗学术研讨会
地点：上海国际展览中心，上海
内容：宠物食品、宠物用品、宠物医疗、水族产品、园艺产品、马术产品、活体宠物、其他：宠物杂志/宠物网站/宠物摄影/宠物俱乐部/宠物爱好者社团等
始办年份：2009
周期：每年一届
市场范围：全国性
入场券价格：30元/张
上届规模 2010：展览面积3,000m²(国外展商260m²)，参展商100家（国外展商18家，来自10个国家），参观人数32,000人（专业贸易观众3,500人）
主办：上海万耀企龙展览有限公司
地址：上海市徐汇区田林路140号26A栋万耀企龙办公楼（200233）
联系人：黄小姐

Pet Fair Shanghai 2011
Venue: Shanghai International Exhibition Center, Shanghai
Profile: Pets foods Pet food, pet feed Pets products Pet clothing, pet supplies, pet cages & houses, pet toys, pet grooming products, pet nursing products, pet training products, others Veterinary Products Pet medical treatment facilities, pet health-care products
Established Year: 2009
Frequency: Annual
Market Area: National
Cost to Attend: RMB 30:-
Statistics 2010: Exhibition Area 3,000m²(foreigners 260m²), Exhibitors 100（foreigners 18, came from 10 countries）, Visitors 32,000（trade visitors 3,500）
Organizer: VNU Exhibitions Asia
Address: VNU Exhibitions Asia VNU House, 26A, No.140 Tianlin, Road Shanghai, China
Contact: Cathy Huang

2011/03/11 - 13
☎ 021-2281 7535, 010-8460 0382
🖷 021-5836 1665
✉ overseas@ciec.com.cn huangshihua@ciec.com.cn
www.adc-expo.com
1380

2011第八届中国国际成人保健及生殖健康展览会
地点：上海国际展览中心，上海
内容：成人用品：成人器具/情趣内衣、服饰/SM产品/润滑剂/消毒剂/性功能调节器具；性调节滋补食品及药品；生殖保健产品：安全套/避孕药/节育器/中止妊娠及妊娠诊断的新技术及产品；生殖健康/性健康的各类产品/书籍及音像制品；医疗器械
周期：每年一届
市场范围：国际性
性质：面向贸易观众
上届规模 2010：展览面积6,000m²，参展商136家，参观人数3,014人
主办：中国国际展览中心集团公司
承办：中展海外展览有限公司；上海市计划生育用品管理协会
地址：上海浦东南路1085华申大厦1311上海国际成人展组委会

China Adult-Care Expo
Venue: Shanghai International Exhibition Center, Shanghai
Profile: adult goods and reproductive health trade
Frequency: Annual
Market Area: International
Nature: Trade Only
Statistics 2010: Exhibition Area 6,000m², Exhibitors 136, Visitors 3,014
Organizer: CIEC Overseas Exhibition Co Ltd; Organizing Committee of China Adult-Care Expo

2011/03/15 - 17
☎ 021-5490 0077
🖷 021-5490 4537
✉ yinzhanc@online.sh.cn
www.ying-zhan.com

1390

2011中国国际电子电路展览会
(第二十届中国国际电子电路展览会)
地点：上海新国际博览中心，上海
内容：该展是中国印制电路行业协会每年的例展，2008年被评为"上海市国际展览会优秀展",被评为"上海市国际展览会品牌展"。展览会主要展示各类电子元件材料、印刷电路设计、制造及新产品。展示类别为印制电路板制造；印制电路板设备；印制电路板原物料及化学品；电子组装设备；电子组装原物料；电子制造服务及合约制造；各类电子元件材料；水处理技术及设备；洁净室技术及设备；学术研究机构等
始办年份：1990
周期：每年一届
市场范围：国际性
性质：面向贸易观众
上届规模 2010：展览面积23,000m², 参展商400家（国外展商200家，来自20个国家
主办：上海颖展展览服务有限公司
地址：上海市漕溪北路41号汇嘉大厦23层D座（200030）
联系人：张经华先生,刘海珍女士

2011 International Electronic Circuits Exhibition
(CPCA SHOW 2011)
Venue: Shanghai New International Expo Center, Shanghai
Established Year: 1990
Frequency: Annual
Market Area: International
Nature: Trade Only
Statistics 2010: Exhibition Area 23,000m², Exhibitors 400 (foreigners 200, came from 20 countries)
Organizer: Shanghai Yingzhan Exhibition Service Co Ltd
Address: Unit D, 23/F, Hui-jia Building, No.41, Cao Xi Road (North) Shanghai 200030, China

2011/03/15 - 18
☎ 010-6715 9042, 6715 8723
🖷 010-6715 6913
✉ shfairs-info@yahoo.cn
www.appliance-expo.com

1410

2011年中国家电博览会(上海)
地点：上海新国际博览中心，上海
内容：大型家用电器、厨卫及小家电、家用太阳能产品、家用消费电子、电零配件及配套服务、电子电器回收处理技术与装备。
始办年份：1992
周期：每年一届
市场范围：全国性
入场券价格：免费
参展费用：标准展位9,800元/9m²，净地980元/m²（36m²起）
上届规模 2010：展览面积24,000m², 参观人数30,000人（专业贸易观众24,000人）
主办：中国家用电器协会；中国电子视像行业协会；中国电子音响工业协会
承办：北京协联信息科技公司

China Appliance World Expo-Shanghai 2011
Venue: Shanghai New International Expo Center, Shanghai
Profile: Major Home Appliances, Small and Kitchen Appliances, Solar Energy Products, Home Electronics Products, Accessories and Components, E-waste Recycling Technology and Equipment
Established Year: 1992
Frequency: Annual
Market Area: National
Cost to Attend: Free
Participated Fee: Standard Booth RMB 9,800/9m², Raw Space RMB 980/m² (min 36m²)
Statistics 2010: Exhibition Area 24,000m², Visitors 30,000 (trade visitors 24,000)
Organizer：China Household Electrical Appliances Association; China Video Industry Association; China Audio Industry Association
Contact：Beijing United Information Technology Co Ltd

2011/03/17 - 20
☎ 021-6195 6088转ext 903
🖷 021-6195 6099
✉ sam.shen@vnuexhibitions.com.cn
www.vnuexhibitionsasia.com

1420

上海之春房产展示交易会
地点：上海展览中心，上海
内容：上海之春·房产展示交易会是上海乃至华东区最具影响力的大型的房产展。经过数十年的打造和运作，该展已成为上海楼市的风向标。每年，超过200家房地产商借助新年伊始的上海之春把握先机、推出新盘、展示形象、拓展市场、主力营销。接近13万的高质量购房人群保证了这一互动平台的高效运行，上海之春也因此受到房产界的一致好评和忠诚青睐。
始办年份：1998
周期：每年一届
性质：面向公众
入场券价格：10元
参展费用：东西平台、东一馆、西一馆二层12,000元/9m²，中央大厅、序馆 20,000元/9m²，海外置业专区2,200元/m²
上届规模 2010：展览面积20,000m², 参展商200家（国外展商6家，来自4个国家），参观人数130,000人
主办：上海万耀企龙展览有限公司
地址：上海市田林路140号26A栋（200233）
联系人：沈先生

Shanghai Spring Real Estate Market
Venue: Shanghai Exhibition Center, Shanghai
Profile: Spring Real Estate Shanghai is one of the most influential large-scale real estate exhibitions in China. With the booming of china's economy and the development of real estate industry, spring real estate market shanghai has developed into an annual event with broad scale, wide range, outstanding influence and high public participation over the past ten years.
Established Year: 1998
Frequency: Annual
Nature: Open to Public
Cost to Attend: RMB 10:-
Participated Fee: Standard Booth RMB 12,000～20,000/9m²
Statistics 2010: Exhibition Area 20,000m², Exhibitors 200 (foreigners 6, came from 4 countries), Visitors 130,000
Organizer: Vnu Exhibitions Asia
Address: VNU House, 26A, No. 140 Tianlin Road, Shanghai
Contact: Sam

2011/03/20 - 22
☎ 010-6879 9042/43
🖷 010-6879 9050
✉ zhanwg@cmes.org
liusl@cmes.org

1430

2011中国国际机器视觉展览会
地点：上海光大展览中心，上海
内容：机器视觉部件、机器视觉辅件、机器视觉系统：
始办年份：2006
周期：每年一届
市场范围：国际性
性质：面向公众
上届规模 2010：展览面积7,000m²(国外展商2,200m²), 参展商110家（国外展商27家，来自14个国家），参观人数3,030人
主办：中国机械工程学会
地址：北京市海淀区首体南路9号主语国际4号楼11层（100048）
联系人：张伟光，刘锁来

China International Machine Vision Exhibition 2011
Venue: Shanghai Everbright Convention & Exhibition Center, Shanghai
Profile: Part, Accessories, System
Established Year: 2006
Frequency: Annual
Market Area: International
Nature: Open to Public
Statistics 2010: Exhibition Area 7,000m²(foreigners 2,200m²), Exhibitors 110 (foreigners 27, came from 14 countries), Visitors 3,030
Organizer: Chinese Mechanical Engineering Society
Contact: Zhang Weiguang, Liu Suolai

2011/03/22 - 24
☎ 021-6195 6088
🖷 021-6195 6099
✉ kitty.bai@vnuexhibitions.com.cn
www.domotexasiachinafloor.com
1440

第十三届中国国际地面材料及铺装技术展览会
地点：上海新国际博览中心，上海
内容：地板、地毯、纤维、木材原料、地毯生产技术、地面材料生产技术、木工机械、地坪、地暖
始办年份：1999
周期：每年一届
市场范围：国际性
性质：面向贸易观众
入场券价格：预登记观众免费，现场200元
上届规模 2010：展览面积51,425m²，参展商966家，专业贸易观众41,040人
主办：上海万耀企龙展览有限公司；德国汉诺威展览公司
地址：上海市田林路140号26A万耀企龙办公楼（200052）
联系人：白皎

DOMOTEX asia/CHINAFLOOR
Venue: Shanghai New International Expo Center, Shanghai
Profile: Wood flooring, Carpet, Fibers, Raw material of wood, Carpet production technology, Floor technology, Wood working machinery, Industrial flooring, Heating system
Established Year: 1999
Frequency: Annual
Market Area: International
Nature: Trade Only
Cost to Attend: Pre-registration Free, On-site RMB 200:-
Statistics 2010: Exhibition Area 51,425m², Exhibitors 966, Trade Visitors 41,040
Organizer: VNU Exhibitions Asia
Address: VNU House, 26A, No. 140 Tianlin Road, Shanghai 200233, China
Contact: Kitty

2011/03/22 - 24
☎ 021-6195 6088
🖷 021-6195 6099
✉ ronnie.chen@vnuexhibitions.com.cn
www.vnuexhibitionsasia.com
1450

第九届上海国际园林景观设计及城市建设展览会
地点：上海新国际博览中心，上海
内容：园林景观规划及设计，园林绿化工程，防腐木、木塑，屋顶绿化材料、屋面系统工程，灌溉及防腐产品，休闲游乐设备、站点设备，户外家具及装饰，户外景观照明，艺植被、园林机械
始办年份：2002
周期：每年一届
市场范围：国际性
性质：面向公众
上届规模 2010：展览面积1,000m²，参展商40家，参观人数5,000人（专业贸易观众3,000人）
主办：上海万耀企龙展览有限公司
地址：上海市徐汇区田林路140号26A栋万耀企龙办公楼（200233）
联系人：陈融

The 9th Shanghai Intl Landscape Design & Urban Construction Expo
Venue: Shanghai New International Expo Center, Shanghai
Profile: Landscape Design Landscape Design of Urban Open Spaces and Residential Quarters, Planning, Construction, Maintenance and Governing of Environmental Landscape, Water Landscape and Environment Design, City Landscape Illumination Design Projects, Landscape Design Landscape Design of Urban Open Spaces and Residential Quarters, Planning, Construction, Maintenance and Governing of Environmental Landscape, Water Landscape and Environment Design, City Landscape Illumination Design Projects, Tourism Development Planning, etc Garden and Urban Green Construction Design and Construction of Urban Green Project, Design and Construction of Villa Garden, Roof Green Technology, etc Landscape & Garden Building Materials and Facilities Antiseptic Wood products, Wood-Plastic Composites, Waterscape Fountain, Landscape Illumination System, Outdoor Furniture, Children Playground Facilities, Colorful Bricks, Membrane Floors, Garden Bricks & Tiles, Water Treatment Technology
Established Year: 2002
Frequency: Annual
Market Area: International
Nature: Open to Public
Statistics 2010: Exhibition Area 1,000m², Exhibitors 40, Visitors 5,000 (trade visitors 3,000)
Organizer: VNU Exhibitions Asia
Address: VNU House, 26A, No. 140 Tianlin Road, Shanghai 200233, China
Contact: Ronnie

2011/03/22 - 24
☎ 021-6195 6088
🖷 021-6195 6099
✉ ronnie.chen@vnuexhibitions.com.cn
www.vnuexhibitionsasia.com
1460

2011中国可持续建筑国家大会&展览会
地点：上海新国际博览中心，上海
内容：绿色建筑设计、技术；外墙保温技术和产品；绿色照明技术与产品；低碳生态环保技术与产品；绿色建材技术与产品；绿色建筑智能化技术与产品；建筑节能技术和产品；可再生能源利用
始办年份：2009
周期：每年一届
市场范围：国际性
性质：面向公众
上届规模 2010：展览面积1,000m²，参展商40家，参观人数5,000人（专业贸易观众2,000人）
主办：上海万耀企龙展览有限公司
地址：上海市徐汇区田林路140号26A栋 万耀企龙办公楼（200233）
联系人：陈融

China Sustainable Building Forum (CSB 2010)
Venue: Shanghai New International Expo Center, Shanghai
Profile: Architectural design and construction services, Acoustical systems, Adhesives/Coatings/Sealants, Air conditioning systems, Appliances BIPV, Blinds & shading, Building Automation & Controls, Ceilings, Cladding & curtain walling Coatings & paints, Commercial real estate.
Established Year: 2009
Frequency: Annual
Market Area: International
Nature: Open to Public
Statistics 2010: Exhibition Area 1,000m², Exhibitors 40, Visitors 5,000 (trade visitors 2,000)
Organizer: VNU Exhibitions Asia
Address: VNU House, 26A, No. 140 Tianlin Road, Shanghai 200233, China
Contact: Ronnie

2011/03/22 - 24
☎ 021-6195 6088
🖷 021-6195 6099
✉ fox.tang@vnuexhibitions.com.cn
lavigne.sheng@vnuexhibitions.com.cn
www.rtasia.org
1470

中国国际遮阳与节能技术博览会
中国国际门及门禁系统展览会
地点：上海新国际博览中心，上海
内容：作为亚洲最大的卷帘门窗、自动门、车库门、遮阳专业贸易展。R+T Asia不仅为参展商提供了展示最新产品和技术的机会，还为零售商、代理商、经销商提供了寻求新客户、新商机和交流的平台。
始办年份：2005
周期：每年一届
市场范围：国际性
入场券价格：200元
参展费用：标准展位(12m²起) 1,500元/m²，净地(36m²起)1,350元/m²，净地(100m²起)1,300元/m²

R+T Asia
Venue: Shanghai New International Expo Center, Shanghai
Profile: R+T Asia - staged on an annual basis - is the professional trade show on shutters, sun protection, rolling doors and garage doors in Asia. As the Chinese subsidiary of R+T in Stuttgart, the leading global trade fair for roller shutters, doors/gates and sun protection systems, R+T Asia is the only trade fair of its kind in Asia to make a name for itself.
Established Year: 2005
Frequency: Annual
Market Area: International
Cost to Attend: RMB 200
Participated Fee: Standard Booth (min 12m²) RMB 1,500/m², Raw

上届规模 2010：展览面积13,275m²(国外展商3,200m²)，参展商318家（国外展商33家，来自26个国家），专业贸易观众14,651人
主办：上海万耀企龙展览有限公司；德国斯图加特国际展览公司
地址：上海市徐汇区田林路140号26A栋万耀企龙办公楼（200233）
联系人：项目负责人(汤伟权先生)，市场及媒体(盛新颖女士)
QQ：270274828

Space (min 36m²) RMB 1,350/m², (100m² and up) RMB 1,300/m²
Statistics 2010: Exhibition Area 13275m²(foreigners 3200m²), Exhibitors 318 (foreigners 33, came from 26 countries), Trade Visitors 14,651
Organizer: VNU Asia; Messe Stuttgart GmbH
Address: VNUBuilding, 26A, No. 140 Tianlin Road, Shanghai 200233, China
Contact: Fox Tang (Project Dir), Lavigne Sheng (Marketing & Media)

2011/03/23 – 25
☎ 010-5979 5833, 6839 6330
🖷 010-5907 1335, 5907 1336, 6839 6422
✉ cfaa1990@yahoo.com.cn
ccpitsli@public3.bta.net.cn
www.ChinaFoodAdditives.com
1480

第十五届中国国际食品添加剂和配料展览会暨
第二十一届全国食品添加剂生产应用技术展示会
地点：上海光大会展中心、上海世贸商城、上海国际展览中心，上海
内容：食品添加剂：酸味剂、抗结剂、消泡剂、抗氧化剂、漂白剂、膨松剂、被膜剂、着色剂、护色剂、复合食品添加剂、乳化剂、酶制剂、食用香精香料、增味剂、面粉处理剂、水分保持剂、营养强化剂、防腐剂、稳定和凝固剂、甜味剂、增稠剂、胶姆糖基础剂；
食品配料：淀粉、变性淀粉、淀粉糖、糖醇、低聚糖、食用油脂及油脂替代品、专用面粉、酵母制品、植物蛋白、脱水果蔬及肉类、冷冻冷藏食品、馅料、调味料、香辛料、调味品、乳制品、保健食品、动植物提取物、饮料浓缩液、腌制剂；大豆制品、坚果、速溶茶、功能性食品配料、可可制品、膳食纤维、蛋制品、蜂产品、豆类、炒货；
食品加工助剂：各类食品加工助剂；
相关材料、设备、仪器与技术：食品包装机械、包装材料、食品加工设备、食品添加剂和配料生产应用技术、食品检测设备和技术、专业刊物和媒体
周期：每年一届
市场范围：国际性
性质：面向贸易观众
上届规模 2010：展览面积58,000m²，参展商1,058家（国外展商223家，来自21个国家），专业贸易观众76,570人
主办：中国食品添加剂和配料协会/《中国食品添加剂》杂志社；中国贸促会轻工业行业分会
参展联络：中国食品添加剂和配料协会/《中国食品添加剂》杂志社
地址：北京朝外大街甲6号万通中心3座1402（100020）
联系人：张越宸、陈艳燕、尹胜利
参展联络：中国贸促会轻工行业分会
地址：北京市阜外大街乙22号（100833）
联系人：张昕

Food Ingredients China 2011
(FIC 2011)
Venue: Shanghai Everbright Convention & Exhibition Center; Shanghai Mart; Shanghai International Exhibition Center, Shanghai
Profile: FIC is the biggest food ingredients & additives exhibition in Asia. The exhibits cover 22 categories of food additives, 33 categories of food ingredients, food processing aides and techniques, equipments and magazines.
Established Year: 1997
Frequency: Annual
Market Area: International
Nature: Trade Only
Statistics 2010: Exhibition Area 58,000m², Exhibitors 1,058 (foreigners 223, came from 21 countries), Trade Visitors 76,570
Organizer: China Food Additives & Ingredients Association; CCPIT Sub-Council of Light Industry
Address: Rm. 430, 22B, Fuwai Dajie, Beijing, China

2011/03/28 - 30
☎ 021-3351 8238, 3351 9437
🖷 021-3351 8239
✉ zyexpo@163.com
www.zyexpo.com
1510

第四届国际光学膜及高机能薄膜(上海)展览会
地点：上海国际展览中心，上海
内容：光学膜：偏光膜、背光用膜、粘着膜、ITO膜、LCD用光学补偿膜、特性提高膜；高机能薄膜：以PI、PC、PET、PEN等薄膜基材为主，主要包括工业用保护膜、离型膜（硅油膜）等；膜成形/加工技术；原料及化工产品；洁净工程 洁净、防护系统，屏蔽防护产品等
始办年份：2007
周期：每年一届
市场范围：国际性
性质：面向贸易观众
参展费用：A区8,800元/9m²，净地900元/m²；B区8,000元/9m²，净地800元/m²；国际T区2,000美元/9m²,净地200美元/m²
上届规模 2010：参展商281家，参观人数17,645人
主办：正亚展览机构
承办：上海富亚展览有限公司；广州正亚展览有限公司
地址：上海市曹安路1855号曹安国际商城10楼1035室正亚展览有限公司上海会展部

FILMEXPO
Venue: Shanghai International Exhibition Center, Shanghai
Established Year: 2007
Frequency: Annual
Market Area: International
Nature: Trade Only
Participated Fee: USD 2,000/booth, Raw Space USD 900/m²
Statistics 2010: Exhibitors 281, Visitors 17,645
Organizer: Zhengya Exhibition Co Ltd; Shanghai Fuya Exhibition Co Ltd

---

2011/03/28 - 30
☎ 021-3351 8238, 3351 9437
🖷 021-3351 8239
✉ zyexpo@163.com
www.zyexpo.com
1530

第六届国际胶粘带、保护膜及光学膜（上海）展览会
地点：上海国际展览中心，上海
内容：胶粘带：各种薄膜类、纸类、布类、箔类、泡棉类等基材的胶粘带制品，主要包括工业胶带、光学胶带等；保护膜：PE、PVC、PET、BOPP、LDPE保护膜等；光学膜：偏光膜、反射膜，扩散膜等；生产设备及仪器：各种胶粘制品与光学膜制造加工过程上料、涂布、干燥等及；原料及化工产品：各类胶粘制品生产用原料及化工产品
周期：每年一届
市场范围：国际性
性质：面向贸易观众
上届规模 2010：参观人数17,465人
主办：广州正亚展览有限公司；上海富亚展览有限公司
联络：正亚展览有限公司上海会展部
地址：上海市曹安路1855号曹安国际商城10楼1035室
联系人：潘先生，雷先生*

The 6th International Adhesive Tape Protective Films & Optical Film (Shanghai) Expo
Venue: Shanghai International Exhibition Center, Shanghai
Frequency: Annual
Market Area: International
Nature: Trade Only
Statistics 2010: Visitors 17,465
Organizer: Zhengya Exhibition Co Ltd; Shanghai Fuya Exhibition Co Ltd

2011/03/29 - 31
☎ 021-6432 9266, 6432 9301
🖷 021-5171 4528
✉ adexpo-sh@163.com
www.expo-ad.com

1540

2011第十二届中国（上海）广告四新展览会
地点： 上海光大会展中心，上海
内容： 广告制作设备，广告材料、物料，展览展示系统及广告标识，多媒体及触摸技术与设备
始办年份： 1999
周期： 每年一届
市场范围： 全国性
性质： 面向贸易观众
入场券价格： 免费
参展费用： 标准展位8,800元，净地800元/m²
上届规模 2010：展览面积8,000m²(国外展商876m²)，参展商217家（国外展商37家，来自11个国家），参观人数9,763人（专业贸易观众8,153人）
主办： 中国商务广告协会；中国广告协会霓虹灯广告分会；中国同源有限公司
承办： 上海秀博展览有限公司；上海威棱展览有限公司
地址： 上海市漕宝路82号E座1905室（200235）
联系人： 李小姐,江先生
MSN：bjslfengqi@hotmail.com
QQ：49565551

The 12th China (Shanghai) Advertising Four New Expo
Venue: Shanghai Everbright Convention & Exhibition Center, Shanghai
Profile: Advertising Production Equipment, Advertising Materials and Articles, Exhibition and Displaying System and Advertising Marking, Multimedia and Touch Technology and Equipment
Established Year: 1999
Frequency: Annual
Market Area: National
Nature: Trade Only
Cost to Attend: Free
Participated Fee: Standard Booth RMB 8,800/booth, Raw Space USD 800/m²
Statistics 2010: Exhibition Area 8,000m²(foreigners 876m²), Exhibitors 217 (foreigners 37, came from 11 countries), Visitors 9,763 (trade visitors 8,153)
Sponsor: China Advertising Assn of Commerce; The Neon Lamp Advertising Committee of China Advertising Assn; China Tong Yuan Co Ltd
Organizer: Shanghai Xiubo Exhibition Co Ltd; Shanghai Weiling Exhibition Co Ltd
Address: Room 1905, Unit E, No. 82, Caobao Road, Shanghai
Contact: Miss Li, Mr Jiang
MSN: bjslfengqi@hotmail.com
www.expo-ad.com

2011/03/29 – 04/01
☎ 021-6437 1178, 020-8667 9383
🖷 021-6437 0982, 020-8667 9396
✉ ceramics@ubmsinoexpo.com
www.ceramics-china.cn

1550

第十二届中国国际建筑陶瓷及卫浴科技精品展览会
地点： 上海新国际博览中心，上海
内容： 第十二届中国国际建筑陶瓷及卫浴科技精品展览会”联袂同期举办的第十九届中国国际建筑装饰展览会、上海国际酒店用品博览会等，总展出面积将超过165,000平方米，其展出场馆将遍及上海新国际展览中心13个室内展馆以及多个户外展馆，预计届时将有超过2,000家展商，为到访的80,000名买家提供全方位、一站式的消费采购服务 展出范围：建筑陶瓷产品系列、卫生陶瓷和浴室精品系列、卫浴配件系列、厨房设施系列
始办年份： 1999
周期： 每年一届
市场范围： 国际性
性质： 面向贸易观众
入场券价格： 免费
参展费用： 标准展位1,100元/m²，净地1,000元/m²
主办： 上海博华国际展览有限公司/上海博建国际会展有限公司
地址： 上海市襄阳南路218号现代大厦8楼（200031）
联系人： 田晓俊,金卿

Ceramics, Tile & Sanitary Ware China 2011
Venue: Shanghai New International Expo Center, Shanghai
Profile: Ceramics, Tile & Sanitary Ware China 2011 Showcases premium and innovative products that set the trend for the ceramic, tile & sanitary ware industry. It is a one-stop platform for building and hospitality industries in a 165,000sqm venue, showcasing colorful mosaic designs with different traditional and modern textures, due to increase in demand for Mosaic. With UBM's international marketing initiatives, Ceramics China gathers over 70,000 global visitors like; industry professionals, traders, agents, designers, hotel owners and developers. Ceramics, Tile & Sanitary Ware China 2011 has powerful media partnerships, support from government and other international and local associations, and presents extensive, in-depth & related events, featuring China International Building & Interior Design Festival and other matchmaking and networking events. Exhibit Category: Building Ceramic Products, Sanitary Ceramics and Bathroom fixtures, Kitchen Facilities, Stones, Glaze and Pigment
Established Year: 1999
Frequency: Annual
Market Area: International
Nature: Trade Only
Cost to Attend: Free
Participated Fee: Standard Booth RMB 1,100/m², Raw Space RMB 1,000/m²
Organizer: Shanghai Expobuild International Exhibition Co Ltd
Address: 8/F Xian Dai Mansion, 218 Xiang Yang Road(S)
Contact: Spric Tian, Jimmy Jin

2011/03/29 – 04/01
☎ 021-6437 1178
🖷 021-6437 0982
✉ expobuild@ubmsinoexpo.com
www.ceramics-china.cn
www.expobuild.com

1560

第十九届中国国际建筑装饰展览会
- 中国国际门窗、幕墙、结构与遮阳产品展览会
- 中国国际马赛克、装饰艺术砖进出口展览会
- 中国国际建筑陶瓷色釉料及原辅材料展览会
- 中国(上海)国际石材进出口及工程设计展览会

地点： 上海新国际博览中心，上海
内容： 全球地产商、建材商、酒店业主、设计师广泛参与，是海外国际建材品牌开拓中国市场以及中国精品建材走向国际的首选建材盛会。展会整合酒店、建材、照明、家具、清洁等空间环境设计综合领域与装饰产业链。2011届建材展联袂同期举办的上海国际酒店用品博览会等，总展出面积将超过165,000平方米，其展出场馆将遍及上海新国际展览中心13个室内展馆以及多个户外展馆，预计届时将有超过2,000家展商，为到访的80,000名买家提供全方位、一站式的消费采购服务。
展出范围：门窗遮阳、屋面结构、玻璃制品、墙体材料、木制品、室内装饰、化学建材、园林石材、陶瓷卫浴、智能化楼宇、建筑安全、通风设备与技术、电梯、地暖、太阳能系统、水处理设备、工程设计
始办年份： 1992
周期： 每年一届
市场范围： 国际性
性质： 面向贸易观众
参展费用： 标准展位1,100元/m²，净地展位1,000元/m²
上届规模 2010：展览面积51,750m²，参展商438家，专业贸易观众29,874人

Expo Build China 2011:
- Doors, Windows, Structure & Sunshades China
- Expo Mosaic China
- Building Ceramic Glaze & Pigment China

Venue: Shanghai New International Expo Center, Shanghai
Profile: Expo Build China is the only comprehensive building show in China that showcases premium and innovative products and sets the trend for the industry. Expo Build China incorporates building industry with other related industries in a 165,000sqm venue, providing one-stop solutions to building and hospitality industries. With UBM's international marketing initiatives, Expo Build China gathers over 70,000 global visitors consisting of industry professionals, traders, agents, designers, hotel owners and developers. Expo Build China presents extensive, in-depth & related events, featuring China International Building & Interior Design Festival and other matchmaking and networking events.
Exhibit Category: Premium building material and interior decoration Doors, windows, sunshade, roofing, hardware, Accessories Building intelligence & automation, Flooring, Wall covering, ceiling, kitchen cabinet, wardrobe, partition, glass, heating, home furnishing, lighting Wooden products, coating & chemical building materials Ceramics, tile & sanitary ware Stone Architecture & design
Established Year: 1992
Frequency: Annual
Market Area: International

主办：上海博华国际展览有限公司/上海博建国际会展有限公司
地址：上海市襄阳南路218号现代大厦8楼（200031）
联系人：田晓俊，金卿

Nature: Trade Only
Participated Fee: Standard Booth RMB 1,100/m^2, Raw Space RMB 1,000/m^2
Statistics 2010: Exhibition Area 51,750m^2, Exhibitors 438, Trade Visitors 29,874
Organizer: Shanghai Expobuild International Exhibition Co Ltd
Address: 8/F Xian Dai Mansion, 218 Xiang Yang Road(S), Shanghai 200031, China
Contact: Spric Tian, Jimmy Jin

2011/03/29 - 01
☎ 021-6437 1178转ext 392
🖷 021-6437 0982转ext 392
✉ sean.song@ubmsinoexpo.com
www.chinacleanexpo.com
1570

中国清洁博览会
地点：上海新国际博览中心，上海
内容：具权威和规模的亚洲清洁行业展。范围有清洁机械与设备，清洁工具及零配件、卫生用品，清洁剂，室内环境净化技术及产品，洗涤、干洗及熨烫设备，净水设备，环卫及固体废弃物处理技术及设备，消毒抗菌用品，汽车清洗美容设备
周期：每年一届
上届规模 2010：参展商177家（来自20个国家），专业贸易观众6,904人
主办：上海博华国际展览有限公司

12th China Clean Expo
Venue: Shanghai New International Expo Center, Shanghai
Profile: The only international cleaning expo in China with excellent reputation over 9 years, held annually in March in Shanghai. Categories: Cleaning Machines and Accessories; Cleaning Tools and Sanitary Appliance, Cleaning Tools and Sanitary Appliance, Cleaning chemicals, Indoor environment purifier, Solid waste disposal; Antimicrobial and disinfectant, Laundry, Water purifier.
Frequency: Annual
Statistics 2010: Exhibitors 177 came from 20 countries, Buyers 6,904
Organizer: Shanghai UBM Sinoexpo Intl Exhibition Co Ltd
Address: 218 Xiang Yang Road (S), Shanghai 200031, PR China

2011/03/29 – 04/01
☎ 021-6467 1178
🖷 021-6437 1196
✉ helen.lei@ubmsinoexpo.com
info-trust@ubm.com
www.expobuild.com
www.ubmtrust.com
1580

中国(上海)国际建筑涂料展览会
地点：上海新国际博览中心，上海
始办年份：2006
周期：每年一届
上届规模 2010：展览面积51,750m^2，参展商438家（来自20个国家），专业贸易观众29,874人（来自70个国家）人）
主办：上海博华国际展览有限公司
承办：上海博建国际会展有限公司
地址：上海市襄阳路218号现代大厦8楼

Expo Coat
Venue: Shanghai New International Expo Center, Shanghai
Established Year: 2006
Frequency: Annual
Statistics 2010: Exhibition Area 51,750m^2, Exhibitors 438 (came from 20 countries), Trade Visitors 29,874 (came from 70 countries)
Organizer: Shanghai UBM Sinoexpo Intl Exhibition Co Ltd; Shanghai Expobuild Intl Exhibition Co Ltd
Address: 8F, Xiandai Mansion, 218 Xiang Yang Road (S), Shanghai 200031

2011/03/29 – 04/01
☎ 021-6437 1178
🖷 021-6437 1196
✉ expobuild@ubmsinoexpo.com
www.expobuild.com
1590

W3国际精品设计展
地点：上海新国际博览中心，上海
周期：每年一届
主办：上海博华国际展览有限公司
地址：上海市襄阳路218号现代大厦8楼

Expo Deco
Venue: Shanghai New International Expo Center, Shanghai
Frequency: Annual
Organizer: Shanghai UBM Sinoexpo Intl Exhibition Co Ltd
Address: 8F, Xiandai Mansion, 218 Xiang Yang Road (S), Shanghai 200031

2011/03/29 – 04/01
☎ 021-6467 1178
🖷 021-6437 0982
✉ hotelex@ubmsinoexpo.com
jojo.zhang@ubmsinoexpo.com
info-trust@ubm.com
www.hotelex.cn
www.hotelexchina.com
www.ubmtrust.com
1620

中国国际咖啡与茶用品展览会
地点：上海新国际博览中心，上海
周期：每年一届
上届规模 2010：展览面积60,000m^2，参展商885家（国外展商24家），专业贸易观众43,288人
主办：上海博华国际展览有限公司
地址：上海市襄阳路218号现代大厦8楼

Coffee & Tea China
Venue: Shanghai New International Expo Center, Shanghai
Frequency: Annual
Statistics 2010: Exhibition Area 60,000m^2, Exhibitors 885 (foreigners 24), Trade Visitors 43,288
Organizer: Shanghai UBM Sinoexpo International Exhibition Co Ltd
Address: 8F, Xiandai Mansion, 218 Xiang Yang Road (S), Shanghai 200031

2011/03/29 – 04/01
☎ 021-6437 1178
🖷 021-6437 0982
✉ hotelex@ubmsinoexpo.com
www.hotelexchina.com
1630

上海国际酒店用品博览会：
- 中国(上海)国际酒店与建筑照明展览会
- 中国国际康体健身，休闲娱乐与运动器材展览会

地点：上海新国际博览中心，上海
内容：酒店、餐饮、酒吧一站式的采购平台，提供建材、清洁、照明整体的解决方案。同时举办的展览有：餐饮设备及供应展、烘焙展、桌面用品展、咖啡与茶用品展、食品及饮料展、康体健身与休闲娱乐展、布草及纺织品展、酒店家具展、客房电器及用品展、酒店智能产品及安全防卫设备展
周期：每年一届
市场范围：国际性
性质：面向贸易观众
上届规模 2010：展览面积60,000m^2，参展商885家（来自78个国家），专业贸易观众43,288人
主办：上海博华国际展览有限公司
地址：上海市襄阳路218号现代大厦8楼

Hotelex Shanghai：
- Expo Light
- Fitness, Sports & Leisure China

Venue: Shanghai New International Expo Center, Shanghai
Profile: Together with other three related shows "Expo Build China 2011", "China Clean Expo 2011" and "Expo Light 2011" four expos under one roof will offer total solutions provided from building, cleaning and lighting suppliers.
Frequency: Annual
Market Area: International
Nature: Trade Only
Statistics 2010: Exhibition Area 60,000m^2, Exhibitors 885 (came from 78 countries), Trade Visitors 43,288
Organizer: Shanghai UBM Sinoexpo International Exhibition Co Ltd
Address: 8/F, Xian Dai Mansion, 218 Xiang Yang Road (s), Shanghai, 200031, China

2011/04/02 - 04
☎ 010-8522 9506, 8522 9504, 8522 9505
🖷 010-8522 9300
✉ intertextile_home@ccpittex.com
www.intertextile-home.com.cn
1640

中国国际家用纺织品及辅料（春夏）博览会
地点：上海国际展览中心及上海世贸商城，上海
内容：各类家用纺织品及辅料,计算机辅助设计与制造,相关出版物及网络
预计规模：总面积30,000m^2
主办：中国纺织工业协会
承办：中国贸促会纺织行业分会；中国家用纺织品行业协会；法兰克福展览（香港）有限公司
联系人：朱勤，林英华，郭亮，何磊，罗洁

China International Trade Fair for Home Textiles and Accessories
Venue: Shanghai International Exhibition Center, Shanghai
Sponsor: China National Textile & Apparel Council
Organizers: The Sub-Council of Textile Industry CCPIT; China Home Textile Association; Messe Frankfurt (HK) Ltd

2011/04/06 - 09
☎ 021-5153 5228
🖷 021-5153 5234
✉ Thomas.huang@reedexpo.com.cn
www.sino-corrugated.com
1660

2011中国国际瓦楞展
地点：上海新国际博览中心，上海
内容：全球领先的专业瓦楞设备、耗材及技术展，致力于通过集中呈现大量并且多样的高性价比设备、耗材，协助全球瓦楞纸箱厂做出不同的采购决策，为其提供获知新产品、新技术发展和市场动态的渠道，搭建与不同供应商进行极富价值的沟通交流的独特平台。内容包括纸板加工设备及零配件，纸箱加工设备及零配件，印后设备，纸箱加工各类工业用纸，纸箱加工相关耗材纸箱加工软件，纸箱加工服务类
始办年份：2001
上届规模 2010：展览面积50,000m^2，参展商550家（国外展商50家），参观人数23,000人
主办：励展博览集团
地址：上海市淮海中路775号新华联大厦8楼（201204）
联系人：黄兆君

SinoCorrugated 2011
Venue: Shanghai New International Expo Center, Shanghai
Profile: SinoCorrugated is one of the world's largest business platforms for the global corrugated manufacturing industry. This corrugated show not only highlights the latest global corrugated equipment and consumables on the market, it also helps carton box manufacturers to make informed purchasing decisions by alerting them to new products, the latest technologies and emerging market trends.
Established Year: 2001
Statistics 2010: Exhibition Area 50,000m^2, Exhibitors 550 (foreigners 50), Visitors 23,000
Organizer: Reed Exhibitions

2011/04/07 - 09
☎ 010-5856 5888
🖷 010-5856 6000
✉ wangping@biec.com.cn
www.cr-expo.com
1670

第二十二届国际制冷、空调、供暖、通风及食品冷冻加工展览会
(中国制冷展)
地点：上海新国际博览中心，上海
内容：全球制冷空调暖通行业规模最大的专业展览会之一。展览会经由国际展览业协会(UFI)和美国商务部(US FCS)两项国际认证，已跻身全球领先的制冷空调暖通展之列，更是亚洲规模最大的同类专业展览会。始终致力于在全球范围内拓展终端用户和专业买家群体。每年世界各地的制冷空调暖通专业组织都会齐聚"中国制冷展"。此展为行业提供高品质的展示交流场所和全球专业贸易采购平台，每年都吸引超过三万来自百余个国家的专业观众和买家。
始办年份：1987
周期：每年一届
市场范围：国际性
性质：面向公众
入场券价格：免费
上届规模 2010：展览面积31,360m^2(国外展商9,187m^2)，参展商1,006家（国外展商238家，来自33个国家），专业贸易观众46,671人
主办：北京国际展览中心
地址：北京市西城区月坛北街26号恒华国际大厦6层601室（100045）
联系人：王平

(China Refrigeration Expo)
The 22nd International Exhibition for Refrigeration, Air-conditioning, Heating and Ventilation, Frozen Food Processing, Packaging and Storage
Venue: Shanghai New International Expo Center, Shanghai
Profile: China Refrigeration Expo has become one of the most successful global exhibitions in its industry. For years, "China Refrigeration Expo" devotes every effort to establishing a quality platform for displaying, trading and networking marketplace for the industry all over the world.
Established Year: 1987
Frequency: Annual
Market Area: International
Nature: Open to Public
Cost to Attend: Free
Statistics 2010: Exhibition Area 31,360m^2(foreigners 9,187m^2), Exhibitors 1,006 (foreigners 238, came from 33 countries), Trade Visitors 46,671
Organizer: Beijing International Exhibition Center
Address: Room601, F/6, Henghua International Mansion, 26 Yuetanbeijie, Xicheng Dist. Beijing, China
Contact: Wang Ping

2011/04/07 - 09
☎ 021-5415 2384
📠 021-6129 4111
✉ skzl@skzl.net
www.skzl.net

1680

2011国际表面工程展览会
第3届上海国际耐磨材料及工业陶瓷展览会及矿山装备展览会
地点：上海国际展览中心，上海
内容：电镀、精饰工艺、涂装与涂料、研磨去毛刺、热喷涂、磨光抛光、特种涂层、喷砂及喷丸设备、防锈防腐蚀、热浸镀、转化膜、浸渗、环保及安全技术及设备、镀膜、贸易协会、咨询服务、工程设计及服务、表面热处理、出版、宣传或电子媒体、涂装设备、涂料及化工原材料
始办年份：2010
周期：每年一届
上届规模 2010：展览面积9000m^2，参展商118家（来自18个国家），参观人数8910人
主办：上海时空展览服务有限公司；中国表面工程协会
地址：上海市都市路4418号金铭大厦3A

Coating Expo
Venue: Shanghai International Exhibition Center, Shanghai
Established Year: 2010
Frequency: Annual
Statistics 2010: Exhibition Area 9,000m^2, Exhibitors 118（came from 18 countries）, Visitors 8,910
Organizer: Time & Space Exhibition Co Ltd

2011/04/07 - 09
☎ 021-3770 4068
📠 021-6086 1336
✉ sk2@skzl.net
www.skzl.net

1690

第三届上海国际搪瓷工业展览会
地点：上海国际展览中心，上海
内容：瓷制品：工业搪瓷、卫生搪瓷、特种搪瓷、日用搪瓷、建筑搪瓷、艺术搪瓷及各种辅助材料等；搪玻璃设备：搪玻璃反应釜、搪玻璃反应罐、搪玻璃搅拌器、搪玻璃储罐、搪玻璃冷凝器、搪玻璃换热器、搪玻璃附件、填料密封、四氟配件、球阀、管件；生产技术及设备：搪瓷涂装生产线、搪瓷涂层、搪瓷粉末喷涂、搪瓷静电和非静电喷涂设备；搪瓷的瓷釉原料：矿物原料、化工原料和色素原料；检测分析仪器及其他理化分析仪器；搪瓷的各种新工艺、新技术、新材料、新产品及科研成果
始办年份：2009
周期：每年一届
市场范围：国际性
上届规模 2010：展览面积3,000m^2，参展商来自18个国家，参观人数8,910人
主办：中国搪瓷工业协会；中国硅酸盐学会搪瓷分会
承办：上海时空展览服务有限公司

The International Ceramics Industry Forum Held Concurrently 2011
Venue: Shanghai International Exhibition Center, Shanghai
Established Year: 2009
Frequency: Annual
Market Area: International
Statistics 2010: Exhibition Area 3000m^2, Exhibitors came from 18 countries, Visitors 8,910
Organizer: Time & Space Exhibition Co Ltd

2011/04/08 - 10
☎ 021-5266 5938, 5266 5618
📠 021-5266 8178, 5266 6815
✉ realexpo@sh163.net
www.realexhibition.cn/cooc

1710

第十一届中国国际眼科和视光技术及设备展览会
地点：上海光大会展中心，上海
内容：展示各类眼科与视光相关的医疗产品及相关设备等
始办年份：1999
周期：每年一届
市场范围：国际性
性质：面向贸易观众
入场券价格：凭相关邀请函或现场凭专业名片
参展费用：国外展商4,000美元/展位，合资企业3,200美元/展位，国内展商11,000元/展位
上届规模 2010：展览面积3,500m^2(国外展商1,000m^2)，参展商120家（国外展商35家，来自8个国家）
主办：上海、安徽、福建、山东、江苏、江西、浙江、湖南、湖北省医学会眼科分会；复旦大学附属眼耳鼻喉科医院
承办：上海瑞欧展览服务有限公司
地址：上海市中山北路2790号杰地大厦1007室（200063）
联系人：陈静娴 宋欢
QQ：982562505

The 11th International Congress of Ophthalmology and Optometry China
Venue: Shanghai Everbright Convention & Exhibition Center, Shanghai
Established Year: 1999
Frequency: Annual
Market Area: International
Nature: Trade Only
Cost to Attend: Free
Participated Fee: USD 4,000/booth
Statistics 2010: Exhibition Area 3,500m^2(foreigners 1,000m^2), Exhibitors 120（foreigners 35, came from 8 countries）
Organizer: Shanghai Real Exhibition Service Co Ltd
Address: Room 1007, Jie Di Plaza, No.2790 Zhong Shan North Road, Shanghai
Contact: Amy Chen, Sofy Song

2011/04/08 - 10
☎ 021-5197 8780, 5197 8781
📠 021-5197 8782, 5197 8784
✉ zhangying@dr-expo.com.cn
www.powerchinashow.com

1720

第五届中国（上海）国际风能展览会暨研讨会
地点：上海新国际博览中心，上海
内容：中国具权威性、有规模、覆盖面广的专业品牌风能展览会之一。
始办年份：2007
周期：每年一届
市场范围：国际性
性质：面向贸易观众
入场券价格：专业的名片免费换入场券
参展费用：标准展位9,600元，净地900元/m^2
上届规模 2010：展览面积21,200m^2(国外展商5,000m^2)，参展商312家（国外展商80家，来自30个国家），参观人数20,734人（专业贸易观众18,000人）
主办：中国农机工业协会风能设备分会(风力机械分会)、中国电机工程学会风力与潮汐发电专业委员会
承办：上海德瑞展览策划有限公司
地址：上海浦东金桥金豫路100号1号926-927室（201206）
联系人：张颖，余洋
QQ：154895951

China (Shanghai) International Wind Energy Exhibition and Conference 2011
Venue: Shanghai New International Expo Center, Shanghai
Profile: Will be held regularly in April every year in Shanghai, taking "Cooperation, Win-win, Practicality, Innovation" as philosophy of running exhibition, CWEE wins many praise and favor from exhibitions and visitors. CWEE wind energy exhibition has become one of the most authoritative, the largest and the most extensive professional wind energy exhibitions in China.
Established Year: 2007
Frequency: Annual
Market Area: International
Nature: Trade Only
Cost to Attend: Free
Statistics 2010: Exhibition Area 21,200m^2(foreigners 5,000m^2), Exhibitors 312（foreigners 80, came from 30 countries）, Visitors 20,734（trade visitors 18,000）
Sponsor: Chinese Wind Energy Equipment Association; Wind & Tidal Committee of Chinese Society for Electrical Engineering; World Wind Energy Association; Shanghai International Sourcing Promotion Center
Organizer：Shanghai Deray Exhibition Planning Co Ltd
Address：Room 926、927 Block1, #100 Jinyu Road, Pudong, Shanghai, China 201206

2011/04/13 - 16
☎ 021-6295 8367，6295 6677 转ext 8367
℻ 021-6278 0038
✉ intexcl@sh163.net
intexcyw@sh163.net
www.hortiflorexpo.com
www.intex-sh.com
1740

第十三届中国国际花卉园艺展览会
地点：上海国际展览中心有限公司，上海
内容：花卉、花艺器皿、花店展示与设计、花卉包装；种子、种球(苗)、盆栽蔬菜、水果、园艺资材；草种、草坪建造养护、绿化工程；观赏植物、仿真植物、干花工艺；温室、冷藏、保鲜技术与设备；生物组培、生物防治、花卉营养；花园家具、户外地板、防腐木、喷泉、雕塑、大型游乐玩具等。 园林景观专区：园林小品、户外家具、水景、景观建筑材料、防腐木类、园艺工具、园林机械、喷灌、灌溉设施等
周期：每年一届
主办：中国花卉协会
承办：上海国际展览中心有限公司；长城国际展览有限责任公司
地址：上海市娄山关路55号新虹桥大厦801-804室上海国际展览中心有限公司

The 13th Hortiflorexpo China
Venue: Shanghai International Exhibition Center, Shanghai
Frequency: Annual
Organizer: INTEX Shanghai Co Ltd

2011/04/14 - 17
☎ 021-6437 1178
℻ 021-6467 5683
✉ helena.gao@ubmsinoexpo.com
www.boatshowchina.com
1750

中国(上海)国际游艇展
第十六届中国国际船艇及其技术设备展览会
地点：上海展览中心，上海
内容：船艇及豪华游艇：动力艇及帆船、豪华及超豪华游艇、橡皮艇、充气艇、游览船 码头、休闲；活动及服务：房产公司、码头开发商、港口和船坞设备、码头设备、出版发行公司、信息顾问服务公司、行业标准机构、船艇设计公司；复合材料及设备：动力装置、推进系统、配套设备、硬件、便携式设备、通讯导航设备、发动机/驱动器、救生装置；水上运动：独木舟和皮筏、潜水、帆船运动、帆板、水橇设备、潜水装置、航行及帆船驾驶课程，便携式健康运动设备；观光：旅游局、旅馆及观净地、水岸别墅、租赁公司等；生活方式：时尚、奢侈品、高级内部装饰及家具公司
周期：每年一届
主办：中国船舶工业行业协会船艇分会；上海船舶工业行业协会；上海博华国际展览有限公司；上海对外科学技术交流中心
地址：上海市襄阳南路218号现代大厦8楼上海博华国际展览有限公司（200031）
联系人：高海燕小姐

China (Shanghai) International Boat Show
Venue: Shanghai Exhibition Center, Shanghai
Profile: China biggest international boat show. CIBS is the most comprehensive and longest established boat & yacht exhibition in China, covering displays of its whole industry chain since its launch in 1996. CIBS has progressively established itself as the endorser and facilitator for yachting culture in 16 years. CIBS provides a platform for all the industry products, but also continues to further explore opportunities to popularize maritime lifestyle and yachting culture.
Frequency: Annual
Organizer: Shanghai UBM Sinoexpo International Exhibition Co Ltd
Address: 8F Xian Dai Mansion, 218 Xiang Yang Road (S), Shanghai 200030, China

2011/04/18 - 20
☎ 010-5919 4402
℻ 010-6591 8986
1760

中国国际食用油及橄榄油展览会
地点：上海光大会展中心，上海
内容：各种食用油、橄榄油及相关产品
始办年份：2005
周期：每年一届
市场范围：国际性
性质：面向公众
上届规模 2010：展览面积3,000m^2，参展商102家（来自15个国家）
主办：中国贸促会农业行业分会
地址：北京市朝阳区麦子店街20号楼805（100125）
联系人：江月朋

China International Exhibition of Olive Oil & Edible Oil
Venue: Shanghai Everbright Convention & Exhibition Center, Shanghai
Profile: Edible oil, olive oil and related products
Established Year: 2005
Frequency: Annual
Market Area: International
Nature: Open to Public
Statistics 2010: Exhibition Area 3,000m^2, Exhibitors 102（came from 15 countries）
Organizer: CCPIT-SSA
Address: Room 805, Building 20，Maizidian Street, Chaoyang District，Beijing
Contact: Linda Jiang

2011/04/20 - 22
☎ 021-6289 5385
℻ 021-6247 2950
✉ info@rechinaexpo.com.cn
info@rechinaexpo.com
www.rechinaexpo.com.cn
1770

第八届ReChina亚洲打印耗材展览会(春季)
地点：上海展览中心，上海
内容：墨盒、硒鼓、色带、碳粉、墨水及连续供墨系统兼容，再生、循环使用的打印机和复印机通用耗材 芯片、感光鼓、各类辊、膜、空盒等配件和原材料，打印耗材的制造、翻新、灌装、测试等设备和工具，相纸、票据纸、彩喷纸、热敏纸等办公打印用纸，打印设备与耗材技术、信息、包装等服务类产品
始办年份：2004
周期：两年一届
市场范围：国际性
性质：面向贸易观众
入场券价格：50元
参展费用：标准展位（9m^2）14,400元或2,250美元；净地1,520元/m^{2}或240美元/m^2
上届规模 2010：展览面积17,000m^2(国外展商1,162m^2)，参展商322家（国外展商40家），参观人数7,200人（专业贸易观众5,600人）
主办：上海广会会展有限公司
承办：Rechina Expo Inc(USA); Recharger Magazine(USA)
地址：上海市镇宁路200号东峰18B（20040）
联系人：陈金祥,陈文瑾
MSN：aprilellios@163.com
QQ：1193882389

ReChina Asia Expo 2011(Spring Session)
Venue: Shanghai Exhibition Center, Shanghai
Profile: Ink cartridges, toner cartridges, ribbons, toner, ink and CISS Compatible, remanufactured and renewable consumables for printers and materials Chips, OPC drums, various, rollers, sleeves, empties and other components and materials Manufacturing
Established Year: 2004
Frequency: Biennial
Market Area: International
Nature: Trade Only
Cost to Attend: RMB 50:-
Participated Fee: Standard Booth USD 2,250/9m^2，Raw Space USD 240/m^2
Statistics 2010: Exhibition Area 17,000m^2(foreigners 1,162m^2), Exhibitors 322（foreigners 40），Visitors 7,200（trade visitors 5,600）
Organizer: Shanghai Grand Expo Co Ltd; Rechina Expo Inc (USA); Recharger Magazine (USA)
Address: 18B East Wing, No.200 Zhenning Rd, Shanghai, China
Contact: Peter Chen, Cheyenne Chen
MSN: aprilellios@163.com
www.rechinaexpo.com.cn

2011/04/20 - 22
☎ 021-6247 3100
🖷 021-6247 0085
✉ info@all-in-office.com
www.officeworldexpo.com

1780

Office World办公设备展览会

地点：上海展览中心，上海

内容：涵盖办公设备、办公耗材、办公数码产品、办公信息系统。产品包括打印机、复印机、一体机、扫描仪、投影仪、碎纸机、装订机、考勤机、点钞机、传真机、交换机、电脑及外设、电纸书及其它数码设备等；打印复印传真等各类办公用纸及硒鼓、墨盒、连供、墨水、色带、碳带等办公耗材;以及各类制造设备与零部件等。

周期：每年一届

市场范围：国际性

性质：面向贸易观众

入场券价格：50元

参展费用：标准展位1,200元/m^2，净地1,100元/m^2

预计规模：展出面积10,000平方米;参展厂商300家，参观人数8,000人

主办：上海广会文化传媒有限公司；Grand Expo Inc (USA)

承办：上海市计算机行业协会；上海文化用品行业协会

地址：上海镇宁路200好欣安大厦东峰18C（200040）

联系人：林莉梅,王瑶

Office World Expo

Venue: Shanghai Exhibition Center, Shanghai

Profile: It is an international trade show focusing on office equipment and office supplies. It provides a great marketplace for business and trade in the office products

Frequency: Annual

Market Area: International

Nature: Trade Only

Cost to Attend: RMB 50；-

Participated Fee: Standard Booth RMB 1,200/m^2, Raw Space RMB 1,100/m^2

Sponsor: Shanghai Grand Culture Media Co Ltd; Grand Expo Inc (USA)

Organizer: Shanghai Computer Association; Shanghai Stationery Association

Address: 18C East Wing, Xin'An Building, 200 Zhen Ning Rd, Shanghai, China

Contact: Jennifer Lin, Eiffe Wang

2011/04/21 - 28
☎ 021-6279 2828
🖷 021-6545 5124
✉ guchunting@hotmail.com
xiaocong@siec-ccpit.com
www.autoshanghai.org

1790 

第十四届上海国际汽车工业展览会

地点：上海新国际博览中心，上海

内容：各类轿车、商务车、客车、卡车、特种车、汽车设计及新概念产品、各类汽车零部件、汽车音响、轮胎、汽车检测维修设备、汽车用品等

始办年份：1985

周期：两年一届

市场范围：国际性

主办：中国汽车工业协会；中国贸促会上海市分会；中国贸促会汽车行业分会

承办：上海市国际展览有限公司；德国慕尼黑国际博览集团；IMAG国际交易会及展览会有限公司

地址：上海市延安中路841号8楼（200040）

联系人：顾春霆先生，陈晓聪女士

AUTO SHANGHAI 2011

Venue: Shanghai New International Expo Center, Shanghai

Profile: All kinds of concept cars, saloon cars, sports car, passenger cars, commercial vehicles, parts and fittings of autos, acoustics of autos, inspection and maintenance equipments of auto, auto article

Established Year: 1985

Frequency: Biennial

Market Area: International

Sponsor: China Association of Automobile Manufacturers; CCPIT Shanghai Sub-Council; CCPIT Automotive Sub-Council

Organizer: Shanghai International Exhibition Co Ltd; MMG-Messe Muenchen International/ IMAG-International Messe-und Ausstellungsdienst GmbH

Address: 8/F, No.841 Yan An Zhong Road, Shanghai 200040, China

Contact: Mr Gu Chunting, Ms Chen Xiaocong

2011/04/22 - 24
☎ 010-6211 5995, 6211 5791
🖷 010-6211 7993
✉ show@interweighing.com
www.weighment.com

1800

2011中国国际衡器展览会

地点：上海光大会展中心，上海

内容：近年来国内外企业研制、开发的衡器新产品、新技术，各种衡器，天平，称重传感器，称重显示控制器及相关检测仪器、仪表，元器件、材料等。

始办年份：1995

周期：每年一届

性质：面向贸易观众

入场券价格：免费

上届规模 2010：展览面积8,800m^2，参展商290家

主办：中国衡器协会

地址：北京市北三环西路43号青云当代大厦806室

InterWeighing2011

2011 China International Weighing Instrument Exhibition

Venue: Shanghai Everbright Convention & Exhibition Center, Shanghai

Profile: All kinds of scales, balance, weighing system, indicator, load cell, testing instrument and device, electronic component and materials used in weighing instrument.

Established Year: 1995

Frequency: Annual

Nature: Trade Only

Cost to Attend: Free

Statistics 2010: Exhibition Area 8,800m^2, Exhibitors 290

Organizer: China Weighing Instrument Association (CWIA)

Address: Rm.806 Qingyun Dangdai Building, 43 N.3rd Ring Rd West, Beijing 100086, China

2011/04/26 - 28
☎ 021-6279 2828, 6289 3343
🖷 021-6386 6972
✉ zlei@siec-ccpit.com
chinainterdye@siec-ccpit.com
www.chinainterdye.com
www.siec-ccpit.com
1810

第十一届中国国际染料工业暨有机颜料、纺织化学品展览会
同期举办：2011中国国际印花技术及设备展览会
地点：上海国际展览中心、上海世贸商城，上海
内容：各类染料、中间体、有机颜料和纺织化学品、各类助剂和整理助剂、各种纺织用化学制品、配套生产、分析检测和监控设备以及印染设备和三废处理设备，印花材料，印花相关设备等
始办年份：2001
周期：每年一届
市场范围：国际性
性质：面向贸易观众
上届规模 2010：展览面积22000m^2，参展商428家（来自14个国家），参观人数39284人
主办：中国染料工业协会；中国印染行业协会；中国贸促会上海市分会；中国国际商会上海商会
承办：上海国际展览服务有限公司
地址：上海市延安中路841号8楼2503室（200040）
联系人：朱磊小姐，陈颖小姐，顾捷先生

CHINA INTERDYE 2011
11th China Intl Dye Industry Pigments and Textile Chemicals Exhibition/ 2011 China Intl Textile Printing Technology & Equipment Exhibition
Venue: Shanghai International Exhibition Center, Shanghai Mart, Shanghai
Profile: Dyestuff, intermediates, organic pigments, textile chemicals, various auxiliaries and finishing agents, various chemicals for textiles, and equipment for related production, analysis, inspection, testing, and monitoring, as well as dyeing and printing equipment and the equipment for the treatment of "three wastes", Printing materials, printing-related equipment, etc.
Established Year: 2001
Frequency: Annual
Market Area: International
Nature: Trade Only
Statistics 2010：Exhibition Area 22,000m^2, Exhibitors 428（came from 14 countries）, Buyers 39,284
Sponsor: China Dyestuff Industry Association; China Dyeing and Printing Association; CCPIT Shanghai Sub-Council; Shanghai Chamber of Commerce of China Chamber of International Commerce
Organizer: Shanghai International Exhibition Service Co Ltd
Address: 8/F, No. 841 Yan An Zhong Road, Shanghai 200040, China
Contact: Ms Julia Zhu

2011/04/30 - 03
☎ 021-6195 6088转ext 903
🖷 021-6195 6099
✉ sam.shen@vnuexhibitions.com.cn
www.vnuexhibitionsasia.com
1840

2011上海房地产展示会——假日楼市
地点：上海展览中心，上海
内容：是上海乃至华东区具影响力的大型的房产展。经过数十年的打造和运作，该展已成为上海楼市的风向标。每年，超过200家房地产商借助新年伊始的上海之春把握先机、推出新盘、展示形象、拓展市场、主力营销。接近13万的高质量购房人群保证了这一互动平台的高效运行，上海之春也因此受到房产界的一致好评和忠诚青睐。
始办年份：1997
周期：每年两届
性质：面向公众
入场券价格：10元
参展费用：12,000元/9m^2(西一馆一层)
上届规模 2010：展览面积2,200m^2，参展商200家（国外展商5家，来自4个国家），参观人数120,000人
主办：上海万耀企龙展览有限公司
地址：上海市田林路140号26A栋（200233）
联系人：沈先生

2011 Holiday Real Estate Market
Venue: Shanghai Exhibition Center, Shanghai
Profile: Holiday real estate Shanghai is one of the most influential large-scale real estate exhibitions in china. After decades of experiences, it has become the vital benchmark in shanghai real estate market.
Established Year: 1997
Frequency: Biannual
Nature: Open to Public
Cost to Attend: RMB 10:-
Participated Fee: RMB 12,000/9m^2
Statistics 2010: Exhibition Area 2,200m^2, Exhibitors 200（foreigners 5, came from 4 countries）, Visitors 120,000
Organizer: VNU Exhibitions Asia
Address: VNU House, 26A, No. 140 Tianlin Road, Shanghai
Contact: Sam

2011/05/04 - 07
☎ 021-6279 2828
🖷 021-6545 5124
✉ xls@siec-ccpit.com
www.chinacycle.com.cn
1860

第二十一届中国国际自行车展览会
2011中国国际摩托车及零部件交易会
地点：上海新国际博览中心，上海
内容：CHINA CYCLE云集了所有在中国自行车市场上的知名品牌。品牌企业的高到位率和高质量的专业观众，保证了展会的规模和层次，体现了展会的影响力和号召力。CHINA CYCLE由于"自行车王国"的特殊地位，历来都受到海内外业界人士的广泛关注。CHINA CYCLE将继续印证：自行车可以让城市更环保，让生活更健康；随着绿色环保、健康生活的理念越来越深入人心，中国的自行车企业必将拥有更为辉煌、广阔的未来。不断创新是CHINA CYCLE发展的动力，有助于展商更好地了解自行车行业的品牌导向、流行趋势和贸易信息；有利于推进展会在创意中不断升华。在中国培育全球顶级的自行车展览会，这既是中国自行车协会的工作目标，也是全行业的共同追求。展会组委会将继续完善展会各项服务功能，不断提高展会整体服务水平。

在中国，绿色出行、低碳生活方式正受到越来越多人的推崇。"低碳"已成为自行车产业转型升级的新引擎，第21届以"低碳出行、骑乐无穷"为主题的CHINA CYCLE 2011又将让我们相聚上海，共筑业界新的辉煌。范围有自行车及零部件，电动自行车及零部件，摩托车及零部件、童车及零部件，相关设备、工艺、材料及相关出版物，相关旅游运动休闲用品

CHINA CYCLE 2011
2011 Motor Fair
Venue: Shanghai New International Expo Center, Shanghai
Profile: Bicycles, bicycle parts and accessories
Established Year: 1990
Frequency: Annual
Market Area: International
Organizer: Shanghai International Exhibition Co Ltd; Shanghai Xiesheng Exhibition Co Ltd
Address: 8/F, No.841 Yan An Zhong Road, Shanghai, 200040, China
Contact: Mr Xie Longsheng

始办年份：1990
周期：每年一届
市场范围：国际性
上届规模 2010：展览面积100,000m²，参展商1,117家（国外展商61家），参观人数102,022人
主办：中国自行车协会
地址：北京市丰台区顺三条21号嘉业大厦1号楼16层（100079）
联系人：贾刚，范震 电话：010-6766 2159 电子邮箱cbike@public2.bta.net.cn
www.china-bicycle.com
承办：上海市国际展览有限公司；上海协升展览有限公司
地址：上海市延安中路841号8楼（200040）
联系人：谢龙生先生

2011/05/05 - 07
☎ 13816943887
🖷 021-5171 4505
✉ xialin_1120@163.com
www.RFHSexpo.com
1870

2011上海国际室内供暖、通风及净化产品展览会
地点：上海新国际展览中心，上海
内容：中央新风展示区：中央新风系统、新风换气设备、空气置换系统、空气处理设备、循环水系统设备、风机、风管、风幕、热交换器、热恢复系统、通风和窗体技术；空调清洗检测维修设备。 中央吸尘展示区，空气净化产品展示区；家庭水净化系统；控制系统：照明控制开关、温控器、分集水器、阀门、热计量、循环泵等。
周期：每年一届
主办：中国建筑金属结构协会地面供暖委员会，中国贸促会上海浦东分会
承办：上海展业展览有限公司
地址：上海市虹漕南路99弄1号1楼A座
联系人：夏小姐

2011 Shanghai International Residential Comfort System Expo
Venue: Shanghai New International Expo Center, Shanghai
Frequency: Annual
Organizer: Shanghai International Service Corporation
Address: 1-1-A, 99 South Hongchao Road, Shanghai
Contact: Ms Xia

2011/05/05 - 07
☎ 021-5459 2323
🖷 021-5425 3480
✉ liuyun@zhongmao.com.cn
www.eptee.com
1880

（第十二届）2011中国国际环保、废弃物及资源利用展览会
地点：上海新国际博览中心，上海
内容：水和污水：水萃取、海水淡化，水和污水处理，机械－物理工艺，化学－物理工艺，生化工艺，污泥及残渣处理，排水及下水道，水管，管道、泵；垃圾：箱、运输车及车厢结构、机械及生物处理、热量利用；道路清洁及冬季路面服务；新能源；测量，控制和实验室技术；烟气净化和空气抽取；工业旧区净化、土壤处理；降噪和减振；服务；教育和科研
始办年份：2000
周期：每年一届
市场范围：国际性
上届规模 2010：展览面积40,000m²，参展商839家，参观人数22,000人
主办：中国环境科学学会；上海中贸国际展览有限公司；德国慕尼黑国际博览集团；慕尼黑展览（上海）有限公司
地址：上海市中山西路2368号华鼎大厦10A（200235）
联系人：刘云

IFAT CHINA+EPTEE+CWS 2011
International Trade Fair for Water, Sewage, Refuse, Recycling and Natural Energy Sources
Venue: Shanghai New International Expo Center, Shanghai
Established Year: 2000
Frequency: Annual
Market Area: International
Statistics 2010: Exhibition Area 40,000m², Exhibitors 839, Visitors 22,000
Organizer: Messe Muenchen International; MMI (Shanghai) Co Ltd; Shanghai ZM International Exhibition

---

2011/05/11 - 13
☎ 021-5153 5100
🖷 021-5153 5248
✉ mike.deng@reedexpo.com.cn
kerry.fan@reedexpo.com.cn
www.nepconchina.com
1890

中国国际电子生产设备暨微电子工业展
地点：上海光大会展中心，上海
内容：SMT展品包括黏合剂与分离剂、仪表控制传输系统与配件、化学制品、芯片载体、元件输送系统等；焊接专区；元器件生产包括PCB及相关产品、放电加工切线设备、模具制造、数控钻头等；电子制造服务包括外包生产、常规印刷电路板组装等；测试与测量等。
周期：每年一届
上届规模：参观人数14,310人
主办：励展博览集团；北京励德展览有限公司上海分公司
地址：上海市淮海中路775号新华联大厦8楼励展博览集团上海分公司

NEPCON China 2011
Venue: Shanghai Everbright Convention & Exhibition Center, Shanghai
Profile: NEPCON China is one of the biggest and longest standing trading and sourcing platform for SMT industry in China featuring all major brands in the SMT world; it is also a leading platform for brand building, leads generation and networking for global SMT equipment and products suppliers. The event enables you to stay ahead of competition in China by bringing you focused access to customers and connecting you with the SMT Community.
Frequency: Annual
Statistics 2010: Visitors 14,310
Organizer: Reed Exhibition China
Address: Reed Exhibitions Shanghai Branch, 8th Floor, New Hua Lian Mansion, No.775 Middle Huai Hai Road, Shanghai, China 200020

2011/05/11 - 13
☎ 021-5153 5110, 5153 5122
🖷 021-5153 5248
✉ selina.wang@reedexpo.com.cn
lingguo.kong@reedexpo.com.cn
www.greenlightingchina.com
1910

2011上海国际新光源、新能源照明展览会暨论坛
地点：上海国际展览中心，上海
内容：以"深化产业联动，引导技术创新"为纲，细心雕琢行业上、中、下游的各个细分市场， 本次展会共规划以下五大专区，芯片/外延片生产及制造设备和材料专区，封装企业及封装设备、配件、材料专区，LED照明产品应用专区，LED照明技术研发成果展示专区，散热驱动及解决方案专区。专区覆盖了LED照明行业全产业链从材料、生产检测设备、产品应用、解决方案到科研成果的主要领域，其专业化程度堪称国内顶尖。与展会同期举行由CSA主办的高端技术论坛，更将在：外延片生长技术、芯片封装技术中的散热管理、提高光通量、防电击穿、配色技术、大功率LED封装技术等众多领域进行深入研讨，预计本次论坛将吸引

Green Lighting Shanghai Expo and Forum 2011
Venue: Shanghai International Exhibition Center, Shanghai
Profile: Green Lighting China is dedicated to exploring every segment of the novel energy and light source industry. The show is a key connector for industry professionals and serves as a valuable guide to emerging technological innovations. The Five Functional Zones: Chip/Epitaxy Manufacturing Equipment and Material Zone, Packaging Equipment/Components/Material Zone, Lighting Devices/LED Application Zone, LED Technology R&D Results Display Zone, Thermal Drive & Solution Zone
Nature: Trade Only
Organizer: Reed Exhibitions China

超过1200位国内外行业专才、专家及行业领军人物与会。论坛规格之高也是在国内首屈一指的。
性质：面向贸易观众
主办：国家半导体照明工程研发及产业联盟（CSA）；励展博览集团中国公司
地址：上海市淮海中路775号新华联大厦8楼励展博览集团中国公司上海分公司
联系人：王桦,孔令国

Address: Reed Exhibitions Shanghai Branch, 8th Floor, New Hua Lian Mansion, No.775 Middle Huai Hai Road, Shanghai, China 200020
Contact: Selina Wang, Darren Kong

2011/05/11 - 14
☎ 010-6343 0880, 6343 0990
🖷 010-6343 0660
✉ chinabakery@126.com
www.cnbakery.com
1920

2011第十四届中国国际焙烤展览会
地点：上海新国际博览中心，上海
内容：凡从事食品、糕点用原辅材料、装饰品及食品代加工（OEM），辅料、焙烤设备及器具、自动计量包装机械、模具及生产设备，展示柜、储藏与冷藏柜、店面装饰；饼房、厨房、西餐厅、咖啡厅生产设备、原辅料及用品等；仿真食品模型等蛋糕装饰材料；咖啡、咖啡制品、咖啡机、咖啡加工设备
周期：每年一届
市场范围：国际性
性质：面向贸易观众
上届规模 2010：展览面积80,000m^2(国外展商1,000m^2)，参展商986家（国外展商22家，来自12个国家），专业贸易观众86,000
主办：中国焙烤食品糖制品工业协会；中国贸促会轻工行业分会
地址：北京市海淀区北蜂窝2号中盛大厦1305A（100038）
联系人：李翔

The 14th China International Trade Fair For Bakery & Confectionery
Venue: Shanghai New International Expo Center, Shanghai
Profile: Baking ovens and accessories, baking and pastry-making machinery, refrigeration, fermenting and air conditioning technology, baking agents, raw materials and ingredients, semi-finished and finished products, ice cream manufacturing, pasta making, etc.
Frequency: Annual
Market Area: International
Nature: Trade Only
Statistics 2010: Exhibition Area 80,000m^2(foreigners 1,000m^2), Exhibitors 986（foreigners 22, came from 12 countries）, Trade Visitors 86,000
Organizer: China Association of Bakery & Confectionery Industry; CCPIT Sub-council of Light Industry
Address: 1305A Rm.1305A Zhongsheng Mansion, NO.2 Beifengwo, Beijing
Contact: Li Xiang

2011/05/12 - 15
☎ 021-6195 6088
🖷 021-6195 6099
✉ stephanie.xu@vnuexhibitions.com.cn
1930

上海世界旅游资源博览会
地点：上海展览中心，上海
内容：国家及地方旅游局、旅行社、地接社、航空公司、邮轮公司、景点、酒店度假村等
始办年份：2004
周期：每年一届
市场范围：国际性
入场券价格：20元
参展费用：净地展位2,150元/m^2，标准展位2,550元/m^2
上届规模 2010：展览面积4,000m^2(国外展商3,000m^2)，参展商500家（国外展商420家，来自45个国家），参观人数20,000人（专业贸易观众6,000人）
主办：上海万耀企龙展览有限公司
地址：上海市田林路140号26A（200233）
联系人：徐洁

World Travel Fair
Venue: Shanghai Exhibition Center, Shanghai
Profile: NTO/RTO, Travel agency, tour operator, airlines, cruises, scenery attractions, hotel & resort and etc.
Established Year: 2004
Frequency: Annual
Market Area: International
Cost to Attend: RMB 20:-
Participated Fee: Raw Space RMB 2,150/m^2, Standard Booth RMB 2,550/m^2
Statistics 2010: Exhibition Area 4,000m^2(foreigners 3,000m^2), Exhibitors 500（foreigners 420, came from 45 countries）, Visitors 20,000（trade visitors 6,000）
Organizer: VNU Exhibitions Asia
Address: 26A, No.140, Tianlin Rd., Shanghai
Contact: Stephanie Xu

2011/05/16 - 18
☎ 021-6295 2131
6295 6677转ext 2131
🖷 021-6278 0038
✉ intexzxm@sh163.net
www.china-aid.com
www.intex-sh.com
1940

2011中国国际康复护理展览会
第六届中国国际老年人和残疾人康复护理技术及辅助器具展览会
地点：上海新国际博览中心，上海
内容：康复辅具、行动辅具、矫形器和假肢、生活辅具、家具和配件、文化通讯、日常护理用品、休闲娱乐、其他
始办年份：2000
周期：每年一届
市场范围：国际性
上届规模 2010：参展商100家（来自11个国家）
主办：上海国际展览中心有限公司
联系人：李菊盛

China Aid 2011
The 6th China International Exhibition of Rehabilitation, Nursing & Health care
Venue: Shanghai New International Expo Center, Shanghai
Established Year: 2000
Frequency: Annual
Market Area: International
Statistics 2010: Exhibitors 100（came from 11 countries）
Organizer: INTEX Shanghai Co Ltd

2011/05/17 - 19
☎ 021-2653 3789, 15221727644
🖷 021-5171 4666
✉ 649871707@qq.com
www.siscf.com
1950

2011第八届上海国际箱包皮具手袋展览会
地点：上海光大会展中心，上海
内容：箱包手袋：箱包 时款包；女士包、男包、背包 旅行包；登山包；腰包、钱包、CD包、冰袋、笔袋、夹包、跨包、运动包、休闲包、手提包、公文包、电脑包、保暖包、手腕包、拉杆箱、拉杆包、学生包、化妆包、帆布包、编织包、草编包、保暖包、礼品袋、晚宴包、工具箱包、挎包、环保袋、无纺不袋、珠绣包；皮件/腰带：皮帽、皮件、票夹、皮套、表带、吊带、腰链、腰带、男女士皮带、各类皮具礼品、钱夹、皮手套、钥匙包、硬币包、皮饰品、名片夹、时装带、自动带、编织带、金属带、胶带、工业皮带、真皮带、PU/PVC带；配件/辅料；刀模冲床；箱包机械/五金；箱包皮具专用加工设备、计算机辅助设计制造。
参展费用：外资企业22,000元/9m^2, 18,000元/9m^2,净地2,000元/m^2；国内企业13,800元/9m^2，10,800元/9m^2, 净地800元/m^2
主办：上海市皮革技术协会
承办：上海雅辉展览服务有限公司
地址：上海漕溪路251弄望族城5号楼20F室（200235）
联系人：金锐

2011 The 8th Shanghai International Cases & Boxes and Handbags Exhibition
Venue: Shanghai Everbright Convention & Exhibition Center, Shanghai
Participated Fee: RMB 22,000/9m^2, 18,000/9m^2, Raw Space RMB 2,000/m^2
Organizer: Shanghai YH Exhibition Service Co
Address: F/20,No.5 Building, Lane 251, Caoxi Rd., Shanghai 200235

2011/05/17 - 19
☎ 021-2653 3789, 15221727644
🖷 021-5171 4666
✉ 649871707@qq.com
www.siscf.com
1960

2011第五届上海国际环保购物袋、包装袋展览会
地点：上海光大会展中心，上海
内容：环保购物袋、超市购物袋、无纺布袋、礼品袋、包装袋、彩印袋、塑料包装袋、食品包装袋、日用品包装袋、环保布袋、背心袋、折叠袋、手提袋、纸袋、纸塑袋、塑料袋(PE,PP,PVC袋)、复合编织袋、垃圾袋、降解塑料袋、生物降解购物袋、降解一次性餐饮具、环保塑料制品；无纺布制品、服装袋、西装套、床上用品袋、广告围裙、鞋套、酒袋、广告袋、收纳袋、包装盒、购物篮、购物车；材料及加工机械类
周期：每年一届
市场范围：国际性
参展费用：外资企业22,000元/9m^2, 18,000元/9m^2,净地2,000元/m^2；国内企业13,800元/9m^2, 10,800元/9m^2, 净地800元/m^2
主办：上海市皮革技术协会
承办：上海雅辉展览服务有限公司
地址：上海漕溪路251弄望族城5号楼20F室（200235）
联系人：金锐

The 5th Shanghai Intl Shopping Bags and Package Bags Expo
Venue: Shanghai Everbright Convention & Exhibition Center, Shanghai
Frequency: Annual
Market Area: International
Participated Fee: RMB 22,000/9m^2, 18,000/9m^2, Raw Space RMB 2,000/m^2
Organizer: Shanghai YH Exhibition Service Co
Address: F/20, No.5 Building, Lane 251, Caoxi Rd., Shanghai 200235

2011/05/17 - 19
☎ 021-2653 3789, 15221727644
🖷 021-5171 4666
✉ 649871707@qq.com
www.siscf.com
1970

2011中国（上海）产业用纺织品、非织造布及无纺布展览会
地点：上海光大会展中心，上海
内容：非织造材料及相关深加工产品，纤维原料及化学助剂；产业用布；非织造材料及深加工技术与设备；涂层、叠层、静电施加(驻极)、静电植绒、模压、包装等设备；非织造布；生产设备、深加工设计、设备、辅助设备及仪器
主办：上海市皮革技术协会
承办：上海雅辉展览服务有限公司
地址：上海漕溪路251弄望族城5号楼20F室（200235）
联系人：金锐

2011 Shanghai Textile, Non-woven Exhibition
Venue: Shanghai Everbright Convention & Exhibition Center, Shanghai
Participated Fee: RMB 22,000/9m^2, 18,000/9m^2, Raw Space RMB 2,000/m^2
Organizer: Shanghai YH Exhibition Service Co
Address: F/20, No.5 Building, Lane 251, Caoxi Rd., Shanghai 200235

2011/05/18 - 20
☎ 021-5308 9900
🖷 021-5308 2151
✉ sun@chinabeautyexpo.com
www.CBEbaiwen.com
1980

第十六届中国美容博览会（上海CBE）
地点：上海新国际博览中心，上海
内容：成品制造商：香水、彩妆、护肤品、洗涤、个人护理用品、专业美容及水疗产品及仪器、专业美发产品及仪器等 化妆品供应商：OEM、ODM、原材料、包装及机械、化妆品制造商相关服务
始办年份：1998
周期：每年一届
市场范围：国际性
性质：面向贸易观众
入场券价格：50元
参展费用：8,000～20,000元/9m^2
上届规模 2010：展览面积34,200m^2(国外展商6,156m^2)，参展商1,257家（国外展商351家，来自19个国家），参观人数201,600人（专业贸易观众95%人）
主办：中国贸促会轻工分会；上海百文会展有限公司
地址：上海市西藏中路728号23F（200001）
联系人：孙旦

China Beauty Expo
Venue: Shanghai New International Expo Center, Shanghai
Profile: Manufacturers of finished products: perfumery, color cosmetics, skincare, detergents, personal care, professional beauty and SPA products and equipment, professional hair products and equipment and etc. Cosmetics supplier: OEM, ODM, raw materials, packaging etc.
Established Year: 1998
Frequency: Annual
Market Area: International
Nature: Trade Only
Cost to Attend: RMB 50:-
Participated Fee: RMB 8,000-20,000/9m^2
Statistics 2010: Exhibition Area 34,200m^2(foreigners 6,156m^2), Exhibitors 1,257（foreigners 351, came from 19 countries）, Visitors 201,600（trade visitors 95%）
Organizer: CCPIT Light Industry Branch; Shanghai Baiwen Exhibition Co Ltd
Address: Suite 23F, 728 Central Tibet Road, Shanghai 200001, China
Contact: Sun

2011/05/18 - 20
☎ 010-6588 6235, 6588 6236
🖷 010-6588 6233
✉ info@sialchina.cn
1990

第十二届中国国际食品和饮料展览会
地点：上海新国际博览中心，上海
内容：食品、酒、酒店餐饮服务、烘焙与糕点、食品加工技术。同时有国内外著名品牌企业和超市参展，发布食品大趋势报告会和新产品评比，推出国内外新产品。
展品范围：食品添加剂；乳制品，蛋类；新鲜肉类；新鲜禽类；新鲜及半腌制鱼及海鲜、贝类制品；新鲜水果、蔬菜、干果；糖果、饼干、烘焙类、休闲食品；腌制肉类；新鲜半成品、速成品、即食食品；罐头食品；宠物食品；速冻食品；有机食品；减肥食品、儿童食品及保健品；杂货食品（调味品、食用油、粮食类）；酒类；酒精饮料；非酒精饮料；专业服务机构与媒体；政府促进机构、信息组织、协会；酒店设备，餐具、酒吧及咖啡设备、一次性用品、餐饮设备、连锁、技术及网络
性质：仅对专业贸易观众
始办年份：2000
周期：每年一届
市场范围：国际性
性质：面向贸易观众
上届规模 2010：参展商1,339家（国外展商550家，来自76个国家），专业贸易观众30,518人
主办：法国高美爱博展览集团；商业发展中心
地址：北京市朝外大街22号泛利大厦1605室
联系人：侯旭，李波

SIAL China 2011
Venue: Shanghai New International Expo Center, Shanghai
Profile: packaging machinery, container making machinery, packing material making machinery, food making machinery, drink machinery and the relative products and equipments
Established Year: 2000
Frequency: Annual
Market Area: International
Nature: Trade Only
Statistics 2010: Exhibitors 1,339（foreigners 550, came from 76 countries）, Trade Visitors 30,518
Organizer: Comexposium; CCDC; Exposium-Sial Exhibition Co
Address: Suite 1605, Prime Tower, No.22 Chaoyangmenwai Dajie, Chaoyang District, Beijing

2011/05/20 - 22
☎ 021-5216 4993
🖷 021-5218 9400
✉ sandy@neon-expo.com
www.kidsedu.cn
2000

第六届上海国际幼儿教育展
地点：上海世博商城，上海
内容：教育类：早教机构、幼儿园、少儿培训机构等；玩具类：益智玩具、婴儿玩具、木制玩具、毛绒玩具、电子玩具等；书籍类：图书、出版社、幼儿杂志等；游乐设施类：幼儿园设施、游乐设备、幼儿活动中心设施、课桌椅等；儿童家具类：儿童成长家居、童床、桌椅、婴儿床上用品、婴儿房配套家具等；服务机构类：月子中心、孕婴护理培训机构、儿童摄影机构、婴童店等
始办年份：2006
周期：每年一届
市场范围：国际性
性质：面向公众
入场券价格：30
参展费用：8,800元/9m²
上届规模 2010：展览面积8,000m²,参展商150家，参观人数17,584人
主办：上海市创意产业协会；上海里扬展览服务有限公司
地址：上海市长宁区协和路1158号鑫达大厦2号楼2层

The 6th Education Expo 2011 Shanghai
Venue: Shanghai Mart, Shanghai
Established Year: 2006
Frequency: Annual
Market Area: International
Nature: Open to Public
Cost to Attend: RMB 30:-
Participated Fee: RMB 8,800/booth (9m²)
Statistics 2010: Exhibition Area 8,000m², Exhibitors 150, Visitors 17,584
Organizer: Shanghai Neon Exhibition Services Ltd
Address: 2/F, Bldg 2, 1158 Xiehe Road, Changning District, Shanghai
Contact: Sandy

2011/05/20 - 23
☎ 021-5266 5938, 5266 5708
🖷 021-5266 8178, 5266 6815
✉ realexpo@sh163.net
www.antiquefurniturefair.com
2010

第十届中国国际古典家具展览会
2011上海国际古董及艺术品展览会（春季展）
地点：上海展览中心，上海
内容：主要展示以明清古典家具，中式红木古典家具为主，涵盖了以中式家居饰品及古董、古玩收藏类艺术品；各类欧洲各时期的古董家具，油画艺术品，古董等；
始办年份：2000
周期：每年两届
上届规模 2010：展览面积12,000m²(国外展商4,200m²)，参展商260家（国外展商60家，来自10个国家），参观人数42,000人（专业贸易观众24,000人）
主办：上海瑞欧展览服务有限公司
地址：上海市中山北路2790号杰地大厦1007室（200063）
联系人：陈静娴 宋薇
QQ：982562505

Antique Furniture China 2011
Antiques & Arts Shanghai 2011
Venue: Shanghai Exhibition Center, Shanghai
Profile: All kinds of antique furniture of Ming & Qing Dynasties, decoration and other artworks, Classical Rose wood and curios; European antique furniture, decoration, oil painting and artworks, etc.
Established Year: 2000
Frequency: Biannual
Statistics 2010: Exhibition Area 12,000m²(foreigners 4,200m²), Exhibitors 260（foreigners 60, came from 10 countries）, Visitors 42,000（trade visitors 24000）
Organizer: Shanghai Real Exhibition Service Co Ltd
Address: Room 1007, Jie Di Plaza, No.2790 Zhong Shan North Road, Shanghai
Contact: Amy Chen, Amanda Song

2011/05/20 - 23
☎ 021-6475 2979, 6475 2907
🖷 021-6475 2907
✉ chenjiedm@163.com
www.tea-shexpo.com
2020

2011中国（上海）国际茶业博览会
地点：上海国际展览中心，上海
内容：六大茶类：绿茶、白茶、黄茶、红茶、乌龙茶（青茶）、黑茶；再生茶类：花（草）茶、紧压茶、萃取茶、浓缩茶、果味茶、保健茶、茶饮料；茶具产品；茶叶包装；泡茶水及净水设备；茶叶加工；茶叶销售；茶工艺品、茶家具及茶科技衍生品
始办年份：2004
周期：每年一届
上届规模 2010：参展商731家（来自30个国家），参观人数53,000人
主办：国茶叶流通协会；中国长三角茶业合作（上海）组织
承办：上海东贸展览服务有限公司
联系人：陈洁

China Tea Expo, Shanghai
2011 China (Shanghai) International Tea Exhibition
Venue: Shanghai International Exhibition Center, Shanghai
Established Year: 2004
Frequency: Annual
Statistics 2010: Exhibitors 731（came from 30 countries）, Visitors 53,000
Organizer: Shanghai Dongmao Exhibition Service Co Ltd

2011/05/26 - 28
☎ 021-5228 4021
🖷 021-5228 4011
✉ ethan.shi@nm-china.com.cn
www.biofachchina.com/index.asp
2040

2011中国国际有机食品博览会
地点：上海国际展览中心，上海
内容：有机食品：有机原料和半成品，有机蔬菜和水果，有机肉类、牛奶、海鲜产品，有机方便食品，有机冷冻食品，有机儿童食品，有机健康食品以及熟食；有机饮料；有机生产资料：种苗和种子，杀虫剂和土地保护产品，土壤改良用品，饲料；服务行业；有机原料制成的药物和芳香剂产品，天然化妆品及个人护理产品，有机棉制品，天然纤维和纺织品，生产加工及市场
始办年份：2007
周期：每年一届
上届规模 2010：参展商313家（来自17个国家），参观人数11,526人
主办：德国纽伦堡展览公司；中国绿色食品发展中心
承办：纽伦堡会展服务（上海）有限公司；中绿华夏有机认证中心
地址：上海市青海路118号云海苑18楼
联系人：施佳卿先生

BioFach China 2011
Venue: Shanghai International Exhibition Center, Shanghai
Established Year: 2007
Frequency: Annual
Statistics 2010: Exhibitors 313（came from 17 countries）, Visitors 11,526
Organizer: NURNBERG MESSE CHINA
Address: 18/Fl., 118 Qinhai Road, Shanghai

2011/06/01 - 03
☎ 021-3251 6618, 3251 6628
🖷 021-3251 6698
✉ expo@vtexpo.com.cn
www.emcexpo.com
2050

2011中国（上海）国际电池展览会
地点：上海世贸商城，上海
内容：各系列电池：锂一次电池、锂离子电池、锂聚合物电池、铅酸蓄电池/阀控式密封铅酸蓄电池、镉镍蓄电池、金属氢化物镍蓄电池、太阳能电池、锌空气电池、锌锰电池、碱锰电池、锌镍蓄电池、锌银电池；各种组合电池：手机、对讲机、无绳电话、笔记本电脑、摄录一体机等；各类电池用原材料、零配件；各类电池制造设备、测试仪器和充电器
周期：每年一届
市场范围：国际性
性质：面向贸易观众
入场券价格：免费
参展费用：外商2,970美元/9m²，国内企业8,100元/9m²，净地：外商280美元/m²，国内企业800元/m²
主办：中国电子学会
承办：上海优创展览服务有限公司
地址：上海市曹杨路505号尚诚国际大厦505室（20063）
联系人：徐以敏先生，沈晓蓉小姐

China (Shanghai) Battery Exhibition
Venue: Shanghai Mart, Shanghai
Frequency: Annual
Market Area: International
Nature: Trade Only
Cost to Attend: Free
Participated Fee: USD 2,970/9m², Raw Space USD 280/m²
Organizer: Shanghai Viewtran Exhibition Service Co Ltd

2011/06/01 - 03
☎ 021-5499 9745, 13044112901
🖷 021-5499 3541
✉ shfairs-info@yahoo.cn
www.shcnlm.com
2060

2011年第99届中国鞋业皮具商品博览会 暨"名品名店"对接展会
地点：上海光大会展中心，上海
内容：品牌鞋
周期：每年一届
市场范围：全国性
入场券价格：免费
参展费用：标准展位：9,800元/9m^2，净地980元/m^2（36m^{2}起）
上届规模 2010：展览面积20,000m^2，参观人数30,000人（专业贸易观众24,000人）
主办：中国百货商业协会
承办：上海百承商务服务有限公司
联系人：刘铭
MSN：shlmcn@hotmail.com
QQ：1187 230 500

99th China Shoes & Leather Commodity Expo and "WELL-KNOWN BRANDS & FAMOUS SHOPS" Exposition
Venue: Shanghai Everbright Convention & Exhibition Center, Shanghai
Profile: Brand shoes
Frequency: Annual
Market Area: National
Cost to Attend: Free
Participated Fee: Standard Booth RMB 9,800/9m^2, Raw Space RMB 980/m^2 (36m^2)
Statistics 2010: Exhibition Area 20,000m^2, Visitors 30,000 (trade visitors 24,000)
Sponsor: China Commerce Association for General Merchandise
Organizer: Shanghai Baicheng Commerce Service Co Ltd
Address: Room 701, No 58, 1108 Lane, LianHua South Rd, Minghang Area, Shanghai, China
Contact: Mr Liu Ming
MSN: shlmcn@hotmail.com

2011/06/01 - 03
☎ 021-6328 8899
🖷 021-6374 9188
2070

2011中国国际生物技术和仪器设备博览会
地点：世博主题馆，上海
内容：生物技术、生物技术相关的仪器设备、生物信息、生物工程、服务、生物技术的其他应用
周期：每年一届
市场范围：国际性
性质：面向贸易观众
上届规模 2010：展览面积6,000m^2，参观人数4,000人
主办：上海现代国际展览有限公司
地址：上海市盛泽路8号18楼（200002）
联系人：生物展项目组

BIOTECH CHINA 2011
Venue: World Expo Theme Pavilion, Shanghai
Frequency: Annual
Market Area: International
Nature: Trade Only
Statistics 2010: Exhibition Area 6000m^2, Visitors 4,000
Organizer: Shanghai Modern Intl Exhibition Co Ltd
Address: 18F No.8 Sheng Ze Road, Shanghai
Contact: Alfred Wang

2011/06/01 - 03
☎ 021-6439 6190, 5013 1760
🖷 021-5013 1761
✉ winefairs@yahoo.com.cn
www.winefair.com.cn
2090

2011第六届上海酒类商品交易博览会
地点：上海国际展览中心，上海
内容：国产酒展区：白酒、啤酒、黄酒、葡萄酒、果露酒、保健酒等；进口酒展区：葡萄酒；香槟；威士忌；伏特加；白兰地；鸡尾酒；龙舌兰酒；其他酒类等。
周期：每年两届
市场范围：国际性
主办：上海市酿酒专业协会
承办：上海高登商业展览有限公司
联系人：杨鹏先生

The 6th Shanghai Wine Trade Fair 2011
Venue: Shanghai International Exhibition Center, Shanghai
Frequency: Biannual
Market Area: International
Organizer: Shanghai Golden Commercial Exhibition Co Ltd

2011/06/01 - 03
☎ 021-5109 7799, 5450 0848
🖷 021-5171 4505
✉ zhanye@vip.sina.com
www.BWTexpo.com
2100

2011上海建筑给排水处理技术及设备展览会
地点：上海国际展览中心，上海
内容：系统类：建筑给水供水设备：叠压供水设备（包括无负压供水设备）、变频调速供水设备、气压给水装置及产品；给水处理设备；太阳能热水系统与建筑一体化系统；生活污水排水系统、同层排水系统等；建筑消防给水技术及设备；屋面雨水排放系统、雨水综合利用系统；建筑热水及饮用水；给水的计量；游泳池给排水系统；产品及配件类：新型管道，各类管件；储水系统；节水型器具；密封类
主办：中国建筑金属结构协会给水排水设备分会；中国建筑学会建筑给水排水研究分会；中国工程建设标准化协会建筑给水排水专业委员会；中国贸促会上海浦东分会
承办：上海展业展览有限公司
地址：上海市虹漕南路99弄1号1楼A座（200233）
联系人：周军

Shanghai Building Water, Water Treatment Technology and Equipment Expo
Venue: Shanghai International Exhibition Center, Shanghai
Organizer: Shanghai International Service Corporation

2011/06/02 - 04
☎ 021-5197 8780, 5197 8781
🖷 021-5197 8782, 5197 8784
✉ zhangying@dr-expo.com.cn
www.powerchinashow.com/index.asp
2110

第十届中国（上海）国际动力设备及发电机组展览会
地点：上海新国际博览中心，上海
内容：国际化、专业化程度最高的行业展会，创新谋变，POWER 2011整合行业资源、扩大展品范围。吸引产业链间的相关企业共同参与、促进展商与观众的良性互动，进一步实现上下游产业一站式采购，搭建独一无二的行业关联纽带。
始办年份：2003
周期：每年一届
市场范围：国际性
性质：面向贸易观众
入场券价格：专业的名片免费换入场券

The 10th China (Shanghai) International Power and Generating Sets Exhibition
Venue: Shanghai New International Expo Center, Shanghai
Profile: it is a grand gathering that the manufacturing, distribution, purchasing generators managers need to take part in. If you are making efforts to establishing your own brand or doing the annually most important purchasing activities to select better suppliers in the booming Chinese market, it will be your best choice through participating in the POWER2011
Established Year: 2003
Frequency: Annual

参展费用：国内企业9,600元/标准展位,净地900元/m²
上届规模 2010：展览面积10,000m²(国外展商3,500m²)，参展商150家（国外展商40家）
主办：中国内燃机工业协会
承办：上海德瑞展览策划有限公司
地址：上海浦东金桥金豫路100号1号926-927室（201206）
联系人：张颖，余洋
QQ：154895951

Market Area: International
Nature: Trade Only
Cost to Attend: Free
Statistics 2010: Exhibition Area 10,000m²(foreigners 3,500m²), Exhibitors 150（foreigners 40）
Sponsor: China Internal Combustion Engine Industry Association
Organizer: Shanghai Deray Exhibition Planning Co Ltd
Address: Room 926/927 Block 1, #100 Jinyu Road, Pudong, Shanghai, China 201206

2011/06/02 - 05
☎ 010-6397 2404
🖷 010-6398 0554
✉ Yannan@cmes.org
www.beijing-essen-welding.com
2120

第十六届北京-埃森焊接与切割展览会

地点：上海新国际博览中心，上海
内容：焊接、切割、钎焊及粘接；消耗材料与其制备和原材料；检测设备及其耗材；焊前准备与焊后处理设备与技术；焊工安全和环境保护
始办年份：1987
周期：每年一届
市场范围：国际性
入场券价格：免费
参展费用：标准展位6,900～16,200元/展位，净地6,200～14,400元/展位
上届规模 2010：展览面积92,400m²(国外展商21,376m²)，参展商973家（国外展商225家，来自30个国家），专业贸易观众42,852人
主办：中国机械工程学会及其焊接分会；中国焊接协会；中国电器工业协会电焊机分会；德国焊接学会；德国埃森展览公司
地址：北京市海淀区莲花小区2-5-1607（100036）
联系人：闫楠
MSN：yannan0012@yahoo.com.cn
QQ：1395364399

The 16th Beijing Essen Welding & Cutting Fair

Venue: Shanghai New International Expo Center, Shanghai
Profile: Welding, Cutting, Brazing and Adhesive bonding; Consumable Materials and their Manufacturing Equipment and Raw Materials; Inspection Equipment and Related Consumables; Pre- and Post-welding Treatment Equipment and Technology; Safety and Health for Welder & Environment Protection
Established Year: 1987
Frequency: Annual
Market Area: International
Cost to Attend: Free
Participated Fee: Standard Booth RMB 6,900-16,200/booth, Raw Space RMB 6,200-14,400/booth
Statistics 2010: Exhibition Area 92,400m²(foreigners 21,376m²), Exhibitors 973（foreigners 225, came from 30 countries），Trade Visitors 42,852
Organizer: Chinese Mechanical Engineering Society; Welding Institution of CMES, China Welding Association; Welding Machine Committee of CEEIA; German Welding Society(DVS); Messe Essen GmbH
Address: 2-5-1607 Lianhuaxiaoqu, Haidian District, Beijing 100036, China
Contact: Yan Nan
MSN: yannan0012@yahoo.com.cn

2011/06/02 - 05
☎ 021-6279 2828
🖷 021-6545 5124
✉ slp@siec-ccpit.com
www.dmcexpo.com
2130

2011中国国际模具、制造应用设备及相关工业展览会

地点：上海新国际博览中心，上海
内容：加工中心，数控铣床、磨床、镗床、车床、钻床等精密加工各类金切机床；各类电加工机床，激光加工设备，雕刻机；三坐标测量机及其它测量设备等；模具及模具制品，模具标准件；压铸机、冲床、各类压力机床等成形设备；塑料机械及橡胶机械；模具CAD / CAM / CAE等计算机集成制造技术；CAPP, PDM, ERP等模具生产管理技术；模具材料、冶金制品；工具、刃具，以及与模具相关的其它产品；各类模具生产用的辅料、辅助设备、包括抛光、研磨、装配夹具等
始办年份：1986
周期：每年一届
市场范围：国际性
性质：面向贸易观众
主办：中国模具工业协会；上海市国际展览有限公司
地址：上海市延安中路841号8楼（200040）
联系人：盛来平先生

DMC 2011

(China International Exhibition on Die & Mould, Metal Processing and Forming Industry)
Venue: Shanghai New International Expo Center, Shanghai
Profile: Machining Center, CNC milling machining, Jig grinding machines, Boring machines, Drilling machines, etc. EDM machines, Laser processing; Coordinate measuring systems die & mould, Standard die & mould components; Various kinds of presses, Punch, die casting machines, etc. Injection Molding machines, Extruders, Blow; Molding machines, Injection & compression moulds, Hot runner system; Die & mould CAD/CAE/CAM, computer integrated manufacturing technology, etc. CAPP, PDM, ERP, etc. Cutting tools, spare parts and components, etc. Die & mould materials; Die spotter system, Polishing system, NC tooling system, Jig & fixture, Engraving machines, etc. Auxiliary equipment for die & mould making; Lubricant, Remover, Rust remover, etc. Heating & cooling units for die & mould
Established Year: 1986
Frequency: Annual
Market Area: International
Nature: Trade Only
Organizer: China Die & Mould Industry Association; Shanghai International Exhibition Co Ltd
Address: 8/F, No.841 Yan An Zhong Road, Shanghai, 200040, China
Contact: Mr Sheng Laiping

2011/06/08 - 10
☎ 021-5406 5152
🖷 021-5406 5150
✉ mshuan@hotmail.com
www.no-digsh.com
2140

2010上海国际非开挖技术展览会暨研讨会

地点：东亚展览馆，上海
内容：机械设备，探测设备，管材，技术，咨询服务，其它设备
始办年份：2004
市场范围：国际性
性质：面向公众
入场券价格：免费
上届规模 2008：展览面积5,500m²(国外展商2,500m²)，参展商73家（国外展商39家，来自10个国家），参观人数3,300人
主办：上海非开挖协会；上海科技会展有限公司
地址：上海市徐汇区钦州路100号2号楼3楼（200235）
联系人：宓晟欢,陈皓

2010 No-Dig Shanghai

Venue: East Asia Exhibition Hall, Shanghai
Established Year: 2004
Frequency: Biannual
Market Area: International
Nature: Open to Public
Cost to Attend: Free
Statistics 2008: Exhibition Area 5,500m²(foreigners 2,500m²), Exhibitors 73（foreigners 39, came from 10 countries），Visitors 3,300
Organizer: Shanghai Society for Trenchless Technology; Shanghai Technology Convention & Exhibition Co Ltd
Contact: Michelle Mi, Howard

2011/06/09 - 11
☎ 010-8496 6538
🖷 010-8496 4056
✉ yfyh519@163.com
www.chmexpo.com
2150

2011中国（上海）国际重型机械装备展览会
地点：上海国际展览中心 上海世贸商城，上海
内容：冶金机械：炼钢设备、连铸设备、轧钢设备、钢材精整深加工设备、炼焦设备、烧浇结设备、高炉炼铁设备、电渣重溶炉及相关辅助配套设备 矿山机械：矿用挖掘机、掘进机、刨煤机、采煤机、刮板输送机、液压支架、矿用提升机、矿用自卸车、露天矿破碎站、破碎机、矿磨机（球磨机、磨煤机等）、筛分设备、洗选设备及其他矿山机械；起重机械：轻小型起重设备；散料装卸输送机械；工业车辆；物流仓储设备；润滑液压设备；起重运输机械配套件
周期：每年一届
市场范围：国际性
上届规模 2010：展览面积20,000 m²，参展商400家
主办：中国机械工业联合会（原国家机械工业部）；中国重型机械工业协会
承办：中国重型机械工业协会；北京五洲卓越国际展览有限公司
地址：北京五洲卓越国际展览有限公司北京市朝阳区北苑家园清友园2号楼1608室
联系人：杨帆

4th International Hoisting Machinery & Fittings Expo (Shanghai), China
Venue: Shanghai International Exhibition Center, Shanghai
Frequency: Annual
Market Area: International
Statistics 2010: Exhibition Area 20,000m², Exhibitors 400
Organizer: Beijing Euzhou Zhuoyue International Show Co Ltd

2011/06/09 - 11
☎ 021-5445 1965,
5445 1166转ext 1965
🖷 021-5445 1968,
5445 1166转ext 1968
✉ ghzlwg@126.com
www.shssny.com
2160

2011中国（上海）国际纺织品面辅料博览会
地点：上海新国际博览中心，上海
内容：面料、辅料、纱线、家用纺织品、纺织原料
始办年份：2002
周期：每年一届
市场范围：国际性
参展费用：标准展位8,800元/9m²，净地880元/m²
上届规模 2010：展览面积30,000m²(国外展商4,300m²)，参展商640家（国外展商66家，来自11个国家），参观人数29,053人（专业贸易观众24,682人）
主办：中国同源有限公司
承办：上海歌华展览服务有限公司
地址：上海市田州路99号新安大楼1206-1208室（200233）
联系人：王刚，梁婷
MSN：ghzlwg@126.com
QQ：524234216

2011 China（Shanghai）International Textiles, Fabrics & Accessories Exhibition
Venue: Shanghai New International Expo Center, Shanghai
Established Year: 2002
Frequency: Annual
Market Area: International
Participated Fee: RMB 8,800/9m², Raw Space RMB 880/m²
Statistics 2010: Exhibition Area 30,000m²(foreigners 4,300m²), Exhibitors 640（foreigners 66, came from 11 countries）, Visitors 29,053（trade visitors 24,682）
Sponsor: China Tongyuan I/E Group
Organizer: Shanghai Gehua Exhibition Service Co Ltd
Address: Rm. 1206-08, Xin'an Mansion, No.99 Tianzhou Road, Shanghai, China
Contact: Wang Gang, Liang Ting
MSN: ghzlwg@126.com

2011/06/13 - 16
☎ 852-3111 9971, 9502 2170
🖷 852-3111 3312
✉ grace.zhang@reedexpo.com.cn
clau@pprgreaterchina.com
2170

国际豪华旅游博览-亚洲站
-全球豪华旅游产品及服务
地点：上海
主办：励展旅游展览集团

International Luxury Travel Market Asia
Venue: Shanghai
Profile: ILTM Asia is a "by invitation only" event, offering a tailor-made diary of one-to-one meetings, exclusive insight into luxury travel trends and developments, plus an enviable business and social networking calendar of events to help you engage with your luxury travel's elite.
Organizer: Reed Exhibitions China
Contact: CC Lau

2011/06/14 - 17
☎ 021-6279 2828
🖷 021-6545 5124
✉ yxf@siec-ccpit.com
www.shanghaitex.cn
2180

SHANGHAITEX
上海国际纺织工业展

第十五届上海国际纺织工业展览会
地点：上海新国际博览中心，上海
内容：针织及织袜机械、印花、染整机械、纺纱、产业用布及非织造布机械、织造机械等不同的设备和技术
始办年份：1984
周期：每年两届
市场范围：国际性
性质：面向贸易观众
预计规模：展览面积92,000m²
主办：上海纺织控股（集团）公司；中国贸促会上海市分会；中国国际商会上海商会
承办：上海市国际展览有限公司
地址：上海市延安中路841号8楼（200040）
联系人：姚秀芳女士

SHANGHAITEX 2011
The 15th International Exhibition on Textile Industry
Venue: Shanghai New International Expo Center, Shanghai
Profile: Knitting machine and hosiery machine; printing machine and dyeing and finishing machine; spinning machine, industry-used cloth machine and non-weaving machine; weaving machine and spare parts
Established Year: 1984
Frequency: Biannual
Market Area: International
Nature: Trade Only
Expectation: Exhibition Area 92,000m²
Sponsor: Shanghai Textile Holding (Group) Corporation; CCPIT Shanghai Sub-Council; Shanghai Chamber of Commerce of China Chamber of International Commerce
Organizer: Shanghai International Exhibition Co Ltd; Shanghai Textile Technology Service Exhibition Center; Adsale Exhibition Services Ltd
Address: Shanghai International Exhibition Co Ltd, 8/F, No.841 Yan An Zhong Road, Shanghai 200040, China
Contact: Ms Yao Xiufang

2011/06/15 - 17
☎ 021-6279 2828
🖷 021-6545 5124
✉ fjy@siec-ccpit.com
www.offshorewindchina.com
2190

2011上海国际海上风电及风电产业链大会暨展览会

地点：上海新国际博览中心，上海
内容：亚洲首个聚焦海上风电市场的专业展览会，海内外风电设备制造商、产业链配套商将云集上海新国际博览中心。展览会为参展商和观众提供了一个极具前瞻性的平台，为相关企业就海上风电项目的设计、安装、运营，海上风电机组的研发、配套等提供互相见面、交换信息、展示产品的机会，推动中国风电市场和行业的健康发展。范围包括风电设备、风电配套服务、风电场开发、风电项目工程施工、储能设备等
周期：每年一届
市场范围：国际性
性质：面向贸易观众
预计规模：展览面积23,000m^2
主办：中国资源综合利用协会可再生能源专业委员会；中国可再生能源学会产业工业委员会；上海市国际展览有限公司
地址：上海市延安中路841号8楼上海市国际展览有限公司（200040）
联系人：费嘉奕女士

Offshore Wind China 2011

Venue: Shanghai New International Expo Center, Shanghai
Profile: will present you the latest technology and innovations in China and the world. Visitors come from government officials, decision makers, buyers, project developers and investors, wind farm designers and operators, electricity company, wind turbine installers, association members, component manufacturers and suppliers to visit the exhibition.
Exhibits: Equipment, services, wind farm development, construction and installation, energy storage equipment
Frequency: Annual
Market Area: International
Nature: Trade Only
Expectation: Exhibition Area 23,000m^2
Organizer: Chinese Renewable Energy Industries Association, Shanghai International Exhibition Co Ltd
Address: 8/F, No.841 Yan An Zhong Road, Shanghai, 200040, China
Contact: Ms Fei Jiayi

2011/06/15 - 17
☎ 021-6426 1858，6426 0525
🖷 021-6426 1858，
6426 0555转ext 816
✉ info@expotop.com.cn
www.expotop.com.cn
2200

2011上海涂料原材料展

地点：上海国际展览中心，上海
内容：涂料、油墨及粘合剂的原材料、辅材：天然树脂、合成树脂、溶剂、颜料、填料、填充剂、助剂（包括增稠剂、表面活性剂、颜料分散剂、乳化剂、交联剂、消泡剂/防泡剂、防结皮剂、流平剂、杀菌剂、催干剂、稳定剂、蜡类）；生产及包装设备：调色系统、混料器/搅拌机、连续式混料器、间歇式混料器、实验室混料器、高速分散机、挤压机/挤出机/捏合机、研磨机及其配件、过滤器、泵、计量仪/称重装置、分料及装料系统、包装机、贴标签机、研磨及分散介质、整厂设备及工程设计服务；测试仪器；安全及环保设备
主办：上海易涂展览有限公司
地址：上海易涂展览有限公司
地址：上海市徐汇区斜土路2601号嘉汇广场T3栋18楼C座

All coat 2011

Venue: Shanghai International Exhibition Center, Shanghai
Organizer: Shanghai Top Expo Co Ltd
Address: T3-18-C, 2601 Xietu Road, Xuhui Dist., Shanghai

2011/06/16 - 17
☎ 021-6279 2828
🖷 021-6545 5124
✉ cxp@siec-ccpit.com
hanmh@siec-ccpit.com
www.itsshanghai.org
2210

2011上海国际智能交通与车联网科技发展论坛暨展览会

地点：上海国际会议中心，上海
内容：交通安全、交通执法、3S产品、道路收费、智能公交、交通控制及诱导、停车管理系统、信息采集、交通工程、通信设施、车辆检测及导航、智能车辆等、停车设备、停车设备零部件及其他、停车场（库）安全设施、道路停车管理系统、停车相关软件及服务
周期：每年一届
市场范围：国际性
性质：面向贸易观众
主办：中国贸促会上海市分会；上海市国际展览有限公司
地址：上海市延安中路841号8楼（200040）
联系人：陈小平先生 韩鸣辉先生

ITS Shanghai 2011

Venue: Shanghai Intl Convention Center, Shanghai
Profile: Traffic safety, traffic enforcement, 3S product, payment & toll systems, intelligent public traffic, traffic control & guidance, parking management system, traffic information system, traffic engineering, telecommunication, vehicle detection & navigation, intelligent vehicle, parking equipment, components, parking safety system, on-street parking management, intelligent transport system, parking software and service, others
Frequency: Annual
Market Area: International
Nature: Trade Only
Organizer: CCPIT Shanghai Sub-Council; Shanghai International Exhibition Co Ltd
Address: 8/F, No.841 Yan An Zhong Road, Shanghai, 200040, China
Contact: Mr Chen Xiaoping, Mr Han Minghui

2011/06/16 - 17
☎ 021-6279 2828
🖷 021-6545 5124
✉ zhoucy@siec-ccpit.com
www.iotconference.com
2220

2011中国国际物联网大会暨展览会

地点：上海环球金融中心会议中心；上海国际会议中心，上海
内容：政策及市场、物联网标准、物联网核心技术、行业应用及商业模式等
周期：每年一届
市场范围：国际性
性质：面向贸易观众
主办：中国贸促会上海市分会；上海市国际展览有限公司
地址：上海市延安中路841号8楼（200040）
联系人：周琤瀛先生

IOT China Conference & Exhibition 2011

Venue: Shanghai World Financial Center; Shanghai Intl Convention Center, Shanghai
Profile: Policy and market, IoT standards, IoT key technology, industry application and business model
Frequency: Annual
Market Area: International
Nature: Trade Only
Organizer: CCPIT Shanghai Sub-Council; Shanghai International Exhibition：Co Ltd
Address: 8/F, No.841 Yan An Zhong Road, Shanghai, 200040, China
Contact: Mr Kevin Zhou

2011/06/16 - 19
☎ 010-5827 6063, 5827 6062
🖷 010-5827 60604
✉ panmx@Jewelry.org.cn
www.chinajewelryshow.com
2230

2011上海国际珠宝首饰展览会

地点：上海新国际博览中心，上海
内容：珠宝首饰类：钻石首饰、黄金首饰、翡翠首饰、珍珠首饰、彩色宝石首饰、铂金首饰、白银首饰、玉石首饰、艺术首饰等 宝石及原料类：钻石、翡翠、白玉、珍珠、红蓝宝石、祖母绿、碧玺、水晶、绿松石、海蓝宝石、珊瑚、琥珀、玛瑙、贵金属等 相关产品：玉石、水晶雕件、流行饰品、矿物标本、机械、设备、工具及包装、行业机构、鉴定机构、媒体等
始办年份：2006
市场范围：国际性

Jewelry Shanghai 2011

Venue: Shanghai New International Expo Center, Shanghai
Profile: Jewelries: Diamond Jewelry; Gold Jewelry; Jade Jewelry; Pearl Jewelry; Gemstone jewelry; Platinum Jewelry; Silver Jewelry; Art Jewelry, and etc. Gems and raw materials: Diamonds; Jade; Pearl; Ruby; Sapphire; Emerald; Tourmaline; Amethyst; etc.
Established Year: 2006
Market Area: International
Nature: Open to Public
Participated Fee: RMB 12,000/booth, Raw Space RMB 11,000/m^2

性质：面向公众
参展费用：12,000元/展位，净地11,000元/展位
上届规模 2010：展览面积23,000m²(国外展商8,000m²)，参展商600家（国外展商180家，来自15个国家），参观人数38,000人（专业贸易观众15,000人）
主办：中国珠宝玉石首饰行业协会
承办：北京中宝协展览有限公司
地址：北京市东城区北三环东路36号环球贸易中心C座2215（100013）
联系人：潘沐闲,易晓
MSN：mumuanais@hotmail.com
QQ：1499102596

Statistics 2010: Exhibition Area 23,000m²(foreigners 8,000m²), Exhibitors 600（foreigners 180, came from 15 countries）, Visitors 38,000（trade visitors 15,000）
Sponsor: Gems & Jewelry Trade Association of China;
Organizer：Beijing Zhongbaoxie Exhibition Center Co Ltd
Address: Rm 2215, Tower C, Global Trade Center, No.36, North Third Ring Road, Dongcheng District, Beijing, China
Contact: Anais Pan, Yi Xiao
MSN: mumuanais@hotmail.com

2011/06/21 - 23
☎ 021-6437 1178
🖷 021-6437 0982
✉ essica.lin@ubmsinoexpo.com
vivian.jiang@ubmsinoexpo.com
www.fia-china.com
2240

第十三届亚洲食品配料
第十三届亚洲天然食品原料、亚洲健康食品原料展览会
地点：上海新国际博览中心，上海
内容：食品添加剂与配料、健康天然原料、食品包装设备、检测设备食品分析与实验室检验服务、食品安全与卫生管理、食品贮存与保护、供应品技术
市场范围：国际性
性质：面向贸易观众
上届规模 2010：参展商2109家，参观人数42,755人
主办：上海博华国际展览有限公司；CCCMHPIE中国医药保健品进出口商会；欧洲博闻展览咨询有限公司
地址：上海市襄阳南路218号现代大厦8楼（200031）
联系人：林克飞,姜薇薇

Fi Asia - China 2011
Health Ingredients China
Hi China 2011
Ni China 2011
Venue: Shanghai New International Expo Center, Shanghai
Frequency: Annual
Market Area: International
Nature: Trade Only
Statistics 2010: Exhibitors 2,109，Visitors 42,755
Organizer: UBM International Media

2011/06/21 - 23
☎ 021-6437 1178
🖷 021-6437 0982
✉ zing.zhou@ubmsinoexpo.com
www.cphi-china.cn
2250

世界制药原料中国展
地点：上海新国际博览中心，上海
内容：原料药、中间体、辅料与剂型、天然提取物、生物产品（试剂、技术服务）、合同外包、定制服务及咨询（精细及专用化学品、定制化学品、外包、服务、咨询）
始办年份：2010
周期：每年一届
市场范围：国际性
性质：面向贸易观众
上届规模 2010：展览面积63,000m²，参展商330家（来自17个国家），参观人数26,547人
主办：上海博华国际展览有限公司
地址：上海市襄阳南路218号现代大厦8楼（200031）
联系人：周幸，冯婷婷，居箴

CPhI China
Venue: Shanghai New International Expo Center, Shanghai
Established Year: 2010
Frequency: Annual
Market Area: International
Nature: Trade Only
Statistics 2010: Exhibition Area 63,000m², Exhibitors 330（came from 17 countries）, Visitors 26,547
Organizer: UBM International Media

2011/06/21 - 23
☎ 021-6437 1178
🖷 021-6467 5683
www.cphi-china.cn
2260

世界合同定制服务中国展
地点：上海新国际博览中心，上海
内容：合同研发外包：合成定制、药物化学、分子药代动力学研究、制剂处方前及处方开发、临床前试验、临床试验、生物制药服务、计算机辅助的药物设计、工艺放大生产、生物检测、高效力药物开发、数据管理、新药申请等。合同生产外包：工艺开发/优化、配方开发/优化、临床试验用药、化学或生物的原料药生产、中间体制造、制剂生产以及包装等。咨询与服务：临床试验管理、咨询、资金和金融服务、一般商业顾问、法律服务、物流分析、法规咨询、训练；分析与检测、医疗器械定制服务等。
始办年份：2005
主办：上海博华国际展览有限公司
地址：上海市襄阳南路218号现代大厦8楼（200031）

ICSE China
Venue: Shanghai New International Expo Center, Shanghai
Profile: Besides contract manufacturing and contract research, other main services provided are packaging, clinical trials, laboratory services, drug discovery and marketing services. Whatever your function within the biotechnology or pharmaceutical industry, ICSE will show you how your organization can benefit from outsourcing to China and enable you to arrange it.
Established Year: 2005
Organizer: UBM International Media

2011/06/21 - 23
☎ 021-6437 1178
🖷 021-6437 0982
✉ zing.zhou@ubmsinoexpo.com
www.p-mec.cn
2270

世界制药机械、包装设备与材料中国展
地点：上海新国际博览中心，上海
内容：生化仪器、分析仪器、实验室成套设备、行业专用仪器设备等产品
周期：每年一届
市场范围：国际性
性质：面向贸易观众
上届规模 2010：展览面积22,000m²，参展商350家，参观人数26,547人
主办：上海博华国际展览有限公司
地址：上海市襄阳南路218号现代大厦8楼（200031）
联系人：周幸，冯婷婷,居箴

P-MEC China
Pharmaceutical Machinery & Equipment Convention China
Venue: Shanghai New International Expo Center, Shanghai
Frequency: Annual
Market Area: International
Nature: Trade Only
Statistics 2010: Exhibition Area 22,000m², Exhibitors 350，Visitors 26,547
Organizer: UBM International Media

2011/06/22 - 24
☎ 021-3408 0278
🖷 021-5430 6576
✉ info@chinadigitalsignage.org
www.chinadigitalsignage.org
2280

2011年第三届上海国际数字标牌展览会
地点：上海国际展览中心，上海
内容：数字告示、数位电子看板、网络广告机、多媒体信息发布系统、高清联网信息发布系统、嵌入式流媒体播放系统。液晶广告机、触控一体机、互动式广告载体。内容软件、远程监控。LCD液晶显示器、等离子显示器、LED全彩显示屏、LCD液晶拼接、3D裸眼立体显示器、LED背光液晶显示器、OLED、柔性显示设备。高清传输、无线传输系统、VGA传输器、KVM延长器、矩阵、多屏处理及控制系统、边缘融合、液晶支架、设备安装。触摸查询产品；软件开发商、通信/网络连通技术、公共互联网接入技术
主办：中国电子视像行业协会大屏幕投影显示设备分会；上海市多媒体行业协会；上海通信广播电视行业协会
承办：上海天盛会展服务有限公司
地址：上海市罗阳路168号C座303室

Shanghai International Digital Signage & Touch Inquiry Technology Show 2011
Venue: Shanghai International Exhibition Center, Shanghai
Organizer: Shanghai Tiansheng Exhibition Service CO Ltd
Address: C-303, 168 Luoyang Road, Shanghai

2011/06/28 - 30
☎ 010-5836 2058，5836 2059
🖷 010-5836 2058，5836 2059
✉ qinger6@hotmail.com
www.csfair.org.cn
2310

第105届中国文化用品商品交易会
地点：上海新国际博览中心，上海
内容：学生用品、文教用品、现代办公及教学仪器设备、办公用品、电脑及IT数码产品、纸与纸制品、文房四宝、印刷与包装用品、照像器材、测量测绘用品、体育与健身器材、休闲娱乐用品、文具礼品与赠品、旅游用品、美术绘画用品、书写工具及生产设备、配件、办公耗材、办公家具、办公室用品、办公日杂品等
周期：每年一届
市场范围：全国性
性质：面向贸易观众
入场券价格：免费
参展费用：净地6,000～12,000元/展位
主办：中国百货商业协会
承办：中百协（北京）会展有限公司
地址：北京市西城区丰汇园11号楼丰汇时代大厦东翼12层（100032）
联系人：杨国庆，梁智青
MSN：qinger6@hotmail.com
QQ：419348810

The 105th China Stationery Fair
Venue: Shanghai New International Expo Center, Shanghai
Profile: Education Products, Office Automation Related Products and Accessories, Data Processing Accessories, Planning, Presentation and Conference materials, Office Supplies, Financial Organization Systems, Organizing Systems, Adhesives, Rubber Stamps, Promotional Materials, Technical Stationery Paper, Writing Instruments and Accessories, Technical Drawing Material, Desk Accessories, Business Luggage, Calendars, School supplies, Albums, Postcards and Greeting Cards, Packaging, Gift Wrap Papers, Graphic Arts and Artists Materials
Frequency: Annual
Market Area: National
Nature: Trade Only
Cost to Attend: Free
Participated Fee: Raw Space RMB 6,000-12,000/booth
Sponsor: China Commerce Association for General Merchandise
Organizer: CCAGM（Beijing）Exhibition Co Ltd
MSN: qinger6@hotmail.com

2011/06/28 - 01
☎ 021-5239 6345
🖷 021-5101 0002
✉ marketing@eastpo.net
www.eastpo.net
2320

第13届上海国际机床展
地点：上海新国际博览中心，上海
内容：金切机床、功能部件及配件、锻冲压、激光钣金、刀具测量仪；自动化控制与动力传动；机床热加工技术与设备；相关制造技术与设备等
始办年份：1998
周期：每年一届
市场范围：国际性
性质：面向贸易观众
入场券价格：专业观众免费
参展费用：标准展位10,800元/9m^2
上届规模 2010：展览面积80,000m^2(国外展商32,000m^2)，参展商1,028家（国外展商348家，来自48个国家），参观人数92,374人（专业贸易观众27,712人）
主办：国家国防科技工业局信息中心
承办：东博展览有限公司
地址：上海市愚园路1258号绿地商务大厦1201室
联系人：高玉晓 杨洋

13th Shanghai Intl Machine Tool Fair
Venue: Shanghai New International Expo Center, Shanghai
Profile: Metal cutting machine, Metal forming machine, Manufacturing cell/systems and automation device, Machine tool accessories and auxiliaries, Specialized equipment, Other related manufacturing technology and equipment
Established Year: 1998
Frequency: Annual
Market Area: International
Nature: Trade Only
Cost to Attend: Free
Participated Fee: Standard Booth RMB 10,800/9m^2
Statistics 2010: Exhibition Area 80,000m^2(foreigners 32,000m^2), Exhibitors 1,028（foreigners 348, came from 48 countries）, Visitors 92,374（trade visitors 27,712）
Sponsor: Information Center of General Administration of Science, Technology and Industry National Defence
Organizer: EASTPO International Expo Co Ltd
Address: Rm.1201 Greenland Business Center, 1258 Yu Yuan Rd., Shanghai

2011/07/06 - 09
☎ 021-6328 8899
🖷 021-6374 9188
2330

2011上海国际广告技术设备展览会
地点：上海新国际博览中心，上海
内容：广告设计制作技术、设备、材料、展示器材
始办年份：1993
周期：每年一届
市场范围：国际性
性质：面向贸易观众
入场券价格：20元
上届规模 2010：展览面积65,000m^2，参展商1,200家，参观人数100,000人
主办：上海现代国际展览有限公司
地址：上海市盛泽路8号18楼（200002）
联系人：广告展项目组

Shanghai Intl AD & Sign Technology Equipment Exhibition 2011
Venue: Shanghai New International Expo Center, Shanghai
Established Year: 1993
Frequency: Annual
Market Area: International
Nature: Trade Only
Cost to Attend: RMB 20:-
Statistics 2010: Exhibition Area 65,000m^2, Exhibitors 1,200, Visitors 100,000
Organizer: Shanghai Modern International Exhibition Co Ltd
Address: 18F No.8 Sheng Ze Road, Shanghai
Contact: Everlin Luo

2011/07/06 - 09
☎ 021-6328 8899
🖷 021-6374 9188

2360

2011上海国际数码及快速印刷设备展览会
地点：上海新国际博览中心，上海
内容：数码及快速印刷设备
始办年份：2006
周期：每年一届
市场范围：国际性
性质：面向贸易观众
入场券价格：20元
上届规模 2010：展览面积10,000m²
主办：上海现代国际展览有限公司
地址：上海市盛泽路8号18楼（200002）
联系人：广告展项目组

Shanghai Intl Digital & Express Printing Exhibition 2011
Venue: Shanghai New International Expo Center, Shanghai
Established Year: 2006
Frequency: Annual
Market Area: International
Nature: Trade Only
Cost to Attend: RMB 20:-
Statistics 2010: Exhibition Area 10,000m²
Organizer: Shanghai Modern International Exhibition Co Ltd
Address: 18F No.8 Sheng Ze Road, Shanghai
Contact: Everlin Luo

2011/07/06 - 09
☎ 021-6328 8899
🖷 021-6374 9188

2370

2011上海国际照明技术设备展览会
地点：上海新国际博览中心，上海
内容：专业、户外照明、室内照明（室内灯饰、灯具）、专业灯光、光源、电灯附件、照明生产设备、仪器、照明控制系统
始办年份：2008
周期：每年一届
市场范围：国际性
性质：面向贸易观众
入场券价格：20元
上届规模 2010：展览面积10,000m²
主办：上海现代国际展览有限公司
地址：上海市盛泽路8号18楼（200002）
联系人：广告展项目组

Shanghai Intl Lighting Technology & Equipment Exhibition 2011
Venue: Shanghai New International Expo Center, Shanghai
Established Year: 2008
Frequency: Annual
Market Area: International
Nature: Trade Only
Cost to Attend: RMB 20:-
Statistics 2010: Exhibition Area 10,000m²
Organizer: Shanghai Modern International Exhibition Co Ltd
Address: 18F No.8 Sheng Ze Road, Shanghai
Contact: Everlin Luo

2011/07/06 - 09
☎ 021-6328 8899
🖷 021-6374 9188

2380

2011上海国际印刷包装纸业展览会
地点：上海新国际博览中心，上海
内容：印刷包装技术、设备、材料、纸业、纸制品加工技术、设备及纸制品
始办年份：1993
周期：每年一届
市场范围：国际性
性质：面向贸易观众
入场券价格：20元
上届规模 2010：展览面积39,000m², 参观人数100,000人
主办：上海现代国际展览有限公司
地址：上海市盛泽路8号18楼（200002）
联系人：广告展项目组

Shanghai Intl Print Pack & Paper Exhibition 2011
Venue: Shanghai New International Expo Center, Shanghai
Established Year: 1993
Frequency: Annual
Market Area: International
Nature: Trade Only
Cost to Attend: RMB 20:-
Statistics 2010: Exhibition Area 39,000m², Visitors 100,000
Organizer: Shanghai Modern International Exhibition Co Ltd
Address: 18F No.8 Sheng Ze Road, Shanghai
Contact: Everlin Luo

2011/07/06 - 09
☎ 021-6328 8899
🖷 021-6374 9188

2390

2011上海国际LED产业展暨LED发光体及城市照明展
地点：上海新国际博览中心，上海
内容：LED大屏幕显示技术及应用系统设备，城市景观照明，LED封装设备、检测仪器等
始办年份：2008
周期：每年一届
市场范围：国际性
性质：面向贸易观众
入场券价格：20元
上届规模 2010：展览面积16,000m², 参观人数100,000人
主办：上海现代国际展览有限公司
地址：上海市盛泽路8号18楼（200002）
联系人：广告展项目组

Shanghai Intl LED Industry & City Lighting Exhibition 2011
Venue: Shanghai New International Expo Center, Shanghai
Established Year: 2008
Frequency: Annual
Market Area: International
Nature: Trade Only
Cost to Attend: RMB 20:-
Statistics 2010: Exhibition Area 16,000m², Visitors 100,000
Organizer: Shanghai Modern International Exhibition Co Ltd
Address: 18F No.8 Sheng Ze Road, Shanghai
Contact: Everlin Luo

2011/07/07 - 10
☎ 021-6279 2828
🖷 021-6545 5124
✉ interphoto@siec-ccpit.com
www.interphoto.com.cn

2410

第十三届中国（上海）国际摄影器材和数码影像展览会
地点：上海光大会展中心，上海
内容：影像输入、相机零件及附件、摄影器材及耗材、影像存储、影像处理、影像输出、数码影像等设备、产品、技术及服务等
始办年份：1998
周期：每年一届
市场范围：国际性
主办：中国贸促会上海市分会；中国国际商会上海商会；中国信息产业商会数字影像产业分会；上海市摄影家协会；上海市国际展览有限公司
承办：上海国际展览服务有限公司
地址：上海市延安中路841号8楼（200040）
联系人：任浩先生

PHOTO & IMAGING SHANGHAI 2011
Venue: Shanghai Everbright Convention & Exhibition Center, Shanghai
Profile: Equipment for image input, camera parts & accessories, photographic equipment and consumables, image storing, image editing, image processing, image output, digital imaging and related products, technologies and services
Established Year: 1998
Frequency: Annual
Market Area: International
Organizer: CCPIT Shanghai Sub-Council; Shanghai Chamber of Commerce of China Chamber of International Commerce; China Information Industry Trade Association; Digital Image Committee; Shanghai Photographers' Association; Shanghai International Exhibition Co Ltd
Address: Shanghai International Exhibition Service Co Ltd, 8/F, No.841 Yan An Zhong Road, Shanghai 200040, China
Contact: Mr Andy Ren

2011/07/07 - 10
☎ 021-6279 2828
📠 021-6386 6972
✉ lina@siec-ccpit.com
www.chinaweddingexpo.com.cn
2420

上海国际婚纱摄影器材展览会暨国际儿童摄影、主题摄影、相册相框展览会
地点：上海国际展览中心、上海世贸商城、上海光大会展中心，上海
内容：婚纱、礼服、相册、相框、彩妆、饰品、婚庆用品、背景、后期制作、冲印彩扩、主题摄影、儿童摄影、影楼培训以及婚纱摄影网络和出版物
始办年份：2002
周期：每年两届
市场范围：国际性
性质：面向贸易观众
主办：中国贸促会上海市分会；中国人像摄影学会；上海市摄影家协会
承办：上海国际展览服务有限公司
地址：上海市延安中路841号8楼（200040）
联系人：张莉娜女士

China Wedding Expo 2011
Venue: Shanghai Intl Exhibition Center, Shanghai Mart, Shanghai Everbright Convention & Exhibition Center, Shanghai
Profile: Wedding related products including wedding gowns, formal attires, photo albums & frames, cosmetics, accessories, wedding supplies, backgrounds, post-production photographic products, lighting, developing techniques, printing and enlarging color photos, thematic photography, children's photography, studio-training programs, wedding photography networks and related publications
Established Year: 2002
Frequency: Biannual
Market Area: International
Nature: Trade Only
Sponsor: CCPIT Shanghai Sub-Council; China Portrait Photography Society; Shanghai Photographers' Association
Organizer: Shanghai International Exhibition Service Co Ltd
Address: 8/F, No.841 Yan An Zhong Road, Shanghai, 200040, China
Contact: Ms Zhang Lina

2011/07/13 - 15
☎ 010-5933 9357
✉ chris.zang@reedexpo.com.cn
www.composites-china.cn
2440

上海国际工业材料展览会 • 复合材料

2011 年上海国际工业材料展览会 · 复合材料
地点：上海新国际博览中心，上海
内容：原材料：树脂、纤维、添加剂、调节剂、填充剂；中间产品：片状膜塑料、团状膜塑料、预侵材料、衬料、纤维增加热塑片材、粒料；半成品与成品：型材、管材、铸件、板材等；加工处理技术与设备：铸造、压缩模塑、注塑成型层压、拉挤成型轧制、缠绕树脂传递；各类服务：软件与程序、研究与开发、专业服务、信息、媒体
周期：每年一届
性质：面向贸易观众
主办：励展博览集团（中国）公司
地址：上海浦东新区龙阳路2345号（201204）
联系人：臧先生

Composites China
Venue: Shanghai New International Expo Center, Shanghai
Profile: The debut of COMPOSITES CHINA will facilitate a world class business platform for trade, networking and educational opportunities, catering to the entire composites community and its major application industries.
Exhibits: Raw Materials, Intermediate Products, Semi-finished and Finished Products, Processing Technology and Equipment, Services
Frequency: Annual
Nature: Trade Only
Organizer: Reed Exhibitions

2011/07/13 - 15
☎ 010-5933 9379
✉ johnson.qin@reedexpo.com.cn
www.magnesiumexpo.com
2450

2011 年上海国际工业材料展览会 · 镁
地点：上海新国际博览中心，上海
内容：镁矿，氧化镁，镁锭、镁合金、镁粉、镁粒，镁合金加工及零部件，镁冶炼设备、镁加工设备，辅助设备及材料，镁质耐火材料
周期：每年一届
性质：面向贸易观众
主办：励展博览集团（中国）公司
地址：上海浦东新区龙阳路2345号（201204）
联系人：秦立强

Magnesium China
Venue: Shanghai New International Expo Center, Shanghai
Profile: Magnesium raw materials, Magnesia, Magnesium ingot, alloy, powder and granule, Magnesium alloy processing and parts, Equipments for Magnesium smelting and processing, Accessories, Magnesium, fireproof materials
Frequency: Annual
Nature: Trade Only
Organizer: Reed Exhibitions

2011/07/13 - 15
☎ 010-5933 9344
✉ Kevin.kang@reedexpo.com.cn
www.industrialmaterials.cn
2460

上海国际工业材料展览会
Industrial Materials China

2011 年上海国际工业材料展览会 · 资源再生及利用
地点：上海新国际博览中心，上海
内容：原材料收购商、质量控制服务商、加工处理服务商；废料经销商和贸易商；金属废料分离/加工商；再生设备制造商/供应商——此类设施包括过滤器、精炼炉、重熔炉及相关设备；金属回收服务公司；尖端回收技术与系统方面的专家；专业咨询和服务公司；行业协会
周期：每年一届
性质：面向贸易观众
主办：励展博览集团（中国）公司
地址：上海浦东新区龙阳路2345号（201204）
联系人：康先生

Industrial Material China
- Green Processing China 2011
Venue: Shanghai New International Expo Center, Shanghai
Profile: Green Processing China is a show that focuses on the sustainable development of global environment. Integrating with ALUMINIUM CHINA 2011 and INDUSTRY MATERIAL CHINA 2011
Frequency: Annual
Nature: Trade Only
Organizer: Reed Exhibitions

2011/07/13 - 15
☎ 021-6209 5209
📠 021-6209 5210
✉ tara@chinaallworld.com
www.woodmacchina.net
2470

第十七届中国国际加工、包装及印刷科技展览
地点：上海新国际博览中心，上海
内容：食品、肉类、乳制品、化妆品、消费品、饮料、液体科技及原料和工业用品塑料、纸张、金属、玻璃和药品等加工、包装及印刷科技
周期：每年一届
市场范围：国际性
性质：面向贸易观众
上届规模 2010：展览面积28,750m^2(国外展商20,000m^2)，参展商530家（来自19个国家），专业贸易观众14,754人
主办：华汉国际会议展览（上海）有限公司
地址：上海市长宁区仙霞路318-320号2402室（200336）
联系人：蔡祎

ProPak China 2011
Venue: Shanghai New International Expo Center, Shanghai
Profile: Food, Meat, Dairy, Cosmetic, Consumer, Beverage and Liquid Technology& Materials & Industrial, Plastic, Paper, Metal, Glass & Pharmaceutical Processing, Packaging & Printing Technology
Frequency: Annual
Market Area: International
Nature: Trade Only
Statistics 2010: Exhibition Area 28,750m^2(foreigners 20,000m^2), Exhibitors 530（came from 19 countries）, Trade Visitors 14,754
Organizer: China International Exhibitions Ltd
Address: Room 2402, No.320 Xian Xia Road, Shanghai 200336
Contact: Tara Cai

2011/07/13 - 15
☎ 010-5933 9317
✉ Jessica.yun@reedexpo.com.cn
www.copperexpo.com.cn
2480

2011 年上海国际工业材料展览会 · 铜
地点：上海新国际博览中心，上海
内容：铜及铜质合金材料、初级金属产品：半成品、半合成品、铸件、管、板、带、箔、棒、线等；应用于相关领域的铜及铜质合金产品；铜冶炼设备；铜加工系统与设备（热处理、自动化控制、检测、表面处理、涂装、包装等）；铜材生产用辅助材料；废旧铜材再生回收技术与设备；铜业相关工程、技术服务与咨询
周期：每年一届
主办：励展博览集团（中国）公司
地址：上海浦东新区龙阳路2345号（201204）
联系人：云洁女士

Copper China 2011
Venue: Shanghai New International Expo Center, Shanghai
Profile: Catering for the entire copper industry chain and its major application industries, the event will facilitate a world class business platform of trade, networking and educational opportunities, and for the first time bring together leading copper processors and technology, equipment providers from both international and domestic markets to seamlessly combine the huge demand in Asia.
Frequency: Annual
Organizer: Reed Exhibitions

2011/07/13 - 15
☎ 010-5933 9000
🖷 010-5933 9333
✉ alu@reedexpo.com.cn
www.aluminiumchina.com
2490

2011 年中国国际铝工业展览会
地点：上海新国际博览中心，上海
内容：2011年中国国际铝工业展览会集全球重要铝企业展示和中国领先铝行业论坛于一身，将服务于来自80多个国家的超过10,000名专业观众与买家，倾力打造亚洲第一铝工业商务社交、业务拓展、信息交流平台。2011年展会的展出范围将扩充至铜、镁以及复合材料等领域，以期打造中国乃至亚洲范围内首届一指的工业材料集群展会
性质：面向贸易观众
上届规模 2010：与会者9,059人
主办：励展博览集团
地址：北京市朝阳区新源南路1-3号平安国际金融中心A座15层01-03,05（100027）
联系人：张岚，张静

Aluminum China 2011
Venue: Shanghai New International Expo Center, Shanghai
Profile: It is the international platform for suppliers of aluminum raw material, semi-finished and finished products, surface treatment and producers of machinery, plant and equipment for aluminium processing and manufacturing. Light-metals trade, consultancy and expert opinions.
Nature: Trade Only
Statistics 2010: Attendees 9,059
Organizer: Reed Exhibitions

2011/07/14 – 16
☎ 010-5836 2071, 5836 2053
🖷 010-5836 2506, 5836 2050
✉ bhzh@ccagm.org.cn
www.zbfair.com.cn
2500

2011第105届中国日用百货商品交易会、中国现代家庭用品博览会
地点：上海新国际博览中心，上海
内容：家用塑料制品；炊具、厨具、餐具、杯壶；清洁用具用品；家用陶瓷及搪瓷制品、玻璃制品；家用衡器；家用竹木制品；家用金属制；品婴童用品；厨用纺织品；保温容器；浴室用品；雨具、衣架、衣夹，烟具、玩具；礼品、工艺品、赠品；以及上列用品的生产设备及原材料。
主办：中国百货商业协会
承办：中百会展（北京）股份有限公司
地址：北京市西城区丰汇园11号丰汇时代大厦东翼12层(100032)

The 105 China Daily-use Articles Trade Fair & China Modern Home Expo
Venue: Shanghai New International Expo Center, Shanghai
Sponsor: China Commerce Association for General Merchandise
Organizer: CCAGM Exhibition (Beijing) Holding Co Ltd

2011/07/20 - 22
☎ 0571-8839 5884
🖷 0571-8838 8829
www.cbmexpo.com/index.asp
2530

上海国际儿童、婴儿、孕妇产品博览会
地点：上海新国际博览中心，上海
内容：车床、汽座及家具、童装、婴装、童鞋及配饰、孕装、内衣及配饰、母婴用品、玩具、教育及纪念品、孕婴童食品、保健品
始办年份：2000
周期：每年一届
市场范围：国际性
性质：面向贸易观众
上届规模 2010：展览面积69000m^2，参展商950家（国外展商384家），专业贸易观众81,539人）
主办：博闻中国(杭州)
地址：浙江省杭州市拱墅区温州路69号南北商务港2-11F（310015）

Children Baby Maternity Expo
Venue: Shanghai New International Expo Center, Shanghai
Established Year: 2000
Frequency: Annual
Market Area: International
Nature: Trade Only
Statistics 2010: Exhibition Area 69,000m^2, Exhibitors 950（foreigners 384），Trade Visitors 81,539
Organizer: UBM China (Hangzhou)
Address: 2-11F South West Business Center, No 69 Wenzhou Road, Gong Shu District, Hangzhou 310015, China

2011/08/16 - 19
☎ 021-6468 1300
🖷 021-6416 8064
✉ service@for-expo.com
www.shanghaiamts.com
2550

AMTS2011
上海国际汽车制造技术及装备与材料展览会
地点：上海新国际博览中心，上海
内容：汽车材料、汽车设计、金属切削机床生产线、车身制造工艺与装备、装配与质量、OEM-电动车技术、相关新材料、新工艺、新技术、相关检测、监控、实验、安全防护装备、维修、制造设备和工具、相关基础设施建设等
始办年份：2004
周期：每年一届
参展费用：11,800元/9m^2
上届规模 2010：参展商257家，专业贸易观众13,807人
主办：中国汽车工程学会；上海恒进展览有限公司
地址：上海市中山南二路440号中粮大厦603室（200032）
联系人：杨梅
MSN：forever.expo516@sina.com
QQ：375105874

Shanghai International Automotive Manufacturing Technology & Material Show
Venue: Shanghai New International Expo Center, Shanghai
Profile: AMTS 2011 aims to exhibit the applications and innovations in the aspects of automotive material and design, automobile manufacturing technology equipment, automobile assembly tech and quality and automobile engineering service
Established Year: 2004
Frequency: Annual
Participated Fee: RMB 11,800/9m^2
Statistics 2010: Exhibitors 257，Trade Visitors 13,807
Organizer: Society of Automotive Engineers of China (SAE-CHINA); Shanghai Forever Exhibition Co Ltd
Address: Room 603, Zhongliang Building, No.440 Zhongshan Road (South-2), Shanghai 200032, China
Contact: Berry Yang
MSN: forever.expo516@sina.com

2011/08/16 - 19
☎ 021-6468 1300
🖷 021-6416 8064
✉ service@for-expo.com
www.shanghaiamts.com
2560

第五届上海国际工业装配与传输技术展览会
地点：上海新国际博览中心，上海
内容：AHTE2011以自动化、机器人、控制技术、传感器、开关、发动机、驱动、运动控制、视觉检测系统等一系列最新技术发展为特色。同期举办"AMTS上海国际汽车制造技术及装备与材料展览会"，展示汽车材料与设计、汽车制造工艺与装备、汽

2011 AHTE
5th Shanghai Intl Assembly & Handling Technology Exhibition
Venue: Shanghai New International Expo Center, Shanghai
Profile: AHTE 2011 is considered to be the leading assembly technology exhibition. It attracts many famous exhibitors to come to attend the event

车装配与质量、汽车工程与服务等各个领域的应用和创新。
始办年份：2004
周期：每年一届
参展费用：国外企业3,200美元/9m^2, B区国内企业13,980元/9m^2, C区国内企业11,800元/9m^2, D区国内企业10,900元/9m^2
主办：中国汽车工程学会；上海恒进展览有限公司
地址：上海市中山南二路440号中粮大厦603室（200032）
联系人：杨梅
MSN：forever.expo516@sina.com
QQ：375105874

Established Year: 2004
Frequency: Annual
Participated Fee: USD 3,200/9m^2
Organizer: Society of Automotive Engineers of China(SAE-CHINA); Shanghai Forever Exhibition Co Ltd
Address: Room 603, Zhongliang Building, No.440 Zhongshan Road (South-2), Shanghai 200032, China
Contact: Berry Yang
MSN: forever.expo516@sina.com

2011/08/16 - 19
☎ 021-6328 8899
🖷 021-6374 9188

2570

2011中国（上海）国际建材及室内装饰展览会
地点：上海新国际博览中心，上海
内容：建筑材料
周期：每年一届
市场范围：国际性
性质：面向贸易观众
上届规模 2010：展览面积25,000m^2
主办：上海现代国际展览有限公司
地址：上海市盛泽路8号18楼（200002）
联系人：建材展项目组

2011 Shanghai International Construction Material and Indoor Decoration Exhibition
Venue: Shanghai New International Expo Center, Shanghai
Frequency: Annual
Market Area: International
Nature: Trade Only
Statistics 2010: Exhibition Area 25,000m^2
Organizer: Shanghai Modern International Exhibition Co Ltd
Address: 18F No.8 Sheng Ze Road, Shanghai
Contact: Herbstone Shi

2011/08/16 - 19
☎ 021-6328 8899
🖷 021-6374 9188
✉ herbstone@126.com
www.expojc.com

2580

第二十二届中国（上海）国际建材及室内装饰展览会
地点：上海新国际博览中心，上海
内容：建筑四节产品展区：节能保温材料、节水技术及设备、新能源利用、节材产品及设备、节地技术及产品；室内装饰精品展区：门窗精品、地板精品、厨卫精品、综合精品、化学建材；建筑及装饰石材；建筑装饰五金；楼宇智能设备；楼宇通风空调系统；建筑幕墙；建筑设备及施工机具、消防设备；建材流通市场
始办年份：1999
周期：每年一届
市场范围：国际性
性质：面向公众
入场券价格：免费
参展费用：10,000元/标准展位
上届规模 2010：展览面积24,000m^2(国外展商4,500m^2), 参展商518家（国外展商76家，来自15个国家），参观人数23,484人（专业贸易观众13,582人）
主办：世博集团上海现代国际展览有限公司；上海市建筑材料行业协会
地址：上海市黄浦区盛泽路8号18楼（200002）
联系人：石卉先生

The 22nd Shanghai International Construction Material and Indoor Decoration Exhibition
Venue: Shanghai New International Expo Center, Shanghai
Profile: Energy-saving & Advanced Wall Material: Energy-saving & Insulation Materials, Water-saving Technology & Equipment, Using of New Energy Resources, Materials-saving Products & Energy-saving Equipments, Land-saving Technology; Indoor Decoration: Windows & Doors, Floor Material, Kitchen and Bathroom Equipment, Integration
Established Year: 1999
Frequency: Annual
Market Area: International
Nature: Open to Public
Cost to Attend: Free
Participated Fee: RMB 10,000/booth
Statistics 2010: Exhibition Area 24,000m^2(foreigners 4,500m^2), Exhibitors 518（foreigners 76, came from 15 countries）, Visitors 23,484（trade visitors 13,582）
Organizer: World Expo Group Shanghai Modern International Exhibition Co Ltd; Shanghai Building Materials Industry Association
Address: 18F, No.8 Shengze Road, Huangpu, Shanghai 200002, China
Contact: Mr Herbstone Shi

2011/08/16 - 19
☎ 021-6328 8899
🖷 021-6374 9188

2590

2011上海国际建筑节能及新型建材展览会
地点：上海新国际博览中心，上海
内容：节能建筑
周期：每年一届
市场范围：国际性
性质：面向贸易观众
上届规模 2010：展览面积15,000m^2
主办：上海现代国际展览有限公司
地址：上海市盛泽路8号18楼（200002）
联系人：建材展项目组

2011 Shanghai International Energy-saving & Advanced Building Materials Exhibition
Venue: Shanghai New International Expo Center, Shanghai
Frequency: Annual
Market Area: International
Nature: Trade Only
Statistics 2010: Exhibition Area 15,000m^2
Organizer: Shanghai Modern International Exhibition Co Ltd
Address: 18F No.8 Sheng Ze Road, Shanghai
Contact: Herbstone Shi

2011/08/18 - 20
☎ 021-6275 5800
🖷 021-6275 7210

2600

第七届中国商业地产博览会
地点：上海国际展览中心，上海
主办：上海华源商务展览有限公司

China Commercial Property Exhibition
Venue: Shanghai International Exhibition Center, Shanghai
Organizer: Shanghai Hua Yuan Trade Exhibition Co Ltd

2011/08/23 - 25
☎ 021-3218 0566, 6253 9759, 6253 0197
🖷 021-6215 3669
✉ controlchina@dragon-invest.com
www.control-china.cn

2610

2011国际质量检测分析技术及测量测试仪器仪表展览会
地点：上海国际展览中心，上海
内容：质量控制系统产品：程序控制系统；智能化质量控制系统；自动系统；质量控制数据处理；鉴定系统；质量管理系统；环境管理系统。光电子产品：感应器；光纤技术测试产品；工业图像分析及处理系统；光电子测量系统。材料测试仪器及设备：破坏性（有损）检测仪器及设备：测试张力、扭转力、压力、弯曲度、阻力的仪器；非破坏性（无损）测试仪器；材料测试仪器度量衡，测量及测试仪器及设备：测量设备；测量机器人；机械测量仪器；测量系统、零部件和附件
参展费用：标准展位：1,600元/m^2，二面开1,700元/m^2，三面开1,800元/m^2, 四面开1,900元/m^2，标准搭建费300元/m^2，展商登录费2,000元
上届规模 2010：参展商70家（来自11个国家），参观人数2,106人
主办：上海天贵德商务咨询有限公司
地址：上海昌平路556弄2号金昌大厦2703室

The International Trade Fair for Quality Assurance 2011
Venue: Shanghai International Exhibition Center, Shanghai
Participated Fee: Standard RMB 1,600/m^2, Corner unit RMB 1,700/m^2, Peninsula unit RMB 1,800/m^2, Island unit RMB 1,900/m^2
Statistics 2010: Exhibitors 70（came from 11 countries）, Visitors 2,106
Organizer: Dragon Invest Shanghai Co Ltd

2011/08/29 - 31
☎ 010-8522 9506, 8522 9504, 8522 9505
🖷 010-8522 9300
✉ intertextile_home@ccpittex.com
www.intertextile-home.com.cn
2630

中国国际家用纺织品及辅料博览会
地点：上海新国际博览中心，上海
内容：各类家用纺织品及辅料,计算机辅助设计与制造,相关出版物及网络
预计规模：总面积126,500m^2
主办：中国纺织工业协会
承办：中国贸促会纺织行业分会；中国家用纺织品行业协会；法兰克福展览（香港）有限公司
联系人：朱勤，林英华，郭亮，何磊，罗洁

China International Trade Fair for Home Textiles and Accessories
Venue: Shanghai New International Expo Center, Shanghai
Expectation: Gross Area 126,500m^2
Sponsor: China National Textile & Apparel Council
Organizers: The Sub-Council of Textile Industry; CCPIT China Home Textile Association; Messe Frankfurt (HK) Ltd

2011/08/29 - 31
☎ 010-8522 9098, 8522 9436, 8522 9701
🖷 010-8522 9059
✉ chinaknitting@ccpittex.com
www.chinaknitting.com.cn
2640

中国国际针织博览会
地点：上海新国际博览中心，上海
内容：内衣、文胸、毛衫、针织休闲装/运动装/T恤、塑身/健身服、泳装/沙滩装、家居服/睡衣、袜类、针织面料、针织辅料、针织机械
预计规模：12,000m^2
主办：中国纺织工业协会
承办：中国针织工业协会；中国贸促会纺织行业分会
联系人：陈博，金俊，徐超

China International Knitting Trade Fair
Venue: Shanghai New International Expo Center, Shanghai
Sponsor: China National Textile & Apparel Council
Organizers: China Knitting Industry Association; Sub-Council of Textile Industry, CCPIT

2011/08/31 - 03
☎ 021-6280 0000
🖷 021-5258 1892
✉ steo@steo.net
www.shanghai-fair.org
2660

2011第五届上海进口商品博览会
地点：上海展览中心，上海
内容：上海进口商品博览会是上海首个以进口消费品为主的博览会，她的成功举办，迎合了中国市场对进口消费品的需求，也为各国中小企业的成熟品牌及产品进入上海市场构筑起一个高效快速的商务平台。2010年中国年进口额突破万亿美元，已连续举办了三届的上海进口商品博览会将继续吸引更多的各国中小企业参展，让更多的适合中国市场的进口商品通过博览会进入上海市场，进而辐射到华东地区和中国内地各省市
始办年份：2007
周期：每年一届
市场范围：国际性
性质：面向公众
主办：上海市商务委员会
承办：上海商展办展览有限公司
地址：上海市长宁区定西路788号7A（200052）
联系人：詹宜青,洪天祥

The 5th Shanghai Imports Expo 2011
Venue: Shanghai Exhibition Center, Shanghai
Profile: The Shanghai Import Expo is the first import expo in Shanghai facing to all the Chinese markets. Shanghai is the biggest economic central city in China and the imported commodities may, through the Shanghai market, enter the East China Area, then, radiate to other inland provinces cities.
Established Year: 2007
Frequency: Annual
Market Area: International
Nature: Open to Public
Sponsor: Shanghai Municipal Commission of Commerce
Organizer: Shanghai STEO Exhibition Co Ltd
Address: Rm 7A No.788, Dingxilu Road, Shanghai, China
Contact: Zhan Yiqing, Hong Tianxiang

2011/09 -
☎ 021-5499 9745, 13044112901
🖷 021-5499 3541
✉ shfairs-info@yahoo.cn
http://fair.sourcing.org.cn
2670

2011年中国（上海）国际跨国采购大会
地点：上海世贸商城，上海
内容：综合类，逆向采购。采购商设展位，供应商现场洽谈。
始办年份：2002
周期：每年一届
市场范围：国际性
性质：面向贸易观众
入场券价格：300元
参展费用：采购商8,000元/9m^2，供应商8,000～20,000元
上届规模 2009：展览面积30,000m^2(国外展商26,000m^2)，参展商300家（国外展商260家，来自12个国家），参观人数6,000人（专业贸易观众5,800人）
主办：中华人民共和国商务部；上海市人民政府
承办：上海跨国采购中心有限公司
地址：上海闵行区莲花南路1108弄58栋701室（201100）
联系人：刘铭
MSN：shlmcn@hotmail.com
QQ：1187 230 500

2011 International Sourcing Fair (Shanghai, China)
Venue: Shanghai Mart, Shanghai
Profile: Comprehensive Options，Reverse Exhibition Comprehensive
Established Year: 2002
Frequency: Annual
Market Area: International
Nature: Trade Only
Cost to Attend: RMB 300/pp
Participated Fee: Buyers RMB 8,000/9m^2, Suppliers RMB 8,000-20,000/booth
Statistics 2009: Exhibition Area 30,000m^2(foreigners 26,000m^2), Exhibitors 300（foreigners 260, came from 12 countries）, Visitors 6,000（trade visitors 5,800）
Sponsor: Ministry of Commerce; Shanghai Municipal Government
Organizer：Shanghai International Sourcing Promotion Center Co Ltd
Contact: Mr Liu Ming
MSN: shlmcn@hotmail.com

2011/09/01 - 04
☎ 010-5933 9166
🖷 010-5933 9199
✉ amy.xie@reedhuaqun.com
ada.zhang@reedhuaqun.com
www.reedhuaqun.com
2680

中国上海礼品、赠品及家居用品展览会
地点：上海
内容：华东地区领先的礼品、家居用品展览会
主办：北京励展华群展览有限公司
地址：北京市朝阳区新源南路1-3号平安国际金融中心A座15层01-03，05（100027）
联系人：谢辉

China Shanghai International Gifts, Premium and Houseware Exhibition
Venue: Shanghai
Organizer: Reed Huaqun Exhibitions
Address: Unit 01-03,05, 15th Floor, Tower A, Ping An International Finance Center, No.1-3, Xinyuan South Road, Chaoyang District, Beijing 100027,China

2011/09/02 - 04
☎ 021-6275 5800
🖷 021-6275 7210

2690

2011第八届上海国际模型展览会展
地点：上海国际展览中心，上海
主办：上海好博塔苏斯展览有限公司

2011 The 8th Shanghai International Model
Venue: Shanghai International Exhibition Center, Shanghai
Organizer: Tarsus Shanghai Hope Exhibition Co Ltd

2011/09/06 - 08
☎ 852-2827 6211
🖷 852-3749 7346
✉ info@aplf.com
sales@aplf.com
www.ciffchina.com
www.aclechina.com

2700

中国国际箱包、裘革服装及服饰展
地点：上海新国际博览中心，上海
内容：鞋类 手袋及皮具 皮衣 时尚配饰 行李箱包 业内相关服务
市场范围：国际性
性质：面向贸易观众
主办：亚太区皮革展有限公司；中国皮革协会
承办：博闻中国有限公司
地址：香港湾仔港湾道26号华润大厦17楼

Moda Shanghai
Venue: Shanghai New International Expo Center, Shanghai
Market Area: International
Nature: Trade Only
Organizer: UBM Asia

2011/09/06 - 08
☎ 010-6522 0753, 8511 1723
🖷 010-8511 1723
✉ expo@mc-ccpit.com
www.stexpo.com.cn

2710

第七届上海国际不锈钢展览会
地点：上海新国际博览中心，上海
内容：不锈钢原料及原料加工设备，不锈钢生产技术及设备，不锈钢产品及辅助材料，不锈钢深加工技术及设备，不锈钢制品，不锈钢技术出版物及相关媒体
始办年份：1999
周期：两年一届
市场范围：国际性
性质：面向贸易观众
入场券价格：免费
上届规模 2009：展览面积3,876m^2(国外展商417m^2)，参展商119家（国外展商9家，来自9个国家），参观人数5,012人
主办：中国钢铁工业协会；中国贸促会冶金行业分会
承办：中国贸促会冶金行业分会
地址：北京东四西大街46号（100711）
联系人：章亦飞，仲文

STEXPO 2011
Venue: Shanghai New International Expo Center, Shanghai
Profile: Stainless steel raw materials and its processing equipment, Technology and equipment for stainless steel production, Stainless steel products and auxiliary materials, Downstream processing technology and equipment, Stainless steel products, Professional magazines, publications and other media.
Established Year: 1999
Frequency: Biennial
Market Area: International
Nature: Trade Only
Cost to Attend: Free
Statistics 2009: Exhibition Area 3,876m^2(foreigners 417m^2), Exhibitors 119 (foreigners 9, came from 9 countries), Visitors 5,012
Sponsor: China Iron & Steel Association; Metallurgical Council of CCPIT
Organizer: Metallurgical Council of CCPIT
Address: 46 Dongsi Xidajie, Dongcheng District, Beijing, China
Contact: Zhang Yifei, Zhong Wen

2011/09/06 - 08
☎ 852-2827 6211
🖷 852-3749 7346
✉ info@aplf.com
sales@aplf.com
www.ciffchina.com
www.aplf.com

2720

中国国际鞋类展
地点：上海新国际博览中心，上海
内容：鞋类、手袋及皮具、皮衣、时尚配饰、行李箱包、业内相关服务
市场范围：国际性
性质：面向贸易观众
主办：亚太区皮革展有限公司；中国皮革协会
承办：博闻中国有限公司
地址：香港湾仔港湾道26号华润大厦17楼

China International Footwear Fair
Venue: Shanghai New International Expo Center, Shanghai
Frequency: Annual
Market Area: International
Nature: Trade Only
Organizer: UBM Asia

2011/09/06 - 08
☎ 852-2827 6211
🖷 852-3749 7346
✉ info@aplf.com
sales@aplf.com
www.ciffchina.com
www.aclechina.com

2730

中国国际皮革展
地点：上海新国际博览中心，上海
内容：生皮及原皮、半制成革及制成革、稀有皮革、人造革、合成/天然物料、化工原料及染料、配件及配饰、部件及工具、制革机器、生产技术(如：电脑辅助设计及生産系统)
市场范围：国际性
性质：面向贸易观众
主办：亚太区皮革展有限公司；中国皮革协会
承办：博闻中国有限公司
地址：香港湾仔港湾道26号华润大厦17楼

All China Leather Exhibition
Venue: Shanghai New International Expo Center, Shanghai
Market Area: International
Nature: Trade Only
Organizer: UBM Asia

2011/09/06 - 09
☎ 010-6606 7682, 6603 9043
🖷 010-6606 7681
✉ applas@applas.com
www.applas.com
2740

亚太国际塑料橡胶工业展览会
地点：上海新国际博览中心，上海
内容：经过12年的发展，"APPLAS"已成为中国重要的塑料橡胶专业展。APPLAS 2011将接待包括世界前30名跨国零售集团在内的4,000多名海外买家，专业观众将达50,000人次。APPLAS已成为我国塑料橡胶企业寻求和增加出口的主渠道之一
始办年份：1997
周期：两年一届
市场范围：国际性
性质：面向贸易观众
参展费用：净地1,100元/m^2，标准展位1,200元/m^2
上届规模 2009：展览面积45,000m^2，参展商773家，参观人数39,588人
主办：中国轻工业联合会；中国石油和化学工业协会；中国机电产品进出口商会；中国轻工业机械总公司
承办：北京中轻亚泰塑料科技有限公司
地址：北京市西城区西黄城根南街33号（100032）
联系人：张晓晨,陈红

Asian-Pacific Intl Plastics and Rubber Industry Exhibition
Venue: Shanghai New International Expo Center, Shanghai
Profile: With 12 years development, APPLAS has been an important show in plastics and rubber industry. 40,000 overseas buyers and 50,000 visitors come to APPLAS' 09, including the front 30 retail groups in the world. In China, for plastics and rubber enterprises, APPLAS will be one of the channels to find and increase export
Established Year: 1997
Frequency: Biennial
Market Area: International
Nature: Trade Only
Participated Fee: Raw Space RMB 1,100/m^2, Standard Booth RMB 1,200/m^2
Statistics 2009: Exhibition Area 45,000m^2, Exhibitors 773, Visitors 39,588
Organizer: China National Light Industry Council; China Petroleum and Chemical Industry Association; China Chamber of Commerce for Import & Export of Machinery & Electronic Products; China National Light Industry Machinery Corp.
Address: No.33 Xihuangchenggen South Street, Xicheng Dist., Beijing 100032, China **Contact**: Xiao Chen, Chen Hong

2011/09/07 - 08
☎ 021-6275 5800
🖷 021-6275 7210
✉ frank.boeser@cancom.com
www.canontradeshows.com
2760

2011上海国际医疗设备设计和技术展览会暨研讨会
地点：上海国际展览中心，上海

MEDTEC China 2011
Venue: Shanghai International Exhibition Center, Shanghai
Organizer: Canon Communications LLC

2011/09/14 - 17
☎ 021-6437 1178
🖷 021-6115 4988转ext 160
✉ william.yuan@ubmsinoexpo.com
bill.zhang@ubmsinoexpo.com
www.ubmsinoexpo.com
2770

第十七届中国国际家具展览会
地点：上海新国际博览中心，上海
内容：卧房家具、餐厅家具、客厅家具、卫浴家具、儿童家具、休闲家具、户外家具、酒店家具、餐饮家具、学校家具、医院家具机场家具、其他
始办年份：1993
周期：每年一届
市场范围：国际性
性质：面向贸易观众
上届规模 2010：参展商2,000家，参观人数80,000人
主办：中国家具协会；上海博华国际展览有限公司
地址：上海襄阳南路218号现代大厦8楼（200031）
联系人：袁林先生、章瑜先生

Furniture China 2011
Venue: Shanghai New International Expo Center, Shanghai
Established Year: 1993
Frequency: Annual
Market Area: International
Nature: Trade Only
Statistics 2010: Exhibitors 2,000, Visitors 80,000
Organizer: UBM Sinoexpo

2011/09/14 - 17
☎ 021-6437 1178
🖷 021-6115 4988转ext 160
✉ william.yuan@ubmsinoexpo.com
bill.zhang@ubmsinoexpo.com
www.ubmsinoexpo.com
2780

中国国际橱柜展览会
地点：上海新国际博览中心，上海
主办：中国家具协会；上海博华国际展览有限公司
地址：上海襄阳南路218号现代大厦8楼（200031）
联系人：袁林先生、章瑜先生

Kitchen & Cabinet China
Venue: Shanghai New International Expo Center, Shanghai
Organizer: UBM Sinoexpo

2011/09/14 - 17
☎ 021-6437 1178
🖷 021-6115 4988转ext 160
✉ william.yuan@ubmsinoexpo.com
bill.zhang@ubmsinoexpo.com
www.ubmsinoexpo.com
2790

FURNISHINGS
FABRICS
& LIGHTINGS
CHINA 2011

中国国际家居布艺饰品展览会
地点：上海新国际博览中心，上海
主办：上海博华国际展览有限公司
地址：上海襄阳南路218号现代大厦8楼（200031）
联系人：袁林先生、章瑜先生

Furnishings, Fabrics & Lightings China
Venue: Shanghai New International Expo Center, Shanghai
Organizer: UBM Sinoexpo

2011/09/14 - 17
☎ 021-6437 1178
🖷 021-6115 4988转ext 160
✉ william.yuan@ubmsinoexpo.com
bill.zhang@ubmsinoexpo.com
www.ubmsinoexpo.com

2800

中国国际办公家具展览会
地点：上海新国际博览中心，上海
内容：办公家具；商用家具：公共座椅，公共交通用家具，机场家具，影剧院/礼堂家具，运动场馆家具，医院家具，学校家具，图书馆家具，实验室家具，定制及其他商用家具
周期：每年一届
上届规模 2010：展览面积30,000m^2，参展商300家，参观人数60,000人
主办：中国家具协会；上海博华国际展览有限公司
地址：上海襄阳南路218号现代大厦8楼（200031）
联系人：袁林先生、章瑜先生

Office Furniture China
Venue: Shanghai New International Expo Center, Shanghai
Frequency: Annual
Statistics 2010: Exhibition Area 30,000m^2, Exhibitors 300，Visitors 60,000
Organizer: UBM Sinoexpo

2011/09/14 - 17
☎ 021-6437 1178
🖷 021-6115 4988转ext 160
✉ william.yuan@ubmsinoexpo.com
bill.zhang@ubmsinoexpo.com
www.ubmsinoexpo.com

2810

第十七届中国国际家具生产设备及原辅材料展览会
地点：上海世博主题馆，上海
内容：家具制造设备、工具与部件、家具制作设备与配件、原辅材料
始办年份：1993
周期：每年一届
市场范围：国际性
性质：面向贸易观众
上届规模 2010：参展商650家，参观人数25,300人
主办：中国家具协会；上海博华国际展览有限公司
地址：上海襄阳南路218号现代大厦8楼（200031）
联系人：袁林先生、章瑜先生

FMC China 2011
Venue: World Expo Theme Pavilion, Shanghai
Established Year: 1993
Frequency: Annual
Market Area: International
Nature: Trade Only
Statistics 2010: Exhibitors 650，Visitors 25,300
Organizer: UBM Sinoexpo

2011/09/14 - 17
☎ 021-6437 1178
🖷 021-6115 4988转ext 160
✉ william.yuan@ubmsinoexpo.com
bill.zhang@ubmsinoexpo.com
www.ubmsinoexpo.com

2820

中国国际家具配件及材料精品展览会
地点：上海世博主题馆，上海
内容：家具生产材料与配件、家具配件、原木、木材、家具生产材料、家具五金、家具装饰材料、家具商标牌、清洗剂、家具制造检测、设计与工程服务
周期：每年一届
性质：面向贸易观众
上届规模 2010：展览面积10,000m^2，参展商200家，专业贸易观众20,000人）
主办：中国家具协会；上海博华国际展览有限公司
地址：上海襄阳南路218号现代大厦8楼（200031）
联系人：袁林先生、章瑜先生

FMC PREMIUM 2011
Venue: World Expo Theme Pavilion, Shanghai
Frequency: Annual
Nature: Trade Only
Statistics 2010: Exhibition Area 10,000m^2, Exhibitors 200，Trade Visitors 20,000）
Organizer: UBM Sinoexpo

2011/09/15 - 17
☎ 010-6478 8342
🖷 010-5804 3750
✉ fengfeng99@vip.163.com
www.coldchainexpo.com

2830

第三届上海国际冷冻保鲜及冷链物流技术设备展览会
地点：上海光大会展中心，上海
内容：全力打造一个国际领先专业、专注、权威、高端的冷链行业的盛会；冷库工程专题展；果蔬、花卉、水产、肉禽蛋及加工食品保鲜冷冻冷藏技术设备；冰箱、冷柜专题展；医药、生化、实验室行业低温冷藏设备专题展；冷链物流技术设备等
始办年份：2009
周期：每年一届
市场范围：国际性
性质：面向贸易观众
参展费用：标准展位：国内企业9,800元/9m^2，合资企业12,800元/9m^2，境外企业3,000美元/9m^2，双开口加收10%；净地（36m^2）：国内企业1,000元/m^2，合资企业1,200元/m^2,外资企业300美元/m^2
上届规模 2010：展览面积10,000m^2(国外展商2,000m^2)，参展商137家（国外展商38家，来自12个国家），参观人数9,921人（专业贸易观众6,347人）
主办：北京新京贸国际展览有限公司
地址：北京市朝阳区望京西路48号金隅国际G座2705（100102）
联系人：霍丽

2011 The 3th Shanghai International Exhibition of Food Frozen & Fresh and Cold Chain Logistics Technology Equipment
Venue: Shanghai Everbright Convention & Exhibition Center, Shanghai
Profile: To build an international leader in professional, focused, authoritative, high-end of the cold chain industry event; Cold storage thematic exhibition; fruits and vegetables, flowers, fish, meat, eggs and processed food preservation refrigeration equipment; refrigerator, freezer thematic exhibitions; Medicine, biochemistry, laboratory equipment, cold storage industry, thematic exhibition; cold-chain logistics, and technical equipment
Established Year: 2009
Frequency: Annual
Market Area: International
Nature: Trade Only
Participated Fee: USB 3,000/9m^2, Corner unit add 10%, Raw Space USD 300/m^2
Statistics 2010: Exhibition Area 10,000m^2(foreigners 2,000m^2), Exhibitors 137（foreigners 38, came from 12 countries），Visitors 9,921（trade visitors 6,347）
Organizer: Beijing Gold Trade International Exhibition Co Ltd
Address: Room 2705, G Block of city one 48#, Wangjing West Road, Beijing, China
Contact: Huo Li

2011/09/15 - 17
☎ 010-6478 7342
🖷 010-8441 4052
✉ huoli88@163.com
www.IceCream-expo.com
2860

2011第二届中国上海国际冰淇淋冷冻食品工业展览会
地点：上海光大会展中心，上海
内容：CICE必将为国内外的企业增添更多商业机会，领进全世界冰淇淋、冷冻食品产业进行贸易洽谈、经销合作、信息交流最快捷、高效的首选平台；冰淇淋、软冰淇淋生产设备及器具；冷冻食品自动生产设备、器具；面食加工成套设备；冰淇淋、冷冻食品技术、科技成果、书刊、与其相关的食品设备、器具、工具等
始办年份：2010
周期：每年一届
市场范围：国际性
性质：面向贸易观众
入场券价格：20元
参展费用：标准展位9,800元，净地1,000元/m^2
上届规模 2010：展览面积5,000m^2(国外展商820m^2)，参展商100家（国外展商20家，来自12个国家），参观人数9,921人（专业贸易观众4,030人）
主办：中国食品工业协会；中食协冷冻食品专业委员会
承办：北京新京贸国际展览有限公司；中国食品工业协会市场发展部
地址：北京市朝阳区望京西路48号金隅国际大厦G座2705（100102）
联系人：霍丽
QQ：1355348329

2011 Second China Shanghai Intl Ice Frozen Food Industry Exhibition
Venue: Shanghai Everbright Convention & Exhibition Center, Shanghai
Profile: CICE for domestic and foreign enterprises will add more business opportunities. Exhibits: Ice cream, soft ice cream production equipment and apparatus; frozen Food automated production equipment, apparatus; pasta processing equipment; ice cream, frozen food technology. scientific and technological achievements, publications, and associated food equipment, utensils, tools
Established Year: 2010
Frequency: Annual
Market Area: International
Nature: Trade Only
Cost to Attend: RMB 20:-
Participated Fee: RMB 9,800/booth, Raw Space RMB 1,000/m^2
Statistics 2010: Exhibition Area 5,000m^2(foreigners 820m^2), Exhibitors 100（foreigners 20, came from 12 countries）, Visitors 9,921（trade visitors 4,030）
Organizer: Beijing Gold Trade International Exhibition Co Ltd
Address: Room 2705, G Block of city one 48#, Wangjing West Road, Beijing, China
Contact: Huo Li

2011/09/17 - 19
☎ 010-6878 4991, 6878 4992
🖷 010-6878 4978
✉ hyq@ccfa.org.cn
ccfahy@126.com
www.chinafranchiseexpo.com
2870

2011国际特许加盟（上海）展览会
（2011年中国特许展上海站）
地点：上海国际展览中心，上海
内容：国际特许加盟（上海）展览会作为中国特许展的系列展览之一，已经成功举办六届。以沪、苏、浙等"长三角"一带的区域特许加盟为先导，辐射华东、华南东部沿海经济带，成为影响中国东部地区的重要的、有代表性的国际化展览会之一。
始办年份：2004
周期：每年一届
参展费用：12,000元/展位，净地1,200元/m^2
上届规模 2010：展览面积2,800m^2(国外展商576m^2)，参展商238家（国外展商60家，来自8个国家），参观人数8,000人
主办：中国连锁经营协会
承办：北京尚智联协会展咨询有限公司
地址：北京市西城区阜外大街22号外经贸大厦811-815号（100037）
联系人：郝永强,何勇
MSN：haoyqjob@hotmail.com

Shanghai International Franchiseexpo.com Exhibition
Venue: Shanghai International Exhibition Center, Shanghai
Profile: China Franchise Expo has developed into the most influential franchise event in China and is considered as the most efficient way to pursue new franchising opportunity. During 3 days exhibition, there will be about 30,000 individual or institutional investors coming to seek the franchise business and exchange new concepts
Established Year: 2004
Frequency: Annual
Participated Fee: RMB 12,000/booth, Raw Space RMB 1,200/m^2
Statistics 2010: Exhibition Area 2,800m^2(foreigners 576m^2), Exhibitors 238（foreigners 60, came from 8 countries）, Visitors 8,000
Organizer: China Chain Store & Franchise Association; Beijing Shine Co Ltd
Address: Room 811,8th floor, Foreign Economic & Trade Plaza, No 22 Fuchengmenwai Str., Xicheng District, Beijing 100037, China
Contact: Evan Hao, John He
MSN: haoyqjob@hotmail.com

2011/09/19 - 21
☎ 020-8989 9266
🖷 020-8989 9050
✉ cnibf@zhenweiexpo.com
www.cnibf.net
2890

第三届中国（上海）国际电池产品及技术展览会
地点：上海光大会展中心，上海
内容：各系列电池、新能源汽车、各种组合电池、各类电池用制造设备、测试仪器、原材料、零部件和充电器；新型电池材料、新型电池技术、新型电池产品；系列二次电池使用充电器；电池工业用三废处理设备；废旧电池回收处理技术与设备。
始办年份：2009
周期：每年一届
市场范围：全国性
性质：面向贸易观众
入场券价格：免费
参展费用：7800元/展位
上届规模 2010：展览面积12,000m^2(国外展商500m^2)，参展商250家（国外展商14家，来自6个国家），参观人数7,000人（专业贸易观众5,000人）
主办：中国电子学会；广东省电源行业协会；振威展览集团
地址：广州市海珠区琶洲大道东1号保利国际广场南塔5楼（510308）
联系人：牛松

The 3rd China (Shanghai) International Battery Industry Fair
Venue: Shanghai Everbright Convention & Exhibition Center, Shanghai
Profile: Batteries for manufacture equipment, testing equipment, materials and chargers, etc. Series of batteries lead-acid storage batteries/Valve-control Sealed Lead Acid Battery, cadmium-nickel storage batteries, Ni-MH recharge battery, Primary batteries
Established Year: 2009
Frequency: Annual
Market Area: National
Nature: Trade Only
Cost to Attend: Free
Participated Fee: RMB 7,800/booth
Statistics 2010: Exhibition Area 12,000m^2(foreigners 500m^2), Exhibitors 250（foreigners 14, came from 6 countries）, Visitors 7,000（trade visitors 5,000）
Organizer: Chinese Institute of Electronics; Guangdong Power Supply Association; Zhenwei Exhibition Group
Address: Unit 501-504 South Tower Poly Intl Plaza, No.688 Middle Yuejiang Road（East of Pazhou Complex）, Haizhu District, Guangzhou 510308,China
Contact: Niu Song

2011/09/21 - 23
☎ 021-6160 8555转ext 231
🖷 021-5876 9332
✉ susan.wang@china.messefrankfurt.com
www.messefrankfurt.com.hk
2895

中国国际文具及办公用品展览会
地点：上海新国际博览中心，上海
周期：每年一届
性质：面向贸易观众
主办：法兰克福展览（上海）有限公司
地址：上海浦东新区浦东南路999号上海联合广场32层
联系人：汪静

China International Stationery & Office Supplies Exhibition
Venue: Shanghai New International Expo Center, Shanghai
Organizer: Messe Frankfurt (Shanghai) Co Ltd
Address: 32nd Floor, Shanghai Union Square, 999, South Pudong Road, Pudong New Area, Shanghai, 200120, China

2011/09/21 - 23
☎ 010-6590 7766
🖷 010-6590 6139
✉ h.chen@koelnmesse.cn
www.cihs.com.cn
www.cihs-practicalworld.com
2900

2011 中国国际五金展
“科隆国际五金展”强力推动
地点：上海新国际博览中心，上海
内容：工具；建筑五金及DIY家装；锁具、安防产品及配件
始办年份：2001
周期：每年一届
市场范围：国际性
性质：面向贸易观众
入场券价格：10元
参展费用：国际：标准展位195欧元/m^2，净地145欧元/m^2；国内：标准展位1,450元/m^2，净地900元/m^2
上届规模 2010：展览面积110,000m^2，参展商2,300家（来自19个国家），参观人数45,000人
主办：中国五金制品协会；德国科隆国际展览有限公司；全国工商联五金机电商会；中国贸促会轻工行业分会；北京时瑞展览有限公司；上海大陆工具发展有限公司
联络：科隆国际展览有限公司
地址：北京市朝阳区东三环北路8号亮马河大厦二座1018室（100004）
联系人：陈晗,田雅妮

China International Hardware Show
— Powered by PRACTICAL WORLD
Venue: Shanghai New International Expo Center, Shanghai
Profile: Tools; DIY and Building Hardware; Security, Locks and Fittings
Established Year: 2001
Frequency: Annual
Market Area: International
Nature: Trade Only
Cost to Attend: RMB 10:-
Participated Fee: Standard Booth EURO 195/m^2, Raw Space EURO 145/m^2
Statistics 2010: Exhibition Area 110,000m^2, Exhibitors 2,300（came from 19 countries）, Visitors 45,000
Organizer: China National Hardware Association; Koelnmesse; All-China Chamber of Commerce in Hardware, Mechanical and Electric Industry; Light Industry Sub-Council, CCPIT; Beijing Triuni Exhibition Co Ltd
Address: Koelnmesse, Unit 1018, Landmark Tower Ⅱ, No. 8 Dongsanhuan North Rd,, Beijing 100004, China
Contact: Helen Chen, Emily Tian

2011/09/22 - 24
☎ 021-6390 6161
🖷 021-6390 6858
✉ m.miao@koelnmesse.cn
www.sweets-china.cn
2910

2011中国糖果文化节暨
第七届中国国际甜食及休闲食品展览会
地点：上海国际展览中心，上海
内容：糖果、巧克力和休闲食品；咖啡与茶；添加剂和原料；包装材料；包装、加工技术与设备
始办年份：2004
周期：每年一届
市场范围：国际性
性质：面向公众
参展费用：国际展区：净地190欧元/m^2（24m^{2}起）,标准展位230欧元/m^2（9m^{2}起），国内展区：净地850元/m^2（24m^{2}起），标准展位1,100元/m^2（9m^2）
上届规模 2009：展览面积3,500m^2(国外展商1,800m^2)，参展商147家（国外展商75家，来自22个国家），参观人数47,500人（专业贸易观众7,500人）
主办：科隆展览(中国)有限公司；中国食品工业协会糖果专业委员会
承办：科隆展览(中国)有限公司
地址：上海市淮海中路283号香港广场南楼1202室（200021）
联系人：缪骏，仇蓓莉

China Confectionery Culture Festival 2011,
Sweets & Snacks China 2011
Venue: Shanghai International Exhibition Center, Shanghai
Profile: Candy, chocolate, snack food; Coffee and tea; Addictive and raw material; Packaging material; Packaging, processing technology and equipment
Established Year: 2004
Frequency: Annual
Market Area: International
Nature: Open to Public
Participated Fee: Raw Space EURO 190/m^2（min 24m^2）, Standard Booth EURO 230/m^2（min 9m^2）
Statistics 2009: Exhibition Area 3,500m^2(foreigners 1,800m^2), Exhibitors 147（foreigners 75, came from 22 countries）, Visitors 47,500（trade visitors 7,500）
Organizer: Koelnmesse Co Ltd; China National Candy Association
Address: Koelnmesse Co Ltd, Rm 1202, No.283, Hong Kong Plaza, South, Middle Huai Hai Rd, Shanghai
Contact: Max Miao, Jasmine Qiu

2011/09/24 - 27
☎ 021-6195 6088
🖷 021-6195 6099
✉ cathy.huang@vnuexhibitions.com.cn
www.petfairasia.com
2930

第十四届亚洲宠物展览会
地点：上海光大会展中心，上海
内容：宠物食品、宠物用品、宠物医疗、水族产品、园艺产品、马术产品、活体宠物：各种犬/猫/鸟/观赏鱼/兔/仓鼠/龟/蜥蜴以及其他活体动物等。其他：宠物杂志/宠物网站/宠物摄影/宠物俱乐部/宠物爱好者社团
始办年份：1997
周期：每年一届
市场范围：国际性
入场券价格：50元
上届规模 2010：展览面积8,000m^2(国外展商1,000m^2)，参展商400家（国外展商80家，来自20个国家），参观人数30,100人（专业贸易观众9,273人）
主办：上海万耀企龙展览有限公司
地址：上海市徐汇区田林路140号26A栋万耀企龙办公楼（200233）
联系人：黄小姐

Pet Fair Asia 2011
Venue: Shanghai Everbright Convention & Exhibition Center, Shanghai
Profile: Pet food, pet feed, Pets products, Pet clothing, pet supplies, pet cages & houses, pet toys, pet grooming products, pet nursing products, pet training products, others Veterinary Products, Pet medical treatment facilities, pet health-care products
Established Year: 1997
Frequency: Annual
Market Area: International
Cost to Attend: RMB 50:-
Statistics 2010: Exhibition Area 8,000m^2(foreigners 1,000m^2), Exhibitors 400（foreigners 80, came from 20 countries）, Visitors 30,100（trade visitors 9,273）
Organizer: VNU Exhibitions Asia
Address: VNU Exhibitions Asia VNU House, 26A, No.140 Tianlin Road Shanghai, China
Contact: Cathy Huang

2011/09/27 - 29
☎ 021-6275 5800
🖷 021-6275 7210
2940

第九届国际粉体工业/散装技术展览会暨会议
地点：上海国际展览中心，上海
主办：纽伯伦会展服务(上海)有限公司

9th International Powder/Bulk Conference & Exhibition
Venue: Shanghai International Exhibition Center, Shanghai
Organizer: NURNBERG MESSE CHINA

2011/10/03 - 06
☎ 021-6195 6088转ext 903
🖷 021-6195 6099
✉ sam.shen@vnuexhibitions.com.cn
www.vnuexhibitionsasia.com
2950

2011上海房地产春季展示会——假日楼市
地点：上海展览中心，上海
内容：房产展示交易会是国内首个专业房产展示会。伴随着中国经济起飞和房产行业的迅猛发展，已成为规模庞大，覆盖面广泛、影响力巨大、民众参与度极高的年度盛会。把握先机、推出新盘、展示形象、拓展市场、主力营销。
始办年份：1997
周期：每年两届
性质：面向公众

2011 Holiday Real Estate Market
Venue: Shanghai Exhibition Center, Shanghai
Profile: One of the most influential large-scale real estate exhibitions in Shanghai. It has become the vital benchmark in shanghai real estate market.
Established Year: 1997
Frequency: Biannual
Nature: Open to Public
Cost to Attend: RMB 10:-

入场券价格：10元
参展费用：12,000元/9m^2
上届规模 2010：展览面积2,200m^2，参展商200家（来自4个国家），参观人数120,000人
主办：上海万耀企龙展览有限公司
地址：上海市田林路140号26A栋（200233）
联系人：沈先生

Participated Fee: RMB 12,000/9m^2
Statistics 2010: Exhibition Area 2,200m^2, Exhibitors 200（came from 4 countries）, Visitors 120,000
Organizer: VNU Exhibitions Asia
Address: VNU House, 26A, No. 140 Tianlin Road, Shanghai
Contact: Sam

2011/10/11 - 14
☎ 021-6160 8555转ext 231
🖷 021-5876 9332
✉ susan.wang@china.messefrankfurt.com
www.messefrankfurt.com.hk
2960

上海国际专业灯光音响展览会
地点：上海新国际博览中心，上海
周期：每年一届
性质：面向贸易观众
主办：法兰克福展览（上海）有限公司
地址：上海浦东新区浦东南路999号上海联合广场32层
联系人：汪静

Prolight + Sound Shanghai
Venue: Shanghai New International Expo Center, Shanghai
Frequency: Annual
Nature: Trade Only
Organizer: Messe Frankfurt (Shanghai) Co Ltd
Address: 32nd Floor, Shanghai Union Square, 999, South Pudong Road, Pudong New Area, Shanghai, 200120, China

2011/10/11 - 14
☎ 021-6160 8555转ext 231
🖷 021-5876 9332
✉ susan.wang@china.messefrankfurt.com
www.messefrankfurt.com.hk
2970

中国（上海）国际乐器展览会
地点：上海新国际展览中心，上海
周期：每年一届
主办：法兰克福展览（上海）有限公司
地址：上海浦东新区浦东南路999号上海联合广场32层
联系人：汪静

China International Exhibition for Musical Instruments and Services
Venue: Shanghai New International Expo Center, Shanghai
Frequency: Annual
Organizer: Messe Frankfurt (Shanghai) Co Ltd
Address: 32nd Floor, Shanghai Union Square, 999, South Pudong Road, Pudong New Area, Shanghai, 200120, China

2011/10/12 - 14
☎ 010-6603 8881
🖷 010-6603 3964
2980

第十届中国国际玩具及模型展览会
地点：上海新国际博览中心，上海
内容：每年10月在上海定期举办。展会坚持双向国际化的市场定位，促进企业外贸、内销两个市场平衡发展，是中国大陆第一、亚洲第二的玩具模型专业贸易展会。经过10年持续、快速发展，展会已成为企业拓展国内外业务不可或缺的主要平台
始办年份：2001
周期：每年一届
市场范围：国际性
性质：面向贸易观众
入场券价格：免费
参展费用：10,000元/9m^2
上届规模 2010：展览面积43,500m^2，参展商786家，参观人数50,712人
主办：中国玩具协会
地址：北京复兴门内大街101号 百盛写字楼8009室（100031）

10th International Trade Fair for Toys and Hobby
Venue: Shanghai New International Expo Center, Shanghai
Profile: The China Toy Expo is the leading industry-wide trade fair in Asia that focuses on toys, hobby and baby articles. It is no doubt to have been the preeminent marketplace event for buyers with various target to source directly from new, quality factories in China and Asia. Also, it is China's leading market platform and gives international manufacturers access to the booming Chinese market. Since 2011, China Toy Expo will held concurrently with China International Baby Carrier & Baby Articles Fair and China International Licensing Show. Visitors could find a wide range of sourcing opportunities in toys, hobby, baby products and licensing.
Established Year: 2001
Frequency: Annual
Market Area: International
Nature: Trade Only
Cost to Attend: Free
Participated Fee: RMB 10,000/9m^2
Statistics 2010: Exhibition Area 43,500m^2, Exhibitors 786, Visitors 50,712
Organizer: China Toy Association
Address: No. 101 Fu Xing Men Nei Street Beijing 100031, China

2011/10/12 - 14
☎ 021-6275 5800
🖷 021-6275 7210
✉ sxbeijing@263.com
2985

2011上海防伪技术暨证卡票券、RFID、商标标签、包装、可变条码印刷设备展览会
地点：上海国际展览中心，上海
主办：北京四星展览服务有限公司；上海泉涌文化传播有限公司

Shanghai RFID, Barcode and Packaging Exhibition
Venue: Shanghai International Exhibition Center, Shanghai
Organizer: Beijing 4 Star Exhibition Co Ltd

2011/10/12 - 14
☎ 021-6275 5800
🖷 021-6275 7210
✉ sxbeijing@262.net
2990

2011上海司法警用及安全防范技术产品博览会
地点：上海国际展览中心，上海
主办：北京四星展览服务有限公司,上海泉涌文化传播有限公司

Shanghai Security Exhibition
Venue: Shanghai International Exhibition Center, Shanghai
Organizer: Beijing 4 Star Exhibition Co Ltd

2011/10/12 - 15
☎ 021-6160 8555转ext 231
🖷 021-5876 9332
✉ susan.wang@china.messefrankfurt.com
www.messefrankfurt.com.hk
2995

中国（上海）国际时尚家居用品展览会
地点：上海展览中心，上海
周期：每年一届
主办：法兰克福展览（上海）有限公司
地址：上海浦东新区浦东南路999号上海联合广场32层
联系人：汪静

Interior Lifestyle China
Venue: Shanghai Exhibition Center, Shanghai
Frequency: Annual
Organizer: Messe Frankfurt (Shanghai) Co Ltd
Address: 32nd Floor, Shanghai Union Square, 999, South Pudong Road, Pudong New Area, Shanghai, 200120, China

2011/10/18 - 20
☎ 021-6275 5800
🖷 021-6275 7210
✉ sxbeijing@263.com
2998

2011国际真空展览会
地点：上海国际展览中心，上海
主办：北京四星展览服务有限公司；上海泉涌文化传播有限公司

2011International Vacuum Exhibition
Venue: Shanghai International Exhibition Center, Shanghai
Organizer: Beijing 4 Star Exhibition Co Ltd

2011/10/25 - 28
☎ 021-5045 6700
🖷 021-5045 9355, 6886 2355
✉ ptc-asia@hmf-china.com
www.ptc-asia.com
3000

2011亚洲国际动力传动与控制技术展览会
地点：上海新国际博览中心，上海
内容：亚洲国际动力传动与控制技术展览会是关于机械和电气传动、流体传动与控制、压缩空气技术、机械零部件、紧固件、弹簧、轴承、内燃机和燃汽轮机的国际盛会，旨在为制造商、销售商、采购商及业内人士提供一个交流和贸易的平台
周期：每年一届
市场范围：国际性
性质：面向贸易观众
上届规模 2010：展览面积6,900m^2，参展商1,249家（国外展商435家，来自26个国家），参观人数42,933人（专业贸易观众7,596人）
主办：汉诺威米兰展览（上海）有限公司；德国汉诺威展览公司；中国液压气动密封件工业协会；中国机械通用零部件工业协会
地址：上海市浦东新区银霄路393号百安居浦东商务大厦301室（201204）
联系人：黄荔小姐，汤建国先生

PTC ASIA 2011
Venue: Shanghai New International Expo Center, Shanghai
Profile: PTC ASIA is a leading trade fair designed to bring together manufacturers and suppliers, investors, trade buyers, industry professionals and other interested parties. So it is the perfect export platform in Asia for companies involved in Electrical and Mechanical Power Transmission, Fluid Power, Compressed Air Technology, Machine Parts, Bearings, Internal Combustion Engines and Gas Turbines
Frequency: Annual
Market Area: International
Nature: Trade Only
Statistics 2010: Exhibition Area 6,900m^2, Exhibitors 1249（foreigners 435, came from 26 countries）, Visitors 42,933（trade visitors 7,596）
Organizer: Hannover Milano Fairs Shanghai Ltd; Deutsche Messe AG; China hydraulics Pneumatics & Seals Association; China General Machine Components Industry Association
Address: 301B&Q Office Tower 393 Yinxiao Road, Pudong, Shanghai, China
Contact: Ms Ally Huang, Mr Evan Tang

2011/10/25 - 28
☎ 021-5045 6700
🖷 021-5045 9355
✉ cemat-asia@hmf-china.com
www.cemat-asia.com
3010

2011亚洲国际物流技术与运输系统展览会
地点：上海新国际博览中心，上海
内容：2010亚洲国际物流技术与运输系统展览会是关于物料搬运、自动化技术、运输技术和物流的国际盛会，旨在为制造商、销售商、采购商及业内人士提供一个交流和贸易的平台
始办年份：1999
周期：每年一届
市场范围：国际性
性质：面向贸易观众
上届规模 2010：展览面积26,000m^2(国外展商1,534m^2)，参展商402家（国外展商68家，来自26个国家），专业贸易观众42,933人
主办：中国物流与采购联合会；中国机械工程学会；德国汉诺威展览公司；汉诺威米兰展览（上海）有限公司
地址：上海市浦东新区银霄路393号百安居浦东商务大厦301室（201204）

CeMAT ASIA 2011
Venue: Shanghai New International Expo Center, Shanghai
Profile: CeMAT ASIA is a leading trade fair designed to bring together manufacturers and suppliers, investors, trade buyers, industry professionals and other interested parties. So it is the perfect export platform in Asia for companies involved in mechanical handling technology and equipment, cranes and accessories, entire systems for material handling and warehouse, material flow control and software
Established Year: 1999
Frequency: Annual
Market Area: International
Nature: Trade Only
Statistics 2010: Exhibition Area 26,000m^2(foreigners 1,534m^2), Exhibitors 402（foreigners 68, came from 26 countries）, Trade Visitors 42,933
Organizer: Deutsche Messe AG；China Federation of Logistics & Purchasing (CFLP)；Chinese Mechanical Engineering Society (CMES)；Hannover Milano Fairs Shanghai Ltd
Address: 301 B&Q Pudong Office Tower 393 Yinxiao Road, Pudong, Shanghai, China

2011/10/25 - 28
☎ 021-6169 8300
🖷 021-6169 8301
✉ shanghai@mdc.com.cn
3015

第十六届中国国际医药（工业）展览会暨技术交流会
地点：上海新国际博览中心，上海
主办：杜塞尔多夫展览（上海）有限公司
地址：上海市浦东新区张江高科技园区科苑路88号上海德意志工商中心1号楼307室

The 16th China International Pharmaceutical Industry Exhibition
Venue: Shanghai New International Expo Center, Shanghai
Organizer: Messe Dusseldorf (Shanghai) Co Ltd
Address: Unit 307, Tower 1 German Center for Industry and Trade Shanghai, 88 Keyuan Road, Zhangjiang Hi-Tech Park Pudong, Shanghai 201203, China

2011/10/26 - 27
www.tfmchina.com
3020

营销和广告创新技术展示会暨研讨会
地点：浦东展览馆，上海
主办：亚洲博闻

Technology For Marketing & Advertising China
Venue: Pudong Exhibition Center, Shanghai
Organizer: UBM Asia

2011/10/26 - 27
☎ 021-6278 7488
转ext 8905/8504
✉ jodi.wang@ubm.com
crystal.yang@ubm.com
www.ccc-expo.com
3030

中国呼叫中心技术设备及解决方案博览会
地点：上海世贸商城，上海
内容：全面汇聚呼叫中心解决方案和产品、应用案例及专业人士的顶级盛会，这将是中国本土首届一指、以中高层决策者为导向的专业展览/会议，旨在有效提升客户联络及整合客户管理。本次大会将和业内人士分享整合的客户解决方案、业内领先的培训活动并提供独特的交流空间。范围包括金融、保险，医药，建设/工程/建筑，制造，电子商务/邮购，旅游/休闲/酒店，教育/政府/培训，IT/高科技制造和服务，物流，营销/传媒/广告代理，慈善机构，自建呼叫中心运营商，服务供应商和外包呼叫中心
市场范围：国际性
性质：面向贸易观众
预计规模：专业观众30,000人
主办：亚洲博闻上海博华国际展览有限公司
地址：上海襄阳南路218号现代大厦8楼（200031）
联系人：王小娟，杨燕

Call Center Expo China
Venue: Shanghai Mart, Shanghai
Profile: Call Center Expo has enjoyed a successful track record in UK & Japan for over 10 years', covering the complete value chain of the call center industry. Our China Call Center Expo will also showcase the entire spectrum of call center industry products and services whilst also showcasing real life case studies maximize implementation effectiveness.
Market Area: International
Nature: Trade Only
Expectation: Trade Visitors 3,000
Organizer: UBM Asia
Contact: Jodi Wang, Crystal Yang

2011/10/26 - 29
☎ 010-6218 0723
3040

第十五届中国国际口腔器材展览会
地点：世博会主题馆，上海
上届规模 2010：展览面积10,000m^2
主办：中国国际科技会议中心

DenTech China 2011
Venue: World Expo Theme Pavilion, Shanghai
Statistics 2010: Exhibition Area 10,000m^2
Organizer: China International Conference Center for Science and Technology

2011/11/01 - 05
☎ 021-5045 6700转ext 259/313
🖷 021-5045 9355
✉ es@hmf-china.com
www.energyasia.com.cn
3050

新能源与电力电工展
地点：上海新国际博览中心，上海
内容：发电设备；电力、电工技术；电力测控仪器；电气自动化技术与设备；输电、配电设备及附件
周期：每年一届
市场范围：国际性
性质：面向贸易观众
上届规模 2010：参展商80家，参观人数102,900人
主办：上海世博（集团）有限公司；中国电器工业协会、德国汉诺威展览公司、汉诺威米兰展览（上海）有限公司
地址：上海市浦东新区银霄路393号百安居浦东商务大厦301室
联系人：夏薇女士，赵梅萍女士

Energy Show
Venue: Shanghai New International Expo Center, Shanghai
Profile: Power Generation Technology & Equipment; Electrical Technology; Electricity Measurement and Control; Electrical Automation; Power Transmission and Distribution
Frequency: Annual
Market Area: International
Nature: Trade Only
Statistics 2010: Exhibitors 80, Visitors 102,900
Organizer: Deutsche Messe; Hannover Milano Fairs Shanghai Ltd; Shanghai World Expo (Group) Co Ltd; China Electrical Equipment Industrial Association (CEEIA)
Address: 301 B&Q Pudong Office Tower 393 Yinxiao Rd, Pudong, Shanghai
Contact: Ms Maggie XIA, Ms Ava ZHAO

2011/11/01 - 05
☎ 021-5045 6700转ext 284/222
🖷 021-5045 9355
✉ mwcs@hmf-china.com
www.metalworkingchina.com
3060

数控机床与金属加工展
地点：上海新国际博览中心，上海
内容：金属切削机床；金属成形机床；特种加工机床；数控系统、数显装置和机床电器；机床零部件及辅助设备；磨料磨具、刀具、工夹具及相关产品；检验和测量设备
周期：每年一届
市场范围：国际性
性质：面向贸易观众
上届规模 2010：参展商400家，参观人数102,900人
主办：上海世博（集团）有限公司；德国汉诺威展览公司；汉诺威米兰展览（上海）有限公司
地址：上海市浦东新区银霄路393号百安居浦东商务大厦301室（201204）
联系人：邵琦先生，沈运先生

Metalworking and CNC Machine Tool Show
Venue: Shanghai New International Expo Center, Shanghai
Profile: Metal Cutting Machine Tools; Metal Forming Machines; Non-traditional machines and special purpose machines; Numerical control systems, digital readout units, machine tool apparatus; Machine Toll Components And Auxiliary Equipments; Abrasive, cutting tools, tooling; jig fixture &related products; Inspection, measuring equipments
Frequency: Annual
Market Area: International
Nature: Trade Only
Statistics 2010: Exhibitors 400, Visitors 102,900
Organizer: Deutsche Messe; Hannover Milano Fairs Shanghai Ltd; Shanghai World Expo (Group) Co Ltd
Address: 301 B&Q Pudong Office Tower 393 Yinxiao Rd, Pudong, Shanghai
Contact: Mr Simon Shao, Mr Vincent Shen

2011/11/01 - 05
☎ 021-5045 6700转ext 259/280
🖷 021-5045 9355
✉ ias@hmf-china.com
www.industrial-automation-show.com
3070

工业自动化展
地点：上海新国际博览中心，上海
内容：工业自动化（生产及过程自动化）；电气系统；机器人技术；工业自动化信息技术及软件
周期：每年一届
市场范围：国际性
性质：面向贸易观众
上届规模 2010：参展商439家，参观人数102,900人
主办：上海世博（集团）有限公司；德国汉诺威展览公司；汉诺威米兰展览（上海）有限公司
地址：上海市浦东新区银霄路393号百安居浦东商务大厦301室（201204）
联系人：夏薇女士，李翔先生

Industrial Automation Show
Venue: Shanghai New International Expo Center, Shanghai
Profile: Industrial Automation (Production and Process Automation); Electrical Systems; Robotics; Industrial Automation IT & Software
Frequency: Annual
Market Area: International
Nature: Trade Only
Statistics 2010: Exhibitors 439, Visitors 102,900
Organizer: Deutsche Messe; Hannover Milano Fairs Shanghai Ltd; Shanghai World Expo (Group) Co Ltd
Address: 301 B&Q Pudong Office Tower 393 Yinxiao Rd, Pudong, Shanghai
Contact: Ms Maggie XIA, Mr Edison LI

2011/11/02 - 04
☎ 021-3251 6618, 3251 6628
🖷 021-3251 6698
✉ expo@vtexpo.com.cn
www.emcexpo.com
3090

第十届电磁兼容与安规认证暨微波展览会
地点：上海光大会展中心，上海
内容：一切用于通讯、电子、电器、航空航天、军工、计算机、网络、无线电、仪器仪表、汽车、交通、医疗、船舶、电力等领域的电磁兼容设备、测试仪器、材料、元件及检测中心、实验室和认证机构等
始办年份：2002
周期：每年一届
市场范围：国际性
性质：面向贸易观众
参展费用：外商24,300元/9m^2，国内企业15,000元/9m^2，净地：外商2,300元/m^2，国内企业1,500元/m^2
主办：中国电子学会
承办：上海优创展览服务有限公司
地址：上海市曹杨路505号尚诚国际大厦505室（20063）
联系人：徐以敏先生,沈晓蓉小姐

China International Conference & Exhibition on Electromagnetic Compatibility
(EMC/China 2011)
Venue: Shanghai Everbright Convention & Exhibition Center, Shanghai
Established Year: 2002
Frequency: Annual
Market Area: International
Nature: Trade Only
Participated Fee: RMB 24,300/9m^2, Raw Space RMB 2,300/m^2
Organizer: Shanghai Viewtran Exhibition Service Co Ltd

2011/11/02 - 04
☎ 021-3251 6618, 3251 6628
🖷 021-3251 6698
✉ expo@vtexpo.com.cn
www.emcexpo.com
3100

第六届微波及天线技术展览会
地点：上海光大会展中心，上海
内容：放大器、混频器、微波开关、振荡器组件等微波有源部件；滤波器、双工器、耦合器、衰减器、隔离器、环形器等微波无源部件；射频同轴连接器、微波电缆组件、硅/砷化镓、PCB材料、集成电路、电阻、电容等微波元件；测试仪器等各类微波毫米波专用仪器仪表；微波吸收材料及相关电子材料；移动通信、扩频微波、微波点对点、寻呼相关等微波通信及其配套和辅助产品；天线产品、材料及配件；微波毫米波专用软件，电磁场仿真软件；电磁兼容产品及技术。
始办年份：2002
周期：每年一届
市场范围：国际性
性质：面向贸易观众
主办：中国电子学会
承办：上海优创展览服务有限公司
地址：上海市曹杨路505号尚诚国际大厦505室（20063）
联系人：徐以敏先生,沈晓蓉小姐

6th Microwave and antenna technology Exhibition
Venue: Shanghai Everbright Convention & Exhibition Center, Shanghai
Established Year: 2002
Frequency: Annual
Market Area: International
Nature: Trade Only
Organizer: Shanghai Viewtran Exhibition Service Co Ltd

2011/11/02 - 04
☎ 021-6275 5800
🖷 021-6275 7210
✉ info@icsc.org.sg
www.icsc.org
3110

ICSC RECON ASIA 2011
地点：上海国际展览中心，上海
主办：icsc

ICSC RECON ASIA 2011
Venue: Shanghai International Exhibition Center, Shanghai
Organizer: International Council of Shopping Centers, Inc

2011/11/03 - 05
☎ 021-5153 5130, 5153 5139
✉ grace.zhang@reedexpo.com.cn
www.100percentdesign.com.cn
3120

100%design
shanghai

"100% 设计" 上海展
- 中国领先当代室内设计采购交流平台
地点：上海展览中心，上海
内容："100%设计"上海展是一个独特的中国当代室内设计领先展会，展示由设计评委会精选出的当代室内设计领先品牌。展会展示一系列原创的家具，灯饰，厨卫设备及地面和墙面装饰。旨在创造一个激发灵感的观展氛围，展示设计的创新和最新理念。"100%设计"上海展是室内设计师，建筑师，业内人士，房地产开发商，酒店业主及高端消费者与供应商开展商业会面，互动并满足其购买需求的首选平台。
上届规模 2010：专业贸易观众11,953人（比2009年增加23.3%）
主办：励展博览集团
联系人：张萱

100% design shanghai
Venue: Shanghai Exhibition Center, Shanghai
Profile: 100% Design Shanghai is a unique exhibition in China featuring leading brands of contemporary interior design products which are strictly qualified by a Design Advisory Panel. The exhibition showcases original designs of furniture, lighting, bathroom/kitchen and floor/wall coverings and it seeks to create a dynamic atmosphere for the proliferation of innovative and trendsetting ideas. 100% Design Shanghai is the premiere venue for the exhibitors to interact and meet the buying needs of key specifiers and buyers.
Statistics 2010: Trade Visitors 11,953
Organizer: Reed Exhibitions China
Contact: Grace Zhang

2011/11/03 - 05
☎ 021-5153 5130, 5153 5139
✉ xianjun.song@reedexpo.com.cn
grace.zhang@reedexpo.com.cn
www.home-decor.net
3130

国际家居装饰艺术展
- 相约奢华·生活·艺术
地点：上海展览中心，上海
内容：代表着高贵、优雅和富有品味的生活态度，国际家居装饰艺术展是一个独特的贸易展会，将一系列高质量的高端品牌带来中国的国际性大都市-上海。它展示高质量室内设计装饰产品、配饰和家具，是业内人士、设计界专业人士、酒店业主及买手必须参加的盛会，为其提供了一个与供应商开展交流，采购和商务洽谈的有效平台。
周期：每年一届
上届规模 2009：参观人数9,692人（来自35个国家）
主办：励展中国
联系人：宋贤军，张萱

International Home Decor & Design
Venue: Shanghai Exhibition Center, Shanghai
Profile: Representing an attitude of elegance and stylishness, International Home Décor & Design is a unique trade exhibition, which brings together a comprehensive range of high-quality and premium brands in the most cosmopolitan city of China – Shanghai, showcasing high quality interior home decoration products and accessories. It is a must-attend event for specifies, design professionals, hoteliers and buyers to network, source and establish business contacts.
Frequency: Annual
Statistics 2009: Visitors 9,692（came from 35 countries）
Organizer: Reed Exhibitions China
Contact: Xianjun Song, Grace Zhang

2011/11/09 - 11
☎ 010-5166 2329转ext 16/22/58
🖷 010-6813 2578, 6818 9519
✉ chenzhy@ceac.com.cn
www.iCEF.com.cn
3140

第78届中国电子展
2011亚洲电子展
地点：上海新国际博览中心，上海
内容：中国历史悠久、权威的电子行业展会。中国电子展以领先的基础电子技术，促进中国电子产业自主创新，与中国电子产业共同成长。
始办年份：1964
主办：中电会展与信息传播有限公司
地址：北京市复兴路49号（100036）
联系人：陈震宇

China Electronics Fair
Asia Electronics Exhibition in Shanghai
Venue: Shanghai New International Expo Center, Shanghai
Profile: A Gateway to Enter the World's Fastest Growing Electronics & ICT Markets
Established Year: 1964
Organizer: China Electronics Appliance Corp.

2011/11/10 - 13
☎ 021-6275 5800
🖷 021-6275 7210
✉ cec@shanghai-cec.com
www.shanghai-cec.com
3150

2011日本消费品展
地点：上海国际展览中心，上海
主办：上海会展有限公司

japan-made Fair
Venue: Shanghai International Exhibition Center, Shanghai
Organizer: Shanghai Intl Convention & Exhibition Corp Ltd

2011/11/11 - 13
☎ 021-6353 9977转ext 1236
🖷 021-3303 0254
✉ lydiali@itpc.com.cn
www.kidsfashionsh.com

3160

上海国际少年儿童服装及用品博览会
同期：上海国际优生优育暨孕婴童产品博览会
地点：上海光大会展中心，上海
内容：上海国际优生优育暨孕婴童产品博览会自2005年首次举办以来一直茁壮成长，现已成为中国最具影响力的婴童行业盛会之一。在此基础上，上海外经贸商务展览有限公司，携手上海市计划生育用品管理协会、上海服装行业协会共同主办上海国际少年儿童服装及用品博览会。上海童装展与优生优育展同期举办。展品范围有儿童服装 儿童鞋类、儿童配饰、儿童箱包、儿童文体用品、婴幼儿服装服饰、孕妇服装服饰、出版物及相关组织机构
始办年份：2010
周期：每年一届
市场范围：国际性
参展费用：标准展台9,000元/9m^2,净地（36m^{2}起）900元/m^2，豪华标摊（36m^{2}起）1,050元/m^2 (2011年6月30日前签约可享10%优惠,或凡已参加上海外经贸商务展览有限公司举办展会的展商，可享10%优惠)
上届规模 2010：展览面积10,000m^2(国外展商3,000m^2)，参展商166家（国外展商38家，来自15个国家），参观人数27,600人（专业贸易观众8,105人）
主办：上海外经贸商务展览有限公司；上海市计划生育用品管理协会；上海服装行业协会
地址：上海外经贸商务展览有限公司上海市天目西路511号锦程大厦12楼（200070）
联系人：李佳

Kids Fashion Shanghai
Mom Baby Shanghai
Venue: Shanghai Everbright Convention & Exhibition Center, Shanghai
Profile: Strategic Platform to Grasp Abundant Business Opportunities in the Strong China Market Since its first edition in 2005, with steady growth, Mom Baby Shanghai has become one of the most influential events of the baby products industry in China. On this basis, Shanghai International Trade Promotion Co Ltd, together with Shanghai Family Planning Services Association and Shanghai Garment Trade Association, organizes Kids Fashion Shanghai, held concurrently with Mom Baby Shanghai. Exhibits: Children's Wear, Shoes for Children, Children's Fashion Accessories, Bags for Children, Stationery & Sports Goods, Baby's Wear & Fashion Accessories, Maternity Wear & Fashion Accessories Publications & Organizations
Established Year: 2010
Frequency: Annual
Market Area: International
Participated Fee: Standard Booth RMB 9,000元/9m^2, Raw Space (min 36m^2) RMB 900/m^2 (10% off before June 30, 2011)
Statistics 2010: Exhibition Area 10,000m^2(foreigners 3,000m^2), Exhibitors 166 (foreigners 38, came from 15 countries), Visitors 27,600 (trade visitors 8,105)
Organizer: Shanghai International Trade Promotion Co Ltd; Shanghai Family Planning Services Association; Shanghai Garment Trade Association
Address: Shanghai International Trade Promotion Co Ltd, 12F. 511 West TianMu Road, Shanghai 200070, China
Contact: Ms Lydia Li

2011/11/12 - 13
☎ 021-5266 5618，5266 2368
🖷 021-5266 8178，5266 6815
✉ realexpo@sh163.net
www.oto-hns.org.cn

3180

2011上海国际耳鼻咽喉头颈外科论坛
2011上海国际耳鼻咽喉头颈外科医疗设备及药品展览会
地点：上海展览中心，上海
内容：展示各类耳鼻咽喉头颈外科相关的医疗产品及相关设备等
始办年份：2009
周期：每年两届
市场范围：国际性
性质：面向贸易观众
入场券价格：凭相关邀请函或现场凭专业名片
参展费用：外商25,000元/展位，合资企业20,000元/展位，国内代理商/贸易公司18,000元/展位，国内厂商15,000元/展位
预计规模：展出面积2,600m^2, 参展商50家，参观人数5,000人
主办：复旦大学附属眼耳鼻喉科医院
承办：上海瑞欧展览服务有限公司
地址：上海市中山北路2790号杰地大厦1007室（200063）
联系人：宋欢，汤雅萍
MSN：982562505

2011 Shanghai International Conference of Otorhinolaryngology and Head & Neck Surgery
Venue: Shanghai Exhibition Center, Shanghai
Profile: All kinds of otorhinolaryngology-head and neck surgery microsurgical appliance and equipment etc.
Established Year: 2009
Frequency: Biannual
Market Area: International
Nature: Trade Only
Cost to Attend: Free
Participated Fee: RMB 25,000/booth
Sponsor: EENT Hospital of Fudan University
Organizer: Shanghai Real Exhibition Service Co Ltd
Address: Room 1007, Jie Di Plaza, No.2790 Zhong Shan North Road, Shanghai
Contact: Sofy Song, Sindy Tang
MSN: 982562505

2011/11/14 - 17
☎ 010-8827 5616
🖷 010-8827 5616
✉ zhangxiaonong@keyin.cn
www.allinprint.com

3190

中国国际全印展
地点：上海新国际博览中心，上海
始办年份：2003
市场范围：国际性
性质：面向贸易观众
入场券价格：免费
预计规模：展出面积100,000m^2，参展商800家，参观人数100,000人
主办：中国印刷技术协会；中国印刷科学技术研究所；杜塞尔多夫展览（中国）有限公司
承办：中国印刷技术协会；科印传媒；杜塞尔多夫展览（中国）有限公司
地址：北京市海淀区翠微路2号（100036）
联系人：张晓农

All in Print
The 4th China International Exhibition for All Printing Technology and Equipment
Venue: Shanghai New International Expo Center, Shanghai
Established Year: 2003
Market Area: International
Nature: Trade Only
Cost to Attend: Free
Sponsor：Printing Technology Association of China; China Academy of Printing Technology; Messe Düsseldorf China Ltd
Organizer：Printing Technology Association of China; KeyinPrint Media China; Messe Düsseldorf (Shanghai) Co Ltd
Address: No.2 CuiweiLu, Haidian District, Beijing
Contact: Zhang Xiaonong

2011/11/15 - 17
☎ 021-6289 5385
🖷 021-62472950
✉ info@rechinaexpo.com.cn
info@rechinaexpo.com
www.rechinaexpo.com.cn

3200

第九届ReChina亚洲打印耗材展览会(秋季)
地点：上海展览中心，上海
内容：墨盒、硒鼓、色带、碳粉、墨水及连续供墨系统，兼容、再生、循环使用的打印机和复印机通用耗材，芯片、感光鼓、各类辊、膜、空盒等配件和原材料，打印耗材的制造、翻新、灌装、测试等设备和工具，相纸、票据纸、彩喷纸、热敏纸等办公打印用纸，打印设备与耗材技术、信息、包装等服务类产品
始办年份：2004
周期：每年两届
市场范围：国际性
性质：面向贸易观众
入场券价格：50元

ReChina Asia Expo 2011(Autumn Session)
Venue: Shanghai Exhibition Center, Shanghai
Profile: Ink cartridges, toner cartridges, ribbons, toner, ink and CISS Compatible, remanufactured and renewable consumables for printers and materials Chips, OPC drums, various, rollers, sleeves, empties and other components and materials Manufacturing **Established Year**: 2004
Frequency: Biannual
Market Area: International
Nature: Trade Only
Cost to Attend: RMB 50:-
Participated Fee: USD 2,250/booth, Raw Space USD 240/m^2
Statistics 2010: Exhibition Area 17,000m^2(foreigners 1,162m^2),

参展费用：标准展位（$9m^2$）14,400元或2,250美元，净地1,520元/m^2或240美元/m^2
上届规模 2010：展览面积17,000m^2(国外展商1,162m^2)，参展商322家（国外展商40家，来自67个国家），参观人数7,200人（专业贸易观众5,600人）
主办：上海广会会展有限公司
承办： Rechina Expo Inc(USA); Recharger Magazine(USA)
地址：上海市镇宁路200号东峰18B（20040）
联系人：陈金祥,陈文瑾
MSN：aprilellios@163.com
QQ：1193882389

Exhibitors 322（foreigners 40, came from 67 countries）, Visitors 7,200（trade visitors 5,600）
Sponsor: Shanghai Grand Expo Co Ltd
Organizer: Rechina Expo Inc (USA); Recharger Magazine (USA)
Address: 18B East Wing, No.200 Zhenning Rd, Shanghai, China
Contact: Peter Chen, Cheyenne Chen
MSN: aprilellios@163.com

2011/11/16 - 18
☎ 021-6209 5209
📠 021-6209 5210
✉ tara@chinaallworld.com
www.woodmacchina.net
3205

第十五届国际食品、饮料、酒店设备、餐饮设备、烘焙及服务展览
地点：上海新国际博览中心，上海
内容：食品、饮料、酒店设备、餐饮设备、烘焙及服务；葡萄酒、烈酒及啤酒；肉类
周期：每年一届
市场范围：国际性
性质：面向贸易观众
主办：华汉国际会议展览（上海）有限公司
地址：上海市长宁区仙霞路318-320号2402室（200336）
联系人：蔡祎

FHC China 2011
Venue: Shanghai New International Expo Center, Shanghai
Profile: Food, Drink, Hospitality, Foodservice, Bakery & Retail Industries, Wine & Spirits; Meat, Meat Products & Equipment
Frequency: Annual
Market Area: International
Nature: Trade Only
Organizer: China International Exhibitions Ltd
Address: Room 2402, No.320 Xian Xia Road, Shanghai 200336
Contact: Tara Cai

2011/11/18 - 20
☎ 021-6195 6088
📠 021-6195 6099
✉ stephanie.xu@vnuexhibitions.com.cn
3210

上海理财博览会
地点：上海展览中心，上海
内容：银行、保险、基金、证券、黄金、外汇、房产、典当、第三方理财等
始办年份：2003
周期：每年一届
市场范围：全国性
性质：面向公众
参展费用：优越展位: 净地2,080元/m^2，标准展位2,350元/m^2，普通展位：净地1,280元/m^2，标准展位1,380元/m^2
上届规模 2010：展览面积4,500m^2(国外展商1,000m^2)，参展商200家（国外展商40家，来自15个国家），参观人数150,000人
主办：上海万耀企龙展览有限公司
地址：上海市田林路140号26A（200233）
联系人：徐洁

Money Fair
Venue: Shanghai Exhibition Center, Shanghai
Profile: Bank, Insurance, Fund, Securities, Gold, Foreign Exchange, Real Estate and etc.
Established Year: 2003
Frequency: Annual
Market Area: National
Nature: Open to Public
Participated Fee: Raw Space RMB 2,080/m^2, Standard Booth RMB 2,350/m^2
Statistics 2010: Exhibition Area 4,500m^2(foreigners 1,000m^2), Exhibitors 200（foreigners 40, came from 15 countries）, Visitors 150,000
Organizer: VNU Exhibitions Asia
Address: 26A, No.140, Tianlin Rd., Shanghai
Contact: Stephanie Xu

2011/11/23 - 25
☎ 021-6279 2828
📠 021-6545 5124
✉ yilei@siec-ccpit.com
www.sfchina.net
3220

第二十四届中国国际表面处理展览会
地点：上海新国际博览中心，上海
内容：机械式精饰工艺、电镀及化学式处理、涂装及涂料产品、涂料原材料、仪器、设备及服务
始办年份：1983
周期：两年一届
市场范围：国际性
性质：面向贸易观众
主办：中贸推广国际有限公司；新展星展览（深圳）有限公司上海分公司
承办：上海市国际展览有限公司
地址：上海市延安中路841号8楼（200040）
联系人：益磊女士

SFCHINA 2011
Venue: Shanghai New International Expo Center, Shanghai
Profile: Mechanical finishing, chemical finishing & electroplating, coating applications and coating products, raw materials, machinery, services and others
Established Year: 1983
Frequency: Biennial
Market Area: International
Nature: Trade Only
Sponsor: Sinostar International Ltd; New Expostar (SZ) Co Ltd Shanghai Branch
Organizer: Shanghai International Exhibition Co Ltd,
Address: 8/F, No.841 Yan An Zhong Road, Shanghai 200040, China
Contact: Ms Carrie Yi

2011/11/23 - 25
☎ 021-6279 2828
📠 021-6545 5124
✉ yilei@siec-ccpit.com
www.sfchina.net
3230

第十六届中国国际涂料展览会
地点：上海新国际博览中心，上海
内容：机械式精饰工艺、电镀及化学式处理、涂装及涂料产品、涂料原材料、仪器、设备及服务
始办年份：1996
周期：两届一届
市场范围：国际性
性质：面向贸易观众
主办：中贸推广国际有限公司；新展星展览（深圳）有限公司上海分公司
承办：上海市国际展览有限公司
地址：上海市延安中路841号8楼（200040）
联系人：益磊女士

CHINACOAT 2011
Venue: Shanghai New International Expo Center, Shanghai
Profile: Mechanical finishing, chemical finishing & electroplating, coating applications and coating products, raw materials, machinery, services and others
Established Year: 1996
Frequency: Biannual
Market Area: International
Nature: Trade Only
Sponsor: Sinostar International Ltd; New Expostar (SZ) Co Ltd Shanghai Branch
Organizer: Shanghai International Exhibition Co Ltd
Address: 8/F, No.841 Yan An Zhong Road, Shanghai 200040, China
Contact: Ms Carrie Yi

2011/11/25 - 28
☎ 021-5266 5938, 5266 5708
📠 021-5266 8178, 5266 6815
✉ realexpo@sh163.net
www.antiquefurniturefair.com
3240

第十届中国国际古典家具展览会&
2011上海国际古董及艺术品展览会（秋季展）
地点：上海国际展览中心，上海
内容：主要展示以明清古典家具，中式红木古典家具为主，涵盖了以中式家居饰品及古董、古玩收藏类艺术品；各类欧洲各时期的古董家具，油画艺术品，古董

Antique Furniture China 2011
Antiques & Arts Shanghai 2011
Venue: Shanghai International Exhibition Center, Shanghai
Profile: All kinds of antique furniture of Ming & Qing Dynasties, decoration and other artworks, Classical Rose wood and curios; European antique furniture, decoration, oil painting and artworks.

周期：每年两届
市场范围：国际性
上届规模 2010：展览面积12,000m²(国外展商4,200m²)，参展商260家（国外展商60家，来自10个国家），参观人数42,000人（专业贸易观众24,000人）
主办：上海瑞欧展览服务有限公司
地址：上海市中山北路2790号杰地大厦1007室（200063）
联系人：陈静娴 宋薇
QQ：982562505

Frequency: Biannual
Market Area: International
Statistics 2010: Exhibition Area 12,000m²(foreigners 4,200m²), Exhibitors 260（foreigners 60, came from 10 countries）, Visitors 42,000（trade visitors 24000）
Organizer: Shanghai Real Exhibition Service Co Ltd
Address: Room 1007, Jie Di Plaza, No.2790 Zhong Shan North Road, Shanghai
Contact: Amy Chen Amanda Song

2011/11/29 - 02
☎ 852-2827 6211
🖷 852-3749 7347
✉ marintec-hk@ubm.com
www.marintecchina.com
3250

中国国际海事技术学术会议和展览会
地点：上海新国际博览中心，上海
内容：船级社，计算机系统、网络和软件，咨询服务，疏浚设备，环境保护装备和设施，起重和升降设备，轮机工程和船用设备，补给和物流，海事出版，导航和通讯系统，离岸工程，滑油和润滑 油漆和涂料，港口和码头设备，港口和水路工程，港务局和码头作业公司，港口建设，港口设施，推进系统/泵和阀，冷冻系统，安全、救援和保护设备，船舶设计和建造，船舶工程，船舶营运和管理，船舶登记和检验，船坞和修船厂，电讯，贸易协会和出口委员会，仓库和配货系统
周期：两年一届
市场范围：国际性
性质：面向贸易观众
上届规模 2009：展览面积超过5,000m²，参展商1,483家（来自28个国家），参观人数42,689人
主办：中华人民共和国工信部；中华人民共和国交通运输部；上海市人民政府
承办：亚洲博闻；上海市造船工程学会
地址：香港湾仔港湾道26号华润大厦17楼亚洲博闻有限公司（200031）
联系人：冯静娴女士

Marintec China
Venue: Shanghai New International Expo Center, Shanghai
Profile: With the increasing global reputation among industry professionals, Marintec China has showed its strength and adaptability to the global economic changes. The proactive policies from the Chinese government in the maritime industry further enhance the leadership position of China in the international maritime industry as well as the tremendous support from the Chinese government, overseas government officials, renowned maritime organizations and communities. All those attributes are the key to the success of the Chinese shipbuilding industry.
Frequency: Biennial
Market Area: International
Nature: Trade Only
Statistics 2009: Exhibition Area 5,000m², Exhibitors 1,483（came from 28 countries）, Visitors 42,689
Organizer: UBM Asia Ltd
Address: 17/F China Resources Building, 26 Harbour Road, Wanchai, Hong Kong
Contact: Ms Stella Fung

2011/12/01 - 03
☎ 021-6275 5800
🖷 021-6275 7210
✉ ayexpo@163.com
www.ayexpo.com
3260

2011上海金属暨冶金工业博览会
2011上海铸件、锻件、产品展览会
地点：上海国际展览中心，上海
主办：上海奥亚展览有限公司

2011Shanghai Metal & Metallurgy Exhibition
2011 Shanghai Intl Casting, Forging
Venue: Shanghai International Exhibition Center, Shanghai
Organizer: Aoya Exhibition Co Ltd

2011/12/07 - 10
☎ 021-6160 8555转ext 231
010-8260 6880转ext 91
🖷 010-8260 6883
✉ susan.wang@china.messefrankfurt.com
ciccyhuang@cnaico.com.cn
www.messefrankfurt.com.hk
3265

2011年上海国际汽车零配件、维修检测诊断设备及服务用品展览会
地点：上海新国际展览中心，上海
周期：每年一届
主办：法兰克福展览（上海）有限公司
地址：上海浦东新区浦东南路999号上海联合广场32层
联系人：汪静（上海）

Shanghai International Trade Fair for Automotive Parts, Equipment and Service Suppliers
Venue: Shanghai New International Expo Center, Shanghai
Organizer: Messe Frankfurt (Shanghai) Co Ltd
Address: 32nd Floor, Shanghai Union Square, 999, South Pudong Road, Pudong New Area, Shanghai, 200120, China

2012/02/27 - 28
☎ 010-5933 9336
🖷 010-5933 9333
✉ karen.fu@reedexpo.com.cn
www.iscchina.com.cn
3270

上海国际城市安全及防护设备展览会
地点：世博主题馆，上海
内容：ISC全球系列展会是安防行业内最具权威及影响力的展会品牌之一，是励展博览集团依托旗下成熟的全球安防展品牌（ISC系列）及其运作模式，于2012年2月在中国上海推出的全新概念国际安防展览及会议。此次展会将引入国际化的运作模式，借助方案演示，产品陈列、系列研讨会等多种形式的现场活动，生动直观地展示国内外安防企业的优秀产品及服务，为安防产品生产、服务企业展示自身优势，吸引行业及客户关注搭建一个独一无二的平台。展会同期的各类行业交流活动，也将是您结识全新合作伙伴，巩固已有商业联系，融入国际安防行业的绝佳机会。
主办：励展博览集团中国公司
地址：北京市朝阳区新源南路1-3号平安国际金融中心A座15层01-03,05（100027）
联系人：傅妍

ISC CHINA
Intl Security Conference & Exposition China
Venue: World Expo Theme Pavilion, Shanghai
Profile: ISC CHINA is an extension of the ISC Expo, the leading global security event. This international event provides all the key elements to establish strong business partnerships in China's competitive security market including the key sectors. Exhibits: Video Surveillance, Access Control, Safety Alarm, Accessories, Home & Building Automation, Intelligent Traffic System, Security Inspection Equipment, Information Security, Solutions Supplier, Constructor
Organizer: Reed Exhibitions
Address: Unit 01-03, 05, 15th Floor, Tower A, Ping An International Finance Center, No.1-3 Xinyuan South Road, Chaoyang District, Beijing 100027, China
Contact: Karen Fu

2012/07/17 - 19
☎ 021-6209 5209
🖷 021-6209 5210
✉ tara@chinaallworld.com
www.woodmacchina.net
3280

第十八届中国国际加工、包装及印刷科技展览
地点：上海新国际博览中心，上海
内容：食品、肉类、乳制品、化妆品、消费品、饮料、液体科技及原料和工业用品塑料、纸张、金属、玻璃和药品等加工、包装及印刷科技
周期：每年一届
市场范围：国际性
性质：面向贸易观众
主办：华汉国际会议展览（上海）有限公司
地址：上海市长宁区仙霞路318-320号2402室（200336）
联系人：蔡祎

ProPak China 2012
Venue: Shanghai New International Expo Center, Shanghai
Profile: Food, Meat, Dairy, Cosmetic, Consumer & Industrial, Plastic, Paper, Metal, Glass, Beverage and Liquid Technology & Materials, Pharmaceutical Processing, Packaging & Printing Technology
Frequency: Annual
Market Area: International
Nature: Trade Only
Organizer: China International Exhibitions Ltd
Address: Room 2402, No.320 Xian Xia Road, Shanghai 200336
Contact: Tara Cai

3290
2012/09/25 - 28
☎ 010-6522 0753, 8511 1723
🖷 010-8511 1723
✉ expo@mc-ccpit.com
www.tubechina.com

第五届中国国际管材展览会
地点：上海新国际博览中心，上海
内容：管、管道原材料及配件，管道加工机械，二手机械，加工机械及辅助设备，测控技术，检测工程，相关领域（特殊用途管、业内研究与咨询等），其它管道贸易，管道及石油专用管材技术
始办年份：2004
周期：两年一届
市场范围：国际性
性质：面向贸易观众
入场券价格：免费
上届规模 2009：展览面积16,695m²(国外展商1,604m²)，参展商412家（国外展商81家，来自18个国家），参观人数26,035人
主办：中国钢铁工业协会；中国贸促会冶金行业分会
承办：中国贸促会冶金行业分会
地址：北京东四西大街46号（100711）
联系人：朱晓光 仲文

TUBE CHINA 2012
Venue: Shanghai New International Expo Center, Shanghai
Profile: Raw materials, tubes and accessories; Tube manufacturing machinery; Rebuilt and reconditioned machinery; Process technology tools and auxiliaries; Measuring and control technology; Test engineering; Specialist areas; Trading with tubes of all kinds; Pipeline and OCTG technology
Established Year: 2004
Frequency: Biennial
Market Area: International
Nature: Trade Only
Cost to Attend: Free
Statistics 2009: Exhibition Area 16,695m²(foreigners 1,604m²), Exhibitors 412 (foreigners 81, came from 18 countries), Visitors 26,035
Sponsor: China Iron & Steel Association; Metallurgical Council of CCPIT
Organizer: Metallurgical Council of CCPIT
Address: 46 Dongsi Xidajie, Dongcheng District, Beijing, China
Contact: Zhu Xiaoguang, Zhong Wen

3300
2012/11/15 - 17
☎ 021-6209 5209
🖷 021-6209 5210
✉ tara@chinaallworld.com
www.woodmacchina.net

第十六届国际食品、饮料、酒店设备、餐饮设备、烘焙及服务展览
地点：上海新国际博览中心，上海
内容：食品、饮料、酒店设备、餐饮设备、烘焙及服务；葡萄酒、烈酒及啤酒；肉类
周期：每年一届
市场范围：国际性
性质：面向贸易观众
主办：华汉国际会议展览（上海）有限公司
地址：上海市长宁区仙霞路318-320号2402室（200336）
联系人：蔡祎

FHC China 2012
Venue: Shanghai New International Expo Center, Shanghai
Profile: Food, Drink, Hospitality, Foodservice, Bakery & Retail Industries, Wine & Spirits; Meat, Meat Products & Equipment
Frequency: Annual
Market Area: International
Nature: Trade Only
Organizer: China International Exhibitions Ltd
Address: Room 2402, No.320 Xian Xia Road, Shanghai 200336
Contact: Tara Cai

天津 Tianjin

3330
2011/03/19 - 21
☎ 010-6841 4609, 6841 6664, 6870 0060
🖷 010-6841 4610
✉ wisdom.zhao@126.com

2011第十届中国（天津）国际客车及零部件展览会
地点：天津梅江国际会展中心，天津
内容：城市公交客车，节能和新能源客车，旅游客车，客车底盘，城市公交专用车辆设备，客车零部件，新能源客车零部件，3G及公交信息化设施，燃气客车的配套设施、加气站设备等，各型公交客车维修设备与配件
参展费用：国内企业：净地甲区800元/m²、乙区700元/m²,标准展位8,000元/9m²
预计规模：15000m²
主办：中国城市公共交通协会；住房和城乡建设部科学技术委员会城市车辆专家委员会；中国旅游车船协会；中国城市公共交通协会科学技术分会；天津市公共交通集团（控股）有限公司
承办：北京建通国豪广告有限公司；天津市公交物资有限公司
地址：北京市海淀区车公庄西路甲19号华通大厦A座831室，邮编：100048
联系人：吴崇筑、李金、陈迎祥

10th China (Tianjin) Bus and Parts Exhibition
Venue: Meijiang Convention and Exhibition Center, Tianjin
Organizer: Beijing Jiantong Guo Hao Ad Co Ltd

3340
2011/03/31 - 02
☎ 022-2643 7460
🖷 022-2643 4768
✉ hualunzhanlan@163.com
www.norbicycle.cn

中国北方国际自行车电动车展览会
地点：天津梅江国际会展中心，天津国展中心，天津
内容：自行车、电动车、零配件、设备、材料、专业媒体、相关运动休闲用品
始办年份：2001
周期：每年一届
市场范围：国际性
性质：面向公众
参展费用：6,500元/展位，净地750元/m²
上届规模 2010：展览面积70,000m²，参展商550家，参观人数100,000人（专业贸易观众30,000人）
主办：天津市华轮展览有限公司；天津国展中心股份有限公司
地址：天津市河北区金钟河大街战备路天华雅园35号楼3楼（300241）
联系人：李福成

China North Intl Bicycle & E-bike Exhibition
Venue: Meijiang Convention and Exhibition Center, Tianjin Intl Exhibition Center, Tianjin
Profile: Bicycles, e-bikes, parts, equipments, materials, media, correlation luggage belt
Established Year: 2001
Frequency: Annual
Market Area: International
Nature: Open to Public
Participated Fee: RMB 6,500/booth, Raw Space RMB 750/m²
Statistics 2010: Exhibition Area 70,000m², Exhibitors 550, Visitors 100,000 (trade visitors 30,000)
Organizer: Tianjin Hualun Exhibition Co Ltd; Tianjin International Exhibition Center Co Ltd
Address: 3F, No.35 Building, Tianhuayayuan, Zhanbei Rd, Jinzhonghe Street, Hebei District, Tianjin
Contact: Li Fucheng

2011/05/18 - 20
☎ 022-2311 5536
✉ kenwall@163.com
3350

2011中国（天津）国际医疗仪器与设备展览会
地点：天津体育中心，天津
内容：放射线设备、超声诊断仪；心电监护设备；内窥镜、生化检验分析设备及试剂、医用实验室设备；呼吸、麻醉机；急救设备、救护设备及车辆；齿科、眼科设备及材料；手术室设备；医用影像设备、康复理疗设备、整形外科设备；医疗消毒灭菌设备；通讯信息设备，医用软件、数字化应用技术及其它医疗设备与耗材等
参展费用：国内企业：标准展位A区5,200元/9m^2，B区4,200元/9m^2，C区3,600元/9m^2；净地（36m^{2}起）国内企业600元/m^2；国际展商1,700美元/m^2
主办：天津市卫生局；天津市机电设备招标局
承办：天津市泰和新侨科技园区管委会；天津市新侨集团；天津建和国际贸易展览有限公司
地址：天津市和平区开封道2号明源（300042）
联系人：赵小姐，张小姐

China (Tianjin) Intl Medical Instruments and Equipment Exhibition
Venue: Tianjin Sport Center, Tianjin
Participated Fee: USD 1,700/9m^2
Organizer: Tianjin Jianhe Intl Trade and Exhibition Co Ltd

2011/06 -
☎ 010-6609 4505
✉ hetian112@sina.com
www.tjqth.cn
3360

中国天津第十八届贸易投资洽谈会
地点：天津
主办：中国商业联合会；天津市人民政府；中国外商投资企业协会；中国外经贸企业协会
联系人：何天

China Tianjin Trade Fair & Investment Talk
Venue: Tianjin
Organizer: China General Chamber of Commerce; Tianjin Government

2011/07 -
☎ 010-6609 4505
✉ hetian112@sina.com
3370

2011中国天津啤酒节
地点：天津
主办：中国商业联合会；天津市人民政府
联系人：何天

Tianjin Beer Festival
Venue: Tianjin
Organizer: China General Chamber of Commerce; Tianjin Government

2011/08 -
☎ 010-6859 4811, 6859 4994, 6859 4910
📠 010-6859 4995
✉ zhangyuhui@ccpitmsc.org
www.chinamachine.org.cn
3380

天津国际工业装备展览会
地点：天津
周期：每年一届
市场范围：全国性
主办：中国贸促会机械行业分会
地址：北京市西城区三里河路46号（100823）
联系人：张玉惠,郭旭萍,吕春丽

Tianjin International Industry Fair
Venue: Tianjin
Frequency: Annual
Market Area: National
Organizer: CCPIT Machinery Sub-Council

安徽-合肥 Anhui-Hefei

2011/03/25 - 27
☎ 0551-2307 222, 2307 263
📠 0551-2307 110, 2152 220
✉ zhong_yi9999@126.com
3390

2011第二届中国(安徽)节能、新能源汽车展览会
地点：安徽国际会展中心，安徽合肥
内容：同期举办新能源汽车新产品发布会，节能、新能源汽车高峰论坛，关键零部件技术创新研讨会
市场范围：国际性
主办：合肥市人民政府；安徽省新能源协会
承办：新能源车网；合肥中亿展览有限公司
地址：合肥市匡河路浅水湾A座709室（230031）
联系人：王晓虎

2011 The 2nd China (Anhui) Energy Saving, New Energy Vehicles Expo
Venue: Anhui Exhibition and Conference Center, Hefei, Anhui
Market Area: International
Organizer: Hefei Zhong Yi Exhibition Co Ltd

2011/03/25 - 27
☎ 0551-2307 222
📠 0551-2152 220
✉ zhong_yi9999@126.com
3400

2010第二届中国（安徽）新能源与光伏展览会
地点：安徽国际会展中心，安徽合肥
主办：中国国际经济贸易促进会,安徽省新能源协会,安徽工业经济联合会
承办：合肥中亿展览有限公司
地址：合肥市匡河路浅水湾A座709室（230031）
联系人：王晓虎

The 2nd China (Anhui) New Energy and Photovoltaic Exhibition
Venue: Anhui Exhibition and Conference Center, Hefei, Anhui
Organizer: Hefei Zhong Yi Exhibition Co Ltd

安徽-淮南 Anhui-Hainan

2011/09 -
☎ 010-6609 4505
✉ hetian112@sina.com
3410

第十八届中国豆腐文化节
地点：安徽淮南
主办：中国商业联合会；安徽省人民政府
联系人：何天

18th China Tofu Culture Festival
Venue: Huainan, Anhui
Organizer: China General Chamber of Commerce; Anhui Provincial Government

福建-福州 Fujian-Fuzhou

2011/03/01 - 03
☎ 022-2311 5536, 2331 2556
✉ kenwall@163.com
3420

2011福建（第二十二届）国际医疗仪器与设备展览会
地点：福建经贸会展中心，福建福州
内容：放射线设备、超声诊断仪；心电监护设备；内窥镜、生化检验分析设备及试剂、医用实验室设备；呼吸、麻醉机；急救设备、救护设备及车辆；齿科、眼科设备及材料；手术室设备；医用影像设备、康复理疗设备、整形外科设备；医疗消毒灭菌设备；中央吸引供氧设备、血库设备、通讯信息设备，医用软件、数字化应用技术及其它医疗设备与耗材等
参展费用：标准展位：国内4,500元/9m^2，国外1,700美元/9m^2
主办：福建省医学装备协会；福建省机电进出口商会；中国贸促会福建省分会
承办：福建经贸会展中心；天津建和国贸易展览有限公司；福州建和展览有限公司
地址：天津市和平区开封道2号明源（300042）

Fujian Intl Medical Instruments and Equipment Exhibition
Venue: Fujian Economic-Trade Conference and Exhibition Center, Fuzhou, Fujian
Participated Fee: Standard Booth USD 1,700美元/9m^2
Organizer: Tianjin Jianhe Intl Trade and Exhibition Co Ltd

2011/04/29 - 03
☎ 010-8260 6880转ext 91
🖷 010-8260 6883
✉ ciccyhuang@cnaico.com.cn
www.cnaico.com.cn
www.autochina.com.cn
3430

第十七届福州国际汽车展览会
地点：福建福州
主办：中国汽车工业国际合作总公司
地址：北京市海淀区中关村丹棱街3号A座

17th Auto Fuzhou
Venue: Fuzhou, Fujian
Organizer: China National Automotive Industry International Corp

福建-晋江 Fujian-Jinjiang

2011/04/18 - 21
☎ 0595-8566 4572, 8560 0609
🖷 0595-8567 4572
✉ jif@cn-jif.com
www.cn-jif.com
3440

第十三届中国（晋江）国际鞋业博览会
地点：晋江市美旗城2号展馆，福建晋江
内容：鞋类制成品（包括运动鞋、休闲鞋、帆布鞋、凉鞋、拖鞋、工作鞋、登山鞋、童鞋、皮鞋、足球鞋等）、鞋材及配件、皮革（含合成革、人造革、PU等）、化工原料、制鞋制革 机械设备及相关科研、设计、信息刊物、图书等
始办年份：1999
周期：每年一届
市场范围：国际性
性质：面向贸易观众
上届规模 2010：展览面积50,000m^2，参展商500家，参观人数50,000人
主办：福建省人民政府；中国贸促会；中国轻工业联合会
承办：晋江市人民政府；晋江市制鞋工业协会
地址：福建省晋江青阳外经贸大厦3楼（362200）
联系人：李志达，丁燕燕
MSN：michelleding79@hotmail.com
QQ：723972

The 13th China (Jinjiang) International Footwear Exhibition
Venue: Jinjiang, Fujian
Profile: Footwear products (include sport shoes, casual shoes, canvas shoes, sandals& slippers working shoes and football shoes of various kinds),shoes materials & accessories, leathers (synthetic and imitation leather, PU , all kinds of leather), chemical raw materials, shoe-making & leather-making equipment, and relative researches, designs, information journals & books ,etc.
Established Year: 1999
Frequency: Annual
Market Area: International
Nature: Trade Only
Statistics 2010: Exhibition Area 50,000m^2, Exhibitors 500, Visitors 50,000
Organizer: Fujian Province Government; CCPIT; China National Light Industry Council
Address: 3F Foreign Economy & Trade Bldg., Qingyang, Jinjiang, Fujian
Contact: Michelle Ding, Lyttans Li
MSN: michelleding79@hotmail.com

福建-石狮 Fujian-Shishi

3450

2011/04/18 - 21
☎ 0595-8870 3999
🖷 0595-8300 2316
✉ stcf01@126.com
www.stcf.com.cn

第十四届海峡两岸纺织服装博览会
暨2011休闲服装博览会
地点：石狮服装城展览艺术中心，福建石狮
始办年份：1998
周期：每年一届
市场范围：国际性
主办：福建省政府；中国纺织工业协会；中国服装协会；台湾纺拓会；台湾针织工业同业公会
承办：石狮市政府；泉州市政府
地址：石狮市南洋路石狮服装城综合服务大楼（362700）
联系人：纪雅辉，林永腾，邱安妮

Straits Textile & Clothing Fair
2011 Casual Wear Expo
Venue: Shishi Fashion City Art Center, Shishi, Fujian
Established Year: 1998
Frequency: Annual
Market Area: International
Organizer: Shishi Municipal Government

福建-厦门 Fujian-Xiamen

3470

2011/01/21 - 24
☎ 0592-595 9898

第三届厦门特色农产品展销会
地点：厦门国际会展中心，福建厦门

3rd Agricultural product Sales
Venue: Xiamen Intl Conference & Exhibition Center, Xiamen, Fujian

3480

2011/03/06 - 09
☎ 0592-595 9898

中国厦门国际石材展览会
地点：厦门国际会展中心，福建厦门

China (Xiamen) Stone Exhibition
Venue: Xiamen Intl Conference & Exhibition Center, Xiamen, Fujian

3490

2011/04/08 - 11
☎ 0592-266 9865, 266 9866
🖷 0592-266 9868
✉ zwl@chinafair.org.cn
ciipc18@chinafair.org.cn
www.straitsfair.org.cn

第十五届对台出口商品交易会
海峡两岸机械电子商品交易会暨厦门对台进出口商品交易会
地点：厦门国际会展中心，福建厦门
主办：厦门市对台贸易促进中心

The 15th China Xiamen Machinery and Electronics Exhibition (CXMEE)
Venue: Xiamen Intl Conference & Exhibition Center, Xiamen, Fujian
Organizer: Xiamen Promotion Center for Trade to Taiwan

3500

2011/05/20 - 22
☎ 0592-508 3677
🖷 0592-291 9751
www.xmrjz.com

第八届厦门人居环境展示会
地点：厦门国际会展中心，福建厦门
主办：厦门华览商务会展有限公司

8th Living Environment Exhibition
Venue: Xiamen Intl Conference & Exhibition Center, Xiamen, Fujian
Profile: Xiamen Hualan Business and Exhibition Co Ltd

3510

2011/05/20 - 22
☎ 0592-291 9753
🖷 0592-291 9751
✉ xmjnz@163.com
www.xmrjz.com/building

第六届中国（厦门）国际建筑节能博览会
地点：厦门国际会展中心，福建厦门
内容：低碳生态城建设规划、可再生能源、绿色照明与节能光电、门窗钢构、建筑节水、新型墙体材料、隔热与防水材料、电气智能化、绿色科技
始办年份：2005
周期：每年一届
市场范围：国际性
性质：面向贸易观众
参展费用：5,800元/标准展位
上届规模 2010：展览面积10,000m²(国外展商2,000m²)，参展商300家（国外展商80家，来自12个国家），参观人数90,000人（专业贸易观众11,200人）
主办：厦门市人民政府；住房和城乡建设部建筑节能与科技司；福建省住房和城乡建设厅
地址：厦门市厦禾路建设大厦19楼（361003）
联系人：薛小姐

The 6th China (Xiamen) International Energy Efficiency in Buildings Expo
Venue: Xiamen Intl Conference & Exhibition Center, Xiamen, Fujian
Profile: Innovative Wall Materials, Doors and windows, Water Efficiency in Buildings, Renewable Energy, Electric Intelligence, Air-conditioning, Green Technology, Coatings and Heat-insulation Films
Established Year: 2005
Frequency: Annual
Market Area: International
Nature: Trade Only
Participated Fee: RMB 5,800/booth
Statistics 2010: Exhibition Area 10,000m²(foreigners 2,000m²), Exhibitors 300（foreigners 80, came from 12 countries）, Visitors 90,000（trade visitors 11,200）
Organizer: Xiamen Municipal Government；Science and Technology Agency of Ministry of Housing and Urban-Rural Development of China
Address: 19/F, Construction Building, Xiahe Road, Xiamen, China
Contact: Ms Xue

2011/05/27 - 29
☎ 0592-595 9898
3520

第九届中国（厦门）食品交易博览会
地点：厦门国际会展中心，福建厦门

9th China (Xiamen) Food Expo
Venue: Xiamen Intl Conference & Exhibition Center, Xiamen, Fujian

2011/07/01 - 04
☎ 0592-595 9898
3530

2011海峡西岸汽车博览会
地点：厦门国际会展中心，福建厦门

2011/07/14 - 17
☎ 010-6609 4505
✉ hetian112@sina.com
3540

第二届海峡两岸烘焙展
第二届海西烘焙暨咖啡展览会
地点：厦门国际会展中心，福建厦门
主办：中国商业联合会；厦门市贸易发展局
联系人：何天

2nd Baking and Coffee Exhibition
Venue: Xiamen Intl Conference & Exhibition Center, Xiamen, Fujian
Organizer: China General Chamber of Commerce

2011/09/08 - 13
☎ 0592-506 5632, 18906032531
3570

2011中国创业项目投资博览会
地点：厦门国际会展中心，福建厦门
内容：餐饮食品项目展区：教育培训项目展区：教育培训、成人专业教育、儿童智力开发、网络游戏、动漫、管理软件开发及其他文化创意项目；服务行业项目展区：洗衣洗染、洗涤设备、零售（便利店、超市、医药店）、汽车服务、汽车护理美容、汽车保养维修、房产中介、物业管理、形象设计、速印冲印、美体、休闲健身、美容美发、化妆品、保健等连锁机构；生活品牌连锁展区；科技成果展区；创业服务展区：行政服务中心、会计服务、法律服务、保险公司、银行
主办：中国投资贸易洽谈会组委会；厦门市人民政府
承办：博源会展（厦门）有限公司
联系人：张经理
QQ：361496921

2011 Entrepreneurship and Investment Exhibition
Venue: Xiamen Intl Conference & Exhibition Center, Xiamen, Fujian
Organizer: Boyuan Conference & Exhibition Co Ltd (Xiamen)

2011/09/08 - 11
☎ 0592-266 9851
🖷 0592-266 9855
✉ chenwenshui@cifit.cn
www.chinafair.org.cn
3580

中国国际投资贸易洽谈会
地点：厦门国际会展中心，福建厦门
内容：简称“投洽会”经中华人民共和国国务院批准，于每年9月8日至11日在中国厦门举办。投洽会以“引进来”和“走出去”为主题，以“突出全国性和国际性，突出投资洽谈和投资政策宣传，突出国家区域经济协调发展，突出对台经贸交流”为主要特色，是中国目前唯一以促进双向投资为目的的国际投资促进活动，通过国际展览业协会（UFI）认证。投洽会主要内容包括：投资和贸易展览、国际投资论坛及系列投资热点问题研讨会和以项目对接会为载体的投资洽谈。投洽会不仅全面展示和介绍中国及中国大陆各省、自治区、直辖市和香港特别行政区、澳门特别行政区的投资环境、投资政策、招商项目和企业产品，同时也吸引了数十个国家和地区的投资促进机构纷纷前来参展并举办投资说明会、推介会。
始办年份：1997
周期：每年一届
市场范围：国际性
性质：面向公众
入场券价格：30元
参展费用：12,000元/展位
上届规模 2010：展览面积60,000m^2(国外展商20,000m^2)，参展商2,000家（国外展商800家，来自45个国家），参观人数200,000人（专业贸易观众100,000人）
主办：中华人民共和国商务部
地址：中国厦门市湖滨北路108号振业大厦8-10层（361012）
联系人：陈文水
MSN：nanjing076@hotmail.com
QQ：406245108

The China International Fair for Investment and Trade
Venue: Xiamen Intl Conference & Exhibition Center, Xiamen, Fujian
Profile: CIFIT approved by the State Council of the People's Republic of China, takes place on September 8-11 every year in Xiamen, China. Themed on “Introducing FDI" and “Going Global", CIFIT features a focus upon nationality and internationality, upon investment negotiation and investment policy promotion, upon coordinated development of national and regional economy, and upon economic and trade exchanges across the Taiwan Strait. CIFIT is currently China's only international investment promotion event aimed at facilitating bilateral investment. It's also the largest global investment event approved by UFI. CIFIT has the following major contents: investment and trade exhibition, the International Investment Forum and serial seminars on hot investment issues, and investment project matchmaking symposia.
Established Year: 1997
Frequency: Annual
Market Area: International
Nature: Open to Public
Cost to Attend: RMB 30:-
Participated Fee: RMB 12,000/booth
Statistics 2010: Exhibition Area 60,000m^2(foreigners 20,000m^2), Exhibitors 2000（foreigners 800, came from 45 countries）, Visitors 200,000（trade visitors 100,000）
Organizer: MOFCOM
Address: 7/F, Bldg. A, Yujingyuan, 2 South Hubin Road, Xiamen, China 361012
Contact: Wenish Chen
MSN: nanjing076@hotmail.com

2011/09/21 - 25
☎ 0592-595 9898
3600

第四届海峡两岸文博会
地点：厦门国际会展中心，福建厦门

4th Straits Culture Expo
Venue: Xiamen Intl Conference & Exhibition Center, Xiamen, Fujian

2011/10/12 - 14
☎ 010-8451 1832
🖷 010-8451 1829
✉ peter@ejkbeijing.com

3610

2011中国（厦门）国际航空维修工程及服务技术展览会
地点：厦门国际会展中心，福建厦门
内容：航空维修类：飞机机体定检；航线定检；发动机定检；发动机修理及翻修；飞机部件维修；客机改货机技术及设备；飞机结构修理与改装；机内设备及用品等。航材及辅设类：新航材及二手航材；PMA件；航材库；消耗件；飞机零备件；发动机部件；机体维修主件和零备件；合材料；润滑油、油漆；个人安全防护产品等。设备类：机库、维修库工程与技术支持及解决方案；测量与检测设备；维修设备及工具；监控设备及仪器等；机场地面勤务设备；特种专用车辆；物流传送系统及处理设备；登机桥；活动梯；升降机；牵引机；辅助动力（APU）设备；地面支持设备；飞机清洗及除冰设备等。航空电子及电气类；信息技术类；培训类
始办年份：2011
首届
周期：每年一届
市场范围：国际性
性质：面向贸易观众
预计规模：总面积20,000m^2
主办：中国民用航空总局；厦门市人民政府；中国航空工业集团公司；中航文化股份有限公司；中航传媒集团
海外合作单位：美国克劳斯公司
地址：北京朝阳区新源南路6号京城大厦2005室（100004）
联系人：姬振鹏

MRO EXPO CHINA 2011
Venue: Xiamen Intl Conference & Exhibition Center, Xiamen, Fujian
Profile: The aviation maintenance, aviation equipment and accessories, Scheduled maintenance of airframe; Regular check of air route; Regular check of engine; Repair and renovation of engine; Maintenance of aircraft components; Technology and equipment for passenger plane converted to cargo aircraft; Repair and modification of aircraft structure; Build-in equipment and articles. New and used aviation equipment; PMA item; Aviation equipment warehouse; Consumptive parts; Aircraft spare parts; Engine parts; Main parts and spare parts for airframe maintenance; Composite material; Lubricating oil and paint; Personal protection products. Engineering and technology supporting and solutions for airplane shed and repair bay; Measuring and testing equipment; Maintenance facilities and tools; Airport ground handling equipment
Established Year: 2011
First Session
Frequency: Annual
Market Area: International
Nature: Trade Only
Organizer: Civil Aviation Administration of China (CAAC); Xiamen Municipal Government; Aviation Industry Corporation of China; AVIC Culture Co. Ltd; China Aviation Media Group
Overseas Organizer: E. J. Krause & Associates Inc
Address: Room 2005 Capital Mansion, 6 Xinyuan Nan Road, Chaoyang District Beijing, China
Contact: Peter

2011/10/20 - 23
☎ 0592-595 9898

3620

中国厦门国际素食养生展览会
地点：厦门国际会展中心，福建厦门

Xiamen Vegetarian food and Health Exhibition
Venue: Xiamen Intl Conference & Exhibition Center, Xiamen, Fujian

2011/10/20 - 23
☎ 0592-595 9898

3630

中国厦门国际茶业展览会
地点：厦门国际会展中心，福建厦门

Xiamen Tea Expo
Venue: Xiamen Intl Conference & Exhibition Center, Xiamen, Fujian

2011/10/20 - 23
☎ 0592-595 9618
🖷 0592-595 9611
✉ info@buddhafair.com
www.buddhafair.com

3640

第六届中国厦门国际佛事用品展览会
地点：厦门国际会议展览中心，福建厦门
内容：佛像、佛具、香、蜡烛、灯具、纸制品、素食、僧服绣品、书画音像、法器法物、密宗用品、佛教生活用品、佛教工艺品、礼品、寺院建筑及装饰、素食原料、制香机械及原料、蜡烛机械及原料、制纸机械及原料、其他设备及原料、其他未分类佛事用品。
始办年份：2006
周期：每年一届
市场范围：国际性
性质：面向公众
入场券价格：免费
上届规模 '09：展览面积34,000m^2(国外展商面积8,500m^2)，参展商500家（国外展商180家，来自10个国家），参观人数80,000人（专业贸易观众26,386人）
主办：厦门会展金泓信展览有限公司
地址：厦门国际会议展览中心（361008）

The 5th China Xiamen International Buddhist Items & Crafts Fair
Venue: Xiamen International Conference & Exhibition Center, Xiamen, Fujian
Profile: Buddhist statues, Buddhist Instrument, Incense, Candles, Buddhist Lamps & Lanterns, Paper Products, Natural Vegetarian Food, Monk Apparel & Embroidery, Buddhist Books, Painting & Music, Buddhist Implements, Vajayana Supplies, Buddhism Supplies, Temple Architecture & Decoration, Incense Machine & Raw Materials, Candle Machine & Raw Materials, Paper Machine & Raw Materials, other related Raw Materials & Machine, Buddhist Crafts, Gifts and other Buddhist Articles.
Established Year: 2006
Frequency: Annual
Market Area: International
Nature: Open to public
Cost to Attend: Free
Statistics '09: Exhibition Area 34,000m^2(foreigners 8,500m^2), Exhibitors 500（foreigners 180, came from 10 countries）, Visitors 80,000（trade visitors 26,386）
Organizer: Xiamen Jinhongxin Exhibition Co
Address: Xiamen International Conference & Exhibition Center, China

2011/10/27 - 31
☎ 0592-595 9898

3650

厦门日报房车大联展
地点：厦门国际会展中心，福建厦门
主办：厦门日报社

Xiamen Housing and Automotive Exhibition
Venue: Xiamen International Conference & Exhibition Center, Xiamen, Fujian
Organizer: Xiamen Daily

2011/11/03 - 07
☎ 0592-595 9898
3660
海峡两岸图书交易会
地点：厦门国际会展中心，福建厦门
Straits Book Fair
Venue: Xiamen Intl Conference & Exhibition Center, Xiamen, Fujian

2011/11/05 - 08
☎ 0592-595 9898
3670
中国厦门国际门窗木业展览会
地点：厦门国际会展中心，福建厦门
China (Xiamen) Door, Window & Wood Industry Exhibition
Venue: Xiamen Intl Conference & Exhibition Center, Xiamen, Fujian

2011/11/05 - 08
☎ 0592-595 9898
3680
中国厦门厨房卫浴用品展览会
地点：厦门国际会展中心，福建厦门
China (Xiamen) Kitchen and Bathroom Product Exhibition
Venue: Xiamen Intl Conference & Exhibition Center, Xiamen, Fujian

2011/11/18 - 02
☎ 0592-595 9898
3690
大连品牌服装服饰博览会
地点：厦门国际会展中心，福建厦门
Dalian Clothing Expo
Venue: Xiamen Intl Conference & Exhibition Center, Xiamen, Fujian

2011/12/03 - 16
☎ 0592-595 9898
3700
"缤纷冬"日厦门购物节
地点：厦门国际会展中心，福建厦门
Xiamen Shopping Festival
Venue: Xiamen Intl Conference & Exhibition Center, Xiamen, Fujian

2011/12/18 - 01
☎ 0592-595 9898
3710
内蒙古羊绒羊毛制品服装展
地点：厦门国际会展中心，福建厦门
Inner Mongolia Wool, Cashmere and Clothing Show
Venue: Xiamen Intl Conference & Exhibition Center, Xiamen, Fujian

甘肃-兰州 Gansu-Lanzhou

2011/08/20 - 30
☎ 010-8260 6880转ext 91
℻ 010-8260 6883
✉ ciccyhuang@cnaico.com.cn
3720
2011中国西部（兰州）国际汽车博览
地点：甘肃兰州
主办：中国汽车工业国际合作总公司
地址：北京市海淀区中关村丹棱街3号A座
West China (Lanzhou) Automobile Expo
Venue: Lanzhou, Gansu
Organizer: China National Automotive Industry International Corp

广东-东莞 Guangdong-Dongguan

2011/02/28 - 04
☎ 020-3802 3852
℻ 020-3802 3815
www.chinasignexpo.com
3725
2011东莞数字喷印及广告技术展览会
地点：广东现代国际展览中心，广东东莞
内容：户内外数码打印喷绘设备、写真机、UV平板打印机、条幅机、冷裱机、接驳机、覆膜机、印花机、热转印机、丝网印刷设备、数码影像技术输出设备等；各类喷墨写真墨水及喷绘布、车身贴、即时贴、冷裱膜、反光材料、写真相纸、压克力板材、PVC发泡板、铝塑板等耗材；广告雕刻机、激光雕刻机、木工雕刻机、CNC雕刻系统、切割机、刻字机、抛光机、弯字机、吸塑机、标牌设备、亚克力设备及刀具、相关配件等；展览展示器材、便携式展具系列、舞台架及其它POP产品；灯箱、发光产品、LCD广告机、三面及多面翻等；标牌、标识产品；3D立体产品、网络媒体、互动媒体、户外媒体、后期制作技术；LED显示屏、LED芯片、LED封装、LED设备
周期：每年一届
市场范围：国际性
性质：面向贸易观众
入场券价格：10元
主办：广州市轩华展览有限公司
地址：广州市天河区中山大道华港东街4号2706A-B室
China Sign Expo Dongguan 2011
Venue: Guangdong Modern International Exhibition Center, Dongguan, Guangdong
Frequency: Annual
Market Area: International
Nature: Trade Only
Cost to Attend: RMB 10:-
Organizer: Shine China Exhibition Co Ltd
Address: 2706A-B, 4 Huagang Dong Xian, Zhongshan Avenue, Tianhe Dist., Guangzhou

2011/03/16 - 20
☎ 0769-8590 0111
℻ 0769-8558 8780
www.3f.net.cn
3728

第二十五届国际名家具（东莞）展览会
地点：广东现代国际展览中心，广东东莞
内容：各类家具、家居饰品、木工机械及原辅材料
始办年份：1999
周期：每年两届
市场范围：国际性
性质：面向贸易观众
入场券价格：50元
参展费用：730元/m^2
上届规模 2010：展览面积260,000m^2(国外展商面积m^2)，参展商915家，专业贸易观众112,000人
主办：东莞市人民政府
承办：东莞市厚街镇人民政府；香港家私协会；东莞名家具俱乐部；广东现代国际展览中心
地址：广州市天河区中山大道华港东街4号2706A-B室
联系人：方润忠

The 25th International Famous Furniture Fair (Dongguan)
Venue: Guangdong Modern International Exhibition Center, Dongguan, Guangdong
Established Year: 1999
Frequency: Biannual
Market Area: International
Nature: Trade Only
Cost to Attend: RMB 50:-
Participated Fee: RMB 730/m^2
Statistics 2010: Exhibition Area 260,000m^2, Exhibitors 915, Trade Visitors 112,000
Organizer：GD Modern International Exhibition Center

2011/03/28 – 31
☎ 0755-2591 1739
852-2763 9011
℻ 0755-8212 9416
852-2341 0379
✉ jenny@paper-con.com.hk
www.scef.com.cn
www.paper-com.com.hk
3730

第十二届中国(东莞)国际纺织制衣工业技术展
地点：广东现代国际展览中心，广东东莞
内容：辅料、辅助品、缝后、刺绣、编织、信息服务/杂志 圆筒针织、缝前/剪裁、横机针织、缝制、物流、CAM/CAD系统/吊挂系统、印花设备、企业信息管理系统、超声波设备、激光设备 **周期**：每年一届
市场范围：国际性
上届规模 2010：展览面积35,000m^2，参展商350家，参观人数33,720人
主办：星球国际资讯（香港）有限公司
地址：深圳市福田区上步南路国企大厦A座11楼11D室
主办：通讯展览公司
地址：香港九龙观塘成业街11号华成工商中心5字楼15室

The 12th China (Dongguan) Intl Textile & Clothing Industry Fair
Venue: Guangdong Modern International Exhibition Center, Dongguan, Guangdong
Frequency: Annual
Market Area: International
Statistics 2010: Exhibition Area 35,000m^2, Exhibitors 350, Visitors 33,720
Organizer: Electronics Fair Service Co Ltd
Organizer: Paper Communication Exhibition Service
Address: Rm. 15, 5/F. Wha Shing Center, 11 Shing Ypi St. Kwun Tong, Kowloon, Hong Kong
Contact: Jenny Leung

2011/03/28 - 31
☎ 852-2763 9011
℻ 852-2341 0379
✉ jenny@paper-con.com.hk
www.paper-com.com.hk
3735

第十二届中国(东莞)国际鞋机鞋材工业技术展
地点：广东现代国际展览中心，广东东莞
主办：通讯展览公司
地址：香港九龙观塘成业街11号华成工商中心5字楼15室

The 12th China (Dongguan) Intl Footwear Machinery & Material Industry Fair
Venue: Guangdong Modern International Exhibition Center, Dongguan, Guangdong
Organizer: Paper Communication Exhibition Service
Address: Rm. 15, 5/F. Wha Shing Center, 11 Shing Ypi St. Kwun Tong, Kowloon, Hong Kong
Contact: Jenny Leung

2011/04/09 - 13
☎ 010-6315 4070
0769-8558 8658
℻ 010-6316 2123
0769-8583 0618
✉ zhangna@printchina.org
www.chinaprint.org.cn
www.printchina.org
3740

第二届中国(广东)国际印刷技术展览会
地点：广东现代国际展览中心，广东东莞
内容：印前处理系统与软件，数码印刷及打样设备，各种柔、凹设备及标签印刷技术设备，喷墨印刷及广告制作技术设备及器材，各类包装印刷设备，瓦楞纸箱及纸品加工、包装加工设备，各种制版设备，各类胶印设备，丝网印刷及各类特种印刷技术设备，印后加工、整饰及装潢设备，各类办公印刷技术设备，各类邮政印刷技术设备，检测仪器仪表、自控设备及配套机电产品，各类纸张、油墨、版材、橡皮布等耗材
始办年份：2007
市场范围：国际性
性质：面向公众
入场券价格：10元
参展费用：A：1,800元/m^2，B：1,200元/m^2，C：1,000元/m^2
上届规模 2007：展览面积80,000m^2(国外展商30,000m^2)，参展商1,047家（国外展商282家，来自31个国家），参观人数104,204人（专业贸易观众50,000人）
主办：中国印刷及设备器材工业协会
承办：中印协国际展览有限公司
地址：北京宣武区永安路106号2层
主办：中印协国际展览有限公司
地址：广东东莞厚街康乐北路明珠花园C13（523962）
联系人：张娜
MSN：zhangna@hotmial.com

2nd International Printing Technology Exhibition of China (Guangdong)
Venue: Guangdong Modern International Exhibition Center, Dongguan, Guangdong
Profile: Prepress: Multi-media Technology, Digital Publishing Systems, Prepress Systems and Software Printing Equipment: Printing Machinery and Accessories Postpress Equipment: Machinery and Accessories Paper Converting Machinery Packaging and Finishing Equipment
Established Year: 2007
Market Area: International
Nature: Open to Public
Cost to Attend: RMB 10:-
Participated Fee: RMB 1,800/m^2
Statistics 2007: Exhibition Area 80,000m^2(foreigners 30,000m^2), Exhibitors 1,047（foreigners 282, came from 31 countries）, Visitors 104,204（trade visitors 50,000）
Sponsor: The Printing Equipment Industries Association of China
Organizer: Print China Show Company
Address: 2nd Floor, 106, Yongan Road, Xuanwu District, Beijing,China
Organizer: Print China Show Company Ltd
Address: House C-13, Ming Zhu Garden, Hou Jie Town, Dongguan, Guangdong 523962, China
Contact: Zhang Na
MSN: zhangna@hotmial.com

2011/04/28 - 30
☎ 021-6169 8300
℻ 021-6169 8301
✉ shanghai@mdc.com.cn
www.mdc.com.cn
3745

第十三届中国东莞国际鞋展 · 鞋机展 · 鞋材展（春季）
地点：广东现代国际展览中心，广东东莞
主办：杜塞尔多夫展览（上海）有限公司
地址：上海市浦东新区张江高科技园区科苑路88号，上海德意志工商中心1号楼307室

The 13th Dongguan China Shoes · China Shoetec
Venue: Guangdong Modern International Exhibition Center, Dongguan, Guangdong
Organizer: Messe Dusseldorf (Shanghai) Co Ltd
Address: Unit 307, Tower 1 German Center for Industry and Trade Shanghai, 88 Keyuan Road, Zhangjiang Hi-Tech Park Pudong, Shanghai 201203, China

3745-1

2011/05/04 - 06
☎ 852-2800 8897
🖷 852-2516 5119
www.adsale.com.hk

中国东莞国际鞋展、鞋机展、手袋展
地点：广东现代国际展览中心，广东东莞
始办年份：2003
周期：每年两届
市场范围：国际性
上届规模 2010：展览面积20,000m²
主办：雅式展览服务有限公司；杜塞尔多夫展览（中国）有限公司
地址：香港北角渣华道321号6楼

Dongguan Shoes, China Shoetes, China Bags
Venue: Guangdong Modern International Exhibition Center, Dongguan, Guangdong
Established Year: 2003
Frequency: Biannual
Market Area: International
Statistics 2010: Exhibition Area 20,000m²
Organizer: Adsale Exhibition Services Ltd; Messe Düsseldorf China Ltd.
Address: 6th Floor, 321 Java Road, North Point, Hong Kong

3745-2

2011/05/14 - 16
☎ 0755-2591 1739
🖷 0755-8212 9416
www.scef.com.cn

第二十届华南(东莞)国际电子制造采购博览会
地点：广东现代国际展览中心，广东东莞
内容：电子元器件展区：致力国际电子制造企业获得先进元器件技术的沟通平台，其中包括从有源、无源与机电元器件至连接器、半导体与紧固件、器件，以及电子生产设备与原材料。电子化学品及SMT应用技术展区：覆盖了从电子化学品在绿色表面组装技术行业应用、微焊接技术质量控制到转包服务的整个产业链。仪器仪表展区：是华南地区专注于电子测量仪器、环境检测设备，生产品质和服务方面的国际会议，为您创造一个在整个制造行业中建立密集商业联系，并提升强大品牌价值的有利平台。激光加工技术展区：是全球激光加工装备及上、下游企业云集东莞，激光加工企业难得高度集中的时刻。著名品牌采购展区。
始办年份：1998
周期：每年一届
市场范围：国际性
主办：星球国际资讯（香港）有限公司
地址：深圳市福田区上步南路国企大厦A座11楼11D室

The 20th (Dongguan) South China Electronic Fair
Venue: Guangdong Modern International Exhibition Center, Dongguan, Guangdong
Established Year: 1998
Frequency: Annual
Market Area: International
Organizer: Electronics Fair Service Co Ltd

3746

2011/05/20 - 22
☎ 020-8359 9695, 852-2318 1867
🖷 020-8358 9272, 852-2318 1967
http://hk.allallinfo.com

2011东莞国际纺织品印花工业技术展览会
地点：广东现代国际展览中心，广东东莞
周期：每年一届
市场范围：国际性
主办：香港浩瀚资讯传媒集团有限公司
地址：香港湾仔骆克道369号国家大厦8楼805室

2011 China International Textile Printing Industrial Technology Exposition
Venue: Guangdong Modern International Exhibition Center, Dongguan, Guangdong
Frequency: Annual
Market Area: International
Organizer: Hong Kong Allallinfo Media Group Ltd
Address: Room 805, 8/Fl Federal Building, 369 Lockhart Road, Wanchai, Hong Kong

3747

2011/06/15 - 18
☎ 0769-8598 1609, 8598 1610
🖷 0769-8598 1696, 8598 1889
✉ gdfecf@vip.163.com
www.gdfecf.com

广东外商投资企业产品（内销）博览会
地点：广东现代国际展览中心，广东东莞
内容：消费电子、鞋帽、家居饰品、日用品、餐厨用品、食品饮品、玩具礼品家用电子，卫浴饰品等
周期：每年一届
市场范围：国际性
主办：广东外商投资企业产品（内销）博览会组委会秘书处
地址：广东省东莞市厚街镇家具大道广东现代国际展览中心12号门三楼

Guangdong Foreign-invested Enterprises Commodities Fair
Venue: Guangdong Modern International Exhibition Center, Dongguan, Guangdong
Profile: Consumer electronics products, footwear and headwear, household products, kitchenware, food and beverage, home decorations, toys and gifts, home appliances, sanitary decorations
Frequency: Annual
Market Area: International
Organizer: Organizing Committee of Guangdong Foreign-invested Enterprises Commodities Fair

3748

2011/09/01 - 05
☎ 0769-8590 0111
🖷 0769-8558 8780
www.3f.net.cn

第二十六届国际名家具（东莞）展览会
地点：广东现代国际展览中心，广东东莞
内容：各类家具、家居饰品、木工机械及原辅材料
始办年份：1999
周期：每年两届
市场范围：国际性
性质：面向贸易观众
入场券价格：50元
参展费用：730元/m²
上届规模 2010：展览面积260,000m²，参展商915家，专业贸易观众112,000人
主办：东莞市人民政府
承办：东莞市厚街镇人民政府；香港家私协会；东莞名家具俱乐部 广东现代国际展览中心
地址：广州市天河区中山大道华港东街4号2706A-B室
联系人：方润忠

The 26th International Famous Furniture Fair (Dongguan)
Venue: GD Modern International Exhibition Center, Dongguan, Guangdong
Established Year: 1999
Frequency: Biannual
Market Area: International
Nature: Trade Only
Cost to Attend: RMB 50:-
Participated Fee: RMB 730/m²
Statistics 2010: Exhibition Area 260,000m², Exhibitors 915, Trade Visitors 112,000
Organizer: Guangdong Modern International Exhibition Center

2011/09/21 - 23
☎ 024-2585 0149
🖷 024-2585 5793
✉ cxm@foundrynations.com
www.foundrynations.com
3750

2011亚太地区压铸工业展览会
地点：广东现代国际展览中心，广东东莞
内容：凡与压铸、低压铸造、挤压铸造、差压铸造、及半固态加工领域等有关项目皆可展示。各类铝、镁、锌、铜合金压铸件；压铸机及其周边处理装备；压铸模具的设计与制造技术；铝、镁、锌、铜等合金和合金锭及其复合材料；压铸后续装备包括清整、涂装、热处理、电镀及钝化等装备；熔化及保温系列装置；压铸新技术包括充氧、真空、CAD/CAE/CAM等应用技术；压铸工艺材料包括涂料、溶剂、变质剂及脱模剂；压铸检测及过程控制装备；压铸环保技术及设备
始办年份：1997
周期：每年一届
市场范围：国际性
上届规模 2010：展览面积4,560m^2(国外展商2,134m^2)，参展商154家（国外展商82家，来自18个国家），专业贸易观众5,632人
主办：中国机械工程学会铸造分会
地址：辽宁省沈阳市铁西区云峰南街17号（110022）
联系人：曹秀梅
QQ：460361759

2011 Asia-Pacific Die-casting Industry Exhibition
Venue: Guangdong Modern International Exhibition Center, Dongguan, Guangdong
Profile: New materials, equipment, technology and technique for die-casting (HP, LP, Grav), differential-pressure die-casting, squeeze casting, semi-solid processing.
Established Year: 1997
Frequency: Annual
Market Area: International
Statistics 2010: Exhibition Area 4,560m^2(foreigners 2,134m^2), Exhibitors 154 (foreigners 82, came from 18 countries), Trade Visitors 5,632
Organizer: Foundry Institution of Chinese Mechanical Engineering Society
Address: 17 South Yunfeng Street Tiexi District, Shenyang 110022, Liaoning, China
Contact: Cao Xiumei

2011/09/29 – 10/04
☎ 0769-8598 1555
010-8260 6880转ext 91
🖷 010-8260 6883
0769-2299 2793
✉ ciccyhuang@cnaico.com.cn
www.gdauto.cc
3755

第十一届广东国际汽车展示交易会
地点：广东现代国际展览中心，广东东莞
内容：汽车（含轿车、越野车、商用车及特种车）；汽车及其零部件；汽车生产制造设备、工艺装备；各种检测、测试、试验仪器和设备；计算机开发设计系统及应用技术；汽车工业生产的新工艺、新材料；汽车工业新能源技术与产品；汽车工业环保技术与产品；汽车用品、装饰件、美容品；汽车维修设备。
周期：每年一届
市场范围：国际性
主办：中国汽车工业国际合作总公司、东莞中汽会展有限公司

The 11th Guangdong International Auto Exhibition & Trade fair
Venue: Guangdong Modern International Exhibition Center, Dongguan, Guangdong
Frequency: Annual
Market Area: International
Organizer: China National Automotive Industry International Corp

---

2011/10/12 - 14
3756

中国国际老龄产业博览会
地点：广东现代国际展览中心，广东东莞
周期：每年一届
市场范围：国际性
主办：北京中经高科科技发展有限公司

China International Industry Expo Ageing
Venue: Guangdong Modern International Exhibition Center, Dongguan, Guangdong
Frequency: Annual
Market Area: International

2011/10/20 - 22
☎ 020-8555 7219
www.dgys8.cn
3757

第十一届东莞国际印刷造纸胶粘带及广告展览会
地点：广东现代国际展览中心，广东东莞
周期：每年一届
市场范围：国际性
主办：广东省印刷包装行业商会

The 11th Dongguan International Printing and Packaging and paper advertising, adhesive tape, protective film exhibition
Venue: Guangdong Modern International Exhibition Center, Dongguan, Guangdong
Frequency: Annual
Market Area: International
Organizer: Guangdong Printing and Packaging Association

2011/10/28 - 30
☎ 852-2800 8897
021-6169 8300
🖷 852-2516 5119
021-6169 8301
✉ shanghai@mdc.com.cn
www.adsale.com.hk
3758

2011中国东莞国际鞋展
地点：广东现代国际展览中心，广东东莞
周期：每年两届
市场范围：国际性
主办：雅式展览服务有限公司；杜塞尔多夫展览（中国）有限公司
地址：香港北角渣华道321号6楼
主办：杜塞尔多夫展览（上海）有限公司
地址：上海市浦东新区张江高科技园区科苑路88号上海德意志工商中心1号楼307室

Dongguan Shoes & China Shoeter
Venue: Guangdong Modern International Exhibition Center, Dongguan, Guangdong
Frequency: Biannual
Market Area: International
Organizer: Adsale Exhibition Services Ltd
Address: 6th Floor, 321 Java Road, North Point, Hong Kong
Organizer: Messe Dusseldorf (Shanghai) Co Ltd
Address: Unit 307, Tower 1 German Center for Industry and Trade Shanghai, 88 Keyuan Road, Zhangjiang Hi-Tech Park Pudong, Shanghai 201203, China

---

2011/11 -
☎ 010-6609 4505
✉ hetian112@sina.com
3760

2011中国高尔夫球用品博览会
地点：广东东莞
主办：中国商业联合会；东莞市人民政府
联系人：何天

China Golf Expo
Venue: Dongguan, Guangdong
Organizer: China General Chamber of Commerce; Gongguan Municipal Government

---

2011/11/09 - 11
☎ 010-8471 0628, 6445 3178
🖷 010-8472 3019, 6441 0962
www.auto-maintenance.com.cn
3765

第56届全国汽车保修检测诊断设备（秋季）展览会
地点：广东现代国际展览中心，广东东莞
内容：汽车维修设备及产品 汽车检测诊断设备及产品 汽车维修工具(手动、气动、电动) 汽车美容养护设备及产品 汽车喷涂设备及产品 汽车维修教学教具 轮胎翻新与循环利用设备及修补产品 加油站设备及产品 汽车环保服务及节能产品 汽车服务用品 汽车连锁经营
周期：每年一届
市场范围：全国性
主办：中国汽车保修行业协会；中国汽车维修行业协会

AMR 2011-Auto Maintenance & Repair
Venue: Guangdong Modern International Exhibition Center, Dongguan, Guangdong
Frequency: Annual
Market Area: National
Organizer: China Auto Maintenance Equipment Industry Association; China Automotive Maintenance and Repair Trade Association

2011/11/16 - 19
☎ 852-2763 9011
🖷 852-2341 0379
✉ jenny@paper-con.com.hk
www.paper-com.com.hk
3770

第十三届东莞国际模具及金属加工展
地点：广东现代国际展览中心，广东东莞
周期：每年一届
主办：通讯展览公司
地址：香港九龙观塘成业街11号华成工商中心5字楼15室

13th China Dongguan International Mould & Metalworking Exhibition
Venue: Guangdong Modern International Exhibition Center, Dongguan, Guangdong
Frequency: Annual
Organizer: Paper Communication Exhibition Service
Address: Rm. 15, 5/F. Wha Shing Center, 11 Shing Ypi St. Kwun Tong, Kowloon, Hong Kong
Contact: Jenny Leung

2011/11/16 - 19
☎ 852-2763 9011
🖷 852-2341 0379
✉ jenny@paper-con.com.hk
www.paper-com.com.hk
3780

第十三届东莞国际橡塑胶及包装展
地点：广东现代国际展览中心，广东东莞
主办：通讯展览公司
地址：香港九龙观塘成业街11号华成工商中心5字楼15室

13th China Dongguan International Plastics, Packaging & Rubber Exhibition
Venue: Guangdong Modern International Exhibition Center, Dongguan, Guangdong
Organizer: Paper Communication Exhibition Service
Address: Rm. 15, 5/F. Wha Shing Center, 11 Shing Ypi St. Kwun Tong, Kowloon, Hong Kong
Contact: Jenny Leung

2011/12/10 - 13
☎ 852-8211 2668
🖷 852-3405 8801
www.tick-fair.com
3870

广东（厚街）茶叶博览会
地点：广东现代国际展览中心，广东东莞
周期：每年一届
市场范围：国际性
主办：迪亿会展(香港)有限公司
地址：香港中环德辅道161－167号香港贸易中心402室

Guangdong (Houjie) Tea Expo
Venue: Guangdong Modern International Exhibition Center, Dongguan, Guangdong
Frequency: Annual
Market Area: International
Organizer: Tick Fair Company Limited
Address: RM 402-40,3 4/F Hong Kong Trade Center, No 161-167 Des Voeux Road Central, Hong Kong

2011/12/24 - 08
☎ 0769-8590 9009
🖷 0769-8583 0960, 8583 0970
3890

2011第11届东莞嘉年华时尚生活用品购物节
地点：广东现代国际展览中心，广东东莞
周期：每年一届
主办：奥华国际展览有限公司

11th Dongguan Shopping Festival
Venue: Guangdong Modern International Exhibition Center, Dongguan, Guangdong
Organizer: Auwa International Exhibition Co Ltd

广东-佛山 Guangdong-Foshan

2011/05 -
☎ 010-8260 6880转ext 91
🖷 010-8260 6883
✉ ciccyhuang@cnaico.com.cn
www.cnaico.com.cn
www.autochina.com.cn
3900

2011佛山国际汽车展览会
地点：广东佛山
主办：中国汽车工业国际合作总公司
地址：北京市海淀区中关村丹棱街3号A座

Foshan Intl Automobile Exhibition
Venue: Foshan, Guangdong
Organizer: China National Automotive Industry International Corp

广东-广州 Guangdong-Guangzhou

2011/02/24 - 26
☎ 020-3404 1988
🖷 020-8637 4257
✉ bestguangzhou@vip.163.com
www.84t.cn
3920

第八届广州(国际)车用空调及冷藏链技术展览会
地点：中国进出口商品交易会琶洲展馆，广东广州
内容：整车空调系统：各种轿车空调、客车空调、卡车空调、工程车空调、火车空调、轮船、飞机空调；车用空调配件：各种车用空调压缩机、电动机、暖风机、空调器、冷凝器、蒸发器、散热器、调温器、加热器、中冷器、空气干燥器、冷却风扇控制器、内部热交换器、暖风装置、各种冷凝器电子扇、贮液灌、热力膨胀阀；各种车用空调管路、生产设备、检测设备。车用空调用品：冷冻油、制冷剂、冷媒、清洁养护剂；冷冻冷藏设备：冷藏汽车、冷藏运输
周期：每年一届
市场范围：国际性
参展费用：8,800元/展位
主办：广州巴斯特展览有限公司
地址：广州新港东路238号世港国际公寓B栋601-604室（510308）

8th Guangzhou Intl Automotive Air-conditioning & Cold Chain Technology Exhibition
Venue: Chinese Import and Export Fair Pazhou Complex, Guangzhou, Guangdong
Profile: Vehicle air conditioning system: automotive air-conditioners, bus air-conditioners, truck air-conditioners, engineering truck air-conditioners, train air-conditioners, ship air conditioners, plane air-conditioners. Auto air-conditioning spare parts
Frequency: Annual
Market Area: International
Participated Fee: RMB 8,800/booth
Organizer: Guangzhou Best Exhibition Co Ltd
Address: Room 601-604, Flat B, Citycoin International Apartment, 238 Xingang East Road, Guangzhou

2011/03 -
☎ 010-6609 4505
✉ hetian112@sina.com
3930

第十届中国广州鞋业展览会
地点：广东广州
主办：中国商业联合会；广东省连锁经营协会
联系人：何天

10th Guangzhou Shoes Exhibition
Venue: Guangzhou, Guangdong
Organizer: China General Chamber of Commerce

2011/03/01 - 04
☎ 020-3810 6261, 3810 6263
🖷 020-3810 6200
✉ led-trust@ubm.com
info-trust@ubm.com
www.ledlightingchina-gz.com
3935

广州国际LED照明展
地点：中国进出口商品交易会琶洲展馆，广东广州
内容：LED室内照明，LED户外照明，LED装饰照明，LED交通灯，LED车用灯，LED显示屏，LED广告光源，LED芯片，LED封装及配套材料，LED背光源，LED制造设备及测试仪器，OLED（有机发光二极管）、LD（激光二极管）、EL（冷光源）、激光传感器等。
周期：每年一届
市场范围：国际性
上届规模 2010：展览面积30,000m²，参展商513家，参观人数42,524+7,150人
主办：广州闻信展览服务有限公司
地址：广州市天河区林和东华庭路4号富力天河商务大厦1306室（510610）

LED Lighting China
Venue: Chinese Import and Export Fair Pazhou Complex, Guangzhou, Guangdong
Profile: LED CHINA provides a perfect purchasing chain for global buyers, which gathers the leading LED enterprises with the most advanced products in China.
Frequency: Annual
Market Area: International
Statistics 2010: Exhibition Area 30,000m², Exhibitors 513, Visitors 42,524+7,150
Organizer: UBM Trust Co Ltd
Address: Rm 1306 Fu Li Tian He Business Mansion No 4 Hua Ting Rd Lin He Dong Rd, Guangzhou 510610, China

2011/03/01 - 04
☎ 020-3810 6261, 3810 6263
🖷 020-3810 6200
✉ led-trust@ubm.com
info-trust@ubm.com
www.signchina-gz.com
www.ubmtrust.com
3940

广东国际广告展
地点：中国进出口商品交易会琶洲展馆，广东广州
内容：展览展示器材、便携式展具系列、舞台架及其它POP产品；灯箱、发光产品、LCD广告机、三面及多面翻等；标牌、标识产品；3D立体产品、网络媒体、互动媒体、户外媒体、后期制作技术及其他各类广告媒体；广告礼品、书籍、图库、软件等；户内外数码打印喷绘设备、广告雕刻机等。
周期：每年一届
主办：广州闻信展览服务有限公司
地址：广州市天河区林和东华庭路4号富力天河商务大厦1306室（510610）

Sign China
Venue: Chinese Import and Export Fair Pazhou Complex, Guangzhou, Guangdong
Profile: Exhibition and Display Equipment, Light box, Signage, LCD, Acrylic Panel, Other POP Items; Large Format Printer, Printing Equipment, Miscellaneous Sign Materials & Components; Engraver, Laser, Cutters and Cutting Components; LED Lighting, LED Display, LED
Frequency: Annual
Organizer: UBM Trust Co Ltd
Address: Rm 1306 Fu Li Tian He Business Mansion, No 4 Hua Ting Rd, Lin He Dong Rd, Guangzhou 510610, China

2011/03/09 - 11
☎ 020-8912 8282
🖷 020-8912 8300
✉ zhangh@fairwindow.com.cn
http://siaf.fairwindow.com
3950

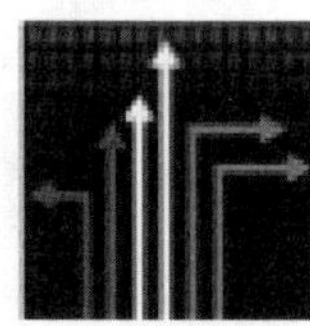

中国广州国际工业自动化技术及装备展览会
地点：中国进出口商品交易会琶洲展馆，广东广州
内容：传动、机械驱动系统及零部件、人机界面装置、工业机器人、电子零部件及辅助设备、工业通讯、机电零部件及辅助设备、培训及咨询、辅助设备、组装系统、感应技术（传感器）、材料处理装置、控制系统、连动技术、工业用电脑装备、微系统技术、低电压开关装置、机器零部件、仪器仪表
周期：每年一届
市场范围：国际性
性质：面向公众
入场券价格：业内观众凭名片登记进场
参展费用：标准展位：A区12,000/9m²，B区8,500/9m²
上届规模 2010：展览面积20,000m²，参展商317家，参观人数16,715人
主办：中国对外贸易中心（集团）；德国法兰克福展览有限公司；广州光亚法兰克福展览有限公司；德国美赛高法兰克福展览有限公司；广州富洋展览有限公司
承办：中国对外贸易广州展览公司
地址：广州市海珠区新港东路980号广交会展馆C区16号馆A层（510000）
联系人：张华

SPS
- Industrial Automation Fair Guangzhou
Venue: Chinese Import and Export Fair Pazhou Complex, Guangzhou, Guangdong
Profile: Drive Systems and Components, Human-Machine-Interface Devices, Industrial Robot, Electromechanical Components and Peripheral Equipment, Training and Consulting, Peripheral Equipment, Assembling System, Sensor Technology(Transducer), Materials Handling Devices, Controlling System, Interlock Technology, Industrial Computer Equipment, Micro-System Technology, Low-Voltage Switch Devices, Machine Components, Instruments and Meters.
Frequency: Annual
Market Area: International
Nature: Open to Public
Cost to Attend: Free to Trade Visitors
Participated Fee: Standard Booth RMB 12,000/9m²
Statistics 2010: Exhibition Area 20,000m², Exhibitors 317, Visitors 16,715
Organizer: China Foreign Trade Center (Group); Messe Frankfurt Exhibition GmbH; Guangzhou Guangya Messe Frankfurt Co Ltd; Mesago Messe Frankfurt GmbH; Guangzhou Overseas Trade Fairs Ltd
Contact：China Foreign Trade Guangzhou Exhibition General Corp
Address: Floor A, Hall 16, Area C, Canton Fair Complex, No.980 Xingang Dong Road, Haizhu District, Guangzhou, China
Contact: Bobby

2011/03/09 - 11
☎ 020-8625 9008, 8625 8323, 8625 7099
🖷 020-8625 9533
✉ info@gzbeautyexpo.com
www.gzbeautyexpo.com
3970

第34届广州国际美博会
地点：中国进出口商品交易会琶洲展馆，广东广州
内容：国际品牌、美容院、日化洗涤、养生、发廊、包装
始办年份：1989
周期：每年两届
市场范围：国际性
上届规模 2010：参展商2,000家（来自18个国家），参观人数310,000人
主办：广东省美容美发化妆品行业协会；广东博环美国际展览有限公司
地址：广东省广州市广园西路121号美博城A座写字楼五楼（510400）

34th Guangzhou International Beauty Expo - Spring 2011
Venue: Chinese Import and Export Fair Pazhou Complex, Guangzhou, Guangdong
Profile: International brands, beauty salons, personal care, nature health, hair salons, packaging.
Established Year: 1989
Frequency: Biannual
Market Area: International
Statistics 2010: Exhibitors 2,000 (came from 18 countries), Visitors 310,000
Organizer: Guangdong International Exhibitions Limited; Guangdong Beauty & Cosmetic Association
Address: 5th Floor, Building A121 Guang Yuan Road (West), Guangzhou 510400, China

2011/03/09 - 11
☎ 020-8912 8266, 8912 8281
🖷 020-8912 8082
转501, 8912 8300
✉ project2@fairwindow.com
www.waterchina-gz.com
3980

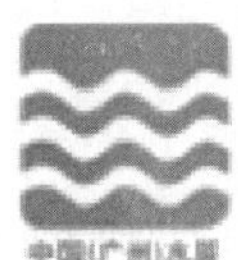

第12届中国（广州）国际给排水、水处理技术设备展览会
2011中国（广州）国际泵、阀门、管道展览会
地点：中国进出口商品交易会琶洲展馆，广东广州
内容：给水排水设备，水处理技术，水处理设备；泵设备,阀门设备,管道设备等
始办年份：2000
周期：每年一届
市场范围：国际性
性质：面向贸易观众
入场券价格：业内观众凭名片登记进场
参展费用：A区：净地1,100元/m^2（48m^2起），标准展位15,000元/12m^2；B区：净地830元/m^2（36m^2起），标准展位7,800元/9m^2
上届规模 2010：展览面积12,000m^2，参展商500家（国外展商60家，来自20个国家），参观人数15,000人（专业贸易观众70,000人）
主办：中国对外贸易中心(集团)
承办：中国对外贸易广州展览总公司
地址：广州市海珠区新港东路980号广交会展馆C区16号馆A层（510014）
联系人：梁兵，黄炜坚

Water, Wastewater & Water Treatment China 2011
Pump, Vale & Pipe China 2011
Venue: Chinese Import and Export Fair Pazhou Complex, Guangzhou, Guangdong
Profile: Water & Wastewater Water Treatment Equipment Industrial Water Treatment Drinking Water Treatment Equipment/ Process Water Filtration/Disinfection Equipment Membrane Separation Technology Instruments, Controls and Automation Sewer Inspection, Cleaning, Maintenance
Established Year: 2000
Frequency: Annual
Market Area: International
Nature: Trade Only
Cost to Attend: Free
Participated Fee: Raw Space RMB 1,100/m^2（min 48m^2）, Standard Booth (min 12m^2) RMB 15,000/booth
Statistics 2010: Exhibition Area 12,000m^2, Exhibitors 500（foreigners 60, came from 20 countries）, Visitors 15,000（trade visitors 70,000）
Sponsor: China Foreign Trade Center (Group)(CFTC)
Organizer: China Foreign Trade Guangzhou Exhibition General Corp
Address: Floor A, Hall 16, Area C, Canton Fair Complex, No.980 Xingang Dong Road, Haizhu District, Guangzhou, China
Contact: Ms Liang Bing, Mr Huang Weijian

2011/03/09 - 11
☎ 020-8912 8263,
8912 8268/8269
🖷 020-8912 8082 转ext 501,
8912 8300
✉ pfp@fairwindow.com.cn
http://sinoprint.fairwindow.com
3990

第十八届华南国际印刷工业展览会
2011中国国际标签印刷技术展览会
地点：中国进出口商品交易会琶洲展馆，广东广州
内容：印前设备、数码印刷设备、标签、柔性及凹性印刷设备、胶印设备及机械、丝网印刷、包装印刷设备、装订机械设备、印刷物料及配件、耗材
始办年份：1994
市场范围：国际性
性质：面向贸易观众
入场券价格：业内观众凭名片登记进场
参展费用：标准展台：A区18,450元/9m^2，B区12,000元/9m^2，C区7,800元/9m^2
上届规模 2010：展览面积45,000m^2，参展商627家（来自16个国家），参观人数45,362人
主办：中国对外贸易广州展览总公司；中国对外贸易广州展览总公司；北京雅展展览服务有限公司；广东省出版印刷物资有限公司
联络：中国对外贸易广州展览总公司
地址：广州市海珠区新港东路980号广交会展馆C区16号馆A层（510335）
联系人：杨先生

The 18th South China International Exhibition on Printing Industry
The China International Exhibition on Label Printing Technology
Venue: Chinese Import and Export Fair Pazhou Complex, Guangzhou, Guangdong
Profile: Pre-press Equipment & Software, Digital Printing Equipment, Label, Flexor & Gravure Printing Equipment, Offset Printing Equipment & Machinery, Screen Printing, Package Printing, Binding Equipment, Printing Materials & Accessories, Consumables
Established Year: 1994
Market Area: International
Nature: Trade Only
Cost to Attend: Free to Trade Visitors
Participated Fee: Standard Booth RMB 18,450/9m^2
Statistics 2010: Exhibition Area 45,000m^2, Exhibitors 627（came from 16 countries）, Visitors 45,362
Organizer: China Foreign Trade Guangzhou Exhibition General Corp; China Foreign Trade Guangzhou Exhibition Corp; Beijing Adsale Exhibition Services Ltd; Guangdong Provincial Publishing & Printing Materials Co Ltd
Contact: China Foreign Trade Guangzhou Exhibition General Corp
Address: Floor A, Hall 16, Area C, Canton Fair Complex, No.980 Xingang Dong Road, Haizhu District, Guangzhou, China
Contact: Bobby

2011/03/18 - 21
☎ 020-8912 8023, 8912 8016
🖷 020-8912 8251转ext 101
✉ hhc@fairwindow.com.cn
http://hhc.fairwindow.com
http://officefurniture.fairwindow.com
4010

中国广州国际家居饰品/用品展览会
地点：中国进出口商品交易会琶洲展馆，广东广州
内容：地毯、挂毯、画、镜及相框、陶瓷、玻璃、树脂、塑料、金属等制品、人造花卉、木/石雕（刻）制品、灯饰、钟、电话、其他
始办年份：2005
周期：每年一届
市场范围：国际性
性质：面向贸易观众
入场券价格：20元
参展费用：净地790元/m^2，7,900元/标准展位
上届规模 2010：展览面积35,000m^2，参观人数37,775人
主办：中国对外贸易中心（集团）
承办：中国对外贸易广州展览总公司
地址：广州市海珠区新港东路980号广交会展馆C区16号馆A层（510036）
联系人：何思慧，于雯

Homedecor & Housewares China 2010
Venue: Chinese Import and Export Fair Pazhou Complex, Guangzhou, Guangdong
Profile: Carpets, Rugs, Picture, Mirrors, Frames, Pottery, Glassware, Artificial Flowers, Lighting, Clock, Stone Carving, Accessories, Others
Established Year: 2005
Frequency: Annual
Market Area: International
Nature: Trade Only
Cost to Attend: RMB 20:-
Participated Fee: Raw Space RMB 790/m^2, Standard Booth RMB 7,900/booth
Statistics 2010: Exhibition Area 35,000m^2, Visitors 37,775
Sponsor: China Foreign Trade Center (Group)
Organizer: China Foreign Trade Guangzhou Exhibition General Corporation
Address: Floor A, Hall 16, Area C, Canton Fair Complex, No.980 Xingang Dong Road, Haizhu District, Guangzhou, China
Contact: Gina Ho, Stephanie Yu

2011/03/18 - 21
☎ 020-8912 8023, 8912 8016
🖷 020-8912 8251转ext 101
✉ hhc@fairwindow.com.cn
http://htc.fairwindow.com
http://officefurniture.fairwindow.com
4020

hometextile
intertextile
GUANGZHOU, CHINA

中国（广州）国际家用纺织品及辅料博览会
地点：中国进出口商品交易会琶洲展馆，广东广州
内容：家居用装饰布及装饰品，床/浴室用/桌用/厨房用纺织品，地毯及地面覆盖物，各类室内配件、靠垫、抱枕及挂件，装饰专供纺织品，纺织类工艺品，其它家用纺织品，家用纺织品相关产品及服务
始办年份：1999
周期：每年一届
市场范围：国际性
性质：面向贸易观众
入场券价格：20元
参展费用：净地790元/m²，7,900元/标准展位
上届规模 2010：展览面积20,000m²
主办：中国纺织工业协会；中国对外贸易中心（集团）
承办：中国对外贸易广州展览总公司
地址：广州市海珠区新港东路980号广交会展馆C区16号馆A层（510036）
联系人：何思慧，于雯

China (Guangzhou) International Trade Fair for Home Textiles
Venue: Chinese Import and Export Fair Pazhou Complex, Guangzhou, Guangdong
Profile: Wall and window decorations, Upholstery fabric, Textiles for contract market, Interior design and textile handicrafts, Accessories, Carpets and rugs, Home textile related products and services, Home textile design
Established Year: 1999
Frequency: Annual
Market Area: International
Nature: Trade Only
Cost to Attend: RMB 20:-
Participated Fee: Raw Space RMB 790/m², Standard Booth RMB 7,900/booth
Statistics 2010: Exhibition Area 20,000m²
Sponsor: China National Textile & Apparel Council; China Foreign Trade Center (Group)
Organizer: China Foreign Trade Guangzhou Exhibition General Corporation
Address: Floor A, Hall 16, Area C, Canton Fair Complex, No.980 Xingang Dong Road, Haizhu District, Guangzhou, China
Contact: Gina Ho, Stephanie Yu

2011/03/18 - 21
☎ 020-8912 8023, 8912 8016
🖷 020-8912 8251转ext 101
✉ ciff@fairwindow.com.cn
http://outdoor.fairwindow.com
http://officefurniture.fairwindow.com
4030

中国广州户外及休闲展览会
地点：中国进出口商品交易会琶洲展馆，广东广州
内容：庭园家具、休闲桌椅、遮阳设备、户外摆设和用品；户外烧烤工具、帐篷、篷方、花园规划与维护、花植物养护器材设备、园林工具、其他
始办年份：2008
周期：每年一届
市场范围：国际性
性质：面向贸易观众
入场券价格：20元
参展费用：净地790元/m²，标准展位7,900元/9m²
上届规模 2010：展览面积15,000m²
主办：中国对外贸易中心（集团）；中国食品土畜进出口商会
承办：中国对外贸易广州展览总公司
地址：广州市海珠区新港东路980号广交会展馆C区16号馆A层（510036）
联系人：何思慧，于雯

China International Outdoor & Leisure Fair
Venue: Chinese Import and Export Fair Pazhou Complex, Guangzhou, Guangdong
Profile: Garden Furniture, Leisure Tables & Chairs, Sun-shading Equipment, Outdoor Items, Garden Design & Maintenance, Plants & Plant Care, Garden Care & Accessories, Others
Established Year: 2008
Frequency: Annual
Market Area: International
Nature: Trade Only
Cost to Attend: RMB 20:-
Participated Fee: Raw Space RMB 790/m², Standard Booth RMB 7,900/booth
Statistics 2010: Exhibition Area 15,000m²
Sponsor: China Foreign Trade Center (Group); China Chamber of Commerce of Import & Export of Food Stuffs, Native Produce & Animal By Products
Organizer: China Foreign Trade Guangzhou Exhibition General Corporation
Address: Floor A, Hall 16, Area C, Canton Fair Complex, No.980 Xingang Dong Road, Haizhu District, Guangzhou, China
Contact: Gina Ho, Stephanie Yu

2011/03/18 - 21
☎ 020-8912 8016, 8912 8062
🖷 020-8912 8251转ext 102
✉ ciff@fairwindow.com.cn
www.ciff-gz.com
4040

中国广州国际家具博览会(民用家具展)
地点：中国进出口商品交易会琶洲展馆，广东广州
内容：现代家具、客厅家具、厨房家具、传统家具、卧室家具、户外家具、软体家具、餐厅家具、儿童家具、其它；古典家具、欧式家具、美式家具、新古典家具、古典软体家具、中式红木家具、其它
始办年份：1998
周期：每年两届
市场范围：国际性
性质：面向贸易观众
入场券价格：20元
参展费用：净地790元/m²，7,900元/标准展位
上届规模 2010：展览面积240,000m²，参展商785家，参观人数82,204人
主办：中国家具协会；中国对外贸易中心（集团）；广东省家具协会；香港家私装饰厂商总会
承办：中国对外贸易广州展览总公司
地址：广州市海珠区新港东路980号广交会展馆C区16号馆A层（510014）
联系人：何思慧，于雯

China International Furniture Fair (Guangzhou)
– Home Furniture
Venue: Chinese Import and Export Fair Pazhou Complex, Guangzhou, Guangdong
Profile: Modern Furniture, Living Room Furniture, Kitchen Furniture, Traditional Furniture, Bedroom Furniture, Outdoor Furniture, Soft Furniture, Dining Room Furniture, Children Furniture, Others; Classical Furniture, European Style Furniture, American Style Furniture, Neo-classical Furniture, Classical Soft Furniture, Chinese Mahogany Furniture, Others
Established Year: 1998
Frequency: Biannual
Market Area: International
Nature: Trade Only
Cost to Attend: RMB 20:-
Participated Fee: Raw Space RMB 790/m², Standard Booth RMB 7,900/booth
Statistics 2010: Exhibition Area 240,000m², Exhibitors 785, Visitors 82,204
Sponsor: China National Furniture Association, China Foreign Trade Center (Group), Guangdong Furniture Association, Hong Kong Furniture & Decoration Trade Association
Organizer: China Foreign Trade Guangzhou Exhibition General Corporation
Address: Floor A, Hall 16, Area C, Canton Fair Complex, No.980 Xingang Dong Road, Haizhu District, Guangzhou, China
Contact: Gina Ho, Stephanie Yu

2011/03/24 - 26
☎ 020-8667 7763
🖷 020-8667 4041
✉ hkbissenli@163.com
4050

2011广州国际个人医疗保健器械及用品展览会
地点：保利世贸博览馆，广东广州
内容：自检类产品区：各类家用电子检测仪（血压仪、血糖仪、体温计、脂肪测试仪）、远程监测、治疗预警器材、心脏及生命特征监测仪；理疗类产品区：各类物理家用理疗器材、磁场、水

2011 Guangzhou Personal healthcare Exhibition
Venue: Poly World Trade Expo Center, Guangzhou, Guangdong
First Session
Frequency: Annual
Market Area: National

质量改善器具、居家生活改善型电子电器；康复类产品区：各类助行器材、康复牵引辅具、护理辅助器具等；养生类产品区:天然保健提取物品、药妆个人护理用品、口腔护理产品。
首届
周期：每年一届
市场范围：全国性
性质：面向公众
入场券价格：10元
预计规模：总面积20,000m²
主办：中国国际经济技术交流中心；广州市医疗器械行业协会；广州市医药质量管理协会
承办：广州市金晔展览有限公司
地址：广东省广州市越秀区流花路119号（510620）
联系人：李晓冬

Nature: Open to Public
Cost to Attend: RMB 10:-
Expectation: Gross Area 20,000m²
Organizer: Guangzhou Jinye Exhibition Co Ltd

2011/03/24 - 26
☎ 021-5045 6700转ext 223
🖷 021-5045 9355
✉ gitf@hmf-china.com
www.gitf.com.cn
4060

广州国际旅游展览会
地点：广州锦汉展览中心，广东广州
内容：国家、地区旅游局及旅游协会；出入境旅行社；酒店、酒店集团及度假中心；旅游景点、主题公园、高尔夫俱乐部；豪华旅行房车租赁及销售、自驾游用品及装备、自驾游服务、自驾游俱乐部；旅游休闲地产；旅游户外用品及装备；航空公司、航空联盟；游览车、汽车租赁及铁路机构；旅游相关服务公司；旅游纪念品；旅游媒体、网络及电子商务；邮轮及海上游；商务及奖励旅游；教育与培训旅游
周期：每年一届
市场范围：国际性
上届规模 2010：参展商506家，参观人数60,000人
主办：汉诺威米兰展览(上海)有限公司
地址：上海市浦东新区银霄路393号百安居浦东商务大厦301室（201204）
联系人：汪村彦先生

Guangzhou International Travel Fair
Venue: Guangzhou Jinhan Exhibition Center, Guangzhou, Guangdong
Profile: National/Region Travel Organizations and Tourist Association; Travel agencies; Hotel, hotel group and holiday camps; Recreation vehicle and sedan rental and sales; Self-driving equipment, self-driving service, self-driving club; Leisure real estate; Tour Equipment; Tourism Attractions such as Theme parks; Resorts & golf courses; Airlines; Coach, car rental and railways companies; Cruise ship and operators; Business and incentive travel; Travel education and training; Travel related companies; Souvenir manufacturers and dealers; Tourism media, network companies/E-commerce enterprises
Frequency: Annual
Market Area: International
Statistics 2010: Exhibitors 506, Visitors 60,000
Organizer: Hannover Milano Fairs Shanghai Ltd
Address: 301 B&Q Pudong Office Tower 393 Yinxiao Rd, Pudong, Shanghai
Contact: Mr Austin Wang

2011/03/27 - 30
☎ 020-8755 2468转ext 12, 8755 2468转ext 15
🖷 020-8755 2970
✉ k.lee@koelnmesse.cn
www.interzum-guangzhou.com
4070

中国广州国际木工机械、家具配料展览会
地点：中国进出口商品交易会琶洲展馆，广东广州
内容：家具生产原料及配件；软体家具和床具生产机械、原料及配件；室内装饰机械、材料及组件、木工、家具生产机械及辅助设备；其它：媒体、贸易推广机构
始办年份：2004
周期：每年一届
市场范围：国际性
性质：面向贸易观众
参展费用：净地（24m²起）1,300元/m²，普通标摊（9m²起）1,500元/m²，高级标摊（18m²起）1,700元/m²，联合参展费2,500元/每一家联合参展商
上届规模 2010：展览面积100,000m²，参展商887家（国外展商198家，来自24个国家），参观人数43,709人
主办：科隆国际展览有限公司；中国对外贸易中心（集团）
承办：科隆展览有限公司；中国对外贸易广州展览总公司
地址：广州市天河区天河北路183号大都会广场3311室科隆展览有限公司（510620）
联系人：李伟莉,梁绍俊

interzum guangzhou
Venue: Chinese Import and Export Fair Pazhou Complex, Guangzhou, Guangdong
Profile: Materials and Components for Furniture Production; Machines, Materials and Components for Upholstery and Bedding; Machines, Materials and Components for Interior Works; Machines and Auxiliary Machines for Woodworking and Furniture Production
Established Year: 2004
Frequency: Annual
Market Area: International
Nature: Trade Only
Participated Fee: Raw Space RMB 1,700/m²(min 24m²2)
Statistics 2010: Exhibition Area 100,000m², Exhibitors 887 (foreigners 198, came from 24 countries), Visitors 43,709
Sponsor: Koelnmesse GmbH; China Foreign Trade Center (Group)
Organizer: Koelnmesse Co Ltd; China Foreign Trade Guangzhou Exhibition Corp.
Address: Koelnmesse Co Ltd, Room 3311, Metro Plaza, No.183 Tianhe Road (North), TianHe District, Guangzhou
Contact: Karen Lee, Mattis Liang

2011/03/27 - 30
☎ 020-8912 8023, 8912 8016
🖷 020-8912 8251转ext 101
✉ ciff@fairwindow.com.cn
www.ciffgz.com
http://officefurniture.fairwindow.com
4080

中国广州国际家具博览会（办公环境展）
地点：中国进出口商品交易会琶洲展馆，广东广州
内容：办公家具：办公坐具、书柜、办公桌、保险柜、屏风、储物柜、高隔段、文件柜、办公配件、其他；公共场所家具：机场家具、剧院/礼堂家具等；公共座椅系列：学校家具、实验室家具；酒店、宾馆、承造家具及其他商用家具；办公场所相关设施：照明系列、墙材系列、铺地材料系列、办公设备和技术
始办年份：2005
周期：每年一届
市场范围：国际性
性质：面向贸易观众
入场券价格：20元
参展费用：净地790元/m²，7,900元/标准展位
上届规模 2010：展览面积130,000m²，参展商610家（国外展商42家），参观人数52,648人
主办：中国家具协会；中国对外贸易中心（集团）；广东省家具协会；香港家私装饰厂商总会
承办：中国对外贸易广州展览总公司
地址：广州市海珠区新港东路980号广交会展馆C区16号馆A层（510036）
联系人：谭洁莹，周文缨

China International Furniture Fair (Guangzhou)
– Office Show
Venue: Chinese Import and Export Fair Pazhou Complex, Guangzhou, Guangdong
Profile:Office Furniture: Office Seating, Book Shelves, Office Desk/Table, Safe, Cabinets, Partition Storage Units, Partitioning Wall Filing, Cabinets, Office Accessories, Others; Public Furniture: Airport Furniture, Theatre/Auditoria Furniture, Public Seating, School Furniture, Laboratory Furniture; Hotel\Restaurant\Contract Furniture, Interiors Lightings, Wall Coverings, Floor Coverings, Office-Related Equipment & Technology
Established Year: 2005
Frequency: Annual
Market Area: International
Nature: Trade Only
Cost to Attend: RMB 20:-
Participated Fee: Raw Space RMB 790/m², Standard Booth RMB 7,900/booth
Statistics 2010: Exhibition Area 130,000m², Exhibitors 610 (foreigners 42), Visitors 52,648
Sponsor: China National Furniture Association; China Foreign Trade Center (Group); Guangdong Furniture Association; Hong Kong Furniture & Decoration Trade Association
Organizer: China Foreign Trade Guangzhou Exhibition General Corporation
Address: Floor A, Hall 16, Area C, Canton Fair Complex, No.980 Xingang Dong Road, Haizhu District, Guangzhou, China
Contact: Tan Jieying, Zhou Wenying

2011/03/29 - 31
☎ 020-6107 8749, 6107 8749, 6107 8749
🖷 020-6108 9459
✉ gzyfzl2001@163.com
www.gzyfzl.com
4090

2011广州药交会第十八届全国药品保健品（广州）交易会
地点：广州锦汉展览中心，广东广州
内容：药品类：医药新特品种、处方药品、ＯＴＣ药品、中西成药、生物制药、中药饮片、植物提取物、民族医药、原料药、医药中间体、消毒液。保健品类：营养保健食品、保健饮料、保健茶、保健酒、微量元素制品、特殊用途化妆品、减增肥保健品、性保健、保健用品、保健治疗仪、保健器具等。药店（房）设施：旋转盘药架、库房药架、调剂台、中药台柜、中药饮片柜、自动药品分包机、全自动预包机、自动数药机、剥药机、中药煎药机、药店管理系统等。医药保健品生产包装类：医药保健生产设备、包装设备、喷码设备、医药包装材料。
始办年份：2002
周期：每年两届
市场范围：全国性
性质：面向公众
参展费用：8,000元/展位
上届规模：展览面积29,800m²，参展商872家，参观人数32,600人
主办：中国医药保健国际贸易促进会；广东省保健食品行业协会
承办：广州市艺帆展览服务有限公司
地址：广州市天河区燕岭路25-27号银燕大厦201室（510507）
联系人：江桂发 13710502143
QQ: 1405764838

The 18 China Medicine and Healthcare Products (Guangzhou) Exhibition 2011
Venue: Guangzhou Jinhan Exhibition Center, Guangzhou, Guangdong
Established Year: 2002
Frequency: Biannual
Market Area: National
Nature: Open to Public
Participated Fee: RMB 8,000/booth
Statistics 2010: Exhibition Area 29,800m², Exhibitors 872, Visitors 32,600
Organizer: Guangzhou Yifan Exhibition Service Co

2011/03/29 - 31
☎ 020-6107 8749, 6107 8749, 6107 8749
🖷 020-6108 9459
✉ gzyfzl2001@163.com
www.gzyfzl.com
4100

2011广州国际食品展暨广州进口食品展览会
地点：广州锦汉展览中心，广东广州
内容：进口食品展区、食品饮料区；饮料饮品、餐饮食品、休闲食品、方便食品、糖果糕点、调味品、水产品、海产品、酒类、茶；生鲜水果蔬菜、干鲜蔬菜；营养品健康食品区；优质农产品及精品粮油区；食品添加剂及配料；食品加工及包装设备区：食品加工设备、肉类加工设备、金属探测器、果蔬加工设备、冷藏技术、发酵生物**始办年份**：2002
周期：每年两届
市场范围：国际性
性质：面向公众
主办：中国医药保健国际贸易促进会；广东省保健食品行业协会
承办：广州市艺帆展览服务有限公司
地址：广州市天河区燕岭路25-27号银燕大厦201室（510507）
联系人：江桂发 13710502143
QQ: 1405764838

Guangzhou Food Fair
Venue: Guangzhou Jinhan Exhibition Center, Guangzhou, Guangdong
Established Year: 2002
Frequency: Biannual
Market Area: International
Nature: Open to Public
Organizer: Guangzhou Yifan Exhibition Service Co

2011/03/29 - 31
☎ 020-6107 8749, 6107 8749, 6107 8749
🖷 020-6108 9459
✉ gzyfzl2001@163.com
www.gzyfzl.com
4110

2011第十届中国（广州）国际营养品/健康食品及有机产品展览会
地点：广州锦汉展览中心，广东广州
内容：营养品与健康食品、营养素、营养补充剂、营养强化食品、富营养食品、功能（保健）食品、天然滋补品、有机产品与绿色食品。
论坛主题：中国营养产业发展的前景；营养产业品牌发展论坛；有机食品安全生产管理与认证。
始办年份：2002
周期：每年两届
市场范围：国际性
性质：面向公众
参展费用：8,000元/展位
主办：中国医药保健国际贸易促进会；广东省保健食品行业协会
承办：广州市艺帆展览服务有限公司
地址：广州市天河区燕岭路25-27号银燕大厦201室（510507）
联系人：江桂发 13710502143
QQ: 1405764838

CINHOE
Guangzhou Nutrition and Organic Food Exhibition
Venue: Guangzhou Jinhan Exhibition Center, Guangzhou, Guangdong
Established Year: 2002
Frequency: Biannual
Market Area: International
Nature: Open to Public
Participated Fee: RMB 8,000/booth
Organizer: Guangzhou Yifan Exhibition Service Co

2011/04/08 - 10
☎ 020-8358 7012, 8358 7037
🖷 020-8358 7016
✉ expo@ctoy.cn
babyfair@ctoy.cn
www.chinababyfair.com
4120

第2届广州国际婴童用品展
地点：广州保利世贸博览馆，广东广州
内容：广东是婴童用品的主要产区，在广州举办婴童用品展有着得天独厚的地域优势，加之与中国内地业界第一展"广州国际玩具及模型展"同期举办，更是资源共享，为参展商和采购商提供更多的商机，两个展会的互动优势十分明显。范围有婴儿推车、座椅、幼儿学步车、童车、奶瓶奶嘴、婴童床及用品、婴儿纸尿片、婴童服、鞋、帽、婴儿电子用品、婴童护肤及沐浴品、婴儿食品、保健品、婴童教育用品、婴儿玩具
周期：每年一届
市场范围：国际性
性质：面向贸易观众
参展费用：标准展位7000元/9m²，净地730元/m²
预计规模：展出面积15,000m²，参展商300家，参观人数5,000人

The 2nd Guangzhou Intl Baby Product Fair
Venue: Poly World Trade Expo Center, Guangzhou, Guangdong
Profile: As the key production base for baby products, Guangdong is endowed with edge in geography for a show in this realm. Since Guangzhou Intl Baby Product Fair is held at the same period with Guangzhou Intl Toy and Hobby Fair, the largest toy fair in mainland China, the two share resource with each other, providing greater trade opportunity for exhibitors and buyers. Exhibits: Baby Strollers, Seats, Baby Walkers, Ride-ons, Diapers, Baby Electronic Products, Baby Foods, Baby Health Products, Baby Toys, Nursing Bottles, Soothers, Cribs and Related Articles, Apparel, Shoes and Hats, Skin-Caring and Bathing Articles, Baby Educational Products.
Frequency: Annual
Market Area: International

主办：广东省玩具协会；广东玩具文化经济发展研究会
地址：广州市淘金北路正平南街1号2楼F室（510095）
联系人：郑小姐,王小姐
QQ：1253936471

Nature: Trade Only
Participated Fee: Standard Booth RMB 7,000/booth, Raw Space RMB 730/m^2
Organizer: Guangdong Toy Association; Guangdong Research Council of Toy Cultural & Economic Development
Address: 2/F, 1 Zhengping St. S., Taojin Road N, Guangzhou, China
Contact: Ms Zheng, Ms Wang

2011/04/08 - 10
☎ 020-8358 7012, 8358 7037
🖷 020-8358 7016
✉ expo@ctoy.cn
fair@ctoy.cn
www.chinababyfair.com

4130

广州玩具展

第23届广州国际玩具及模型展览会

地点：保利世贸博览馆，广东广州
内容：此展地处全球最大的玩具和模型产区，加之毗邻港、澳，有着无可比拟的地利办展优势。展会历经二十多年的发展和积淀，以其专业化、国际化和卓著成效受到了业界的首肯，成为亚洲第二大、中国内地最具影响力的业界展会。由于与“广州国际婴童用品展”同期举办，强化资源共享，为展商和买家拓展了更广泛的商贸领域、提供了更多商机，充分显示了两个展会的互动优势。 展品范围：电子电动玩具、塑胶玩具、布毛绒玩具、娃娃、充气玩具、木制、纸品玩具、学习机、游乐设施、模型、动漫品牌授权
始办年份：1989
周期：每年一届
市场范围：国际性
性质：面向贸易观众
参展费用：标准展位7,000元/9m^2，净地730元/m^2
预计规模：展出面积45,200m^2，参展商750家，参观人数27,000人
主办：广东省玩具协会；广东玩具文化经济发展研究会
地址：广州市淘金北路正平南街1号2楼F室（510095）
联系人：郑小姐,王小姐
QQ：1253936471

23rd Guangzhou Intl Toy & Hobby Fair

Venue: Poly World Trade Expo Center, Guangzhou, Guangdong
Profile: Founded in the largest toy and model production base and adjacent to Hong Kong and Macau, Guangzhou Intl Toy & Hobby Fair sees incomparable location superiority. With development of over 20 years, it has been highly recognized for its specialism, globalization and efficiency and grown into the second-largest toy fair in Asia and the largest one in China. Concurrent with the Guangzhou Intl Baby Product Fair, it shares more resources and explores wider business prospect for exhibitors and buyers. Fully displaying their interactive power, the two Fairs will provide greater opportunity for the trade. Exhibits: Electronic and Electrical Toys ,Amusement Play-sets ,Plastic Toys ,Baby Strollers, Ride-ons, Cribs Plush and Cloth Toys ,Toy and Model Supporting Products ,Dolls ,Animation and Comic Character Licensing, Inflatable Toys ,Airplane, Boat and Car Models ,Wooden and Paper Toys ,Various Miniature Action and Fixed Models ,Learning Systems
Established Year: 1989
Frequency: Annual
Market Area: International
Nature: Trade Only
Participated Fee: Standard Booth RMB 7,000/9m^2, Raw Space RMB 730/m^2
Organizer: Guangdong Toy Association; Guangdong Research Council of Toy Cultural & Economic Development
Address: 2/F, 1 Zhengping St. S., Taojin Road N, Guangzhou, China
Contact: Ms Zheng, Ms Wang

2011/04/14 - 18
☎ 020-2831 9715
🖷 020-2831 9715
✉ gzkhzl3618@126.com

4140

第六届中国（广州）国际建材交易会暨红星美凯龙直销周

地点：广州国际采购中心，广东广州
内容：卫浴陶瓷类、地面铺装材料、建筑装饰五金类、整体橱柜与材料、整体家居类、建筑装饰玻璃类，各种门窗、天花吊顶及幕墙类、墙纸/布艺/室内装饰及材料类、涂料、化学建材类、石材
参展费用：B1区：标准展位15,000元(双面开加收1,500元），净地(36m^{2}起)1,300元/m^2；B2区：标准展位13,800元(双面开加收1,300元），净地(36m^{2}起)1,200元/m^2
主办：广州国际采购中心
承办：广州科汉展览有限公司
地址：广州市天河区东圃大观南路18号挚晟大厦B栋403室（510660）
联系人：宋漫辉

6th China (Guangzhou) Building Materials Fair

Venue: Guangzhou Mart, Guangzhou, Guangdong
Participated Fee: Standard Booth RMB 15,000, Corner unit add RMB 1,500, Raw Space (min 36m^2) RMB 1,300/m^2
Organizer: Guangzhou Kehan Exhibition Co Ltd

2011/04/21 - 27
☎ 020-2894 6525
🖷 020-2894 6456
✉ chenjin666@163.com

4150

2011第六届广州国际采购博览会

地点：广州国际采购中心，广东广州
内容：现代家具：客厅家具、卧室家具、软体/沙发、酒店家具、藤制家具、餐厅家具、儿童家具、办公家具、户外/休闲家具、教育家具、厨房家具、金属家具、其它家具；古典家具：欧式家具、美式家具、新古典家具、古典软体家具、中式红木家具、其它家具；家居用品展区 餐具器皿：陶瓷、玻璃、金属、塑料器皿、餐桌装饰品、餐具、小家电、厨房电器等礼品摆设：手工艺品、礼品文具、花艺、熏香、蜡烛、限量版设计品、节能环保用品等居家艺术：家具及配饰、灯饰、家居挂饰/装饰画及配件、镜子、花园用品等
始办年份：2006
周期：每年一届
市场范围：地区性
性质：面向公众
上届规模 2010：展览面积76,000m^2，参展商3,000家
主办：广州国际采购中心，广州华亚展览服务有限公司
地址：广东省广州市天河区涌东路30号德添商务中心215室（510665）
联系人：陈晋

6th Guangzhou Purchasing Fair

Venue: Guangzhou Mart, Guangzhou, Guangdong
Established Year: 2006
Frequency: Annual
Market Area: Regional
Nature: Open to Public
Statistics 2010: Exhibition Area 76,000m^2, Exhibitors 3,000
Organizer: Guangzhou Mart

2011/04/15 – 19
☎ 400-888 999
+86-20-28 888 999
(境外overseas)
www.cantonfair.org.cn
4145

第109届中国进出口商品交易会（第一期）
地点：中国进出口商品交易会展馆，广东广州
内容：电子及家电、照明、车辆及配件、机械、五金工具、建材、化工产品、进口产品
承办：中国对外贸易中心

107th China Import and Export Fair Phase 1
Venue: China Import and Export Fair Complex, Guangzhou, Guangdong
Profile: Large Machinery and Equipment, Small Machinery, Bicycles, Motorcycles, Vehicle Spare Parts, Chemical Products, Hardware, Tools, Vehicles (Outdoor), Construction Machinery (Outdoor), Household Electrical Appliances, Consumer Electronics, Electronic and Electrical Products, Computer and Communication Products, Lighting Equipment, Building and Decoration? Materials, Sanitary and Bathroom Equipment, International Pavilion
Organizer: China Foreign Trade Centre

2011/04/23 – 27
☎ 400-888 999
+86-20-28 888 999
(境外overseas)
www.cantonfair.org.cn
4155

第109届中国进出口商品交易会（第二期）
地点：中国进出口商品交易会展馆，广东广州
内容：日用消费品、礼品、家居装饰品
承办：中国对外贸易中心

107th China Import and Export Fair Phase 2
Venue: China Import and Export Fair Complex, Guangzhou, Guangdong
Profile: Kitchen & Tableware, General Ceramics, Art Ceramics, Home Decorations, Glass Artware,
Furniture, Weaving, Rattan and Iron Arts, Gardening Products, Stone and Iron Products (Outdoor)
Household Items, Personal Care Products, Toiletries, Clocks, Watches & Optical Instruments,
Toys, Gifts and Premiums, Festival Products
Organizer: China Foreign Trade Centre

2011/05/01 – 05
☎ 400-888 999
+86-20-28 888 999
(境外overseas)
www.cantonfair.org.cn
4156

第109届中国进出口商品交易会（第三期）
地点：中国进出口商品交易会展馆，广东广州
内容：纺织服装、鞋类、办公箱包及休闲用品、医药及医疗保健、食品及土特产品
承办：中国对外贸易中心

107th China Import and Export Fair Phase 3
Venue: China Import and Export Fair Complex, Guangzhou, Guangdong
Profile: Men and Women's Clothes, Kid's Wear, Underwear, Sports and Casual Wear, Furs, Leather, Down & Related Products, Fashion Accessories and Fittings, Home Textiles, Textile Raw Materials & Fabrics, Carpets & Tapestries, Food, Native Produce, Medicines and Health Products, Medical Devices, Disposables and Dressings, Sports, Travel and Recreation Products, Office Supplies, Shoes
Cases and Bags
Organizer: China Foreign Trade Centre

2011/05/08 - 11
☎ 010-8351 1589, 8353 3198
🖷 010-8353 3198
✉ liuqsh@northexpo.com.cn
laurence@northexpo.com.cn
www.cipas.com.cn
4160

第四届广州国际宠物水族用品展
地点：保利世贸博览馆，广东广州
内容：以宠物水族用品生产商、贸易商及观赏鱼供应商为展商主体，以构建国内外宠物水族用品贸易桥梁为宗旨，以促进中国宠物水族产业健康发展为目的的专业贸易展览会。
始办年份：2008
周期：每年一届
市场范围：国际性
上届规模 2010：展览面积$7,000m^2$(国外展商$200m^2$)，参展商170家（国外展商10家，来自6个国家），参观人数4,000人（专业贸易观众1,000人）
主办：北方国际展览有限公司；广东省水族协会
地址：北京市宣武区菜园街1号1102室（100053）
联系人：刘强顺先生，王薇薇小姐
MSN：izumars@gmail.com
QQ：315547962

The 4th Guangzhou International Pet & Aquarium Show
Venue: Poly World Trade Expo Center, Guangzhou, Guangdong
Profile: CIPAS is a professional commercial exhibition of pet and aquarium. The major exhibitors of CIPAS are manufacturers and merchants in the aquarium and pet industry and the Suppliers of live pet. The aim of the show is to boost the export and import
Established Year: 2008
Frequency: Annual
Market Area: International
Statistics 2010: Exhibition Area $7,000m^2$(foreigners $200m^2$), Exhibitors 170 (foreigners 10, came from 6 countries), Visitors 4,000 (trade visitors 1,000)
Organizer: North International Exhibition Co Ltd; Guangdong Aquarists' Association
Address: Room 1102, No. 1 Caiyuan Street, Beijing, China
Contact: Liu Qiangshun
MSN: izumars@gmail.com

2011/05/11 - 13
☎ 020-3759 9008
🖷 020-3759 9151
✉ coatexpo@126.com
www.coatexpo.cn
4170

第九届广州国际涂料、油墨、胶粘剂展览会
地点：中国进出口商品交易会琶洲展馆，广东广州
内容：COAT EXPO 是由广东智展展览公司、广东省涂料行业协会、顺德涂料商会、美国粉末涂料涂装协会联合主办的行业盛会，得到了十多个境外协会的协作及国内五十多个相关协会的参与协办，是国际涂料、油墨、胶粘剂原材料及设备供应商拓展和巩固中国市场的最佳营销平台之一。
始办年份：2000
周期：两年一届

The 9th Guangzhou (China) International Coatings, Printing Inks & Adhesives Exhibition
Venue: Chinese Import and Export Fair Pazhou Complex, Guangzhou, Guangdong
Profile: Biennial Held, Industry Pageant, Endless Opportunities, Never Miss COAT EXPO is the best marketing and sales platform for the international raw material and equipment suppliers of coating, printing ink and adhesive etc. to consolidate and develop China market.
Established Year: 2000

市场范围：国际性
参展费用：12,800元/展位
上届规模 2010：展览面积15,000m²，参展商300家，参观人数18,000人
主办：广东省涂料行业协会；广东智展展览有限公司
地址：广州市寺右新马路5号华友大厦1802室（510000）
联系人：练文良

Frequency: Biennial
Market Area: International
Participated Fee: RMB 12800
Statistics 2010: Exhibition Area 15,000m², Exhibitors 300, Visitors 18,000
Organizer: Wise Exhibition (Guangdong) Co Ltd

2011/05/11 - 13
☎ 020-3759 9008
🖷 020-3759 9151
✉ ex360s@126.com
www.sf-expo.cn

4180

第九届广州国际表面处理、电镀、涂装展览会
地点：中国进出口商品交易会琶洲展馆，广东广州
内容：SF EXPO 2011将以"全面提升表面处理业水平"为已任，由中国表面工程协会电镀分会、美国粉末涂料涂装协会、广东电镀协会、广东省涂料行业协会、广东智展展览有限公司联手举办
始办年份：2000
周期：两年一届
市场范围：国际性
参展费用：12,800元/展位
上届规模 2009：展览面积15,000m²，参展商300家，参观人数18,000人
主办：广东省涂料行业协会；广东智展展览有限公司
地址：广州市寺右新马路5号华友大厦1802室（510000）
联系人：陈燕慧

The 9th Guangzhou International Surface Finishing, Electroplating and Coating Exhibition
Venue: Chinese Import and Export Fair Pazhou Complex, Guangzhou, Guangdong
Profile: SF EXPO China 2011 is a premier surface finishing industry's event jointly organized by China Surface Engineering Association Electroplating Branch, Powder Coating Institute, Guangdong Electroplating Association, Guangdong Coating Industry Association
Established Year: 2000
Frequency: Biannual
Market Area: International
Participated Fee: RMB 12,800/booth
Statistics 2009: Exhibition Area 15,000m², Exhibitors 300, Visitors 18,000
Organizer: China Surface Engineering Association Electroplating Branch; Wise Exhibition (Guangdong) Co Ltd
Address: Room 1802 Huayou Building, No.5 Si You Xin Road, Guangzhou, Guangdong Province, China

2011/05/12 - 14
☎ 010-6522 0753, 8511 1723
🖷 010-8511 1723
✉ expo@mc-ccpit.com
www.metalsfair.com

4190

第五届中国国际金属工业博览会
地点：中国进出口商品交易会琶洲展馆，广东广州
内容：冶金设备技术及产品、金属深加工设备及金属制品、冶金环保技术及设备、废旧金属回收、加工处理及检测设备、管材及管件制品、不锈钢原料、生产技术设备及不锈钢制品。
始办年份：2003
市场范围：国际性
性质：面向贸易观众
入场券价格：免费
上届规模 2009：展览面积8,000m²(国外展商145m²)，参展商366家（国外展商9家，来自6个国家），参观人数6,055人
主办：中国钢铁工业协会；中国有色金属工业协会；中国贸促会冶金行业分会
承办：中国贸促会冶金行业分会
地址：北京东四西大街46号（100711）
联系人：章亦飞 仲文

The 5th China International Metals Industry Trade Fair
Venue: Chinese Import and Export Fair Pazhou Complex, Guangzhou, Guangdong
Profile: Production technology & equipment for Ferrous & Non-ferrous metals and product showcase; Pollutant monitoring, environmental protection technology & equipment for metal production; Deep processing technology, equipment & downstream products; Metal scrap collecting, cutting, sorting, baling, refining & detecting technology and equipment; Stainless steel raw materials, production & processing equipment, stainless steel products; Tube & pipe production technology, equipment & products showcase.
Established Year: 2003
Market Area: International
Nature: Trade Only
Cost to Attend: Free
Statistics 2009: Exhibition Area 8,000m²(foreigners 145m²), Exhibitors 366 (foreigners 9, came from 6 countries), Visitors 6,055
Organizer: China Iron & Steel Association; China Non-ferrous Metals Industry Association; Metallurgical Council of CCPIT
Address: Metallurgical Council of CCPIT, 46 Dongsi Xidajie, Dongcheng District, Beijing, China
Contact: Zhang Yifei, Zhong Wen

2011/05/16 - 18
☎ 010-8455 6622, 8455 6623
🖷 010-6237 3998
✉ expolab@reedsinopharm.com
www.expolab.com.cn

4200

中国实验室技术及装备交易会
EXPO LAB

中国实验室技术及装备交易会
地点：广州锦汉展览中心，广东广州
内容：中国实验室技术及装备交易会（Expolab）围绕实验室研究与应用范畴，通过展示各类实验室试剂耗材、通用仪器以及其它相关产品和服务，反映中国实验室领域在各方面的技术及装备发展方向，特别专注于食品药品研发及质量检测、疾病控制、检验检疫以及实验室基础建设等领域，是中国实验室相关产品服务采购和技术交流的最佳商务平台。
周期：每年一届
主办：国药励展展览有限责任公司
联系人：魏小姐，王小姐

61th Expolab
The 61th China Laboratory Technology and Equipment Exhibition
Venue: Guangzhou Jinhan Exhibition Center, Guangzhou, Guangdong
Profile: Expolab serves exclusively as the best commercial platform for the procurement of laboratory product & related services, and the most efficient platform for laboratory technology exchange. Keeping its eye upon laboratory technology development, it brings together the alternative laboratory instruments, scientific instruments, reagents and other related products (services),catering to the development of food & drug R&D and quality control, disease control, inspection & quarantine and laboratory furniture
Frequency: Annual
Organizer: Reed Sinopharm Exhibitions

2011/05/17 - 20
☎ 021-6169 8300
🖷 021-6169 8301
✉ shanghai@mdc.com.cn
4210

第二十五届中国国际塑料橡胶工业展览会
地点：中国进出口商品交易会琶洲展馆，广东广州
主办：杜塞尔多夫展览（上海）有限公司
地址：上海市浦东新区张江高科技园区科苑路88号上海德意志工商中心1号楼307室

The 25th International Exhibition on Plastics and Rubber Industries
Venue: China Import and Export Fair Pazhou Complex, Guangzhou, Guangdong
Organizer: Messe Dusseldorf (Shanghai) Co Ltd
Address: Unit 307, Tower 1 German Center for Industry and Trade Shanghai, 88 Keyuan Road, Zhangjiang Hi-Tech Park Pudong, Shanghai 201203, China

2011/05/26 - 28
☎ 020-2200 5175
🖷 020-3886 1722
✉ 1251761299@qq.com
www.jinnuo-gzjc.com
4220

2011广州国际机床模具展览会
地点：中国进出口商品交易会琶洲展馆，广东广州
内容：机床展,机床功能部件、工具及附件展,锻压机械展,模具及配套件展
市场范围：国际性
参展费用：标准展位：A类10,800元/9m^2，B类8,800元/9m^2，双开口加收10%；净地（36m^{2}起）A类1,100元/m^2，B类900元/m^2
上届规模 2010：展览面积10,000m^2
主办：中国机电产品流通协会；中国贸促会机械行业分会
承办：广州金诺展览有限公司；青岛金诺会展有限公司
地址：广州市天河北路609号华标广场荟华阁901室
联系人：刘静

2011 Guangzhou International Machine Tools & moulds Exhibition
Venue: Chinese Import and Export Fair Pazhou Complex, Guangzhou, Guangdong
Market Area: International
Participated Fee: Standard Booth RMB 10800/9m^2, Corner unit add 10%, Raw Space（min 36m^2）RMB 1,100/m^2
Statistics 2010: Exhibition Area 10,000m^2
Organizer: Jinnoc Expo

2011/05/26 - 28
☎ 010-5979 2007, 6580 1456
🖷 010-8721 3827
✉ lixia@baking-china.com
www.baking-china.org
4225

2011第15届中国烘焙展览会
地点：中国进出口商品交易会琶洲展馆，广东广州
内容：烘焙生产设备；包装设备；烘焙业产品；食品添加剂；烘焙原料辅料；烘焙书籍、教育和培训机构
始办年份：1996
周期：每年一届
市场范围：国际性
性质：面向公众
参展费用：国内企业：标准展位6,200元，净地600元/m^2；国际企业：标准展位2,500欧元/个;特展位250欧元/m^2
上届规模 2010：展览面积40,000m^2，参展商600家（来自50个国家）
主办：中华全国工商业联合会烘焙业公会
承办：北京中连鼎和烘焙食品技术有限公司
地址：北京市朝阳区广渠路3号竞园38A（100124）
联系人：张伟,李夏
QQ：1356529521

The 15th China Bakery Exhibition
Venue: Chinese Import and Export Fair Pazhou Complex, Guangzhou, Guangdong
Profile: Bakery and pastry-making machinery, Packaging machinery, equipment and material, Pasta manufacturing, Cleaning and hygiene, Laboratory and measuring equipment, EDP hardware and software, Bakery books, institution of education& training, etc
Established Year: 1996
Frequency: Annual
Market Area: International
Nature: Open to Public
Participated Fee: Standard Booth EURO 2,500/booth, Raw Space EURO 250/m^2
Statistics 2010: Exhibition Area 40,000m^2, Exhibitors 600（came from 50 countries）
Sponsor: All China Bakery Association
Organizer: Beijing Zhonglian Dinghe Bakery Technology Co Ltd
Address: 38A，Jingyuan, No.3, Guangqu Road, Chaoyang District, Beijing
Contact: Zhang Wei, Li Xia

2011/05/28 - 29
☎ 0571-8839 3239, 8839 3237, 8839 3235
✉ fashion_baby@163.com
http://party.baby023.com
4230

时尚育儿 嘉年华

时尚育儿广州嘉年华
地点：广州锦汉展览中心，广东广州
内容：玩具系列、孕妇用品、车床系列、食品保健品、童装系列、早教用品、婴幼儿用品
周期：每年一届
上届规模 2010：展览面积6,000m^2
主办：博闻中国(杭州)
地址：浙江省杭州市拱墅区温州路69号南北商务港2-11F（310015）

Fashion baby Guangzhou Carnival
Venue: Guangzhou Jinhan Exhibition Center, Guangzhou, Guangdong
Frequency: Annual
Statistics 2010: Exhibition Area 6,000m^2
Organizer: UBM China (Hangzhou)
Address: 2-11F South West Business Center, No 69 Wenzhou Road, Gong Shu District, Hangzhou 310015, China

2011/06/01 - 03
☎ 852-2851 8603
🖷 852-2851 8637
✉ topreput@top-repute.com
www.shoesleather-guangzhou.com/index.html
4240

SHOES & LEATHER GUANGZHOU

广州国际鞋类、皮革及工业设备展览会
地点：中国进出口商品交易会琶洲展馆，广东广州
内容：鞋类机械、制革机、皮具机、皮革、原皮料、鞋材、化工、配件/辅料
周期：每年一届
市场范围：国际性
参展费用：标准展位3,000美元/9m^2
上届规模 2010：参展商875家，参观人数36,000人
主办：显辉国际展览有限公司；广州市显辉展览服务有限公司
地址：香港上环禧利街27号富辉商业中心2403室
联系人：郭小姐

The International Shoes & Leather Exhibition
(Machinery & Raw Material)
Venue: Chinese Import and Export Fair Pazhou Complex, Guangzhou, Guangdong
Profile: Tanning machinery, shoes machinery, raw materials, leather, etc.
Frequency: Annual
Market Area: International
Participated Fee: Standard Booth USD 3,000/9m^2
Statistics 2010: Exhibitors 875，Visitors 36,000
Organizer: Top Repute Co Ltd; Top Repute Co Ltd (Guangzhou)
Address: Rm 2403, Fu Fai Commercial Center, 27 Hillier Street, Sheung Wan, Hong Kong
Contact: Ms Kwok

2011/06/09 - 11
☎ 020-2896 5742
🖷 020-2887 9080
✉ qifaexpo@126.com
www.itsguangzhou.org
4250

2011第十一届中国（广州）国际自动识别与物联网应用展览会
地点：保利世贸博览馆，广东广州
内容：生物识别技术、图像识别技术、语音识别技术、条码打印机、数据采集器、扫描枪、不干胶标签、耗材DCR及光电识别技术及产品、打标设备、标签生产材料、标签天线、电子标签封装设备、应用软件以及集成服务、各领域的成功案例展示
始办年份：2001
周期：每年一届
性质：面向公众
入场券价格：15元
参展费用：标准展位16,000元/展位
上届规模 2010：展览面积100,000m^2
主办：广东省交通厅；广东省科学技术厅；广东省公路管理局；香港物流及供应链管理应用技术研发中心、广东省经济和信息化委员会、广东省质量监督管理局，
承办：广州思齐展览有限公司
地址：广东省广州市天河区中山大道龙怡苑A座407室（510000）
联系人：王忠发

China (Guangzhou) Automatic Identification and IOT Exhibition
Venue: Poly World Trade Expo Center, Guangzhou, Guangdong
Established Year: 2001
Frequency: Annual
Nature: Open to Public
Cost to Attend: RMB 15:-
Participated Fee: Standard Booth：RMB 16,000/9m^2
Organizer: Guangzhou Siqi Exhibition Co Ltd

2011/06/09 - 11
☎ 021-6160 8555转ext 231
🖷 021-5876 9332
✉ susan.wang@china.messefrankfurt.com
www.messefrankfurt.com.hk
4255

广州国际照明展览会
地点：中国进出口商品交易会展馆，广东广州
周期：每年一届
性质：面向贸易观众
主办：法兰克福展览（上海）有限公司
地址：上海浦东新区浦东南路999号上海联合广场32层
联系人：汪静

Guangzhou International Lighting Exhibition
Venue: China Import and Export Fair Pazhou Complex, Guangzhou, Guangdong
Frequency: Annual
Nature: Trade Only
Organizer: Messe Frankfurt (Shanghai) Co Ltd
Address: 32nd Floor, Shanghai Union Square, 999, South Pudong Road, Pudong New Area, Shanghai, 200120, China

2011/06/09 - 12
☎ 021-6160 8555转ext 231
🖷 021-5876 9332
✉ susan.wang@china.messefrankfurt.com
www.messefrankfurt.com.hk
4256

广州国际建筑电气技术展览会
地点：中国进出口商品交易会展馆，广东广州
周期：每年一届
性质：面向贸易观众
主办：法兰克福展览（上海）有限公司
地址：上海浦东新区浦东南路999号上海联合广场32层
联系人：汪静

Electrical Building Technology Guangzhou
Venue: China Import and Export Fair Pazhou Complex, Guangzhou, Guangdong
Frequency: Annual
Nature: Trade Only
Organizer: Messe Frankfurt (Shanghai) Co Ltd
Address: 32nd Floor, Shanghai Union Square, 999, South Pudong Road, Pudong New Area, Shanghai, 200120, China

2011/06/17 - 20
☎ 020-8666 0158
852-2585 6179
🖷 020-8667 7120
852-3749 7542
✉ info-china@ubm.com
salescjgf-hk@ubm.com
http://exhibitions.Jewelrynetasia.com
4260

中国(广州)国际黄金珠宝玉石展览会
珠光魅影-广州
艺术广东-国际收藏品及艺术品博览会
地点：广州锦汉展览中心，广东广州
内容：黄金、珠宝、玉石、铂金、珍珠。
珠光魅影-广州：这个专为珠宝收藏家、高端消费者及高级珠宝零售商而设的国际展会，将为您带来崭新的体验，缔造源源商机。珠光魅影-广州将邀请近百家世界知名、专门销售高级珠宝的公司参与，展示华丽夺目、设计独特的名贵 钻饰、珍珠首饰、手表、古董首饰、以及稀有矜贵的有色宝石及钻石。展品全属收藏鉴赏的上佳之选，必 定能令与会者大饱眼福。
始办年份：2003
周期：每年一届
入场券价格：消费者50元。业内人士免费
参展费用：特装展位：1,345元或195美元/m^2(9m^{2}起)，净地1,210元或175美元/m^2 (36m^{2}起)，高级展位，标准展位1,060元或155美元/m^2(9m^{2}起)，净地955元或140美元/m^2(36m^{2}起)
上届规模 2010：参展商150家，专业贸易观众7,260人
主办：亚洲博闻有限公司
联络：博闻(广州)展览有限公司
地址：中国广州市流花路中国大酒店商业大厦1151-1153室(510015)

China International Gold, Jewelry & Gem Fair – Guangzhou
Treasures Guangzhou
Art Canton International Art & Collection Fair
Venue: Guangzhou Jinhan Exhibition Center, Guangzhou, Guangdong
Profile: Provides consumers and collectors with unmatched opportunity to buy luxurious Jewelry, including Jewelry sets with rare diamonds, lustrous pearls, be-jeweled watches, antique and estate Jewelry and other exclusive one-offs of highest quality from about 100 esteemed Jewelry companies from around the world.
Established Year: 2003
Frequency: Annual
Cost to Attend: Public RMB 50:-, Free to Trade Visitors
Participated Fee: USD 140-195/m^2
Statistics 2010: Exhibitors 150，Trade Visitors 7,260
Organizer: UBM Asia Limited
Contact: UBM China (Guangzhou) Co Ltd

2011/06/22 - 24
☎ 020-3404 1988
🖷 020-8637 4257
✉ bestguangzhou@vip.163.com
www.84t.cn
4270

第二届广州国际物流装备与技术展览会
地点：中国进出口商品交易会琶洲展馆，广东广州
内容：仓储物流装备展区，自动识别RFID与物联网展区，物流信息化展区，物流运输车辆展区，物品分拣/自动化/包装设备展区、脚轮展区、升降平台展区，危险品、安全物流装备展区，工业门展区,冷链物流装备展区，起重设备及葫芦工具展区，港口物流装备展区，航空物流装备展区，物流供应链及服务展区，应急物流装备展区
周期：每年一届
市场范围：国际性
主办：广州巴斯特展览有限公司
地址：广州新港东路238号世港国际公寓B栋601-604室（510308）

The 2nd Guangzhou International Logistics Equipment & Technology Exhibition
Venue: Chinese Import and Export Fair Pazhou Complex, Guangzhou, Guangdong
Profile: Logistics Warehousing Equipments, Automatic Recognition RFID and Internet of Things, Logistics Information, Logistics Vehicles, Articles Separation/Automation/Packaging Equipment
Frequency: Annual
Market Area: International
Organizer: Guangzhou Best Exhibition Co Ltd
Address: Room 601-604, Flat B, Citycoin International Apartment, No. 238, Xingang East Road, Guangzhou

2011/06/22 - 24
☎ 020-3404 1988
🖷 020-8637 4257
✉ bestguangzhou@vip.163.com
www.84t.cn
4280

第七届广州国际品牌叉车及配件展览会
地点：中国进出口商品交易会琶洲展馆，广东广州
内容：叉车展区：内燃式叉车、电瓶叉车、电力叉车、电动托盘搬运车、电动托盘堆垛车、前移式叉车、侧面叉车、牵引车、固定平台搬运车、集装箱叉车、集装箱正面吊、手动托盘叉车、手动叉车、伸缩叉式巷道堆垛叉车。
始办年份：2005
周期：每年一届
市场范围：国际性
主办：广州巴斯特展览有限公司
地址：广州新港东路238号世港国际公寓B栋601-604室（510308）

The 7th Guangzhou International Brand Forklift & Accessory Exhibition
Venue: Chinese Import and Export Fair Pazhou Complex, Guangzhou, Guangdong
Profile: Exhibition Range Display Area of Forklift: Diesel trucks, battery trucks, electric trucks, electric pallet trucks, electric pallet handlers, telescopic trucks, side forklift trucks, truck tractors, container trucks, container front suspension, hand pallet.
Established Year: 2005
Frequency: Annual
Market Area: International
Organizer: Guangzhou Best Exhibition Co Ltd
Address: Room 601-604, Flat B, Citycoin International Apartment, No. 238, Xingang East Road, Guangzhou

2011/06/23 - 25
☎ 020-3862 1295
🖷 020-38620781
✉ julangmeiwen@126.com
www.julang.com.cn
4300

第十二届广州国际管材展
地点：中国进出口商品交易会琶洲展馆，广东广州
内容：管件产品、管道配件、法兰、管件设备、钢管产品、钢管设备、焊管机组、无缝钢管机组：三辊管机组、五辊冷轧管机组、周期轧管机组、钢管矫直机、穿孔机、连轧机组、连轧管机组、两辊冷轧管机组、冷拔机、自动轧管机组、顶管机组、钢管挤压机组、张力减径机等加工工艺设备等各类钢管精整设备等。
始办年份：2000
市场范围：国际性
性质：面向贸易观众
入场券价格：30元
参展费用：11,000元/9m²
主办：广州巨浪展览策划有限公司
地址：广州市天河区珠江新城华明路29号星汇源A1座3A04-06（510623）
联系人：梅文
MSN：julangmeiwen
QQ：992662913

The 12th China (Guangzhou) Intl Tube & Pipe Industry Exhibition
Venue: Chinese Import and Export Fair Pazhou Complex, Guangzhou, Guangdong
Profile: Raw materials, tubes and accessories, Tube manufacturing machinery, Rebuilt and reconditioned machinery, Process technology tools and auxiliaries, Measuring and control technology, Testing, Specialist areas, Trading stockiest of tubes, Pip
Established Year: 2000
Market Area: International
Nature: Trade Only
Cost to Attend: RMB 30:-
Participated Fee: RMB 11,000/9m²
Organizer: Guangzhou Julang Exhibition Co Ltd
Address: Suite 3A04-06, Building A1, Galaxy City, Pearl River New City, Tianhe, Guangzhou, China
Contact: Mei Wen
MSN: julangmeiwen

2011/06/23 - 25
☎ 020-3862 1295
🖷 020-3862 0781
✉ julangmeiwen@126.com
www.julang.com.cn
4310

第十二届广州国际紧固件、弹簧及设备展
地点：中国进出口商品交易会琶洲展馆，广东广州
内容：汽车、摩托车、家电紧固件；紧固件、配件及连接产品类；紧固件生产设备及螺丝模具。弹簧及紧固件材料；弹簧设备；紧固件使用工具、紧固系统。检测仪器机械、各种零部件及相关技术设备。
周期：每年一届
市场范围：国际性
性质：面向贸易观众
入场券价格：30元
参展费用：11,000元/9m²
主办：广州巨浪展览策划有限公司
地址：广州市天河区珠江新城华明路29号星汇源A1座3A04-06（510623）
联系人：梅文
MSN：julangmeiwen
QQ：992662913

12th China (Guangzhou) Intl Fasteners, Spring & Equipment Exhibition
Venue: Chinese Import and Export Fair Pazhou Complex, Guangzhou, Guangdong
Profile: Fasteners, parts and products for linking; Fastener production equipment and screw mould; Matching raw materials for fasteners and spring production; spring equipment; Tools for fastener application and fastening system; Detecting apparatus and machinery, all kinds of parts and the related technology and equipments; Washer and equipment
Frequency: Annual
Market Area: International
Nature: Trade Only
Cost to Attend: RMB 30:-
Participated Fee: RMB 11,000/9m²
Organizer: Guangzhou Julang Exhibition Co Ltd
Address: Suite 3A04-06, Building A1, Galaxy City, Pearl River New City, Tianhe, Guangzhou, China
Contact: Mei Wen
MSN: julangmeiwen

2011/06/23 - 25
☎ 020-3862 1295
🖷 020-3862 0781
✉ julangmeiwen@126.com
www.julang.com.cn
4320

第十二届广州国际铸件产品及工艺技术研讨展
地点：中国进出口商品交易会琶洲展馆，广东广州
内容：压铸产品：汽车、摩托车零件、机动车缸盖（体）车轮毂、发动机马达箱体边盖及配件，家电、燃气具件，机械零件、梯级，五金件、工艺品、锁具，各种建筑装饰件、浴室配件，电脑、电讯、电子、3C产品零件等铜、铝、锌、镁合金压铸件及其他有色合金压铸件，压铸模具、模具钢；泵、阀体、管件、汽车配件、灯饰、家具配件、家电配件、电子通讯类、电动工具、电机、工艺品（钟表、首饰等）、五金、高尔夫球具及配件、集装箱角件、炉具、水暖器材、水龙头、机床、液压设备、注塑机、柴油机、内燃机、压缩机、建设机械、风机配件、纺机、缝纫机、电梯、园林机械等通用机械等各类零部件铸件、精密铸造件、铸钢件、铸铁件、灰铁铸件、球墨铸件、耐磨耐热铸件、合金铸铁件及其它铸件
始办年份：2000
周期：每年一届
市场范围：国际性
性质：面向贸易观众
入场券价格：30元
参展费用：11,000元/9m²
主办：广州巨浪展览策划有限公司
地址：广州市天河区珠江新城华明路29号星汇源A1座3A04-06（510623）
联系人：梅文
MSN：julangmeiwen
QQ：992662913

The 12th China (Guangzhou) Intl Exhibition of Casting Products and Technology Symposium
Venue: Chinese Import and Export Fair Pazhou Complex, Guangzhou, Guangdong
Profile: Casting of Cu, Al, Zn, Mg alloy and other non-ferrous alloy, mould, stainless steel casting; The cylinder cover of Automobile, motorcycle, hub, automobile engine organism, cylinder and casting parts; Casting for general use such as , pump, valve, electron, computer, lighting, electric appliance, electric tools, furniture; Casting for machine tool, textile/garden/agriculture machinery, elevator, hardware cast; Casting raw materials: Cu/Al/Zn/Mg alloy ingot; Casting materials: mould release agent, precoated sand, curative agent , lubricant, refine agent, zircon sand/powder
Established Year: 2000
Frequency: Annual
Market Area: International
Nature: Trade Only
Cost to Attend: 30:-
Participated Fee: RMB 11,000/9m²
Organizer: Guangzhou Julang Exhibition Co Ltd
Address: Suite 3A04-06 Building A1, Galaxy City, Pearl River New City, Tianhe, Guangzhou, China
Contact: Mei Wen
MSN: julangmeiwen

2011/06/23 - 25
☎ 020-3862 1295
🖷 020-3862 0781
✉ julangmeiwen@126.com
www.julang.com.cn
4330

第十二届广州国际金属暨冶金工业展览会
地点：中国进出口商品交易会琶洲展馆，广东广州
内容：金属板材、棒材、线材、钢格板及金属加工、配套设备；管材工业；不锈钢工业；钢丝、钢绳、钢绞线、金属制品 五、铸件、压铸、铸造、工业炉及热处理；紧固件、弹簧及设备；钣金、锻压产品及设备；矿石、铜工业
始办年份：2000
周期：每年一届
市场范围：国际性
性质：面向贸易观众
入场券价格：30元
参展费用：11,000元/9m^2，净地960元/m^2
上届规模 2009：展览面积30,000m^2(国外展商5,000m^2)，参展商680家（国外展商65家，来自15个国家），参观人数23,893人（专业贸易观众5,679人）
主办：广州巨浪展览策划有限公司
地址：广州市天河区珠江新城华明路29号星汇源A1座3A04-06（510623）
联系人：梅文
MSN：julangmeiwen
QQ：992662913

The 12th China (Guangzhou) Intl Metal & Metallurgy Exhibition
Venue: Chinese Import and Export Fair Pazhou Complex, Guangzhou, Guangdong
Profile: Plate metal, Bar, Wire, Grating, Metal Processing and Setting Equipment, Tube & Pipe Industry; Stainless Steel Industry; Steel Wire, Steel Rope, Metal Products; Casting, Die casting, Foundry, Heat Treatment
Established Year: 2000
Frequency: Annual
Market Area: International
Nature: Trade Only
Cost to Attend: RMB 30:-
Participated Fee: RMB 11,000/9m^2, Raw Space RMB 960/m^2
Statistics 2009: Exhibition Area 30,000m^2(foreigners 5,000m^2), Exhibitors 680（foreigners 65, came from 15 countries）, Visitors 23,893（trade visitors 5,679）
Organizer: Guangzhou Julang Exhibition Co Ltd
Address: Suite 3A04-06, Building A1, Galaxy City, Pearl River New City, Tianhe, Guangzhou, China
Contact: Mei Wen
MSN: julangmeiwen

2011/06/23 - 25
☎ 020-3862 1295
🖷 020-3862 0781
✉ julangmeiwen@126.com
www.julang.com.cn
4340

第十二届广州国际不锈钢工业展
地点：中国进出口商品交易会琶洲展馆，广东广州
内容：大型不锈钢企业形象展示；不锈钢生产工艺、技术设备；不锈钢原材料、型材；不锈钢生产、加工、检测设备；不锈钢复合管、复合板及其生产加工设备；特殊钢；不锈钢打磨、抛光、切割设备及材料配件；高附加值不锈钢产品及不锈钢制品。
始办年份：2000
周期：每年一届
市场范围：国际性
性质：面向贸易观众
入场券价格：30元
主办：广州巨浪展览策划有限公司
地址：广州市天河区珠江新城华明路29号星汇源A1座3A04-06（510623）
联系人：梅文
MSN：julangmeiwen
QQ：992662913

The 12th China (Guangzhou) Intl Stainless Steel Industry Exhibition
Venue: Chinese Import and Export Fair Pazhou Complex, Guangzhou, Guangdong
Profile: Display of big stainless steel enterprises. Arts and crafts, technology and equipments of stainless steel production; Raw materials of stainless steel, section; Equipments of stainless steel production, processing and detecting. Stainless steel duplex tube, clad plate and the processing equipments; Special steel; Stainless steel burnish/polish/cutting equipment & fittings; Stainless steel products and high value added stainless steel products.
Established Year: 2000
Frequency: Annual
Market Area: International
Nature: Trade Only
Cost to Attend: RMB 30:-
Organizer: Guangzhou Julang Exhibition Co Ltd
Address: Suite 3A04-06, Building A1, Galaxy City, Pearl River New City, Tianhe, Guangzhou, China
Contact: Mei Wen
MSN: julangmeiwen

2011/06/23 - 25
☎ 020-3862 1295
🖷 020-3862 0781
✉ julangmeiwen@126.com
www.julang.com.cn
4350

第十二届广州国际压铸，铸造及工业炉展
地点：中国进出口商品交易会琶洲展馆，广东广州
内容：压铸设备；熔炼设备；压铸合金；压铸造涂料；压铸模具；工艺控制及挤压铸造；低压铸造；重力金属模铸造；离心铸造；连续铸造；壳型铸造；消失模铸造。砂处理设备；落砂设备；造型制芯设备；抛喷丸清理强化设备；金属型铸造设备；熔炼烧注设备；熔模设备；输送设备；检测设备；时效处理设备；涂料设备；型芯烘干设备；特种铸造设备；铸造用炉及配件；燃烧器及铁嘴；无损探伤；耐火材料；铸造材料；铸造用树脂、铸造修补材料及设备等辅助产品；控制设备；测试仪器（测温仪等），锻造设备等
始办年份：2000
周期：每年一届
市场范围：国际性
性质：面向贸易观众
入场券价格：30元
参展费用：11,000元/9m^2
主办：广州巨浪展览策划有限公司
地址：广州市天河区珠江新城华明路29号星汇源A1座3A04-06（510623）
联系人：梅文
MSN：julangmeiwen
QQ：992662913

12th China (Guangzhou) Intl Exhibition on Die Casting Foundry and Industrial Furnace
Venue: Chinese Import and Export Fair Pazhou Complex, Guangzhou, Guangdong
Profile: Pressure Die-Casting; high-pressure die-casting; Low-pressure die-casting; Squeeze casting; Precision Casting; Lost wax casting; Plaster mould casting; Ceramic mould casting; Vacuum casting; Casting technology; Foam pattern; Centrifugal Casting;
Established Year: 2000
Frequency: Annual
Market Area: International
Nature: Trade Only
Cost to Attend: RMB 30:-
Participated Fee: RMB 11,000/9m^2
Organizer: Guangzhou Julang Exhibition Co Ltd
Address: Suite 3A04-06, Building A1, Galaxy City, Pearl River New City, Tianhe, Guangzhou, China
Contact: Mei Wen
MSN: julangmeiwen

2011/07/08 - 11
☎ 020-8912 8206
🖷 020-8912 8251
✉ leo@fairwindow.com.cn
www.cbd-china.com
4360

2011中国（广州）国际地面铺装材料展
地点：中国进出口商品交易会琶洲展馆，广东广州
内容：实木地板、实木复合地板、强化木地板、软木地板、竹地板，各种地板材料；手工、机制地毯及纺织地铺材料；地面石材等；其它地面铺装材料；地面材料原料、配件、用品等
始办年份：2007
周期：每年一届
市场范围：国际性
性质：面向公众
参展费用：10,000元/展位，净地900元/m^2（36m^{2}起）
上届规模 2010：展览面积250,000m^2，参展商2,157家（国外展商99家），参观人数113,625人

China (Guangzhou) Intl Floor Covering Fair 2011
Venue: Chinese Import and Export Fair Pazhou Complex, Guangzhou, Guangdong
Profile: Solid wood flooring, Engineered wood flooring, Laminate flooring, Cork flooring, Bamboo flooring, Carpets and textile flooring covering(Handmade or machine made). Stone flooring Material etc. Other floor covering materials, Fittings and products etc.
Established Year: 2007
Frequency: Annual
Market Area: International
Nature: Open to Public
Participated Fee: RMB 10,000/booth, RMB 900/m^2（min 36m^2）

主办：中国对外贸易中心（集团）；中国林产工业协会
承办：广州中贸华建展览有限公司；广州博亚展览发展有限公司
地址：广州市海珠区新港东路980号广交会展馆C区16号馆A层（510335）
联系人：陈羿

Statistics 2010: Exhibition Area 250,000m², Exhibitors 2,157 (foreigners 99), Visitors 113,625
Sponsor: China Foreign Trade Center (Group), China National Forest Product Industry Association
Organizer: China Foreign Trade Building Decoration Exhibition Co Ltd; Guangzhou Boya Exhibition Development Co Ltd
Address: #980, Xingang East Road, Guangzhou 510335, China
Contact: Leo Chan

4370

2011/07/08 - 11
☎ 020-8912 8206
🖷 020-8912 8251
✉ leo@fairwindow.com.cn
www.cbd-china.com

2011中国（广州）国际厨房设备及配件展

地点：中国进出口商品交易会琶洲展馆，广东广州
内容：整体橱柜、橱柜配件及材料、厨房配件、厨房电器设备、软件及出版物等
始办年份：2010
周期：每年一届
市场范围：国际性
性质：面向贸易观众
参展费用：10,000元/展位，净地900元/m²（36m²起）
上届规模 2010：展览面积250,000m²，参展商2,157家（国外展商99家），参观人数113,625人（专业贸易观众101,586人）
主办：中国对外贸易中心（集团）；全国工商联家具装饰业商会
承办：广州中贸华建展览有限公司
地址：广州市海珠区新港东路980号广交会展馆C区16号馆A层（510335）
联系人：陈羿

China (Guangzhou) Intl Kitchen Fair 2011

Venue: Chinese Import and Export Fair Pazhou Complex, Guangzhou, Guangdong
Profile: Unit Kitchen Cabinets, Cabinet Accessories & Materials, Kitchen Accessories, Kitchen Appliance & Equipments, Software & Publications etc.
Established Year: 2010
Frequency: Annual
Market Area: International
Nature: Trade Only
Participated Fee: RMB 10,000/booth, RMB 900/m² (min 36m²)
Statistics 2010: Exhibition Area 250,000m², Exhibitors 2,157 (foreigners 99), Visitors 113,625
Sponsor: China Foreign Trade Center (Group); China Furniture & Decoration Chamber of Commerce
Organizer: China Foreign Trade Building Decoration Exhibition Co Ltd; Guangzhou Boya Exhibition Development Co Ltd
Address: #980, Xingang East Road, Guangzhou 510335, China
Contact: Leo Chan

4380

2011/07/08 - 11
☎ 020-8912 8206
🖷 020-8912 8251
✉ leo@fairwindow.com.cn
www.cbd-china.com

第十三届中国（广州）国际建筑装饰博览会

地点：中国进出口商品交易会琶洲展馆，广东广州
内容：建筑装饰五金、装饰玻璃/移门、天花吊顶、墙纸/布艺及辅料、楼梯、建筑装饰照明、建筑涂料及化学建材、石材等
始办年份：1999
周期：每年一届
市场范围：国际性
性质：面向贸易观众
入场券价格：待定
参展费用：10,000/展位，净地900元/m²（36m²起）
上届规模 2010：展览面积250,000m²，参展商2,157家（国外展商99家），参观人数113,625人（专业贸易观众101,586人）
主办：中国对外贸易中心（集团）；中国建筑装饰协会
承办：广州中贸华建展览有限公司；广州博亚展览发展有限公司
地址：广州市海珠区新港东路980号广交会展馆C区16号馆A层（510335）
联系人：陈羿

The 13th China (Guangzhou) International Building Decoration Fair

Venue: Chinese Import and Export Fair Pazhou Complex, Guangzhou, Guangdong
Profile: Decorative Hardware, Decorative Glass/Slide Door, Ceiling, Wallpaper & Fabric, Stairs, Decorative Lighting, Coating & Chemicals, Stone and so on
Established Year: 1999
Frequency: Annual
Market Area: International
Nature: Trade Only
Participated Fee: RMB 10,000/booth, RMB 900/m² (min 36m²)
Statistics 2010: Exhibition Area 250,000m², Exhibitors 2,157 (foreigners 99), Visitors 113,625 (trade visitors 101,586)
Sponsor: China Foreign Trade Center (Group); China Building Decoration Association;
Organizer: China Foreign Trade Building Decoration Exhibition Co Ltd; Guangzhou Boya Exhibition Development Co Ltd
Address: Floor A, Hall 16, Area C, Canton Fair Complex, No.980 Xingang Dong Road, Haizhu District, Guangzhou, China
Contact: Leo Chan

4390

2011/07/08 - 11
☎ 020-8912 8206
🖷 020-8912 8251
✉ leo@fairwindow.com.cn
www.cbd-china.com

2011中国（广州）国际卫浴及建筑陶瓷展

地点：中国进出口商品交易会琶洲展馆，广东广州
内容：整体浴室、浴缸类、淋浴类、座便器、台盆、浴室五金/配件类、卫浴镜、浴室取暖器、浴室柜、间隔、泳池设施、各类墙砖、地砖、屋顶砖、空心砖、原辅材料及生产设备、泳池水处理设备、循环过滤、清洁保养系统、防滑设施、泳池外围设施、泳池配件、SPA设备、水疗工程、桑拿设备、恒温器、各类热水设备、节水系列产品等
始办年份：2008
周期：每年一届
市场范围：国际性
性质：面向公众
参展费用：10,000元/展位，净地900元/m²（36m²起）
主办：中国对外贸易中心（集团）；中国建筑卫生陶瓷协会
承办：广州中贸华建展览有限公司；广州博亚展览发展有限公司
地址：广州市海珠区新港东路980号广交会展馆C区16号馆A层（510335）
联系人：陈羿

China (Guangzhou) Intl Exhibition for Sanitary Ware and Building Ceramics 2011

Venue: Chinese Import and Export Fair Pazhou Complex, Guangzhou, Guangdong
Profile: Integrated bathroom, bathtub, shower, faucet, water closet, shower cubicle, shower basin, bathroom hardware and accessories, bathroom mirror, bathroom heater, bathroom cabinet, shelf, Wall tile, ground tile, brick, roof tile, hollow tile, raw material, auxiliary material, and production facility, Pool water process equipment, circulation filter, cleaning and maintaining system, antiskid facility, pool periphery facility, pool accessory, SPA equipment, sauna equipment, thermostat, water heater, water saving products.
Established Year: 2008
Frequency: Annual
Market Area: International
Nature: Open to Public
Participated Fee: RMB 10,000/booth, RMB 900/m² (min 36m²)
Sponsor: Chinese Foreign Trade Center (Group); China Building Ceramic & Sanitary Ware Association
Organizer: China Foreign Trade Building Decoration Exhibition Co Ltd; Guangzhou Boya Exhibition Development Co Ltd
Address: #980, Xingang East Road, Guangzhou 510335, China
Contact: Leo Chan

2011/07/08 - 11
☎ 020-8912 8206
🖷 020-8912 8251
✉ leo@fairwindow.com.cn
www.cbd-china.com

4400

2011中国(广州)国际门窗展览会
地点：中国进出口商品交易会琶洲展馆，广东广州
内容：铝合金门、实木门、实木复合门、生态门、钢木门、钢门窗、安全门、防盗门、防火门、仿古铜门、艺术玻璃门、模压门、塑钢门窗、防蚊纱窗、百叶窗、模压木门、隔断门、橱柜门、折叠门、木塑门、百叶门、镶嵌玻璃木门、门板；门窗专业配件及机械、木门成套生产及加工设备；木皮、木塑、高分子材料、密封材料等门业新材料等
始办年份：2011
周期：每年一届
市场范围：国际性
性质：面向贸易观众
参展费用：10,000/展位，净地900元/m^2（$36m^2$起）
预计规模：展出面积300,000m^2，参展商2,300家，参观人数120,000人
主办：中国对外贸易中心(集团)
承办：广州中贸华建展览有限公司；广州博亚展览发展有限公司
地址：广州市海珠区新港东路980号广交会展馆C区16号馆A层（510335）
联系人：陈羿

CBD-Windoor 2011
Venue: Chinese Import and Export Fair Pazhou Complex, Guangzhou, Guangdong
Profile: Steel doors, aluminum doors, steel doors, security doors, security doors , fire doors, insulation doors, antique copper door, art glass doors, molded doors, steel windows, steel windows, aluminum windows, mosquito screen window, shutters, doors, windows dedicated equipment, Solid wood door, composite doors, molded doors, partition doors, cabinet doors, folding doors, wood doors, sliding doors, shutter doors, glazing wooden doors, door; Door and window fittings and machines, wooden doors production and processing equipment; Door auxiliary materials: veneer, wood, polymer materials, sealing materials, new materials such as doors.
Established Year: 2011
Frequency: Annual
Market Area: International
Nature: Trade Only
Participated Fee: RMB 10,000/booth, RMB 900/m^2（min $36m^2$）
Organizer: China Foreign Trade Center (Group);China Foreign Trade Building Decoration Exhibition Co Ltd , Guangzhou Boya Exhibition Development Co Ltd
Address: #980, Xingang East Road, Guangzhou 510335, China
Contact: Leo Chan

2011/07/08 - 11
☎ 020-8912 8206
🖷 020-8912 8251
✉ leo@fairwindow.com.cn
www.cbd-china.com

4410

2011中国（广州）国际衣柜展览会
地点：中国进出口商品交易会琶洲展馆，广东广州
内容：入墙柜、衣柜、书柜、组合柜等；隔断门、移门、移动隔间、衣帽间、滑动门等；衣柜系统五金配件；板材、涂料及其他辅材等；木工机械等
始办年份：2011
周期：每年一届
市场范围：国际性
性质：面向贸易观众
参展费用：10,000/展位，净地900元/m^2（$36m^2$起）
预计规模：展出面积300,000m^2，参展商2,300家，参观人数120,000人
主办：中国对外贸易中心(集团)
承办：广州中贸华建展览有限公司；广州博亚展览发展有限公司
地址：广州市海珠区新港东路980号广交会展馆C区16号馆A层（510335）
联系人：陈羿

CBD-Wardrobe 2011
Venue: Chinese Import and Export Fair Pazhou Complex, Guangzhou, Guangdong
Profile: Of Household Cloakroom, Wardrobe, Wall Cabinet, Sliding Door, Cut Off etc.
Established Year: 2011
Frequency: Annual
Market Area: International
Nature: Trade Only
Participated Fee: RMB 10,000/booth, RMB 900/m^2（min $36m^2$）
Expectation: Gross Area 300,000m^2, Exhibitors 2,300, Visitors 120,000
Sponsor: China Foreign Trade Center (Group)
Organizer: China Foreign Trade Building Decoration Exhibition Co Ltd; Guangzhou Boya Exhibition Development Co Ltd
Address: #980, Xingang East Road, Guangzhou 510335, China
Contact: Leo Chan

2011/07/15 - 17
☎ 020-3220 5179
🖷 020-3220 5179
✉ gdjdexpo@163.com
www.gdjdexpo.com

4420

2011广东国际家电配件采购展览会
地点：中国进出口商品交易会琶洲展馆，广东广州
内容：家电原材料；金属、塑料、玻璃制品、化学品、通用件及模具；智能家电解决方案；电子元器件、电气；包装、印刷材料及设备；生产设备与辅助材料；OEM及服务商；采购洽谈
始办年份：2009
周期：每年一届
市场范围：国际性
性质：面向贸易观众
入场券价格：免费
参展费用：8,800元/展位，净地900元/m^2
上届规模 2010：展览面积15,000m^2(国外展商3,500m^2)，参展商402家（国外展商102家，来自12个国家），参观人数18,000人
主办：广东省家用电器行业协会
承办：广州博优会展服务有限公司
地址：广州市中山大道中368号华金盾大酒店附一楼全层（510660）
联系人：邓波，刘敢
QQ：52129808

2011 Guangdong Intl Appliance Parts Procurement Fair
Venue: Chinese Import and Export Fair Pazhou Complex, Guangzhou, Guangdong
Profile: Home appliance raw materials; Metals, plastics, glass products, chemicals, using common standard spare and die; Intelligent home appliance solutions; Electronic components, electric; Packaging, printing materials and equipment ; Production equipment and auxiliary materials; OEM and service providers; Purchasing negotiation
Established Year: 2009
Frequency: Annual
Market Area: International
Nature: Trade Only
Cost to Attend: Free
Participated Fee: RMB 8,800/booth, Raw Space RMB 900/m^2
Statistics 2010: Exhibition Area 15,000m^2(foreigners 3,500m^2), Exhibitors 402（foreigners 102, came from 12 countries）, Visitors 18,000
Organizer: Guangdong Boyou Conference and Exhibition Co Ltd
Address: 1st Floor, 368 Zhongshan Road (M), Guangzhou 510660, Guangdong

2011/07/20 - 22
☎ 020-3220 5850
🖷 020-8256 2179
✉ buexpo@163.com

4430

2011广州国际电线电缆专用设备及原辅材料采购展览会
地点：中国进出口商品交易会琶洲展馆，广东广州
内容：种线缆制造及精加工机械，包括线缆处理设备；各种电线电缆材料，辅助加工材料；检测仪器、测控技术；光纤光缆制造设备及材料；相关领域；支撑线缆设备及材料生产加工的相关配套设备、配件等
始办年份：2009
周期：每年一届
市场范围：国际性
性质：面向贸易观众
入场券价格：专业人士免费
参展费用：8,800元/展位，双开口另加1,000元，外资企业2,800美

2011 GZ International Wire & Cable Equipment and Raw & Auxiliary Material Purchase Fair
Venue: Chinese Import and Export Fair Pazhou Complex, Guangzhou, Guangdong
Profile: Wire & cable equipment; Wire & cable material; Detecting instrument, observation and control technology
Established Year: 2009
Frequency: Annual
Market Area: International
Nature: Trade Only
Cost to Attend: Free
Participated Fee: Standard Booth USD 2,800/booth, Raw Space

元/展位；净地（36m²起）国内企业900元/m²，外资企业280美元/m²
上届规模 2010：展览面积13,000m²(国外展商3,200m²)，参展商402家（国外展商68家，来自12个国家），参观人数11,000人（专业贸易观众1,532人）
主办：广州博优会展服务有限公司
承办：广州博优会展服务有限公司
地址：广州市中山大道中368号华金盾大酒店附一楼全层（510660）
联系人：刘敢，高勇

USD 280/m² (min 36m²)
Statistics 2010: Exhibition Area 13,000m²(foreigners 3,200m²), Exhibitors 402（foreigners 68, came from 12 countries），Visitors 11,000（trade visitors 1,532）
Organizer: Guangzhou Boyou Exhibition Service Co Ltd
Address: 1st Floor, 368 Zhongshan Road (M), Guangzhou 510660, Guangdong

2011/08/17 - 20
☎ 852-2763 9011
🖷 852-2341 0379
✉ jenny@paper-con.com.hk
www.paper-com.com.hk
4440

广州国际机床及加工装备展
地点：中国进出口商品交易会琶洲展馆，广东广州
主办：通讯展览公司
地址：香港九龙观塘成业街11号华成工商中心5字楼15室

Guangzhou International Machine Tools & Machinery Show
Venue: Chinese Import and Export Fair Pazhou Complex, Guangzhou, Guangdong
Organizer: Paper Communication Exhibition Service
Address: Rm. 15, 5/F. Wha Shing Center, 11 Shing Ypi St. Kwun Tong, Kowloon, Hong Kong
Contact: Jenny Leung

2011/09/01 - 03
☎ 020-8989 9266
🖷 020-8989 9050
✉ ns@zhenweiexpo.com
www.cneici.net
4450

2011中国（广州）国际化工技术装备展览会
地点：中国进出口商品交易会琶洲展馆，广东广州
内容：化工单元设备；化工非标专用设备；通用机械；仪器仪表；专用设备：化工、石化设备、压力容器；搪瓷、搪玻璃设备，化工机械及备品配件，橡胶塑料机械，安全生产技术设备，化工环保设备，医药化工、制药与生物工程专用设备，电子化工专用设备，化工成套装置和设备；化工、石化设备贸易及营销代理机构。
始办年份：2011
首届
周期：每年一届
性质：面向贸易观众
入场券价格：免费
参展费用：8,800元/展位
预计规模：总面积7,000m²
主办：广东省化工学会；广东省石油和化学工业协会；振威展览集团
地址：广州市海珠区琶洲大道东1号保利国际广场南塔5楼（510308）
联系人：牛松

China (Guangzhou) International Chemical Technology & Equipment Exhibition
Venue: Chinese Import and Export Fair Pazhou Complex, Guangzhou, Guangdong
Profile: Chemical engineering unit operation, Chemical unstandard equipment, General machinery, Instruments, Special equipment：special chemical equipment, petrochemical equipment, pressure vessel; chemical enamel equipment, glass-lined equipment; chemical machinery and equipment spare parts; rubber & plastics machinery; safety in production technology and equipments; chemical environmental protection equipment; pharmaceutical chemical equipments, pharmaceutical equipments and biological engineering special equipment, etc
Established Year: 2011
First Session
Frequency: Annual
Nature: Trade Only
Cost to Attend: Free
Participated Fee: RMB 8,800/booth
Organizer: Chemical Industry and Engineering Society of Guangdong; Guangdong Petroleum and Chemical Industry Association; Zhenwei Exhibition Group
Address: Unit 501-504 South Tower Poly International Plaza,No.688,Middle Yuejiang Road（East of Pazhou Complex）, Haizhu District, Guangzhou, China
Contact: Niu Song

2011/09/01 - 03
☎ 020-8989 9266
🖷 020-8989 9050
✉ ns@zhenweiexpo.com
www.cneici.net
4460

2011中国（广州）国际电子化学品展览会
地点：中国进出口商品交易会琶洲展馆，广东广州
内容：集成电路电子化学品；印刷电路板电子化学品；平板显示产业电子化学品；新能源电池电子化学品：锂电电池材料、太阳能光伏电池用电子化学品、电容器化学品；含氟、含硅电子化学品；其他电子化学品及专用设备
始办年份：2011
首届
周期：每年一届
性质：面向贸易观众
入场券价格：免费
参展费用：8,800元/展位
预计规模：总面积7,000m²
主办：广东省化工学会；广东省石油和化学工业协会；振威展览集团
地址：广州市海珠区琶洲大道东1号保利国际广场南塔5楼（510308）
联系人：牛松

China (Guangzhou) Intl Electronic Chemicals Exhibition
Venue: Chinese Import and Export Fair Pazhou Complex, Guangzhou, Guangdong
Profile: Integrated circuit electronics chemical; PCB electronic chemicals; Flat panel display industrial electronics chemical; New energy battery electronic chemicals：lithium electricity battery material, cathode material, anode materials, the diaphragm and electrolyte, solar cells with electronic chemicals, capacitor chemicals; Containing fluorine, containing silicon electronics chemical; Other electronic chemicals and special equipment
Established Year: 2011
First Session
Frequency: Annual
Nature: Trade Only
Cost to Attend: Free
Participated Fee: RMB 8,800/booth
Organizer: Chemical Industry and Engineering Society of Guang Dong; Guangdong Petroleum and Chemical Industry Association; Zhenwei Exhibition Group
Address: Unit 501-504 South Tower Poly International Plaza,No.688,Middle Yuejiang Road（East of Pazhou Complex）, Haizhu District, Guangzhou, China
Contact: Niu Song

2011/09/01 - 03
☎ 020-8989 9266
🖷 020-8989 9050
✉ ns@zhenweiexpo.com
www.cneici.net
4470

2011中国（广州）国际车用化工产品及技术展览会
地点：中国进出口商品交易会琶洲展馆，广东广州
内容：润滑系统用化学品：汽车机油、柴油机油、发动机油、火花机油、内燃机油、汽轮机油、冷冻机油、压缩机油、刹车及离合系统用油、波箱油、齿轮油、链条油、润滑脂、润滑油添加剂及其他。汽车用清洗剂；汽车用防护用品；汽车用涂料；汽车用粘结剂；汽车皮革、橡胶、塑料及其化学品；汽车空气清新剂；车用化工材料

China (Guangzhou) International Automotive Chemical Products & Technology Exhibition
Venue: Chinese Import and Export Fair Pazhou Complex, Guangzhou, Guangdong
Profile: Specialty Chemicals for Lubrication system, Automobile cleaner, Automobile use protective appliances, Automotive paint, Automobile use binder, Automotive leather, rubber, plastic and chemicals, Auto air freshener, Vehicle chemical materials

始办年份：2011
首届
周期：每年一届
性质：面向贸易观众
入场券价格：免费
参展费用：8,800元/展位
预计规模：展览面积7,000m²
主办：广东省化工学会；广东省石油和化学工业协会；振威展览集团
地址：广州市海珠区琶洲大道东1号保利国际广场南塔5楼（510308）
联系人：牛松

Established Year: 2011
First Session
Frequency: Annual
Nature: Trade Only
Cost to Attend: Free
Participated Fee: RMB 8,800/booth
Organizer: Chemical Industry and Engineering Society of Guang Dong; Guangdong Petroleum and Chemical Industry Association; Zhenwei Exhibition Group
Address: Unit 501-504 South Tower Poly International Plaza,No.688, Middle Yuejiang Road（East of Pazhou Complex）, Haizhu District, Guangzhou, China
Contact: Niu Song

2011/09/02 - 04
☎ 852-2811 8897
📠 852-2516 5024
✉ publicity@adsale.com.hk
www.adsale.com.hk
4480

中国（广东）国际旅游产业博览会
地点：保利世贸博览馆，广东广州
内容：唯一由国家旅游局及广东省人民政府荣誉主办的旅游展览会。秉承其优良B2B及B2C的销售和推广基础以及政府的积极参与，CITE 每年也成功吸引数以万计中外人士参观展会。
周期：每年一届
市场范围：国际性
上届规模 2010：展览面积30,000m²，参展商1,015家，参观人数150,000人
承办：广东省旅游协会；广州广之旅国际旅行社股份有限公司；雅式展览服务有限公司
地址：香港北角渣华道321号6楼雅式展览服务有限公司
联系人：曾慧怡小姐，黄嘉欣小姐

China International Travel Expo (CITE) 2011
Venue: Poly World Trade Expo Center, Guangzhou, Guangdong
Profile: The only tourism expo sponsored by National Tourism Administration & People's Government of Guangdong Province. Contributing from its well-established B-To-B and B-To-C sales and marketing foundation as well as the strong support and involvement of the government, CITE is well-attended by thousands of international and Chinese trade and public visitors annually.
Frequency: Annual
Market Area: International
Statistics 2010: Exhibition Area 30,000m², Exhibitors 1015, Visitors 150,000
Organizer: Guangdong Tourism Association; GZL International Travel Service Ltd; Adsale Exhibition Services Ltd
Address: 6th Floor, 321 Java Road, North Point, Hong Kong
Contact: Ms Alice Tsang, Ms Cat Wong

2011/09/07 - 09
☎ 020-3877 3839
📠 020-3877 3345
✉ swgl2tc@163.com
4490

2011第二届广州整体橱柜、壁柜及生产设备展览会
地点：中国进出口商品交易会琶洲展馆，广东广州
内容：整体橱柜、橱柜、集成厨房，消毒柜、吊柜、橱柜板材、橱柜门板、防火门板、人造石台面、不锈钢台面；整体衣柜、整体书柜、衣帽间、浴室柜、组合柜、移门、推拉门、隔断、配套系列、内门系统、壁柜板材、滑轨、合页、把手等五金配件；橱柜生产设备、壁柜生产设备
始办年份：2010
周期：每年一届
市场范围：全国性
性质：面向公众
主办：广东省木材行业协会；广州市博展展览有限公司
地址：广东省广州市林和西横路121号恒康阁409室（510610）
联系人：倪晓勉

Guangzhou whole cabinet, Closet and Equipment Exhibition
Venue: Chinese Import and Export Fair Pazhou Complex, Guangzhou, Guangdong
Established Year: 2010
Frequency: Annual
Market Area: National
Nature: Open to Public
Organizer: Guangzhou Bo Zhan Exhibition Co Ltd

2011/09/07 - 09
☎ 020-3877 3615
📠 020-3877 3623
✉ liqiang8088@126.com
4500

2011第十一届广州木材、人造板、木地板、木门及设备展览会
地点：中国进出口商品交易会琶洲展馆，广东广州
内容：木材类，人造板类，木地板类，木材干燥设备、木材旋切设备、木板激光雕刻设备、人造板材生产设备；木门生产成套生产及加工设备、人造板热压设备、木地板生产设备；木业涂装设备、木业淋漆设备、板材UV涂装生产线、木材及人造板检测仪器；木工刀具、木业包装机械、喷码机、除尘设备。木业用胶、胶粘剂、助剂
始办年份：2000
周期：每年一届
市场范围：全国性
性质：面向公众
主办：广东省木材行业协会；广州市博展展览有限公司
地址：广东省广州市林和西横路121号恒康阁409室（510610）
联系人：李强

11th Guangzhou Lumber, Building board, Wood floor, Door and Equipment Exhibitio
Venue: Chinese Import and Export Fair Pazhou Complex, Guangzhou, Guangdong
Established Year: 2000
Frequency: Annual
Market Area: National
Nature: Open to Public
Organizer: Guangzhou Bo Zhan Exhibition Co Ltd

2011/09/07 - 10
☎ 020-8912 8016, 8912 8062
📠 020-8912 8251转ext 102
✉ ciff@fairwindow.com.cn
www.ciff-gz.com
4510

中国广州国际家具博览会(民用家具展)
地点：中国进出口商品交易会琶洲展馆，广东广州
内容：现代家具、客厅家具、厨房家具、传统家具、卧室家具、户外家具、软体家具、餐厅家具、儿童家具、其它；古典家具、欧式家具、美式家具、新古典家具、古典软体家具、中式红木家具、其它
始办年份：1998
周期：每年两届
市场范围：国际性
性质：面向贸易观众
入场券价格：20元
参展费用：净地790元/m²，标准展位7,900元/9m²
上届规模 2010：展览面积150,000m²，参展商517家，参观人数33,982人
主办：中国对外贸易中心（集团）
承办：中国对外贸易广州展览总公司

China International Furniture Fair (Guangzhou) – Home Furniture
Venue: Chinese Import and Export Fair Pazhou Complex, Guangzhou, Guangdong
Profile: Modern Furniture, Living Room Furniture, Kitchen Furniture, Traditional Furniture, Bedroom Furniture, Outdoor Furniture, Soft Furniture, Dining Room Furniture, Children Furniture, Others; Classical Furniture, European Style Furniture, American Style Furniture, Neo-classical Furniture, Classical Soft Furniture, Chinese Mahogany Furniture, Others
Established Year: 1998
Frequency: Biannual
Market Area: International
Nature: Trade Only
Cost to Attend: RMB 20:-
Participated Fee: Raw Space RMB 790/m², Standard Booth RMB 7,900/9m²

地址：广州市海珠区新港东路980号广交会展馆C区16号馆A层（510014）
联系人：何思慧，于雯

Statistics 2010: Exhibition Area 150,000m², Exhibitors 517, Visitors 33,982
Sponsor: China Foreign Trade Center (Group)
Organizer: China Foreign Trade Guangzhou Exhibition General Corporation
Address: Floor A, Hall 16, Area C, Canton Fair Complex, No.980 Xingang Dong Road, Haizhu District, Guangzhou, China
Contact: Gina Ho, Stephanie Yu

2011/09/07 - 10
☎ 020-8912 8023, 8912 8016
🖷 020-8912 8251转ext 101
✉ hhc@fairwindow.com.cn
hhc.fairwindow.com
4520

中国广州国际家居饰品、家纺布艺展览会
地点：中国进出口商品交易会琶洲展馆，广东广州
内容：家居饰品、家纺布艺
始办年份：2005
周期：每年一届
市场范围：国际性
入场券价格：20元
参展费用：净地790元/m²，标准展位7,900元/9m²
上届规模 2010：展览面积40,000m²，参观人数13,526人
主办：中国对外贸易中心（集团）
承办：中国对外贸易广州展览总公司
地址：广州市海珠区新港东路980号广交会展馆C区16号馆A层（510036）
联系人：何思慧，于雯

Homedecor + Hometextile China 2011
Venue: Chinese Import and Export Fair Pazhou Complex, Guangzhou, Guangdong
Profile: Home decor, Home textile.
Established Year: 2005
Frequency: Annual
Market Area: International
Cost to Attend: RMB 20:-
Participated Fee: Raw Space RMB 790/m², Standard Booth RMB 7,900/booth
Statistics 2010: Exhibition Area 40,000m², Visitors 13,526
Sponsor: China Foreign Trade Center (Group)
Organizer: China Foreign Trade Guangzhou Exhibition General Corporation
Address: Floor A, Hall 16, Area C, Canton Fair Complex, No.980 Xingang Dong Road, Haizhu District, Guangzhou, China
Contact: Gina Ho, Stephanie Yu

2011/09/08 - 10
☎ 020-3409 5949
🖷 020-3409 5856
✉ zengsisi44@139.com
4530

2011第2届华南医疗器械（广州）展览会
地点：中国进出口商品交易会琶洲展馆，广东广州
内容：诊断、影像设备：CT、X线机、核磁共振、B超、洗片机、镜类设备、图像记录仪及图像处理系统、远程诊断系统；心脑电监护设备：遥测监护系统、除颤监护仪、胎儿监护仪、运动平板心电系统、动态血压、脑电图机、肌电头机、诱发电仪、血氧饱和度监护仪及辅助诊断设备；生化及试验室设备：生化分析仪、血球计数仪、尿分析仪、血液透析仪、流式细胞仪、电解质分析仪、酶标仪、色谱仪、PCR仪、微生物鉴定分析系统、血库冰箱和培养箱；医用辅助设备。
始办年份：2010
市场范围：全国性
性质：面向公众
上届规模 2010：展览面积15,000m²
主办：广州市医疗器械行业协会；香港巴斯特国际会展集团公司；广州益发展览有限公司
地址：广东省广州市新港东路238号世港国际公寓B栋403（510405）
联系人：曾思思

South China Medical Equipment Exhibition
Venue: Chinese Import and Export Fair Pazhou Complex, Guangzhou, Guangdong
Established Year: 2010
Market Area: National
Nature: Open to Public
Statistics 2010: Exhibition Area 15,000m²
Organizer: Guangzhou Yifa Exhibition Co Ltd

2011/09/15 - 17
☎ 020-6107 8749, 6107 8749, 6107 8749
🖷 020-6108 9459
✉ gzyfzl2001@163.com
www.gzyfzl.com
4540

2011广州国际食品展暨广州进口食品展览会
地点：广州锦汉展览中心，广东广州
内容：进口食品展区、食品饮料区、营养品健康食品区、优质农产品及精品粮油区、食品添加剂及配料、食品加工及包装设备区
始办年份：2002
周期：每年两届
市场范围：国际性
性质：面向公众
参展费用：8,000元/展位
主办：中国医药保健国际贸易促进会；广东省保健食品行业协会
联络：广州市艺帆展览服务有限公司
地址：广州市天河区燕岭路25-27号银燕大厦201室（510507）
联系人：江桂发，13710502143
QQ：1405764838

Guangzhou Food Fair
Venue: Guangzhou Jinhan Exhibition Center, Guangzhou, Guangdong
Established Year: 2002
Frequency: Biannual
Market Area: International
Nature: Open to Public
Participated Fee: RMB 8,000/booth
Organizer: Guangzhou Yifa Exhibition Co Ltd

2011/09/15 - 17
☎ 020-6107 8749, 6107 8749, 6107 8749
🖷 020-6108 9459
✉ gzyfzl2001@163.com
www.gzyfzl.com
4560

2011广州药交会第19届全国药品保健品（广州）交易会
地点：广州锦汉展览中心，广东广州
内容：药品类：医药新特品种、处方药品、ＯＴＣ药品、中西成药、生物制药、中药饮片、植物提取物、民族医药、原料药、医药中间体、消毒液。保健品类：营养保健食品、保健饮料、保健茶、保健酒、微量元素制品、特殊用途化妆品、减增肥保健品、性保健、保健用品、保健治疗仪、保健器具等。药店（房）设施；医药保健品生产包装类
始办年份：2002
周期：每年两届
市场范围：全国性
性质：面向公众
参展费用：8,000元/展位
主办：中国医药保健国际贸易促进会；广东省保健食品行业协会
联络：广州市艺帆展览服务有限公司
地址：广州市天河区燕岭路25-27号银燕大厦201室（510507）
联系人：江桂发，13710502143
QQ：1405764838

18th China Medicine and Healthcare Products (Guangzhou) Exhibition 2011
Venue: Guangzhou Jinhan Exhibition Center, Guangzhou, Guangdong
Established Year: 2002
Frequency: Biannual
Market Area: National
Nature: Open to Public
Participated Fee: RMB 8,000/booth
Organizer: Guangzhou Yifa Exhibition Co Ltd

2011/09/15 - 17
☎ 020-61078749, 6107 8749, 6107 8749
🖷 020-6108 9459
✉ gzyfzl2001@163.com
www.gzyfzl.com
4570

第11届中国（广州）国际营养品/健康食品及有机产品展览会
地点：广州锦汉展览中心，广东广州
内容：营养品与健康食品：营养素、营养补充剂、营养强化食品、富营养食品、功能（保健）食品；天然滋补品：花粉产品、蜂产品、人参产品、鱼油产品、酶化产品、绿藻产品、胚芽产品、叶绿素产品、芦荟产品、植物提取物产品、菌类产品；有机产品与绿色食品。
论坛主题：中国营养产业发展的前景；营养产业品牌发展论坛；有机食品安全生产管理与认证。
始办年份：2002
周期：每年两届
市场范围：国际性
性质：面向公众
参展费用：8,000元/展位
主办：中国医药保健国际贸易促进会；广东省保健食品行业协会
联络：广州市艺帆展览服务有限公司
地址：广州市天河区燕岭路25-27号银燕大厦201室（510507）
联系人：江桂发
QQ：1405764838

CINHOE
Guangzhou Nutrition and Organic Food Exhibition
Venue: Guangzhou Jinhan Exhibition Center, Guangzhou, Guangdong
Established Year: 2002
Frequency: Biannual
Market Area: International
Nature: Open to Public
Participated Fee: RMB 8,000/booth
Organizer: Guangzhou Yifan Exhibition Co Ltd

2011/09/19 - 21
☎ 020-8625 9008, 8625 8323, 8625 7099
🖷 020-8625 9533
✉ info@gzbeautyexpo.com
www.gzbeautyexpo.com
4580

第35届广州国际美博会
地点：中国进出口商品交易会琶洲展馆，广东广州
内容：国际品牌、美容院、日化洗涤、养生、发廊、包装。护肤品、化妆品、美发品、天然保健品、身心健康产品、美甲用品、彩绘文绣用品、美容院发廊的仪器家具及配套品、日用洗涤品、卫生产品、女性内衣、婚纱、时尚饰品、香水、香精、香料、包装材料、设备、机械、原料、代客加工（OEM）
始办年份：1989
周期：每年两届
市场范围：国际性
性质：面向贸易观众
上届规模 2010：参展商2,000家（来自18个国家），参观人数310,000人
主办：广东省美容美发化妆品行业协会；广东博环美国际展览有限公司
地址：广东省广州市广园西路121号美博城A座写字楼五楼（510400）

The 35th Guangzhou International Beauty Expo - Autumn 2011
Venue: Chinese Import and Export Fair Pazhou Complex, Guangzhou, Guangdong
Profile: International brands, beauty salons, personal care, nature health, hair salons, packaging.
Established Year: 1989
Frequency: Biannual
Market Area: International
Nature: Trade Only
Statistics 2010: Exhibitors 2,000（came from 18 countries）, Visitors 310,000
Organizer: Guangdong International Exhibitions Limited; Guangdong Beauty & Cosmetic Association
Address: 5th Floor, Building A121 Guang Yuan Road (West), Guangzhou 510400, China

2011/09/21 - 23
☎ 021-6160 8555转ext 231
🖷 021-5876 9332
✉ susan.wang@china.messefrankfurt.com
www.messefrankfurt.com.hk
4583

广州国际模具展览会
地点：保利世贸博览馆，广东广州
周期：每年一届
性质：面向贸易观众
主办：法兰克福展览（上海）有限公司
地址：上海浦东新区浦东南路999号上海联合广场32层
联系人：汪静

Guangzhou International Mould & Die Exhibition
Venue: Poly World Trade Center Expo, Guangzhou, Guangdong
Frequency: Annual
Nature: Trade Only
Organizer: Messe Frankfurt (Shanghai) Ltd

2011/10/15 – 30
☎ 400-888 999
+86-20-28 888 999
(境外overseas)
www.cantonfair.org.cn
4585

第108届中国进出口商品交易会
地点：中国进出口商品交易会展馆，广东广州
承办：中国对外贸易中心

108th China Import and Export Fair
Venue: China Import and Export Fair Complex, Guangzhou, Guangdong
Organizer: China Foreign Trade Centre

2011/10/20 - 22
☎ 010-5933 9495
🖷 010-5933 9494
✉ info@reedguanghe.com
www.chinagolfshow.com
4590

CHINA GOLF SHOW

亚洲国际高尔夫球博览会
地点：广州锦汉展览中心，广东广州
内容：球场及练习场设施设备及建设用品、高尔夫个人用品消费品及OEM生产展区、高尔夫设计建造行业/服务及媒体区、高尔夫球具特卖区。
始办年份：2004
周期：每年两届
市场范围：国际性
主办：北京励展光合展览有限公司
地址：北京市朝阳区新源南路1-3号平安国际金融中心A座15层01-03,05（100027）

China Golf Show, Guangzhou
Venue: Guangzhou Jinhan Exhibition Center, Guangzhou, Guangdong
Profile: Golf Merchandise, Golf Course Equipment and Applications, Golf Industry services, Golf Life Style
Established Year: 2004
Frequency: Biannual
Market Area: International
Organizer: Reed Guanghe Exhibition Co Ltd
Address: Unit 01-03, 05, 15th Floor, Tower A, Ping An International Finance Center, No.1-3 Xinyuan South Road, Chaoyang District, Beijing 100027, China

2011/11/01 - 03
☎ 852-2851 8603
🖷 852-2851 8637
✉ topreput@top-repute.com
www.ifle-china.com
4600

广州国际鞋类、皮革制成品展览会
地点：中国进出口商品交易会琶洲展馆，广东广州
内容：所有鞋类、皮包和箱包、皮革衣服和产品、时尚皮制饰物配件、知名品牌产品
周期：每年一届
市场范围：国际性
参展费用：标准展位1,800美元/9m²
主办：显辉国际展览有限公司；广州市显辉展览服务有限公司
地址：香港上环禧利街27号富辉商业中心2403室
联系人：林生先，刘小姐

International Footwear & Leather Products Exhibition – Guangzhou
Venue: Chinese Import and Export Fair Pazhou Complex, Guangzhou, Guangdong
Profile: All kinds of footwear, Bags & Suitcases, Leather Garments & Leather Product, Fashion Accessories, Brand Name Products
Frequency: Annual
Market Area: International
Participated Fee: Standard Booth USD 1,800/9m²
Organizer: Top Repute Co Ltd; Top Repute Co Ltd (Guangzhou)
Address: Rm 2403, Fu Fai Commercial Center, 27 Hillier Street, Sheung Wan, Hong Kong
Contact: Mr Lam, Ms Lau

2011/11/09 - 11
☎ 020-8989 9266
🖷 020-8989 9050
✉ ns@zhenweiexpo.com
www.cantontex.com.cn

4610

第十一届中国（广州）国际纺织机械展览会
地点：中国进出口商品交易会琶洲展馆，广东广州
内容：针织机械：圆型针织机、提花机、织袜机、电脑横编机、手套机、经编机、钩编机、编织机。纺纱机械：粗纱机、细纱机、捻线机、络筒机、倍捻机、并条机、摇纱机、化纤机械设备。织造机械：剑杆织机、喷气织机、梭织机、织带机、商标机、整经机、验布卷布机。染整机械：各种漂泊、染色、整理机、定型机、烘干机、预缩机、印花机。绣花机：各种电脑刺绣机、飞梭刺绣机、绣花机配件。制衣设备：设计、裁剪、激光、CAD/CAM系统；缝前、缝纫设备；刺绣、绣花、绗缝设备；缝后、配送、整熨设备；其它相关设备、辅料、辅助服务、信息服务
始办年份：2000
周期：每年一届
市场范围：全国性
性质：面向贸易观众
入场券价格：免费
参展费用：10,000元/展期
上届规模 2010：展览面积10,000m^2(国外展商2,000m^2)，参展商309家（国外展商35家，来自12个国家），参观人数11,000人（专业贸易观众8,000人）
主办：广东振威国展展览有限公司
地址：广州市海珠区琶洲大道东1号保利国际广场南塔5楼（510308）
联系人：牛松

The 11th China (Guangzhou) International Exhibition For Textile Machinery
Venue: Chinese Import and Export Fair Pazhou Complex, Guangzhou, Guangdong
Profile: Weaving preparatory machinery, weaving machinery Loom, rapier loom, air jet loom, jacquard, non-woven fabric machine, and weft accumulator Non-woven fabric line, spinning machine for environment protect Preparatory and auxiliary machine for knitting and hosiery industry. Circular knitting machine, knitting machine, hosiery machine. Washing, bleaching, dyeing machine, printing, finishing, sewing-thread machine Crabbing, bleach, washing, filling, dyeing, printing, raising, dryer, damping ager, steaming machine and apparatus, raising, polishing machine, grinding machine for shearing-blade and shearing cylinder, suede finishing machine, other finishing machine
Established Year: 2000
Frequency: Annual
Market Area: National
Nature: Trade Only
Cost to Attend: Free
Participated Fee: RMB 10,000/booth
Statistics 2010: Exhibition Area 10,000m^2(foreigners 2,000m^2), Exhibitors 309 (foreigners 35, came from 12 countries), Visitors 11,000 (trade visitors 8,000)
Organizer: Guangdong Zhenwei Guozhan Exhibition Co Ltd
Address: Unit 501-504 South Tower Poly Intl Plaza, No.688 Middle Yuejiang Road (East of Pazhou Complex), Haizhu District, Guangzhou,China
Contact: Niu Song

2011/11/09 - 11
☎ 020-8989 9266
🖷 020-8989 9050
✉ ns@zhenweiexpo.com
www.cantondye.com.cn

4620

第十一届中国国际染料工业及纺织化学品展览会
地点：中国进出口商品交易会琶洲展馆，广东广州
内容：染料：分散染料、酸性染料、活性染料、碱性染料、直接染料、还原染料、硫化染料、靛蓝、硫化黑；有机颜料；涂料印花浆、色母料；中间体；助剂；印染前处理助剂、着色剂、分散剂、柔软剂、渗透剂、稳定剂、均染剂、增稠剂、粘合剂及各种整理助剂；化纤单体、催化剂、化纤油剂、生物酶制品及其他各种纺织用化学制品；纺织行业环保技术、质量认证体系及分析检测和监控、配套生产、印染、三废处理设备
始办年份：2000
周期：每年一届
市场范围：全国性
性质：面向贸易观众
入场券价格：免费
参展费用：10,000元/展位
上届规模 2010：展览面积9,000m^2(国外展商2,500m^2)，参展商175家（国外展商45家，来自10个国家），参观人数11,000人（专业贸易观众8,700人）
主办：中国纺织报社；中国服饰报社；振威展览集团
地址：广州市海珠区琶洲大道东1号保利国际广场南塔5楼（510308）
联系人：牛松

The 11th China International Exhibition for Dye Industry & Textile Chemical
Venue: Chinese Import and Export Fair Pazhou Complex, Guangzhou, Guangdong
Profile: Dyes: disperse dye, acid dye, reactive dyes, basic dye, vat dye, sulfur dye, Indigo, sulphur black; Organic pigments: coating printing paste, color master-batch, kinds of intermediates; Textile auxiliaries, before printing & dyeing auxiliaries, colorants, dispersant, softener, stabilizer, dye, thickener, adhesives and various finishing auxiliary; Fiber-grademonomer, catalyst, preparation agent, enzyme products and other various textile chemicals; Textile industry environmental technology, quality certification system and analytical testing and monitoring
Established Year: 2000
Frequency: Annual
Market Area: National
Nature: Trade Only
Cost to Attend: Free
Participated Fee: RMB 10,000/booth
Statistics 2010: Exhibition Area 9,000m^2(foreigners 2,500m^2), Exhibitors 175 (foreigners 45, came from 10 countries), Visitors 11,000 (trade visitors 8,700)
Organizer: Zhenwei Exhibition Group
Address: Unit 501-504 South Tower Poly Intl Plaza, No.688 Middle Yuejiang Road (East of Pazhou Complex), Haizhu Dist, Guangzhou City,China
Contact: Niu Song

2011/11/09 - 11
☎ 020-8989 9266
🖷 020-8989 9050
✉ ns@zhenweiexpo.com
www.cantondye.com.cn

4630

第十一届中国（广州）国际纺织面辅料及纱线展览会
地点：中国进出口商品交易会琶洲展馆，广东广州
内容：面料：麻织、丝织、棉织、化纤类梭织、毛织、针织及涂层织物、各类复合织物、防静电、防油、防水、阻燃、防辐射织物、丝光、反光织物、弹力织物、无纺布、及纳米技术；纱线、纤维：圆编及横编针织/梭织纱线、织袜纱线、制衣纱线、花式纱线；天然/合成纤维；辅料：刺绣、花边、衬里、纽扣、线带、商标、配件、拉链、衣架；家用纺织品：各类床上用品、厨卫用纺织品、窗帘布艺及相关面料、辅料、各类服装及设计、相关系统；纺织原料：助剂；设计及生产系统
始办年份：2000
周期：每年一届
性质：面向贸易观众
入场券价格：免费
参展费用：10,000元/展位
上届规模 2010：展览面积9,000m^2(国外展商3000m^2)，参展商305家（国外展商32家，来自8个国家），参观人数12,000人（专业贸

The 11th Guangzhou International Exhibition for Apparel Fabric, Accessories & Yarns
Venue: Chinese Import and Export Fair Pazhou Complex, Guangzhou, Guangdong
Profile: Fabric: Linen, Silk, Cotton, Chemical Fibre, Wool, Knitting, Coating Fabric, all kinds of complex fabric, functional fabric, defend static, defend oil, waterproof, firre-retardant, radiation protection fabric, silky luster of mercerized fabric, glisten. Fabric: Linen, Silk, Cotton, Chemical Fibre, Wool, Knitting, Coating Fabric, all kinds of complex fabric, functional fabric, defend static, defend oil, waterproof, firre-retardant, radiation protection fabric,etc **Established Year**: 2000
Frequency: Annual
Nature: Trade Only
Cost to Attend: Free
Participated Fee: RMB 10,000/booth
Statistics 2010: Exhibition Area 9,000m^2(foreigners 3,000m^2),

易观众7,800人）
主办：中国纺织报社；中国服饰报社；振威展览集团
地址：广州市海珠区琶洲大道东1号保利国际广场南塔5楼（510308）
联系人：牛松

Exhibitors 305（foreigners 32, came from 8 countries），Visitors 12,000（trade visitors 7,800）
Organizer: Zhenwei Exhibition Group
Address: Unit 501-504 South Tower Poly Intl Plaza,No.688,Middle Yuejiang Road（East of Pazhou Complex），Haizhu District, Guangzhou, China
Contact: Niu Song

2011/11/22 – 28
☎ 020-8912 8222
📠 020-8912 8240
✉ caoyw@fairwindow.com.cn
www. Autoshow-gz.com
4635

第九届中国（广州）国际汽车展览会
地点：中国进出口商品交易会展馆，广东广州
内容：乘用车、商用车、汽车零部件、汽车用品。
始办年份：2003
周期：每年一届
市场范围：国际性
性质：面向公众
入场价格：60元\天，40元\天
参展费用：乘用车展区1,600/m²（200m²起），商用车展区1,600元/m²（100m²起）；汽车零部件及用品展区：9,000元/展位，净地900元/m²（36m²起）
上届规模 2010：展览面积160,000m²，参展商687家（来自20个国家），参观人数487,615人
主办：广州市人民政府；广东省经济贸易委员会；中国对外贸易中心；中国机械工业联合会；中国汽车工业协会
承办：中国对外贸易广州展览总公司；中国国际贸易促进委员会汽车行业分会；广州汽车工业集团有限公司；中国汽车工程学会；广州联合展贸有限公司；中国国际贸易促进委员会广州市分会；广州汽车销售行业协会；广州工业经济联合会
地址：广州市海珠区新港东路980号广交会展馆C区16号馆A层（510335）
联系人：曹育武，刘少璞

The 9th China (Guangzhou) Intl Automobile Exhibition
Venue: China Import & Export Complex, Guangzhou, Guangdong
Profile: Passenger Cars\commercial vehicles\auto parts\auto accessories.
Established Year: 2003
Frequency: Annual
Market Area: International
Nature: Open to Public
Cost to Attend: RMB 40-60/m²
Participated Fee: RMB 1,600/m²(min 200m²)
Statistics 2010: Exhibition Area 160,000m², Exhibitors 687(came from 20 countries), Visitors 487,615
Sponsor: Municipal People's Government of Guangzhou; The Economic & Trade Commission of Guangdong Province; China Foreign Trade Center; China Machinery Industry Federation; China Association of Automobile Manufacturers
Organizer: China Foreign Trade Guangzhou Exhibition General Corporation; CCPIT Automotive Sub-Council; Guangzhou Automobile Industry Group Co., Ltd. (GAIG); The Society of Automotive Engineers of China (SAE-China),Union Fair and Trade Co., Ltd.; CCPIT Guangzhou Sub-Council; Guangzhou Association of Auto-marketing Industry; Guangzhou Industrial Economy Federation
Address: #980, Xin'gang East Road, Guangzhou 510335, China
Contact: Cao Yuwu, Liu Shaopu

2012/03/27 - 30
☎ 020-8755 2468转ext 12/15
📠 020-8755 2970
✉ k.lee@koelnmesse.cn
www.interzum-guangzhou.com
4640

中国广州国际木工机械、家具配料展览会
地点：中国进出口商品交易会琶洲展馆，广东广州
内容：家具生产原料及配件；软体家具和床具生产机械、原料及配件；室内装饰机械、材料及组件；木工、家具生产机械及辅助设备；其它：媒体、贸易推广机构
始办年份：2004
周期：每年一届
市场范围：国际性
性质：面向贸易观众
参展费用：净地（24m²起）1,300元/m²，普通标准展位（min 9m²）1,500元/m²，高级标摊（18m²起）1,700元/m²，联合参展费2,500元/每一家联合参展商
上届规模 2010：展览面积100,000m²，参展商887家（国外展商198家，来自24个国家），参观人数43,709人
主办：科隆国际展览有限公司；中国对外贸易中心（集团）
承办：科隆展览有限公司；中国对外贸易广州展览总公司
地址：广州市天河区天河北路183号大都会广场3311室科隆展览有限公司（510620）
联系人：李伟莉，梁绍俊

interzum guangzhou
Venue: Chinese Import and Export Fair Pazhou Complex, Guangzhou, Guangdong
Profile: Materials and Components for Furniture Production; Machines, Materials and Components for Upholstery and Bedding; Machines, Materials and Components for Interior Works; Machines and Auxiliary Machines for Woodworking and Furniture Production
Established Year: 2004
Frequency: Annual
Market Area: International
Nature: Trade Only
Participated Fee: Raw Space（min 24m²）RMB 1,300/m², Standard Booth（min 9m²）RMB 1,500/m²
Statistics 2010: Exhibition Area 100,000m², Exhibitors 887（foreigners 198, came from 24 countries），Visitors 43,709
Sponsor: Koelnmesse GmbH; China Foreign Trade Center (Group)
Organizer: Koelnmesse Co Ltd; China Foreign Trade Guangzhou Exhibition Corp
Address: Koelnmesse Co Ltd, Unit 1018, Landmark Tower 2, No.8 Dongsanhuan North Rd., Beijing
Contact: Karen Lee, Mattis Liang

广东-惠州 Guangdong-Huizhou

2011/08 -
☎ 010-8260 6880转ext 91
📠 010-8260 6883
✉ ciccyhuang@cnaico.com.cn
www.cnaico.com.cn
www.autochina.com.cn
4645

2011惠州国际汽车展览会
地点：广东惠州
主办：中国汽车工业国际合作总公司
地址：北京市海淀区中关村丹棱街3号A座

Huizhou International Automobile Exhibition
Venue: HuizhouGuangdong
Organizer: China National Automotive Industry International Corp

广东-深圳 Guangdong-Shenzhen

2011/02/22 - 24
☎ 010-8455 6632
🖷 010-6235 8292
✉ lin.xu@reedsinopharm.com
www.pchi-china.com
4650

2011（深圳）国家化妆品、个人及家庭护理用品原料展览会
地点：深圳会展中心，广东深圳
内容：化妆品、洗浴用品、个人护理及家庭护理用品原材料、辅料加工和包装材料、设备
周期：每年一届
主办：国药励展展览有限责任公司
地址：北京朝阳区新源南路1-3号平安国际金融中心B座15层（100027）
联系人：徐琳

Personal Care and Homecare ingredients Fair (PCHI)
Venue: Shenzhen Convention & Exhibition Center, Shenzhen, Guangdong
Profile: The Personal Care and Homecare Ingredients (PCHi) trade show is China's dedicated trade event for ingredient suppliers to engage manufacturers of cosmetics, personal care and homecare goods to meet their growing production demands. PCHI is the one stop platform for peer-to-peer information exchange of emerging market trends, technological innovations, new scientific developments and updates on international regulations, underpinned by quality service standards.
Frequency: Annual
Organizer: Reed Sinopharm Exhibitions
Address: 15th Floor Tower B, Ping An International Financial Center, No.1-3 Xinyuan South Road, Chaoyang District. Beijing, China
Contact: Lynn Xu

2011/03/19 - 22
☎ 0755-2601 8222, 2601 8333
🖷 0755-2601 8179, 2601 8152
✉ sevices@szfa.com
www.sifechina.cn
4660

第26深圳国际家具展
地点：深圳会展中心，广东深圳
内容：实木家具展、现代板式家具展、软体家具展、金属玻璃家具展、户外家具展、缤纷家居饰品展、设计论坛
始办年份：1996
周期：每年一届
市场范围：国际性
性质：面向贸易观众
入场券价格：50RMB
参展费用：标准展位7,900元，净地790元/m²
上届规模 2010：展览面积200,000m²(国外展商500m²)，参观人数120,000人
主办：深圳市家具行业协会；深圳市德赛展览有限公司
地址：深圳市南山区西丽沙河西路家具研发基地（518055）
联系人：郑昊

Shenzhen International Furniture Exhibition
Venue: Shenzhen Convention & Exhibition Center, Shenzhen, Guangdong
Established Year: 1996
Frequency: Annual
Market Area: International
Nature: Trade Only
Cost to Attend: RMB 50:-
Participated Fee: Standard Booth RMB 7,900, Raw Space RMB 790/m²
Statistics 2010: Exhibition Area 200,000m²(foreigners 500m²), Visitors 120,000
Organizer: Shenzhen Furniture Trade Association
Address: The Furniture Research Base, Shahe West Rd., Shenzhen, China
Contact: Suny Zheng

2011/03/28 - 31
☎ 0755-8345 9957
🖷 0755-8347 7946
✉ vipyshen@yahoo.com.cn
4670

2011第12届深圳国际机械、模具及制品、塑胶工业展览会
地点：深圳会展中心，广东深圳
内容：作为全球国际展览联盟（UFI）在中国华南地区首家认可的品牌展览会，已成为中国最具影响和辐射力的专业代表展，为来自全球的供应商、经销代理商、用户及行业专家提供了业务洽谈、项目投资、技术合作、学术讨论的舞台。
始办年份：2000
周期：每年一届
市场范围：国际性
性质：面向贸易观众
入场券价格：专业免费
参展费用：标准展位15,000元，净地1,500元/m²
上届规模 2010：展览面积29,268m²(国外展商5,580m²)，参展商984家（国外展商131家，来自22个国家），参观人数97,184人（专业贸易观众28,232人）
主办：深圳市机械行业协会
承办：深圳市协广机械有限公司
地址：广东省深圳市福田区深南大道6021号喜年中心A座517室（518040）
联系人：尹惠斌
MSN：yshen@126.com
QQ：770353181

China Shenzhen International Machinery Manufacturing Industry Exhibition （SIM2011）
Venue: Shenzhen Convention & Exhibition Center, Shenzhen, Guangdong
Profile: Approved by UFI, SIMM & S. Mould & S. Plas firstly gained this honor in south of China, winning the recognition from the exhibitors and buyers home and aboard, and has become the most influential professional exhibitions in China.
Established Year: 2000
Frequency: Annual
Market Area: International
Nature: Trade Only
Cost to Attend: Free
Participated Fee: Standard Booth RMB 15,000, Raw Space RMB 1,500/m²
Statistics 2010: Exhibition Area 29,268m² (foreigners 5,580m²), Exhibitors 984（foreigners 131, came from 22 countries）, Visitors 97,184（trade visitors 28,232）
Sponsor: Shenzhen Machinery Association
Organizer: Shenzhen Xieguang Machinery Co Ltd
Address: Rm.1204, 12/F., Hailrun Complex, No.6021 Shennan Blvd, Futian District, Shenzhen, China
Contact: Kevin Yin
MSN: yshen@126.com

2011/04/03 - 05
☎ 0755-8364 3424, 13798342253
🖷 0755-8364 3450
www.china-wed.com
4680

2011深圳春季婚博会暨婚庆文化节
地点：深圳会展中心，广东深圳
内容：婚纱摄影、工作室精品区：最新风格婚纱摄影、主题婚纱摄影、个性婚纱摄影、儿童摄影；酒店、酒楼婚宴精品区：豪华婚宴、中西式婚宴、个性婚宴、精品百姓婚宴；婚礼策划及服务精品区：时尚特色定制婚礼、婚典花艺、蜜月旅游、婚车租赁；

Shenzhen International Wedding Exhibition &Wedding Cultural Festival 2010
Venue: Shenzhen Convention & Exhibition Center, Shenzhen, Guangdong
Participated Fee: 1st Floor: Standard Booth RMB 8,800/9m², Raw Space RMB 880/m²; 2nd Floor: Standard Booth RMB 6,800/9m², Raw

婚礼庆典精品区：喜糖、喜烟、喜酒、喜帖、喜品、工艺品、相框、相册、化妆品；结婚首饰精品区：钻石对戒、黄金饰品、各类首饰；婚纱礼服精品区：2011国际流行最新婚纱礼服、中式礼服、修身内衣；新婚服务精品区：新婚理财、蜜月旅游、新婚化美容纤体、色彩设计与咨询；新婚家居精品区
参展费用：一楼：标准展位8,800元/9m²，净地880元/m²，二楼标准展位6,800元/9m²，净地680元/m²
主办：深圳市商业联合会
承办：深圳市美博会展有限公司
地址：深圳市福田区莲花支路公交大厦1808
联系人：李想

Space RMB 680/m²
Organizer: Shenzhen Meibo Exhibition Co Ltd

2011/04/08 - 10
☎ 010-5166 2329转ext 16/22/58
🖷 010-6813 2578, 6818 9519
✉ liuhong@ceac.com.cn
www.icef.com.cn

4690

第77届中国电子展
地点：深圳会展中心，广东深圳
内容：电子元器件、光电器件、LED显示、集成电路、电源模块、新型传感器、嵌入式系统、电子材料、电子生产设备、电子工具、电子测量仪器及工控自动化系统
始办年份：1964
参展费用：境外企业：标准展位2,520美元，净地260美元/m²；国际展区：标准展位15,000元，净地1,300元/m²；国内企业：标准展位10,000元，净地1,000元/m²
上届规模 2010：展览面积70,000m²，参展商1,400家（国外展商140家），参观人数92,357人
主办：中国电子器材总公司
承办：中电会展与信息传播有限公司；深圳市创意时代会展有限公司
地址：北京市复兴路49号（100036）
联系人：崔承哲、陈震宇、刘洪

77th China Electronics Fair
Venue: Shenzhen Convention & Exhibition Center, Shenzhen, Guangdong
Established Year: 1964
Participated Fee: Standard Booth USD 2,520, Raw Space 260/m²
Statistics 2010: Exhibition Area 70,000m², Exhibitors 1,400 (foreigners 140), Visitors 92,357
Organizer: Creativity Convention & Exhibition Co Ltd

2011/04/16 - 19
☎ 010-8455 6611, 8455 6602
🖷 010-8202 2922, 6203 3210
✉ chuanjun.ding@reedsinopharm.com
xiaojing.zhang@reedsinopharm.com
www.cmef.com.cn

4700

第65届中国国际医疗器械博览会
第12届中国国际医疗器械设计与制造技术展览会
地点：深圳会展中心，广东深圳
内容：展出内容全面涵盖了包括医用影像、体外诊断、电子、光学、急救、康复护理以及医疗信息技术、外包服务等上万种产品，直接并全面服务于医疗器械行业从源头到终端整条医疗产业链。
始办年份：1979
周期：每年两届
主办：国药励展展览有限责任公司
地址：北京市朝阳区新源南路1-3号平安国际金融大厦B座15层（100027）

China International Medical Equipment Fair
Venue: Shenzhen Convention & Exhibition Center, Shenzhen, Guangdong
Profile: After 30 years of continuous innovation and self-improvement, CMEF has become the largest exhibition of medical equipment, related products and services in the Asia-Pacific region. The exhibition widely covers ten thousands of products such as medical imaging, in vitro diagnosis, electronics, optics, first aid, rehabilitation nursing, medical information technology and outsourcing services, and it provides services to the entire medical industry chain from the source to the end of the medical equipment industry in a direct and all-round way.
Established Year: 1979
Frequency: Biannual
Organizer: Reed Sinopharm Exhibitions
Address: 15th Floor Tower B, Ping An Intl Finance Center, No.1-3, Xinyuan South Road, Chaoyang District, Beijing 100027, China

---

2011/04/24 - 27
☎ 0755-3398 9211, 3398 9230
🖷 0755-3333 1168
www.reedhuabo.com

4710

GIFTS& HOME
礼品|家居·中国

第十九届中国（深圳）国际礼品、工艺品、钟表及家庭用品展
地点：深圳会展中心，广东深圳
内容：中国最大规模的礼品家居用品展之一。展会每年吸引十余万专业买家前来采购各种商务礼赠品及时尚消费品，买家包括代理商、分销商、批发商、礼品公司、百货商场、集团采购及终端用户。来自各行业的制造商以最具竞争力的价格、品种繁多的优质产品、创新的原创设计为买家提供丰富的选择。
周期：每年一届
性质：面向贸易观众
入场券价格：20元
预计规模：展览面积20,000m²，参展商2,800家，贸易观众120,000人
主办：励展华博展览（深圳）有限公司
地址：深圳市中心区福华三路深圳国际商会中心1801、1802室（518048）
联系人：袁文军，王清林

Gifts and Home China
The 19th China (Shenzhen) International Gifts, Handicrafts, Watches & Houseware Fair
Venue: Shenzhen Convention & Exhibition Center, Shenzhen, Guangdong
Profile: Reed Huabo's China Gifts and Home Fair is the largest trade show of its kind in Mainland China. Held in Shenzhen during the best buying seasons in April and October every year, the fair offers the widest selection of business gifts, premiums and consumer products, and attracts tens of thousands of buyers from across the country.
Frequency: Annual
Nature: Trade Only
Cost to Attend: RMB 20:-
Statistics 2010: 2,800 exhibitors and over 120,000 visitors
Organizer: Reed Huabo Exhibitions (Shenzhen) Co Ltd

2011/05/13 – 16
✉ wbh@cnicif.com
www.cnci.gov.cn
www.cnicif.com

4715

中国（深圳）国际文化产业博览交易会
地点：深圳会展中心，广东深圳
始办年份：2004
周期：每年一届
市场范围：全国性
性质：面向公众
承办：深圳报业集团；深圳广电集团；深圳出版发行集团公司；深圳国际文化产业博览交易会有限公司
地址：深圳市福田区商报路奥林匹克大厦10楼（518034）

China (Shenzhen) Intl Cultural Industries Fair
Venue: Shenzhen Convention and Exhibition Center, Shenzhen, Guangdong
Established Year: 2004
Frequency: Annual
Market Area: National
Nature: Open to public
Organizer: Ministry of Culture; Ministry of Commerce; State Administration of Radio, Film and Television; General Administration of Press and Publication; CCPIT

2011/05/13 - 16
☎ 0755-2516 0148
🖷 0755-2516 0449
✉ 224458338@qq.com
www.cnicif.com
4720

第七届中国（深圳）国际文化产业博览交易会
暨第二届中国国际新媒体影视动漫节
地点：深圳会展中心，广东深圳
始办年份：2004
周期：每年一届
市场范围：国际性
性质：面向公众
入场券价格：50元
上届规模 2010：展览面积4,014m²(国外展商1,338m²)，参展商23家，参观人数160,000人（专业贸易观众20,324人）
主办：国家广播电影电视总局；深圳市人民政府
承办：深圳市文体旅游局；深圳广播电影电视集团

China (Shenzhen) Intl Cultural Industries Fair
- Games & Cartoons
Venue: Shenzhen Convention & Exhibition Center, Shenzhen, Guangdong
Established Year: 2004
Frequency: Annual
Market Area: International
Nature: Open to Public
Cost to Attend: RMB 50:-
Statistics 2010: Exhibition Area 4,014m²(foreigners 1,338m²), Exhibitors 23, Visitors 160,000 (trade visitors 20,324)
Organizer: Organizing Committee of China (Shenzhen) International Cultural Industries Fair

2011/05/30 - 10
☎ 010-8260 6880转ext 91
🖷 010-8260 6883
✉ ciccyhuang@cnaico.com.cn
www.cnaico.com.cn
www.autochina.com.cn
4725

第十五届深圳-香港-澳门国际汽车博览会
地点：广东深圳
主办：中国汽车工业国际合作总公司
地址：北京市海淀区中关村丹棱街3号A座

15th Shenzhen-Hong Kong-Macao Intl Automobile Expo
Venue: Shenzhen, Guangdong
Organizer: China National Automotive Industry International Corp

2011/06/17 - 19
☎ 020-8555 6058
🖷 020-8555 6137
✉ denkohuang@163.com
4730

2011第四届中国（深圳）国际胶粘带及保护膜展览会
地点：深圳会展中心，广东深圳
内容：胶粘带：工业胶带、光学胶带、电子胶带、电工/气胶带、聚酰亚胺胶带、双面胶带、BOPP封箱胶带、包装胶带、印刷胶带、化工胶带、文具胶带、医疗胶带、美纹纸胶带、牛皮纸胶带、布基胶带、金属箔胶带、防腐胶带、塑料薄膜胶带、压敏胶片贴等胶带及其模切产品。保护膜：PE、PET、PVC、BOPP、LDPE保护膜，包括光学保护膜、表面保护膜、LCD保护膜、手机保护膜、汽车保护膜、建筑膜、玻璃膜，静电保护膜、耐高温膜、PET镀铝膜、缠绕膜、拉伸膜及包装带/膜、热熔胶膜、冲压膜、复合膜等各类保护用薄膜。生产设备及仪器：各种胶粘带、工业薄膜、保护膜相关设备，包括涂布机、分切机、复合机、模切设备、模压机制胶设备、涂布设备、测试仪器及分析、施胶工具及技术、贴标机、相关包装及印刷设备等。原料及化工产品：各种生产用原料及化工产品，包括胶粘剂、离型剂、树脂、硅胶、压敏胶、热熔胶、助剂、油墨及各类辅助材料等。
始办年份：2008
周期：每年一届
性质：面向公众
入场券价格：20元
参展费用：标准展位 国内企业8,800元，角位（双开口、三面开口）加收500元，境外企业1,800美元，净地：国内企业780元/m²
上届规模 2010：展览面积10,000m²，参观人数12,000人
主办：德国多特蒙德展览集团；会多展览（深圳）有限公司
地址：广东省广州市天河区建中路7号广海大厦17层（510665）
联系人：黄登科

Shenzhen Adhesive Tape, Protective Film Exhibition
Venue: Shenzhen Convention & Exhibition Center, Shenzhen, Guangdong
Established Year: 2008
Frequency: Annual
Nature: Open to Public
Cost to Attend: RMB 20:-
Participated Fee: Standard Booth USD 1,800/booth
Statistics 2010: Exhibition Area 10000m², Visitors 12,000
Organizer: Huiduo Exhibition (Shenzhen) Co Ltd

2011/06/29 - 01
☎ 020-6119 8862, 6119 8871
🖷 020-6119 8841
✉ hjh-76@163.com
water@waterexpo.org
www.waterexpo.org
4740

第十三届华南水展
地点：深圳会展中心，广东深圳
内容：污水和工业水处理；膜分离技术与设备；饮水、净水技术与设备；给排水与管道；流体设备、泵、阀门；仪器仪表与自控系统；工程及服务；水处理化药剂及学品；节水设备。
始办年份：1999
周期：每年一届
市场范围：国际性
性质：面向贸易观众
入场券价格：免费
参展费用：8,000元/展位
上届规模 2010：展览面积1,908m²(国外展商495m²)，参展商147家（国外展商32家，来自19个国家），参观人数12,892人（专业贸易观众12,247人）
主办：广东会展推广有限公司
地址：广州市远景路168-170号时代新都汇B栋812室（510403）
联系人：罗燕

13th Intl Water Treatment & Fluid, Pump, Valve & Pipe Exhibition for South China
Venue: Shenzhen Convention & Exhibition Center, Shenzhen, Guangdong
Profile: Sewage/ wastewater treatment equipment; Water treatment agent/ reagent, Water supply and drainage, Water tank equipment/ cleaning equipment, Membrane technology/ membrane processing equipment, Filtering equipment
Established Year: 1999
Frequency: Annual
Market Area: International
Nature: Trade Only
Cost to Attend: Free
Participated Fee: RMB 8,000/booth
Statistics 2010: Exhibition Area 1,908m²(foreigners 495m²), Exhibitors 147 (foreigners 32, came from 19 countries), Visitors 12,892 (trade visitors 12,247)
Organizer: Guangdong Convention & Exhibition Promotion Ltd
Address: #.812, Tower B, Times Focus, 168-170 Yuanjing Road Guangzhou 510403,PRC

2011/06/29 - 01
☎ 020-6119 8876, 6119 8879
🖷 020-6119 8841
✉ hjh-76@163.com
61198879@iaexpo.org
www.iaexpo.org
4750

第十五届华南工业控制自动化国际展览会
地点：深圳会展中心，广东深圳
内容：工业自动化（生产及过程自动化），电气系统，工业自动化信息技术及软件，机器人技术，机器视觉技术，接口技术（连接器），电子零部件及辅助设备等
始办年份：1997
周期：每年一届

15th Intl Industrial Control & Automation Exhibition for South China
Venue: Shenzhen Convention & Exhibition Center, Shenzhen, Guangdong
Established Year: 1997
Frequency: Annual
Market Area: International

市场范围：国际性
性质：面向贸易观众
入场券价格：免费
参展费用：8,200元/展位
上届规模 2010：展览面积5,499m²(国外展商1,287m²)，参展商328家（国外展商62家，来自33个国家），参观人数21,037人（专业贸易观众19,985人）
主办：广东会展推广有限公司
地址：广州市远景路168-170号时代新都汇B栋812室（510403）
联系人：韩建华、林萍

Nature: Trade Only
Cost to Attend: Free
Participated Fee: RMB 8,200/booth
Statistics 2010: Exhibition Area 5,499m²(foreigners 1,287m²), Exhibitors 328 (foreigners 62, came from 33 countries), Visitors 21,037 (trade visitors 19,985)
Organizer: Guangdong Convention & Exhibition Promotion Ltd
Address: #.812, Tower B, Times Focus, 168-170 Yuanjing Road, Guangzhou 510403

2011/06/30 - 03
☎ 0755-8294 9443
🖷 0755-8294 9700
✉ oversea@ewatch.cn
www.fair.ewatch.cn

4760

第22届中国（深圳）国际钟表展览会
地点：深圳会展中心，广东深圳
内容：成钟、成表、机心、配件、包装、机械等钟表配套产品。
始办年份：1988
周期：每年一届
市场范围：国际性
性质：面向贸易观众
入场券价格：免费
参展费用：760元/m²
上届规模 2010：展览面积30,000m²(国外展商5,000m²)，参展商500家（国外展商100家，来自30个国家），参观人数56,638人（专业贸易观众45,635人）
主办：深圳市钟表行业协会；深圳市晶品会展文化传播有限公司
地址：深圳市福田区新闻路深茂商业中心815室（518034）
联系人：陈小姐

22nd China Watch & Clock Fair
Venue: Shenzhen Convention & Exhibition Center, Shenzhen, Guangdong
Profile: Watches & Clocks, Movement, Parts, Electronic Calendar, Radio Controlled Clock, Packaging, Machinery & Equipment, etc.
Established Year: 1988
Frequency: Annual
Market Area: International
Nature: Trade Only
Cost to Attend: Free
Participated Fee: RMB 760/m²
Statistics 2010: Exhibition Area 30,000m²(foreigners 5,000m²), Exhibitors 500 (foreigners 100, came from 30 countries), Visitors 56,638 (trade visitors 45,635)
Organizer: Shenzhen Watch & Clock Association; Shenzhen Fitime Conference & Exhibition Culture Co Ltd
Address: Room 815, Shenmao Commerce Center, News Rd., Shenzhen, China
Contact: Pauline Chen

2011/07/07 - 09
☎ 0755-8347 2856
🖷 0755-8347 2852, 8347 2956
www.szic.cn

4770

中国（深圳）国际品牌服装服饰交易会
地点：深圳会展中心，广东深圳
内容：具影响力、专业化程度最高的服装展会之一，深受业界推崇，担当着一个举足轻重的商贸平台角色。深圳服交会首度举办由最初的15000平方米展览面积，190个参展商，4万人次专业观众，发展到第十届的7万平方米展览面积，800家海内外展商以及10万余人次的专业观众，规模迅速扩大，影响力不断提升。秉承过往十届的辉煌业绩，2011年深圳服交会继续为展商与专业买家提供商贸合作的重要平台。
始办年份：2001
周期：每年一届
市场范围：国际性
性质：面向贸易观众
入场券价格：20元
参展费用：10,000元/9m²
上届规模 2010：展览面积70,000m²，参展商800家，参观人数100,000人（专业贸易观众80,000人）
主办：深圳市服装行业协会；时尚汇品牌管理有限公司
地址：广东省深圳市福田区车公庙泰然工业区中国有色大厦11楼（518000）
联系人：雷先生

11th China (Shenzhen) International Brand Clothing & Accessories Fair
Venue: Shenzhen Convention & Exhibition Center, Shenzhen, Guangdong
Established Year: 2001
Frequency: Annual
Market Area: International
Nature: Trade Only
Cost to Attend: RMB 20:-
Participated Fee: RMB 10,000/9m²
Statistics 2010: Exhibition Area 70,000m², Exhibitors 800, Visitors 100,000 (trade visitors 80,000)
Organizer: Shenzhen Garment Industry Assn
Contact: Mr Lei

2011/07/07 - 09
☎ 010-8522 9208, 8522 9702, 8522 9488
🖷 010-8522 9296

4780

深圳国际纺织面料及辅料博览会
地点：深圳会展中心，广东深圳
内容：各类服装面料、辅料、计算机CAD/CAM系统，相关出版物及网络
预计规模：展览面积9,000m²
主办：中国纺织工业协会
承办：中国贸促会纺织行业分会；法兰克福展览（香港）有限公司；深圳市服装行业协会
联系人：马一丹，吴知真，黎明家

Shenzhen International Trade Fair for Apparel Fabrics and Accessories
Venue: Shenzhen Convention & Exhibition Center, Shenzhen, Guangdong
Sponsors: China National Textile & Apparel Council
Organizers: The Sub-Council of Textile Industry, CCPIT; Messe Frankfurt (HK) Ltd; Shenzhen Garment Industry Association

2011/07/21 - 25
☎ 0755-2516 0148
🖷 0755-2516 0449
✉ 224458338@qq.com
www.szicie.com

4790

第三届深圳动漫节
地点：深圳会展中心，广东深圳
内容：体验区：让观众在体验的过程中更为感性的体会动漫的乐趣。展示区：以动漫系列产品形象展示、销售和交易为主。活动区：突出互动和参与，以精彩表演、比赛、反斗乐园游戏区等各种项目带动现场人气。
始办年份：2009
周期：每年一届
市场范围：国际性
性质：面向公众
入场券价格：25元/张
上届规模 2010：参展商116家，参观人数500,000人
主办：深圳广播电影电视集团
承办：深圳市文化产业（国际）会展有限公司；深圳国家动漫画产业基地
地址：（518000）
联系人：罗清

3rd Shenzhen Animation Festival
Venue: Shenzhen Convention & Exhibition Center, Shenzhen, Guangdong
Established Year: 2009
Frequency: Annual
Market Area: International
Nature: Open to Public
Cost to Attend: RMB 25:-
Statistics 2010: Exhibitors 116, Visitors 500,000
Organizer: Shenzhen Media Group Intl Cultural Industry Fair Co Ltd

2011/08/25 - 27
☎ 852-2763 9011
🖷 852-2341 0379
✉ jenny@paper-con.com.hk
www.paper-com.com.hk
4800

毛织设计及工艺展
地点： 深圳会展中心，广东深圳
主办： 通讯展览公司
地址： 香港九龙观塘成业街11号华成工商中心5字楼15室

Knitwear Design and Technology Fair (KDT)
Venue: Shenzhen Convention & Exhibition Center, Shenzhen, Guangdong
Organizer: Paper Communication Exhibition Service
Address: Rm. 15, 5/F. Wha Shing Center, 11 Shing Ypi St. Kwun Tong, Kowloon, Hong Kong
Contact: Jenny Leung

2011/08/30 - 01
☎ 852-2965 1661
🖷 852-2824 0178, 2824 0246
✉ vera.ng@reedexpo.com.hk
www.nepconchina.com
4810

第十七届华南国际电子生产设备暨微电子工业展
地点： 深圳会展中心，广东深圳
内容： NEPCON China是亚洲地区最大的电子制造与表面贴装行业盛会之一，它涵盖了该行业在全球范围的创新产品和技术，将全世界表面贴装品牌呈现在您的面前。NEPCON China为您建立一个最佳交流平台，帮助您提高行业竞争优势，有效物色新供应商，收集最新市场信息，寻找技术解决方案以及学习最新技术。
上届规模 2010：展览面积30,000m^2，参展商282家（来自15个国家），参观人数24,241人
主办： 励展博览集团；中国贸促会电子信息行业分会
地址： 香港湾仔皇后大道东183号合和中心39写字楼
联系人： 吴欐芬

NEPCON/ EMT China 2011
Venue: Shenzhen Convention & Exhibition Center, Shenzhen, Guangdong
Profile: NEPCON China is one of the largest and longest standing trading and sourcing platforms for the SMT industry in China. Featuring a comprehensive range of innovative SMT products and technology, it brings the entire world of SMT to your door step.
The event provides a sourcing platform for new suppliers gathers new market information and displays the latest technologies to help you enhance your competitiveness in the electronics manufacturing industry.
Statistics 2010: Exhibition Area 30,000m^2, Exhibitors 282（came from 15 countries）, Visitors 24,241
Organizer: Reed Exhibitions

2011/08/30 - 01
☎ 852-2965 1661
🖷 852-2824 0178, 2824 0246
✉ vera.ng@reedexpo.com.hk
www.atexpochina.com
4820

2011华南国际电子组装及包装技术展览会
地点： 深圳会展中心，广东深圳
内容： 组装设备及材料：接合剂、胶带、密封胶和分离设备、承载带、盖带、薄膜（光学膜、保护膜）、泡沫塑料、塑料片材、绝缘、导电、屏蔽材料、防静电、防电磁辐射产品及与电子相关的包装技术设备；工具：电动工具、电批、电动螺丝刀、电动起子、焊台、气动工具和手动工具；机器视觉系统：电子组装检测系统、印刷电路板检测方案、SMT生产线检测方案、焊膏检测、自动光学检测（AOI）、汽车制造检测系统、非接触性传感器、机器视觉工具软件、智能相机；电子包装：电子包装材料，密封电子包装，罐封，电子胶埋，绝缘漆，覆膜，敷形涂覆材料，防潮绝缘保护漆，金属/陶瓷封接，SMD包装载带，上带，胶盘，纸盘，卷轮，塑料盘，电子元件包装机
性质： 面向贸易观众
入场券价格： 免费
参展费用： 净地3,400元/m^2(24m^{2}起)，标准展位4,000元/m^2(12m^{2}起)，角位费830元/角位，注册费664元/展商，电子营销700元/展商
主办： 励展博览集团
地址： 香港湾仔皇后大道东183号，合和中心39写字楼
联系人： 吴欐芬

ATE 2011
Electronics Assembly and Packaging Technology Expo 2011
Venue: Shenzhen Convention & Exhibition Center, Shenzhen, Guangdong
Profile: ATE 2011 main exhibit **profile:** Assembly system and materials, tools, machine vision systems, electronic packaging
Nature: Trade Only
Cost to Attend: Free
Participated Fee: Raw Space RMB 3,400/m^2 (min 24m^2), Standard Booth RMB 4,000/m^2 (min 12m^2), Corner unit add RMB 830/unit
Organizer: Reed Exhibitions

2011/08/30 - 02
☎ 010-5933 9062, 5933 9000
🖷 010-5933 9099
✉ shirley.chan@reedhuayin.com.cn
www.mtcsouth.com.cn
4830

中国（南部）机床展览会
地点： 深圳会展中心，广东深圳
内容： 华南国际机床展览会2011为全球机床供应商在中国华南地区扩展分销网络，寻找新的合作伙伴及寻求新的商业契机，提供了一个绝佳的交易平台和专业途径。
首届
始办年份： 2011
预计规模： 展览面积15,000m^2，参展商300家，参观人数10,000人
主办： 励展博览集团
地址： 北京市朝阳区新源南路1-3号平安国际金融中心A座15层01-03（201204）

Machine Tool China – South 2011
Venue: Shenzhen Convention & Exhibition Center, Shenzhen, Guangdong
Profile: MTC SOUTH provides an excellent trading platform and gateway for global machine tool suppliers to expand distribution network, meet new partners and look for new business opportunities in South China.
First Session
Expectation: Exhibition Area 15,000m^2, Exhibitors 300, Visitors 10,000
Organizer: Reed Exhibitions China
Address: Unit 01-03,05, 15th Floor, Tower A, Ping An International Finance Center, No.1-3, Xinyuan South Road, Chaoyang District, Beijing 100027, China
Contact: Shirley Chan

2011/09/16 - 18
☎ 010-8455 6608, 8455 6525
🖷 010-8444 2080
✉ heng.sun@reedsinopharm.com
yu1.wang@reedsinopharm.com
www.inter-health.com.cn
4840

第11 届中国国际保健博览会
2011中国（深圳）保健节
地点： 深圳会展中心，广东深圳
内容： 精品展区、保健食品区、终端洽谈区、健康体验区、媒体传播区
周期： 每年一届
上届规模 2010：展览面积10,000m^2，参展商300家，专业贸易观众17,000人）
主办： 国药励展展览有限责任公司
地址： 北京市朝阳区新源南路1—3号 平安国际金融中心B座15层（100027）

11th China Intl Healthcare Expo
2011 China (Shenzhen) Healthcare Festival
Venue: Shenzhen Convention & Exhibition Center, Shenzhen, Guangdong
Frequency: Annual
Statistics 2010: Exhibition Area 10,000m^2, Exhibitors 300，Trade Visitors 17,000）
Organizer: Reed Sinopharm Exhibitions

2011/09/23 - 25
☎ 0755-3398 9211, 3398 9230
🖷 0755-3333 1168
✉ info@reedhuabo.com
www.reedhuabo.com
4850

华南国际孕婴童用品展览会
地点：深圳会展中心，广东深圳
内容：进口孕婴童品牌产品，婴儿用品及孕妇用品，孕婴童食品及保健品、婴幼儿护理用品，婴儿鞋帽及服饰、儿童鞋帽及服饰、孕妇休闲服饰、孕婴童摄影。
周期：每年一届
性质：面向贸易观众
预计规模：展览面积15,000m^2, 参展商250家
主办：励展华博展览（深圳）有限公司
地址：深圳市中心区福华三路深圳国际商会中心1801、1802室（518048）
联系人：袁文军，王清林

Southern China Intl Maternity, Baby & Children Products Exhibition
Venue: Shenzhen Convention & Exhibition Center, Shenzhen, Guangdong
Profile: the fair offers the widest selection of maternity, baby and children products, and is poised to attract quality global buyers, including distributors, agents, department stores, wholesalers, online stores, and investors. Exhibitors are primarily manufacturers, promising the best design and quality at competitive prices. The fair enables key market players to meet and trade, form partnerships and preview industry trends.
Frequency: Annual
Nature: Trade Only
Expectation: Exhibition Area 15,000m^2, Exhibitors 250
Organizer: Reed Huabo Exhibitions (Shenzhen) Co Ltd

2011/10/20 - 23
☎ 0755-3398 9211, 3398 9230
🖷 0755-3333 1168
✉ info@reedhuabo.com
www.reedhuabo.com
4860

GIFTS& HOME
礼品|家居·中国

第十九届中国（深圳）国际玩具及礼品展览会
地点：深圳会展中心，广东深圳
内容：中国最大规模的礼品家居用品展之一。
周期：每年一届
市场范围：国际性
性质：面向贸易观众
预计规模：展览面积100,000m^2, 参展商2,800家, 买家120,000人
主办：励展华博展览（深圳）有限公司
地址：深圳市中心区福华三路深圳国际商会中心1801、1802室（518048）
联系人：袁文军, 王清林

Gifts & Home China
Venue: Shenzhen Convention & Exhibition Center, Shenzhen, Guangdong
Profile: Held in Shenzhen during the best buying seasons in April and October every year, the fair offers the widest selection of business gifts, premiums and consumer products, and attracts tens of thousands of buyers from across the country. They include distributors, agents, premium houses, department stores and large corporate end users. Exhibitors are primarily manufacturers, promising the best design and quality at competitive prices
Frequency: Annual
Market Area: International
Nature: Trade Only
Organizer: Reed Huabo Exhibitions (Shenzhen) Co Ltd

2011/11/16 - 21
☎ 0755-8284 8900, 8284 8800
✉ chtf@chtf.com
www.chtf.com
4870

第13届中国国际高新技术成果交易会信息技术与产品展
地点：深圳会展中心，广东深圳
始办年份：1999
周期：每年一届
市场范围：国际性
主办：中华人民共和国商务部；技术部；工信部；发展和改革委员会；教育部；人力资源和社会保障部；国家知识产权局；中国科学院；中国工程院；深圳市政府
承办：深圳市中国国际高新技术成果交易中心

China Hi-Tech Fair
Venue: Shenzhen Convention and Exhibition Center, Shenzhen, Guangdong
Established Year: 1999
Frequency: Annual
Market Area: International
Organizer: Shenzhen China Hi-Tech Fair Center

2012/03/28 - 30
☎ 021-6195 6088转ext 919
🖷 021-6195 6099
✉ tom.cao@vnuexhibitions.com.cn
www.cwiemechina.com
4880

中国（深圳）国际绕线设备展览会
地点：深圳会展中心，广东深圳
内容：各类电磁线圈、磁性材料、电机与变压器制造设备、绕线机、插片机、浸漆机、测试仪器、电气绝缘材料、电机叠片和普通金属冲压工具类、永磁材料、电磁线、线轴和连接器、晶粒取向硅钢用纵剪作业线、线形、螺旋和环状线圈绕线机械类、变压器进线套管和陶瓷绝缘子类等。
始办年份：2012
首届
周期：每年一届
市场范围：国际性
性质：面向贸易观众
参展费用：360欧元/m^2
预计规模：展览面积4,500m^2，参观人数20,000人
主办：英国国际线圈展有限公司；VNU亚洲展览集团；上海万耀企龙展览有限公司
地址：上海市徐汇区田林路140号26A栋万耀企龙办公楼（200233）
联系人：曹锋

CWIEME SHENZHEN
Venue: Shenzhen Convention & Exhibition Center, Shenzhen, Guangdong
Profile: Coils & Transformer Manufacture, insulation materials Laminations & Cores, Magnet Wire, Magnet & magnetizing Equipment.
Established Year: 2012
First Session
Frequency: Annual
Market Area: International
Nature: Trade Only
Participated Fee: EURO 360/m^2
Organizer: CWIEME Ltd; VNU Exhibitions Asia
Contact: Tom Cao

广东-顺德 Guangdong-Shunde

2011/10/17 – 20
☎ 020-8755 2468转ext 11/ 19
🖷 020-8755 2970
✉ e.cheung@koelnmesse.cn
g.liu@koelnmesse.cn
www.shundeexpo.cn
www.shundeexpo.com

4900

2011中国顺德国际家用电器博览会
地点： 顺德展览中心，广东顺德
内容： 在各界商家及合作机构的积极参与和支持下，第十届中国顺德国际家用电器博览会（简称：顺德家电展）以"光耀亚洲，经典十年"为主题的盛会盛况空前，展会于2010年10月21日在广东顺德展览中心圆满闭幕。

第十一届顺德家电展将于2011年10月17-20日在广东顺德展览中心继续举办。预计展会规模达30，000平方米，参展商近500家。相信您绝对不会错过这个了解家电行业最新潮流、最新技术以及开拓海内外销售渠道的最佳电器贸易平台。展品范围包括：黑色家电、白色家电、小家电、厨房家电、水家电，卫浴家电、家电配件以及家电相关服务与刊物等。
始办年份： 2001
周期： 每年一届
市场范围： 国际性
入场券价格： 20元
参展费用： 净地（27m^{2}起）880元/m^2; 普通标准展位（9m^{2}起）900元/m^2,高级标准展位（18m^{2}起）1,200元/m^2
上届规模 2010：展览面积30,000m^2，参展商502家（来自10个国家），专业贸易观众24,573人
主办： 科隆展览有限公司；中国机电产品进出口商会；中国国际贸易促进委员会广东省分会；顺德区人民政府
承办： 科隆展览有限公司
地址： 中国广东省广州市天河区天河北路183号大都会广场3311室（510620）
联系人： 张井飞先生，刘桂宜女士

China Shunde International Exposition for Household Electrical Appliances 2011
Venue: Shunde Exhibition Center, Guangdong Province, PR China
Profile: Shunde Expo 2011 will take place again on 17-20 October 2011 at the Shunde Exhibition Center. The floor space is expected to grow up to 30,000sqm with around 500 exhibitors. Please don't miss this golden opportunity to keep up to date on the latest industry trends and developments network and do business with the local and international players in the household appliance industry. Exhibit profile includes: Black home appliances, white home appliances, small home appliances, kitchen and bathroom home appliances, water appliances, accessories and components, services and publications etc.
Established Year: 2001
Frequency: Annual
Market Area: International
Nature:
Cost to Attend: RMB 20:-
Participated Fee: Raw Space RMB 880/m^2 (min 27m^2), Standard Booth RMB 900/m^2
Statistics 2010: Exhibition Area 30,000sqm, Exhibitors 502(came from 10 countries), Trade Visitors 24,573
Sponsor: Koelnmesse Co Ltd; China Chamber of Commerce for Import and Export of Machinery and Electronic Products (CCCME); China Council for the Promotion of International Trade Guangdong Sub-council (CCPIT GD); The People's Government of Shunde
Organizer: Koelnmesse Co Ltd
Address: Rm3311 Metro Plaza, No. 183 Tianhebei Road, Tianhe District, Guangzhou, 510620 China
Contact: Mr Eric Cheung , Ms Grace Liu

广西-南宁 Guangxi-Nanning

2011/03/18 - 20
☎ 0771-564 9131
🖷 0771-584 0017
✉ lomhuizhan@163.com
www.gxkMscom

4910

2011第二届泛北部湾（广西）粮油、食品、农产品及其生产加工机械设备博览会
地点： 南宁国际会展中心，广西南宁
内容： 粮油产品及加工设备类，各种粮油精深加工产品，仓储设备，输送设备，面粉设备，大米设备，玉米设备，面条设备，粮油烘干设备等。食品类：各种名特优食品、绿色食品、粮油食品、保健食品、休闲食品、速冻食品、烘焙食品、肉禽产品、水产品、调味品、乳制品、干果炒货、土特产品、农产品、糖、烟；糖、酒、茶类。饮品类；食品原料、添加剂类。食品饮品生产加工机械类；农副产品及加工生产设备类；高新食品；果蔬栽培技术与设备、包装材料与设备、自动化控制与温室工程、无公害化技术设备、生物组培、防治技术、园艺工具、采收、保鲜储藏技术等。
始办年份： 2010
周期： 每年一届
市场范围： 全国性
性质： 面向公众
主办： 广西县域经济研究会、粮油行业分会
承办： 广西南宁凯姆斯展览有限公司
地址： 广西南宁市园湖南路25号新源大厦四单元607室（530023）
联系人： 马薇

2nd Guangxi Exhibition on Food, Agricultural Products and Processing Machinery
Venue: Nanning Intl Convention & Exhibition Center, Nanning, Guangxi
Established Year: 2010
Frequency: Annual
Market Area: National
Nature: Open to Public
Organizer: Guangxi Nanning Kames Exhibition Co Ltd

2011/03/18 - 20
☎ 0771-586 3039
🖷 0771-584 0017
✉ kms@gxkMscom
www.gxkMscom

4915

2011第七届泛北部湾（广西）畜牧水产行业博览会
地点：南宁国际会展中心，广西南宁
内容：畜禽类：禽畜类、特种养殖类；畜牧业及药品类：畜牧繁殖、畜禽良种培育技术；动物饲养技术及孵化育种设备、兽药生产设备、畜禽渔药品、生物制品、疫苗、动物保健品、兽医器械；
始办年份：2005
周期：每年一届
市场范围：全国性
性质：面向公众
主办：广西县域经济研究会；畜牧行业分会
承办：广西南宁凯姆斯展览有限公司
地址：广西南宁市园湖南路25号新源大厦四单元607室（530023）
联系人：廖德远

7th Guangxi Livestock, Fisheries Expo
Venue: Nanning Intl Convention & Exhibition Center, Nanning, Guangxi
Established Year: 2005
Frequency: Annual
Market Area: National
Nature: Open to Public
Organizer: Guangxi Nanning Kames Exhibition Co Ltd

2011/03/25 - 27
☎ 0771-236 8926
🖷 0771-555 2402
✉ nanningnanchun@163.com
www.nanchunhz.com

4920

2011第12届广西广告技术设备展览会
地点：南宁国际会展中心，广西南宁
内容：广告制作设备：喷绘设备、写真设备、雕刻设备、条幅制作设备、喷墨打印设备、吸塑成型设备、制卡设备、装裱设备、覆膜机、热转印设备、烫印设备、图文制作设备、数码快印设备、数码影像设备；广告器材材料：广告标识、广告灯箱、LED光源、霓虹灯、电子显示屏、标牌加工制作、视觉导向系统、展览展示器材、商业展示设施器材、发光字、广告材料、反光材料、板材、喷绘墨水、广告礼品；广告媒体：新型广告户外媒体、三面翻广告设备、新型显示载体、充气媒体、广告公司作品、广告公司形象展示等。
始办年份：1999
周期：每年一届
市场范围：全国性
主办：广西机械工程学会
承办：南宁南春展览服务有限公司
地址：广西南宁市金洲路11号金旺角B1002室（530028）
联系人：王燕君

12th Guangxi Advertising Technology & Equipment Exhibition
Venue: Nanning Intl Convention & Exhibition Center, Nanning, Guangxi
Established Year: 1999
Frequency: Annual
Market Area: National
Organizer: Guangxi Nanchun Exhibition Service Co Ltd

2011/03/25 - 27
☎ 0771-236 8926
🖷 0771-236 8401
✉ zzhygs@tom.com
www.nanchunhz.com

4930

2011第五届广西国际糖业技术设备展览会
地点：南宁国际会展中心，广西南宁
内容：制糖设备及技术：输送设备、压榨设备及驱动装置、撕解设备、压滤设备、过滤设备、清洗设备、蒸发器、冷却设备、结晶机、助晶机、分蜜设备、离心机、筛分设备、干燥设备、减速机、齿轮箱、糖厂自动控制系统、压力容器；制糖生物助剂、添加剂等。配套设备器材：糖厂专用泵阀、自动控制设备、电气设备、焊接设备及材料、糖厂窑炉、乳化设备、糖机专用链条、糖机配件、润滑油脂、糖度检测仪器仪表、计量仪器、糖厂监控设备、发电设备、装卸设备
始办年份：2007
周期：每年一届
市场范围：全国性
主办：广西机械工程学会
承办：南宁南春展览服务有限公司
地址：广西南宁市金洲路11号金旺角B座1002室（530028）
联系人：辜洪潮

5th Guangxi Intl Sugar Industry Exhibition
Venue: Nanning Intl Convention & Exhibition Center, Nanning, Guangxi
Established Year: 2007
Frequency: Annual
Market Area: National
Organizer: Guangxi Nanchun Exhibition Service Co Ltd

2011/10/21 - 26
☎ 0771-581 3111, 581 3116, 581 3315（参展）
🖷 0771-581 3388, 581 3114
✉ zszz@caexpo.org
www.caexpo.org

4940

中国—东盟博览会
地点：南宁国际会展中心，广西南宁
内容：商品贸易专题、投资合作专题、先进技术专题、服务贸易专题、魅力之城专题，每届博览会围绕中国与东盟重点合作领域举办系列高层次论坛及专题活动，每届博览会同期举办文化体育交流活动
始办年份：2004
周期：每年一届
市场范围：国际性
性质：面向贸易观众
参展费用：主会场(南宁国际会展中心)标准展位10,000元/9m^2，室内净地（36m^{2}起）1,000元/m^2，室外净地500元/m^2；分会场(广西展览馆)标准展位5,000元/9m^2，室内净地500元/m^2
上届规模 2010：参展商2,200家（来自11个国家），专业贸易观众49,000人
主办：中国商务部；文莱工业和初级资源部；柬埔寨商业部；印度尼西亚贸易部；老挝工业和贸易部；马来西亚国际贸易和工业部；缅甸商务部；菲律宾贸易和工业部；新加坡贸易和工业部；泰国商业部；越南工业贸易部；东盟秘书处
承办：广西壮族自治区人民政府
地址：中国广西南宁市竹溪大道98号（530021）

CHINA-ASEAN EXPO
Venue: Nanning Intl Convention & Exhibition Center, Nanning, Guangxi
Profile: Pavilion of Commodity Trade, Pavilion of Investment Cooperation, Pavilion of Advanced Technologies, Pavilion of Trade in Services, Pavilion of Cities of Charm. Series of high-end forums and theme programs on the key cooperation fields by China and the 10 ASEAN countries. Concurrent cultural, sports exchange programs held during each CAEXPO
Established Year: 2004
Frequency: Annual
Market Area: International
Nature: Trade Only
Participated Fee: Standard Booth RMB 10,000/9m^2, Indoor Raw Space (min 36m^2) , Outdoor Raw Space RMB 500/m^2
Statistics 2010: Exhibitors 2200（came from 11 countries）, Trade Visitors 49,000）
Organizer: Ministry of Commerce of the People’s Republic of China, Ministry of Industry and Primary Resources of Brunei Darussalam, Ministry of Commerce of the Kingdom of Cambodia, Ministry of Trade of the Republic of Indonesia, Ministry of Industry and Commerce of the Lao People’s Democratic Republic, Ministry of International Trade and Industry of Malaysia, Ministry of Commerce of the Union of Myanmar, Department of Trade and Industry of the Republic of Philippines, Ministry of Trade and Industry of the Republic of Singapore, Ministry of Commerce of the Kingdom of Thailand, Ministry of Industry and Trade of the Socialist Republic of Viet Nam, The ASEAN Secretariat;
Sponsor：People’s Government of Guangxi Zhuang Autonomous Region
Address: No. 98, Zhuxi Avenue, Nanning, Guangxi, China

2011/12/01 - 05
☎ 010-8260 6880转ext 91
🖷 010-8260 6883
✉ ciccyhuang@cnaico.com.cn
www.cnaico.com.cn
www.autochina.com.cn
4945

2011中国-东盟第四届南宁国际汽车展览会
地点：广西南宁
主办：中国汽车工业国际合作总公司
地址：北京市海淀区中关村丹棱街3号A座

Nanning International Automobile Exhibition
Venue: Nanning, Guangxi
Organizer: China National Automotive Industry International Corp

贵州-贵阳 Guizhou-Guiyang

2011/04/15 - 19
☎ 010-8260 6880转ext 91
🖷 010-8260 6883
✉ ciccyhuang@cnaico.com.cn
www.cnaico.com.cn
www.autochina.com.cn
4950

2011首届.贵阳国际汽车展览会
地点：贵州贵阳
主办：中国汽车工业国际合作总公司
地址：北京市海淀区中关村丹棱街3号A座

2011 Guiyang Intl Automobile Exhibition
Venue: Guiyang, Guizhou
Organizer: China National Automotive Industry International Corp

2011/05/13 - 16
☎ 0851-689 4453
🖷 0851-685 2878
✉ yaogan888@126.com
4960

2011第二届中国（贵州）国际铁路、城市轨道交通技术与装备展览会
地点：贵州省展览馆，贵州贵阳
内容：铁路、地铁、轻轨机车车辆；车辆成套设备、配套设施及相关配件；轨道交通系统及安全设施、通讯信号系统、照明系统、集成控制系统、减振系统、指示系统、电气系统、动力供应系统、安全防护设施、光纤电缆、防火及报警系统；车站设备：自动售检票系统、屏蔽门系统、电子显示屏、空调及通风设备、自动扶梯及输送带设备；铁路的信息自动化、铁道养路机械、安全、检测技术及轨道的防震技术；轨道车辆内部装饰材料、城轨工程材料及防水材料；隧道掘进（盾构）机械；曲线钻进机、定向钻机、旋挖钻机；防水堵漏密封材料；勘察测量仪器；城市规划机构、设计研究院、工程勘察单位、投融资机构、相关媒体等。
始办年份：2010
周期：每年一届
市场范围：全国性
性质：面向公众
主办：中国机械工业联合会；贵州省人民政府；贵州省经济和信息化委员会；贵州省电力行业协会；贵州省机械工程学会
承办：贵州科博展览广告有限公司
地址：贵州省贵阳市中华北路181号省经信委干部培训中心5楼（550004）
联系人：姚竿

2nd China (Guizhou) Exhibition on Railway, Urban Rail, Transport Technology and Equipment
Venue: Guizhou Exhibition Hall, Guiyang, Guizhou
Established Year: 2010
Frequency: Annual
Market Area: National
Nature: Open to Public
Organizer: Kebo Exhibition & Ad Co Ltd

2011/05/13 - 16
☎ 0851-689 4453
🖷 0851-685 2878
✉ yaogan888@126.com
4970

2011第六届中国（贵州）国际装备制造业博览会
地点：贵州省展览馆，贵州贵阳
内容：航空航天及先进制造技术设备，数控机床及工模具，工业自动化及仪器仪表，新能源、电力电工及电网技术设备，工业安全、真空设备及特种设备，表面处理技术设备，品牌汽车、节能与新能源汽车展，通用机械，流体机械及泵、阀，五金工具、焊接设备，锻造、冲压、锻压、工业炉，工程机械、建材机械、农机、叉车、物流运输，轴承、动力传动及控制技术设备
始办年份：2006
周期：每年一届
性质：面向公众
入场券价格：20元
主办：中国机械工业联合会；贵州省人民政府；贵州省经济和信息化委员会；贵州省电力行业协会；贵州省机械工程学会
承办：贵州科博展览广告有限公司
地址：贵州省贵阳市中华北路181号省经信委干部培训中心5楼（550004）
联系人：宁田峰

6th China (Guizhou) Intl Industry Equipment Fair
Venue: Guizhou Exhibition Hall, Guiyang, Guizhou
Established Year: 2006
Frequency: Annual
Nature: Open to Public
Cost to Attend: RMB 20:-
Organizer: Kebo Exhibition & Ad Co Ltd

海南-海口 Hainan-Haikou

2011/02/25 - 27
☎ 0898-3159 6939
🖷 0898-3198 3099
✉ yangjunexpo@yeah.net
4980

2011中国（海南）国际海钓装备暨用品展览会
地点：海口会展中心，海南海口
内容：钓鱼装备：钓鱼船艇、橡皮船艇、游艇、钓鱼俱乐部、钓鱼服饰、钓鱼眼镜、钓鱼包、帐篷、钓鱼床、钓鱼刀具、太阳伞、钓鱼椅、夜钓灯具、视频用品、渔猎日历、钓鱼书刊、音像制品及相关产品。钓鱼用品：鱼钩、鱼线、鱼网、鱼杆、鱼袋、钓鱼用线轴、鱼线轮、浮漂及附件、钓饵、鱼篮、咬钩指示器、咬钩传感器、抄网、钓鱼支架、鱼类探测器、探鱼机、铅皮座、工具盒、太空豆、专业漂盒、仕挂、封口器、钓台。
始办年份：2008
周期：每年一届
市场范围：全国性
性质：面向公众
主办：海南省贸促会；海口市贸促会；海南省海钓协会；海南省文化促进会
承办：海口博慧展览有限公司
地址：海南省海口市国贸大道北侧16-2号帝国大厦B座1103室（570125）
联系人：杨军

2011 China (Hainan) Sea Fishing Equipment Exhibition
Venue: Haikou Convention Center, Haikou, Hainan
Established Year: 2008
Frequency: Annual
Market Area: National
Nature: Open to Public
Organizer: Haikou Bohui Exhibition Co Ltd

2011/03/25 - 27
☎ 0898-6625 2360
🖷 0898-3638 6318
✉ wanggang7212@126.com
www.haikouxianhui.cn
4990

2011第二届海南国际葡萄酒博览会
地点：海口会展中心，海南海口
内容：品牌葡萄酒、果酒及原酒展示，酿酒工艺技术及设备，灌充、包装工艺技术及设备，葡萄酒、果酒陈列设备，酒礼品、艺术品，葡萄酒文化活动，葡萄酒图书、杂志信息等。
始办年份：2010
周期：每年一届
主办：中国贸促会海南省分会；海口显辉展览有限公司
地址：海南省海口市海甸三东路金苑别墅10号（570203）
联系人：王纲先生

2nd Hainan Wine Expo
Venue: Haikou Convention Center, Haikou, Hainan
Established Year: 2010
Frequency: Annual
Organizer: Haikou Xianhui

河北-唐山 Hebei-Tangshan

2011/04/20 - 22
☎ 010-8260 6880转ext 91
🖷 010-8260 6883
✉ ciccyhuang@cnaico.com.cn
www.cnaico.com.cn
www.autochina.com.cn
5000

2011中国唐山专（商）用车暨现代物流博览会
地点：河北唐山
主办：中国汽车工业国际合作总公司
地址：北京市海淀区中关村丹棱街3号A座

2011 China (Tanshan) Special Purpose Vehicle & Logistic Expo
Venue: Tangshan, Hebei
Organizer: China National Automotive Industry International Corp

2011/05/27 - 01
☎ 010-8260 6880转ext 91
🖷 010-8260 6883
✉ ciccyhuang@cnaico.com.cn
www.cnaico.com.cn
www.autochina.com.cn
5010

2011第七届中国（唐山）国际汽车博览会
地点：河北唐山
主办：中国汽车工业国际合作总公司
地址：北京市海淀区中关村丹棱街3号A座

7th China (Tangshan) Intl Automobile Expo
Venue: Tangshan, Hebei
Organizer: China National Automotive Industry International Corp

黑龙江-哈尔滨 Heilongjiang-Harbin

2011/01/21 - 24
☎ 0755-2516 0148
🖷 0755-2516 0449
✉ 224458338@qq.com

首届中国冰雪动漫展
地点：哈尔滨国际会展体育中心，黑龙江哈尔滨
内容："中国冰雪动漫展"将以打造大规模、娱乐性和最具人气的动漫展会为目标，设置丰富的内容，主要分为展示区和活
5015 动区。八大主题活动 开幕式、国内外动漫名家冰雕作品花车巡游、俄罗斯主题日、全国COSPLAY挑战赛、城际街舞大赛、电子竞技大赛、摄影大赛、漫画名家签售会；展示区 ："中国原创动漫推广计划"、全国动漫基地发展成果、中国优秀动漫成果、粤港澳品牌动漫企业、国际品牌动漫企业、国内知名动漫企业、全国动漫基地、动漫衍生品产品销售、创意地摊区、游艺体验区
首届
周期：每年一届
市场范围：国际性
性质：面向公众
入场券价格：25元
预计规模：总面积12,020m^2
主办：文化部文化产业司；黑龙江省委宣传部；哈尔滨市人民政府；中国（深圳）国际文化产业博览交易会组委会办公室
承办：黑龙江日报报业集团；深圳广播电影电视集团；哈尔滨工大集团
联系人：罗清

The 1st China Ice & Snow Comic-Con
Venue: Harbin Intl Conference Exhibition and Sport Center, Harbin, Heilongjiang
First Session
Frequency: Annual
Market Area: International
Nature: Open to Public
Cost to Attend: RMB 25:-
Organizer: Organizing Committee of China (Shenzhen) International Cultural Industries Fair

2011/04/21 - 23
☎ 0451-8238 8901, 8238 8902, 8238 8904
🖷 0451-8238 8903
✉ 0451zxzl@163.com
zxwyzl@163.com

中国哈尔滨国际生态城市建设博览会：
第9届中国哈尔滨国际绿色环保建筑装饰展
第12届中国哈尔滨国际城市供热供暖锅炉空调制冷燃气及地面供暖技术设备展
第11届中国哈尔滨国际环境保护与水工业展
第7届中国哈尔滨国际城市照明及LED展
5020 **地点**：哈尔滨国际会展中心，黑龙江哈尔滨
内容：哈尔滨建博会设4大专题展同时展出
始办年份：2000
周期：每年一届
市场范围：国际性
性质：面向贸易观众
入场券价格：免费
参展费用：标准展位：国内企业6,800元，三资企业1,800美元，国外企业2,500美元；室内净地：国内企业680元/m^2，三资企业180美元/m^2，国外企业255美元/m^2；室外净地：国内企业300元/m^2，三资企业100美元/m^2，国外企业130美元/m^2
上届规模 2010：展览面积22,000m^2(国外展商4,200m^2)，参展商470家（国外展商96家，来自9个国家），参观人数17,300人（专业贸易观众16,600人）
主办：哈尔滨市建设委员会/环境保护局、哈尔滨市贸促会、哈尔滨市城管局/水务局/质量技术监督局/城市规划局/电业局、哈尔滨市卫生局/供排水集团
承办：哈尔滨中信伟业展览有限公司
联系人：梁伟先生，刘红梅女士
QQ：120495099

China (Harbin) Urban Eco Construction Expo:
9th Green Building and Decoration Exhibition
12th Urban Heating, Air-conditioning, Gas Technology and Equipment Exhibition
11th Environment Protection and Water Industry Exhibition
7th Urban Lighting and LED Exhibition
Venue: Harbin Intl Conference Exhibition and Sport Center, Harbin, Heilongjiang
Established Year: 2000
Frequency: Annual
Market Area: International
Nature: Trade Only
Cost to Attend: Free
Participated Fee: Standard Booth USD 2,500/booth, Raw Space USD 255/m^2, Outdoor USD 130/m^2
Statistics 2010: Exhibition Area 22,000m^2(foreigners 4,200m^2), Exhibitors 470 (foreigners 96, came from 9 countries) , Visitors 17,300 (trade visitors 16,600)
Organizer: Harbin Zhongxin Weiye Exhibition Co Ltd

2011/04/27 - 29
☎ 0451-8238 8901, 8238 8902, 8238 8904
🖷 0451-8238 8903
✉ 0451zxzl@163.com
zxwyzl@163.com

第11届中国哈尔滨国际装备制造业博览会
地点：哈尔滨国际会展中心，黑龙江哈尔滨
内容：哈尔滨制博会设7大展区：机械加工设备展区；工业自动化及仪器仪表与发供电及电工技术设备展区；动力传动设备与控制技术展区；物流技术与运输系统展区；五金工具及焊接设备展区；石油化工技术设备展区；工程机械、建筑机械、园林机械、
5030 专用汽车及矿山机械设备展区
始办年份：2001
周期：每年一届
市场范围：国际性
性质：面向贸易观众
入场券价格：免费
参展费用：室内展位：国内企业6,500元，三资企业2,000美元，国外企业2,500美元；室内净地：国内企业650元/m^2，三资企业200美元/m^2，国外企业260美元/m^2；室外净地：国内企业300元/m^2，三资企业90美元/m^2，国外企业125美元/m^2

The 11th China Harbin International Manufacture Exhibition
Venue: Harbin Intl Conference Exhibition and Sport Center, Harbin, Heilongjiang
Profile: Machinery processing equipments; Industrial automation and the instrumentation and meters; Tools of hardware and the welding equipments; Power conveying and controlling equipments, fluid machinery; Logistics technique and transportation system; Plastic machinery and packing equipments; Engineering machinery, constructing machinery, gardening devices, appropriation automobile and large machinery equipments.
Established Year: 2001
Frequency: Annual
Market Area: International
Nature: Trade Only
Cost to Attend: Free
Participated Fee: Standard Booth USD 2,500, Raw Space USD

上届规模 2010：展览面积20,000m²(国外展商6,800m²)，参展商460家（国外展商102家，来自11个国家），参观人数26,000人（专业贸易观众23,600人）
承办：中国贸促会黑龙江省分会；哈尔滨市工业和信息化委员会；中国贸促会哈尔滨市分会；哈尔滨中信伟业展览有限公司
地址：哈尔滨市黄河路99号黄河绿园小区黄河大厦805室（150090）
联系人：梁伟先生，刘红梅女士
QQ：120495099

260/m², Outdoor USD 125/m² **Statistics 2010**: Exhibition Area 20,000m²(foreigners 6,800m²), Exhibitors 460（foreigners 102, came from 11 countries）, Visitors 26,000（trade visitors 23,600）
Organizer: Heilongjiang Harbin CCPIT; Committee of Industry and Information Technology of Harbin City; Harbin CCPIT; Harbin Zhongxinweiye Exhibition Ltd Co

2011/06/15 - 19
☎ 0451-8234 0100
🖷 0451-8234 0226
✉ chn@ichtf.com
eng@ichtf.com
kor@ichtf.com
jpn@ichtf.com
www.ichtf.com
5050

第二十二届中国哈尔滨国际经济贸易洽谈会
地点：哈尔滨国际会展体育中心，黑龙江哈尔滨
内容：中国哈尔滨国际经济贸易洽谈会（简称哈洽会）是中国政府批准举办的大型对外交易会之一。已连续成功举办了21届，累计有80多个国家和地区的近160万中外客商参会参展，总成交额逾千亿美元。已发展成为拥有3000个国际标准展位、10多个专业展区（馆）的国际性大型经贸洽谈会，其中有现代农业展区、高新技术展区、新兴产业展区、金融产业展区、经济合作展区、龙江制造展区、旅游产业展区、建材与家居展区、轻工展区、文化产业展区、机电展区、家具馆、港澳台展区和俄罗斯等外国展区。哈洽会是对俄经贸科技合作的最大展会，东北亚区域合作的重要平台，中国全面开拓多元化国际市场的窗口
始办年份：1990
周期：每年一届
市场范围：国际性
性质：面向公众
入场券价格：50元
参展费用：室内国际标准展位（3mx3m）：A、B、C厅展位6,000元/9m²、D厅展位5000元/9m²；室内净地（36m²起）：A、B、C厅展位620元/m²、D厅展位520元/m²，按9m²递增；机电馆（展览篷房）标准展位4,000元/9m²（3mx3m）；室外大型机械展区120元/m²(25m²起)
上届规模 2010：展览面积86,000m²(国外展商10,000m²)，参展商2,200家（国外展商220家，来自21个国家），参观人数32人（专业贸易观众12人）
主办：中华人民共和国商务部；中华人民共和国国家发展和改革委员会；中国贸促会；黑龙江省人民政府；浙江省人民政府；哈尔滨市人民政府
承办：中国哈尔滨经济贸易洽谈会办公室
地址：中国哈尔滨市南岗区美顺街35号（150090）
联系人：景林，张玉虹

Harbin Trade Fair
The 22nd China Harbin International Economic and Trade Fair
Venue: Harbin Intl Conference Exhibition and Sport Center, Harbin, Heilongjiang
Profile: China Harbin International Economic and Trade Fair (Harbin Trade Fair) is one of the large-scale foreign trade fairs authorized by the Chinese government. Since its first session in 1990, the Fair has been successfully held for 20 consecutive years. Over the years, 1.6 million Chinese and foreign visitors from 80 countries participated and visited the fair, the total trade volume reached 100 billion USD. Harbin Trade Fair is a large scale international trade fair that can provide 3000 international standard booths, with over 10 professional exhibition areas（pavilions）including Modern Agricultural Exhibition Area, High Tech Exhibition Area, New Emerging Industry Exhibition Area, Financial Industry Exhibition Area, Economic Cooperation Exhibition Area, Heilongjiang Manufacturing Industry Exhibition Area, Tourism Industry Exhibition Area, Construction and Household Material Exhibition Area, Light Industry Exhibition Area, Cultural Industry Exhibition Area, Machinery and Electric Products Exhibition Area, Furniture Pavilion, Hong Kong, Macao and Taiwan Exhibition Area, Russian Exhibition Area, Foreign Countries Exhibition Area. Harbin Trade Fair is the largest fair for China–Russian economic and trade cooperation, the significant platform for regional cooperation with Northeast Asian countries, the window for China to fully develop diversified international market
Established Year: 1990
Frequency: Annual
Market Area: International
Nature: Open to Public
Cost to Attend: RMB 50:-
Participated Fee: Standard Booth（3mx3m）: Hall A, B, C RMB 6,000/9m², Hall D RMB 5,000/9m²; Raw Space (min 36m²) Hall A、B、C RMB 620/m², Hall D RMB 520/m²; Machinery and Electric Pavilions RMB 4,000/9m²; Outdoor RMB 120/m²(min 25m²)
Statistics 2010: Exhibition Area 86,000m²(foreigners 10,000m²), Exhibitors 2,200（foreigners 220, came from 21 countries）, Visitors 32（trade visitors 12）
Sponsor: Ministry of Commerce of the People' s Republic of China; National Development and Reform Commission; CCPIT; The People' s Government of Heilongjiang Province; The People' s Government of Zhejiang Province; The People' s Government of Harbin Municipality
Organizer: The Administration Office of China Harbin Economic and Trade Fair
Address: No.35 Meishun St., Nangang Dist., Harbin, China
Contact: Jing Lin, Zhang Yuhong

2011/08/01 - 08
☎ 0451-8755 8666, 8755 8685
🖷 0451-8626 8632, 8755 8688
✉ zwh1000@126.com
www.autoharbin.org
5055

哈尔滨国际车展
（第14届哈尔滨国际汽车工业展览会）
地点：哈尔滨国际会展中心，黑龙江哈尔滨
内容：各种类型的汽车、摩托车；各种汽车、摩托车总成及其零部件；各种汽车、零部件生产制造设备、工艺设备；各种汽车维修工具及设备；各种检测、测试、测验仪器和设备；各种汽车美容护理用品、装饰件；各种汽车音响、车载电话、电视、汽车导航系统；立体停车设备；汽车工业生产的新技术、新工艺、新材料；汽车工业新能源技术与产品；汽车工业环保技术与产品；计算机开发设计系统及应用技术；汽车专业杂志、科技资讯、网络以及先进的设计、管理技术。
始办年份：1998
周期：每年一届
市场范围：国际性
性质：面向公众
上届规模 '09：展览面积95,000m²，参展商458家(来自11个国家)
主办：中国汽车工业协会；中国汽车工程学会；黑龙江省人民政府；哈尔滨市人民政府；哈尔滨长城国际展览有限公司
联系人：高笑怡，吴涛

The 14th Harbin International Automobile Exhibition
Venue: Harbin International Conference Exhibition and Sports Center, Harbin, Heilongjiang
Profile: Automobiles and motorcycles; Automobiles, motorcycle assemblies and their components, parts; Automobiles, motorcycle manufacture equipment and workmanship equipment; Maintenance & repair tools and equipment for automobiles; Detection, test, inspection devices and equipment; Automobile beauty & care articles and decoration articles; Sound equipment, automobile telephones, TVs and automobile navigation systems; Three-dimensional parking equipment; New technique, new workmanship and new materials for the production in automobile industry; New energy technique and products in automobile industry; Environment protection technique and products in automobile industry.
Established Year: 1998
Frequency: Annual
Market Area: International
Nature: Open to public
Statistics '09: Exhibition Area 95,000m², Exhibitors 458 (came from 11 countries)
Organizer: China Automobile Industry Assn; China Automobile Engineering Academy; Heilongjiang People' s Government; Harbin Municipal People' s Government; Harbin Great Wall International Exhibition Co Ltd
Contact: Gao Xiao Yi, Wu Tao

河南-漯河 Henan-Luohe

2011/05 -
☎ 010-6609 4505
✉ hetian112@sina.com
5060

第九届中国（漯河）食品博览会
地点：河南漯河
主办：中国商业联合会；河南省人民政府；中国食品工业协会
联系人：何天

9th China (Luohe) Food Fair
Venue: Luohe, Henan
Organizer: China General Chamber of Commerce

河南-洛阳 Henan-Luoyang

2011/04/08 - 11
☎ 010-8260 6880转ext 91
🖷 010-8260 6883
✉ ciccyhuang@cnaico.com.cn
www.cnaico.com.cn
www.autochina.com.cn
5070

2011年中国洛阳国际汽车展览会
地点：河南洛阳
主办：中国汽车工业国际合作总公司
地址：北京市海淀区中关村丹棱街3号A座

China Luoyang Intl Automobile Exhibition
Venue: Luoyang, Henan
Organizer: China National Automotive Industry International Corp

河南-郑州 Henan-Zhengzhou

2011/02/18 - 21
☎ 0371-6808 9866
🖷 0371-6808 9835
✉ sales@zzicec.com
www.zzicec.com
5080

2011年（春季）中国郑州第十八届中原广告展暨
2011年中国中部LED霓虹灯展
地点：郑州国际会展中心，河南郑州
预计规模：总面积22,500m²

Zhengzhou Central China Advertising Exhibition
2011 Central China LED Neon Exhibition
Venue: Zhengzhou International Convention & Exhibition Center, Zhengzhou, Henan
Expectation: Gross Area 22,500m²

2011/02/23 - 26
☎ 0371-6808 9866
🖷 0371-6808 9835
✉ sales@zzicec.com
www.zzicec.com
5090

2011太阳能展（春交会）
地点：郑州国际会展中心，河南郑州
预计规模：总面积12,000m²

2011 Solar Energy
Venue: Zhengzhou International Convention & Exhibition Center, Zhengzhou, Henan
Expectation: Gross Area 12,000m²

2011/03/07 - 12
☎ 0371-6808 9866
🖷 0371-6808 9835
✉ sales@zzicec.com
www.zzicec.com
5100

2011年中国郑州微型汽车配件展
地点：郑州国际会展中心，河南郑州
预计规模：总面积18,000m²

2011 China (Zhengzhou) Mini Automobile and Parts Exhibition
Venue: Zhengzhou International Convention & Exhibition Center, Zhengzhou, Henan
Expectation: Gross Area 18,000m²

2011/03/14 - 18
☎ 0371-6808 9866
🖷 0371-6808 9835
✉ sales@zzicec.com
www.zzicec.com
5110

第二十届中原国际医疗器械展览会
地点：郑州国际会展中心，河南郑州
预计规模：18,000m²

20th Central China Medical Equipment Exhibition
Venue: Zhengzhou International Convention & Exhibition Center, Zhengzhou, Henan
Expectation: Gross Area 18,000m²

2011/03/21 - 26
☎ 0371-6808 9866
🖷 0371-6808 9835
✉ sales@zzicec.com
www.zzicec.com
5120

2011中国中部（郑州）国际装备制造业博览会
地点：郑州国际会展中心，河南郑州
预计规模：总面积12,000m²

2011 Central China (Zhengzhou) Equipment and Manufacturing Expo
Venue: Zhengzhou International Convention & Exhibition Center, Zhengzhou, Henan
Expectation: Gross Area 18,000m²

2011/03/30 - 03
☎ 0371-6808 9866
🖷 0371-6808 9835
✉ sales@zzicec.com
www.zzicec.com
5130

中国古玩展览会
地点：郑州国际会展中心，河南郑州
预计规模：总面积6,000m²

China Antique Exhibition
Venue: Zhengzhou International Convention & Exhibition Center, Zhengzhou, Henan
Expectation: Gross Area 6,000m²

2011/03/30 - 03
☎ 0371-6808 9866
🖷 0371-6808 9835
✉ sales@zzicec.com
www.zzicec.com
5140

第二届华夏有机肥展示会暨第七届中原肥料双交会
地点：郑州国际会展中心，河南郑州
预计规模：总面积12,000m²

2nd China Organic Fertilizer Show
7th Central China Fertilizer Fair
Venue: Zhengzhou International Convention & Exhibition Center, Zhengzhou, Henan
Expectation: Gross Area 12,000m²

2011/04/06 - 10
☎ 0371-6808 9866
🖷 0371-6808 9835
✉ sales@zzicec.com
www.zzicec.com
5150

第二届大河汽车博览会
地点：郑州国际会展中心，河南郑州
预计规模：总面积22,500m²

2nd Giant River Automobile Expo
Venue: Zhengzhou International Convention & Exhibition Center, Zhengzhou, Henan
Expectation: Gross Area 22,500m²

2011/04/11 - 15
☎ 0371-6808 9866
🖷 0371-6808 9835
✉ sales@zzicec.com
www.zzicec.com
5160

2011年中国郑州烘焙展览会
地点：郑州国际会展中心，河南郑州
预计规模：总面积6,000m²

2011 China (Zhengzhou) Baking Exhibition
Venue: Zhengzhou International Convention & Exhibition Center, Zhengzhou, Henan
Expectation: Gross Area 6,000m²

2011/04/12 - 16
☎ 0371-6808 9866
🖷 0371-6808 9835
✉ sales@zzicec.com
www.zzicec.com
5170

2011第九届郑州社会公共安全产品博览会
地点：郑州国际会展中心，河南郑州
预计规模：总面积12,000m²

9th Zhengzhou Public Safety and Security Products Expo
Venue: Zhengzhou International Convention & Exhibition Center, Zhengzhou, Henan
Expectation: Gross Area 12,000m²

2011/04/24 - 28
☎ 0371-6808 9866
🖷 0371-6808 9835
✉ sales@zzicec.com
www.zzicec.com
5180

2011首届中国（郑州）国际孕婴童用品博览会
地点：郑州国际会展中心，河南郑州
预计规模：总面积6,000m²

1st China (Zhengzhou) Expo for Baby, Kids and Mother-to-be Products
Venue: Zhengzhou International Convention & Exhibition Center, Zhengzhou, Henan
Expectation: Gross Area 6,000m²

2011/05/18 - 23
☎ 0371-6808 9866
🖷 0371-6808 9835
✉ sales@zzicec.com
www.zzicec.com
5190

2011年中国郑州渔具用品展览会
地点：郑州国际会展中心，河南郑州
预计规模：总面积6,000m²

2011 China (Zhengzhou) Fishing Equipment Exhibition
Venue: Zhengzhou International Convention & Exhibition Center, Zhengzhou, Henan
Expectation: Gross Area 6,000m²

2011/05/25 - 29
☎ 0371-6808 9866
🖷 0371-6808 9835
✉ sales@zzicec.com
www.zzicec.com
5200

2011中国（郑州）国际缝制设备展览会
暨2011中国（郑州）国际纺织面料、辅料及纱线展览会
地点：郑州国际会展中心，河南郑州
预计规模：总面积10,500m²

China (Zhengzhou) Sewing Machines Exhibition
Textile, Yarn and Supplementary Material Exhibition
Venue: Zhengzhou International Convention & Exhibition Center, Zhengzhou, Henan
Expectation: Gross Area 10,500m²

2011/06/01 - 05
☎ 0371-6808 9866
🖷 0371-6808 9835
✉ sales@zzicec.com
www.zzicec.com
5210

第六届中国（郑州）国际酒店、餐饮、泳池沐浴SPA设备及用品博览会/第六届中国（郑州）国际家纺、布艺及工艺品、礼品家居装饰博览会
地点：郑州国际会展中心，河南郑州
预计规模：总面积18,000m²

6th China (Zhengzhou) Hospitality, Swimming Pool and Spa Expo
Grafts, Gifts and Home-ware Expo
Venue: Zhengzhou International Convention & Exhibition Center, Zhengzhou, Henan
Expectation: Gross Area 18,000m²

2011/06/08 - 12
☎ 0371-6808 9866
🖷 0371-6808 9835
✉ sales@zzicec.com
www.zzicec.com
5220

中国郑州裤业博览会
地点：郑州国际会展中心，河南郑州
预计规模：总面积22,500m²

China (Zhengzhou) Pants Show
Venue: Zhengzhou International Convention & Exhibition Center, Zhengzhou, Henan
Expectation: Gross Area 22,500m²

2011/06/23 - 02
☎ 0371-6808 9866
🖷 0371-6808 9835
✉ sales@zzicec.com
www.zzicec.com
5230

2011第八届汽车用品交易会
暨第八届汽车羊剪绒产品订货会
地点：郑州国际会展中心，河南郑州
预计规模：总面积65,000m²

8th Automobile Products Fair
Venue: Zhengzhou International Convention & Exhibition Center, Zhengzhou, Henan
Expectation: Gross Area 65,000m²

2011/08/23 - 28
☎ 0371-6808 9866
🖷 0371-6808 9835
✉ sales@zzicec.com
www.zzicec.com
5240

惠州商品展
地点：郑州国际会展中心，河南郑州
预计规模：总面积12,000m²

Huizhou Commodity Fair
Venue: Zhengzhou International Convention & Exhibition Center, Zhengzhou, Henan
Expectation: Gross Area 12,000m²

2011/09/05 - 09
☎ 0371-6808 9866
🖷 0371-6808 9835
✉ sales@zzicec.com
www.zzicec.com
5250

第二十一届中原国际医疗器械(秋季)展览会
中国中部郑州（秋季）国际装备制造业博览会
地点：郑州国际会展中心，河南郑州
预计规模：总面积18,000m²

21st Central China Autumn Medical Equipment Exhibition
Central China Industrial Equipment Expo - Autumn
Venue: Zhengzhou International Convention & Exhibition Center, Zhengzhou, Henan
Expectation: Gross Area 18,000m²

2011/09/12 - 18
☎ 0371-6808 9866
🖷 0371-6808 9835
✉ sales@zzicec.com
www.zzicec.com
5260

2011郑州全国商品交易会
地点：郑州国际会展中心，河南郑州
预计规模：总面积65,000m²

Zhengzhou Commodity Fair
Venue: Zhengzhou International Convention & Exhibition Center, Zhengzhou, Henan
Expectation: Gross Area 65,000m²

2011/09/19 - 22
☎ 0371-6808 9866
🖷 0371-6808 9835
✉ sales@zzicec.com
www.zzicec.com
5270

家禽交易会
地点：郑州国际会展中心，河南郑州
预计规模：总面积33,000m²

Poultry Fair
Venue: Zhengzhou International Convention & Exhibition Center, Zhengzhou, Henan
Expectation: Gross Area 33,000m²

2011/10/12 - 14
☎ 010-6343 0880, 6343 0990
🖷 010-6343 0660
✉ cn870870@126.com
www.cn870.com
5290

2011第7届中国冰淇淋冷冻食品工业展览会
地点：郑州国际会展中心，河南郑州
内容：冰淇淋生产设备及器具、软冰淇淋生产设备及器具；冰淇淋、冷冻食品的原辅材料、食品代加工（OEM）；冰淇淋专用油脂、奶油、专用粉、奶乳清粉、蛋白粉、豆粉、淀粉、；冰淇淋专用香草香精香料，复合乳化稳定剂，纯天然色素，食用色素，甜蜜素，乳酸菌，植脂末奶精，乳清粉、天然果粉，浓缩果汁果浆，巧克力、咖啡，可可制品，代可可脂，果仁、干果等；分馅机、成型机、包馅机；展示柜、储藏；冰淇淋、冷冻食品包装机械，纸包装、复合软包装。塑料封口和商标印刷、自动打码机等；冰淇淋连锁店、加盟店等；冷冻食品自动生产设备、器具；面食加工成套设备；冷冻食品专用油脂、专用面粉、糯米粉、酵母、奶粉、蛋白粉、豆粉、淀粉及辅料；冷冻食品专用馅料、干果等农产品；专业水处理、环保设备；冷食专用运输车、冷冻冷藏设备及金属探测设备；冰淇淋、冷冻食品技术
周期：每年一届
市场范围：全国性
性质：面向贸易观众
上届规模 2010：展览面积13,000m², 参展商130家，专业贸易观众8,000人
主办：全国冷冻饮品专业委员会
地址：北京市海淀区北蜂窝2号中盛大厦1305A（100038）
联系人：李翔，李娟

China Ice-Cream & Frozen Foods Exposition
Venue: Zhengzhou International Convention & Exhibition Center, Zhengzhou, Henan
Frequency: Annual
Market Area: National
Nature: Trade Only
Statistics 2010: Exhibition Area 13,000m², Exhibitors 130, Trade Visitors 8,000
Organizer: National Frozen Food Professional Committee
Address: 1305A Rm.1305A Zhangshang Mansion, 2 Beifengwo, Beijing

2011/11/11 - 15
☎ 010-8260 6880转ext 91
🖷 010-8260 6883
✉ ciccyhuang@cnaico.com.cn
www.cnaico.com.cn
www.autochina.com.cn
5300

2011年第四届郑州国际汽车展览会
地点：郑州国际会展中心，河南郑州
预计规模：总面积39,500m²
主办：中国汽车工业国际合作总公司
地址：北京市海淀区中关村丹棱街3号A座

2011 China (Zhengzhou) Intl Automobile Expo
Venue: Zhengzhou International Convention & Exhibition Center, Zhengzhou, Henan
Expectation: Gross Area 39,500m²
Organizer: China National Automotive Industry International Corp

湖北-武汉 Hubei-Wuhan

2011/05/13 - 16
☎ 027-6560 2827
🖷 027-6560 3179
✉ teaexpo@qq.com
www.hzteaexpo.com
5310

2011第四届中国武汉茶业博览会暨陆羽国际茶文化节
地点：武汉国际会展中心，湖北武汉
内容：茶叶：绿茶、红茶、青茶、白茶、黄茶、黑茶；茶具：陶瓷、紫砂、茶盘、煮茶器、冲茶具、玻璃器皿、茶家具、根雕；茶包装：茶叶罐、茶叶盒及相关包装类制品；茶机械：茶叶生产加工机械，茶叶干燥、微波与保鲜设备；茶流通企业：茶叶经销代理、连锁经营企业、茶庄、茶馆、茶楼、茶店；其他：茶业媒体、茶饮食品、茶工艺品及茶衍生品。
始办年份：2008
周期：每年一届
市场范围：全国性
性质：面向公众
主办：湖北省茶叶学会；湖北省陆羽茶文化研究会；湖北省茶叶协会武汉茶业协会
联络：武汉中兴恒远展览会议有限公司
地址：湖北省武汉市新华路385号南达大楼（430015）
联系人：吴远志

4th China Wuhan Tea Expo
Luyu Tea Culture Festival
Venue: Wuhan Intl Conference & Exhibition Center, Wuhan, Hubei
Established Year: 2008
Frequency: Annual
Market Area: National
Nature: Open to Public
Organizer: Wuhan Zhongxing Hengyuan Exh & Con. Co Ltd

2011/05/20 - 24
☎ 010-8260 6880转ext 91
🖷 010-8260 6883
✉ ciccyhuang@cnaico.com.cn
www.cnaico.com.cn
www.autochina.com.cn
5320

2011年第九届华中国际汽车展览会
地点：湖北武汉
主办：中国汽车工业国际合作总公司
地址：北京市海淀区中关村丹棱街3号A座

9th Central China Automobile Exhibition
Venue: Wuhan, Hubei
Organizer: China National Automotive Industry International Corp

2011/06/10 - 12
☎ 027-8228 8759, 8228 8716, 8228 8725
🖷 027-8228 8715, 8228 8759
www.whcciec.com
5325

2011中国湖北国际专业灯光、音响、视听集成技术、乐器及设备博览会
地点：武汉国际会展中心，湖北武汉
内容：钢琴和键盘乐器、电声乐器、打击乐器、铜管乐器、木管乐器、弦乐器、民族乐器、乐器配件和加工机械、乐谱和书籍、音乐相关电脑硬件和软件、音乐相关服务、协会和媒体。音响、KTV展区：专业音响、KTV、舞台机械与设备；灯光、LED展区：专业灯光、LED、以下设备的制造商、供应商、经销商、系统集成商：视听设备、指挥及控制系统、视频会议设备、监视器及显示屏、数字广告系统、投影系统、大屏幕系统集成、家庭娱乐、安全与自动化系统、商业、零售业、娱乐设施及公共场所
主办：湖北省演出中心湖北省演出协会
承办： 湖北省文化厅大型活动策划制作中心；武汉传承文化展览有限公司
地址：武汉市江岸区黄浦大街88号黄浦东宫B座2106室
联系人：杨永金

China Hubei PLAV (Lighting, Audio, Video, Musical Instrument) Expo
Venue: Wuhan Intl Conference & Exhibition Center, Wuhan, Hubei
Organizer: Wuhan Chuancheng Culture Exhibition Co Ltd

2011/06/25 - 26
☎ 027-8228 8759 822 8871
🖷 027-8228 8716
✉ whciee2006@yahoo.com.cn
www.ChinaEducationExhibition.com
5330

2011第七届中国（武汉）国际教育展
地点：武汉国际会展中心，湖北武汉
内容：海外预科学校、学院和大学（学历、学位经所在国家政府教育主管部门或其授权的权威机构承认或注册，以及具有接收海外国学生资质的院校）；海外职业培训学校；海外语言培训学校和机构；海外政府教育机构；使（领）馆；留学相关服务（银行、住宿、航空公司）；留学中介及中外合作办学项目
参展费用：国外机构1,800美元/标准展位（双面开口加收10%），会务费30美元/人；国内企业8,000元/标准展位（双面开口加收10%），会务费200元/人
上届规模 2010：参观人数30,000人
主办：武汉市出入境中介服务行业协会
承办：湖北金茂出国咨询顾问管理有限公司；武汉传承文化展览有限公司
联系人：杨永金
MSN：yangyongjin2008@hotmail.com

7th China (Wuhan) Intl Education Exhibition
Venue: Wuhan Intl Conference & Exhibition Center, Wuhan, Hubei
Participated Fee: Standard Booth USD 1,800/9m², Corner unit add 10%
Statistics 2010: Visitors 30,000
Organizer: HuBei Jinmao Foreign Consultants Management Co Ltd; Wuhan Chuancheng Culture Exhibition Co Ltd
MSN: yangyongjin2008@hotmail.com

2011/09/01 - 06
☎ 027-8577 7921, 8577 8685, 6333 2561
🖷 027-8573 3284
✉ expowh@ccpit.org
www.autowuhan.com.cn
5340

第十二届中国（湖北武汉）国际汽车工业展览会
地点：武汉国际博览中心，湖北武汉
内容：整车：乘用车、商用车、特种车；汽车零部件：发动机、传动系统、行驶系统、转向系统、制动系统、车身附件、电器设备、汽车轮胎；汽车用品：汽车内饰、汽车音响系统、通信导航系统、空调系统、汽车安全系统、车载电子产品、汽车美容及养护用品、油漆、润滑剂、添加剂；汽车维修检测设备：诊断设备、维修工具、汽车喷烤漆、洗车及其它相关设备；汽车相关制造设备、技术和工具；其它相关产品和服务
周期：每年一届
市场范围：国际性
性质：面向公众
入场券价格：30元
参展费用：900元/m^2
上届规模 2010：展览面积17,000m^2(国外展商2,500m^2)，参展商257家（国外展商33家，来自8个国家），参观人数280,000人（专业贸易观众30,000人）
主办：中国机械工业联合会；中国贸促会；湖北省人民政府；武汉市人民政府
承办：中国贸促会武汉市分会；湖北省机械汽车行业协会
地址：武汉市汉口台北路217号8楼（430015）
联系人：喻金富,章劲
MSN：zlwhcn@hotmail.com
QQ：34698629

The 12th China (Hubei/Wuhan) International Auto Industry Exhibition
Venue: Wuhan Intl Expo Center, Wuhan, Hubei
Profile: Vehicles: Passenger cars, commercial vehicles, special-purpose vehicles, etc. Automotive Parts: Engines & mechanical system, Gearbox, Exhaust, Axle, Steering, Brakes, Suspension system, Body system, Electric and electronic system, Tire and wheels. Automotive Accessories: Interior trimmings, Car audio system, Navigation and telecom system, Air conditioning system, Safety and vehicle security system, Vehicle mounted electronic products, Car care products, paints, lubricants, additives. Measuring, testing and control devices & systems, Related manufacturing technology, machinery, equipment and tools.
Frequency: Annual
Market Area: International
Nature: Open to Public
Cost to Attend: RMB 30:-
Participated Fee: RMB 900/m^2
Statistics 2010: Exhibition Area 17,000m^2(foreigners 2,500m^2), Exhibitors 257（foreigners 33, came from 8 countries）, Visitors 280,000（trade visitors 30,000）
Sponsor: China Machinery Industry Federation; CCPIT; Hubei Provincial People's Government; Wuhan Municipal People's Government
Organizer: CCPIT Wuhan Sub-Council; Hubei Provincial Machinery & Automotive Industry Association
Address: 8/Fl., 217 Tabei Road, Hankou, Wuhan 430015, China
Contact: Yu Jinfu, Zhang Jin
MSN: zlwhcn@hotmail.com

2011/09/23 - 26
☎ 852-2763 9011
🖷 852-2341 0379
✉ jenny@paper-con.com.hk
www.paper-com.com.hk
5350

第十二届中国国际机电产品博览会-武汉
地点：武汉国际博览中心(新馆)，湖北武汉
主办：通讯展览公司
地址：香港九龙观塘成业街11号华成工商中心5字楼15室

12th China International Machinery & Electronic Products Expo, Wuhan
Venue: Wuhan Expo Center, Wuhan, Hubei
Organizer: Paper Communication Exhibition Service
Address: Rm. 15, 5/F. Wha Shing Center, 11 Shing Ypi St. Kwun Tong, Kowloon, Hong Kong
Contact: Jenny Leung

2011/10/12 - 14
☎ 010-6876 7728, 6837 3982
🖷 010-6876 7765
✉ sunth@autoid-chian.com.cn
www.aimchina.org.cn
5360

国际自动识别技术展览会
地点：武汉科技会展中心，湖北武汉
内容：从应用推广、技术探讨、产业发展以及国际交流等方面着手，致力于促进中国自动识别技术的应用与发展，"展示产业新技术/新产品，倡导自主知识产权，推动产业健康发展"。以展览和论坛为载体，整合流通、连锁零售、制造、医疗、食品、制造、电子商务与现代物流等行业、领域资源，为自动识别技术研发商、产品制造商、系统集成商、自动识别技术相关的信息化解决方案提供商以及广大用户，构建了交流、发展的平台
始办年份：1994
周期：每年一届
市场范围：国际性
性质：面向贸易观众
入场券价格：免费
参展费用：国内企业800～1,200元/m^2, 国外企业260～300美元/m^2
上届规模 2010：展览面积8,000m^2(国外展商2,000m^2)，参展商100家（国外展商20家，来自5个国家），参观人数10,000人（专业贸易观众1,000人）
主办：中国物品编码中心/中国自动识别技术协会
承办：北京源智天成科技有限公司
地址：北京市海淀区阜成路16号航天科技大厦附楼401室（100048）
联系人：王灿，孙天慧

International Exhibition of Automatic Identification Technology
Venue: Wuhan Science and Technology Conference and Exhibition Center, Wuhan, Hubei
Established Year: 1994
Frequency: Annual
Market Area: International
Nature: Trade Only
Cost to Attend: Free
Participated Fee: USD 260-300/m^2
Statistics 2010: Exhibition Area 8,000m^2(foreigners 2,000m^2), Exhibitors 100（foreigners 20, came from 5 countries）, Visitors 10,000（trade visitors 1,000）
Organizer: Automatic Identification Manufacture Association of China

2011/12 -
☎ 010-6609 4505
✉ hetian112@sina.com
5370

中国国际进出口食品交易会
第二十届中国食品博览会暨交易会
地点：湖北武汉
主办：中国商业联合会；湖北省人民政府；武汉市人民政府
联系人：何天

China Intl Food Fair
Venue: Wuhan, Hubei
Organizer: China General Chamber of Commerce

湖南-长沙 Hunan-Changsha

2011/03/21 - 23
☎ 0731-8559 6322, 8218 6792
🖷 0731-8218 6793
✉ 1311024636@qq.com
5390

2011湖南环境保护产业博览会
地点：长沙红星国际会展中心，湖南长沙
内容：纯净水设备、纯水机、直饮水设备、供水设备、成套设备、工业用水设备、污水与污泥处理设备、中水回用、泵、阀门、管道、膜产品、过滤、消毒设备、给排水设备、节水产品、水利水电设备与工程装备及材料，防洪抗旱装备、仪器仪表；市容环卫机械及设施
始办年份：2009
周期：每年一届
市场范围：地区性
主办：湖南省循环经济研究会；湖南省环境工作协会；湖南省生态环保建筑装饰委员会
承办：长沙支点展览策划有限公司
地址：湖南省长沙市八一路59号湖南省科技厅二院（410000）
联系人：王经理

Hunan Changsha Environment Protection Expo
Venue: Changsha Hongxing Intl Exhibition Center, Changsha, Hunan
Established Year: 2009
Frequency: Annual
Market Area: Regional
Organizer: Changsha Zhidian Exhibition Co Ltd

2011/05/25 - 27
☎ 0731-8283 6020
🖷 0731-8283 6036
✉ zmm51888@163.com
5400

2011第6届湖南电力新技术新装备展览会
地点：湖南国际会展中心，湖南长沙
内容：发电技术及设备：火电、核电、光伏发电技术及设备、热电联产技术及装置。输配电设备：电力电缆、高压断路器、变压器、接触器、断路器、继电器、起动器、互感器、电容器、整流器、电力稳压器、电抗器、终端电器等、接地开关及高压绝缘设备、高低压成套产品、电源柜、配电箱柜、控制箱柜、各类绝缘子、各式开关电器。电气自动化技术与设备：中低压电网配备产品，电气控制与自动化成套设备、配网自动化、电力通信设备、负荷控制设备、电力信息技术和IT集成产品、电力电子产品与技术。电工器材产品；电力施工设备/电力金具
始办年份：2004
周期：每年一届
市场范围：全国性
性质：面向公众
主办：湖南省电力行业协会；长沙好博塔苏斯展览有限公司
地址：湖南省长沙市芙蓉中路一段468号湖南财富中心富1904（410005）
联系人：张明敏

Hunan Electric Power Technology and Equipment Exhibition
Venue: Hunan International Convention & Exhibition Center, Changsha, Hunan
Established Year: 2004
Frequency: Annual
Market Area: National
Nature: Open to Public
Organizer: Changshai Tarsus Hope Exhibition Co Ltd

2011/05/25 - 27
☎ 0731-8283 6020
🖷 0731-8283 6036
✉ zmm51888@163.com
5410

2011第12届湖南工控自动化及仪器仪表展览会
地点：湖南国际会展中心，湖南长沙
内容：传感器、变频器、连接器、端子、变送器、编码器、定位器、互感器、继电器；工控机、嵌入式、伺服控制及驱动系统、数控数显系统及设备、机械驱动系统；传动、液压气动及元件、马达、步进机电、自动化器件、密封件装置和辅助设备；三坐标测量仪、温湿度仪、流体控制、各类阀、执行器、流量计、计量测试设备；信号处理器、指示器、监控器、记录器、检测/计量分析/质量控制/测试仪器仪表；非标自动化设备、激光技术、组装及搬运和线性定位系统、电子零部件
始办年份：1999
周期：每年一届
市场范围：全国性
性质：面向公众
主办：湖南省自动化学会；湖南省仪器仪表行业协会；湖南省国防科技工业办公室；湖南省仪器仪表学会
承办：长沙好博塔苏斯展览有限公司
地址：湖南省长沙市芙蓉中路一段468号湖南财富中心富1904（410005）
联系人：张明敏

12th Industrial Control, Automation, Instrument Exhibition
Venue: Hunan Intl Convention & Exhibition Center, Changsha, Hunan
Established Year: 1999
Frequency: Annual
Market Area: National
Nature: Open to Public
Organizer: Changshai Tarsus Hope Exhibition Co Ltd

2011/11/04 - 06
☎ 010-6878 4991, 6878 4992
🖷 010-6878 4978
✉ yw@ccfa.org.cn
5420

第十三届中国连锁业会议暨
第十三届中国连锁店展览会
地点：湖南国际会展中心，湖南长沙
内容：作为中国零售业规模最大、权威性最强，具有前瞻性的展会活动，中国连锁业会议，中国连锁店展览会一直是相关行业人士年度关注的重点活动，她汇聚了国内外零售业的最新模式、最新技术和产品；加强了海内外零售商、供应商以及同行业之间的交流与合作；真实展示了中国现代流通业的飞速发展

The 13th China Retail Industry Convention &
The 13th China Chain Store Expo
Venue: Hunan International Convention & Exhibition Center, Changsha, Hunan
Profile: China Chain Store Expo (China Store)is the Largest, most influential and forward-looking event in China, due to the attraction and support from thousands of retails and suppliers every year. Based on the past eleven successful sessions, China Store not only gathered

和辉煌成就；在推动中国零售业管理创新和技术进步中扮演着重要的角色。
始办年份：1999
周期：每年一届
市场范围：国际性
性质：面向贸易观众
参展费用：标准展位7,200元，净地720元/m²
上届规模 2010：展览面积8,200m²，参展商248家，参观人数12,000人
主办：中国连锁经营协会
承办：北京尚智联协会展咨询有限公司
地址：北京市西城区阜外大街22号外经贸大厦811-815号（100037）
联系人：沈静小姐、杨雯小姐
MSN：embun332002@hotmail.com

the latest models, technologies and products from China and abroad, enhanced and improved the international exchange and cooperation, but also showed the rapid development and brilliant achievements of modern circulation industry in China. There is no doubt that China Store has been at the forefront of the world retail industry.
Established Year: 1999
Frequency: Annual
Market Area: International
Nature: Trade Only
Participated Fee: Standard Booth RMB 7,200/m², Raw Space RMB 720/m²
Statistics 2010: Exhibition Area 8,200m², Exhibitors 248, Visitors 12,000
Sponsor: China Chain Store & Franchise Association
Organizer: Beijing Shine Co Ltd
Address: Room 811,8th floor, Foreign Economic & Trade Plaza, No 22 Fuchengmenwai Str., Xicheng District, Beijing, China 100037
Contact: Sharon Yang
MSN: embun332002@hotmail.com

内蒙古-包头 Inner Mongolia-Baotou

2011 -
☎ 010-8260 6880转ext 91
🖷 010-8260 6883
✉ ciccyhuang@cnaico.com.cn
www.cnaico.com.cn
www.autochina.com.cn
5430

2011中国包头国际汽车展览会
地点：内蒙古包头
主办：中国汽车工业国际合作总公司
地址：北京市海淀区中关村丹棱街3号A座

China Baotou Intl Automobile Exhibition
Venue: Baotou, Inner Mongolia
Organizer: China National Automotive Industry International Corp

内蒙古-呼和浩特 Inner Mongolia-Hohhot

2011/07/15 - 19
☎ 010-8260 6880转ext 91
🖷 010-8260 6883
✉ ciccyhuang@cnaico.com.cn
www.cnaico.com.cn,
www.autochina.com.cn
5435

2011年第三届呼和浩特国际汽车展览会
地点：内蒙古呼和浩特
主办：中国汽车工业国际合作总公司
地址：北京市海淀区中关村丹棱街3号A座

3rd Hohhot Intl Automobile Exhibition
Venue: Hohhot, Inner Mongolia
Organizer: China National Automotive Industry International Corp

内蒙古-鄂尔多斯 Inner Mongolia-Ordos

2011/09/01 - 05
☎ 010-8260 6880转ext 91
🖷 010-8260 6883
✉ ciccyhuang@cnaico.com.cn
www.cnaico.com.cn
www.autochina.com.cn
5438

2011第二届鄂尔多斯国际汽车展览会
地点：内蒙古鄂尔多斯
主办：中国汽车工业国际合作总公司
地址：北京市海淀区中关村丹棱街3号A座

Ordos International Automobile Exhibition
Venue: Ordos, Inner Mongolia
Organizer: China National Automotive Industry International Corp

江苏-常州 Jiangsu-Changzhou

2011/03/25 - 27
☎ 0519-8985 1052
🖷 0519-8985 1052

5440 **2011中国（常州）国际摩托车零部件及后用品交易会**
地点：常州国际会展中心，江苏常州
内容：摩托车零部件、改装件后用品新技术的展示与洽谈
始办年份：2011
周期：每年一届
市场范围：全国性
入场券价格：免费
预计规模：展出面积20,000m^2，参展商250家，参观人数60,000人
主办：中华全国工商联汽车摩托车配件用品业商会
地址：常州市晋陵北路3号（奥体中心内）（213022）

China (Changzhou) Intl Motorbike, Parts and Services Fair
Venue: Changzhou Intl Exhibition Center, Changzhou, Jiangsu
Established Year: 2011
Frequency: Annual
Market Area: National
Cost to Attend: Free
Organizer: China Federation of Industry and Commerce - Auto & Motorbike Parts & Accessories Chamber of Commerce

2011/05/01 - 03
☎ 0519-8985 1052
🖷 0519-8985 1052
www.0519car.net

5450 **第三届常州春季汽车博览会**
地点：常州国际会展中心，江苏常州
内容：汽车整车销售及新品发布
始办年份：2009
周期：每年两届
市场范围：地区性
入场券价格：免费
上届规模 2010：展览面积20,000m^2，参展商150家，参观人数100,000人
主办：常州汽车流通协会；常州日报社；常州广播电视台
承办：常州车网；常州国际会展中心；常州上游文化传媒有限公司
地址：常州市晋陵北路3号（奥体中心内）（213022）

3rd Changzhou Spring Automobile Expo
Venue: Changzhou Intl Exhibition Center, Changzhou, Jiangsu
Established Year: 2009
Frequency: Biannual
Market Area: Regional
Cost to Attend: Free
Statistics 2010: Exhibition Area 20,000m^2, Exhibitors 150, Visitors 100,000
Organizer: Changzhou Shangyou Culture Media Co Ltd

2011/05/18 - 22
☎ 0519-8985 1052
🖷 0519-8985 1052

5460 **2011常州住宅产品交易会**
地点：常州国际会展中心，江苏常州
内容：房地产信息发布及交易
始办年份：2005
周期：每年一届
市场范围：地区性
入场券价格：免费
上届规模 2010：展览面积15,000m^2，参展商150家，参观人数80,000人
主办：常州市政府
承办：常州市房管局

Changzhou Housing Fair
Venue: Changzhou Intl Exhibition Center, Changzhou, Jiangsu
Established Year: 2005
Frequency: Annual
Market Area: Regional
Cost to Attend: Free
Statistics 2010: Exhibition Area 15,000m^2, Exhibitors 150, Visitors 80,000
Organizer: Changzhou Housing Authority

2011/06/23 - 25
☎ 0519-8985 1052
🖷 0519-8985 1052

5470 **第五届中国（常州）电动车燃油助力车及零部件展览会**
地点：常州国际会展中心，江苏常州
内容：各类电动自行车、燃油助力车电动汽车等，各类电动车部件及零配件类，生产及检测设备等**始办年份**：2007
周期：每年一届
市场范围：全国性
入场券价格：免费
上届规模 2010：展览面积25,000m^2，参展商250家，参观人数60,000人（专业贸易观众30,000人）
主办：电动车商情
承办：青岛金奥广告策划有限公司
地址：常州市晋陵北路3号（奥体中心内）（213022）

5th China (Changzhou) Electric Car, Hibrid Car and Parts Exhibition
Venue: Changzhou Intl Exhibition Center, Changzhou, Jiangsu
Established Year: 2007
Frequency: Annual
Market Area: National
Cost to Attend: Free
Statistics 2010: Exhibition Area 25000m^2, Exhibitors 250, Visitors 60,000（trade visitors 30,000）
Organizer: Qingdao Jinao Advertising Co Ltd

2011/08/26 - 30
☎ 0519-8985 1052
🖷 0519-8985 1052

5480 **2011年中国（常州）国际动漫艺术周**
地点：常州国际会展中心，江苏常州
内容：国内外动漫画基地、知名动画频道、原创机构等展示，网络游戏互动、动漫衍生产品的展示及交易，大赛作品的展示及动漫影片的放映
始办年份：2009
周期：每年一届
市场范围：地区性
入场券价格：20元
上届规模 2010：展览面积15,000m^2(国外展商5,000m^2)，参展商150家（国外展商20家，来自8个国家），参观人数50,000人（专业贸易观众5,000人）
主办：中华人民共和国文化部；江苏省人民政府
承办：中华人民共和国文化部中外文化交流中心；江苏省委宣传部；常州市人民政府有限公司
地址：常州市晋陵北路3号（奥体中心内）（213022）

China (Changzhou) Intl Comic and Animation Week
Venue: Changzhou Intl Exhibition Center, Changzhou, Jiangsu
Established Year: 2009
Frequency: Annual
Market Area: Regional
Cost to Attend: RMB 20:-
Statistics 2010: Exhibition Area 15,000m^2(foreigners 5,000m^2), Exhibitors 150（foreigners 20, came from 8 countries）, Visitors 50,000（trade visitors 5,000）
Organizer: Changzhou Municipal Government

江苏-连云港 Jiangsu-Lianyungang

2011/06/03 - 06
☎ 010-8260 6880转ext 91
🖷 010-8260 6883
✉ ciccyhuang@cnaico.com.cn
www.cnaico.com.cn
www.autochina.com.cn
5490

第三届连云港-大陆桥汽车贸易博览会
地点：江苏连云港
主办：中国汽车工业国际合作总公司
地址：北京市海淀区中关村丹棱街3号A座

3rd Lianyugang-Continental Bridge Automobile Expo
Venue: Lianyungang, Jiangsu
Organizer: China National Automotive Industry International Corp

江苏-南京 Jiangsu-Nanjing

2011/04/12 - 14
☎ 010-8851 4541,
8899转ext 669
🖷 010-6845 8356
✉ wangkunyi@foundry.com.cn
www.expochina.cn
5500

第八届中国国际有及及特种铸造展览会
暨中国铸造零部件展览会
地点：南京国际博览中心，江苏南京
内容：应用于汽车、机床、风电、船舶、通用机械、工程机械、能源电力、轨道交通等领域的各种铸件产品、零部件产品、总成；各类精密、实型、压力、低压、金属型、消失模等各类有色铸造装备、铸件深加工设备及铸造原辅材料等。
周期：两年一届
市场范围：国际性
性质：面向贸易观众
参展费用：标准展位9,000元/9m^2，净地900元/m^2
上届规模 2009：展览面积6,000m^2(国外展商200m^2)，参展商350家（国外展商20家，来自8个国家），参观人数7,800人（专业贸易观众200人）
主办：中国铸造协会
地址：北京市海淀区紫竹院路甲32号（100048）
联系人：王坤毅，范琦

2011 Non-ferrous & Special foundry and China Cast-part Exhibition
Venue: Nanjing International Expo Center, Nanjing, Jiangsu
Profile: Non-ferrous & Ferrous semi-finished, finished casting, cast parts; Foundry Equipment; Consumable Materials; Casting Processing Equipment; Scientific results, periodicals, website and other services.
Frequency: Biennial
Market Area: International
Nature: Trade Only
Participated Fee: Standard Booth RMB 9,000/9m^2, Raw Space RMB 900/m^2
Statistics 2009: Exhibition Area 6,000m^2(foreigners 200m^2), Exhibitors 350（foreigners 20, came from 8 countries）, Visitors 7,800（trade visitors 200）
Organizer：China Foundry Association
Address: Jia 32 Zizhuyuan Road, Haidian District, Beijing 100048
Contact: Wang Kun, Yi Fanqi

2011/04/12 - 14
☎ 025-8452 1101转ext 869
🖷 025-8469 2610
✉ info@china-ship.com
www.china-ship.com
5510

2011中国国际船舶工业博览会
地点：南京国际博览中心，江苏南京
内容：船舶技术：船舶修造：造船厂、修船厂、拆船厂；船厂装备：船厂建造装备与设备；造修船装备与设备；焊接与切割：焊接机械、焊接配套设备、焊接材料、焊接辅机具；切割装备；探伤材料技术；船用钢材与造船材料：船用钢材；造船用金属、非金属材料；涂装防腐材料及设备：船用油漆及涂料、涂装设备及技术。船舶配套：动力设备，舾装件，科研院所、设计单位。海洋工程；通讯导航；港口技术；物流运输；仓储码头项目。
参展费用：B区（标准展区）6,800元/12m^2，净地510/m^2（36m^{2}起）；A区（优越展区）8,500元/12m^2，净地640元/m^2；境外展区22,200元/12m^2，净地1,600元/m^2，双面开口24m^{2}起；室外500元/m^2
上届规模 2010：展览面积24,000m^2，参展商1,200家（国外展商416家，来自18个国家），参观人数22,941人
承办：江苏省经济和信息化委员会；江苏省商务厅；南京市人民政府

China International Marine, Port & Shipbuilding Fair
Venue: Nanjing International Expo Center, Nanjing, Jiangsu
Participated Fee: RMB 22,200/12m^2, Raw Space (min 36m^2) RMB 1,600/m^2, Outdoor RMB 500/m^2
Statistics 2010: Exhibition Area 24,000m^2, Exhibitors 1,200（foreigners 416, came from 18 countries）, Visitors 22,941
Organizer: Jiangsu United Asia Intl Exhibition Co Ltd

2011/04/30 - 04
☎ 010-8260 6880转ext 91
🖷 010-8260 6883
✉ ciccyhuang@cnaico.com.cn
www.cnaico.com.cn
www.autochina.com.cn
5515

2011年第四届中国（南京）国际汽车博览会
地点：江苏南京
主办：中国汽车工业国际合作总公司
地址：北京市海淀区中关村丹棱街3号A座

4th China (Nanjing) Intl Automobile Expo
Venue: Nanjing, Jiangsu
Organizer: China National Automotive Industry International Corp

2011/09 -
☎ 010-6609 4505
✉ hetian112@sina.com
5520

2011南京台湾名品交易会
地点：江苏南京
主办：南京市人民政府；台北世界贸易中心
联系人：何天

2011 Taiwan Brand Name Product Sales
Venue: Nanjing, Jiangsu
Organizer: Taibei Word Trade Center

2011/09/23 - 26
☎ 010-8455 6613, 8455 6617
✉ yuhui.wang@reedsinopharm.com
fan.liu@reedsinopharm.com
www.gccd2010.org
5530

全球华人口腔医学大会暨
中国国际口腔医学大会
地点：南京国际博览中心，江苏南京
内容：亚太地区首选口腔领域高层学术和技术交流、商务社交、产品采购的国际 化平台
周期：每年一届
主办：国药励展
联系人：王宇辉, 刘繁

4th CSA General Assembly & Annual Meeting
China Dental Show
Venue: Nanjing International Expo Center, Nanjing, Jiangsu
Frequency: Annual
Organizer: Reed Sinopharm Exhibitions

江苏-苏州 Jiangsu-Suzhou

2011/05/11 - 13
☎ 852-2763 9011
🖷 852-2341 0379
✉ jenny@paper-con.com.hk
www.paper-com.com.hk
5540

苏州电路板展览会
地点：苏州国际博览中心，江苏苏州
主办：通讯展览公司
地址：香港九龙观塘成业街11号华成工商中心5字楼15室

Suzhou PCB / SMT Show
Venue: Suzhou International Expo Center, Suzhou, Jiangsu
Organizer: Paper Communication Exhibition Service
Address: Rm. 15, 5/F. Wha Shing Center, 11 Shing Ypi St. Kwun Tong, Kowloon, Hong Kong
Contact: Jenny Leung

2011/05/11 - 13
☎ 852-2763 9011
🖷 852-2341 0379
✉ jenny@paper-con.com.hk
www.paper-com.com.hk
5550

2011苏州自动化产业设备展览会
地点：苏州国际博览中心，江苏苏州
主办：通讯展览公司
地址：香港九龙观塘成业街11号华成工商中心5字楼15室

2011 Suzhou Automation Industry Exhibition
Venue: Suzhou International Expo Center, Suzhou, Jiangsu
Organizer: Paper Communication Exhibition Service
Address: Rm. 15, 5/F. Wha Shing Center, 11 Shing Ypi St. Kwun Tong, Kowloon, Hong Kong
Contact: Jenny Leung

2011/09/09 - 13
☎ 010-8260 6880转ext 91
🖷 010-8260 6883
✉ ciccyhuang@cnaico.com.cn
www.cnaico.com.cn
www.autochina.com.cn
5553

2011第八届中国（苏州）国际汽车工业博会
地点：江苏苏州
主办：中国汽车工业国际合作总公司
地址：北京市海淀区中关村丹棱街3号A座

8th China (Suzhou) Intl Automobile Show
Venue: Suzhou, Jiangsu
Organizer: China National Automotive Industry International Corp

江西-南昌 Jiangxi-Nanchang

2011/10/22 - 25
☎ 010-8260 6880转ext 91
🖷 010-8260 6883
✉ ciccyhuang@cnaico.com.cn
5555

2011年第六届南昌国际汽车展览会
地点：江西南昌
主办：中国汽车工业国际合作总公司
地址：北京市海淀区中关村丹棱街3号A座

6th Nanchang International Automobile Exhibition
Venue: Nanchang, Jiangxi
Organizer: China National Automotive Industry International Corp

吉林-长春 Jilin-Changchun

2011/03/08 - 10
☎ 0431-8460 6572, 8460 6571
🖷 0431-8460 6147
✉ weidagg2008@163.com
www.wdexpo.com.cn
5560

2011年长春国际灯饰博览会暨LED应用展
地点：长春国际会展中心，吉林长春
内容：四方宾客齐聚长春，共赴一场集合渠道、品牌、资源、资讯的风云际会，我们期待此展为厂商带来更丰硕的收获，为行业带来更广阔的发展空间，为中国灯饰行业带来更多的惊喜*
始办年份：1997
周期：每年一届
市场范围：全国性
参展费用：4,800元/展位
上届规模 2010：展览面积10,000m²，参展商200家，参观人数20,000人（专业贸易观众12,000人）
主办：长春市灯饰协会
承办：长春维达展览服务有限公司
地址：长春市会展大街100号会展中心110室（130033）
联系人：李经理，董先生
QQ：422399672

Changchun Intl Lighting and LED Exhibition
Venue: Changchun Intl Conference & Exhibition Center, Changchun, Jilin
Established Year: 1997
Frequency: Annual
Market Area: National
Participated Fee: RMB 4,800/booth
Statistics 2010: Exhibition Area 10,000m², Exhibitors 200家, Visitors 20,000（trade visitors 12,000）
Organizer: Changchun Weida Exhibition Co Ltd

2011/03/08 - 10
☎ 0431-8460 6572, 8460 6571
🖷 0431-8460 6147
✉ weidagg2008@163.com
www.wdexpo.com.cn
5570

2011长春第十四届广告博览会
地点：长春国际会展中心，吉林长春
内容：本届展会将展出更多的广告新媒体、新材料、新设备、新技术，产品丰富，规模宏大，欢迎各界人士光临展会，同享商机，共谋发展，实现新跨越！
始办年份：1997
周期：每年一届
市场范围：全国性
参展费用：4,800元/展位
上届规模 2010：展览面积10,000m²，参展商200家，参观人数20,000人（专业贸易观众12,000人）
主办：长春市灯饰协会
承办：长春维达展览服务有限公司
地址：长春市会展大街100号会展中心110室（130033）
联系人：李经理，董先生
QQ：422399672

14th Changchun Advertising Expo
Venue: Changchun Intl Conference & Exhibition Center, Changchun, Jilin
Established Year: 1997
Frequency: Annual
Market Area: National
Participated Fee: RMB 4,800/booth
Statistics 2010: Exhibition Area 10,000m², Exhibitors 200家, Visitors 20,000（trade visitors 12,000）
Organizer: Changchun Weida Exhibition Co Ltd

2011/03/09 - 10
☎ 0431-8783 5764
🖷 0431-8783 5765
✉ ntcpjg@126.com
www.nongtewang.com
5580

第六届全国粳稻米大会
地点：长春市华苑宾馆，吉林长春
内容：粳稻米2010年生产情况与2011年行情报告会；状元米、金奖大米、优质食味米评选推介；新米品尝与产品展洽订货会；首届粳稻米期货与电子商务展销会；全国粳稻米联盟年会
始办年份：2002
周期：每年一届
市场范围：全国性
性质：面向贸易观众
入场券价格：900元/人
上届规模 2010：展览面积300m²，参展商100家，专业贸易观众350人
主办：全国粳稻米联盟；中国农业科技东北创新中心；吉林农特产品加工协会
承办：长春区宇特产食品推广中心
地址：长春市西安大路5333号吉林大学军需科技学院104室（130062）

6th Countrywide Rice Convention
Venue: Changchun Huayuan Hotel, Changchun, Jilin
Established Year: 2002
Frequency: Annual
Market Area: National
Nature: Trade Only
Cost to Attend: RMB 900/pp
Statistics 2010: Exhibition Area 300m², Exhibitors 100, Trade Visitors 350
Organizer: Jilin Agricultural Product Processing Assn

2011/07/15 – 24
☎ 0431-8273 0386
www.auto-changchun.com
5585

中国长春国际汽车博览会
地点：长春国际会展中心，吉林长春
主办：中国贸促会长春分会

China Changchun International Automobile Fair
Venue: Changchun Intl Conference & Exhibition Center, Changchun, Jilin
Organizer: CCPIT Changchun Sub-council

辽宁-大连 Liaoning-Dalian

2011/04/08 - 11
☎ 0411-8253 8642
🖷 0411-8253 8678
✉ my12336@126.com

5590

第十六届中国国际建筑装饰材料展览会
地点：大连星海会展中心，辽宁大连
内容：门窗、幕墙、五金及设备、工程公司；洁具、陶瓷、石材、水泥制品；铺地材料、铺装技术及设备；橱柜及厨房电器、配套用品；各类油漆、涂料、防水材料、橡塑制品；采暖、空调、通风、燃气技术及太阳能产品；照明灯饰、LED显示器、美化工程及园林设施；大型工艺品、室内装饰用品及居室用品；管材、管件、阀门；智能小区、监控系统、楼宇对讲设备；建筑五金、电动工具展区
始办年份：1995
周期：每年一届
市场范围：国际性
性质：面向公众
入场券价格：免费
参展费用：国外展商2,000美元/展位；国内展商5,500元/展位，净场550元/m^2（54m^2起）
主办：中国室内装饰协会；大连市人民政府；大连北展豪迈集团
承办：大连北方国际展览股份有限公司
地址：大连市中山区同兴街二十五号世贸大厦二十五楼（116000）
联系人：王常虹
MSN：my12336@hotmail.com

16th China Intl Construction & Decoration Materials Exhibition
Venue: Dalian Xinghai Convention and Exhibition Center, Dalian, Liaoning
Profile: Energy-saving technology products, Intelligent community, monitoring systems, building interphone equipment, building hardware, power tools, Wood Construction; Kitchen cabinets and appliances, supporting supplies, Pipes, fittings, valves, color light
Established Year: 1995
Frequency: Annual
Market Area: International
Nature: Open to Public
Cost to Attend: Free
Participated Fee: USD 2,000/booth
Organizer: Dalian Northern International Exhibition Limited Company
Contact: Rainbow
MSN: my12336@hotmail.com

2011/05/19 - 21
☎ 0411-8253 2825
🖷 0411-8265 2581
✉ dl82532825@126.com
www.industry-expo.com

5600

2011第九届大连国际印刷及包装工业展览会
地点：大连世界博览广场，辽宁大连
内容：印前、印中及印后设备：晒版机、拷贝机、打样机、制版机、柔性制版系统、扫描仪、轻印设备、胶印机、不干胶印刷机、数码印刷机、切纸机、装订机、复膜机、糊盒机、折页机、上光机、贴面机、模切机、压痕机、烫金机等。特种印刷设备：丝网印刷技术及器材、凹印机、凸印机、柔印机、丝印机、移印机、名片印刷机、不干胶印刷机、商标印刷机。
周期：每年一届
性质：面向公众
主办：大连市人民政府；中国贸促会大连市分会
地址：大连市中山区解放街万达大厦1004室（116001）
联系人：王小姐
QQ：339559640

9th Dalian Intl Printing and Packaging Exhibition
Venue: Dalian World Expo Center, Dalian, Liaoning
Frequency: Annual
Nature: Open to Public
Organizer: CCPIT Dalian Sub-council

2011/05/19 - 21
☎ 0411-8378 7049, 8231 0682/ 72
🖷 0411-8378 7049, 8231 0692
✉ sandy8176@163.com
www.dongbeizhanlan.com

5610

2011（第十三届）大连国际自动化、仪表展览会
地点：大连星海会展中心，辽宁大连
内容：工控机、数据采集系统，软硬件；可编程控制器（PLC）、分布式控制系统（DCS），现场总线系统；过程自动控制系统、监控系统；低压电器；电气传动装置、动力传动设备；各种仪表：流量仪表、计量测试器具设备、性能试验设备；测试测量、科学分析仪器等。
始办年份：1999
周期：每年一届
市场范围：国际性
性质：面向贸易观众
入场券价格：免费
参展费用：标准展位3x3m（主通道两侧加价20%）：国内企业6,000元，国外企业2,000美元；净地（36m^2起）(主通道两侧加价20%)：国内企业600元/m^2，国外企业200美元/m^2
主办：辽宁省机械工程学会自动化分会
承办：大连华展展览服务有限公司
地址：大连市中山区友好路211号商务特区1203室（116001）
联系人：王晓峰，魏娟
QQ：13491902

2011（13th）Dalian International Automation & Instrumentation Exhibition
Venue: Dalian Xinghai Convention and Exhibition Center, Dalian, Liaoning
Established Year: 1999
Frequency: Annual
Market Area: International
Nature: Trade Only
Cost to Attend: Free
Participated Fee: Standard Booth 3x3m USD 2,000, Raw Space (min 36m^2) USD 200/m^2
Organizer: Liaoning Provincial Institute of Mechanical Engineering; Dalian Hua Zhan Exhibition & Service Co Ltd
Contact: Xiao Fengwang, Juan Wei

2011/05/19 - 21
☎ 0411-8231 0625
🖷 0411-8231 0692
✉ dlhuazhan@sina.com

5620

2011第九届大连国际焊接工业展览会
地点：大连星海会展中心，辽宁大连
始办年份：2003
周期：每年一届
市场范围：国际性
性质：面向贸易观众
入场券价格：免费
参展费用：6,000元/展位，净地600元/m^2
主办：辽宁省焊接学会；大连市焊接协会
承办：大连华展展览服务有限公司
地址：大连市中山区友好路211号商务特区1203室（116001）
联系人：高杰

9th Dalian Intl Welding Exhibition
Venue: Dalian Xinghai Convention and Exhibition Center, Dalian, Liaoning
Established Year: 2003
Frequency: Annual
Market Area: International
Nature: Trade Only
Cost to Attend: Free
Participated Fee: RMB 6,000/booth, Raw Space RMB 600/m^2
Organizer: Dalian Hua Zhan Exhibition & Service Co Ltd

2011/06/16 - 19
☎ 0411-8362 8908
📠 0411-8363 5468
✉ wangjl@cisis.com.cn
www.cisis.com.cn

5630

第九届中国国际软件和信息服务交易会
地点：大连世界博览广场，辽宁大连
内容：中国软交会全面展示软件和信息服务业最新的产品、技术和服务。内容包括展览、会议论坛、重要活动三个组成部分，展示内容包括系统软件、支撑软件、应用软件、嵌入式软件等；会议论坛由主论坛、主题分论坛和行业信息化应用论坛、专题技术研讨会及区域合作对接会组成，涉及供热、航空、农业、物流、零售、教育、制造业、生物等领域，三网融合、物联网等热门话题，以及日本、韩国、美国、新加坡、爱尔兰、芬兰等国家和地区；重要活动包括人才招聘洽谈会、IT人摄影大赛及油画、艺术品展等。
始办年份：2003
周期：每年一届
市场范围：国际性
性质：面向贸易观众
参展费用：国内企业：标准展位 9,000元，特装净地900元/m^2，国际企业：标准展位3,000美元， 特装净地300美元/m^2
上届规模 2010：展览面积30,000m^2(国外展商7,500m^2)，参展商711家（国外展商102家，来自20个国家），参观人数30,000人（专业贸易观众20,000人）
主办：中华人民共和国商务部；中华人民共和国工业和信息化部；中华人民共和国教育部；中华人民共和国科学技术部；中国贸促会；辽宁省人民政府
承办：大连市人民政府；中国服务贸易协会
地址：大连市西岗区胜利路38号（116011）
联系人：王建莉

China International Software & Information Service Fair 2011
Venue: Dalian World Expo Center, Dalian, Liaoning
Profile: China International Software & Information Service Fair (CISIS for short) comprehensively displays the latest products, technology and service in the software and information industry. The event consists of exhibition, conferences and activities. The exhibition displays system software, supporting software, application software, embedded software, etc; The conferences are composed of main forum, thematic forum, industry application seminars, technical seminars and regional seminars, those include Heating industry, Aviation, Agriculture, Logistics, Retail, Education, Manufacturing, and Biology, and hot topics of "Convergence of Internet, Telecommunication, and Cable TV network" and "Internet of Things". There will be foreign pavilions from Japan, Korea, the U.S.A, Singapore, Ireland, Finland, and other countries and areas; The activities consists of Job Hunting Fair, Photo Competition of IT people, paintings and artwork exhibitions.
Established Year: 2003
Frequency: Annual
Market Area: International
Nature: Trade Only
Participated Fee: Standard Booth USD 3,000, Raw Space USD 300/m^2
Statistics 2010: Exhibition Area 30,000m^2(foreigners 7,500m^2), Exhibitors 711 (foreigners 102, came from 20 countries) , Visitors 30,000 (trade visitors 20,000)
Sponsors: Ministry of Commerce; Ministry of Industry and Information Technology; Ministry of Education; Ministry of Science and Technology; CCPIT Liaoning; Liaoning Provincial People' s Government
Organizer: Dalian Municipal People' s Government; China Association of Trade in Service
Address: No.38 Shengli, Xigang District, Dalian, Liaoning

2011/08/17 - 21
☎ 0411-8282 2356
📠 0411-8265 0186
✉ autodalian@163.com
www.auto-show.com.cn

5640

2011（第十六届）大连国际汽车展览会
地点：大连星海会展中心和大连世界博览广场，辽宁大连
内容：乘用车（各种基本型乘用车、SUV、MPV、改装车型等）、新能源汽车、房车、游艇。商用车（卡车、客车、半挂车、牵引车、货车）、叉车。汽车零部件、汽车维护保养设备及工具、汽车用品、汽车改装配件及用品等。
始办年份：1996
周期：每年一届
市场范围：国际性
上届规模 2010：展览面积120,000m^2，参观人数350,000人
主办：中国贸促会；中国贸促会汽车行业分会；中国汽车工业协会；中国汽车工程学会；中国汽车工业进出口总公司；大连市人民政府
地址：大连市中山区解放街9号万达大厦1006房间（116001）
联系人：姜先生
MSN：dltyc@hotmail.com

The 16th Dalian International Automotive Exhibition
Venue: Dalian World Expo Center, Dalian Xinghai Convention and Exhibition Center, Dalian, Liaoning
Profile: Various passenger cars, new energy vehicles, commercial vehicles, special vehicles, etc; Automobile parts and automobile accessories; Automobile repair equipments and tools; Automobile modifying equipments and automobile electronic and automobile ornaments. e. Automobile use oils and auto-care products.
Established Year: 1996
Frequency: Annual
Market Area: International
Statistics 2010: Exhibition Area 120,000m^2, Visitors 350,000
Organizer: CCPIT; CCPIT Automotive Sub-Council; China Association of Automobile Manufacturers; Society of Automotive Engineers of China; China National Automotive Industry
Address: Room 1006, Wanda Building, No.9 Jiefang Street, Zhongshan District, Dalian 116001, Liaoning
Contact: Mr Jiang
MSN: dltyc@hotmail.com

2011/09/01 - 03
☎ 0411-8231 0627, 8231 0681
📠 0411-8231 0627
✉ dlylz@126.com
www.dlshuangxin.com

5650

2011大连国际医疗器械展览会
地点：大连星海会展中心，辽宁大连
内容：医用影像类：X线诊断设备、CT、MRI、超声诊断设备、核医学设备。监护类：各种动态监护、血氧监护、胎儿监护。手术类：无影灯、手术床、麻醉机、呼吸机。医用光学仪器：各种显微镜，眼、耳鼻喉光学仪器。检测类：血球计数仪、免疫分析仪、酶标分析仪、生化分析仪及试剂。仪器及辅助类：病床、产床、婴儿床、输液泵等护理设备。口腔、眼科类：牙科椅、口腔各种治疗仪器及材料；眼科专用设备及配套产品。医用车辆类：救护车、防疫车、卫生监督车、采血车、送血车。 医用耗材：注射器、输液袋，注谢泵、棉签、纱布绷带、石膏等一次性耗材，医用敷料包。
始办年份：2006
周期：每年一届
市场范围：全国性
性质：面向贸易观众
入场券价格：免费
主办：大连市卫生局
承办：大连双新展览策划有限公司
地址：大连市中山区友好路211号商务特区1203室（116001）
联系人：周英,刘阳
QQ：1183754295

2010 Dalian Intl Exhibition for Medical Instrument
Venue: Dalian Xinghai Convention and Exhibition Center, Dalian, Liaoning
Established Year: 2006
Frequency: Annual
Market Area: National
Nature: Trade Only
Cost to Attend: Free
Organizer: Liaoning Provincial Institute of Mechanical Engineering; China National Automotive Industry
Contact: Zhou Yang, Liu Yang

2011/09/01 - 03
☎ 0411-8231 0653, 8231 0681
🖷 0411-8231 0692, 8231 0653
✉ liuyegeng@hotmail.com
www.dongbeizhanlan.com
5660

大连国际广告技术与设备展览会
地点：大连星海会展中心，辽宁大连
内容：广告制作技术设备；广告材料及物料；户内外广告媒体；广告摄影技术及设备；标识系统；展览展示器材；新媒体技术设备，创意创新设计产业；大屏幕及户外媒体；城市景观照明；LED显示技术及应用系统设备_
始办年份：2008
周期：每年一届
性质：面向贸易观众
参展费用：4,800元/9 m^2，450元/m^2
主办：大连华展展览服务有限公司
地址：辽宁省大连市中山区友好路211号商务特区1203室（116001）
联系人：刘烨赓，王晓峰
MSN：liuyegeng@hotmail.com
QQ：125116113

Dalian Advertising Technology and Equipment Exhibition
Venue: Dalian Xinghai Convention and Exhibition Center, Dalian, Liaoning
Established Year: 2008
Frequency: Annual
Nature: Trade Only
Participated Fee: Standard Booth RMB 4,800/9m^2, Raw Space RMB 450/m^2
Organizer: Dalian Huazhan Exhibition Service Co Ltd; Dalian Huazhan Exhibition Service Co Ltd
Contact: Liu Yegeng, Wang Xiaofeng
MSN: liuyegeng@hotmail.com

2011/09/01 - 05
☎ 0411-8253 2833, 8253 2852
🖷 0411-8265 2581, 8264 4331
✉ 41580408@QQ.COM
5680

第五届大连进出口企业产品展销会
地点：大连星海会展中心，辽宁大连
内容：日用消费品、服装、轻工产品、食品、水产品等
市场范围：国际性
性质：面向公众
参展费用：本地企业2,000元/展位，外埠企业4,000元/展览
上届规模 2010：展览面积7,500m^2，参展商200家（来自1个国家），参观人数50,000人
主办：大连市人民政府
承办：中国贸促会大连市分会；中国国际商会大连商会
地址：大连市中山区解放街9号万达大厦1004室
联系人：叶丽兰,杨虹
QQ：41580408

5th Dalian Import and Export Product Fair
Venue: Dalian Xinghai Convention and Exhibition Center, Dalian, Liaoning
Market Area: International
Nature: Open to Public
Participated Fee: Local Companies RMB 2,000/booth, Other Companies RMB 4,000/booth
Statistics 2010: Exhibition Area 7500m^2, Exhibitors 200, Visitors 50,000
Organizer: CCPIT Dalian Sub-council

2012/10/23 - 26
☎ 0411-3991 6916, 3991 6999
🖷 0411-8480 9988
✉ Terryhan522@gmail.com
5685

第八届中国大连国际海事展览会
地点：大连世界博览广场，辽宁大连
内容：船舶设计、建造、修理；造船工艺装备；港口、港口机械、航运、疏浚；海洋工程装备；船舶配套；海事管理、服务；社团组织；贸易、物流、金融、保险；海事媒体、院校、咨询机构
始办年份：1992
周期：两年一届
市场范围：国际性
入场券价格：免费
上届规模 2010：展览面积20,300m^2(国外展商面积5,000m^2)，参展商436家（国外展商135家，来自18个国家），专业贸易观众11,500人
主办：中国船舶工业行业协会
承办：大连星海会展商务有限公司
地址：大连市沙河口区会展路18号东区14号门
联系人：韩倩倩
MSN：hanqianqian0522@126.com
QQ：327188068

The 8th International Shipping Building, Ports and Marine Equipment Exhibition for China
Venue: Dalian World Exhibition Center, Dalian, Liaoning
Profile: Ship Design, Ship Building and Repairing；Ports and Technology；Offshore Engineering；Ship Fittings and Equipment；Marine Management, Service；Trade, Logistics, Finance, Insurance；Association；Maritime Media, Educational Institutions, Consulting Institutes.
Established Year: 1992
Frequency: Biennial
Market Area: International
Cost to Attend: Free
Statistics 2010: Exhibition Area 20,300m^2(foreigners 5,000m^2), Exhibitors 436（foreigners 135, came from 18 countries）, Trade Visitors 11,500
Organizer: China Association of National Shipbuilding Industry; Dalian Xinghai Exhibition Co Ltd
Address: No.18 Huizhan Road Dalian China
Contact: Terry Han

辽宁-沈阳 Liaoning-Shenyang

2011/03 -
☎ 024-8956 6755
🖷 024-8956 6778
✉ marketing@shenyang-expo.com
www.shenyang-expo.com
5690

2011中国沈阳春季房地产展示交易会
地点：沈阳国际展览中心，辽宁沈阳

China Shenyang Spring Real Estate Fair
Venue: Shenyang International Exhibition Center, Shenyang, Liaoning

2011/03/22 - 24
☎ 024-2397 4279
🖷 024-2392 2432
✉ bfzlzhong@126.com
www.bfexpo.com.cn
5700

2011年第四届中国东北流体机械展览会
（暨泵阀管、压缩机、风机展览会）
地点：辽宁工业展览馆，辽宁沈阳
内容：流体工程及流程工业：流体输送及存储系统、压缩机、过滤与分离设备、真空设备、干燥设备等流体机械专业技术与产品，风机、压力容器及配件、流体传动及控制系统、密封系统、流体处理、过滤、流体测量及控制系统。泵：水泵及供水设备、叶片式泵、容积式泵、真空泵及其它泵类产品。阀：球阀、蝶

2011 China (Northeast) 3rd Fluid Machinery Exhibition
Venue: Liaoning Industrial Exhibition Hall, Shenyang, Liaoning
Frequency: Annual
Market Area: International
Nature: Open to Public
Cost to Attend: Free
Participated Fee: Raw Space RMB 700/m^2 (min 36m^2), Standard Booth RMB 6,500, Corner Unit add 10%

阀、闸阀、柱塞阀、电磁阀、调节阀、止回阀、阀门配件、阀门及驱动装置。管材、管件、管道、接头、水箱及配件。流量计：超声流量计、涡轮与射流流量计、差压式流量计、电磁流量计。污水处理、空气净化、脱硫除尘、环保过程装备
周期：每年一届
市场范围：国际性
性质：面向公众
入场券价格：免费
参展费用：净地700元/m²(36m²起)，标准展位6,500元，角位上浮10%
上届规模 2010：展览面积20,000m²(国外展商500m²)，参展商463家（国外展商10家，来自6个国家），参观人数300,000人
主办：辽宁北方工商业展览服务有限公司
地址：辽宁省沈阳市和平区三好街93号金源大厦5楼（110004）
联系人：仲照宇
QQ：149802689

Statistics 2010: Exhibition Area 20,000m²(foreigners 500m²), Exhibitors 463 (foreigners 10, came from 6 countries), Visitors 300,000
Sponsor: Shenyang Municipal Government
Organizer: Northern Industrial & Commercial Exhibition Co Ltd

2011/03/22 - 24
☎ 024-2392 1795
🖷 024-2392 2432
✉ rocklee101@163.com
www.bfexpo.com.cn

5710

2011第十四届中国东北国际仪器仪表及工业自动化展览会
地点：辽宁工业展览馆，辽宁沈阳
内容：东北自动化展凭借着"全面展示工业自动化产品，推动东北制造业创新发展"这一明确定位和服务至上的办展理念，在东北地区各级政府部分鼎力支持下，在各工业协会学会热心帮助下，经过13年历练和培育，不论是展览规模、展览面积、企业数量、企业档次、观众质量数量都稳步提升，成为国内外企业踊跃参与的专业盛会。已在东北及行业内确定了权威地位，享有崇高信誉。
始办年份：1998
周期：每年一届
市场范围：国际性
入场券价格：免费
参展费用：6,500元/展位
上届规模 2010：展览面积10,000m²(国外展商2,000m²)，参展商300家（国外展商50家，来自10个国家），参观人数15,600人（专业贸易观众10,000人）
主办：沈阳市装备制造行业协会
承办：北方工商业展览有限公司
地址：沈阳市三好街93号金源大厦5楼（110004）
联系人：李瑶，刘丽
QQ：790402038

Northeast 14th International Instrument & Automation Exhibition China
Venue: Liaoning Industrial Exhibition Hall, Shenyang, Liaoning
Established Year: 1998
Frequency: Annual
Market Area: International
Cost to Attend: Free
Participated Fee: RMB 6,500/booth
Statistics 2010: Exhibition Area 10,000m²(foreigners 2,000m²), Exhibitors 300 (foreigners 50, came from 10 countries), Visitors 15,600 (trade visitors10,000)
Organizer: Shenyang Equipment Manufacturing Industry Association; Northern Industry and Commerce Exhibition Co Ltd

2011/03/22 - 24
☎ 024-2392 1795
🖷 024-2392 2432
✉ iepe2011@163.com
www.bfexpo.com.cn

5720

2011第十四届中国东北国际电力电工技术设备展览会暨
东北国际节电、节能及新能源技术设备展览会
地点：辽宁工业展览馆，辽宁沈阳
内容："全面展示电力电工先进技术设备，推动东北电力电工创新发展"这一准确定位和服务至上的办展理念，在东北地区国家电力有关部门和各省市政府有关部门的鼎力支持下，在各省市电力企业协会的热心帮助下，经过了13年的历程，不论是展览规模、展览面积、企业数量、观众的质量都稳步提升，成为国内外电力电工企业及专业人士踊跃参与的专业盛会。成为东北电力第一展，享有崇高信誉。
始办年份：1998
周期：每年一届
市场范围：国际性
入场券价格：免费
参展费用：6,500元/展位
上届规模 2010：展览面积10,000m²(国外展商2,000m²)，参展商300家（国外展商50家，来自10个国家），参观人数15,600人（专业贸易观众10,000人）
主办：沈阳市装备制造行业协会
承办：北方工商业展览有限公司
地址：沈阳市和平区三好街93号金源大厦5楼（110004）
联系人：李瑶 刘丽
QQ：790402038

Northeast 14th International Electro Technology Equipment Exhibition China 2011
Venue: Liaoning Industrial Exhibition Hall, Shenyang, Liaoning
Established Year: 1998
Frequency: Annual
Market Area: International
Cost to Attend: Free
Participated Fee: RMB 6,500/booth
Statistics 2010: Exhibition Area 10,000m²(foreigners 2000m²), Exhibitors 300 (foreigners 50, came from 10个 countries), Visitors 15,600 (trade visitors 10,000)
Organizer: Shenyang Equipment Manufacturing Industry Association; Northern Industry and Commerce Exhibition Co Ltd

2011/03/27 - 29
☎ 024-3188 1727
🖷 024-2392 2432
✉ zhkmaster@163.com
www.bfexpo.com.cn

5730

2011中国（沈阳）第九届建筑节能、墙体保温材料及设备展览会
地点：辽宁工业展览馆，辽宁沈阳
内容：节能保温材料：建筑保温系统，保温、隔热材料，添加剂，涂料，屋面系统及防水材料，化学建材；节材产品：新型墙体材料，结构材料；节电设备；设备：砂浆设备，其他设备；新型建筑施工设备：模板类，脚手架类，思杠类，高空施工技术平台类
始办年份：2003
周期：每年一届
入场券价格：免费
参展费用：5,800 元
上届规模 2010：展览面积30,000m²(国外展商10,000m²)，参展商853家（国外展商215家，来自个国家），参观人数31,584人（专业贸易观众24,587人）
主办：沈阳市城乡建设委员会
地址：沈阳市和平区三好街93号金源大厦5楼（110004）
联系人：赵坤
QQ：32555934

2011 The 9th China (Shenyang) International Energy-saving & New Wall Material and Equipment Exhibition
Venue: Liaoning Industrial Exhibition Hall, Shenyang, Liaoning
Established Year: 2003
Frequency: Annual
Cost to Attend: Free
Participated Fee: RMB 5,800/booth
Statistics 2010: Exhibition Area 30,000m²(foreigners 10,000m²), Exhibitors 853 (foreigners 215), Visitors 31,584 (trade visitors 24,587)
Organizer: Northern Industrial & Commercial Exhibition Co Ltd

2011/03/27 - 29
☎ 024-2397 5522, 3188 1708
🖷 024-2392 2432
✉ bfcd@163.com
www.bfexpo.com.cn
5740

第十一届东北国际给排水、水处理技术设备及泵、阀、管道展览会
地点：辽宁工业展览馆，辽宁沈阳
内容：已拥有十余年历史，经过十余年的精心打造，"东北水展"已成为行业公认的品牌水展，在东北地区享有盛誉，"东北水展"不仅吸引了全国各地区的参展商和观众，而且也成为日本、韩国等邻国客商的重要交流平台。
始办年份：2000
周期：每年一届
市场范围：国际性
性质：面向公众
上届规模 2010：展览面积15,000m²(国外展商1,100m²)，参展商300家（国外展商6家，来自4个国家），参观人数30,000人
主办：沈阳市人民政府；沈阳市城乡建设委员会
承办：北方工商业展览有限公司
地址：沈阳市三好街93号金源大厦5楼（110004）
联系人：盖晓乐 13516038521

The 12th Northeast International, Water Disposal Technique & Equipment and Pump & Value and Pipeline Exhibition
Venue: Liaoning Industrial Exhibition Hall, Shenyang, Liaoning
Established Year: 2000
Frequency: Annual
Market Area: International
Nature: Open to Public
Statistics 2010: Exhibition Area 15,000m²(foreigners 1,100m²), Exhibitors 300（foreigners 6, came from 4 countries）, Visitors 30,000
Organizer: Northern Industrial & Commercial Exhibition Co Ltd
Contact: Gai Xiaole

2011/03/27 - 29
☎ 024-2397 5522, 3188 1708
🖷 024-2392 2432
✉ bfcd@163.com
www.bfexpo.com.cn
5750

2011中国东北第十四届国际供热供暖、空调、热泵技术设备展览会
地点：辽宁工业展览馆，辽宁沈阳
内容：东北供热展已连续举办了12届，得到了政府相关部门、行业协会及东北三省国内外燃气、环保、水领域专业人士的大力支持和协助，取得了圆满成功。以其规模宏大、专业性强、参展商多、影响面广、展出产品档次高，展出效果好，在专业界影响深远，声誉卓著，成为每年东北地区唯一的行业盛会，不可或缺的行业例会，被誉为"东北供热第一展"。
始办年份：1998
周期：每年一届
性质：面向公众
上届规模 2010：展览面积15,000m²(国外展商1,000m²)，参展商300家，参观人数30,000人
主办：沈阳市人民政府；沈阳市城乡建设委员会
承办：北方工商业展览有限公司
地址：沈阳市三好街93号金源大厦5楼（110004）
联系人：盖晓乐 13516038521

14th China (Northeast) International Equipments of Heating, Air-Condition & New Energy Sources Exhibition
Venue: Liaoning Industrial Exhibition Hall, Shenyang, Liaoning
Established Year: 1998
Frequency: Annual
Nature: Open to Public
Statistics 2010: Exhibition Area 15,000m²(foreigners 1,000m²), Exhibitors 300, Visitors 30,000
Organizer: Northern Industrial & Commercial Exhibition Co Ltd
Contact: Gai Xiaole

2011/04/01 - 04
☎ 024-2392 0245
🖷 024-2392 2432
✉ sjzx1985@163.com
www.bfexpo.com.cn
5760

2011年中国东北第十三届国际口腔器材展览会暨学术交流会
第三届口腔保健护理用品展览会
第一届义齿加工产品展览会
地点：辽宁工业展览馆，辽宁沈阳
内容：口腔诊断设备 口腔治疗设备 数字化口腔 口腔辅助设备 口腔材料 口腔技工器材与设备 口腔药品、清洁剂、消毒剂、口腔实验室设备、家具及实验所需原材料 口腔卫生用品、口腔保健食品、口腔牙外科器材及材料、口腔清洁用品、口腔学会、杂志、宣传刊物、挂图、教学用器、技术软件等
始办年份：1999
周期：每年一届
市场范围：国际性
性质：面向贸易观众
入场券价格：免费
参展费用：6,800元/展位
上届规模 2010：展览面积10,000m²(国外展商3,000m²)，参展商315家（国外展商53家，来自12个国家），参观人数20,000人（专业贸易观众14,000人）
主办：北方工商业展览有限公司；辽宁省口腔医学会
地址：沈阳市和平区三好街93号金源大厦5F（110004）
联系人：纪晓帆
QQ：1211355649

13th China Northeast International Dental Equipment & Affiliated Facilities Exhibition
Venue: Liaoning Industrial Exhibition Hall, Shenyang, Liaoning
Profile: Dental diagnostic equipment, dental treatment equipment, digital oral cavity, dental assistant equipment, dental materials, equipment and facility
Established Year: 1999
Frequency: Annual
Market Area: International
Nature: Trade Only
Cost to Attend: Free
Participated Fee: RMB 6,800/booth
Statistics 2010: Exhibition Area 10,000m²(foreigners 3,000m²), Exhibitors 315（foreigners 53, came from 12 countries）, Visitors 20,000（trade visitors 14,000）
Organizer: Northern Industrial & Commercial Exhibition Co Ltd; Liaoning provincial Stomatological Association
Address: 5th Floor, Jinyun Mansion, 93 Sanhao Street, Heping District, Shenyang, China
Contact: Xiaofan Ji

2011/04/07 - 11
☎ 024-8956 6755
🖷 024-8956 6778
✉ marketing@shenyang-expo.com
www.shenyang-expo.com
5770

第五届中国（沈阳）汽车交易博览会
地点：沈阳国际展览中心，辽宁沈阳

5th China (Shenyang) Automobile Fair
Venue: Shenyang International Exhibition Center, Shenyang, Liaoning

2011/04/08 - 10
☎ 024-2397 4769, 13804040384
🖷 024-2392 2432, 3188 1716
✉ lxlbf2007@163.com
www.bfexpo.com.cn
5780

第十四届中国东北国际五金工具展览会
地点：辽宁工业展览馆，辽宁沈阳
内容：工具五金：手动工具、电动工具、气动工具、风动工具、液压工具、汽保工具、机械工具、量具刃具、磨具磨料、园林园艺工具；五金机械设备：空压机、电动机、发电机、液压机械及配件、金属加工机械、压铸机、雕刻打标机、喷涂设备、起重吊索具、木工机械、仓储设备、机电产品、冲压锻造铸造设备各种机床及五金专用生产设备；焊接切割设备：焊接切割设备及技术、电焊机、焊割炬、焊机配套件、焊接材料及消耗品；建筑五金：五金制品、标准紧固件、金属门窗五金配件、铁艺及金属制品、泵阀、管道、水暖器材、化工材料、卫生陶瓷五金、家具五

14th China (Northeast) International Hardware and Tool Exhibition
Venue: Liaoning Industrial Exhibition Hall, Shenyang, Liaoning
Profile: Tool and Hardware: hand tool, power tool, air-driven tool, pneumatic tool, hydraulic tool, automobile maintenance tool, mechanical tool, measuring and cutting tool, grinding material and grinding tool, garden tool and so on; Hardware Machinery and Equipment; Welding and Cutting Equipment; Construction Hardware; Civil Hardware
Established Year: 1998
Frequency: Annual

金件、照明灯具、电工电料、钉丝网类、装饰用具、梯子及施工架、DIY产品；民用五金
始办年份：1998
周期：每年一届
市场范围：全国性
性质：面向公众
参展费用：品牌展区800元/m^2；2号大厅（36m^{2}起）700元/m^2；标准展区（1、3号厅）5,500元/9m^2，角位上浮10%
上届规模 2010：展览面积15,000m^2(国外展商1,400m^2)，参展商807家（国外展商34家，来自7个国家），参观人数68,977人（专业贸易观众5,788人）
主办：沈阳市人民政府
地址：沈阳市和平区三好街93号金源大厦5F（110004）
联系人：刘秀丽
QQ：1150658640

Market Area: National
Nature: Open to Public
Participated Fee: Raw Space RMB 700/m^2 (min 36m^2), Standard Booth RMB 5,500, Corner unit add 10%
Statistics 2010: Exhibition Area 15,000m^2(foreigners 1,400m^2), Exhibitors 807 (foreigners 34, came from 7 countries), Visitors 68,977 (trade visitors 5,788) **Sponsor**: People's Government of Shenyang City
Organizer: Northern Industrial & Commercial Exhibition Co Ltd
Address: 5F Jinyuan Building, No. 93 in Sanhao Street, Heping District, Shenyang
Contact: Liu Xiuli

2011/04/13 - 15
☎ 024-3188 1720
🖷 024-2392 2432
✉ sunlijingbf@163.com
5790

2011第十三届东北国际汽车用品展览会
地点：辽宁工业展览馆，辽宁沈阳
内容：东北地区包括辽宁、吉林、黑龙江省及内蒙古四市，管辖面积62.6万平方里，人口约1.5亿，是我国经济实力雄厚发展趋势强劲的大经济区域。大会主题：新面貌、新商机、国际化、专业化、品牌化。展区划分：精品区、养护区、电子区、影音区、座垫区、改装区、汽保展区、汽车零部件展区等。
周期：每年一届
入场券价格：免费
参展费用：4,800元/展位
上届规模 2010：展览面积5,000m^2，参展商306家，参观人数30,000人
主办：辽宁北方工商业展览公司
地址：辽宁省沈阳市和平区三好街93号5F（110004）
联系人：孙李晶
QQ：174817958

Shenyang China Car Expo
Venue: Liaoning Industrial Exhibition Hall, Shenyang, Liaoning
Frequency: Annual
Cost to Attend: Free
Participated Fee: RMB 4,800/booth
Statistics 2010: Exhibition Area 5,000m^2, Exhibitors 306, Visitors 30,000
Organizer: Northern Industrial & Commercial Exhibition Co Ltd

---

2011/04/22 - 25
☎ 024-2397 4189
🖷 024-2392 2432
✉ 15940093590@163.com
wwww.bfexpo.com.cn
5800

第十二届中国东北国际物流技术及运输系统展览会
地点：沈阳国际展览中心，辽宁沈阳
内容：与第69届全国汽配展同期举办
周期：每年一届
市场范围：国际性
性质：面向公众
入场券价格：免费
参展费用：标准展位6,500元/9m^2
上届规模 2010：展览面积10,000m^2，参展商326家，参观人数15,600人
主办：北方工商业展览有限公司
地址：沈阳市三好街93号金源大厦5F（110004）
联系人：于晶晶
QQ：413527141

12th Northeast Intl Physical Distribution & Transport System Exhibition
Venue: Shenyang International Exhibition Center, Shenyang, Liaoning
Frequency: Annual
Market Area: International
Nature: Open to Public
Cost to Attend: Free
Participated Fee: Standard Booth RMB 6,500/9m^2
Statistics 2010: Exhibition Area 10,000m^2, Exhibitors 326, Visitors 15,600
Organizer: Northern Industrial & Commercial Exhibition Co Ltd

---

2011/04/22 - 25
☎ 024-8956 6755
🖷 024-8956 6778
✉ marketing@shenyang-expo.com
www.shenyang-expo.com
5820

第69届全国汽车配件交易会暨全国汽车配件采购交易会
地点：沈阳国际展览中心，辽宁沈阳

National Auto Parts Fair
Venue: Shenyang International Exhibition Center, Shenyang, Liaoning

---

2011/04/22 - 25
☎ 024-2391 4926
🖷 024-2392 2432
✉ expo-sy@163.com
www.bfexpo.com.cn
5830

2011年第12届中国东北国际机床、工模具技术展览会
地点：沈阳国际展览中心，辽宁沈阳
内容：机床类：车床、铣床、刨床、磨床、钻床、镗床、锯床；加工中心、数控设备；电加工机床、激光设备、非标设备；锻压机械、冲压设备、管材加工设备；攻丝机。机床附件、配件、辅助设备与材料、机床电器；数控系统及数控装置；刀具、量具、夹具：车刀、铣刀、镗刀、镗头、钻头、砂轮、锯片、螺纹刀具、可转位刀片、工夹具；测量仪器、测量工具及三座标测量机；磨具磨料、研磨工具、攻牙机。工具柜、刀具储运及工作桌等工具配套产品。模具类，模具软件，相关制造技术与设备。
始办年份：1999
周期：每年一届
市场范围：国际性
性质：面向贸易观众
入场券价格：免费
参展费用：6,500元/展位
上届规模 2010：展览面积10,000m^2，参展商500家，参观人数38,625人
主办：沈阳市人民政府
承办：北方工商业展览有限公司
地址：沈阳市和平区三好街93号金源大厦5F（110004）
联系人：张秀双
QQ：55675994

2011 The 12th International Machine Tool and Tools & Moulds Technique Exhibition in Northeast of China
Venue: Shenyang International Exhibition Center, Shenyang, Liaoning
Profile: Machine tools: Various lathes, milling machines, planers, drill presses, boring machines, grinding machines, gear-processing machines and grinders. The various N.C equipments, processing centers. The various electrical processing machine tools. Cutting tools, gauges, and the various fixtures; Models; Mould standard items; Mould products.
Established Year: 1999
Frequency: Annual
Market Area: International
Nature: Trade Only
Cost to Attend: Free
Participated Fee: RMB 6,500/booth
Statistics 2010: Exhibition Area 10,000m^2, Exhibitors 500, Visitors 38,625
Sponsor: People's Government of Shenyang
Organizer: Liaoning Northern Industry & Business Exhibition Service Co Ltd
Address: 5F, No.93 Sanhao Street, Heping District, Shenyang
Contact: Zhang Xiushuang

2011/04/22 - 25
☎ 024-3188 1707, 2391 3336
🖷 024-2392 2432
✉ soppert@163.com
www.bfexpo.com.cn
5850

中国东北第15届国际焊接、切割、激光技术设备展览会
地点：沈阳国际展览中心，辽宁沈阳
内容：焊机、焊接设备、Brazing及锡焊、焊接材料、焊接关联自动化设备、焊接机器人、焊接用装置及器械、焊接关联卫生、安全保护用具、焊接线、焊接构造物流程用机械、非破坏检查装置及试验器械、表面处理装置、焊接原副材料、关联器械及材料。数控切割机、等离子切割机设备、火焰切割机、Plasma & CO2折机、坡口机、金属加工折机、切割自动化设备、切割装置及器械、锯齿、切割工具；激光加工设备、激光打标机、激光焊接机、激光切割机、激光雕刻机、激光数控机床、激光热处理机、激光打（钻）孔机、激光模具雕刻机、激光内雕机、激光划片机、激光雕铣机、激光雕版机、CO2激光标刻机、激光防伪喷码机、激光喷码技术、激光辅助设备及配件、激光和光导发光元。
始办年份：1997
周期：每年一届
市场范围：国际性
性质：面向公众
入场券价格：免费
参展费用：6,500元/展期
上届规模 2010：展览面积10,000m^2，参展商326家，参观人数28,546人
主办：沈阳市人民政府
承办：辽宁省焊接协会；沈阳市焊接协会；沈阳装备制造行业学会；北方工商业展览有限公司
地址：沈阳市和平区三好街93号5F北方工商业展览有限公司（110004）
联系人：韩雪梅
QQ：359435020

15th China (Northeast) International Welding, Cutting & Laser Technology and Equipment Exhibition
Venue: Shenyang International Exhibition Center, Shenyang, Liaoning
Established Year: 1997
Frequency: Annual
Market Area: International
Nature: Open to Public
Cost to Attend: Free
Participated Fee: RMB 6,500/booth
Statistics 2010: Exhibition Area 10,000m^2, Exhibitors 326, Visitors 28,546
Organizer: Northern Industrial & Commercial Exhibition Co Ltd

2011/04/22 - 25
☎ 024-2384 8943, 2392 1795
🖷 024-2392 2432
✉ nipm@163.com
www.bfexpo.com.cn
5860

2011第12届中国东北国际塑胶机械及包装展览会
地点：沈阳国际展览中心，辽宁沈阳
内容：注塑机，挤出机及挤出机生产线，吹瓶机&包装机械，中空吹塑机，后加工及其它加工机械，计算器辅助设计及生产系统，模具及零部件，预加工、回收利用机械及设备，原料、辅料，装潢、修饰、印刷及印标机械设备，半成品等
周期：每年一届
市场范围：全国性
性质：面向公众
入场券价格：免费
参展费用：国际名牌展区：室内净地800元/m^2（36m^{2}起）；国内展区：室内净地700元/m^2(36m^{2}起)，标准展位：6,500元/9m^2，角位上浮10%
上届规模 2010：展览面积10,000m^2，参展商326家，参观人数15,600人
主办：沈阳市人民政府
承办：沈阳装备制造业行业协会；沈阳市工装模具协会；北方工商业展览有限公司
地址：沈阳市和平区三好街93号金源大厦5F（110004）
联系人：江月

12th Northeast International Plastics Machinery & Packaging Exhibition China 2011
Venue: Injection Molding machines, Ancillary equipment, Extruders & extrusion lines, Blow Molding machines, IT applications/ CAD-CAM, Machines & equipment for preprocessing, recycling, Packaging machines, Machinery & plant for finishing, decorating, printing & marking, Moulds & dies, Parts & components, Post processing & other processing machines, Raw materials, auxiliaries, Semi-finishes products
Frequency: Annual
Market Area: National
Nature: Open to Public
Cost to Attend: Free
Participated Fee: Raw Space RMB 800/m^2 (min 36m^2), Standard Booth RMB 6,500, Corner Unit add 10%
Statistics 2010: Exhibition Area 10,000m^2, Exhibitors 326, Visitors 15,600
Sponsor: People's Government of Shenyang
Organizer: Shenyang Tool & Mould Industry Association; Liaoning Northern Industry & Business Exhibition Service Co Ltd; Shenyang Equipment Manufacturing Industry Association
Address: 5F, No.93, Sanhao Street, Heping District, Shenyang
Contact: Moon River

2011/05/29 - 01
☎ 024-8956 6755
🖷 024-8956 6778
✉ marketing@shenyang-expo.com
www.shenyang-expo.com
5865

第41届全国制药机械博览会
地点：沈阳国际展览中心，辽宁沈阳

41th National Pharmaceutical Machinery Expo
Venue: Shenyang International Exhibition Center, Shenyang, Liaoning

2011/06 -
☎ 024-8956 6755
🖷 024-8956 6778
✉ marketing@shenyang-expo.com
www.shenyang-expo.com
5870

2011辽宁（沈阳）台湾名品博览会
地点：沈阳国际展览中心，辽宁沈阳

Liaoning (Shenyang) Taiwan Brand Name Product Expo
Venue: Shenyang International Exhibition Center, Shenyang, Liaoning

2011/06/16 - 20
☎ 024-8956 6755
🖷 024-8956 6778
✉ marketing@shenyang-expo.com
www.shenyang-expo.com
5890

首届中国沈阳国际家具及木工机械、原辅材料展览会
地点：沈阳国际展览中心，辽宁沈阳

1st China (Shenyang) Intl Furniture & Woodworking Exhibition
Venue: Shenyang International Exhibition Center, Shenyang, Liaoning

2011/06/30 - 05
☎ 010-8260 6880转ext 91
🖷 010-8260 6883
✉ ciccyhuang@cnaico.com.cn
www.cnaico.com.cn
www.autochina.com.cn
5900

2011年第十届中国沈阳汽车工业博览会
地点：沈阳国际展览中心，辽宁沈阳
主办：中国汽车工业国际合作总公司
地址：北京市海淀区中关村丹棱街3号A座

10th China (Shenyang) Automobile Industry Expo
Venue: Shenyang International Exhibition Center, Shenyang, Liaoning
Organizer: China National Automotive Industry International Corp

2011/07/21 - 25
☎ 024-8956 6755
🖷 024-8956 6778
✉ marketing@shenyang-expo.com
www.shenyang-expo.com
5920

第三届中国（沈阳）食品博览会
地点：沈阳国际展览中心，辽宁沈阳

3rd China (Shenyang) Food Expo
Venue: Shenyang International Exhibition Center, Shenyang, Liaoning

2011/08 –
☎ 024-2325 6988
🖷 024-2325 6988
✉ iecsy@126.com
www.neimme.cn
5930

2011第十一届中国东北国际冶金及金属工业展览会暨中国?东北钢铁市场论坛
地点：辽宁沈阳
内容：冶金及金属工业
始办年份：1994
周期：每年一届
市场范围：国际性
主办：鞍山钢铁集团公司；沈阳国际展览公司
承办：沈阳国际展览公司
地址：沈阳市和平区十一纬路云集东巷32号经纬大厦1-8-1（110003）
联系人：李男

11th Northeast China Metal Expo
Venue: Shenyang, Liaoning
Established Year: 1994
Frequency: Annual
Market Area: International
Statistics '08: Exhibition Area 10,000m^2, Exhibitors 300，Visitors 40,000，Trade Visitors 20,000
Organizer: Shenyang Intl Exhibition Co

2011/08/25 - 28
☎ 024-2272 9975, 2272 9972
🖷 024-2272 9975
✉ ccpitmail@163.com
www.northeastasiafair.cn
5950

第五届中国东北亚（沈阳）进出口商品博览会
地点：辽宁工业展览馆，辽宁沈阳
内容：纺织品、服装；日用商品（化妆品、饰品、工艺品、杂品）；餐饮、食品、保健品；IT电子、电器产品；动漫、电玩；文化、旅游、教育
始办年份：2007
周期：每年一届
市场范围：国际性
性质：面向公众
上届规模 2010：展览面积12,000m^2(国外展商7,200m^2)，参展商237家（国外展商142家，来自18个国家），参观人数60,000人（专业贸易观众6,000人）
主办：中国贸促会；沈阳市人民政府
承办：沈阳国际商会；沈阳市贸促会
地址：辽宁省沈阳市沈河区青年大街35号国际贸易大厦4楼（110014）
联系人：王海军

The 5th China Northeast Asia (Shenyang) Import & Export Fair
Venue: Liaoning Industrial Exhibition Hall, Shenyang, Liaoning
Profile: Textiles, clothing; daily use commodities (cosmetics, jewelry, handicrafts, groceries); catering, food, health care products; IT electronic & electrical appliances products; animation & videogame; culture, tourism & education
Established Year: 2007
Frequency: Annual
Market Area: International
Nature: Open to Public
Statistics 2010: Exhibition Area 12,000m^2(foreigners 7,200m^2), Exhibitors 237（foreigners 142, came from 18 countries），Visitors 60,000（trade visitors 6,000）
Sponsor: CCPIT; Shenyang Municipal People' s Government
Organizers: Shenyang Chamber of International Commerce; Shenyang Sub-council of CCPIT
Address: 4/F. Intl Trade Building, No. 35 Youth Street, Shenhe District, Shenyang, Liaoning, China
Contact: Mr Wang Haijun

2011/09 -
☎ 024-8956 6755
🖷 024-8956 6778
✉ marketing@shenyang-expo.com
www.shenyang-expo.com
5960

2011中国沈阳秋季房地产展示交易会
地点：沈阳国际展览中心，辽宁沈阳

China (Shenyang) Autumn Real Estate Fair
Venue: Shenyang International Exhibition Center, Shenyang, Liaoning

2011/09/01 - 05
☎ 024-6265 1059
🖷 024-6265 1059
✉ cieme@zxexpo.com
www.zxexpo.com
5970

第十届中国国际装备制造业博览会
地点：沈阳国际展览中心，辽宁沈阳
内容：机床及功能部件：数控机床及功能部件。数控机床：车、铣、刨、镗、磨、钻等金属切削机床及冲压、锻压、挤压等压力成型机床，数控系统、各类机床附件、机床电器、模具、模具设备、模具配件。工业自动化与仪器仪表、动力传动与控制技术：变频器、传感器、安全系统、伺服系统、工业以太网、现场总线、人机界面、工控机、仪器仪表、液压技术、气动技术、密封技术、机械传动、电气传动、电机、压缩机、轴承、工业基础件。专用设备与通用设备等综合：过滤与分离设备、气体净化设备、泵、阀门、管道、风机等流体机械；焊接与切割、物流、变压器、互感器等通用设备；包装机械、铸造技术与设备；冶金、环保、重矿等专用设备。能源技术装备：输变电设备、工程机械
始办年份：2002
周期：每年一届
市场范围：国际性

The 10th China International Equipment Manufacturing Exposition
Venue: Shenyang International Exhibition Center, Shenyang, Liaoning
Profile: CNC machine tools and accessories, Industrial automation & PTC, New energy equipment, General & specialized equipment, Construction & engineering machine
Established Year: 2002
Frequency: Annual
Market Area: International
Participated Fee: Standard Booth RMB 7,000, Raw Space RMB 700/m^2（min 36m^2）
Sponsor: The Ministry of Commerce of the People's Republic of China National Development and Reform Commission; CCPIT Liaoning; Provincial People's Government
Organizer: Shenyang Municipal People's Government; CCPIT Liaoning Sub-Council; Liaoning Provincial Economic Commission

参展费用：标准展位7,000元，净地700元/m^2（36m^{2}起）
主办：商务部；国家发展和改革委员会；中国贸促会；辽宁省人民政府
承办：沈阳市人民政府；中国贸促会辽宁省分会；辽宁省经济和信息化委员会
地址：沈阳市沈河区北站路72号格林大饭店7楼（110013）
联系人：李克忠，马凯

Address: 7F Green Hotel, No. 72 Beizhan Road, Shenhe District, Shenyang, China

2011/09/15 - 18
☎ 024-8956 6755
🖷 024-8956 6778
✉ marketing@shenyang-expo.com
www.shenyang-expo.com
5990

第八届中国辽宁（沈阳）国际农业博览会
地点：沈阳国际展览中心，辽宁沈阳

8th Liaoning (Shenyang) Intl Agriculture Expo
Venue: Shenyang International Exhibition Center, Shenyang, Liaoning

2011/09/26 - 28
☎ 024-8956 6755
🖷 024-8956 6778
✉ marketing@shenyang-expo.com
www.shenyang-expo.com
5995

第18届中国国际广告节
地点：沈阳国际展览中心，辽宁沈阳

18th China International Advertising Festival
Venue: Shenyang International Exhibition Center, Shenyang, Liaoning

2011/10 -
☎ 024-8956 6755
🖷 024-8956 6778
✉ marketing@shenyang-expo.com
www.shenyang-expo.com
6000

第六届中国（沈阳）汽车交易博览会
地点：沈阳国际展览中心，辽宁沈阳

6th China (Shenyang) Automobile Fair
Venue: Shenyang International Exhibition Center, Shenyang, Liaoning

2011/11 -
☎ 024-2325 6988
🖷 024-2325 6988
✉ iecsy@126.com
www.iecsy.com
6005

2011中国东北（沈阳）政府采购暨节能减排展览会
地点：沈阳市科学宫会展中心，辽宁沈阳
内容：政府采购用品、节能减排产品
始办年份：2006
周期：每年一届
市场范围：国际性
主办：沈阳国际展览公司
地址：沈阳市和平区十一纬路云集东巷32号经纬大厦1-8-1（110003）
联系人：李男

Northeast China (Shenyang) International Exhibition for Government Purchase
Venue: Liaoning Industrial Exhibition Hall, Shenyang, Liaoning
Established Year: 2006
Frequency: Annual
Market Area: National
Statistics '09: Exhibition Area 4,000m^2(foreigners 400m^2), Exhibitors 140（foreigners 17）, Trade Visitors 20,000
Organizer: Shenyang Intl Exhibition Co

宁夏-银川 | Ningxia-Yinchuan

2011/06/12 -
☎ 0951-505 5836
🖷 0951-567 3900
✉ xbkylhh@126.com
6010

2011第七届中国·宁夏国际能源装备与节能减排科技博览会
地点：银川国际会展中心，宁夏银川
内容：大型能源企业形象展示、能源产业项目推介以及投融资项目推介；为能源企业服务的投融资机构；重点节能减排企业成果展示；宁夏相关节能单位和五市组织的节能减排成果展。煤炭技术、设备、产品展示：国内外煤炭资源勘探、采掘、运输、洗选；煤矿安全预警监测与自动控制系统、矿山消防系统与设备、矿山安全生产监督管理的新产品新技术；矿用通讯技术装备与矿业管理软件、井下个人安全防护新产品；地质勘测、基建施工技术装备；矿井电气、供配电、电线、电缆；矿山工程机械设备。
始办年份：2005
周期：每年一届
市场范围：全国性
性质：面向公众
主办：宁夏回族自治区经济与信息化委员会；宁夏回族自治区财政厅；宁夏回族自治区科技厅；宁夏回族自治区环保厅；宁夏至尊展览广告有限公司
地址：宁夏银川金凤区紫荆花商务中心B座1303室（750002）
联系人：王经理

Ningxia Energy, Energy Saving and Emission Reduction Expo
Venue: Yinchuan Intl Convention and Exhibition Center, Yinchuan, Ningxia
Established Year: 2005
Frequency: Annual
Market Area: National
Nature: Open to Public
Organizer: Ningxia Zhizhun Exhibition & Advertising Co Ltd

陕西-西安 Shaanxi-Xi'an

2011 -
☎ 010-8260 6880转ext 91
🖷 010-8260 6883
✉ ciccyhuang@cnaico.com.cn
www.cnaico.com.cn
www.autochina.com.cn
6015

2011西安国际汽车展览会
地点：陕西西安
主办：中国汽车工业国际合作总公司
地址：北京市海淀区中关村丹棱街3号A座

Xi'an International Automobile Exhibition
Venue: Xi'an, Shaanxi
Organizer: China National Automotive Industry International Corp

2011/03/09 - 11
☎ 029-8556 0026/27
🖷 029-8556 0028
✉ qiushui10532@163.com
xacaame@126.com
6020

第四届西安国际汽车用品展览会暨
2011西部汽车用品订货交易会
地点：西安曲江国际会展中心，陕西西安
内容：汽车电子电器：汽车音响、车载导航、汽车电视、安全防盗、车载电话、定位监控、电动门窗、空调冰箱、倒车雷达、车灯及照明系统；汽车半导体、电子元器件、传感器。汽车内外装饰品：汽车地毯、空中放电、桃木饰件、方向盘套、防爆膜、纸巾盒、手机架、眼镜架、保温壶、钥匙扣、温度计、遮阳挡、气压表、靠垫、靠枕、座套、窗帘、晴雨档、备胎罩、看位灯、雨刮器、冷光灯、轮眉；车用美容护理用品；汽车环保；改装部件
始办年份：2008
周期：每年一届
市场范围：全国性
性质：面向公众
主办：陕西省汽车工程学会；陕西省汽车工业协会
承办：西安联方会展有限公司
地址：陕西省西安市长安南路3号蓝山国际公馆410室（710061）
联系人：焦香枝，吴松

4th Xi'an Intl Automobile Accessories Fair
Venue: Xi' an Qujiang Intl Conference and Exhibition Center, Xi' an, Shaanxi
Established Year: 2008
Frequency: Annual
Market Area: National
Nature: Open to Public
Organizer: Xi' an Lianfang Conference & Exhibition Co Ltd
Address: Room 410, 3 South Chang' an Road, Xi' an, Shaanxi 710061

2011/05/07 - 11
☎ 010-6651 6617
🖷 010-6651 9145
✉ ceieaweb@yahoo.com.cn
www.ceiea.com
6040

第61届中国教育装备展示会
地点：西安曲江国际会展中心，陕西西安
内容：各级各类教育所需仪器、设备、教具、标本、模型、计算机及软件、电教器材及软件、教学用图书、挂图等的全面展示；技术交流
始办年份：1980
周期：每年两届
市场范围：全国性
性质：面向贸易观众
参展费用：会员2,800元；非会员4,200元
上届规模 2010：展览面积15,000m^2(国外展商500m^2)，参展商700家（国外展商5家，来自3个国家），参观人数50,000人（专业贸易观众30,000人）
主办：中国教学仪器设备行业协会
承办：陕西省教育厅；西安市人民政府
地址：北京市西城区辟才胡同丰汇园小区8号楼1101室（100032）
联系人：张继芳,王文声

61th China Education Equipment Exhibition
Venue: Xi' an Qujiang Intl Conference and Exhibition Center, Xi' an, Shaanxi
Established Year: 1980
Frequency: Biannual
Market Area: National
Nature: Trade Only
Participated Fee: Member RMB 2,800, Non-member RMB 4,200*
Statistics 2010: Exhibition Area 15,000m^2(foreigners 500m^2), Exhibitors 700（foreigners 5, came from 3 countries）, Visitors 50,000（trade visitors 30,000）
Organizer: China Educational Instrument & Equipment Association
Address: 8-1101#Building Fenghuiyuan, Picai Hutong, Xicheng District, Beijing, China
Contact: Zhang Jifang, Wan Wensheng

2011/05/18 - 20
☎ 020-3882 3237
🖷 020-2222 3568
✉ lxlovemn_2008@126.com
www.hosfair.com
6060

2011第12届西安国际酒店设备及用品展览会
2011西安国际食品、葡萄酒、饮料及餐饮服务展览会
西安国际烘培、咖啡、茶展览会
地点：西安曲江国际会展中心，陕西西安
内容：餐饮厨房设备用品区：厨房炉灶、中西厨设备、制冷设备、电磁炉、食品展示柜、冷藏柜、保鲜柜、食品机械、洗碗机、制冰机、铁板烧、不锈钢厨具、火锅加热设备、厨房刀具、热水器、厨用刀具、排风设备、环保设备
始办年份：2000
周期：每年一届
市场范围：全国性
性质：面向公众
入场券价格：30元
主办：陕西省旅游局；陕西省旅游协会；陕西旅游饭店协会；陕西省烹饪餐饮行业协会陕西省饭店协会；陕西省烘焙行业协会；西安市咖啡专业委员会
承办：西安华展展览有限公司；广州华展展览策划有限公司
地址：广东省广州市广州大道中900号金穗大厦9楼H座；（510620）
联系人：刘经理

12th Xi'an Intl Hospitality Equipment & Supplies Fair
Venue: Xi' an Qujiang Intl Conference and Exhibition Center, Xi' an, Shaanxi
Established Year: 2000
Frequency: Annual
Market Area: National
Nature: Open to Public
Cost to Attend: 30
Organizer: Xi'an Huazhan Exhibition Co Ltd

2011/05/18 - 21
☎ 029-8311 8366
🖷 029-8311 8365
✉ 1448569986@qq.com
www.cibes.com.cn
6070

第五届中国（西安）建筑节能节新型建材博览会
地点：西安曲江国际会展中心，陕西西安
内容：建筑保温系统、干混砂浆、保温、隔热材料、屋面系统、建筑陶瓷节能系列产品、节电设备及能源统计监测、新型墙体材料、可再生能源展区、节能电气、节水技术及设备、涂料及防水产品
始办年份：2007
周期：每年一届
参展费用：6,800元/展位
主办：陕西振威国际会展有限公司
地址：西安市长安北路91号富城大厦806（710061）
QQ：144856986

The 5th China (Xi'an) International Energy-saving & Advanced Building Materials Exhibition
Venue: Xi' an Qujiang Intl Conference and Exhibition Center, Xi' an, Shaanxi
Established Year: 2007
Frequency: Annual
Participated Fee: RMB 6,800/booth
Organizer: Xi' an Zhenwei Exhibition Co Ltd
Address: 806，901 North Chang' an Road, Xi' an, Shaanxi 710061

2011/05/18 - 21
☎ 029-8311 8366
🖷 029-8311 8365
✉ 1448569986@qq.com
www.cibes.com.cn
6080

第十一届中国（西安）门窗幕墙及设备展览会
地点：西安曲江国际会展中心，陕西西安
内容：窗系列、门系列、幕墙、钢结构类、玻璃类、门窗幕墙系统、各类生产、加工、安装机器、各类遮阳产品和通风设备、各类结构胶、密封产品、清洁用品等、电建筑一体化应用**周期**：每年一届
主办：陕西振威国际会展有限公司
地址：西安市长安北路91号富城大厦806（710061）
QQ：144856986

10th China (Xi'an) Fenestration and Equipment Exhibition
Venue: Xi' an Qujiang Intl Conference and Exhibition Center, Xi' an, Shaanxi
Frequency: Annual
Organizer: Xi' an Zhenwei Exhibition Co Ltd
Address: 806，901 North Chang' an Road, Xi' an, Shaanxi 710061

2011/05/18 - 21
☎ 029-8311 8366
🖷 029-8311 8365
✉ 1448569986@qq.com
www.cibes.com.cn
6090

第3届中国(西安)国际桥梁、建筑模板及生产设备展览会
地点：西安曲江国际会展中心，陕西西安
内容：模板类：路、桥梁、隧道模板；新型墙体模板、脚手架类、模板生产设备及原材料、高空施工设备类
周期：每年一届
主办：陕西振威国际会展有限公司
地址：西安市长安北路91号富城大厦806（710061）
QQ：144856986

3rd China (Xi'an) Intl Building Formwork Scaffolding & Construction Technology Exhibition
Venue: Xi' an Qujiang Intl Conference and Exhibition Center, Xi' an, Shaanxi
Frequency: Annual
Organizer: Xi' an Zhenwei Exhibition Co Ltd
Address: 806，901 North Chang' an Road, Xi' an, Shaanxi 710061

2011/08/25 - 27
☎ 010-5166 2329转ext 16/ 22/ 58
🖷 010-6813 2578, 6818 9519
✉ chenzhy@ceac.com.cn
www.iCEF.com.cn
6100

2011年中国（西安）电子展
地点：西安曲江国际会展中心，陕西西安
始办年份：1964
性质：面向贸易观众
上届规模 2008：展览面积10,000m^2，参展商400家，专业贸易观众10,211人）
主办：四川省经济和信息化委员会；中国电子器材总公司
承办：中电会展与信息传播有限公司
地址：北京市复兴路49号（100036）
联系人：陈震宇

China Electronic Fair
CEF Summer Xi' an
Venue: Xi' an Qujiang Intl Conference and Exhibition Center, Xi' an, Shaanxi
Profile:
Established Year: 1964
Frequency:
Nature: Trade Only
Statistics 2008: Exhibition Area 10,000m^2, Exhibitors 400，Trade Visitors 10,211
Organizer: China Electronics Appliance Corp.
Address: 49 Fuxing Road, Beijing 100036

陕西-杨凌 Shaanxi-Yangling

2011/11/05 - 09
☎ 029-8703 6998, 8703 6991
🖷 029-8703 6994
www.agri-fair.com
6110

中国杨凌农业高新科技成果博览会
地点：陕西杨凌
内容："科技创新、示范推广、现代农业"为主题，集中举行了展览展示、国际合作交流、中国农业科技创新创业大赛项目对接、科技成果信息发布、农业实用技术咨询培训、项目洽谈与交易6大板块。展览分为室内展馆、室外展场和室外展区三大区域。其中室内展馆面积近9万平米，集中展示了农作物良种、设施农业、农业机械、畜牧、农产品加工、林果园艺、节水灌溉、农业信息化等领域的技术、产品与项目，以及发展现代农业的新品种、新技术和新模式。
始办年份：1994
周期：每年一届
入场券价格：50元
参展费用：5,300元
上届规模 2010：展览面积98,000m^2(国外展商1,000m^2)，参展商1,500家（国外展商86家，来自25个国家），参观人数60人（专业贸易观众15人）
主办：国家科技部、农业部、教育部、商务部等19个部委和陕西省人民政府
地址：陕西省杨凌示范区产业路国际馆（712100）
联系人：贾团利
QQ：554326924

China Yangling Agricultural Hi-Tech Fair
Venue: Yangling, Shaanxi
Established Year: 1994
Frequency: Annual
Cost to Attend: RMB 50:-
Participated Fee: RMB 5,300
Statistics 2010: Exhibition Area 98,000m^2(foreigners 1,000m^2), Exhibitors 1,500（foreigners 86, came from 25 countries），Visitors 60（trade visitors 15）
Organizer: CAF Organizing Committee

山东-济南 Shandong-Jinan

2011/02/26 - 28
☎ 0531-8238 5199
🖷 0531-8238 5199转ext 808
✉ 79155623@qq.com
6120

2011第五届山东国际自行车电动车及零部件展览会
地点：济南国际会展中心，山东济南
内容：各种普通自行车、运动自行车、折叠自行车、儿童车、滑板车；电单车、轻型电动两轮车、电动摩托车、电动三轮车、电动轿车、摩托车、燃油助力车、特种电动车；电源、电机、控制器、轮胎等零部件，电池修复仪等配套辅助产品；机械加工、流水线、检测仪器等配套设备；行业协会、检测中心及行业媒体
始办年份：2007
周期：每年一届
市场范围：全国性
性质：面向公众
主办：济南市人民政府；山东省自行车电动车行业协会；济南世博展览策划有限公司
地址：山东省济南市花园路189-1号334室（250013）
联系人：张迪

5th Shandong Bike, Electric-Bike and Parts Exhibition
Venue: Jinan Intl Convention & Exhibition Center, Jinan, Shandong
Established Year: 2007
Frequency: Annual
Market Area: National
Nature: Open to Public
Organizer: Jinan Shibo Exhibition Co Ltd
Address: Room 334, 189-1 Huanyuan Road, Jinan, Shandong 250013

2011/03/03 - 05
☎ 0531-8353 2222
www.jn-smtm.com
6130

2011济南国际机床模具展览会
地点：济南国际会展中心，山东济南
内容：机床展区,机床功能部件、工具及附件展区,锻压机械展区,模具及配套件展区
市场范围：国际性
参展费用：标准展位(3x3m)国内企业6,800元，国外企业1,500美元，双开口展位加收10%；净地(36m^{2}起)国内企业700元/m^2, 国外企业150美元/m^2；室外空地(36m^{2}起)国内企业500元/m^2，国外企业100美元/m^2
上届规模 2010：展览面积30,000m^2, 参展商426家，参观人数26,626人
主办：中国贸促会机械行业分会；中国国际商会机械行业商会；济南市人民政府；山东省自动化学会
承办：中国贸促会济南市分会；青岛金诺会展有限公司；济南华展展览有限公司

2011 Jinan International Machine Tools & moulds Exhibition
Venue: Jinan Intl Convention & Exhibition Center, Jinan, Shandong
Market Area: International
Participated Fee: Standard Booth (3x3m) USD 1,500, Corner unit add 10%, Raw Space (min 36m^2) USD 150/m^2, Outdoor USD 100/m^2
Statistics 2010: Exhibition Area 30,000m^2, Exhibitors 426, Visitors 26,626
Organizer: Jinan Huazhan Exhibition Co Ltd

2011/03/23 - 25
☎ 0531-8716 3048, 8716 3049
🖷 0531-8797 1298
✉ mamin4253@163.com
6140

2011第十届国际公共安全防范产品（济南）展览会
地点：济南舜耕国际会展中心，山东济南
内容：防盗报警器材：报警系统视频监控设备；报警系统出入口控制设备；智能楼宇对讲（可视）系统；机动车防盗报警系统；液晶拼接大屏显示系统，多媒体视频处理技术、多媒体网络应用技术；门禁、一卡通、停车场管理系统、巡更巡检系统、防盗门、锁、保险柜（箱）、防弹复合玻璃；警用装备器材、警用车辆、刑侦器材、无线对讲机、GPS卫星定位系统、交通安全产品、防伪技术；智能公共广播、综合布线、紧急消防广播及背景音乐音响、防雷产品、专业安防市场
始办年份：2002
周期：每年一届
上届规模：展览面积18,000m^2，参观人数50,000人
主办：山东省公安厅
承办：上海汇展商贸有限公司
地址：山东省济南市槐村街25号3F（250022）
联系人：马民

10th Jinan Intl Public Security Product Exhibition
Venue: Jinan Shungeng Intl Convention & Exhibition Center, Jinan, Shandong
Established Year: 2002
Frequency: Annual
Statistics 2010: Exhibition Area 18000m^2, Visitors 50,000
Organizer: Shanghai Huizhan Trade Co Ltd
Address: 3F, 25 Huai Cun Street, Jinan 250022, Shandong

2011/03/28 - 30
☎ 0531-8796 1189
🖷 0531-8718 2646
✉ wm87961189@163.com
www.shhzexpo.com
6150

2011中国（济南）国际打印耗材及办公设备展览会
地点：济南舜耕国际会展中心，山东济南
内容：打印耗材：墨盒、硒鼓、色带、碳粉、墨水及连续供墨系统、兼容、再生、循环使用的打印机和复印机通用耗材、芯片、感光鼓，打印耗材的制造、翻新、测试等设备和工具、相纸、票据纸、彩喷纸、热敏纸等办公用纸、打印设备与耗材。办公设备：保险柜、办公家具、验钞机、捆钞机、传真机、运钞箱、收款机、办公自动化；文件管理设备：大幅面绘图仪、各种打印机、复印机、胶印机、一体化机、速印机；文件储存类：纸制品，书写工具及修改用品，财会用品，带模机，计算器，U盘
首届
周期：每年一届
市场范围：全国性
性质：面向公众
主办：中国贸促会济南分会；上海汇展商贸有限公司
地址：山东省济南市槐村街25号3楼（250022）
联系人：吴明

China (Jinan) Printer Accessories and Office Equipment Exhibition
Venue: Jinan Shungeng Intl Convention & Exhibition Center, Jinan, Shandong
Profile: Printers, printer accessories, office supplies, office equipment and furniture
First Session
Frequency: Annual
Market Area: National
Nature: Open to Public
Organizer: Shanghai Huizhan Trade Co Ltd
Address: 3F, 25 Huai Cun Street, Jinan 250022, Shandong

2011/04/15 - 17
☎ 0531-8816 0483
🖷 0531-8816 0489
✉ jhlhaoyun@126.com

6160

2011年中国济南建筑装饰玻璃及艺术玻璃展会
地点：济南国际会展中心，山东济南
内容：建筑装饰玻璃：节能隔热玻璃、幕墙玻璃、光伏玻璃、中空玻璃、夹胶玻璃、夹层玻璃、钢化玻璃、LOW-E玻璃、安全玻璃、热反射玻璃、防盗玻璃、玻璃贴膜涂料；玻璃门窗：玻璃移门、玻璃隔断、艺术屏风、门窗玻璃、推拉门、自动门、金属型材、车刻玻璃、玻璃贴膜、玻璃喷绘机、喷画机、艺术玻璃写真机；艺术玻璃：装饰玻璃、卫浴玻璃、玻璃马赛克、玻璃护角、开关贴、玻璃背景墙、玻璃地台、压花玻璃、镶嵌玻璃、琉璃玻璃、玻璃艺术品、彩绘玻璃、丝印玻璃、玻璃砖（瓦）等；喷砂、激光雕刻、彩绘等冷加工设备等。
始办年份：2007
周期：每年一届
市场范围：全国性
性质：面向公众
主办：中国建筑装饰协会；济南信展展览有限公司
地址：山东省济南市华龙路28号智能园五层（250100）
联系人：靳焕丽

China Jinan Architecture Glass and Art Glass Exhibition
Venue: Jinan Intl Convention & Exhibition Center, Jinan, Shandong
Established Year: 2007
Frequency: Annual
Market Area: National
Nature: Open to Public
Organizer: Jinan Xinzhan Exhibition Co Ltd

2011/04/15 - 17
☎ 0531-8816 0493
🖷 0531-8816 0483
✉ wu_wei310@163.com
www.sdcf-xz.cn

6170

2011第十二届中国济南国际门窗、型材及配套实施展览会
地点：济南国际会展中心，山东济南
内容：型材：各种铝型材、铝合金型材、塑钢型材、塑料型材、玻璃钢型材、PVC型材、彩色塑钢型材、木塑型材、异型材及各种门窗型材；建筑门窗：实木门窗、铝合金门窗、塑钢门窗、彩板门窗、不锈钢门窗、玻璃钢门窗、隐形纱窗及其他金属门窗、斜屋顶窗、各种新型节能门窗。
始办年份：1999
周期：每年一届
市场范围：全国性
性质：面向公众
主办：全国高科技建筑建材产业化委员会；中国建筑装饰协会；亚洲经贸发展促进中心；亚洲新型建筑材料产业促进会；山东省建材工业协会
承办：济南信展展览有限公司
地址：山东省济南市华龙路28号智能园五层（250100）
联系人：吴薇

Jinan Intl Doors and Windows, Profiles and Facilities Exhibition
12th China Jinan Intl Door and Decorative Hardware Exhibition
Venue: Jinan Intl Convention & Exhibition Center, Jinan, Shandong
Established Year: 1999
Frequency: Annual
Market Area: National
Nature: Open to Public
Organizer: Jinan Xinzhan Exhibition Co Ltd

2011/09/16 - 18
☎ 010-6879 9043
🖷 010-6879 9050
✉ liusl@cmes.org

6180

2011中国国际制造技术及设备展览会
地点：济南国际会展中心，山东济南
内容：机床模具、铸造锻压、橡塑设备、涂装电镀、工业自动化、五金工具等专题。
始办年份：2006
周期：每年一届
性质：面向公众
上届规模 2010：展览面积18,000m^2，参展商470家，参观人数23,000人
主办：中国机械工程学会
地址：北京市海淀区首都体育馆南路9号4号楼11层（100048）
联系人：刘锁来

2011 China Intl Mechanical Manufacturing Technology& Equipment Exhibition
Venue: Jinan Intl Convention & Exhibition Center, Jinan, Shandong
Established Year: 2006
Frequency: Annual
Nature: Open to Public
Statistics 2010: Exhibition Area 18,000m^2, Exhibitors 470, Visitors 23,000
Organizer: Chinese Mechanical Engineering Society
Contact: Liu Suolai

山东-临沂 Shandong-Linyi

2011/04/10 - 12
☎ 0539-310 8125
🖷 0539-310 8135
✉ 406642655@qq.com

6190

2011中国（临沂）酒店用品及设备博览会
地点：中国商城会展中心，山东临沂
内容：厨房餐饮设备用品区；桌面用品区；酒店家具区；纺织布艺、制服区；清洁及洗衣设备区；客房用品、配套电器及大堂用品区；清洁及洗涤设备用品区；酒店智能系统区；咖啡和茶、食品区；综合区：台球、桌球、全自动麻将桌、舞台音响、卡拉OK娱乐设施、泳池设备、桑拿设备、商用、家用健身器械/器材、隔断、墙纸、布艺、地毯、浴缸、旅游商品。
始办年份：2007
周期：每年一届
市场范围：全国性
性质：面向公众
参展费用：标准展位3,600元（3x3m）双开口展位加收1,000元
主办：山东省烹饪协会；临沂市经济贸易委员会；临沂鹏展会展服务有限公司
地址：山东省临沂市新华一路和开阳路交汇处向南20米路西（金叶烟草院内）（276000）
联系人：王树梅

China (Linyi) Hotel Supplies and Equipment Exhibition
Venue: China Mall Conference and Exhibition Center, Linyi, Shandong
Established Year: 2007
Frequency: Annual
Market Area: National
Nature: Open to Public
Participated Fee: Standard Booth RMB 3,600/9m^2, Corner unit add RMB 1,000
Organizer: Linyi Pengzhan Conference and Exhibition Co Ltd

2011/05/17 - 19
☎ 0539-252 2267
🖷 0539-252 2269
✉ zq207374@126.com
6200

2011第六届中国临沂塑料机械暨塑料包装展览会
地点：山东临沂鲁信国际会展中心，山东临沂
内容：注射成型生产技术设备、机械手臂（取出机）、中央供料及辅机设备、模具及模具零组件制造设备。挤出生产技术及设备：发泡板材、吹膜/袋、管材、异型材、片材、合塑、圆丝、扁丝、电线电缆、混炼、造粒等生产设备。塑胶机械、橡胶/轮胎机械及配套产品、测试及控制仪器、表面处理、打光设备、后处理设备。中空成型生产技术及设备。相关配套设备及各类零件
始办年份：2005
周期：每年一届
市场范围：全国性
性质：面向公众
主办：中国塑料包装协会；山东省塑料协会；临沂市国际贸易促进委员会；临沂恒展展览有限公司
地址：山东省临沂市通达路与陶然路交汇处锦绣蓝山
联系人：赵经理

6th China Linyi Plastic Machinery and Plastic Packaging Exhibition
Venue: Luxin Intl Conference & Exhibition Center, Linyi, Shandong
Established Year: 2005
Frequency: Annual
Market Area: National
Nature: Open to Public
Organizer: Linyi Hengxin Exhibition Co Ltd

山东-青岛 Shandong-Qingdao

2011/03/10 - 12
☎ 0532-8299 5726
🖷 0532-8299 5720
✉ zongliang0530@163.com
6220

2011青岛（春季）国际照明暨LED展览会
地点：青岛国际会展中心，山东青岛
内容：LED显示类：LED显示屏；触摸屏；LED立体发光字；LED芯片、外延片、磊晶片及相关基材；LED发光二极管及大功率器件；LED封装及配套材料；LED产品控制系统及IC；LED背光源；LED制造设备及测试仪器；OLED（有机发光二级管）、LD（激光二极管）、EL（冷光源）；LED点阵、数码管。LED灯类；LED交通照明灯具；其他相关产品，如变压器镇流器、触发器、控制箱等
首届
周期：每年一届
市场范围：全国性
主办：青岛市人民政府会展发展办公室；山东省照明学会；青岛市照明协会；青岛国际会展中心；青岛外经贸商务展览有限公司
联系人：牟宗良

Qingdao （Spring） Lighting and LED Exhibition
Venue: Qingdao Intl Convention & Exhibition Center, Qingdao, Shandong
First Session
Frequency: Annual
Market Area: National
Organizer: Qingdao Trade and Exhibition Co Ltd
Contact: Mou Zongliang

2011/03/15 - 17
☎ 0532-5555 2963, 5555 2955
🖷 0532-5555 2960
✉ qdjinnuo @126.com
www.mwexpo.com
6230

第九届青岛国际金属加工技术设备展览会
地点：青岛国际会展中心，山东青岛
内容：金属成形机床,金属切削机床,特种加工机床,数控系统、数显装置和机床电器；机床零部件及辅助设备；磨料磨具、刀具、工夹具及相关产品;检验和测量设备
市场范围：国际性
参展费用：标准展位（3x3m）国内企业6,800元，国外企业1,500美元，双开口展位另加10%；净地（36m^{2}起）国内企业700元/m^2，国外企业150美元/m^2；技术讲座5,000元/每场
上届规模 2010：展览面积20,000m^2，参观人数18,983人
主办：中国金属学会,青岛市人民政府
承办：青岛金诺会展有限公司
地址：青岛市福州南路87号福林大厦902室（266071）
联系人：臧勇华,李萍

The 9th Qingdao International Metal Processing Technology and Equipment Exhibition
Venue: Qingdao Intl Convention & Exhibition Center, Qingdao, Shandong
Market Area: International
Participated Fee: Standard Booth (3x3m) USD 1,500, Corner unit add 10%; Raw Space (min 36m^2) USD 150元/m^2
Statistics 2010: Exhibition Area 20,000m^2, Visitors 18,983
Organizer: Qingdao Jinnoc Exhibition Co Ltd
Address: Room 902, 807 South Fuzhou Road, Qingdao 266071, Shandong
Contact: Zang Yonghua, Li Ping

2011/03/25 - 27
☎ 0532-8501 2515
🖷 0532-8501 2916
✉ qdlanbozxn@163.com
www.qdlanbo.com
6240

2011第二届中国（青岛）国际重型汽车、卡车、挂车及零部件展览会
地点：青岛国际会展中心，山东青岛
内容：整车展区：各类重卡、中卡、轻卡、货车、挂车、客车、公交车、旅行房车；汽车配件及用品展区：柴油发动机、电子电气系统、驾驶室、汽车仪表、变速箱；各种汽车生产制造设备；轮胎类展区；汽车维修检测展区；润滑油及汽保展区：各类润滑油（齿轮油、传动油、冷却油等）、油品添加剂、节油产品、相关养护产品、安全防盗、汽车通讯等产品与技术
始办年份：2010
周期：每年一届
市场范围：全国性
主办：中国国际机械工业协会；青岛蓝博会展有限公司
地址：山东省青岛市山东路46号华宇大厦605室（266071）
联系人：赵旭娜

2nd China (Qingdao) Intl Exhibition on Heavy Cars, Trucks and Special Vehicles and Parts
Venue: Qingdao Intl Convention & Exhibition Center, Qingdao, Shandong
Established Year: 2010
Frequency: Annual
Market Area: National
Organizer: Qingdao Lanbo Exhibition Co Ltd
Address: Room 605, 46 East Shandong Road, Qingdao 266071, Shandong
Contact: Zhao Xuna

2011/04/27 - 29
☎ 0532-8501 9533
🖷 0532-8501 2624
✉ kakaxizhanshi@126.com
6250

2011第13届山东口腔器械与齿科材料（青岛）展览会
地点：青岛国际会展中心，山东青岛
内容：口腔器械及齿科材料专区：牙科综合治疗设备；牙科影像设备；牙科治疗所需材料；牙科技工设备；牙科用药品、清洁剂、消毒剂；牙科设备零配件；牙外科器械及材料；牙科消毒设备；牙科实验室设备及实验所需原材料；口腔保健用品专区：牙膏（药物牙膏、漂白牙膏）、保健牙刷、专用牙刷、漱口水、润喉品、香口胶、牙齿漂白剂、牙线、假牙清洁剂、假牙固定剂、牙粉
始办年份：2000
周期：每年一届
市场范围：全国性
入场券价格：15元
上届规模 2010：展览面积13,000m^2
主办：亚洲经贸发展促进中心；青岛市口腔医学会；青岛海名国际会展有限公司
地址：山东省青岛市山东路52号华嘉大厦4楼（266072）
联系人：王小姐
2011第13届山东口腔器械与齿科材料（青岛）展览会

13th Shandong Exhibition on Dental & Denture Equipment and Materials
Venue: Qingdao Intl Convention & Exhibition Center, Qingdao, Shandong
Established Year: 2000
Frequency: Annual
Market Area: National
Cost to Attend: 15
Statistics 2010: Exhibition Area 13,000m^2, Exhibitors
Organizer: Qingdao Haiming Exhibition Co Ltd

2011/06/03 - 06
☎ 0532-8299 5616
🖷 0532-8889 4849
✉ qingdaozhanlan@163.com
www.qdteafair.com
6260

2011第五届中国（青岛）国际茶文化博览会暨紫砂艺术展
地点：青岛国际会展中心，山东青岛
内容：茶叶类企业：全国茶叶产销企业（红茶、绿茶、黑茶、白茶、黄茶、青茶、花茶）；茶叶经销代理加盟、茶叶连锁经营企业、茶叶进出口公司；茶具类企业：紫砂、陶瓷、煮茶器、冲茶具、金属、竹木等其它附属茶具；茶食品类企业：茶饮料、茶糖果、茶点、茶保健食品、茶叶提取物
始办年份：2007
周期：每年一届
市场范围：全国性
性质：面向公众
主办：青岛市农业委员会崂山区人民政府；青岛国际会展中心；青岛外经贸商务展览有限公司
地址：山东省青岛市崂山区苗岭路9号青岛国际会展中心5号馆11楼（266061）
联系人：王振才

5th China （Qingdao） Tea Culture Fair
Purple Clay Teapot Art Show
Venue: Qingdao Intl Convention & Exhibition Center, Qingdao, Shandong
Established Year: 2007
Frequency: Annual
Market Area: National
Nature: Open to Public
Organizer: Qingdao Trade and Exhibition Co Ltd
Address: 11/Fl, Hall 5, 9 Miaoling Road, Qingdao, Shandong 266061
Contact: Wang Zhencai

2010/07/07 – 10
☎ 0532-8197 8685, 8197 8683
🖷 0532-8197 8692
✉ sinoceszl@sinoces.com
www.sinoces.com
6270

2010中国国际消费电子博览会
地点：青岛国际会展中心，山东青岛
内容：家庭影音产品、数字家庭产品、数字内容支持、工业设计、存储解决方案、便携办公设备、家用电器产品、汽车电子、数字娱乐产品、软件应用方案、移动无线通信、安防产品
始办年份：2001
周期：每年一届
市场范围：国际性
上届规模 ‘09：展览面积39,000m^2，参展商451家（国外展商76家），参观人数92,760人（专业贸易观众41,529人）
主办：国家商务部；工业和信息化部；科学技术部；山东省人民政府
承办：中国电子商会；中国机电产品进出口商会；青岛市人民政府
地址：青岛市山东路2号甲华仁国际大厦19层A（266071）

2010 China Intl Consumer Electronics Show (SINOCES)
Venue: Qingdao International Convention & Exhibition Center, Qingdao, Shandong
Profile: Home Entertainment, Smart Home Products, Mobile Communications, Mobile Office, Automotive Electronics, Storage Solutions & Application
Established Year: 2001
Frequency: Annual
Market Area: International
Statistics ‘09: Exhibition Area 39,000m^2, Exhibitors 451（foreigners 76）, Visitors 92,760（trade visitors 41,529）
Organizer: China Electronic Chamber of Commerce; China Chamber of Commerce for Import and Export of Machinery

2011/07/21 - 24
☎ 0532-8079 1051
🖷 0532-8384 1887
✉ hcservice3@gmail.com
www.cbe-qd.com
6280

第七届中国(青岛)国际建筑材料及装饰材料博览会
地点：青岛国际会展中心，山东青岛
内容：地面铺装材料,卫浴陶瓷专业,建筑装饰五金,整体橱柜与材料及相关设备,自动门及门控五金、铝型材,门、窗,玻璃,天花吊顶及幕墙,墙纸/布艺/室内装饰及材料
市场范围：国际性
参展费用：标准展位7,200元/9m^2，异型展位8,200元/9m^2，净地700元/m^2（36m^{2}起）
主办：中国建筑材料联合会；中国建筑金属结构协会；联合国工业发展组织国际环境资源监督管理机构；青岛市人民政府
承办：青岛市城乡建设委员会；山东省建设机械行业协会,青岛海宸国际会展有限公司
地址：中国青岛国际会展中心5-8F（苗岭路9号）（266061）
联系人：刘娜

The 7th China (Qingdao) International Construction & Decoration Materials Exhibition
Venue: Qingdao Intl Convention & Exhibition Center, Qingdao, Shandong
Market Area: International
Participated Fee: Standard Booth RMB 7,200/9m^2, Raw Space RMB 700/m^2（min 36m^2）**Organizer**: Qingdao Haichen International Expo Co Ltd

2011/07/21 - 24
☎ 0532-8079 1096
🖷 0532-8395 1085
✉ qdcese@163.com
www.qdcese.com
6290

第五届中国（青岛）国际建筑节能和可再生能源建筑应用博览会
地点：青岛国际会展中心，山东青岛
内容：建筑节能保温系统,新型墙体材料，建筑、装饰涂料类，干混砂浆产品、添加剂及技术设备，屋面系统，化学建材，防水材料，太阳能，供热采暖，热泵空调技术及产品，能源统计监测,绿色照明,环保木制、木塑产品，节地技术
市场范围：国际性
参展费用：标准展位6,800元/9m^2，异型展位8,200元/9m^2，净地700元/m^2（36m^{2}起）
主办：住房和城乡建设部科技发展促进中心；住房和城乡建设部建筑节能中心；青岛市城乡建设委员会
承办：青岛市建筑节能与墙体材料革新办公室；青岛市建筑节能协会;青岛海宸国际会展有限公司
地址：山东青岛国际会展中心5-8F（苗岭路9号）
联系人：公言

2011 China (Qingdao) Intl Building Energy Saving Fair
Venue: Qingdao Intl Convention & Exhibition Center, Qingdao, Shandong
Market Area: International
Participated Fee: Standard Booth RMB 6,800/9m^2, Raw Space RMB 700/m^2（min 36m^2）
Organizer: Qingdao Haichen International Expo Co Ltd
Address: 5-8F, Miaoling Road, Qingdao, Shandong
Contact: Gong Yan

2011/07/21 - 24
☎ 0532-8501 8671, 13656423086
🖷 0532-8395 1189
www.cbe-qd.com

6300 **第七届中国(青岛)国际门窗幕墙及相关设备展览会**
地点：青岛国际会展中心，山东青岛
内容：窗系列，门系列，幕墙、钢结构类，玻璃类，五金胶粘剂类，遮阳系统，相关加工设备
市场范围：国际性
性质：门窗幕墙建材
参展费用：标准展位:A区7,600元，B区7,200元，C区6,800元；异型标展:A区8,000元，B区7,600元，C区7,200元；净地：A区820元/m^2，B区760元/m^2，C区700元/m^2；国际展区：标准展位1,800美元,净地180美元/m^2
主办：中国建筑金属结构协会；全国建筑幕墙门窗标准化技术委员会；青岛市建设委员会；山东省建设机械行业协会
地址：山东青岛国际会展中心5-8F（苗岭路9号）（266061）
联系人：任翔

The 7th China (Qingdao) International Doors, Windows, Curtain Exhibition
Venue: Qingdao Intl Convention & Exhibition Center, Qingdao, Shandong
Market Area: International
Participated Fee: Standard Booth USD 7,600/9m^2, Raw Space USD 180/m^2 (min 36m^2)
Organizer: Qingdao Haichen International Expo Co Ltd
Address: 5-8F, Miaoling Road, Qingdao, Shandong
Contact: Ren Xiang

2011/07/21 - 24
☎ 0532-8079 1050
🖷 0532-8384 1887
✉ wooddoorqd@163.com
www.wooddoorqd.cn

6310 **第七届中国（青岛）国际木门展览会**
地点：青岛国际会展中心，山东青岛
市场范围：国际性
参展费用：标准展位6,800元/9m^2，异型展位7,200元/9m^2，净地760元/m^2（36m^{2}起）
主办：中国木材与木制品流通协会木门专业委员会；青岛市建设委员会
承办：青岛海宸国际会展有限公司
地址：青岛国际会展中心5-8F（苗岭路9号）（266061）
联系人：张东

Qingdao Intl Wooden Door Exhibition
Venue: Qingdao Intl Convention & Exhibition Center, Qingdao, Shandong
Market Area: International
Participated Fee: Standard Booth RMB 8,600 (3m × 3m), Raw Space RMB 760/m^2 (min 36m^2)
Organizer: Qingdao Haichen International Expo Co Ltd
Address: 5-8F, Miaoling Road, Qingdao, Shandong

2011/07/21 - 24
☎ 0532-8079 1056
🖷 0532-8395 1197
✉ expotuliao@163.com
www.expotuliao.com

6320 **2011中国（青岛）国际建筑防水及屋面系统展览会**
地点：青岛国际会展中心，山东青岛
内容：防水卷材，防水涂料，密封材料，刚性防水及堵漏材料，屋面防水系统，各种防水瓦材，防水材料的原辅材料及配件/设备，其他防水材料，相关防水技术科研成果、管理软件及防水专业书刊
市场范围：国际性
性质：面向公众
参展费用：标准展位6,800元/9m^2，异型展位8,200元/9m^2，净地700元/m^2（36m^{2}起）
主办：住房和城乡建设部科技发展促进中心；住房和城乡建设部建筑节能中心；青岛市建设委员会
承办：青岛市建筑节能与墙体材料革新办公室；青岛市建筑节能协会；青岛海宸国际会展有限公司
地址：山东青岛国际会展中心5-8F
联系人：杨光

Qingdao Building Waterproof Exhibition
Venue: Qingdao Intl Convention & Exhibition Center, Qingdao, Shandong
Market Area: International
Nature: Open to Public
Participated Fee: Standard Booth RMB 6,800/9m^2, Raw Space RMB 700/m^2 (min 36m^2)
Organizer: Qingdao Haichen International Expo Co Ltd
Address: 5-8F, Miaoling Road, Qingdao, Shandong
Contact: Yang Guang

2011/07/21 - 24
☎ 0532-8395 1011
🖷 0532-8384 1887
✉ qdtyn2009@163.com
www.qdcese.cn

6330 **第四届中国（青岛）国际太阳能与建筑一体化应用产品技术展览会**
地点：青岛国际会展中心，山东青岛
内容：太阳能热利用,太阳能光伏、光电,太阳能空调,太阳能配件
市场范围：国际性
参展费用：标准展位6,800元/9m^2，异型展位8,200元/9m^2，净地700元/m^2（36m^{2}起）
主办：中国建筑材料联合会；青岛市人民政府；山东省石材行业协会
承办：青岛海宸国际会展有限公司
地址：山东青岛国际会展中心5-8F（苗岭路9号）（266061）
联系人：郑阳

Qingdao Solar Energy and BIPV Exhibition
Venue: Qingdao Intl Convention & Exhibition Center, Qingdao, Shandong
Market Area: International
Participated Fee: Standard Booth RMB 6,800/9m^2, Raw Space RMB 700/m^2 (min 36m^2)
Organizer: Qingdao Haichen International Expo Co Ltd
Address: 5-8F, Miaoling Road, Qingdao, Shandong
Contact: Zheng Yang

2011/07/21 - 24
☎ 0532-8079 1055
🖷 0532-8395 1197, 83951132
✉ qdjbhcsk@163.com

6340 **2011中国（青岛）国际陶瓷卫浴及厨房设备展览会**
地点：青岛国际会展中心，山东青岛
内容：卫浴产品,卫浴配套五金,卫浴技术及其他,建筑陶瓷及产品,厨房产品
市场范围：国际性
参展费用：标准展位7,200元/9m^2，异型展位8,200元/9m^2，净地700元/m^2（36m^{2}起）
主办：青岛市人民政府；中国建筑材料联合会
承办：青岛市城乡建设委员会；青岛海宸国际会展有限公司
地址：中国青岛国际会展中心5-8F（苗岭路9号）（266061）
联系人：梅舭

2011 China (Qingdao) International Ceramics Sanitary Ware and Kitchen Facilities Fair
Venue: Qingdao Intl Convention & Exhibition Center, Qingdao, Shandong
Market Area: International
Participated Fee: Standard Booth RMB 7,200/9m^2, Raw Space RMB 700/m^2 (min 36m^2)
Organizer: Qingdao Haichen International Expo Co Ltd
Address: 5-8F, Miaoling Road, Qingdao, Shandong
Contact: Mei Bi

2011/07/21 - 24
☎ 0532-8079 1070
🖷 0532-8384 1887
✉ zhaoshilei7788@126.com
www.floorqd.cn

6350 **第五届中国(青岛)国际地板及木制品展览会**
地点：青岛国际会展中心，山东青岛
内容：中国是国际最大的地板消费市场之一，近年来，越来越多的一线品牌、新兴品牌、新兴产品凭借“绿色”的特质、时尚的款式、卓越的品质和快速拓展的渠道得到广大消费者的认可与信赖。2011年，第五届青岛国际地板展以“科技与时尚”为主题，聚焦行业新产品、新技术、新品牌，全面加大地板代理商、房地

China (Qingdao) Intl Floor Exhibition
Venue: Qingdao Intl Convention & Exhibition Center, Qingdao, Shandong
Participated Fee: Standard Booth RMB 7,200/9m^2, Raw Space RMB 700/m^2 (min 36m^2)
Organizer: Qingdao Haichen International Expo Co Ltd

产商、外贸公司、海外采购商到会，为国内外地板企业与专业买家搭建快捷、高效的精准对接平台，寻找最佳的合作伙伴！
参展费用： 标准展位7,200元/9m²，异型展位8,200元/9m²，净地700元/m²（36m²起）
主办： 青岛市人民政府；中国建筑材料联合会；联合国工业发展组织国际环境资源监督管理机构
承办： 青岛市城乡建设委员会；青岛海宸国际会展有限公司
地址： 山东青岛国际会展中心5-8F（266061）
联系人： 赵世磊

Address: 5-8F, Miaoling Road, Qingdao, Shandong
Contact: Liu Nian

6360

2011/07/21 - 24
☎ 0532-8079 1060
🖷 0532-8384 1887
✉ qdscz2009@163.cn

第五届中国(青岛)国际石材工业及机械设备展览会
地点： 青岛国际会展中心，山东青岛
内容： 石材类,板材类,人造石类,墓碑类,石雕制品类,环境装饰类,石材机械及加工设备,养护材料及设备
市场范围： 国际性
参展费用： 标准展位6,800元/9m²，异型展位8,200元/9m²，净地700元/m²（36m²起）
主办： 中国建筑材料联合会；青岛市人民政府；山东省石材行业协会
承办： 青岛海宸国际会展有限公司
地址： 青岛国际会展中心5-8F（苗岭路9号）
联系人： 公正

The 5th China (Qingdao) International Stone Products & Machinery Exhibition
Venue: Qingdao Intl Convention & Exhibition Center, Qingdao, Shandong
Market Area: International
Participated Fee: Standard Booth RMB 6,800/9m², Raw Space RMB 700/m² (min 36m²)
Organizer: Qingdao Haichen International Expo Co Ltd
Address: 5-8F, Miaoling Road, Qingdao, Shandong
Contact: Gong Zheng

6370

2011/07/21 - 24
☎ 0532-8079 1058
🖷 0532-8395 1101
✉ qdlszm@163.com

2011中国（青岛）国际绿色照明产品及技术应用展览会
地点： 青岛国际会展中心，山东青岛
内容： LED照明，庭院及景观灯，户外照明系列，室内照明（室内灯饰、灯具）,各类电光源产品，照明电工产品及附件，城市亮化工程技术设备
市场范围： 国际性
参展费用： 标准展位6,800元/9m²，异型展位8,200元/9m²，净地700元/m²（36m²起）
承办： 青岛市建筑节能与墙体材料革新办公室；青岛市建筑节能协会；青岛海宸国际会展有限公司
地址： 青岛国际会展中心5-8F（苗岭路9号）
联系人： 王帅

Qingdao Green Lighting Exhibition
Venue: Qingdao Intl Convention & Exhibition Center, Qingdao, Shandong
Market Area: International
Participated Fee: Standard Booth RMB 6,800/9m², Raw Space RMB 700/m² (min 36m²)
Organizer: Qingdao Haichen International Expo Co Ltd
Address: 5-8F, Miaoling Road, Qingdao, Shandong

6380

2011/07/21 - 24
☎ 0532-8079 1056
🖷 0532-838 4887
✉ expotuliao@163.com
www.expotuliao.com

2011中国（青岛）国际建筑装饰涂料及化学建材展览会
地点： 青岛国际会展中心，山东青岛
内容： 涂料/涂膜/贴膜产品,涂料原材料与胶粘剂,防水材料、系统及设备,涂料相关工具、设备,行业相关服务
市场范围： 国际性
参展费用： 标准展位6,800元/9m²，异型展位8,200元/9m²，净地700元/m²（36m²起）
主办： 住房和城乡建设部科技发展促进中心；住房和城乡建设部建筑节能中心；青岛市城乡建设委员会
承办： 青岛市建筑节能与墙体材料革新办公室；青岛市建筑节能协会；青岛海宸国际会展有限公司
地址： 青岛国际会展中心5-8F（苗岭路9号）
联系人： 杨光

Qingdao Architectural coatings and Chemical Building Materials
Venue: Qingdao Intl Convention & Exhibition Center, Qingdao, Shandong
Market Area: International
Participated Fee: Standard Booth RMB 6,800/9m², Raw Space RMB 700/m² (min 36m²)
Organizer: Qingdao Haichen International Expo Co Ltd
Address: 5-8F, Miaoling Road, Qingdao, Shandong
Contact: Yang Guang

6390

2011/07/21 - 24
☎ 0532-8395 1161
🖷 0532-8384 1887
✉ qdcainuan@163.com
www.qdcainuan.com

第二届中国（青岛）国际供热采暖系统产品及技术应用展览会
地点： 青岛国际会展中心，山东青岛
内容： 地面供暖产品及设备;供热采暖技术设备;供暖系统自动化与配套设备;空调制冷通风及热泵节能技术设备;新技术产品推介交流与研讨
市场范围： 国际性
参展费用： 标准展位6,800元/9m²，异型展位8,200元/9m²，净地700元/m²（36m²起）
主办： 住房和城乡建设部科技发展促进中心；住房和城乡建设部建筑节能中心；青岛市建设委员会
承办： 青岛市建筑节能与墙体材料革新办公室；青岛市建筑节能协会；青岛海宸国际会展有限公司
地址： 山东青岛国际会展中心5-8F
联系人： 孟翔

Qingdao Heating Supply System and Technology Exhibition
Venue: Qingdao Intl Convention & Exhibition Center, Qingdao, Shandong
Market Area: International
Participated Fee: Standard Booth RMB 6,800/9m², Raw Space RMB 700/m² (min 36m²)
Organizer: Qingdao Haichen International Expo Co Ltd
Address: 5-8F, Miaoling Road, Qingdao, Shandong
Contact: Meng Xiang

6395

2011/07/21 - 24
☎ 0532-8395 1195
🖷 0532-8384 1887

中国（青岛）国际窗帘布艺及产品展览会
地点： 青岛国际会展中心，山东青岛
内容： 窗帘，窗纱，布艺，布艺，窗饰配件，家纺产品及辅料
市场范围： 国际性
性质： 面向公众
参展费用： 标准展位6,800元/9m²，异型展位8,200元/9m²，净地700元/m²（36m²起）
主办： 青岛市人民政府;中国建筑材料联合会；联合国工业发展组织国际环境资源监督管理机构
承办： 青岛市城乡建设委员会；青岛海宸国际会展有限公司
地址： 山东青岛国际会展中心5-8F
联系人： 刘念

Qingdao Window Covering Exhibition
Venue: Qingdao Intl Convention & Exhibition Center, Qingdao, Shandong
Market Area: International
Nature: Open to Public
Participated Fee: Standard Booth RMB 6,800/9m², Raw Space RMB 700/m² (min 36m²)
Organizer: Qingdao Haichen International Expo Co Ltd
Address: 5-8F, Miaoling Road, Qingdao, Shandong
Contact: Liu Nian

2011/07/21 - 24
☎ 0532-8079 1096
🖷 0532-8395 1085
✉ qdcese@163.com
www.qdcese.com

6398

第五届中国（青岛）国际外墙保温及新型墙体产品技术展览会
地点：青岛国际会展中心，山东青岛
内容：建筑保温系统,屋面保温系统,保温、隔热材料,新型墙体材料,干混砂浆产品、添加剂及技术设备,节能建筑、绿色工程示范成果展示,住宅产业化部品
市场范围：国际性
参展费用：标准展位6,800元/9m^2，异型展位8,200元/9m^2，净地700元/m^2（36m^{2}起）
主办：住房和城乡建设部科技发展促进中心；住房和城乡建设部建筑节能中心；青岛市建设委员会
承办：青岛市建筑节能与墙体材料革新办公室；青岛市建筑节能协会；青岛海宸国际会展有限公司
地址：山东青岛国际会展中心5-8F（苗岭路9号）（266061）
联系人：公言

Qingdao Building External wall insulation and New Wall Materials Exhibition
Venue: Qingdao Intl Convention & Exhibition Center, Qingdao, Shandong
Market Area: International
Participated Fee: Standard Booth RMB 6,800/9m^2, Raw Space RMB 700/m^2 (min 36m^2)
Organizer: Qingdao Haichen International Expo Co Ltd
Address: 5-8F, Miaoling Road, Qingdao, Shandong
Contact: Gong Yan

2011/07/28 - 30
☎ 0532-8537 6392, 18754238417
🖷 0532-8537 6167
✉ uhaipeng333@sina.com

6400

2011第六届中国青岛国际电力电工及电气自动化展览会
地点：山东青岛
内容：电力、电工产品展区：发电设备：火电/水电/核能；新能源发电技术及设备：风能、太阳能、地热及潮汐发电设备。输配电设备：整厂设备及工程、电力调度系统设备（SCADA /DMS/ EMS系统）、机箱、机柜、控制及测试电力设备及仪器、自动化控制设备、电力资讯科技、控制面板、探测及安全报警系统。建筑电气及机电装置：楼宇管理及控制系统、开关设备、照明系统等。工业用电设备：不间断电源、柴油发电机及交流发电机等、环保技术及设备。
始办年份：2005
周期：每年一届
市场范围：地区性
性质：面向公众
主办：中国国际贸易促进联合会亚洲经贸发展促进中心；山东省电器行业协会
承办：青岛德尔展览有限公司
地址：山东省青岛市华嘉大厦201（266071）
联系人：卢鹏

Qingdao Electrical power and Electrical Automation Exhibition
Venue: Qingdao, Shandong
Established Year: 2005
Frequency: Annual
Market Area: Regional
Nature: Open to Public
Organizer: Qingdao Deer Exhibition Co Ltd

2011/08 -
☎ 010-6859 4811, 6859 4994, 6859 4910
🖷 010-6859 4995
✉ zhangyuhui@ccpitmsc.org
www.chinamachine.org.cn

6410

中国国际工业装备(青岛)博览会
地点：山东青岛
周期：每年一届
市场范围：全国性
主办：中国贸促会机械行业分会
地址：北京市西城区三里河路46号（100823）
联系人：张玉惠,郭旭萍,吕春丽

China (Qingdao) Industry Fair
Venue: Qingdao, Shandong
Frequency: Annual
Market Area: National
Organizer: CCPIT–Machinery Sub-Council

2011/08/04 - 07
☎ 0532-5555 2936, 5555 2955
🖷 0532-5555 2960
✉ qdjinnuo@126.com
www.jch-mj.com

6420

2011青岛国际机床模具展览会
地点：青岛国际会展中心，山东青岛
内容：机床展,机床功能部件、工具及附件展,锻压机械展,模具及配套件展
性质：机床模具
参展费用：国内企业6,800/9m^2，净地700元/m^2；国外企业2,000美元/9m^2，净地200美元/m^2，角位加收10%，净地36m^{2}起
主办：青岛金诺会展有限公司
地址：青岛市福州南路87号福林大厦902室（266071）
联系人：杨晓华

2011 Qingdao International Machine Tools & Moulds Exhibition
Venue: Qingdao Intl Convention & Exhibition Center, Qingdao, Shandong
Participated Fee:
Standard Booth USD 2,000/9m^2, Raw Space USD 200/m^2(min 36m^2)
Organizer: Qingdao Jinnoc Exhibition Co Ltd
Address: Room 902, 87 South Fouzhou Road, Qingdao 266071, Shandong
Contact: Yang Xiaohua

2011/11/01 - 03
☎ 010-5919 4405
🖷 010-6591 8986

6430

中国国际渔业博览会
地点：青岛国际会展中心，山东青岛
内容：水产品加工及贸易、渔业机械设备、海洋捕捞、养殖饲料及病害防治、质量控制、相关服务及媒体
始办年份：1996
周期：每年一届
市场范围：国际性
性质：面向贸易观众
入场券价格：100元
上届规模 2010：展览面积40,000m^2(国外展商15,000m^2)，参展商近800家（国外展商近400家，来自35个国家），专业贸易观众20,000人
主办：中国贸促会农业行业分会
地址：北京市朝阳区麦子店街20号楼805（100125）
联系人：张晓颖

China Fisheries & Seafood Expo
Venue: Qingdao Intl Convention & Exhibition Center, Qingdao, Shandong
Profile: Seafood products, seafood processing equipment, aquaculture products and supplies, fishing equipment, associated services
Established Year: 1996
Frequency: Annual
Market Area: International
Nature: Trade Only
Cost to Attend: RMB 100:-
Statistics 2010: Exhibition Area 40,000m^2 (foreigners 15,000m^2), Exhibitors 800 (foreigners 400, came from 35 countries), Trade Visitors 20,000
Organizer: CCPIT-SSA
Address: Room 805, Building 20, Maizidian Street, Chaoyang District, Beijing
Contact: Joy Zhang

山东-烟台 Shandong-Yantai

2011/04/15 - 17
☎ 010-8260 6880转ext 91
🖷 010-8260 6883
✉ ciccyhuang@cnaico.com.cn
www.cnaico.com.cn
www.autochina.com.cn
6440

2011年烟台春季汽车展销会
地点：山东烟台
主办：中国汽车工业国际合作总公司
地址：北京市海淀区中关村丹棱街3号A座

2011 Spring Yantai Automobile Show
Venue: Yantai, Shandong
Organizer: China National Automotive Industry International Corp

2011/05/19 - 21
☎ 0532-5555 2936, 5555 2955
🖷 0535-666 3138
✉ qdjinnuo @126.com
www.mwexpo.com
6450

2011烟台国际机床暨工模具技术设备展览会
地点：烟台国际博览中心，山东烟台
内容：机床类,机床零部件及辅助设备类,锻压机械类,模具及配套件类
始办年份：2003
周期：每年一届
市场范围：国际性
性质：机床暨工模具技术设
参展费用：国内企业：5,800元/展位，净地600元/m^2，室外净地500元/m^2；国外企业1,200美元/展位，净地120美元/m^2，室外净地100美元/m^2
上届规模 2010：展览面积10,000m^2, 参展商400家
主办：中国机电产品流通协会；烟台市人民政府；青岛金诺会展有限公司
承办：烟台金诺会展有限公司
地址：烟台市南大街117号文化宫大厦2218室（264000）
联系人：康杰

2011 Yantai International Machine Tools & Industrial Moulds Equipment Exhibition
Venue: Yantai International Expo Center, Yantai, Shandong
Established Year: 2003
Frequency: Annual
Market Area: International
Participated Fee: Standard Booth USD 1,200/booth, Raw Space USD 120/m^2, Outdoor USD 100/m^2
Statistics 2010: Exhibition Area 10,000m^2, Exhibitors 400
Organizer: Yantai Jinnoc Exhibition Co Ltd
Address: Room 2218, 117 Nan Da Jie, Yantai, Shandong

2011/05/19 - 21
☎ 0535-666 3138
🖷 0535-886 8272
✉ ytjn6663198@163.com
www.ytjinnuo.com
6460

2011年烟台国际物流及仓储设备展览会
地点：烟台国际博览中心，山东烟台
内容：物料搬运设备、仓储设备、起重设备、包装设备、输送设备及物流系统、港口设备与技术、物流配送车辆、物流控制和软件
始办年份：2011
首届
周期：每年一届
市场范围：全国性
性质：面向贸易观众
主办：中国机电产品流通协会；烟台市人民政府；青岛金诺会展有限公司
地址：烟台市芝罘区南大街117号文化宫大厦2218房间（264000）
联系人：刘肖

Yantai Logistics and Storage Equipment Exhibition
Venue: Yantai International Expo Center, Yantai, Shandong
Established Year: 2011
First Session
Frequency: Annual
Market Area: National
Nature: Trade Only
Organizer: Yantai Jinnoc Exhibition Co Ltd
Address: Room 2218, 117 Nan Da Jie, Yantai, Shandong

2011/05/19 - 21
☎ 0535-666 3138
🖷 0535-668 6272
✉ yanglie1023@163.com
www.ytjinnuo.com
6470

2011第九届烟台国际工业自动化及仪器仪表展览会
地点：烟台国际博览中心，山东烟台
内容：仪器仪表：传感器、调节器、敏感元件及测量装置、变送器、传感器、测试仪、计量仪、指示器、电子测量 仪器、电工仪表、执行器及调节阀、定位器、称重装置、信号处理器、智能化仪表、分析和光学仪器、实验 室仪器及设备；控制系统：变频器、监控及数据采集系统、过程自动化控制系统、工厂自动化控制系统、混合控制系统、现 场总线控制系统、安全及危险系统、工业以太网、IPC及嵌入式控制系统、过程控制用OLE、电气传动及运动 控制系统、无线电系统；仪表材料元器件及附件；工业机器人及相关技术；自动化及IT解决方案
始办年份：2003
周期：每年一届
市场范围：国际性
性质：面向公众
入场券价格：免费
参展费用：5,800元/展位
主办：烟台金诺会展有限公司
地址：烟台市南大街117号文化宫大厦2218室
联系人：杨丽娥
QQ：113084384

2011 The 9th Yantai International Industrial Automation & Instrument Exhibition
Venue: Yantai International Expo Center, Yantai, Shandong
Established Year: 2003
Frequency: Annual
Market Area: International
Nature: Open to Public
Cost to Attend: Free
Participated Fee: RMB 5,800/booth
Organizer: Yantai Jinnoc Exhibition Co Ltd
Address: Room 2218, 117 Nan Da Jie, Yantai, Shandong

2011/05/19 - 21
☎ 0535-666 3138
🖷 0535-668 6272
✉ yanglie1023@163.com
www.ytjinnuo.com
6480

第九届烟台国际动力传动及控制技术展览会
地点：烟台国际博览中心，山东烟台
内容：液压元件，气动元件，流体动力元件，压缩空气技术，密封技术，阀门，减速机，机械传动元件，传动配件，机械传动元件，轴承，电能传动。
始办年份：2003
周期：每年一届
市场范围：国际性
主办：烟台金诺会展有限公司
地址：烟台市南大街117号文化宫大厦2218室
联系人：杨丽娥
QQ：113084384

Yantai Power Transmission and Control Technology Exhibition
Venue: Yantai International Expo Center, Yantai, Shandong
Established Year: 2003
Frequency: Annual
Market Area: International
Organizer: Yantai Jinnoc Exhibition Co Ltd
Address: Room 2218, 117 Nan Da Jie, Yantai, Shandong

2011/05/19 - 21
☎ 0535-666 3138
🖷 0535-668 6272
✉ ytzhanhui@163.com
www.ytjinnuo.com
6490

第九届烟台国际机床暨工模具技术设备展览会
地点：烟台国际博览中心，山东烟台
内容：机床类；机床零部件及辅助设备类 ；锻压机械类；模具及配套件类等。
始办年份：2003
周期：每年一届
市场范围：国际性
性质：面向公众
入场券价格：免费
参展费用：5,800元/展位
上届规模 2010：展览面积20,000m²(国外展商5,000m²)，参展商400家（国外展商50家，来自3个国家），参观人数50,000人（专业贸易观众9,000人）
主办：中国机电产品流通协会
地址：烟台市南大街117号文化宫大厦2218室（264000）
联系人：李欣
QQ：1256156378

The 9th Yantai International Machine Tools & Industrial Mould Technology and Equipment Exhibition
Venue: Yantai International Expo Center, Yantai, Shandong
Established Year: 2003
Frequency: Annual
Market Area: International
Nature: Open to Public
Cost to Attend: Free
Participated Fee: RMB 5,800/booth
Statistics 2010: Exhibition Area 20,000m²(foreigners 5000m²), Exhibitors 400（foreigners 50, came from 3 countries）, Visitors 50,000（trade visitors 9,000）**Organizer**: Yantai Jinnoc Exhibition Co Ltd
Contact: Li Xin

2011/09/01 - 05
☎ 010-8260 6880转ext 91
🖷 010-8260 6883
✉ ciccyhuang@cnaico.com.cn
www.cnaico.com.cn
www.autochina.com.cn
6495

2011（第七届）烟台国际汽车展示交易会
地点：山东烟台
主办：中国汽车工业国际合作总公司
地址：北京市海淀区中关村丹棱街3号A座

7th Yantai Intl Automobile Show
Venue: Yantai, Shandong
Organizer: China National Automotive Industry International Corp

2011/10/18 - 21
☎ 0535-6611 833, 6280 001
🖷 0535-6280 002
✉ yantai@fruitveg-expo.cn
www.fruitveg-expo.cn
6498

第十一届国际果蔬、食品博览会
地点：烟台国际博览中心，山东烟台
内容：专业设备展区、北方果蔬展区、东盟果蔬展区：东盟国家特色干果、鲜果及制成品、蔬菜及加工产品等；台湾果蔬展区、江南果蔬展区、食品展区、水产品展区；饮料、茶叶、酒类展区、农用资料展区；种苗、花卉展区 农机展区
始办年份：1999
周期：每年两届
市场范围：国际性
性质：面向公众
上届规模 ‘08：展览面积6,000m²(国外展商面积1,200m²)，参展商480家（国外展商100家，来自15个国家），参观人数60,000人（专业贸易观众50,000人）
主办：联合国亚洲及太平洋经济社会委员会；联合国亚太农业工程与机械中心；联合国亚太技术转让中心
承办：烟台市政府；山东省商务厅；山东省科学技术厅；山东省农业厅；山东省林业局；山东省供销合作社联合社；山东省农业机械管理办公室
地址：山东省烟台市朝阳街80号绮丽大厦三楼（294008）
联系人：王晓燕，孔艳玲
QQ: 20584045

11th International Fruit/Vegetable/Food Exposition
Venue: Yantai International Expo Center, Yantai, Shandong
Profile: The Machinery Equipments Featured Exhibition The Northern Fruit and Vegetable Pavilion The Assn of Southeast Asian Nations (ASEAN) Fruit and Vegetable Pavilion The Chinese Taipei Fruit and Vegetable Pavilion The Southern Fruit and Vegetable Pavilion The Food Pavilion The Aquatic Products Pavilion The Beverage Pavilion. The Agricultural Materials Pavilion The Seeds and Seedlings, Flowers Pavilion The Agricultural Machinery Pavilion
Established Year: 1999
Frequency: Biannual
Market Area: International
Nature: Open to public
Statistics‘08: Exhibition Area 6,000m²(foreigners 1,200m²), Exhibitors 480（foreigners 100, came from 15 countries）, Trade Visitors 50,000
Organizer: United Nations Economic and Social Commission for Asia; Pacific (ESCAP); United Nations Asian and Pacific Center for Agricultural Engineering and Machinery (APCAEM-ESCAP), Asian and Pacific Center for Transfer of Technology (APCTT-ESCAP)
Address: 3rd Fl, Qili Mansion, 80 Chaoyang St, Yantai 264001, Shandong, China
Contact: Ms Amanda Wang, Ms Kerry Kong

山西-太原 Shanxi-Taiyuan

2011/05/12 - 14
☎ 0351-562 4103, 562 4104, 562 4105
🖷 0351-562 4101
✉ xinte@hope-tarsus.com
www.cwmee.com
6500

2011中国中西部（太原）医疗器械展览会
地点：山西省展览馆国际馆，山西太原
内容：诊断设备：超声诊断设备、X线影像诊断设备、心脑电监护设备、扫描设备、生化检测设备、康复理疗设备、功能检查设备、病理诊断设备、内窥镜检查设备、光学仪器及神经科、骨科、五官科、眼科、骨科等检查诊断设备。治疗设备：内外科手术设备、放射治疗设备、核医学治疗设备、激光设备、理疗设备、低温冷冻治疗设备、透析治疗设备、急救设备、麻醉和止痛设备及病房护理设备。辅助设备；卫生材料及用品；口腔设备及用品
市场范围：全国性
参展费用：净地6,800元/9m^2（36m^{2}起），标准展位：A区5,800元/9m^2，B区4,800元/9m^2
主办：全国医药技术市场协会；山西省医疗器械工业公司；中英合资好博塔苏斯展览公司
承办：湖北好博塔苏斯展览有限公司；太原新特展贸策划有限公司
联系人：吴怀顺

Taiyuan Medical Equipment Exhibition
Venue: Shanxi Exhibition Hall, Taiyuan, Shanxi
Market Area: National
Participated Fee: Raw Space Raw Space RMB 6,800/9m^2（min 36m^2），Standard Booth RMB 5,800/booth
Organizer: Taiyuan Xinte Exhibition Co

2011/06/03 - 05
☎ 010-8260 6880转ext 91
🖷 010-8260 6883
✉ ciccyhuang@cnaico.com.cn
www.cnaico.com.cn
www.autochina.com.cn
6510

第三届中国(太原)国际卡车暨物流展览会
地点：山西太原
主办：中国汽车工业国际合作总公司
地址：北京市海淀区中关村丹棱街3号A座

3rd China (Taiyuan) Truck and Logistics Exhibition
Venue: Taiyuan, Shanxi
Organizer: China National Automotive Industry International Corp

2011/06/03 - 06
☎ 010-8260 6880转ext 91
🖷 010-8260 6883
✉ ciccyhuang@cnaico.com.cn
www.cnaico.com.cn
www.autochina.com.cn
6520

2011第二届中国(太原)国际汽车展览
地点：山西太原
主办：中国汽车工业国际合作总公司
地址：北京市海淀区中关村丹棱街3号A座

2nd China (Taiyuan) Intl Automobile Exhibition
Venue: Taiyuan, Shanxi
Organizer: China National Automotive Industry International Corp

四川-成都 Sichuan-Chengdu

2011 -
☎ 010-8455 6677
🖷 010-6202 3887
www.pharmchina.com.cn
6530

第65 届全国药品交易会
地点：成都世纪城国际会展中心，四川成都
内容：中国最大规模的医药制剂及相关技术、服务交易会之一。范围有化学药品展区、中成药展区、生物制药展区、医药软技术展区、非处方药展示区、健康产品展区
周期：每年两届
主办：国药励展展览有限责任公司
地址：北京朝阳区新源南路1-3号平安国际金融中心B座15层（100027）

65th PharmChina
Venue: City-New International Exhibition & Convention Center, Chengdu, Sichuan, Chengdu, Sichuan
Profile: PHARMCHINA is the largest exhibition in Chinese pharmaceutical industry. Product & Service: Chemical Pharmaceuticals, Chinese patent medicines, Traditional Chinese Medicine, Biopharmaceuticals, OTC medicines, Healthcare products, PharmSoft (Pharmaceutical technologies & services)
Frequency: Biannual
Organizer: Reed Sinopharm Exhibitions

2011/02/20 - 22
☎ 028-8600 8777转ext 811
🖷 028-8600 9111
✉ sc8y@163.com
6540

2011德纳成都国际LED展览会及四新广告展览会
地点：成都世纪城新国际会展中心，四川成都
内容：LED照明：LED路灯/隧道灯、LED户外/室内照明、LED交通/汽车灯、太阳能LED灯及L饰配件等；LED显示屏：户外/室内显示屏、全彩/双色/单色显示屏、控制系统、LED/LCD电视等；LED广告光源：发光字、标识、招牌、模组、灯箱、灯条、护栏管、霓虹灯、控制器等；LED封装及配套材料：贴片LED、大功

Chengdu LED and Advertising Exhibition
Venue: City-New International Exhibition & Convention Center, Chengdu, Sichuan, Chengdu, Sichuan
Established Year: 2011
First Session
Frequency: Annual
Market Area: National

率LED、数码管、点阵模块、有机硅、环氧胶、荧光粉等；LED背光源、LED芯片、外延片、磊晶片及相关基材等；LED制造设备及测试仪器
始办年份：2011
首届
周期：每年一届
市场范围：全国性
性质：面向公众
主办：中国轻工业对外经济技术合作公司；德纳展览集团
地址：四川省成都市锦江区橡树林路166号1栋1单元3305（629010）
联系人：袁旭成

Nature: Open to Public
Organizer: 2011 Donnor Exhibition Group
Address: 1-1-335, 166 Xiangshulin Road, Jinjiang District, Chengdu 629010, Sichuan

2011/03/25 - 28
☎ 010-6831 2733, 6836 0997, 6836 5088
🖷 010-6831 7408
✉ info@qgtjh.com
www.qgtjh.com

6550

2011年春季全国糖酒会
地点：成都世纪城新国际会展中心，四川成都
内容：全国食品行业的重要经济活动。于每年春、秋两季举办两次。糖业及其制品、酒类、各类饮料和粮酿制品以及各类食品、添加剂、食品包装、加工机械的销售或生产
始办年份：1955年
周期：每年两届
性质：面向贸易观众
参展费用：葡萄酒及国际烈酒馆，葡萄酒、国际烈酒、进口食品馆：特优净地560元/m²，简特展位5,000元/9m²；非葡萄酒、国际烈酒、进口食品馆、非食品机械展区：特优净地370元/m²，普通净地340元/m²，标准展位3,200元/9m²，简特展位3,600元/9m²；食品机械展区：标准展位4,000元/9m²；包装展区：标准展位3,000元/9m²
主办：全国糖酒商品交易会办公室；中国副食流通协会
承办：全国糖酒商品交易会办公室
地址：北京西城区西外大街110号中糖大厦3层（100044）

China National Sugar and Alcoholic Commodities Fair
Venue: City-New International Exhibition & Convention Center, Chengdu, Sichuan, Chengdu, Sichuan
Established Year: 1995
Frequency: Biannual
Nature: Trade Only
Participated Fee: RMB 560/m², RMB 5,000/booth (9m²)
Organizer: Chengdu Municipal Government; Office of China National Sugar and Alcoholic Commodities Fair
Address: 3/Fl, 110 Xi Wai Street, Xicheng District, Beijing 100044

2011/03/29 - 31
☎ 028-8408 7596
🖷 028-8408 7059
✉ cdfxb100@qq.com
www.zxbyq.com

6560

2011第四届成都国际教育技术装备及高教仪器展览会
地点：成都世纪城新国际会展中心，四川成都
内容：各种适用于基础教育、职业教育、高等教育的教育技术装备、仪器和材料：教学仪器及成套设备、实验室与教室专用器具、图书馆设备、教学用标本模型、教具、教学用品印刷及复印设备、教育图书教材、教学资源光盘、优秀教学课件、学校用家具、学生公寓用品、学校体育用品 设施、特殊教育设备仪器等。IT信息技术设备及软件；电化教学及影音视频设备；远距离教育设备；实验室仪器、设备与材料
周期：每年一届
市场范围：全国性
入场券价格：免费
参展费用：标准展位6,800元/9m²，净地800元/m²
上届规模 2010：展览面积12,000m²，参展商200家（国外展商20家，来自个国家
主办：中国教育技术协会职业教育技术专业委员会；中国电子视像行业协会大屏幕显示设备分会；成都市教学仪器设备行业协会；四川省分析测试学会
承办：成都风向标科技展览有限公司
地址：成都市锦华路8号万达广场一单元2903室（610021）
联系人：文敏小姐，梅荣志先生
QQ：39979639

2011 4th Chengdu International Education and Higher Education Exhibition on Technology and Equipment
Venue: City-New International Exhibition & Convention Center, Chengdu, Sichuan, Chengdu, Sichuan
Frequency: Annual
Market Area: National
Cost to Attend: Free
Participated Fee: Standard Booth RMB 6,800/9m², Raw Space RMB 800/m²
Statistics 2010: Exhibition Area 12,000m², Exhibitors 200 (foreigners 20)
Organizer: Chengdu Fengxiaobiao Exhibition Co Ltd

2011/03/29 - 31
☎ 028-8408 7596
🖷 028-8408 7059
✉ cdfxb100@qq.com
www.zxbyq.com

6570

2011第六届中国西部国际科学仪器及实验室装备展览会
地点：成都世纪城新国际会展中心，四川成都
内容：分析测试仪器：光学仪器及设备、电子光学仪器；实验室仪器与设备、实验室家具及配套设备；生化仪器、生命科学及微生物检测仪器；材料力学性能试验设备、无损检测仪器 食品安全检测仪器；石油、化工及矿用仪器；环境监测仪器；计量仪器、电工测量仪表；测绘勘探仪器；化学试剂和标准物质
周期：每年一届
市场范围：全国性
入场券价格：免费
参展费用：标准展位6,800元/9m²，净地800元/m²
上届规模 2010：展览面积12,000m²，参展商200家（国外展商20家）
主办：四川省分析测试学会；四川省分析测试服务中心；中国仪器仪表学会科学仪器学术工作专委会
承办：四川省分析测试学会；成都风向标科技展览有限公司
地址：成都市锦华路8号万达广场一单元2903室（610021）
联系人：文敏小姐，梅荣志先生
QQ：39979639

2011 6th Western China International Exhibition for Scientific Instruments and Laboratory Equipment, IESILE
Venue: City-New International Exhibition & Convention Center, Chengdu, Sichuan, Chengdu, Sichuan
Frequency: Annual
Market Area: National
Cost to Attend: Free
Participated Fee: Standard Booth RMB 6,800/9m², Raw Space RMB 800/m²
Statistics 2010: Exhibition Area 12,000m², Exhibitors 200 (foreigners 20)
Organizer: Chengdu Fengxiaobiao Exhibition Co Ltd
Address: Room 2903, 8 Jinhua Road, Chengdu 610021, Sichuan

2011/03/29 - 31
☎ 028-6827 6845
🖷 028-6816 8911
✉ 68168911@vip.163.com
www.chengdulighting.com
6580

2011第11届中国成都国际照明博览会
地点：成都世纪城新国际会展中心，四川成都
内容：专业/户外照明：室外/街道照明，办公室及工厂照明，建筑照明、商业照明、工程照明，体育馆照明、园林、公共场所照明，防爆、工矿照明；室内照明（室内灯饰、灯具）：吊灯，落地灯、台灯、壁灯，现代与传统照明；LED照明：LED灯具，LED芯片、外延片、磊晶片及相关基材，LED封装及器件，LED显示屏，LED生产及研发设备和测试仪器；光源：电灯泡，节能灯泡，发光二极管技术，电灯附件，灯罩，原材料与组装技术；照明电工产品及附件；专业灯光及其它照明控制系统、生产设备、仪器、新闻媒体。
始办年份：2001
周期：每年一届
市场范围：全国性
主办：四川省市政市容协会；重庆市城市道路照明协会；四川省照明电器协会；四川新中联展览服务有限公司
地址：四川省成都市抚琴西路181号群益大厦7楼A座（610072）
联系人：张赫

2011 Chengdu International Lighting Fair
Venue: City-New International Exhibition & Convention Center, Chengdu, Sichuan, Chengdu, Sichuan
Established Year: 2001
Frequency: Annual
Market Area: National
Organizer: Sichuan Xin Zhong Lian Exhibition Services Co Ltd

2011/04/15 - 18
☎ 028-8612 5488, 8612 6488
🖷 028-8612 7488, 8612 9488
✉ fengqianying2004@163.com
www.meibohui.com
6590

2011第25届(春季)成都美容美发节
地点：四川科技馆(原四川省展览馆)，四川成都
内容：专业美容产品、护肤品、美容仪器设备及技术；医学整形产品、设备、技术及材料；美发用品和仪器、纹绣、纹刺、美甲、彩妆及化妆用品；日化洗涤产品及足疗产品；OEM加工、美容美发产品的包装、原料、机械；美容美发行业媒体
始办年份：1997
周期：每年两届
性质：面向贸易观众
参展费用：4,000～8,000元
上届规模 2010：展览面积10,000m²(国外展商36m²)，参展商252家（国外展商2家，来自2个国家），参观人数30,000人（专业贸易观众26,000人）
主办：四川美容美发行业商会；成都市美发美容协会
地址：四川省成都市上南大街2号长富花园2栋16楼5号（610041）
联系人：冯小姐
QQ：345219351

25th Spring Chengdu Beauty, Hairdressing and Cosmetics Festival
Venue: Sichuan Science Center, Chengdu, Sichuan
Established Year: 1997
Frequency: Biannual
Nature: Trade Only
Participated Fee: RMB 4,000-8,000/booth
Statistics 2010: Exhibition Area 10,000m²(foreigners 36m²), Exhibitors 252（foreigners 2, came from 2 countries）, Visitors 30,000（trade visitors 26,000）
Organizer: Chengdu Hairdressing and Beauty Association

2011/04/21 - 23
☎ 010-8455 6677
🖷 010-6235 8733
✉ yini.zhang@reedsinopharm.com
xinwei.zhao@reedsinopharm.com
www.interphexchina.com
6600

世界制药工业展中国展区
（原包装材料、制药设备区）
地点：成都世纪城国际会展中心，四川成都
内容：医药包装与机械。医药原料药、中间体、化工原料、药用辅料、药品包装、制药设备、天然原料和中药设备等相关领域的展览集中展示，现与世界制药工业展中国展区联合举办，力图使国内外参展企业和专业观众尽享"一站式"集中采购、服务、信息交流的便利。
周期：每年两届
上届规模 2010：展览面积55,000m²，参展商1,400家，参观人数30,000人
主办：国药励展展览有限责任公司
地址：北京朝阳区新源南路1-3号平安国际金融中心B座15层（100027）

INTERPHEX CHINA
Conference & Exhibition
Venue: City-New International Exhibition & Convention Center, Chengdu, Sichuan **Profile**: Benefiting from being co-located with API China's over 800 pharmaceutical ingredients, intermediate and fine chemicals manufacturers which attracts 35,000 visitors, INTERPHEX CHINA will provide a unique platform for its exhibitors to see significant buyers from all parts of the pharmaceutical manufacturing chain.
Frequency: Biannual
Statistics 2010: Exhibition Area 55,000m², Exhibitors 1,400, Visitors 30,000
Organizer: Reed Sinopharm Exhibitions
Address: 15th Floor Tower B, Ping An International Financial Center, No.1-3 Xinyuan South Road, Chaoyang District. Beijing, China

2011/04/21 - 23
☎ 010-8455 6677, 8455 6536
🖷 010-6235 8733
✉ yini.zhang@reedsinopharm.com
xinwei.zhao@reedsinopharm.com
www.apichina.com.cn
6620

第66届中国国际医药原料药、中间体、包装、设备交易会
地点：成都世纪城国际会展中心，四川成都
内容：原料药、中间体、化工原料、药用辅料、药品包装、制药设备等。API CHINA & INTERPHEX CHINA专注于提高中国医药原料药、中间体、医药包装材料、制药设备企业生产、研发的整体水平，为公众提供安全、健康的用药保障。已形成1000余家原料药生产企业、300余家医药包装企业、200余家制药设备企业及3万余名海内外专业观众的规模。API CHINA 和 INTERPHEX CHINA的联合举办。
周期：每年两届
市场范围：国际性
性质：面向公众
主办：国药励展展览有限责任公司
地址：朝阳区新源南路1-3号平安国际金融中心B座15层（100027）
联系人：张旖旎

The 66th API China
INTERPHEX China
Venue: City-New International Exhibition & Convention Center, Chengdu, Sichuan, Chengdu, Sichuan
Profile: API China is China's leading exhibition for the pharmaceutical manufacturing sector covering the complete spectrum of products from raw material, fine chemical, intermediate, ingredients, processing machinery and packaging machinery. It is an event for international buyers to meet Asian sellers especially Chinese ingredients manufacturers.
Frequency: Biannual
Organizer: Reed Sinopharm Exhibitions
Address: 15th Floor Tower B, Ping An International Financial Center, No.1-3 Xinyuan South Road, Chaoyang District. Beijing, China
Contact: Yini Zhang

2011/05/13 - 16
☎ 010-8718 3962
🖷 010-6710 2689, 6719 2832
✉ info@sportshow.com.cn
www.sportshow.com.cn

6630

2011(第28届)中国国际体育用品博览会
地点：成都世纪城新国际会展中心，四川成都
内容：国家体育总局扶持培育的品牌展会。亚太规模最大，最权威的体育用品专业展，是全球买家采购的中心，是民族产品拓展国际市场的桥梁，是经销代理商采购与合作的平台。展会涵盖运动服饰和水上装备，户外休闲运动用品，健身器材及配件，网羽、球类运动，场馆器材/设施，轮滑和自行车运动
始办年份：1993
周期：每年两届
上届规模 2010：展览面积100,000m^2，参展商1,000家（来自30个国家），参观人数150,000人（专业贸易观众50,000人）
主办：国家体育总局；中华全国体育总会；中国奥林匹克委员会；中国体育用品业联合会；中国体育科学学会；国家体育总局体育器材装备中心；成都市人民政府；华兴体育用品发展中心
地址：北京市崇文区体育馆路3号（100763）
联系人：侯亮
MSN：hou1978@hotmail.com
QQ：11779441

China Sport Show 2011
Venue: City-New International Exhibition & Convention Center, Chengdu, Sichuan
Profile: The only national-class internationalized and professionalized trade show for the sports industry. It is also the largest and most influential sporting goods show in the Asia-Pacific region. As a fast developing brand show, depending on the organizers' strong industry resources, China Sport Show is helping to boost the sports brands. Take the advantage of China Sport Show, present your brands, and promote your business worldwide. Categories: Sportswear and leisure apparel, Outdoor sports equipment, Cycling equipment & accessories, Skates & boards equipment, Fitness equipment and accessories, Stadium and gym facilities, Ball game and racket equipment
Established Year: 1993
Frequency: Biannual
Statistics 2010: Exhibition Area 100,000m^2, Exhibitors 1,000（came from 30 countries）, Visitors 150,000（trade visitors 50,000）
Sponsor: China General Administration of Sport All-China Sports Federation Chinese Olympic Committee China Sporting Goods Federation China Sports Science Society
Organizer: Sports Equipment Administrative Center of China General Administration of Sport; Chengdu Municipal Government
Address: Address：No.3, Tiyuguan Road, Chongwen District, Beijing, 100763, China
Contact: Hou Liang
MSN: hou1978@hotmail.com

2011/05/23 - 25
☎ 028-8777 9557
🖷 028-6817 9768
✉ djzl888@126.com

6640

2011中国西部工程机械建筑机械及混凝土设备展览会
地点：成都世纪城新国际会展中心，四川成都
内容：工程机械及设备：挖掘机械、装载机、路面机械、压实机械、桩工机械、起重机械、路桥设备、起重运输设备、平地机、铲土运输机械、凿岩机械、钢筋机械、筑桥机械设备、沥青搅拌站、沥青摊铺机、市政工程机械及其它成套焊接设备、空压机设备、柴油发电机组、风动工具、水中控井、隧道施工用成套设备与机械、钻机、打桩机、拔桩机、各种零件及附件、维修检测与技术设备；工程专用车辆；建筑机械及设备；混凝土生产及运输设备；路桥检测和试验仪器。
市场范围：全国性
性质：面向贸易观众
参展费用：总冠名费39万元，协办赞助 28万元/18万元/10万元；标准展位(3x3m)A区6,800元，B区5,800元；双开A区7,480元，B区6,380元；净地800元/m^2（36m^{2}起），室外600元/m^2
上届规模 2010：展览面积32,000m^2，参观人数30,000人
主办：四川省工商联工程机械行业商会；中国矿山物资流通协会
承办：成都鼎坚展览服务有限公司
地址：成都市永陵路17号11F-G座
联系人：王简

West China Construction Machinery and Concrete Machinery Exhibition
Venue: City-New International Exhibition & Convention Center, Chengdu, Sichuan
Market Area: National
Nature: Trade Only
Participated Fee: Standard Booth RMB 6,800/9m^2, Raw Space (min 36m^2) Indoor RMB 800/m^2, Outdoor RMB 600/m^2
Statistics 2010: Exhibition Area 32,000m^2, Visitors 30,000
Organizer: Chengdu Ding Jian Exhibition and Service Co Ltd
Address: 11F-G, 17 Yongling Road, Chengdu, Sichuan
Contact: Wang Jian

2011/06/17 - 19
☎ 0755-3398 9211, 3398 9230
🖷 0755-3333 1168
www.reedhuabo.com

6650

成都家居、休闲用品及礼品展览会
地点：成都世纪城新国际会展中心，四川成都
内容：礼品家居用品行业拓展中国西部市场的专业平台。
周期：每年一届
性质：面向贸易观众
预计规模：展览面积16,000m^2，参展商500家
主办：励展华博展览（深圳）有限公司
地址：深圳市中心区福华三路深圳国际商会中心1801、1802室（518048）
联系人：袁文军，王清林

2011 Chengdu Houseware, Leisure Goods & Gifts Fair
Venue: City-New International Exhibition & Convention Center, Chengdu, Sichuan
Profile: The perfect trade show if you are an distributor, trader or large-scale retailer who buys products in volume, Meet with the manufacturers from China who supply international quality OEM and finished products to buyers around the world
Frequency: Annual
Nature: Trade Only
Organizer: Reed Sinopharm Exhibitions
Contact: Yuan Wenjun, Wang Qinglin

2011/06/23 - 25
☎ 028-6196 3015, 6196 3056
🖷 028-6196 3056
✉ sch@ccpit.org
yangduanjie529@yahoo.com.cn
www.ccpit-sichuan.org

6660

第三届中国国际名酒博览会
地点：成都世纪城新国际会展中心，四川成都
内容：酒类产品：白酒、红酒、黄酒、洋酒、果露酒、保健酒。酒类设备：生产设备、贮藏设备、运输设备。酒文化及酒具：酒标、酒产品收藏、酒具。名酒名镇、酒类工业发展园区。
始办年份：2004
周期：两年一届
市场范围：国际性
上届规模 2007：展览面积8,000m^2，专业贸易观众80,000人
主办：中国贸促会；四川省人民政府；四川省贸促会
地址：四川成都市蜀兴西街36号国际商会大楼10-12楼（610036）
联系人：杨端洁

3rd China International Premier Wine & Spirits Exhibition
Venue: City-New International Exhibition & Convention Center, Chengdu, Sichuan
Profile: Wine Product: liquor, white wine, red wine, beer, brandy, yellow wine, healthy wine, champagne, shirley, sparkling wine, sweet wine, vermouth, peter snow liquor etc. Wine Equipment: wine packaging, wine transportation, wine storage technology, wine producing machinery. Wine Culture & Tool: label, wine collection, vessel of wine; Others：Famous wine brands and towns, wine industry development zones
Established Year: 2004
Frequency: Biennial
Market Area: International
Statistics 2007: Exhibition Area 8,000m^2, Trade Visitors 80,000
Organizer: CCPIT; People's Government of Sichuan Province; CCPIT Sichuan Council
Address: 10-12/F, Sichuan Chamber of International Commerce Building, No.36, Shuxing Street West, Chengdu, Sichuan, China
Contact: Catherine Yang

2011/07/03 - 06
☎ 028 -8628 0489
🖷 028-86280 491
✉ cdiff@neweastfair.com
www.iffcd.com
6670

第12届成都国际家具工业展览会
地点： 成都世纪城新国际会展中心，四川成都
内容： 民用家具、家居饰品、木工机械
始办年份： 2000
周期： 每年一届
市场范围： 国际性
参展费用： 标准展位4,500元/9m^2，净地500元/m^2
上届规模 2010：展览面积110,000m^2，参展商600家，参观人数110,000人（专业贸易观众60,000人）
主办： 成都市人民政府；四川省商务厅
承办： 中国贸促会成都市分会；四川省家具进出口商会
地址： 成都市人民中路一段28号房地大厦1601室（610015）
联系人： 姜华
QQ：735520965

International Furniture Fair Chengdu
Venue: City-New International Exhibition & Convention Center, Chengdu, Sichuan
Established Year: 2000
Frequency: Annual
Market Area: International
Participated Fee: Standard Booth RMB 4,500/9m^2，Raw Space RMB 500/m^2
Statistics 2010: Exhibition Area 11,0000m^2, Exhibitors 600，Visitors 110,000（trade visitors 60,000）
Organizer: Committee of Furniture Fair
Address: Room 1601, 28 Yiduan, Middle Renmin Road, Chengdu 610015, Sichuan

2011/08/12 - 15
☎ 028-6196 3041, 6196 3055, 6196 3046
🖷 028-6196 3041, 6196 3046
www.ccpit-sichuan.org
6680

2011中国西部国际服装服饰博览会
地点： 成都世纪城新国际会展中心，四川成都
内容： 国际著名高端品牌服装服饰展区主要展示国际著名高端品牌服装、箱包、饰品。创意设计展区主要展示国际国内纺织服装院校、纺织服装设计创意专业公司、工作室等，拟展出面积1000平方米。国内品牌服装服饰展区主要展示国内著名服装服饰品牌。纺织面、辅料展区主要展示各种纺织面料、针织面料和辅助材料。服装加工制造与纺织机械展区主要展示服装加工厂商、纺织服装加工机械和工具。
始办年份： 2011
首届
周期： 每年一届
市场范围： 国际性
预计规模： 展览面积20,000m^2
主办： 中国贸促会；四川省人民政府；中国服装协会；中国贸促会纺织行业分会；四川省贸促会
地址： 成都市蜀兴西街36号四川省贸促会10楼（610036）
联系人： 唐友均，谭朝宏，程欣，张金蝶

Western China International Clothing & Accessories Fair
Venue: City-New International Exhibition & Convention Center, Chengdu, Sichuan
Profile: Overseas Brands International Clothing & Accessories Companies; Innovative Design Textile-Apparel Related Institute, school, company, studio; Chinese Famous Brands Domestic Clothing & Accessories Companies; Fabrics and Accessories; Textile Machinery
Established Year: 2011
First Session
Frequency: Annual
Market Area: International
Organizer: CCPIT; People's Government of Sichuan Province; China National Garment Association; CCPIT Textile Council; CCPIT Sichuan Council
Address: 10/F, Sichuan Chamber of Intl Commerce Bldg, 36 Shuxing Street West, Chengdu, Sichuan, China
Contact: Mr Tang Youjun, Mr Tan Chaohong, Ms Cheng Xin, Ms Zhang Jindie

2011/09/17 - 25
☎ 021-5045 6700转ext 255, 028-8538 0305
🖷 021-5045 9355, 028-8538 3218
✉ cdms@hmf-china.com
✉ cdms@live.cn
www.cd-motorshow.com
6690

成都国际汽车展览会
地点： 成都世纪城新国际会展中心，四川成都
内容： 各类整车，汽车零部件，汽车售后相关产品，汽车技术展示，汽车专业媒体、俱乐部、协会和服务
周期： 每年一届
市场范围： 国际性
上届规模 2010：参展商399家，参观人数456,850人
主办： 成都市人民政府
承办： 汉诺威米兰展览会（中国）有限公司
地址： 上海市浦东新区银霄路393号百安居浦东商务大厦301室
联系人： 王飞先生
承办： 成都世纪城新国际会展中心
地址： 四川省成都市世纪城路198号世纪城国际会议中心7楼（610041）
联系人： 王渝 女士

Chengdu Motor Show
Venue: City-New International Exhibition & Convention Center, Chengdu, Sichuan
Profile: Autos, Auto Components, After Sales Products, Automobile Technologies, Media, Organizations & Associations, Services
Frequency: Annual
Market Area: International
Statistics 2010: Exhibitors 399，Visitors 456,850
Sponsor: Chengdu People's Municipal Government
Organizer: Hannover Milano Fairs China Ltd；Chengdu International Exhibition & Convention Center
Address: 301 B&Q Pudong Office Tower 393 Yinxiao Rd, Pudong
Contact: Karl Wang

2011/11 -
☎ 010-8455 6510, 13910380501
✉ bingchuan.liu@reedsinopharm.com
www.tcmex.cn
6700

中医药国际科技博览会
地点： 四川成都
内容： 全面覆盖中医中药产业链的贸易平台
主办： 国药励展展览有限责任公司
地址： 北京市朝阳区新源南路1—3号 平安国际金融中心B座15层（100027）
联系人： 刘冰川
QQ：244296719

Traditional Chinese Medicine Exposition
Venue: Chengdu, Sichuan
Organizer: Reed Sinopharm Exhibitions
Address: 15th Floor Tower B, Ping An International Financial Center, No.1-3 Xinyuan South Road, Chaoyang District. Beijing,China

2011/11/15 – 17
☎ 010- 6620 6773，6620 6619，6620 5556
🖷 010-6620 6773
✉ zhanlan@chinagas.org.cn
www.gaschina2011.com
6710

2011年中国国际燃气、供热技术与设备展览会
地点： 成都世纪城新国际会展中心，四川成都
内容： 燃气输配系统新技术及维护管理技术、燃气应用技术；燃气控制检测技术与设备、燃气自动化控制、报警系统、燃气表；天然气存储技术、煤气净化与回收技术；燃气新型专用管材与设备、管道的防腐技术、燃气阀门；燃气锅炉、燃气供热（水）设备、各类燃气用具及零配件等；燃气采暖技术设备、燃气中央空调；地下管线探测、检测、泄漏监测技术设备； 城市燃气领域综合信息管理系统、软件系统；其它与城市燃气有关的技术、设备。
始办年份： 1994
周期： 每年一届
市场范围： 国际性
性质： 面向贸易观众
入场券价格： 免费
参展费用： 10,000元
主办： 中华人民共和国住房和城乡建设部
承办： 中国城市燃气协会
地址： 北京市西城区西直门南小街22号（100035）

Gas & Heating China 2011
Venue: City-New International Exhibition & Convention Center, Chengdu, Sichuan
Established Year: 1994
Frequency: Annual
Market Area: International
Nature: Trade Only
Cost to Attend: Free
Participated Fee: Standard Booth RMB 10,000:-
Organizer: China Gas Association
Address: 22 Nanxiaojie, Xizhimeng, Xicheng District, Beijing 100035

新疆-乌鲁木齐 Xinjiang-Urumqi

2011/05/14 - 16
☎ 0757-2238 1815
🖷 0757-2238 1816
✉ sdpink777@gmail.com
6720

2011年新疆－中亚家用电器、厨卫及消费电子展
地点：新疆国际博览中心，新疆乌鲁木齐
内容：家用电器：冰箱、空调、洗衣机、电暖器、电风扇、微波炉、电烤箱、吸尘器、饮水机、净水装置、测量工具、空气净化器、缝纫设备、灯具、咖啡机、车载电子用品、电熨斗及其他小家电；厨房橱柜：不锈钢橱柜、木质橱柜、防火板橱柜、钢板橱柜、整体橱柜、整体厨房、集成厨房、橱柜台面、智能设备；消费电子；数码影像。
始办年份：2007
周期：每年一届
市场范围：全国性
性质：面向公众
主办：中国贸促会新疆分会；佛山市世博展览有限公司
地址：广东省佛山市顺德区大良宜新路1号银海大厦8楼（528300）
联系人：胡先生

Xinjiang Central Asia Home Appliances and Consumer Electronic
Venue: Xinjiang Intl Exhibition Center, Urumqi, Xinjiang
Established Year: 2007
Frequency: Annual
Market Area: National
Nature: Open to Public
Organizer: Foshan World Expo Co Ltd
Address: 8/Fl, 1 Daliang Yixin Road, Shunde, Foshan, Guangdong 528300

2011/05/19 - 21
☎ 0991-286 6318
🖷 0991-853 1318
✉ ite928@sohu.com
www.xjite.com
6730

2011新疆国际建筑材料博览会
地点：新疆国际博览中心，新疆乌鲁木齐
内容：节能保温材料：建筑保温系统、地面供暖系统、节能门窗、保温、隔热材料、遮阳系统、屋面系统、节电设备、建筑陶瓷节能系列产品、节水技术及设备；新能源利用：太阳能利用、热泵技术；节材产品及设备；门窗；地板；厨卫；建筑陶瓷；配套设施；化学建材；建筑及装饰石材；建筑装饰五金；整体家居；建筑设备及施工机具；消防设备；建材流通市场；建筑幕墙楼宇智能设备
周期：每年一届
市场范围：全国性
性质：面向公众
参展费用：标准展位 5,000元/9mm^2
主办：新疆国际贸易展览公司
地址：新疆乌鲁木齐市新华南路835号（830049）
联系人：林春叶
QQ：84778082

2011 Xinjiang International Building Fair
Venue: Xinjiang Intl Exhibition Center, Urumqi, Xinjiang
Frequency: Annual
Market Area: National
Nature: Open to Public
Participated Fee: Standard Booth RMB 5,000/9m^2
Organizer: Xinjiang International Trade-Exhibition Co
Contact: Lin Chunye

2011/07/22 - 22
☎ 0991-232 1006
🖷 0991-232 1606
✉ liuyang@zhenweiexpo.com
www.xjicme.com.cn
6740

2011第八届中国新疆国际煤炭工业博览会
地点：新疆国际博览中心，新疆乌鲁木齐
内容：大型能源企业形象展示；大型煤矿高产高效及安全生产示范形象展示；煤电、煤化工、煤层气开发项目展示；煤矿工程与设计成果专利展示；煤矿开采技术设备与矿山服务设备展示；煤矿安全技术设备及其他辅助设备展示；矿用防爆产品、救援设施及应急设施设备；八、工程机械及专用车辆展示
始办年份：2003
周期：每年一届
市场范围：全国性
主办：新疆维吾尔自治区经济和信息化委员会；新疆维吾尔自治区招商发展局（自治区经协办）；新疆维吾尔自治区煤炭工业管理局；新疆煤矿安全监察局；新疆生产建设兵团安全生产监督管理局；振威展览集团新疆振威国际展览有限公司
地址：新疆乌鲁木齐市政协巷56号汇丰大厦15层M/N座（830002）
联系人：刘洋

Xinjiang Intl Coal Industry Exhibition
Xinjiang International Coal, Mining and Exploration Technology & Equipment Exhibition
Venue: Xinjiang Intl Exhibition Center, Urumqi, Xinjiang
Profile: The government of Xinjiang Uygur Autonomous Region will expedite the construction of the 13 key mining areas and the four bases of coal and electricity, coal chemicals and coal coking in Zhundong,Yili, Tuha and Kubai.
Established Year: 2003
Frequency: Annual
Market Area: National
Organizer: Zhenwei Exhibition Group

2011/08/05 - 07
☎ 020-2336 7917
🖷 020-8216 1389
✉ cailing_2009@yahoo.cn
6750

2011年亚欧照明展
地点：新疆国际会展中心，新疆乌鲁木齐
内容：太阳能照明、LED照明、奈米高效节能照明、户外照明、工业照明、商业照明、室内灯饰照明、电光源、舞台灯光、应急、防爆灯具、特种灯具、电子
始办年份：2010
周期：每年一届
市场范围：地区性
主办：新疆维吾尔自治区住房和城乡建设厅；新疆维吾尔自治区商务厅；中国贸促会新疆分会；乌鲁木齐市商务局；广州利峰展览科技有限公司
地址：广东省广州市天河区车陂路美东花园1号楼903室（510660）
联系人：蔡乃玲

Xinjiang Lighting Exhibition
Venue: Xinjiang Intl Exhibition Center, Urumqi, Xinjiang
Profile: Solar power lighting, LED, industry and commercial lighting, indoor and outdoor lighting, stage and emergency lighting, etc.
Established Year: 2010
Frequency: Annual
Market Area: regional
Organizer: Guangzhou Lifeng Exhibition & Technology Co Ltd

2011/08/12 - 14
☎ 0991-2321 006
🖷 0991-2321 606
✉ y13118@126.com
www.cxiaf.com.cn

6760

2011第11届中国新疆国际农业博览会
地点： 新疆国际博览中心，新疆乌鲁木齐
内容： 氮肥、磷肥、钾肥、生物肥、复合肥、生态肥、有机天然肥、控释肥、复混肥、叶面肥、液肥、冲施肥、微肥、育苗肥、各种菌肥、专用肥料、环保肥料、土壤改良剂、表面活性剂、以及有利于作物增产和改善品质的生物技术和产品。种子、种苗加工、包装、包衣剂机、包装机械设备，穴盘、苗盘、水稻育秧钵体软，种子新品种、新技术及农副相关产品。
始办年份： 2000
周期： 每年一届
市场范围： 全国性
性质： 面向公众
主办： 新疆维吾尔自治区农业厅新疆维吾尔自治区畜牧厅；新疆维吾尔自治区农机局；新疆维吾尔自治区林业厅；新疆生产建设兵团农业局；新疆维吾尔自治区科技厅；新疆生产建设兵团经协办；新疆维吾尔自治区招商发展局（经协办）；新疆维吾尔自治区供销社；新疆维吾尔自治区乡企局；新疆振威国际展览有限公司
地址： 新疆乌鲁木齐市政协巷56号汇丰大厦15层M/N座（830002）
联系人： 刘英

11th Xinjiang Intl Agriculture Fair
Venue: Xinjiang Intl Exhibition Center, Urumqi, Xinjiang
Established Year: 2000
Frequency: Annual
Market Area: National
Nature: Open to Public
Organizer: Zhenwei Exhibition Group
www.cxiaf.com.cn

2010/09/01 - 05
☎ 0991-285 0497, 287 9890
🖷 0991-287 9890, 285 0497
✉ urumqifairoffice@163.com
www.urumqifair.com

6770

中国—亚欧博览会
（乌鲁木齐对外经济贸易洽谈会）
地点： 新疆国际博览中心，新疆乌鲁木齐
内容： 1、面向中西南亚、俄罗斯市场展示中国名优商品； 2、展示中亚及周边国家的资源优势和特色商品； 3、展示中国及周边国家的投资环境和项目，吸引外商投资，鼓励中国企业投资中西亚及俄罗斯市场； 4、展示新疆和内地省市的投资环境和投资合作项目，促进内联合作； 5、举办中西南亚区域经济高层论坛、中外企业家见面会等系列交流活动。
始办年份： 1992
周期： 每年一届
市场范围： 国际性
性质： 面向公众
主办： 中国商务部；中国贸促会；新疆维吾尔自治区人民政府
承办： 中国商务部外贸发展事务局；新疆商务厅；新疆生产建设兵团；新疆招商发展局；乌鲁木齐市人民政府
地址： 新疆乌鲁木齐市新华南路1292号乌洽会办公室（830049）

China Urumqi Foreign Economic Relations & Trade Fair
Venue: Xinjiang International Exhibition Center, Urumqi, Xinjiang
Profile: 1. Showcase the import &export commodities from China and Central, West and South Asian countries; 2. Showcase the advantageous resources and special products from neighboring countries; 3. Showcase the investment environment and cooperation projects from China and neighboring countries, attract foreign investment and encourage Chinese enterprises to invest in Middle, South and West Asian Countries; 4. Showcase the investment environment and cooperation projects of Xinjiang and other provinces in China, promote the domestic cooperation; 5. Hold a series of exchange activities such as Regional Economic Cooperation Forum and business matching.
Established Year: 1992
Frequency: Annual
Market Area: International
Nature: Open to public
Sponsor: Ministry of Commerce of China; China Council for the Promotion of International Trade; The People' s Government of Xinjiang; Uygur Autonomous Region
Organizer: Trade Development Bureau of Ministry of Commerce, PRC; Xinjiang Commerce Department; Urumqi Fair Office of Xinjiang Department of Foreign Trade and Economic Cooperation
Address: Urumqi Fair Office, No. 1292, South Xinhua Road, Urumqi, Xinjiang

云南-昆明 Yunnan-Kunming

2011/03/18 - 20
☎ 028-6697 0755
🖷 028-6196 2761
✉ tryone333@sina.com
www.schzex.com

6780

第四届华展云南广告四新暨LED照明展览会
地点： 昆明国际会展中心，云南昆明
内容： 合巴蜀联谊云贵，促四新搭共享平台"四川广告设备器材展"、"云南广告四新展"、"贵州广告四新展"，资源共享、三地联办、巡回展示。内容包含：广告制作及设备材料、LED显示技术及应用系统设备、广告摄影、影视广告制作及设备、媒体广告设计制作技术及设备、广告传媒
始办年份： 2008
周期： 每年一届
市场范围： 全国性
参展费用： 4,500 元/展位
上届规模 2010：展览面积5,000m^2，参展商80家，参观人数20,000人（专业贸易观众500人）
主办： 四川省包装装潢印刷工业协会
承办： 四川华展文化传播有限公司
地址： 四川省成都市蜀源路1号华府金沙4-2903
联系人： 罗先生,庹先生
QQ：8510867

4th Yunnan Advertising New Technology and New Media Exhibition/ LED Lighting Exhibition
Venue: Kunming Intl Convention & Exhibition Center, Kunming, Yunnan
Established Year: 2008
Frequency: Annual
Market Area: National
Participated Fee: RMB 4,500/booth
Statistics 2010: Exhibition Area 5,000m^2, Exhibitors 80（came from 1 countries）, Visitors 20,000（trade visitors 500）
Organizer: Sichuan Huazhan Cultural Diffusion Co Ltd
Address: 4-2903, 1 Shuyuan Road, Chengdu, Sichuan

2011/06/06 - 10
☎ 0871-313 9277, 316 4305
🖷 0871-316 4304, 316 4305
✉ kmfair@kmfair.org
www.kmsacc.com
6790

第四届南亚展
第四届南亚国家商品展
地点：昆明国际会展中心，云南昆明
内容：第四届南亚国家商品展（简称“南亚展”）是为扩大自南亚进口，平衡双边贸易为目的的进口商品交易会。展洽内容包括纺织服装、矿业资源、医疗制药、仪表仪器、珠宝首饰、工艺制品、海产品、家装建材、软件信息、旅游服务等10大类别，规模达400个标准展位
始办年份：2007
周期：每年一届
市场范围：国际性
性质：面向公众
入场券价格：30元
参展费用：南亚国家展商免展位费
主办：中国商务部；云南省人民政府
承办：云南省人民政府
地址：云南省昆明市北京路175号（650011）
联系人：刘浏,王凡
QQ：55454271

The 4th SACTF Fair
The 4th South Asian Countries Trade Fair
Venue: Kunming Intl Convention & Exhibition Center, Kunming, Yunnan
Profile: The 4th South Asian Countries Trade Fair (The SACTF Fair) is an import trade fair, aimed at enlarging import from South Asian countries and balancing the bilateral trade. There are more than ten kinds of exhibition products, including Textiles & Clothing; Minerals; Medical Devices & Pharmaceutical
Established Year: 2007
Frequency: Annual
Market Area: International
Nature: Open to Public
Cost to Attend: RMB 30:-
Participated Fee: Free to South Asian Countries' Exhibitors
Sponsor: The Ministry of Commerce of the People Republic of China (MOFCOM), the People's Government of Yunnan Province
Organizer: The People's Government of Yunnan Province
Address: Beijing Road 175, Kunming 650011, Yunnan, China
Contact: Liu Liu, Wang Fan

2011/06/06 - 10
☎ 0871-313 9277, 316 4305
🖷 0871-316 4304, 316 4305
✉ kmfair@kmfair.org
www.kmfair.org
6800

第十九届昆交会
– 第十九届中国昆明进出口商品交易会
地点：昆明国际会展中心，云南昆明
内容：第十九届中国昆明进出口商品交易会（简称“第十九届昆交会”）展洽内容包括商品、技术进出口、国内外招商引资及经济技术合作项目洽谈等，设有机电、生物资源、化工矿业等商品专业馆和投资促进、境外来展等专题展馆
始办年份：1993
周期：每年一届
市场范围：国际性
性质：面向公众
入场券价格：30元
参展费用：标准展位5,000元（3x3=9m^2）
主办：商务部；云南、四川、重庆、贵州、广西、西藏六省（区、市）及成都市人民政府
承办：云南省人民政府
地址：云南省昆明市北京路175号（650011）
联系人：刘浏,王凡
QQ：55454271

The 19th Kunming Fair
- The 19th China Import & Export Fair, Kunming
Venue: Kunming Intl Convention & Exhibition Center, Kunming, Yunnan
Profile: Kunming Fair covers import and export trade and technology, investment promotion, and economic and technological cooperation. There are pavilions for all sectors from Machinery & Electronics; Biological Resources; Chemicals & Minerals. There are also them
Established Year: 1993
Frequency: Annual
Market Area: International
Nature: Open to Public
Cost to Attend: RMB 30:-
Participated Fee: Standard Booth RMB 5,000 (3x3=9m^2)
Sponsors: Ministry of Commerce of the People's Republic of China and seven of China's provincial governments – Yunnan, Sichuan, Guizhou, Guangxi, Tibet, Chongqing and Chengdu
Organizer: The People's Government of Yunnan Province
Address: Beijing Road 175, Kunming 650011, Yunnan, China
Contact: Liu Liu, Wang Fan

浙江 Zhejiang

2011/04 -
☎ 010-8260 6880转ext 91
🖷 010-8260 6883
✉ ciccyhuang@cnaico.com.cn
www.cnaico.com.cn
www.autochina.com.cn
6801

品质生活.精品汽车浙江巡回展
地点：浙江
主办：中国汽车工业国际合作总公司
地址：北京市海淀区中关村丹棱街3号A座

Automobile Zhejiang Road Show
Venue: Zhejiang
Organizer: China National Automotive Industry International Corp

2011/05 -
☎ 010-8260 6880转ext 91
🖷 010-8260 6883
✉ ciccyhuang@cnaico.com.cn
www.cnaico.com.cn
www.autochina.com.cn
6802

品质生活.精品汽车浙江巡回展
地点：浙江
主办：中国汽车工业国际合作总公司
地址：北京市海淀区中关村丹棱街3号A座

Automobile Zhejiang Road Show
Venue: Zhejiang
Organizer: China National Automotive Industry International Corp

2011/06 -
☎ 010-8260 6880转ext 91
🖷 010-8260 6883
✉ ciccyhuang@cnaico.com.cn
www.cnaico.com.cn
www.autochina.com.cn
6803

品质生活.精品汽车浙江巡回展
地点：浙江
主办：中国汽车工业国际合作总公司
地址：北京市海淀区中关村丹棱街3号A座

Automobile Zhejiang Road Show
Venue: Zhejiang
Organizer: China National Automotive Industry International Corp

2011/11 -
☎ 010-8260 6880转ext 91
🖷 010-8260 6883
✉ ciccyhuang@cnaico.com.cn
www.cnaico.com.cn
www.autochina.com.cn
6804

品质生活.精品汽车浙江巡回展
地点：浙江
主办：中国汽车工业国际合作总公司
地址：北京市海淀区中关村丹棱街3号A座

Automobile Zhejiang Road Show
Venue: Zhejiang
Organizer: China National Automotive Industry International Corp

2011/12 -
☎ 010-8260 6880转ext 91
🖷 010-8260 6883
✉ ciccyhuang@cnaico.com.cn
www.cnaico.com.cn
www.autochina.com.cn
6805

品质生活.精品汽车浙江巡回展
地点：浙江
主办：中国汽车工业国际合作总公司
地址：北京市海淀区中关村丹棱街3号A座

Automobile Zhejiang Road Show
Venue: Zhejiang
Organizer: China National Automotive Industry International Corp

浙江-杭州 Zhejiang-Hangzhou

2011/04 -
☎ 010-8260 6880转ext 91
🖷 010-8260 6883
✉ ciccyhuang@cnaico.com.cn
www.cnaico.com.cn
www.autochina.com.cn
6810

2011年第五届杭州春季汽车展销会
地点：浙江杭州
主办：中国汽车工业国际合作总公司
地址：北京市海淀区中关村丹棱街3号A座

5th Spring Hangzhou Automobile Fair
Venue: Hangzhou, Zhejiang
Organizer: China National Automotive Industry International Corp

2011/04 -
☎ 010-8260 6880转ext 91
🖷 010-8260 6883
✉ ciccyhuang@cnaico.com.cn
www.cnaico.com.cn
www.autochina.com.cn
6820

2011中国（浙江）改装车、专用车博览会
地点：浙江杭州
主办：中国汽车工业国际合作总公司
地址：北京市海淀区中关村丹棱街3号A座

China (Hangzhou) Modified Mobile and Special Purpose Vehicle Expo
Venue: Hangzhou, Zhejiang
Organizer: China National Automotive Industry International Corp

2011/05/28 - 29
☎ 010-8260 6880转ext 91
🖷 010-8260 6883
✉ ciccyhuang@cnaico.com.cn
www.cnaico.com.cn
www.autochina.com.cn
6830

2011年第二届中国（浙江）汽配交易会
地点：浙江杭州
主办：中国汽车工业国际合作总公司
地址：北京市海淀区中关村丹棱街3号A座

2nd China (Hangzhou) Auto Part Fair
Venue: Hangzhou, Zhejiang
Organizer: China National Automotive Industry International Corp

2011/10/20 - 24
☎ 010-8260 6880转91
🖷 010-8260 6883
✉ ciccyhuang@cnaico.com.cn
www.cnaico.com.cn
www.autochina.com.cn
6835

2011年第十二届中国杭州国际汽车工业展览会
地点：浙江杭州
主办：中国汽车工业国际合作总公司
地址：北京市海淀区中关村丹棱街3号A座

12nd China Hangzhou Intl Automobile Industry Exhibition
Venue: Hangzhou, Zhejiang
Organizer: China National Automotive Industry International Corp

2011/11/03 - 05
☎ 0571-8577 9755
🖷 0571-8577 9709
✉ ecsef@sinobal.com
expo.ecsef-hz.com

6840

第五届中国（杭州）国际清洁能源与环保产业展览会
地点：浙江世贸中心，浙江杭州
内容：清洁能源：太阳能光伏发电设备及零部、风力发电设备及零部件、生物质能、地热能、清洁煤技术；节能技术与产品：节能建筑及新型建材、绿色照明、太阳能热水器及零部件、节能电器；环境监测与评估：监测分析仪器、空气净化、环境信息系统；低碳技术：碳捕捉与存放技术、碳交易服务商；固体废弃物处理：废弃物收集和运输、转运装置和转运站、固废能源化利用、资源回收和再利用；污泥、水处理
始办年份：2007
周期：每年一届
市场范围：国际性
上届规模 2010：展览面积5,000m²(国外展商2,000m²)，参展商300家（国外展商120家，来自17个国家），参观人数12,000人（专业贸易观众3,500人）
主办：杭州市政府；中节能实业发展有限公司；欧中联合商会
承办：杭州思诺博会展服务有限公司
地址：杭州市体育场路229号浙江粮油大厦12楼（310003）
联系人：肖倩

The 5th China Intl Clean Energy & Environment Protection Industry Fair
Venue: Intl Exhibition Center World Trade Center Zhejiang, Hangzhou, Zhejiang
Profile: Clean Energy; Low Carbon Emission Technologies, Carbon Capture and Storage Carbon Traders; Energy-saving Technology and Products, Energy-saving Architecture, Innovative Building Materials, Lighting, Solar Water Heaters, Energy-saving Home Appliance; Environment Inspection and Evaluation Inspecting and Analyzing Instruments; Solid Waste Treatment; Sludge and Water Treatment, Water and Sewage Treatment, Water Disinfection and Softening Equipment Sludge and Residues Treatment
Established Year: 2007
Frequency: Annual
Market Area: International
Statistics 2010: Exhibition Area 5,000m²(foreigners 2,000m²), Exhibitors 300（foreigners 120, came from 17 countries）, Visitors 12,000（trade visitors 3,500）
Organizers: Hangzhou Municipal Government; China Energy Conservation Investment Corp; Europe-China Commercial Union
Hosted: Hangzhou SINOBAL Convention & Exhibition Service Co Ltd
Address: Room 1206 Zhejiang Liangyou Building, 229 Tiyuchang Road, Hangzhou, Zhejiang 310003, China
Contact: Ms Sandra Xia

浙江-宁波 Zhejiang-Ningbo

2011/03/17 - 19
☎ 0574-8784 9308, 2771 6605
🖷 0574-8784 9306
✉ younage@younage.com
www.china-mts.com

6850

2011宁波国际海事展览会
地点：宁波国际会展中心，浙江宁波
内容：港口、航运与海事安全；船艇及技术设备；海洋工程装备与技术；物流技术与设备；海事服务：金融、保险、法律、培训与租赁
首届
市场范围：国际性
性质：面向贸易观众
入场券价格：免费
参展费用：标准展位：海外企业2,800美元/9m²，国内企业9,000元/9m²；净地：海外企业260美元/m²，国内企业850元/m²
预计规模：展出面积12,000m²，参展商300家，专业观众10,000名
主办：浙江省船舶工业协会；中华人民共和国宁波海事局；宁波市江东区人民政府；宁波市现代物流发展领导小组办公室
承办：美国克劳斯展览公司；雅卓展览服务有限公司；宁波市船舶工业行业协会
地址：宁波市江东区百丈东路650号7楼（315040）
联系人：王银辉，赵清华
MSN：wangyinhui1984@sina.com
QQ：199461938

China Maritime Tech & Security Expo 2011
Venue: Ningbo Intl Conference & Exhibition Center, Ningbo, Zhejiang
Profile: 1. Port, Shipping and Marine Security; 2. Boat and Ship Making Technology and Equipment; 3. Oceanographic Equipment and Technology; 4. Logistics Technology and Equipment; 5. Maritime Service: Finance, Insurance, law, Training and Lease
First Session
Market Area: International
Nature: Trade Only
Cost to Attend: Free
Participated Fee: Standard Booth USD 2,800/9m², Raw Space USD 260/m²
Expectation: Gross Area 12,000m², Exhibitors 300, Trade Visitors 10,000
Organizer: E. J. Krause & Associates, Inc; Younage Exhibition Co Ltd; Ningbo Association of Shipbuilding Industry
Address: 7 Floor, No.650 East Bai Zhang Road, Ningbo, China
Contact: Yinhui Wang, Qianghua Zhao
MSN: wangyinhui1984@sina.com

2011/03/17 - 19
☎ 0574-8725 4009
🖷 0574-8725 4017
✉ 87254009@163.com
expo.21wenju.com

6860

第八届中国国际文具礼品博览会
地点：宁波国际会展中心，浙江宁波
内容：文具及办公用品（书写工具、纸及纸制品、桌面办公用品、文件整理用品、学生及学校用品、美术用品）；文具生产加工设备、零部件；办公设备及电脑周边产品、耗材；文具礼品
始办年份：2004
周期：每年一届
市场范围：国际性
性质：面向贸易观众
入场券价格：20元
参展费用：标准展位7,500元/9m²，角位8,000元/9m²，净地750元/m²
上届规模 2010：展览面积25,000m²(国外展商2,500m²)，参展商488家（国外展商56家，来自47个国家），参观人数17,664人（专业贸易观众15,500人）
主办：中国贸促会；宁波市人民政府

（CNISE）
The 8th China International Stationery & Gifts Exposition
Venue: Ningbo Intl Conference & Exhibition Center, Ningbo, Zhejiang
Profile: Stationery and Office Supplies: Writing Instruments, Paper & Paper Products, Desk Supplies, Stationery for Document Management, School & Student Stationery, Drawing Products; Stationery Producing and Processing Machines, Parts & Accessories; Office Equipments and Appending Device, Exhaustible Materials of Computers; Stationery Gifts
Established Year: 2004
Frequency: Annual
Market Area: International
Nature: Trade Only
Cost to Attend: RMB 20:-
Participated Fee: Standard Booth RMB 7,500/9m², Corner unit RMB 8,000, Raw Space RMB 750/m²

承办：中国贸促会宁波分会；宁海县人民政府
地址：宁波高新区创苑路750号软件产业园B幢8层（315040）
联系人：陈淑飞，周华杰

Statistics 2010: Exhibition Area 25,000m²(foreigners 2,500m²), Exhibitors 488（foreigners 56, came from 47 countries）, Visitors 17,664（trade visitors 15,500）
Organizer: CCPIT Ningbo; Ninghai Municipal Government
Address: 8/F,Area-B,No.750,ChuangyuanRd.Ningbo Hi-Tech Zone, Zhejiang, China
Contact: Chen Shufei, Zhou Huajie

2011/03/17 - 20
☎ 0574-2771 6625, 2771 6601
🖷 0574-8784 9306, 2771 6613
✉ younage@younage.com
www.chinamaching.cn
6870

第十二届中国国际机械工业展览会
地点：宁波国际会展中心，浙江宁波
内容：金属加工机床；金属成型机床：电加工、线切割机床；工控自动化、数控系统、检测设备、数显装置、机床工具及附件；焊接切割设备；塑料机械及配件
始办年份：2000
周期：每年一届
市场范围：国际性
性质：面向贸易观众
入场券价格：免费
参展费用：标准展位6,800元/个，净地680元/m²
主办：中国机械设备进出口总公司
承办：宁波市经济委员会；雅卓展览服务有限公司
地址：宁波市江东区百丈东路650号7楼（315040）
联系人：施国平,郑岗

The 12th China Intl Machinery Industry Exhibition
Venue: Ningbo Intl Conference & Exhibition Center, Ningbo, Zhejiang
Profile: Metalworking machine tools; Mold machinery; Molding machine; Die mold technical equipment and assistive devices; Die supporting materials; Die heat treatment and surface treatment equipment; Die items;
Established Year: 2000
Frequency: Annual
Market Area: International
Nature: Trade Only
Cost to Attend: Free
Participated Fee: Standard Booth RMB 6,800/booth, Raw Space RMB 680/m²
Sponsor: China National Machinery & Equipment Import & Export Corporation
Organizer: Ningbo Economic Committee; Younage Exhibition Co Ltd
Address: 7/F, No.650.Baizhang East Road, Jiangdong District, Ningbo China
Contact: Shi Guoping, Zheng Gang

2011/06/08 - 11
☎ 0574-8717 8074
🖷 0574-8732 7443
✉ trade@cicgf.com
www.cicgf.com
6880

中国国际日用消费品博览会
（简称“消博会”）
地点：宁波国际会展中心，浙江宁波
内容：由国家商务部和浙江省人民政府共同主办的中国国际日用消费品博览会是中国年中规模最大的日用消费品专业博览会，每年6月在著名的港口城市宁波举办。第十届“消博会”（CICGF 2011）设置家电电子、家纺服装、文体及户外休闲用品、家居用品及礼品四大展区。 展会之前和展会期间，将开通上海浦东国际机场至宁波的穿梭巴士，免费接送到会的境外客商。
始办年份：2002
周期：每年一届
市场范围：国际性
性质：面向贸易观众
参展费用：1,200美元/展位
上届规模 2010：展览面积90,000m²(国外展商10,000m²)，参展商5,000家（国外展商500家，来自110个国家），参观人数50,000人（专业贸易观众6,023人）
主办：宁波市对外贸易服务中心有限公司
地址：宁波市海曙区灵桥路190号中国国际日用消费品博览会组委会（315000）
联系人：池俏瑜，唐鑫

China International Consumer Goods Fair
Venue: Ningbo Intl Conference & Exhibition Center, Ningbo, Zhejiang
Profile: CICGF, co-sponsored by Ministry of Commerce PRC and Zhejiang Provincial People's Government, is one of the largest consumer goods fair in China, which is held in the famous harbor city of Ningbo in June every year. The 10th CICGF (CICGF 2011) will be divided into 4 sections: Home Appliances and Electronics; Household Textiles and Garments; Sport Products, Outdoors and Recreational Products; Household Articles and Gifts. Free shuttle buses will be available for overseas visitors between Shanghai Pudong International Airport and Ningbo
Established Year: 2002
Frequency: Annual
Market Area: International
Nature: Trade Only
Participated Fee: USD 1,200/booth
Statistics 2010: Exhibition Area 90,000m²(foreigners 10,000m²), Exhibitors 5000（foreigners 500, came from 110 countries）, Visitors 50,000（trade visitors 6023）
Organizer: Ningbo Foreign Trade Service Center Co Ltd
Address: Organizing Committee, CICGF, 190 Lingqiao Road, Haishu District, Ningbo, 315000, China
Contact: Ms Yang, Mr Pei, Ms Chi

2011/09 -
☎ 0574-2771 6603, 2771 6605
🖷 0574-8784 9306
✉ younage@younage.com
www.widfair.com
6890

2011中国宁波国际工业设计博览会
地点：宁波国际会展中心，浙江宁波
内容：1.设计公司、制造业企业、设计师包括：产品设计、环境设计、视觉设计；2.设计组织、设计院校；3.设计奖项，设计大赛；4.设计软件，涉及专利、涉及器材、快速成形设备，模型制作，新材料，新工艺，相关媒体
始办年份：2006
周期：每年一届
市场范围：国际性
性质：面向公众
入场券价格：免费
主办：中国机械设备进出口总公司
承办：宁波市经济委员会；雅卓展览服务有限公司
地址：宁波市江东区百丈东路650号7楼（315040）
联系人：薛层,王银辉
MSN：casey_xue@163.com
QQ：274392563

2011 International Industry Design Fair Ningbo China
Venue: Ningbo Intl Conference & Exhibition Center, Ningbo, Zhejiang
Profile: Product design, environmental design, visual design
Established Year: 2006
Frequency: Annual
Market Area: International
Nature: Open to Public
Cost to Attend: Free
Sponsor: China National Machinery & Equipment Import & Export Corporation
Organizer: Ningbo Economic Committee; Younage Exhibition Co Ltd
Address: 7Floor, No.650 East Bai Zhang Road, Ningbo, China
Contact: Casey; Yinhui Wang
MSN: casey_xue@163.com

2011/10/28 - 31
☎ 0574-8791 1562, 8791 1560
🖷 0574-8791 1559
✉ wyj3401@126.com
www.nbdcj.com
6900

第十六届中国宁波国际住宅产品博览
地点：宁波国际会展中心，浙江宁波
内容：房产置业、家装设计、厨具、陶瓷玻艺、油漆涂料、门窗地板、管道型材、家具布艺 家具用品、新型建材、房顶幕墙、空调能源、防水保温、智能安防、网络信息、五金灯具、国艺绿化
始办年份：1996
周期：每年一届
市场范围：国际性
性质：面向贸易观众
入场券价格：10元
参展费用：房产展区7,500元/展位，其他5,700元/展位
上届规模 2010：展览面积55,000m^2(国外展商9,800m^2)，参展商780家（国外展商198家，来自23个国家），参观人数390,000人（专业贸易观众50,000人）
主办：住房和城乡建设部住宅产业化促进中心；宁波市人民政府
承办：宁波市建设委员会；宁波市城之新展览有限公司
地址：浙江省宁波市院士路66号203（315040）
联系人：戴勇勤，吴伊君

The 16th China international Exhibition on Housing Industry Product
Venue: Ningbo Intl Conference & Exhibition Center, Ningbo, Zhejiang
Profile: Real estate, Interior design and decoration, Kitchen and bath, Painting, Machinery and materials for days, gates, roofs and walls, Pipe, Housing and furnishing, New building materials, Construction energy-saving, thermal protection and waterproof technology and pro
Established Year: 1996
Frequency: Annual
Market Area: International
Nature: Trade Only
Cost to Attend: RMB 10:-
Participated Fee: RMB 7,500/booth
Statistics 2010: Exhibition Area 55,000m^2(foreigners 9,800m^2), Exhibitors 780（foreigners 198, came from 23 countries）, Visitors 390,000（trade visitors 50,000）
Sponsor: The Center For Hosing Industrialization; Ningbo Municipal People's Government
Organizer：Ningbo Construction Committee；Ningbo Chengzhixin Exhibition Co Ltd
Address: 66 Yuanshi Road, Ningbo, China

浙江-绍兴 Zhejiang-Shaoxing

2011/10 -
☎ 010-6609 4505
✉ hetian112@sina.com
6910

2011中国柯桥国际纺织品博览会
地点：浙江绍兴
主办：中国商业联合会；中国纺织工业协会
联系人：何天

Heqiao Textile Expo
Venue: Shaoxing, Zhejiang
Organizer: China General Chamber of Commerce

浙江-台州 Zhejiang-Taizhou

2011/05/11 - 13
☎ 020-3835 8081, 3837 3263
🖷 020-3835 8082
✉ shipbuildex@126.com
www.shipbuildex.cn
6920

2011第四届中国（台州）国际船舶工业博览会
地点：台州国际会展中心，浙江台州
内容：台州、舟山、宁波和温州四市联合打造2011年浙江唯一船舶展。展览内容包括船舶及船舶配套产品、造船装备、海洋工程技术及装备、船舶技术及海事技术
始办年份：2007
周期：每年两届
市场范围：国际性
性质：面向贸易观众
入场券价格：免费
参展费用：国内：标准展位6,800元，净地680元/m^2，国际：标准展位2,500美元，净地250美元/m^2
上届规模 2009：展览面积15,000m^2(国外展商2,000m^2)，参展商304家（国外展商20家，来自5个国家），参观人数18,052人（专业贸易观众6,018人）
主办：台州市人民政府
承办：台州市经济委员会 广州汇成展览服务公司
地址：广州市中山大道190号骏景花园骏御轩G座18B（510665）
联系人：谭飞荣
MSN：mfjyf021@hotmail.com
QQ：874722692

The 4th Session China (Taizhou) International Shipbuilding Exposition in 2011
Venue: Taizhou Intl Convention & Exhibition Center, Taizhou, Zhejiang
Profile: Taizhou, Zhoushan, Ningbo and Wenzhou Jointly Organize the Only Shipbuilding Expo in Zhejiang in 2011. Exhibits: Supporting Products of Ships, Shipbuilding Equipment, Marine Engineering Technologies and Equipment, Shipbuilding Technology and Marine Technology
Established Year: 2007
Frequency: Biannual
Market Area: International
Nature: Trade Only
Cost to Attend: Free
Participated Fee: Standard Booth USD 2,500，Raw Space USD 250/m^2
Statistics 2009: Exhibition Area 15,000m^2(foreigners 2,000m^2), Exhibitors 304（foreigners 20, came from 5 countries）, Visitors 18,052（trade visitors 6,018）
Sponsor: Taizhou Municipal People’s Government
Organizer: Taizhou Economic Commission; Guangzhou Wellexpo Exhibition Service Co Ltd
Address: Room 18B, Building G, Junyuxuan, Junjing Garden, 190 Zhongshan Avenue, Guangzhou, Guangdong
Contact: Feirong Tan
MSN: mfjyf021@hotmail.com

浙江-温州 Zhejiang-Wenzhou

2011/03/11 - 13
☎ 0577-8890 2222
🖷 0577-8890 1788
✉ ce@donnor.com
www.donnor.com/china/mould/
6930

第十八届中国（温州）国际机床、工模具展览会
地点：温州国际会展中心，浙江温州
内容：金切机床，特种加工机床及专用设备，金属成型机床，制造单元/系统及自动化设备，工夹具及检测仪器，机床零部件及辅助设备，模具与加工设备，塑胶加工设备与原材料，相关制造技术与设备
始办年份：1992
周期：每年一届
市场范围：全国性
性质：面向贸易观众
入场券价格：免费
参展费用：5,500～6,000元/展位
上届规模 2010：展览面积30,000m²，参展商300家，参观人数40,000人
主办：温州市人民政府；中国机床总公司；德纳展览集团
承办：北京火花机床集团；温州市模具协会；德纳展览有限公司；温州雅博展览有限公司
地址：浙江省温州市新城大道晚报大厦7楼（325001）
联系人：石宪伟，林超凡*
QQ：947035604

The 18th China (Wenzhou) Intl Machine Tool Exhibition
Venue: Wenzhou Intl Conference and Exhibition Center, Ningbo, Zhejiang
Profile: Metal Cutting Machine; non-traditional machine & special equipment; Metal forming machine; manufacturing cell/system & automated equipment; clamping apparatus & inspection device; machine parts & auxiliary equipment; mould & processing equipment; plastics processing equipment & raw materials; related manufacturing technologies & equipment
Established Year: 1992
Frequency: Annual
Market Area: National
Nature: Trade Only
Cost to Attend: Free
Participated Fee: RMB 5,500-6,000/booth
Statistics 2010: Exhibition Area 30,000m², Exhibitors 300, Visitors 40,000
Organizer: Wenzhou Municipal People's Government, China National Machine Tool Corp. (CNMTC), China Donnor Exhibition Group
Address: 7F Wanbao Mansion, 296 Xincheng Road, Wenzhou, Zhejiang
Contact: Mr Xianwei Shi, Ms Chaofan Lin

2011/04/07 - 10
☎ 0577-8890 2222, 8890 2168
🖷 0577-8890 1788
✉ auot@donnor.net
http://auto.donnor.com
6940

2011第九届中国（温州）汽车展览会
地点：温州国际会展中心，浙江温州
内容：各类轿车、商务车、越野车、改装车、各类汽车零部件、各种汽车生产制造设备、工艺装备、检测维修设备、各种汽车维护保养用品、美容用品等
始办年份：2003
周期：每年一届
市场范围：国际性
入场券价格：40元
参展费用：标准展位5,000元/9m²，室外净地150元/m²（100m²起），室内净地420元/m²
上届规模 2010：展览面积38,000m²
主办：温州市汽车流通行业协会
承办：温州德纳展览有限公司
地址：浙江省温州市新城大道晚报大厦（325000）
联系人：苏苗守，江瑞
QQ：1113783308

9th Wenzhou Intl Auto Expo
Venue: Wenzhou Intl Conference and Exhibition Center, Ningbo, Zhejiang
Profile: Full range of automobiles, auto parts & components, auto manufacture equipment, tools, auto maintenance products.
Established Year: 2003
Frequency: Annual
Market Area: International
Cost to Attend: RMB 40:-
Participated Fee: Standard Booth RMB 5,000/9m², Raw Space: outdoor RMB 150/m² (min 100m²), Indoor RMB 420/m²
Statistics 2010: Exhibition Area 38,000m²
Sponsor: Wenzhou Automobile Dealers Association
Organizer: Wenzhou Donnor Exhibition Co Ltd
Address: 7Fl, Wanbao Mansion,No.296 Xincheng Road, Wenzhou,China
Contact: Su Miaoshou, Angela

2011/04/08 - 10
☎ 0577-8890 2222, 8890 2168
🖷 0577-8890 1788, 8890 5178
✉ donnor2@donnor.com
http://wzestate.donnor.com
www.donnor.com
6950

"魅力之都"2011温州房产展
地点：温州国际会展中心，浙江温州
内容：各种商品房、商铺、写字楼、二手房、投资公司、中介代理、房产模型制作、专业房产网站、室内设计与装潢、房产专业媒体等
始办年份：2011
首届
市场范围：全国性
入场券价格：40元
参展费用：18,000元/展位
主办：温州市工商联房地产商会
承办：温州德纳展览有限公司
地址：浙江省温州市新城大道晚报大厦7楼（325000）
联系人：苏苗守先生，江瑞女士
MSN：angel_715_163@hotmail.com
QQ：1113783302

2011 Wenzhou Real Estate Exhibition
Venue: Wenzhou Intl Conference and Exhibition Center, Ningbo, Zhejiang
Profile: Residential building, Commercial building, Office building, Second-hand house, Investment company, Agency, Property modeling, Interior design & decoration, Professional real estate portal.
Established Year: 2011
First Session
Frequency:
Market Area: National
Cost to Attend: RMB 40:-
Participated Fee: RMB 18,000/booth
Organizer: Wenzhou Donnor Exhibition Co Ltd
Address: 7Fl,Wanbao Mansion,No.296 Xincheng Road, Wenzhou, China
Contact: Su Miaoshou Angela Jiang
MSN: angel_715_163@hotmail.com

2011/07/06 - 08
☎ 0577-8890 2222, 8890 2168
🖷 0577-8890 1788
✉ optics@donnor.com
www.opticsfair.cn
6960

2011第九届中国（温州）国际眼镜业展览会暨
首届中国眼镜品牌连锁加盟会
地点：温州国际会展中心，浙江温州
内容：太阳镜及运动眼镜、老视镜、镜片及毛坯 、眼镜零配件 、眼镜专用工具 、眼镜制造设备、验光配镜的仪器及设备、眼镜原辅材料、隐形眼镜及眼镜护理产品、眼镜电镀、零售及店铺设计、眼镜陈列设备及技术、眼镜包装、眼镜连锁品牌、眼镜店设备及家具、眼镜电镀设备及材料等

9th Wenzhou Intl Optics Fair, China incorporating
The 1st Franchisee Meeting for China Optical Brands
Venue: Wenzhou Intl Conference and Exhibition Center, Ningbo, Zhejiang
Profile: Sunglasses and Sports Spectacles, Pre synoptic Glasses, Lens, Frames, Glasses Spare Parts, Optical Tools, Optical Manufacturing Equipments, Optometry Instruments, Optical Raw Materials, Contact Lens & Care, Optical Plating, Equipments & Raw Materials, Optical Chain Brands, Retailer and Shop Designing, Display Equipment and

始办年份：2003
周期：每年一届
市场范围：国际性
入场券价格：免费
参展费用：国内企业：标准展位5,800元/9m²，净地600元/m²；海外企业：标准展位1,800美元/9m²，净地180美元/m²
上届规模 2010：展览面积20,000m²，参展商300家，专业贸易观众242,027人
主办：温州市人民政府；浙江省中小型企业局；浙江省眼镜行业协会；德纳展览集团
承办：温州市眼镜商会；温州德纳展览有限公司
地址：浙江省温州市新城大道晚报大厦7楼（325000）
联系人：苏苗守，江瑞
QQ：1113783308

Technology, Optical Packages
Established Year: 2003
Frequency: Annual
Market Area: International
Cost to Attend: Free
Participated Fee: Standard Booth USD 1,800/9m², Raw Space USD 180/m²
Statistics 2010: Exhibition Area 20,000m², Exhibitors 300, Trade Visitors 242,027
Sponsor: Wenzhou Municipal People' s Government; Zhejiang SME Bureau; Zhejiang Optometric & Optical Association; Wenzhou Donnor Exhibition Co Ltd
Organizer: Wenzhou Glasses Chamber of Commerce; Wenzhou Donnor Exhibition Co Ltd
Address: 7Fl, Wanbao Mansion,No.296 Xincheng Road, Wenzhou, China
Contact: Su Miaoshou, Angela

2011/08/26 - 28
☎ 0577-8890 2222, 8890 5881
🖷 0577-8890 1788
✉ leather@donnor.com
www.chinaleatherfair.cn

6970

2011中国国际合成革展览会
（CSLF2011）
地点：温州国际会展中心，浙江温州
内容：中国首个专业合成革展览会。由中国塑料加工工业协会主办，中国塑协人造革合成革专业委员会、温州市合成革商会、温州德纳展览有限公司联合承办。
展品范围：PVC/PU、超细纤维、合成革、人造革、革基布、化工原辅材料、机械设备和环保机械等产品。
始办年份：2010
周期：每年一届
市场范围：国际性
性质：面向贸易观众
入场券价格：免费
参展费用：标准展位（3x3m）7,800元/展位，（3x4m）9,800元/展位，净地800元/m²(36m²起)
上届规模 2010：展览面积12,000m²(国外展商208m²)，参展商187家（国外展商6家，来自5个国家），专业贸易观众25,875人
主办：中国塑料加工工业协会
承办：中塑协人造革合成革专业委员会；温州市合成革商会；温州德纳展览有限公司
地址：浙江省温州市新城大道晚报大厦7楼（325000）
联系人：林先生，廖小姐
MSN：sring1982@yahoo.com.cn
QQ：林先生1353606820，廖小姐765167797

2011 China Intl Synthetic Leather Fair
Venue: Wenzhou Intl Conference and Exhibition Center, Ningbo, Zhejiang
Profile: CSLF is the first professional trade fair for synthetic leather industry. Exhibits: PVC/PU, Superfine fibre, Synthetic leather, Artificial leather, Leather fibre, Chemical & raw material, Machinery, Environmental-friendly machinery
Established Year: 2010
Frequency: Annual
Market Area: International
Nature: Trade Only
Cost to Attend: Free
Participated Fee: Standard Booth（3m × 3m）RMB 7,800,（3x4m）RMB 9,800, Raw Space RMB 800/m² (min 36m²)
Statistics 2010: Exhibition Area 12,000m²(foreigners 208m²), Exhibitors 187（foreigners 6, came from 5 countries）, Trade Visitors 25,875
Organizer: Artificial & Synthetic Leather Committee of CPPIA；Wenzhou Synthetic Leather Chamber of Commerce；Wenzhou Donnor Exhibition Co Ltd
Address: 7Fl, Wanbao Mansion, No.296 Xincheng Road, Wenzhou, China
Contact: Andrew Suki
MSN: sring1982@yahoo.com.cn

2011/08/26 - 28
☎ 0577-8890 2222, 8890 5881
🖷 0577-8890 1788
✉ leather@donnor.com
www.chinaleatherfair.cn

6980

第16届中国（温州）国际皮革、鞋材、鞋机展览会
地点：温州国际会展中心，浙江温州
内容：现已成为国内首屈一指的皮革、鞋材、鞋机行业专业展会，每年吸引近30000位来自60多个国家和地区的海内外人士前来参观、采购。 展品范围：皮革、鞋材、鞋类化工、鞋类五金/配件、制鞋机械、CAD/CAM系统等
始办年份：1996
周期：每年一届
市场范围：国际性
性质：面向贸易观众
入场券价格：免费
参展费用：普装区：（3x3m）7,800元，（3x4m）9,800元；净地：800元/m²(36m²起)；精装区（3.5x3m）9,800元；国际区：（3x3m）15,000元，（3x4m）20,000元，净地1,500元/m²(36m²起)；国际鞋机/皮机馆A区9,800元/展位，净地 1,000元/m²(36m²起)，B/C区7,800元/展位，净地800元/m² (36m²起)
上届规模 2010：展览面积32,000m²(国外展商1,100m²)，参展商627家（国外展商51家，来自21个国家），专业贸易观众25,875人
主办：温州市鞋革行业协会
承办：温州德纳展览有限公司
地址：浙江省温州市新城大道晚报大厦7楼（325000）
联系人：林先生，廖小姐
MSN：sring1982@yahoo.com.cn
QQ：林先生：1353606820 廖小姐：765167797

The 16th China (Wenzhou) Intl Leather, Shoe Material & Shoe Machinery Fair
Venue: Wenzhou Intl Conference and Exhibition Center, Ningbo, Zhejiang
Profile: With years' efforts and recent leaps in brand promotion, China (Wenzhou) Intl Leather, Shoe Material & Shoe Machinery Fair (ALL CHINA SHOE-TECH) has become the premier professional trade fair in leather and shoe manufacture industry. Exhibits: All Kinds of Leather, Shoe Machinery, Raw Materials, Vamp Finishing, Shoe-Making Accessories & Components, CAD/CAM system
Established Year: 1996
Frequency: Annual
Market Area: International
Nature: Trade Only
Cost to Attend: Free
Participated Fee: RMB 15,000(3x3m), RMB 20,000(3x4m)，Raw Space RMB 1,500/m²(min 36m²)
Statistics 2010: Exhibition Area 32,000m²(foreigners 1,100m²), Exhibitors 627（foreigners 51, came from 21 countries）, Trade Visitors 25,875
Organizer: Wenzhou Donnor Exhibition Co Ltd
Address: 7Fl, Wanbao Mansion, No.296 Xincheng Road, Wenzhou, China
Contact: Andrew, Suki
MSN: sring1982@yahoo.com.cn

浙江-义乌 Zhejiang-Yiwu

2011/04/20 - 23
☎ 0579-8541 5444, 8541 5803/268/477/406
🖷 0579-8541 5386
✉ expo@chinafairs.org
www.ssofair.com
6990

中国义乌文化产品交易博览会

地点： 义乌国际博览中心，浙江义乌
内容： 文体用品、工艺品、印刷包装、文化创意产品、工艺美术、书画、古玩
始办年份： 2004
周期： 每年一届
市场范围： 国际性
性质： 面向贸易观众
上届规模 2010：2,000个国际标准展位，专业贸易观众62,000人
主办： 中华人民共和国文化部；浙江省人民政府
承办： 浙江省文化厅；浙江省文化产业促进会；义乌市人民政府
地址： 浙江省义乌市宾王路301号梅湖会展中心义乌中国小商品城展览有限公司展览四部（322000）
联系人： 陈经理
MSN：yiwufair@hotmail.com

China Yiwu Cultural Products Trade Fair

Venue: Yiwu International Exhibition Center, Yiwu, Zhejiang
Profile: Stationery & Sports Products, Handicraft Articles, Printing & Packing, Originative Cultural Products, Handicrafts & Arts, Antique & Collections
Established Year: 2004
Frequency: Annual
Market Area: International
Nature: Trade Only
Statistics 2010: 2,000 booths, Trade Visitors 62,000
Sponsor: Ministry of Culture of the People's Republic of China; Zhejiang Provincial People's Government
Organizer: Department of Culture of Zhejiang Province; Zhejiang Association for Promoting Culture Industry; Yiwu Municipal People's Government
Address: Yiwu China Commodities City Exhibition Co Ltd, 1/F, Hall 1, Sales 4 Dept., Meihu Exhibition Center, No. 301 Binwang Road, Yiwu, Zhejiang
MSN: yiwufair@hotmail.com

2011/04/28 - 30
☎ 0579-8541 5030, 8541 5003, 8541 5026, 8541 5262
🖷 0579-8541 5004
✉ Hardwareexpo2010@163.com
www.hardwareexpo.cn
7000

第八届中国国际五金电器博览会

地点： 义乌国际博览中心，浙江义乌
内容： 五金工具、建筑五金、礼品五金、日用五金、厨卫酒店用品、五金休闲用品、电器产品、电子产品、电气电工、配件器材、加工机械、机械设备、五金机床、机电产品、模具产品等
始办年份： 2004
周期： 每年一届
市场范围： 国际性
性质： 面向贸易观众
上届规模 2010：1,000个国际标准展位，专业贸易观众46,102人
主办： 中国五金交电化工商业协会；义乌市人民政府
承办： 浙江中国小商品城集团股份有限公司；义乌市五金家电行业协会
地址： 中国国际五金电器博览会组委会办公室 浙江省义乌市宾王路301号梅湖会展中心3号馆一楼（322000）
联系人： 贾文俊
MSN：yiwufair@hotmail.com
QQ：435708

The 8th China International Hardware & Electrical Appliances Trade Fair

Venue: Yiwu International Exhibition Center, Yiwu, Zhejiang
Profile: Hardware tools, architectural hardware, hardware gifts, daily-use hardware, hotel kitchen supplies, hardware leisure products, electrical products, electronics, electric-engineering and electrization, equipment and accessory, processing machinery, mechanical equipment, metal machine tool, mechanical and electrical products, mold products
Established Year: 2004
Frequency: Annual
Market Area: International
Nature: Trade Only
Statistics 2010: 1,000 booths, Trade Visitors 46,102
Sponsor: China National Hardware Electric and Chemical Products Commercial Association; Yiwu Municipal People's Government
Organizer: Zhejiang China Commodities City Group Co Ltd; Yiwu Hardware & Electrical Appliances Trade Association
Address: 1/F, Hall 3, Meihu Exhibition Center, No.301 Binwang Road, Yiwu, Zhejiang
MSN: yiwufair@hotmail.com

2011/04/28 - 30
☎ 0579-8541 5333, 8541 5266, 8541 5277, 8541 5288
🖷 0579-8541 5244
✉ expo@chinafairs.org
www.yiwusourcingfair.com
7010

义乌消费品交易会

地点： 义乌国际博览中心，浙江义乌
内容： 家用纺织品、家居用品、礼品及喜庆用品
始办年份： 2006
周期： 每年一届
市场范围： 国际性
性质： 面向贸易观众
上届规模 2010：展览面积15,000m^2，参展商433家，境外观众5,886人
主办： 中华人民共和国商务部外贸发展事务局；义乌市人民政府
承办： 浙江中国小商品城集团股份有限公司
地址： 义乌中国小商品城展览有限公司 浙江省义乌市宾王路301号梅湖会展中心展览四部（322000）
联系人： 陈经理，黄小姐，吴先生
MSN：yiwufair@hotmail.com
QQ：435708

Yiwu Sourcing Fair: Consumer Goods

Venue: Yiwu International Exhibition Center, Yiwu, Zhejiang
Profile: Household textiles, household commodities, gifts & festival products
Established Year: 2006
Frequency: Annual
Market Area: International
Nature: Trade Only
Statistics 2010: Exhibition Area 15,000m^2, Exhibitors 433, Foreign Visitors 5,886
Sponsor: Trade Development Bureau of Ministry of Commerce, PRC; Yiwu Municipal People's Government
Organizer: Zhejiang China Commodities City Group Co Ltd
Address: Sales Dept. 4, Yiwu China Commodities City Exhibition Co Ltd, 1/F, Hall 1, Meihu Exhibition Center, No.301 Binwang Road, Yiwu, Zhejiang 322000
MSN: yiwufair@hotmail.com

2011/05/06 - 08
☎ 010-8260 6880转ext 91
🖷 010-8260 6883
✉ ciccyhuang@cnaico.com.cn
www.cnaico.com.cn
www.autochina.com.cn
7020

2011年第六届义乌汽车展览会

地点： 浙江义乌
主办： 中国汽车工业国际合作总公司
地址： 北京市海淀区中关村丹棱街3号A座

6th Yiwu Automobile Exhibition

Venue: Yiwu, Zhejiang
Organizer: China National Automotive Industry International Corp

2011/05/26 - 29
☎ 0579-8541 5258转ext 002
🖷 0579-8541 5005
✉ expo@chinafairs.org
www.tourismfair.cn
7030

中国国际旅游商品博览会
地点：义乌国际博览中心，浙江义乌
内容：旅游装备品、酒店用品、户外休闲用品、旅游纪念品
始办年份：2009
周期：每年一届
市场范围：国际性
性质：面向贸易观众
上届规模 2010：2,256个标准展位，参观人数100,000人
主办：国家旅游局；浙江省人民政府
承办：中国旅游协会；浙江省旅游局；义乌市人民政府
地址：浙江省义乌市宾王路301号梅湖会展中心一楼义乌中国小商品城展览有限公司展览部（322000）
联系人：何经理
MSN：yiwufair@hotmail.com
QQ：435708

China International Tourism Commodities Fair
Venue: Yiwu International Exhibition Center, Yiwu, Zhejiang
Profile: Tourism equipment, hotel products, outdoor leisure products, tourism souvenir
Established Year: 2009
Frequency: Annual
Market Area: International
Nature: Trade Only
Statistics 2010: 2,256 booths, Visitors 100,000
Sponsor: National Tourism Administration Zhejiang Provincial People' s Government
Organizer: China Tourism Association; Zhejiang Tourism Bureau; Yiwu Municipal People' s Government
Address: 1/F, Hall 1, Sale Dept., Meihu Exhibition Center, No.301 Binwang Road, Yiwu, Zhejiang
MSN: yiwufair@hotmail.com

2011/10/21 - 25
☎ 0579-8541 5222, 8541 5111, 8541 5333, 8541 5444
🖷 0579-8541 5777, 8541 5402
✉ expo@chinafairs.org
www.yiwufair.com
7050

中国义乌国际小商品博览会
地点：义乌国际博览中心，浙江义乌
内容：五金、汽摩配件及用品、电子电器、工艺品、水晶及玻璃制品、文化办公用品、体育及休闲用品、箱包皮具、日用品、化妆洗涤用品、饰品及饰品配件、针织；服装及辅料、家用纺织品、玩具及儿童用品、电子商务及贸易服务、境外商品
始办年份：1995
周期：每年一届
市场范围：国际性
性质：面向贸易观众
上届规模 2010：展览面积120,000m²，专业贸易观众134,393人
主办：中华人民共和国商务部；浙江省人民政府；中国贸促会；中国轻工业联合会；中国商业联合会
承办：浙江省商务厅；义乌市人民政府
地址：义乌中国小商品城展览有限公司，浙江省义乌市宾王路301号梅湖会展中心一楼展览部（322000）
联系人：虞先生
MSN：yiwufair@hotmail.com
QQ：435708

China Yiwu International Commodities Fair
Venue: Yiwu International Exhibition Center, Yiwu, Zhejiang
Profile: Hardware, Auto Supplies, Electronic & Electrical Appliances, Crafts, Crystal & Glass Products, Stationery & Office Supplies, Sports & Recreation Articles, Leather, Cases & Bags, Daily Necessity, Cosmetics & Cleaning Products, Jewelry & Accessories, Knitting Accessories & Garment, Household Textiles, Toys & Children' s Products, Electronic Commerce & Trade Services, Foreign Goods
Established Year: 1995
Frequency: Annual
Market Area: International
Nature: Trade Only
Statistics 2010: Exhibition Area 120,000m², Trade Visitors 134,393
Sponsor: Ministry of Commerce of the P.R.C; Zhejiang Provincial People' s Government; CCPIT China National Light Industry Council; China General Chamber of Commerce
Organizer: Department of Commerce of Zhejiang Province; Yiwu Municipal People' s Government
Address: 1/F, Hall 1, Sale Dept., Meihu Exhibition Center, No.301 Binwang Road, Yiwu, Zhejiang
MSN: yiwufair@hotmail.com

2011/11/01 - 04
☎ 0579-8541 5255, 8541 5277
🖷 0579-8541 5244
✉ expo@chinafairs.org
www.forestryfair.com
7060

第4届中国义乌国际森林产品博览会
地点：义乌国际博览中心，浙江义乌
内容：森林食品类,竹木工艺品类,竹木日用品类,林业装备类,竹木家居类,花卉园艺类,森林休闲用品类
始办年份：2008
周期：每年一届
市场范围：国际性
性质：面向贸易观众
上届规模 2010：2,160个国际标准展位，参展商1,200家，专业贸易观众100,000人
主办：国家林业局；浙江省人民政府
承办：浙江省林业厅；义乌市人民政府
地址：义乌中国小商品城展览有限公司，浙江省义乌市宾王路301号梅湖会展中心一楼展览部（322000）
联系人：陈经理
MSN：yiwufair@hotmail.com
QQ：435708

The 4th China Yiwu International Forest Products Fair
Venue: Yiwu International Exhibition Center, Yiwu, Zhejiang
Profile: Forest food products, Bamboo & wood handicrafts, Bamboo & wood articles for daily use, Forestry equipments, Bamboo & wood household supplies, Flower and gardening products, Forest leisure products
Established Year: 2008
Frequency: Annual
Market Area: International
Nature: Trade Only
Statistics 2010: 2,160 booths, Exhibitors 1,200, Trade Visitors 100,000
Sponsor: State Forestry Administration PRC; Zhejiang Provincial People' s Government
Organizer: Department of Forestry of Zhejiang Province; Yiwu Municipal People Government
Address: 1/F, Hall 1, Sale Dept., Meihu Exhibition Center, No.301 Binwang Road, Yiwu, Zhejiang
MSN: yiwufair@hotmail.com

浙江-永康 Zhejiang-Yongkang

2011/03/31 - 02
☎ 0579-8711 7335, 8711 7336
📠 0579-8711 7336
www.donnor.com/china/moul/
7090

2011第四届中国（永康）五金装备、机床及工模具展览会
地点：永康科技五金城，浙江永康
内容：金属加工机床；五金技术及装备机械；各种测量仪器、仪表及精密工具、刀刃具、量具、卡（夹）具；模具技术及辅助装置设备，各类模具、标准件及相关辅助材料；涂料、涂装及表面处理设备和技术；塑胶、塑料机械及相关配套产品。
始办年份：1992
周期：每年一届
市场范围：全国性
性质：面向贸易观众
参展费用：4,200元
上届规模 2010：展览面积15,000m^2，参展商200余家家，参观人数30,000人
主办：永康市人民政府
承办：永康市经贸局；永康市模具行业协会
地址：永康市九铃东路3090号邮政大楼1206室（325001）
联系人：夏天 林超凡
QQ：1349002115

2011 The 4th China (Yongkang) Hardware Equipment & Machine Tools Exhibition
Venue: Yongkang Hardware City, Yongknag, Zhejiang
Profile: Metal processing machine; hardware technology & machine tool; measuring device & apparatus, precision instrument, cutting tool, measuring apparatus & clamping tools; mould technologies & auxiliary device, all kinds of mould, standard parts & accessories; coating, painting & surface finishing equipment & technologies; plastic machine & complementary products.
Established Year: 1992
Frequency: Annual
Market Area: National
Nature: Trade Only
Participated Fee: RMB 4,200/booth
Statistics 2010: Exhibition Area 15,000m^2, Exhibitors 200, Visitors 30,000
Sponsor: Yongkang People's Govenment
Organizer: Yongkang Economy & Trade Bureau; Yongkang Mould Industry Association
Address: Rm 1206, Postal Service Building, No. 3090 East Jiuling Road, Yongkang
Contact: Mr Tian Xia, Ms Chaofan Lin

2011/05/26 - 28
☎ 010-6601 4062
📠 010-6601 4062
✉ wangying_kk@sina.com
www.chidf.com
7100

第二届中国国际门业博览会
地点：科技五金城，浙江永康
内容：建筑房屋门类、自动门类、车库门类、围墙大门及门禁系统、建筑门窗类、设备
始办年份：2010
周期：每年一届
市场范围：国际性
性质：面向公众
入场券价格：20元
参展费用：800/m^2
上届规模 2010：参展商486家（国外展商23家，来自8个国家），参观人数100,000人（专业贸易观众40,000人）
主办：中国建筑金属结构协会；中国商业联合会；中国房地产业协会；永康市人民政府
承办：浙江中国科技五金城集团有限公司；中国建筑金属结构协会钢木门窗委员会；永康市钢门窗行业协会
地址：北京市西地区在酱坊胡同3号207（100032）
联系人：王颖
MSN：wangying_kk@hotmail.com
QQ：68598408

China International Door Industry Fair
Venue: Yongkang Hardware City, Yongknag, Zhejiang
Established Year: 2010
Frequency: Annual
Market Area: International
Nature: Open to Public
Cost to Attend: RMB 20:-
Participated Fee: 800/m^2
Statistics 2010: Exhibitors 486 (foreigners 23, came from 8 countries), Visitors 100,000 (trade visitors 40,000)
Organizer: Zhejiang China Technology Hardware City Group Co Ltd
MSN: wangying_kk@hotmail.com

2011/09 -
☎ 0579-8707 1588, 8707 1595
010-6609 4505
📠 0579-8707 1597
✉ hetian112@sina.com
ch@chhwf.com
www.hardwarefair.cn
7105

第十六届中国五金博览会
地点：中国科技五金城，浙江永康
主办：中国商业联合会；贸促总会
承办：永康市政府

China Hardware Fair
Venue: Yongkang, Zhejiang
Organizer: China General Chamber of Commerce; Yongkong Government

浙江-余姚 Zhejiang-Yuyao

2011/11 -
☎ 010-6609 4505
✉ hetian112@sina.com
7110

2011中国裘皮服装节
地点：浙江余姚
主办：中国商业联合会；中国皮革协会；余姚市人民政府
联系人：何天

China Fur Fashion Festival
Venue: Yuyao, Zhejiang
Organizer: China General Chamber of Commerce

其他 Others

2011/06 -
☎ 010-6202 8899
🖷 010-8202 2922
www.dsshow.cn
7140

中国药店展览会
中国国际家庭医疗用品展览会
地点：待定
内容：服务于健康产品终端市场
周期：每年一届
上届规模 2010：参展商315家
主办：国药励展展览有限责任公司
地址：北京海淀区知春路20号中国医药大厦11层（100088）

China Drug Store Show
Venue: undetermined
Frequency: Annual
Statistics 2010: Exhibitors 315
Organizer: Reed Sinopharm Exhibitions

2011/11 -
☎ 010-8455 6677
🖷 010-6202 3887
www.pharmchina.com.cn
7170

第66届全国药品交易会
地点：待定
周期：每年两届
主办：国药励展展览有限责任公司
地址：北京朝阳区新源南路1-3号平安国际金融中心B座15层（100027）

66th PHARMCHINA
Venue: undetermined
Profile: Chemical Pharmaceuticals, Chinese patent medicines, Traditional Chinese Medicine, Biopharmaceuticals, OTC medicines, Healthcare products, PharmSoft (Pharmaceutical technologies & services)
Frequency: Biannual
Organizer: Reed Sinopharm Exhibitions

2011/11 -
☎ 010-8455 6677, 8455 6536
🖷 010-6235 8733
✉ yini.zhang@reedsinopharm.com
xinwei.zhao@reedsinopharm.com
www.apichina.com.cn
7180

第67届中国国际医药原料药、中间体、包装、设备交易会
地点：待定
内容：医药制造及活性原料药解决方案
周期：每年两届
主办：国药励展展览有限责任公司
地址：北京朝阳区新源南路1-3号平安国际金融中心B座15层（100027）

API China
Venue: undetermined
Profile: API China is China's leading exhibition for the pharmaceutical manufacturing sector covering the complete spectrum of products from raw material, fine chemical, intermediate, ingredients, processing machinery and packaging machinery. It is an event for international buyers to meet Asian sellers especially Chinese ingredients manufacturers.
Frequency: Biannual
Organizer: Reed Sinopharm Exhibitions

2011/11 -
☎ 010-8455 6677
🖷 010-6235 8733
✉ yini.zhang@reedsinopharm.com
xinwei.zhao@reedsinopharm.com
www.interphexchina.com
7190

世界制药工业展中国展区
地点：待定
内容：医药包装与机械。
周期：每年两届
市场范围：国际性
主办：国药励展展览有限责任公司
地址：北京朝阳区新源南路1-3号平安国际金融中心B座15层（100027）

INTERPHEX China
Venue: undetermined
Profile: Benefiting from being co-located with API China's over 800 pharmaceutical ingredient, intermediate and fine chemicals manufacturers which attracts 35,000 visitors, INTERPHEX CHINA will provide a unique platform for its exhibitors to see significant buyers from all parts of the pharmaceutical manufacturing chain.
Frequency: Biannual
Market Area: International
Organizer: Reed Sinopharm Exhibitions

国内展览会议

日期索引

Exhibitions and Conferences in Chronological Order

2011

2011-
中国国际纺织面料及辅料（秋冬）博览会
China Intl Trade Fair for Apparel Fabrics and Accessories
上海Shanghai
118

2011-
第65届全国药品交易会
65th PharmChina
四川成都Sichuan-Chengdu
6530

2011-
2011西安国际汽车展览会
Xi' an Intl Automobile Exhibition
陕西西安Shaanxi-Xi'an
6015

2011-
中国国际纺织纱线（秋冬）展览会
China Intl Trade Fair for Fibres and Yarns
上海Shanghai
1190

2011-
中国国际加油加气站高新技术及设备暨便利店业务博览会
Gas station
北京Beijing
10

January 2011 一月

2011/01/11-14
中国国际裘皮革皮制品交易会
China Fur and Leather Products Fair
北京Beijing
30

2011/01/21-24
首届中国冰雪动漫展
1st China Ice & Snow Comic-Con
黑龙江哈尔滨Heilongjiang-Harbin
5015

2011/01/21-24
第三届厦门特色农产品展销会
3rd Agricultural product Sales
福建厦门Fujian-Xiamen
3470

February 2011 二月

2011/02/17-19
第21届中国国际钓鱼用品贸易展览会
21st Intl Fishing Tackle Trade Exhibition
北京Beijing
40

2011/02/18-21
（春季）中国郑州第18届中原广告展
暨2011年中国中部LED霓虹灯展
Zhengzhou Central China Advertising Exhibition
Central China LED Neon Exhibition
河南郑州Henan-Zhengzhou
5080

2011/02/20-22
德纳成都国际LED展览会及四新广告展览会
Chengdu LED and Advertising Exhibition
四川成都Sichuan-Chengdu
6540

2011/02/22-24
惠州国际汽车展览会
Huizhou Intl Automobile Exhibition
广东惠州Guangdong-Huizhou
4645

2011/02/22-24
（深圳）国家化妆品、个人及家庭护理用品原料展览会
Personal Care and Homecare ingredients Fair (PCHI)
广东深圳Guangdong-Shenzhen
4650

2011/02/23-25
中国中西部（重庆）医疗器械展览会
第19届中国重庆国际医疗器械展览会
China (Chongqing) Medical Equipment Exhibition
重庆Chongqing
1100

2011/02/23-26
上海市高校毕业生就业招聘会
Shanghai Job Fair for University graduates
上海Shanghai
1200

2011/02/23-26
第19届中国（上海）国际婚纱摄影器材展览会
19th China (Shanghai) Intl Wedding Photographic Equipment Exhibition
上海Shanghai
1210

2011/02/23-26
2011太阳能展（春交会）
Solar Energy
河南郑州Henan-Zhengzhou
5090

2011/02/23-26
上海国际婚纱摄影器材展览会暨
国际儿童摄影、主题摄影、相册相框展览会
China Wedding Expo 2011
上海Shanghai
1230

2011/02/24-26
2011佛山国际汽车展览会
Foshan Intl Automobile Exhibition
广东佛山Guangdong-Foshan
3900

2011/02/24-26
第八届广州(国际)车用空调及冷藏链技术展览会
8th Guangzhou Intl Automotive Air-conditioning & Cold Chain Technology Exhibition
广东广州Guangdong-Guangzhou
3920

2011/02/25-27
中国（海南）国际海钓装备暨用品展览会
China (Hainan) Sea Fishing Equipment Exhibition
海南海口Hainan-Haikou
4980

2011/02/25-27
第12届汽车用品暨改装汽车展览会
12th China Intl Expo for Auto Electronics, Accessories, Tuning & Car Care products
北京Beijing
50

2011/02/26-28
第五届山东国际自行车电动车及零部件展览会
5th Shandong Bike, Electric-Bike and Parts Exhibition
山东济南Shandong-Jinan
6120

2011/02/28-04
2011东莞数字喷印及广告技术展览会
China Sign Expo Dongguan 2011
广东东莞-Dongguan
3725

March 2011 三月

2011/03/01-05
第21届中国华东进出口商品交易会
East China Fair
上海Shanghai
1250

2011/03/01-04
第十届中国广州鞋业展览会
10th Guangzhou Shoes Exhibition
广东广州Guangdong-Guangzhou
3930

2011/03/01-03
第十八届中国豆腐文化节
18th China Tofu Culture Festival
安徽淮南Anhui-Huainan
3410

2011/03/01-03
福建（第22届）国际医疗仪器与设备展览会
Fujian Intl Medical Instruments and Equipment Exhibition
福建福州Fujian-Fuzhou
3420

2011/03/01-04
广州国际LED照明展
LED Lighting China
广东广州Guangdong-Guangzhou
3935

2011/03/01-04
第11届中国国际林业、木业机械与供应展览
WoodMac China 2011
上海Shanghai
1240

2011/03/01-04
广东国际广告展
Sign China
广东广州Guangdong-Guangzhou
3940

2011/03/02-05
第十届中国国际橱柜、壁柜、隔断、木业展览会
10th China Cupboard, Closet, Wood Exhibition
北京Beijing
100

2011/03/02-05
中国（北京）国际集成吊顶及天花材料博览会
China (Beijing) Intl Ceiling and Materials Expo
北京Beijing
80

2011/03/02-05
M.Y.COMIC 游园会
M.Y.COMIC
北京Beijing
60

2011/03/02-05
北京建材展览会-第18届中国（北京）国际建筑装饰及材料博览会
China Intl Building Decorations and Building Materials Exposition
北京Beijing
70

2011/03/02-05
第11届中国（北京）国际墙纸布艺展览会
11th China (Beijing) Wallpaper Exhibition
北京Beijing
90

2011/03/02-05
北京玻璃展览会-中国国际建筑装饰艺术玻璃及技术博览会
Beijing Glass Exhibition
北京Beijing
110

2011/03/03-05
济南国际机床模具展览会
Jinan Intl Machine Tools & Moulds Exhibition
山东济南Shandong-Jinan
6130

2011/03/03-05
中国(北京)国际供热空调、卫生洁具及城建设备与技术展览会
China Intl Trade Fair for Sanitation, Heating & Air-Conditioning
北京Beijing
120

2011/03/05-08
北京国际创意礼品及工艺品展览会
Beijing Intl Creative Gift & Craftwork Exhibition
北京Beijing
130

2011/03/06-08
中国（上海）第16届国际玩具展
暨上海玩具第47届博览会
Toy China 2011 (Spring)
上海Shanghai
1250

2011/03/06-09
中国厦门国际石材展览会
China (Xiamen) Stone Exhibition
福建厦门Fujian-Xiamen
3480

2011/03/07-12
年中国郑州微型汽车配件展
China (Zhengzhou) Mini Automobile and Parts Exhibition
河南郑州Henan-Zhengzhou
5100

2011/03/08-10
长春国际灯饰博览会暨LED应用展
Changchun Intl Lighting and LED Exhibition
吉林长春Jilin-Changchun
5560

2011/03/08-10
长春第十四届广告博览会
14th Changchun Advertising Expo
吉林长春Jilin-Changchun
5570

2011/03/09-10
第六届全国粳稻米大会
6th Countrywide Rice Convention
吉林长春Jilin-Changchun
5580

2011/03/09-11
第四届西安国际汽车用品展览会暨
2011西部汽车用品订货交易会
4th Xi' an Intl Automobile Accessories Fai
陕西西安Shaanxi-Xi'an
6020

2011/03/09-11
第17届上海国际服装纺织品贸易博览会
Shanghai Intl Clothing & Textile Expo
上海Shanghai
1280

2011/03/09-11
第18届华南国际印刷工业展览会
中国国际标签印刷技术展览会
18th South China Intl Exhibition on Printing Industry
China Intl Exhibition on Label Printing Technology
广东广州Guangdong-Guangzhou
3990

2011/03/09-11
中国广州国际工业自动化技术及装备展览会
SPS-Industrial Automation Fair-Guangzhou
广东广州Guangdong-Guangzhou
3960

2011/03/09-11
中国广州国际工业自动化技术及装备展览会
SPS - Industrial Automation Fair Guangzhou
广东广州Guangdong-Guangzhou
3950

2011/03/09-11
第34届广州国际美博会
34th Guangzhou Intl Beauty Expo - Spring 2011
广东广州Guangdong-Guangzhou
3970

2011/03/09-11
第12届中国（广州）国际给排水、水处理技术设备展览会/中国（广州）国际泵、阀门、管道展览会
Water Waster water & Water Treatment China
Pump, Vale & Pipe China
广东广州Guangdong-Guangzhou
3980

2011/03/09-11
第93届中国针棉织品交易会
第23届中国丝绸交易会
93rd China Intl Trade Fair for Mode
上海Shanghai
1330

2011/03/09-11
第19届中国国际五金博览会
19th China Intl Hardware Fair
上海Shanghai
1290

2011/03/09-12
CIDE-2011
第十届中国国际门业展览会
10th China Intl Door Industry Exhibition
北京Beijing
140

2011/03/10-12
第二届上海国际教育技术装备及高职教仪器展览会
2nd Shanghai Intl Educational Equipment Exhibition
上海Shanghai
1340

2011/03/10-12
青岛（春季）国际照明暨LED展览会
2nd Shanghai Intl Educational Equipment Exhibition
山东青岛Shandong-Qingdao
6220

2011/03/10-12
中国重庆第16届仪器仪表工业控制自动化国际展览会
Intl Automation& Instrument Exhibition Central & Western China
重庆Chongqing
1110

2011/03/11-13
上海宠物大会暨第四届上海宠物医疗学术研讨会
Pet Fair Shanghai 2011
上海Shanghai
1360

2011/03/11-13
第8届中国国际成人保健及生殖健康展览会
China Adult-Care Expo
上海Shanghai
1380

2011/03/11-13
第18届中国（温州）国际机床、工模具展览会
18th China (Wenzhou) Intl Machine Tool Exhibition
浙江温州Zhejiang-Wenzhou
6930

2011/03/12-13
第16届中国国际教育巡回展
16th China Intl Education Exhibition Tour
北京Beijing
150

2011/03/14-18
第20届中原国际医疗器械展览会
20th Central China Medical Equipment Exhibition
河南郑州Henan-Zhengzhou
5110

2011/03/15-17
第9届青岛国际金属加工技术设备展览会
9th Qingdao Intl Metal Processing Technology and Equipment Exhibition
山东青岛Shandong-Qingdao
6230

2011/03/15-17
中国国际电子电路展览会
(第20届中国国际电子电路展览会)
Intl Electronic Circuits Exhibition
(CPCA SHOW 2011)
上海Shanghai
1390

2011/03/15-18
中国家电博览会(上海)
China Appliance World Expo-Shanghai
上海Shanghai
1410

2011/03/16-19
第24届北京国际礼品、赠品及家庭用品展览会
China Beijing Intl Gifts, Premium & Houseware Exhibition
北京Beijing
170

2011/03/16-20
第25届国际名家具（东莞）展览会
25th Intl Famous Furniture Fair (Dongguan)
广东东莞Guangdong-Dongguan
3728

2011/03/17-19
第八届中国国际文具礼品博览会
（CNISE 2011）
8th China Intl Stationery & Gifts Exposition
浙江宁波Zhejiang-Ningbo
6860

2011/03/17-19
宁波国际海事展览会
China Maritime Tech & Security Expo 2011
浙江宁波Zhejiang-Ningbo
6850

2011/03/17-20
第12届中国国际机械工业展览会
12th China Intl Machinery Industry Exhibition
浙江宁波Zhejiang-Ningbo
6870

2011/03/17-20
上海之春房产展示交易会
shanghai spring real estate market
上海Shanghai
1420

2011/03/18-20
第四届华展云南广告四新暨LED照明展览会
4th Yunnan Advertising New Technology and New Media Exhibition/ LED Lighting Exhibition
云南昆明Yunnan-Kunming
6770

2011/03/18-20
第2届泛北部湾(广西)粮油、食品、农产品及其生产加工机械设备博览会
2nd Guangxi Exhibition on Food, Agricultural Products and Processing Machinery
广西南宁Guangxi-Nanning
4910

2011/03/18-20
第七届泛北部湾（广西）畜牧水产行业博览会
7th Guangxi Livestock, Fisheries Expo
广西南宁Guangxi-Nanning
4915

2011/03/18-20
第四届华展云南广告四新暨LED照明展览会
4th Yunnan Advertising New Technology and New Media Exhibition/ LED Lighting Exhibition
云南昆明Yunnan-Kunming
6780

2011/03/18-20
中国-亚欧博览会
（乌洽会）
China Urumqi Foreign Economic Relations & Trade Fair
新疆乌鲁木齐 Xinjiang- Urumqi
6770

2011/03/18-20
中国国际高尔夫球博览会
China Golf Show
北京Beijing
180

2011/03/18-21
中国广州国际家居饰品/用品展览会
Homedecor & Housewares China
广东广州Guangdong-Guangzhou
4010

2011/03/18-21
中国（广州）国际家用纺织品及辅料博览会
China (Guangzhou) Intl Trade Fair for Home Textiles
广东广州Guangdong-Guangzhou
4020

2011/03/18-21
中国广州户外及休闲展览会
China Intl Outdoor & Leisure Fair
广东广州Guangdong-Guangzhou
4030

2011/03/18-21
中国广州国际家具博览会(民用家具展
China Intl Furniture Fair (Guangzhou) – Home Furniture
广东广州Guangdong-Guangzhou
4040

2011/03/19-21
第十届中国（天津）国际客车及零部件展览会
10th China (Tianjin) Bus and Parts Exhibition
天津Tianjin
3330

2011/03/19-22
第26深圳国际家具展
Shenzhen Intl Furniture Exhibition
广东深圳Guangdong-Shenzhen
4660

2011/03/20-22
中国国际机器视觉展览会
China Intl Machine Vision Exhibition
上海Shanghai
1430

2011/03/20-23
中国国际婚纱及摄影器材博览会
China Wedding 2011
北京Beijing
190

2011/03/21-23
湖南环境保护产业博览会
Hunan Changsha Environment Protection Expo
湖南长沙Hunan-Changsha
5390

2011/03/21-26
中国中部（郑州）国际装备制造业博览会
Central China (Zhengzhou) Equipment and Manufacturing Expo
河南郑州Henan-Zhengzhou
5120

2011/03/22-24
第14届中国东北国际电力电工技术设备展览会暨东北国际节电、节能及新能源技术设备展览会
Northeast 14th Intl Electeotechnology Equipment Exhibition China 2011
辽宁沈阳Liaoning-Shenyang
5720

2011/03/22-24
中国国际遮阳与节能技术博览会
中国国际门及门禁系统展览会
R+T Asia
上海Shanghai
1470

2011/03/22-24
第9届上海国际园林景观设计及城市建设展览会
9th shanghai intl landscape design & urban construction expo
上海Shanghai
1450

2011/03/22-24
第四届中国东北流体机械展览会
（暨泵阀管、压缩机、风机展览会）
China (Northeast) 3rd Fluid Machinery Exhibition
辽宁沈阳Liaoning-Shenyang
5700

2011/03/22-24
中国沈阳春季房地产展示交易会
China Shenyang Spring Real Estate Fair
辽宁沈阳Liaoning-Shenyang
5690

2011/03/22-24
第14届中国东北国际仪器仪表及工业自动化展览会
Northeast 14th Intl Instrument & Automation Exhibition China
辽宁沈阳Liaoning-Shenyang
5710

2011/03/22-24
中国可持续建筑国家大会&展览会
China Sustainable Building Forum
(CSB 2011)
上海Shanghai
1460

2011/03/22-24
第13届中国国际地面材料及铺装技术展览会
DOMOTEX asia/CHINAFLOOR
上海Shanghai
1440

2011/03/23-25
第15届中国国际食品添加剂和配料展览会暨第21届全国食品添加剂生产应用技术展示会
Food Ingredients China
(FIC 2011)
上海Shanghai
1480

2011/03/23-25
第十届国际公共安全防范产品（济南）展览会
10th Jinan Intl Public Security Product Exhibition
山东济南Shandong-Jinan
6140

2011/03/24-26
广州国际个人医疗保健器械及用品展览会
Guangzhou Personal healthcare Exhibition
广东广州Guangdong-Guangzhou
4050

2011/03/24-26
广州国际旅游展览会
Guangzhou Intl Travel Fair
广东广州Guangdong-Guangzhou
4060

2011/03/25-27
天津国际工业装备展览会
Tianjin Intl Industry Fair
天津Tianjin
3380

2011/03/25-27
第2届中国(青岛)国际重型汽车、卡车、挂车及零部件展览会
2nd China (Qingdao) Intl Exhibition on Heavy Cars, Trucks and Special Vehicles and Parts
山东青岛Shandong-Qingdao
6240

2011/03/25-27
西部汽车用品订货交易会
4th Xi' an Intl Automobile Accessories Fair
陕西西安Shaanxi-Xi'an
6030

2011/03/25-27
第二届海南国际葡萄酒博览会
2nd Hainan Wine Expo
海南海口Hainan-Haikou
4990

2011/03/25-27
第12届广西广告技术设备展览会
12th Guangxi Advertising Technology & Equipment Exhibition
广西南宁Guangxi-Nanning
4920

2011/03/25-27
第23届国际医疗仪器设备展览会
23rd Intl Medical Instruments and Equipment Exhibition
北京Beijing
200

2011/03/25-27
第5届广西国际糖业技术设备展览会
5th Guangxi Intl Sugar Industry Exhibition
广西南宁Guangxi-Nanning
4930

2011/03/25-27
中国（常州）国际摩托车零部件及后用品交易会
China (Changzhou) Intl Motorbike, Parts and Services Fair
江苏常州Jiangsu-Changzhou
5440

2011/03/25-27
北京旅居人士服务展览会
Expat Show
北京Beijing
210

2011/03/25-27
第2届中国（安徽）新能源与光伏展览会
2nd China (Anhui) New Energy and Photovoltaic Exhibition
安徽合肥Anhui-Hefei
3400

2011/03/25-27
第2届中国(安徽)节能、新能源汽车展览会
2nd China (Anhui) Energy Saving, New Energy VehiclesExpo
安徽合肥Anhui-Hefei
3390

2011/03/25-28
春季全国糖酒会
China National Sugar and Alcoholic Commodities Fair
四川成都Sichuan-Chengdu
6550

2011/03/27-29
中国（沈阳）第九届建筑节能、墙体保温材料及设备展览会
9th china (shenyang) Intl energy-saving & new wall material and equipment exhibition.
辽宁沈阳Liaoning-Shenyang
2730

2011/03/27-29
中国东北第14届国际供热供暖、空调、热泵技术设备展览会
China (Northeast) 14th Intl Equipments of Heating, Air-Condition & New Energy Sources Exhibition
辽宁沈阳Liaoning-Shenyang
5750

2011/03/27-29
第12届东北国际给排水、水处理技术设备及泵、阀、管道展览会
12th Northeast Intl water disposal technique & equipment and pump & value and pipeline exhibition
辽宁沈阳Liaoning-Shenyang
5740

2011/03/27-30
中国广州国际木工机械、家具配料展览会
interzum guangzhou
广东广州Guangdong-Guangzhou
4070

2011/03/27-30
中国广州国际家具博览会 （办公环境展）
China Intl Furniture Fair (Guangzhou) – Office Show
广东广州Guangdong-Guangzhou
4080

2011/03/28-30
中国（济南）国际打印耗材及办公设备展览会
China (Jinan) Printer Accessories and Office Equipment Exhibition
山东济南Shandong-Jinan
6150

2011/03/28-30
第6届国际胶粘带、保护膜及光学膜（上海）展览会
6th Intl Adhesive tape Protective Films & Optical Film (Shanghai) Expo
上海Shanghai
1530

2011/03/28-30
第4届国际光学膜及高机能薄膜(上海)展览会
FILMEXPO
上海Shanghai
1510

2011/03/28-31
第12届深圳国际机械、模具及制品、塑胶工业展览会
China Shenzhen Intl Machinery Manufacturing Industry Exhibition
（SIMM2011）
广东深圳Guangdong-Shenzhen
4670

2011/03/28-31
第19届中国国际服装服饰博览会
19th China Intl Clothing & Accessories Fair
(CHIC2011)
北京Beijing
230

2011/03/28-31
第12届中国(东莞)国际鞋机鞋材工业技术展
12th China (Dongguan) Intl Footwear Machinery & Material Industry Fair
广东东莞Guangdong-Dongguan
3720

2011/03/28-31
第12届中国(东莞)国际纺织制衣工业技术展
12th China (Dongguan) Intl Textile & Clothing Industry Fair
广东东莞Guangdong-Dongguan
3730

2011/03/29-30
第3届全国杂粮产业大会
3rd Natl Grain Industry Conference
北京Beijing
240

2011/03/29-31
广州国际食品展暨广州进口食品展览会
Guangzhou Food Fair
广东广州Guangdong-Guangzhou
4100

2011/03/29-31
第6届中国西部国际科学仪器及实验室装备展览会
6th Western China Intl Exhibition for Scientific Instruments and Laboratory Equipments, IESILE
四川成都Sichuan-Chengdu
6570

2011/03/29-31
第4届成都国际教育技术装备及高教仪器展览会
4th Chengdu Intl Education and Higher Education Exhibition on Technology and Equipment
四川成都Sichuan-Chengdu
6560

2011/03/29-31
广州药交会
第18届全国药品保健品（广州）交易会
18 China Medicine and Healthcare Products (Guangzhou) Exhibition
广东广州Guangdong-Guangzhou
4090

2011/03/29-31
CINHOE 2011
第十届中国（广州）国际营养品/健康食品及有机产品展览会
Guangzhou Nutrition and Organic Food Exhibition
广东广州Guangdong-Guangzhou
4110

2011/03/29-31
第12届中国国际天然气汽车、加气站设备展览会
12th China Intl Natural Gas Automobile and Gas Station Equipment Exhibition
北京Beijing
250

2011/03/29-31
第12届中国（上海）广告四新展览会
12th China (Shanghai) Advertising Four New Expo
上海Shanghai
1540

2011/03/29-31
第11届中国成都国际照明博览会
Chengdu Intl Lighting Fair
四川成都Sichuan-Chengdu
6580

2011/03/29-01
中国(上海)国际建筑涂料展览会
Expo Coat
上海Shanghai
1580

2011/03/29-01
中国清洁博览会
China Clean Expo
上海Shanghai
1570

2011/03/29-01
W3国际精品设计展
Expo Deco
上海Shanghai
1590

2011/03/29-01
第12届中国国际建筑陶瓷及卫浴科技精品展览会
Ceramics, Tile & Sanitary Ware China
上海Shanghai
1550

2011/03/29-03
上海国际酒店用品博览会：
- 中国(上海)国际酒店与建筑照明展览会
- 中国国际康体健身、休闲娱乐与运动器材展览会
Hotelex Shanghai：
- Expo Light
- Fitness, Sports & Leisure China
上海Shanghai
1630

2011/03/29-03
中国国际咖啡与茶用品展览会
Coffee & Tea China
上海Shanghai
1620

2011/03/30-01
中国国际纺织面料及辅料（春夏）博览会
China Intl Trade Fair for Apparel Fabrics and Accessories
北京Beijing
260

2011/03/30-03
第二届华夏有机肥展示会暨
第七届中原肥料双交会
2nd China Organic Fertilizer Show
河南郑州Henan-Zhengzhou
5140

2011/03/30-03
中国古玩展览会
China Antique Exhibition
河南郑州Henan-Zhengzhou
5130

2011/03/31-02
中国北方国际自行车电动车展览会
China North Intl Bicycle & E-bike Exhibition
天津Tianjin
3340

2011/03/31-02
中国国际纺织纱线（春夏）展览会
China Intl Trade Fair for Fibres and Yarns
北京Beijing
270

2011/03/31-02
第4届中国（永康）五金装备、机床及工模具展览会
4th China (Yongkang) Hardware Equipment & Machine Tools Exhibition
浙江永康Zhejiang-Yongknag
7090

April 2011 四月

2011/04 -
2011年第五届杭州春季汽车展销会
5th Spring Hangzhou Automobile Fair
浙江杭州Zhejiang-Hangzhou
6810

2011/04 -
品质生活.精品汽车浙江巡回展
Automobile Zhejiang Road Show
浙江Zhejiang-
6801

2011/04/01-04
中国东北第13届国际口腔器材展览会暨学术交流会/第三届口腔保健护理用品展览会/第一届义齿加工产品展览会
13 China Northeast Intl Dental Equipment & Affiliated Facilities Exhibition
辽宁沈阳Liaoning-Shenyang
5760

2011/04/02-04
中国国际家用纺织品及辅料（春夏）博览会
China Intl Trade Fair for Home Textiles and Accessories
上海Shanghai
1640

2011/04/03-05
深圳春季婚博会暨婚庆文化节
Shenzhen Intl Wedding Exhibition &Wedding Cultural Festival
广东深圳Guangdong-Shenzhen
4680

2011/04/06-09
中国国际瓦楞展
SinoCorrugated
上海Shanghai
1660

2011/04/06-10
第2届大河汽车博览会
2nd Giant River Automobile Expo
河南郑州Henan-Zhengzhou
5150

2011/04/07-09
第22届国际制冷、空调、供暖、通风及食品冷冻加工展览会
22nd Intl Exhibition for Refrigeration, Air-conditioning, Heating and Ventilation, Frozen Food Processing, Packaging and Storage
上海Shanghai
1670

2011/04/07-09
国际表面工程展览会
seexpo
上海Shanghai
1680

2011/04/07-09
第3届上海国际搪瓷工业展览会
Intl Ceramics Industry Forum Held Concurrently 2011
上海Shanghai
16R90

2011/04/07-10
第九届中国（温州）汽车展览会
9th Wenzhou Intl Auto Expo
浙江温州Zhejiang-Wenzhou
6940

2011/04/07-10
中国北京春季房地产展示交易会
Springtime Real Estate Trade Fair Beijing China
北京Beijing
290

2011/04/07-11
第五届中国（沈阳）汽车交易博览会
5th China (Shenyang) Automobile Fair
辽宁沈阳Liaoning-Shenyang
5770

2011/04/08-10
北京国际美容美发化妆用品博览会
Chinese Intl Beauty, Hairdressing & Cosmetics Expo in Beijing
北京Beijing
300

2011/04/08-10
第11届中国国际眼科和视光技术及设备展览会
11th Intl Congress of Ophthalmology and Optometry China
上海Shanghai
1710

2011/04/08-10
第14届中国东北国际五金工具展览会
14 China (Northeast) Intl Hardware and Tool Exhibition
辽宁沈阳Liaoning-Shenyang
5780

2011/04/08-10
第77届中国电子展
77th China Electronics Fair
广东深圳Guangdong-Shenzhen
4690

2011/04/08-10
第23届广州国际玩具及模型展览会
23rd Guangzhou Intl Toy & Hobby Fair
广东广州Guangdong-Guangzhou
4130

2011/04/08-10
第5届中国（上海）国际风能展览会暨研讨会
China (Shanghai) Intl Wind Energy Exhibition and Conference
上海Shanghai
1720

2011/04/08-10
“魅力之都”2011温州房产展
Wenzhou Real Estate Exhibition
浙江温州Zhejiang-Wenzhou
6950

2011/04/08-10
第2届广州国际婴童用品展
2nd Guangzhou Intl Baby Product Fair
广东广州Guangdong-Guangzhou
4120

2011/04/8-11
第9届中国（漯河）食品博览会
9th China (Luohe) Food Fair
河南漯河Henan-Luohe
5060

2011/04/08-11
第16届中国国际建筑装饰材料展览会
16th China Intl Construction & Decoration Materials Exhibition
辽宁大连Liaoning-Dalian
5590

2011/04/08-11
第15届对台出口商品交易会
15th China Xiamen Machinery and Electronics Exhibition (CXMEE)
福建厦门Fujian-Xiamen
3490

2011/04/08-11
中国洛阳国际汽车展览会
China Luoyang Intl Automobile Exhibition
河南洛阳Henan-Luoyang
5070

2011/04/09-13
第二届中国(广东)国际印刷技术展览会
2nd Intl Printing Technology Exhibition of China(Guangdong)
广东东莞Guangdong-Dongguan
3740

2011/04/10-12
中国（临沂）酒店用品及设备博览会
China (Linyi) Hotel Supplies and Equipment Exhibition
山东临沂Shandong-Linyi
6190

2011/04/11-15
中国郑州烘焙展览会
China (Zhengzhou) Baking Exhibition
河南郑州Henan-Zhengzhou
5160

2011/04/11-16
第12届中国国际机床展览会
12th China Intl Machine Tool Show
北京Beijing
310

2011/04/12-14
第8届中国国际有及特种铸造展览会暨中国铸造零部件展览会
Non-ferrous & Special foundry and China Cast-part Exhibition
江苏南京Jiangsu-Nanjing
5500

2011/04/12-14
中国国际船舶工业博览会
China Intl Marine, Port & Shipbuilding Fair
江苏南京Jiangsu-Nanjing
5510

2011/04/12-16
第9届郑州社会公共安全产品博览会
9th Zhengzhou Public Safety and Security Products Expo
河南郑州Henan-Zhengzhou
5170

2011/04/13-15
第13届东北国际汽车用品展览会
Shenyang China Car Expo
辽宁沈阳Liaoning-Shenyang
5790

2011/04/13-15
中国出境旅游交易会
China Outbound Travel and Tourism Market
北京Beijing
330

2011/04/13-15
第7届全国（北京）焙烤展览会
China Intl Trade Fair for Bakery & Confectionery
北京Beijing
320

2011/04/13-16
第13届中国国际花卉园艺展览会
13th Hortiflorexpo China
上海Shanghai
1740

2011/04/14-16
第2届中国（重庆）国际电子信息产业展览会
2nd China (Chongqing) Electronic Information Industry Exhibition
重庆Chongqing
1120

2011/04/14-16
中国（重庆）国际物联网技术与应用展览会
China (Chongqing) Exhibition on Internet of Things
重庆Chongqing
1130

2011/04/14-17
中国(上海)国际游艇展
China (Shanghai) Intl Boat Show
上海Shanghai
1750

2011/04/14-18
第6届中国(广州)国际建材交易会暨红星美凯龙直销周
6th China (Guangzhou) Building Materials Fair
广东广州Guangdong-Guangzhou
4140

2011/04/15-17
中国济南建筑装饰玻璃及艺术玻璃展会
China Jinan Architecture Glass and Art Glass Exhibition
山东济南Shandong-Jinan
6160

2011/04/15-17
第12届中国济南国际门窗、型材及配套实施展览会
Jinan Intl Doors and Windows, Profiles and Facilities Exhibition
12th China Jinan Intl Door and Decorative Hardware Exhibition
山东济南Shandong-Jinan
6170

2011/04/15-17
烟台春季汽车展销会
山东烟台Shandong-Yantai
6440

2011/04/15-18
第25届(春季)成都美容美发节
2011 Spring Yantai Automobile Show
四川成都Sichuan-Chengdu
6590

2011/04/15-19
中国东北（沈阳）政府采购暨节能减排展览会
Northeast China (Shenyang) Intl Exhibition for Government Purchase
辽宁沈阳Liaoning-Shenyang
6005

2011/04/15-19
首届.贵阳国际汽车展览会
Guiyang Intl Automobile Exhibition
贵州贵阳Guizhou-Guiyang
4950

2010/04/15-19
第109届中国进出口商品交易会（第一期）
109th China Import and Export Fair Phase 1
广东广州Guangdong-Guangzhou
4145

2011/04/16-19
第65届中国国际医疗器械博览会
第12届中国国际医疗器械设计与制造技术展览会
China Intl Medical Equipment Fair
广东深圳Guangdong-Shenzhen
4700

2011/04/17-19
中国国际葡萄酒及烈酒展览会
China Intl Wine & Spirits Exhibition
北京Beijing
340

2011/04/18-20
中国国际食用油及橄榄油展览会
China Intl Exhibition of Olive Oil & Edible Oi
上海Shanghai
1760

2011/04/18-21
第14届海峡两岸纺织服装博览会暨2011休闲服装博览会
Straits Textile & Clothing Fair
2011 Casual Wear Expo
福建石狮Fujian-Shishi
3450

2011/04/18-21
第13届中国（晋江）国际鞋业博览会
13th China (Jinjiang) Intl Footwear Exhibition
福建晋江Fujian-Jinjiang
3440

2011/04/20-22
第18届中国国际工业装备展览会
18th China Intl Industry Fair（CIF）
重庆Chongqing
1150

2011/04/20-22
第8届ReChina亚洲打印耗材展览会(春季)
ReChina Asia Expo 2011(Spring Session)
上海Shanghai
1770

2011/04/20-22
中国唐山专（商）用车暨现代物流博览会
China (Tanshan) Special Purpose Vehicle & Logistic Expo
河北唐山Hebei-Tangshan
5000

2011/04/20-22
Office World办公设备展览会
Office World Expo
上海Shanghai
1780

2011/04/20-23
中国义乌文化产品交易博览会
China Yiwu Cultural Products Trade Fair
浙江义乌Zhejiang-Yiwu
6990

2011/04/20-23
第18届中国（北京）国际石材产品及石材技术装备展览会
18th China Intl Stone Processing Machinery, Equipment and Products Exhibition
北京Beijing
350

2011/04/20-24
中艺博国际画廊博览会
China Intl Gallery Exposition
北京Beijing
360

2011/04/21-23
中国哈尔滨国际生态城市建设博览会
China (Harbin) Urban Eco Construction Expo
黑龙江哈尔滨Heilongjiang-Haerbin
5020

2011/04/21-23
世界制药工业展中国展区（原包装材料、制药设备区）
INTERPHEX CHINA Conference & Exhibition
四川成都Sichuan-Chengdu
6600

2011/04/21-23
第66届中国国际医药原料药、中间体、包装、设备交易会
66th API China & INTERPHEX China
四川成都Sichuan-Chengdu
6620

2011/04/21-24
中国国际照相机械影像器材与技术博览会
China Intl Photograph & Electrical Imaging Machinery and Technology Fair
北京Beijing
370

2011/04/21-27
第6届广州国际采购博览会
6th Guangzhou Purchasing Fair
广东广州Guangdong-Guangzhou
4150

2011/04/21-28
第14届上海国际汽车工业展览会
AUTO SHANGHAI 2011
上海Shanghai
1790

2011/04/22-25
第12届中国东北国际物流技术及运输系统展览会
12th Northeast Intl Physical Distribution & Transport System Exhibition
辽宁沈阳Liaoning-Shenyang
5800

2011/04/22-24
2011中国国际衡器展览会
InterWeighing2011
上海Shanghai
1800

2011/04/22-25
中国东北第15届国际焊接、切割、激光技术设备展览会
15th China (Northeast) Intl Welding, Cutting & Laser Technology and Equipment Exhibition
辽宁沈阳Liaoning-Shenyang
5850

2011/04/22-25
第12届中国东北国际机床、工模具技术展览会
12th Intl Machine Tool and Tools & Moulds Technique Exhibition in Northeast of China
辽宁沈阳Liaoning-Shenyang
5810

2011/04/22-25
第12届中国东北国际机床、工模具技术展览会
12th Intl Machine Tool and Tools & Moulds Technique Exhibition in Northeast Of China
辽宁沈阳Liaoning-Shenyang
5830

2011/04/22-25
第12届中国东北国际物流技术及运输系统展览会
12th Northeast Intl Physical Distribution & Transport System Exhibition
辽宁沈阳Liaoning-Shenyang
5820

2011/04/22-25
第69届全国汽车配件交易会暨全国汽车配件采购交易会
National Auto Parts Fair
待定undetermined
5820

2011/04/22-25
第12届中国东北国际塑胶机械及包装展览会
Northeast 12th Intl Plastics Machinery & Packaging Exhibition China
辽宁沈阳Liaoning-Shenyang
5860

2011/04/23-27
第109届中国进出口商品交易会（第二期）
109th China Import and Export Fair Phase II
广东广州Guangdong-Guangzhou
4155

2011/04/24-27
第19届中国（深圳）国际礼品、工艺品、钟表及家庭用品展览会
19th China (Shenzhen) Intl Gifts, Handicrafts, Watches & Houseware Fair
广东深圳Guangdong-Shenzhen
4710

2011/04/24-28
首届中国（郑州）国际孕婴童用品博览会
1st China (Zhengzhou) Expo for Baby, Kids and Mother-to-be Products
河南郑州Henan-Zhengzhou
5180

2011/04/25-27
第9届中国国际科学仪器及实验室装备展览会
9th China Intl Scientific Instrument and Laboratory Equipment
北京Beijing
380

2011/04/26-28
北京酒店用品、厨房设备、清洁用品、咖啡展览会（第十四届北京酒店设备用品展览会）
14th Beijing Hospitality Equipment & Supplies Exhibition
北京Beijing
390

2011/04/26-28
第11届中国国际染料工业暨有机颜料、纺织化学品展览会
CHINA INTERDYE 2011
上海Shanghai
1810

2011/04/27-29
第13届山东口腔器械与齿科材料（青岛）展览会
13th Shandong Exhibition on Dental & Denture Equipment and Materials
山东青岛Shandong-Qingdao
6250

2011/04/27-29
北京国际隧道地下工程、喷涂聚脲、土工材料、工程纤维及建筑化学品展览会
Beijing Intl Tunnel Underground Project, Spray Polyurea, Geo-technical Material, Engineering Fiber and Construction Chemicals Exhibition
北京Beijing
400

2011/04/27-29
第11届中国哈尔滨国际装备制造业博览会
11th China Harbin Intl Manufacture Exhibition
黑龙江哈尔滨Heilongjiang-Harbin
5030

2011/04/28-30
第13届中国东莞国际鞋展·鞋机展·鞋材展（春季）
13th Dongguan China Shoes · China Shoetec
广东东莞Guangdong-Dongguan
3745

2011/04/28-30
第8届中国国际五金电器博览会
8th China Intl Hardware & Electrical Appliances Trade Fair
浙江义乌Zhejiang-Yiwu
7000

2011/04/28-30
义乌消费品交易会
Yiwu Sourcing Fair: Consumer Goods
浙江义乌Zhejiang-Yiwu
7010

2011/04/29-05/02
艺术北京-当代艺术博览会
Art Beijing Contemporary Art Fair
北京Beijing
410

2011/04/29-05/03
第17届福州国际汽车展览会
17th Auto Fuzhou
福建福州Fujian-Fuzhou
3430

2011/04/30-05/03
上海房地产展示会-假日楼市
holiday real estate market
上海Shanghai
1840

2011/04/30-05/04
第4届中国（南京）国际汽车博览会
4th China (Nanjing) Intl Automobile Expo
江苏南京Jiangsu-Nanjing
5515

May 2011 五月

2011/05-
第二届中国国际门业博览会
China Intl Door Industry Fair
浙江永康Zhejiang-Yongkang
7070

2011/05-
品质生活.精品汽车浙江巡回展
Automobile Zhejiang Road Show
浙江Zhejiang
6802

2011/05/01-03
第3届常州春季汽车博览会
3rd Changzhou Spring Automobile Expo
江苏常州Jiangsu-Changzhou
5450

2011/05/01-05
第109届中国进出口商品交易会（第三期）
109th China Import and Export Fair Phase 3
广东广州Guangdong-Guangzhou
4156

2011/05/04-06
中国东莞国际鞋展-鞋机展-手袋展
Dongguan Shoes-China Shoetes-China Bags
广东东莞Guangdong-Dongguan
3745-1

2011/05/04-07
第21届中国国际自行车展览会
CHINA CYCLE 2011
上海Shanghai
1860

2011/05/05-07
上海国际室内供暖、通风及净化产品展览会
Shanghai Intl Residential Comfort System Expo
上海Shanghai
1870

2011/05/05-07
（第12届）中国国际环保、废弃物及资源利用展览会
IFAT CHINA+EPTEE+CWS 2011
上海Shanghai
1880

2011/05/06-08
第6届义乌汽车展览会
6th Yiwu Automobile Exhibition
浙江义乌Zhejiang-Yiwu
7020

2011/05/07-09
COMIC.G.U动漫交流会
COMIC.G.U
北京Beijing
420

2011/05/07-09
中国特许展-第13届中国特许加盟展览会
China Franchise Expo 2011
北京Beijing
430

2011/05/07-11
第61届中国教育装备展示会
61st China Education Equipment Exhibition
陕西西安Shaanxi-Xi'an
6040

2011/05/08-10
北京国际减灾应急技术设备博览会
Disaster Reduction and Emergency Technology Exhibition
北京Beijing
440

2011/05/08-11
第4届广州国际宠物水族用品展
4th Guangzhou Intl Pet & Aquarium Show
广东广州Guangdong-Guangzhou
4160

2011/05/11-13
第9届广州国际表面处理 电镀 涂装展览会
9th Guangzhou Intl Surface Finishing, Electroplating and Coating Exhibition
广东广州Guangdong-Guangzhou
4180

2011/05/11-13
中国柯桥国际纺织品博览会
Heqiao Textile Expo
浙江绍兴Zhejiang-Shaoxing
6910

2011/05/11-13
第4届中国（台州）国际船舶工业博览会
4th Session China (Taizhou) Intl Shipbuilding Exposition in 2011
浙江台州Zhejiang-Taizhou
6920

2011/05/11-13
中国国际电子生产设备暨微电子工业展
NEPCON China 2011
上海Shanghai
1890

2011/05/11-13
上海国际新光源&新能源照明展览会暨论坛
Green Lighting Shanghai Expo and Forum
上海Shanghai
1910

2011/05/11-13
苏州自动化产业设备展览会
Suzhou Automation Industry Exhibition
江苏苏州Jiangsu-Suzhou
5550

2011/05/11-13
苏州电路板展览会
Suzhou PCB / SMT Show
江苏苏州Jiangsu-Suzhou
5540

2011/05/11-13
第9届广州国际涂料 油墨 胶粘剂展览会
9th Guangzhou (China) Intl Coatings, Printing Inks & Adhesives Exhibition
广东广州Guangdong-Guangzhou
4170

2011/05/11-14
第14届中国国际焙烤展览会
14th China Intl Trade Fair For Bakery & Confectionery
上海Shanghai
1920

2011/05/12-14
第5届中国国际新型墙体材料技术装备及产品展览会暨中国散装水泥暨预拌混凝土与预拌砂浆技术装备及产品展览会
WALLEXPO CHINA 2011
北京Beijing
450

2011/05/12-14
中国中西部（太原）医疗器械展览会
Taiyuan Medical Equipment Exhibition
山西太原Shanxi-Taiyuan
6500

2011/05/12-14
第15届中国国际软件博览会
INTL SOFT CHINA 2011
北京Beijing
460

2011/05/12-14
第5届中国国际金属工业博览会
5th China Intl Metals Industry Trade Fair
广东广州Guangdong-Guangzhou
4190

2011/05/12-15
上海世界旅游资源博览会
World Travel Fair
上海Shanghai
1930

2011/05/13-15
第13届北京国际玩具及幼教用品展览会暨北京国际婴幼童用品展览会
Beijing Intl Toys & Preschool Tools Exhibition, China Intl Pregnancy and Baby Show
北京Beijing
480

2011/05/13-16
2011 (第28届) 中国国际体育用品博览会
China Sport Show 2011
四川成都Sichuan-Chengdu
6630

2011/05/13-16
第4届中国武汉茶业博览会暨陆羽国际茶文化节
4th China Wuhan Tea Expo
湖北武汉Hubei-Wuhan
5310

2011/05/13-16
第7届中国（深圳）国际文化产业博览交易会暨第2届中国国际新媒体影视动漫节
China (Shenzhen) Intl Cultural Industries Fair
广东深圳Guangdong-Shenzhen
4715

2011/05/13-16
第2届中国（贵州）国际铁路、城市轨道交通技术与装备展览会
2nd China (Guizhou) Exhibition on Railway, Urban Rail, Transport Technology and Equipment
贵州贵阳Guizhou-Guiyang
4960

2011/05/13-16
第6届中国（贵州）国际装备制造业博览会
6th China (Guizhou) Intl Industry Equipment Fair
贵州贵阳Guizhou-Guiyang
4970

2011/05/14-16
第20届华南(东莞)国际电子制造采购博览会
20th (Dongguan) south China Electronic Fair
广东东莞Guangdong-Dongguan
3745-2

2011/05/14-16
新疆－中亚家用电器、厨卫及消费电子展
Xinjiang Central Asia Home Appliances and Consumer Electronic
新疆乌鲁木齐Xinjiang-Urumuqi
6720

2011/05/16-18
中国国际康复护理展览会
第六届中国国际老年人和残疾人康复护理技术及辅助器具展览会
China Aid 2011
6th China Intl Exhibition of Rehabilitation, Nursing & Health care
上海Shanghai
1940

2011/05/16-18
中国实验室技术及装备交易会
61th China Laboratory Technology and Equipment Exhibition
广东广州Guangdong-Guangzhou
4200

2011/05/17-19
第8届上海国际箱包皮具手袋展览会
8th Shanghai Intl Cases & Boxes And Handbags Exhibition
上海Shanghai
1950

2011/05/17-19
中国（上海）产业用纺织品、非织造布及无纺布展览会
Shanghai Textile, Non-woven Exhibition
上海Shanghai
1970

2011/05/17-19
第6届中国临沂塑料机械暨塑料包装展览会
6th China Linyi Plastic Machinery and Plastic Packaging Exhibition
山东临沂Shandong-Linyi
6200

2011/05/17-19
第5届上海国际环保购物袋、包装袋展览会
5th Shanghai Intl Shopping Bags and Package Bags Expo
上海Shanghai
1960

2011/05/17-20
第25届中国国际塑料橡胶工业展览会
25th Intl Exhibition on Plastics and Rubber Industries
广东广州Guangdong-Guangzhou
4210

2011/05/18-20
中国国际酒店博览会
Hotel China 2011
北京Beijing
490

2011/05/18-20
第16届中国美容博览会
（上海CBE）
China Beauty Expo
上海Shanghai
1980

2011/05/18-20
第12届中国国际食品和饮料展览会
SIAL China 2011
上海Shanghai
1990

2011/05/18-20
国际现代工厂/过程自动化技术与装备展览会
FA/PA 2011
北京Beijing
500

2011/05/18-20
第12届西安国际酒店设备及用品展览会
12th Xi' an Intl Hospitality Equipment & Supplies Fair
陕西西安Shaanxi-Xi'an
6060

2011/05/18-20
2011中国（天津）国际医疗仪器与设备展览会
China (Tianjin) Intl Medical Instruments and Equipment Exhibition
天津Tianjin
3350

2011/05/18-21
第3届中国(西安)国际桥梁、建筑模板及生产设备展览会
3rd China (Xi'an) Intl Building Formwork Scaffolding & Construction Technology Exhibition
陕西西安Shaanxi-Xi'an
6090

2011/05/18-21
第11届中国（西安）门窗幕墙及设备展览会
10th China (Xi' an) Fenestration and Equipment Exhibition
陕西西安Shaanxi-Xi'an
6080

2011/05/18-21
第5届中国（西安）建筑节能节新型建材博览会
5th China (Xi'an) Intl Energy-saving & Advanced Building Materials Exhibition
陕西西安Shaanxi-Xi'an
6070

2011/05/18-21
第14届中国北京国际科技产业博览会
14th China Beijing Intl High-Tech Expo
北京Beijing
510

2011/05/18-22
常州住宅产品交易会
Changzhou Housing Fair
江苏常州Jiangsu-Changzhou
5460

2011/05/18-23
中国郑州渔具用品展览会
China (Zhengzhou) Fishing Equipment Exhibition
河南郑州Henan-Zhengzhou
5190

2011/05/19-21
第9届大连国际印刷及包装工业展览会
9th Dalian Intl Printing and Packaging Exhibition
辽宁大连Liaoning-Dalian
5600

2011/05/19-21
新疆国际建筑材料博览会
Xinjiang Intl Building Fair
新疆乌鲁木齐Xinjiang-Urumuqi
6730

2011/05/19-21
（第13届）大连国际自动化、仪表展览会
13th Dalian Intl Automation & Instrumentation Exhibition
辽宁大连Liaoning-Dalian
5610

2011/05/19-21
烟台国际物流及仓储设备展览会
Yantai Logistics and Storage Equipment Exhibition
山东烟台Shandong-Yantai
6460

2011/05/19-21
烟台国际机床暨工模具技术设备展览会
Yantai Intl Machine Tools & Industrial Moulds Equipment Exhibition
山东烟台Shandong-Yantai
6450

2011/05/19-21
第9届烟台国际动力传动及控制技术展览会
Yantai Power Transmission and Control Technology Exhibition
山东烟台Shandong-Yantai
6480

2011/05/19-21
第9届大连国际焊接工业展览会
9th Dalian Intl Welding Exhibition
辽宁大连Liaoning-Dalian
5620

2011/05/19-21
第9届烟台国际工业自动化及仪器仪表展览会
9th Yantai Intl Industrial Automation & Instrument Exhibition
山东烟台Shandong-Yantai
6470

2011/05/19-21
第9届烟台国际机床暨工模具技术设备展览会
9th Yantai Intl Machine Tools & Industrial Mould Technology and Equipment Exhibition
山东烟台Shandong-Yantai
6490

2011/05/20-22
第6届上海国际幼儿教育展
6th education expo 2011 shanghai
上海Shanghai
2000

2011/05/20-22
东莞国际纺织品印花工业技术展览会
China Intl Textile Printing Industrial Technology Exposition
广东东莞Guangdong-Dongguan
3746

2011/05/20-22
第8届厦门人居环境展示会
8th Living Environment Exhibition
福建厦门Fujian-Xiamen
3500

2011/05/20-22
第6届中国（厦门）国际建筑节能博览会
6th China (Xiamen) Intl Energy Efficiency in Buildings Expo
福建厦门Fujian-Xiamen
3510

2011/05/20-23
中国（上海）国际茶业博览会
China Tea Expo, Shanghai
上海Shanghai
2020

2011/05/20-23
第10届中国国际古典家具展览
2011上海国际古董及艺术品展览会（春季展）
Antique Furniture China 2011
Antiques & Arts Shanghai
上海Shanghai
2010

2011/05/20-24
第9届华中国际汽车展览会
9th Central China Automobile Exhibition
湖北武汉Hubei-Wuhan
5320

2011/05/23-25
中国西部工程机械建筑机械及混凝土设备展览会
West China Construction Machinery and Concrete Machinery Exhibition
四川成都Sichuan-Chengdu
6640

2011/05/23-26
中国国际葡萄酒博览会
TopWine China 2011
北京Beijing
530

2011/05/25-27
第12届湖南工控自动化及仪器仪表展览会
12th Industrial Control, Automation, Instrument Exhibition
湖南长沙Hunan-Changsha
5410

2011/05/25-27
第6届湖南电力新技术新装备展览会
Hunan Electric Power Technology and Equipment Exhibition
湖南长沙Hunan-Changsha
5400

2011/05/25-29
中国（郑州）国际缝制设备展览会暨
2011中国（郑州）国际纺织面料、辅料及纱线展览会
Hunan Electric Power Technology and Equipment Exhibition
河南郑州Henan-Zhengzhou
5200

2011/05/26-28
中国国际有机食品博览会
BioFach China 2011
上海Shanghai
2040

2011/05/26-28
广州国际机床模具展览会
Guangzhou Intl Machine Tools & moulds Exhibition
广东广州Guangdong-Guangzhou
4220

2011/05/26-28
第15届中国烘焙展览会
15th China Bakery Exhibition
广东广州Guangdong-Guangzhou
4225

2011/05/26-28
第2届中国国际门业博览会
china Intl door industry fair
浙江永康Zhejiang-Yongknag
7100

2011/05/26-29
中国国际旅游商品博览会
China Intl Tourism Commodities Fair
浙江义乌Zhejiang-Yiwu
7030

2011/05/26-29
第20届中国国际专业音响·灯光·乐器及技术展览会
20th China Intl Exhibition on Pro Audio, Light, Music & Technology
北京Beijing
540

2011/05/27-29
第9届中国（厦门）食品交易博览会
9th China (Xiamen) Food Expo
福建厦门Fujian-Xiamen
3520

2011/05/27-01
第7届中国（唐山）国际汽车博览会
7th China (Tangshan) Intl Automobile Expo
河北唐山Hebei-Tangshan
5010

2011/05/28-29
中国新能源战略与“十二五”新能源发展高峰论坛暨新能源产业十一五成就盘点
New Energy Strategy Summit
北京Beijing
550

2011/05/28-29
第2届中国（浙江）汽配交易会
2nd China (Hangzhou) Auto Part Fair
浙江杭州Zhejiang-Hangzhou
6830

2011/05/28-29
中国（浙江）改装车、专用车博览会
China (Hangzhou) Modified Mobile and Special Purpose Vehicle Expo
浙江杭州Zhejiang-Hangzhou
6820

2011/05/28-29
时尚育儿广州嘉年华
Fashionbaby Guangzhou Carnival
广东广州Guangdong-Guangzhou
4230

2011/05/29-01
第41届全国制药机械博览会
41st National Pharmaceutical Machinery Expo
待定undetermined
5865

2011/05/30-10
第15届深圳-香港-澳门国际汽车博览会
15th Shenzhen-Hong Kong-Macao Intl Automobile Expo
深圳-Shenzhen
4725

June 2011 六月

2011/06-
品质生活.精品汽车浙江巡回展
Automobile Zhejiang Road Show
浙江Zhejiang-
6803

2011/06-
中国天津第十八届贸易投资洽谈会
China Tianjin Trade Fair & Investment Talk
天津Tianjin
3360

2011/06-
中国药店展览会
China Drug Store Show
待定undetermined
7140

2011/06/01-03
广州国际鞋类、皮革及工业设备展览会
Intl Shoes & Leather Exhibition
(Machinery & Raw Material)
广东广州Guangdong-Guangzhou
4240

2011/06/01-03
中国（上海）国际电池展览会
China (Shanghai) Battery Exhibition
上海Shanghai
2050

2011/06/01-03
年第99届中国鞋业皮具商品博览会暨“名品名店”对接展会
99th China Shoes & Leather Commodity Expo and “WELL-KNOWN BRANDS & FAMOUS SHOPS” Exposition
上海Shanghai
2060

2011/06/01-03
中国国际生物技术和仪器设备博览会
BIOTECH CHINA 2011
上海Shanghai
2070

2011/06/01-03
第6届上海酒类商品交易博览会
6th Shanghai Wine Trade Fair
上海Shanghai
2090

2011/06/01-03
上海建筑给排水处理技术及设备展览会
Shanghai Building Water, Water Treatment Technology and Equipment Expo
上海Shanghai
2100

2011/06/01-05
第6届中国（郑州）国际酒店、餐饮、泳池沐浴SPA设备及用品博览会/第6届中国（郑州）国际家纺、布艺及工艺品、礼品家居装饰博览会
6th China (Zhengzhou) Hospitality, Swimming Pool and Spa Expo
Grafts, Gifts and Home-ware Expo
河南郑州Henan-Zhengzhou
5210

2011/06/02-04
第10届中国（上海）国际动力设备及发电机组展览会
10th China (Shanghai) Intl Power and Generating sets Exhibition
上海Shanghai
2110

2011/06/02-05
中国国际模具、制造应用设备及相关工业展览会
DMC 2011
(China Intl Exhibition on Die & Mould, Metal Processing and Forming Industry)
上海Shanghai
2130

2011/06/02-05
第16届北京-埃森焊接与切割展览会
16th Beijing Essen Welding & Cutting Fair
上海Shanghai
2120

2011/06/03-05
第3届中国(太原)国际卡车暨物流展览会
3rd China (Taiyuan) Truck and Logistics Exhibition
山西太原Shanxi-Taiyuan
6510

2011/06/03-06
第5届中国（青岛）国际茶文化博览会暨紫砂艺术展
5th China (Qingdao) Tea Culture Fair
山东青岛Shandong-Qingdao
6260

2011/06/03-06
第2届中国(太原)国际汽车展览
2nd China (Taiyuan) Intl Automobile Exhibition
山西太原Shanxi-Taiyuan
6520

2011/06/03-06
第3届连云港-大陆桥汽车贸易博览会
3rd Lianyungang-Continental Bridge Automobile Expo
江苏连云港Jiangsu-Lianyungang
5490

2011/06/06-10
第19届中国昆明进出口商品交易会
（简称“第十九届昆交会”）
19th China Import & Export Fair, Kunming
(The 19th Kunming Fair)
云南昆明Yunnan-Kunming
6800

2011/06/06-10
第4届南亚国家商品展
（简称“第四届南亚展”）
4th South Asian Countries Trade Fair
(The 4th SACTF Fair)
云南昆明Yunnan-Kunming
6790

2011/06/08-10
上海国际非开挖技术展览会暨研讨会
No-Dig Shanghai
上海Shanghai
2140

2011/06/08-11
中国国际日用消费品博览会
China Intl Consumer Goods Fair
浙江宁波Zhejiang-Ningbo
6880

2011/06/08-12
中国郑州裤业博览会
China (Zhengzhou) Pants Show
河南郑州Henan-Zhengzhou
5220

2011/06/09-11
广州国际照明展览会
Guangzhou Intl Lighting Exhibition
广东广州Guangdong-Guangzhou
4255

2011/06/09-11
中国（上海）国际纺织品面辅料博览会
China (Shanghai) Intl Textiles, Fabrics & Accessories Exhibition
上海Shanghai
2160

2011/06/09-11
中国（上海）国际重型机械装备展览会
4th Intl Hoisting Machinery & Fittings Expo (Shanghai), China
上海Shanghai
2150

2011/06/09-11
第11届中国（广州）国际自动识别与物联网应用展览会
China (Guangzhou) Automatic Identification and IOT Exhibition
广东广州Guangdong-Guangzhou
4250

2011/06/09-12
广州国际建筑电气技术展览会
Electrical Building Technology Guangzhou
广东广州Guangdong-Guangzhou
4256

2011/06/09-12
第15届中国国际口腔设备材料展览会暨技术交流会
SINO-DENTAL
北京Beijing
560

2011/06/10-12
中国湖北国际专业灯光、音响、视听集成技术、乐器及设备博览会
China Hubei PLAV (Lighting, Audio, Video, Musical Instrument) Expo
湖北武汉Hubei-Wuhan
5325

2011/06/12-
第7届中国·宁夏国际能源装备与节能减排科技博览会
Ningxia Energy, Energy Saving and Emission Reduction Expo
宁夏银川Ningxia-Yinchuan
6010

2011/06/12-16
第11届中国国际机床工具展览会
10th China Intl Machine Tool & Tools Exhibition
北京Beijing
570

2011/06/13-16
国际豪华旅游博览- 亚洲站-全球豪华旅游产品及服务
Intl Luxury Travel Market Asia
上海Shanghai
2170

2011/06/14-17
第15届上海国际纺织工业展览会
SHANGHAITEX 2011
上海Shanghai
2180

2011/06/15-17
上海涂料原材料展
All coat 2011
上海Shanghai
2200

2011/06/15-17
上海国际海上风电及风电产业链大会暨展览会
Offshore Wind China 2011
上海Shanghai
2190

2011/06/15-18
广东外商投资企业产品（内销）博览会
Guangdong Foreign-invested Enterprises Commodities Fair
广东东莞Guangdong-Dongguan
3747

2011/06/15-19
第22届中国哈尔滨国际经济贸易洽谈会
22nd China Harbin Intl Economic and Trade Fair
黑龙江哈尔滨Heilongjiang-Harbin
5050

2011/06/16-17
中国国际物联网大会暨展览会
IOT China Conference & Exhibition 2011
上海Shanghai
2220

2011/06/16-17
上海国际智能交通与车联网科技发展论坛暨展览会
ITS Shanghai 2011
上海Shanghai
2210

2011/06/16-19
第9届中国国际软件和信息服务交易会
China Intl Software & Information Service Fair
辽宁大连Liaoning-Dalian
5630

2011/06/16-19
上海国际珠宝首饰展览会
Jewelry Shanghai 2011
上海Shanghai
2230

2011/06/16-20
首届中国沈阳国家家具及木工机械、原辅材料展览会
1st China (Shenyang) Intl Furniture & Woodworking Exhibition
辽宁沈阳Liaoning-Shenyang
5890

2011/06/16-20
辽宁（沈阳）台湾名品博览会
Liaoning (Shenyang) Taiwan Brand Name Product Expo
辽宁沈阳Liaoning-Shenyang
5870

2011/06/17-19
成都家居、休闲用品及礼品展览会
Chengdu Houseware, Leisure Goods & Gifts Fair
四川成都Sichuan-Chengdu
6650

2011/06/17-19
第4届中国（深圳）国际胶粘带及保护膜展览会
Shenzhen Adhesive Tape, Protective Film Exhibition
广东深圳Guangdong-Shenzhen
4730

2011/06/17-20
中国(广州)国际黄金珠宝玉石展览会
China Intl Gold, Jewelry & Gem Fair - Guangzhou
广东广州Guangdong-Guangzhou
4260

2011/06/18-20
北京国际咖啡博览会
China Intl Coffee Industry Exhibition
北京Beijing
580

2011/06/21-23
世界合同定制服务中国展
ICSE China
上海Shanghai
2260

2011/06/21-23
亚洲食品配料、亚洲天然食品原料、亚洲健康食品原料展览会
Fi Asia - China 2011
Hi China 2011
Ni China 2011
上海Shanghai
2240

2011/06/21-23
世界制药原料中国展
CPhI China
上海Shanghai
2250

2011/06/21-23
世界制药机械、包装设备与材料中国展
P-MEC China
上海Shanghai
2270

2011/06/22-24
亚洲风能大会暨国际风能设备展览会
Wind Power Asia
- Asian Wind Energy Exhibition & Conference
北京Beijing
585

2011/06/22-24
中国国际清洁能源博览会
Clean Energy Expo China
北京Beijing
586

2011/06/22-24
第7届广州国际品牌叉车及配件展览会
7th Guangzhou Intl Brand Forklift & Accessory Exhibition
广东广州Guangdong-Guangzhou
4280

2011/06/22-24
第2届广州国际物流装备与技术展览会
2nd Guangzhou Intl Logistics Equipment & Technology Exhibition
广东广州Guangdong-Guangzhou
4270

2011/06/22-24
第3届上海国际数字标牌展览会
Shanghai Intl Digital Signage & Touch Inquiry Technology Show 2011
上海Shanghai
2280

2011/06/23-25
第3届中国国际名酒博览会
3rd China Intl Premier Wine&Spirits Exhibition
四川成都Sichuan-Chengdu
6660

2011/06/23-25
第5届中国（常州）电动车燃油助力车及零部件展览会
5th China (Changzhou) Electric Car, Hibrid Car and Parts Exhibition
江苏常州Jiangsu-Changzhou
5470

2011/06/23-25
第12届广州国际压铸、铸造及工业炉展
12th China (Guangzhou) Intl Exhibition on Die Casting Foundry and Industry Furnace
广东广州Guangdong-Guangzhou
4350

2011/06/23-25
第12届广州国际紧固件、弹簧及设备展
12th China (Guangzhou) Intl Fasteners, Spring & Equipment Exhibition
广东广州Guangdong-Guangzhou
4310

2011/06/23-25
第12届广州国际金属暨冶金工业展览会
12th China (Guangzhou) Intl Metal & Metallurgy Exhibition
广东广州Guangdong-Guangzhou
4330

2011/06/23-25
第12届广州国际铸件产品及工艺技术研讨展
12th China (Guangzhou) Intl Exhibition on Casting Products and Technology Symposium
广东广州Guangdong-Guangzhou
4320

2011/06/23-25
第12届广州国际管材展
12th China (Guangzhou) Intl Tube & Pipe Industry Exhibition
广东广州Guangdong-Guangzhou
4300

2011/06/23-25
第12届广州国际不锈钢工业展
12th China (Guangzhou) Intl Stainless Steel Industry Exhibition
广东广州Guangdong-Guangzhou
4340

2011/06/23-26
中国北京夏季房地产展示交易会
Summertime Real Estate Trade Fair Beijing China
北京Beijing
590

2011/06/23-02
第8届汽车用品交易会暨
第8届汽车羊剪绒产品订货会
8th Automobile Products Fair
河南郑州Henan-Zhengzhou
5230

2011/06/25-26
2011第7届中国（武汉）国际教育展
7th China (Wuhan) Intl Education Exhibition
湖北武汉Hubei-Wuhan
5330

2011/06/28-30
第105届中国文化用品商品交易会
105th China Stationery Fair
上海Shanghai
2310

2011/06/28-30
中国国际美发美容博览会
China Hair & Beauty
北京Beijing
600

2011/06/28-01
第13届上海国际机床展
13th SHANGHAI INTL MACHINE TOOL FAIR
上海Shanghai
2320

2011/06/29-01
第15届华南工业控制自动化国际展览会
15th Intl Industrial Control & Automation Exhibition for South China
广东深圳Guangdong-Shenzhen
4750

2011/06/29-01
第十三届华南水展
13th Intl Water Treatment & Fluid, Pump, Valve & Pipe Exhibition for South China
广东深圳Guangdong-Shenzhen
4740

2011/06/30-03
第22届中国（深圳）国际钟表展览会
22nd China Watch & Clock Fair
广东深圳Guangdong-Shenzhen
4760

2011/06/30-05
第10届中国沈阳汽车工业博览会
10th China (Shenyang) Automobile Industry Expo
辽宁沈阳Liaoning-Shenyang
5900

July 2011 七月

2011/07-
中国天津啤酒节
Tianjin Beer Festival
天津Tianjin
3370

2011/07/01-10
北京欧美超级家具展览会
Beijing Intl Luxury Furniture Expo
北京Beijing
610

2011/07/03-06
第12届成都国际家具工业展览会
Intl Furniture Fair Chengdu
四川成都Sichuan-Chengdu
6670

2011/07/06-08
中国国际彩盒展
SinoFoldingCarton
北京Beijing
620

2011/07/06-08
第9届中国（温州）国际眼镜业展览会暨首届中国眼镜品牌连锁加盟会
9th Wenzhou Intl Optics Fair, China incorporating 1st franchisee meeting for China Optical Brands
浙江温州Zhejiang-Wenzhou
6960

2011/07/06-09
上海国际印刷包装纸业展览会
Shanghai Intl Print Pack & Paper Exhibition
上海Shanghai
2380

2011/07/06-09
上海国际照明技术设备展览会
Shanghai Intl Lighting Technology & Equipment Exhibition
上海Shanghai
2370

2011/07/06-09
上海国际LED产业展暨LED发光体及城市照明展
Shanghai Intl LED Industry& City Lighting Exhibition
上海Shanghai
2390

2011/07/06-09
上海国际广告技术设备展览会
Shanghai Intl AD & Sign Technology Equipment Exhibition
上海Shanghai
2330

2011/07/07-09
中国（深圳）国际品牌服装服饰交易会
11th China (Shenzhen) Intl Brand Clothing & Accessories Fair
广东深圳Guangdong-Shenzhen
4770

2011/07/07-09
深圳国际纺织面料及辅料博览会
Shenzhen Intl Trade Fair for Apparel Fabrics and Accessories
广东深圳Guangdong-Shenzhen
4780

2011/07/07-10
第13届中国（上海）国际摄影器材和数码影像展览会
PHOTO & IMAGING SHANGHAI
上海Shanghai
2410

2011/07/07-10
上海国际婚纱摄影器材展览会暨国际儿童摄影、主题摄影、相册相框展览会
China Wedding Expo 2011
上海Shanghai
2420

2011/07/07 – 10
中国国际消费电子博览会
China Intl Consumer Electronics Show (SINOCES)
山东青岛Shandong-Qingdao
6270

2011/07/08-11
中国（广州）国际厨房设备及配件展
China (Guangzhou) Intl Kitchen Fair
广东广州Guangdong-Guangzhou
4370

2011/07/08-11
中国(广州)国际衣柜展览会
CBD-Wardrobe 2011
广东广州Guangdong-Guangzhou
4410

2011/07/08-11
中国(广州)国际门窗展览会
CBD-Windoor 2011
广东广州Guangdong-Guangzhou
4400

2011/07/08-11
第13届中国（广州）国际建筑装饰博览会
13th China (Guangzhou) Intl Building Decoration Fair
广东广州Guangdong-Guangzhou
4380

2011/07/08-11
中国（广州）国际地面铺装材料展
China (Guangzhou) Intl Floor Covering Fair
广东广州Guangdong-Guangzhou
4360

2011/07/08-11
中国（广州）国际卫浴及建筑陶瓷展
China (Guangzhou) Intl Exhibition for Sanitary Ware and Building Ceramics
广东广州Guangdong-Guangzhou
4390

2011/07/13-15
年上海国际工业材料展览会·复合材料
Composites China
上海Shanghai
2440

2011/07/13-15
中国国际铝工业展览会
Aluminum China 2011
上海Shanghai
2490

2011/07/13-15
第17届中国国际加工、包装及印刷科技展览
ProPak China 2011
上海Shanghai
2470

2011/07/13-15
上海国际工业材料展览会·镁
Magnesium China
上海Shanghai
2450

2011/07/13-15
上海国际工业材料展览会·资源再生及利用
Industrial Material China
上海Shanghai
2460

2011/07/13-15
上海国际工业材料展览会·铜
Copper China 2011
上海Shanghai
2480

2011/07/14-16
第105届中国日用百货商品交易会、中国现代家庭用品博览会
105th China Daily-use Articles Trade Fair & China Modern Home Expo
上海Shanghai
2500

2011/07/14-17
第2届海峡两岸烘焙展
2nd Baking and Coffee Exhibition
福建厦门Fujian-Xiamen
3540

2011/07/15-17
广东国际家电配件采购展览会
Guandong Intl appliance parts procurement fair
广东广州Guangdong-Guangzhou
4420

2011/07/15-18
北京国际珠宝展览会
11th Beijing Intl Jewelry Fair
北京Beijing
630

2011/07/15-19
中国包头国际汽车展览会
China Baotou Intl Automobile Exhibition
内蒙古包头Inner Mongolia-Baotou
5430

2011/07/15-19
第3届呼和浩特国际汽车展览会
3rd Hohhot Intl Automobile Exhibition
内蒙古呼和浩特Inner Mongolia-Hohhot
5435

2011/07/15-24
中国长春国际汽车博览会
China Changchun Intl Automobile Fair
吉林长春Jilin-Changchun
5585

2011/07/20-22
上海国际儿童、婴儿、孕妇产品博览会
Children Baby Maternity Expo
上海Shanghai
2530

2011/07/20-22
广州国际电线电缆专用设备及原辅材料采购展览会
GZ Intl Wire & Cable Equipment and Raw & Auxiliary Material Purchase Fair
广东广州Guangdong-Guangzhou
4430

2011/07/21-24
第5届中国（青岛）国际建筑节能和可再生能源建筑应用博览会
China (Qingdao) Intl Building Energy Saving Fair
山东青岛Shandong-Qingdao
6290

2011/07/21-24
第5届中国（青岛）国际外墙保温及新型墙体产品技术展览会
Qingdao Building External wall insulation and New Wall Materials Exhibition
山东青岛Shandong-Qingdao
6398

2011/07/21-24
第7届中国(青岛)国际建筑材料及装饰材料博览会
7th China (Qingdao) Intl Construction & Decoration Materials Exhibition
山东青岛Shandong-Qingdao
6280

2011/07/21-24
第4届中国（青岛）国际太阳能与建筑一体化应用产品技术展览会
Qingdao Solar Energy and BIPV Exhibition
山东青岛Shandong-Qingdao
6330

2011/07/21-24
第7届中国（青岛）国际木门展览会
Qingdao Intl Wooden Door Exhibition
山东青岛Shandong-Qingdao
6310

2011/07/21-24
中国（青岛）国际绿色照明产品及技术应用展览会
Qingdao Green Lighting Exhibition
山东青岛Shandong-Qingdao
6370

2011/07/21-24
中国（青岛）国际陶瓷卫浴及厨房设备展览会
China (Qingdao) Intl Ceramics Sanitary Ware and Kitchen Facilities Fair
山东青岛Shandong-Qingdao
6340

2011/07/21-24
中国（青岛）国际建筑装饰涂料及化学建材展览会
Qingdao Architectural coatings and Chemical Building Materials
山东青岛Shandong-Qingdao
6380

2011/07/21-24
第5届中国(青岛)国际石材工业及机械设备展览会
5th China (Qingdao) Intl Stone Products & Machinery Exhibition
山东青岛Shandong-Qingdao
6360

2011/07/21-24
中国（青岛）国际建筑防水及屋面系统展览会
Qingdao Building Waterproof Exhibition
山东青岛Shandong-Qingdao
6320

2011/07/21-24
第二届中国（青岛）国际供热采暖系统产品及技术应用展览会
2nd China (Qingdao) Intl Heating Product and Technology Exhibition
山东青岛Shandong-Qingdao
6390

2011/07/21-24
第5届中国(青岛)国际地板及木制品展览会
China (Qingdao) Intl Floor Exhibition
山东青岛Shandong-Qingdao
6350

2011/07/21-24
中国（青岛）国际窗帘布艺及产品展览会
Qingdao Window Covering Exhibition
山东青岛Shandong-Qingdao
6370

2011/07/21-24
第7届中国(青岛)国际门窗幕墙及相关设备展览会
7th China (Qingdao) Intl Doors windows Curtain Exhibition
山东青岛Shandong-Qingdao
6300

2011/07/21-25
第3届深圳动漫节
3rd Shenzhen Animation Festival
广东深圳Guangdong-Shenzhen
4790

2011/07/21-25
第3届中国（沈阳）食品博览会
3rd China (Shenyang) Food Expo
辽宁沈阳Liaoning-Shenyang
5920

2011/07/22-22
第8届中国新疆国际煤炭工业博览会
Xinjiang Intl Coal Industry Exhibition
新疆乌鲁木齐Xinjiang-Urumqi
6740

2011/07/28-30
第6届中国青岛国际电力电工及电气自动化展览会
Qingdao Electrical power and Electrical Automation Exhibition
山东青岛Shandong-Qingdao
6400

2011/07/29-01
中国（北京）玩具动漫教育文化博览会
China Toys & Animation Educational Expo
北京Beijing
650

August 2011 八月

2011/08 –
第11届中国东北国际冶金及金属工业展览会暨中国-东北钢铁市场论坛
11th Northeast China Metal Expo
辽宁沈阳Liaoning-Shenyang
5930

2011/08/01-08
哈尔滨国际车展
14th Harbin Intl Automobile Exhibition
北京Beijing
5055

2011/08/04-07
中国国际工业装备(青岛)博览会
China (Qingdao) Industry Fair
山东青岛Shandong-Qingdao
6410

2011/08/04-07
青岛国际机床模具展览会
Qingdao Intl Machine Tools & Moulds Exhibition
山东青岛Shandong-Qingdao
6420

2011/08/05-07
亚欧照明展
Xinjiang Lighting Exhibition
新疆乌鲁木齐Xinjiang-Urumqi
6750

2011/08/10-12
第8届中国(北京)国际冶金工业博览会
8th China (Beijing) Intl Metallurgy Industry Expo 2011
北京Beijing
670

2011/08/10-12
第8届中国(北京)国际铸造展览会
8th China (Beijing) Intl Casting Industry Expo 2011
北京Beijing
660

2011/08/11-13
第3届中国（北京）国际路灯.庭院灯暨户外照明展览会
3th China Intl Road Lamp, Patio Lamp & Outdoor Lights Exhibition
北京Beijing
680

2011/08/11-14
北京国际创意礼品及工艺品展览会
Beijing Intl Creative Gift & Craftwork Exhibition
北京Beijing
690

2011/08/12-14
第11届中国新疆国际农业博览会
11th Xinjiang Intl Agriculture Fair
新疆乌鲁木齐Xinjiang-Urumqi
6760

2011/08/12-15
中国西部国际服装服饰博览会
Western China Intl Clothing & Accessories Fair
四川成都Sichuan-Chengdu
6680

2011/08/16-19
AMTS2011
上海国际汽车制造技术及装备与材料展览会
Shanghai Intl Automotive Manufacturing Technology & Material Show
上海Shanghai
2550

2011/08/16-19
第22届中国（上海）国际建材及室内装饰展览会
22nd Shanghai Intl Construction Material and Indoor Decoration Exhibition
上海Shanghai
2580

2011/08/16-19
上海国际建筑节能及新型建材展览会
Shanghai Intl Energy-saving & Advanced Building Materials Exhibition
上海Shanghai
2590

2011/08/16-19
AHTE2011
第5届上海国际工业装配与传输技术展览会
5th Shanghai Intl Assembly & Handling Technology Exhibition
上海Shanghai
2560

2011/08/16-19
中国（上海）国际建材及室内装饰展览会
Shanghai Intl Construction Material and Indoor Decoration Exhibition
上海Shanghai
2570

2011/08/17-20
第24届中国北京国际礼品、赠品及家庭用品展览会
24th China Beijing Intl Gifts, Premium & Houseware Exhibition
北京Beijing
700

2011/08/17-20
广州国际机床及加工装备展
Guangzhou Intl Machine Tools & Machinery Show
广东广州Guangdong-Guangzhou
4440

2011/08/17-21
（第16届）大连国际汽车展览会
16th Dalian Intl Automotive Exhibition
辽宁大连Liaoning-Dalian
5640

2011/08/18-20
第20届中国国际医用仪器设备展览会暨技术交流会
CHINA-HOSPEQ 2011
北京Beijing
710

2011/08/18-20
第7届中国商业地产博览会
China Commercial Property Exhibition
上海Shanghai
2600

2011/08/18-22
北京国际艺术博览会
Beijing Intl Art Exposition
北京Beijing
720

2011/08/20-30
中国西部（兰州）国际汽车博览
West China (Lanzhou) Automobile Expo
甘肃兰州Gansu-Lanzhou
3720

2011/08/23-25
国际质量检测分析技术及测量测试仪器仪表展览会
Intl Trade Fair for Quality Assurance
上海Shanghai
2610

2011/08/23-28
惠州商品展
Huizhou Commodity Fair
河南郑州Henan-Zhengzhou
5240

2011/08/24 – 27
第二十届北京国际广播电影电视设备展览会
Beijing International Radio, TV & Film Equipment Exhibition
(BIRTV2011)
北京Beijing
725

2011/08/25-27
中国（西安）电子展
China Electronic Fair
陕西西安Shaanxi-Xi'an
6100

2011/08/25-27
毛织设计及工艺展
Knitwear Design and Technology Fair (KDT)
广东深圳Guangdong-Shenzhen
4800

2011/08/25-28
第11届中国东北国际冶金及金属工业展览会暨中国-东北钢铁市场论坛
11th Northeast China Metal Expo
辽宁 沈阳 Liaoning-Shenyang
5930

2011/08/25-28
第5届中国东北亚（沈阳）进出口商品博览会
5th China Northeast Asia (Shenyang) Import & Export Fair
辽宁沈阳Liaoning-Shenyang
5950

2011/08/26-28
第16届中国（温州）国际皮革、鞋材、鞋机展览会
16th China (Wenzhou) Intl Leather, Shoe Material & Shoe Machinery Fair
浙江温州Zhejiang-Wenzhou
6980

2011/08/26-28
中国国际合成革展览会
（CSLF2011）
China Intl Synthetic Leather Fair
浙江温州Zhejiang-Wenzhou
6970

2011/08/26-30
中国（常州）国际动漫艺术周
China (Changzhou) Intl Comic and Animation Week
江苏常州Jiangsu-Changzhou
5480

2011/08/29-31
中国国际针织博览会
China Intl Knitting Trade Fair
上海Shanghai
2640

2011/08/29-31
中国国际家用纺织品及辅料博览会
China Intl Trade Fair for Home Textiles and Accessories
上海Shanghai
2630

2011/08/30-09/01
第17届华南国际电子生产设备暨微电子工业展
NEPCON/ EMT China 2011
广东深圳Guangdong-Shenzhen
4810

2011/08/30-09/01
中国（北京）国际商务及会奖旅游展览会
China Incentive, Business Travel & Meetings Exhibition
北京Beijing
730

2011/08/30-01
华南国际电子组装及包装技术展览会
Electronics Assembly and Packaging Technology Expo
广东深圳Guangdong-Shenzhen
4820

2011/08/30-02
第22届多国仪器仪表学术会议暨展览会
22nd Intl Conference and Fair for Measurement Instrumentation and Automation
北京Beijing
740

2011/08/30-02
中国（南部）机床展览会
Machine Tool China – South
广东深圳Guangdong-Shenzhen
4830

2011/08/31-03
第5届上海进口商品博览会
5th Shanghai Imports Expo
上海Shanghai
2660

September 2011 九月

2011/09-
第16届中国五金博览会
China Hardware Fair
浙江永康Zhejiang-Yongkang
7105

2011/09/01-04
中国（上海）国际跨国采购大会
Intl Sourcing Fair (Shanghai, China)
上海Shanghai
2670

2011/09/01 - 05
中国-亚欧博览会
（乌鲁木齐对外经济贸易洽谈会）
China Urumqi Foreign Economic Relations & Trade Fair
新疆乌鲁木齐Xinjiang-Urumqi
6770

2011/09/08-10
第2届北京王府井国际品牌节
2nd Beijing Wangfujing Brand Festival
北京Beijing
750

2011/09-
中国沈阳秋季房地产展示交易会
China (Shenyang) Autumn Real Estate Fair
辽宁沈阳Liaoning-Shenyang
5960

2011/09/01-03
大连国际广告技术与设备展览会
Dalian Advertising Technology and Equipment Exhibition
辽宁大连Liaoning-Dalian
5660

2011/09/01-03
大连国际医疗器械展览会
Dalian Intl Exhibition for Medical Instrument
辽宁大连Liaoning-Dalian
5650

2011/09/01-03
中国（广州）国际车用化工产品及技术展览会
China (Guangzhou) Intl Automotive Chemical Products & Technology Exhibition
广东广州Guangdong-Guangzhou
4470

2011/09/01-03
中国（广州）国际电子化学品展览会
China (Guangzhou) Intl Electronic Chemicals Exhibition
广东广州Guangdong-Guangzhou
4460

2011/09/01-03
中国（广州）国际化工技术装备展览会
China (Guangzhou) Intl Chemical Technology & Equipment Exhibition
广东广州Guangdong-Guangzhou
4450

2011/09/01-04
中国上海礼品、赠品及家居用品展览会
China Shanghai Intl Gifts, Premium and Houseware Exhibition
上海Shanghai
2680

2011/09/01-05
第5届大连进出口企业产品展销会
5th Dalian Import and Export Product Fair
辽宁大连Liaoning-Dalian
5680

2011/09/01-05
第5届大连进出口企业产品展销会
5th Dalian Import and Export Product Fair
辽宁大连Liaoning-Dalian
5670

2011/09/01-05
(第7届)烟台国际汽车展示交易会
7th Yantai Intl Automobile Show
山东烟台Shandong-Yantai
6495

2011/09/01-05
第10届中国国际装备制造业博览会
10th China Intl Equipment Manufacturing Exposition
辽宁沈阳Liaoning-Shenyang
5970

2011/09/01-05
第10届中国国际装备制造业博览会
10th China Intl Equipment Manufacturing Exposition
辽宁沈阳Liaoning-Shenyang
5980

2011/09/01-05
第2届鄂尔多斯国际汽车展览会
Ordos Intl Automobile Exhibition
内蒙古鄂尔多斯Inner Mongolia-Ordos
5438

2011/09/01-05
第26届国际名家具（东莞）展览会
26th Intl Famous Furniture Fair (Dongguan)
广东东莞Guangdong-Dongguan
3748

2011/09/01-06
第12届中国（湖北-武汉）国际汽车工业展览会
12th China (Hubei/Wuhan) Intl Auto Industry Exhibition
湖北武汉Hubei-Wuhan
5340

2011/09/02-04
中国(广东)国际旅游产业博览会
China Intl Travel Expo (CITE) 2011
广东广州Guangdong-Guangzhou
4480

2011/09/02-04
第8届上海国际模型展览会展
8th Shanghai Intl Model
上海Shanghai
2690

2011/09/05-09
第21届中原国际医疗器械(秋季)展览会
中国中部郑州（秋季）国际装备制造业博览会
21st Central China Autumn Medical Equipment Exhibition
河南郑州Henan-Zhengzhou
5250

2011/09/06-08
中国国际箱包、裘革服装及服饰展
Moda Shanghai
上海Shanghai
2700

2011/09/06-08
中国国际鞋类展
China Intl Footwear Fair
上海Shanghai
2720

2011/09/06-08
第7届上海国际不锈钢展览会
STEXPO 2011
上海Shanghai
2710

2011/09/06-08
中国国际皮革展
All China Leather Exhibition
上海Shanghai
2730

2011/09/06-09
亚太国际塑料橡胶工业展览会
Asian-Pacific Intl Plastics & Rubber Industry Exhibition
上海Shanghai
2740

2011/09/07-08
上海国际医疗设备设计和技术展览会暨研讨会
MEDTEC China 2011
上海Shanghai
2760

2011/09/07-09
第11届广州木材、人造板、木地板、木门及设备展览会
11th Guangzhou Lumber, Building board, Wood floor, Door and Equipment Exhibition
广东广州Guangdong-Guangzhou
4500

2011/09/07-09
第2届广州整体橱柜、壁柜及生产设备展览会
Guangzhou whole cabinet, Closet and Equipment Exhibition
广东广州Guangdong-Guangzhou
4490

2011/09/07-10
中国广州国际家居饰品、家纺布艺展览会
Homedecor + Hometextile China 2011
广东广州Guangdong-Guangzhou
4520

2011/09/07-10
中国广州国际家具博览会(民用家具展)
China Intl Furniture Fair (Guangzhou) – Home Furniture
广东广州Guangdong-Guangzhou
4510

2011/09/08-13
中国创业项目投资博览会
Entrepreneurship and Investment Exhibition
福建厦门Fujian-Xiamen
3570

2011/09/08-10
CIAPE
中国国际汽车零部件博览会
China Intl Auto Parts Expo
北京Beijing
760

2011/09/08-10
第2届华南医疗器械（广州）展览会
South China Medical Equipment Exhibition
广东广州Guangdong-Guangzhou
4530

2011/09/08-11
中国国际投资贸易洽谈会
China Intl Fair for Investment and Trade
福建厦门Fujian-Xiamen
3580

2011/09/09-13
第8届中国（苏州）国际汽车工业博会
8th China (Suzhou) Intl Automobile Show
江苏苏州Jiangsu-Suzhou
5553

2011/09/10-11
时尚育儿北京嘉年华
Fashion baby Beijing Carnival
北京Beijing
770

2011/09/12-18
郑州全国商品交易会
Zhengzhou Commodity Fair
河南郑州Henan-Zhengzhou
5260

2011/09/14-17
中国国际办公家具展览会
Office Furniture China
上海Shanghai
2800

2011/09/14-17
中国国际家具配件及材料精品展览会
FMC PREMIUM 2011
上海Shanghai
2820

2011/09/14-17
第17届中国国际家具生产设备及原辅材料展览会
FMC China 2011
上海Shanghai
2810

2011/09/14-17
中国国际家居布艺饰品展览会
Furnishings, Fabrics & Lightings China
上海Shanghai
2790

2011/09/14-17
中国国际橱柜展览会
Kitchen & Cabinet China
上海Shanghai
2780

2011/09/14-17
第17届中国国际家具展览会
Furniture China 2011
上海Shanghai
2770

2011/09/15-17
广州药交会
第19届全国药品保健品（广州）交易会
19th China Medicine and Healthcare Products (Guangzhou) Exhibition
广东广州Guangdong-Guangzhou
4560

2011/09/15-17
第3届上海国际冷冻保鲜及冷链物流技术设备展览会
3rd Shanghai Intl Exhibition of Food Frozen & Fresh and Cold Chain Logistics Technology Equipment
上海Shanghai
2830

2011/09/15-17
广州国际食品展暨广州进口食品展览会
Guangzhou Food Fair
广东广州Guangdong-Guangzhou
4540

2011/09/15-17
CINHOE 2011
第11届中国（广州）国际营养品/健康食品及有机产品展览会
Guangzhou Food Fair
广东广州Guangdong-Guangzhou
4570

2011/09/15-17
第2届中国上海国际冰淇淋冷冻食品工业展览会
2nd China Shanghai Intl Ice Frozen Food Industry Exhibition
上海Shanghai
2860

2011/09/15-18
第8届中国辽宁（沈阳）国际农业博览会
8th Liaoning (Shenyang) Intl Agriculture Expo
辽宁沈阳Liaoning-Shenyang
5990

2011/09/15-18
中国北京秋季房地产展示交易会
Autumn time Real Estate Trade Fair Beijing China
北京Beijing
790

2011/09/16-18
第11 届中国国际保健博览会
2011中国（深圳）保健节
11th China Intl Healthcare Expo
2011 China (Shenzhen) Healthcare Festival
广东深圳Guangdong-Shenzhen
4840

2011/09/16-18
中国国际制造技术及设备展览会
China Intl Mechanical Manufacturing Technology & Equipment Exhibition
山东济南Shandong-Jinan
6180

2011/09/17-19
国际特许加盟（上海）展览会
（2011年中国特许展上海站）
Shanghai Intl Franchiseexpo.com Exhibition
上海Shanghai
2870

2011/09/17-25
成都国际汽车展览会
Chengdu Motor Show
四川成都Sichuan-Chengdu
6690

2011/09/19-21
第19届中国国际纸浆造纸、林业展览会及会议
China Paper / China Forest 2011
北京Beijing
800

2011/09/19-21
第35届广州国际美博会
35th Guangzhou Intl Beauty Expo - Autumn
广东广州Guangdong-Guangzhou
4580

2011/09/19-21
第3届中国（上海）国际电池产品及技术展览会
3rd China (Shanghai) Intl Battery Industry Fair
上海Shanghai
2890

2011/09/19-22
家禽交易会
Poultry Fair
河南郑州Henan-Zhengzhou
5270

2011/09/21-23
广州国际模具展览会
Guangzhou Intl Mould & Die Exhibition
广东广州Guangdong-Guangzhou
4583

2011/09/21-23
亚太地区压铸工业展览会
Asia-Pacific Die0casting Industry Exhibition&&
广东东莞Guangdong-Dongguan
3750

2011/09/21-23
中国国际五金展
－"科隆国际五金展"强力推动
China Intl Hardware Show
—Powered by PRACTICAL WORLD
上海Shanghai
2900

2011/09/21-23
中国国际文具及办公用品展览会
China Intl Stationery & Office Supplies Exhibition
上海Shanghai
2895

2011/09/21-25
首届中国国际名表展
China Intl Watch Exhibition
北京Beijing
810

2011/09/21-25
第4届海峡两岸文博会
4th Straits Culture Expo
福建厦门Fujian-Xiamen
3600

2011/09/22-24
中国糖果文化节暨
第七届中国国际甜食及休闲食品展览会
China Confectionery Culture Festival,
Sweets & Snacks China
上海Shanghai
2910

2011/09/23-25
华南国际孕婴童用品展览会
Southern China Intl Maternity, Baby & Children Products Exhibition
广东深圳Guangdong-Shenzhen
4850

2011/09/23-26
第12届中国国际机电产品博览会-武汉
12th China Intl Machinery & Electronic Products Expo, Wuhan
湖北武汉Hubei-Wuhan
5350

2011/09/23-26
南京台湾名品交易会
Taiwan Brand Name Product Sales
江苏南京Jiangsu-Nanjing
5520

2011/09/23-26
全球华人口腔医学大会
暨中国国际口腔医学大会
4th CSA General Assembly & Annual Meeting/ China Dental Show
江苏南京Jiangsu-Nanjing
5530

2011/09/24-27
第14届亚洲宠物展览会
Pet Fair Asia 2011
上海Shanghai
2930

2011/09/26-28
第5届中国中部投资贸易博览会
Expo Central China 2011
北京Beijing
820

2011/09/26-28
第18届中国国际广告节
18th China Intl Advertising Festival
待定undetermined-
5995

2011/09/26-30
中国国际信息通信展览会
PT / EXPO COMM CHINA
北京Beijing
830

2011/09/27-29
第9届国际粉体工业/散装技术展览会暨会议
9th Intl Powder/Bulk Conference & Exhibition
上海Shanghai
2940

2011/09/29-04
第11届广东国际汽车展示交易会
11th Guangdong Intl Auto Exhibition & Trade fair
广东东莞Guangdong-Dongguan
3755

October 2011 十月

2011/10-
第六届中国（沈阳）汽车交易博览会
辽宁沈阳Liaoning-Shenyang
6000

2011/10/03-06
上海房地产展示会-假日楼市
holiday real estate market
上海Shanghai
2950

2011/10/11-14
上海国际专业灯光音响展览会
Prolight + Sound Shanghai
上海Shanghai
2960

2011/10/12-14
中国国际老龄产业博览会
China Intl Industry Expo Ageing
广东东莞Guangdong-Dongguan
3756

2011/10/12-14
第7届中国冰淇淋冷冻食品工业展览会
China Ice-Cream & Frozen Foods Exposition
河南郑州Henan-Zhengzhou
5290

2011/10/12-14
上海司法警用及安全防范技术产品博览会
Shanghai Security Exhibition
上海Shanghai
2970

2011/10/12-14
国际自动识别技术展览会
Intl Exhibition of Automatic Identification Technology
湖北武汉Hubei-Wuhan
5360

2011/10/12-14
中国（厦门）国际航空维修工程及服务技术展览会
MRO EXPO CHINA 2011
福建厦门Fujian-Xiamen
3610

2011/10/12-14
第10届中国国际玩具及模型展览会
10th Intl Trade Fair for Toys and Hobby
上海Shanghai
2980

2011/10/12-14
上海防伪技术暨证卡票券、RFID、商标标签、包装、可变条码印刷设备展览会
Shanghai RFID, Barcode and Packaging Exhibition
上海Shanghai
2960

2011/10/12-15
中国（上海）国际时尚家居用品展览会
Interior Lifestyle China
上海Shanghai
2980

2011/10/13-15
中国水博览会暨中国国际膜与水处理技术装备展览会
Water Expo China + Water & Membrane China
北京Beijing
835

2011/10/14-16
第2届中国国际建筑高科技及城市建设博览会
2nd China Intl Building Hi-tech and Urban Construction Expo
北京Beijing
840

2011/10/15-16
中国国际教育展
China Education Expo
北京Beijing
850

2011/10/15-30
第110届中国进出口商品交易会
110th China Import and Export Fair
广东广州Guangdong-Guangzhou
4585

2011/10/17-20
中国顺德国际家用电器博览会
China Shunde Intl Exposition for Household Electrical Appliances
广东顺德Guangdong-Shunde
4900

2011/10/18-20
国际真空展览会
Intl Vacuum Exhibition
上海Shanghai
2990

2011/10/18-21
第11届中国(北京)国际工程机械、建材机械及矿山机械展览与技术交流会
Beijing Intl Construction Machinery Exhibition & Seminar
北京Beijing
870

2011/10/18-21
第11届国际果蔬、食品博览会
11th Intl Fruit/Vegetable/Food Expo
山东烟台 Shandong-Yantai
6498

2011/10/20-22
第11届东莞国际印刷造纸胶粘带及广告展览会
11th Dongguan Intl Printing and Packaging and Paper Advertising, Adhesive Tape, Protective Film Exhibition
广东东莞Guangdong-Dongguan
3757

2011/10/20-22
亚洲国际高尔夫球博览会
China Golf Show, Guangzhou
广东广州Guangdong-Guangzhou
4590

2011/10/20-23
第19届中国（深圳）国际玩具及礼品展览会
Gifts & Home China
广东深圳Guangdong-Shenzhen
4860

2011/10/20-23
中国厦门国际茶业展览会
Xiamen Tea Expo
福建厦门Fujian-Xiamen
3630

2011/10/20-23
中国厦门国际素食养生展览会
Xiamen Vegetarian food and Health Exhibition
福建厦门Fujian-Xiamen
3620

2011/10/20-23
中国厦门国际佛事用品展览会
5th China Xiamen Intl Buddhist Items & Crafts Fair
福建厦门Fujian-Xiamen
3640

2011/10/20-24
第12届中国杭州国际汽车工业展览会
5th China Xiamen Intl Buddhist Items & Crafts Fair
浙江杭州Zhejiang-Hangzhou
6835

2011/10/21-25
中国义乌国际小商品博览会
China Yiwu Intl Commodities Fair
浙江义乌Zhejiang-Yiwu
7050

2011/10/21-26
中国—东盟博览会
CHINA-ASEAN EXPO
广西南宁Guangxi-Nanning
4940

2011/10/22-25
第6届南昌国际汽车展览会
6th Nanchang Intl Automobile Exhibition
江西南昌Jiangxi-Nanchang
5555

2011/10/25-28
第16届中国国际医药（工业）展览会暨技术交流会
16th China Intl Pharmaceutical Industry Exhibition
上海Shanghai
3015

2011/10/25-28
亚洲国际动力传动与控制技术展览会
PTC ASIA 2011
上海Shanghai
3000

2011/10/25-28
亚洲国际物流技术与运输系统展览会
CeMAT ASIA 2011
上海Shanghai
3010

2011/10/15-30
第109届中国进出口商品交易会（第三期）
109th China Import and Export Fair Phase 3
广东广州Guangdong-Guangzhou
4156

2011/10/26-27
营销和广告创新技术展示会暨研讨会
Technology for Marketing & Advertising China
上海Shanghai
3020

2011/10/26-27
中国呼叫中心技术设备及解决方案博览会
Call Center Expo China
上海Shanghai
3030

2011/10/26-28
第8届中国国际机器视觉展览会暨机器视觉技术及工业应用研讨会
8th China Intl Machine Vision Exhibition and Machine Vision Technology & Application Conference
北京Beijing
880

2011/10/26-28
中国光电周暨
第16届中国国际激光、光电子及LED光显示产品展览会
16th China Intl Lasers, Optoelectronics and Photonics Exhibition
北京Beijing
890

2011/10/26-29
第15届中国国际口腔器材展览会
DenTech China 2011
上海Shanghai
3040

2011/10/27-31
厦门日报房车大联展
Xiamen Housing and Automotive Exhibition
福建厦门Fujian-Xiamen
3650

2011/10/28-30
中国东莞国际鞋展
Dongguan Shoes-China Shoetes
广东东莞Guangdong-Dongguan
3758

2011/10/28-31
第16届中国宁波国际住宅产品博览
16th China Intl Exhibition on Housing Industry Product
浙江宁波Zhejiang-Ningbo
6900

2011/10/28-31
中国宁波国际工业设计博览会
Intl Industry Design Fair Ningbo China
浙江宁波Zhejiang-Ningbo
6890

第8届中国国际茶业博览会
CHINA TEA EXPO 2011
北京Beijing
900

November 2011 十一月

2011/11-
2011中国裘皮服装节
China Fur Fashion Festival
浙江余姚Zhejiang-Yuyao
7110

2011/11-
第66届全国药品交易会
66th PHARMCHINA
待定undetermined
7170

2011/11/09-11
中国高尔夫球用品博览会
China Golf Expo
广东东莞Guangdong-Dongguan
3760

2011/11-
品质生活.精品汽车浙江巡回展
Automobile Zhejiang Road Show
浙江Zhejiang
6804

2011/11-
第67届中国国际医药原料药、中间体、包装、设备交易会
API China
待定undetermined
7180

2011/11-
世界制药工业展中国展区
INTERPHEX China
待定undetermined
7190

2011/11 -
中国东北（沈阳）政府采购暨节能减排展览会
Northeast China (Shenyang) Intl Exhibition for Government Purchase
辽宁沈阳Liaoning-Shenyang
6005

2011/11/01-03
广州国际鞋类、皮革制成品展览会
Intl Footwear & Leather Products Exhibition – Guangzhou
广东广州Guangdong-Guangzhou
4600

2011/11/01-03
中国国际渔业博览会
China Fisheries & Seafood Expo
山东青岛Shandong-Qingdao
6430

2011/11/01-04
第4届中国义乌国际森林产品博览会
4th China Yiwu Intl Forest Products Fair
浙江义乌Zhejiang-Yiwu
7060

2011/11/01-05
新能源与电力电工展
Energy Show
上海Shanghai
3050

2011/11/01-05
工业自动化展
Industrial Automation Show
上海Shanghai
3070

2011/11/01-05
数控机床与金属加工展
Metalworking and CNC Machine Tool Show
上海Shanghai
3060

2011/11/02-04
第9届中国国际门窗幕墙博览会
Fenestration china 2011
北京Beijing
910

2011/11/02-04
ICSC RECON ASIA 2011
上海Shanghai
3110

2011/11/02-04
第6届微波及天线技术展览会
6th Microwave and Antenna Technology Exhibition
上海Shanghai
3100

2011/11/02-04
第10届电磁兼容与安规认证暨微波展览会
China International Conference & Exhibition on Electromagnetic Compatibility
(EMC/China 2011)
上海Shanghai
3090

2011/11/03-05
"100% 设计"上海展
-中国领先当代室内设计采购交流平台
100% design shanghai
上海Shanghai
3120

2011/11/03-05
国际家居装饰艺术展
-相约奢华·生活·艺术
Intl Home Decor & Design
上海Shanghai
3130

2011/11/03-05
第5届中国（杭州）国际清洁能源与环保产业展览会
5th China Intl Clean Energy & Environment Protection Industry Fair
浙江杭州Zhejiang-Hangzhou
6840

2011/11/03-07
海峡两岸图书交易会
Straits Book Fair
福建厦门Fujian-Xiamen
3660

2011/11/04-06
北京国际钱币博览会
Beijing Intl Coins Exposition
北京Beijing
915

2011/11/04-06
第13届中国连锁业会议暨
第13届中国连锁店展览会
13th China Retail Industry Convention &
13th China Chain Store Expo
湖南长沙Hunan-Changsha
5420

2011/11/05-08
中国厦门国际门窗木业展览会
China (Xiamen) Door, Window & Wood Industry Exhibition
福建厦门Fujian-Xiamen
3670

2011/11/05-08
中国厦门厨房卫浴用品展览会暨
China (Xiamen) Kitchen and Bathroom Product Exhibition
福建厦门Fujian-Xiamen
3680

2011/11/05-09
中国杨凌农业高新科技成果博览会
China Yangling Agricultural Hi-tich Fair
陕西杨凌Shaanxi-Yangling
6110

2011/11/08-09
中国对外投资合作洽谈会
2nd China Overseas Investment Fair
北京Beijing
930

2011/11/09-11
第78届中国电子展
China Electronics Fair
上海Shanghai
3140

2011/11/09-11
北京国际日化产品原料及设备包装展览会
Cosmetics, Personal Care & Detergents Expo
北京Beijing
950

2011/11/09-11
第56届全国汽车保修检测诊断设备（秋季）展览会
AMR 2011-
Auto Maintenance & Repair
广东东莞Guangdong-Dongguan
3765

2011/11/09-11
第11届中国（广州）国际纺织面辅料及纱线展览会
11th Guangzhou Intl Exhibition for Apparel Fabric, Accessories & Yarns
广东广州Guangdong-Guangzhou
4630

2011/11/09-11
第11届中国（广州）国际纺织机械展览会
11th China (Guangzhou) Intl Exhibition for Textile Machinery
广东广州Guangdong-Guangzhou
4610

2011/11/09-11
第11届中国国际染料工业及纺织化学品展览会
11th China Intl Exhibition for Dye Industry & Textile Chemical
广东广州Guangdong-Guangzhou
4620

2011/11/09-11
北京国际酒店用品展览会
Hotelex Beijing
北京Beijing
940

2011/11/10-13
第6届中国北京国际文化创意产业博览会
6th China Intl Culture & Creative Industry Expo
北京Beijing
960

2011/11/10-13
日本消费品展
japan-made Fair
上海Shanghai
3150

2011/11/11-13
上海国际少年儿童服装及用品博览会
Kids Fashion Shanghai
上海Shanghai
3160

2011/11/11-15
第4届郑州国际汽车展览会
China (Zhengzhou) Intl Automobile Expo
河南郑州Henan-Zhengzhou
5300

2011/11/12-13
上海国际耳鼻咽喉头颈外科论坛
上海国际耳鼻咽喉头颈外科医疗设备及药品展览会
Shanghai Intl Conference of Otorhinolaryngology and Head & Neck Surgery
上海Shanghai
3170

2011/11/14-17
中国国际全印展
All in Print
上海Shanghai
3190

2011/11/15-17
第9届ReChina亚洲打印耗材展览会(秋季)
ReChina Asia Expo 2011(Autumn Session)
上海Shanghai
3200

2011/11/15-17
中医药国际科技博览会
Traditional Chinese Medicine Exposition
四川成都Sichuan-Chengdu
6700

2011/11/15-17
中国国际燃气、供热技术与设备展览会
Gas & heating china 2011
四川成都Sichuan-Chengdu
6710

2011/11/16-19
第13届东莞国际模具及金属加工展
13th China Dongguan Intl Mould & Metalworking Exhibition
广东东莞Guangdong-Dongguan
3770

2011/11/16-19
第13届东莞国际橡塑胶及包装展
13th China Dongguan Intl Plastics, Packaging & Rubber Exhibition
广东东莞Guangdong-Dongguan
3780

2011/11/16-21
第13届中国国际高新技术成果交易会信息技术与产品展
China Hi-Tech Fair
广东深圳Guangdong-Shenzhen
4870

2011/11/17-19
中国国际有机食品和绿色食品博览会
ORGANIC CHINA EXPO BEIJING 2011
北京Beijing
970

2011/11/18-20
上海理财博览会
Money Fair
上海Shanghai
3210

2011/11/18-02
大连品牌服装服饰博览会
Dalian Clothing Expo
福建厦门Fujian-Xiamen
3690

2011/11/22-28
第9届中国（广州）国际汽车展览会
9th China (Guangzhou) Intl Automobile Exhibition
广东广州Guangdong-Guangzhou
4630

2011/11/23-25
第16届中国国际涂料展览会
CHINA COAT 2011
上海Shanghai
3230

2011/11/23-25
第24届中国国际表面处理展览会
SFCHINA 2011
上海Shanghai
3220

2011/11/23-27
中国国际珠宝展
China Intl Jewelry Fair
北京Beijing
1000

2011/11/25-27
北京国际礼品、赠品及家用精品（年底）采购订货会
22nd China Intl Gifts, Premium & Houseware Exhibition
北京Beijing
1020

2011/11/25-28
第10届中国国际古典家具展览会
上海国际古董及艺术品展览会（秋季展）
Antique Furniture China 2011
Antiques & Arts Shanghai
上海Shanghai
3240

2011/11/22-28
第9届中国（广州）国际汽车展览会
9th China（Guangzhou）Intl Automobile Exhibition
广东广州Guangdong-Guangzhou
4635

2011/11/29-12/02
中国国际海事技术学术会议和展览会
Marintec China
上海Shanghai
3250

2011/11/30-12/02
第12届中国国际食品加工和包装机械展览会
12th China Intl Food Processing and Packaging Machinery Exhibition
北京Beijing
1030

December 2011 十二月

2011/12-
中国国际进出口食品交易会
第二十届中国食品博览会暨交易会
China Intl Food Fair
湖北武汉Hubei-Wuhan
5370

2011/12-
品质生活.精品汽车浙江巡回展
Automobile Zhejiang Road Show
浙江Zhejiang
6805

2011/12/01-03
上海金属暨冶金工业博览会
上海铸件、锻件、产品展览会
Shanghai Metal & Metallurgy Exhibition
Shanghai Intl Casting, Forging Exhibition
上海Shanghai
3260

2011/12/01-05
中国-东盟第四届南宁国际汽车展览会
Nanning Intl Automobile Exhibition
广西南宁Guangxi-Nanning
4945

2011/12/03-16
“缤纷冬”日厦门购物节
Xiamen Shopping Festival
福建厦门Fujian-Xiamen
3700

2011/12/07-10
上海国际汽车零配件、维修检测诊断设备及服务用品展览会
Shanghai Intl Trade Fair for Automotive Parts, Equipment and Service Suppliers
上海Shanghai
3265

2011/12/09-18
北京欧美超级家具展览会
Beijing Intl Luxury Furniture Expo
北京Beijing
1040

2011/12/10-13
广东（厚街）茶叶博览会
Guangdong (Houjie) Tea Expo
广东东莞Guangdong-Dongguan
3870

2011/12/16-18
第15届国际食品、饮料、酒店设备、餐饮设备、烘焙及服务展览
FHC China 2011
上海Shanghai
3205

2011/12/18-01
内蒙古羊绒羊毛制品服装展
Inner Mongolia Wool, Cashmere and Clothing Show
福建厦门Fujian-Xiamen
3710

2011/12/24-08
第11届东莞嘉年华时尚生活用品购物节
11th Dongguan Shopping Festival
广东东莞Guangdong-Dongguan
3890

February 2012 二月

2012/02/27-28
上海国际城市安全及防护设备展览会
ISC CHINA (Intl Security Conference & Exposition China)
上海Shanghai
3270

March 2012 三月

2012/03/27-30
中国广州国际木工械、家具配料展览会
interzum guangzhou
广东广州Guangdong-Guangzhou
4640

2012/03/28-30
中国（深圳）国际绕线设备展览会
CWIEME Shenzhen
广东深圳Guangdong-Shenzhen
4880

April 2012 四月

2012/04-
(第十二届) 北京国际汽车展览会
2012 BEIJING INTL AUTOMOTIVE EXHIBITION
北京Beijing
1050

May 2012 五月

2012/05/09-12
2012中国国际铸造博览会
2012 China Intl Foundry Expo (CIFEX)
北京Beijing
1060

2012/05/09-12
第13届中国国际冶金工业展览会
Metallurgy China 2012
北京Beijing
1070

July 2012 七月

2012/07/17-19
第18届中国国际加工、包装及印刷科技展览
ProPak China 2012
上海Shanghai
3280

September 2012 九月

2012/09/25-28
第5届中国国际管材展览会
TUBE CHINA 2012
上海Shanghai
3290

Octomber 2012 十月

2012/10/23-26
第8届中国大连国际海事展览会
8th Intl Shippingbuilding,Ports and Marine Equipment Exhibition for China
辽宁大连Liaoning-Dalian
5685

November 2012 十一月

2012/11/15-17
第16届国际食品、饮料、酒店设备、餐饮设备、烘焙及服务展览
FHC China 2012
上海Shanghai
3300

国内展览会议
行业索引

1. 综合博览会

A

2. 安全

B

保健(见医药)
3. 包装
玻璃（见陶瓷 玻璃）

C

仓储 (见物流 运输 仓储)
茶(见 食品 饮料 茶 酒及设备)
4. 材料
5. 宠物
6. 船艇 海事 港口

D

7. 灯光照明 灯饰
8. 电池 电源
9. 电力 电工
电视 电影 (见广播电影电视舞台及设备)
10. 电子
11. 动漫 游戏

E

儿童用品 (见 玩具 婴儿 儿童用品)

F

12. 防务 警用设备
13. 房地产
14. 纺织 服装 服饰 及生产机械

G

15. 高新技术
16. 工程机械
工具 (见 五金 工具)
17. 古玩 收藏
18. 管道 管材 泵 阀门
19. 广播电影电视舞台及设备
20. 光电
21. 广告 媒介

H

22. 航空航天 机场
23. 焊接
24. 化工
25. 环境保护
26. 婚庆

J

27. 家具 木制品 木工机械
家居 (见消费品 家具用品)
28. 建筑 建材 装饰材料及机械
29. 交通 轨道 航运 公路 桥梁
30. 教育
31. 教学设备
家用电器 (见 消费电子 家用电器)
节能(见能源 新能源 节能)
金融(见投资 金融)
32. 金属加工 冶金 锻造 锻造技术及设备
33. 酒店业
酒(见视频 饮料 茶 酒 及生产)
34. 机械 制造 工业装备 自动化

K

35. 空调 制冷 供暖 通风
36. 矿业

L

连锁加盟 (见 特许经营 连锁加盟)
37. 零售业 营销
38. 礼品
39. 铝业
40. 旅游

M

41. 美容美发 化妆品 水疗
摩托车 (见汽车 摩托车 电动车)
42. 模具
木工机械 (见家居 木制品 木工机械)
43. 模型

N

44. 能源 新能源 节能
45. 农业 林业 渔业 畜牧业

Q

46. 汽车 摩托车 电动车
47. 清洁

R

燃气 (见石油 天然气 燃气)

S

48. 设计
生物 (见医药 医疗器械 生物 保健)
49. 摄影 影像
50. 食品 饮料 茶 酒及生产
51. 实验室设备
52. 石油 石化 燃气 天然气
53. 水 水处理
54. 塑料 橡胶

T

55. 陶瓷 玻璃
56. 特许经营 连锁加盟
57. 体育 休闲
58. 投资 金融
59. 图书

W

60. 玩具 儿童用品
61. 文化产业
62. 文具 办公用品
63. 五金工具
64. 物流 仓储 运输
舞台 (见 广播电影电视舞台)

X

橡胶 (见塑料 橡胶)
65. 线 缆
66. 消费电子 家用电器
67. 消费品 家居用品
68. 鞋 皮革
新能源(见 能源 新能源 节能)
69. 信息技术 通信技术
休闲 (见 体育 休闲)

Y

眼镜 (见 钟表 眼镜)
饮料 (见 食品 饮料 茶 酒及生产)
70. 印刷
71. 仪器仪表
72. 艺术
73. 医药 医疗设备 生物 保健
游戏 (见 动漫 游戏)
74. 乐器
运输 (见 物流 仓储 运输)

Z

75. 纸业
76. 钟表 眼镜
77. 珠宝
78. 自行车 电动自行车
79. 其他

Exhibitions and Conferences in Mainland China
Index of Industry/ Profession – Classification

1. General Fair

A
21. Advertising & Media
45. Agriculture, Forestry, Fishery & Animal Husbandry
35. Air-conditioning, Heating, Refrigeration, Ventilation
39. Aluminum Industry
17. Antique and Collection
72. Arts
46. Automobiles and Motorcycles
22. Aviation, Aerospace & Airport

B
8. Battery & Power Supply
41. Beauty, Cosmetics, Hairdressing, Personal Care & Spa
78. Bikes
6. Boats, Ship Building, Ports and Marine
59. Books
19. Broadcasting, Film, Television & Stage
28. Building, Construction, Decoration, Materials and Materials

C
65. Cable and Wire
55. Ceramic and Glass
24. Chemical Industry
47. Cleaning
14. Clothing, Textile and Related Machinery
11. Comics and Games
16. Construction Machinery
66. Consumer Electronics & Appliances
67. Consumer Goods
61. Culture Industry

D
12. Defense and Police Equipment
48. Design

E
30. Education
9. Electric Power, Electrical Engineering
10. Electronics
24. Environment Protection

F
50. Food, Beverage, Tea, Spirit and Processing
56. Franchising
27. Furniture, Woodworking

G
38. Gifts

H
63. Hardware & Tools
33. Hotel & Restaurant

I
69. Information Technology & Communication Technology
71. Instrument
58. Investment and Finance

J
77. Jewelry

L
50. Laboratory Equipment
7. Lighting (including LED)
64. Logistics

M
34. Machinery, Machine Tools and Technology & Automation
73. Medical Equipment, Pharmaceuticals and Health Care
32. Metalworking, Metallurgy and Foundry
4. Materials
36. Mining
43. Models
42. Mold
74. Music Instrument

N
15. New & Hi-Tech
44. New Energy and Energy-Saving

O
20. Opto-Electronic
79. Others

P
3. Packaging
75. Paper
52. Petroleum, Gas, Petrochemical
5. Pets
49. Photography and Image
18. Pipeline, Pump and Value
54. Plastics and Rubbers
70. Printing

R
13. Real Estate
37. Retail

S
2. Safety and Security
68. Shoes & Leather
57. Sports and Leisure
62. Stationery & Offices Supplies

T
31. Teaching Instrument
40. Tourism
60. Toys and Children' s Products
29. Transportation, Road, Bridge, Railway

W
76. Watches, Clocks & Optics
53. Water Treatment
26. Wedding Show
23. Welding

1、综合博览会 General Fair

第21届中国华东进出口商品交易会
East China Fair
2011/03/01-05
上海Shanghai
1250

第十五届对台出口商品交易会
The 15th China Xiamen Machinery and Electronics Exhibition (CXMEE)
2011/04/08-11
福建厦门Fujian-Xiamen
3490

第109届中国进出口商品交易会（第一期）
107th China Import and Export Fair Phase 1
2011/04/15-19
广东广州Guangdong-Guangzhou
4145

2011第六届广州国际采购博览会
6th Guangzhou Purchasing Fair
2011/04/21-27
广东广州Guangdong-Guangzhou
4150

第109届中国进出口商品交易会（第二期）
109th China Import and Export Fair Phase 2
2011/04/23-27
广东广州Guangdong-Guangzhou
4155

第109届中国进出口商品交易会（第三期）
109th China Import and Export Fair Phase 3
2011/05/01-05
广东广州Guangdong-Guangzhou
4156

中国天津第十八届贸易投资洽谈会
China Tianjin Trade Fair & Investment Talk
2011/06-
天津Tianjin
3360

2011辽宁（沈阳）台湾名品博览会
Liaoning (Shenyang) Taiwan Brand Name Product Expo
2011/06/16-20
辽宁沈阳Liaoning-Shenyang
5870

第十九届中国昆明进出口商品交易会
（简称“第十九届昆交会”）
The 19th China Import & Export Fair, Kunming
(The 19th Kunming Fair)
2011/06/06-10
云南昆明Yunnan-Kunming
6800

第四届南亚国家商品展
（简称“第四届南亚展”）
The 4th South Asian Countries Trade Fair
(The 4th SACTF Fair)
2011/06/06-10
云南昆明Yunnan-Kunming
6790

第22届中国哈尔滨国际经济贸易洽谈会
The 22nd China Harbin Intl Economic and Trade Fair
2011/06/15-19
黑龙江哈尔滨Heilongjiang-Harbin
5050

广东外商投资企业产品（内销）博览会
Guangdong Foreign-invested Enterprises Commodities Fair
2011/06/15-18
广东东莞Guangdong-Dongguan
3747

惠州商品展
Huizhou Commodity Fair
2011/08/23-28
河南郑州Henan-Zhengzhou
5240

第五届中国东北亚（沈阳）进出口商品博览会
5th China Northeast Asia (Shenyang) Import & Export Fair
2011/08/25-28
辽宁沈阳Liaoning-Shenyang
5950

2011第五届上海进口商品博览会
5th Shanghai Imports Expo 2011
2011/08/31-03
上海Shanghai
2660

2011南京台湾名品交易会
Taiwan Brand Name Product Sales
2011/09/23-26
江苏南京Jiangsu-Nanjing
5520

中国（上海）国际跨国采购大会
Intl Sourcing Fair (Shanghai, China)
2011/09/01-04
上海Shanghai
2670

第五届大连进出口企业产品展销会
5th Dalian Import and Export Product Fair
2011/09/01-05
辽宁大连Liaoning-Dalian
5680

中国-亚欧博览会
（乌鲁木齐对外经济贸易洽谈会）
China Urumqi Foreign Economic Relations & Trade Fair
2011/09/01 - 05
新疆乌鲁木齐Xinjiang-Urumqi
6770

中国国际投资贸易洽谈会
The China Intl Fair for Investment and Trade
2011/09/08-11
福建厦门Fujian-Xiamen
3580

2011郑州全国商品交易会
Zhengzhou Commodity Fair
2011/09/12-18
河南郑州Henan-Zhengzhou
5260

第110届中国进出口商品交易会
110th China Import and Export Fair
2011/10/15-30
广东广州Guangdong-Guangzhou
4585

中国—东盟博览会
CHINA-ASEAN EXPO
2011/10/21-26
广西南宁Guangxi-Nanning
4940

中国义乌国际小商品博览会
China Yiwu Intl Commodities Fair
2011/10/21-25
浙江义乌Zhejiang-Yiwu
7050

中国东北（沈阳）政府采购暨节能减排展览会
Northeast China (Shenyang) Intl Exhibition for Government Purchase
2011/11 –
辽宁沈阳Liaoning-Shenyang
6005

2、安全 Safety and Security

2011第十届国际公共安全防范产品（济南）展览会
10th Jinan Intl Public Security Product Exhibition
2011/03/23-25
山东济南Shandong-Jinan
6140

2011第九届郑州社会公共安全产品博览会
9th Zhengzhou Public Safety and Security Products Expo
2011/04/12-16
河南郑州Henan-Zhengzhou
5170

北京国际减灾应急技术设备博览会
Disaster Reduction and Emergency Technology Exhibition
2011/05/08-10
北京Beijing
440

2011上海国际智能交通与车联网科技发展论坛暨展览会
ITS Shanghai 2011
2011/06/16-17
上海Shanghai
2210

2011上海司法警用及安全防范技术产品博览会
Shanghai Security Exhibition
2011/10/12-14
上海Shanghai
2970

上海国际城市安全及防护设备展览会
ISC CHINA (Intl Secutiry Conference & Exposition China)
2012/02/27-28
上海Shanghai
3270

3、包装 Packaging

2011第12届中国东北国际塑胶机械及包装展览会
Northeast The 12th Intl Plastics Machinery & Packaging

Exhibition China 2011
2011/04/22-25
辽宁沈阳Liaoning-Shenyang
5860

2011第五届上海国际环保购物袋、包装袋展览会
The 5th Shanghai Intl Shopping Bags and Package Bags Expo
2011/05/17-19
上海Shanghai
1960

2011第九届大连国际印刷及包装工业展览会
9th Dalian Intl Printing and Packaging Exhibition
2011/05/19-21
辽宁大连Liaoning-Dalian
5600

2011上海国际印刷包装纸业展览会
Shanghai Intl Print Pack & Paper Exhibition
2011/07/06-09
上海Shanghai
2380

2011中国国际彩盒展
SinoFoldingCarton 2011
2011/07/06-08
北京Beijing
620

第17届中国国际加工、包装及印刷科技展览
ProPak China 2011
2011/07/13-15
上海Shanghai
2470

2011华南国际电子组装及包装技术展览会
Electronics Assembly and paekaging Technology Expo
2011/08/30-01
广东深圳Guangdong-Shenzhen
4820

2011北京国际日化产品原料及设备包装展览会
Cosmetics, Personal Care & Detergents Expo
2011/11/09-11
北京Beijing
950

第13届东莞国际橡塑胶及包装展
13th China Dongguan Intl Plastics, Packaging & Rubber Exhibition
2011/11/16-19
广东东莞Guangdong-Dongguan
3780

第12届中国国际食品加工和包装机械展览会
12thChina Intl Food Processing and Packaging Machinery Exhibition
2011/11/30-02
北京Beijing
1030

第18届中国国际加工、包装及印刷科技展览
ProPak China 2012
2012/07/17-19
上海Shanghai
3280

4、材料 Materials

第18届中国（北京）国际石材产品及石材技术装备展览会
18th China Intl Stone Processing Machinery, Equipment and Products Exhibition
2011/04/20-23
北京Beijing
350

2011北京国际隧道地下工程、喷涂聚脲、土工材料、工程纤维及建筑化学品展览会
Beijing Intl Tunnel Underground Project, Spray Polyurea, Geo-technical Material, Engineering Fiber and Construction Chemicals Exhibition
2011/04/27-29
北京Beijing
400

2011 年上海国际工业材料展览会·资源再生及利用
Industrial Material China
2011/07/13-15
上海Shanghai
2460

2011 年上海国际工业材料展览会·镁
Magnesium China
2011/07/13-15
上海Shanghai
2450

2011 年上海国际工业材料展览会·铜
Copper China 2011
2011/07/13-15
上海Shanghai
2480

2011 年上海国际工业材料展览会·复合材料
Composites China
2011/07/13-15
上海Shanghai
2440

第九届国际粉体工业/散装技术展览会暨会议
9th Intl Powder/Bulk Conference & Exhibition
2011/09/27-29
上海Shanghai
2940

5、宠物 Pets

上海宠物大会暨第四届上海宠物医疗学术研讨会
Pet Fair Shanghai 2011
2011/03/11-13
上海Shanghai
1360

第四届广州国际宠物水族用品展
The 4th Guangzhou Intl Pet & Aquarium Show
2011/05/08-11
广东广州Guangdong-Guangzhou
4160

第十四届亚洲宠物展览会
Pet Fair Asia 2011
2011/09/24-27
上海Shanghai
2930

6、船艇 海事 港口 Boats, Ship Building, Ports and Marine

2011宁波国际海事展览会
China Maritme Tech&Security Expo 2011
2011/03/17-19
浙江宁波Zhejiang-Ningbo
6850

2011中国国际船舶工业博览会
China Intl Marine, Port & Shipbuilding Fair
2011/04/12-14
江苏南京Jiangsu-Nanjing
5510

中国(上海)国际游艇展
China (Shanghai) Intl Boat Show
2011/04/14-17
上海Shanghai
1750

2011第四届中国（台州）国际船舶工业博览会
The 4th Session China (Taizhou) Intl Shipbuilding Exposition in 2011
2011/05/11-13
浙江台州Zhejiang-Taizhou
6920

中国国际海事技术学术会议和展览会
Marintec China
2011/11/29-02
上海Shanghai
3250

第八届中国大连国际海事展览会
The 8th Intl Shippingbuilding,Ports and Marine Equipment Exhibition for China
2012/10/23-26
辽宁大连Liaoning-Dalian
5685

7、灯光照明 灯饰 Lighting (including LED)

2011年（春季）中国郑州第十八届中原广告展暨2011年中国中部LED霓虹灯展
Zhengzhou Central China Advertising Exhibition
2011/02/18-21
河南郑州Henan-Zhengzhou
5080

广州国际LED照明展
LED Lighting China
2011/03/01-04
广东广州Guangdong-Guangzhou
3935

2011年长春国际灯饰博览会暨LED应用展
Changchun Intl Lighting and LED Exhibition
2011/03/08-10
吉林长春Jilin-Changchun
5560

2011青岛（春季）国际照明暨LED展览会
Qingdao (Spring) Lighting and LED Exhibition
2011/03/10-12
山东青岛Shandong-Qingdao
6220

2011第11届中国成都国际照明博览会
2011 Chengdu International Lighting Fair
2011/03/29-31
四川成都Sichuan-Chengdu
6580

广州国际照明展览会
Guangzhou Intl Lighting Exhibition
2011/06/09-11
广东广州Guangdong-Guangzhou
4255

2011上海国际照明技术设备展览会
Shanghai Intl Lighting Technology & Equipment Exhibition
2011/07/06-09
上海Shanghai
2370

中国长春国际汽车博览会
China Changchun Intl Automobile Fair
2011/07/15-24
吉林长春Jilin-Changchun
5585

2011中国（青岛）国际绿色照明产品及技术应用展览会
Qingdao Green Lighting Exhibition
2011/07/21-24
山东青岛Shandong-Qingdao
6370

2011年亚欧照明展
Xinjiang Lighting Exhibition
2011/08/05-07
新疆乌鲁木齐Xinjiang-Urumuqi
6750

2011第3届中国（北京）国际路灯.庭院灯暨户外照明展览会
3th ChinaINTL Road Lamp\Patio Lamp & Outdoor Lights Exhibition
2011/08/11-13
北京Beijing
680

上海国际专业灯光音响展览会
Prolight + Sound Shanghai
2011/10/11-14
上海Shanghai
2960

8、电池 电源 Battery & Power Supply

2011中国（上海）国际电池展览会
China (Shanghai) Battery Exhibition
2011/06/01-03
上海Shanghai
2050

第3届中国（上海）国际电池产品及技术展览会
The 3rd China (ShangHai) Intl Battery Industry Fair
2011/09/19-21
上海Shanghai
2890

9、电力 电工 Electric Power, Electrical Engineering

第14届中国东北国际电力电工技术设备展览会暨东北国际节电、节能及新能源技术设备展览会
Northeast The 14th International Electeotechnology Equipment Exhibition China 2011
2011/03/22-24
辽宁沈阳Liaoning-Shenyang
5720

2011第6届湖南电力新技术新装备展览会
Hunan Electric Power Technology and Equipment Exhibition
2011/05/25-27
湖南长沙Hunan-Changsha
5400

第10届中国（上海）国际动力设备及发电机组展览会
10th China(shanghai) Intl Power and Generating sets Exhibition
2011/06/02-04
上海Shanghai
2110

上海国际海上风电及风电产业链大会暨展览会
Offshore Wind China 2011
2011/06/15-17
上海Shanghai
2190

2011第六届中国青岛国际电力电工及电气自动化展览会
Qingdao Electrical power and Electrical Automation Exhibition
2011/07/28-30
山东青岛Shandong-Qingdao
6400

第12届中国国际机电产品博览会-武汉
12th China Intl Machinery & Electronic Products Expo, Wuhan
2011/09/23-26
湖北武汉Hubei-Wuhan
5350

新能源与电力电工展
Energy Show
2011/11/01-05
上海Shanghai
3050

10、电子 Electronics

中国国际电子电路展览会
(第20届中国国际电子电路展览会)
2011 Intl Electronic Circuits Exhibition
(CPCA SHOW 2011)
2011/03/15-17
上海Shanghai
1390

2011中国（济南）国际打印耗材及办公设备展览会
China (Jinan) Printer Accessories and Office Equipment Exhibition
2011/03/28-30
山东济南Shandong-Jinan
6150

第77届中国电子展
77th China Electronics Fair
2011/04/08-10
广东深圳Guangdong-Shenzhen
4690

2011第二届中国（重庆）国际电子信息产业展览会
2nd China (Chongqing) Electronic Information Industry Exhibition
2011/04/14-16
重庆Chongqing
1120

第八届ReChina亚洲打印耗材展览会(春季)
ReChina Asia Expo 2011(Spring Session)
2011/04/20-22
上海Shanghai
1770

2011上海国际新光源& 新能源照明展 览会暨论坛
Green Lighting Shanghai Expo and Forum 2011
2011/05/11-13
上海Shanghai
1910

苏州电路板展览会
Suzhou PCB / SMT Show
2011/05/11-13
江苏苏州Jiangsu-Suzhou
5540

中国国际电子生产设备暨微电子工业展
NEPCON China 2011
2011/05/11-13
上海Shanghai
1890

第20届华南(东莞)国际电子制造采购博览会
The 20th (Dongguan) south China Electronic Fair
2011/05/14-16
广东东莞Guangdong-Dongguan
3745-2

2011年第三届上海国际数字标牌展览会
Shanghai Intl Digital Signage & Touch Inquiry Technology Show
2011/06/22-24
上海Shanghai
2280

2011年中国（西安）电子展
China Electronic Fair
2011/08/25-27
陕西西安Shaanxi-Xi'an
6100

第十七届华南国际电子生产设备暨微电 子工业展
NEPCON/ EMT China 2011
2011/08/30-01
广东深圳Guangdong-Shenzhen
4810

2011华南国际电子组装及包装技术展览会
Electronics Assembly and paekaging Technology Expo
2011/08/30-01
广东深圳Guangdong-Shenzhen
4820

第十二届中国国际机电产品博览会-武汉
12th China Intl Machinery & Electronic Products Expo, Wuhan
2011/09/23-26
湖北武汉Hubei-Wuhan
5350

中国光电周暨
第十六届中国国际激光、光电子及LED光显示产品展览会
The 16th China Intl Lasers, Optoelectronics and Photonics Exhibition
2011/10/26-28
北京Beijing
890

第十届电磁兼容与安规认证暨微波展览会
China International Conference & Exhibition on Electromagnetic Compatibility
2011/11/02-04
上海Shanghai
3090

第六届微波及天线技术展览会
6th Microwave and antenna technology Exhibition
2011/11/02-04
上海Shanghai
3100

第78届中国电子展
China Electronics Fair
2011/11/09-11
上海Shanghai
3140

第九届ReChina亚洲打印耗材展览会(秋季)
ReChina Asia Expo 2011(Autumn Session)
2011/11/15-17
上海Shanghai
3200

中国（深圳）国际绕线设备展览会
CWIEME SHENZHEN
2012/03/28-30
广东深圳Guangdong-Shenzhen
4880

11、动漫 游戏 Comics and Games

首届中国冰雪动漫展
The 1st China ice & Snow Comic-Con
2011/01/21-24
黑龙江哈尔滨Heilongjiang-Harbin
5015

M.Y.COMIC 游园会
M.Y.COMIC
2011/03/02- 05
北京Beijing
60

COMIC.G.U动漫交流会
COMIC.G.U
2011/05/07-09-
北京Beijing
420

第三届深圳动漫节
3rd Shenzhen Animation Festival
2011/07/21-25
广东深圳Guangdong-Shenzhen
4790

中国（北京）玩具动漫教育文化博览会
China Toys & Animation Educational Expo
2011/07/29-01
北京Beijing
640

中国（北京）玩具动漫教育文化博览会
China Toys & Animation Educational Expo
2011/07/29-01
北京Beijing
650

2011年中国（常州）国际动漫艺术周
China (Changzhou) Intl Comic and Animation Week
2011/08/26-30
江苏常州Jiangsu-Changzhou
480

12、防务 警用设备 Defense & Police Equipment

2011第十届国际公共安全防范产品（济南）展览会
10th Jinan Intl Public Security Product Exhibition
2011/03/23-25
山东济南Shandong-Jinan
6140

2011上海司法警用及安全防范技术产品博览会
Shanghai Security Exhibition
2011/10/12-14
上海Shanghai
2970

13、房地产 Real Estate

2011中国沈阳春季房地产展示交易会
China Shenyang Spring Real Estate Fair
2011/03/22-24
辽宁沈阳Liaoning-Shenyang
5690

上海之春房产展示交易会
shanghai spring real estate market
2011/03/17-20
上海Shanghai
1420

2011年中国北京春季房地产展示交易会
2011 Springtime Real Estate Trade Fair Beijing China
2011/04/07-10
北京Beijing
290

"魅力之都"2011温州房产展
2011 Wenzhou Real Estate Exhibition
2011/04/08-10
浙江温州Zhejiang-Wenzhou
6950

上海房地产春季展示会-假日楼市
2011 holiday real estate market
2011/04/30-03
上海Shanghai
1840

2011常州住宅产品交易会
Changzhou Housing Fair
2011/05/18-22
江苏常州Jiangsu-Changzhou
5460

2011年中国北京夏季房地产展示交易会
Summertime Real Estate Trade Fair Beijing China
2011/06/23-26
北京Beijing
590

第七届中国商业地产博览会
China Commercial Property Exhibition
2011/08/18-20
上海Shanghai
2600

2011中国沈阳秋季房地产展示交易会
China (Shenyang) Autumn Real Estate Fair
2011/09/01 - 05
辽宁沈阳Liaoning-Shenyang
5960

2011年中国北京秋季房地产展示交易会
Autumntime Real Estate Trade Fair Beijing China
2011/09/15-18
北京Beijing
790

2011上海房地产秋季展示会-假日楼市
2011 holiday real estate market
2011/10/03-06
上海Shanghai
2950

厦门日报房车大联展
Xiamen Housing and Automotive Exhibition
2011/10/27-31
福建厦门Fujian-Xiamen
3650

14、纺织 服装 服饰及生产机械 Clothing, Textile and Related Machinery

中国国际纺织面料及辅料（秋冬）博览会
China Intl Trade Fair for Apparel Fabrics and Accessories
2011 –
上海Shanghai
1180

中国国际纺织纱线（秋冬）展览会
China Intl Trade Fair for Fibres and Yarns
2011/01/08 –
上海Shanghai
1190

大连服装展
2011/01/09-26
福建厦门Fujian-Xiamen
3460

第93届中国针棉织品交易会 第23届中国丝绸交易会
The 93rd China Intl Trade Fair for Mode
2011/03/09-11
上海Shanghai
1330

2011年第17届上海国际服装纺织品贸易博览会
Shanghai Intl Clothing & Textile Expo
2011/03/09-11
上海Shanghai
1280

中国（广州）国际家用纺织品及辅料博览会
China (Guangzhou) Intl Trade Fair for Home Textiles
2011/03/18-21
广东广州Guangdong-Guangzhou
4020

第十九届中国国际服装服饰博览会
The 19th China Intl Clothing & Accessories Fair (CHIC2011)
2011/03/28-31
北京Beijing
230

第十二届中国(东莞)国际纺织制衣工业技术展
The 12th China (Dongguan) Intl Textile & Clothing Industry Fair
2011/03/28-31
广东东莞Guangdong-Dongguan
3730

中国国际纺织面料及辅料（春夏）博览会
China Intl Trade Fair for Apparel Fabrics and Accessories
2011/03/30-01
北京Beijing
260

中国国际纺织纱线（春夏）展览会
China Intl Trade Fair for Fibres and Yarns
2011/03/31-02
北京Beijing
270

中国国际家用纺织品及辅料（春夏）博览会
China International Trade Fair for Home Textiles and Accessories
2011/04/02-04
上海Shanghai
1640

第十四届海峡两岸纺织服装博览会暨2011休闲服装博览会
Straits Textile & Clothing Fair
2011/04/18-21
福建石狮Fujian-Shishi
3450

第十一届中国国际染料工业暨有机颜料、纺织化学品展览会
CHINA INTERDYE 2011
2011/04/26-28
上海Shanghai
1810

2011中国（上海）产业用纺织品、非织造布及无纺布展览会
2011 Shanghai Textile, Non-woven Exhibition
2011/05/17-19
上海Shanghai
1970

2011东莞国际纺织品印花工业技术展览会
2011 China Intl Textile Printing Industrial Technology Exposition
2011/05/20-22
广东东莞Guangdong-Dongguan
3746

2011中国（郑州）国际缝制设备展览会暨2011中国（郑州）国际纺织面料、辅料及纱线展览会
China (Zhengzhou) Sewing Machines Exhibition
2011/05/25-29
河南郑州Henan-Zhengzhou
5200

中国郑州裤业博览会
China (Zhengzhou) Pants Show
2011/06/08-12
河南郑州Henan-Zhengzhou
5220

2011中国（上海）国际纺织品面辅料博览会
2011China（Shanghai）Intl Textiles, Fabrics & Accessories Exhibition
2011/06/09-11
上海Shanghai
2160

第十五届上海国际纺织工业展览会
SHANGHAITEX 2011
2011/06/14-17
上海Shanghai
2180

深圳国际纺织面料及辅料博览会
Shenzhen Intl Trade Fair for Apparel Fabrics and Accessories
2011/07/07-09
广东深圳Guangdong-Shenzhen
4780

中国（深圳）国际品牌服装服饰交易会
The 11th china (shenzhen) Intl Brand Clothing & Accessories Fair
2011/07/07-09
广东深圳Guangdong-Shenzhen
4770

中国（青岛）国际窗帘布艺及产品展览会
Qingdao Window Covering Exhibition
2011/07/21-24
山东青岛Shandong-Qingdao
6370

2011中国西部国际服装服饰博览会
Western China Intl Clothing & Accessories Fair
2011/08/12-15
四川成都Sichuan-Chengdu
6680

毛织设计及工艺展
Knitwear Design and Technology Fair (KDT)
2011/08/25-27
广东深圳Guangdong-Shenzhen
4800

中国国际针织博览会
China Intl Knitting Trade Fair
2011/08/29-31
上海Shanghai
2640

中国国际家用纺织品及辅料博览会
China Intl Trade Fair for Home Textiles and Accessories
2011/08/29-31
上海Shanghai
2630

中国国际箱包、裘革服装及服饰展
Moda Shanghai
2011/09/06-08
上海Shanghai
2700

中国广州国际家居饰品、家纺布艺展览会 Homedecor + Hometextile China 2011
Homedecor + Hometextile China 2011
2011/09/07-10
广东广州Guangdong-Guangzhou
4520

中国国际家居布艺饰品展览会
Furnishings, Fabrics & Lightings China
2011/09/14-17
上海Shanghai
2790

2011中国柯桥国际纺织品博览会
Heqiao Textile Expo
2011/05/11-13
浙江绍兴Zhejiang-Shaoxing
6910

2011中国裘皮服装节
China Fur Fashion Festival
2011/11-
浙江余姚Zhejiang-Yuyao
7110

第十一届中国国际染料工业及纺织化学品展览会
The 11th China Intl Exhibition for Dye Industry & Textile Chemical
2011/11/09-11
广东广州Guangdong-Guangzhou
4620

第十一届中国（广州）国际纺织面辅料及纱线展览会
The 11th Guangzhou Intl Exhibition For Apparel Fabric, Accessories & Yarns
2011/11/09-11
广东广州Guangdong-Guangzhou
4630

第十一届中国（广州）国际纺织机械展览会
The 11th China (Guangzhou) Intl Exhibition For Textile Machinery
2011/11/09-11
广东广州Guangdong-Guangzhou
4610

上海国际少年儿童服装及用品博览会
Kids Fashion Shanghai
2011/11/11-13
上海Shanghai
3160

大连品牌服装服饰博览会
Dalian Clothing Expo
2011/11/18-02
福建厦门Fujian-Xiamen
3690

内蒙古羊绒羊毛制品服装展
Inner Mongolia Wool, Cashmere and Clothing Show
2011/12/18-01
福建厦门Fujian-Xiamen
3710

15、高新技术 New Hi-Tech

2011第十五届中国国际软件博览会
INTL SOFT CHINA 2011
2011/05/12-14
北京Beijing
460

第十四届中国北京国际科技产业博览会
THE 14th CHINA BEIJING Intl HIGH-TECH EXPO
2011/05/18-21
北京Beijing
510

第九届中国国际软件和信息服务交易会
China Intl Software & Information Service Fair 2011
2011/06/16-19
辽宁大连Liaoning-Dalian
5630

第13届中国国际高新技术成果交易会信息技术与产品展
China Hi-Tech Fair
2011/11/16-21
广东深圳Guangdong-Shenzhen
4870

16、工程机械 Construction Machinery

2011中国西部工程机械建筑机械及混凝土设备展览会
West China Construction Machinery and Concrete Machinery Exhibition
2011/05/23-25
四川成都Sichuan-Chengdu
6640

上海国际非开挖技术展览会暨研讨会
No-Dig Shanghai
2011/06/08-10
上海Shanghai
2140

2011中国（上海）国际重型机械装备展览会
4th International Hoisting Machinery & Fittings Expo (Shanghai), China
2011/06/09-11
上海Shanghai
2150

第五届中国(青岛)国际石材工业及机械设备展览会
The 5th China(Qingdao) Intl Stone Products & Machinery Exhibition
2011/07/21-24
山东青岛Shandong-Qingdao
6360

第十一届中国(北京)国际工程机械、建材机械及矿山机械展览与技术交流会
2011 Beijing International Construction Machinery Exhibition & Seminar
2011/10/18-21
北京Beijing
870

17、古玩 收藏 Antique and Collection

中国古玩展览会
China Antique Exhibition
2011/03/30-03
河南郑州Henan-Zhengzhou
5130

第十届中国国际古典家具展览会 & 2011上海国际古董及艺术品展览会（春季展）
Antique Furniture China 2011, Antiques & Arts Shanghai 2011
2011/05/20-23
上海Shanghai
2010

2011北京国际钱币博览会
Beijing Intl Coins Exposition 2011
2011/11/04-06
北京-Biejing
1090

第十届中国国际古典家具展览会
上海国际古董及艺术品展览会（秋季展）
Antique Furniture China 2011, Antiques & Arts Shanghai 2011
2011/11/25-28
上海Shanghai
3240

18、管道 管材 泵 阀门 Pipeline, Pump & Value

第12届中国（广州）国际给排水、水处理技术设备展览会
中国（广州）国际泵、阀门、管道展览会
Water Wasterwater & Water Treatment China2011
Pump, Vale & Pipe China 2011
2011/03/09-11
广东广州Guangdong-Guangzhou
3980

2011年第四届中国东北流体机械展览会（暨泵阀管、压缩机、风机展览会）
2011 China (Northeast) 3rd Fluid Machinery Exhibition
2011/03/22-24
辽宁沈阳Liaoning-Shenyang
5700

第十一届东北国际给排水、水处理技术设备及泵、阀、管道展览会
The 12th Northeast Intl, water disposal technique & equipment and pump & value and pipeline exhibition
2011/03/27-29
辽宁沈阳Liaoning-Shenyang
5740

第十二届广州国际管材展
12th China (Guangzhou) Intl Tube&Pipe Industry Exhibition
2011/06/23-25
广东广州Guangdong-Guangzhou
4300

第五届中国国际管材展览会
TUBE CHINA 2012
2012/09/25-28
上海Shanghai
3290

19、广播 电影 电视 舞台设备 Broadcasting, Film, Television & Stage Equipment

2011中国国际机器视觉展览会
China Intl Machine Vision Exhibition 2011
2011/03/20-22
上海Shanghai
1430

第二十届中国国际专业音响-灯光-乐器及技术展览会
20th China Intl Exhibition on Pro Audio, Light, Music & Technology
2011/05/26-29
北京Beijing
540

2011中国湖北国际专业灯光、音响、视听集成技术、乐器及设备博览会
China Hubei PLAV (Lighting, Audio, Video, Musical Instrument) Expo
2011/06/10-12
湖北武汉Hubei-Wuhan
5325

第十三届中国（上海）国际摄影器材和数码影像展览会
PHOTO & IMAGING SHANGHAI 2011
2011/07/07-10
上海Shanghai
2410

第二十届北京国际广播电影电视设备展览会
Beijing Intl Radio, TV & Film Equipment Exhibition (BIRTV2011)
2011/08/24-27
725

20、光电 Opto-Electronic

2011第2届中国（安徽）新能源与光伏展览会
2nd China (Anhui) New Energy and Photovoltaic Exhibition
2011/03/25-27
安徽合肥Anhui-Hefei
3400

中国光电周暨
第16届中国国际激光、光电子及LED光显示产品展览会
16th China Intl Lasers, Optoelectronics and Photonics Exhibition
2011/10/26-28
北京Beijing
890

21、广告 媒介 Advertising & Media

2011德纳成都国际LED展览会及四新广告展览会
Chengdu LED and Advertising Exhibition
2011/02/20-22
四川成都Sichuan-Chengdu
6540

2011东莞数字喷印及广告技术展览会
China Sign Expo Dongguan 2011
2011/02/28-04
广东东莞Guangdong-Dongguan
3725

广东国际广告展
Sign China
2011/03/01-04
广东广州Guangdong-Guangzhou
3940

2011长春第十四届广告博览会
14th Changchun Advertising Expo
2011/03/08-10
吉林长春Jilin-Changchun
5570

第四届华展云南广告四新暨LED照明展览会
4th Yunnan Advertising New Technology and New Media Exhibition/ LED Lighting Exhibition
2011/03/18-20
云南昆明Yunnan-Kunming
6780

2011第12届广西广告技术设备展览会
12th Guangxi Advertising Technology & Equipment Exhibition
2011/03/25-27
广西南宁Guangxi-Nanning
4920

2011第十二届中国（上海）广告四新展览会
12th China (Shanghai) Advertising Four New Expo
2011/03/29-31
上海Shanghai
1540

2011上海国际LED产业展暨LED发光体及城市照明展
Shanghai Intl LED Industry& City Lighting Exhibition 2011
2011/07/06-09
上海Shanghai
2390

2011上海国际广告技术设备展览会
Shanghai Intl AD & Sign Technology Equipment Exhibition
2011/07/06-09
上海Shanghai
2330

大连国际广告技术与设备展览会
Dalian Advertising Technology and Equipment Exhibition
2011/09/01-03
辽宁大连Liaoning-Dalian
5660

第18届中国国际广告节
18th China International Advertising Festival
2011/09/26-28
待定undetermined
5995

营销和广告创新技术展示会暨研讨会
Technology for Marketing & Advertising China
2011/10/26-27
上海Shanghai
3020

22、航空 航天 机场 Aviation, Aerospace & Airport

2011中国（厦门）国际航空维修工程及服务技术展览会
MRO EXPO CHINA 2011
2011/10/12-14
福建厦门Fujian-Xiamen
3610

23、焊接 Welding

中国东北第15届国际焊接、切割、激光技术设备展览会
15th China (Northeast) Intl Welding, Cutting & Laser Technology and Equipment Exhibition
2011/04/22-25
辽宁沈阳Liaoning-Shenyang
5850

2011第九届大连国际焊接工业展览会
9th Dalian Intl Welding Exhibition
2011/05/19-21
辽宁大连Liaoning-Dalian
5620

第十六届北京-埃森焊接与切割展览会
The 16th Beijing Essen Welding & Cutting Fair
2011/06/02-05
上海Shanghai
2120

24、化工 Chemical Industry

第六届国际胶粘带、保护膜及光学膜（上海）展览会
6th Intl Adhesive tape Protective Films & Optical Film (Shanghai) Expo
2011/03/28-30
上海Shanghai
1530

第四届国际光学膜及高机能薄膜(上海)展览会
FILMEXPO
2011/03/28-30
上海Shanghai
1510

中国(上海)国际建筑涂料展览会
Expo Coat
2011/03/29-01
上海Shanghai
1580

2011国际表面工程展览会
seexpo
2011/04/07-09
上海Shanghai
1680

第十一届中国国际染料工业暨有机颜料、纺织化学品展览会
CHINA INTERDYE 2011
2011/04/26-28
上海Shanghai
1810

2011北京国际隧道地下工程、喷涂聚脲、土工材料、工程纤维及建筑化学品展览会
Beijing Intl Tunnel Underground Project, Spray Polyurea, Geo-technical Material, Engineering Fiber and Construction Chemicals Exhibition
2011/04/27-29
北京Beijing
400

第九届广州国际涂料 油墨胶粘剂展览会
9th Guangzhou (China) Intl Coatings, Printing Inks & Adhesives Exhibition
2011/05/11-13
广东广州Guangdong-Guangzhou
4170

2011上海涂料原材料展
All coat 2011
2011/06/15-17
上海Shanghai
2200

2011第四届中国（深圳）国际胶粘带及保护膜展览会
Shenzhen Adhesive Tape, Protective Film Exhibition
2011/06/17-19
广东深圳Guangdong-Shenzhen
4730

2011中国（青岛）国际建筑装饰涂料及化学建材展览会
Qingdao Architectural coatings and Chemical Building Materials
2011/07/21-24
山东青岛Shandong-Qingdao
6380

2011中国（广州）国际化工技术装备展览会
China (Guangzhou) Intl Chemical Technology & Equipment Exhibition
2011/09/01-03
广东广州Guangdong-Guangzhou
4450

2011中国（广州）国际电子化学品展览会
China (Guangzhou) Intl Electronic Chemicals Exhibition
2011/09/01-03
广东广州Guangdong-Guangzhou
4460

2011中国（广州）国际车用化工产品及技术展览会
China (Guangzhou) Intl Automotive Chemical Products & Technology Exhibition
2011/09/01-03
广东广州Guangdong-Guangzhou
4470

2011北京国际日化产品原料及设备包装展览会
Cosmetics, Personal Care & Detergents Expo
2011/11/09-11
北京Beijing
950

第十一届中国国际染料工业及纺织化学品展览会
11th China Intl Exhibition for Dye Industry & Textile Chemical
2011/11/09-11
广东广州Guangdong-Guangzhou
4620

第十六届届中国国际涂料展览会
CHINACOAT 2011
2011/11/23-25
上海Shanghai
3230

第二十四届中国国际表面处理展览会
SFCHINA 2011
2011/11/23-25
上海Shanghai
3220

25、环境保护 Environment Protection

2011湖南环境保护产业博览会
Hunan Changsha Environment Protection Expo
2011/03/21-23
湖南长沙Hunan-Changsha
5390

第十二届东北国际给排水、水处理技术设备及泵、阀、管道展览会
12th northeast Intl, water disposal technique & equipment and pump & value and pipeline exhibition
2011/03/27-29
辽宁沈阳Liaoning-Shenyang
5740

2011中国东北第十四届国际供热供暖、空调、热泵技术设备展览会
China (Northeast) 14th Intl Equipments of Heating,Air-Condition & New Energy Sources Exhibition
2011/03/27-29
辽宁沈阳Liaoning-Shenyang
5750

中国哈尔滨国际生态城市建设博览会
China (Harbin) Urban Eco Construction Expo
2011/04/21-23
黑龙江哈尔滨Heilongjiang-Haerbin
5020

第12届中国国际环保、废弃物及资源利用展览会
IFAT CHINA+EPTEE+CWS 2011
2011/05/05-07
上海Shanghai
1880

第十三届华南水展
13th Intl Water Treatment & Fluid, Pump, Valve & Pipe Exhibition For South China
2011/06/29-01
广东深圳Guangdong-Shenzhen
4740

2011 年上海国际工业材料展览会
-资源再生及利用
Industrial Material China
2011/07/13-15
上海Shanghai
2460

第五届中国（青岛）国际外墙保温及新型墙体产品技术展览会
Qingdao Building External wall insulation and New Wall Materials Exhibition
2011/07/21-24
山东青岛Shandong-Qingdao
6325

第五届中国（杭州）国际清洁能源与环保产业展览会
5th China Intl Clean Energy & Environment Protection Industry Fair
2011/11/03-05
浙江杭州Zhejiang-Hangzhou
6840

26、婚庆 Wedding Shows

第19届中国（上海）国际婚纱摄影器材展览会
19th China (Shanghai) Intl Wedding Photographic Equipment Exhibition
2011/02/23-26
上海Shanghai
1210

上海国际婚纱摄影器材展览会暨
国际儿童摄影、主题摄影、相册相框展览会
China Wedding Expo 2011
2011/02/23-26
上海Shanghai
1230

中国国际婚纱及摄影器材博览会
China Wedding 2011
2011/03/20-23
北京Beijing
190

2011深圳春季婚博会暨婚庆文化节
Shenzhen International Wedding Exhibition &Wedding Cultural Festival 2010
2011/04/03-05
广东深圳Guangdong-Shenzhen
4680

上海国际婚纱摄影器材展览会暨
国际儿童摄影、主题摄影、相册相框展览会
China Wedding Expo 2011
2011/07/07-10
上海Shanghai
2420

27、家具 木制品 木工机械 Furniture, Woodworking

第11届中国国际林业、木业机械与供应展览
WoodMac China 2011
2011/03/01-04
上海Shanghai
1240

第10届中国国际橱柜、壁柜、隔断、木业展览会
10th China Cupboard, Closet，Wood Exhibition
2011/03/02-05
北京Beijing
100

第二十五届国际名家具（东莞）展览会
25th Intl Famous Furniture Fair (Dongguan)
2011/03/16-20
广东东莞Guangdong-Dongguan
3728

中国广州国际家具博览会(民用家具展
China Intl Furniture Fair (Guangzhou) – Home Furniture
2011/03/18-21
广东广州Guangdong-Guangzhou
4040

第26深圳国际家具展
Shenzhen Intl Furniture Exhibition
2011/03/19-22
广东深圳Guangdong-Shenzhen
4660

第十三届中国国际地面材料及铺装技术展览会
DOMOTEX asia/CHINAFLOOR
2011/03/22-24
上海Shanghai
1440

中国广州国际木工机械、家具配料展览会
interzum guangzhou
2011/03/27-30
广东广州Guangdong-Guangzhou
4070

首届中国沈阳国家家具及木工机械、原辅材料展览会
1st China (Shenyang) Intl Furniture & Woodworking Exhibition
2011/06/16-20
辽宁沈阳Liaoning-Shenyang
5890

2011年北京欧美超级家具展览会
Beijing Intl Luxury Furniture Expo
2011/07/01-10
北京Beijing
610

第12届成都国际家具工业展览会
International Furniture Fair Chengdu
2011/07/03-06
四川成都Sichuan-Chengdu
6670

2011中国(广州)国际衣柜展览会
CBD-Wardrobe 2011
2011/07/08-11
广东广州Guangdong-Guangzhou
4410

第七届中国（青岛）国际木门展览会
Qingdao Intl Wooden Door Exhibition
2011/07/21-24
山东青岛Shandong-Qingdao
6310

第五届中国(青岛)国际地板及木制品展览会
China (Qingdao) Intl Floor Exhibition
2011/07/21-24
山东青岛Shandong-Qingdao
6350

第二十六届国际名家具（东莞）展览会
The 26th Intl Famous Furniture Fair (Dongguan)
2011/09/01-05
广东东莞Guangdong-Dongguan
3748

2011第二届广州整体橱柜、壁柜及生产设备展览会
Guangzhou whole cabinet, Closet and Equipment Exhibition
2011/09/07-09
广东广州Guangdong-Guangzhou
4490

中国广州国际家具博览会(民用家具展)
China Intl Furniture Fair (Guangzhou) – Home Furniture
2011/09/07-10
广东广州Guangdong-Guangzhou
4510

2011第十一届广州木材、人造板、木地板、木门及设备展览会
11th Guangzhou Lumber, Building board, Wood floor, Door and Equipment Exhibitio
2011/09/07-09
广东广州Guangdong-Guangzhou
4500

第十七届中国国际家具生产设备及原辅材料展览会
FMC China 2011
2011/09/14-17
上海Shanghai
2810

中国国际家具配件及材料精品展览会
FMC PREMIUM 2011
2011/09/14-17
上海Shanghai
2820

中国国际办公家具展览会
Office Furniture China
2011/09/14-17
上海Shanghai
2800

第十七届中国国际家具展览会
Furniture China 2011
2011/09/14-17
上海Shanghai
2770

中国国际橱柜展览会
Kitchen & Cabinet China
2011/09/14-17
上海Shanghai
2780

第十届中国国际古典家具展览会&
2011上海国际古董及艺术品展览会 （秋季展）
Antique Furniture China 2011,
Antiques & Arts Shanghai
2011/11/25-28
上海Shanghai
3240

2011年北京欧美超级家具展览会
Beijing Intl Luxury Furniture Expo
2011/12/09-18
北京Beijing
1040

中国广州国际木工机械、家具配料展览会
interzum guangzhou
2012/03/27-30
广东广州Guangdong-Guangzhou
4640

28、建筑 建材 装饰材料及机械 Building, Construction, Decoration, Materials and Machinery

2011北京玻璃展览会-中国国际建筑装饰艺术玻璃及技术博览会
2011 Beijing Glass Exhibition
2011/03/02-05
北京Beijing
110

第十届中国国际橱柜、壁柜、隔断、木业展览会
10th China Cupboard, Closet，Wood Exhibition
2011/03/02-05
北京Beijing
100

第十一届中国（北京）国际墙纸布艺展览会
11th China (Beijing) Wallpaper Exhibition
2011/03/02-05
北京Beijing
90

中国（北京）国际集成吊顶及天花材料博览会
China (Beijing) Intl Ceiling and Material Expo
2011/03/02-05
北京Beijing
80

2011北京建材展览会-第十八届中国（北京）国际建筑装饰及材料博览会
China International Building Decorations and Building Materials Exposition
2011/03/02-05
北京Beijing
70

中国(北京)国际供热空调、卫生洁具及城建设备与技术展览会
China Intl Trade Fair for Sanitation, Heating & Air-Conditioning
2011/03/03-05
北京Beijing
120

中国厦门国际石材展览会
China (Xiamen) Stone Exhibition
2011/03/06-09
福建厦门Fujian-Xiamen
3480

CIDE-2011
第十届中国国际门业展览会
10th China Intl Door Industry Exhibition
2011/03/09-12
北京Beijing
140

第13届中国国际地面材料及铺装技术展览会
DOMOTEX asia/CHINAFLOOR
2011/03/22-24
上海Shanghai
1440

中国国际遮阳与节能技术博览会
中国国际门及门禁系统展览会
R+T Asia
2011/03/22-24
上海Shanghai
1470

2011中国可持续建筑国际大会&展览会
China Sustainable Building Forum (CSB 2011)
2011/03/22-24
上海Shanghai
1460

第9届上海国际园林景观设计及城市建设展览会
9th shanghai intl landscape design & urban construction expo
2011/03/22-24
上海Shanghai
1450

2011中国（沈阳）第九届建筑节能、墙体保温材料及设备展览会
9th china (shenyang) Intl energy-saving &new wall material and equipment exhibition
2011/03/27-29
辽宁沈阳Liaoning-Shenyang
5730

第12届中国国际建筑陶瓷及卫浴科技精品展览会
Ceramics, Tile & Sanitary Ware China 2011
2011/03/29-01
上海Shanghai
1550

中国(上海)国际建筑涂料展览会
Expo Coat
2011/03/29-01
上海Shanghai
1580

第16届中国国际建筑装饰材料展览会
16th China Intl Construction & Decoration Materials Exhibition
2011/04/08-11
辽宁大连Liaoning-Dalian
5590

第六届中国（广州）国际建材交易会暨红星美凯龙直销周
6th China (Guangzhou) Building Materials Fair
2011/04/14-18
广东广州Guangdong-Guangzhou
4140

2011年中国济南建筑装饰玻璃及艺术玻璃展会
China Jinan Architecture Glass and Art Glass Exhibition
2011/04/15-17
山东济南Shandong-Jinan
6160

2011第十二届中国济南国际门窗、型材及配套实施展览会
China Jinan Architecture Glass and Art Glass Exhibition
2011/04/15-17
山东济南Shandong-Jinan
6170

第18届中国（北京）国际石材产品及石材技术装备展览会
18th China Intl Stone Processing Machinery, Equipment and Products Exhibition
2011/04/20-23
北京Beijing
350

中国哈尔滨国际生态城市建设博览会
China (Harbin) Urban Eco Construction Expo:
2011/04/21-23
黑龙江哈尔滨Heilongjiang-Haerbin
5020

2011北京国际隧道地下工程、喷涂聚脲、土工材料、工程纤维及建筑化学品展览会
Beijing Intl Tunnel Underground Project, Spray Polyurea, Geo-technical Material, Engineering Fiber and Construction Chemicals Exhibition
2011/04/27-29
北京Beijing
400

第二届中国国际门业博览会
China International Door Industry Fair
2011/05/26-28
浙江永康Zhejiang-Yongkang
7070

第九届广州国际涂料 油墨 胶粘剂展览会
9th Guangzhou(China) Intl Coatings,Printing Inks & Adhesives Exhibition
2011/05/11-13
广东广州Guangdong-Guangzhou
4170

第五届中国国际新型墙体材料技术装备及产品展览会暨中国散装水泥暨预拌混凝土与预拌砂浆技术装备及产品展览会
WALLEXPO CHINA 2011
2011/05/12-14
北京Beijing
450

第五届中国（西安）建筑节能节新型建材博览会
5th China (Xi'an) Intl Energy-saving & Advanced Building Materials Exhibition
2011/05/18-21
陕西西安Shaanxi-Xi'an
6070

第3届中国(西安)国际桥梁、建筑模板及生产设备展览会
The 3rd China (Xi'an) ntemational Building Fomwork Scaffolding & Construction Technology Exhibition
2011/05/18-21
陕西西安Shaanxi-Xi'an
6090

第十一届中国（西安）门窗幕墙及设备展览会
The Tenth China (Xi' an) Fenestration and Equipment Exhibition
2011/05/18-21
陕西西安Shaanxi-Xi'an
6080

2011新疆国际建筑材料博览会
2011 Xinjiang Intl Building Fair
2011/05/19-21
新疆乌鲁木齐Xinjiang-Urumuqi
6730

第六届中国（厦门）国际建筑节能博览会
The 6th China (Xiamen) Intl Energy Efficiency in Buildings Expo
2011/05/20-22
福建厦门Fujian-Xiamen
3510

第八届厦门人居环境展示会
8th Living Environment Exhibition
2011/05/20-22
福建厦门Fujian-Xiamen
3500

2011中国西部工程机械建筑机械及混凝土设备展览会
West China Construction Machinery and Concrete Machinery Exhibition
2011/05/23-25
四川成都Sichuan-Chengdu
6640

第二届中国国际门业博览会
china Intl door industry fair
2011/05/26-28
浙江永康Zhejiang-Yongknag
7100

2011上海建筑给排水处理技术及设备展览会
Shanghai Building Water, Water Treatment Technology and Equipment Expo
2011/06/01-03
上海Shanghai
2100

广州国际建筑电气技术展览会
Electrical Building Technology Guangzhou
2011/06/09-12
广东广州Guangdong-Guangzhou
4256

2011上海涂料原材料展
All coat 2011
2011/06/15-17
上海Shanghai
2200

2011第四届中国（深圳）国际胶粘带及保护膜展览会
Shenzhen Adhesive Tape, Protective Film Exhibition
2011/06/17-19
广东深圳Guangdong-Shenzhen
4730

2011中国(广州)国际门窗展览会
CBD-Windoor 2011
2011/07/08-11
广东广州Guangdong-Guangzhou
4400

2011中国（广州）国际卫浴及建筑陶瓷展
China(Guangzhou) Intl Exhibition for Sanitary Ware and Building Ceramics 2011
2011/07/08-11
广东广州Guangdong-Guangzhou
4390

2011中国（广州）国际地面铺装材料展
China(Guangzhou) Intl Floor Covering Fair 2011
2011/07/08-11
广东广州Guangdong-Guangzhou
4360

第十三届中国（广州）国际建筑装饰博览会
The 13th China(Guangzhou) Intl Building Decoration Fair
2011/07/08-11
广东广州Guangdong-Guangzhou
4380

2011中国（青岛）国际陶瓷卫浴及厨房设备展览会
2011 China (Qingdao) Intl Ceramics Sanitary Ware and Kitchen Facilities Fair
2011/07/21-24
山东青岛Shandong-Qingdao
6340

第五届中国（青岛）国际外墙保温及新型墙体产品技术展览会
Qingdao Building External wall insulation and New Wall Materials Exhibition
2011/07/21-24
山东青岛Shandong-Qingdao
6398

2011中国（青岛）国际建筑防水及屋面系统展览会
Qingdao Building Waterproof Exhibition
2011/07/21-24
山东青岛Shandong-Qingdao
6320

第五届中国（青岛）国际建筑节能和可再生能源建筑应用博览会
2011 China (Qingdao) Intl Building Energy Saving Fair
2011/07/21-24
山东青岛Shandong-Qingdao
6290

2011中国（青岛）国际建筑装饰涂料及化学建材展览会
Qingdao Architectural coatings and Chemical Building Materials
2011/07/21-24
山东青岛Shandong-Qingdao
6380

第五届中国(青岛)国际石材工业及机械设备展览会
The 5th China(Qingdao) Intl Stone Products & Machinery Exhibition
2011/07/21-24
山东青岛Shandong-Qingdao
6360

第四届中国（青岛）国际太阳能与建筑一体化应用产品技术展览会
Qingdao Solar Energy and BIPV Exhibition
2011/07/21-24
山东青岛Shandong-Qingdao
6330

第七届中国(青岛)国际建筑材料及装饰材料博览会
The 7th China (Qingdao) Intl Construction & Decoration Materials Exhibition
2011/07/21-24
山东青岛Shandong-Qingdao
6280

第七届中国（青岛）国际木门展览会
Qingdao Intl Wooden Door Exhibition
2011/07/21-24
山东青岛Shandong-Qingdao
6310

第五届中国(青岛)国际地板及木制品展览会
China (Qingdao) Intl Floor Exhibition
2011/07/21-24
山东青岛Shandong-Qingdao
6350

第七届中国(青岛)国际门窗幕墙及相关设备展览会
The 7th China(Qingdao) Intl Doors windows Curtain Exhibition
2011/07/21-24
山东青岛Shandong-Qingdao
6300

2011上海国际建筑节能及新型建材展览会
2011 Shanghai Intl Energy-saving & Advanced Building Materials Exhibition
2011/08/16-19
上海Shanghai
2590

2011中国（上海）国际建材及室内装饰展览会
2011 Shanghai Intl Construction Material and Indoor Decoration Exhibition
2011/08/16-19
上海Shanghai
2570

第二十二届中国（上海）国际建材及室内装饰展览会
The 22nd Shanghai Intl Construction Material and Indoor Decoration Exhibition
2011/08/16-19
上海Shanghai
2580

2011第十一届广州木材、人造板、木地板、木门及设备展览会
11th Guangzhou Lumber, Building board, Wood floor, Door and Equipment Exhibitio 2011/09/07-09
广东广州Guangdong-Guangzhou
4500

2011第二届广州整体橱柜、壁柜及生产设备展览会
Guangzhou whole cabinet, Closet and Equipment Exhibition
2011/09/07-09
广东广州Guangdong-Guangzhou
4490

中国国际橱柜展览会
Kitchen & Cabinet China
2011/09/14-17
上海Shanghai
2780

2011第二届中国国际建筑高科技及城市建设博览会
The 2th China Intl Building Hi-tech and Urban Construction Expo,2011
2011/10/14-16
北京Beijing
840

2011第九届中国国际门窗幕墙博览会
Fenestration china 2011
2011/11/02-04
北京Beijing
910

中国厦门国际门窗木业展览会
China (Xiamen) Door, Window & Wood Industry Exhibition
2011/11/05-08
福建厦门Fujian-Xiamen
3670

中国厦门厨房卫浴用品展览会暨
China (Xiamen) Kitchen and Bathroom Product Exhibition
2011/11/05-08
福建厦门Fujian-Xiamen
3680

第十六届届中国国际涂料展览会
CHINACOAT 2011
2011/11/23-25
上海Shanghai
3230

29、交通 轨道 航运 公路 桥梁 Transportation, Road, Bridge, Railway

2011第二届中国（贵州）国际铁路、城市轨道交通技术与装备展览会
2nd China (Guizhou) Exhibition on Railway, Urban Rail, Transport Technology and Equipment
2011/05/13-16
贵州贵阳Guizhou-Guiyang
4960

2011上海国际智能交通与车联网科技发展论坛暨展览会
ITS Shanghai 2011
2011/06/16-17
上海Shanghai
2210

海峡两岸轨道科技展览暨研讨会_(RAILTEC 2011)
Taiwan Intl Exhibition and Conference on Railway Technology (RAILTEC 2011)
2011/08/04-05
台北Fujian-Xiamen
3560

30、教育 Education

上海市高校毕业生就业招聘会
Shanghai Job Fair for University graduates
2011/02/23-26
上海Shanghai
1200

第十六届中国国际教育巡回展
The 16th China Intl Education Exhibition Tour
2011/03/12-13
北京Beijing
150

第六届上海国际幼儿教育展
the 6th education expo 2011 shanghai
2011/05/20-22
上海Shanghai
2000

2011第七届中国（武汉）国际教育展
7th China (Wuhan) Intl Education Exhibition
2011/06/25-26
湖北武汉Hubei-Wuhan
5330

中国（北京）玩具动漫教育文化博览会
China Toys & Animation Educational Expo
2011/07/29-01
北京Beijing
650

2011中国国际教育展
China Education EXPO 2011
2011/10/15-16
北京Beijing
850

31、教学设备 Teaching Instrument

20011第二届上海国际教育技术装备及高职教仪器展览会
7th China (Wuhan) Intl Education Exhibition
2011/03/10-12
上海Shanghai
1340

第61届中国教育装备展示会
61st China Education Equipment Exhibition
2011/05/07-11
陕西西安Shaanxi-Xi'an
6040

32、金属加工 冶金 铸造锻造技术设备 Metalworking, Metallurgy & Foundry

第九届青岛国际金属加工技术设备展览会
The 9th Qingdao Intl Metal Processing Technology And Equipment Exhibition
2011/03/15-17
山东青岛Shandong-Qingdao
6230

第八届中国国际有及及特种铸造展览会暨中国铸造零部件展览会
2011 Non-ferrous & Special foundry and China Castpart Exhibition
2011/04/12-14
江苏南京Jiangsu-Nanjing
5500

第五届中国国际金属工业博览会
The 5th China Intl Metals Industry Trade Fair
2011/05/12-14
广东广州Guangdong-Guangzhou
4190

第十六届北京-埃森焊接与切割展览会
The 16th Beijing Essen Welding & Cutting Fair
2011/06/02-05
上海Shanghai
2120

第十二届广州国际管材展
12th China (Guangzhou) Intl Tube&Pipe Industry Exhibition
2011/06/23-25
广东广州Guangdong-Guangzhou
4300

第十二届广州国际压铸，铸造及工业炉展
12th CHINA (GUANGZHOU) INTL EXHIBITION ON DIE CASTING FOUNDRY AND INDUSTRIAL FURNACE
2011/06/23-25
广东广州Guangdong-Guangzhou
4350

第十二届广州国际不锈钢工业展
12th China (Guangzhou) Intl Stainless Steel Industry Exhibition
2011/06/23-25
广东广州Guangdong-Guangzhou
4340

第十二届广州国际铸件产品及工艺技术研讨展
THE 12th CHINA (GUANGZHOU) INT" L EXHIBITION OF CASTING PRODUCTS AND TECHNOLOGY SYMPOSIUM
2011/06/23-25
广东广州Guangdong-Guangzhou
4320

第十二届广州国际金属暨冶金工业展览会
12th China (Guangzhou) Intl Metal & Metallurgy Exhibition
2011/06/23-25
广东广州Guangdong-Guangzhou
4330

2011 年上海国际工业材料展览会-镁
Magnesium China
2011/07/13-15
上海Shanghai
2450

2011 年上海国际工业材料展览会-铜
Copper China 2011
2011/07/13-15
上海Shanghai
2480

2011 年上海国际工业材料展览会
-资源再生及利用
Industrial Material China
2011/07/13-15
上海Shanghai
2460

2011 年中国国际铝工业展览会
Aluminum China 2011
2011/07/13-15
上海Shanghai
2490

2011第11届中国东北国际冶金及金属工业展览会暨中国-东北钢铁市场论坛
11th Northeast China Metal Expo
2011/08-
辽宁沈阳
Liaoning-Shenyang
5930

2011第八届中国(北京)国际铸造展览会
The 8th China (Beijing) Intl Casting Industry Expo 2011
2011/08/10-12
北京Beijing
660

2011第八届中国(北京)国际冶金工业博览会
The 8th China (Beijing) Intl Metallurgy Industry Expo 2011
2011/08/10-12
北京Beijing
670

第十六届中国五金博览会
China Hardware Fair
2011/09-
浙江永康Zhejiang-Yongkang
7105

第七届上海国际不锈钢展览会
STEXPO 2011
2011/09/06-08
上海Shanghai
2710

2011亚太地区压铸工业展览会
2011 Asia-Pacific Diecasting Industry Exhibition
2011/09/21-23
广东东莞Guangdong-Dongguan
3750

数控机床与金属加工展
Metalworking and CNC Machine Tool Show
2011/11/01-05
上海Shanghai
3060

第十三届东莞国际模具及金属加工展
13th China Dongguan Intl Mould & Metalworking Exhibition
2011/11/16-19
广东东莞Guangdong-Dongguan
3770

2011上海金属暨冶金工业博览会、2011上海铸件、锻件、产品展览会
2011Shanghai Metal & Metallurgy Exhibition、2011 Shanghai INT ' T Casting , Forging
2011/12/01-03
上海Shanghai
3260

2012中国国际铸造博览会
2012 China Intl Foundry Expo (CIFEX)
2012/05/09-12
北京Beijing
1060

第十三届中国国际冶金工业展览会
Metallurgy China 2012
2012/05/09-12
北京Beijing
1070

第五届中国国际管材展览会
TUBE CHINA 2012
2012/09/25-28
上海Shanghai
3290

33、酒店业 Hotel & Restaurant

中国清洁博览会
China Clean Expo
2011/03/29-01
上海Shanghai
1570

上海国际酒店用品博览会：
-中国(上海)国际酒店与建筑照明展览会
-中国国际康体健身、休闲娱乐与运动器材展览会
Hotelex Shanghai：
- Expo Light
- Fitness, Sports & Leisure China
2011/03/29-03
上海Shanghai
1630

2011中国（临沂）酒店用品及设备博览会
China (Linyi) Hotel Supplies and Equipment Exhibition
2011/04/10-12
山东临沂Shandong-Linyi
6190

2011北京酒店用品、厨房设备、清洁用品、咖啡展览会（第十四届北京酒店设备用品展览会）
14th Beijing Hospitality Equipment & Supplies Exhibition
2011/04/26-28
北京Beijing
390

2011第十二届西安国际酒店设备及用品展览会
12th Xi' an Intl Hospitality Equipment & Supplies Fair
2011/05/18-20
陕西西安Shaanxi-Xi'an
6060

2011中国国际酒店博览会
Hotel China 2011
2011/05/18-20
北京Beijing
490

中国国际旅游商品博览会
China Intl Tourism Commodities Fair
2011/05/26-29
浙江义乌Zhejiang-Yiwu
7030

第六届中国（郑州）国际酒店、餐饮、泳池沐浴SPA设备及用品博览会/第六届中国（郑州）国际家纺、布艺及工艺品、礼品家居装饰博览会
6th China (Zhengzhou) Hospitality, Swimming Pool and Spa Expo
Grafts, Gifts and Home-ware Expo
2011/06/01-05
河南郑州Henan-Zhengzhou
5210

北京国际酒店用品展览会
Hotelex Beijing
2011/11/09-11
北京Beijing
940

第十五届国际食品、饮料、酒店设备、餐饮设备、烘焙及服务展览
FHC China 2011
2011/11/16-18
上海Shanghai
3205

第十六届国际食品、饮料、酒店设备、餐饮设备、烘焙及服务展览
FHC China 2012
2012/11/15-17
上海Shanghai
3300

34、机械 制造 工业装备 自动化 Machinery, Machine Tools and Technology & Automation

2011济南国际机床模具展览会
2011 Jinan Intl Machine Tools & Moulds Exhibition
2011/03/03-05
山东济南Shandong-Jinan
6130

中国广州国际工业自动化技术及装备展览会
SPS - Industrial Automation Fair Guangzhou
2011/03/09-11
广东广州Guangdong-Guangzhou
3950

中国广州国际工业自动化技术及装备展览会
SPS-Industrial Automation Fair Guangzhou
2011/03/09-11
广东广州Guangdong-Guangzhou
3960

中国重庆第16届仪器仪表工业控制自动化国际展览会
Intl Automation& Instrument Exhibition Central & Western China
2011/03/10-12
重庆Chongqing
1110

第18届中国（温州）国际机床、工模具展览会
18th China (Wenzhou) Intl Machine Tool Exhibition
2011/03/11-13
浙江温州Zhejiang-Wenzhou
6930

第12届中国国际机械工业展览会
12th China Intl Machinery Industry Exhibition
2011/03/17-20
浙江宁波Zhejiang-Ningbo
6870

2011中国国际机器视觉展览会
China Intl Machine Vision Exhibition
2011/03/20-22
上海Shanghai
1430

2011中国中部（郑州）国际装备制造业博览会
Central China (Zhengzhou) Equipment and Manufacturing Expo
2011/03/21-26
河南郑州Henan-Zhengzhou
5120

第14届中国东北国际仪器仪表及工业自动化展览会
Northeast 14th Intl Instrument & Automation Exhibition China
2011/03/22-24
辽宁沈阳Liaoning-Shenyang
5710

第12届深圳国际机械、模具及制品、塑胶工业展览会
China Shenzhen Intl Machinery Manufacturing Industry Exhibition
（SIMM2011）
2011/03/28-31
广东深圳Guangdong-Shenzhen
4670

国际表面工程展览会
Seexpo 2011
2011/04/07-09
上海Shanghai
1680

第12届中国国际机床展览会
12th China Intl Machine Tool Show
2011/04/11-16
北京-Beijing
310

第18届中国国际工业装备展览会
18th China Intl Industry Fair（CIF）
2011/04/20-22
重庆Chongqing
1150

第12届中国东北国际机床、工模具技术展览会
12th Intl Machine Tool and Tools & Moulds Technique Exhibition in Northeast China
2011/04/22-25
辽宁沈阳Liaoning-Shenyang
5830

中国东北第15届国际焊接、切割、激光技术设备展览会
15th China (Northeast) Intl Welding, Cutting & Laser Technology and Equipment Exhibition
2011/04/22-25
辽宁沈阳Liaoning-Shenyang
5850

第11届中国哈尔滨国际装备制造业博览会
11th China Harbin Intl Manufacture Exhibition
2011/04/27-29
黑龙江哈尔滨Heilongjiang-Harbin
5030

2011苏州自动化产业设备展览会
2011 Suzhou Automation Industry Exhibition
2011/05/11-13
江苏苏州Jiangsu-Suzhou
5550

第9届广州国际表面处理、电镀、涂装展览会
9th Guangzhou Intl Surface Finishing, Electroplating and Coating Exhibition
2011/05/11-13
广东广州Guangdong-Guangzhou
4180

第6届中国（贵州）国际装备制造业博览会
6th China (Guizhou) Intl Manufacture Exhibition
2011/05/13-16
贵州贵阳Guizhou-Guiyang
4970

2011国际现代工厂/过程自动化技术与装备展览会
FA/PA 2011
2011/05/18-20
北京Beijing
500

第9届烟台国际动力传动及控制技术展览会
Yantai Power Transmission and Control Technology Exhibition
2011/05/19-21
山东烟台Shandong-Yantai
6480

第9届烟台国际工业自动化及仪器仪表展览会
9th Yantai Intl Industrial Automation & Instrument Exhibition
2011/05/19-21
山东烟台Shandong-Yantai
6470

第九届烟台国际机床暨工模具技术设备展览会
9th Yantai Intl Machine Tools & Industrial Mould Technology and Equipment Exhibition
2011/05/19-21
山东烟台Shandong-Yantai
6490

第13届大连国际自动化、仪表展览会
13th Dalian Intl Automation & Instrumentation Exhibition
2011/05/19-21
辽宁大连Liaoning-Dalian
5610

烟台国际机床暨工模具技术设备展览会
Yantai Intl Machine Tools & Industrial Moulds Equipment Exhibition
2011/05/19-21
山东烟台Shandong-Yantai
6450

第12届湖南工控自动化及仪器仪表展览会
12th Industrial Control, Automation, Instrument Exhibition
2011/05/25-27
湖南长沙Hunan-Changsha
5410

广州国际机床模具展览会
Guangzhou Intl Machine Tools & Moulds Exhibition
2011/05/26-28
广东广州Guangdong-Guangzhou
4220

中国国际模具、制造应用设备及相关工业展览会
DMC 2011-China Intl Exhibition on Die & Mould, Metal Processing and Forming Industry
2011/06/02-05
上海Shanghai
2130

第16届北京-埃森焊接与切割展览会
16th Beijing Essen Welding & Cutting Fair
2011/06/02-05
上海Shanghai
2120

第7届广州国际品牌叉车及配件展览会
7th Guangzhou Intl Brand Forklift & Accessory Exhibition
2011/06/22-24
广东广州Guangdong-Guangzhou
4280

第13届上海国际机床展
13th Shanghai Intl Machine Tool Fair
2011/06/28-01
上海Shanghai
2320

第15届华南工业控制自动化国际展览会
15th Intl Industrial Control & Automation Exhibition for South China
2011/06/29-01
广东深圳Guangdong-Shenzhen
4750

2011 年上海国际工业材料展览会?复合材料
Composites China
2011/07/13-15
上海Shanghai
2440

天津国际工业装备展览会
Tianjin International Industry Fair
2011/08-
天津Tianjin
3380

中国国际工业装备(青岛)博览会
China (Qingdao) Industry Fair
2011/08/04-07
山东青岛Shandong-Qingdao
6410

青岛国际机床模具展览会
Qingdao Intl Machine Tools & Moulds Exhibition
2011/08/04-07
山东青岛Shandong-Qingdao
6420

第5届上海国际工业装配与传输技术展览会
2011 AHTE-5th Shanghai Intl Assembly & Handling Technology Exhibition
2011/08/16-19
上海Shanghai
2560

广州国际机床及加工装备展
Guangzhou Intl Machine Tools & Machinery Show
2011/08/17-20
广东广州Guangdong-Guangzhou
4440

中国（南部）机床展览会
Machine Tool China-South 2011
2011/08/30-02
广东深圳Guangdong-Shenzhen
4830

第10届中国国际装备制造业博览会
10th China Intl Equipment Manufacturing Exposition
2011/09/01-05
辽宁沈阳Liaoning-Shenyang
5970

第10届中国国际装备制造业博览会
10th China Intl Equipment Manufacturing Expo
2011/09/01-05
辽宁沈阳Liaoning-Shenyang
5980

中国国际制造技术及设备展览会
China Intl Mechanical Manufacturing Technology & Equipment Exhibition
2011/09/16-18
山东济南Shandong-Jinan
6180

第12届中国国际机电产品博览会-武汉
12th China Intl Machinery & Electronic Products Expo, Wuhan
2011/09/23-26
湖北武汉Hubei-Wuhan
5350

第9届国际粉体工业/散装技术展览会暨会议
9th Intl Powder/Bulk Conference & Exhibition
2011/09/27-29
上海Shanghai
2940

国际自动识别技术展览会
Intl Exhibition of Automatic Identification Technology
2011/10/12-14
湖北武汉Hubei-Wuhan
5360

亚洲国际动力传动与控制技术展览会
PTC ASIA 2011
2011/10/25-28
上海Shanghai
3000

第8届中国国际机器视觉展览会暨机器视觉技术及工业应用研讨会
8th China Intl Machine Vision Exhibition and Machine Vision Technology & Application Conference
2011/10/26-28
北京Beijing
880

数控机床与金属加工展
Metalworking and CNC Machine Tool Show
2011/11/01-05
上海Shanghai
3060

工业自动化展
Industrial Automation Show
2011/11/01-05
上海Shanghai
3070

第24届中国国际表面处理展览会
SFCHINA 2011
2011/11/23-25
上海Shanghai
3220

第11届中国国际机床工具展览会
11th China Intl Machine Tool & Tools Exhibition
2012/06/12-16
北京Beijing
1075

35、空调 制冷 供暖 通风 Air-conditioning, Heating, Refrigeration & Ventilation

中国(北京)国际供热空调、卫生洁具及城建设备与技术展览会
China Intl Trade Fair for Sanitation, Heating & Air-Conditioning
2011/03/03-05
北京Beijing
120

2011中国东北第十四届国际供热供暖、空调、热泵技术设备展览会
china(Northeast)The 14th Intl Equipments of Heating,Air-Condition & New Energy Sources Exhibition
2011/03/27-29
辽宁沈阳Liaoning-Shenyang
5750

第二十二届国际制冷、空调、供暖、通风及食品冷冻加工展览会
The 22nd Intl Exhibition for Refrigeration, Air-conditioning, Heating and Ventilation, Frozen Food Processing, Packaging and Storage
2011/04/07-09
上海Shanghai
1670

2011上海国际室内供暖、通风及净化产品展览会
2011 Shanghai Intl Residential Comfort System Expo
2011/05/05-07
上海Shanghai
1870

第二届中国（青岛）国际供热采暖系统产品及技术应用展览会
Qingdao Heating Supply System and Technology Exhibition
2011/07/21-24
山东青岛Shandong-Qingdao
6390

第三届上海国际冷冻保鲜及冷链物流技术设备展览会
2011 The 3th Shanghai Intl Exhibition of Food Frozen & Fresh and Cold Chain Logistics Technology Equipment
2011/09/15-17
上海Shanghai
2830

36、矿业 Mining

2011第八届中国新疆国际煤炭工业博览会
Xinjiang Intl Coal Industry Exhibition
2011/08/05 - 07
新疆乌鲁木齐Xinjiang-Urumuqi
6740

第十一届中国(北京)国际工程机械、建材机械及矿山机械展览与技术交流会
2011 Beijing International Construction Machinery Exhibition & Seminar
2011/10/18-21
北京Beijing
870

37、零售业 营销 Retail

2011中国特许展——第13届中国特许加盟展览会
China Franchise Expo 2011
2011/05/07-09
北京Beijing
430

2011中国创业项目投资博览会
2011 Entrepreneurship and Investment Exhibition
2011/09/08-13
福建厦门Fujian-Xiamen
3570

国际特许加盟（上海）展览会
（2011年中国特许展上海站）
Shanghai Intl Franchiseexpo.com Exhibition
2011/09/17-19
上海Shanghai
2870

营销和广告创新技术展示会暨研讨会
Technology for Marketing & Advertising China
2011/10/26-27
上海Shanghai
3020

第十三届中国连锁业会议暨
第十三届中国连锁店展览会
The 13th China Retail Industry Convention
13th China Chain Store Expo
2011/11/04-06
湖南长沙Hunan-Changsha
5420

38、礼品 Gifts

2011北京国际创意礼品及工艺品展览会
2011 Beijing Intl Creative Gift & Craftwork Exhibition
2011/03/05-08
北京Beijing
130

第24届北京国际礼品、赠品及家庭用品展览会
China Beijing Intl Gifts, Premium & Houseware Exhibition
2011/03/16-19
北京Beijing
170

第八届中国国际文具礼品博览会（CNISE 2011）
8th China Intl Stationery & Gifts Exposition
2011/03/17-19
浙江宁波Zhejiang-Ningbo
6860

第十九届中国（深圳）国际礼品、工艺 品、钟表及家庭用品展览会
Gifts and Home China
2011/04/24-27
广东深圳Guangdong-Shenzhen
4710

成都家居、休闲用品及礼品展览会
2011 Chengdu Houseware, Leisure Goods & Gifts Fair
2011/06/17-19
四川成都Sichuan-Chengdu
6650

2011中国国际彩盒展
SinoFoldingCarton 2011
2011/07/06-08
北京Beijing
620

2011北京国际创意礼品及工艺品展览会
2011 Beijing Intl Creative Gift & Craftwork Exhibition
2011/08/11-14
北京Beijing
690

第24 届中国北京国际礼品、赠品及 家庭用品展览会
24th China Beijing Intl Gifts, Premium & Houseware Exhibition
2011/08/17-20
北京Beijing
700

中国上海礼品、赠品及家居用品展览会
China Shanghai International Gifts, Premium and Houseware Exhibition 2011/09/01-04
2011/09/02 - 04
上海Shanghai
2680

第十九届中国（深圳）国际玩具及礼品展览会
Gifts & Home China
2011/10/20-23
广东深圳Guangdong-Shenzhen
4860

北京国际礼品、赠品及家用精品（年底） 采购订货会
The 22nd China International Gifts, Premium & Houseware Exhibition
2011/11/25-27
北京Beijing
1020

39、铝业 Aluminum Industry

2011年中国国际铝工业展览会
Aluminum China 2011
2011/07/13-15
2490

40、旅游 Tourism

中国广州户外及休闲展览会
China Intl Outdoor & Leisure Fair
2011/03/18-21
广东广州Guangdong-Guangzhou
4030

广州国际旅游展览会
Guangzhou Intl Travel Fair
2011/03/24-26
广东广州Guangdong-Guangzhou
4060

2011中国出境旅游交易会
China Outbound Travel and Tourism Market 2011
2011/04/13-15
北京Beijing
330

上海世界旅游资源博览会
World Travel Fair
2011/05/12-15
上海Shanghai
1930

中国国际旅游商品博览会
China Intl Tourism Commodities Fair
2011/05/26-29
浙江义乌Zhejiang-Yiwu
7030

国际豪华旅游博览- 亚洲站-全球豪华旅游产品及服务
Intl Luxury Travel Market Asia
2011/06/13-16
上海Shanghai
2170

中国（北京）国际商务及会奖旅游展览会
China Incentive, Business Travel & Meetings Exhibition
2011/08/30-01
北京Beijing
730

中国(广东)国际旅游产业博览会
China Intl Travel Expo (CITE) 2011
2011/09/02-04
广东广州Guangdong-Guangzhou
4480

41、美容美发 化妆品 个人护理用品 水疗 Beauty, Cosmetics, Hairdressing, Personal Care, Spa

2011（深圳）国家化妆品、个人及家庭护理用品原料展览会
Personal Care and Homecare ingredients Fair(PCHI)
2011/02/22-24
广东深圳Guangdong-Shenzhen
4650

第十九届中国（上海）国际婚纱摄影器材展览会
The 19th China (Shanghai) Intl Wedding Photographic Equipment Exhibition
2011/02/23-26
上海Shanghai
1210

第34届广州国际美博会
34th Guangzhou Intl Beauty Expo - Spring 2011
2011/03/09-11
广东广州Guangdong-Guangzhou
3970

2011北京国际美容美发化妆用品博览会
Chinese Intl Beauty, Hairdressing & Cosmetics Expo in Beijing 2011
2011/04/08-10
北京Beijing
300

2011第25届(春季)成都美容美发节
25th Spring Chengdu Beauty, Hairdressing and Cosmetics Festival
2011/04/15-18
四川成都Sichuan-Chengdu
6590

第十六届中国美容博览会（上海CBE）
China Beauty Expo
2011/05/18-20
上海Shanghai
1980

中国国际美发美容博览会
China Hair & Beauty
2011/06/28-30
北京Beijing
600

第35届广州国际美博会
The 35th Guangzhou Intl Beauty Expo - Autumn 2011
2011/09/19-21
广东广州Guangdong-Guangzhou
4580

42、模具 Mold

2011济南国际机床模具展览会
2011 Jinan Intl Machine Tools & moulds Exhibition
2011/03/03-05
山东济南Shandong-Jinan
6130

第十八届中国（温州）国际机床、工模具展览会
The 18th China (Wenzhou) Intl Machine Tool Exhibition
2011/03/11-13
浙江温州Zhejiang-Wenzhou
6930

2011第12届深圳国际机械、模具及制品、塑胶工业展览会
China Shenzhen Intl Machinery Manufacturing Industry Exhibition （SIMM2011）
2011/03/28-31
广东深圳Guangdong-Shenzhen
4670

2011烟台国际机床暨工模具技术设备展览会
2011 Yantai Intl Machine Tools & Industria Moulds Equipment Exhibition
2011/05/19-21
山东烟台Shandong-Yantai
6450

第九届烟台国际机床暨工模具技术设备展览会
The 9th Yantai Intl Machine Tools & Industrial Mould Technology and Equipment Exhibition
2011/05/19-21
山东烟台Shandong-Yantai
6490

2011广州国际机床模具展览会
2011 Guangzhou Intl Machine Tools & moulds Exhibition
2011/05/26-28
广东广州Guangdong-Guangzhou
4220

2011中国国际模具、制造应用设备及相关工业展览会
DMC 2011 (China Intl Exhibition on Die & Mould, Metal Processing and Forming Industry)
2011/06/02-05
上海Shanghai
2130

2011青岛国际机床模具展览会
2011 Qingdao Intl Machine Tools & Moulds Exhibition
2011/08/04-07
山东青岛Shandong-Qingdao
6420

广州国际模具展览会
Guangzhou Intl Mould & Die Exhibition
2011/09/21-23
广东广州Guangdong-Guangzhou
4583

第十三届东莞国际模具及金属加工展
13th China Dongguan Intl Mould & Metalworking Exhibition
2011/11/16-19
广东东莞Guangdong-Dongguan
3770

43、模型 Models

第23届广州国际玩具及模型展览会
23rd Guangzhou Intl Toy & Hobby Fair
2011/04/08-10
广东广州Guangdong-Guangzhou
4130

2011第八届上海国际模型展览会展
2011The 8th Shanghai Intl Model
2011/09/02-04
上海Shanghai
2690

第十届中国国际玩具及模型展览会
10th Intl Trade Fair for Toys and Hobby
2011/10/12-14
上海Shanghai
2980

44、能源 新能源 节能 New Energy, Energy-Saving

2011太阳能展（春交会）
2011 Solar Energy
2011/02/23-26
河南郑州Henan-Zhengzhou
5090

第12届中国（广州）国际给排水、水处理技术设备展览会
2011中国（广州）国际泵、阀门、管道展览会
Water Wasterwater & Water Treatment China 2011
Pump, Vale & Pipe China 2011
2011/03/09-11
广东广州Guangdong-Guangzhou
3980

中国国际遮阳与节能技术博览会
中国国际门及门禁系统展览会
R+T Asia
2011/03/22-24
上海Shanghai
1470

第2届中国（安徽）新能源与光伏展览会
2nd China (Anhui) New Energy and Photovoltaic Exhibition
2011/03/25-27
安徽合肥Anhui-Hefei
3400

2011第二届中国(安徽)节能、新能源汽车展览会
2nd China (Anhui) Energy Saving、 New Energy VehiclesExpo
2011/03/25-27
安徽合肥Anhui-Hefei
3390

2011中国（沈阳）第九届建筑节能、墙体保温材料及设备展览会
9th china (shenyang) Intl energy-saving & new wall material and equipment exhibition.
2011/03/27-29
辽宁沈阳Liaoning-Shenyang
5730

第五届中国（上海）国际风能展览会暨研讨会
China (Shanghai) Intl Wind Energy Exhibition and Conference 2011
2011/04/08-10
上海Shanghai
1720

第五届中国（西安）建筑节能节新型建材博览会
5th China (Xi'an) Intl Energy-saving & Advanced Building Materials Exhibition
2011/05/18-21
陕西西安Shaanxi-Xi'an
6070

第六届中国（厦门）国际建筑节能博览会
6th China (Xiamen) Intl Energy Efficiency in Buildings Expo
2011/05/20-22
福建厦门Fujian-Xiamen
3510

2011中国新能源战略与“十二五”新能源发展高峰论坛暨新能源产业十一五成就盘点
2011 New Energy Strategy Summit
2011/05/28-29
北京Beijing
550

2011第七届中国-宁夏国际能源装备与节能减排科技博览会
Ningxia Energy, Energy Saving and Emission Reduction Expo
2011/06/12-
宁夏银川Ningxia-Yinchuan
6010

亚洲风能大会暨国际风能设备展览会
Wind Power Asia - Asian Wind Energy Exhibition & Conference
2011/06/22-24
北京Beijing
585

中国国际清洁能源博览会
Clean Energy Expo China
2011/06/22-24
北京Beijing
586

第四届中国（青岛）国际太阳能与建筑一体化应用产品技术展览会
Qingdao Solar Energy and BIPV Exhibition
2011/07/21-24
山东青岛Shandong-Qingdao
6330

第五届中国（青岛）国际建筑节能和可再生能源建筑应用博览会
2011 China (Qingdao) Intl Building Energy Saving Fair
2011/07/21-24
山东青岛Shandong-Qingdao
6290

2011第八届中国新疆国际煤炭工业博览会
Xinjiang Intl Coal Industry Exhibition
2011/07/22-22
新疆乌鲁木齐Xinjiang-Urumuqi
6740

新能源与电力电工展
Energy Show
2011/11/01-05
上海Shanghai
3050

2011中国东北（沈阳）政府采购暨节能减排展览会
Northeast China (Shenyang) Intl Exhibition for Government Purchase
2011/11-
辽宁沈阳Liaoning-Shenyang
6005

第五届中国（杭州）国际清洁能源与环保产业展览会
5th China Intl Clean Energy & Environment Protection Industry Fair
2011/11/03-05
浙江杭州Zhejiang-Hangzhou
6840

45、农业 林业 渔业 畜牧业 Agriculture, Forestry, Fishery & Animal Husbandry

第三届厦门特色农产品展销会
3rd Agricultural product Sales
2011/01/21-24
福建厦门Fujian-Xiamen
3470

第六届全国粳稻米大会
6th Countrywide Rice Convention
2011/03/09-10
吉林长春Jilin-Changchun
5580

2011第七届泛北部湾（广西）畜牧水产行业博览会
7th Guangxi Livestock, Fisheries Expo
2011/03/18-20
广西南宁Guangxi-Nanning
4900

2011第二届泛北部湾(广西)粮油、食品、农产品及其生产加工机械设备博览会
2nd Guangxi Exhibition on Food, Agricultural Products and Processing Machinery
2011/03/18-20
广西南宁Guangxi-Nanning
4910

第九届上海国际园林景观设计及城市建设展览会
9th shanghai intl landscape design&urban construction expo
2011/03/22-24
上海Shanghai
1450

第三届全国杂粮产业大会
3rd National Grain Industry Conference
2011/03/29-30
北京Beijing
240

第二届华夏有机肥展示会暨第七届中原肥料双交会
2nd China Organic Fertilizer Show
2011/03/30-03
河南郑州Henan-Zhengzhou
5140

第13届中国国际花卉园艺展览会
13th Hortiflorexpo China
2011/04/13-16
上海Shanghai
1740

2011第11届中国新疆国际农业博览会
11th Xinjiang Intl Agriculture Fair
2011/08/12-14
新疆乌鲁木齐Xinjiang-Urumuqi
6760

第八届中国辽宁（沈阳）国际农业博览会
8th Liaoning (Shenyang) Intl Agriculture Expo
2011/09/15-18
辽宁沈阳Liaoning-Shenyang
5990

家禽交易会
Poultry Fair
2011/09/19-22
河南郑州Henan-Zhengzhou
5270

第十九届中国国际纸浆造纸、林业展览会及会议
China Paper / China Forest 2011
2011/09/19-21
北京Beijing
800

第11届国际果蔬、食品博览会
11th Intl Fruit/Vegetable/Food Expo
2011/10/18-21
6495

第4届中国义乌国际森林产品博览会
4th China Yiwu Intl Forest Products Fair
2011/11/01-04
浙江义乌Zhejiang-Yiwu
7060

中国国际渔业博览会
China Fisheries & Seafood Expo
2011/11/01-03
山东青岛Shandong-Qingdao
6430

中国杨凌农业高新科技成果博览会
China Yangling Agricultural Hi-tich Fair
2011/11/05-09
陕西杨凌Shaanxi-Yangling
6110

46、汽车 摩托车 电动车 Automobiles and Motorcycles

2011惠州国际汽车展览会
Huizhou International Automobile Exhibition
2011/02/22-24
广东惠州Guangdong-Huizhou
4645

2011佛山国际汽车展览会
Foshan Intl Automobile Exhibition
2011/02/24-26
广东佛山Guangdong-Foshan
3900

第八届广州(国际)车用空调及冷藏链技术展览会
8th Guangzhou Intl Automotive Air-conditioning & Cold Chain Technology Exhibition
2011/02/24-26
广东广州Guangdong-Guangzhou
3920

第12届汽车用品暨改装汽车展览会
12th China Intl Expo for Auto Electronics, Accessories, Tuning & Car Care products
2011/02/25-27
北京Beijing
50

2011年中国郑州微型汽车配件展
2011 China (Zhengzhou) Mini Automobile and Parts Exhibition
2011/03/07-12
河南郑州Henan-Zhengzhou
5100

2011西安国际汽车展览会
Xi' an International Automobile Exhibition
2011/03/09-11
陕西西安Shaanxi-Xi'an
6015

第四届西安国际汽车用品展览会暨2011西部汽车用品订货交易会
4th Xi' an Intl Automobile Accessories Fair
2011/05/07-11
陕西西安Shaanxi-Xi'an
6020

2011第十届中国（天津）国际客车及零部件展览会
10th China (Tianjin) Bus and Parts Exhibition
2011/03/19-21
天津Tianjin
3330

2011中国（常州）国际摩托车零部件及后用品交易会
China (Changzhou) Intl Motorbike, Parts and Services Fair
2011/03/25-27
江苏常州Jiangsu-Changzhou
5440

2011第二届中国(安徽)节能、新能源汽车展览会
2nd China (Anhui) Energy Saving, New Energy VehiclesExpo
2011/03/25-27
安徽合肥Anhui-Hefei
3390

2011西部汽车用品订货交易会
4th Xi' an Intl Automobile Accessories Fair
2011/03/25-27
陕西西安Shaanxi-Xi'an
6030

2011第二届中国(青岛)国际重型汽车、卡车、挂车及零部件展览会
2nd China (Qingdao) Intl Exhibition on Heavy Cars, Trucks and Special Vehicles and Parts
2011/03/25-27
山东青岛Shandong-Qingdao
6240

第12届中国国际天然气汽车、加气站设备展览会
12th China Intl Natural Gas Automobile and Gas Station Equipment Exhibition
2011/03/29-31
北京Beijing
250

品质生活、精品汽车浙江巡回展
Automobile Zhejiang Rood Show
2011/04-
浙江Zhejiang
6801

2011年第五届杭州春季汽车展销会
5th Spring Hangzhou Automobile Fair
2011/04-
浙江杭州Zhejiang-Hangzhou
6810

2011中国（浙江）改装车、专用车博览会
China (Hangzhou) Modified Mobile and Special Purpose Vehicle Expo
2011/05/28-29
浙江杭州Zhejiang-Hangzhou
6820

第二届大河汽车博览会
2nd Giant River Automobile Expo
2011/04/06-10
河南郑州Henan-Zhengzhou
5150

第五届中国（沈阳）汽车交易博览会
5th China (Shenyang) Automobile Fair
2011/04/07-11
辽宁沈阳Liaoning-Shenyang
5770

2011第九届中国（温州）汽车展览会
9th Wenzhou Intl Auto Expo
2011/04/07-10
浙江温州Zhejiang-Wenzhou
6940

2011年中国洛阳国际汽车展览会
China Luoyang Intl Automobile Exhibition
2011/04/08-11
河南洛阳Henan-Luoyang
5070

2011第十三届东北国际汽车用品展览会
Shenyang China Car Expo
2011/04/13-15
辽宁沈阳Liaoning-Shenyang
5790

2011首届.贵阳国际汽车展览会
2011 Guiyang Intl Automobile Exhibition
2011/04/15-19
贵州贵阳Guizhou-Guiyang
4950

2011年烟台春季汽车展销会
2011 Spring Yantai Automobile Show
2011/04/15-17
山东烟台Shandong-Yantai
6440

2011中国唐山专（商）用车暨现代物流博览会
2011 China (Tanshan) Special Purpose Vehicle & Logistic Expo
2011/04/20-22
河北唐山Hebei-Tangshan
5000

第十四届上海国际汽车工业展览会
AUTO SHANGHAI 2011
2011/04/21-28
上海Shanghai
1790

第69届全国汽车配件交易会暨全国汽车配件采购交易会
National Auto Parts Fair
2011/04/22-25
待定undetermined
5820

第十七届福州国际汽车展览会
17th Auto Fuzhou
2011/04/29-03
福建福州Fujian-Fuzhou
3430

2011年第四届中国（南京）国际汽车博览会
4th China (Nanjing) Intl Automobile Expo
2011/04/30-04
江苏南京Zhejiang-Nanjing
5515

品质生活、精品汽车浙江巡回展
Automobile Zhejiang Rood Show
2011/05-
浙江Zhejiang
6802

第三届常州春季汽车博览会
3rd Changzhou Spring Automobile Expo
2011/05/01-03
江苏常州Jiangsu-Changzhou
5450

2011年第六届义乌汽车展览会
6th Yiwu Automobile Exhibition
2011/05/06-08
浙江义乌Zhejiang-Yiwu
7020

2011年第九届华中国际汽车展览会
9th Central China Automobile Exhibition
2011/05/20-24
湖北武汉Hubei-Wuhan
5320

2011第七届中国（唐山）国际汽车博览会
7th China (Tangshan) Intl Automobile Expo
2011/05/27-06/01
河北唐山Hebei-Tangshan
5010

2011年第二届中国（浙江）汽配交易会
2nd China (Hangzhou) Auto Part Fair
2011/05/28-29
浙江杭州Zhejiang-Hangzhou
6830

第十五届深圳-香港-澳门国际汽车博览会
15th Shenzhen-Hong Kong-Macao Intl Automobile Expo
2011/05/30-10
深圳-Shenzhen
4725

品质生活、精品汽车浙江巡回展
Automobile Zhejiang Rood Show
2011/06-
浙江Zhejiang
6803

2011第二届中国(太原)国际汽车展览
2nd China (Taiyuan) Intl Automobile Exhibition
2011/06/03-06
山西太原Shanxi-Taiyuan
6520

第三届中国(太原)国际卡车暨物流展览会
3rd China (Taiyuan) Truck and Logistics Exhibition
2011/06/03-05
山西太原Shanxi-Taiyuan
6510

第三届连云港-大陆桥汽车贸易博览会
3rd Lianyugang-Continental Bridge Automobile Expo
2011/06/03-06
江苏连云港Jiangsu-Lianyungang
5490

第7届广州国际品牌叉车及配件展览会
7th Guangzhou Intl Brand Forklift & Accessory Exhibition
2011/06/22-24
广东广州Guangdong-Guangzhou
4280

第五届中国（常州）电动车燃油助力车及零部件展览会
5th China (Changzhou) Electric Car, Hibrid Car and Parts Exhibition
2011/06/23-25
江苏常州Jiangsu-Changzhou
5470

2011第八届汽车用品交易会暨第八届汽车羊剪绒产品订货会
8th Automobile Products Fair
2011/06/23-02
河南郑州Henan-Zhengzhou
5230

2011年第十届中国沈阳汽车工业博览会
10th China (Shenyang) Automobile Industry Expo
2011/06/30-05
辽宁沈阳Liaoning-Shenyang
5900

2011年第三届呼和浩特国际汽车展览会
3rd Hohhot Intl Automobile Exhibition
2011/07/15-19
内蒙古呼和浩特Inner Mongolia-Hohhot
5435

2011中国包头国际汽车展览会
China Baotou Intl Automobile Exhibition
2011/07/15-19
内蒙古包头Inner Mogolia-Baotou
5430

哈尔滨国际车展
（第14届哈尔滨国际汽车工业展览会）
The 14th Harbin Intl Automobile Exhibition
2011/08/01 - 08
黑龙江哈尔滨Heilongjiang-Harbin
5055

AMTS2011
上海国际汽车制造技术及装备与材料展览会
Shanghai Intl Automotive Manufacturing Technology & Material Show
2011/08/16-19
上海Shanghai
2550

2011（第十六届）大连国际汽车展览会
16th Dalian Intl Automotive Exhibition
2011/08/17-21
辽宁大连Liaoning-Dalian
5640

2011中国西部（兰州）国际汽车博览
West China (Lanzhou) Automobile Expo
2011/08/20-30
甘肃兰州Gansu-Lanzhou
3720

2011（第七届）烟台国际汽车展示交易会
7th Yantai Intl Automobile Show
2011/09/01-05
山东烟台Shandong-Yantai
6495

第17届中国（湖北-武汉）国际汽车工业展览会
12th China (Hubei/Wuhan) Intl Auto Industry Exhibition
2011/09/01-06
湖北武汉Hubei-Wuhan
5340

2011第二届鄂尔多斯国际汽车展览会
Ordos International Automobile Exhibition
2011/09/01-05
内蒙古鄂尔多斯Inner Mongolia-Ordos
5438

CIAPE中国国际汽车零部件博览会
China Lnternational Auto Parts Expo
2011/09/08-10
北京Beijing
760

2011第八届中国（苏州）国际汽车工业博会
8th China (Suzhou) Intl Automobile Show
2011/09/09-13
江苏苏州Jiangsu-Suzhou
5553

成都国际汽车展览会
Chengdu Motor Show
2011/09/17-25
四川成都Sichuan-Chengdu
6690

第十一届广东国际汽车展示交易会
11th Guangdong Internarional Auto Exhibition & Trade Fair
2011/09/29-04
广东东莞Guangdong-Dongguan
3755

第六届中国（沈阳）汽车交易博览会
6th China (Shenyang) Automobile Fair
2011/10-
辽宁沈阳Liaoning-Shenyang
6000

2011年第十二届中国杭州国际汽车工业展览会
12nd China Hangzhou Intl Automobile Industry Exhibition
2011/10/20-24
浙江杭州Zhejiang-Hangzhou
6835

2011年第六届南昌国际汽车展览会
6th Nanchang International Automobile Exhibition
2011/10/22-25
江西南昌Jiangxi-Nanchang
5555

品质生活、精品汽车浙江巡回展
Automobile Zhejiang Rood Show
2011/11-
浙江Zhejiang
6804

厦门日报房车大联展
Xiamen Housing and Automotive Exhibition
2011/10/27-31
福建厦门Fujian-Xiamen
3650

第56届全国汽车保修检测诊断设备（秋季）展览会
AMR 2011-Auto Maintenance & Repair
2011/11/09-11
广东东莞Guangdong-Dongguan
3765

2011年第四届郑州国际汽车展览会
2011 China (Zhengzhou) Intl Automobile Expo
2011/11/11-15
河南郑州He'nan-Zhengzhou
5300

第九届中国（广州）国际汽车展览会
The 9th China (Guangzhou) Intl Automobile Exhibition
2011/11/22-28
广东广州Guangdong-Guangzhou
4635

品质生活、精品汽车浙江巡回展
Automobile Zhejiang Rood Show
2011/12-
浙江Zhejiang
6805

2011中国-东盟第四届南宁国际汽车展览会
Nanning International Automobile Exhibition
2011/12/01-05
广西南宁Guangxi-Nanning
4945

2011年上海国际汽车零配件、维修检测诊断设备及服务用品展览会
Shanghai Intl Trade Fair for Automotive Parts, Equipment and Service Suppliers
2011/12/07-10
上海Shanghai
3265

2012（第12届）北京国际汽车展览会
Beijing Intl Automotive Exhibition
2012/04-
北京Beijing
1050

47、清洁 Cleaning

中国清洁博览会
China Clean Expo
2011/03/29-04/01
上海Shanghai
1570

2011北京酒店用品、厨房设备、清洁用品、咖啡展览会
（第十四届北京酒店设备用品展览会）
14th Beijing Hospitality Equipment & Supplies Exhibition
2011/04/26-28
北京Beijing
390

48、设计 Design

第九届上海国际园林景观设计及城市建设展览会
9th shanghai intl landscape design & urban construction expo
2011/03/22-24
上海Shanghai
1450

W3国际精品设计展
Expo Deco
2011/03/29-01
上海Shanghai
1590

毛织设计及工艺展
Knitwear Design and Technology Fair (KDT)
2011/08/25-27
广东深圳Guangdong-Shenzhen
4800

2011中国宁波国际工业设计博览会
Intl Industry Design Fair Ningbo China
2011/10/28-31
浙江宁波Zhejiang-Ningbo
6890

"100% 设计"上海展-
中国领先当代室内设计采购交流平台
100% design shanghai
2011/11/03-05
上海Shanghai
3120

49、摄影 影像 Photography & Image

第19届中国（上海）国际婚纱摄影器材展览会
19th China (Shanghai) Intl Wedding Photographic Equipment Exhibition
2011/02/23-26
上海Shanghai
1210

上海国际婚纱摄影器材展览会暨国际儿童摄影、主题摄影、相册相框展览会
China Wedding Expo 2011
2011/02/23-26
上海Shanghai
1230

2011中国国际婚纱及摄影器材博览会
China Wedding 2011
2011/03/20-23
北京Beijing
190

中国国际照相机械影像器材与技术博览会
China Intl Photograph & Electrical Imaging Machinery and Technology Fair
2011/04/21-24
北京Beijing
370

第七届中国（深圳）国际文化产业博览交易会 暨第二届中国国际新媒体影视动漫节
China (Shenzhen) Intl Cultural Industries Fair
2011/05/13-16
广东深圳Guangdong-Shenzhen
4720

第13届中国（上海）国际摄影器材和数码影像展览会
PHOTO & IMAGING SHANGHAI 2011
2011/07/07-10
上海Shanghai
2410

50、食品 饮料 茶酒及生产机械 Food, Beverage, Tea, Spirit & Processing

2011第二届泛北部湾(广西)粮油、食品、农产品及其生产加工机械设备博览会
2nd Guangxi Exhibition on Food, Agricultural Products and Processing Machinery
2011/03/18-20
广西南宁Guangxi-Nanning
4915

第15届中国国际食品添加剂和配料展览会暨第21届全国食品添加剂生产应用技术展示会
Food Ingredients China 2011 (FIC 2011)
2011/03/23-25
上海Shanghai
1480

2011年春季全国糖酒会
China National Sugar and Alcoholic Commodities Fair
2011/03/25-28
四川成都Sichuan-Chengdu
6550

2011第二届海南国际葡萄酒博览会
2nd Hainan Wine Expo
2011/03/25-27
海南海口Hainan-Haikou
4990

2011第五届广西国际糖业技术设备展览会
5th Guangxi Intl Sugar Industry Exhibition
2011/03/25-27
广西南宁Guangxi-Nanning
4930

2011广州国际食品展暨广州进口食品展览会
Guangzhou Food Fair
2011/03/29-31
广东广州Guangdong-Guangzhou
4100

中国国际咖啡与茶用品展览会
Coffee & Tea China
2011/03/29-03
上海Shanghai
1620

CINHOE 2011第十届中国（广州）国际营养品/健康食品及有机产品展览会
Guangzhou Nutrition and Organic Food Exhibition
2011/03/29-31
广东广州Guangdong-Guangzhou
4110

2011年中国郑州烘焙展览会
2011 China (Zhengzhou) Baking Exhibition
2011/04/11-15
河南郑州Henan-Zhengzhou
5160

第七届全国（北京）焙烤展览会
China International Trade Fair for Bakery & Confectionery
2011/04/13-15
北京Beijing
320

中国国际葡萄酒及烈酒展览会
China Intl Wine & Spirits Exhibition
2011/04/17-19
北京Beijing
340

中国国际食用油及橄榄油展览会
China Intl Exhibition of Olive Oil & Edible Oi
2011/04/18-20
上海Shanghai
1760

2011北京酒店用品、厨房设备、清洁用品、咖啡展览会（第十四届北京酒店设备用品展览会）
14th Beijing Hospitality Equipment & Supplies Exhibition
2011/04/26-28
北京Beijing
390

第九届中国（漯河）食品博览会
9th China (Luohe) Food Fair
2011/04/08-11
河南漯河Henan-Luohe
5060

2011第十四届中国国际焙烤展览会
14th China Intl Trade Fair For Bakery & Confectionery
2011/05/11-14
上海Shanghai
1920

2011第四届中国武汉茶业博览会暨陆羽国际茶文化节
4th China Wuhan Tea Expo
2011/05/13-16
湖北武汉Hubei-Wuhan
5310

第十二届中国国际食品和饮料展览会
SIAL China 2011
2011/05/18-20
上海Shanghai
1990

2011中国（上海）国际茶业博览会
China Tea Expo, Shanghai
2011/05/20-23
上海Shanghai
2020

2011年中国国际葡萄酒博览会
TopWine China 2011
2011/05/23-26
北京Beijing
530

2011第15届中国烘焙展览会
15th China Bakery Exhibition
2011/05/26-28
广东广州Guangdong-Guangzhou
4225

2011中国国际有机食品博览会
BioFach China 2011
2011/05/26-28
上海Shanghai
2040

第九届中国（厦门）食品交易博览会
9th China (Xiamen) Food Expo
2011/05/27-29
福建厦门Fujian-Xiamen
3520

2011第6届上海酒类商品交易博览会
6th Shanghai Wine Trade Fair 2011
2011/06/01-03
上海Shanghai
2090

2011第五届中国（青岛）国际茶文化博览会暨紫砂艺术展
5th China （Qingdao） Tea Culture Fair
2011/06/03-06
山东青岛Shandong-Qingdao
6260

2011北京国际咖啡博览会
China Intl Coffee Industry Exhibition
2011/06/18-20
北京Beijing
580

亚洲食品配料、亚洲天然食品原料、亚洲健康食品原料展览会
Fi Asia - China 2011
Hi China 2011
Ni China 2011
2011/06/21-23
上海Shanghai
2240

第三届中国国际名酒博览会
3rd China Intl Premier Wine&Spirits Exhibition
2011/06/23-25
四川成都Sichuan-Chengdu
6660

2011中国天津啤酒节
Tianjin Beer Festival
2011/07-
天津Tianjin
3370

第二届海峡两岸烘焙展
2nd Baking and Coffee Exhibition
2011/07/14-17
福建厦门Fujian-Xiamen
3540

第三届中国（沈阳）食品博览会
3rd China (Shenyang) Food Expo
2011/07/21-25
辽宁沈阳Liaoning-Shenyang
5920

第十八届中国豆腐文化节
18th China Tofu Culture Festival
2011/03/01-03
安徽淮南Anhui-Huainan
3410

2011第二届中国上海国际冰淇淋冷冻食品工业展览会
2nd China Shanghai Intl Ice Frozen Food Industry Exhibition
2011/09/15-17
上海Shanghai
2860

2011广州国际食品展暨广州进口食品展览会
Guangzhou Food Fair
2011/09/15-17
广东广州Guangdong-Guangzhou
4540

CINHOE 2011
第十一届中国（广州）国际营养品/健康食品及有机产品展览会
Guangzhou Nutrition and Organic Food Exhibition
2011/09/15-17
广东广州Guangdong-Guangzhou
4570

2011中国糖果文化节暨第七届中国国际甜食及休闲食品展览会
China Confectionery Culture Festival
Sweets & Snacks China
2011/09/22-24
上海Shanghai
2910

2011第7届中国冰淇淋冷冻食品工业展览会
China Ice-Cream & Frozen Foods Exposition
2011/10/12-14
河南郑州Henan-Zhengzhou
5290

中国厦门国际素食养生展览会
Xiamen Vegetarian food and Health Exhibition
2011/10/20-23
福建厦门Fujian-Xiamen
3620

中国厦门国际茶业展览会
Xiamen Tea Expo
2011/10/20-23
福建厦门Fujian-Xiamen
3630

第八届中国国际茶业博览会
CHINA TEA EXPO 2011
2011/10/28-31
北京Beijing
900

第15届国际食品、饮料、酒店设备、餐饮设备、烘焙及服务展览
FHC China 2011
2011/11/16-18
上海 Shanghai
3205

第16届国际食品、饮料、酒店设备、餐饮设备、烘焙及服务展览
FHC China 2012
2011/11/15-17
上海 Shanghai
3300

中国国际有机食品和绿色食品博览会
Organic China Expo Beijing 2011
2011/11/17-19
北京Beijing
970

第十二届中国国际食品加工和包装机械展览会
12th China Intl Food Processing and Packaging Machinery Exhibition
2011/11/30-02
北京Beijing
1030

第二十届中国食品博览会暨交易会
中国国际进出口食品交易会
China Intl Food Fair
2011/12-
湖北武汉Hubei-Wuhan
5370

广东（厚街）茶叶博览会
Guangdong (Houjie) Tea Expo
2011/12/10-13
广东东莞Guangdong-Dongguan
3870

第16届国际食品、饮料、酒店设备、餐饮设备、烘焙及服务展览
FHC China 2012
2012/11/15-17
上海Shanghai
3300

51、实验室设备 Laboratory Equipment

2011第六届中国西部国际科学仪器及实验室装备展览会
6th Western China Intl Exhibition for Scientific Instruments and Laboratory Equipments,IESILE
2011/03/29-31
四川成都Sichuan-Chengdu
6570

第九届中国国际科学仪器及实验室装备展览会
9th China Intl Scientific Instrument and Laboratory Equipment
2011/04/25-27
北京Beijing
380

中国实验室技术及装备交易会
61st China Laboratory Technology and Equipment Exhibition
2011/05/16-18
广东广州Guangdong-Guangzhou
4200

52、石油 石化 燃气 天然气 Petroleusm, Gas, Petrochemical

2011年中国国际燃气、供热技术与设备展览会
gas & heating china 2011
2011/11/15-17
四川 成都 Sichuan-Chengdu
6710

53、水 水处理 Water Treatment

第12届中国（广州）国际给排水、水处理技术设备展览会
2011中国（广州）国际泵、阀门、管道展览会
Water Wasterwater & Water Treatment China 2011
Pump, Vale & Pipe China 2011
2011/03/09-11
广东广州Guangdong-Guangzhou
3980

第11届东北国际给排水、水处理技术设备及泵、阀、管道展览会
12th Northeast Intl Water Disposal Technique & Equipment and Pump & Value and Pipeline Exhibition
2011/03/27-29
辽宁沈阳Liaoning-Shenyang
5740

2011上海建筑给排水处理技术及设备展览会
Shanghai Building Water, Water Treatment Technology and Equipment Expo
2011/06/01-03
上海Shanghai
2100

第13届华南水展
13th Intl Water Treatment & Fluid, Pump, Valve & Pipe Exhibition for South China
2011/06/29-01
广东深圳Guangdong-Shenzhen
4740

中国水博览会暨中国国际膜与水处理技术装备展览会
Water Expo China + Water & Membrane China
2011/10/13-15
北京Beijing
835

54、塑料 橡胶 Plastics & Rubbers

2011第12届深圳国际机械、模具及制品、塑胶工业展览会
China Shenzhen Intl Machinery Manufacturing Industry Exhibition （SIMM2011）
2011/03/28-31
广东深圳Guangdong-Shenzhen
4670

2011第12届中国东北国际塑胶机械及包装展览会
Northeast The 12th Intl Plastics Machinery & Packaging Exhibition China
2011/04/22-25
辽宁沈阳Liaoning-Shenyang
5860

第25届中国国际塑料橡胶工业展览会
25th Intl Exhibition on Plastics and Rubber Industries
2011/05/17-20
广东广州Guangdong-Guangzhou
4210

2011第六届中国临沂塑料机械暨塑料包装展览会
6th China Linyi Plastic Machinery and Plastic Packaging Exhibition
2011/05/17-19
山东临沂Shandong-Linyi
6200

亚太国际塑料橡胶工业展览会
Asian-Pacific Intl Plastic & Rubber Industry Exhibition
2011/09/06-09
上海Shanghai
2740

第十三届东莞国际橡塑胶及包装展
13th China Dongguan Intl Plastics, Packaging & Rubber Exhibition
2011/11/16-19
广东东莞Guangdong-Dongguan
3780

55、陶瓷 玻璃 Ceramic and Glass

第十二届中国国际建筑陶瓷及卫浴科技精品展览会
Ceramics, Tile & Sanitary Ware China 2011
2011/03/29-01
上海Shanghai
1550

第三届上海国际搪瓷工业展览会
Intl Ceramics Industry Forum Held Concurrently
2011/04/07-09
上海Shanghai
1690

2011年中国济南建筑装饰玻璃及艺术玻璃展会
China Jinan Architecture Glass and Art Glass Exhibition
2011/04/15-17
山东济南Shandong-Jinan
6160

2011中国（广州）国际卫浴及建筑陶瓷展
China(Guangzhou) Intl Exhibition for Sanitary Ware and Building Ceramics
2011/07/08-11
广东广州Guangdong-Guangzhou
4390

2011中国（青岛）国际陶瓷卫浴及厨房设备展览会
China (Qingdao) Intl Ceramics Sanitary Ware and Kitchen Facilities Fair
2011/07/21-24
山东青岛Shandong-Qingdao
6340

56、特许经营 连锁加盟 Franchising

2011中国特许展
- 第13届中国特许加盟展览会
China Franchise Expo 2011
2011/05/07-09
北京Beijing
430

2011国际特许加盟（上海）展览会
（2011年中国特许展上海站）
Shanghai Intl Franchiseexpo.com Exhibition
2011/09/17-19
2870

57、体育 休闲 Sports & Leisure

第21届中国国际钓鱼用品贸易展览会
21st Intl Fishing Tackle Trade Exhibition
2011/02/17-19
北京Beijing
40

2011中国（海南）国际海钓装备暨用品展览会
2011 China (Hainan) Sea Fishing Equipment Exhibition
2011/02/25-27
海南海口Hainan-Haikou
4980

中国广州户外及休闲展览会
China Intl Outdoor & Leisure Fair
2011/03/18-21
广东广州Guangdong-Guangzhou
4030

中国国际高尔夫球博览会
China Golf Show
2011/03/18-20
北京Beijing
180

2011(第28届)中国国际体育用品博览会
China Sport Show 2011
2011/05/13-16
四川成都Sichuan-Chengdu
6630

2011年中国郑州渔具用品展览会
2011 China (Zhengzhou) Fishing Equipment Exhibition
2011/05/18-23
河南郑州Henan-Zhengzhou
5190

成都家居、休闲用品及礼品展览会
2011 Chengdu Houseware, Leisure Goods & Gifts Fair
2011/06/17-19
四川成都Sichuan-Chengdu
6650

亚洲国际高尔夫球博览会
China Golf Show, Guangzhou
2011/10/20-22
广东广州Guangdong-Guangzhou
4590

2011中国高尔夫球用品博览会
China Golf Expo
2011/11/09 - 11
广东东莞Guangdong-Dongguan
3760

58、投资、金融、理财、保险 Investment & Finance

中国天津第十八届贸易投资洽谈会
China Tianjin Trade Fair & Investment Talk
2011/06-
天津Tianjin
3360

2011中国创业项目投资博览会
2011 Entrepreneurship and Investment Exhibition
2011/09/08-13
福建厦门Fujian-Xiamen
3570

中国国际投资贸易洽谈会
China Intl Fair for Investment and Trade
2011/09/08-11
福建厦门Fujian-Xiamen
3580

第五届中国中部投资贸易博览会
Expo Central China 2011
2011/09/26-28
北京Beijing
820

北京国际钱币博览会
Beijing Intl Coins Expo
2011/11/04-06
北京Beijing
915

中国对外投资合作洽谈会
2nd China Overseas Investment Fair
2011/11/08-09
北京Beijing
930

上海理财博览会
Money Fair
2011/11/18-20
上海Shanghai
3210

59、图书 Books

海峡两岸图书交易会
Straits Book Fair
厦门 Xiamen
2011/11/03-07
3660

60、玩具 婴幼儿童用品 Toys & Children'sProducts

中国（上海）第16届国际玩具展暨
上海玩具第47届博览会
Toy China 2011 (Spring)
2011/03/06-08
上海Shanghai
1250

第23届广州国际玩具及模型展览会
23rd Guangzhou Intl Toy & Hobby Fair
2011/04/08-10
广东广州Guangdong-Guangzhou
4130

第2届广州国际婴童用品展
2nd Guangzhou Intl Baby Product Fair
2011/04/08-10
广东广州Guangdong-Guangzhou
4120

2011首届中国（郑州）国际孕婴童用品博览会
1st China (Zhengzhou) Expo for Baby, Kids and Mother-to-be Products
2011/04/24-28
河南郑州Henan-Zhengzhou
5180

第13届北京国际玩具及幼教用品展览会
暨北京国际婴幼童用品展览会
Beijing Intl Toys & Preschool Tools Exhibition
China Intl Pregnancy and Baby Show
2011/05/13-15
北京Beijing
480

第六届上海国际幼儿教育展
6th education expo 2011 shanghai
2011/05/20-22
上海Shanghai
2000

时尚育儿广州嘉年华
Fashionbaby Guangzhou Carnival
2011/05/28-29
广东广州Guangdong-Guangzhou
4230

上海国际儿童、婴儿、孕妇产品博览会
Children Baby Maternity Expo
2011/07/20-22
上海Shanghai
2530

时尚育儿北京嘉年华
Fashionbaby Beijing Carnival
2011/09/10-11
北京Beijing
770

华南国际孕婴童用品展览会
Southern China Intl Maternity, Baby & Children Products Exhibition
2011/09/23-25
广东深圳Guangdong-Shenzhen
4850

第十届中国国际玩具及模型展览会
10th Intl Trade Fair for Toys and Hobby
2011/10/12-14
上海Shanghai
2980

第十九届中国（深圳）国际玩具及礼品展览会
Gifts & Home China
2011/10/20-23
广东深圳Guangdong-Shenzhen
4860

上海国际少年儿童服装及用品博览会
Kids Fashion Shanghai
2011/11/11-13
上海Shanghai
3160

61、文化产业 Culture Industry

中国义乌文化产品交易博览会
China Yiwu Cultural Products Trade Fair
2011/04/20-23
浙江义乌Zhejiang-Yiwu
6990

第七届中国（深圳）国际文化产业博览交易会 暨第二届中国国际新媒体影视动漫节
China (Shenzhen) Intl Cultural Industries Fair
2011/05/13-16
广东深圳Guangdong-Shenzhen
4715

第四届海峡两岸文博会
4th Straits Culture Expo
2011/09/21-25
福建厦门Fujian-Xiamen
3600

中国厦门国际佛事用品展览会
The 5th China Xiamen International Buddhist Items & Crafts Fair
2011/10/20-23
福建厦门Fujian-Xiamen
3640

第6届中国北京国际文化创意产业博览会
6th China Beijing Intl Culture & Creative Industy Expo
2011/11/10-13
北京Beijing
960

62、文具 办公用品 Stationery & Office Supplies

第8届中国国际文具礼品博览会（CNISE 2011）
8th China Intl Stationery & Gifts Exposition
2011/03/17-19
浙江宁波Zhejiang-Ningbo
6860

中国广州国际家具博览会（办公环境展）
China Intl Furniture Fair (Guangzhou) – Office Show
2011/03/27-30
广东广州Guangdong-Guangzhou
4080

2011中国（济南）国际打印耗材及办公设备展览会
China (Jinan) Printer Accessories and Office Equipment Exhibition
2011/03/28-30
山东济南Shandong-Jinan
6150

Office World办公设备展览会
Office World Expo
2011/04/20-22
上海Shanghai
1780

第105届中国文化用品商品交易会
105th China Stationery Fair
2011/06/28-30
上海Shanghai
2310

中国国际办公家具展览会
Office Furniture China
2011/09/14-17
上海Shanghai
2800

中国国际文具及办公用品展览会
China Intl Stationery & Office Supplies Exhibition
2011/09/21-23
上海Shanghai
2895

第九届ReChina亚洲打印耗材展览会(秋季)
ReChina Asia Expo 2011(Autumn Session)
2011/11/15-17
上海Shanghai
3200

63、五金 工具 Hardware and Tools

第19届中国国际五金博览会
19th China Intl Hardware Fair
2011/03/09-11
上海Shanghai
1290

2011第4届中国（永康）五金装备、机床及工模具展览会
4th China (Yongkang) Hardware Equipment & Machine Toolds Exhibition
2011/03/31-02
浙江永康Zhejiang-Yongknag
7090

第14届中国东北国际五金工具展览会
14th China (Northeast) Intl Hardware and Tool Exhibition
2011/04/08-10
辽宁沈阳Liaoning-Shenyang
5780

第8届中国国际五金电器博览会
8th China Intl Hardware & Electrical Appliances Trade Fair
2011/04/28-30
浙江义乌Zhejiang-Yiwu
7000

第12届广州国际紧固件、弹簧及设备展
12th China (Guangzhou) Intl Fasterners, Spring & Equipment Exhibition
2011/06/23-25
广东广州Guangdong-Guangzhou
4310

第十六届中国五金博览会
China Hardware Fair
2011/09-
浙江永康Zhejiang-Yongkang
7105

2011 中国国际五金展
－科隆国际五金展-强力推动
China Intl Hardware Show
—Powered by PRACTICAL WORLD
2011/09/21-23
上海Shanghai
2900

64、物流 运输 仓储 Logistics

2011中国（重庆）国际物联网技术与应用展览会
China (Chongqing) Exhibition on Internet of Things
2011/04/14-16
重庆Chongqing
1130

第12届中国东北国际物流技术及运输系统展览会
12th Northeast Intl Physical Distribution & Transport System Exhibition
2011/04/22-25
辽宁沈阳Liaoning-Shenyang
5820

2011年烟台国际物流及仓储设备展览会
Yantai Logistics and Storage Equipment Exhibition
2011/05/19-21
山东烟台Shandong-Yantai
6460

第三届中国(太原)国际卡车暨物流展览会
3rd China (Taiyuan) Truck and Logistics Exhibition
2011/06/03-05
山西太原Shanxi-Taiyuan
6510

2011第十一届中国（广州）国际自动识别与物联网应用展览会
China (Guangzhou) Automatic Identification and IOT Exhibition
2011/06/09-11
广东广州Guangdong-Guangzhou
4250

2011中国国际物联网大会暨展览会
IOT China Conference & Exhibition 2011
2011/06/16-17
上海Shanghai
2220

第2届广州国际物流装备与技术展览会
2nd Guangzhou Intl Logistics Equipment & Technology Exhibition
2011/06/22-24
广东广州Guangdong-Guangzhou
4270

第3届上海国际冷冻保鲜及冷链物流技术设备展览会
3th Shanghai Intl Exhibition of Food Frozen & Fresh and Cold Chain Logistics Technology Equipment
2011/09/15-17
上海Shanghai
2830

2011亚洲国际物流技术与运输系统展览会
CeMAT ASIA 2011
2011/10/25-28
上海Shanghai
3010

65、线、缆 Cable & Wire

2011广州国际电线电缆专用设备及原辅材料采购展览会
GZ Intl Wire & Cable Equipment and Raw & Auxiliary Material Purchase Fair
2011/07/20-22
广东广州 Guangdong-Guangzhou
4430

中国（深圳）国际绕线设备展览会
CWIEME SHENZHEN
2012/03/28-30
深圳 Shenzhen
4880

66、消费电子 家用电器 Consumer Electronics & Appliances

2011年中国家电博览会(上海)
China Appliance World Expo-Shanghai
2011/03/15-18
上海Shanghai
1410

2011年新疆－中亚家用电器、厨卫及消费电子展
Xinjiang Central Asia Home Appliances and Consumer Electronic
2011/05/14-16
新疆乌鲁木齐Xinjiang-Urumuqi
6720

2011中国国际消费电子博览会
China Intl Consumer Electronics Show (SINOCES)
2011/07/07-10
山东青岛Shandong-Qingdao
6270

2011中国（广州）国际厨房设备及配件展
China (Guangzhou) Intl Kitchen Fair 2011
2011/07/08-11
广东广州Guangdong-Guangzhou
4370

广东国际家电配件采购展览会
Guandong Intl appliance parts procurement fair
2011/07/15-17
广东广州Guangdong-Guangzhou
4420

2011中国顺德国际家用电器博览会
China Shunde Intl Exposition for Household Electrical Appliances
2011/10/17-20
广东顺德Guangdong-Shunde
4900

67、消费品 家居用品 Consumer Goods

第24届北京国际礼品、赠品及家庭用品展览会
China Beijing Intl Gifts, Premium & Houseware Exhibition
2011/03/16-19
北京Beijing
170

中国广州国际家居饰品/用品展览会
Homedecor & Housewares China 2011
2011/03/18-21
广东广州Guangdong-Guangzhou
4010

2011北京旅居人士服务展览会
Expat Show
2011/03/25-27
北京Beijing
210

义乌消费品交易会
Yiwu Sourcing Fair: Consumer Goods
2011/04/28-30
浙江义乌Zhejiang-Yiwu
7010

第十届中国国际古典家具展览会 & 2011上海国际古董及艺术品展览会 （春季展）
Antique Furniture China 2011, Antiques & Arts Shanghai 2011
2011/05/20-23
上海Shanghai
2010

中国国际日用消费品博览会
China Intl Consumer Goods Fair
2011/06/08-11
浙江宁波Zhejiang-Ningbo
6880

广东外商投资企业产品（内销）博览会
Guangdong Foreign-invested Enterprises Commodities Fair
2011/06/15-18
广东东莞Guangdong-Dongguan
3747

成都家居、休闲用品及礼品展览会
2011 Chengdu Houseware, Leisure Goods & Gifts Fair
2011/06/17-19
四川成都Sichuan-Chengdu
6650

2011中国（广州）国际厨房设备及配件展
China (Guangzhou) Intl Kitchen Fair 2011
2011/07/08-11
广东广州Guangdong-Guangzhou
4370

2011第105届中国日用百货商品交易会、中国现代家庭用品博览会
The 105 China Daily-use Articles Trade Fair & China Modern Home Expo
2011/07/14-16
上海Shanghai
2500

第24届中国北京国际礼品、赠品及 家庭用品展览会
24th China Beijing Intl Gifts, Premium & Houseware Exhibition
2011/08/17-20
北京Beijing
700

第二届北京王府井国际品牌节
2nd Beijing Wangfujing Brand Festival
2011/09/08-10
北京Beijing
750

中国上海礼品、赠品及家居用品展览会
China Shanghai International Gifts, Premium and Houseware Exhibition
2011/09/01-04
上海Shanghai
2680

中国国际老龄产业博览会
China Intl Industry Expo Ageing
2011/10/12-14
广东东莞Guangdong-Dongguan
3756

中国（上海）国际时尚家居用品展览会
Interior Lifestyle China
2011/10/12-15
上海Shanghai
2980

国际家居装饰艺术展
-相约奢华-生活-艺术
Intl Home Decor & Design
2011/11/03-05
上海Shanghai
3130

2011日本消费品展
japan-made Fair
2011/11/10-13
上海Shanghai
3150

北京国际礼品、赠品及家用精品（年底） 采购订货会
The 22nd China International Gifts, Premium & Houseware Exhibition
2011/11/25-27
北京Beijing
1020

“缤纷冬”日厦门购物节
Xiamen Shopping Festival
2011/12/03-16
福建厦门Fujian-Xiamen
3700

2011第11届东莞嘉年华时尚生活用品购物节
11th Dongguan Shopping Festival
2011/12/24-08
广东东莞Guangdong-Dongguan
3890

68、鞋 皮革 及相关机械 Shoes & Leather

第十届中国广州鞋业展览会
10th Guangzhou Shoes Exhibition
2011/03/01- 04
广东广州Guangdong-Guangzhou
3930

第十三届中国（晋江）国际鞋业博览会
The 13th China (Jinjiang) Intl Footwear Exhibition
2011/04/18-21
福建晋江Fujian-Jinjiang
3440

第十三届中国东莞国际鞋展-鞋机展-鞋材展（春季）
The 13th Dongguan China Shoes
China Shoetec
2011/04/28-30
广东东莞Guangdong-Dongguan
3745

中国东莞国际鞋展 - 鞋机展 - 手袋展
Dongguan Shoes-China Shoetes- China Bags
2011/05/04-06
广东东莞Guangdong-Dongguan
3745-1

广州国际鞋类、皮革及工业设备展览会
The Intl Shoes & Leather Exhibition (Machinery & Raw Material)
2011/06/01-03
广东广州Guangdong-Guangzhou
4240

2011年第99届中国鞋业皮具商品博览会 暨“名品名店”对接展会
The 99th China Shoes & Leather Commodity Expo And “WELL-KNOWN BRANDS & FAMOUS SHOPS” Exposition
2011/06/01-03
上海Shanghai
2060

第16届中国（温州）国际皮革、鞋材、鞋机展览会
The 16th China (Wenzhou) Intl Leather, Shoe Material & Shoe Machinery Fair
2011/08/26-28
浙江温州Zhejiang-Wenzhou
6980

2011中国国际合成革展览会 （CSLF2011）
2011 China Intl Synthetic Leather Fair
2011/08/26-28
浙江温州Zhejiang-Wenzhou
6970

中国国际箱包、裘革服装及服饰展
Moda Shanghai
2011/09/06-08
上海Shanghai
2700

中国国际皮革展
All China Leather Exhibition
2011/09/06-08
上海Shanghai
2730

中国国际鞋类展
China Intl Footwear Fair
2011/09/06-08
上海Shanghai
2720

2011中国东莞国际鞋展
Dongguan Shoes-China Shoetes
2011/10/28-30
广东东莞Guangdong-Dongguan
3758

广州国际鞋类、皮革制成品展览会
Intl Footwear & Leather Products Exhibition – Guangzhou
2011/11/01-03
广东广州Guangdong-Guangzhou
4600

69、信息技术 通信技术 Information Technology & Communication Technology

2011中国（重庆）国际物联网技术与应用展览会
China (Chongqing) Exhibition on Internet of Things
2011/04/14-16
重庆Chongqing
1130

2011第二届中国（重庆）国际电子信息产业展览会
2nd China (Chongqing) Electronic Information Industry Exhibition
2011/04/14-16
重庆Chongqing
1120

2011第十五届中国国际软件博览会
INTL SOFT CHINA 2011
2011/05/12-14
北京Beijing
460

第十四届中国北京国际科技产业博览会
THE 14th CHINA BEIJING Intl HIGH-TECH EXPO
2011/05/18-21
北京Beijing
510

2011第十一届中国（广州）国际自动识别与物联网应用展览会
China (Guangzhou) Automatic Identification and IOT Exhibition
2011/06/09-11
广东广州Guangdong-Guangzhou
4250

第九届中国国际软件和信息服务交易会
China Intl Software & Information Service Fair 2011
2011/06/16-19
辽宁大连Liaoning-Dalian
5630

2011上海国际智能交通与车联网科技发展论坛暨展览会
ITS Shanghai 2011
2011/06/16-17
上海Shanghai
2210

2011中国国际物联网大会暨展览会
IOT China Conference & Exhibition 2011
2011/06/16-17
上海Shanghai
2220

2011年中国国际信息通信展览会
PT / EXPO COMM CHINA 2011
2011/09/26-30
北京Beijing
830

2011上海防伪技术暨证卡票券、RFID、商标标签、包装、可变条码印刷设备展览会
Shanghai RFID, Barcode and Packaging Exhibition
2011/10/12-14
上海Shanghai
2960

国际自动识别技术展览会
Intl Exhibition of Automatic Identification Technology
2011/10/12-14
湖北武汉Hubei-Wuhan
5360

中国呼叫中心技术设备及解决方案博览会
Call Center Expo China
2011/10/26-27
上海Shanghai
3030

第八届中国国际机器视觉展览会暨机器视觉技术及工业应用研讨会
The 8th China Intl Machine Vision Exhibition and Machine Vision Technology & Application Conference
2011/10/26-28
北京Beijing
880

第六届微波及天线技术展览会
6th Microwave and antenna technology Exhibition
2011/11/02-04
上海Shanghai
3100

70、印刷 Printing

2011东莞数字喷印及广告技术展览会
China Sign Expo Dongguan 2011
2011/02/28-04
广东东莞Guangdong-Dongguan
3725

第十八届华南国际印刷工业展览会
2011中国国际标签印刷技术展览会
18th South China Intl Exhibition on Printing Industry
China Intl Exhibition on Label Printing Technology
2011/03/09-11
广东广州Guangdong-Guangzhou
3990

2011中国国际瓦楞展
SinoCorrugated 2011
2011/04/06-09
上海Shanghai
1660

第二届中国(广东)国际印刷技术展览会
The second Intl Printing Technology Exhibition of China(Guangdong)
2011/04/09-13
广东东莞Guangdong-Dongguan
3740

2011第九届大连国际印刷及包装工业展览会
9th Dalian Intl Printing and Packaging Exhibition
2011/05/19-21
辽宁大连Liaoning-Dalian
5600

2011上海国际印刷包装纸业展览会
Shanghai Intl Print Pack & Paper Exhibition 2011
2011/07/06-09
上海Shanghai
2380

第十七届中国国际加工、包装及印刷科技展览
ProPak China 2011
2011/07/13-15
上海Shanghai
2470

2011上海防伪技术暨证卡票券、RFID、商标标签、包装、可变条码印刷设备展览会
Shanghai RFID, Barcode and Packaging Exhibition
2011/10/12-14
上海Shanghai
2960

中国国际全印展
All in Print
2011/11/14-17
上海Shanghai
3190

第十八届中国国际加工、包装及印刷科技展览
ProPak China 2012
2012/07/17-19
上海Shanghai
3280

71、仪器仪表 Instrument

中国广州国际工业自动化技术及装备展览会
SPS - Industrial Automation Fair Guangzhou
2011/03/09-11
广东广州Guangdong-Guangzhou
3950

2011中国重庆第十六届仪器仪表工业控制自动化国际展览会
International Automation& Instrument Exhibition Central & Western China
2011/03/10-12
重庆Chongqing
1110

2011中国国际机器视觉展览会
China Intl Machine Vision Exhibition 2011
2011/03/20-22
上海Shanghai
1430

2011第十四届中国东北国际仪器仪表及工业自动化展览会
Northeast The 14th Intl Instrument & Automation Exhibition China
2011/03/22-24
辽宁沈阳Liaoning-Shenyang
5710

第23届国际医疗仪器设备展览会
The 23rd Intl Medical Instruments and Equipment Exhibition
2011/03/25-27
北京Beijing
200

2011第四届成都国际教育技术装备及高教仪器展览会
2011 4th Chengdu Intl Education and Higher Education Exhibition on Technology and Equipment
2011/03/29-31
四川成都Sichuan-Chengdu
6560

2011第六届中国西部国际科学仪器及实验室装备展览会
6th Western China Intl Exhibition for Scientific Instruments and Laboratory Equipments, IESILE
2011/03/29-31
四川成都Sichuan-Chengdu
6570

2011中国国际衡器展览会
InterWeighing2011
2011/04/22-24
上海Shanghai
1800

第九届中国国际科学仪器及实验室装备展览会
The 9th China Intl Scientific Instrument and Laboratory Equipment
2011/04/25-27
北京Beijing
380

2011国际现代工厂/过程自动化技术与装备展览会
FA/PA 2011
2011/05/18-20
北京Beijing
500

2011（第十三届）大连国际自动化、仪表展览会
2011（13th）Dalian Intl Automation&Instrumentation Exhibition
2011/05/19-21
辽宁大连Liaoning-Dalian
5610

2011第九届烟台国际工业自动化及仪器仪表展览会
2011 The 9th Yantai Intl Industrial Automation & Instrument Exhibition
2011/05/19-21
山东烟台Shandong-Yantai
6470

2011第12届湖南工控自动化及仪器仪表展览会
12th Industrial Control, Automation, Instrument Exhibition
2011/05/25-27
湖南长沙Hunan-Changsha
5410

2011国际质量检测分析技术及测量测试仪器仪表展览会
The Intl Trade Fair for Quality Assurance 2011
2011/08/23-25
上海Shanghai
2610

第二十二届多国仪器仪表学术会议暨展览会
The 22nd Intl Conference and Fair for Measurement Instrumentation and Automation
2011/08/30-02
北京Beijing
740

72、艺术 Arts

2011中艺博国际画廊博览会
China Intl Gallery Exposition 2011
2011/04/20-24
北京Beijing
360

艺术北京-当代艺术博览会
Art Beijing Contemporary Art Fair
2011/04/29-02
北京Beijing
410

第十届中国国际古典家具展览会 & 2011上海国际古董及艺术品展览会（春季展）
Antique Furniture China 2011, Antiques & Arts Shanghai 2011
2011/05/20-23
上海Shanghai
2010

2011北京国际艺术博览会
2011 Beijing Intl Art Exposition
2011/08/18-22
北京Beijing
720

国际家居装饰艺术展
-相约奢华-生活-艺术
Intl Home Decor & Design
2011/11/03-05
上海Shanghai
3130

73、医药 医疗设备 生物 保健 Medical Equipment, Pharmaceuticals & Health Care

第65届全国药品交易会
65th PharmChina
2011/02/20-22
四川成都Sichuan-Chengdu
6530

2011中国中西部（重庆）医疗器械展览会第19届中国重庆国际医疗器械展览会
China (Chongqing) Medical Equipment Exhibition
2011/02/23-25
重庆Chongqing
1100

2011福建（第二十二届）国际医疗仪器与设备展览会
Fujian Intl Medical Instruments and Equipment Exhibition
2011/03/01-03
福建福州Fujian-Fuzhou
3420

2011第八届中国国际成人保健及生殖健康展览会
China Adult-Care Expo
2011/03/11-13
上海Shanghai
1380

第二十届中原国际医疗器械展览会
20th Central China Medical Equipment Exhibition
2011/03/14-18
河南郑州Henan-Zhengzhou
5110

2011广州国际个人医疗保健器械及用品展览会
2011 Guangzhou Personal healthcare Exhibition
2011/03/24-26
广东广州Guangdong-Guangzhou
4050

第23届国际医疗仪器设备展览会
The 23rd Intl Medical Instruments and Equipment Exhibition
2011/03/25-27
北京Beijing
200

2011广州药交会第十八届全国药品保健品（广州）交易会
The 18 China Medicine and Healthcare Products (Guangzhou) Exhibition 2011
2011/03/29-31
广东广州Guangdong-Guangzhou
4090

2011年中国东北第十三届国际口腔器材展览会暨学术交流会 第三届口腔保健护理用品展览会第一届义齿加工产品展览会
2011the 13 China Northeast Intl Dental Equipment&Affiliated Facilities Exhibition
2011/04/01-04
辽宁沈阳Liaoning-Shenyang
5760

第十一届中国国际眼科和视光技术及设备展览会
The 11th Intl Congress of Ophthalmology and Optometry China
2011/04/08-10
上海Shanghai
1710

第65届中国国际医疗器械博览会 第12届中国国际医疗器械设计与制造技术展览会
China Intl Medical Equipment Fair
2011/04/16-19
广东深圳Guangdong-Shenzhen
4700

世界制药工业展中国展区（原包装材料、制药设备区）
INTERPHEX CHINA Conference & Exhibition
2011/04/21-23
四川成都Sichuan-Chengdu
6600

第66届中国国际医药原料药、中间体、包装、设备交易会
The 66th API China & INTERPHEX China
2011/04/21-23
四川成都Sichuan-Chengdu
6620

2011第13届山东口腔器械与齿科材料（青岛）展览会
13th Shandong Exhibition on Dental & Denture Equipment and Materials
2011/04/27-29
山东青岛Shandong-Qingdao
6250

2011中国中西部（太原）医疗器械展览会
Taiyuan Medical Equipment Exhibition
2011/05/12-14
山西太原Shanxi-Taiyuan
6500

2011中国国际康复护理展览会 第六届中国国际老年人和残疾人康复护理技术及辅助器具展览会
China Aid 2011 The 6th China Intl Exhibition of Rehabilitation, Nursing & Health care
2011/05/16-18
上海Shanghai
1940

中国实验室技术及装备交易会
The 61th China Laboratory Technology and Equipment Exhibition
2011/05/16-18
广东广州Guangdong-Guangzhou
4200

2011中国（天津）国际医疗仪器与设备展览会
China (Tianjin) Intl Medical Instruments and Equipment Exhibition
2011/05/18-20
天津Tianjin
3350

第41届全国制药机械博览会
41st National Pharmaceutical Machinery Expo
2011/05/29-01
待定undetermined
5865

中国药店展览会
China Drug Store Show
2011/06-
待定undetermined
7140

2011中国国际生物技术和仪器设备博览会
BIOTECH CHINA 2011
2011/06/01-03
上海Shanghai
2070

第15届中国国际口腔设备材料展览会暨技术交流会
SINO-DENTAL 2011
2011/06/09-12
北京Beijing
560

世界合同定制服务中国展
ICSE China
2011/06/21-23
上海Shanghai
2260

世界制药机械、包装设备与材料中国展
P-MEC China
2011/06/21-23
上海Shanghai
2270

世界制药原料中国展
CPhI China
2011/06/21-23
上海Shanghai
2250

第20届中国国际医用仪器设备展览会暨技术交流会
CHINA-HOSPEQ 2011
2011/08/18-20
北京Beijing
710

2011大连国际医疗器械展览会
2010 Dalian Intl Exhibition for Medical Instrument
2011/09/01-03
辽宁大连Liaoning-Dalian
5650

第21届中原国际医疗器械(秋季)展览会
中国中部郑州（秋季）国际装备制造业博览会
21st Central China Autumn Medical Equipment Exhibition
2011/09/05-09
河南郑州Henan-Zhengzhou
5250

2011上海国际医疗设备设计和技术展览会暨研讨会
MEDTEC China 2011
2011/09/07-08
上海Shanghai
2760

2011第2届华南医疗器械（广州）展览会
South China Medical Equipment Exhibition
2011/09/08-10
广东广州Guangdong-Guangzhou
4530

2011广州药交会第19届全国药品保健品（广州）交易会
18th China Medicine and Healthcare Products (Guangzhou) Exhibition 2011
2011/09/15-17
广东广州Guangdong-Guangzhou
4560

第11 届中国国际保健博览会
2011中国（深圳）保健节
11th China Intl Healthcare Expo
China (Shenzhen) Healthcare Festival
2011/09/16-18
广东深圳Guangdong-Shenzhen
4840

全球华人口腔医学大会暨
中国国际口 腔医学大会
4th CSA General Assembly & Annual Meeting
China Dental Show
2011/09/23-26
江苏南京Jiangsu-Nanjing
5530

第16届中国国际医药（工业）展览会暨技术交流会
16th China Intl Pharmaceutical Industry Exhibition
2011/10/25-28
上海Shanghai
3015

第15届中国国际口腔器材展览会
DenTech China 2011
2011/10/26-29
上海Shanghai
3040

第66届全国药品交易会
66th PHARMCHINA
2011/11-
待定undetermined
7170

世界制药工业展中国展区
INTERPHEX China
2011/11-
待定undetermined
7190

中医药国际科技博览会
Traditional Chinese Medicine Exposition
2011/11/15 – 17
四川成都Sichuan-Chengdu
6700

第67届中国国际医药原料药、中间体、包装、设备交易会
Traditional Chinese Medicine Exposition
2011/11/15-17
成都 Chengdu
7180

2011上海国际耳鼻咽喉头颈外科论坛
上海国际耳鼻咽喉头颈外科医疗设备及药品展览会
Shanghai Intl Conference of Otorhinolaryngology and Head & Neck Surgery
2011/11/12-13
上海Shanghai
3170

74、乐器 Musical Instrument

第二十届中国国际专业音响·灯光·乐器及技术展览会
20th China Intl Exhibition on Pro Audio, Light, Music & Technology
2011/05/26-29
北京Beijing
540

2011中国湖北国际专业灯光、音响、视听集成技术、乐器及设备博览会
China Hubei PLAV (Lighting, Audio, Video, Musical Instrument) Expo
2011/06/10-12
湖北 武汉 Hubei-Wuhan
5325

中国（上海）国际乐器展览会
China Intl Exhibition for Musical Instruments and Services
2011/10/11 - 14
上海Shanghai
2970

75、纸业 Paper

2011中国国际瓦楞展
SinoCorrugated 2011
2011/04/06-09
上海Shanghai
1660

2011上海国际印刷包装纸业展览会
Shanghai Intl Print Pack & Paper Exhibition
2011/07/06-09
上海Shanghai
2380

第19届中国国际纸浆造纸、林业展览会及会议
China Paper / China Forest 2011
2011/09/19-21
北京Beijing
800

第11届东莞国际印刷造纸胶粘带及广告展览会
11th Dongguan Intl Printing and Packaging and Paper Advertising, Adhesive Tape, Protective Film Exhibition
2011/10/20-22
广东东莞Guangdong-Dongguan
3757

76、钟表 眼镜 Watches, Clocks, Optics

第十九届中国（深圳）国际礼品、工艺 品、钟表及家庭用品展览会
Gifts and Home China
2011/04/24-27
广东深圳Guangdong-Shenzhen
4710

第22届中国（深圳）国际钟表展览会
22nd CHINA WATCH & CLOCK FAIR
2011/06/30-03
广东深圳Guangdong-Shenzhen
4760

2011第9届中国（温州）国际眼镜业展览会暨首届中国眼镜品牌连锁加盟会
9th Wenzhou Intl Optics Fair China
incorporating The 1st franchisee meeting for China Optical Brands
2011/07/06-08
浙江温州Zhejiang-Wenzhou
6960

首届中国国际名表展
2011 China Intl Watch Exhibition
2011/09/21-25
北京Beijing
810

77、珠宝 Jewelry

2011上海国际珠宝首饰展览会
Jewelry Shanghai 2011
2011/06/16-19
上海Shanghai
2230

中国(广州)国际黄金珠宝玉石展览会
China Intl Gold, Jewellery & Gem Fair - Guangzhou
2011/06/17-20
广东广州Guangdong-Guangzhou
4260

2011北京国际珠宝展览会
11th Beijing Intl Jewellery Fair
2011/07/15-18
北京Beijing
630

2011中国国际珠宝展
China Intl Jewellery Fair
2011/11/23-27
北京Beijing
1000

78、自行车 电动车 Bikes

2011第五届山东国际自行车电动车及零部件展览会
5th Shandong Bike, Electric-Bike and Parts Exhibition
2011/02/26-28
山东济南Shandong-Jinan
6120

中国北方国际自行车电动车展览会
China North Intl Bicycle & E-bike Exhibition
2011/03/31-02
天津Tianjin
3340

第21届中国国际自行车展览会
CHINA CYCLE 2011
2011/05/04-07
上海Shanghai
1860

79、其他 Others

中国厦门国际佛事用品展览会
The 5th China Xiamen International Buddhist Items & Crafts Fair
2011/10/20-24
福建厦门Fujian-Xiamen
3640

ICSC RECON ASIA 2011
2011/11/02-04
上海Shanghai
3110

中国香港展览会议

Exhibitions and Conferences in Hong Kong, China

日期 Date	展览会议 Event	地点 Venue	主办 Organizer
2011.1.8-9	2nd Asia Pacific Congenital & Structural Heart Intervention Symposium 2011 (APCASH 2011)	香港喜来登酒店 Sheraton Hong Kong Hotel & Towers	
2011.1.8-9	春季宠物展 Hong Kong Intl Pet Accessory Expo	香港国际展贸中心 Hong Kong Intl Trade & Exhibition Center	讯通展览公司 Paper Communication Exhibition Services ☎ 852-2763 9011 🖷 852-2341 0379 ✉ petexpo@paper-com.com.hk www.petexpo.hk
2011.1.8-9	亦轩高级耳机大会2010-2011 Mingo-headphone Festival 2011~2011	香港国际展贸中心 Hong Kong Intl Trade & Exhibition Center	www.mingo-headphone-festival.com
2011.1.10-12	香港贸发局香港国际授权展 HKTDC Hong Kong International Licensing Show	香港会议展览中心 Hong Kong Convention and Exhibition Centre	香港贸易发展局 Hong Kong Trade Development Council ☎ 852-1830 668 🖷 852-2824 0249 ✉ hktdc@hktdc.org www.hktdc.com/hklicensingshow 详细介绍见☆1 Detail See ☆1
2011.1.10-13	香港贸发局香港玩具展 HKTDC Hong Kong Toys & Games Fair	香港会议展览中心 Hong Kong Convention and Exhibition Centre	香港贸易发展局 Hong Kong Trade Development Council ☎ 852-1830 668 🖷 852-2824 0249 ✉ hktdc@hktdc.org www.hktdc.com/hktoyfair 详细介绍见☆2 Detail See ☆2
2011.1.10-13	香港贸发局香港婴儿用品展 HKTDC Hong Kong Baby Products Fair	香港会议展览中心 Hong Kong Convention and Exhibition Centre	香港贸易发展局 Hong Kong Trade Development Council ☎ 852-1830 668 🖷 852-2824 0249 ✉ hktdc@hktdc.org www.hktdc.com/hkbabyfair 详细介绍见☆3 Detail See ☆3
2011.1.10-13	香港国际文具展 Hong Kong International Stationery Fair	香港会议展览中心 Hong Kong Convention and Exhibition Centre	香港贸易发展局 Hong Kong Trade Development Council ☎ 852-1830 668 🖷 852-2824 0249 ✉ exhibitions@hktdc.org www.hkstationeryfair.com 详细介绍见☆4 Detail See ☆4

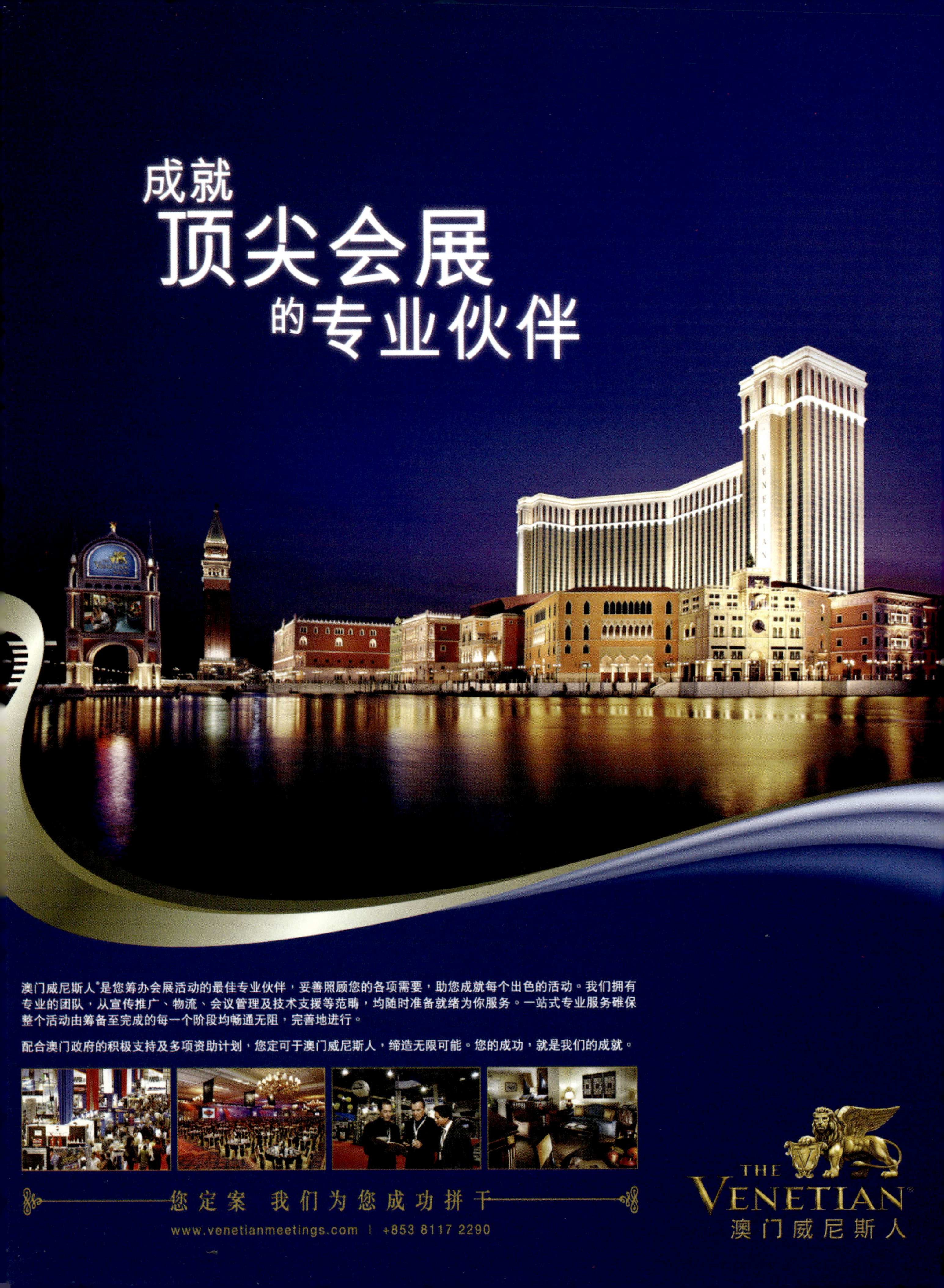
成就
顶尖会展
的专业伙伴
澳门威尼斯人®是您筹办会展活动的最佳专业伙伴，妥善照顾您的各项需要，助您成就每个出色的活动。我们拥有专业的团队，从宣传推广、物流、会议管理及技术支援等范畴，均随时准备就绪为你服务。一站式专业服务确保整个活动由筹备至完成的每一个阶段均畅通无阻，完善地进行。
配合澳门政府的积极支持及多项资助计划，您定可于澳门威尼斯人，缔造无限可能。您的成功，就是我们的成就。
您定案 我们为您成功拼干
www.venetianmeetings.com | +853 8117 2290
THE VENETIAN®
澳门威尼斯人

日期 Date	展览会议 Event	地点 Venue	主办 Organizer
2011.1.17-19	LINC Asia-Pacific 2011	亚洲博览馆 AsiaWorld-Expo	CongO Congress Organisation and more GmbH ☎ 011-498 912 954 40 ✉ toniejaeger@aol.com www.lincasiapacific.com
2011.1.17-20	香港贸发局香港时装节秋冬系列 HKTDC Hong Kong Fashion Week for Fall/Winter	香港会议展览中心 Hong Kong Convention and Exhibition Centre	香港贸易发展局 Hong Kong Trade Development Council ☎ 852-1830 668 🖷 852-2824 0249 ✉ exhibitions@hktdc.org www.hktdc.com/hkfashionweekfw 详细介绍见☆5 Detail See ☆5
2011.1.17-20	香港贸发局香港国际时尚荟萃 HKTDC World Boutique, Hong Kong	香港会议展览中心 Hong Kong Convention and Exhibition Centre	香港贸易发展局 Hong Kong Trade Development Council ☎ 852-1830 668 🖷 852-2824 0249 ✉ exhibitions@hktdc.org www.hktdc.com/worldboutiquehk 详细介绍见☆6 Detail See ☆6
2011.1.18-19	Asian Business Aviation Conference & Exhibition (ABACE 2011)	香港商用航空中心有限公司 Hong Kong Business Aviation Centre Ltd	National Business Aviation Association ☎ +1 (202) 478 7760 🖷 +1 (202) 862 5552 ✉ draphael@nabb.org www.abace.aero/2011/
2011.1.26-28	The Twelfth East Asia-Pacific Conference on Structural Engineering and Construction (EASEC-12)	香港会议展览中心 Hong Kong Convention and Exhibition Centre	Department of Building and Construction, City University of Hong Kong ☎ 852-2788 7303 🖷 852-27887612 ✉ paullam@cityu.edu.hk
2011.1.29-30	英国教育展 Education UK Exhibition 2011	香港会议展览中心 Hong Kong Convention and Exhibition Centre	英国文化协会 The British Council ☎ 852-2913 5100 🖷 852-2913 5102 ✉ enquiries@britishcouncil.org.hk www.britishcouncil.org.hk
2011.1.31-2.2	Overseas CBMC Korea Convention 2011	香港会议展览中心 Hong Kong Convention and Exhibition Centre	CBMC Korea (China) ☎ 852 6384 5555 🖷 852 2886 5002 ✉ cmre001@gmail.com cbmc.or.kr/main/main.php
2011.2.11-13	第62届情人节婚纱、婚宴及结婚服务博览 62nd Valentine's Wedding Service & Banquet Expo	香港会议展览中心 Hong Kong Convention and Exhibition Centre	香港亚洲展览(集团)有限公司 Hongkong-Asia Exhibition (Holdings) Ltd ☎ 852-2591 9823 🖷 852-2573 3311 ✉ hkexhi@hka.com.hk www.iweddingclub.com

日期 Date	展览会议 Event	地点 Venue	主办 Organizer
2011.2.13	Comic World 香港 31	香港国际展贸中心 Hong Kong Intl Trade & Exhibition Center	Comic World Hong Kong Ltd www.cwhk.org
2011.2.17-20	香港贸发局教育及职业博览 HKTDC Education & Careers Expo	香港会议展览中心 Hong Kong Convention and Exhibition Centre	香港贸易发展局 Hong Kong Trade Development Council ☎ 852-1830 668 🖷 852-2824 0249 ✉ exhibitions@hktdc.org www.hktdc.com/hkeducationexpo 详细介绍见☆7 Detail See ☆7
2011.2.18-20	第六届香港宠物节 6th Hong Kong Pet Show	香港会议展览中心 Hong Kong Convention and Exhibition Centre	World Hong Kong Investment Limited ☎ 852-2424 1188 🖷 852-2424 8077 ✉ marketing@petshow.com.hk www.petshow.com.hk
2011.2.21-25	APRICOT - APAN 2011 Hong Kong	香港会议展览中心 Hong Kong Convention and Exhibition Centre	DotAsia Organisation Limited ☎ 852-3520 2635 🖷 852-3520 2634 ✉ sec@apricot-apan.asia www.apricot-apan.asia
2011.2.25-27	Asia Top Gallery Hotel Art Fair 2011	香港文华东方酒店 Mandarin Oriental Hotel, Hong Kong	Asia Top Gallery Hotel Art Fair Committee ☎ +82 2 741 6320 🖷 +82 2 741 6319 ✉ hotelartfair@nate.com www.hotelartfair.kr
2011.2.25-27	2011 BB春季购物节 暨儿童成长教育展 2011 Baby Show in Spring & Child Growth Education Show	香港会议展览中心 Hong Kong Convention and Exhibition Centre	荷花集团 ☎ 852-2811 4522 🖷 852-2565 0258 ✉ marketing@eugenegroup.com.hk www.eugenegroup.com.hk
2011.2.25-27	香港心律失常学术论坛 2011 CardioRhythm 2011	香港会议展览中心 Hong Kong Convention and Exhibition Centre	香港心脏专科院及中华医学会心电生理和起搏分会 Hong Kong College of Cardiology and the Chinese Society of Pacing and Electrophysiology ☎ 852-2294 4468 🖷 852-2294 4489 ✉ info@cardiorhythm.com www.cardiorhythm.com
2011.2.25-28	2011香港国际毛皮时装展览会 2011 Hong Kong International Fur & Fashion Fair	香港会议展览中心 Hong Kong Convention and Exhibition Centre	香港毛皮业协会 Hong Kong Fur Federation ☎ 852 2367 4646 🖷 852 2739 0799 ✉ fur@hkff.org www.hkff.org

日期 Date	展览会议 Event	地点 Venue	主办 Organizer
2011.2.26-27	香港药剂学术年会 2011 Hong Kong Pharmacy Conference 2011	香港会议展览中心 Hong Kong Convention and Exhibition Centre	✉ hkpharmacyconference@gmail.com www.pharmacyconference.org
2011.3.3-6	三月亚洲时尚首饰及配饰展 Asia's Fashion Jewellery & Accessories Fair – March	亚洲国际博览馆 AsiaWorld-Expo	亚洲博闻有限公司 UBM Asia Limited ☎ 852-2585 6179, 2516 1677 🖷 852-3749 7542 ✉ salesafj-hk@ubm.com www.asiafja.com 详细介绍见☆8 Detail See ☆8
2011.3.4-8	香港贸发局香港国际珠宝展 HKTDC Hong Kong International Jewellery Show	香港会议展览中心 Hong Kong Convention and Exhibition Centre	香港贸易发展局 Hong Kong Trade Development Council ☎ 852-1830 668 🖷 852-2824 0249 ✉ exhibitions@hktdc.org www.hktdc.com/hkjewelleryshow 详细介绍见☆9 Detail See ☆9
2011.3.7-8	国际管线管理及安全会议 The Second International Conference on Utility Management and Safety (ICUMAS)	如心海景酒店暨会议中心 L'hotel Nina et Convention Centre	Hong Kong Institute of Utility Specialists ☎ 852 2494 5922 🖷 852 2618 4500 ✉ conference@uti.hk www.hkius.org.hk
2011.3.8-10	2011年亚洲航空物流技术展览会暨论坛 Air Freight Asia 2011	亚洲国际博览馆 AsiaWorld-Expo	励展博览集团 Reed Exhibitions 详细介绍见☆10 Detail See ☆10
2011.3.8-10	2011年亚太区航空公司培训研讨会 Asia Pacific Airline Training Symposium (APATS 2011)	亚洲国际博览馆 AsiaWorld-Expo	励展博览集团 Reed Exhibitions 详细介绍见☆10 Detail See ☆10
2011.3.8-10	2011年亚洲国际航空展览会暨论坛 Asian Aerospace International Expo and Congress 2011	亚洲国际博览馆 AsiaWorld-Expo	励展博览集团 Reed Exhibitions 详细介绍见☆10 Detail See ☆10
2011.3.8-10	2011年亚洲商用航空展览会 Asian Business Aviation 2011	亚洲国际博览馆 AsiaWorld-Expo	励展博览集团 Reed Exhibitions 详细介绍见☆10 Detail See ☆10
2011.3.10-12	Going Global 2011	香港会议展览中心 Hong Kong Convention and Exhibition Centre	British Council ☎ +44 (0)207 389 3118 www.britishcouncil.org/goingglobal

日期 Date	展览会议 Event	地点 Venue	主办 Organizer
2011.3.11-13	香港婚纱暨海外婚礼博览2011 Hong Kong Wedding & Overseas Wedding Expo 2011	香港会议展览中心 Hong Kong Convention and Exhibition Centre	隽杰国际展览有限公司 Audace International Fairs Limited ☎ 852-2367 8385 🖷 852-2367 8488 ✉ info@expo.com.hk www.wedding.expo.com.hk
2011.3.11-13	香港婚宴暨世界名酒博览2011 Hong Kong Wedding Banquet & World Wine Expo	香港会议展览中心 Hong Kong Convention and Exhibition Centre	隽杰国际展览有限公司 Audace International Fairs Limited ☎ 852-2367 8385 🖷 852-2367 8488 ✉ info@expo.com.hk www.wedding.expo.com.hk
2011.3.11-13	C3 日本动玩博览 C3 in Hong Kong 2011	香港会议展览中心 Hong Kong Convention and Exhibition Centre	SOTSU CO LTD
2011.3.15-19	USANA Asia Pacific Convention 2011	亚洲博览馆 AsiaWorld-Expo	Usana HK Ltd
2011.3.16-18	香港国际春季成衣及时装材料展 Interstoff Asia Essential - Spring 2011	香港会议展览中心 Hong Kong Convention and Exhibition Centre	法兰克福展览(香港)有限公司 Messe Frankfurt (HK) Ltd ☎ 852 2238 9932 🖷 852 2598 8771 ✉ olivia.ho@hongkong.messefrankfurt.com www.messefrankfurt.com.hk
2011.3.21-24	香港贸发局香港国际影视展 HKTDC Hong Kong Intl Film & TV Market (FILMART)	香港会议展览中心 Hong Kong Convention and Exhibition Centre	香港贸易发展局 Hong Kong Trade Development Council ☎ 852-1830 668 🖷 852-2824 0249 ✉ hktdc@hktdc.org www.hktdc.com/hkfilmart 详细介绍见☆11 Detail See ☆11
2011.3.23-24	亚太区网上资讯展览2011 Online Information Asia-Pacific 2011	香港会议展览中心 Hong Kong Convention and Exhibition Centre	Incisive Media ☎ 852 3411 4983 🖷 852 3411 4811 ✉ jonathon.whiteley@incisivemedia.com www.online-information.asia
2011/03/26 – 27	CUHK-Mayo Clinic-Asia Cardiovascular Summit	威尔斯亲王医院 Prince of Wales Hospital	香港中文大学 The Chinese University of Hong Kong ☎ 852 2647 6639 🖷 852 2144 5343 ✉ cardiology@cuhk.edu.hk www.mect.cuhk.edu.hk
2011/03/28 – 04/01	Association of Independently Owned Financial Planners (AIOFP) Conference 2011	香港君悦酒店 Grand Hyatt Hong Kong	Association of Independently Owned Financial Planners ☎ +61 08 8274 3777 🖷 +61 08 8373 4606 ✉ pjohnston@aiofp.net.au www.aiofp.net.au

日期 Date	展览会议 Event	地点 Venue	主办 Organizer
2011/03/29 – 31	亚洲智能卡工业展 Cartes in Asia 2011	亚洲国际博览馆 AsiaWorld-Expo	Comexposium ☎ +33-06 2397 0698 🖷 +33-01 5330 9514 ✉ Slobodan.PETROVIC@comexposium.com www.cartes-asia.com
2011.3.30-4.1	亚太区皮革展 - 原料及制造技术展 APLF - Materials, Manufacturing & Technology	香港会议展览中心 Hong Kong Convention and Exhibition Centre	亚太区皮革展有限公司 APLF Limited ☎ 852-2827 6211 🖷 852-3749 7346 ✉ sales@aplf.com www.aplf.com 详细介绍见☆12 Detail See ☆12
2011.3.30-4.1	时尚汇集 Fashion Access	香港会议展览中心 Hong Kong Convention and Exhibition Centre	亚太区皮革展有限公司 APLF Limited ☎ 852-2827 6211 🖷 852-2827 7831 ✉ info@aplf.com www.fashionaccess.aplf.com 详细介绍见☆13 Detail See ☆13
2011.3.30-4.1	国际服装业高峰论坛 Prime Source Forum	香港会议展览中心 Hong Kong Convention and Exhibition Centre	APLF Ltd ☎ 852-2827 6211 🖷 852-2827 7831 ✉ info@primesourceforum.com www.primesourceforum.com 详细介绍见☆14 Detail See ☆14
2011/03/30 - 31	香港国际时尚内衣展 Hong Kong Mode Lingerie	香港会议展览中心 Hong Kong Convention and Exhibition Centre	欧罗维特 Eurovet Asia Ltd ☎ 852-2815 0667 🖷 852-2815 0691 ✉ vbonnet@la-federation.com www.hongkong-mode-lingerie.com
2011.4.12-15	环球资源电子产品及零件采购交易会 环球资源安防产品采购交易会 环球资源安防产品采购交易会 环球资源韩国电子产品及零件采购交易会 China Sourcing Fair – Electronics & Components – Security Products – Solar & Energy Saving Products Korea Sourcing Fair – Electronics & Components	亚洲国际博览馆 AsiaWorld-Expo	环球资源 Global Sources ☎ 852-8199 7308 🖷 852-8199 7628 ✉ visit@chinasourcingfair.com www.chinasourcingfair.com
2011.4.13-16	香港贸发局香港春季电子产品展 HKTDC Hong Kong Electronics Fair (Spring Edition)	香港会议展览中心 Hong Kong Convention and Exhibition Centre	香港贸易发展局 Hong Kong Trade Development Council ☎ 852-1830 668 🖷 852-2824 0249 ✉ exhibitions@hktdc.org www.hktdc.com/hkelectronicsfairse 详细介绍见☆15 Detail See ☆15

日期 Date	展览会议 Event	地点 Venue	主办 Organizer
2011.4.13-16	香港贸发局国际资讯科技博览 HKTDC Intl ICT Expo	香港会议展览中心 Hong Kong Convention and Exhibition Centre	香港贸易发展局 Hong Kong Trade Development Council ☎ 852-1830 668 🖷 852-2824 0249 ✉ exhibitions@hktdc.org www.hktdc.com/ictexpo 详细介绍见☆16 Detail See ☆16
2011.4.13-16	香港贸发局香港国际春季灯饰展 HKTDC Hong Kong Intl Lighting Fair (Spring Edition)	香港会议展览中心 Hong Kong Convention and Exhibition Centre	香港贸易发展局 Hong Kong Trade Development Council ☎ 852-1830 668 🖷 852-2824 0249 ✉ exhibitions@hktdc.org www.hktdc.com/hklightingfairse 详细介绍见☆17 Detail See ☆17
2011.4.16-17	Wedding Expo	香港国际展贸中心 Hong Kong Intl Trade & Exhibition Center	Audace International Faris Ltd ☎ 852-2367 8385 www.wedding.expo.com.hk
2011.4.20-23	香港贸发局香港家庭用品展 HKTDC Hong Kong Houseware Fair	香港会议展览中心 Hong Kong Convention and Exhibition Centre	香港贸易发展局 Hong Kong Trade Development Council ☎ 852-1830 668 🖷 852-2824 0249 ✉ exhibitions@hktdc.org www.hktdc.com/hkhousewarefair 详细介绍见☆18 Detail See ☆18
2011.4.20-23	香港贸发局香港国际家用纺织品展 HKTDC Hong Kong Intl Home Textiles Fair	香港会议展览中心 Hong Kong Convention and Exhibition Centre	香港贸易发展局 Hong Kong Trade Development Council ☎ 852-1830 668 🖷 852-2824 0249 ✉ exhibitions@hktdc.org www.hktdc.com/hkhometextilesfair 详细介绍见☆19 Detail See ☆19
2011.4.20-23	环球资源婴儿及儿童产品采购交易会 环球资源家居用品采购交易会 环球资源医疗用品及供应采购交易会 环球资源礼品及赠品采购交易会 环球资源印度家居用品采购交易会 China Sourcing Fair – Baby & Children’ s Products – Home Products – Medical Products & Supplies – Gifts & Premiums India Sourcing Fair – Home Products	亚洲国际博览馆 AsiaWorld-Expo	环球资源 Global Sources ☎ 852-8199 7308 🖷 852-8199 7628 ✉ visit@chinasourcingfair.com www.chinasourcingfair.com
2011/04/22 - 25	Database Systems for Advanced Applications 2011 (DASFAA)		香港中文大学 The Chinese University of Hong Kong ☎ 852 2609 8218 🖷 852 2603 7327 ✉ sytam@cuhk.edu.hk

日期 Date	展览会议 Event	地点 Venue	主办 Organizer
2011.4.27-30	香港贸发局香港礼品及赠品展 HKTDC Hong Kong Gifts & Premium Fair	香港会议展览中心 Hong Kong Convention and Exhibition Centre	香港贸易发展局 Hong Kong Trade Development Council ☎ 852-1830 668 🖷 852-2824 0249 ✉ exhibitions@hktdc.org www.hktdc.com/hkgiftspremiumfair 详细介绍见☆20 Detail See ☆20
2011.4.27-30	香港国际印刷及包装展 Hong Kong Intl Printing & Packaging Fair	香港会议展览中心 Hong Kong Convention and Exhibition Centre	香港贸易发展局 Hong Kong Trade Development Council ☎ 852-1830 668 🖷 852-2824 0249 ✉ exhibitions@hktdc.org www.hkprintpackfair.com 详细介绍见☆21 Detail See ☆21
2011.4.27-30	环球资源流行服饰配件采购交易会 环球资源内衣及泳衣采购交易会 环球资源印度服装及配饰采购交易会 China Sourcing Fair – Fashion Accessories China Sourcing Fair - Garments & Textiles China Sourcing Fair – Underwear & Swimwear	亚洲国际博览馆 AsiaWorld-Expo	环球资源 Global Sources ☎ 852-8199 7308 🖷 852-8199 7628 ✉ visit@chinasourcingfair.com www.chinasourcingfair.com
2011.5.4-6	International Conference on Solid Waste 2011 Moving Towards Sustainable Resource Management	香港会议展览中心 Hong Kong Convention and Exhibition Centre	嘉汉林业珠三角环境应用研究中心 香港浸会大学 Sino-Forest Applied Research Centre for Pearl River Delta Environment (ARCPE), Hong Kong Baptist University ☎ 852-3411 2537 🖷 852-3411 2095 ✉ arcpe@hkbu.edu.hk http://arcpe.hkbu.edu.hk/conf2011
2011/05/08 - 10	香港国际佛教用品博览会 Hong Kong International Buddhist Products Fair	香港会议展览中心 Hong Kong Convention and Exhibition Centre	Kenfair Exhibition (Hong Kong) Limited ☎ 852-3588 9688 🖷 852-3588 5448 ✉ cs@mega-show.com www.buddhistfair.com
2011/05/11 - 14	第十四届亚洲国际食品及饮料、酒店、餐厅及餐饮设备、供应及服务展览会 HOFEX 2011 - 14th Intl Exhibition of Food & Drink, Hotel, Restaurant & Food Service Equipment, Supplies & Services	香港会议展览中心 Hong Kong Convention and Exhibition Centre	香港展览服务有限公司 Hong Kong Exhibition Services Ltd ☎ 852-2804 1500 🖷 852-2528 3103 ✉ exhibit@hkesallworld.com www.hofex.com
2011/05/14 - 17	Combined Scientific Meeting 2011	香港会议展览中心 Hong Kong Convention and Exhibition Centre	International Conference Consultants Ltd ☎ 852-2559 9973 🖷 852-2547 9528 ✉ info@csm2011.com www.csm2011.com

日期 Date	展览会议 Event	地点 Venue	主办 Organizer
2011/05/19 - 21	2011 亚洲殡仪博览 Asia Funeral Expo 2011	香港会议展览中心 Hong Kong Convention and Exhibition Centre	Vertical Expo Services Company Limited ☎ 852-2528 0062 🖷 852-2528 0072 ✉ afe@verticalexpo.com www.asiafuneralexpo.com
2011.5.20-21	OOTR 7th Annual Conference - Future in Oncology: What's in it for us?		e21 Magicmedia ☎ 852-2960 1820 🖷 852-2960 1830 ✉ tammmy.tsui@e21mm.com www.ootr.org
2011.5.20-22	第10届育儿天地博览 10th Parents' Journal Baby, Children & Family Expo	香港会议展览中心 Hong Kong Convention and Exhibition Centre	百家宝集团有限公司 Peegaboo Corp Ltd ☎ 852-3741 1720 🖷 852-3741 1725 ✉ info@peegaboo.com www.peegaboo.com
2011.5.20-22	香港长者博览2011 Hong Kong Senior Fair	香港会议展览中心 Hong Kong Convention and Exhibition Centre	纵延展业有限公司 Vertical Expo Services Co Ltd ☎ 852-2528 0062 🖷 852-2528 0072 ✉ hksf@verticalexpo.com www.hkseniorfair.com
2011.5.23-27	14th Asian Regional Conference on Soil Mechanics and Geotechnical Engineering	香港理工大学 The Hong Kong Polytechnic University	香港理工大学 The Hong Kong Polytechnic University ☎ 852-2766 6065 🖷 852-2334 6389 ✉ cejhyin@polyu.edu.hk www.cse.polyu.edu.hk/14arc
2011.5.26-29	香港国际艺术展11 ART HK	香港会议展览中心 Hong Kong Convention and Exhibition Centre	Asian Art Fairs Ltd ☎ 852-2918 8793 🖷 852-2918 8794 ✉ info@hongkongartfair.com www.hongkongartfair.com
2011.5.27-29	8th Conference of the Pacific Rim Society for Fertility & Sterility (PRSFS 2011)	香港会议展览中心 Hong Kong Convention and Exhibition Centre	Hong Kong Society for Reproductive Medicine ☎ 852-2559 9973 🖷 852-2547 9528 ✉ Prsfs2011@icc.com.hk www.prsfs2011.hk
2011.5.27-29	第六届亚洲国际艺术古董展 6th Asia International Arts & Antiques Fair 2011	国际展贸中心 Hongkong International Trade and Exhibition Centre	讯通展览公司(香港) Paper Communication Exhibition Services ☎ 852-2950 1999 🖷 852-2341 0379 ✉ shirley@paper-com.com.hk www.aiaa.com.hk

日期 Date	展览会议 Event	地点 Venue	主办 Organizer
2011.6.2-3	第三届亚太区问题赌博及成瘾问题研讨会2011 3rd Asian Pacific Problem Gambling and Addictions Conference	The Mira Hong Kong	Tung Wah Group of Hospitals ☎ 852-2827 4567 🖷 852-2827 4884 ✉ info@appgac.org www.appgac.org
2011.6.4-5	SMART Investment and International Property Expo 2011	香港会议展览中心 Hong Kong Convention and Exhibition Centre	Corporate Consumer Communications Limited ☎ 852-2944 6430 🖷 852-2944 6424 www.smartexpos.com
2011.6.4-6	第63届夏日婚纱、婚宴及结婚服务博览暨 第12届美容健身及化妆节2011 63rd Summer Wedding Service & Banquet Expo incorporating 12th HK Beauty Fitness & Makeup Fiesta	香港会议展览中心 Hong Kong Convention and Exhibition Centre	香港亚洲展览(集团)有限公司 Hongkong-Asia Exhibition (Holdings) Ltd ☎ 852-2591 9823 🖷 852-2573 3311 ✉ hkexhi@hka.com.hk www.iweddingclub.com
2011.6.9-12	Evolution Asia Yoga Conference	香港会议展览中心 Hong Kong Convention and Exhibition Centre	Asia Yoga Conference Ltd ☎ 852-3691 3981 🖷 852-3520 4999 ✉ info@asiayogaconference.com www.asiayogaconference.com
2011.6.9-12	第6届商务会奖旅游展 6th M.I.C.E. Travel Expo	香港会议展览中心 Hong Kong Convention and Exhibition Centre	汇众展览服务有限公司 TKS Exhibition Services Ltd ☎ 852-3155 0600 🖷 852-3520 1500 ✉ travel@tkshk.com www.itehkmice.com
2011.6.9-12	第25届香港国际旅游展 25th International Travel Expo	香港会议展览中心 Hong Kong Convention and Exhibition Centre	汇众展览服务有限公司 TKS Exhibition Services Ltd ☎ 852-3155 0600 🖷 852-3520 1500 ✉ travel@tkshk.com www.itehkmice.com
2011.6.11-12	2011 The International Digestive Disease Forum (The IDD Forum)	香港会议展览中心 Hong Kong Convention and Exhibition Centre	Elsevier (Singapore) Pte Ltd ☎ 852-2965 1311 🖷 852-2976 0778 ✉ d.chang@elsevier.com www.hkcec.com.hk
2011.6.11-12	第二届妇产科焦点暨香港妇产科学会50周年 FOCUS in Obstetrics and Gynaecology	如心海景酒店暨会议中心 L'hotel Nina et Convention Centre	香港中文大学 The Chinese University of Hong Kong ☎ 852-2632 1535 🖷 852-2636 0008 ✉ focus@med.cuhk.edu.hk http://department.obg.cuhk.hk/focus

日期 Date	展览会议 Event	地点 Venue	主办 Organizer
2011.6.14-16	Retail Asia Expo 2011	香港会议展览中心 Hong Kong Convention and Exhibition Centre	Diversified Events Hong Kong LLC ☎ 852-3105 3970 🖷 852-3105 3974 ✉ info@retailasiaexpo.com www.retailasiaexpo.com
2011.6.21-24	六月亚洲时尚首饰及配饰展 Asia's Fashion Jewellery & Accessories Fair - June	香港会议展览中心 Hong Kong Convention and Exhibition Centre	亚洲博闻有限公司 UBM Asia Limited ☎ 852-2585 6179, 2516 1677 🖷 852-3749 7542 ✉ salesafj-hk@ubm.com www.asiafja.com 详细介绍见☆22 Detail See ☆22
2011.6.23-26	六月香港珠宝首饰展览会 June Hong Kong Jewellery & Gem Fair 2011	香港会议展览中心 Hong Kong Convention and Exhibition Centre	亚洲博闻有限公司 UBM Asia Limited ☎ 852-2516 1677, 2585 6179 🖷 852-3749 7542 ✉ salesjgf-hk@ubm.com www.jewellerynetasia.com 详细介绍见☆23 Detail See ☆23
2011.6.28-29	学与教博览2011 Learning & Teaching Expo 2011	香港会议展览中心 Hong Kong Convention and Exhibition Centre	香港教育城有限公司 Hong Kong Education City Limited
2011.7.3-9	15th Intl Symposium on Toxicity Assessment		香港城市大学 City University of Hong Kong ☎ 852-2788 9710 🖷 852-2788 7406 ✉ bhdwtau@cityu.edu.hk
2011.7.4-7	香港贸发局香港夏季礼品、家庭用品及玩具展 HKTDC Summer Sourcing Show for Gifts, Houseware & Toys	香港会议展览中心 Hong Kong Convention & Exhibition Centre	香港贸易发展局 Hong Kong Trade Development Council ☎ 852-1830 668 🖷 852-2824 0249 ✉ exhibitions@hktdc.org www.hktdc.com/summersourcingshow 详细介绍见☆24 Detail See ☆24
2011.7.4-7	香港贸发局香港时装节春夏系列 HKTDC Hong Kong Fashion Week for Spring/Summer	香港会议展览中心 Hong Kong Convention & Exhibition Centre	香港贸易发展局 Hong Kong Trade Development Council ☎ 852-1830 668 🖷 852-2824 0249 ✉ exhibitions@hktdc.org www.hktdc.com/hkfashionweekss 详细介绍见☆25 Detail See ☆25
2011.7.4-8	9th Intl Conference on Computer Supported Collaborative Learning CSCL2011: Connecting computer supported collaborative learning to policy and practice	香港大学 The University of Hong Kong	香港大学 The University of Hong Kong 🖷 852 2517 7194 ✉ cite@hkucc.hku.hk www.cite.hku.hk

日期 Date	展览会议 Event	地点 Venue	主办 Organizer
2011.7.8-11	国际防痨联盟亚太区第三届学术会议 3rd Asia Pacific Region Conference of the Intl Union Against Tuberculosis and Lung Disease	香港会议展览中心 Hong Kong Convention and Exhibition Centre	香港防痨心脏及胸病协会 The Hong Kong Tuberculosis, Chest and Heart Diseases Association ☎ 852-2572 3466 🖷 852-2834 0711 ✉ antitb@ha.org.hk www.2011apr-unionc.org.hk
2011.7.9-10	第十届香港国际教育展 10th Hong Kong International Education Expo	香港会议展览中心 Hong Kong Convention and Exhibition Centre	立新国际展览有限公司 Neway Intl Trade Faris Ltd ☎ 852-2561 5566 🖷 852-2561 5566 ✉ info@newayfairs.com
2011.7.10-14	国际电机工程会议 2011 Intl Conference on Electrical Engineering (ICEE 2011)		香港工程师学会 The Hong Kong Institution of Engineers ☎ 852-2859 4446 🖷 852-2203 4133 ✉ conf3@hkie.org.hk www.icee-hk.org
2011.7.15-17	香港婚纱暨结婚礼品博览2011 Hong Kong Wedding & Wedding Gifts Expo	香港会议展览中心 Hong Kong Convention and Exhibition Centre	隽杰国际展览有限公司 Audace International Fairs Limited ☎ 852-2367 8385 🖷 852-2367 8488 ✉ info@expo.com.hk www.wedding.expo.com.hk
2011.7.15-17	香港婚宴暨结婚服务博览2011 Hong Kong Wedding Banquet & Wedding Services Expo	香港会议展览中心 Hong Kong Convention and Exhibition Centre	隽杰国际展览有限公司 Audace International Fairs Limited ☎ 852-2367 8385 🖷 852-2367 8488 ✉ info@expo.com.hk www.wedding.expo.com.hk
2011.7.20-26	香港贸发局香港书展 HKTDC Hong Kong Book Fair	香港会议展览中心 Hong Kong Convention and Exhibition Centre	香港贸易发展局 Hong Kong Trade Development Council ☎ 852-1830 668 🖷 852-2824 0249 ✉ exhibitions@hktdc.org www.hkbookfair.com 详细介绍见☆26 Detail See ☆26
2011.7.22–24	优质生活展览-美容及养生、休闲及培育、开学用品及精明消费 Better Living Expo - for Beauty & Well-Being, Hobbies & Learning, Back-to-school and Value Shopping	亚洲国际展览馆 Asia World-Expo	通讯展览公司 Paper Communication Exhibition Service ☎ 852-2763 9011 🖷 852-2341 0379 ✉ jenny@paper-con.com.hk www.paper-com.com.hk

日期 Date	展览会议 Event	地点 Venue	主办 Organizer
2011.7.25-29	The School Nurses Intl 16th Biennial Conference 2011	香港理工大学 The Hong Kong Polytechnic University	香港理工大学 The Hong Kong Polytechnic University ☎ 852-2766 4147 ✉ hspamela@inet.polyu.edu.hk
2011.7.29-31	第七届香港国际宠物用品展暨水族博览 7th Hong Kong International Pet Accessory & Aqua Expo	香港国际展贸中心 International Trade & Exhibition Center	通讯展览公司 Paper Communication Exhibition Service ☎ 852-2763 9011 🖷 852-2341 0379 ✉ jenny@paper-con.com.hk www.paper-com.com.hk
2011.8	香港国际茶展 Hong Kong Intl Tea Fair	香港会议展览中心 Hong Kong Convention and Exhibition Centre	香港贸易发展局 Hong Kong Trade Development Council ☎ 852-1830 668 🖷 852-2824 0249 ✉ exhibitions@hktdc.org www.hktdc.com/hkfoodexpo 详细介绍见☆27 Detail See ☆27
2011.8	国际现代化中医药及健康产品展览会暨会议 Intl Conference & Exhibition of the Modernization of Chinese Medicine & Health Products	香港会议展览中心 Hong Kong Convention and Exhibition Centre	香港贸易发展局 Hong Kong Trade Development Council ☎ 852-1830 668 🖷 852-2824 0249 ✉ exhibitions@hktdc.org www.hktdc.com/icmcm 详细介绍见☆28 Detail See ☆28
2011.8.5-7	2011香港高级视听展 Hong Kong High-End Audio-Visual Show	香港会议展览中心 Hong Kong Convention and Exhibition Centre	音响技术 Audio Technique ☎ 852-2881 1252 🖷 852-2890 3999 ✉ mag@audiotechnique.com www.audiotechnique.com
2011.8.11-15	香港贸发局美食博览 HKTDC Food Expo	香港会议展览中心 Hong Kong Convention and Exhibition Centre	香港贸易发展局 Hong Kong Trade Development Council ☎ 852-1830 668 🖷 852-2824 0249 ✉ exhibitions@hktdc.org www.hktdc.com/hkfoodexpo 详细介绍见☆29 Detail See ☆29
2011.8.16-21	The 17th Intl Congress of Phonetic Sciences	Hong Kong Convention and Exhibition Centre	香港城市大学 City University of Hong Kong ☎ 852-2788 7594 🖷 852-2788 7594 ✉ ctlzee@cityu.edu.hk

日期 Date	展览会议 Event	地点 Venue	主办 Organizer
2011.8.25-27	第九届亚洲天然产品博览 New Hope Natural Media, a division of Penton Media	香港会议展览中心 Hong Kong Convention and Exhibition Centre	New Hope Natural Media, a division of Penton Media ☎ 852-2975 9051 🖷 852-2857 6144 ✉ expoasia@penton.com www.naturalproductsasia.com
2011.9.6-8	国际佳肴、餐饮、酒廊设备博览会 Restaurant & Bar 2011	香港会议展览中心 Hong Kong Convention and Exhibition Centre	Diversified Events Hong Kong LLC ☎ 852-3105 3970 🖷 852-3105 3974 ✉ info@restaurantandbarhk.com www.restaurantandbarhk.com
2011.9.6-8	亚洲海鲜展 Asian Seafood Exposition 2011	香港会议展览中心 Hong Kong Convention and Exhibition Centre	Diversified Events Hong Kong LLC ☎ 852-3105 3970 🖷 852-3105 3974 www.asianseafoodexpo.com
2011.9.7-9	Vitafoods Asia 2011	亚洲博览馆 AsiaWorld-Expo	IIR Exhibitions
2011.9.7-9	Asia Fruit Logistica Asiafruit Congress 2011	香港会议展览中心 Hong Kong Convention and Exhibition Centre	Global Produce Events GmbH ☎ +49 30 3038 2178 🖷 +49 30 3038 7060 ✉ info@asiafruitlogistica.com
2011.9.7-11	香港贸发局香港钟表展 HKTDC Hong Kong Watch & Clock Fair	香港会议展览中心 Hong Kong Convention and Exhibition Centre	香港贸易发展局 香港表厂商会有限公司 香港钟表业总会有限公司 Hong Kong Trade Development Council, Hong Kong Watch Manufacturers Association Ltd., The Federation of Hong Kong Watch Trades and Industries Ltd ☎ 852-1830 668 🖷 852-2824 0249 ✉ info@asiafruitlogistica.com www.hktdc.com/hkwatchfair 详细介绍见☆30 Detail See ☆30
2011.9.14-17	ISQua's 28th Intl Conference, Hong Kong, China 2011, Patient Safety: Sustaining the Global Momentum	香港会议展览中心 Hong Kong Convention and Exhibition Centre	The Intl Society for Quality in Health Care (ISQua) ☎ +353-1-8717049 🖷 +353-1-8783845 ✉ isqua@isqua.org www.isqua.org

日期 Date	展览会议 Event	地点 Venue	主办 Organizer
2011.9.19-22	九月亚洲时尚首饰及配饰展 Asia' s Fashion Jewellery & Accessories Fair – September	亚洲国际博览馆 AsiaWorld-Expo	亚洲博闻有限公司 UBM Asia Limited ☎ 852- 2585 6179, 2516 1677 🖷 852-3749 7542 ✉ salesafj-hk@ubm.com www.asiafja.com 详细介绍见☆31 Detail See ☆31
2011.9.19-23	九月香港珠宝首饰展览会 September Hong Kong Jewellery & Gem Fair 2011	亚洲国际博览馆 AsiaWorld-Expo	亚洲博闻有限公司 UBM Asia Limited ☎ 852-2827 6211 🖷 852-2827 7831 ✉ salesjwf@cmpasia.com exhibitions.jewellerynetasia.com 详细介绍见☆32 Detail See ☆32
2011.9.21-25	九月香港珠宝首饰展览会 September Hong Kong Jewellery & Gem Fair 2011	香港会议展览中心 Hong Kong Convention and Exhibition Centre	亚洲博闻有限公司 UBM Asia Limited ☎ 852-2827 6211 🖷 852-2827 7831 ✉ salesjwf@cmpasia.com exhibitions.jewellerynetasia.com 详细介绍见☆33 Detail See ☆33
2011.9.22-24	Fifth Pan- Pacific Nursing Conference and Seventh Nursing Symposium on Cancer Care	帝京酒店 Royal Plaza Hotel	香港中文大学 The Chinese University of Hong Kong ☎ 852 2696 1237 🖷 852 2603 5520 ✉ tiffanyli@cuhk.edu.hk www.nur.cuhk.edu.hk
2011.9.28-30	时尚汇集 Fashion Access	香港会议展览中心 Hong Kong Convention and Exhibition Centre	亚洲博闻有限公司 APLF Limited ☎ 852-2827 6211 🖷 852-3749 7346 ✉ salesf@aplf.com www.fashionaccess.aplf.com 详细介绍见☆34 Detail See ☆34
2011.10.6-8	香港国际秋季成衣及时装材料展 Interstoff Asia Essential - Autumn 2011	香港会议展览中心 Hong Kong Convention and Exhibition Centre	☎ 852-2802 7728 🖷 852-2598 8771 ✉ textile@hongkong.messefrankfurt.com www.interstoff-asia.com

日期 Date	展览会议 Event	地点 Venue	主办 Organizer
2011.10.12-15	环球资源电子产品及零件采购交易会 环球资源安防产品采购交易会/环球资源太阳能及节能产品采购交易会/环球资源韩国电子产品及零件采购交易会 China Sourcing Fair – Electronics & Components – Security Products – Solar & Energy Saving Products Korea Sourcing Fair – Electronics & Components	亚洲国际博览馆 AsiaWorld-Expo	环球资源 ☎ 852-8199 7308 🖷 852-8199 7628 ✉ visit@chinasourcingfair.com www.chinasourcingfair.com
2011.10.13-16	香港贸发局香港秋季电子产品展 HKTDC Hong Kong Electronics Fair (Autumn Edition)	香港会议展览中心 Hong Kong Convention and Exhibition Centre	香港贸易发展局 Hong Kong Trade Development Council ☎ 852-1830 668 🖷 852-2824 0249 ✉ exhibitions@hktdc.org www.hktdc.com/hkelectronicsfairae 详细介绍见☆35 Detail See ☆35
2011.10.13-16	国际电子组件及生产技术展 electronicAsia	香港会议展览中心 Hong Kong Convention and Exhibition Centre	香港贸易发展局 Hong Kong Trade Development Council ☎ 852-1830 668 🖷 852-2824 0249 ✉ exhibitions@hktdc.org www.electronicasia.com 详细介绍见☆36 Detail See ☆36
2011.10.13-16	亚洲展览盛事第一部分 Mega Show Part 1	香港会议展览中心 Hong Kong Convention and Exhibition Centre	Group Idea International Limited ☎ 852-3588 9688 🖷 852-3588 5448 ✉ cs@mega-show.com http://mega-show.com
2011.10.20-23	环球资源印度家居用品采购交易会 环球资源医疗用品及供应采购交易会 环球资源家居用品采购交易会 环球资源礼品及赠品采购交易会 环球资源婴儿及儿童产品采购交易会 China Sourcing Fair – Baby & Children’s Products – Gifts & Premiums – Home Products – Medical Products & Supplies India Sourcing Fair – Home Products	亚洲国际博览馆 AsiaWorld-Expo	环球资源 Global Sources ☎ 852-8199 7308 🖷 852-8199 7628 ✉ visit@chinasourcingfair.com www.chinasourcingfair.com

日期 Date	展览会议 Event	地点 Venue	主办 Organizer
2011.10.27-30	香港贸发局香港国际秋季灯饰展 HKTDC Hong Kong International Lighting Fair (Autumn Edition)	香港会议展览中心 Hong Kong Convention and Exhibition Centre	香港贸易发展局 Hong Kong Trade Development Council ☎ 852-1830 668 🖷 852-2824 0249 ✉ exhibitions@hktdc.org www.hktdc.com/hklightingfairae 详细介绍见☆37 Detail See ☆37
2011.10.27-30	亚洲运动用品展 Sports Source Asia	亚洲国际博览馆 AsiaWorld-Expo, Hong Kong	香港贸易发展局 Hong Kong Trade Development Council ☎ 852-1830 668 🖷 852-2824 0249 ✉ exhibitions@hktdc.org www.sportssource-asia.com 详细介绍见☆38 Detail See ☆38
2011.10	香港贸发局香港国际建筑装饰材料及五金展 HKTDC Hong Kong Intl Building and Decoration Materials & Hardware Fair	亚洲国际博览馆 AsiaWorld-Expo, Hong Kong	香港贸易发展局 Hong Kong Trade Development Council ☎ 852-1830 668 🖷 852-2824 0249 ✉ exhibitions@hktdc.org www.hktdc.com/hkbdh 详细介绍见☆39 Detail See ☆39
2011.10.27-30	国际环保博览 Eco Expo Asia – Intl Trade Fair on Environmental Protection	亚洲国际博览馆 AsiaWorld-Expo, Hong Kong	香港贸易发展局 Hong Kong Trade Development Council ☎ 852-1830 668 🖷 852-2824 0249 ✉ exhibitions@hktdc.org www.ecoexpoasia.com 详细介绍见☆40 Detail See ☆40
2011.10.27-30	环球资源流行服饰配件采购交易会 环球资源内衣及泳衣采购交易会 环球资源服装及面料采购交易会 环球资源印度服装及配饰采购交易会 China Sourcing Fair – Fashion Accessories – Underwear & Swimwear – Garments & Textiles India Sourcing Fair - Garments & Accessories	亚洲国际博览馆 AsiaWorld-Expo	环球资源 Global Sources ☎ 852-8199 7308 🖷 852-8199 7628 ✉ visit@chinasourcingfair.com www.chinasourcingfair.com
2011.10.28-30	亚洲展览盛事第二部分 Mega Show Part 2 - Gifts, Décor & Home	香港会议展览中心 Hong Kong Convention and Exhibition Centre	Group Idea International Limited ☎ 852-3588 9688 🖷 852-3588 5448 ✉ cs@mega-show.com http://mega-show.com

日期 Date	展览会议 Event	地点 Venue	主办 Organizer
2011.11.3-5	香港贸发局香港国际医疗器材及用品展 HKTDC Hong Kong Intl Medical Devices and Supplies Fair	香港会议展览中心 Hong Kong Convention and Exhibition Centre	香港贸易发展局 Hong Kong Trade Development Council ☎ 852-1830 668 🖷 852-2824 0249 ✉ exhibitions@hktdc.org www.hktdc.com/hkmedicalfair 详细介绍见☆41 Detail See ☆41
2011.11.3-5	香港贸发局香港国际美酒展 HKTDC Hong Kong Intl Wine & Spirits Fair	香港会议展览中心 Hong Kong Convention and Exhibition Centre	香港贸易发展局 Hong Kong Trade Development Council ☎ 852-1830 668 🖷 852-2824 0249 ✉ exhibitions@hktdc.org www.hktdc.com/hkwinefair 详细介绍见☆42 Detail See ☆42
2011.11.3-5	香港贸发局香港眼镜展 HKTDC Hong Kong Optical Fair	香港会议展览中心 Hong Kong Convention and Exhibition Centre	香港贸易发展局 Hong Kong Trade Development Council ☎ 852-1830 668 🖷 852-2824 0249 ✉ exhibitions@hktdc.org www.hktdc.com/hkopticalfair 详细介绍见☆43 Detail See ☆43
2011.11.4-6	香港婚纱暨结婚博览2011 Hong Kong Wedding Expo 2011	香港会议展览中心 Hong Kong Convention and Exhibition Centre	隽杰国际展览有限公司 Audace International Fairs Limited ☎ 852-2367 8385 🖷 852-2367 8488 ✉ info@expo.com.hk www.wedding.expo.com.hk
2011.11.9-11	2011年亚太区美容展 Cosmoprof Asia 2011	香港会议展览中心 Hong Kong Convention and Exhibition Centre	Cosmoprof Asia Ltd ☎ 852-2827 6211 020-8666 0158 🖷 852-3749 7345 020-8667 2235 ✉ cosmasia-hk@ubm.com www.cosmoprof-asia.com 详细介绍见☆44 Detail See ☆44
2011.11.10-12	Asian Epilepsy Surgery Congress	香港医学专科学院 Hong Kong Academy of Medicine	香港医学专科学院 Hong Kong Academy of Medicine ☎ 852-2871 8841 🖷 852-2871 8898 ✉ lenora@hkam.org.hk www.hkam.org.hk
2011.11.23-27	The Gospel for China 2011	亚洲博览馆 AsiaWorld-Expo	Christian Life Press USA (HK) Limited

日期 Date	展览会议 Event	地点 Venue	主办 Organizer
2011.12	香港贸发局国际中小企博览 HKTDC World SME Expo	香港会议展览中心 Hong Kong Convention and Exhibition Centre	香港贸易发展局 Hong Kong Trade Development Council ☎ 852-1830 668 🖷 852-2824 0249 ✉ exhibitions@hktdc.org www.hktdc.com/worldsmeexpo 详细介绍见☆45 Detail See ☆45
2011.12.1-3	香港贸发局创新科技及设计博览 HKTDC Inno Design Tech Expo	香港会议展览中心 Hong Kong Convention and Exhibition Centre	香港贸易发展局 Hong Kong Trade Development Council ☎ 852-1830 668 🖷 852-2824 0249 ✉ hktdc@hktdc.org www.hktdc.com/innodesigntechexpo 详细介绍见☆46 Detail See ☆46
2011.12.5-7	第12届世界海南乡团联谊大会暨 第3届世界海南青年大会 12th Congress of the World Federation of Hainanese Associations 3rd World Forum for Hainanese Youth	香港会议展览中心 Hong Kong Convention and Exhibition Centre	香港海南商会 ☎ 852-2891 4941 🖷 852-2836 3500 ✉ info@hkhnca.com.hk
2011.6.6-8	CineAsia 2011	香港会议展览中心 Hong Kong Convention and Exhibition Centre	E5 Global Medai ☎ +1-646 654 5164 🖷 +1-646 654 7694 www.cineasia.com
2012.2.25-28	2012香港国际毛皮时装展览会 2012 Hong Kong International Fur & Fashion Fair	香港会议展览中心 Hong Kong Convention and Exhibition Centre	香港毛皮业协会 Hong Kong Fur Federation ☎ 852-2367 4646 🖷 852-2739 0799 ✉ fur@hkff.org www.hkff.org
2012.8.19-25	CIRP General Assembly	香港会议展览中心 Hong Kong Convention and Exhibition Centre	CIRP ☎ +33 1 4526 2180 🖷 +33 1 4526 9215 ✉ cirp@cirp.net www.cirp.net
2013.9.25-28	国际小儿肿瘤会第45次年会 45th Congress of the International Society of Paediatric Oncology	香港会议展览中心 Hong Kong Convention and Exhibition Centre	威尔斯亲王医院 Prince of Wales Hospital ☎ 852-2632 1019 🖷 852-2649 7859 ✉ ckli@cuhk.edu.hk www.fmshk.com
2014.6.3-8	Intl Conference on Emergency Medicine	香港会议展览中心 Hong Kong Convention and Exhibition Centre	香港急症科医学院 Hong Kong College of Emergency Medicine ☎ +61 3 9320 0444 🖷 +61 3 9320 0400 ✉ ifem@acem.org.au www.ifem.cc

☆1
2011/01/10-12
☎ 852-1830 668
🖷 852-2824 0249
✉ hktdc@hktdc.org
www.hktdc.com/hklicensingshow

HKTDC

Hong Kong International Licensing Show
香港國際授權展

香港贸发局香港国际授权展
地点：　香港会议展览中心，香港
内容：　产品、设计等授权活动包括 品牌或设计、卡通人物、动漫及数码娱乐、艺术设计、专上学府品牌、知名企业品牌、娱乐名人、生活时尚及服饰、运动品牌、设计及市场推广服务、法律及专业顾问服务
上届规模2010：　展出面积4,456平方米，参展商143家
主办：　香港贸易发展局
地址：　香港湾仔港湾道一号会展广场办公大楼38字楼

HKTDC Hong Kong International Licensing Show
Venue: Hsong Kong Convention & Exhibition Center, Hong Kong
Profile: Properties and brands for licensing, animation & digital entertainment, art & design, characters, collegiate, corporate brands, entertainment, fashion & lifestyle, sports, design & marketing services, legal & professional services
Statistics 2010: Gross Area 4,456m^2, Exhibitors 143
Organizer: Hong Kong Trade Development Council
Address: 38/F, Office Tower, Convention Plaza, 1 Harbour Road, Wan Chai, Hong Kong

☆2
2011/01/10-13
☎ 852-1830 668
🖷 852-2824 0249
✉ exhibitions@hktdc.org
www.hktdc.com/hktoyfair

HKTDC

Hong Kong Toys & Games Fair
香港玩具展

香港贸发局香港玩具展
地点：　香港会议展览中心，香港
内容：　糖果玩具、益智玩具及游戏、电子及遥控玩具、嗜好玩具、魔术用具、户外及运动用品、纸品及玩具包装、派对用品、玩具零件及配件、软身玩具及洋娃娃、检测及认证服务、模型、机械玩具及动作玩偶、电玩游戏
上届规模2010：　展出面积57,532平方米，参展商1,915家
主办：　香港贸易发展局
地址：　香港湾仔博览道1号香港会议展览中心博览商场13号展览事务部

HKTDC Hong Kong Toys & Games Fair
Venue: Hong Kong Convention & Exhibition Center, Hong Kong
Profile: Candy toys, educational toys & games, electronic & remote control toys, hobby goods, magic items, outdoor & sporting items, paper products & toy packaging, party items, toy parts & accessories, soft toys & dolls, testing, inspection and certification, vehicles, mechanical toys & action figures, video games
Statistics 2010: Gross Area 57,532m^2, Exhibitors 1,915
Organizer: Hong Kong Trade Development Council
Address: Exhibitions Department, Unit 13, Expo Galleria, Hong Kong Convention and Exhibition Center, 1 Expo Drive, Wan Chai, Hong Kong

☆3
2011/01/10-13
☎ 852-1830 668
🖷 852-2824 0249
✉ exhibitions@hktdc.org
www.hktdc.com/hkbabyfair

HKTDC

Hong Kong Baby Products Fair
香港嬰兒用品展

香港贸发局香港婴儿用品展
地点：　香港会议展览中心，香港
内容：　品牌廊，婴儿寝具及家具、婴儿玩具及游戏用品、婴儿衣服及鞋、育婴产品、婴儿礼品及纪念品、孕妇用品、育婴电器、护肤及沐浴产品、婴儿手推车及婴儿椅
上届规模 2010：　展出面积9,963平方米，参展商308家
主办：　香港贸易发展局
地址：　香港湾仔博览道1号香港会议展览中心博览商场13号展览事务部

HKTDC Hong Kong Baby Products Fair
Venue: Hong Kong Convention & Exhibition Center, Hong Kong
Profile: Brand Name Gallery, baby bedding and furniture, baby toys and activities, baby wear and footwear, feeding and nursery, gift sets and souvenirs, maternity products, nursery electrical appliances, skincare and bath products, strollers and gear
Statistics 2010: Gross Area 9,963m^2, Exhibitors 308
Organizer: Hong Kong Trade Development Council
Address: Exhibitions Department, Unit 13, Expo Galleria, Hong Kong Convention and Exhibition Center, 1 Expo Drive, Wan Chai, Hong Kong

☆4
2011/01/10-13
☎ 852-1830 668
🖷 852-2824 0249
✉ exhibitions@hktdc.org
www.hkstationeryfair.com

香港国际文具展
地点： 香港会议展览中心，香港
内容： 美术用品、儿童文具及学校用品、电脑周边设备及配件、办公室设备用消耗品、礼品文具、办公室设备、纸品及印刷品、书写设备
上届规模 2010： 展出面积5,101平方米，参展商243家
主办： 香港贸易发展局，法兰克福展览(香港)有限公司
地址： 香港湾仔博览道1号香港会议展览中心博览商场13号展览事务部

Hong Kong International Stationery Fair
Venue: Hong Kong Convention & Exhibition Center, Hong Kong
Profile: Artist supplies, children' s stationery & school supplies, computer peripherals & related accessories, consumables for office equipment, gift stationery, office equipment, paper & printing products, writing equipment
Statistics 2010: Gross Area 5,101m^2, Exhibitors 243
Organizers: Hong Kong Trade Development Council, Messe Frankfurt (HK) Ltd
Address: Exhibitions Department, Unit 13, Expo Galleria, Hong Kong Convention and Exhibition Center, 1 Expo Drive, Wan Chai, Hong Kong

☆5
2011/01/17-20
☎ 852-1830 668
🖷 852-2824 0249
✉ exhibitions@hktdc.org
www.hktdc.com/hkfashionweekfw

HKTDC
Hong Kong Fashion Week for Fall/Winter
香港時裝節秋冬系列

香港贸发局香港时装节秋冬系列
地点： 香港会议展览中心，香港
内容： 女装、男装、婴儿服装、运动服装、内衣、泳衣、新娘礼服及晚礼服、手袋、鞋、流行饰物、布料及纱线、钮扣、唛头、时装杂志、专业商贸服务
上届规模 2010： 展出面积50,748平方米，参展商1,714家
主办： 香港贸易发展局
地址： 香港湾仔博览道1号香港会议展览中心博览商场13号展览事务部

HKTDC Hong Kong Fashion Week for Fall/Winter
Venue: Hong Kong Convention & Exhibition Center, Hong Kong
Profile: Ladies' wear, men' s wear, babies and children' s wear, sportswear, lingerie, swimwear, bridal & evening wear, handbags, shoes, costume jewellery, fabric & yarn, buttons, labels, fashion magazines, trade services
Statistics 2010: Gross Area 50,748m^2, Exhibitors 1,714
Organizer: Hong Kong Trade Development Council
Address: Exhibitions Department, Unit 13, Expo Galleria, Hong Kong Convention and Exhibition Center, 1 Expo Drive, Wan Chai, Hong Kong

☆6
2011/01/17-20
☎ 852-1830 668
🖷 852-2824 0249
✉ exhibitions@hktdc.org
www.hktdc.com/worldboutiquehk

HKTDC
Hong Kong Fashion Week for Fall/Winter
香港時裝節秋冬系列

香港贸发局香港国际时尚荟萃
地点： 香港会议展览中心，香港
内容： 品牌时装及设计师系列、时装饰品、家居时尚用品及赠品
上届规模 2010： 展出面积 8,917平方米，参展商256家
主办： 香港贸易发展局
地址： 香港湾仔博览道1号香港会议展览中心博览商场13号展览事务部

HKTDC World Boutique, Hong Kong
Venue: Hong Kong Convention & Exhibition Center, Hong Kong
Profile: Fashion designers' collection, branded fashion products, home fashion & lifestyle products, small gifts
Statistics 2010: Gross Area 8,917m^2, Exhibitors 256
Organizer: Hong Kong Trade Development Council
Address: Exhibitions Department, Unit 13, Expo Galleria, Hong Kong Convention and Exhibition Center, 1 Expo Drive, Wan Chai, Hong Kong

☆7
2011/02/17-20
☎ 852-1830 668
🖷 852-2824 0249
✉ exhibitions@hktdc.org

HKTDC

Education & Careers Expo
教育及職業博覽

香港贸发局教育及职业博览

地点：	香港会议展览中心，香港
内容：	大专院校及理工、大学、专科及进修学校、职业训练机构、语文学校、外地教育机构、政府部门、半政府机构、专业学会、私人机构、出版商及书店、教学／学习辅助器材
上届规模 2010：	展出面积9,481平方米，参展商547家
主办：	香港贸易发展局
地址：	香港湾仔博览道1号香港会议展览中心博览商场13号展览事务部

HKTDC Education & Careers Expo

Venue:	Hong Kong Convention & Exhibition Center, Hong Kong
Profile:	Colleges & polytechnics, universities, school for continue education, vocational training, language schools, outside Hong Kong educational institutions, government departments, semi-government organizations, professional associations, private enterprises, book publishers/book stores, learning aids/educational equipment
Statistics 2010:	Gross Area 9,481m^2, Exhibitors 547
Organizer:	Hong Kong Trade Development Council
Address:	Exhibitions Department, Unit 13, Expo Galleria, Hong Kong Convention and Exhibition Center, 1 Expo Drive, Wan Chai, Hong Kong

☆8
2010/03/03 – 06
☎ 852-2585 6179, 2516 1677
🖷 852-3749 7542
✉ salesafj-hk@ubm.com
www.asiafja.com

3 - 6 March 2011
二〇一一年三月三至六日

三月亚洲时尚首饰及配饰展

地点：	亚洲国际博览馆, 香港
内容：	时尚首饰：非贵金属首饰、珠子首饰、珐琅及白蜡首饰、宝石首饰、半宝石首饰、合成宝石或仿宝石首饰、玻璃首饰、天然物料首饰、塑料首饰、纯银首饰及配饰 时尚配饰：皮带及配饰、时尚手表、发饰、手袋、钱包、头饰及颈饰 时尚首饰原料：珠子、宝石—未经打磨及打磨宝石、半宝石、合成宝石或仿宝石、首饰配件及组件、天然物料 陈列及包装：陈列物料、礼盒
周期：	每年三届（三月、六月、九月）
市场范围：	国际性
展览性质：	只对专业观众开放
上届规模2010：	展商总数300家（来自15国家），贸易观众4151人(来自83个国家)
主办：	亚洲博闻有限公司

Asia's Fashion Jewellery & Accessories Fair - March

Venue:	AsiaWorld-Expo, Hong Kong
Profile:	Fashion Jewellery, Fashion Jewellery Materials, Fashion accessories, Display and packaging
Frequency:	Three times a year (March, June, September)
Market Area:	International
Nature:	Trade only
Statistics 2010:	Exhibitors 300 (came from 15 countries）, Trade Visitors 4,151
Organizer:	UBM Asia Limited

☆9
2011/03/04-08
☎ 852-1830 668
🖷 852-2824 0249
✉ exhibitions@hktdc.org
www.hktdc.com/hkjewelleryshow

HKTDC

Hong Kong International Jewellery Show
香港國際珠寶展

香港贸发局香港国际珠宝展

地点：	香港会议展览中心，香港
内容：	珠宝首饰、银首饰、制成首饰、古董首饰、翡翠首饰、钻石、贵重宝石、南洋珠及大溪地珍珠、淡水珠及养珠、半宝石、珠宝配件、宝石陈列及包装用品、工具及仪器、珠宝刊物及服务、贸易商会、品牌表及时钟、成表及时钟
上届规模2010：	展出面积88,550平方米，参展商2,673家
主办：	香港贸易发展局
地址：	香港湾仔博览道1号香港会议展览中心博览商场13号展览事务部

HKTDC Hong Kong International Jewellery Show

Venue: Hong Kong Convention & Exhibition Center, Hong Kong

Profile: Fine jewellery, silver jewellery, finished jewellery, antique jewellery, jade jewellery, diamonds, precious stones, south sea pearls & Tahiti pearls, fresh water & cultured pearls, semi-precious stones, jewellery accessories, jewellery display & packaging material, jewellery tools & equipment, trade publications & services, trade associations, brand name watches & clocks, complete watches & clocks

Statistics 2010: Gross Area 88,550m^2, Exhibitors 2,673

Organizer: Hong Kong Trade Development Council

Address: Exhibitions Department, Unit 13, Expo Galleria, Hong Kong Convention and Exhibition Center, 1 Expo Drive, Wan Chai, Hong Kong

☆10
2011/03/08-10
☎ 010-5933 9288
🖷 010-5933 9233
✉ liang.wang@reedexpo.com.cn
www.asianaerospace.com

亚洲国际航空展览会暨论坛

- 100%商用及民用航空的B2B平台

地点： 亚洲国际博览馆，香港

内容： 亚洲国际航空展览会暨论坛是世界上最大的专著于商用和民用航空市场的单一主题展览会和论坛。作为过去25年来亚洲的首要航空盛会，亚洲国际航空展览会将整合行业资源突出体现世界航空业对亚洲行业发展的高度关注，为那些具有远景规划的商业航空企业及专业人士提供独一无二的“一站式采购”机会，从而继续助力航空企业发展重要的战略伙伴关系，拉近中国，亚洲与世界的距离。

产品及服务： 飞机包租、运输服务，航空货运公司，航空物流、供应链管理，空中交通管制系统，飞机经纪人、经销商和分销商，飞机、机身构造制造商，飞机室内设计及设备-设备与服务，飞机零件和附件，航空公司，机场、航站楼管理，机场系统/基础设施、服务，航空电子设备及雷达系统，餐饮设备、服务，化学品、油漆、涂料，民用飞机设计与工程，元件工程维修和检查，复合材料/航空材料，顾问、代理，引擎制造商、零部件，金融、银行、租赁、保险服务，固定基地运营商、燃油供应商，航班规划和气象服务，飞行培训、学校与服务机构、研究院，政府部门、立法机构，机场航空管理局、运营商、行政管理部门，地面支持设备、运输，直升飞机，航载娱乐、通信系统，维护、修理和检修、工程，媒体、出版，医疗、救援，安全、逃生、急救，安全系统、服务-飞机/机场，软件系统、服务与应用，模拟、培训设备与服务，太空、卫星设备与服务，系统制造商，测试设备与服务，行业协会、其他工业组织。

周期： 两年一届

上届规模 2009： 展商总数356家，观众总数12,615人

主办： 励展博览集团

地址： 北京市朝阳区新源南路1-3号平安国际金融中心A座15层01-03,05（100027）
www.reedexport.cn

Asian Aerospace International Expo & Congress :

100% B2B Platform for Commercial Aerospace & Civil Aviation

Venue: AsiaWorld-Expo, Hong Kong

Profile: Asian Aerospace 2011 (Asian Aerospace International Expo and Congress) is the leading B2B commercial aerospace event embraces key sectors – MRO, manufacturing, business aviation, interiors and training.

Asian Aerospace 2011 will also feature the popular AA Congress, in conjunction with Airline Business - the must attend event for lively discussion and engaging debate on air transport trends and infrastructure.

Frequency: Biennial

Statistics 2009: Exhibitors 356, Visitors 12,615

Organizer: Reed Exhibitions Ltd

☆10
2011/03/08 - 10
☎ +65-9125 5124,
852-2965 1668
✉ vid.lim@reedexpo.com.sg,
✉ jellis.kan@reedexpo.com.hk
www.airfreightasia.com

2011亚洲航空物流技术展览会

地点： 亚洲国际博览馆，香港

内容： 亚洲航空物流技术展览会暨论坛是两年一届并致力于全球航空货运行业的盛会。亚洲航空物流技术展览会暨论坛将在2011年竭诚为所有参与者提供一个宝贵的机会与业界同仁直面交流。香港是一处东方航空运输及供应链管理的物流企业与西方同行交流的理想之地。位于中国南大门，香港地理位置优越，是亚洲乃至世界各国进入中国巨大市场的跳板。

周期： 两年一届

性质： 面向贸易观众

主办： 励展博览集团

地址： 香港湾仔皇后大道东183号合和中心39字楼

联系人： 林源和，简明茵

Air Freight Asia 2011

Venue: AsiaWorld-Expo, Hong Kong

Profile: The Air Freight Asia Conference and Exhibition is a biennial event for the global air freight industry. In 2011, logistics in supply chain management will be new element at the event. Hong Kong is where Eastern air freight and logistics business involved in supply chain management engage with their Western counterparts. Strategically located in South China, Hong Kong is the gateway to the China market or industries from across the globe.

Frequency: Biennial

Nature: Trade Only

Organizer: Reed Exhibitions

Address: 39/F, Hopewell Centre, 183 Queen's Road East, Wanchai, Hong Kong**

Contact: David Lim

☆10

2011/03/08 - 10

☎ +65-9125 5124

+44-208 9107821**

✉ david.lim@reedexpo.com.sg**

www.asianbusinessav.com

2011亚洲商务航空展览会

地点： 香港机场商用航空中心

内容： 亚洲商务航空展（ABA）以香港的战略性位置为依托，让参与者在商用航空领域有效拓展人脉联系，汇聚来自世界顶级买家和服务提供商的无限商机。ABA将展览、静态展示、专属派对和会议整合一处，为从业者搭建完美的一体化平台，不仅能够满足顶级买家需求、建立全新联系，更可紧随市场趋势，并在中国乃至整个亚洲地区——世界发展最快的商用航空市场上构建全新的合作伙伴关系。

产品及服务： 飞机内部设计、飞机维护与运营、飞机制造、飞机市场销售、管理和相关服务、机身和飞机组件、机场和机场运营、私人飞机运营、固定基地运营、商务和金融服务、教育培训、电子 航空电子设备和仪器、发动机和推进器、飞行计划和导航、地面运营、行业组织、飞机中产区和服务，出版，安全、安保和应急准备，工具和测试设备，交通服务。

主办： 励展博览集团

Asian business Aviation 2011

Venue: Hong Kong-Business Aviation Center, Hong Kong

Profile: Strategically located in Hong Kong, Asian Business Aviation (ABA) fuels an effective networking and information gathering opportunity for the world' s top-tier buyers and service providers within the business-aviation sector. Combining exhibition, static displays, exclusive parties and conferences at a single event, ABA is the perfect place for industry players. Participants will be able to meet the top-tier buyers, generate new contacts, get market information, and establish new partnerships in China as well as other destinations in Asia – the world' s fastest-growing market in business aviation.

Exhibits: Aircraft interior, Aircraft maintenance and operations, Aircraft manufacturers, Aircraft market sales, Management and related services, Airframe and aircraft components, Airports and airport operations, Private jet operators, FBOs, Business and financial services, Education training, Electronics Avionics and instrumentation, Engines and propellers, Flight planning and navigation, Ground operations, Industry organizations, In-flight products and services, Publications Safety, security and emergency preparation, Tools and test equipment, Transportation services.

Organizer: Reed Exhibitions

☆11

2011/03/21-24

☎ 852-1830 668

🖷 852-2824 0249

✉ hktdc@hktdc.org

www.hktdc.com/hkfilmart

HKTDC

Hong Kong International Film & TV Market (FILMART)

香港國際影視展

香港贸发局香港国际影视展

地点： 香港会议展览中心，香港

内容： 电影、电视节目、动画、数码娱乐、有关产品及服务

上届规模 2010： 展出面积13,684平方米，参展商548家

主办： 香港贸易发展局

地址： 香港湾仔港湾道1号会展广场办公大楼38楼

HKTDC Hong Kong International Film & TV Market (FILMART)

Venue: Hong Kong Convention & Exhibition Center, Hong Kong

Profile: Movies, TV programmes, animation, digital entertainment, related products & services.

Statistics 2010: Gross Area 13,684m^2, Exhibitors 548

Organizer: Hong Kong Trade Development Council

Address: 38/F, Office Tower, Convention Plaza, 1 Harbour Road, Wan Chai, Hong Kong

☆12
2010/03/30 - 04/01
☎ 852-2827 6211
🖷 852-3749 7346
✉ sales@aplf.com
www.mmt.aplf.com

亚太区皮革展 – 原料及制造技术展(APLF–MMT)

地点：　香港会议展览中心, 香港
内容：　全球皮革业每年一度的盛会。建基於香港，是皮革相关行业中最具国际性的集中地，也是时尚界专业人士不可错过的采购平台。亚太区皮革展 - 原料及制造技术展与一如以往，将与“时尚汇集”及“国际服装业高峰论坛”同期举行。
产品种类　皮革；化工；机械；配件等皮革原料;生产技术/品质认证及检测、其他服务。
周期：　每年一届
市场范围：　国际性
展览性质：　面向贸易观众
上届规模 2010：　贸易观众17,907人来自88个国家及地区
主办：　亚太区皮革展有限公司

APLF-MM&T

APLF - Materials, Manufacturing & Technology
Asia Pacific Leather Fair – Materials ,Manufacturing and Technology
Venue: Hong Kong Convention and Exhibition Center, Hong Kong
Profile: the annual premier event for the global leather industry. Based in Hong Kong, the fair serves as the most international hub for the leather-related business and a must-attend buying platform for fashion professionals. Raw Materials; Synthetic /Textiles; Chemicals & Dyes; Tanning & Footwear Machinery; Components & Accessories; Technology, Testing Laboratories and Other Services
Frequency: Annual
Market Area: International
Nature: Trade only
Statistics 2010: Trade Visitors 17,907 came from 88 countires
Organizer: APLF Limited

☆13
2011/03/30- 04/01
☎ 852-2827 6211
🖷 852-2827 7831
✉ sales@aplf.com
www.fashionaccess.aplf.com

时尚汇集春季展

地点：　香港会议展览中心, 香港
内容：　以其国际参展商的全方位品质和“从头到脚”的时尚系列的时尚汇集吸引众多买家，比去年三月份多出18%。作为国际主要的时尚展会，时尚汇集的核心优势亦同时得到了证明，七成的买家来自国外，来自意大利和法国的来自日本、韩国、中国的亚洲买家同行进行切磋。
展品范围：　各类鞋类、箱包、手袋、皮带、钱包、皮衣、时尚配饰、传播媒介及其他
周期：　每年两届
市场范围：　国际性
展览性质：　仅向贸易观众开放
上届规模 2010：　买家33,272人比上届增加18%
主办：　亚太区皮革展有限公司（亚洲博闻有限公司和巴黎SIC SA公司的合资公司）

Fashion Access - Spring Show

Handbags/ Travelware/ Footwear/ Leather Garments and Fashion Accessories
Venue: Hong Kong Convention & Exhibition Center, Hong Kong
Profile: FASHION ACCESS is the must-attend international fashion fair for high quality, affordable bags and footwear, plus small leather goods, lifestyle accessories, apparel and more. The march fair showcases collections for the upcoming autumn-winter season, while the September fair focuses on spring-summer offerings.
Exhibitors' Profile: Bags & Leather Goods, Footwear, Apparel, Travelware, Fashion & Lifestyle Accessories, Components & Accessories.
Frequency: Biannual
Market Area: International
Nature: Trade only
Statistics 2010: Buyers 33,272
Organizer: APLF Limited

☆14
2011/03/30 - 04/01
☎ 852-2827 6211
🖷 852-2827 7831
✉ info@primesourceforum.com
www.primesourceforum.com

PRIME SOURCE FORUM HONG KONG
THE ANNUAL MEETING PLACE FOR THE APPAREL INDUSTRY

国际服装业高峰论坛

地点： 香港会议展览中心，香港
内容： 与会代表之业务领域：服装，纺织品，零件和附件，服装加工，相关的技术及设备，产品生命周期管理，物流及供应链管理、设计、咨询、金融服务、法律服务、出版、联会及政府组织、教育机构。
与会代表： 学术界，品牌商，顾问，金融界、投资银行服务，行业协会，法律专业人士，厂商，零售商、连锁店、百货公司，商贸组织或政府官员，批发商，代理人，商行
周期： 每年一届
市场范围： 国际性
主办： 亚太区皮革展有限公司（亚洲博闻有限公司和巴黎SIC SA公司的合资公司）

Prime Source Forum

Venue: Hong Kong Convention & Exhibition Center, Hong Kong
Profile: Delegate business sectors: Apparel, Textile and fabrics, Components and Accessories, Garment Manufacturing-Related Technology & Equipment, Product Lifecycle Management, Logistics & Supply Chain Management, Design, Consultation, Financial Services, Legal Services, Press, Associations & Government Organisations, Educational Institutes
Delegate Profiles: Manufacturer, Wholesaler, Buying Agent, Trading Firm, Retailer, Chain Stores, Department Stores, Industrial Association Representative, Brand Owner, Consultant, Financial, Investment or Banking Service Provider, Legal Professional, Trade Organization Representative/Government Official, Academic
Frequency: Annual
Market Area: International
Nature: Trade only
Organizer: APLF Limited

☆15
2011/04/13-16
☎ 852-1830 668
🖷 852-2824 0249
✉ exhibitions@hktdc.org
www.hktdc.com/hkelectronicsfairse

HKTDC

Hong Kong Electronics Fair (Spring Edition)
香港春季電子產品展

香港贸发局香港春季电子产品展

地点： 香港会议展览中心，香港
内容： 品牌荟萃廊(品牌电子产品)、视听产品、数码影像产品、电子配件、电子游戏产品、电子制造服务、电子组件及生产技术、电子保健产品、家用电器、汽车电子及导航系统、办公室自动化及设备、个人电子产品、保安产品、检测和认证服务、电子产品保护／储存设备、电讯产品、商贸服务
上届规模 2010： 展出面积60,235平方米，参展商2,305家
主办： 香港贸易发展局
地址： 香港湾仔博览道1号香港会议展览中心博览商场13号展览事务部

HKTDC Hong Kong Electronics Fair (Spring Edition)

Venue: Hong Kong Convention & Exhibition Center, Hong Kong
Profile: Hall of fame (branded electronic products), audio & visual, digital imaging, electronic accessories, electronic gaming, electronic manufacturing services (EMS), electronic parts, components and production technology, healthcare electronics, home appliances, in-vehicle electronics & navigation systems, office automation & equipment, personal electronics, security products, testing and certification, protective & storage solutions for electronics, telecommunication products, trade services
Statistics 2010: Gross Area 60,235m^2, Exhibitors 2,305
Organizer: Hong Kong Trade Development Council
Address: Exhibitions Department, Unit 13, Expo Galleria, Hong Kong Convention and Exhibition Center, 1 Expo Drive, Wan Chai, Hong Kong

☆16
2011/04/13-16
☎ 852-1830 668
🖷 852-2824 0249
✉ exhibitions@hktdc.org
www.hktdc.com/ictexpo

HKTDC

International ICT Expo
國際資訊科技博覽

香港贸发局国际资讯科技博览
地点：香港会议展览中心，香港
内容：云端运算及开放源码、电讯、网络及无线方案、企业解决方案、电脑及周边产品、数码娱乐及多媒体、电子物流及零售科技、本土创意科技、资讯科技外包服务、智能电话、商贸服务
上届规模 2010：展出面积9,109平方米，参展商571家
主办：香港贸易发展局
地址：香港湾仔博览道1号香港会议展览中心博览商场13号展览事务部

HKTDC International ICT Expo
Venue: Hong Kong Convention & Exhibition Center, Hong Kong
Profile: Cloud computing & open source, telecom, networking & wireless technology, enterprise solutions, computer & peripherals, digital entertainment & multimedia, e-logistics & retail technologies, home-grown innovations, IT outsourcing, Smartphone, trade services
Statistics 2010: Gross Area 9,109m^2, Exhibitors 571
Organizer: Hong Kong Trade Development Council
Address: Exhibitions Department, Unit 13, Expo Galleria, Hong Kong Convention and Exhibition Center, 1 Expo Drive, Wan Chai, Hong Kong

☆17
2011/04/13-16
☎ 852-1830 668
🖷 852-2824 0249
✉ exhibitions@hktdc.org
www.hktdc.com/hklightingfairse

HKTDC

Hong Kong International Lighting Fair (Spring Edition)
香港國際春季燈飾展

香港贸发局香港国际春季灯饰展
地点：香港会议展览中心，香港
内容：商业照明、环保照明、家居照明、LED照明、户外灯饰、灯饰配件及零件、灯饰管理、设计及技术
上届规模 2010：展出面积8,917平方米，参展商381家
主办：香港贸易发展局
地址：香港湾仔博览道1号香港会议展览中心博览商场13号展览事务部

HKTDC Hong Kong International Lighting Fair (Spring Edition)
Venue: Hong Kong Convention & Exhibition Center, Hong Kong
Profile: Commercial lighting, green lighting, household lighting, LED lighting, outdoor lighting, lighting accessories, parts & components, lighting management, design & technology
Statistics 2010: Gross Area 8,917m^2, Exhibitors 381
Organizer: Hong Kong Trade Development Council
Address: Exhibitions Department, Unit 13, Expo Galleria, Hong Kong Convention and Exhibition Center, 1 Expo Drive, Wan Chai, Hong Kong

☆18
2011/04/20-23
☎ 852-1830 668
🖷 852-2824 0249
✉ exhibitions@hktdc.org
www.hktdc.com/hkhousewarefair

HKTDC

Hong Kong Houseware Fair
香港家庭用品展

香港贸发局香港家庭用品展
地点：香港会议展览中心，香港
内容：人造花饰、酒吧用具、浴室用具、美容及健身用品、蜡烛及香熏饰品、清洁用品、家具、园艺及户外用品、手工艺品、五金用具及自行装配产品、保健及个人护理产品、家居装饰品、厨具及厨房小器具、油画及艺术作品、宠物用品、长者用品、小型家庭电器、餐具、商贸服务
上届规模 2010：展出面积58,255平方米，参展商2,149家
主办：香港贸易发展局
地址：香港湾仔博览道1号香港会议展览中心博览商场13号展览事务部

HKTDC Hong Kong Houseware Fair
Venue: Hong Kong Convention & Exhibition Center, Hong Kong
Profile: Artificial flowers, bar accessories, bathroom accessories, beauty & fitness, candles & scent sensation, cleaning & supplies, furniture, gardening & outdoor accessories, handicrafts, hardware & DIY products, health & personal care items, home decorations, kitchenware and gadgets, paintings & objets d' Art, pet supplies, silver generation products, small electrical appliances, tableware, trade services
Statistics 2010: Gross Area 58,255m^2, Exhibitors 2,149
Organizer: Hong Kong Trade Development Council
Address: Exhibitions Department, Unit 13, Expo Galleria, Hong Kong Convention and Exhibition Center, 1 Expo Drive, Wan Chai, Hong Kong

☆19
2011/04/20-23
☎ 852-1830 668
🖷 852-2824 0249
✉ exhibitions@hktdc.org
www.hktdc.com/hkhometextilesfair

Hong Kong International Home Textiles Fair
香港國際家用紡織品展

香港贸发局香港国际家用纺织品展

地点： 香港会议展览中心，香港
内容： 浴室纺织品、寝室纺织品、地毡及铺地制品、家居饰品、餐桌及厨房纺织品、铺墙制品、婴儿纺织品、家用纺织相关产品、设计及贸易服务
上届规模 2010： 展出面积5,671平方米，参展商243家
主办： 香港贸易发展局
地址： 香港湾仔博览道1号香港会议展览中心博览商场13号展览事务部

HKTDC Hong Kong International Home Textiles Fair

Venue: Hong Kong Convention & Exhibition Center, Hong Kong
Profile: Bathroom textiles, bedroom textiles, carpet & floor coverings, interior & décor, table & kitchen textiles, wall coverings, baby textiles, home textile related products, design & trade services
Statistics 2010: Gross Area 5,671m^2, Exhibitors 243
Organizer: Hong Kong Trade Development Council
Address: Exhibitions Department, Unit 13, Expo Galleria, Hong Kong Convention and Exhibition Center, 1 Expo Drive, Wan Chai, Hong Kong

☆20
2011/04/27-30
☎ 852-1830 668
🖷 852-2824 0249
✉ exhibitions@hktdc.org
www.hktdc.com/hkgiftspremiumfair

HKTDC
Hong Kong Gifts & Premium Fair
香港禮品及贈品展

香港贸发局香港礼品及赠品展

地点： 香港会议展览中心，香港
内容： 宣传赠品及赠品、公司礼品、时尚首饰及饰品、小型摆设及装饰品、综合礼品、绿色礼品、行李及旅游用品、包装产品、派对及节庆用品/新婚贺礼及用品、个人及健康礼品、画框及相架、文具及纸品、科技礼品、玩具及体育用品、雨伞及户外用品、钟表、商贸服务
上届规模 2010： 展出面积88,143平方米，参展商4,016家
主办： 香港贸易发展局
地址： 香港湾仔博览道1号香港会议展览中心博览商场13号展览事务部

HKTDC Hong Kong Gifts & Premium Fair

Venue: Hong Kong Convention & Exhibition Center, Hong Kong
Profile: Advertising gifts & premium, corporate gifts, fashion jewellery & accessories, figurines & decorations, general gift items, green gifts, luggage & travel goods, packaging, party & festive items/wedding favours, personal & well-being gifts, pictures & photo frames, stationery & paper, tech gifts, toys & sporting goods, umbrella and outdoor goods, watches & clocks, trade services
Statistics 2010: Gross Area 88,143m^2, Exhibitors 4,016
Organizer: Hong Kong Trade Development Council
Address: Exhibitions Department, Unit 13, Expo Galleria, Hong Kong Convention and Exhibition Center, 1 Expo Drive, Wan Chai, Hong Kong

☆21
2011/04/27-30
☎ 852-1830 668
🖷 852-2824 0249
✉ exhibitions@hktdc.org
www.hkprintpackfair.com

香港国际印刷及包装展

地点： 香港亚洲国际博览馆，香港
内容： 印刷服务、包装服务、印刷耗材、包装材料及配件、印刷及包装机械及设备、书刊印刷、印前处理、图像及设计服务、整饰及纸品加工服务、多谋体印刷科技及服务、电脑喷画及广告牌印刷服、设备及配件、机器设备维修及保养服务、咨询及培训服务
上届规模 2010： 展出面积6,480平方米，参展商263家
主办： 香港贸易发展局，华港国际展览有限公司
地址： 香港湾仔博览道1号香港会议展览中心博览商场13号展览事务部

Hong Kong International Printing & Packaging Fair

Venue: AsiaWorld-Expo, Hong Kong
Profile: Printing services, packaging services, printing consumables, packaging materials & accessories, printing & packaging equipment & systems, book printing, pre-press services, graphic arts and design services, finishing & converting services, multimedia technologies and services, inkjet printing & signage production services, equipment & accessories, equipment repair and maintenance services, consultancy and training services
Statistics 2010: Gross Area 6,480m^2, Exhibitors 263
Organizer: Hong Kong Trade Development Council, CIEC Exhibition Company (HK) Ltd.
Address: Exhibitions Department, Unit 13, Expo Galleria, Hong Kong Convention and Exhibition Center, 1 Expo Drive, Wan Chai, Hong Kong

☆22
2011/06/21 – 24
☎ 852-2585 6179, 2516 1677
📠 852-3749 7542
✉ salesafj-hk@ubm.com
www.asiafja.com

六月亚洲时尚首饰及配饰展
地点：香港会议展览中心，香港
内容：亚洲区内唯一以时尚首饰及配饰为主题的商贸展会。自1998年创办以来一直深得参展商及买家支持，规模不断扩充。展出的时尚首饰及配饰包括非贵金属首饰、珠子首饰、水晶首饰、方晶锆石首饰、莱茵石首饰、玻璃首饰、塑料首饰、发饰及时尚首饰物料等。
六月亚洲时尚首饰及配饰展与六月香港珠宝首饰展览会同步举行。
周期：每年三届(三月、六月、九月)
市场范围：国际性
性质：只对贸易观众开放
上届规模 2009：展商总数430家（来自18国家），贸易买家4,200人（来自83个国家）
主办：亚洲博闻有限公司

Asia's Fashion Jewellery & Accessories Fair - June
Venue: Hong Kong Convention and Exhibition Center, Hong Kong
Profile: Asia's Fashion Jewellery & Accessories Fair (AFJ) is the only international trade event dedicated to fashion jewellery and accessories industry in Asia. The Fair has received enormous support from exhibitors and visitors, and had been expanding in size since its inception in 1998. Products on display included base metal jewellery, bead jewellery, crystal jewellery, cubic zirconia jewellery, rhinestone jewellery, glass jewellery, plastic jewellery, hair accessories and fashion jewellery materials etc.
Frequency: Three times a year (March, June, September)
Market Area: International
Nature: Trade only
Statistics ‘09: Exhibitors 430 (came from 18 countries）, buyers 4,200 (came from 83 countries)
Organizer: UBM Asia Ltd

☆23
2011/06/23 -26
☎ 852-2516 1677, 2585 6179
📠 852-3749 7542
✉ salesjgf-hk@ubm.com
www.jewellerynetasia.com

六月香港珠宝首饰展览会
地点：香港会议展览中心，香港
内容：大会逐步发展成为亚洲三大珠宝展之一。大会特设多个主题展区，方便买家选购心仪产品。除尊贵展区和香港艺粹馆外，其他专题展区包括名贵珠宝首饰、钻石、珍珠、宝石，还有银饰、包装、工具和仪器展区，以及翡翠廊。
产品类别：珠宝首饰，宝石，珍珠，钻石，银及银饰，设备及包装，其它。
周期：每年一届
市场范围：国际性
上届规模 2010：展览面积40,000m^2，展商总数1,283家（来自31国家），贸易观众19,094人(海外观众9,950人来自100个国家和地区)
主办：亚洲博闻有限公司

June Hong Kong Jewellery & Gem Fair
Venue: Hong Kong Convention and Exhibition Center, Hong Kong
Profile: Wide range of products from fine finished jewellery, polished diamonds and gemstones, to all varieties of pearls, jewellery timepieces, packaging, displays, as well as jewellery-making equipment, tools and machinery.
Frequency: Annual
Market Area: International
Statistics 2010: Exhibition Area 40,000m^2, Exhibitors 1,283 (came from 31 countries）, Trade Visitors 19,094 came from 100 countires and regions
Organizer: UBM Asia Limited

☆24
2011/07/04-07
☎ 852-1830 668
🖷 852-2824 0249
✉ exhibitions@hktdc.org
www.hktdc.com/summersourcingshow

HKTDC

Summer Sourcing Show for Gifts, Houseware & Toys
香港夏季禮品、家庭用品及玩具展

香港贸发局香港夏季礼品、家庭用品及玩具展
地点：香港会议展览中心，香港
内容：设计服务、礼品及赠品、环保及家庭用品、家居电器、家居装饰品、玩具及游戏、节日及派对装饰品
上届规模 2010：展出面积8,671平方米，参展商409家
主办：香港贸易发展局
地址：香港湾仔博览道1号香港会议展览中心博览商场13号展览事务部

HKTDC Summer Sourcing Show for Gifts, Houseware & Toys
Venue: Hong Kong Convention & Exhibition Center, Hong Kong
Profile: Design service, gifts and premium, green gifts and houseware, home appliance, household products, home decorations, toys and games, festive and party items
Statistics 2010: Gross Area 8,671m^2, Exhibitors 409
Organizer: Hong Kong Trade Development Council
Address: Exhibitions Department, Unit 13, Expo Galleria, Hong Kong Convention and Exhibition Center, 1 Expo Drive, Wan Chai, Hong Kong

☆25
2011/07/04-07
☎ 852-1830 668
🖷 852-2824 0249
✉ exhibitions@hktdc.org
www.hktdc.com/hkfashionweekss

HKTDC

Hong Kong Fashion Week for Spring/Summer
香港時裝節春夏系列

香港贸发局香港时装节春夏系列
地点：香港会议展览中心，香港
内容：女装、男装、婴儿服装、运动服装、内衣、新娘礼服及晚礼服、泳衣、手袋、鞋、流行饰物、眼镜、布料及纱线、钮扣、唛头、时装杂志、专业商贸服务
上届规模2010：展出面积36,003平方米，参展商1,294家
主办：香港贸易发展局
地址：香港湾仔博览道1号香港会议展览中心博览商场13号展览事务部

HKTDC Hong Kong Fashion Week for Spring/Summer
Venue: Hong Kong Convention & Exhibition Center, Hong Kong
Profile: Ladies' wear, men's wear, babies and children's wear, sportswear, lingerie, bridal & evening wear, swimwear, handbags, shoes, costume jewellery, eyewear, fabrics & yarns, buttons, labels, fashion magazines, trade services
Statistics 2010: Gross Area 36,003m^2, Exhibitors 1,294
Organizer: Hong Kong Trade Development Council
Address: Exhibitions Department, Unit 13, Expo Galleria, Hong Kong Convention and Exhibition Center, 1 Expo Drive, Wan Chai, Hong Kong

☆26
2011/07/20-26
☎ 852-1830 668
🖷 852-2824 0249
✉ exhibitions@hktdc.org
www.hkbookfair.com

HKTDC

Hong Kong Book Fair
香港書展

香港贸发局香港书展
地点：香港会议展览中心，香港
内容：各类书籍及刊物、儿童及青少年图书、宗教书籍、电子学习资源: 电子书、电子阅读器、数码出版、视听教材、教育软件、多媒体产品、各类文具及印刷品
上届规模 2010：展出面积45,608平方米，参展商510家
主办：香港贸易发展局
地址：香港湾仔博览道1号香港会议展览中心博览商场13号展览事务部

HKTDC Hong Kong Book Fair
Venue: Hong Kong Convention & Exhibition Center, Hong Kong
Profile: Books and publications, children's and teen's books, religious books, e-learning resources: eBooks, eBook reader, digital publishing, audio-visual learning aids, educational software, multimedia products, stationery and printing products
Statistics 2010: Gross Area 45,608m^2, Exhibitors 510
Organizer: Hong Kong Trade Development Council
Address: Exhibitions Department, Unit 13, Expo Galleria, Hong Kong Convention and Exhibition Center, 1 Expo Drive, Wan Chai, Hong Kong

☆27
2011/08
☎ 852-1830 668
🖷 852-2824 0249
✉ exhibitions@hkteafair.org
www.hkteafair.com

香港国际茶展
地点： 香港会议展览中心，香港
内容： 各地名茶、加工茶、茶饮料、茶食品、各种茶相关加工产品、茶叶包装、茶叶机械及检测、茶具、茶业机构、茶叶技术、茶工ā品、茶叶媒体、茗茶之友(包括伴茶食品及茶食品等)
上届规模 2010： 展出面积9,128平方米，参展商315家
主办： 香港贸易发展局，中国茶文化国际交流协会
地址： 香港湾仔博览道1号香港会议展览中心博览商场13号展览事务部

Hong Kong International Tea Fair
Venue: Hong Kong Convention & Exhibition Center, Hong Kong
Profile: Tea, processed tea and tea product, tea packaging, tea processing equipment and testing service, tea ware, tea bar/organization, tea technology, tea craft, tea media, friends of tea (confectionery, bakery products, etc.)
Statistics 2010: Gross Area 9,128m^2, Exhibitors 315
Organizers: Hong Kong Trade Development Council, Chinese Tea Culture International Exchange Association
Address: Exhibitions Department, Unit 13, Expo Galleria, Hong Kong Convention and Exhibition Center, 1 Expo Drive, Wan Chai, Hong Kong

☆29
2011/08
☎ 852-1830 668
🖷 852-2824 0249
✉ exhibitions@hktdc.org
www.hktdc.com/icmcm

HKTDC
International Conference & Exhibition of the Modernization of Chinese Medicine & Health Products
國際現代化中醫藥及健康產品展覽會暨會議

国际现代化中医药及健康产品展览会暨会议
地点： 香港会议展览中心，香港
内容： 中药、保健食品、健康护理及疗法、原料、设备及相关服务、科研及开发、商会
上届规模 2010： 展出面积4,231平方米，参展商133家
主办： 香港贸易发展局
地址： 香港湾仔博览道1号香港会议展览中心博览商场13号展览事务部

International Conference & Exhibition of the Modernization of Chinese Medicine & Health Products
Venue: Hong Kong Convention & Exhibition Center, Hong Kong
Profile: Chinese medicine, health supplement, health care & therapy, raw material, equipment & related services, research & development, trade association
Statistics 2010: Gross Area 4,231m^2, Exhibitors 133
Organizer: Hong Kong Trade Development Council
Address: Exhibitions Department, Unit 13, Expo Galleria, Hong Kong Convention and Exhibition Center, 1 Expo Drive, Wan Chai, Hong Kong

☆28
2011/08/11-15
☎ 852-1830 668
🖷 852-2824 0249
✉ exhibitions@hktdc.org
www.hktdc.com/hkfoodexpo

HKTDC
Food Expo
美食博覽

香港贸发局美食博览
地点： 香港会议展览中心，香港
内容： 食品及饮品、厨具、食品包装、标签、物流及相关服务、食品处理产品、食品科技、机械及服务、政府机构及食品业商会
上届规模 2010： 展出面积31,784平方米，参展商741家
主办： 香港贸易发展局
地址： 香港湾仔博览道1号香港会议展览中心博览商场13号展览事务部

HKTDC Food Expo
Venue: Hong Kong Convention & Exhibition Center, Hong Kong
Profile: Food & beverage products, kitchenware, food packaging, labelling, safety & logistic products & services, food processing products, machinery & related services and government organizations & trade associations
Statistics 2010: Gross Area 31,784m^2, Exhibitors 741
Organizer: Hong Kong Trade Development Council
Address: Exhibitions Department, Unit 13, Expo Galleria, Hong Kong Convention and Exhibition Center, 1 Expo Drive, Wan Chai, Hong Kong

☆30
2011/09/07-11
☎ 852-1830 668
🖷 852-2824 0249
✉ exhibitions@hktdc.org
www.hktdc.com/hkwatchfair

HKTDC

Hong Kong Watch & Clock Fair
香港鐘表展

香港贸发局香港钟表展

地点：香港会议展览中心，香港
内容：品牌钟表、表及钟、配件及零件、设备、机械、包装用品、商贸服务
上届规模 2010：展出面积32,608平方米，参展商700家
主办：香港贸易发展局，香港表厂商会有限公司，香港钟表业总会有限公司
地址：香港湾仔博览道1号香港会议展览中心博览商场13号展览事务部

HKTDC Hong Kong Watch & Clock Fair

Venue: Hong Kong Convention & Exhibition Center, Hong Kong
Profile: Brand name watches & clocks, complete watches & clocks, parts & components, equipment, machinery, packaging, trade services
Statistics 2010: Gross Area 32,608m^2, Exhibitors 700
Organizers: Hong Kong Trade Development Council, Hong Kong Watch Manufacturers Association Ltd. The Federation of Hong Kong Watch Trades and Industries Ltd.
Address: Exhibitions Department, Unit 13, Expo Galleria, Hong Kong Convention and Exhibition Center, 1 Expo Drive, Wan Chai, Hong Kong

☆31
2011/09/19 - 22
☎ 852-2585 6179, 2516 1677
🖷 852-3749 7542
✉ salesafj-hk@ubm.com
www.asiafja.com

Asia's
Fashion Jewellery
& Accessories Fair
亞洲時尚首飾及配飾展
19 - 22 September 2011
二〇一一年九月十九至廿二日

九月亚洲时尚首饰及配饰展

地点：亚洲国际博览馆, 香港
内容：九月亚洲时尚首饰展公认为业界下半年度最瞩目的盛事，是接洽来年春夏季订 单的黄金机会。九月亚洲时尚首饰及配饰展，将与亚洲最大型的国际珠宝展及全球三 大珠宝展之一的九月香港珠宝首饰展览会同期举行。展品种类繁多，包括珠宝首饰、钻石、珍珠、宝石、珠宝钟表、相关设备、包装及科技等。
周期：每年三届（三月、六月、九月）
市场范围：国际性
展览性质：仅向贸易观众开放
上届规模 2010：展览面积11,000m^2, 展商总数370家（来自17国家）, 贸易观众5,104人(来自99个国家)
主办：亚洲博闻有限公司

Asia's Fashion Jewellery & Accessories Fair - September

Venue: Asia World – Expo, Hong Kong
Profile: Recognized as the leading event in the fashion jewellery and accessories industry for the second half of the year in Asia, Asia's Fashion Jewellery & Accessories Fair - September (9FJ) is an ideal platform for volume business to be done in preparation for the following Spring/Summer.
Products Profile: Fashion Jewellery, Fashion Jewellery Materials, Fashion Accessories
Frequency: Three times a year (March, June, September)
Market Area: International
Nature: Trade Only
Statistics 2010: Exhibition Area 11,000m^2, Exhibitors 370 came from 17 countries, Trade Visitors 5,104 came from 99 countries
Organizer: UBM Asia Limited

☆32
2011/09/19 - 23
☎ 852-2827 6211
🖷 852-2827 7831
✉ salesjwf@cmpasia.com
http://exhibitions.jewellerynetasia.com

九月香港珠宝首饰展览会
——裸钻、珍珠、有色宝石、工具设备及包装

地点： 亚洲国际博览馆, 香港
内容： 过去28年，九月香港珠宝首饰展览会不断推陈出新，致力为业界导航，2009年，九月展成为全球最大型珠宝展，也是香港展览史上最具规模的展览会，占用两大场馆。2011年，九月展将进一步扩充，亚洲国际博览馆展出部份由八个展馆增加至九个，连同香港会议展览中心的占地，九月展的总展览面积将达130,000平方米。
展品范围包括： 贵重成品首饰、已打磨钻石及有色宝石、不同类型的珍珠、首饰表、包装陈列用品，以及首饰制造设备、工具及机器。
周期： 每年一届
市场范围： 国际性
展览性质： 仅向贸易观众开放
上届规模 2010： 展览面积130,000m^2, 展商总数3,300家（来自45国家），贸易观众44,000人（来自135个国家和地区）
主办： 亚洲博闻有限公司

September Hong Kong Jewellery & Gem Fair
– Diamonds, Pearls, Gemstones, Tools, Equipment and Packaging

Venue: AsiaWorld-Expo, Hong Kong
Profile: The world' s number one fine jewellery event in 2009 and also the largest fair ever in terms of exhibition space – in any industry – in Hong Kong. The September Fair, which occupies two world-class venues, will further expand in 2011 from eight halls to nine halls in AsiaWorld-Expo (AWE), together with the Fair in the Hong Kong Convention & Exhibition Centre (HKCEC), the September Fair occupies a record 130,000 square metres of exhibition space.
Exhibits: Wide range of products from fine finished jewellery, polished diamonds and gemstones, to all varieties of pearls, jewellery timepieces, packaging, displays, as well as jewellery-making equipment, tools and machinery.
Frequency: Annual
Market Area: International
Nature: Trade only
Statistics 2010: Exhibition Area 130,000m^2, Exhibitors 3,300 (came from 45 countries）, Trade Visitors 44,000 came from 135 countries and regions
Organizer: UBM Asia Limited

☆33
2011/09/21 - 25
☎ 852-2827 6211
🖷 852-2827 7831
✉ salesjwf@cmpasia.com
http://exhibitions.jewellerynetasia.com

九月香港珠宝首饰展览会——珠宝首饰成品

地点： 香港会议展览中心, 香港
内容： 贵重成品首饰、已打磨钻石及有色宝石、不同类型的珍珠、首饰表、包装陈列用品，以及首饰制造设备、工具及机器。
周期： 每年一届
市场范围： 国际性
展览性质： 仅向贸易观众开放
上届规模 2010： 展览面积130,000m^2, 展商总数3,300家（来自45国家），贸易观众44,000人
主办： 亚洲博闻有限公司

September Hong Kong Jewellery & Gem Fair -

Venue: Hong Kong Convention and Exhibition Center, Hong Kong
Profile: Wide range of products from fine finished jewellery, polished diamonds and gemstones, to all varieties of pearls, jewellery timepieces, packaging, displays, as well as jewellery-making equipment, tools and machinery.
Frequency: Annual
Market Area: International
Nature: Trade only
Statistics 2010: Exhibition Area 130,000m^2, Exhibitors 3,300 (came from 45 countries), Trade Visitors 44,000
Organizer: UBM Asia Limited

☆34
2011/09/28-30
☎ 852-2827 6211
🖷 852-3749 7346
✉ salesf@aplf.com
www.fashionaccess.aplf.com

FASHION ACCESS

时尚汇集秋季展
——手袋、行李箱包、鞋类、皮衣、裘皮服装及时尚配饰展-秋季展(FAA)

地点：	香港会议展览中心，香港
内容：	“时尚汇集”是必须参加的国际性时尚配饰展，展品包括优质的手袋、鞋履，加上小型皮革制品、品味配饰、服装
周期：	每年两届
市场范围：	国际性
展览性质：	仅向贸易观众开放
上届规模 2010：	展商总数656家（来自22国家），买家14,000人
主办：	亚太区皮革展有限公司(由亚洲博闻有限公司及SIC集团合资)

Fashion Access - Autumn Show
- Handbags/ Travelware/ Footwear/ Leather Garments and Fashion Accessories

Venue:	Hong Kong Convention & Exhibition Center, Hong Kong
Profile:	FASHION ACCESS is the twice-a-year, must-attend international fashion fair in Hong Kong for bags, footwear, leather goods, garments and a full range of lifestyle accessories.
Frequency:	Biannual
Market Area:	International
Nature:	Trade only
Statistics 2010:	Exhibitors 656 (came from 22 countries），Buyers 14,000
Organizer:	APLF Limited (JV with CMP Asia Ltd. & SIC Group)

☆35
2011/10/13-16
☎ 852-1830 668
🖷 852-2824 0249
✉ exhibitions@hktdc.org
www.hktdc.com/hkelectronicsfairae

HKTDC
Hong Kong Electronics Fair (Autumn Edition)
香港秋季電子產品展

香港贸发局香港秋季电子产品展

地点：	香港会议展览中心，香港
内容：	品牌荟萃廊(品牌电子产品)、视听产品、电脑及周边产品、数码影像产品、电子配件、电子游戏产品、家用电器、电子保健产品、汽车电子及导航系统、办公室自动化及设备、个人电子产品、保安产品、电讯产品、商贸服务
上届规模 2010：	展出面积78,300平方米，参展商2,988家
主办：	香港贸易发展局
地址：	香港湾仔博览道1号香港会议展览中心博览商场13号展览事务部

HKTDC Hong Kong Electronics Fair (Autumn Edition)

Venue:	Hong Kong Convention & Exhibition Center, Hong Kong
Profile:	Hall of fame (branded electronic products), audio visual products, computer & peripherals, digital imaging, electronic accessories, electronic gaming, home appliances, healthcare electronics, in-vehicle electronics and navigation systems, office automation, personal electronics, security products, telecommunications products, trade services
Statistics 2010:	Gross Area 78,300m^2, Exhibitors 2,988
Organizer:	Hong Kong Trade Development Council
Address:	Exhibitions Department, Unit 13, Expo Galleria, Hong Kong Convention and Exhibition Center, 1 Expo Drive, Wan Chai, Hong Kong

☆36
2011/10/13-16
☎ 852-1830 668
🖷 852-2824 0249
✉ exhibitions@hktdc.org
www.electronicasia.com

electronicAsia
國際電子組件及生產技術展

国际电子组件及生产技术展

地点：	香港会议展览中心，香港
内容：	电子科技、元器件、组件、显示技术、太阳能光伏电子技术
上届规模 2010：	展出面积12,119平方米，参展商606家
主办：	香港贸易发展局
地址：	香港湾仔博览道1号香港会议展览中心博览商场13号展览事务部

electronicAsia

Venue:	Hong Kong Convention & Exhibition Center, Hong Kong
Profile:	Electronic components, assemblies, electronics production, display technologies, photovoltaic technology
Statistics 2010:	Gross Area 12,119m^2, Exhibitors 606
Organizer:	Hong Kong Trade Development Council
Address:	Exhibitions Department, Unit 13, Expo Galleria, Hong Kong Convention and Exhibition Center, 1 Expo Drive, Wan Chai, Hong Kong

☆37
2011/10/27-30
☎ 852-1830 668
🖷 852-2824 0249
✉ exhibitions@hktdc.org
www.hktdc.com/hklightingfairae

HKTDC

Hong Kong International Lighting Fair (Autumn Edition)
香港國際秋季燈飾展

香港贸发局香港国际秋季灯饰展

地点：香港会议展览中心，香港
内容：LED及环保照明、家居照明、商业照明、户外照明、灯饰配件及零件、灯饰管理、设计及技术
上届规模 2010：展出面积66,803平方米，参展商2,028家
主办：香港贸易发展局
地址：香港湾仔博览道1号香港会议展览中心博览商场13号展览事务部

HKTDC Hong Kong International Lighting Fair (Autumn Edition)

Venue: Hong Kong Convention & Exhibition Center, Hong Kong
Profile: LED & green lighting, household lighting, commercial lighting, outdoor lighting, lighting accessories, parts & components, lighting management, design & technology
Statistics 2010: Gross Area 66,803m^2, Exhibitors 2,028
Organizer: Hong Kong Trade Development Council
Address: Exhibitions Department, Unit 13, Expo Galleria, Hong Kong Convention and Exhibition Center, 1 Expo Drive, Wan Chai, Hong Kong

☆38
2011/10/27-29
☎ 852-1830 668
🖷 852-2824 0249
✉ exhibitions@hktdc.org
www.sportssource-asia.com

亚洲运动用品展

地点：亚洲国际博览馆，香港
内容：球类运动装备、自行车运动用品、运动服装布料／物料、健身及健美器材、高尔夫球用品、室内运动、户外运动及休闲用品、球拍运动、滚轴及滑板用品、体育防护配件、运动鞋、运动用品店装置及设备、运动服装及配件、田径运动、水上运动、冰上运动、期刊及服务、运动用品贸易组织、其他
上届规模 2010：展出面积5,680平方米，参展商194家
主办：香港贸易发展局，慕尼黑国际博览亚洲有限公司
地址：香港湾仔博览道1号香港会议展览中心博览商场13号展览事务部

Sports Source Asia

Venue: AsiaWorld-Expo, Hong Kong
Profile: Ball game equipment, cycling, fabrics & materials for sportswear, fitness & gymnastic training equipment, golf equipment & supplies, indoor sports, outdoor sports, racket sports, skating & skateboarding supplies, sports safety & protection gear, sports shoes, sports shop fittings & equipment, sportswear & accessories, track & field sports, water sports, winter sports, publications & services, sporting goods trade organizations
Statistics 2010: Gross Area 5,680m^2, Exhibitors 194
Organizers: Hong Kong Trade Development Council, MMI Asia Pte Ltd
Address: Exhibitions Department, Unit 13, Expo Galleria, Hong Kong Convention and Exhibition Center, 1 Expo Drive, Wan Chai, Hong Kong

☆39
2011/10
☎ 852-1830 668
🖷 852-2824 0249
✉ exhibitions@hktdc.org
www.hktdc.com/hkbdh

HKTDC
Hong Kong International Building and Decoration Materials & Hardware Fair
香港國際建築裝飾材料及五金展

香港贸发局香港国际建筑装饰材料及五金展

地点：亚洲国际博览馆，香港
内容：卫浴/厨房、建筑装饰五金、建筑科技、天花/幕墙、陶瓷/石材、涂料/化学建材、门窗、家居/办公室及户外设备、环保建材、室内装饰材料、检测及认证
上届规模 2010：展出面积5,680平方米，参展商176家
主办：香港贸易发展局
地址：香港湾仔博览道1号香港会议展览中心博览商场13号展览事务部

HKTDC Hong Kong International Building and Decoration Materials & Hardware Fair

Venue: AsiaWorld-Expo, Hong Kong
Profile: Bathroom & kitchen; building & decorative hardware; building technology; ceiling & curtain wall; ceramics, stone & marble; coating & chemicals; door & window; home, office and outdoor accessories; green building; indoor decorative materials; testing, inspection & certification
Statistics 2010: Gross Area 5,680m^2, Exhibitors 176
Organizer: Hong Kong Trade Development Council
Address: Exhibitions Department, Unit 13, Expo Galleria, Hong Kong Convention and Exhibition Center, 1 Expo Drive, Wan Chai, Hong Kong

☆40
2011/10/27-30
☎ 852-1830 668
🖷 852-2824 0249
✉ exhibitions@hktdc.org
www.ecoexpoasia.com

国际环保博览
地点： 亚洲国际博览馆，香港
内容： 空气质素、能源效益及能源、废物处理及循环再造、环保产品
上届规模 2010： 展出面积9,950平方米，参展商266家
主办： 香港贸易发展局，法兰克福展览(香港)有限公司
地址： 香港湾仔博览道1号香港会议展览中心博览商场13号展览事务部

Eco Expo Asia –
International Trade Fair on Environmental Protection
Venue: AsiaWorld-Expo, Hong Kong
Profile: Air quality , energy efficiency & energy, waste & recycling, eco-friendly product
Statistics 2010: Gross Area 9,950m^2, Exhibitors 266
Organizers: Hong Kong Trade Development Council, Messe Frankfurt (HK) Ltd.
Address: Exhibitions Department, Unit 13, Expo Galleria, Hong Kong Convention and Exhibition Center, 1 Expo Drive, Wan Chai, Hong Kong

☆41
2011/11/03-05
☎ 852-1830 668
🖷 852-2824 0249
✉ exhibitions@hktdc.org
www.hktdc.com/hkmedicalfair

香港贸发局香港国际医疗器材及用品展
地点： 香港会议展览中心，香港
内容： 意外及急救设备、建筑科技及医院家具、中医设备、通讯、系统及资讯科技、牙科设备及用品、诊断工具及仪器、电子医疗设备／医疗科技、化验室设备、医疗设备部件及物料、医疗用品及消耗用品、物理治疗／整形外科／复健技术及设备、医疗纺织品
上届规模 2010： 展出面积4,144平方米，参展商140家
主办： 香港贸易发展局
地址： 香港湾仔博览道1号香港会议展览中心博览商场13号展览事务部

HKTDC Hong Kong International Medical Devices and Supplies Fair
Venue: Hong Kong Convention & Exhibition Center, Hong Kong
Profile: Accident and emergency equipment, building technology and hospital furniture, Chinese medical devices, communication, systems and information technology, dental equipment and supplies, diagnostics, electro-medical equipment/medical technology, laboratory equipment, medical components and materials, medical supplies and disposables, physiotherapy / orthopaedic / rehabilitation technology, textiles
Statistics 2010: Gross Area 4,144m^2, Exhibitors 140
Organizer: Hong Kong Trade Development Council
Address: Exhibitions Department, Unit 13, Expo Galleria, Hong Kong Convention and Exhibition Center, 1 Expo Drive, Wan Chai, Hong Kong

☆42
2011/11/03-05
☎ 852-1830 668
🖷 852-2824 0249
✉ exhibitions@hktdc.org
www.hktdc.com/hkwinefair

HKTDC
Hong Kong International Wine & Spirits Fair
香港國際美酒展

香港贸发局香港国际美酒展
地点： 香港会议展览中心，香港
内容： 含酒精饮品、酒业服务、酒类配件及器具、美酒之友
上届规模 2010： 展出面积16,114平方米，参展商680家
主办： 香港贸易发展局
地址： 香港湾仔博览道1号香港会议展览中心博览商场13号展览事务部

HKTDC Hong Kong International Wine & Spirits Fair
Venue: Hong Kong Convention & Exhibition Center, Hong Kong
Profile: Liquor & beverage products, wine services, wine accessories & equipment, friends of wine
Statistics 2010: Gross Area 16,114m^2, Exhibitors 680
Organizer: Hong Kong Trade Development Council
Address: Exhibitions Department, Unit 13, Expo Galleria, Hong Kong Convention and Exhibition Center, 1 Expo Drive, Wan Chai, Hong Kong

☆43
2011/11/03-05
☎ 852-1830 668
🖷 852-2824 0249
✉ exhibitions@hktdc.org
www.hktdc.com/hkopticalfair

HKTDC
Hong Kong Optical Fair
香港眼鏡展

香港贸发局香港眼镜展
地点：　香港会议展览中心，香港
内容：　隐形眼镜、镜框及镜架、镜片、眼镜配件、护目镜、运动眼镜、太阳眼镜、视光仪器、眼镜盒及眼镜袋、相关之机械及技术、相关之化学原料、相关之包装物料、相关之服务及专业刊物、零售及店铺设计、陈列设备及技术
上届规模 2010：　展出面积25,009平方米，参展商584家
主办：　香港贸易发展局
地址：　香港湾仔博览道1号香港会议展览中心博览商场13号展览事务部

HKTDC Hong Kong Optical Fair
Venue: Hong Kong Convention & Exhibition Center, Hong Kong
Profile: Contact lenses, frames & mountings, lenses, parts & accessories, safety eyewear, sportswear, sunglasses, optometric instruments, spectacle cases & holders, related equipment & technology, related chemical & materials, related packaging materials, related services and publications, retail & shop design, equipment & technology
Statistics 2010: Gross Area 25,009m^2, Exhibitors 584
Organizer: Hong Kong Trade Development Council
Address: Exhibitions Department, Unit 13, Expo Galleria, Hong Kong Convention and Exhibition Center, 1 Expo Drive, Wan Chai, Hong Kong

☆44
2011/11/09-11
☎ 852-2827 6211
🖷 852-3749 7345, 3749 7310
✉ cosmasia-hk@ubm.com
www.cosmoprof-asia.com
中国内地
☎ 020 8666 0158
🖷 020 8667 2235, 8667 7120
✉ info-china@ubm.com

COSMOPROF
ASIA HONG KONG
亞太區美容展

亚太区美容展
地点：　香港会议展览中心, 香港
内容：　亚太区美容展是亚洲领先b2b专业美容贸易展览。展馆划分为5个主题展区—零 售分销(香水、化妆品及护肤品)、包装、美容院、美发及天然保健，让参观者尽览美容及身心健康产业的最新潮流、产品及尖端技术。国家及团体展馆强势列阵，展现环球美 容趋势，突显国际氛围，成为展会ā目亮点。除产品展览外，3天的展会期间将举办各类特备节目，让参加者与同业及客户聚首交流，同时可建立新业务联系，发掘商机。
周期：　每年一届
市场范围：　国际性
展览性质：　仅向贸易观众开放
上届规模：　展览面积57,400m^2, 展商总数1,633家（来自34国家），贸易观众45,100人
主办：　亚太区美容展有限公司（由亚洲博闻有限公司与BolognaFiere合办）

Cosmoprof Asia
Venue: Hong Kong Convention and Exhibition Center, Hong Kong
Profile: The most prestigious and trendsetting beauty event in Asia that offers unique business chances in the entire region. The most complete showcase for every facets of the beauty and health industry.
Exhibits Sectors: Retail, Natural health, Pack, Beauty Salon, Hair salon.
Frequency: Annual
Market Area: International
Nature: Trade only
Statistics: Exhibition Area 57,400m^2, Exhibitors 1,633 (came from 34 countries) , Trade Visitors 45,200
Organizer: Cosmoprof Asia Ltd. (JV by CMP Asia and BolognaFiere)

☆45
2011/12
☎ 852-1830 668
🖷 852-2824 0249
✉ hktdc@hktdc.org
www.hktdc.com/worldsmeexpo

HKTDC
World SME Expo
國際中小企博覽

香港贸发局国际中小企博览
地点：　香港会议展览中心，香港
内容：　一站式国际商贸平台，提供中小企业支援服务及环球商机：中国及海外市场商机、中国商务策略、企业顾问、市场推广、理财融资、电子商贸、法律、会计、创业营商、特许经营商机、商业资讯及支援机构
上届规模 2009：　展出面积10,386平方米，参展商323家
主办：　香港贸易发展局
地址：　香港湾仔港湾道一号会展广场办公大楼38字楼

HKTDC World SME Expo

Venue: Hong Kong Convention & Exhibition Center, Hong Kong

Profile: A one-stop international marketplace for SMEs, providing business solutions and market opportunities: China and overseas opportunities, China trade strategies, corporate management consultancy and marketing services, financial services, IT and e-Business, legal and accounting, new start-up and franchising, business intelligence, institutional support

Statistics 2009: Gross Area 10,386m^2, Exhibitors 323

Organizer: Hong Kong Trade Development Council

Address: 38/F, Office Tower, Convention Plaza, 1 Harbour Road, Wan Chai, Hong Kong

☆46
2011/12/01-03
☎ 852-1830 668
🖷 852-2824 0249
✉ hktdc@hktdc.org
www.hktdc.com/innodesigntechexpo

HKTDC
Inno Design Tech Expo
創新科技及設計博覽

香港贸发局创新科技及设计博览

地点：香港会议展览中心，香港

内容：“创新科技及设计博览”是创意及科技业界发掘生意契机、物色合适商贸伙伴的理想平台。

上届规模 2009：展出面积15,004平方米，参展商345家

主办：香港贸易发展局

地址：香港湾仔港湾道一号会展广场办公大楼38字楼

HKTDC Inno Design Tech Expo

Venue: Hong Kong Convention & Exhibition Center, Hong Kong

Profile: Inno Design Tech Expo (IDT Expo) provides a unique platform for creative and technology professionals to exchange ideas and explore business opportunities.

Statistics 2009: Gross Area 15,004m^2, Exhibitors 345

Organizer: Hong Kong Trade Development Council

Address: 38/F, Office Tower, Convention Plaza, 1 Harbour Road, Wan Chai, Hong Kong

中国澳门展览会议

Exhibitions in Macao China

2011/06/07 - 09
☎ 010-5933 9288
🖷 010-5933 9233
✉ liang.wang@reedexpo.com.cn
www.G2EAsia.com

global gaming expo
G2E ASIA

亚洲全球博彩业博览会

地点：	澳门威尼斯人度假村Cotai Strip会展中心
内容：	亚洲全球博彩业博览会是亚洲博彩市场的首要行业展会兼研讨会。展会集中展现亚洲博彩行业的迅猛发展、最新产品及最新潮流，吸引优质买家，且创造亚太地区博彩业最好的互联氛围。作为全球博彩业博览会（G2E）系列展会的一部分，亚洲全球博彩业博览会是来自博彩行业且专为博彩行业主办的展会。
产品及服务：	博彩行业各方面的产品及服务，包括赌场管理、电子游戏及设备、博彩软件、老虎机、桌上博彩及附件、电子博彩机、安保及监视、网络博彩等。
周期：	每年一届
参展费用：	标准展位445美元/m²，光地展位395美元/m²
上届规模 2009：	展览面积6,261m²，参展商135家，专业贸易观众4,304人）
主办：	励展香港国内公司
地址：	励展博览集团国际销售部（中国），北京市朝阳区新源南路1-3号平安国际金融中心A座15层01-03,05 （100027）

www.reedexport.cn

G2E Asia : The Premier Gaming Trade Show & Conference

- The Premier Gaming Trade Show & Conference

Venue:	Cotai Strip® CotaiExpo™, The Venetian®
Profile:	G2E Asia is the event for the Asian gaming and the best place to help you succeed in this rapidly growing and dynamic industry. Join us in June as casino-entertainment professionals from Asia and around the globe will gather in Macau—a world-class destination.
Frequency:	Annual
Participation Fee:	Standard Booth USD 445/m², Raw Space USD 395/m²
Statistics 2009:	Net Area 6,261m², Exhibitors 135, Visitors 4,304
Organizer:	Reed Exhibitions Hong Kong

2011/11-
☎ 010-8260 6881, 6891
6893, 6874
🖷 010-8260 6883, 8260 6790
✉ exhibition@cnaico.com.cn
www.autochina.com.cn

2011年澳门国际汽车展览会

地点：	澳门
联络：	中国汽车工业国际合作总公司
地址：	北京市海淀区中关村丹棱街3号A座国机大厦（100080）
联系人：	马蓉，刘岩，娄杰，杨菁

2011/11/02-04
☎ 010-6590 7766 转ext 715
🖷 010-6590 6139
✉ g.pan@koelnmesse.cn
www.wineandgourmetasia.cn

亚洲美食佳酿暨酒店及餐饮设备展

地点：	澳门威尼斯人会议展览中心
内容：	亚洲美食佳酿暨酒店及餐饮设备展是亚洲地区唯一致力于国际精制食品与高级葡萄酒，酒店与餐饮设备及供应与服务行业的专业展览会。同期举办丰富活动，是美食主义者的盛会
主要展品：	酒店设备与服务、葡萄酒和烈酒、食品和饮料
周期：	每年一届
性质：	仅对专业贸易观众开放
上届规模：	展览面积7,000m²，参展商100家（来自11个国家），贸易观众7,163人
主办：	科隆展览国际有限公司
地址：	北京市东三环北路8号亮马河大厦2座1018室（100004）
联系人：	潘容

Wine & Gourmet Asia

Venue:	Cotai Strip® CotaiExpo™, The Venetian®
Frequency:	Annual
Nature:	Trade Only
Statistics 2010:	Exhibition Area 7,000m², Exhibitors 100, Buyers 7,163
Organizer:	Koelnmesse
Contact:	Grace Pan

台湾展览信息

Exhibitions in Taiwan

2011/06/24 - 26
☎ 886-2-2595-4212
🖷 886-2-2595-5726
✉ cynthiayen@kaigo.com.tw
www.homelifestyle.com.tw

居家生活时尚展

地点：台湾台北世界贸易中心
内容：台湾唯一以高档次居家生活为主轴的B2C展会。内容涵盖八大展区：SPA美容香氛区、起居用品区、烹调/厨房用品区、生活家电区、创意摆饰礼品区、休闲/健身区、园艺户外区、孩童宠物区，是注重品味生活的台湾消费者不可错过的年度盛会。
始办年份：2008
周期：每年一届
市场范围：地区性
性质：面向公众
入场券价格：新台币100元
参展费用：新台币40,000～45,000元
主办：开国有限公司
地址：台北市10461 德惠街9号8楼之3（10461）
联系人：颜慧娟，蔡郁洁

Home & Life Style Fair

Venue: Taiwan World Trade Center (TWTC)
Profile: The only one high-quality lifestyle show in Taiwan. Eight topics in exhibition: SPA & Fragrance, Home Living Products, Gourmet & Kitchenware , Home Electronics, Décor & Gift, Leisure & Fitness, Gardening & Outdoor, Kids & Pets.
Established Year: 2008
Frequency: Annual
Market Area: Regional
Nature: Open to public
Cost to Attend: NTD 100
Participated Fee: NTD 40,000-45,000
Organizer: Kaigo Co Ltd
Address: 8th Fl.-3, 9 Dehuei Street, Taipei 104, Taiwan
Contact: Cynthia Yen, Eva Tsai

2011/06/25 - 26
☎ 886-2-2595-4212
🖷 886-2-2595-5726
✉ cynthiayen@kaigo.com.tw
www.homelifestyle.com.tw

台北葡萄酒展

地点：台湾台北世界贸易中心三馆
内容：台湾唯一、规模最大、最完整葡萄酒产业消费供应链的专业级展会。展出项目包含最受欢迎葡萄酒品项，如红酒、白酒、冰酒、香槟、波特酒、雪利酒等酒品外，同时也展出专业饮酒用品及配件，如酒杯、醒酒瓶、酒柜、制酒架、酒柜等，与顶级美食共襄盛举，展出如奶酪、鱼子酱、生蚝、火腿与熏鲑鱼等老饕精选。展中同时举办葡萄酒大师讲堂、限量酒款品酒活动、酒庄新酒发布会等，提供专业酒商、进出口业者、餐饮相关业者及消费者最佳采购平台，是台湾葡萄酒产业中最受瞩目的年度盛会！
首届
周期：每年一届
市场范围：地区性
性质：面向公众
入场券价格：新台币300元
预计规模：参展厂商100家，参观人数10,000人
主办：开国有限公司
地址：台北市10461 德惠街9号8楼之3（10461）
联系人：颜慧娟,蔡郁洁

Wine & Gourmet, Taipei

Venue: Taiwan World Trade Center (TWTC), Taiwan
Profile: Taipei is set to be the largest, most highly anticipated event dedicated to connecting Taiwanese wine enthusiasts with purveyors of every wine imaginable. The full spectrum of both new and old world wines will be on full display at Wine & Gourmet Taipei.
Established Year: 2011
First Session
Frequency: Annual
Market Area: Regional
Nature: Open to public

Cost to Attend: NTD 300
Organizer: Kaigo Co Ltd
Address: 8th Fl.-3, 9 Dehuei Street, Taipei 104, Taiwan
Contact: Cynthia Yen, Eva Tsai

2011/08/04 - 05
☎ 886-2-2595-4212
🖷 886-2-2595-5726
✉ exhibition@railtec-taiwan.com
www.railtec-taiwan.com

海峡两岸轨道科技展览暨研讨会

地点： 台湾台北世贸中心一馆
内容： 本展会举办之目的为将全球轨道科技及产业最新趋势全面呈现给国内、外轨道业者，提供无限跨国商机与合作的机会。展品主题包含轨道车辆、轨道及基础公共建设、信号及无线通讯系统、电气化、票务及乘客信息、信息科技系统、电缆系统、安全防护系统、内装、供电、铁路工程及机械系统、验证与认证、咨询/顾问及培训公司。
始办年份： 2010
周期： 每年两届
市场范围： 国际性
性质： 面向公众
入场券价格： 免费
参展费用： 标准展位新台币68,000(未税)，光地新台币6,650(未税)/m2
主办： 开国有限公司
地址： 台北市10461 德惠街9号8楼之3（10461）
联系人： 陈秋萍,颜慧娟

(RAILTEC 2011)

Taiwan International Exhibition and Conference on Railway Technology (RAILTEC 2011)
Venue: Taipei World Trade Center (Hall 1, TWTC), Taiwan
Profile: RAILTEC aims to promote both horizontal and vertical information sharing and open the doors to forming cross-country partnerships. By forming strategic alliances and creating more integrated supply chains, businesses can better serve the global market
Established Year: 2010
Frequency: Biannual
Market Area: International
Nature: Open to public
Cost to Attend: Free
Participated Fee: NTD 68,000/Booth, NTD 650/m2
Organizer: Kaigo Co Ltd
Address: 8th Fl.-3, 9 Dehuei Street, Taipei 104, Taiwan
Contact: Silvia Chen, Cynthia Yen

2011/10/20 - 22
☎ 886-2-2595-4212
🖷 886-2-2595-5726
✉ exhibition@kaigo.com.tw
www.hardwareshow.com.tw

台湾五金展

地点： 中国台湾
内容： 国际专业买主必访之年度亚洲五金重点采购会，此次展出八大展品，包括专业五金工具、锁具、紧固扣件、建材零配件、园艺工具、汽车修护配件、五金机械厂房设备以及安全防护设备
始办年份： 2000
周期： 每年一届
市场范围： 国际性
性质： 面向贸易观众
入场券价格： 免费
参展费用： 新台币57,000元整(未税)、新台币52,400元整(未税)
主办： 开国有限公司
地址： 台北市10461 德惠街9号8楼之3（10461）
联系人： 黄玉真,陈静音

Taiwan Hardware Show

Venue: Taiwan
Profile: Taiwan Hardware Show (THS) is the first choice for international buyers to source quality hardware in Asia. There are eight exhibit groups in THS 2011: Tools & Accessories, Locks & Fittings, Fasteners & Fittings, Builders' Supplies, Garden
Established Year: 2000
Frequency: Annual
Market Area: International
Nature: Trade only
Cost to Attend: Free
Participated Fee: NTD 52,400-57,000
Organizer: Kaigo Co Ltd
Address: 8th Fl.-3, 9 Dehuei Street, Taipei 104, Taiwan
Contact: Gina Huang,Cela Chen

CHOICE DESIGN CONSULTANT

维创企划公司是多美维创传媒旗下品牌，是全国首屈一指的会展设计规划供应商。为多家位列财富500排行榜的公司、政府机关及非政府组织度身订造全方位品牌激活方案。

秉承十二年的丰富经验，维创精于把抽象概念活灵活现地展现在世人面前，在业界早已享负盛名。维创凭借非凡创意、专业知识及可靠信誉为客户与合作伙伴提供服务，并持之以恒，以取得今天的丰盛成果。

维创既提供一站式全方位品牌启动方案，同时擅长满足客户在个别专业领域上的需要。我们的核心业务包括为主办机构提供主场承建及技术支持服务；会展场馆及设施之管理服务；设计及承建展台；活动、会议及展览策划；为活动场地提供装置及临时设施；为博物馆及主题环境设计及装置永久性展品陈列；品牌标识规划。

成立于1999年的上海维创是维创在中国区的总部。10年来，维创不断在中国扩展业务范围，先后在北京、上海、广州、成都成立了分公司和办事处。

目前，维创拥有200余员工，其业务及生产网络覆盖全国30多个主要城市以及香港、拉斯维加斯、法兰克福、新加坡等国际都市。为此，维创所具备的资源、技术和经验可为我们的客户提供最佳的服务。

海外展览会议

Exhibitions and Fairs Overseas

阿尔及利亚
Algeria........250

安哥拉
Angola........250

阿根廷
Argentina........250

澳大利亚
Australia........250

奥地利
Austria........252

阿塞拜疆
Azerbaijan........252

孟加拉
Bangladesh........252

比利时
Belgium........252

巴西
Brazil........252

加拿大
Canada........257

哥伦比亚
Colombia........257

捷克
Czech Republic........258

丹麦
Denmark........258

埃及
Egypt........258

法国
France........259

德国
Germany........263

危地马拉
Guatemala........272

洪都拉斯
Honduras........272

印度
India........272

印度尼西亚
Indonesia........275

意大利
Italy........276

日本
Japan........277

哈萨克斯坦
Kazakhstan........282

肯尼亚
Kenya........283

利比亚
Libya........283

马来西亚
Malaysia........283

墨西哥
Mexico........283

摩洛哥
Morocco........283

尼日利亚
Nigeria........283

荷兰
Netherlands........283

朝鲜
North Korea........283

挪威
Norway........283

巴基斯坦
Pakistan........283

巴拿马
Panama........285

秘鲁
Peru........285

菲律宾
Philippines........285

波兰
Poland........285

葡萄牙
Portugal........285

波多黎各
Puerto Rico........286

俄罗斯
Russia........286

沙特阿拉伯
Saudi Arabia........288

新加坡
Singapore........289

南非
South Africa........290

韩国
South Korea........290

西班牙
Spain........293

斯里兰卡
Sri Lanka........294

瑞典
Sweden........294

瑞士
Switzerland........294

叙利亚
Syria........294

坦桑尼亚
Tanzania........294

泰国
Thailand........294

土耳其
Turkey........298

乌克兰
Ukraine........298

阿联酋
United Arab Emirates........299

英国
United Kingdom........303

美国
USA........305

乌兹别克斯坦
Uzbekistan........309

委内瑞拉
Venezuela........309

越南
Vietnam........309

阿尔及利亚
Algeria

2011年第四届阿尔及利亚汽配展

日期：2011/04/03 - 07
地点：阿尔及利亚SAFEX展览中心
内容：阿尔及利亚唯一一个专注于汽车后市场、汽车维护维修和工业车辆的专业展会。展会将为致力于在阿尔及利亚及北非和南欧这个发展中的市场进行投资的有识之士提供信息来源和寻找合作伙伴的机会。展出内容有轻型车、工业用车及售后网络所需设备和配件；汽车维修设备和相关服务；石油产品—润滑油和保养品；车身所需设备和产品；轮胎和轮辋；汽车服务场所所需设备、产品和配件；个人保护设备 市场分析
始办年份：2006
周期：每年一届
市场范围：国际性
性质：面向公众
主办：中国贸促会建设行业分会
联系人：全静
☎ 010-5979 9850转808
℻ 010-5885 7468
✉ quanjing@top-fairs.com.cn
MSN：quanjing@top-fairs.com.cn
QQ：602693071
www.build-ccpit.org
www.btfi.cn

阿尔及利亚环保及水处理设备展

SIEE–Pollutec 2011:

6th International Exhibition of Equipment & Services for Water

日期：2011/05 -
地点：阿尔及利亚阿尔及尔
内容：其境内业界唯一的专业展览，展示来自世界各地的不同水处理装备，服务，和技术解决方案，同时将有6,000多名有业务意向的观众在4天的时间里寻觅绝佳商机。SIEE – Pollutec一年一届，致力于提供广泛技术方案，解决各国所遇到的各种水处理问题，并且辅以高质量的会议日程，覆盖所有重要主题，这对于在阿尔及利亚的水处理行业专业人士是必不可少的。
周期：每年一届
市场范围：国际性
性质：面向贸易观众
上届规模 2009：参展商319家，参观人数6,411人
赞助：阿尔及利亚水资源部
主办：励展法国公司
联络：励展博览集团国际销售部
地址：北京市朝阳区新源南路1-3号平安国际金融中心A座15层01-03,05
联系人：王亮 @@@
☎ 010-5933 9268
℻ 010-5933 9233
✉ david.gong@reedexpo.com.cn
www.reedexport.cn
www.siee-pollutec.com

第四十四届北非阿尔及尔国际博览

日期：2011/06/01 - 06
地点：阿尔及利亚阿尔及尔展览中心
内容：北非最大、最有影响力的综合性展览会。内容包括各类电子家电和轻工产品；机械五金卫浴产品包括：摩托车、五金制品、汽车及零部件、环保及水处理系统、自动化技术、建筑材料、消费品、手工艺品、自行车、玩具、文具等五金工具、生活用品，装饰用品；机械设备，其中工程机械、建筑修路机械（多数国际知名的工程机械行业都参加，占据了室外全部场地）、和重型卡车、农业机械、客车及相关产品展出面积较多。
始办年份：1963
周期：每年一届
市场范围：国际性
上届规模：展览面积70,000m²（室内50,000m²），参展商来自30个国家
主办：阿尔及利亚国家展览和出口公司（SAFEX）
联络：北京麦田通会国际展览有限公司
地址：北京海淀区海淀中街中关村公馆B座1603室
联系人：吴珊
☎ 010-8248 4014转801
℻ 010-5165 9302转8004
✉ xiaoxiangzhishui@yahoo.com.cn
MSN：xiaoxiangzhishui@hotmail.com
QQ：48916458

阿尔及利亚国际工程及施工设备展览会

SITP

日期：2011/11 -
地点：阿尔及利亚阿尔及尔
周期：每年一届
主办：中国贸促会
地址：北京市西城区三里河路46号（100823）
联系人：张玉惠, 郭旭萍, 吕春丽
☎ 010-6859 4811, 6859 4994, 6859 4910
℻ 010-6859 4995
✉ zhangyuhui@ccpitmsc.org
www.chinamachine.org.cn

安哥拉
Angola

2011年安哥拉国际贸易博览会

日期：2011/07/14 - 21
地点：安哥拉罗安达国际展览中心
内容：展会共分为6个室内展馆和室外面积。安哥拉经过长年内战，交通运输基础设施遭到严重破坏，水电、通信网络都在兴建之中，工程及路面机械及建筑原材料，大型农用机械需求量非常大。生产和生活物资及原材料急缺，物价及其高昂。对于我国产品进入安哥拉市场及在安哥拉市场获得长足发展是非常好的时机。 展品范围有工程机械、电力产品、技术及机械设备、建筑材料、轻工产品及日常用品、家电类、音像视听类产品、通讯产品类、动力机械类、农用机械、医疗器械
周期：每年一届
市场范围：国际性
性质：面向公众
主办：中国贸促会建设行业分会会展部；北京中杰城设国际展览有限公司
地址：北京市海淀区紫竹院路31号华澳中心嘉慧苑1703（100089）
联系人：全静
☎ 010-5979 9850转808，13693550328
℻ 010-5885 7468
✉ quanjing@top-fairs.com.cn
MSN：quanjing@top-fairs.com.cn
QQ：602693071
www.build-ccpit.org
www.btfi.cn

安哥拉国际工程机械与建材机械展览会

CONSTROI ANGOLA

日期：2011/10 -
地点：安哥拉罗安达
周期：每年一届
主办：中国贸促会
地址：北京市西城区三里河路46号（100823）
联系人：张玉惠, 郭旭萍, 吕春丽
☎ 010-6859 4811, 6859 4994, 6859 4910
℻ 010-6859 4995
✉ zhangyuhui@ccpitmsc.org
www.chinamachine.org.cn

阿根廷
Argentina

阿根廷国际机床工具展览会

EMAQH

日期：2011/03/25 - 30
地点：阿根廷布宜诺斯艾利斯
周期：每年两届
主办：中国贸促会
地址：北京市西城区三里河路46号（100823）
联系人：张玉惠, 郭旭萍, 吕春丽
☎ 010-6859 4811, 6859 4994, 6859 4910
℻ 010-6859 4995
✉ zhangyuhui@ccpitmsc.org
www.chinamachine.org.cn

2011年第八届阿根廷国际矿业博览会

日期：2011/05/04 - 06
地点：阿根廷Buenos Aires, Argentinien Centro Costa Salguero
内容：阿根廷国际矿业博览会是阿根廷及南美最有影响的矿业展览之一，2011年将是第八届。2009年有来自智利，玻利维亚，巴西，加拿大，美国，芬兰，英国，墨西哥，秘鲁，波兰，俄罗斯和南非的矿业相关企业参加了展览，取得了非常好的效果。矿业是目前阿根廷发展速度最快的行业，展览会推动了这一发展。
周期：两年一届
市场范围：国际性
上届规模 2009：展览面积12,000m², 参展商350家
主办：Viewpoint S.A.
承办：北京麦田通会国际展览有限公司
联系人：吴珊
☎ 010-8248 4014转801, 5165 9302转8005
℻ 010-5165 9302转8004
✉ xiaoxiangzhishui@yahoo.com.cn
MSN：xiaoxiangzhishui@hotmail.com
www.cornfairs.com

阿根廷面料服装展

EMITEX

日期：2011/05/10 - 12
地点：阿根廷
联络：上海比天展览服务有限公司
地址：上海市中山北路900号加禾商务中心3号楼303室(200070)
联系人：刘先生
☎ 021-5655 2843
℻ 021-5655 9981
www.betium.com

澳大利亚
Australia

澳大利亚悉尼国际家具展

AIFF2011

日期：2011/02/02 - 04
地点：澳大利亚
☎ 0411-8378 8831
℻ 0411-8378 8830

2011年澳大利亚全球商品采购交易会

2011 The Global Sourcing & Merchandising Expo

日期：2011/05 -
地点：澳大利亚墨尔本展览中心
内容：服装纺织：日常服装、婚礼服装、布料、鞋类、手提包、时尚配件、皮革制品、孕妇服装、

运动装；男士用品：日常用品、随身小器具及漫画书、五金工具；家居园艺：家具、手工艺品、家庭及厨房用具、家庭防护、灯具、户外及休闲产品、季节性装饰品、家居储藏；企业商品：小礼品、促销礼品、IT系统、办公家具、办公用品、包装及纸质用品、印刷出版物、安全装置、通信、制服；休闲用品：汽车相关、化妆品、消费电子及电脑产品、眼镜、礼品、珠宝手表、奢侈品、个人护理用品、运动器具；自主品牌：服饰、化妆品、食品、健康产品、家居服装、护肤品、软件；0-12岁：婴儿用品、儿童服装、玩具。
周期：每年一届
市场范围：国际性
性质：面向公众
主办：International Conferences & Exhibitions LLC（IC&E）；杭州思诺博会展服务有限公司
地址：杭州市体育场路229号浙江粮油大厦1202室展览部（310003）
☎ 0571-8577 8500
🖷 0571-8577 9709
✉ expo@sinobal.com
www.sinobal.com

澳大利亚国际机械制造周

AIEE

日期：2011/05 -
地点：澳大利亚墨尔本
周期：每年一届
主办：中国贸促会机械行业分会
地址：北京市西城区三里河路46号（100823）
联系人：张玉惠,郭旭萍,吕春丽
☎ 010-6859 4811, 6859 4994, 6859 4910
🖷 010-6859 4995
✉ zhangyuhui@ccpitmsc.org
www.chinamachine.org.cn

澳大利亚汽车配件及售后服务博览会

Australian AUTO aftermarket EXPO

日期：2011/05/12 - 14
地点：澳大利亚墨尔本展览中心
内容：四驱车配件、汽车空调、影音设备、刹车片、导航系统、动力传动系统、点火系统、引擎、传动装置、排气系统、润滑剂、滤波器、汽车漆、散热系统、挡风玻璃、轮胎轮毂、汽车环保设备、汽车服务与维修设备、汽车保养及清洗、车间设备。

澳大利亚的汽车的配件附件市场在60亿美元左右。如果加上轮胎、引擎以及引擎的零配件，价值就增加到了120亿美元左右。澳大利亚的汽配售后服务市场在过去9年里保持了5%的平均增长率。澳大利亚的汽车配件市场充分对国外开放，2010年起关税降至5%。目前澳大利亚与中国的FTA自由贸易的谈判正在加紧进行，今后中国的制造业产品进入澳大利亚将更加便利并具有竞争性。
周期：两年一届
市场范围：国际性
性质：面向公众
上届规模 2009：展览面积22,000m²，参观人数8100人
主办：澳大利亚汽车售后协会
联络：杭州思诺博会展服务有限公司
地址：浙江省杭州市体育场路229号浙江粮油大厦1202室（310003）
联系人：金赛琼小姐
☎ 0571-8577 9914
🖷 0571-8577 9709
✉ expo@sinobal.com

澳大利亚机械制造周

National Manufacturing Week

NMW
NATIONAL MANUFACTURING WEEK

日期：2011/05/24 - 27
地点：澳大利亚悉尼奥林匹克公园 悉尼展览中心
内容：澳大利亚国际机械制造周（National Manufacturing Week）是大洋州规模最大、水平最高、涉及范围最广的工业技术展示与交易场所，分别在悉尼和墨尔本两个城市轮回展出。澳大利亚国际机械制造周展览会围绕10大主题：澳大利亚国际工程展、焊接热处理展；气动液压技术；物料搬运；计算机控制；安保展；流程与控制展及机床工具展等。

中国参展展品主要有机床、剪板机、电机、柴油机、机械零配件、五金工具、电动工具、轴承、搬运车、摩托车、割草机、小五金等。澳大利亚国际机械制造周展览会的展品范围极其广泛，几乎涵盖了工业制造流程的各个方面。
周期：每年一届
市场范围：国际性
性质：面向贸易观众
上届规模 2008：展览面积12,000m²，参展商400家
主办：励展博览集团国际销售部
地址：北京市朝阳区新源南路1-3号平安国际金融中心A座15层01-03,05
联系人：李悦
☎ 010－5933 9298
🖷 010－5933 9233
✉ anna.li@reedexpo.com.cn
www.reedexport.cn
www.nationalmanufacturingweek.com.au

澳大利亚国际美发展览会

Hair Expo Australia: Expo, Education, Galas – Australia's Top Hairdressing Event

日期：2011/06 -
地点：澳大利亚悉尼情人港悉尼会展中心
内容：澳大利亚国际美发展览会是南半球最大的美发行业展会，定于每年6月的一个周末举办。在展会上参展商把各自的产品与服务一一展示，观众因此可以了解到新产品、资源以及采购行情。通过产品销售以及为买卖双方搭桥，展会使得参展商在美发沙龙、美发行业的地位得到提升，在决定购买之前展会为其提供了看、闻、触、比的机会。产品与服务有美发用具（电动产品）、美发店家具、美容美发市场/软件/网站、媒体及媒体协会、接发/辫子/发具、美甲产品与设备、美容/护肤用品与设备、美发与时尚配饰、教学
周期：每年一届
市场范围：国际性
性质：面向贸易观众
主办：励展澳大利亚公司
联络：励展博览集团国际销售部
地址：北京市朝阳区新源南路1-3号平安国际金融中心A座15层01-03,05
联系人：申健
☎ 010-5933 9299
🖷 010-5933 9233
✉ jerry.shen@reedexpo.com.cn
www.hairexpoaustralia.com

悉尼国际SPA及美容展览会

Sydney International Spa & Beauty Expo: Australia's Premier Spa & Beauty Event

sydney international
spa & beauty
expo

日期：2011/08/13 - 14
地点：澳大利亚悉尼达令港悉尼会展中心
内容：悉尼国际SPA及美容展览会是澳大利亚SPA及美容行业最大的专业展览会。展会汇集了众多知名美容品牌和供货商。他们为美容及SPA中心经营者、美容师、水疗师、美甲师、化妆师、美发师和其他美容行业专业人士提供了独一无二的机会去了解最新的美容产品、治疗方法并方便行业人士采购产品。产品及服务有最新技术、治疗方法、沙龙服务、设备、传统面部美容、蜜蜡脱毛、全身护理、非外科面部整容、健康项目、全自由体验
周期：每年一届
市场范围：国际性
性质：面向贸易观众
参展费用：标准展位534澳大利亚元
主办：励展澳大利亚公司
联络：励展博览国际展览部
地址：北京市朝阳区新源南路1-3号平安国际金融中心A座15层01-03,05
联系人：申健
☎ 010-5933 9299
🖷 010-5933 9233
✉ jerry.shen@reedexpo.com.cn
www.internationalbeautyexpo.com.au

悉尼亚太国际矿业展

AIMEX: Asia Pacific's International Mining Exhibition

日期：2011/09/06 - 09
地点：澳大利亚悉尼奥林匹克公园悉尼展览场
内容：面向世界采矿以及相关工程行业最大的产品及服务展会之一。产品及服务有采矿设备、供应及服务、计算机-软件及硬件、传送装置及相关操作设备、电子设备、消防设备、安全设备、地下采矿、运输、环境保护及尘埃控制、露天采矿、矿物开采、矿物加工及选煤、粉碎、碾压及筛选设备、发电、传送、布缆、能源系统、进程控制、水泵及阀门。
周期：四年一届
市场范围：国际性
性质：面向贸易观众
上届规模 2007：展览面积18,600m²，参展商519家，参观人数10,947人
赞助：澳大利亚采矿设备及服务委员会（MESCA），建筑及采矿设备工业集团（CMEIG），澳大拉西亚采矿及冶金学院(AUSIMM)，澳大利亚采矿设备技术及服务（AUSTMINE），澳大利亚贸易委员会（AUSTRADE）
主办：励展博览集团国际销售部
地址：北京市朝阳区新源南路1-3号平安国际金融中心A座15层01-03,05
联系人：张志超
☎ 010-5933 9266
🖷 010-5933 9233
✉ ivy.zhang@reedexpo.com.cn
www.reedexport.cn

澳大利亚中国纺织服装展

CTAF(Australia)

日期：2011/11/17 - 19
地点：澳大利亚
联络：上海比天展览服务有限公司
地址：上海市中山北路900号加禾商务中心3号楼303室(200070)
联系人：刘先生
☎ 021-5655 2843
🖷 021-5655 9981
www.betium.com

澳大利亚国际采购展

AISF

日期：2011/11/17 - 19
地点：澳大利亚
联络：上海比天展览服务有限公司

地址：上海市中山北路900号加禾商务中心3号楼303室(200070)
联系人：刘先生
☎ 021-5655 2843
🖷 021-5655 9981
www.betium.com

澳大利亚昆士兰采矿机械展

QME- Queensland Mining & Engineering Exhibition

日期：2012/07 -
地点：澳大利亚昆士兰
内容：是在煤矿开采区的核心地区举办的最大的区域性展会，主要展出采矿、矿物加工、发电、糖类加工及金属熔炼业的产品及服务。QME2006 是第二次与QCME(Queensland Construction & Machinery Exhibition)合办的展会。
周期：两年一届
市场范围：国际性
性质：面向贸易观众
主办：澳大利亚励展博览集团；励展博览集团国际销售部
地址：北京市朝阳区新源南路1-3号平安国际金融中心A座15层01-03,05
联系人：张志超
☎ 010- 5933 9266
🖷 010- 5933 9233
✉ ivy.zhang@reedexpo.com.cn
www.reedexport.cn
www.queenslandminingexpo.com.au

悉尼亚太国际矿业展

AIMEX: Asia Pacific's International Mining Exhibition

日期：2014 -
地点：澳大利亚悉尼奥林匹克公园悉尼展览场
内容：面向世界采矿以及相关工程行业最大的产品及服务展会之一。产品及服务有采矿设备、供应及服务、计算机-软件及硬件、传送装置及相关操作设备、电子设备、消防设备、安全设备、地下采矿、运输、环境保护及尘埃控制、露天采矿、矿物开采、矿物加工及选煤、粉碎、碾压及筛选设备、发电、传送、布缆、能源系统、进程控制、水泵及阀门。
市场范围：国际性
性质：面向贸易观众
赞助：澳大利亚采矿设备及服务委员会 (MESCA), 建筑及采矿设备工业集团 (CMEIG), 澳大拉西亚采矿及冶金学院(AUSIMM), 澳大利亚采矿设备技术及服务(AUSTMINE), 澳大利亚贸易委员会(AUSTRADE)
主办：励展博览集团国际销售部
地址：北京市朝阳区新源南路1-3号平安国际金融中心A座15层01-03,05
联系人：张志超
☎ 010-5933 9266
🖷 010-5933 9233
✉ ivy.zhang@reedexpo.com.cn
www.reedexport.cn
www.aimex.reedexhibitions.com.au

奥地利
Austria

Auto Zum:

奥地利国际汽车生产设备及加油站设备、化学品及环境技术展

Intl Trade Fair for Car Workshop & Petrol Station Equipment

AutoZum Salzburg

日期：2011/01/12 - 15
地点：奥地利萨尔斯堡贸易展览中心 Salzburg Trade Fair Center, Austria
内容：汽车附件、备件，汽车维修设备、器材，轮胎、轮圈，汽车电子，售后服务产品，汽车美容产品、加油站产品及修理设备，环境保护和技术，清洗，洁净技术，化学用品，汽车服务行业，汽车IT技术，EDP解决方案
周期：每年两届
上届规模 2009：展览面积20,667m²，参展商320家，参观人数23,929人
主办：励展奥地利公司
联络：励展博览集团国际销售部
地址：北京市朝阳区新源南路1-3号平安国际金融中心A座15层01-03,05
联系人：杜一鸣
☎ 010-5933 9209
🖷 010-5933 9233
✉ martin.du@reedexpo.com.cn
www.reedexport.cn

奥地利国际食品技术及制造展览会

L-TEC

The Trade Fair for Food Technology & Manufacturing

日期：2011/03 -
地点：奥地利萨尔茨堡 Messezentrum Salzburg Exhibition Center, Salzburg, Austria
内容：食品技术和生产所需的产品及服务
始办年份：2005
周期：两年一届
性质：面向贸易观众
上届规模 2008：展览面积102m²，参展商家，参观人数14,908人
主办：励展奥地利公司
联络：励展博览集团国际销售部
地址：北京市朝阳区新源南路1-3号平安国际金融中心A座15层01-03,05
联系人：杜一鸣
☎ 010-5933 9209
🖷 010-5933 9233
✉ martin.du@reedexpo.com.cn
www.ltec.at
www.reedexport.cn

奥地利国际木材加工、处理、装配、木匠用品展

BWS: International Trade Fair for Woodworking

日期：2011/03/23 - 26
地点：奥地利萨尔茨堡展览中心 Exhibition Center, Salzburg, Austria
内容：木工五金配件、防护衣及工作安全用品、铰链和配件、工具、锁具及锁具技术、安全设备、金属加工、紧固及固定技术、环境技术、木具加工及成套设备、木工材料及加工材料、木工及细木供应，表面磨光、加工聚合材料机器和工具、木工及细木机械/工具、锯木技术、锯木机械及工具、门窗设备、结构设备、森林伐木设备，机械，工具
始办年份：1979
周期：两年一届
上届规模 2009：展览面积20,057 m²，参展商329家，参观人数17,879人
主办：励展奥地利公司Messe Salzburg
联络：励展博览集团国际销售部
地址：北京市朝阳区新源南路1-3号平安国际金融中心A座15层01-03,05
联系人：张志超
☎ 010-5933 9266
🖷 010-5933 9233
✉ ivy.zhang@reedexpo.com.cn
www.reedexport.cn
www.bwsmesse.at

维也纳国际汽车展

Vienna Auto Show

日期：2012/01 -
地点：奥地利维也纳
内容：由奥地利汽车进口商支持的汽车展。产品及服务：新汽车产品、轮胎及各类汽车配件。
周期：两年一届
主办：励展奥地利公司
联络：励展博览集团国际销售部
联系人：杜一鸣
☎ 010-5933 9209
🖷 010-5933 9233
✉ martin.du@reedexpo.com.cn
www.reedexport.cn
www.viennaautoshow.at

Auto Zum:

奥地利国际汽车生产设备及加油站设备、化学品及环境技术展

International Trade Fair for the Car & Vehicle Industry

AutoZum Salzburg

日期：2013/01 -
地点：奥地利萨尔斯堡贸易展览中心
内容：AutoZum 是奥地利最大的汽车零部件及加油站设备、汽车化学产品及环保产品国际专业展览会，至今已成功举办了28届。该展是在奥地利地区汽车行业人士汇聚的唯一场所，同时它也无可置疑成为奥地利主要的国际贸易展览会。作为衡量下一个财政年度的标准，该展被称为是在多瑙河和阿尔卑斯山区域的市场指南针。展览会具有明确的主题，高质量的专业讲座、专业的观众，这些都为参展提供了必要的增值服务。
周期：两年一届
市场范围：国际性
性质：面向贸易观众
主办：励展博览集团国际销售部
地址：北京市朝阳区新源南路1-3号平安国际金融中心A座15层01-03,05
联系人：杜一鸣
☎ 010-5933 9209

☎ 010-5933 9233
✉ martin.du@reedexpo.com.cn
www.reedexport.cn

奥地利国际木材加工、处理、装配、木匠用品展

BWS: International Trade Fair for Woodworking

日期： 2013/04 -
地点： 奥地利萨尔茨堡展览中心
内容： BWS是国际顶级的木工机械和金属制品的展览会，和"奥地利五金展"同是木工业和五金业内全国性和国际性供应商和购买商必须参加的盛会。吸引着来自整个欧洲的供货商和采购商。观众主要是欧洲的木工、工匠、门窗制造厂、木制产品加工厂、家具制造商、木工贸易、油漆贸易公司、伐木厂、五金商、建筑公司、钥匙锁具贸易公司、安全科技企业、金属处理加工公司、建筑师。产品和服务有木工五金配件、防护衣及工作安全用品、铰链和配件、工具、锁具及锁具技术、安全设备、金属加工、紧固及固定技术、环境技术、木具加工及成套设备、木工材料&加工材料、木工&细木供应，表面磨光、加工聚合材料机器和工具、木工及细木机械/工具、锯木技术、锯木机械及工具、门窗设备、结构设备、森林伐木设备，机械，工具
周期： 两年一届
市场范围： 国际性
性质： 面向贸易观众
上届规模 2009：展览面积20,057m²，参展商329家，参观人数17,879人
主办： 励展奥地利公司Messe Salzburg
联络： 励展博览集团国际销售部
地址： 北京市朝阳区新源南路1-3号平安国际金融中心A座15层01-03,05
联系人： 张志超
☎ 010-5933 9266
☎ 010-5933 9233
✉ ivy.zhang@reedexpo.com.cn
www.reedexport.cn

阿塞拜疆
Azerbaijan

阿塞拜疆国际家具展

Caspian Mebel Expo2011

日期： 2011/10 -
地点： 阿塞拜疆
☎ 0411-8378 8831
☎ 0411-8378 8830

孟加拉
Bangladesh

孟加拉达卡国际面料展

DIFS

日期： 2011/02/02 - 05
地点： 孟加拉
联络： 上海比天展览服务有限公司
地址： 上海市中山北路900号加禾商务中心3号楼303室(200070)
联系人： 刘先生
☎ 021-5655 2843
☎ 021-5655 9981
www.betium.com

孟加拉达卡国际纺织展

DTG

日期： 2011/02/13 - 16
地点： 孟加拉
联络： 上海比天展览服务有限公司
地址： 上海市中山北路900号加禾商务中心3号楼303室(200070)
联系人： 刘先生
☎ 021-5655 2843
☎ 021-5655 9981
www.betium.com

第12届孟加拉国际纺织机械展览会

日期： 2011/07/20 - 23
地点： 孟加拉达卡
内容： 各类纺织机械、零部件及染化料等
主办： 孟加拉国会议及展览公司
联络： 中国贸促会纺织行业分会
联系人： 高杨，孙培宁
☎ 010-8522 9372，8522 9663
☎ 010-8522 9480

孟加拉达卡国际面料展

DIFS

日期： 2011/07/28 - 31
地点： 孟加拉
联络： 上海比天展览服务有限公司
地址： 上海市中山北路900号加禾商务中心3号楼303室(200070)
联系人： 刘先生
☎ 021-5655 2843
☎ 021-5655 9981
www.betium.com

比利时
Belgium

2011年比利时布鲁塞尔水产展

ESE & SPE

European Seafood Exposition

Seafood Processing Europe

日期： 2011/04/27 - 29
地点： 比利时布鲁塞尔展览中心
内容： 全球最有影响力的水产品贸易展之一。汇集了整个欧洲乃至全世界的水产品行业内的买家和卖家，是全球水产品行业企业维持已有客户、展示新产品、寻找新买家，评估行业发展趋势以及挖掘行业新闻的最有效的途径。涉及产品研究、分销、超市零售、加工与处理、进出口等领域。

09年中国参展商规模近90家，近800平方米的展出面积达到了历届之最。展品范围有水产品、水产服务及组织、水产边缘产品、水产品设备、水产包装运输仓储。
周期： 每年一届
上届规模 2009：展出面积37,600m²，参展商1,980家（来自87个国家），观众47,322人（来自140个国家）
主办： 北京领汇国际展览有限公司
地址： 北京市朝阳区农展馆南路13号瑞辰国际中心719（100125）
联系人： 刘佳
☎ 010-5129 5359转8505
☎ 010-5129 5379转8505
✉ expo8505@worldfairs.cn
MSN：expo8505@worldfairs.cn

巴西
Brazil

巴西国际鞋业、皮革制品及附件展览会

COUROMODA

日期： 2010/01/18 - 21
地点： 巴西圣保罗Sao Paulo, Brazil
内容： 鞋材、制鞋设备、箱包、皮革服饰以及与其相关的皮革制品等
市场范围： 国际性
主办： 京慕国际展览有限公司
地址： 北京市朝阳区北三环东路6号中国国际展览中心服务楼3层
联系人： 李嘉羊，古莹
☎ 010-8460 0551
☎ 010-8460 0394
✉ zhaolingna@ciec.com.cn
www.jingmu.com.cn

巴西国际洗衣及干洗设备展

Expolav:

Laundry & Dry-cleaning Products & Services Trade Fair

日期： 2011/03 -
地点： 巴西圣保罗安年比展览中心Anhembi, Sao Paulo, Brazil
内容： 配件，化学产品，基本输入，软件，服务，其他
始办年份： 2002
周期： 两年一届
上届规模 2009：展览面积52,000m²，参展商602家，参观人数23,609人
主办： 励展巴西公司
联络： 励展博览集团国际销售部
地址： 北京市朝阳区新源南路1-3号平安国际金融中心A座15层01-03,05
联系人： 宫卫
☎ 010-5933 9268
☎ 010-5933 9233
✉ david.gong@reedexpo.com.cn
www.expolav.com.br

Feimaco:
巴西国际服装制造机械及零部件展

International Garment Industry Machinery & Components Trade Fair

日期： 2011/03 -
地点： 巴西圣保罗安年比展览中心
内容： 模具和裁剪设备(CAD/CAM 系统)、工业和半工业缝纫设备、工业和半工业刺绣设备、熨烫设备、装饰配件加工设备
始办年份： 2005
周期： 两年一届
上届规模 2009：展览面积52,000m²，参展商602家，参观人数23,609人
主办： 励展巴西公司
联络： 励展博览集团国际销售部

地址：北京市朝阳区新源南路1-3号平安国际金融中心A座15层01-03,05
联系人：宫卫
☎ 010-5933 9268
🖷 010-5933 9233
✉ david.gong@reedexpo.com.cn
www.feimaco.com.br

巴西国际建筑展

Feicon Batimat

International Construction Industry Trade Fair

FEICON BATIMAT

日期：2011/03/15 - 19
地点：巴西圣保罗市安年比展览中心Anhembi, Sao Paulo, Brazil
内容：FEICON BATIMAT是在建筑业开展业务的最佳平台。它的成功是基于高质量的观众、其传播战略以及参展商的声望。它是建筑业内唯一的综合展会，在国内已经举办了20年，在国际上则已有40年历史。圣保罗的"国际建筑周"集合了拉美建筑业最优秀的项目。这是一个了解世界上最重要、最富盛名的品牌之创新和投资的绝佳机会。
产品及服务：空调，休闲区，挂锁，锁具和配件，金属屋顶和墙体，门窗框，石膏，浮秤，泵，水箱，防水材料，隔热隔音，软百叶窗和遮阳棚，水池，楼板衬料
始办年份：1992
周期：每年一届
上届规模 ：展览面积64,000m²，参展商630家，参观人数132,000人
主办：励展巴西公司
联络：励展博览集团国际销售部
地址：北京市朝阳区新源南路1-3号平安国际金融中心A座15层01-03,05
联系人：宫卫
☎ 010-5933 9268
🖷 010-5933 9233
✉ david.gong@reedexpo.com.cn
www.reedexport.cn
www.feicon.com.br

巴西国际电子展

FIEE Elétrica: International Electrical, Energy & Automation Industry Trade Fair

日期：2011/03/28 – 04/01
地点：巴西圣保罗安年比展览中心 Anhembi, Sao Paulo, Brazil
内容：在过去的42年中，作为巴西最重要的电力工业展，FIEE Elétrica一直给予能源生产，传输和分销领域广泛支持，提供商业机遇，发布前沿科技，与本展同期举行的electronicAmerica——一个集组件、组件生产设备、激光技术和光电业的国际贸易展会。
产品及服务：能源生产，传送和分配装备、GTD必需元件、供电组件、电力安装材料、电力工具和自动控制-公用设施组件、电力工程，安装和维修、银行服务,实体公司，贸易发布及服务。
始办年份：1985
周期：两年一届
参展费用：光地展位260美元，标准展位340美元
上届规模 2009：展览面积60,000m²，参展商1,100家，参观人数53,567人

主办：励展巴西公司
联络：励展博览集团国际销售部
地址：北京市朝阳区新源南路1-3号平安国际金融中心A座15层01-03,05
联系人：宫卫
☎ 010-5933 9268
🖷 010-5933 9233
✉ david.gong@reedexpo.com.cn
www.fiee.com.br
www.reedexport.cn

2011年巴西国际汽车零部件、维修设备及服务贸易展览会

AUTOMEC 2011

日期：2011/04/05-07
地点：巴西圣保罗
Anhembi Park Exhibition Hall, Brizal
内容：各类车、汽车、配件、组件及零部件、汽车修理设备、维修保养产品、车轮轮胎、音箱系统和设备、车内娱乐系统、汽车加工业产品、加油站设备、电池电源、空调制冷系统、汽车装饰产品、电子机械系统、发动机、各种工具、涂料、安全系统等。
周期：两年一届
上届规模 2009：参展商1,400家（国外展商650家，来自30个国家），参观人数150,000人
承办：巴西机械制造商协会
联络：中国汽车工业国际合作总公司
地址：北京市海淀区中关村丹棱街3号A座国机大厦（100080）
☎ 010-8260 6881, 6891, 6893, 6874
🖷 010-8260 6883, 8260 6790
联系人：马蓉，刘岩，娄杰，杨菁
✉ exhibition@cnaico.com.cn
www.autochina.com.cn

巴西国际汽车配件展

Automec：

International Autoparts, Equipment and Services Trade Fair

日期：2011/04/12 - 16
地点：巴西圣保罗Anhembi, Sao Paulo, Brazil
内容：Automec是南美地区最大的也是最专业性的汽车零配件展览会，更是汽车零配件新技术和商业的焦点。是世界5大最好的汽车零配件展会之一，目前为全世界厂商一味难求的热门汽车零配件展。

产品与服务有汽车配件、附件、机器、为汽车行业，经销商，修理厂和服务站提供装备和服务、运输，存储和材料处理、发动机改造、喷漆、焊接、橡胶硫化和轮胎翻新、工具、测量诊断装备及系统、轮胎准线、自动控件（机器人）、信息学、润滑油、润滑油添加剂、银行服务、协会服务、出版服务。
始办年份：2001
周期：两年一届
性质：面向贸易观众
上届规模 ：展览面积50,000m²，参展商968家，参观人数62,314人
主办：励展巴西公司
联络：励展博览集团国际销售部
地址：北京市朝阳区新源南路1-3号平安国际金融中心A座15层01-03,05
联系人：宫卫
☎ 010-5933 9288
🖷 010-5933 9233
✉ david.gong@reedexpo.com.cn
www.automecfeira.com.br

巴西国际安防产品博览会

ISC Brazil:

International Security Conference & Exposition

日期：2011/04/26 - 28
地点：巴西圣保罗北方展览中心Expo Center Norte, Brazil
内容：报警装置，生物统计，TV内电路，存取控制，火焰探测，探测器，通信设备，监视设备和服务，无线设备，整合产品和系统，护栏，个人安防，辨认系统，车辆和特殊交通工具
始办年份：2005
周期：每年一届
参展费用：光地展位280美元，标准展位368美元
上届规模 ：展览面积10,500m²，参展商100家，参观人数6,212人
主办：励展巴西公司
联络：励展博览集团国际销售部
地址：北京市朝阳区新源南路1-3号平安国际金融中心A座15层01-03,05
联系人：张志超
☎ 010-5933 9266
🖷 010-5933 9233
✉ ivy.zhang@reedexpo.com.cn
www.iscexpo.com.br

巴西国际地理信息展览会

GEO Summit Latin America:

International Geoinformation Congress & Exhibition

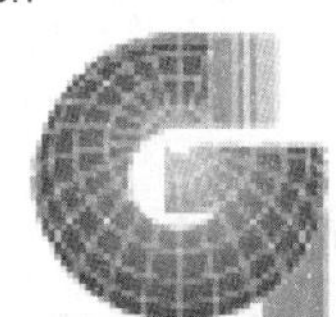

GEO Summit Latin America

日期：2011/05 -
地点：巴西圣保罗Imigrantes展览中心
内容：为您呈现业内最新潮流，产品和服务，特别针对绘图，本地化，导航，地形定位，国营和私营企业管理分析，提供解决方案。展会系列活动：GEO巴西，GEO基础设备，GEO采矿，GEO石油和天然气，GEO城市。
产品和服务：全球导航卫星系统，接收器和配件，陆地和航空传感器，数据收集和PDAs，通信设备，卫星图像，航空拍摄，绘图，土地登记和数据模型，web内容，GIS，导航，设计，监控和追踪，数据模型，IT和数据库，制图，注册登记和地形测量，咨询和地理营销。
周期：每年一届
上届规模 2009：展览面积4,200m²，参展商49家，参观人数3,800人
主办：励展巴西公司（Alcantara Machado）
地址：北京市朝阳区新源南路1-3号平安国际金融中心A座15层01-03,05
联系人：宫卫
☎ 010-5933 9268
🖷 010-5933 9233
✉ david.gong@reedexpo.com.cn
www.vietnammanufacturingexpo.com

巴西国际机床工具及成套设备展

Feimafe:

International Machine Tools and Integrated Manufacturing Systems Trade Fair

FEIMAFE

日期： 2011/05 -
地点： 巴西圣保罗安年比展览中心 Anhembi, Sao Paulo, Brazil
内容： 由于机床市场的快速增长，巴西机械工具展（FEIMAFE）占领了拉丁美洲地区，被认为是该地区最大最重要的展会，展会的发展也非常成功。届时，国际质量控制贸易展览会（QUALIDADE）也将同期举办。
产品及服务： 机床、自动化、质量控制整合生产技术、辅助设备，配件和零部件、工具、服务
周期： 两年一届
上届规模 2009：展览面积72,000m²，参展商1,307家，参观人数67,700人
主办： 励展巴西公司
联络： 励展博览国际展览部
地址： 北京市朝阳区新源南路1-3号平安国际金融中心A座15层01-03,05
联系人： 宫卫
☎ 010-5933 9268
🖷 010-5933 9233
✉ david.gong@reedexpo.com.cn
www.feimafe.com.br
www.reedexport.cn

巴西农业机械展

Agrishow:

International Trade Fair for Agricultural Technology in Action

日期： 2011/05/02 - 06
地点： 巴西圣保罗里贝朗普雷图
内容： 农业机械与零配件（拖拉机、联合收割机、仓储、灌溉及轮胎、泵等其他零配件）；肥料、杀虫剂、种子、动物饲料及矿物质辅料；动物防疫与药品等。
始办年份： 1993
周期： 每年一届
上届规模：展览面积360,000m²，参展商730家，参观人数141,000人
主办： 励展巴西公司
地址： 北京市朝阳区新源南路1-3号平安国际金融中心A座15层01-03,05
联系人： 宫卫
☎ 010-5933 9268
🖷 010-5933 9233
✉ david.gong@reedexpo.com.cn
www.agrishow.com.br

巴西国际塑料机械展览会

Brasilplast:

International Plastic Industry Trade Fair

日期： 2011/05/09 - 13
地点： 巴西圣保罗Anhembi, Sao Paulo, Brazil
内容： 塑料产品生产商、人造树脂、原材料与电子元件塑料衬底、化工产品、机械、设备与零件、模具、仪器、控制与自动设备、服务与技术项目、交易宣传及其他服务。
始办年份： 1998
周期： 两年一届
上届规模： 展览面积76,000m²，参展商1,294家，专业贸易观众62,787人
主办： 励展巴西公司Alcantara Machado
地址： 北京市朝阳区新源南路1-3号平安国际金融中心A座15层01-03,05
联系人： 宫卫
☎ 010-5933 9268
🖷 010-5933 9233
✉ david.gong@reedexpo.com.cn
www.agrishow.com.br

巴西国际食品、饮料工业加工技术和包装工业博览会

Fispal Tecnologia

日期： 2011/06 -
地点： 巴西圣保罗
周期： 每年一届
主办： 中国贸促会机械行业分会
地址： 北京市西城区三里河路46号（100823）
联系人： 张玉惠，郭旭萍，吕春丽
☎ 010-6859 4811, 6859 4994, 6859 4910
🖷 010-6859 4995
✉ zhangyuhui@ccpitmsc.org
www.chinamachine.org.cn

巴西国际海洋石油及天然气工业设备展览会

Brazil Offshore:

International Offshore Oil and Gas Industry Trade Show and Conference

日期： 2011/06/14 - 17
地点： 巴西里约州马珈耶Macaé, Roberto Marinho展览中心
内容： 作为世界第三大海洋石油工业产品贸易展会，巴西国际海洋石油天然气工业设备展是众多成功业内贸易展会之一，在参展公司和观众的数量和质量上有突飞猛进的增长。展会每两年举办一次，举办地点在Macaé，也是Petrobras UNBC的基地。Campos Watershed目前是世界最大的海洋实验室，巨大的投资焦点在于探索新发现并将海洋石油的前沿推向超深水域，而巴西在这一领域正处于世界领先水平。同期举办的展会：- 国际海洋石油与天然气工业会议/IBP-巴西石油及生物燃料研究所/SPE-汽油工程师组织 - 商务谈判/ONIP-国家汽油工业组织/SEBRAE-RJ
周期： 两年一届
市场范围： 国际性
性质： 面向贸易观众
上届规模 2009：参展商636家，参观人数49,224人
主办： 励展巴西公司
赞助： IBP; ONIP; SPE; FIRJAN; Macaé市政厅; 里约州政府; Upstream; Offshore Engineer; Brasil Energia, Click Macaé
联络： 励展博览集团国际销售部
地址： 北京市朝阳区新源南路1-3号平安国际金融中心A座15层01-03,05
联系人： 宫卫
☎ 010-5933 9268
🖷 010-5933 9233
✉ david.gong@reedexpo.com.cn
www.reedexport.cn
www.brasiloffshore.com

巴西圣保罗国际纺织工业及服装贸易博览会

FENIT

日期： 2011/06/17 - 20
地点： 巴西
联络： 上海比天展览服务有限公司
地址： 上海市中山北路900号加禾商务中心3号楼303室(200070)
联系人： 刘先生
☎ 021-5655 2843
🖷 021-5655 9981
www.betium.com

拉美国际环保及卫生展览会

AmbientalExpo:

Latin America Sanitation & Environmental Solutions Fair

Ambientalexpo

日期： 2011/06/28 - 30
地点： 巴西圣保罗Anhembi, Brazil
内容： 拉美国际环保及卫生展览会（Ambiental Expo）将成为新供应商、买家和其它专业人士在圣保罗会面的理想平台。圣保罗市也是整个南美最重要的城市之一。展览将展示最新产品、系统和解决方案，用于水、土壤、空气、滤渣、能源，及嘈音等领域，预计将有来自公共机构和私人公司的近5000名高端访客来此与90多个展出公司洽谈业务。
周期： 每年一届
市场范围： 国际性
性质： 面向贸易观众
上届规模 2010：展览面积7,000m²
主办： 励展巴西公司
联络： 励展博览集团国际销售部
地址： 北京市朝阳区新源南路1-3号平安国际金融中心A座15层01-03,05
联系人： 宫卫
☎ 010-5933 9268
🖷 010-5933 9233
✉ david.gong@reedexpo.com.cn
www.reedexport.cn
www.ambientalexpo.com.br

第27届巴西国际家具工业贸易展览会

ABIMOVEL

Date： 2011/08/09 - 12
地点： 巴西
周期： 两年一届
市场范围： 国际性
性质： 面向贸易观众
主办： 大连上选会展服务有限公司
地址： 大连市西岗区鞍山路13号兴业广场大厦B座508室（116011）
☎ 0411-8378 8326, 8378 8396, 8378 9165
🖷 0411-8378 8830, 8378 8823
✉ cicyhuang@vip.sina.com
MSN：cicyhuang@msn.com
www.sun-show.com

南美国际混凝土设备展览会

Concrete Show South America

日期： 2011/08 -
地点： 巴西圣保罗
周期： 每年一届
主办： 中国贸促会
地址： 北京市西城区三里河路46号（100823）
联系人： 张玉惠，郭旭萍，吕春丽
☎ 010-6859 4811, 6859 4994, 6859 4910
🖷 010-6859 4995
✉ zhangyuhui@ccpitmsc.org
www.chinamachine.org.cn

巴西造船、航运及海事展暨学术研讨会

Navalshore -

Shipbuilding and Offshore Industries Expo and Conference

日期：2011/08/03 - 05
地点：巴西里约热内卢SulAmérica 会议中心 Rio de Janeiro, Brazil
主办：博闻公司
☎ 852-2516 1612
🖷 852-3749 7347
✉ stella.fung@ubm.com
www.ubmnavalshore.com.br

巴西国际工程机械零部件及服务展览会

M&T EXPO PARTS AND SERVICES

日期：2011/08/10 - 13
地点：巴西圣保罗
周期：每年两届
主办：中国贸促会
地址：北京市西城区三里河路46号（100823）
联系人：张玉惠, 郭旭萍, 吕春丽
☎ 010-6859 4811, 6859 4994, 6859 4910
🖷 010-6859 4995
✉ zhangyuhui@ccpitmsc.org
www.chinamachine.org.cn

2011年巴西国际工程机械及矿山机械配件及技术展

日期：2011/08/10 - 13
地点：巴西圣保罗移民展览中心
内容：展会影响力波及巴西及整个南美洲国家。
始办年份：1991
周期：两年一届
市场范围：国际性
上届规模 2009：参展商436家（中国企业100家）
主办：巴西技术与设备维修协会
联络：北京麦田通会国际展览有限公司
联系人：吴珊
☎ 010-8248 4014转801, 5165 9302转8005
🖷 010-5165 9302转8004
✉ xiaoxiangzhishui@yahoo.com.cn
MSN：xiaoxiangzhishui@hotmail.com
www.cornfairs.com

巴西国际影像贸易及消费类电子展

PHOTOIMAGE BRAZIL:

International Image Trade Fair

PHOTOIMAGE BRAZIL
19th International Image Fair

日期：2011/08/16 - 18
地点：巴西圣保罗北方展览中心(Expo Center Norte)
内容：展会将吸引摄影器材及配件的主要厂商、代表及进口商。展会期间举办的业内大会和研讨会，使整个展会充满卓越 的商业机会，长期以来一直是国际知名影像类企业向南美乃至整个美洲市场展示自身最新技术及产品的最佳平台。巴西 — 将成为您打开南美市场的最佳通道。
产品及服务：光学镜头、光学附件、其他光电类产品、传统及数码照相机和摄像机；摄影摄像器材；摄影摄像配件及附件；影像消费品；胶片和数字存储媒介；数字图像处理；家庭 打印；照相亭系统；移动成像；LED显示技术；家庭影院；DVD播放器；幻灯技术和附件；成像服务等；专业照相机和灯光系统；摄影工作室器材；大开本印 刷；照相洗印服务材料；成像服务；数据/录像放映机；交互式演示系统；专业录像/音响技术；控制技术和网络；AV服务等。
周期：每年一届
市场范围：国际性
性质：面向贸易观众
主办：励展澳大利亚公司；励展博览集团巴西Alcantara Machado公司
联络：励展博览集团国际销售部
地址：北京市朝阳区新源南路1-3号平安国际金融中心A座15层01-03,05
联系人：宫卫
☎ 010-5933 9268
🖷 010-5933 9233
✉ david.gong@reedexpo.com.cn
www.photoimagebrazil.com.br

巴西里约热内卢国际汽车配件展览会

Rioparts

日期：2011/09 -
地点：巴西里约热内卢
周期：每年两届
主办：中国贸促会
地址：北京市西城区三里河路46号（100823）
联系人：张玉惠, 郭旭萍, 吕春丽
☎ 010-6859 4811, 6859 4994, 6859 4910
🖷 010-6859 4995
✉ zhangyuhui@ccpitmsc.org
www.chinamachine.org.cn

Febrava: 巴西国际制冷、空调、通风、供暖和空气处理贸易展

International Refrigeration, Air-conditioning, Ventilation, Heating and Air Treatment Trade Fair

FEBRAVA

日期：2011/09/20 - 23
地点：巴西圣保罗Imigrantes会展中心
内容：美洲第二大制冷、空调、通风、供暖和空气处理行业展会。展会吸引来自巴西和国际的业内最重要公司，是发布推动行业发展的解决方案和创新技术的理想场所。
周期：两年一届
市场范围：国际性
性质：面向贸易观众
参展费用：光地展位260美元/m^2, 标准展位340美元/m^2
上届规模 2009：参展商550家，参观人数29,261人
赞助：ABRAVA、SINDRATAR、ABIMAQ
主办：Reed Exhibitions Alcantara Machado BRAZIL
联络：励展博览集团国际销售部
地址：北京市朝阳区新源南路1-3号平安国际金融中心A座15层01-03,05（100738）
联系人：宫卫
☎ 010-5933 9268
🖷 010-5933 9233
✉ david.gong@reedexpo.com.cn
www.reedexport.cn

CASA & DECORACAO SHOW: 第2届巴西国际家居用品、室内装饰及五金工具展

Intl. Trade Fair of Products for Refurbishment & Decoration

日期：2011/09/22 - 25
地点：巴西圣保罗安年比展览中心（Anhembi）
内容：包括室内装饰、家居用品、家庭装修及装修用材料。 产品及服务：装饰品，桌子、床和浴室配件，地毯，垫子，窗帘，灯具，浴室家具，床垫，储藏、储物家具，厨房家具，卧室家具，客厅家具，DVD，音响，电视，通讯工具，办公家具，电子产品，电话，浴室配件， 储藏家具配件，厨房配件，起居室配件，卫生洁具，家居用品，灶台、烤箱，冰柜，冰箱，板材，木材，镶嵌工艺品，墙面装饰品，地板装饰品 金属器皿，涂料
周期：每年一届
主办：励展巴西公司（Reed Exhibitions Alcantara Machado）
联络：励展博览集团国际销售部
地址：北京市朝阳区新源南路1-3号平安国际金融中心A座15层01-03,05 （100027）
☎ 010-5933 9288
🖷 010-5933 9233
✉ liang.wang@reedexpo.com.cn
www.casaedecoracaoshow.com.br/en
www.reedexport.cn

巴西国际管材、配件、管道、阀门及组件展览会

TUBOTECH

日期：2011/10 -
地点：巴西圣保罗
周期：每年两届
主办：中国贸促会机械行业分会
地址：北京市西城区三里河路46号（100823）
联系人：张玉惠, 郭旭萍, 吕春丽
☎ 010-6859 4811, 6859 4994, 6859 4910
🖷 010-68594995
✉ zhangyuhui@ccpitmsc.org
www.chinamachine.org.cn

第11届巴西国际两轮车展览会

Intl Motorcycle, Bicycle, Parts & Equipment Show

日期：2011/10/04 - 09
地点：巴西圣保罗市安年比展览中心（ANHEMBI）
内容：展会吸引业内专家和客户共聚一堂，更多机会面对面交流，掌握国内国际业内资讯，可谓提供一站式服务。展览场地除了室内的部分，还包括室外的场地，其中设有试驾区，观众可以在此体验试驾乐趣及其他互动活动。
周期：两年一届
上届规模 2007：展览面积71,000m^2，参展商375家（国外展商25家），参观人数228,960人
主办：励展巴西公司（Alcantara Machado）
联络：励展博览集团国际销售部
地址：北京市朝阳区新源南路1-3号平安国际金融中心A座15层01-03,05 （100027）
☎ 010-5933 9288
🖷 010-5933 9233
✉ liang.wang@reedexpo.com.cn
www.reedexport.cn

巴西国际旅游展览会

（拉美国际旅游博览会）

Fair of the Americas:

Tourism Industry Trade Fair

日期：2011/10/19 - 21

地点：巴西里约热内卢里约展览中心（Riocentro Exhibition Center）
内容：被公认为是拉丁美洲旅游业最大的贸易展会，也是旅游行业商务与交流的大型论坛，汇集了产业链上所有的展会支持企业。
产品与服务：政府机构，旅游协会，旅游公司，航空公司，旅游操作，旅行社，游轮公司，房车租赁，宾馆酒店，保险公司，旅游资讯以及媒体机构。
周期：每年一届
主办：励展巴西公司（Alcantara Machado）
联络：励展博览集团国际销售部
地址：北京市朝阳区新源南路1-3号平安国际金融中心A座15层01-03,05 （100027）
联系人：宫卫
☎ 010-5933 9268
🖷 010-5933 9233
✉ david.gong@reedexpo.com.cn
www.feiradasamericas.com.br

巴西国际交通展览会

Fenatran:

International Transport Industry Trade Show

日期：2011/10/24 - 28
地点：巴西圣保罗安年比展览中心（Anhembi）
内容：将展示货物运输领域技术的发展状况，为众多观众及买家提供了巨大的商机。巴西国际交通展览会被公认为是拉丁美洲最大的技术性运输方面的展会，本展会将展示国际运输产品与设备，主要涉及公路运输方面。
产品与服务：货物运输企业、交通工具组装、工具制造商、汽车部件制造商、发动机与轮胎生产商、汽油及衍生产品经销商、设备维修站、行业情报。
周期：两年一届
上届规模 2005：展览面积78,000m^2，参展商353家（国外展商49家），参观人数46,718人（国外观众942人）
主办：励展巴西公司（Alcantara Machado）
联络：励展博览集团国际销售部
地址：北京市朝阳区新源南路1-3号平安国际金融中心A座15层01-03,05 （100027）
联系人：宫卫
☎ 010-5933 9268
🖷 010-5933 9233
✉ david.gong@reedexpo.com.cn
www.reedexport.cn

巴西国际铁路工业装备展览会

Business on Rails

日期：2011/11 -
地点：巴西圣保罗
周期：每年一届
主办：中国贸促会机械行业分会
地址：北京市西城区三里河路46号（100823）
联系人：张玉惠,郭旭萍,吕春丽
☎ 010-6859 4811, 6859 4994, 6859 4910
🖷 010-6859 4995
✉ zhangyuhui@ccpitmsc.org
www.chinamachine.org.cn

巴西石油化工设备展

Química & Petroquímica:

International Trade Fair of Machinery & Equipment for the Chemical & Petrochemical Industry

日期：2012/ -
地点：巴西圣保罗
内容：现在石油化工业的发展，在巴西甚至是在世界范围内都十分迅猛。除了世界人口自然增长这个原因之外，另一个原因是由于环境保护和关注意识越来越强，这促使人们去利用可持续资源来改善生活质量。根据相关部门统计：工业的装机容量为87%，年收入已达1,030亿美元，平均增长8%，预期2012年吸引投资200亿美元。本展会将是南美首个专门以石油化工、制药、化妆品、食品饮料、纤维素及纸张、农产品贸易等为内容的展会，在展会中，参展商都是机械、设备、零件及服务的供应商。
周期：两年一届
市场范围：国际性
性质：面向贸易观众
主办：励展巴西公司Alcantara Machado
联络：励展博览集团国际销售部
地址：北京市朝阳区新源南路1-3号平安国际金融中心A座15层01-03,05
联系人：宫卫
☎ 010-5933 9268
🖷 010-5933 9233
✉ david.gong@reedexpo.com.cn
www.reedexport.cn
www.quimica-petroquimica.com.br

巴西国际海洋石油及天然气工业设备展览会

Brazil Offshore:

International Offshore Oil and Gas Industry Trade Show and Conference

日期：2013 -
地点：巴西里约州马珈耶Macaé, Roberto Marinho展览中心
内容：作为世界第三大海洋石油工业产品贸易展会，巴西国际海洋石油天然气工业设备展是众多成功业内贸易展会之一，在参展公司和观众的数量和质量上有突飞猛进的增长。巨大的投资焦点在于探索新发现并将海洋石油的前沿推向超深水域，而巴西在这一领域正处于世界领先水平。
同期举办的展会：国际海洋石油与天然气工业会议、IBP-巴西石油及生物燃料研究所、SPE-汽油工程师组织、商务谈判、ONIP-国家汽油工业组织、SEBRAE-RJ
周期：两年一届
市场范围：国际性
性质：面向贸易观众
赞助：IBP; ONIP; SPE; FIRJAN; Macaé市政厅; 里约州政府; Upstream; Offshore Engineer; Brasil Energia, Click Macaé.
主办：励展巴西公司
联络：励展博览集团国际销售部
地址：北京市朝阳区新源南路1-3号平安国际金融中心A座15层01-03,05 （100027）
联系人：宫卫
☎ 010-5933 9268
🖷 010-5933 9233
✉ david.gong@reedexpo.com.cn
www.reedexport.cn
www.brasiloffshore.com

巴西纺织机械展

ITMEX Americas:

International Textile Machinery Trade Fair

日期：2013 -
地点：巴西圣保罗Anhembi, Brazil
内容：此展再次展出创新型高技术非织造品，机械装备、必需件及零件、卫生用品（尿布、卫生巾、湿纸巾），非织造品转换器，转换用机械及装备，转换必需材料及零件。同时举办的展会还有 Fenatec, Feimaco, Expolav and Ponto Final。
产品及服务：非织造品、高技术纺织品、其它技术纺织品、机械和设备，生产必需品和零件、一次性卫生用品（尿布、卫生巾、湿纸巾）、非织造品转换器、转换机械及设备、转换器必需品及零件。
周期：两年一届
市场范围：国际性
性质：面向贸易观众
参展费用：光地展位260美元，标准展位340美元
主办：励展巴西公司；
联络：励展博览集团国际销售部
地址：北京市朝阳区新源南路1-3号平安国际金融中心A座15层01-03,05 （100027）
联系人：宫卫
☎ 010-5933 9268
🖷 010-5933 9233
✉ david.gong@reedexpo.com.cn
www.reedexport.cn

加拿大
Canada

2011年加拿大蒙特利尔国际食品饮料展览会

2011 SIAL Montreal

日期：2011/04 -
地点：加拿大蒙特利尔展览中心
内容：食品添加剂、佐料、熟食、奶制品、蛋制品、猪肉制品和腌制品、新鲜肉类和肠类、新鲜家禽和野味、海产品、新鲜水果蔬菜、水果干和脱水蔬菜、甜食、饼干、面包、罐头食品、冷冻食品、生物制品、宠物食品、食品杂货、冰淇淋、含酒精饮料、一般饮料等各类食品饮料。
始办年份：2001
周期：每年一届
市场范围：国际性
性质：面向公众
主办：SIAL Montréal
联络：杭州思诺博会展服务有限公司
地址：杭州市体育场路229号浙江粮油大厦1202室（310003）
☎ 0571-8577 8500
🖷 0571-8577 9709
✉ expo@sinobal.com
www.sinobal.com

2011年加拿大国际汽车零配件及售后服务展览会

Automechanika Canada 2011

日期：2011/06/01-04
内容：作为加拿大汽配市场唯一的展览会，为国际供应商进入加拿大市场及巩固现有业务提供了良好的交流平台。观众来自维修商、技术人员、零售商、分销商、批发商、制造厂商、媒体及业内人士。参展范围有部 件及系统，附件及改装，维修及保养，加油站和洗车房
周期：两年一届
上届规模：展览面积3,500m2，参展商202家，专业观众124,900人
联络：中国汽车工业国际合作总公司
地址：北京市海淀区中关村丹棱街3号A座国机大厦（100080）
☎ 010-8260 6881, 6891, 6893, 6874
🖷 010-8260 6883, 8260 6790
联系人：马蓉，刘岩，娄杰，杨菁
✉ exhibition@cnaico.com.cn
www.autochina.com.cn

哥伦比亚
Colombia

哥伦比亚国际纺织服装展

Colombiatex
日期：2011/01/25 - 27

地点：哥伦比亚
联络：上海比天展览服务有限公司
地址：上海市中山北路900号加禾商务中心3号楼303室(200070)
联系人：刘先生
☎ 021-5655 2843
🖷 021-5655 9981
www.betium.com

捷克 Czech Republic

2011年捷克布鲁诺国际汽车展

Autosalon Bron 2011

日期：2011/06/03-09
地点：捷克布鲁诺
内容：中部欧洲唯一针对多用途运载车的博览会。范围有整车类：卡车货车、巴士、拖车；汽车零部件、汽车相关外围产品及设备包括车用装饰品等汽车制造、操作和修理、汽车相关维修设备/工具、手工具；汽车配件、燃油、润滑油和加油站；公路交通服务
上届规模 2010：展览面积90,000平方米，参展商1,000家，参观人数70,765人（来自23个国家）
联络：中国汽车工业国际合作总公司
地址：北京市海淀区中关村丹棱街3号A座国机大厦（100080）
☎ 010-8260 6881, 6891, 6893, 6874
🖷 010-8260 6883, 8260 6790
联系人：马蓉，刘岩，娄杰，杨菁
E-mail: exhibition@cnaico.com.cn
www.autochina.com.cn

捷克布鲁诺国际服装展

Styl & Kabo

日期：2011/08/23 - 25
地点：捷克
联络：上海比天展览服务有限公司
地址：上海市中山北路900号加禾商务中心3号楼303室(200070)
联系人：刘先生
☎ 021-5655 2843
🖷 021-5655 9981
www.betium.com

捷克国际机械博览会 国际机床展览会

MSV & IMT

日期：2011/10/03 - 07
地点：捷克布尔诺
周期：每年一届
主办：中国贸促会机械行业分会
地址：北京市西城区三里河路46号（100823）
联系人：张玉惠,郭旭萍,吕春丽
☎ 010-6859 4811, 6859 4994, 6859 4910
🖷 010-6859 4995
✉ zhangyuhui@ccpitmsc.org
www.chinamachine.org.cn

丹麦 Denmark

哥本哈根国际服装博览会

CIFF

日期：2011/02/11 - 14
地点：丹麦哥本哈根
联络：上海比天展览服务有限公司
地址：上海市中山北路900号加禾商务中心3号楼303室(200070)
联系人：刘先生
☎ 021-5655 2843
🖷 021-5655 9981
www.betium.com

丹麦哥本哈根国际服装展览会

CIFF

日期：2011/08/12 - 15
地点：丹麦哥本哈根
联络：上海比天展览服务有限公司
地址：上海市中山北路900号加禾商务中心3号楼303室(200070)
联系人：刘先生
☎ 021-5655 2843
🖷 021-5655 9981
www.betium.com

丹麦哥本哈根国际家具展

CODE2010

日期：2011/09/01 - 04
地点：丹麦
☎ 0411-8378 8831
🖷 0411-8378 8830

埃及 Egypt

开罗国际博览会

日期：2011/03 -
地点：埃及开罗
周期：三年一届
市场范围：国际性
主办：中国贸促会机械行业分会
地址：北京市西城区三里河路46号（100823）
联系人：张玉惠,郭旭萍,吕春丽
☎ 010-6859 4811, 6859 4994, 6859 4910
🖷 010-6859 4995
✉ zhangyuhui@ccpitmsc.org
www.chinamachine.org.cn

2011年第四十四届埃及开罗贸易展览会

日期：2011/03/06 - 10
地点：埃及开罗国际展览中心
内容：该博览会已成为埃及每年一届的盛会，在非洲具有相当大的影响力。中国主要出口产品为食品、农业机械、工程机械、摩托车、彩电接收机、卡车和汽车零部件、阀门、单相交流电动机、五金件、工具类、计算机、空气调节器、家用电扇、灯具、电缆、餐具、照明器材、计量仪表、水果榨汁机和搅拌机、电话机、电脑零部件、铸塑机、锁具、轴承、收音机、厨房用具、吸尘器、热水器、工业缝纫机、绣花机、插头与插座、扬声器等这些产品在出口数量和出口创汇上都大幅度增长。
周期：每年一届
市场范围：国际性
上届规模：展览面积200,000m^2, 参展商4300家
主办：北京麦田通会国际展览有限公司
联系人：吴珊
☎ 010-8248 4014转801
🖷 010-5165 9302转8004
✉ xiaoxiangzhishui@yahoo.com.cn
MSN：xiaoxiangzhishui@hotmail.com
www.cornfairs.com

2011年第十届埃及食品及食品科技展

Food Fair &Tech

日期：2011/05/23 - 26
地点：埃及开罗国际会议与展览中心
内容：埃及食品加工业中最具发展潜力的行业是对冷冻水果、蔬菜、果汁和果酱以及半成品的加工。罐头类食品、休闲方便食品和快餐的国内需求不断增长。埃及是阿拉伯世界最大的国家，有着充裕的旅游、石油、运河外汇收入，每年要进口大量的消费品和原材料。埃及在经济上与中国互补性强，工业产品价格高，产业与技术梯度低于中国，是中国产品、设备、技术、资本转移的最佳地区。展品范围有食品、食品科技、食品机械。
周期：每年一届
市场范围：国际性
主办：AGD Arabian Group for Development
联络：北京领汇国际展览有限公司
地址：北京市朝阳区农展馆南路13号瑞辰国际中心719（100125）
联系人：刘佳
☎ 010-5129 5359转8505
🖷 010-5129 5379转8505
✉ expo8505@worldfairs.cn
MSN：expo8505@worldfairs.cn

泛阿拉伯/非洲地区国际汽车及零配件展览会

AUTOMECH

日期：2011/06 -
地点：埃及开罗
周期：每年一届
主办：中国贸促会
地址：北京市西城区三里河路46号（100823）
联系人：张玉惠, 郭旭萍, 吕春丽
☎ 010-6859 4811, 6859 4994, 6859 4910
🖷 010-6859 4995
邮箱：zhangyuhui@ccpitmsc.org
www.chinamachine.org.cn

埃及开罗国际建材、家具展

INTER BUILD2011

日期：2011/06/23 - 27
地点：埃及开罗
☎ 0411-8378 8831
🖷 0411-8378 8830

埃及国际机床工具展览会

MACTECH

日期：2011/11 -
地点：埃及开罗
周期：每年一届
主办：中国贸促会
地址：北京市西城区三里河路46号（100823）
联系人：张玉惠, 郭旭萍, 吕春丽
☎ 010-6859 4811, 6859 4994, 6859 4910
🖷 010-6859 4995
✉ zhangyuhui@ccpitmsc.org
www.chinamachine.org.cn

泛阿拉伯/非洲塑料橡胶材料展览会

PLASTEX

日期：2011/11 -
地点：埃及开罗
周期：每年一届
主办：中国贸促会机械行业分会
地址：北京市西城区三里河路46号（100823）
联系人：张玉惠, 郭旭萍, 吕春丽
☎ 010-6859 4811, 6859 4994, 6859 4910
🖷 010-6859 4995
✉ zhangyuhui@ccpitmsc.org
www.chinamachine.org.cn

埃及国际纺织品交易会

EGYTEX

日期：2011/11/02 - 04
地点：埃及
联络：上海比天展览服务有限公司
地址：上海市中山北路900号加禾商务中心3号楼303室(200070)
联系人：刘先生
☎ 021-5655 2843
🖷 021-5655 9981
www.betium.com

法国
France

Eclat de Mode / Bijorhca:
巴黎国际服装、珠宝、银饰及配件展览会
International Event dedicated to the Fashion Jewellery Universe

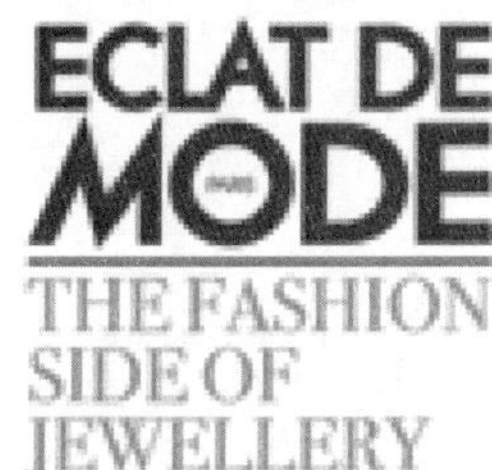

日期：2011/01/21 - 24
地点：法国巴黎凡尔赛门展览中心
内容：服装设计、高级女装珠宝设计、银饰、金饰和金器珠宝、时尚手表、穿刺配饰、时尚配饰、其他（工业和代理）
周期：每年两届
主办：励展法国公司
联络：励展博览集团国际销售部
联系人：申健
☎ 010-5933 9299
🖷 010-5933 9233
✉ jerry.shen@reedexpo.com.cn
www.reedexport.cn

法国巴黎国际家具展
Masion & Objet 2011

日期：2011/01/21 - 25
地点：法国巴黎
☎ 0411-8378 8831
🖷 0411-8378 8830

世界音乐博览会
MIDEM
The World's Music Market

日期：2011/01/22 - 26
地点：法国戛纳Palais des Festivals, France
内容：与音乐产业及其关联产业相关的所有产品与服务。通过丰富的会议与联络活动帮助参会代表全面、深入了解产业与市场的最新资讯和发展趋势。MIDEM国际音乐博览会观众来自93个国家、覆盖各种音乐类别和所有产业细分市场的10,000多名音乐界专业人士。MIDEM致力于为国际音乐产业提供交易、联络、交流、发现新音乐风格与人才、吸取资讯的贸易展会平台。
始办年份：1967
上届规模：展览面积5,930m^2，参展商1,703家，参观人数7,200人
主办：励展法国公司
联络：励展博览集团国际销售部
地址：北京市朝阳区新源南路1-3号平安国际金融中心A座15层01-03,05
联系人：吴祥
☎ 010-5933 9277
🖷 010-5933 9233
✉ ronald.wu@reedexpo.com.cn
www.midem.com

法国国际纺织面料春季博览会
(TEXWORLD)

日期：2011/02/07 - 10
地点：法国巴黎
内容：服装面料、辅料
主办：法兰克福展览(法国)公司
联络：中国贸促会纺织行业分会
联系人：黎明家、沈桢
☎ 010-8522 9062，8522 9463
🖷 010-8522 9296

第一视觉面料博览会（春）
Premiere Vision

日期：2011/02/09 - 12
地点：法国
联络：上海比天展览服务有限公司
地址：上海市中山北路900号加禾商务中心3号楼303室(200070)
联系人：刘先生
☎ 021-5655 2843
🖷 021-5655 9981
www.betium.com

法国国际农牧业设备及技术展览会
SIMA

日期：2011/02/20 - 24
地点：法国巴黎北维勒班展览中心
内容：多功能设备，专业设备。巴黎国际农牧业展览会（SIMAGENA）：畜牧饲养者和育种者的国际商务会晤，再生能源
周期：两年一届
市场范围：国际性
性质：面向公众
上届规模 2009：展览面积122,446m^2，参展商1,323家（国外展商529家），参观人数208,550人
主办：法国爱博西玛公司
地址：北京市朝阳区朝外大街20号联合大厦710室（100020）
联系人：卢晓成
☎ 010-6588 5968, 6588 5969
🖷 010-6588 5970
✉ louislu@promosalons-china.com

法国国际地产投资交易会
MIPIM featuring MIPIM Horizons:
The World's Property Market

日期：2011/03/08 - 11
地点：法国戛纳影节宫Palais des Festivals, France
内容：房地产、建筑。MIPIM是世界上唯一聚集全球房地产界最具影响力的人物的交易会。它创造独一无二的、绝佳的联络、展示以及商业机会。房地产顾问、开发商、地区官员、投资者以及公司最终用户可在展会上搜集新楼信息、开展新交易以及创建新的伙伴关系。
产品及服务：为投资者、公司最终用户、当地及地区官员、开发商、经纪商、资产管理者以及服务供应商提供商业机会。另有内容丰富的研讨会活动以及各种社交联络活动，令参会者深刻理解房地产业并获取国际房地产业的最新资讯动态。
周期：每年一届
市场范围：国际性
性质：面向贸易观众
上届规模：展览面积18,003m^2，参展商8,737家，参观人数17,300人
主办：励展法国展览公司
联络：励展博览集团国际销售部
地址：北京市朝阳区新源南路1-3号平安国际金融中心A座15层01-03,05
联系人：吴祥
☎ 010-5933 9209
🖷 010-5933 9233
✉ ronald.wu@reedexpo.com.cn
www.mipim.com

巴黎国际特许经营展览会
Franchise Expo Paris:
International Franchise Show

日期：2011/03/20 - 23
地点：法国巴黎Porte de Versailles, Paris, France
内容：授予特许经营者，服务供应商及机构
始办年份：1981
周期：每年一届
市场范围：国际性
性质：面向贸易观众
主办：励展法国公司
联络：励展博览集团国际销售部
地址：北京市朝阳区新源南路1-3号平安国际金融中心A座15层01-03,05
联系人：王亮
☎ 010-5933 9288
🖷 010-5933 9233
✉ liang.wang@reedexpo.com.cn
www.reedexport.cn

世界卫生纸展览会
Tissue World

日期：2011/03/29 - 31
地点：法国尼斯卫城展览中心Nice, France
主办：亚洲博闻
电话：+65-6592 0890
传真：+65-6438 6090
邮箱：gwen.ng@ubm.com
联络：博闻（广州）展览有限公司
☎ 020-8666 0158
🖷 020-8667-7120
✉ info-china@ubm.com
www.tissueworld.com

巴黎国际实时运输及物流展
SITL Real Time:
International Logistics Solutions Show

日期：2011/03/29 - 31
地点：法国巴黎凡尔赛门展览馆 Paris Expo - Porte de Versailles, France
内容：SITL Real Time为运输及物流业展览会，旨在向业界展示营销供应链管理中的整套服务及产品，是运输与物流业界必不可少的重要B2B商业平台。观众及参展商通过参加商务会议获得新知，并交流市场的最新动态，以获得提升企业经营及策略规划等竞争优势。
产品与服务：运输与联合运输服务、海外服务、物

流服务、运输、物流设备及服务、运输、物流技术与信息服务、物流基础设施、物流地产、其他相关服务
始办年份：1982
周期：两年一届
性质：面向贸易观众
上届规模 2009：参展商497家，参观人数24,573人
主办：励展法国公司
联络：励展博览集团国际销售部
地址：北京市朝阳区新源南路1-3号平安国际金融中心A座15层01-03,05
联系人：宫卫
☎ 010-5933 9268
🖷 010-5933 9233
✉ david.gong@reedexpo.com.cn
www.sitl.eu
www.reedexport.cn

法国国际批发商博览会
INTERSELECTION

日期：2011/04/04 - 06
地点：法国
联络：上海比天展览服务有限公司
地址：上海市中山北路900号加禾商务中心3号楼303室(200070)
联系人：刘先生
☎ 021-5655 2843
🖷 021-5655 9981
www.betium.com

法国戛纳春季电视节
MIPTV
The World's Entertainment Content Market

日期：2011/04/04 - 08
地点：法国戛纳影节宫Palais des Festivals, Cannes, France
内容：电视，电影，网络和移动视听设备，系列商务交际活动，让参与观众面对面交流，掌握最新行业资讯
始办年份：1963
周期：每年一届
上届规模：展览面积20,256m^2，参展商1,542家，参观人数12,044人
主办：励展法国公司
联络：励展博览集团国际销售部
地址：北京市朝阳区新源南路1-3号平安国际金融中心A座15层01-03,05
联系人：王亮
☎ 010-5933 9288
🖷 010-5933 9233
✉ liang.wang@reedexpo.com.cn
www.mipworld.com

法国国际纺织面料秋季博览会
(TEXWORLD)

日期：2011/09 -
地点：法国巴黎
内容：服装面料、辅料
主办：法兰克福展览(法国)公司
联络：中国贸促会纺织行业分会
联系人：沈桢，黎明家
☎ 010-8522 9463, 8522 9062
🖷 010-8522 9296

中国纺织品服装贸易展览会(巴黎)
CTAF - China Textile and Apparel Trade Fair(Paris)

日期：2011/09 -
地点：法国巴黎
内容：服装、服饰
主办：中国纺织工业协会；中国贸促会纺织行业分会
联系人：王彤、张嘉
☎ 010-8522 9482, 8522 9376
🖷 010-85229544

法国巴黎Masion & Objet 2011

日期：2011/09/09 - 13
地点：法国巴黎
☎ 0411-8378 8831
🖷 0411-8378 8830

2011年第九届法国巴黎国际美容展览会
Beyond Beauty Paris

日期：2011/09/12 - 14
地点：法国巴黎凡尔赛门展览中心
Porte de Versailles, France
内容：COSMEETING展区：香水、化妆品、美容护理、护肤产品、天然化妆品、家用香料、美容配件；CREATIVE展区：包装，设备，私有标牌、定单生产，咨询与设计，促销产品，广告材料，陈列与展示。EUROPEAN SPA展区：专业的皮肤护理产品，专业附件产品，专业设备仪器。

此展是一个汇聚美容市场，产品及经营管理众多资讯的聚会交流平台，提供了对整个美容市场——从原料到成品全方位的视角。

始办年份：2003
周期：每年一届
市场范围：国际性
性质：面向公众
上届规模 2010：参展商530家，参观人数19,500人
主办：ITEC（法国）公司
联络：杭州思诺博会展服务有限公司
地址：浙江省杭州市体育场路229号浙江粮油大厦1202室（310003）
联系人：汪霞小姐
☎ 0571-8577 8500
🖷 0571-8577 9709
✉ expo@sinobal.com
www.sinobal.com

法国第一视觉面料博览会（秋）
Premiere Vision

日期：2011/09/14 - 16
地点：法国
联络：上海比天展览服务有限公司
地址：上海市中山北路900号加禾商务中心3号楼303室(200070)
联系人：刘先生
☎ 021-5655 2843
🖷 021-5655 9981
www.betium.com

Viscom Paris:
第23届法国巴黎国际视觉广告技术及标识制作展
The International Event for Visual Communication

日期：2011/09/27 - 29
地点：法国巴黎维勒班特国际展览中心（Paris Nord Villepinte）
内容：展会汇集了制图行业专家，将所有的最新概念和技术一一呈现，其中涉及数码打印，丝网印刷。展会 针对数码打印和视觉效果，以及丝网印刷和标牌制作的新动态，进行深度挖掘和比较开发。展会范围涉及面广泛，几乎涵盖业内所有竞争力强的技术和极具创新性的产品。
产品及服务：视觉行业的所有生产商、供应商和服务提供商：标志、标牌、数码影像、数字标牌、后期制作、丝网印刷、模切机、雕版印刷。
周期：每年一届
赞助：法国标牌协会（SYNAFEL），法国数字标牌协会（APCAD）
主办：励展法国公司（Reed Expositions France）
联络：励展博览集团国际销售部，
地址：北京市朝阳区新源南路1-3号平安国际金融中心A座15层01-03,05 （100027）
☎ 010-5933 9288
🖷 010-5933 9233
✉ liang.wang@reedexpo.com.cn
www.viscom-paris.com
www.reedexport.cn

巴黎国际汽车工业展
EQUIP'AUTO

日期：2011/10 -
地点：法国巴黎北维勒班展览中心
内容：汽车工程、转包加工项目；汽车零部件和配饰、售后网络；物流；个人防护产品；石化产品、润滑油、护理产品；渠道管理系统、信息技术；维修、护养；车身、油漆；汽车服务；专业人士服务、业务分化；其它相关展示
始办年份：1975
周期：两年一届
市场范围：国际性
性质：面向公众
上届规模 2007：展览面积160,000m^2，参展商2,022家（国外展商1,617家），参观人数106,407人
主办：法国高美爱博展览集团
地址：北京市朝阳区朝外大街20号联合大厦710室（100020）
联系人：卢晓成
☎ 010-6588 5968, 6588 5969
🖷 010-6588 5970
✉ louislu@promosalons-china.com

FIAC:
第38届法国国际当代艺术展览会
International Contemporary Art Fair

日期：2011/10/20 - 23
地点：法国巴黎Grand Palais展览馆及Cour Carree du Louvre展览馆
内容：魅力巴黎：高品质生活方式和富有艺术气息的氛围。FIAC展览场地的世界级品质无人能及，无论是设备还是参展观众，都是超一流的，而且展览场地的设计避免了过度浪费，遵循着以人为本的设计理念。展览范围涉及广泛，包括现代，当代作品以及流行艺术和设计作品。创新理念独占鳌头（创新项目，相关活动和每年举行的各种奖项活动等）。
产品及服务：现代和当代艺术交易市场，展示油画、雕塑、素描、印刷品、纸上作品、摄影、录像及装置艺术。
观众来源：法国及国际艺术品经销商、收集家、展览馆长、博物馆及基金会。
周期：每年一届
主办：励展法国公司
联络：励展博览集团国际销售部
地址：北京市朝阳区新源南路1-3号平安国际金融中心A座15层01-03,05
联系人：李悦
☎ 010-5933 9298
🖷 010-5933 9233
✉ anna.li@reedexpo.com.cn
www.fiac.com

法国国际批发商博览会界音乐博览会
INTERSELECTION

日期：2011/10/19 - 21
地点：法国
联络：上海比天展览服务有限公司
地址：上海市中山北路900号加禾商务中心3号楼303室(200070)
联系人：刘先生
☎ 021-5655 2843
🖷 021-5655 9981
www.betium.com

法国巴黎服装服饰定牌贸易展览会
FATEX

日期：2011/10/20 - 22
地点：法国
联络：上海比天展览服务有限公司
地址：上海市中山北路900号加禾商务中心3号楼303室(200070)
联系人：刘先生
☎ 021-5655 2843
🖷 021-5655 9981
www.betium.com

法国国际葡萄酒及果蔬技术展
SITEVI

日期：2011/11 -
地点：法国蒙彼利埃展览中心
内容：葡萄、果蔬种植设备，葡萄收获，葡萄酒酿制、葡萄酒工艺，包装，水果与蔬菜，灌溉，农用物资和服务类
始办年份：1977
周期：两年一届
市场范围：国际性
性质：面向公众
上届规模 2009：展览面积35,190m^2，参展商720家（国外展商174家），参观人数44,592人
主办：法国爱博西玛公司
地址：北京市朝阳区朝外大街20号联合大厦710室（100020）
联系人：卢晓成
☎ 010-6588 5968, 6588 5969
🖷 010-6588 5970
✉ louislu@promosalons-china.com

巴黎国际殡葬展：
殡葬行业供应商与经销商的展会（第13届）
Funéraire Paris 2011：
The Exhibition for Funeral Suppliers & Distributors

日期：2011/11 -
地点：法国巴黎Paris Le Bourget, France
内容：欧洲及世界范围内殡葬业产品以及与之相配套的服务，包括：纪念碑，墓碑，棺材，骨灰瓮，殡葬服务，殡葬防腐产品，殡仪运输，大理石，专业媒体与组织。
产品及服务：追悼会、仪式、殡葬处理、服务、设备与器具、材料、贸易媒体及专业组织。
参展费用：标准展位269欧元/m^2，光地展位203欧元/m^2
上届规模 2009：展览面积9,500m^2(国外展商面积233m^2)，参展商233家（国外展商65家），参观人数5,639人（国外参观人数1196人）
主办：励展法国公司（Reed Expositions France）
联络：励展博览集团国际销售部
地址：北京市朝阳区新源南路1-3号平安国际金融中心A座15层01-03,05
联系人：王颖
☎ 010-5933 9208
🖷 010-5933 9233
✉ winnie.wang@reedexpo.com.cn
www.reedexport.cn

法国戛纳电视节
MIPCOM:
The World's Entertainment Content Market

日期：2011/11/03 - 06
地点：法国戛纳影节宫（Palais des Festivals）
内容：法国戛纳电视节是世界上领先的电视传媒展会。众多参展商以此为平台满足自己设计、联合制作、购买、出售、融资、发行娱乐产品的市场需求。
产品和服务：展览平台，会议，策划宣传活动，审核机构，网络交流及洽淡 市场中介，俱乐部：VIP俱乐部、购买商俱乐部、参与者俱乐部，在线影视数据库，在线影视媒体中心。 观众来源：广播电台及相关频道，有线/卫星、IPTV运营商，制片、出品、经销商，影视工作室负责人、独立机构，共同出品伙伴、国际金融家，特别委员、影视传媒基金、权利机构，广告公司、品牌公司，授权许可机构负责人，在线媒体、游戏开发人员、社会广播电视网络，发行商、交互技术人员、数字影视创作人员
周期：每年一届
上届规模：展览面积22,218m^2，参展商1,698家（国外展商1,497家），参观人数12,279人
主办：法国Reed MIDEM
联络：励展博览集团国际销售部
地址：北京市朝阳区新源南路1-3号平安国际金融中心A座15层01-03,05 （100027）
☎ 010-5933 9288
🖷 010-5933 9233
✉ liang.wang@reedexpo.com.cn
www.mipworld.com
www.reedexport.cn

BATIMAT:
第28届法国巴黎国际建筑展览会
The World's Leading Construction Exhibition

日期：2011/11/7 - 12
地点：法国巴黎
内容：主体工程区-屋架、结构构件、屋顶、防水材料、保温隔热材料、主体结构材料和构配件、水处理系统、排水系统；门窗及五金区；装饰装修区-各种隔段材料、橱柜、墙地面装饰材料、瓷砖、大理石、花岗石、其它石材、石板、木质板材、木地板、油漆涂料、壁炉及烟道、厨房装饰、照明、装饰材料、游泳池装修及其设备、露天家具及设施、户外运动及娱乐设施；建筑施工设备区。
观众构成：承包商、建筑工匠39%，建筑师、开发商 24%，零售商、分销商17%，制造商15%。
周期：两年一届
上届规模：展览面积220,000m^2，参展商2,382 家（44%来自52个国家），参观人数380,000人（16%来自171个国家）
主办：励展博览集团
联络：励展博览集团国际销售部
地址：北京市朝阳区新源南路1-3号平安国际金融中心A座15层01-03,05
联系人：吴祥
☎ 010-5933 9277
🖷 010-5933 9233
✉ ronald@reedexpo.com.cn
www.batimat.com
www.reedexport.cn

MIDEST:
法国国际工业配件展（第41届）
The World's Leading Industrial Subcontracting Show

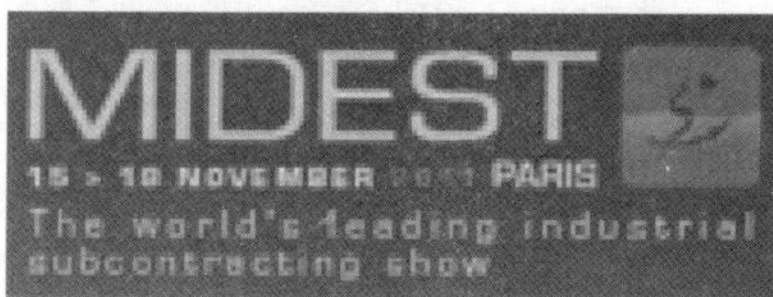

日期：2011/11/15 - 18
地点：法国巴黎维勒班特展览中心（Paris - Nord, Villepinte）
内容：全球规模最大、最著名的工业分包展。MIDEST以承揽来样、来图加工及零配件加工业务，即分包／转包为展会特色，是欧洲主要生产行业制造商、装配商和构件供应商之间面对面交流，共同达成订单交易的一流平台。
市场优势：MIDEST分包专业性强，成交量大，成交后交易延续性好；多数订单是按照来图来样加工，确认样品供货，一旦成交，客户很少更换供货商。
展品范围：金属加工业（铸造、锻造、切割、焊接），金属表面处理及模具 微技术加工，电子加工
观众来源：一般管理层、技术、采购、研发、质量部门。
周期：每年一届
参展费用：标准展位268欧元/m^2，光地展位218欧元/m^2
上届规模 2010：参展商1,710家，参观人数40,424人
主办：励展法国公司（Reed Expositions France）
联络：励展博览集团国际销售部
地址：北京市朝阳区新源南路1-3号平安国际金融中心A座15层01-03,05
联系人：宫卫，刘昫珺
☎ 010-5933 9268，5933 9200
🖷 010-5933 9233
✉ david.gong@reedexpo.com.cn
✉ natalie.liu@reedexpo.com.cn
www.midest.com
www.reedexport.cn

2011欧洲食品及天然配料展
Food ingredients Europe & Natural ingredients

日期：2011/11/29 - 01
地点：法国巴黎
内容：在法国巴黎同期举行两大主题展--欧洲食品配料展、天然原料展，是为欧洲食品配料、食品添加剂及天然原料量身定制的专业展览会，将会汇集世界食品行业的研发、生产、采购分销的专业人士。近年来中国食品配料以其种类丰富、物美价廉的优势逐渐受到国际市场的重视，食品配料企业在引进国外食品配料及添加剂最新技术和产品的同时，也加大了开拓国际市场的力度。
周期：两年一届
市场范围：国际性
上届规模：参展商1,250家，参观人数20,800人
主办：欧洲UBM集团公司
联络：北京领汇国际展览有限公司
地址：北京市朝阳区农展馆南路13号瑞辰国际中心719（100125）
联系人：刘佳
☎ 010-5129 5359转8505
🖷 010-5129 5379转8505
✉ expo8505@worldfairs.cn
MSN：expo8505@worldfairs.cn

国际环保工业展
POLLUTEC

日期：2011/12 -
地点：法国巴黎凡尔赛门展览中心
内容：自来水技术，城市污水处理，工业废水处理，垃圾处理，废物再生利用技术，能源及环境，地面去污，气体污染治理，防治噪声，分析及监测设备，洁净工业技术，景观保护，清洁工业，生态工业区，污染预防，太阳能、风能及小水电站，隔热保温及热能的回收利用，地热，热力网。巴黎展侧重工业环保，里昂展既有工业环保，又有城市环保
周期：每年一届
市场范围：国际性
性质：面向公众
上届规模 2009：展览面积25,800m²，参展商1,451家，参观人数35,890人
主办：法国励展公司
联络：励展博览集团国际销售部
地址：北京市朝阳区信源里南路1-3号平安国际金融中心A座01-03, 05（100020）
联系人：张静
☎ 010-5933 9288
🖷 010-5933 9233

法国国际工业自动化展

SCS

日期：2011/12 -
地点：法国巴黎北维勒班展览中心
内容：自动化：工业自动化设备和系统，自动化零部件，传感器，工业自动化信息技术及软件，有线和无线通讯技术；电气能源：BT 器材和工业检测设备，BT 电气零部件，控制装置和分配系统，能源的持续、质量和转换，功率电子元件，数据的测试、分析和采集，电气能源的制造，电气能源的经营和供给；传动装置： 液压泵、零部件和传动装置，气动压缩机、零部件和传动装置，机械零部件和传动装置，轴承和限位器，H.P.V. 操作和连接
周期：每年一届
市场范围：国际性
性质：面向公众
上届规模 2007：展览面积20,000m²，参展商600家（国外展商121家），参观人数25,000人
主办：法国智奥展览集团
地址：北京市朝阳区朝外大街20号联合大厦710室（100020）
联系人：张静
☎ 010-6588 5968, 6588 5969
🖷 010-6588 5970
✉ jackiezhang@promosalons-china.com

Interclima+elec Home&building

巴黎国际供暖、制冷、空调、新能源及家用电气展览会

日期：2012 /02 -
地点：法国巴黎Paris Expo - Porte de Versailles
内容：由国际知名展览机构--励展博览法国公司主办的Interclima每两年一届，2010年将是第19届，是目前世界上供暖、制冷、空调及智能建筑领域规模最大、影响力最强的专业展会之一。 2008年的Interclima展会，无论是在展出面积还是观众人数上，均又创历史新高。展出净面积超过7万m²，展商则比2004年增加了22.5%。平均每个展商在展出期间建立的有效联系为650个。2008年的Interclima接待观众人数达102620人次，比2006年增加20.5%。其中，来自法国以外的观众有7700多名，占总数的7.53%；贸易商与制造商占35%强，安装商占39%强。 Interclima展的潜力却非常巨大。因为德国、意大利的相关市场已经进入成熟期，而法国却还处于发展期。也正因如此，所以法国政府对建筑住宅用冷凝锅炉、制冷、供暖设备提供高达40%的补贴，对某些太阳能采暖设施及加热泵的补贴更高达50%。另外，法国工业部长亲临参观上届展会也说明了法国政府对新能源技术的高度重视。
周期：两年一届
市场范围：国际性
性质：面向贸易观众
参展费用：光地展位240欧元/m²，标准展位（9m²）325-517欧元/m²（价格不含增值税19%）
主办：励展博览集团国际销售部
地址：北京市朝阳区新源南路1-3号平安国际金融中心A座15层01-03,05
联系人：杜一鸣
☎ 010-5933 9209
🖷 010-5933 9233
✉ martin.du@reedexpo.com.cn
www.reedexport.cn

欧洲国际运输及物流周

SITL Europe:

International Event for Transport & Logistics

日期：2012/03 -
地点：法国巴黎北维勒班特展馆
内容：欧洲国际运输及物流周（SITL Europe）向业界展示营销供应链管理中的整套服务及产品，是运输与物流业界必不可少的重要B2B商业平台。观众及参展商通过参加商务会议获得新知，并交流市场的最新动态，以获得提升企业经营及策略规划等竞争优势。
周期：两年一届
市场范围：国际性
性质：面向贸易观众
主办：励展法国公司
联络：励展博览集团国际销售部
地址：北京市朝阳区新源南路1-3号平安国际金融中心A座15层01-03,05 （100027）
联系人：王亮
☎ 010-5933 9288
🖷 010-5933 9233
✉ liang.wang@reedexpo.com.cn
www.reedexport.cn

法国国际安防展

消防设备展

Expoprotection/Feu:

The Exhibition for Risk Management

日期：2012 /11 -
地点：法国巴黎维勒班特国际展览中心
内容：该展会是安防及消防业界的盛会。届时，安防、消防等领域展品都将在此全面展示，包括工作服、行业风险及自然风险等。
周期：两年一届
市场范围：国际性
性质：面向贸易观众
主办：励展法国公司
联络：励展博览集团国际销售部
地址：北京市朝阳区新源南路1-3号平安国际金融中心A座15层01-03,05 （100027）
联系人：宫卫
☎ 010-5933 9268
🖷 010-5933 9233
✉ david.gong@reedexpo.com.cn
www.reedexport.cn

Equip' Hotel

法国国际酒店及餐饮设备展

The World Class Event for the Restaurant, Hotel, Cafes & Catering Industries

日期：2012/11/11 - 15
地点：法国凡尔赛门巴黎展览馆
内容：餐馆、酒店、咖啡馆与餐饮业的世界级展会。
展品范围：浴室、健身与健美、饮料、建筑装配与翻新、咖啡制作与酒吧、家具与装饰、酒店连锁、厨房设备与材料、洗衣与卫生、服务、点心与简餐、餐具与桌布、技术。
周期：两年一届
市场范围：国际性
性质：面向贸易观众
参展费用：光地展位249欧元/m²，标准展位354欧元/m²
主办：励展法国公司
联络：励展博览集团海外展览部
地址：北京市朝阳区新源南路1-3号平安国际金融中心A座15层01-03,05
联系人：杜一鸣
☎ 010-5933 9209
🖷 010-5933 9233
✉ martin.du@reedexpo.com.cn
www.reedexport.cn
www.equiphotel.com

法国国际建筑门窗展：

汇聚国际领先的门窗、防护和遮阳设备

EQUIP'BAIE

METAL EXPO

International Windows, Doors, Shutters & Solar Protection Exhibition

日期：2012 /11 -
地点：法国凡尔赛门展览中心
内容：作为建筑行业中创新领域的一大亮点，Equip' Baie在业内具有极高地位，展会致力于提高建筑物的能源利用率、安全保障和舒适度。EQUIP' BAIE是致力于建材和建筑的国际型展会，展览范围包括木工类、门窗类、玻璃类和遮阳产品。

Equip' Baie也为制造商和机械设备供应商交流提供了一个绝佳的平台。由于强大的合约促进力，EQUIP' BAIE被业内高度赞誉，展会致力于在一个友好的环境下，将业内专家汇集一堂，把握时机尽情和同行们探讨热点话题。

METAL EXPO是一个致力于建筑行业内的金属产品应用的展会，同时也是EQUIP' BAIE展会的联合主办方。
周期：两年一届
市场范围：国际性
性质：面向贸易观众
参展费用：光地展位205欧元，标准展位286 欧元
主办：法国励展博览集团
联络：励展博览集团国际销售部
地址：北京市朝阳区新源南路1-3号平安国际金融中心A座15层01-03,05
联系人：王颖
☎ 010-5933 9208
🖷 010-5933 9233
✉ winnie.wang@reedexpo.com.cn
www.reedexport.cn

SITL Real Time

巴黎国际实时运输及物流展

International Show for Logistics Solutions

日期：2013/03 -
地点：法国巴黎凡尔赛门展览馆
内容：SITL Real Time为运输及物流业展览会，旨在向业界展示营销供应链管理中的整套服务及产品，是运输与物流业界必不可少的重要B2B商业平台。观众及参展商通过参加商务会议获得新知，并交流市场的最新动态，以获得提升企业经营及策略规划等竞争优势。
产品及服务：运输与联合运输服务、海外服务、物流服务、运输、物流设备及服务、运输、物流技术与信息服务、物流基础设施、物流地产、其他相关服务
周期：两年一届
市场范围：国际性
性质：面向贸易观众
主办：励展法国公司
联络：励展博览集团国际销售部
地址：北京市朝阳区新源南路1-3号平安国际金融中心A座15层01-03,05
联系人：王亮
☎ 010-5933 9288
🖷 010-5933 9233
✉ liang.wang@reedexpo.com.cn
www.reedexport.cn
www.sitl.eu

巴黎国际殡葬展

Funéraire Paris 2013:

The Exhibition for Funeral Suppliers & Distributors

日期：2013/11 -
地点：法国巴黎
主办：励展法国公司（Reed Expositions France）
联络：励展博览集团国际销售部
地址：北京市朝阳区新源南路1-3号平安国际金融中心A座15层01-03,05
联系人：王颖
☎ 010-5933 9208
🖷 010-5933 9233
✉ winnie.wang@reedexpo.com.cn
www.reedexport.cn
www.salon-funeraire.com

德国
Germany

2011年德国科隆国际糖果及休闲食品展览会

2011 ISM

日期：2011/01 -
地点：德国科隆国际展览中心
内容：可可、巧克力和巧克力制品；饼干；休闲食品；糖制品；冰淇淋和糖浆
周期：每年一届
市场范围：国际性
性质：面向公众
上届规模 2009：展览面积110,000m^2，参展商1,593家（国外展商1,274家，来自56个国家），参观人数35,200人
主办：德国科隆国际展览有限公司
联络：杭州思诺博会展服务有限公司
地址：杭州市体育场路229号浙江粮油大厦1202室（310003）
☎ 0571-8577 8500
🖷 0571-8577 9709
✉ expo@sinobal.com
www.sinobal.com

2011年法兰克福国际家用及商用纺织品展览会

Heimtextil

日期：2011/01/12 - 15
地点：德国法兰克福
内容：家用纺织品
主办：法兰克福展览公司 Messe Frankfurt
联络：中国贸促会纺织行业分会
联系人：何磊，朱勤
☎ 010-8522 9446, 8522 9506
🖷 010-8522 9300

科隆国际家具展

imm cologne

日期：2011/01/18 - 23
地点：德国科隆国际展览中心
内容：是当今世界最负盛名的家具展览会。每年一月份在德国科隆国际展览中心举行。展品无以伦比的广度和深度是科隆国际家具展作为全球第一品牌的独特性。在这里，全球的观众将领略到来自世界范围的包罗万象的设计一流的家具以及经典家居用品世界，其间，丰富多彩的配套活动也为科隆国际家具展增色不少。
始办年份：1949
周期：每年一届
市场范围：国际性
性质：面向公众
入场券价格：人民币700元
参展费用：统一特装560欧元/m^2，自行特装155欧元/m^2
上届规模：参展商1,057家（来自49个国家），参观人数250,000人（专业贸易观众100,000人）
主办：德国科隆展览国际有限公司
地址：北京市朝阳区东三环北路8号亮马河大厦二座1018室（100004）
联系人：郑志强
☎ 010-6590 7766转717
🖷 010-6590 6139
✉ info@koelnmesse.cn
www.imm-cologne.cn
www.koelnmesse.cn

柏林绿色周–食品工业、农业及园艺博览会

Internationale GrÜne Woche Berlin

日期：2011/01/21-29
地点：德国柏林
内容：农业机械、农业、啤酒、饮料、烹饪用具、鱼类、粮食、园艺用品、园艺物料、园艺设备、家庭用品、畜产业、肉制品、香肠、汽酒、烈酒、酒类。
周期：每年一届
参展费用：大厅(一面开展台)123-151欧元/m^2
主办：Messe Berlin Gmbh
上届规模：展览面积51,527m^2,参展商1,498家（国外展商464家），参观人数394,590人(国外观众5,130人)
参展联络：德国工商会(香港)南中国办事处/柏林国际展览有限公司香港及中国代表处
☎ 020-8755 2353
🖷 020-8755 1889
✉ meng-sophie@gz.china.ahk.de
www.messe-berlin.de

科隆国际糖果原料和机械展览会

ProSweets Cologne 2010

日期：2011/01/29 - 01
地点：德国科隆国际博览中心Cologne Exhibition Center, Germany
内容：甜食生产原材料、甜食包装材料、甜食包装机械、甜食工业机器与设备、甜食生产中冷藏与空调技术、甜食生产中的食品安全、质量管理、甜食生产中的自动化、数据处理、开环和闭环控制技术 甜食生产用加工设备和辅助装置 服务提供商、组织机构、出版社 垃圾处理、废物循环利用
始办年份：2006
周期：每年一届
市场范围：国际性
性质：面向贸易观众
上届规模 2010：展览面积19,000m^2，参展商325家（国外展商184家，来自60个国家），专业贸易观众19,000人
主办：科隆国际展览有限公司
地址：北京市东三环北路8号亮马河大厦2座1018室（100004）
联系人：潘容
☎ 010-6590 7766转715
🖷 010-6590 6139
✉ g.pan@koelnmesse.cn
www.prosweets.cn

ProSweets Cologne 2010

Date：2011/01/29 - 01
Venue: Cologne Exhibition Center, Germany
Established Year: 2006
Frequency: Annual
Market Area: International
Nature: Trade only
Statistics 2010: Exhibition Area 19,000m^2, Exhibitors 325 (foreigners 184, came from 60 countries), Trade Visitors 19,000
Organizer: Koelnmesse GmbH/ MVK JSC
Address: Unit 1018, Landmark Tower II, No.8 Dongsanhuan North Rd., Beijing 100004
Contact: Grace Pan
☎ 010-6590 7766 ext 715
🖷 010-6590 6139
✉ g.pan@koelnmesse.cn
www.prosweets.cn

科隆国际糖果及休闲食品展

ISM-international Sweets and Biscuits Fair

日期：2011/01/30 – 02/02
地点：德国科隆国际博览中心
内容：ISM全球市场成功的标志，ISM是全球最大、最重要的甜食和休闲食品的展览会。每年，来自全球贸易界的专业人士汇聚在这里，相互介绍、发掘和探讨国际最新流行趋势、最新的产品，寻找最近最好的商机
始办年份：1972
周期：每年一届
市场范围：国际性
性质：面向贸易观众
上届规模 2010：展览面积110,000m^2，参展商1,503家

（国外展商1,228家，来自140个国家），参观人数32,000人
主办：德国科隆展览国际有限公司/ MVK JSC
地址：北京市朝阳区东三环北路8号亮马河大厦二座1018室（100004）
联系人：潘容
☎ 010-6590 7766转715
🖷 010-6590 6139
✉ g.pan@koelnmesse.cn
www.ism-cologne.cn
www.koelnmesse.cn

ISM
-international Sweets and Biscuits Fair

Date: 2011/01/30 – 02/02
Venue: Cologne Exhibition Center, Germany
Profile: ISM is the largest and most important sweets and biscuits fair in the world. Every year the international sector meets to introduce, discover and discuss the latest trends, the newest products and the most up-to-dates perspectives
Established Year: 1972
Frequency: Annual
Market Area: International
Nature: Trade only
Statistics 2010: Exhibition Area 110,000m^2, Exhibitors 1,503（foreigners 1,228, came from 140 countries）, Trade Visitors 32,000
Organizer: Koelnmesse GmbH/ MVK JSC
Address: Unit 1018 Landmark Tower II, No. 8 Dongsanhuan N. Road, Beijing
Contact: Grace Pan
☎ 010-6590 7766 ext 715
🖷 010-6590 6139
✉ g.pan@koelnmesse.cn
www.ism-cologne.cn

国际果蔬展
FRUIT LOGISTICA

日期：2011/02/09-11
地点：德国柏林
内容：生态产品、水果、商品展示、坚果、服务、仓储技术、计算机软件、包装技术、运输、蔬菜、干果。
周期：每年一届
参展费用：大厅(一面开展台)183 欧元/m2
主办：Messe Berlin Gmbh
上届规模：展览面积53,886m2, 参展商2,314家（国外展商2,070家），参观人数54,172人（国外观众42,663人）
参展联络：德国工商会(香港)南中国办事处/柏林国际展览有限公司香港及中国代表处
☎ 020-8755 2353
🖷 020-8755 1889
✉ meng-sophie@gz.china.ahk.de
www.messe-berlin.de

德国慕尼黑国际面料展览会
MUNICH FABRIC START

日期：2011/02/01 - 03
地点：德国
联络：上海比天展览服务有限公司
地址：上海市中山北路900号加禾商务中心3号楼303室(200070)
联系人：刘先生
☎ 021-5655 2843
🖷 021-5655 9981
www.betium.com

春季马术用品展
spoga horse(spring)

日期：2011/02/06 - 08
地点：德国科隆国际展览中心展馆
内容：马术用品及相关服务
始办年份：2008
周期：每年两届
市场范围：国际性
性质：面向贸易观众
上届规模 2008：展览面积28,500m^2, 参展商379家，参观人数38,600人
参展费用：标准摊位381欧元/m^2(最小9m^2)费用包括光地费、摊位搭建费、公共能源费、AUMA费及19%的增值税。不包含基本会刊登录费、垃圾清运及电费；光地136欧元/m^2（最小36m^2）；其它费用包括公共能源费5欧元/m^2、AUMA费0.6欧元/m^2、会刊登录费用167欧元/参展商、缴杂费及19%增值税
上届规模 2008：展览面积28,500m^2, 参展商379家，参观人数38,600人
主办：科隆展览中国有限公司
地址：北京市东三环北路8号亮马河大厦2座1018室（100004）
联系人：张昱,贾宁
☎ 010-6590 7766转738
🖷 010-6590 6139
✉ j.zhang@koelnmesse.cn
www.koelnmesse.cn
www.spogagafa.cn

spoga horse(spring)

Date: 2011/02/06 - 08
Venue: Cologne Exhibition Center, Germany
Established Year: 2008
Frequency: Biannual
Market Area: International
Nature: Trade only
Statistics 2008: Exhibition Area 28,500m^2, Exhibitors 379，Buyers 38,600
Organizer: Koelnmesse GmbH
Address: Unit 1018，Landmark Tower II, No.8 Dongsanhuan North Rd., Beijing 100004
Contact: Joesy Zhang, Maggie Jia
☎ 010-6590 7766 ext 738
🖷 010-6590 6139
✉ j.zhang@koelnmesse.cn
www.spogagafa.cn

科隆亚太采购交易会
—五金、家居、家电、园艺产品
Asia Pacific Sourcing

日期：2011/03/09 - 11
地点：德国科隆国际展览中心
内容：旨在创造新的环太平洋地区与欧洲、北美洲之间的进出口贸易的平台——科隆亚太采购交易会—五金、家居、家电、园艺产品每单数年在科隆国际博览中心举办。APS已经成为亚太地区的制造商向欧洲和北美地区的客户展示自己最新的产品和技术的重要平台。
产品范围：五金及DIY产品包括工具、锁具及安全设备、DIY材料、铁艺制品、丝网制品及紧固件；园林及休闲产品包括花园家具、园艺工具、烧烤用具、露营设备、体育用品、玩具；家居消费品有玻璃制品、陶瓷制品、餐桌灯饰灯具、礼品、季节性礼品等
始办年份：2005
周期：每年两届
市场范围：国际性
性质：面向公众
参展费用：510欧元/m^2，178欧元/m^2
上届规模 2009：展览面积25,000m^2, 参展商406家（来自65个国家），参观人数5,300人
主办：德国科隆展览国际有限公司
地址：北京市朝阳区东三环北路8号亮马河大厦二座1018室（100004）
联系人：陈瑞,郑志强
☎ 010-6590 7766转750
🖷 010-6590 6139
✉ r.chen@koelnmesse.cn
✉ k.zheng@koelnmesse.cn
www.asiapacificsourcing.cn
www.koelnmesse.cn

Asia Pacific Sourcing

Date: 2011/03/09 - 11
Venue: Koelnmesse Trade Fair Center, Germany
Profile: The event is a separate platform presenting Asian products from the house, garden and leisure sector. The aim is to link product ranges from Asian growth markets with the growing demand in Europe and North America, all in a concentrated format in Cologne. This trade fair is scheduled to be held every two years, serving as a multi-lateral hub for the import and export business. Asia-Pacific Sourcing is the ordering and communication platform for products, innovations and trends for the house, garden and leisure segment.
Established Year: 2005
Frequency: Biannual
Market Area: International
Nature: Open to public
Participated Fee: EURO 510/m^2
Statistics 2009: Exhibition Area 25,000m^2, Exhibitors 406（came from 65 countries）, Buyers 5,300
Organizer: Koelnmesse GmbH
Address: Unit 1018, Landmark Tower Ⅱ, No. 8 Dongsanhuan North Rd., Beijing 100004, China
Contact: Ryan Chen, Ken Zheng
☎ 010-6590 7766 ext 750
🖷 010-6590 6139
✉ r.chen@koelnmesse.cn
✉ k.zheng@koelnmesse.cn
www.asiapacificsourcing.cn

柏林国际旅游展
ITB Berlin

日期：2011/03/09-13
地点：德国柏林
内容：旅游设备、信息技术、国际旅游业协会、市政工程、服务、旅游、旅行社讯息、旅行、旅行团。
周期：每年一届
参展费用：大厅(一面开展台)163欧元/平方米
上届规模：展览面积89,227m^2,参展商7,233家（国外展商5,667家），参观人数131,131人
主办：Messe Berlin Gmbh
参展联络：德国工商会(香港)南中国办事处/柏林国际展览有限公司香港及中国代表处
☎ 020-8755 2353
🖷 020-8755 1889
✉ meng-sophie@gz.china.ahk.de
www.messe-berlin.de

科隆国际牙科展
IDS 2011：
International Dental Show 2011

日期：2011/03/22 - 26
地点：德国科隆国际展览中心
内容：牙科临床实践 牙科技工室 感染控制与维护 服务、信息、交流和机构
始办年份：1945
周期：每年两届
市场范围：国际性
性质：面向贸易观众
入场券价格：260 人民币
参展费用：标准展位（最小9m^2）615欧元/m^{2}标准展

位价格含光地租金、摊位装修、公共能源费、会刊费、其它杂费及相关税费；光地（最小36m^2）238欧元/m^2；其它费用有公共能源费6.50欧元/ m^2、会刊登录费349欧元/参展商、缴杂费25欧元/m^2（300m^{2}以上展位另计），及相关税费
上届规模： 展览面积138,000m^2，参展商1,823家（来自57个国家），专业贸易观众106,000人
主办： 科展览有中国限公司
地址： 北京市亮马河大厦2座1018室
联系人： 齐志宇
☎ 010-6590 7766转727
🖷 010-6590 6139
✉ k.qi@koelnmesse.cn
www.ids-cologne.cn
www.koelnmesse.cn

IDS 2011

International Dental Show 2011
Date: 2011/03/22 - 26
Venue: Cologne Exhibition Center, Germany
Profile: Dental practice, Dental laboratory, Infection control and maintenance Services, information, communication and organization
Established Year: 1945
Frequency: Biannual
Market Area: International
Nature: Trade only
Participated Fee: Standard Booth EURO 615/m^2 (min 9m^2), Raw Space EURO 238/m^2 (min 36m^2)
Statistics 2010: Exhibition Area 138,000m^2, Exhibitors 1,823 (came from 57 countries), Trade Visitors 106,000
Organizer: Koelnmesse GmbH
Address: Unit 1018, Landmark Tower 2, No.8 Dongsanhuan North Rd., Beijing
Contact: Kevin Qi
☎ 010-6590 7766 ext 727
🖷 010-6590 6139
✉ k.qi@koelnmesse.cn
www.ids-cologne.cn

2011年汉诺威国际工业展览会

日期： 2011/04/04 - 08
地点： 德国汉诺威展览中心
内容： 作为世界最大的工业博览会，荟萃了各个工业领域的技术，引领世界工业的创新与发展，成为名副其实的“世界工业发展的晴雨表”。
产品范围：过程控制与生产自动化、工业自动化、厂房自动化与工厂清洁、能源、管道传递技术、数字化工业、微系统技术、研究与技术专题、工业设施的管理与服务、动力/传动控制、表面处理技术、压缩空气与真空技术展、风能
始办年份： 1947
周期： 每年一届
市场范围： 国际性
上届规模2010：展览面积224,800m^2，参展商6,150家来自60个国家，观众210,000人,中国展商441家（大陆426家，香港15家）
主办： 北京麦田通会国际展览有限公司
联系人： 吴珊
☎ 010-5165 9302转8005
🖷 010-5165 9302转8004
✉ xiaoxiangzhishui@yahoo.com.cn
MSN：xiaoxiangzhishui@hotmail.com
www.cornfairs.com

2011年德国杜塞尔多夫国际铸造展览会

NEWCAST 2011
日期： 2011/04/04 - 08
地点： 德国杜塞尔多夫展览中心
内容： 当前世界上规模最大的国际铸造展，同期还举办热处理、冶金展览会。2011年该展览会将展出世界各国最先进的铸造设备，仪器仪表和各国质量优秀的铸件及铸造材料，是我国铸造、铸品相关企业了解国际市场变化，展示我们的铸件和相关产品，开拓国际市场，增进我国铸件和铸造材料出口的极好机会。
始办年份： 1969
周期： 四年一届
市场范围： 国际性
性质： 面向公众
上届规模 2007：展览面积40,000m^2(国外展商30,000m^2)，参展商1,000家（国外展商800家，来自69个国家），专业贸易观众70,000人
主办： 德国Messe Dusseldorlf展览公司
联络： 上海达欧展览服务有限公司
地址： 上海市春申路3758弄凯利大楼1号206（201100）
联系人： 朱志强
☎ 021-3412 3509
🖷 021-3412 3496
✉ dail_zhuzhiqiang@yahoo.com.cn
MSN：lyn_zhuzhiqiang@yahoo.com.cn
QQ：417438558
www.dail.com.cn

德国汉堡国际飞机内饰展览会

Aircraft Interiors Expo – Hamburg

AlimentariaLisboa

日期： 2011/04/05 - 07
地点： 德国汉堡会展中心Hamburg Messe, Germany
内容： 设施包括客舱管理系统、清洁处理、驾驶舱舱门、设计工作室、环境系统、固定装置、食物/食物提供设备、地板、装潢、硬件、飞行途中的娱乐和通讯、行李架、维修和修复、指示标志及标牌、地毯及纺织物、制服、窗帘与百叶窗
始办年份： 2000
周期： 每年一届
性质： 面向贸易观众
参展费用： 光地展位310欧元起，标准展位85-100欧元
上届规模： 展览面积15,092m^2，参展商537家，参观人数7,316人
主办： 励展英国公司
联络： 励展博览集团国际销售部
联系人： 宫卫
☎ 010-5933 9268
🖷 010-5933 9233
✉ david.gong@reedexpo.com.cn
www.aircraftinteriorsexpo.com
www.koelnmesse.cn

科隆国际艺术展

ART COLOGNE 2011

日期： 2011/04/13 - 17
地点： 德国科隆国际展览中心
Cologne Exhibition Center, Germany
内容： 科隆艺术展是一个以传播和销售被国际认可的现代及当 代艺术作品展览会。科隆艺术展是世界上最重要的艺术展览会之一。主要展品范围：油画作品、绘图作品、雕塑作品、行为艺术、摄影作品
始办年份： 1967
周期： 每年一届
市场范围： 国际性
性质： 面向贸易观众
上届规模： 展览面积33,200m^2，参展商230家
主办： 科隆展览中国有限公司
地址： 北京市朝阳区东三环北路8号亮马河大厦二座1018室（100004）
联系人： 潘容
☎ 010-6590 7766
🖷 010-6590 6139
✉ g.pan@koelnmesse.cn
www.artcologne.cn
www.koelnmesse.cn

FIBO

国际健身及休闲运动用品博览会
The Leading International Trade Show for Fitness, Wellness & Health

日期： 2011/04/14 - 17
地点： 德国埃森展览中心
内容： 一听到FIBO，健身中心经营者、健身教练、体育医生、理疗师、宾馆经营者、桑拿浴经营者、投资者及多功能健康中心经营者会立刻想到每年春季在埃森举办的世界最专业的健美与健身展会。每年的FIBO都是一个独一无二的思想和创新的市场，涵盖健身器材、服务、营养、健康、美容、服饰、娱乐、运动等领域。
产品及服务： 健身及训练器材、咨询、健康宣传、医疗健身、运动营养、健美及美容器材、桑拿浴、日光浴床、化妆品、健身房器材、电脑软硬件、协会、音乐、运动及健身服饰。
始办年份： 1979
周期： 每年一届
参展费用： 光地展位141-165欧元
主办： 励展德国公司
联络： 励展博览集团海外销售部
联系人： 张志超
☎ 010-5933 9266
🖷 010-5933 9233
✉ ivy.zhang@reedexpo.com.cn
www.fibo.de/en/index.php
www.reedexport.cn

科隆国际牙科展

International Dental Show 2011

日期： 2011/04/22 - 26
地点： 德国科隆国际展览中心
内容： 牙科临床实践；牙科技工室；感染控制与维护；服务、信息、交流和机构
周期： 两年一届
市场范围： 国际性
性质： 面向贸易观众
入场券价格： 人民币260元
参展费用： 标准展位（最小9m^2）545欧元/m^2，标准展位价格含光地租金、摊位装修、公共能源费；光地（最小36m^2）238欧元/m^2，其它费用有公共能源费6欧元/m^2、会刊登录费349欧元/家、暂缴杂费25欧元/m^2（300m^{2}以上展位另计）及19%增值税
上届规模 2009：展览面积138,000m^2，参展商1,820家（来自57个国家），参观人数106,000人
主办： 科展览有中国限公司
地址： 北京市亮马河大厦2座1018室（100004）
联系人： 齐志宇
☎ 010-6590 7766转ext 727
🖷 010-6590 6139
✉ k.qi@koelnmesse.cn
www.ids-cologne.cn
www.koelnmesse.cn

International Dental Show 2011

Date: 2011/04/22 - 26
Venue: Cologne Exhibition Center, Germany
Profile: Dental practice, Dental laboratory, Infection control and maintenance, Services, information, communication and organization
Frequency: Biennial

Market Area: International
Nature: Trade only
Participated Fee: Standard Booth EURO 545欧元/m^2（min $9m^2$），Raw Space EURO 238/m^2 (min $36m^2$)
Statistics 2009: Exhibition Area 138,000m^2, Exhibitors 1,820（came from 57 countries），Visitors 106,000
Organizer: Koelnmesse Co Ltd
Address: Unit 1018, Landmark Tower 2, No.8 Dongsanhuan North Rd., Beijing
Contact: Kevin Qi
☎ 010-6590 7766转ext 727
🖷 010-6590 6139
✉ k.qi@koelnmesse.cn
www.ids-cologne.cn

柏林国际水利技术、污水处理展暨学术会议
WASSER BERLIN INTERNATIONAL

日期：2011/05/02-09
地点：德国柏林
内容：通讯技术、工业设备、信息技术、测量体系、分析技术、泵站技术、驱动技术、调节和控制技术、交流技术、钻井技术、过滤器设备、服务、污水处理技术、污水、游泳池装置、地下工程建筑体系、管道建设、管道及设备、管道、水体保护、洪水防治、供水技术、水处理设备、水处理技术、供水、水流经济。
周期：两年一届
参展费用：大厅(一面开展台)170欧元/m^2，露天站台60欧元/m^2
上届规模：展览面积17,432m^2,参展商662家（国外展商171家），观众24,511人（国外观众5,000人）
主办：Messe Berlin Gmbh
参展联络：德国工商会(香港)南中国办事处/柏林国际展览有限公司香港及中国代表处
☎ 020-8755 2353
🖷 020-8755 1889
✉ meng-sophie@gz.china.ahk.de
www.messe-berlin.de

德国国际包装机械、包装及糖果机械展览会
Interpack

日期：2011/05/12 - 18
地点：德国杜塞尔多夫
周期：三年一届
主办：中国贸促会机械行业分会
地址：北京市西城区三里河路46号（100823）
联系人：张玉惠, 郭旭萍, 吕春丽
☎ 010-6859 4811, 6859 4994, 6859 4910
🖷 010-6859 4995
✉ zhangyuhui@ccpitmsc.org
www.chinamachine.org.cn

汉诺威国际林业木工机械展览会
LIGNA

日期：2011/05/14 - 18
地点：德国汉诺威
周期：每年两届
主办：中国贸促会机械行业分会
地址：北京市西城区三里河路46号（100823）
联系人：张玉惠,郭旭萍,吕春丽
☎ 010-6859 4811, 6859 4994, 6859 4910
🖷 010-6859 4995
✉ zhangyuhui@ccpitmsc.org
www.chinamachine.org.cn

2011法兰克福国际产业用纺织品及非织造布展览会
(TECHTEXTIL)

日期：2011/05/24 - 26
地点：德国法兰克福
内容：农业、建筑、工业、土工、家用纺织品、医疗卫生、交通运输、环保、包装、防护、运动休闲、服装等十二个领域的各种技术纺织品、非织造布及相关的设备、纤维原料、复合材料、粘合技术、化学品、测试仪器等
主办：法兰克福展览公司Messe Frankfurt
联络：中国贸促会纺织行业分会
联系人：王欣，顾萌
☎ 010-8522 9093，8522 9074
🖷 010-8522 9295

科隆国际家具生产、木工及室内装饰展
interzum cologne

日期：2011/05/25 - 28
地点：德国科隆国际展览中心
内容：针对家具生产及其原辅料方面的一个全球性盛会，是目前世界上木工机械、家具生产设备及家具原材料、配件领域规模最大、影响力最大的专业展览会之一，其展品范围之广位居所有同类展会之首。
始办年份：1959（逢当年举办）
周期：两年一届
市场范围：国际性
性质：面向公众
参展费用：标准展位510 欧元/m^2(最小面积$9m^2$)含光地租金、摊位装修、公共能源费、AUMA费、垃圾清运及电费、基本会刊登录费、公共宣传费及19%增值税；光地：一面开口136欧元/m^2，两面开口138欧元/m^2，三面开口140欧元/m^2，四面开口140欧元/m^2(不含标准展位所列各项费用及19%增值税
上届规模 2009：展览面积152,000m^2，参展商1,370家，参观人数47,000人
主办：德国科隆展览国际有限公司/ MVK JSC
地址：北京市朝阳区东三环北路8号亮马河大厦二座1018室（100004）
联系人：贾宁
☎ 010-6590 7766转ext 729
🖷 010-6590 6139
✉ m.jia@koelnmesse
www.interzum.cn
www.koelnmesse.cn

interzum cologne

Date：2011/05/25 - 28
Venue: Koelnmesse Trade Fair Center, Germany
Profile: interzum is the leading global event for the furniture and interior construction industries' supplying sections. This is where the trends and visions that will create future living spaces using modern materials, outstanding design, and exclusive innovations come to life.
Established Year: 1959
Frequency: Biennial
Market Area: International
Nature: Open to public
Participated Fee: EURO 490/m^2，EURO 165/m^2
Organizer: Koelnmesse Co Ltd
Address: Unit 1018 Landmark Tower II, No. 8 Dongsanhuan N. Road, Beijing 100004
Contact: Maggie Jia
☎ 010-6590 7766 ext 729
🖷 010-6590 6139
✉ m.jia@koelnmesse
www.interzum.cn

国际废物处理博览会
ENTECO

日期：2011/06/06 - 09
地点：德国科隆国际博览中心
内容：废物管理和再循环、水处理和废水治理、焚化和可再利用能源、市政及环境服务、环保技术和物流管理、空气质量和污染控制、职业安全和噪音保护、环保调查和组织机构
始办年份：1976
周期：两年一届
市场范围：国际性
性质：面向贸易观众
参展费用：标准展位360欧元/m^2（$12m^2$起），光地（$36m^2$起），一面开口129欧元/m^2，两面开口135欧元/m^2，三面开口139欧元/m^2，岛形展位139欧元/m^2，室外场地70欧元/m^2
上届规模 2009：展览面积72,000m^2，参展商784家，专业贸易观众36,000人
主办：科隆展览国际有限公司
地址：北京东三环北路8号亮马河大厦2座1018室（100004）
联系人：徐畅
☎ 010-6590 7766转715
🖷 010-6590 6139
✉ j.xu@koelnmesse.cn
www.entsorga-enteco.cn
www.koelnmesse.cn

ENTECO

Date：2011/06/06 - 09
Venue: Cologne Exhibition Center, Germany
Profile: Waste Management & Recycling, Health and Safety at Work & Noises Protection, Research & Organization, Local Authority & Environmental Service, Air Quality Control & Emissions Protection, Technology & Logistics, Incineration & Renewable Energy, Water & Liquid Waste
Established Year: 1976
Frequency: Biennial
Market Area: International
Nature: Trade only
Participated Fee: EURO 360/m^2（min $12m^2$），Raw Space (min $36m^2$) EURO 129/m^2, Corner EURO 135/m^2, Peninsula unit euro 139/m^2, Island unit euro 139/m^2, outdoor euro 70/m^2
Statistics 2009: Exhibition Area 72,000m^2, Exhibitors 784, Trade visitors 36,000
Organizer: Koelnmesse Co Ltd
Address: Unit 1018, Landmark Tower Ⅱ, No. 8 Dongsanhuan North Rd., Beijing 100004, China
Contact: Joyce Xu
☎ 010-6590 7766 ext 715
🖷 010-6590 6139
✉ j.xu@koelnmesse.cn
www.entsorga-enteco.cn

柏林国际会展及媒体技术展览会
SHOWTECH:
Intl. Show & Conference for Stage Technology, Eqpt. & Event Svs

SHOWTECH

日期：2011/06/07 - 09
地点：德国柏林展览中心
内容：国际会展技术及媒体技术展览会是针对舞台表演及展会活动行业的著名欧洲展览会，是向业内技术决策人、制造商、展会活动经理人、主办者及经销商展示灯光、音响科技领域最新创新、解决方案及行业潮流的高水平业务交流平台。由展会赞助机构德国影剧院技术协会（DTHG）于展会同期主办的专业会议将邀请顶级业内专家介绍最新的国际影剧院技术及管理经验。
产品及服务：舞台技术、演播室技术、灯光及投影技术、音响及舞台专业音响（PA）技术、影像及通讯技术、展会活动技术、会议技术、影剧院设备及效果、展会活动服务、安全、初级及高级培训学院、媒体、协会机构。
周期：两年一届
性质：面向贸易观众
参展费用：光地展位169-225 欧元
上届规模 2009：展览面积9,431m^2，参展商340家，参观人数7,815人
主办：励展德国公司

联络：励展博览集团国际销售部
地址：北京市朝阳区新源南路1-3号平安国际金融中心A座15层01-03,05
联系人：杜一鸣
☎ 010-5933 9209
🖷 010-5933 9233
✉ martin.du@reedexpo.com.cn
www.showtech.de
www.reedexport.cn

德国国际铸造、铸件展览会

NEWCAST

日期：2011/06/28 - 02
地点：德国杜塞尔多夫
周期：四年一届
主办：中国贸促会机械行业分会
地址：北京市西城区三里河路46号（100823）
联系人：张玉惠, 郭旭萍, 吕春丽
☎ 010-6859 4811, 6859 4994, 6859 4910
🖷 010-6859 4995
✉ zhangyuhui@ccpitmsc.org
www.chinamachine.org.cn

2011年德国菲德列斯哈芬户外运动休闲运动博览会

OutDoor

日期：2011/07/14 - 17
地点：德国菲德列斯哈芬新展览中心
内容：休闲用具：户外家具、花园设备、休闲桌椅；露营器材：睡袋、帐篷、吊床、配件；背包类：旅行袋、旅行帆布背包、越野帆布背包、登山包、攀岩包及配件；运动健身器械：水上运动用具、充气艇、橡皮艇、马具用品、望远镜、球类用品；运动休闲服装：夹克、登山服、羽绒服、自行车服、滑雪服、越野服、休闲运动鞋、帽子。

每年户外用品产业的各领域汇聚在展会举办地腓特烈港市，该地区位于德国南部、邻近瑞士，依山傍水、风景优美、交通便利(地处欧洲中心位置、紧邻瑞士苏黎世机场、市内也有机场)，是最适合展会运动与休闲主题的举办地，给展商和观众带来无与伦比的休闲。

始办年份：1994
周期：每年一届
市场范围：国际性
性质：面向公众
上届规模 2010：参展商868家（来自70个国家），参观人数20,460人
主办：菲德列斯哈芬展览集团
联络：杭州思诺博会展服务有限公司
地址：浙江省杭州市体育场路229号浙江粮油大厦1202室（310003）
联系人：吴蓓小姐
☎ 0571-8577 8500
🖷 0571-8577 9709
✉ expo@sinobal.com
www.sinobal.com

科隆国际游戏展

gamescom

日期：2011/08/17 - 21
地点：德国科隆国际博览中心
内容：由原莱比锡游戏展(Games Convention)发展而来，09年起正式移师科隆，是欧洲最专业的综合性互动式游戏软件、信息软件和硬件设备展览，也是欧洲唯一一个集中了游戏软件、硬件、娱乐设备、信息软件和设备的大型国际性展会。
展品范围：电脑、游戏机、电信设备、掌上电脑、掌上游戏设备、电子玩具、游戏软件、教育软件、家用及其他软件、网络游戏、移动游戏、维修保养机构、媒体、游戏开发商及运营商等
始办年份：2002
周期：每年一届
市场范围：国际性
性质：面向公众
参展费用：标准展位450欧元/m²，光地156欧元/m²
上届规模：展览面积120,000m²，参展商33家（国外展商505家，来自31个国家），参观人数254,000人（专业贸易观众18,900人）
主办：科隆展览中国有限公司
地址：北京市朝阳区东三环北路8号亮马河大厦二座1018室（100004）
联系人：陈瑞
☎ 010-6590 7766 转750
🖷 010-6590 6139
✉ r.chen@koelnmesse.cn
www.gamescom-cologne.cn
www.koelnmesse.cn

国际电子消费品展

IFA

日期：2011/09/02-07
地点：德国柏林
内容：声像技术、嵌入式厨具、电缆技术、计算机软件、计算机技术、家电、数据保护技术、数据传输、电子家电、信息技术、多媒体技术、网络技术、在线服务、电信、电视技术。
周期：每年一届
参展费用：大厅(一面开展台) 171欧元/m²，露天站台139.5欧元/m²
上届规模：展览面积121,000m²，参展商1,164家（国外展商765家），观众224,235人
主办：Messe Berlin Gmbh; guf-Gesellschaft fÜr Unterhaltungs-und Kommunikationselektronik (gfu) mbh
联络：德国工商会(香港)南中国办事处/柏林国际展览有限公司香港及中国代表处
☎ 020-8755 2353
🖷 020-8755 1889
✉ meng-sophie@gz.china.ahk.de
www.messe-berlin.de

秋季马术用品展

spoga horse (Autumn)

日期：2011/09/04 - 06
地点：德国科隆国际展览中心展馆
内容：马术用品及相关服务
始办年份：2008
周期：每年两届
市场范围：国际性
性质：面向贸易观众
参展费用：标准摊位381欧元/m²（最小9m²）费用包括光地费、摊位搭建费、公共能源费、AUMA费及19%的增值税，不包含基本会刊登录费、垃圾清运及电费；光地136欧元/m²（最小36m²），其它费用包括公共能源费5欧元/m²，AUMA费0.6欧元/m²，会刊登录费用167欧元/参展商，暂缴杂费及19%增值税
上届规模 2008：展览面积28,500m²，参展商379家，参观人数38,600人
主办：科隆展览中国有限公司
地址：北京市东三环北路8号亮马河大厦2座1018室（100004）
联系人：张昱，贾宁
☎ 010-6590 7766转738
🖷 010-6590 6139
✉ j.zhang@koelnmesse.cn
www.spogagafa.cn
www.koelnmesse.cn

spoga horse (Autumn)

Date：2011/09/04 - 06
Venue: Cologne Exhibition Center, Germany
Established Year: 2008
Frequency: Biannual
Market Area: International
Nature: Trade only
Participated Fee: Standard Booth euro 381/m²(min 9m²), Raw Space EURO 136/m²（min 36m²）
Statistics 2008: Exhibition Area 28,500m², Exhibitors 379，Visitors 38,600
Organizer: Koelnmesse Co Ltd
Address: Unit 1018，Landmark Tower II, No.8 Dongsanhuan North Rd., Beijing 100004
Contact: Joesy Zhang, Maggie Jia
☎ 010-6590 7766 ext 738
🖷 010-6590 6139
✉ j.zhang@koelnmesse.cn
www.spogagafa.cn

国际体育用品、露营设备及园林生活博览会/国际园艺博览会

spoga/gafa

日期：2011/09/04 - 06
地点：德国科隆国际展览中心
内容：户外生活（户外家具）、户外运动（烧烤设备、露营休闲用品、体育及比赛用品）、户内和户外休闲（植物和植物护理、花卉栽培和装饰、水处理和室外照明、花园规划和维护、其它设备和花园布置、宠物用品）、马术用品及服务
周期：每年一届
上届规模：展览面积265,600m²，参展商2,236家（来自57个国家），参观人数38,433人
主办：科隆展览中国有限公司
地址：北京市东三环北路8号亮马河大厦2座1018室（100004）
联系人：张昱，贾宁
☎ 010-6590 7766转738
🖷 010-6590 6139
✉ j.zhang@koelnmesse.cn
www.spogagafa.cn
www.koelnmesse.cn

spoga/gafa

Date：2011/09/04 - 06
Venue: Cologne Exhibition Center, Germany
Frequency: Annual
Statistics 2010: Exhibition Area 265,600m², Exhibitors 2,236（came from 57 countries），Visitors 38,433
Organizer: Koelnmesse Co Ltd
Address: Unit 1018，Landmark Tower II, No.8 Dongsanhuan North Rd., Beijing 100004
Contact: Joesy Zhang, Maggie Jia
☎ 010-6590 7766 ext 738
🖷 010-6590 6139
✉ j.zhang@koelnmesse.cn
www.spogagafa.cn

欧洲机床展览会

EMO HANNOVER

日期：2011/09/14 - 19
地点：德国汉诺威
周期：每年两届
主办：中国贸促会
地址：北京市西城区三里河路46号（100823）
联系人：张玉惠, 郭旭萍, 吕春丽
☎ 010-6859 4811, 6859 4994, 6859 4910
🖷 010-68594995
✉ zhangyuhui@ccpitmsc.org
www.chinamachine.org.cn

科隆国际少儿用品展

Kind + Jugend

日期：2011/09/15 - 18
地点：德国科隆国际展览中心
内容：儿车及附件，安全座椅及设备，家具及附件，纺织品，婴儿、儿童、青年时装及孕妇装，玩具，育婴用品，电器，出版物，团体及其它
始办年份：1960
周期：每年一届
市场范围：国际性
性质：面向公众
参展费用：展位费415欧元/m²(最小9m²)含光地租金、摊位装修、公共能源费、AUMA 费、基本会刊登录费、垃圾清运费、摊位电费、其它杂费，及相关税费；光地：一面开口132欧元/m²，两面开口138欧元/m²，三面开口141欧元/m2，四面开口144欧元/m²，其它费用包括公共能源费6.95 欧元/m²，AUMA费0.6欧元/m²，会刊登录费用249欧元/参展商，暂缴杂费25 欧元/m²（包括展期垃圾清运费和电费）及相关税费
上届规模 2010：展览面积80,000m²，参展商820家，专业贸易观众19,000人
主办：科隆展览有中国限公司
地址：北京市亮马河大厦2座1018室（510620）
联系人：齐志宇
☎ 010-6590 7766转727
🖷 010-6590 6139
✉ k.lee@koelnmesse.cn
www.kindundjugend.cn
www.koelnmesse.cn

Kind + Jugend

Date：2011/09/15 - 18
Venue: Cologne Exhibition Center, Germany
Profile: Prams, car/bicycle seats, children' s furniture, hygiene articles, electric appliances, textiles, baby cosmetics, toys and games for babies and toddlers, fashion for babies and toddlers, maternity wear, shop equipment, publications, organizations
Established Year: 1960
Frequency: Annual
Market Area: International
Nature: Open to public
Participated Fee: Standard Booth EURO 415/m²(min 9m²), Raw Space EURO 132/m²
Statistics 2010: Exhibition Area 80,000m², Exhibitors 820，Trade Visitors 19,000
Organizer: Koelnmesse Co Ltd
Address: Unit 1018, Landmark Tower 2, No.8 Dongsanhuan North Rd., Beijing
Contact: Kevin Qi
☎ 010-6590 7766 -727
🖷 010-6590 6139
✉ k.lee@koelnmesse.cn
www.kindundjugend.cn

数码管理解决方案展览会

DMS EXPO

日期：2011/09/20 - 22
地点：德国科隆国际博览中心
内容：在线营销、门户网站营销、营销搜索引擎、电子邮件营销、手机营销、媒体宣传策划、游戏内置广告及相关营销、播客平台及推广、公关公司咨询、市场定位跟踪与服务、电子商务
始办年份：1995
周期：每年一届
市场范围：国际性
性质：面向贸易观众
上届规模：参展商309家（来自14个国家），专业贸易观众16,100人
主办：科隆展览国际有限公司
地址：北京市朝阳区东三环北路8号亮马河大厦二座1018室（100004）
联系人：陈瑞
☎ 010-6590 7766 转 750
🖷 010-6590 6139
✉ r.chen@koelnmesse.cn
www.dm-exco.cn
www.koelnmesse.cn

DMS EXPO

Date：2011/09/20 - 22
Venue: Cologne Exhibition Center, Germany
Profile: Hardware and software, complete solutions and services from the following areas: Enterprise content management; Document management ; Web content management; Business process management ; Records management ; Information life-cycle management; Output management ; Input management / Capturing solutions/ Incoming mail processing; Technical documentation; Product information management; Storage management
Established Year: 1995
Frequency: Annual
Market Area: International
Nature: Trade only
Statistics 2010: Exhibitors 309（came from 14 countries）, Trade Visitors 16,100
Organizer: Koelnmesse Co Ltd
Address: Unit 1018, Landmark Tower Ⅱ, No. 8 Dongsanhuan North Rd., Beijing 100004, P.R. China
Contact: Ryan Chen
☎ 010-6590 7766 ext 750
🖷 010-6590 6139
✉ r.chen@koelnmesse.cn
www.dm-exco.cn

数码营销博览会

dmexco

日期：2011/09/21 - 22
地点：德国科隆国际博览中心
内容：在线营销、门户网站营销、营销搜索引擎、电子邮件营销、手机营销、媒体宣传策划、游戏内置广告及相关营销、播客平台及推广、公关公司咨询、市场定位、跟踪与服务、电子商务
始办年份：2009
周期：每年一届
市场范围：国际性
性质：面向贸易观众
上届规模 2010：展览面积25,000m²，参展商355家，专业贸易观众15,800人
主办：科隆展览国际有限公司
地址：北京市朝阳区东三环北路8号亮马河大厦二座1018室（100004）
联系人：陈瑞
☎ 010-6590 7766转750
🖷 010-6590 6139
✉ r.chen@koelnmesse.cn
www.dm-exco.cn
www.koelnmesse.cn

dmexco

Date：2011/09/21 - 22
Venue: Cologne Exhibition Center, Germany
Profile: The dmexco is the leading international event for everyone working in the global digital marketing and media industry. The future of marketing lies in digital, and through its unique combination of an impressive exhibition and cutting-edge conference programme, the event therefore brings together innovative and progressive thinking for this significant growth market. Because today' s marketing is digital!
Established Year: 2009
Frequency: Annual
Market Area: International
Nature: Trade only
Statistics 2010: Exhibition Area 25,000m², Exhibitors 355，Trade Visitors 15,800
Organizer: Koelnmesse Co Ltd
Address: Unit 1018, Landmark Tower Ⅱ, No. 8 Dongsanhuan North Rd., Beijing 100004, P.R. China
Contact: Ryan Chen
☎ 010-6590 7766 ext 750
🖷 010-6590 6139
✉ r.chen@koelnmesse.cn
www.dm-exco.cn

柏林国际建筑物清洁、管理及服务展暨学术会议

CMS-Cleaning.Management.Services

日期：2011/09/20-23
内容：清洁设备、清洁技术、商品清洁、洗涤剂、设备管理、楼层清洁、保养、维修、服务。
周期：两年一届
参展费用：大厅(一面开展台) 154欧元/m²，露天站台83欧元/m²
上届规模：展览面积11,210m²,参展商345家（国外展商86家），参观人数14,384人（国外观众1,323）
主办：Messe Berlin Gmbh
联络：德国工商会(香港)南中国办事处/柏林国际展览有限公司香港及中国代表处
☎ 020-8755 2353
🖷 020-8755 1889
✉ meng-sophie@gz.china.ahk.de
www.messe-berlin.de

欧洲国际复合材料展

COMPOSITES EUROPE:

European Trade Fair for Composites, Technology & Applications

日期：2011/09/27 - 29
地点：德国斯图加特展览中心（Exhibition Center Stuttgart）
内容：涵盖整个复合材料产业的新兴国际性展会，会见该行业高品质观众。 产品及服务：展商涵盖化学制品、原料（树脂、玻璃纤维、碳纤维）、中间产品、混合材料、半成品和成品、技术和设备，以及服务。媒体。
周期：每年一届
参展费用：标准展位222.95欧元/m²起，光地展位172欧元/m²起
上届规模 2010：参展商294家，参观人数8,101人
主办：励展德国公司（Reed Exhibitions Deutschland GmbH）
联络：励展博览集团国际销售部
地址：北京市朝阳区新源南路1-3号平安国际金融中心A座15层01-03,05 （100027）
☎ 010-5933 9288
🖷 010-5933 9233
✉ liang.wang@reedexpo.com.cn
www.composites-europe.com
www.reedexport.cn

柏林国际艺术展

art forum berlin

日期：2011/09/29-10/02
内容：美术、图像、摄影、雕塑、影像艺术、画。
周期：每年一届
参展费用：大厅(一面开展台)250欧元/m²
上届规模：展览面积6,108m²，参展商165家（国外展商84家），观众12,742人
主办：Messe Berlin Gmbh
参展联络：德国工商会(香港)南中国办事处/柏林国际展览有限公司香港及中国代表处
☎ 020-8755 2353
🖷 020-8755 1889
✉ meng-sophie@gz.china.ahk.de
www.messe-berlin.de

世界食品博览会

Anuga

日期： 2011/10/08 - 12
地点： 德国科隆国际博览中心
内容： 全世界的食品展数不胜数，但只有Anuga才是食品和饮料行业规模最大、地位最重要的展览会，也是唯一一个为您的未来精心规划的展览会。
展品范围： 基本食品和精细食品，冷冻食品，肉制品，冷藏食品，奶制品，面包、焙烤食品和热饮，饮料，有机食品，餐饮技术，零售技术。其他包括非处方药OTC论坛、健康及功能性食品论坛、协会、组织、贸易媒体、服务提供商和信息技术
始办年份： 1922
周期： 每年两届
市场范围： 国际性
性质： 面向贸易观众
参展费用： 440欧元/m^2（最小12m^2）含光地租金、摊位装修、公共能源费、AUMA费,不含基本会刊登录费349欧元/参展商、联合参展费250欧元/参展商及19%增值税；垃圾清运及电费25欧元/平方米及19%增值税
上届规模 2010：展览面积287,000m^2, 参展商6,522家（国外展商5,307家），专业贸易观众153,500人
主办： 科隆国际展览有限公司
联络： 科隆展览中国有限公司
地址： 北京东三环北路8号亮马河大厦2座1018室（100004）
联系人： 徐畅,王迎
☎ 010-6590 7766转715
℡ 010-6590 6139
✉ j.xu@koelnmesse.cn
www.anuga.cn
www.koelnmesse.cn

Anuga

Date：2011/10/08 - 12
Venue: Cologne Exhibition Center, Germany
Profile: Trade Fair for the International Food Industry Leading fair for industry, trade and catering trade in the food and beverage sector Manufacturers, importers and wholesalers - of food and drinks - of catering technology - of retail technology/shop fittings - Suppliers of services for the catering sector and the food retail trade - Trade agencies - Suppliers of specialties - Suppliers of fresh convenience products
Established Year: 1922
Frequency: Biannual
Market Area: International
Nature: Trade only
Participated Fee: EURO 440/m^2（min 12m^2）
Statistics 2010: Exhibition Area 287,000m^2, Exhibitors 6,522（foreigners 5,307, came from countries）, Trade Visitors 153,500
Organizer: Koelnmesse Co Ltd
Address: Unit 1018, Landmark Tower Ⅱ, No. 8 Dongsanhuan North Rd., Beijing 100004, China
Contact: Joyce Xu, Elan Wang
☎ 010-6590 7766 ext 715
℡ 010-6590 6139
✉ j.xu@koelnmesse.cn
www.anuga.cn

viscom dusseldorf

德国国际视觉广告技术与标识制作展

International Trade Fair for Visual Communication

日期： 2011/10/13 - 15
地点： 德国杜赛尔多夫
内容： 德国国际视觉广告技术与标识制作展涵盖视觉传播领域的各个方面。该展之前名为PRO SIGN，一直以创新的产品、高质量的展会服务而闻名。
周期： 两年一届
市场范围： 国际性
性质： 面向贸易观众
主办： 励展博览集团
联络： 励展博览集团国际销售部
地址： 北京市朝阳区新源南路1-3号平安国际金融中心A座15层01-03,05
联系人： 张志超
☎ 010-5933 9266
℡ 010-5933 9233
✉ ivy.zhang@reedexpo.com.cn
www.viscom-messe.com
www.reedrxport.cn

德国国际专业电梯设备及配件展览会

Interlift

日期： 2011/10/18 - 21
地点： 德国奥格斯堡
周期： 每年两届
主办： 中国贸促会机械行业分会
地址： 北京市西城区三里河路46号（100823）
联系人： 张玉惠,郭旭萍,吕春丽
☎ 010-6859 4811, 6859 4994, 6859 4910
℡ 010-6859 4995
✉ zhangyuhui@ccpitmsc.org
www.chinamachine.org.cn

科隆国际休闲、体育设施及泳池设备展2011

FSB2011

日期： 2011/10/26 - 28
地点： 德国科隆国际博览中心
内容： 运动设施，公共泳池设施，运动场的规划设计、建设及其配套设施，城市规划、景观建筑、服务及专业媒体
始办年份： 1969
周期： 每年两届
市场范围： 国际性
性质： 面向贸易观众
参展费用： 标准展位495欧元/m^2（最小12m^2）费用包括含光地租金、摊位装修、公共能源费、AUMA费、基本会刊登录费、买家推广费、垃圾清运及电费及19%增值税；光地151欧元/m^2（最小36m^2）其它费用包括公共能源费、AUMA费、会刊登录费用、买家推广费、垃圾清运费、摊位电费、暂缴杂费及19%增值税。光地企业需要自行安排摊位装修
上届规模 2009：展览面积62,000m^2, 参展商572家，参观人数24,568人
主办： 科隆展览中国有限公司
地址： 北京市朝阳区东三环北路8号亮马河大厦二座1018室（100004）
联系人： 贾宁
☎ 010-6590 7766转729
℡ 010-6590 6139
✉ m.jia@koelnmesse.cn
www.fsb-cologne.cn

FSB2011

Date：2011/10/26 - 28
Venue: Cologne Exhibition Center, Germany
Profile: Construction and equipping of sport Construction and equipping of sport, Public pool facilities, Project planning, construction and equipping of playgrounds and leisure facilities, Urban Design/Landscape architecture, Services and media
Established Year: 1969
Frequency: Biannual
Market Area: International
Nature: Trade only
Participated Fee: Standard Booth EURO 495/m^2(min 12m^2), Raw Space EURO 151/m^2(min 36m^2) Statistics 2009: Exhibition Area 62,000m^2, Exhibitors 572, Visitors 24,568
Organizer: Koelnmesse Co Ltd
Address: Unit 1018, Landmark Tower Ⅱ, No. 8 Dongsanhuan North Rd., Beijing 100004, P.R. China
Contact: Maggie Jia
☎ 010-6590 7766 ext 729
℡ 010-6590 6139
✉ m.jia@koelnmesse.cn
www.fsb-cologne.cn

国际桑拿及泳池设备展

Aquanale

日期： 2011/10/26 - 29
地点： 德国科隆国际博览中心
内容： 游泳池、桑拿房的设计、建设及其维护,游泳池、桑拿房相关设施、设备、器材、用品，游泳休闲设备、疗养设备，私人spa，服务、专业媒体及其它，人工日光浴装置包括技术仪器，spa治疗
始办年份： 1953
周期： 每年两届
市场范围： 国际性
性质： 面向贸易观众
参展费用： 标准展位(最小12m^2)495欧元/m^{2}费用包括：含光地租金、摊位装修、公共能源费、AUMA费、基本会刊登录费、买家推广费、垃圾清运及电费及19%增值税；光地(最小36m^2)151欧元/m^{2}其它费用包括公共能源费、AUMA费、会刊登录费用、垃圾清运费、摊位电费、暂缴杂费、买家推广费及19%增值税。光地企业需要自行安排摊位装修
上届规模 2009：展览面积36,000m^2, 参展商271家，参观人数24,568人
主办： 科隆展览中国有限公司
地址： 北京市朝阳区东三环北路8号亮马河大厦二座1018室（100004）
联系人： 贾宁
☎ 010-6590 7766转729
℡ 010-6590 6139
✉ m.jia@koelnmesse.cn
www.aquanale.cn
www.koelnmesse.cn

Aquanale

Date：2011/10/26 - 29
Venue: Cologne Exhibition Center, Germany
Profile: Project planning, construction and equipping of pool facilities; Project planning, construction and equipping of sauna facilities and similar bath shapes; Ambience and fittings for pool and Wellness; Private SPA; Service and media; Synthetic Tanning Devices incl. technical equipment; Spa Treatment
Established Year: 1953
Frequency: Biannual
Market Area: International
Nature: Trade only
Participated Fee: Standard Booth EURO 495/m^2 (min 12m^2), Raw Space EURO 151/m^2 (min 36m^2)
Statistics 2009: Exhibition Area 36,000m^2, Exhibitors 271, Visitors 24,568
Organizer: Koelnmesse Co Ltd
Address: Unit 1018, Landmark Tower Ⅱ, No. 8 Dongsanhuan North Rd., Beijing 100004, China
Contact: Maggie Jia
☎ 010-6590 7766 ext 729
℡ 010-6590 6139
✉ m.jia@koelnmesse.cn
www.aquanale.cn

国际博物馆及展示技术展览会
EXPONATEC

日期： 2011/11/16 - 18
地点： 德国科隆国际展览中心
内容： 国际博物馆及展示技术展览会是全球最大的博物行业的展会。
展品范围： 楼宇新建、重建与规划，人事服务供应商，公共关系，观众研究与定位，展览设计，建筑与展览技术，媒体，入口出口区域，博物馆商店，博物馆餐饮，安全与运输，行政后勤，修复与保存，分解，材料测试，继续教育，研究机构
始办年份： 2004
周期： 两年一届
市场范围： 国际性
性质： 面向贸易观众
主办： 科隆展览国际有限公司
联络： 科隆展览中国有限公司
地址： 北京东三环北路8号亮马河大厦2座1018室（100004）
联系人： 陈瑞
☎ 010-6590 7766转750
🖷 010-6590 6139
✉ r.chen@koelnmesse.cn
www.exponatec.com
www.koelnmesse.cn

科隆国际优秀艺术及古董展
Cologne Fine Art and Antiques

日期： 2011/11/16 - 20
地点： 德国科隆国际展览中心
内容： 取代原西德优秀艺术展，科隆古书籍博览会及国际出 版、原生艺术、摄影作品展等三大春季艺术展，以国际市场为导向、聚焦最优秀而实用艺术精品 科隆国际优 秀艺术展将为国际优秀艺术和古董商提供一个高质量、全新的欧洲艺术平台，并为国际艺术经销商打造出广泛的交易领域。
展品范围： 艺术品及古董：非欧洲艺术、部落艺术、人类学艺术、古代宗教绘画和19世纪艺术、家具、古董、摄影作品、挂毯、地毯、武器装备、军事纪念品、音乐设备、钟表、珠宝、袖珍模型、图示、新近艺术、装饰艺术风格(Art Deco)、包豪 斯风格、现代设计艺术、书籍和艺术杂志；现代艺术：现代古典艺术、战后艺术、当代艺术、艺术版画、摄影 作品、录像、原生艺术（Art Brut）、书籍和艺术杂志 古董书籍 书籍、手稿、地图、图像及印刷品
始办年份： 2006
周期： 每年一届
市场范围： 国际性
性质： 面向公众
上届规模 2010：展览面积23,000m^2，参展商1,579家（国外展商1,029家），专业贸易观众16,249人
主办： 科隆国际展览有限公司
地址： 北京市朝阳区东三环北路8号亮马河大厦二座1018室（100004）
联系人： 潘容
☎ 010-6590 7766
🖷 010-6590 6139
✉ g.pan@koelnmesse.cn
www.cihs.com.cn
www.cihs-practicalworld.com

欧洲模具及机床技术展览会
EuroMold and Turntec

日期： 2011/12 -
地点： 德国法兰克福
周期： 每年一届
主办： 中国贸促会机械行业分会
地址： 北京市西城区三里河路46号（100823）
联系人： 张玉惠，郭旭萍，吕春丽
☎ 010-6859 4811, 6859 4994, 6859 4910
🖷 010-6859 4995
✉ zhangyuhui@ccpitmsc.org
www.chinamachine.org.cn

科隆国际家具展
imm cologne

日期： 2012 /01/17 - 22
地点： 德国科隆国际展览中心
内容： 当今世界最负盛名的家具展览会。每年一月份在德国科隆国际展览中心举行。展品无以伦比的广度和深度是科隆国际家具展作为全球第一品牌的独特性。在这里，全球的观众将领略到来自世界范围的包罗万象的设计一流的家具以及经典家居用品世界，其间，丰富多彩的配套活动也为科隆国际家具展增色不少
始办年份： 1949
周期： 每年一届
市场范围： 国际性
性质： 面向公众
入场券价格： 700RMB
参展费用： 统一特装560欧元/m^2，自行特装155欧元/m^2
主办： 德国科隆展览国际有限公司
地址： 北京市朝阳区东三环北路8号亮马河大厦二座1018室（100004）
联系人： 郑志强
☎ 010-6590 7766转717
🖷 010-6590 6139
✉ info@koelnmesse.cn
www.imm-cologne.cn
www.kolnmesse.cn

imm cologne

Date： 2012 /01/17 - 22
Venue: Koelnmesse Trade Fair Center, Germany
Profile: imm cologne is the international leading trade fair for the furnishing sector. Each year, imm cologne is the first event to present the latest home trends for Europe and overseas. The unparalleled breadth and depth of the exhibits is the trademark and claim to top quality of imm cologne. Here, international trade visitors discover furniture and home style ideas from all
Established Year: 1949
Frequency: Annual
Market Area: International
Nature: Open to public
Organizer: Koelnmesse Co Ltd
Address: Unit 1018 Landmark Tower II, No. 8 Dongsanhuan N. Road, Beijing
Contact: Ken Zheng
☎ 010-6590 7766 ext 717
🖷 010-6590 6139
✉ info@koelnmesse.cn
www.imm-cologne.cn

柏林国际建筑技术展
bautec

日期： 2012/02/21-25
内容： 气象设备、建筑设备、建筑用品、餐馆建筑、建筑系统、建筑化学、城市与区域规划、土木工程、通讯技术、门、大门、热技术、内部建筑、市政大厦、公共卫生技术、脚手架、服务、表面承载技术、窗户、屋顶工程、房屋立面系统、防火、房屋技术、木结构建筑物、护壁板。
周期： 两年一届
参展费用： 大厅(一面开展台)145欧元/m^2，露天站台80 欧元/m^2
上届规模： 展览面积16,236m^2，参展商719家（国外展商58家），观众53,926人（国外观众2,966人）
主办： Messe Berlin Gmbh
参展联络： 德国工商会(香港)南中国办事处/柏林国际展览有限公司香港及中国代表处
☎ 020-8755 2353
🖷 020-8755 1889
✉ meng-sophie@gz.china.ahk.de
www.messe-berlin.de

科隆国际五金博览会
INTERNATIONAL HARDWARE FAIR COLOGNE

日期： 2012/03/04 - 07
地点： 德国科隆国际展览中心
内容： 国际五金行业规模最大最有影响力的盛会，代表着国际化的发展和顶级品质。科隆国际五金博览会在2010 年采用新的LOGO 和名称后，在五金领域将更加专业化。博览会包括三大展品系列－工具、锁具及安全系统、紧固件和家居改进。来自全球相关领域的零售商、供应商及采购商都聚集在此。随着中国产品的国际竞争力的增强以及参展取得的卓越的效果，中国企业参加科隆国际五金博览会的规模和数量也在最近数年内有着突飞猛进的增长。
始办年份： 1952
周期： 两年一届
市场范围： 国际性
性质： 面向公众
参展费用： 标准展位540欧元/m^{2}含光地租金、摊位装修、公共能源费、德国展览业协会费用（AUMA费）、基本会刊登录费用、观众推广费用359欧元/家、垃圾清运费、摊位电费、其它杂费19%增值税
上届规模 2010：展览面积195,000m^2，参展商3,360家（来自61个国家），专业贸易观众70,000人（来自135个国家）
主办： 德国科隆展览国际有限公司
地址： 北京市朝阳区东三环北路8号亮马河大厦二座1018室（100004）
联系人： 郑志强
☎ 010-6590 7766转717
🖷 010-6590 6139
✉ k.zheng@koelnmesse.cn
www.koelnmesse.cn

INTERNATIONAL HARDWARE FAIR COLOGNE

Date： 2012 /03/04 - 07
Venue: Cologne Exhibition Center, Germany
Profile: The world' s leading trade fair for the hardware sector regarding: - Internationality of exhibitors and visitors - Comprehensive survey of the hardware industry: "One-Stop-Shopping". Tools, Industrial supply, Locks & fittings, Fastening & fittings, Home improvement five sectors under one roof.
Established Year: 1952
Frequency: Biannual
Market Area: International
Nature: Open to public
Participated Fee: Standard Booth EURO 540/m^2
Statistics 2010: Exhibition Area 195,000m^2, Exhibitors 3,360（came from 61 countries）, Trade Visitors 70,000
Organizer: Koelnmesse Co Ltd
Address: Unit 1018 Landmark Tower II, No. 8 Dongsanhuan N. Road, Beijing 100004

Contact: Ken Zheng
☎ 010-6590 7766 ext 717
🖷 010-6590 6139
✉ k.zheng@koelnmesse.cn
www.koelnmesse.cn

柏林–勃兰登堡国际航空航天展

LIA-Berlin Air Show

日期：2012/06/19-24
内容：新型材料、航空设备、航空航天研究、航天研究、航天技术、飞机、飞机发电机、飞机维护、机场设备、组件、防御技术、电子设备、电子系统、直升机、电源装置、太空技术。
周期：两年一届
参展费用：大厅(一面开展台)317欧元/m^2，露天站台180欧元/m^2
上届规模：展览面积26,039m^2，参展商1127家展商（国外展商435家），观众241,000人（国外观众228,920人）
主办：Messe Berlin Gmbh；Bunderverband der Deutschen Luft-und Raumfahrtindustrie e.V.(BDLI)
参展联络：德国工商会(香港)南中国办事处/柏林国际展览有限公司香港及中国代表处
☎ 020-8755 2353
🖷 020-8755 1889
✉ meng-sophie@gz.china.ahk.de
www.messe-berlin.de

交通、车辆、组件–革新产品展

InnoTrans

日期：2012/09/18-21
内容：设备、组建、桥梁建造、数据处理设备、铁路建设、铁路、铁路技术、汽车、内部设施、设备维护、网络技术服务、通信技术、信号装置、交通方式、货物运输系统、运输技术、隧道建设、交通控制、交通规划。
周期：两年一届
参展费用：大厅(一面开展台)220/欧元/m^2，露天站台162 欧元/m^2
上届规模：展览面积67,972m^2，参展商1,914家（国外展商987家），观众88,330人（国外观众33,124人）
主办：Messe Berlin Gmbh
参展联络：德国工商会(香港)南中国办事处/柏林国际展览有限公司香港及中国代表处
☎ 020-8755 2353
🖷 020-8755 1889
✉ meng-sophie@gz.china.ahk.de
www.messe-berlin.de

2012德国国际铝工业展览会

ALUMINIUM 2012

日期：2012/10/09 - 11
地点：德国杜塞尔多夫展览中心
内容：ALUMINIUM 2012是铝工业和其相关应用配套设备展览的首选之地。本展览覆盖整个价值链从提炼到成品应用于汽车制造和运输、建筑、机械电机工程、包装设计以及铝加工及精炼技术等主要领域。
产品及服务：来自40多个国家约900个展商将展示近千种创新产品，以及深层技术开发和最新趋势。德国国际铝工业展览会（ALUMINIUM）是铝工业及相关配套应用设备最重要的展示平台。铝生产商、加工商、精炼商以及科技和附加产品供应商，以及各种配套应用产品供应商将于九月汇聚德国埃森。
周期：两年一届
市场范围：国际性
性质：面向贸易观众
参展费用：光地展位185欧元/m^2
主办：励展德国公司
联络：励展博览集团国际销售部
地址：北京市朝阳区新源南路1-3号平安国际金融中心A座15层01-03,05
联系人：王颖
☎ 010- 5933 9208
🖷 010- 5933 9233
✉ winnie.wang@reedexpo.com.cn
www.reedexport.cn
www.aluminium-messe.com

秋季马术用品展

spoga horse (Autumn)

日期：2012 /09/04 - 06
地点：德国科隆国际展览中心
内容：马术用品及相关服务
始办年份：2008
周期：每年两届
市场范围：国际性
性质：面向公众
参展费用：标准展位381欧元/m^2(最小9m^2)费用包括光地费、摊位搭建费、公共能源费、AUMA费及19%的增值税。不包含基本会刊登录费、垃圾清运及电费；光地136欧元/m^2（最小36m^2）其它费用包括公共能源费5欧元/m^2、AUMA费0.6欧元/m^2、会刊登录费167欧元/参展商、暂缴杂费及19%增值税
上届规模 2010：展览面积28,500m^2，参展商379家，参观人数38,600人
主办：科隆展览国际有限公司
地址：北京东三环北路8号亮马河大厦2座1018室（100004）
联系人：张昱，贾宁
☎ 010-6590 7766转738
🖷 010-6590 6139
✉ j.zhang@koelnmesse.cn
www.spogagafa.cn
www.koelnmesse.cn

spoga horse (Autumn)

Date：2012/09/04 - 06
Venue: Cologne Exhibition Center, Germany
Established Year: 2008
Frequency: Biannual
Market Area: International
Nature: Open to public
Participated Fee: Standard Booth EURO 381/m^2(min 9m^2), Raw Space EURO 6/m^2（min 36m^2）
Statistics 2010: Exhibition Area 28,500m^2, Exhibitors 379，Visitors 38,600
Organizer: Koelnmesse Co Ltd
Address: Unit 1018, Landmark Tower Ⅱ, No. 8 Dongsanhuan North Rd., Beijing 100004, China
Contact: Joesy Zhang, Maggie Jia
☎ 010-6590 7766 ext 738
🖷 010-6590 6139
✉ j.zhang@koelnmesse.cn
www.spogagafa.cn

世界影像博览会

photokina

photokina
world of imaging

日期：2012/09/18 - 23
地点：德国科隆国际博览中心
内容：照相与成像工业领域领先的展览会，是世界上唯一的为大众消费者和专业人士提供所有成像介质、成像技术与成像市场综合性展示的展览会。因此，世界影像博览会（photokina）在成像领域具有独特的竞争优势，使其成为所有影像用户提供综合性解决方案的展示平台。世界影像博览会（photokina）不仅为照相与成像产业部门提供新的销售动力，而且是集中展示面向未来的各种技术和产品的趋势论坛
始办年份：1950
周期：两年一届
市场范围：国际性
性质：面向公众
上届规模 2010：展览面积210,000m^2，参展商1,523家（国外展商1,004家，来自161个国家），专业贸易观众169,000人
主办：科隆展览国际有限公司
地址：北京东三环北路8号亮马河大厦2座1018室（100004）
联系人：潘容
☎ 010-6590 7766 转715
🖷 010-6590 6139
✉ g.pan@koelnmesse.cn
www.photokina.cn

photokina

Date：2012 /09/18 - 23
Venue: Cologne Exhibition Center, Germany
Established Year: 1950
Frequency: Biannual
Market Area: International
Nature: Open to public
Statistics 2010: Exhibition Area 210,000m^2, Exhibitors 1,523（foreigners 1,004, came from 161 countries），Visitors 169,000
Organizer: Koelnmesse Co Ltd
Address: Unit 1018, Landmark Tower Ⅱ, No. 8 Dongsanhuan North Rd., Beijing 100004, P.R. China
Contact: Grace Pan
☎ 010-6590 7766 ext 715
🖷 010-6590 6139
✉ g.pan@koelnmesse.cn
www.photokina.cn
www.koelnmesse.cn

科隆国际摩托车、滑板车及自行车展览会

INTERMOT Cologne

日期：2012/10/03 - 07
地点：德国科隆国际展览中心
内容：动力车，拖车和边车，摩托车零件及配件，发动机及组件，电动设备，摩托服及用具、摩托生产工具、车间和商店设备，原材料、半成品、及包装材料，润滑油及防护用品，摩托车旅游及相关户外用品
始办年份：1988
周期：两年一届
市场范围：国际性
性质：面向贸易观众
入场券价格：人民币300元（2010年）
参展费用：标准展位500欧元/m^2（最小9m^2）含光地租金、展位装修、公共能源费、AUMA费、基本会刊登录费、垃圾清运费、展位电费、其它杂费及19%增值税；光地（最小36m^2）：一面开口141.50欧元/m^2，两面开口146.50欧元/m^2，三面开口149.50欧元/m^2，四面开口151.50欧元/m^2，室外场地80欧元/m^2，其他费用AUMA费0.6欧元/m^2、基本会刊登录费299欧元/参展商、买家推广费
上届规模 2009：展览面积110,000m^2，参展商1,107家（国外展商702家，来自40个国家），参观人数210,000人（专业贸易观众195,000人）
主办：科展览有中国限公司
地址：北京市朝阳区东三环北路8号亮马河大厦二座1018室（100004）
联系人：齐志宇
☎ 010-6590 7766转727
🖷 010-6590 6139

✉ k.qi@koelnmesse.cn
www.intermot-koeln.com
www.koelnmesse.cn

INTERMOT Cologne

Date：2012 /10/03 - 07
Venue: Cologne Exhibition Center, Germany
Profile: Motorized vehicles, Trailers and sidecars, Components and accessories for motorcycles, Engines and components, Electrical equipment Clothing, motorcyclists' gear, Machines, tools, workshop and shop equipment, Raw materials, semi-finished products, packaging materials, Lubricants, gear-box/transmission oil, care products, Tourism, Contact groups.
Established Year: 1988
Frequency: Biennial
Market Area: International
Nature: Trade only
Participated Fee: Standard Booth EURO 500/m^2（min 9m^2）; Raw Space EURO 141.50/m^2, Corner Booth EURO 146.50/m^2, Peninsula Unit EURO 149.50/m^2, Island Unit EURO 151.50/m^2; Outdoor EURO 80/m^2
Statistics 2010: Exhibition Area 110,000m^2, Exhibitors 1107（foreigners 702, came from 40 countries）, Visitors 210,000（trade visitors 195,000）
Organizer: Koelnmesse Co Ltd
Address: Unit 1018 Landmark Tower II, No. 8 Dongsanhuan N. Road, Beijing 100004
Contact: Kevin Qi
☎ 010-6590 7766 ext 727
🖷 010-6590 6139
✉ k.qi@koelnmesse.cn
www.intermot-koeln.com

SHOWTECH

柏林国际会展技术及媒体技术展览会

International Trade Show & Conference for Event Technology & Services

SHOWTECH

日期：2013/06 -
地点：德国柏林展览中心
内容：国际会展技术及媒体技术展览会是针对舞台表演及展会活动行业的著名欧洲展览会，是向业内技术决策人、制造商、展会活动经理人、主办者及经销商展示灯光、音响科技领域最新创新、解决方案及行业潮流的高水平业务交流平台。由展会赞助机构德国影剧院技术协会（DTHG）于展会同期主办的专业会议将邀请顶级业内专家介绍最新的国际影剧院技术及管理经验。
周期：两年一届
市场范围：国际性
性质：面向贸易观众
主办：励展德国公司
联络：励展博览集团国际销售部
地址：北京市朝阳区新源南路1-3号平安国际金融中心A座15层01-03,05 （100027）
☎ 010- 5933 9211
🖷 010- 5933 9233
✉ ISGCNmarketing@reedexpo.com.cn
www.reedexport.cn
www.showtech.de

危地马拉 Guatemala

中国贸易展览会

日期：2011/11 -
地点：危地马拉危地马拉城
主办：中国贸促会机械行业分会
地址：北京市西城区三里河路46号（100823）
联系人：张玉惠,郭旭萍,吕春丽
☎ 010-6859 4811, 6859 4994, 6859 4910
🖷 010-6859 4995
✉ zhangyuhui@ccpitmsc.org
www.chinamachine.org.cn

洪都拉斯 Honduras

中国贸易展览会

日期：2011/11 -
地点：洪都拉斯圣佩德罗苏拉
市场范围：国际性
主办：中国贸促会机械行业分会
地址：北京市西城区三里河路46号（100823）
联系人：张玉惠,郭旭萍,吕春丽
☎ 010-6859 4811, 6859 4994, 6859 4910
🖷 010-6859 4995
✉ zhangyuhui@ccpitmsc.org
www.chinamachine.org.cn

印度 India

印度南亚地球勘探科学展览会暨研讨会 (GEO India 2011)

3rd South Asia Geosciences Conference and Exhibition

日期：2011/01/12 - 14
地点：印度新德里New Delhi Expo XXI, India
始办年份：2008
周期：每年一届
市场范围：国际性
性质：面向贸易观众
上届规模 2008：参展商61家，专业贸易观众1,549人
主办：北京邦企展览服务有限公司
地址：北京市朝阳区惠新东街11号紫光发展大厦B1座501室（100029）
联系人：杨先生
☎ 010-6482 3808
🖷 010-6482 3670
✉ bbes@china.com
MSN：bbes13@live.cn
www.bbes.com.cn

印度国际机床工具展览会

IMTEX&TOOLTECH

日期：2011/01/20 - 26
地点：印度班加罗尔
周期：每年一届
主办：中国贸促会
地址：北京市西城区三里河路46号（100823）
联系人：张玉惠, 郭旭萍, 吕春丽
☎ 010-6859 4811, 6859 4994, 6859 4910
🖷 010-6859 4995
邮箱：zhangyuhui@ccpitmsc.org
www.chinamachine.org.cn

印度国际宝石及珠宝展览会

Gem & Jewellery India International Exhibition

日期：2011/02/26 - 28
地点：印度钦奈贸易中心
主办：博闻印度公司
☎ +91 (044) 45530072/73
🖷 +91 (044) 42698747
✉ syedt@ubmindia.com
联络：亚洲博闻
地址：UBM Asia Ltd UBM China Ltd 17/F, China Resources Building 26 Harbor Road, Wanchai, Hong Kong
☎ 852-2516 1634/2197
🖷 852-2802 9934
✉ salesjwf@cmpasia.com
www.JewelleryNetAsia.com
www.jewelleryfair.in/chennai/home.asp

Gem & Jewellery India International Exhibition

Date：2011/02/26 - 28
Venue: Chennai Trade Center, India
Profile: A unique event for the jewellery industry in southern India and is one of the International B-2-B Jewellery Exhibition in the region
Organizer: UBM Asia Ltd
☎ +91 (044) 45530072/73
🖷 +91 (044) 42698747
✉ syedt@ubmindia.com
www.jewelleryfair.in/chennai/home.asp
Contact: UBM China Ltd
Address: 17/F, China Resources Building 26 Harbor Road, Wanchai, Hong Kong
☎ 852-2516 1634/2197
🖷 852-2802 9934
✉ salesjwf@cmpasia.com
www.JewelleryNetAsia.com
www.jewelleryfair.in/chennai/home.asp

印度国际机械工业展览会

India International Machinery and Equipment Exhibition

日期：2011/03 -
地点：印度孟买
周期：每年一届
主办：中国贸促会机械行业分会
地址：北京市西城区三里河路46号（100823）
联系人：张玉惠, 郭旭萍, 吕春丽
☎ 010-6859 4811, 6859 4994, 6859 4910
🖷 010-6859 4995
邮箱：zhangyuhui@ccpitmsc.org
www.chinamachine.org.cn

印度鞋履、原料、制造及技术展览会

Footwear, Materials, Manufacturing and Technology

日期：2011/05/06 - 08
地点：印度诺伊达
上届规模 2010：参展商180家，买家3,500人（来自18个国家）
主办：博闻印度公司；亚太区皮革展
☎ 852-2827 6211
🖷 852-2827 7831
✉ sales@aplf.com
www.aplfindia.com

Footwear, Materials, Manufacturing and Technology

Date：2011/05/06 - 08
Venue: India Expo Center, Expo XXI, Greater Noida, New Delhi, India
Statistics 2010: Exhibitors 180，Buyers 3,500（came from 18 countries）

Organizer: UBM India & APLF Ltd
☎ 852-2827 6211
🖷 852-2827 7831
✉ sales@aplf.com
www.aplfindia.com

南印度国际安全与消防技术设备展览会

IFSEC South India

IFSEC SOUTH INDIA
1 - 3 June 2011
Bangalore International Exhibition Centre,
Bengaluru, India

日期：2011/06/01 - 03
地点：印度班加洛
市场范围：国际性
主办：亚洲博闻
☎ +91(0)11 2376 5554
✉ nigel.brown@ubm.com
www.ifsecsouthindia.com

IFSEC South India

Date：2011/06/01 - 03
Venue: Bangalore Intl Exhibition Center, India
Profile: IFSEC South India will provide the South Indian security market with a platform where security and fire prevention professionals can source the latest security and fire products from the world' s leading companies
Market Area: International
Organizer: UBM Asia
☎ +91(0)11 2376 5554
✉ nigel.brown@ubm.com
www.ifsecsouthindia.com

印度面辅料展

F&A

日期：2011/06/04 - 06
地点：印度
联络：上海比天展览服务有限公司
地址：上海市中山北路900号加禾商务中心3号楼303室(200070)
联系人：刘先生
☎ 021-5655 2843
🖷 021-5655 9981
www.betium.com

海德拉巴珠宝珍珠玉石展览会

Hyderabad Jewellery, Pearl & Gem Fair

日期：2011/07/09 - 11
地点：印度海德拉巴HITEX 展览中心
主办：博闻印度公司
☎ +91(022)6612 2600 转608/688
🖷 +91(022)6612 2626/27
✉ jewellery@ubmindia.com
联络：博闻中国公司
☎ 852-2516 1634/2197
🖷 852-2802 9934
✉ salesjwf@cmpasia.com
www.JewelleryNetAsia.com
www.jewelleryfair.in/hyderabad/home.asp

Hyderabad Jewellery, Pearl & Gem Fair

Date：2011/07/09 - 11
Venue: HITEX Exhibition Center, India
Organizer: UBM India Pvt Ltd
☎ +91(022)6612 2600 ext 608/688
🖷 +91(022)6612 2626/27
✉ jewellery@ubmindia.com
www.jewelleryfair.in/hyderabad/home.asp

嵌入式系统会议

Embedded Systems Conference India

日期：2011/07/20 - 22
地点：印度班加洛
主办：博闻公司
☎ +91 22 6769 2400
🖷 +91 22 6769 2426
✉ esc@ubmindia.com
www.esc-india.com

Embedded Systems Conference India

Date：2011/07/20 - 22
Venue: Nimhans Convention Centerm, Bangalore, India
Organizer: UBM Ltd
☎ +91 22 6769 2400
🖷 +91 22 6769 2426
✉ esc@ubmindia.com
www.esc-india.com

Interop 商业科技印度展

Interop India

日期：2011/09/28 - 30
地点：印度孟买
主办：博闻（印度）公司
☎ +91 22 6769 2400
🖷 +91 22 6769 2426
✉ pankaj.jain@ubm.com
www.interop.in

Interop India

Date：2011/09/28 - 30
Venue: Bombay Exhibition Center, Mumbai, India
Organizer: UBM Ltd
☎ +91 22 6769 2400
🖷 +91 22 6769 2426
✉ pankaj.jain@ubm.com
www.interop.in

印度能源展

India Energy

日期：2011/09/29 - 01
地点：印度孟买
主办：博闻（印度）公司
☎ +91 22 6612 2600/644
🖷 +91 22 6612 2626-27
✉ abhijit.mukherjee@ubm.com
www.interop.in

India Energy

Date：2011/09/29 - 01
Venue: Bombay Exhibition Center, Mumbai, India
Organizer: UBM India Pvt Ltd
☎ +91 22 6612 2600/644
🖷 +91 22 6612 2626-27
✉ abhijit.mukherjee@ubm.com
www.interop.in

第22届印度孟买国际家具展

INDEX MUMBAI2011

日期：2011/09/29 - 02
地点：印度
☎ 0411-8378 8831
🖷 0411-8378 8830

印度食品配料展

Food Ingredients India

日期：2011/10/05 - 07
地点：印度孟买
主办：博闻印度公司
☎ +31(0)20 40 99 544
🖷 +31(0)20 36 32 616
✉ jonathan.vis@ubm.com
www.fi-events.com

Food Ingredients India

Date：2011/10/05 - 07
Venue: Bombay Exhibition Center, Mumbai, India
Organizer: UBM International Media BV
☎ +31(0)20 40 99 544
🖷 +31(0)20 36 32 616
✉ jonathan.vis@ubm.com
www.fi-events.com

印度国际工程机械与技术展览会

EXCON

日期：2011/11 -
地点：印度班加罗尔
周期：每年两届
主办：中国贸促会
地址：北京市西城区三里河路46号（100823）
联系人：张玉惠，郭旭萍，吕春丽
☎ 010-6859 4811, 6859 4994, 6859 4910
🖷 010-6859 4995
✉ zhangyuhui@ccpitmsc.org
www.chinamachine.org.cn

印度国际铝工业展（第三届）

ALUMINIUM INDIA

日期：2011/11/10 - 12
地点：印度孟买展览中心Bombay Exhibition Center）
内容：作为印度领先的铝业生态系统及其应用工业的企业间行业展会，印度国际铝工业展汇聚生产商、加工商、技术供应商和消费用户，从原材料到半成品和成品的完整价值链。第三届展会举办在即，2011年印度国际铝工业展旨在通过聚焦于南亚地区高成长制造业的新兴机遇，彰显印度在全球铝业的重要地位。这些高成长行业包括汽车制造、建筑建材、通信和电力等。每个行业都能够将印度次大陆的铝业提升至从未企及的高度。印度国际铝工业展是一个汇集全球产业巨头的地区性平台，囊括铝业生产商、加工商、原材料制造商、铝部件制作终端产品厂商等。

展会还吸引铝业技术的供应商，铝业生产、加工及精炼领域配件生产商，以及制造加工、建筑建材、包装、五金、汽车运输、电力传输、工厂和机器生产、金属和大宗商品市场等相关行业厂商出席。

展品范围：原材料、原生金属制品；半成品、铸造、薄片、带条、平板、挤出铝制品；适于建筑建造、运输、电子及机械行业应用的铝制品；表面处理及链接技术；铝提取、处理及精炼机械、设备及配件；轻金属贸易及回收再用；服务、咨询、专业意见及信息。
观众来源：铝业（包括设备、技术和供应商），提取、熔炼和铸造
上届规模 2010：展出净面积5,000m²，参展商108家（国外展商75家），专业贸易观众2,309人（国际观众129人）
主办：励展印度公司
联络：励展博览集团国际销售部
北京市朝阳区新源南路1-3号平安国际金融中心A座15层01-03,05
联系人：王颖
☎ 010-5933 9208
🖷 010-5933 9233
✉ winnie.wang@reedexpo.com.cn
www.reedexport.cn

印度食品博览会
Annapoorna -
World of Food India

日期：2011/11/16 - 18
地点：印度孟买
内容：精细食品，果蔬制品，食品配料和添加剂，鱼类、海鲜食品，冷冻食品、冰激凌，肉禽类，饮料，甜食、休闲食品，牛奶及乳制品，面包及焙烤类食品
始办年份：2006
周期：每年一届
市场范围：国际性
性质：面向贸易观众
上届规模 2010：参展商152家（国外展商184家，来自45个国家），专业贸易观众4,736人
主办：科隆国际展览有限公司
地址：北京市东三环北路8号亮马河大厦2座1018室（100004）
联系人：潘容
☎ 010-6590 7766转715
🖷 010-6590 6139
www.worldoffoodindia.cn

Annapoorna
- World of Food India

Date：2011/11/16 - 18
Venue: Mumbai, India
Established Year: 2006
Frequency: Annual
Market Area: International
Nature: Trade only
Statistics 2010: Exhibitors 152 came from 45 countries，Trade Visitors 4,736
Organizer: Koelnmesse GmbH
Address: Landmark Tower II, No.8 Dongsanhuan North Rd., Beijing 100004
Contact: Grace Pan
☎ 010-6590 7766 ext 715
🖷 010-6590 6139
www.worldoffoodindia.cn

世界制药机械、包装设备与材料印度展
P-MEC India

日期：2011/11/30 - 02
地点：印度孟买
主办：博闻公司
☎ +91 22 66122600
🖷 +91 22 66122626
MSN：chaitali.patil@ubm.com
www.pmec-india.com

P-MEC India
Date：2011/11/30 - 02
Venue: Bombay Exhibition Center, Mumbai, India
Profile: Focusing on pharmaceutical machinery, equipment and technology, P-MEC India is part of the largest and most comprehensive pharmaceutical events in South Asia.
Organizer: UBM India Pvt. Ltd
☎ +91 22 66122600
🖷 +91 22 66122626
MSN: chaitali.patil@ubm.com
www.pmec-india.com

世界制药原料印度展
CPhI India

日期：2011/11/30 - 02
地点：印度孟买
主办：博闻公司
☎ +91 22 66122600
🖷 +91 22 66122626
MSN：chaitali.patil@ubm.com
www.cphi-india.com

CPhI India
Date：2011/11/30 - 02
Venue: Bombay Exhibition Center, Mumbai, India
Organizer: UBM Live
☎ +91 22 66122600
🖷 +91 22 66122626
MSN: chaitali.patil@ubm.com
www.cphi-india.com

印度国际合同服务展
ICSE India

icse
bringing outsourcing to CPhI India

日期：2011/11/30 - 02
地点：印度孟买
主办：亚洲博闻
☎ +91 22 66122600
🖷 +91 22 66122626
✉ chaitali.patil@ubm.com
www.callcenter-japan.com

ICSE India
Date：2011/11/30 - 02
Venue: Bombay Exhibition Center, Mumbai, India
Organizer: UBM Live and UBM Asia
☎ +91 22 66122600
🖷 +91 22 66122626
✉ chaitali.patil@ubm.com
www.callcenter-japan.com

孟买珠宝首饰展览会
Mumbai Jewellery & Gem Fair

日期：2011/12 -
地点：印度孟买
主办：博闻印度公司
☎ +91(022)6612 2600转608/688
🖷 +91(022)6612 2626/27
✉ ayesha.salve@ubm.com
www.jewelleryfair.in

Mumbai Jewellery & Gem Fair
Date：2011/12 -
Venue: Bombay Exhibition Center, Mumbai, India
Organizer: UBM India Pvt. Ltd
☎ +91(022)6612 2600 ext 608/688
🖷 +91(022)6612 2626/27
✉ ayesha.salve@ubm.com
www.jewelleryfair.in

印度国际五金工具展览会
日期：2011/12 -
地点：印度孟买
周期：每年一届
主办：中国贸促会机械行业分会
地址：北京市西城区三里河路46号（100823）
联系人：张玉惠，郭旭萍，吕春丽
☎ 010-6859 4811, 6859 4994, 6859 4910
🖷 010-6859 4995
✉ zhangyuhui@ccpitmsc.org
www.chinamachine.org.cn

印度国际工业装备展览会
Industrial Automation INDIA

日期：2011/12 -
地点：印度孟买
周期：每年一届
主办：中国贸促会机械行业分会
地址：北京市西城区三里河路46号（100823）
联系人：张玉惠,郭旭萍,吕春丽
☎ 010-6859 4811, 6859 4994, 6859 4910
🖷 010-6859 4995
✉ zhangyuhui@ccpitmsc.org
www.chinamachine.org.cn

印度国际安全科技及产品大展
IFSEC India

IFSECINDIA
08 - 10 December 2011
Pragati Maidan, New Delhi

日期：2011/12/08 - 12
地点：印度新德里Pragati Maidan国际展览中心
上届规模 2009：参展商220家（来自20个国家），专业贸易观众11,447人
主办：博闻公司
☎ +91(0)11 2376 5554, +91(0)22 6612 2674
✉ nigel.brown@ubm.com,
✉ prashant.bahl@ubm.com
www.ifsecindia.com

IFSEC India
Date：2011/12/08 - 12
Venue: Pragati Maidan, New Delhi, India
Profile: India's largest Intl exhibition for commercial homeland security & fire technology
Statistics 2009: Exhibitors 220（came from 20 countries），Trade Visitors 11,447
Organizer: UBM Live

☎ +91(0)11 2376 5554, +91(0)22 6612 2674
✉ nigel.brown@ubm.com
✉ prashant.bahl@ubm.com
www.ifsecindia.com

2012年印度国际铝展
Aluminium India 2012

日期： 2012/ -
地点： 印度孟买展览中心
内容： 蓬勃发展中的印度铝业市场预计将在未来数年内持续增长。随着印度厂商生产能力的不断扩展、新企业的加入以及当前市场对高品质产品需求的不断增长，印度铝业正在越来越多地采用新科技与新设备以求提升生产质量。为满足印度铝业对国际铝业新技术及新产品的迫切需求，Alcastek（印度国际铝制造技术会议暨贸易展）和励展博览集团将联合举办"印度国际铝展（ALUMINIUM INDIA）"，届时将吸引3,000多名行业决策者、厂商代表、用户及技术研发人员与会观展。而Alcastek印度国际铝制造技术会议也将于同期继续举行，期间将邀请世界级专家共同探讨国际铝业的最新进展、打造高标准的技术交流平台。
周期： 两年一届
市场范围： 国际性
性质： 面向贸易观众
参展费用： 光地展位250美元/m²，标准展位325美元/m²
主办： 励展印度公司
联络： 励展博览集团国际销售部
地址： 北京市朝阳区新源南路1-3号平安国际金融中心A座15层01-03,05 （100027）
☎ 010-5933 9211
🖷 010-5933 9233
✉ ISGCNmarketing@reedexpo.com.cn
www.reedexport.cn
www.aluminium-india.com

印度尼西亚
Indonesia

2011年印尼国际商用车及零配件展
INAPA 2011

日期： 2011/03/23-26
地点： 印度尼西亚雅加达Indonesia-Jakarta
内容： 2011年该展分3个主题展会，分别是INAPA——乘用车配件及附件展、IIBT——商用车及零配件展、INABIKE——摩托车、电动车及零配件展。届时，该展将成为东南亚规模最大的覆盖乘用车、商用车、双轮车及其配件的综合性汽摩配展会。2010年，印尼INAPA展共吸引了62家中国企业。中国企业的参展数量是2009年的3.5倍。
参展范围： 各类汽车零部件、配件、维修工具设备及零件、汽车相关外围产品及设备包括车用装饰品等。
周期： 每年一届
上届规模 2010：展览面积10,000m²，参展商300家，专业买家12,597人（82%本地买家，12%国外买家）
联络： 中国汽车工业国际合作总公司
地址： 北京市海淀区中关村丹棱街3号A座国机大厦（100080）
☎ 010-8260 6881, 6891, 6893, 6874
🖷 010-8260 6883, 8260 6790
联系人： 马蓉，刘岩，娄杰，杨菁
✉ exhibition@cnaico.com.cn
www.autochina.com.cn

2011年印尼国际重型设备及工程机械展览会
Heavy Equipment 2011

日期： 2011/03/23 - 26
地点： 印度尼西亚雅加达国际展览中心JIEXPO, Indonesia
内容： 该展成为东南亚规模重要的重型设备及工程机械展览会。展品范围有工程车辆，工程机械设备及配件；矿业车辆，机械及配件；重型设备，卡车，拖车；农业及林业车辆及配件，拖拉机；液压起重机，工业机械及相关配件；重型车辆配件及设备；轮胎及技术；其他相关机械设备。
始办年份： 2009
周期： 每年一届
市场范围： 国际性
上届规模 2010：参展商300家，买家12,597人（18%来自国外）
主办： 北京麦田通会国际展览有限公司
联系人： 吴珊
☎ 010-8248 4014转801，5165 9302转8005
🖷 010-5165 9302转8004
✉ xiaoxiangzhishui@yahoo.com.cn
MSN：xiaoxiangzhishui@hotmail.com
www.cornfairs.com

印度尼西亚家具制造零配件展

日期： 2011/03/30 – 04/02
地点： 印度雅加达国际展览中心
内容： 本展举办之目的在于引领优质木工机械及家具零配件厂商前往印度尼西亚布局，赢得拓展外贸之先机。展品范围包含木工机械、手工具、家具制造材料与部品零配件、化学粘合剂与塑料、表面处理工具与产品、沙发寝具制造材料与配件、室内装潢设备材料与部品零配件、家具设计与制造相关顾问与服务、家具设计相关软件、媒体公协会首届
市场范围： 国际性
性质： 面向公众
入场券价格： 免费入场
参展费用： 新台币75,000(未税)/标摊；光地新台币7,000(未税)/m²
预计规模： 展出面积2,000m²，参展商70家，参观人数5,000人
主办： 开国有限公司
地址： 台北市10461 德惠街9号8楼之3 （10461）
联系人： 高世娟,周美玉
☎ 886-2-2595-4212
🖷 886-2-2595-5726
✉ sales@kaigo.com.tw
http://ifmac.kaigo.com.tw

iFMAC 2011 - Furniture Manufacturing Components Show

Date： 2011/03/30 - 02
Venue: Jakarta International Expo (JIE), Indonesia
Profile: The purpose of iFMAC 2011 is to assist quality manufacturers of woodworking machines and suppliers of furniture components to increase their brand exposure and expand their business in Indonesia. Exhibit profile includes machines and auxiliary machines for furniture production; materials and components for furniture production; machines/materials/components for upholstery and bedding; machines/materials/components for interior works; media and associations.
Established Year: 2011
First Session
Market Area: International
Nature: Open to public
Cost to Attend: Free
Organizer: Kaigo Co Ltd
Address: 8th Fl.-3, 9 Dehuei Street, Taipei 104, Taiwan
Contact: Jany Kao, Meiyu Chou
☎ 886-2-2595-4212
🖷 886-2-2595-5726
✉ sales@kaigo.com.tw
http://ifmac.kaigo.com.tw

印度尼西亚国际橡塑暨包装展览会
Indoplas 2011

日期： 2011/03/30 – 04/02
地点： 印度尼西亚雅加达会议展览中心_
内容： 机械设备类：塑料相关机械设备、辅助设备、挤压机、挤出机、注塑机、吹塑机、塑料发泡设备、塑料加固机、再生产与循环利用的塑料机械、塑料模具、测试仪器、塑料相关附件、后续加工处理设备等 包装机械及设备材料、包装产品、冲压机、封口机、条形码机、封装机、卷标机、秤重机。相关产品：半成品及技术部件等 原材料：添加剂、粘合剂、覆胶胶料、泡沫塑料、橡胶及合成纤维、人造橡胶、热固塑料等
始办年份： 2005
周期： 每年一届
市场范围： 国际性
性质： 面向贸易观众
上届规模 2009：展览面积8,295m²，参展商120家（国外展商70%家），参观人数16,754人
主办： PT. Wahana Kemalaniaga Makmur (WAKENI)
地址： 上海市浦东新区福山路450号新天国际大厦7楼A座（200122）
联系人： 管婷婷,黎洁
☎ 021-5109 5546
🖷 021-6875 2877
✉ gitty@uniexpo.com.cn
www.indoautomotive.com

Indoplas 2011

Date： 2011/03/30 - 02
Venue: Jakata International Expo Kemayoran, Indonesia
Profile: additives/Adhesive & Glues/Auxiliary/Bag Making Machine/Coating Compounds/Extruders & Extrusion Line/Fillers /Foam, Reactive Resin /Plastic packaging machinery/ Post Processing/ Raw Materials/ Moulds &Dies
Established Year: 2005
Frequency: Annual
Market Area: International
Nature: Trade only
Statistics 2009: Exhibition Area 8,295m², Exhibitors 120（foreigners 70%）, Visitors 16,754
Organizer: PT. Wahana Kemalaniaga Makmur (WAKENI)
Address: 7A, Sun Time International Mansion, No. 450 Fushan Road, Shanghai, China
Contact: Gitty, Yoyo
☎ 021-5109 5546
🖷 021-6875 2877
✉ gitty@uniexpo.com.cn
www.indoautomotive.com

2011第六届印尼国际印刷展
Indoprint

日期： 2011/03/30 – 04/02
地点： 印度尼西亚雅加达国际展览中心
内容： 印前多媒体设计及软件、电子及数据出版印刷、电脑技术类、印刷机械设备、印后加工设备、纸张加工设备、包装生产技术、日用消费品系列、相关服务项
始办年份： 2006
周期： 每年一届
市场范围： 国际性
上届规模 2010：展览面积8,295m²，参展商107家，参观人数16,754人
主办： 德国杜塞尔多夫印尼公司
承办： 印尼印刷技术协会；印尼印刷工会
地址： 上海市浦东新区福山路450号新天国际大厦7楼A座（200122）
联系人： 黎洁
☎ 021-6875 3265, 6875 3267转8006
🖷 021-6875 2877
✉ yoyo@uniexpo.com.cn
www.indoprint.net

Indoprint

Date： 2011/03/30 - 02
Venue: Jakarta International Expo, Indonesia
Profile: Advertising services, Animation, Bookbinding equipment, Computer technologies, Converting, Electronic and database publishing, Labeling and smart labeling, Package production technology, Paper converting equipment
Established Year: 2006
Frequency: Annual
Market Area: International
Statistics 2010: Exhibition Area 8,295m², Exhibitors 107, Visitors 16,754

Organizer: PT.WAKENI (PT.Wahana Kemalaniaga Makmur)
Address: Suit 7A, Sun Time International Mansion No.450 Fushan Road, Shanghai
Contact: YOYO
☎ 021-6875 3265, 6875 3267 ext 8006
📠 021-6875 2877
✉ yoyo@uniexpo.com.cn
www.indoprint.net

中国机械和电子产品展览会

CME

日期：2011/05 -
地点：印度尼西亚雅加达
周期：每年一届
主办：中国贸促会机械行业分会
地址：北京市西城区三里河路46号（100823）
联系人：张玉惠,郭旭萍,吕春丽
☎ 010-6859 4811, 6859 4994, 6859 4910
📠 010-6859 4995
✉ zhangyuhui@ccpitmsc.org
www.chinamachine.org.cn

印尼雅加达国际纺织面料及纱线展

JIFS

日期：2011/05/12 - 14
地点：印度尼西亚
联络：上海比天展览服务有限公司
地址：上海市中山北路900号加禾商务中心3号楼303室(200070)
联系人：刘先生
☎ 021-5655 2843
📠 021-5655 9981
www.betium.com

2011印度尼西亚国际汽车、摩托车及零配件展

日期：2011/05/25 - 28
地点：印度尼西亚雅加达会议展览中心
内容：汽车零配件/车用音响、安全设备等/各式工具、汽修工具、维修相关机械及配件、汽车清洁及汽车烤漆等/燃料、润滑油、加油站设备、车用电子、物流服务等
始办年份：2008
周期：每年一届
市场范围：国际性
性质：面向贸易观众
上届规模 2010：展览面积15,000m^2，参展商250家，专业贸易观众37,500人
主办：PT. Wahana Kemalaniaga Makmur (WAKENI)
地址：上海市浦东新区福山路450号7楼A座（200122）
联系人：管婷婷，黎洁
☎ 021-5109 5546
📠 021-6875 2877
✉ gitty@uniexpo.com.cn
www.indoautomotive.com

Indoautomotive 2011

Date：2011/05/25 - 28
Venue: Jakarta Intl Expo Kemayoran, Indonesia
Profile: Automotive parts & Components/ Automotive Accessories &Tuning/ Machinery, Tool & Equipment/ Repair, Maintenance & Services/ Motorcycle Parts & Accessories
Established Year: 2008
Frequency: Annual
Market Area: International
Nature: Trade only
Statistics 2010: Exhibition Area 15,000m^2, Exhibitors 250, Trade Visitors 37,500
Organizer: PT. Wahana Kemalaniaga Makmur (WAKENI)
Address: 7A, Sun Time International Mansion, No. 450 Fushan Road, Shanghai, China
Contact: Gitty, Yoyo
☎ 021-5109 5546
📠 021-6875 2877
✉ gitty@uniexpo.com.cn
www.indoautomotive.com

2011年印尼中国技术设备和商品展

日期：2011/05/25 - 28
地点：印度尼西亚雅加达国际展览中心
内容：汽车及摩托车零部件，文具及办公用品，仪器仪表及发电设备，建材及设备，新能源技术及设备，IT数码及通讯类产品，机械设备类，轻工产品类，乐器器材及配件
始办年份：2002
周期：每年一届
市场范围：全国性
入场券价格：免费
参展费用：人民币2500元
上届规模 2010：展览面积4,000m^2，参展商150家，参观人数8,000人
主办：上海外经贸商务展览有限公司
地址：上海市雁荡路107号雁荡大厦5楼G座（200020）
联系人：黄慧英
☎ 021-3310 0378
📠 021-6372 2827
MSN：huanghuiying8@hotmail.com

2011 China Technical Equipment & Commodities Exhibition

Date：2011/05/25 - 28
Venue: Jakarta International Expo, Indonesia
Established Year: 2002
Frequency: Annual
Market Area: National
Cost to Attend: Free
Participated Fee: RMB 2,500:-
Statistics 2010: Exhibition Area 4,000m^2, Exhibitors 150，Visitors 8,000
Organizer: Shanghai International Trade Promotion Co Ltd
Address: 5G of No.107 Yandang Road, Shanghai
Contact: Huang Huiying
☎ 021-3310 0378
📠 021-6372 2827
MSN: huanghuiying8@hotmail.com

印度尼西亚国际汽车制造机械及零配件展览会

日期：2011/12 -
地点：印度尼西亚雅加达
周期：每年一届
主办：中国贸促会
地址：北京市西城区三里河路46号（100823）
联系人：张玉惠，郭旭萍，吕春丽
☎ 010-6859 4811, 6859 4994, 6859 4910
📠 010-6859 4995
✉ zhangyuhui@ccpitmsc.org
www.chinamachine.org.cn

印度尼西亚国际机床工具展览会

MACHINE TOOL INDONESIA

日期：2011/12 -
地点：印度尼西亚雅加达
周期：每年一届
主办：中国贸促会
地址：北京市西城区三里河路46号（100823）
联系人：张玉惠，郭旭萍，吕春丽
☎ 010-6859 4811, 6859 4994, 6859 4910
📠 010-6859 4995
✉ zhangyuhui@ccpitmsc.org
www.chinamachine.org.cn

意大利
Italy

意大利米兰国际面料展

INTERTEX MILANO READY TO SHOW

日期：2011/02/08 - 10
地点：意大利
联络：上海比天展览服务有限公司
地址：上海市中山北路900号加禾商务中心3号楼303室(200070)
联系人：刘先生
☎ 021-5655 2843
📠 021-5655 9981
www.betium.com

意大利国际工程机械与建材机械展览会

Samoter

日期：2011/03/02 - 06
地点：意大利维罗纳
周期：三年一届
主办：中国贸促会
地址：北京市西城区三里河路46号（100823）
联系人：张玉惠，郭旭萍，吕春丽
☎ 010-6859 4811, 6859 4994, 6859 4910
📠 010-6859 4995
✉ zhangyuhui@ccpitmsc.org
www.chinamachine.org.cn

in-cosmetics

日期：2011/03/29 - 31
地点：意大利米兰新国际展览中心
内容：in-cosmetics是世界领先的化妆品、化妆用具及个人护理业原料及配料国际展会。产品及服务有化妆品和化妆用具的原料及配料
始办年份：1990
周期：每年一届
参展费用：光地展位514欧元/m^2，标准展位593欧元/m^2
上届规模 2010：展览面积10,265m^2，参展商575家，参观人数7,807人
主办：励展英国公司
联络：励展博览集团国际销售部
联系人：杜一鸣
☎ 010-5933 9209
📠 010-5933 9233
✉ martin.du@reedexpo.com.cn
www.in-cosmetics.com

in-cosmetics

Date：2011/03/29 - 31
Venue: Fiera Milano Exhibition Center, Italy
Profile: Leading Global Business Platform for Personal Care Ingredients
Established Year: 1990
Frequency: Annual
Participated Fee: Raw Space EURO 514/m^2, Standard Booth EURO 593/m^2
Statistics 2010: Exhibition Area 10,265m^2, Exhibitors 575，Visitors 7,807
Organizer: Reed Exhibitions
☎ 010-5933 9209
📠 010-5933 9233
✉ martin.du@reedexpo.com.cn
www.in-cosmetics.com

意大利米兰国际家具展

日期：2011/04/12 - 17
地点：意大利
☎ 0411-8378 8831
📠 0411-8378 8830

意大利米兰国际面料展

INTERTEX MILANO READY TO SHOW

日期：2011/09/08 - 10
地点：意大利
联络：上海比天展览服务有限公司
地址：上海市中山北路900号加禾商务中心3号楼303室(200070)
联系人：刘先生
☎ 021-5655 2843
📠 021-5655 9981
www.betium.com

意大利国际视觉传播展（第23届）

Viscom Visual Communication Italia: Intl Trade Fair for Visual Communication

日期：2011/11/03 - 05
地点：意大利米兰展览中心（Fiera Milano）
内容：欧洲最大型的视觉展览。展会吸引了视觉行业的专家，通过展览提供的平台了解最新行业资讯和营销战略。展览观众来自各个领域，包括现代制图师和决策人，让您有更多机会拓展商务合作。
产品及服务：大幅面数码印刷及成像，标志及标志制作，数码标志制作及媒体，P.O.P/P.O.S制作，丝网印刷及移动印刷，雕版印刷和压制，营销物品及服装，奖品，活动服务。
观众来源：制图商：标志制作，广告牌制作，数字印刷，装潢者，综合印刷，丝网印刷，室内丝网印刷，包装，移印，纸张加工，造纸厂，石板影印，影音和照相店，刺绣工，POP/展览制作，营销物件，LFDP，商场装饰/橱窗装饰，标志租赁公司，看台搭建，供应商/分销商，奖品制作，雕刻师/模具制造，金匠，奖杯和奖章，活动组织者。
周期：每年一届
赞助：A.I.F.I.L.（意大利发光标志协会），ASSOPROM（意大利营销物品生产商和分销商协会），SIOTEC（意大利丝网印刷协会）
主办：励展意大利公司S.r.l
联络：励展博览集团国际销售部
地址：北京市朝阳区新源南路1-3号平安国际金融中心A座15层01-03,05
联系人：张志超
☎ 010-5933 9266
🖷 010-5933 9233
✉ ivy.zhang@reedexpo.com.cn
www.reedexport.cn
www.visualcommunication.it

米兰国际卫浴展

EXPOBAGNO

日期：2012/03/27 - 30
地点：意大利米兰国际展览中心Rho新展馆
内容：国际知名的、新兴的国际卫浴展，主要展出注重精致、现代、舒适和设计的高端产品。EXPOBAGNO展品的设计和风格满足市场需求，引领时尚潮流。首届展会在新米兰展览中心举办。
产品及服务：陶瓷洁具、浴缸、淋浴房及附件、健身设备、按摩浴缸、装饰淋浴隔间、卫浴家具、迷你水疗、贴面材料、瓷砖、大理石、桑拿浴房、龙头及配件、配件、浴室附件以及烘干毛巾架等。
周期：两年一届
市场范围：国际性
主办：励展意大利展览公司（Italia S.r.l.）
联络：励展博览集团国际销售部
地址：北京市朝阳区新源南路1-3号平安国际金融中心A座15层01-03,05
联系人：李悦
☎ 010- 5933 9298
🖷 010- 5933 9233
✉ anna.li@reedexpo.com.cn
www.reedexport.cn
www.expodelbagno.it

意大利米兰供暖、空调、制冷、再生能源及太阳能展

Mostra Convegno Expocomfort: Production & Distribution line for the HVAC & Plumbing Sector

日期：2012/03/27 - 31
地点：意大利米兰国际展览中心Rho新展馆
内容：MCE（Mostra Convegno Expocomfort）是在民用和工业用供暖、再生能源、空调、制冷、通风、水处理、相关服务及零部件领域首屈一指、最具影响力的国际专业展会。作为意大利第一个致力于工业的展览，40多年的发展历程证明了MCE是这个领域的领跑者。
产品及服务：多年来，MCE始终保持着丰富及鲜明的主题，供暖（暖气设备、零部件、工具/器具）；能源(光电、太阳能、热电，生物能源、共生能源、绝缘)；制冷（空调设备、通风装置、商业和工业制冷）；供水(饮水卫生技术、水处理）等四个主要内容历久弥新
始办年份：1960
周期：两年一届
市场范围：国际性
性质：面向贸易观众
参展费用：光地展位189欧元/m²
主办：励展意大利展览公司（Italia S.r.l.）
联络：励展博览集团国际销售部
地址：北京市朝阳区新源南路1-3号平安国际金融中心A座15层01-03,05
联系人：李悦
☎ 010- 5933 9298
🖷 010- 5933 9233
✉ anna.li@reedexpo.com.cn
www.reedexport.cn
www.mcexpocomfort.it

日本 Japan

日本电子展

Electronics Manufacturing & SMT Exhibition

INTERNEPCON JAPAN

日期：2011/01/19 - 21
地点：日本东京有明国际展览中心
内容：电子产品包装和生产，针对电子产品生产和SMT的所有设备、材料以及技术生产线，安装器、丝印机、回流焊机、焊接机、水洗机、分配器，穿孔机，带式载体，产品生产管理系统；焊接区，焊接机、回流焊机、再加工机、烙铁、金属熔化槽，焊剂涂敷器、焊锡及焊用材料/助焊剂；安装专区，贴片机/隔板，厂房设备区，工厂所需的所有设施和供应品生产线，清洗设备和清洁区，配件和相关设备等，EMS/合同加工区
上届规模 2010：参展商1,228家，参观人数63,982人
主办：励展日本公司
联络：励展博览集团国际销售部
联系人：张志超
☎ 010-5933 9266
🖷 010-5933 9233
✉ ivy.zhang@reedexpo.com.cn
www.reedexport.cn

日本EV/MEV驱动系统技术展

EV & HEV Drive System Technology Expo

日期：2011/01/19 - 21
地点：日本东京有明国际展览中心
内容：驱动系统、可充电电池、下一代电池、电机技术、变频器、外围设备、充电器、连接器、线束
周期：每年一届
上届规模 2010：参展商109家，参观人数63,982人
主办：励展日本公司
联络：励展博览集团国际销售部
联系人：张志超
☎ 010-5933 9266
🖷 010-5933 9233
✉ ivy.zhang@reedexpo.com.cn
www.reedexport.cn

日本国际照明展览会

LED/OLED Lighting Technology Expo

LED/OLED Lighting Technology Expo
LIGHTING JAPAN

日期：2011/01/19 - 21
地点：日本东京有明国际展览中心
内容：照明设备、生产设备：照明设备，处理设备，照明模具，组装设备，贴装器件，其他设备、检测、测量、测试、评估设备，元件和材料：照明设备，光学元件，操控元件、设计分析器，软件、光学相关产品和技术、照明模具设备元件、照明系统产品，科技和服务、联络服务、其他技术和服务
上届规模 2010：参展商308家，参观人数20,536人
主办：励展日本公司
联络：励展博览集团国际销售部
联系人：张志超
☎ 010-5933 9266
🖷 010-5933 9233
✉ ivy.zhang@reedexpo.com.cn
www.reedexport.cn

日本汽车电子展

Intl Automotive Electronics Technology Expo

Int'l Automotive Electronics Technology Expo CAR-ELE JAPAN

日期：2011/01/19 - 21
地点：日本东京有明国际展览中心
内容：汽车电子元器件/电子模块、嵌入式系统开发技术、汽车电子材料、汽车电子系统：发动机操纵系统、安全和舒适控制系统、底盘控制系统、通信及智能交通系统和技术、其他汽车系统、汽车网络系统：车身控制网络系统、多媒体网络系统、其他相关汽车网络、汽车软件、制造设备、设计和制造工具、测试/测量/分析装置、其他相关技术和产品
始办年份：2008
周期：每年一届
上届规模 2010：参展商240家，参观人数16,606人
主办：励展日本公司
联络：励展博览集团国际销售部
联系人：张志超
☎ 010-5933 9266
🖷 010-5933 9233
✉ ivy.zhang@reedexpo.com.cn
www.reedexport.cn

东京国际珠宝展

International Jewellery Tokyo

日期：2011/01/26 - 29
地点：日本东京有明展览馆
内容：钻石、天然宝石、人工宝石、黄金、铂金、银饰、手表、钟表、古珠宝、珍珠、湖泊、珊瑚、浮雕、金银成品、宝石（裸石、裸珠、珠子、链子及其他宝石），包装材料、商店展示柜、展示框及部件、生产设备及工具，安全监测设备，OEM/

ODM，加工服务等。
周期：每年一届
上届规模 2010：参展商1,257家，参观人数35,763人
主办：励展日本公司
联络：励展博览集团国际销售部
联系人：申健
☎ 010-5933 9299
🖷 010-5933 9233
✉ jerry.shen@reedexpo.com.cn
www.ijt.jp
www.reedexport.cn

网络及手机直销方案展览会
Net & Mobile Direct Marketing Solution Fair

日期：2011/02/24 - 25
地点：日本东京阳光城市展览中心
主办：博闻日本公司
☎ 03-5296-1020
🖷 03-5296-1018
www.cmptech.jp/tsuhan

2011年第36届日本国际食品饮料展
2011 Foodex Japan

日期：2011/03/01 - 04
地点：日本千叶幕张国际会展中心举办
内容：食品：农产品（新鲜、冷冻、干货）、农产加工品、谷物、畜产品（冷冻、干货）、速冻蔬菜、罐头、肉加工品、乳制品、水产品（新鲜、冷冻、干货）、水产加工品、已加工食品、蒸煮袋食品、副食品、西式副食品、调料、香辣佐料、各种面类、西式糕点、甜食。饮料：含酒精饮料（日本酒、烧酒、啤酒、葡萄酒等）饮料、矿泉水、咖啡、红茶、日本茶、以及其它茶类。
始办年份：1976
周期：每年一届
市场范围：国际性
性质：面向贸易观众
主办：日本能率协会Japan Management Association
联络：杭州思诺博会展服务有限公司
地址：杭州市体育场路229号浙江粮油大厦1202室（310003）
☎ 0571-8577 8500
🖷 0571-8577 9709
✉ expo@sinobal.com
www.sinobal.com
联络：北京领汇国际展览有限公司
地址：北京市朝阳区农展馆南路13号瑞辰国际中心719室（100125）
联系人：陈平
☎ 010-5129 5359转8010，13810365877
🖷 010-5129 5379转8010
✉ chen_sapin@163.com

东京国际光伏发电展览会
PV EXPO 2011: International Photovoltaic Power Generation Expo

Int'l Photovoltaic Power Generation Expo
PV EXPO

日期：2011/03/02 - 04
地点：日本东京有明国际展览中心Tokyo Big Sight, Japan
内容：装置/材料：单晶/多晶硅，非晶硅，符合半导体，模块底片，电极塑料，填充/密封材料，框架材料，互连材料，阵列等。评估/检测/分析：电池测量仪、厚度测量仪、电化测量仪、电子称量仪、电流表/电压表/流量表，温度计/光量计，光感测量仪、光学辐射仪、底片检测仪等。制造设备：熔炉/扩散炉/模具、表面加工机/镀膜机、CVD机、切片/切割机、焊接/波峰焊接机、清洗设备、净化水装置、模块组装设备、晶片制造机械等。光伏系统：电缆/连接器、接线盒、分流器、配电箱、逆变器/转换器、功率调节器、蓄电池、电储藏设备、继电保护、聚光器、电压表、灯泡/泵等。清洁/放电保护设备：清洁室、清洁间、无菌工作服、手套、面罩、放电保护装置/产品，清洁滚轮、橡胶滚轮、各式滚轮、除尘刷、空调设施、过滤器、粒子计数器、其他清洁室相关产品。太阳能电池/模块：单晶太阳能电池/模块、多晶太阳能电池/模块，非晶太阳能电池/模块，薄膜式太阳能电池/模块，其他太阳能电池/模块 各式建筑服务。
周期：每年一届
上届规模 2010：参展商579家，参观人数80,045人
主办：励展日本公司
联络：励展博览集团国际销售部
联系人：杜一鸣
☎ 010-5933 9209
🖷 010-5933 9233
✉ martin.du@reedexpo.com.cn
www.reedexport.cn

日本国际二次电池展
Intl Rechargeable Battery Expo

BATTERY JAPAN

日期：2011/03/02 - 04
地点：日本东京有明国际展览中心Tokyo Big Sight, Japan
内容：原材料/零部件、设备制造、检测/测试/评估、可充电电池、相关仪器
周期：每年一届
上届规模 2010：参展商231家，参观人数80,045人
主办：励展日本公司
联络：励展博览集团国际销售部
联系人：张志超
☎ 010-5933 9266
🖷 010-5933 9233
✉ ivy.zhang@reedexpo.com.cn
www.reedexport.cn

东京健康博览会
Tokyo Health Industry Show

日期：2011/03/16 - 18
地点：日本东京有明国际展览中心
主办：博闻日本公司
☎ +81-3-5296-1025
🖷 +81-3-5296-1018
✉ h-expo-jp@ubm.com
联络：博闻（广州）展览有限公司
☎ 020-8666 0158
🖷 020-8667 7120
✉ info-china@ubm.com
www.this.ne.jp

Tokyo Health Industry Show

Date: 2011/03/16 - 18
Venue: Tokyo Big Sight Exhibition Center, Japan
Profile: The Tokyo Health Industry Show (THIS) is the biggest and longest running health-related products exhibition in Japan. THIS2011 will feature over 550 exhibitors, with 5 main zonings for "Functional Ingredients & OEM", "Health Foods", "Organic & Natural", "Wellness" and "Health & Beauty", and intensive visitor promotion campaign will be conducted for each zone.
Organizer: UBM Media Co Ltd
☎ +81-3-5296-1025
🖷 +81-3-5296-1018
✉ h-expo-jp@ubm.com
www.this.ne.jp

2011年日本东京国际汽车零部件及汽保展

日期：2011/03/16 - 18
地点：日本东京幕张国际展览中心
内容：部件及系统：汽车驾驶之部件及原件、底盘、车身、电子及电器。汽车内部、外部、驾驶、驾驶动力及电子控制；配件及改装：汽车配件、特别设备、改装服务系统及改进设计；修理及保养：汽车保养及修理装备、车间维修及涂漆、维修站建造及管理；加油站及洗车：加油站装备、洗车及护理等。

为了活跃以日本为中心的亚洲地区汽车售后市场，国际汽车售后市场展将努力成为新事业、贸易的新讯息发布中心，而成为亚洲大规模的专业商展。
周期：每年一届
市场范围：国际性
性质：面向公众
上届规模 2010：参展商224家（国外展商占25%），专业贸易观众36,334人
主办：北京中杰城设国际展览有限公司
地址：北京市海淀区紫竹院路31号华澳中心嘉慧苑1703室（100089）
联系人：全静
☎ 010-5979 9850转808
🖷 010-5885 7468
✉ quanjing@top-fairs.com.cn
MSN：quanjing@top-fairs.com.cn
QQ：602693071
www.build-ccpit.org
www.btfi.cn

日本美食佳酿暨酒店及餐饮设备展
Wine & Gourmet Japan 2009

日期：2011/04/06 - 08
地点：日本东京国际展览中心
内容：罐头食品、乳制品、精制烘焙食品、精制特色食品、食品配料、新鲜食品、冷冻、冷藏食品、精制巧克力、鲜美食品、肉禽制品、海鲜、非酒精饮料（茶和咖啡）、休闲食品、糖果、甜食、葡萄酒、烈酒、啤酒、食品招待和餐饮服务相关设备
始办年份：2009
周期：每年一届
市场范围：国际性
性质：面向贸易观众
入场券价格：3000日元
上届规模 2010：展览面积25,690m²，专业贸易观众63,478人
主办：科隆展览国际有限公司
地址：北京东三环北路8号亮马河大厦2座1018室（100004）
联系人：潘容
☎ 010-6590 7766 转 715
🖷 010-6590 6139
✉ g.pan@koelnmesse.cn
www.wineandgourmetasia.cn

Wine & Gourmet Japan 2009

Date: 2011/04/06 - 08
Venue: Tokyo Big Sight, Japan
Established Year: 2009
Frequency: Annual
Market Area: International
Nature: Trade only

Cost to Attend: JPY 3000
Statistics 2010: Exhibition Area 25,690m^2, Trade Visitors 63,478
Organizer: Koelnmesse
Address: Unit 1018, Landmark Tower Ⅱ, No. 8 Dongsanhuan North Rd., Beijing 100004, China
Contact: Grace Pan
☎ 010-6590 7766 ext 715
🖷 010-6590 6139
✉ g.pan@koelnmesse.cn
www.wineandgourmetasia.cn

日本光通信技术展

Fiber Optics Expo

FOE FIBER OPTICS EXPO

日期：2011/04/13 - 15
地点：日本东京有明国际展览中心Tokyo Big Sight, Japan
内容：光通信系统/设备 光学测量/检测设备 光学设备/材料 设备制造/服务 光纤到户/光纤到楼宇（FTTH/ FTTP）展区 连接器展区 光学互联区 光纤电缆和施工区
始办年份：2000
周期：每年一届
性质：面向贸易观众
上届规模 2010：参展商172家，参观人数13,142人
主办：励展日本公司
联络：励展博览集团国际销售部
联系人：张志超
☎ 010-5933 9288
🖷 010-5933 9233
✉ ivy.zhang@reedexpo.com.cn
www.foe.jp
www.reedexport.cn

日本FPD制造设备及技术国际展览会

FPD R&D & Manufacturing Technology Expo & Conference

FINETECH JAPAN

日期：2011/04/13 - 15
地点：日本东京有明国际展示中心
内容：零件和原材料、生产设备、FPD生产的测试设备、生产设备区、清洁/ESD保护装置展示角、检测/修复/测量区、评估/测试/分析区、FPD元件和材料展示、光学薄膜展示角、高功能薄膜技术展示
始办年份：1990
周期：每年一届
性质：面向贸易观众
上届规模 2010：展览面积42,710m^2，参展商584家，参观人数66,739人
主办：励展日本公司
联络：励展博览集团国际销售部
联系人：张志超
☎ 010-5933 9288
🖷 010-5933 9233
✉ ivy.zhang@reedexpo.com.cn
www.ftj.jp
www.reedexport.cn

日本激光光学技术展

An International Event representing Asia's Photonics Industry

日期：2011/04/13 - 15
地点：日本东京有明国际展览中心Tokyo Big Sight, Japan
内容：首届光学传感器技术展、首届医疗光电展（MEDIX）。同期举办第11届光通信技术展、第4届激光应用展、第4届光学展览会
主办：励展日本公司
联络：励展博览集团国际销售部
联系人：张志超
☎ 010-5933 9288
🖷 010-5933 9233
✉ ivy.zhang@reedexpo.com.cn
www.photonix-expo.jp
www.reedexport.cn

世界制药原料日本展览

CPhI Japan

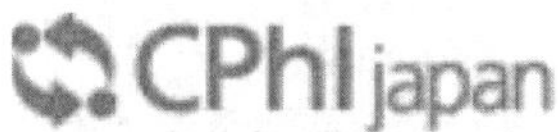

日期：2011/04/18 - 20
地点：日本东京有明国际展览中心
Tokyo Big Sight Exhibition Center, Japan
主办：日本博闻有限公司
☎ +81-3-5296-1020
🖷 +81-3-5296-1018
邮箱：info@cphijapan.com
联络：亚洲博闻有限公司
☎ +852-2827 6211
🖷 +852-2827 7831
✉ candice.Lau@ubm.com
www.cphijapan.com

世界制药机械、设备与材料日本展

P-MEC Japan

日期：2011/04/18 - 20
地点：日本东京有明国际展览中心
主办：日本博闻有限公司
☎ +81-3-5296-1020
🖷 +81-3-5296-1018
✉ info@cphijapan.com
联络：亚洲博闻有限公司
☎ +852-2827 6211
🖷 +852-2827 7831
✉ candice.Lau@ubm.com
www.pmec-japan.com/eng

P-MEC Japan

Date：2011/04/18 - 20
Venue: Tokyo Big Sight Exhibition Center, , Japan
Profile: Japan's APIs and intermediates producers, including pharmaceutical manufacturers who develop these products internally, are always on the lookout for new technologies for enhancing quality control, safety assurance, and increasing production efficiency. Exhibitors include Analyzer, Synthesizer, Chromatography, Concentration System, Centrifugal Separators, Reaction Vessels, Filtration Devices, Granulators, Agitators, Dryers.
Organizer: UBM Asia
☎ +81-3-5296-1020
🖷 +81-3-5296-1018
✉ info@cphijapan.com
☎ +852-2827 6211
🖷 +852-2827 7831
✉ candice.Lau@ubm.com
www.pmec-japan.com/eng

制药业生物解决方案日本展

BioPh Japan

日期：2011/04/18 - 20
地点：日本东京有明国际展览中心
主办：日本博闻有限公司
电话：+81-3-5296-1020
传真：+81-3-5296-1018
邮箱：info@cphijapan.com
联络：亚洲博闻有限公司
☎ +852-2827 6211
🖷 +852-2827 7831
✉ candice.Lau@ubm.com
www.cphijapan.com/bioph-japan

BioPh Japan

Date：2011/04/18 - 20
Venue: Tokyo Big Sight Exhibition Center, Japan
Profile: BioPh brings bio Solutions to CPhI Japan and is for companies and organizations involved in the research and development of new treatment methods arising from biotechnical processes or which are derived from, or use live organisms. If you are a supplier of bio pharma raw materials, services or equipment, don't miss this opportunity to enjoy enhanced visibility by exhibiting in this hot-topic pavilion.
Organizer: UBM Asia
☎ +81-3-5296-1020
🖷 +81-3-5296-1018
✉ info@cphijapan.com
www.cphijapan.com/bioph-japan

国际合同定制服务日本展

ICSE Japan

iCSe bringing outsourcing to CPhI Japan

日期：2011/04/18 - 20
地点：日本东京有明国际展览中心
主办：日本博闻有限公司
☎ +81-3-5296-1020
🖷 +81-3-5296-1018
✉ info@cphijapan.com
联络：亚洲博闻有限公司
☎ +852-2827 6211
🖷 +852-2827 7831
✉ candice.Lau@ubm.com
www.icsejapan.com/eng

ICSE Japan

Date：2011/04/18 - 20
Venue: Tokyo Big Sight Exhibition Center, Japan
Profile: Held alongside CPhI Japan, ICSE attracts international exhibitors who are keen to capitalize on the benefits of doing business in Japan. Besides contract manufacturing and contract research, other main services provided are packaging, clinical trials, laboratory services, drug discovery and marketing services.
Organizer: UBM Asia
☎ +81-3-5296-1020
🖷 +81-3-5296-1018
✉ info@cphijapan.com
www.icsejapan.com/eng

日本国际成衣展（春）

CFF

日期：2011/04/19 - 21
地点：日本
联络：上海比天展览服务有限公司
地址：上海市中山北路900号加禾商务中心3号楼303室(200070)
联系人：刘先生
☎ 021-5655 2843
🖷 021-5655 9981
www.betium.com

日本国际模具暨金属加工展览会
NTERMOLD

日期： 2011/04/20 - 23
地点： 日本东京
周期： 每年两届
主办： 中国贸促会机械行业分会
地址： 北京市西城区三里河路46号（100823）
联系人： 张玉惠，郭旭萍，吕春丽
☎ 010-6859 4811, 6859 4994, 6859 4910
🖷 010-6859 4995
✉ zhangyuhui@ccpitmsc.org
www.chinamachine.org.cn

日本软件开发展览会
SODEC: Software Development Expo

日期： 2011/05/11 - 13
地点： 日本东京国际展览中心
内容： 是亚洲嵌入式软件系统领域规模最大的展览会。众多海外企业已透过该平台顺利进入日本市场。凭借展会所取得的瞩目成绩，东京软件开发展每年都在不断地发展壮大，它将为软件行业参展商及观展群众搭建互相联络的高效平台。
周期： 每年一届
市场范围： 国际性
性质： 面向贸易观众
上届规模 2010：参展商1,206家，参观人数122,371人
主办： 励展日本公司
联络： 励展博览集团国际销售部
地址： 北京市朝阳区新源南路1-3号平安国际金融中心A座15层01-03,05
联系人： 张志超
☎ 010- 5933 9266
🖷 010- 5933 9233
✉ ivy.zhang@reedexpo.com.cn
www.reedexport.cn
www.sodec.jp/en

Imabari 海事展
Imabari Maritime Fair (Bari-Ship)

日期： 2011/05/19 - 21
地点： 日本今治
主办： 博闻日本公司
☎ 03-5296 1020
✉ info@bariship.com
www.bariship.com

Bari-Ship
Imabari Maritime Fair

Date： 2011/05/19 - 21
Venue: Texport Imabari, Imabari-City, Ehime, Japan
Organizer: UBM Japan Co Ltd
☎ 03-5296 1020
✉ info@bariship.com
www.bariship.com
www.thai-exhibition.com/intermach

Interop 商业科技东京展
Interop Tokyo

日期： 2011/06/07 - 10
地点： 日本东京
主办： 亚洲博闻
☎ +81-3-6431-7800
🖷 +81-3-6431-7850
✉ sales-info@f2ff.jp
www.interop.jp

Interop Tokyo
Date： 2011/06/07 - 10
Venue: Makuhari Messe, Chiba, Tokyo, Japan
Profile: Interop is the leading global business technology event. Cloud Computing , Mobile & Wireless , Data Center , Network Security and more.
Organizer: NANO OPT Media, Inc
☎ +81-3-6431-7800
🖷 +81-3-6431-7850
✉ sales-info@f2ff.jp
www.interop.jp

客户服务中心/客户关系管理展览会及会议大阪展
Call Center/
CRM Demo & Conference Osaka

日期： 2011/06/21 - 24
地点： 日本大阪
主办： 亚洲博闻
www.callcenter-japan.com/osaka/index.html

东京机械零部件及材料技术展
M-Tech:
Mechanical Components & Materials Technology Expo

日期： 2011/06/22 - 24
地点： 日本东京Big Sight展览中心
内容： 日本最大的机械零部件、材料及加工装配技术行业贸易展会，是日本机械加工行业的门户平台。
产品及服务： 轴承、齿轮、离合器、传动带/链条、线性传动、减震、轴封、电机、传感器、其它传动相关的机械零部件、紧固件及紧固技术、螺栓、螺母、垫圈、铆钉、粘结剂与粘合剂、种紧固件及相关产品/技术、工程塑料、塑料、聚合物、金属/有色金属、合金、陶瓷、橡胶、人造橡胶、硅零件、塑料零件/技术、金属零件/技术、橡胶零件/技术、其他材质零件/技术、机械加工技术如冲压、轧制、锻造（压模、脱腊、精密铸造及其他铸造工艺）、成形（射出、转送、吹塑及其他成形工艺）、挤出成形（薄膜、型材、片材及其他挤出成形工艺）、机械、轧制、锻造、成型、表面加工、净化材料、润滑剂、去毛刺技术、表面处理技术、出版物、其他机械零部件。
周期： 每年一届
市场范围： 国际性
性质： 面向贸易观众
主办： 励展博览集团国际销售部
地址： 北京市朝阳区新源南路1-3号平安国际金融中心A座15层01-03,05
联系人： 宫卫
☎ 010- 5933 9268
🖷 010- 5933 9233
✉ david.gong@reedexpo.com.cn
www.reedexport.cn
www.mtech-tokyo.jp/english

日本国际制药工业展览会
ASIA'S LARGEST Pharmaceutical Industry

INTERPHEX JAPAN

日期： 2011/06/29 – 07/01
地点： 日本东京有明国际展览中心（Big Sight）
内容： 亚洲最大制药行业盛会，药品生产商和来自世界各地的展商汇聚一堂。展会还包括“科技会议”及一系列研讨会吸引大批参与者共同交流，掌握行业最新资讯。
产品和服务： 材料处理设备，填充设备，设备供应，转移设备，包装，打印设备，灭菌设备，工序检验，测试设备，实验室检测，分析设备，生物设备计算机系统，车间设备，供应和设备工程，外包服务。
周期： 每年一届
市场范围： 国际性
性质： 面向贸易观众
主办： 励展日本公司
联络： 励展博览结果国际销售部
地址： 北京市朝阳区新源南路1-3号平安国际金融中心A座15层01-03,05
联系人： 申健
☎ 010-5933 9299
🖷 010-5933 9233
✉ jerry.shen@reedexpo.com.cn
www.interphex.jp/ipj/english/
www.reedexport.cn

东京国际孕婴童用品展
3rd Baby & Kits Expo
Trade Show Gathering All Kinds of Items for Baby & Kids

Baby & Kids Expo

日期： 2011/07/06 - 08
地点： 日本东京有明国际展览中心（Tokyo Big Sight）
内容： 一站式采购婴幼儿用品、玩具、孕妇用品的绝佳地点。随着市场需求量的增长，孕婴童用品展吸引了更为广泛的目光，本展会展出的产品涵盖所有婴幼儿用品，是日本独一无二的贸易展。
展品范围： 婴幼儿用品 婴儿小推车、汽车座椅、橡皮奶嘴、奶瓶、拨浪鼓、被褥、家具、午餐盒、水壶、餐具、背包、文具、澡盆玩具、婴儿香皂、沐浴露、纪念品、安全用品等 玩具 填充玩具、积木、画册、着色簿、猜谜玩具、棋类、玩具屋、器具、益智玩具、手工材料等 婴幼儿时尚用品 婴儿装、儿童装、内衣、围嘴、裙子、童鞋、睡袋、袜子、紧身裤、帽子、睡衣、有机用品 孕妇用品 尿不湿口袋、吊兜、孕妇装、按摩霜、健康化妆品
周期： 每年一届
市场范围： 国际性
性质： 面向贸易观众
上届规模 2010：参展商187家，参观人数24,891人
主办： 励展日本公司
联络： 励展博览集团国际销售部
地址： 北京市朝阳区新源南路1-3号平安国际金融中心A座15层01-03,05
联系人： 王亮
☎ 010-5933 9288
🖷 010-5933 9233
✉ liang.wang@reedexpo.com.cn
www.bk-w.jp
www.reedexport.cn

东京国际礼品采购展
International Variety –
Gift Expo Tokyo

日期：2011/07/06 - 08
地点：日本东京有明国际展览中心（Tokyo Big Sight）
内容：同期举办的五场展会包括：东京国际孕婴童用品展、东京时尚装饰品展、东京设计精品展、东京餐桌装饰与餐具展、东京国际文具及办公用品展览会。
展品范围：玩具与人偶：玩具、娃娃、人偶、钥匙盒、手机挂绳、新奇产品等。时尚饰品：时尚首饰、配饰、箱包、皮带、钟表、手表、旅行装备等。花卉与仿真花：仿真花、干花与绢花、观叶植物、花瓶、花篮、沙土、园艺用品。香水与芳香剂：香火、蜡烛、香薰精油、香水、草药茶。沐浴与化妆用品：洗浴用品、浴盐、香皂、美甲用品、化妆镜、化妆品盒。餐桌器皿、瓷器、玻璃器皿、刀具、台布、餐桌装饰品、厨具、家用电器。Wazakka（日本现代家居器皿）与工艺品：日式装饰品与餐桌器皿、陶器、漆器、装饰摆件。婴幼儿童用品：人偶、餐具、拨浪鼓、澡盆玩具、婴儿装、其他婴幼儿童产品、玩具、娃娃、棋类、乐器、画册、婴儿护理用品、束身带、按摩膏、胸前婴儿吊带。
周期：每年一届
市场范围：国际性
性质：面向贸易观众
上届规模 2010：参展商577家（来自25个国家和地区），参观人数24,391人
主办：励展日本公司
联络：励展博览集团国际销售部
地址：北京市朝阳区新源南路1-3号平安国际金融中心A座15层01-03,05
联系人：王亮
☎ 010-5933 9288
📠 010-5933 9233
✉ liang.wang@reedexpo.com.cn
www.giftex.jp/giftex/en/
www.reedexport.cn

东京国际办公家具展览会
International Office Furniture Expo

日期：2011/07/06 - 08
地点：日本东京国际展览中心
内容：办公室家具一直吸引着各行各业人士的目光，这是因为办公家具是提高工作效率、优化办公环境、激励员工工作等的一个重要工具。快来加入到东京国际办公家具展览会行列中吧，紧跟销售量上升的趋势，扩展贵公司在日本的市场！
始办年份：2009
周期：每年一届
市场范围：国际性
性质：面向贸易观众
上届规模 2010：参展商40家，参观人数19,514人
主办：励展日本公司
联络：励展博览集团国际销售部
地址：北京市朝阳区新源南路1-3号平安国际金融中心A座15层01-03,05
联系人：张志超
☎ 010-5933 9266
📠 010-5933 9233
✉ ivy.zhang@reedexpo.com.cn
www.reedexport.cn

日本东京国际文具及办公用品展
International Stationery & Office Products Fair Tokyo

日期：2011/07/06 - 08
地点：日本东京有明国际展览中心（Tokyo Big Sight）
内容：世界领先的文具和办公用品贸易展览会之一。该展会为参展商提供了最好的现场销售和签订订单的场所，为您提供与众多核心买家交流的机会，助您打开日本及国际市场。
产品及服务：书写用具、办公用纸、文具、电子及多媒体产品、办公配件、文件、办公自动化产品及配件、绘图仪器、贺卡、办公家具、礼品、礼品包装、书包、公文包、通行证、设计用设备、法用品、电子记事本、环保文具
周期：每年一届
市场范围：国际性
性质：面向贸易观众
主办：励展日本公司
联络：励展博览集团国际销售部
地址：北京市朝阳区新源南路1-3号平安国际金融中心A座15层01-03,05
联系人：王亮
☎ 010-5933 9288
📠 010-5933 9233
✉ liang.wang@reedexpo.com.cn
www.isot-fair.jp/en

东京国际办公机械及设备展览会
OFMEX:
Intl Office Machines & Equipment Expo Tokyo

日期：2011/07/06 - 08
地点：日本东京Big Sight展览中心
内容：亚洲最佳的办公机械及设备行业展会。
产品及服务：复印机、打印机、传真机、电视会议系统、剪裁机、压膜机、装订机、写字板、投影仪、OHP（高架投影仪）、屏幕、工时记录器、磁带复写器、电子文具、空气清新剂、电子打卡机、收银机、计算器、音响系统、电子产品、前台系统、邮寄机、碳粉盒、商业电脑软件、扫描器、办公安全系统。
周期：每年一届
市场范围：国际性
性质：面向贸易观众
上届规模 2010：参展商32家，参观人数41,112人
赞助：日本办公机械经销商协会
主办：励展日本公司
联络：励展博览集团国际销售部
地址：北京市朝阳区新源南路1-3号平安国际金融中心A座15层01-03,05（100738）
联系人：张志超
☎ 010-5933 9266
📠 010-5933 9233
✉ ivy.zhang@reedexpo.com.cn
www.reedexport.cn

东京书展
Tokyo International Book Fair

日期：2011/07/07 - 10
地点：日本东京有明国际展览中心（Tokyo Big Sight）
内容：IBF日本最大的国际图书展会，是版权谈判、合作出版项目、直接出口方面的理想平台。
产品与服务：图书、专业期刊、杂志、报纸、连环画册、期刊、电子出版物、音频与视频、日历、明信片、出版支持系统/服务、版权。六种专业图书展会同时在日本书展上亮相，为商机的把握、国际版权谈判、联合出版项目和直接出口开辟了一条通路。这些专业图书展会包括自然科学书展、人文社科书展、儿童书展、普通编辑出版物书展、数字出版展、教育图书及软件展。
周期：每年一届
市场范围：国际性
性质：面向贸易观众
上届规模 2010：参展商984家，参观人数76,297人
主办：励展日本公司
联络：励展博览集团国际销售部
地址：北京市朝阳区新源南路1-3号平安国际金融中心A座15层01-03,05
联系人：王亮
☎ 010-5933 9288
📠 010-5933 9233
✉ liang.wang@reedexpo.com.cn
www.tibf.jp

日本东京国际五金及DIY展览会
Japan DIY Homecenter Show

日期：2011/08 -
地点：日本东京
周期：每年一届
主办：中国贸促会机械行业分会
地址：北京市西城区三里河路46号（100823）
联系人：张玉惠，郭旭萍，吕春丽
☎ 010-6859 4811, 6859 4994, 6859 4910
📠 010-6859 4995
邮箱：zhangyuhui@ccpitmsc.org
www.chinamachine.org.cn

日本珠宝展
Japan Jewellery Fair

日期：2011/09/01 - 03
地点：日本东京有明国际展览中心
主办：博闻日本公司
☎ +81-3-5296-1020
📠 +81-3-5296-1018
✉ info@japanjewelleryfair.com
联络：亚洲博闻
☎ 852-2516 1655
📠 852-3749 7536
✉ Michael.Tse@ubm.com
www.japanjewelleryfair.com

Japan Jewellery Fair
Date：2011/09/01 - 03
Venue: Tokyo Big Sight Exhibition Center, Japan
Organizer: UBM JAPAN Co Ltd
☎ +81-3-5296-1020
📠 +81-3-5296-1018
✉ info@japanjewelleryfair.com
www.japanjewelleryfair.com

日本国际成衣展（秋）
CFF

日期：2011/09/01 - 03
地点：日本
联络：上海比天展览服务有限公司
地址：上海市中山北路900号加禾商务中心3号楼303室(200070)
联系人：刘先生
☎ 021-5655 2843
📠 021-5655 9981
www.betium.com

日本国际印刷展览会
IGAS

日期：2011/09/16 - 22
地点：日本东京

周期：四年一届
主办：中国贸促会机械行业分会
地址：北京市西城区三里河路46号（100823）
联系人：张玉惠, 郭旭萍, 吕春丽
☎ 010-6859 4811, 6859 4994, 6859 4910
🖷 010-6859 4995
✉ zhangyuhui@ccpitmsc.org
www.chinamachine.org.cn

日本SPA美容展
Spa Japan

日期：2011/09/26 - 28
地点：日本东京有明国际展览中心
主办：博闻（日本）公司
☎ +81-3-5296-1013
🖷 +81-3-5296-1018
邮箱：d-expo-jp@ubm.com
联络：博闻（广州）展览有限公司
☎ 020-8666 0158
🖷 020-8667 7120
✉ info-china@ubm.com
www.spajapan.info/en

Spa Japan
Date：2011/09/26 - 28
Venue: Tokyo Big Sight Exhibition Center, , Japan
Profile: Spa products & devices zone, natural products zone, wellness tourism zone
Organizer: UBM Media Co Ltd
☎ +81-3-5296-1013
🖷 +81-3-5296-1018
✉ d-expo-jp@ubm.com
Contact: Ms. Maggie Ou
Address: UBM China (Guangzhou) Co Ltd, Room1159-1164 China Hotel Office Tower, Liu Hua Road, Guangzhou 510015, China
☎ 020-8666 0158
🖷 020-8667 7120
✉ info-china@ubm.com
www.spajapan.info/en

纤体及美容展 2011（第十届）
Diet & Beauty Fair (10th)

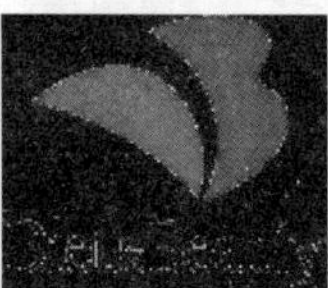

日期：2011/09/26 - 28
地点：日本东京有明国际展览中心
主办：博闻（日本）公司
☎ +81-3-5296-1013
🖷 +81-3-5296-1018
✉ d-expo-jp@ubm.com
联络：博闻（广州）展览有限公司
☎ 020-8666 0158
🖷 020-8667 7120
✉ info-china@ubm.com
www.dietandbeauty.jp

Diet & Beauty Fair (10th)
Date：2011/09/26 - 28
Venue: Tokyo Big Sight Exhibition Center, Japan
Profile: Cosmetics products, inner beauty zone, total beauty zone, OEM-private brand zone, business support zone, new concept zone.
Organizer: UBM Media Co Ltd
☎ +81-3-5296-1013
🖷 +81-3-5296-1018
✉ d-expo-jp@ubm.com
Contact: Ms. Maggie Ou
Address: UBM China (Guangzhou) Co Ltd, Room1159-1164 China Hotel Office Tower, Liu Hua Road , Guangzhou 510015, China
☎ 020-8666 0158
🖷 020-8667 7120
✉ info-china@ubm.com
www.dietandbeauty.jp

日本健康食品原料展/安全及技术展
Health Ingredients Japan / Safety and Technology Japan

日期：2011/10/05 - 07
地点：日本东京有明国际展览中心
主办：博闻公司
☎ +81-3-5296-1017
🖷 +81-3-5296-1018
✉ f-expo-jp@ubm.com
联络：博闻（广州）展览有限公司
☎ 020-8666 0158
🖷 020-8667 7120
www.hijapan.info

Health Ingredients Japan
Safety and Technology Japan
Date：2011/10/05 - 07
Venue: Tokyo Big Sight Exhibition Center, Japan
Organizer: UBM Media Co Ltd
☎ +81-3-5296-1017
🖷 +81-3-5296-1018
✉ f-expo-jp@ubm.com
Contact: UBM China (Guangzhou) Co Ltd
☎ 020-8666 0158
🖷 020-8667 7120
www.hijapan.info

GARDEX：
日本东京国际花卉、园艺及户外用品博览会
International Garden & Exterior Expo Tokyo

GARDEX

日期：2011/10/13 - 15
地点：日本千叶
主办：励展博览集团
联络：励展博览集团国际销售部
地址：北京市朝阳区新源南路1-3号平安国际金融中心A座15层01-03,05
联系人：吴祥
☎ 010-5933 9277
🖷 010-5933 9233
✉ ronald.wu@reedexpo.com.cn
www.gardex.jp/english

第31届日本东京国际家具展
IFFT/ILL2011
日期：2011/11 -
地点：日本东京
☎ 0411-8378 8831
🖷 0411-8378 8830

第24届东京国际眼镜展
IOFT:
International Optical Fair Tokyo

日期：2011/11/11 - 13
地点：日本东京有明国际展览中心（Big Sight）
内容：在日本眼镜人均拥有数量超过2副，对进口眼镜的需求也在不断增加，日本眼镜市场有巨大开发潜力。日本对海外眼镜品牌有很大需求。日本的消费者的时尚品味在世界排名前列，日本人特别钟情于具有创新风格的国外眼镜产品和太阳眼镜产品。IOFT设立了六个专区，包括精品小店，眼镜配饰专区，Fukui专区，奢侈品专区，IT解决方案专区和店铺设计专区。展会构建的一站式平台，满足买家所有需要。
产品和服务：眼镜架、太阳镜、镜头、放大镜、运动眼镜、镜片调整设备、光学元件、镜片加工设备、眼镜架加工设备、眼镜架/镜片材料、隐形眼镜片及相关产品、检查/检测设备、助听器及相关设备、客户管理系统、销售管理系统、眼镜盒、眼镜链、配件、店铺设计、店铺陈列、展示柜、照明器材、促销工具(包装材料、POP、广告牌等)、镜片清洗器、眼镜布、超声波清洗器。
周期：每年一届
上届规模 2010：专业贸易观众16,142人
主办：励展日本公司
联络：励展博览集团国际销售部
地址：北京市朝阳区新源南路1-3号平安国际金融中心A座15层01-03,05
联系人：杜一鸣
☎ 010-5933 9209
🖷 010-5933 9233
✉ martin.du@reedexpo.com.cn
www.ioft.jp/en
www.reedexport.cn

客户服务中心/客户关系管理展览会及会议
Call Center/ CRM Demo & Conference

日期：2011/11/17 - 18
地点：日本东京阳光城市展览中心
主办：亚洲博闻
www.callcenter-japan.com

Call Center
CRM Demo & Conference
Date：2011/11/17 - 18
Venue: Sunshine City Convention Center, Japan
Organizer: UBM Asia
www.callcenter-japan.com

哈萨克斯坦
Kazakhstan

哈萨克斯坦国际矿业和工程机械展览会
Mining World
日期：2011/09 -
地点：哈萨克斯坦阿拉木图
周期：每年一届
主办：中国贸促会
地址：北京市西城区三里河路46号（100823）
联系人：张玉惠, 郭旭萍, 吕春丽
☎ 010-6859 4811, 6859 4994, 6859 4910
🖷 010-68594995
✉ zhangyuhui@ccpitmsc.org
www.chinamachine.org.cn

肯尼亚
Kenya

肯尼亚国际贸易博览会
NITF

日期：2011/09 -
地点：肯尼亚内罗毕
周期：每年一届
市场范围：国际性
主办：中国贸促会机械行业分会
地址：北京市西城区三里河路46号（100823）
联系人：张玉惠,郭旭萍,吕春丽
☎ 010-6859 4811, 6859 4994, 6859 4910
🖷 010-6859 4995
✉ zhangyuhui@ccpitmsc.org
www.chinamachine.org.cn

利比亚
Libya

利比亚国际工程建筑机械与建材机械展览会
Libya Build

日期：2011/05 -
地点：利比亚的黎波里
周期：每年一届
主办：中国贸促会
地址：北京市西城区三里河路46号（100823）
联系人：张玉惠, 郭旭萍, 吕春丽
☎ 010-6859 4811, 6859 4994, 6859 4910
🖷 010-6859 4995
✉ zhangyuhui@ccpitmsc.org
www.chinamachine.org.cn

马来西亚
Malaysia

马来西亚国际家具展
MIFF2011

日期：2011/03/01 - 05
地点：马来西亚
☎ 0411-8378 8831
🖷 0411-8378 8830

2011年马来西亚国际汽车零配件、设备及服务用品展览会
Automechanika Malaysia 2011

日期：2011/03/31-04/02
地点：马来西亚吉隆坡
内容：马来西亚作为东盟自由贸易区中最大的乘用车生产国，汽配行业发展迅速。

参展范围有部件及系统，附件及改装，维修及保养，IT及管理，加油站和洗车房。
周期：两年一届
上届规模 2009：参展商133家（来自14个国家），参观人数4,521人
联络：中国汽车工业国际合作总公司
地址：北京市海淀区中关村丹棱街3号A座国机大厦（100080）
☎ 010-8260 6881, 6891, 6893, 6874
🖷 010-8260 6883, 8260 6790
联系人：马蓉，刘岩，娄杰，杨菁
✉ exhibition@cnaico.com.cn
www.autochina.com.cn

马来西亚槟城电子微电子展览会
NEPCON Malaysia:
Malaysia's Only Event for Electronics Manufacturing Industry

日期：2011/06/14 - 16
地点：马来西亚槟城槟城国际体育场（PISA）
周期：每年一届
市场范围：国际性
性质：面向贸易观众
参展费用：光地展位RM$960，标准展位RM$1,060
主办：Reed Elsevier (Singapore) Pte Ltd
联络：励展博览集团国际销售部
地址：北京市朝阳区新源南路1-3号平安国际金融中心A座15层01-03,05
联系人：张志超
☎ 010-5933 9266
🖷 010-5933 9233
✉ ivy.zhang@reedexpo.com.cn
www.nepcon.com.my

第十三届马来西亚亚洲防务展览会
13th DEFENCE SERVICES ASIA EXHIBITION & CONFERENCE (DSA2012)

日期：2012 /04/16 - 19
地点：马来西亚吉隆坡太子世界贸易中心
内容：已成为世界主要防务工业专业展览盛会之一，范围也不断扩大。2010年防务展除展示三军装备外，还展示警察等单位使用的装备，并设立了装备操作、战地医疗急救等演示中心。在防务展期间，还将举办国际防务研讨会，讨论国际防务发展最新趋势等议题：战地医疗卫生保健-展品将包含所有海、陆、空战地医疗各个方面的产品和服务。国内安全保卫-这一重要部门将会有大量公司展示其产品和服务。
始办年份：1988
周期：两年一届
市场范围：国际性
性质：面向贸易观众
上届规模 2010：展览面积40,000m^2，参展商850家（来自42个国家），专业贸易观众25,000人
主办：北京邦企展览服务有限公司
地址：北京市朝阳区惠新东街11号紫光发展大厦B1座501室（100029）
联系人：杨先生
☎ 010-6482 3808
🖷 010-6482 3670
✉ bbes@china.com
MSN：bbes02@live.cn
www.bbes.com.cn

墨西哥
Mexico

墨西哥服装面料展
INTERMODA

日期：2011/01/18 - 21
地点：墨西哥
联络：上海比天展览服务有限公司
地址：上海市中山北路900号加禾商务中心3号楼303室(200070)
联系人：刘先生
☎ 021-5655 2843
🖷 021-5655 9981
www.betium.com

第17届墨西哥国际家具工业展

日期：2011/01/19 - 22
地点：墨西哥
☎ 0411-8378 8831
🖷 0411-8378 8830

墨西哥国际机床展览会
TECMA

日期：2011/03/08 - 11
地点：墨西哥墨西哥城
周期：每年两届
主办：中国贸促会
地址：北京市西城区三里河路46号（100823）
联系人：张玉惠, 郭旭萍, 吕春丽
☎ 010-6859 4811, 6859 4994, 6859 4910
🖷 010-6859 4995
✉ zhangyuhui@ccpitmsc.org
www.chinamachine.org.cn

墨西哥国际制药工业展览会
Expofarma INTERPHEX Mexico

日期：2011/04 -
地点：墨西哥墨西哥城世界贸易中心
内容：EXPOFARMA是墨西哥医药界负盛名的展会与INTERPHEX这一全球制药业的权威展会将联合打造业内全新的盛会EXPOFARMA INTERPHEX。
产品及服务：加工设备、工程设备、分析设备、器材及控制、代码解决方案、承包制造、设备维护、Contract containment）、自动化加工、卫生调节设备、质量保证、质量控制（QA&QC）、技术认证
周期：每年一届
市场范围：国际性
性质：面向贸易观众
主办：励展美洲公司（美国）
联络：励展博览集团国际销售部
www.reedexport.cn

墨西哥国际食品及饮料展
Alimentaria Mexico: International Food & Beverage Exhibition

MÉXICO Alimentaria

日期：2011/05/31 – 06/02
地点：墨西哥墨西哥城
内容：Alimentaria México每年汇聚大量食品、饮料业者以及墨西哥与国际领先的最新产品，已成为墨西哥食品饮料销售商、零售商、酒店、餐饮业、食品业及款待业专业人士的重要贸易展会平台。Alimentaria México的观众专业程度相当高：80%拥有采购决策权、53%有意寻找新供应商，而且其中大部分为零售商。Alimentaria México共吸引来自28个国家的410家参展公司、近11,500位观众，展品超过5,000，是墨西哥领先的食品与饮料贸易展会。展商来源 食品饮料类 包括以下种类食品饮料的生产商或经销商：肉制品、禽类产品、海产品、农产品、奶制品、冰冻食品、罐装食品、甜味品、面包及糖果类、无酒精饮料、酒类 食品设备类 包括以下种类设备的制造商及经销商：食品饮料制作、储存及售卖设备，餐馆饭店、咖啡 酒吧及其他相关附加服务专用设备件
周期：每年一届
市场范围：国际性
性质：面向贸易观众
参展费用：光地展位315美元/m^2，标准展位3,195美元起(+ VAT)
主办：励展博览集团国际销售部
地址：北京市朝阳区新源南路1-3号平安国际金融中心A座15层01-03,05（100027）
☎ 010-5933 9211
🖷 010- 5933 9233
✉ ISGCNmarketing@reedexpo.com.cn
www.reedexport.cn
www.alimentaria-mexico.com

墨西哥国际包装展览会
Expo Pack

日期：2011/06/23 - 26
地点：墨西哥墨西哥城
周期：每年一届
主办：中国贸促会机械行业分会
地址：北京市西城区三里河路46号（100823）
联系人：张玉惠, 郭旭萍, 吕春丽

☎ 010-6859 4811, 6859 4994, 6859 4910
🖷 010-6859 4995
✉ zhangyuhui@ccpitmsc.org
www.chinamachine.org.cn

2011年中美洲国际汽车零配件、原料加工及售后服务贸易展览会

PAACE Automechanika Mexico 2011

日期：2011/07/13-15
地点：墨西哥墨西哥城
周期：每年一届
性质：仅对专业观众
内容：部件及系统，附件及改装，维修及保养，加油站和洗车房
上届规模 2010：展览面积24,853m2, 参展商650家, 专业观众12,059人
主办：德国法兰克福展览有限公司
联络：中国汽车工业国际合作总公司
地址：北京市海淀区中关村丹棱街3号A座国机大厦（100080）
☎ 010-8260 6881, 6891, 6893, 6874
🖷 010-8260 6883, 8260 6790
联系人：马蓉，刘岩，娄杰，杨菁
✉ exhibition@cnaico.com.cn
www.autochina.com.cn

墨西哥秋季国际服装和面料展

INTERMODA

日期：2011/07/20 - 23
地点：墨西哥
联络：上海比天展览服务有限公司
地址：上海市中山北路900号加禾商务中心3号楼303室(200070)
联系人：刘先生
☎ 021-5655 2843
🖷 021-5655 9981
www.betium.com

墨西哥哈里斯科国际家具展

MUEBLE

日期：2011/08 -
地点：墨西哥
周期：每年一届
☎ 0411-8378 8831
🖷 0411-8378 8830

墨西哥国际五金展览会

Expo National Ferretera

日期：2011/09 -
地点：墨西哥墨西哥城
周期：每年一届
主办：中国贸促会机械行业分会
地址：北京市西城区三里河路46号（100823）
联系人：张玉惠，郭旭萍，吕春丽
☎ 010-6859 4811，6859 4994，6859 4910
🖷 010-6859 4995
✉ zhangyuhui@ccpitmsc.org
www.chinamachine.org.cn

2011年墨西哥国际五金工具展

日期：2011/09/01 - 03
地点：墨西哥瓜达拉哈拉展览中心
内容：瓜达拉哈拉是墨西哥第二大城市。此展是除德国科隆五金博览会外全球第二大规模的五金专业展览会,也是南美及拉丁美洲地区最大的国际五金展览会。虽然墨西哥市场没有欧洲那样广阔，但是中国企业对那里涉足甚少，市场需求旺盛，出口价格令厂商满意。由于墨西哥属于北美自由贸易区，通过墨西哥，可以将商品低关税甚至零关税出口至美国和拉美国家，这将成为中国公司在墨西哥建厂的最大优势。
展品范围：手动工具、电动工具、切削工具、建筑工具、气动工具、粉刷工具、农具、工具箱、测量工具与仪器。锁具各类锁具及家具配件。油漆、化工制品与材料粘合剂、胶粘带、密封剂、防水材料、油漆与清漆、溶解剂与其它化工产品。水暖器材卫浴设备如冲水、淋浴、盆浴设施；水龙头、管件与接头；阀门及其配件。建筑材料与附件卫生间家具与配件、厨具与配件、建材与装饰材料；家用泵、焊接设备与配件。电气与家电产品小家电，厨房电器，照明产品，包括各种灯具、配件及电池。紧固件、磨具与磨料；索具原生与塑料绳、缆索、链条及配件；梯子与脚手架（各种材质）。花园工具与设备包括灌溉设备、工具、水管、栅栏及丝网。机械产品金属加工机械、建筑机械、木工机械、清洗设备及零配件。
始办年份：1989
周期：每年一届
市场范围：国际性
性质：面向贸易观众
上届规模 2010：展览面积60,000m^2，参展商4,000家（来自32个国家），参观人数150,000万
主办：墨西哥国家工业制造发展商会
联络：中国贸促会机械行业分会
地址：北京市西城区三里河路46号（100823）
联系人：张玉惠，郭旭萍，吕春丽
☎ 010-6859 4811，6859 4994，6859 4910
🖷 010-6859 4995
✉ zhangyuhui@ccpitmsc.org
www.chinamachine.org.cn
联络：周文槟
☎ 020-8396 3610转706，13710318991
🖷 020-3887 0797
✉ ynwb88@163.com
MSN：gdwenbin@hotmail.com
QQ：406372636

摩洛哥
Morocco

Pollutec Maroc:

摩洛哥环保及水处理设备展（第三届）

Intl. Environmental Equipment, Technologies & Services Event

Pollutec MAROC

日期：2011/10/26 - 29
地点：摩洛哥卡萨布兰卡国际展览中心
内容：将会吸引400个摩洛哥的生态产业和国际领先企业参展，同时展会还将吸引超过7000名来自环保行业、生态环境保护活动、生态建设、服务行业及地方政府的专业人士，共同为摩洛哥环境挑战问题寻求解决办法。
周期：每年一届
主办：法国Reed Expositions France
联络：励展博览集团国际销售部
地址：北京市朝阳区新源南路1-3号平安国际金融中心A座15层01-03,05
联系人：宫卫
☎ 010-5933 9268
🖷 010-5933 9233
✉ david.gong@reedexpo.com.cn
www.reedexport.cn

尼日利亚
Nigeria

2011年中国工业品（尼日利亚）展览会

Made In China Exhibition 2011

日期：2011/11-
地点：尼日利亚
内容：来自中国十几个省市的60多家企业前来参展，包括沃顿洁具、珠海兴业新能源、郑州日产、中工国际、一拖集团、济南轻骑、河北宣工、济南柴油机等知名企业。尤其是尼日利亚汽车零部件以及改装维修等市场需求量非常大，参展的汽车零部件企业尤其是生产通用件的企业非常受欢迎，
始办年份：2010
上届规模 2010：展览面积2,000m^2，参展商60家，买家3,000人
联络：中国汽车工业国际合作总公司
地址：北京市海淀区中关村丹棱街3号A座国机大厦（100080）
☎ 010-8260 6881, 6891, 6893, 6874
🖷 010-8260 6883, 8260 6790
联系人：马蓉，刘岩，娄杰，杨菁
✉ exhibition@cnaico.com.cn
www.autochina.com.cn

荷兰
Netherlands

荷兰国际不锈钢展览会

STAINLESS STEEL WORLD EXHIBITION

日期：2011/11 -
地点：荷兰马斯特里赫
周期：每年一届
主办：中国贸促会机械行业分会
地址：北京市西城区三里河路46号（100823）
联系人：张玉惠，郭旭萍，吕春丽
☎ 010-6859 4811, 6859 4994, 6859 4910
🖷 010-6859 4995
✉ zhangyuhui@ccpitmsc.org
www.chinamachine.org.cn

朝鲜
North Korea

朝鲜国际商品博览会

International Fair

日期：2011/05 -
地点：朝鲜平壤
周期：每年一届
主办：中国贸促会机械行业分会
地址：北京市西城区三里河路46号（100823）
联系人：张玉惠，郭旭萍，吕春丽
☎ 010-6859 4811, 6859 4994, 6859 4910
🖷 010-6859 4995
✉ zhangyuhui@ccpitmsc.org
www.chinamachine.org.cn

挪威
Norway

挪威国际海事展览会

NOR-Shipping

日期：2011/05/24 - 27
地点：挪威奥斯陆
主办：中国贸促会机械行业分会
地址：北京市西城区三里河路46号（100823）
联系人：张玉惠，郭旭萍，吕春丽
☎ 010-6859 4811, 6859 4994, 6859 4910
🖷 010-6859 4995
✉ zhangyuhui@ccpitmsc.org
www.chinamachine.org.cn

巴基斯坦
Pakistan

巴基斯坦国际机械及汽车工业展览会

MTAP

日期：2011/10 -
地点：巴基斯坦卡拉奇

周期：每年一届
主办：中国贸促会
地址：北京市西城区三里河路46号（100823）
联系人：张玉惠，郭旭萍，吕春丽
☎ 010-6859 4811, 6859 4994, 6859 4910
🖷 010-6859 4995
✉ zhangyuhui@ccpitmsc.org
www.chinamachine.org.cn

巴拿马 Panama

2011巴拿马第29届国际博览会

Expocomer 2011

日期：2011/03/23 - 26
地点：巴拿马
内容：在中南美洲、美国及欧洲地区影响很大。每年均有30多个国家和地区的几百家企业参展。2010年3月的第二十八届博览会参观人数十万人之多，其中各国商人占一半以上。2010年的中国展团总成交额达到1.27亿美元。
展出内容：机械、电子、仪器、化工、五矿、五金工具、食品、服装、轻工产品、照明设备、灯具、建材、消费品、纺织品、家用电器、石油化工、加工机械、农用机械、电子通讯、轻工家电、汽车配件、五矿建材、农机具、文具玩具、体育用品、汽车、摩托车、农产品、畜牧产品等。
始办年份：1982
周期：每年一届
市场范围：国际性
性质：面向公众
上届规模 2010：展览面积35,000m^2
主办：巴拿马农工商协会
联络：周文槟 先生
地址：广州市海珠区江海大道粤信广场观景楼503室（510310）
☎ 13710318991
🖷 020-8417 9290
✉ 1979wenbin@163.com
MSN：gdwenbin@hotmail.com
QQ：406372636

秘鲁 Peru

第30届南美秘鲁国际矿业机械设备展

日期：2011/09 -
地点：秘鲁阿雷基帕
内容：矿业机械设备
市场范围：国际性
主办：北京中仕达兴业展览有限公司
地址：北京市海淀区蓝靛厂东路2号金源时代商务中心2号楼A座11B（100097）
联系人：贾倩，赵仕忱，牟向东，张露
☎ 010-5129 8900
🖷 010-8886 2939
✉ mail@chinstar.cn
www.chinstar.cn

秘鲁纺织展

EXPOtextil Peru

日期：2011/10/21 - 24
地点：秘鲁
联络：上海比天展览服务有限公司
地址：上海市中山北路900号加禾商务中心3号楼303室(200070)
联系人：刘先生
☎ 021-5655 2843
🖷 021-5655 9981
www.betium.com

菲律宾 Philippines

菲律宾食品配料展

Food Ingredients Philippines

日期：2011/07/06 - 08
地点：菲律宾马尼拉SMX 会议中心
主办：亚洲博闻
☎ +31(0)20 40 99 544
🖷 +31(0)20 36 32 616
✉ jonathan.vis@ubm.com
http://fiphilippines.ingredientsnetwork.com

Food Ingredients Philippines

Date：2011/07/06 - 08
Venue: SMX Convention Center, Manila, Philippines
Profile: The first Food Ingredients (Fi) trade show ever held in the Philippines will give the domestic food industry greater access to much needed ingredients and technology from around the world.
Organizer: UBM International Media BV
☎ +31(0)20 40 99 544
🖷 +31(0)20 36 32 616
✉ jonathan.vis@ubm.com
http://fiphilippines.ingredientsnetwork.com/home

波兰 Poland

波兰国际纺织服装展

Tex-Style

日期：2011/03/01 - 03
地点：波兰
联络：上海比天展览服务有限公司
地址：上海市中山北路900号加禾商务中心3号楼303室(200070)
联系人：刘先生
☎ 021-5655 2843
🖷 021-5655 9981
www.betium.com

2011年波兰汽车工业及配件展览会

Automotive Technology Fair

日期：2011/05/13-15
地点：波兰波兹南
内容：现已成为波兰地区最大的专业盛会。展会期间还将举办一系列高层会议专业展示会，包括波兰汽车商会组织的“Auto Event”等。此次展会展出包括工具和轮胎，流动维修配套设备，完整的诊断流程以及个别测试，测量和控制装置的应用设备，汽车零部件，防盗解决方案，配件，以及清洁和保养设备和产品。
始办年份：1992
周期：两年一届
上届规模 2009：参展商350家（来自11个国家）
联络：中国汽车工业国际合作总公司
地址：北京市海淀区中关村丹棱街3号A座国机大厦（100080）
☎ 010-8260 6881, 6891, 6893, 6874
🖷 010-8260 6883, 8260 6790
联系人：马蓉，刘岩，娄杰，杨菁
✉ exhibition@cnaico.com.cn
www.autochina.com.cn

波兰国际机械与创新技术展览会

MACH-TOOL

日期：2011/06 -
地点：波兰波兹南
周期：每年一届
主办：中国贸促会机械行业分会
地址：北京市西城区三里河路46号（100823）
联系人：张玉惠，郭旭萍，吕春丽
☎ 010-6859 4811, 6859 4994, 6859 4910
🖷 010-6859 4995
✉ zhangyuhui@ccpitmsc.org
www.chinamachine.org.cn

波兰国际纺织服装展

Tex-Style

日期：2011/08/29 - 31
地点：波兰
联络：上海比天展览服务有限公司
地址：上海市中山北路900号加禾商务中心3号楼303室(200070)
联系人：刘先生
☎ 021-5655 2843
🖷 021-5655 9981
www.betium.com

葡萄牙 Portugal

里斯本国际食品展

Alimentaria&Horexpo Lisboa

Intl. Exhibition of Food, Food Service & Technology

AlimentariaLisboa

日期：2011/03/27 - 30
地点：葡萄牙里斯本国际展览馆
Feira Internacional de Lisboa, Lisbon, Portugal
内容：食品和饮料产品、食品饮料业设备及技术。
始办年份：2000
周期：两年一届
上届规模 2009：展览面积12,403m^2，参展商346家，参观人数30,438人
主办：励展奥地利公司Messe Salzburg
联络：励展博览集团国际销售部
联系人：杜一鸣
☎ 010-5933 9266
🖷 010-5933 9233
✉ martin.du@reedexpo.com.cn
www.alimentaria-lisboa.com

里斯本国际食品展

Alimentaria Lisboa:

International Food & Beverage Exhibition

AlimentariaLisboa

日期：2013/04 -
地点：葡萄牙里斯本国际展览馆
内容：里斯本国际食品展在葡萄牙食品饮料业的领先地位。每奇数年一次在伊比利亚半岛上举办的食品饮料领域最重要的商业展会。在葡萄牙配销公司协会（APED）以及每个葡萄牙零售渠道的支持下，展会凝聚了食品市场最大最全面的视野，展会期间还为观众和展商提供丰富多彩的活动。
周期：两年一届
市场范围：国际性
性质：面向贸易观众
参展费用：光地展位96.5–121.8欧元/m^2
主办：励展博览集团国际销售部
联系人：杜一鸣
☎ 010-5933 9266
🖷 010-5933 9233
✉ martin.du@reedexpo.com.cn
www.alimentaria-lisboa.com
www.reedexport.cn

波多黎各
Puerto Rico

INTERPHEX Puerto Rico
第8届波多黎各国际制药工业展览会：生物科技及制药商展览会
Featuring Medical Device Puerto Rico

日期：2011/10/20 - 21
地点：波多黎各圣胡安波多黎各会议中心
内容：为加勒比地区最主要的专业性展会，包括：药品的审批，生产，包装，以及生物制药。展览会将展出超过350种设备，技术，另外还有为期两天的教学项目和丰富的网上活动。展会由下列五个不同的展区组成：监管、生产技术、设备/工程、生物技术和包装。届时，波多黎各国际制药工业展览会将与波多黎各供应链及物流展（Supply Chain & Logistics Puerto Rico）和波多黎各医疗仪器展（MEDICAL DEVICE Puerto Rico）同期举办。
产品与服务：最新的信息技术、加工与控制设备、加工与制造、环保/危险材料、贴标签设备、喷码与打码设备、设计设备、包装机、包装材料及零件、厂房工程/厂房维护、加工自动化、加工机器与设备、服务与相关产品、审批支持、仓库、经销与物流。观众来自制药与生物科技产品制造商的重要买家与决策者。
周期：每年一届
上届规模 2010：净展位面积35,650平方英尺，参展商232家，参观人数3,814人
主办：励展美国公司
联络：励展博览集团国际销售部
地址：北京市朝阳区新源南路1-3号平安国际金融中心A座15层01-03,05
联系人：申健
☎ 010-5933 9299
🖷 010-5933 9233
✉ jerry.shen@reedexpo.com.cn
www.interphexpuertorico.com

俄罗斯
Russia

2011年俄罗斯国际食品展
PRODEXPO 2011

日期：2011/02/07 - 11
地点：俄罗斯莫斯科
内容：俄罗斯国际食品展是俄罗斯以及整个东欧地区最大的专业食品展会。17年来，该展会不断发展壮大，出展面积增加了5倍，众多参展商伴随着展会的成长，稳固进入、开拓着俄罗斯广阔市场。该展会对俄罗斯食品工业的发展起到了至关重要的作用。
展品范围：农副产品、罐头食品、休闲食品、肉类品、海产品、调味品、方便食品、粮油制品、速冻食品、绿色食品、保健食品、婴幼儿食品、禽制品、乳制品、干鲜果蔬、烘焙食品、饮料、咖啡、烟酒、饼干、糖果、食用菌、食品原辅料及添加剂、茶叶及土特产品等；食品加工技术、食品机械、冰淇淋生产技术、包装技术。
始办年份：1993
周期：每年一届
市场范围：国际性
上届规模 2010：展览面积80,000m^2(国外展商面积45,000m^2)，参展商2,100家（国外展商1,067家，来自57个国家），参观人数56,000人（专业贸易观众35,000人）
主办：北京领汇国际展览有限公司
地址：北京市朝阳区农展馆南路13号瑞辰国际中心719室（100125）
联系人：简丹
☎ 010-51295359转8616
🖷 010-51295379转8616
✉ jiandanno1@163.com
MSN：expo8616@worldfairs.cn
QQ：815241762
www.worldfairs.cn

aqua-therm Moscow
俄罗斯暖通、制冷、空调、卫浴及水池设备展
International Exhibition for HVAC Sector & Pools

日期：2011/02/8 - 11
地点：俄罗斯莫斯科Crocus Expo会展中心
内容：HVAC（热通风与空调设备）、自动化控制系统、卫浴配件、锅炉设备、能源、燃气供给 环境、水质控制设备、阀门及配件、供热技术、管道管线、泵、卫生技术与设备、热力配件 水、污水处理技术、空调、通风管道及空气过滤器、空气净化器、压缩机、风扇、加湿器、除湿器、制冷、冷藏设备、通风设备、水健身与水疗、化工产品、水上乐园设备、小型游泳池、桑拿设备、水疗设备、游泳池、泳池设备及配件、水净化器、按摩浴缸
周期：每年一届
上届规模：参展商248家（国外展商142家），参观人数15,850人
主办：励展俄罗斯公司，俄罗斯联邦
联络：励展博览集团国际销售部
联系人：李悦
☎ 010-5933 9298
🖷 010-5933 9233
✉ anna.li@reedexpo.com.cn
www.aquatherm-moscow.com
www.reedexport.cn

俄罗斯国际安防技术论坛
Intl Forum & Exhibition on Security and Safety Technologies

日期：2011/02/15 - 18
地点：俄罗斯莫斯科Crocus Expo会展中心
内容：安防系统与解决方案：闭路电视、数字视频录像、四象限分光器、多通道数据采集器、通路审核装置 通讯及IT安全方案：IT软件、数据储存、数据连接、IP技术、生物特征识别技术 机械安全方案：周边安全系统、门禁、保险箱、防弹玻璃 安全系统电子元件：天线、电缆、适配器、放大器、音频信号设备 安防设备与系统：火灾及突发情况报警器、烟气探测器、防火玻璃 运输、反恐怖安防解决方案：公路交通、隧道、轨道、桥梁安全系统 救援与紧急情况设备与方案：个人安防设备、装备、救援仪器
周期：每年一届
上届规模 2010：参展商191家，参观人数15,000人
主办：励展俄罗斯公司，俄罗斯联邦
联络：励展博览集团国际销售部
联系人：张志超
☎ 010-5933 9266
🖷 010-5933 9233
✉ ivy.zhang@reedexpo.com.cn
www.reedexport.cn

俄联邦莫斯科国际轻纺展
Taxtilexpo

日期：2011/02/16 - 19
地点：俄罗斯
联络：上海比天展览服务有限公司
地址：上海市中山北路900号加禾商务中心3号楼303室(200070)
联系人：刘先生
☎ 021-5655 2843
🖷 021-5655 9981
www.betium.com

俄罗斯莫斯科服装博览会
CPM

日期：2011/02/21 - 24
地点：俄罗斯莫斯科
联络：上海比天展览服务有限公司
地址：上海市中山北路900号加禾商务中心3号楼303室(200070)
联系人：刘先生
☎ 021-5655 2843
🖷 021-5655 9981
www.betium.com

2011年俄罗斯莫斯科国际建筑建材展
Mosbuild

日期：2011/04/05 - 08
地点：俄罗斯莫斯科红宝石展馆和奥林匹克展馆
内容：五金：卫浴五金，厨房五金，家具五金，水暖五金，家庭装饰小五金类；地铺：地板，地毯，塑料地面材料，地面材料配件；工程机械：挖掘机械及铲土运输机械、工程车辆、建筑设备和工具，门窗玻璃：门类，窗类，门窗五金及配件，各类玻璃及玻璃生产设备；暖通制冷；园林工具：园艺工具、园林机械及剪草机械，栅栏、丝网、铁艺、五金产品；装饰材料；综合建材；卫浴石材瓷砖
周期：每年一届
市场范围：国际性
性质：面向贸易观众
上届规模 2010：展览面积50,000m^2
主办：英国ITE国际展览集团
地址：北京市朝阳区农展馆南路13号瑞辰国际中心719（100125）
联系人：张爽
☎ 010-51295359转8810
🖷 010-51295379转8810
✉ bangni5858@163.com
MSN：expo8810@worldfairs.cn
QQ：574000135

InterCharm Professional
俄罗斯专业化妆品及美容仪器博览会
Fair for Professional Cosmetics & Equipment for Beauty Salons

日期：2011/04/14 - 16
地点：俄罗斯莫斯科Crocus会展中心
Crocus Expo, Moscow, Russia
内容：专业护肤美容、美容美发设备、美甲、美发等，专业美发、美甲产品与配件，塑料手术器材与服务，晒肤设备与产品、水疗、芳香疗法以及彩妆。
始办年份：2001
周期：每年一届
性质：面向贸易观众
参展费用：光地展位320欧元，标准展位380欧元
上届规模 2010：展览面积7,700m^2，参展商370家，参观人数33,600人
主办：励展德国公司
联络：励展博览集团国际销售部
联系人：张志超
☎ 010-5933 9266
🖷 010-5933 9233
✉ ivy.zhang@reedexpo.com.cn
www.reedexport.cn
www.intercharm.ru

俄罗斯国际机床展览会
METALLOOBRABOTKA

日期：2011/05 -
地点：俄罗斯莫斯科
周期：每年一届
主办：中国贸促会
地址：北京市西城区三里河路46号（100823）
联系人：张玉惠, 郭旭萍, 吕春丽
☎ 010-6859 4811, 6859 4994, 6859 4910
🖷 010-6859 4995
✉ zhangyuhui@ccpitmsc.org
www.chinamachine.org.cn

俄罗斯国际管材线材展览会
Tube & Wire Russia

日期：2011/05 -
地点：俄罗斯莫斯科
周期：每年一届
主办：中国贸促会机械行业分会
地址：北京市西城区三里河路46号（100823）
联系人：张玉惠, 郭旭萍, 吕春丽
☎ 010-6859 4811, 6859 4994, 6859 4910
🖷 010-6859 4995
✉ zhangyuhui@ccpitmsc.org
www.chinamachine.org.cn

俄罗斯春季家具展

莫斯科国际家具生产、木工及室内装饰展
interzum moscow 2011/ EEM/ EuroExpoFurniture 2011

日期：2011/05/12 - 15
地点：俄罗斯莫斯科Crokus博览中心
内容：莫斯科国际家具生产、木工及室内装饰展和俄罗斯春季家具展同期举行，后者是俄罗斯最重要的春季家具展。作为interzum 的系列展会，莫斯科国际家具生产、木工及室内装饰展在展示一系列国际领先的家具生产材料和辅助配件的同时，也让您对俄罗斯及东欧的家具市场及潮流走向拥有更深入的了解
周期：每年两届
市场范围：国际性
性质：面向公众
参展费用：光地（24m²起）260欧元/m²，标准展位（9m²）380欧元/m²，会刊登录费260欧元/展商，联合展商附加登记费240欧元/展商
上届规模 2008：展览面积20,174m², 参展商来自20个国家，专业贸易观众63,700人
主办：德国科隆展览国际有限公司/ MVK JSC
地址：北京市朝阳区东三环北路8号亮马河大厦二座1018室（100004）
联系人：贾宁
☎ 010-6590 7766转729
🖷 010-6590 6139
✉ m.jia@koelnmesse
www.interzum-moscow.cn

interzum moscow 2011

EEM/EuroExpoFurniture 2011

Date：2011/05/12 - 15
Venue: Crokus Expo Exhibition Center, Russia
Profile: interzum moscow / Interkomplekt provides a comprehensive overview into the broad country specific spectrum of the sector, held at the new Crokus Expo Exhibition Center in Moscow. The fair presents an impressive range of materials and components for furniture production as well as an inside view of the Russian furniture market and Russian trends
Frequency: Biannual
Market Area: International
Nature: Open to public
Participated Fee: Raw Space (min 24m²) EURO 260/m², Standard Booth（min 9m²）EURO 380/m²
Statistics 2008: Exhibition Area 20,174m², Exhibitors came from 20 countries，Trade visitors 63,700
Organizer: Koelnmesse GmbH/ MVK JSC
Address: Unit 1018 Landmark Tower II, No. 8 Dongsanhuan N. Road, Beijing, China
Contact: Maggie Jia
☎ 010-6590 7766 ext 729
🖷 010-6590 6139
✉ m.jia@koelnmesse
www.interzum-moscow.cn

俄罗斯国际建筑及工程机械展览会
CTT

日期：2011/06 -
地点：俄罗斯莫斯科
周期：每年一届
主办：中国贸促会
地址：北京市西城区三里河路46号（100823）
联系人：张玉惠, 郭旭萍, 吕春丽
☎ 010-6859 4811, 6859 4994, 68594910
🖷 010-6859 4995
✉ zhangyuhui@ccpitmsc.org
www.chinamachine.org.cn

俄罗斯国际模具制造与技术展览会
Rosmould

日期：2011/06 -
地点：俄罗斯莫斯科
周期：每年一届
主办：中国贸促会机械行业分会
地址：北京市西城区三里河路46号（100823）
联系人：张玉惠, 郭旭萍, 吕春丽
☎ 010-6859 4811, 6859 4994, 6859 4910
🖷 010-6859 4995
✉ zhangyuhui@ccpitmsc.org
www.chinamachine.org.cn

俄罗斯国际包装工业展览会
Rosupak

日期：2011/06 -
地点：俄罗斯莫斯科
周期：每年一届
主办：中国贸促会机械行业分会
地址：北京市西城区三里河路46号（100823）
联系人：张玉惠, 郭旭萍, 吕春丽
☎ 010-6859 4811, 6859 4994, 6859 4910
🖷 010-6859 4995
✉ zhangyuhui@ccpitmsc.org
www.chinamachine.org.cn

莫斯科国际汽车零配件展览会
Moscow International Motor Show

日期：2011/08 -
地点：俄罗斯莫斯科
周期：每年一届
主办：中国贸促会
地址：北京市西城区三里河路46号（100823）
联系人：张玉惠，郭旭萍，吕春丽
☎ 010-6859 4811，6859 4994，6859 4910
🖷 010-68594995
✉ zhangyuhui@ccpitmsc.org
www.chinamachine.org.cn

2011年莫斯科国际汽车零配件、售后服务及设备展览会
MIMS Automechanika Moscow 2011

时间：2011/08/25-29
地点：俄罗斯莫斯科
内容：从 2010 年开始，Automechanika Moscow（莫斯科国际汽车配件、售后服务及设备展览会）同MIMS（莫斯科国际汽车、配件及附件展览会）将强强联合，联袂为制造商和买家提供更佳的平台。此前，这两个展览会都聚焦迅猛发展的俄罗斯汽车市场，包括汽车工业的各个细分市场，从最新的汽车配件、附件，到售后维修设备。俄罗斯汽车及零配件市场是未来最具吸引力的市场之一。
周期：每年一届
上届规模 2010：展览面积18,413m2，参展商593家，采购商30,000人
主办：法兰克福展览公司
联络：中国汽车工业国际合作总公司
地址：北京市海淀区中关村丹棱街3号A座国机大厦（100080）
☎ 010-8260 6881, 6891, 6893, 6874
🖷 010-8260 6883, 8260 6790
联系人：马蓉，刘岩，娄杰，杨菁
✉ exhibition@cnaico.com.cn
www.autochina.com.cn

俄罗斯国际动力传动、表面处理及工业自动化展览会
IA Russia

日期：2011/09 -
地点：俄罗斯莫斯科
周期：每年一届
主办：中国贸促会机械行业分会
地址：北京市西城区三里河路46号（100823）
联系人：张玉惠,郭旭萍,吕春丽
☎ 010-6859 4811, 6859 4994, 6859 4910
🖷 010-6859 4995
✉ zhangyuhui@ccpitmsc.org
www.chinamachine.org.cn

莫斯科国际食品展览会
World Food Moscow

日期：2011/09/13 - 2011-09-16
地点：俄罗斯展览中心
内容：果汁饮料、食品原料、食品配料、罐头食品、肉禽制品、蔬菜水果、海产品、茶叶、食品加工
始办年份：1992
周期：每年一届
市场范围：国际性
性质：面向贸易观众
上届规模 2010：展览面积40,0002m², 参展商1,266家，专业贸易观众60,000人
主办：英国国际贸易与展览有限公司(英国ITE集团)
联络：中企国际展览广告有限公司
☎ 010-6446 6671, 6446 6369
🖷 010-8838 2248
✉ eacieceo@mx.cei.gov.cn

第19届新西伯利亚国际家具及加工设备、室内装饰展
SIBFURNITURE

日期：2011/10/04 - 07
地点：俄罗斯新西伯利亚
☎ 0411-8378 8831
🖷 0411-8378 8830

俄罗斯国际印刷设备及技术展览会
POLYGRAPHINTER

日期：2011/10/04 - 08
地点：俄罗斯莫斯科
周期：每年两届
主办：中国贸促会机械行业分会
地址：北京市西城区三里河路46号（100823）
联系人：张玉惠, 郭旭萍, 吕春丽
☎ 010-6859 4811, 6859 4994, 6859 4910
🖷 010-6859 4995
✉ zhangyuhui@ccpitmsc.org
www.chinamachine.org.cn

InterCHARM

俄罗斯国际化妆品及美容博览会
Largest Perfumery & Cosmetics Exhibition in Russia & E. Europe

日期：2011/10/26 - 29
地点：俄罗斯莫斯科Crocus展览中心
内容：InterCHARM致力于通过丰富的展览及活动安排聚集行业决策者、满足观众及参展商需求、展示市场机会，是美容市场专业人士进行会面交流、寻

求区域与国际合作伙伴、讨论重要话题、发现新产品的领先贸易展会平台。
产品及服务：化妆品、香水、指甲与头发护理产品与配饰、SPA产品、发廊服务与设备、培训学校、洗浴护理、婴儿护理、男性梳妆用品、包装、小众品牌及市场新奇产品等各类美容产品。 观众来源：批发商、采购商、经销商、进口商、零售商、制造商、技术人员、市场人员、美容产业专业人士、设计师、研究机构、行业媒体。
周期：每年一届
参展费用：标准展位405欧元，光地展位310欧元
上届规模 2010：参展商834家，参观人数80,000人（专业贸易观众50,925人）
赞助：俄罗斯联邦商业与工业部、俄罗斯香水与化妆品协会
主办：励展俄罗斯公司
联络：励展博览集团国际销售部
地址：北京市朝阳区新源南路1-3号平安国际金融中心A座15层01-03,05
联系人：张志超
☎ 010-5933 9266
℻ 010-5933 9233
✉ ivy.zhang@reedexpo.com.cn
www.reedexport.cn

第23届俄罗斯国际家具、配件及室内装潢展
MEBEL2011

日期：2011/11 -
地点：俄罗斯
☎ 0411-8378 8831
℻ 0411-8378 8830

俄罗斯石油和天然气技术展览会
SPE Russian Oil & Gas Technical Conference & Exhibition

日期：2012/10 -
地点：俄罗斯莫斯科All-Russian会展中心
内容：石油和天然气勘探及生产业的一次国际盛会，这个以研讨会为主的盛会将主要关注适合世界级工业发展的技术应用方面。
展品范围：钻井、井完成、地质和地球物理、油藏监测、测井与油井地层评价、设施工程、生产运作、渗流机制与原油回收方法、油藏工程、天然气技术、项目管理、出射和外围技术、健康/安全与环境。
周期：两年一届
市场范围：国际性
性质：面向贸易观众
参展费用：光地展位235英磅/m²,标准展位275英磅/m²
主办：励展英国公司
联络：励展博览集团国际销售部
地址：北京市朝阳区新源南路1-3号平安国际金融中心A座15层01-03,05
联系人：宫卫
☎ 010-5933 9268
℻ 010-5933 9233
✉ david.gong@reedexpo.com.cn
www.russianoilgas.com
www.reedexport.cn

PAP-FOR Russia
俄罗斯国际纸浆造纸、林业、生活用纸及纸包装展览会
International Exhibition and Conference for Russia's Pulp & Paper, Forestry, Tissue & Converting & Packaging Industries

日期：2012/11 -
地点：俄罗斯圣彼得堡
Len Expo Exhibition Center, Russia
内容：俄罗斯及独联体地区规模最大、历史最悠久的纸浆造纸、林业、生活用纸及纸包装行业国际贸易博览会。
产品及服务：纸浆、纸板、纸转化产品、造纸系统和产品（储木场、纸浆制造、漂白、浆料准备、纸机、涂层、表面处理、化学材料、计算机、建造、数据处理、能源、工程、环保、仪器、维护、过程控制、质量控制、安全、测试）、纸转化系统和产品（印压、复卷设备、涂层设备、卷纸机、干燥设备、卷筒与卷轴、印刷、检查与扫描设备等）
周期：两年一届
市场范围：国际性
性质：面向贸易观众
参展费用：光地展位430欧元/m²，标准展位711欧元/m²
主办：励展俄罗斯公司
联络：励展博览集团国际销售部
地址：北京市朝阳区新源南路1-3号平安国际金融中心A座15层01-03,05
联系人：宫卫
☎ 010-5933 9268
℻ 010-5933 9233
✉ david.gong@reedexpo.com.cn?
www.reedexport.cn

沙特阿拉伯 Saudi Arabia

2011年沙特阿拉伯国际建筑及工程机械展览会

日期：2011/03/13 - 17
地点：沙特阿拉伯阿卜杜拉国王经济城
内容：该展会是沙特境内唯一的专业工程机械展览会
展品范围：建筑材料类：建筑材料，陶瓷及石材机械，五金，工具，暖通设备，卫浴及配件，玻璃产品及机械，陶瓷石材，门窗及锁具，内部装饰，灯饰，各类板材木结构制品，涂料；建筑工程机械类：压路机及其设备，混凝土，混凝土铺路机，沥青铺路机，履带车辆，运输管道以及道路的养护服务设备，挖掘机，装载机，分类机，推土机，铲土机，起重设备及工具，照明及通风设备，运输以及递送设备
始办年份：1994
周期：每年一届
市场范围：国际性
上届规模：展出面积17,000m²，参展商215家，参观人数20,000人
主办：北京麦田通会国际展览有限公司
联系人：吴珊
☎ 010-8248 4014转801，5165 9302转8005
℻ 010-5165 9302转8004
✉ xiaoxiangzhishui@yahoo.com.cn
MSN：xiaoxiangzhishui@hotmail.com
www.cornfairs.com

第十四届沙特国际医疗及医疗器械展
The 14th International Healthcare, Hospital Supplies and Medical Equipment Show

日期：2011/04/10 - 13
地点：沙特阿拉伯国际展览中心
内容：沙特是中东地区最大的医疗市场，沙特是高福利的国家，而不断增长的人口刺激医疗行业的发展。不断增长的高于65岁的人群，以及不断增多的外籍劳力，且在未来十年里，其人口将增长30%，均刺激着沙特继续扩大其保健服务以满足人们日益增长的需求。政府越来越重视这一行业，采取了一系列的措施，增加支出，努力满足人民增长的需求；预计在2016年支出超过200亿美金。现有79所医院在建设之中，新的工程包括超过250个初级治疗中心和8所医院均计划中
周期：每年一届
市场范围：国际性
主办：IFP集团沙特分公司REC
地址：北京市朝阳区东三环南路19号联合国家大厦1408
联系人：杨亚男
☎ 010-8763 5663
℻ 87635688
✉ ifp5633@ifpchina.com
MSN：laurayangyanana@hotmail.com
QQ：215720839
www.ifpchina.com

沙特（吉达）国际纺织展览会
The Fashion Arabia Exhibition

日期：2011/05/08 - 11
地点：沙特阿拉伯
联络：上海比天展览服务有限公司
地址：上海市中山北路900号加禾商务中心3号楼303室(200070)
联系人：刘先生
☎ 021-5655 2843
℻ 021-5655 9981
www.betium.com

2011年第十届沙特（利雅得）国际电子通讯展
10th Intl Information & Communication Technology Exhibition for Saudi Arabia

日期：2011/05/15 - 19
地点：沙特阿拉伯沙特国际展览中心
内容：是一个通过UFI认证的展会。沙特阿拉伯正进入一个电脑、信息技术飞速发展的时代，利雅得的电信公司已经投资了10亿美元用于建设全国的数据通讯信息服务。12000千米的网络连接已经在沙特阿拉伯的主要城市发展。无线基站、数据中心、光纤环也已经在利雅得中心建立。近期还将建设中东最大的电信基础结构工程，并投资超过60亿美元用于添加安装1,500,000条数字线缆，GSM 网络的 500,000线扩容,对基本配件产品和移动电话及其附件产品都将有大量的需求。
周期：每年一届
市场范围：国际性
性质：面向贸易观众
主办：IFP集团沙特分公司REC
地址：北京市朝阳区东三环南路19号联合国家大厦1408
联系人：杨亚男
☎ 010-8763 5663
℻ 010-8763 5688
✉ ifp5633@ifpchina.com
MSN：laurayangyanana@hotmail.com
QQ：215720839
www.ifpchina.com

2011年沙特国际灯具设备展
11th Intl Lighting Equipment Show

日期：2011/05/30 – 06/02
地点：沙特阿拉伯国际展览中心
内容：沙特是中国在西亚北非的第一大贸易伙伴，两国之间的经贸联系日益紧密，合作前景广阔。当前中沙都处在经济快速发展时期，两国都在紧紧抓住这一有利时机，充分发挥各自优势，提高合作水平，实现共同发展。中沙将继续扩大相互投资规模，重点加强在能源、基础设施建设、信息通信领域的合作。沙特对中国产品的需求广泛
周期：每年一届
市场范围：国际性
主办：IFP集团沙特分公司REC
地址：北京市朝阳区东三环南路19号联合国家大厦1408
联系人：杨亚男
☎ 010-8763 5663
℻ 010-8763 5688
✉ ifp5633@ifpchina.com
MSN：laurayangyanana@hotmail.com
QQ：215720839
www.ifpchina.com

2011年沙特国际空调制冷，暖通设备博览会
12th Intl Air Conditioning, Ventilation, Heating and Refrigeration Show

日期：2011/05/30 – 06/02
地点：沙特阿拉伯国际展览中心
内容：沙特是世界上人口增长最快的国家之一，每

年的人口持续增长幅度在3%以上，人口的大幅度上升推动了市场的活跃度，也使本国旅游业，房地产，宾馆，休闲和购物中心兴旺发展，人们对各种生活必需品的要求也日益上升，房产业出现了供不应求的现象。炎热的气候，以及干旱的环境使得沙特的空调市场前景广阔,为外商带来了独一无二的投资机会。沙特国内生产空调和暖通设备的厂家非常少，所以它需要通过进口来满足本国对空调和暖通设备的需求。沙特阿拉伯的空气调节设备需求量每年增长6%，当前的空调市场价值已达到了五亿美元。

周期：每年一届

市场范围：国际性

主办：IFP集团沙特分公司REC

地址：北京市朝阳区东三环南路19号联合国家大厦1408

联系人：杨亚男

☎ 010-8763 5663

🖷 010-8763 5688

✉ ifp5633@ifpchina.com

MSN：laurayangyanana@hotmail.com

QQ：215720839

www.ifpchina.com

2011年沙特能源电力博览会

14th Intl Electrical Engineering, Power Generation and Distribution Exhibition

日期：2011/05/30 – 06/02

地点：沙特阿拉伯国际展览中心

内容：该展会获得UFI（国际博览会联盟）认证，沙特每年的人口以3%的速度增长着，石油价格和经济的增长，这些因素使得沙特王国呈现出繁荣的景象。建筑物日益增多，住宅区域在不断向外扩张，沙特电力部门每年扩大7%，在未来的20年内，为了满足电力的分配和传输，将耗资1200亿在工程建设上。沙特公报2010年5月13日报道，今年海湾国家能源和能源相关项目投资总额增加了142%，由2009年的950亿美元，增加到2300亿美元。参加2010年沙特能源电力展，你将发现自己在海湾最大的电力市场中心-沙特利雅得占据着一个独特的位置。

周期：每年一届

主办：IFP集团沙特分公司REC

地址：北京市朝阳区东三环南路19号联合国家大厦1408

联系人：杨亚男

☎ 010-8763 5663

🖷 010-8763 5688

✉ ifp5633@ifpchina.com

MSN：laurayangyanana@hotmail.com

QQ：215720839

www.ifpchina.com

沙特国际工程建筑机械与工程车辆展览会

PMV

日期：2011/10 -

地点：沙特阿拉伯利雅得

周期：每年一届

主办：中国贸促会

地址：北京市西城区三里河路46号（100823）

联系人：张玉惠，郭旭萍，吕春丽

☎ 010-6859 4811, 6859 4994, 6859 4910

🖷 010-6859 4995

✉ zhangyuhui@ccpitmsc.org

www.chinamachine.org.cn

新加坡
Singapore

BreakBulk Asia

- 3rd Annual Breakbulk Asia Conference & Exhibition

日期：2011/01/24 - 26

地点：新加坡国际会议展览中心

周期：每年一届

市场范围：国际性

性质：面向贸易观众

上届规模 2010：参展商80家，与会者2,000人

主办：亚洲博闻

☎ +65 6592 0891

🖷 +65 6438 6090

✉ gregory.zheng@ubm.com

http://asia.breakbulk.com

BreakBulk Asia –

3rd Annual Breakbulk Asia Conference & Exhibition

Date：2011/01/24 - 26

Venue: Suntec Singapore Intl Convention & Exhibition Center, Singapore

Profile: The largest and most important gathering in Asia for companies involved in the shipping of heavy-lift, project cargo and traditional breakbulk cargoes. It is where shippers have the opportunity to meet and develop relationships with the leading specialized carriers, forwarders, ports, terminals and packers who have the expertise and resources to handle oversized cargoes with unique handling requirements. Exhibitors include the world' s major carriers, forwarders and ports that handle specialized heavy-lift, project and breakbulk cargoes. The Breakbulk Asia event is an outgrowth of the Breakbulk Conference and Exhibition held in New Orleans, USA since 1989 and the Breakbulk Europe event held in Antwerp since 2006.

Frequency: Annual

Market Area: International

Nature: Trade only

Statistics 2010: Exhibitors 80, Participants 2000)

Organizer: UMB Asia

Contact: Gregory Zheng

☎ +65 6592 0891

🖷 +65 6438 6090

✉ gregory.zheng@ubm.com

http://asia.breakbulk.com

新加坡国际家具展

IFFS2011

日期：2011/03/09 - 12

地点：新加坡

☎ 0411-8378 8831

🖷 0411-8378 8830

新加坡国际缝制设备展览会

International Apparel Machinery Trade Show (JIAM 2011)

日期：2011/05 -

地点：新加坡展览中心

内容：世界三大缝制设备展会之一的JIAM即将于2008年5月13-16日首次在新加坡举行。本届展会为期4天，其主题为"将技术从JIAM推向世界之门"，将展出来自世界领先厂商和供应商的最新、最先进机械及设备，并展示为服装、服饰产业提供解决方案的高度创新、尖端的技术。JIAM 2008在亚洲出口商和世界服装市场间起着关键的桥梁作用。

始办年份：2008

市场范围：国际性

性质：面向贸易观众

参展费用：光地展位（9m²）315,000日元

主办：励展新加坡公司（亚太总部）

联络：励展博览集团国际销售部

www.reedexport.cn

国际观赏鱼及配件展览

Aquarama/Pet Asia 2011

日期：2011/05/26 - 29

地点：新加坡国际会议展览中心

主办：亚洲博闻

☎ +65-6592 0897

🖷 +65-6438 6090

✉ Wein.Ng@ubm.com

联络：博闻（广州）有限公司

☎ 020-8666 0158

🖷 020-8667 7120

email: lauren.cheung@ubm.com

http://aquarama.com.sg

Aquarama/Pet Asia 2011

Date：2011/05/26 - 29

Venue: Suntec, Singapore

Profile: Aquarama is one of Asia' s biggest international ornamental fish and accessories exhibition for the aquatic fish industries and its related sectors.

Organizer: UBM Asia

☎ +65-6592 0897

🖷 +65-6438 6090

✉ Wein.Ng@ubm.com

Contact: UBM China (Guangzhou) Co Ltd

Address: Rm 1159-1164 China Hotel Office Tower, Liu Hua Road Guangzhou 510015, CHINA

☎ 020-8666 0158

🖷 020-8667 7120

✉ lauren.cheung@ubm.com

http://aquarama.com.sg

亚洲制药工业展览会

Interphex Asia:

Asia's Dedicated Sourcing Platform for Pharmaceutical Manufacturing

INTERPHEX ASIA

日期：2011/05/30 - 31

地点：新加坡新达城展览中心

内容：致力于全面展示亚洲制药行业的机械设备与材料新品，展会汇集了许多来自亚太地区的药品生产专家和国际供应商。新加坡作为活动主办地，在地理位置上，处在像印度尼西亚，马来群岛，菲律宾和泰国这样的发展中市场的中心，加之展会中举办的同期会议ISPE Singapore Conference，意味着您将会在展会中与该地区制药生产链上的资深人士不期而遇，与其交换意见并共同探讨亚洲地区的行业发展。

周期：每年一届

市场范围：国际性

性质：面向贸易观众

参展费用：光地展位：485新加坡元 标准展位：585新加坡元

主办：励展新加坡公司

联络：励展博览集团国际销售部

联系人：申健

☎ 010-8518 2644, 8515 1375

🖷 010-8515 1304

✉ jerry.shen@reedexpo.com.cn

www.reedexport.cn

亚洲建筑及室内装饰展览会

Build Eco Xpo Asia（BEX Asia）

日期：2011/09/14 - 16

地点：新加坡新达城会展中心（Suntec）

内容：面向东南亚市场建筑项目的展会，针对环保和可持续发展，展出最新的建筑材料，设计和建筑方案，展会吸引了建筑行业的业内人士，专家和主要买家等。参加展会有机会了解更多业内资讯，建立关系网，挖掘更多东南亚新兴经济带来的商机。展会参与国家众多，包括澳大利亚、中国、德国、香港、印尼、意大利、马来西亚、新加坡、台湾、泰国、英国和越南。展会也吸引了许多业内专家和

决策者，包括建筑师、设计师、承包人、地产开发商、施工技术人员、政府官员和专家及业内人士。参加展会您有机会和同行面对面交流，建立关系网，交换见解，参加一系列行业活动。
产品和服务： 建筑材料、设备，生态区，内部装饰、照明、卫浴，智能家具、安防、建筑系统和解决方案
周期： 每年一届
市场范围： 国际性
性质： 面向贸易观众
参展费用： 光地展位625新加坡元/m²，标准展位755新加坡元/m²
主办： 励德爱思唯尔（新加坡）Reed Elsevier (Singapore)Pte Ltd
联络： 励展博览集团国际销售部
地址： 北京市朝阳区新源南路1-3号平安国际金融中心A座15层01-03,05
联系人： 王颖
☎ 010-5933 9208
🖷 010-5933 9233
✉ winnie.wang@reedexpo.com.cn
www.bex-asia.com

亚洲海上旅游及邮轮展
Cruise Shipping Asia

日期： 2011/11/16 - 18
地点： 新加坡
主办： 亚洲博闻
☎ +65-6592 0897
🖷 +65-6438 6090
✉ Wein.Ng@ubm.com
www.cruiseshippingasia.com

Cruise Shipping Asia
Date：2011/11/16 - 18
Venue: Sands Expo Convention Center, Singapore
Profile: 亚洲海上旅游及邮轮展
Organizer: UBM Asia
☎ +65-6592 0897
🖷 +65-6438 6090
✉ Wein.Ng@ubm.com
www.cruiseshippingasia.com

亚太海事展
Asia Pacific Maritime

Asia Pacific MARITIME

日期： 2012/03/14 - 16
地点： 新加坡博览中心
内容： 亚太海事展是亚太地区海事行业一站式的交易会，展示海事工程及港口科技领域的最新产品和技术。APM被誉为新加坡最重要的国际海事展，它集展会、研讨会和小组讨论为一体，提供完整的行业体验；它的一系列联络活动将亚太地区的高级买家与国际海事供应商联系起来。APM为您节省时间，使您在最快的时间内找到可以让您的公司领先于海事市场的产品。APM也为您提供开拓国际市场和扩展全球业务的机会。
展商来源： 造船、船只维修和改造、海事设备、推进力系统（主推进力和辅助推进力）、船只运行设备、海事技术、电子/电力工程、港口技术、货物传输系统、货代、货代设备、配件及存储、海事服务、海事安全、导航与通讯技术。
周期： 两年一届
市场范围： 国际性
性质： 面向贸易观众
参展费用： 光地展位630新加坡元/m²，标准展位760-800新加坡元/m²
主办： 励展新加坡公司（亚太总部）
联络： 励展博览集团国际销售部
地址： 北京市朝阳区新源南路1-3号平安国际金融中心A座15层01-03,05
联系人： 宫卫
☎ 010-5933 9268
🖷 010-5933 9233
✉ david.gong@reedexpo.com.cn
www.reedexport.cn
www.apmaritime.com

新加坡电子展
GlobalTRONINCS 2012：
featuring Green Technologies for Electronics

日期： 2012/09/19 - 21
地点： 新加坡Suntec展览馆
内容： 东南亚及亚太地区最具影响力、规模最大、专业水平很高的电子专业展。参展商有来自世界各国的千余家企业，观众数万人，其中近半数来自亚太各国。
产品及服务： 应用集成电路、光电半导体器件、功率半导体器件、半导体传感器及固体传感器、各类阻容元件、真空电子器件、光导纤维、封装材料、PCB组件及原材料、电子保护装置、接插件、各种连接器、开关、按键及键盘、无源微波器件、各种显示器件、磁盘驱动器、光盘驱动器及配件、磁性材料、网卡、电机、计算机外部设备及材料、电子工模具、各种电子测量仪器、电子整机配套组件、防静电器材、各种电源等。
周期： 两年一届
市场范围： 国际性
性质： 面向贸易观众
参展费用： 光地展位675新加坡元/m²，标准展位775新加坡元/m²
主办： 励展博览集团国际销售部
联系人： 张志超
地址： 北京市朝阳区新源南路1-3号平安国际金融中心A座15层01-03,05
☎ 010－5933 9266
🖷 010－5933 9233
✉ ivy.zhang@reedexpo.com.cn
www.reedexport.cn
www.globaltronics.com.sg

南非
South Africa

南非国际汽车零部件及售后服务展览会
Automechanika South Africa

日期： 2011/03 -
地点： 南非约翰内斯堡
周期： 每年一届
主办： 中国贸促会
地址： 北京市西城区三里河路46号（100823）
联系人： 张玉惠,郭旭萍,吕春丽
☎ 010-6859 4811, 6859 4994, 6859 4910
🖷 010-6859 4995
✉ zhangyuhui@ccpitmsc.org
www.chinamachine.org.cn

南非约翰内斯堡家具家居及室内装饰展
DECOREX2011

日期： 2011/08/01 - 05
地点： 南非约翰内斯堡
☎ 0411-8378 8831
🖷 0411-8378 8830

南非国际模具展览会
Afrimold

日期： 2011/09/27 - 29
地点： 南非约翰内斯堡
周期： 每年一届
主办： 中国贸促会机械行业分会
地址： 北京市西城区三里河路46号（100823）
联系人： 张玉惠,郭旭萍,吕春丽
☎ 010-6859 4811, 6859 4994, 6859 4910
🖷 010-6859 4995
✉ zhangyuhui@ccpitmsc.org
www.chinamachine.org.cn

南非国际纺织品、纺织机械及鞋类展览会
ATF

日期： 2011/11/24 - 26
地点： 南非
联络： 上海比天展览服务有限公司
地址： 上海市中山北路900号加禾商务中心3号楼303室（200070）
联系人： 刘先生
☎ 021-5655 2843
🖷 021-5655 9981
www.betium.com

韩国
South Korea

韩国大邱国际纤维展览会
Preview In Daegu

日期： 2011/03/10 - 12
地点： 韩国
联络： 上海比天展览服务有限公司
地址： 上海市中山北路900号加禾商务中心3号楼303室(200070)
联系人： 刘先生
☎ 021-5655 2843
🖷 021-5655 9981
www.betium.com

2011韩国太阳能、风能、地能展览会
Solar, Wind & Earth Energy Trade Fair 2011

日期： 2011/03/16 - 18
地点： 韩国韩国光州金大中会展中心
内容： 太阳能类加热设备、太阳能能量发生器、太阳能收集器、太阳能水加热器、太阳能蓄电池、太阳能模块、存储电池、变极器、能量转炉设备等；风能汽车、风力传输设备、风力发电机、风力存储电池和其他相关设备等；地热类快速加热板、压力板、导管、压缩机、循环泵、等其他相关设备等；生物方面淀粉酒精燃料、生物柴油机和其他相关设备等；燃料电池类单节电池、堆栈、变极器等其他相关设备；海洋热交换器、涡轮、低地变电器、存储电池和其他相关设备等；氢燃料汽车、氢发生器、氢电池系统、氢生产设备和其他相关设备等；节能、高效率产品及相关设备；环保、资源再利用产品及相关设备。
始办年份： 2006
周期： 每年一届
市场范围： 国际性
性质： 面向贸易观众
入场券价格： 免费
参展费用： 光地展位（9m²）1,700美元，标准展位（9m²）2,000美元
上届规模 2010：标准展位500个），参展商200家（来自17个国家）
主办： 韩国光州广域市政府
承办: 大韩贸易投资振兴公社；韩国能源经济新闻；金大中会展中心
地址： 上海市兴义路8号万都中心3110室（200336）
联系人： 麻小利
☎ 021-5108 8771转126, 13764378035
🖷 021-6219 6015, 6236 8211
✉ kotra_exhibition@163.com
MSN：kathleen.mxl@hotmail.com
www.sweet.or.kr

Solar, Wind & Earth Energy Trade Fair 2011

Date：2011/03/16 - 18
Venue: Korea Kimdaejung Convention Center, South Korea
Profile: Photovoltaics, Solar Thermal, Wind Power, Hydrogen, Fuel Cell, Geothermal & Unused Energy, Biomass, Marine Energy, Integrated Gasification Combined Cycle, Small Hydro Power, Waste Energy, Eco-environmental Industry
Established Year: 2006
Frequency: Annual
Market Area: International
Nature: Trade Only
Cost to Attend: Free
Participated Fee: Raw Space (9m^2) US$ 1,700, Standard Booth (9m^2) US$ 2,000
Statistics 2010: Standard Booth 500, Exhibitors 200 (came from 17 countries) Sponsor: Gwangju Metropolitan City; Jeollanam-do Province
Organizer: KOTRA; The Energy Economic News,Kimdaejung Convention Center
Address: Room 3110, Maxdo Center, No.8 Xingyi Road, Shanghai, China
Contact: Ms. Ma Xiaoli
☎ 021-5108 8771 ext 126, 13764378035
🖷 021-6219 6015, 6236 8211
✉ kotra_exhibition@163.com
MSN: kathleen.mxl@hotmail.com
www.sweet.or.kr

韩国电子展

SMT/PCB & NEPCON KOREA

국제 표면실장 및 인쇄회로기판 생산기자재전
SMT/PCB & PACKAGING NEPCON KOREA

日期：2011/04/06 - 08
地点：韩国首尔Coex会议及展览中心
Coex Convention and Exhibition Center, Seoul, South Korea
内容：SMT相关设备和材料，PCB生产设备和材料，电子零件生产设备和材料，IT终端产品的自动化生产设备和材料，电子元件和测试检测设备，控制设备和材料，微电子技术和包装技术
始办年份：1990
周期：每年一届
参展费用：光地展位400美元/m^2，标准展位450美元/m^2
主办：励展日本公司
联络：励展博览集团国际销售部
联系人：张志超
☎ 010-5933 9266
🖷 010-5933 9233
✉ ivy.zhang@reedexpo.com.cn
www.smtpcb.org
www.reedexport.cn

2011首尔国际食品产业大展

SEOUL FOOD 2011

首尔国际食品产业大展
Since 1983

日期：2011/04/26 - 29
地点：韩国韩国国际会展中心 1～5厅
内容：农产品/农产加工；水产品/水产加工；畜产品/畜产品加工；谷物、豆、干果、蔬菜、水果、蘑菇、燕麦片、罐装产品等；鱼、贝、甲壳类、海藻、冷冻水产品、罐装水产品；牛肉、猪肉、熏猪肉、火腿、香肠及各类冷冻畜产加工品。家禽类、乳制品、食品材料/添加剂、面包糕点；鸡肉、鸭肉、鸡蛋等各种家禽加工品；牛奶、黄油、奶酪、奶油、酸奶等；调味品、甘味料、香辛料、防氧化剂、天然色素等；点心、面包、饼干、巧克力、糖果、糕点、软糖、冰淇淋。酒类、饮料、咖啡；保健品、有机农产品、传统食品、进口食品等。经销商、外送服务、有关食品信息服务等。食品设备，食品包装，食品安全；
始办年份：1983
周期：每年一届
市场范围：国际性
入场券价格：免费
参展费用：光地展位（9m^2）2,790美元，标准展位（9m^2）3,330美元
上届规模 2010：展览面积53,541m^2，参展商1,095家（来自35个国家），参观人数50,000人（专业贸易观众43,059人）
主办：大韩贸易投资振兴公社
承办：韩国食品工业协会；英国奥伟展览集团；韩国展览管理韩国知识经济部；农林水产食品部；文化体育观光部；保健福利部；农村振兴厅；食品医药品安全厅；韩国食品研究院；韩国食品工程学会
地址：上海市兴义路8号万都中心3110室（200336）
联系人：麻小利
☎ 021-5108 8771转126，13764378035
🖷 021-6219 6015，6236 8211
✉ kotra_exhibition@163.com
MSN：kathleen.mxl@hotmail.com
www.seoulfood.or.kr

SEOUL FOOD 2011

Date：2011/04/26 - 29
Venue: KINTEX, South Korea
Profile: Agricultural Products / Processed & Packaged Foods；Seafood / Processed & Packaged Foods；Meat/ Processed & Packaged Foods；Poultry Products；Dairy Products；Food Additives & Ingredients；Bakery & Confectionery；Wine, Liquor & Beverages；Coffee & Tea；Health & Organic Food；Traditional Foods；Franchise；Catering Service；Food Marketing, Information and Equipment / Others；Food Processing Machinery；Packaging Machinery / Components；Food Sanitation Equipment；Others
Established Year: 1983
Frequency: Annual
Market Area: International
Cost to Attend: Free
Participated Fee: Raw Space (9m^2) US$ 2,790, Standard Booth (9m^2) US $3,330
Statistics 2010: Exhibition Area 53,541m^2, Exhibitors 1,095 (came from 35 countries), Visitors 50,000 (trade visitors 43,059)
Sponsor: KOTRA
Organizer: KFIA;Allworld Exhibitions; KEM; MKE; MIFAFF; MCST; MOHW; RDA
Address: Room 3110, Maxdo Center, No.8 Xingyi Road, Shanghai, China
Contact: Ms. Ma Xiaoli
☎ 021-5108 8771 ext 126, 13764378035
🖷 021-6219 6015, 6236 8211
✉ kotra_exhibition@163.com
MSN: kathleen.mxl@hotmail.com
www.seoulfood.or.kr

2011韩国国际游艇展

Korea International Boat Show 2011

2011경기국제보트쇼& 코리아매치컵 세계요트대회
Korea International Boat Show | World Match Racing Tour Korea Match Cup

日期：2011/06/09 - 13
地点：韩国韩国京畿道华城市全谷港
内容：各式游艇；大型游艇（豪华游艇、机动艇、游览休闲船）；小型游艇（赛艇、摩托艇、橡皮艇）；独木舟、皮划艇、水上摩托、脚踏艇、拖车；船用引擎及配件；发动机、推进装置、零部件、控制盘、通讯大巷设备、电气电子设备、甲板用品、锚链、船内装备；水上运动；尾波、帆板、潜水设备及相关服务、钓具、配件及相关服务、游艇用服装、书籍及安全救生用品
始办年份：2008
周期：每年一届
市场范围：国际性
入场券价格：免费
上届规模 2009：参展商280家，参观人数237,679人
主办：韩国京畿道政府；华城市；安山市
承办：大韩贸易投资振兴公社；韩国国际展览中心
地址：上海市兴义路8号万都中心3110室（200336）
联系人：麻小利
☎ 021-5108 8771转126，13764378035
🖷 021-6219 6015，6236 8211
✉ kotra_exhibition@163.com
MSN：kathleen.mxl@hotmail.com
www.koreaboatshow.org

Korea International Boat Show 2011

Date：2011/06/09 - 13
Venue: Jeongok Marina,Hwaseong City & Tando Port, Ansan City, Gyeonggi Province, South Korea
Profile: Boats/ Yachts; Large boat & yachts (Luxury yachts, sailing yachts, cruise boats)Small boats & yachts (small racing yachts, jetboats, inflatable boats)Canoes, kayaks, row boats, water skis, PWCs, trailers, campers; Marine Engines/ Parts; Marine engines, propulsion engine parts controllersNavigation, communication and electronic equipment Others (outfits, anchors, moorings, transportation equipment);Material & Maintenance (waterproofing material, wood, plywood, plastic);Boat Interiors Water sports
Established Year: 2008
Frequency: Annual
Market Area: International
Cost to Attend: Free
Statistics 2009: Exhibitors 280, Visitors 237,679
Sponsor : Gyeonggi Province, Hwaseong City, Ansan City
Organizer: KOTRA, KINTEX
Address: Room 3110, Maxdo Center, No.8 Xingyi Road, Shanghai, China
Contact: Ms. Ma Xiaoli
☎ 021-5108 8771 ext 126, 13764378035
🖷 021-6219 6015, 6236 8211
✉ kotra_exhibition@163.com
MSN: kathleen.mxl@hotmail.com
www.koreaboatshow.org

2011韩国国际纺织展览会

Preview In Seoul 2011

PRE VIEW IN SEOUL Preview in SEOUL 2011
SEOUL INTERNATIONAL TEXTILE FAIR
Aug 31(Wed)~Sep.2(Fri),2011, B Hall, COEX(Seoul, KOREA)

日期：2011 /08/31 - 02
地点：韩国韩国首尔国际会展中心 COEX
内容：铺地材料、墙布、窗帘、床上及浴用亚麻制、装饰布等B、各类天然原料、面料：丝、棉、麻、毛、羊绒及混纺面料。各种制衣用纱线、面料：针织布、梭织布、坯布、化纤、印染布等。各类服装、成衣等。各种服装辅料、辅件：拉链、扣子、衬、垫、饰物。各类工业用纺织品原料、面料：纤维、线、无纺布、涂层织物、合成织物。各种相关出版物：书籍、图案、软件等
始办年份：2000
周期：每年一届
市场范围：国际性
入场券价格：免费
上届规模 2010：展览面积8,010m^2，参展商230家，参观人数11,500人
主办：韩国纺织业协会；首尔市政府
承办:韩国知识经济部；大邱市政府；大韩贸易投资振兴公社
地址：上海市兴义路8号万都中心3110室（200336）
联系人：麻小利
☎ 021-5108 8771转126，13764378035
🖷 021-6219 6015，6236 8211
✉ kotra_exhibition@163.com
MSN：kathleen.mxl@hotmail.com
http://en.previewinseoul.com

Preview In Seoul 2011

Date：2011/08/31 - 02
Venue: Seoul COEX 1F, South Korea

Profile: Fibers, Cotton, Denim, Embroidery, Functional Fabrics, Knits, Lace, Linen, Prints, Silk, Silky Aspects, Wool, Findings/Trims, Cad/Cam, Accessories, etc
Established Year: 2000
Frequency: Annual
Market Area: International
Cost to Attend: Free
Statistics 2010: Exhibition Area 8,010m^2, Exhibitors 230, Visitors 11,500
Sponsor: Korea Federation of Textile Industries; Seoul Metropolitan Government
Organizer: Ministry of Knowledge Economy; Daegu Metropolitan City; KOTRA
Address: Room 3110, Maxdo Center, No.8 Xingyi Road, Shanghai, China
Contact: Ms. Ma Xiaoli
☎ 021-5108 8771转126, 13764378035
☏ 021-6219 6015, 6236 8211
✉ kotra_exhibition@163.com
MSN: kathleen.mxl@hotmail.com
http://en.previewinseoul.com

2011韩国国际环境能源产业展
ENVIRONMENT & ENERGY TECH 2011

日期：2011/09/01 - 04
地点：韩国韩国釜山国际会展中心
内容：环境：水质、大气、废弃物处理及污染预防等；能源、再生能源：风力、太阳能、燃料电池、潮力、生物质等；电力、发电：燃气、水力、原子能、火力、氢节能设备及产品等；家庭、产业用能源、公共部分；气候；CO 降低技术及产品；
始办年份：2007
周期：每年一届
市场范围：国际性
入场券价格：免费
参展费用：通过KOTRA提前申请，可获得免费展位
上届规模 2009：标准展位450个，参展商200家，参观人数30,000人
主办：釜山广域市政府；国际新闻；大韩贸易投资振兴公社
承办：韩国釜山国际会展中心；今日能源；韩国中小企业振兴公团
地址：上海市兴义路8号万都中心3110室（200336）
联系人：麻小利
☎ 021-5108 8771转126, 13764378035
☏ 021-6219 6015, 6236 8211
✉ kotra_exhibition@163.com
MSN：kathleen.mxl@hotmail.com
www.entechkorea.net

ENVIRONMENT & ENERGY TECH 2011
Date：2011/09/01 - 04
Venue: BEXCO, South Korea
Profile: Environment: Water, Air, Waste, Pollution Prevention etc. Energy: Renewable Energy, Home & Industrial Energy, Transportation Energy, Electricity & ESCO, Petroleum, Atomic Energy, Community Energy, Gas, Public Sector
Established Year: 2007
Frequency: Annual
Market Area: International
Cost to Attend: Free
Statistics 2009: Standard Booth 450, Exhibitors 200, Visitors 30,000
Sponsor: Busan Metropoolitan City; International News; KOTRA
Organizer: BEXCO; TODAY ENERGY
Address: Room 3110, Maxdo Center, No.8 Xingyi Road, Shanghai, China
Contact: Ms. Ma Xiaoli
☎ 021-5108 8771 ext 126, 13764378035
☏ 021-6219 6015, 6236 8211
✉ kotra_exhibition@163.com
MSN: kathleen.mxl@hotmail.com
www.entechkorea.net

2011韩国国际文化创意产业展
Asia Content & Entertainment Industry Fair 2011

日期：2011/09/22 - 2011-09-25
地点：韩国光州金大中国际会展中心
内容：动漫游戏，动漫衍生品（玩具等相关产品），广播电视节目、影视剧、影视动画，新闻出版印刷与版权贸易；工艺美术交易，工业设计（包括包装、产品等设计），建筑设计，服装设计；工艺美术设计，画廊、古玩及艺术品交易，文化演艺产业交易；演出器材、视听等设备，演出团体、演出节目、经纪公司，文化旅游景区与旅游商品等；
始办年份：2006
周期：每年一届
市场范围：国际性
入场券价格：免费
上届规模 2010：参展商325家（国外展商135家），参观人数98,248人
主办：韩国光州广域市
承办：韩国文化体育观光部；韩国文化振兴院；大韩贸易投资振兴公社
联络：大韩贸易投资振兴公社
地址：上海市兴义路8号万都中心3110室（200336）
联系人：麻小利
☎ 021-5108 8771转126, 13764378035
☏ 021-6219 6015, 6236 8211
✉ kotra_exhibition@163.com
MSN：kathleen.mxl@hotmail.com
www.acefair.or.kr

Asia Content & Entertainment Industry Fair 2011
Date：2011 /09/22 - 6499
Venue: Kimdaejung Convention Center, Gwangju, Korea
Profile: Animation; Movie; Games; the press and publishing; Art; Media; Videos; the radio, film and television industries; other cultural products
Established Year: 2006
Frequency: Annual
Market Area: International
Cost to Attend: Free
Statistics 2010: Exhibitors 325（foreigners 135）, Visitors 98,248
Organizer: Korea Gwangju Metropolitan City; KOTRA
Address: KOTRA, Room 3110, Maxdo Center, No.8 Xingyi Road, Shanghai, China
Contact: Ms. Ma Xiaoli
☎ 021-5108 8771 ext 126, 13764378035
☏ 021-6219 6015, 6236 8211
✉ kotra_exhibition@163.com
MSN: kathleen.mxl@hotmail.com
www.acefair.or.kr

2011韩国釜山国际纺织、时装展览会
Busan International Textile & Fashion Show 2011

日期：2011/10/13 - 15
地点：韩国韩国釜山国际会展中心
内容：时装：运动装、时尚女装、时尚男装、青少年服装、童装等；工业纺织品：交通设备的纺织材料和超级纤维（汽车、火车、飞机、船）；面料：粗纺羊毛、羊毛、天然纤维、化学纤维等；纺织机器：染色机、缝纫机、绣花机、织布机、工艺品机器、毡机等；时装附件：时装材料、配件、皮包箱包、钱包、腰带、装饰品等；生态纺织品标签、时装设计、咨询及研究机构、信息服务等
始办年份：2001
周期：每年一届
市场范围：国际性
入场券价格：免费
参展费用：光地展位770美元,标准展位1000美元
上届规模 2010：标准展位500个，参展商250余家
主办：釜山广域市政府
承办：大韩贸易投资振兴公社；釜山国际会展中心；釜山纺织与时装协会
地址：上海市兴义路8号万都中心3110室（200336）
联系人：麻小利
☎ 021-5108 8771转126 13764378035
☏ 021-6219 6015, 6236 8211
✉ kotra_exhibition@163.com
MSN：kathleen.mxl@hotmail.com
www.acefair.or.kr

Busan International Textile & Fashion Show 2011
Date：2011/10/13 -
Venue: BEXCO, Korea
Profile: Fashion (Sportwear; Women' s wear, Men' s wear; Teen Clothing, Children' s Wear.etc.); Industrial Textile (Transportation including Automobiles, rail cars, aircrafts and Marine Equipment Textiles, Super Fabrics, etc.); Machinery (Dyeing Machines, sewing and embroidery machines, weaving machines, handicraft machinery, felting machines etc.); Fashion Accessories and others
Established Year: 2001
Frequency: Annual
Market Area: International
Cost to Attend: Free
Participated Fee: Raw Space USD 770, Standard Booth USD 1,000
Statistics 2010: Standard Booths 500, Exhibitors 250
Sponsor: Busan Metropolitan City
Organizer: KOTRA, BEXCO, Busan Federation of Textile & Fashion Industry
Address: Room 3110, Maxdo Center, No.8 Xingyi Road, Shanghai, China
Contact: Ms. Ma Xiaoli
☎ 021-5108 8771 ext 126, 13764378035
☏ 021-6219 6015, 6236 8211
✉ kotra_exhibition@163.com
MSN: kathleen.mxl@hotmail.com
www.acefair.or.kr

KORMARINE
韩国海事展：韩国国际造船及海事设备展
The Intl Shipbuilding & Marine Equipment Exhibition

日期：2011/10/26 - 29
地点：韩国釜山会展中心（BEXCO）
内容：此展是韩国海事及造船业最主要的展会活动。
产品及服务：船只设计、建造和装备、起重机械、火警与安全系统、烟气探测、防火设备、电子设备、船只及港口导航/通讯系统、引擎、海上防卫系统、分级与出版物。 观众来源：船主、造船公司、船厂采购经理、海事营救单位、海事研究机构、海事防火单位、海事设备厂商、贸易公司、港口部门、设备及配件产商、渔场经理、海运业经理及工程师、巡航及摆渡运营商。
周期：两年一届
主办：励展日本公司
联络：励展博览集团国际销售部（中国）
地址：北京市朝阳区新源南路1-3号平安国际金融中心A座15层01-03,05（100027）
☎ 010-5933 9288
☏ 010-5933 9233
✉ liang.wang@reedexpo.com.cn
www.kormarine.net
www.reedexport.cn

西班牙
Spain

2011年西班牙国际制冷、暖通、泵阀及卫浴管件展（第14届）

日期：2011/03/01 - 04
地点：西班牙马德里
内容：展品包括空调、空调零部件、制冷、供暖设备、泵、阀、管件、卫生洁具、工业和商业冷藏设备、通风设备等。家用和工业用途产品各占50%。该展是欧洲几个主要制冷、泵阀展之一，处在其他几个展会的空档年，且西班牙等南欧国家市场又是欧洲空调制冷、泵阀消费的主要市场，因此，很受国内企业欢迎。展会在空调、暖通和泵阀领域有良好的增长前景，将会成为我国空调制冷、暖通、泵阀企业开拓欧盟市场的又一重要途径
周期：两年一届
市场范围：国际性
性质：面向贸易观众
上届规模 2009：展览面积45269.5m^2，参展商680家，专业贸易观众46899人
联络：周文槟
地址：广州市天河区体育东路122号羊城国际商贸中心东塔1202, 1208, 1209室（510620）
☎ 020-8396 3610转706，13710318991
🖷 020-3887 0797
✉ ynwb88@163.com
MSN：gdwenbin@hotmail.com
QQ：406372636

西班牙毕尔巴鄂国际五金工具展

Ferroforma 2011

日期：2011/03/23 - 26
地点：西班牙毕尔巴鄂展览中心
内容：锁具、安防设备及配件 工具 电动工具和木工机械 建筑五金和建材 工业供应品 劳保用品 紧固件商店、仓储设备与配件 家居用品 装潢五金 电气产品，照明 管件 家居改进和DIY产品 园艺工具和产品
始办年份：1974
周期：每年两届
市场范围：国际性
性质：面向贸易观众
入场券价格：17 欧元
参展费用：标准展位325欧元/m^2，光地135欧元/m^2
上届规模 2009：展览面积12,000m^2，参展商776家（国外展商504家，来自27个国家），参观人数15,172人
主办：科隆国际展览公司；西班牙毕尔巴鄂展览中心
地址：北京市朝阳区东三环北路8号亮马河大厦二座1018室（100004）
联系人：陈瑞
☎ 010-6590 7766 转 750
🖷 010-6590 6139
✉ r.chen@koelnmesse.cn
www.ferroforma.cn

Ferroforma 2011

Date: 2011/03/23 - 26
Venue: Bilbao Exhibition Center, Spain
Established Year: 1974
Frequency: Biannual
Market Area: International
Nature: Trade only
Cost to Attend: EURO 17:-
Participated Fee: Standard Booth EURO 325/m^2, Raw Space EURO 135/m^2
Statistics 2009: Exhibition Area 12,000m^2, Exhibitors 776 (foreigners 504, came from 27 countries), Visitors 15,172
Organizer:
Address: Unit 1018, Landmark Tower Ⅱ, No. 8 Dongsanhuan North Rd., Beijing 100004, China
Contact: Ryan Chen
☎ 010-6590 7766 ext 750
🖷 010-6590 6139
✉ r.chen@koelnmesse.cn
www.ferroforma.cn

2011年伊比利亚汽车零部件、设备及售后服务展览会

Motortec Automechanika Ibérica 2011

日期：2011/03/30-04/02
地点：西班牙马德里
内容：部件及系统：汽车驱动，底盘，车身，顶棚，汽车内饰，通讯设备，电力、电子、传感技术，标准件；老式车的部件及服务；附件及改装：机动车附件，汽车改装、发动机外形优化设计、设计改进、外观改装，改装及选择，轮胎、轮辋、轮辐及轮；配件及改装：汽车配件、特别设备、改装服务系统及改进设计；修理及保养：汽车保养及修理装备、车间维修及涂漆、维修站建造及管理；加油站及洗车：加油站装备、洗车及护理。
始办年份：1991
周期：两年一届
上届规模 2009：展览面积46,720m^2，参展商804家，专业贸易观众51,289人（来自67个国家）
联络：中国汽车工业国际合作总公司
地址：北京市海淀区中关村丹棱街3号A座国机大厦（100080）
☎ 010-8260 6881, 6891, 6893, 6874
🖷 010-8260 6883, 8260 6790
联系人：马蓉，刘岩，娄杰，杨菁
✉ exhibition@cnaico.com.cn
www.autochina.com.cn

西班牙国际工程机械与矿山机械展览会

SMOPYC

日期：2011/04/05 - 09
地点：西班牙萨拉戈萨
周期：三年一届
主办：中国贸促会
地址：北京市西城区三里河路46号（100823）
联系人：张玉惠，郭旭萍，吕春丽
☎ 010-6859 4811, 6859 4994, 6859 4910
🖷 010-6859 4995
✉ zhangyuhui@ccpitmsc.org
www.chinamachine.org.cn

西班牙瓦伦西亚国际家具展

Ideas&Pasion

日期：2011/09/20 - 24
地点：西班牙
☎ 0411-8378 8831
🖷 0411-8378 8830

第11届欧洲国际纺织机械展览会（ITMA2011）

日期：2011/09/22 - 29
地点：西班牙巴塞罗那
内容：各类纺织机械、零部件及染化料等
主办：欧洲纺织机械制造商委员会
联络：中国贸促会纺织行业分会
联系人：高杨 孙培宁
☎ 010-85229372 85229663
🖷 010-85229480

Viscom-Sign Espana

第24届西班牙标识视觉传播及图像设计行业展

International Trade Fair for Visual Communication

日期：2011/10/06 - 08
地点：西班牙马德里IFEMA展览中心
内容：标识视觉传播及图像设计行业展（Viscom）精益求精 - 展品更佳、规模更大、国际化程度更高，正在成为欧洲视觉传播行业的领导型展会，为您展览最新的数码印刷、户外广告、卖场视觉传播产品、服务以及平面设计领域的最新潮流趋势。展品范围：采用新材料和新幅面尺寸的高品质数码印刷技术，使用各类材料和尺寸的创新广告解决方案，专业图像管理服务、图形处理输出设备、专用软件与工具。观众来源：数码印刷、印刷与平面艺术、标识制作、标牌与户外广告、广告与平面设计、丝网印刷广告、广告、移印与烫印、装潢与室内设计、雕刻与广告产品、终端大用户、摄影与数码影像
周期：每年一届
参展费用：光地展位188欧元
主办：励展西班牙公司（Iberia, S.A., SPAIN）
联络：励展博览集团国际销售部
地址：北京市朝阳区新源南路1-3号平安国际金融中心A座15层01-03,05
联系人：张志超
☎ 010-5933 9266
🖷 010-5933 9233
✉ ivy.zhang@reedexpo.com.cn
www.viscomspain.com/en,
www.reedexport.cn

2012年西班牙国际食品饮料展览会

Alimentaria 2012:

International Food & Beverage Exhibition

日期：2012/03 -
地点：西班牙Fira Barcelona展览中心
内容：西班牙最重要的食品饮料展，也是世界范围内重要的展会之一。展会的分区、革新、创造与活力氛围，及其专业精神和国际影响力都是该展会成功的重要因素。展会吸引了5,000家领先的食品饮料制造商和经销商和158,000位来自五大洲的专业采购，它为食品与饮料工业再次提供一个国际经济舞台。
周期：两年一届
市场范围：国际性
性质：面向贸易观众
主办：西班牙Alimentaria Exhibitions S. A.
联络：励展博览集团国际销售部
www.reedexport.cn

巴塞罗那国际食品、饮料设备及技术展

Bta. Barcelona tecnologías de la alimentación:

Bta. Barcelona Food Technology Exhibition

Bta.
Barcelona tecnologías
de la alimentación

日期：2012/05 -
地点：西班牙巴塞罗那
内容：国际食品及饮料加工机械、技术及配料行业展会。一个展览，三个行业子展会，涵盖食品加工行业的所有技术。作为一个重要的国际商贸平台，巴塞罗那国际食品、饮料设备及技术展览会通过其三个子展会——Tecnoalimentaria、Tecnocárnica及Ingretecno——为食品和饮料业的各个领域提供机械及中间食品（调料、添加剂、功能性配料）的技术方案。BTA与HISPACK瞄准同样观众群的两大展会联合同期举办，为顾客带来更高价值，同时为食品和饮料界人士提供满足他们生产需求的从配料到包装所有选择：加工机械、中间食品、容器及包装。产品及服务：食品和饮料业各领域的机械和技术、中间产品（调料、添加剂、功能性配料等）后勤，冷藏、清洁、安全、销售的技术应用。
周期：三年一届
市场范围：国际性
性质：面向贸易观众
参展费用：光地展位135-145欧元/m^2＋增值税

赞助：AMEC、ICEX、IRTA、AECOC
主办：西班牙Alimentaria展览公司
联络：励展博览集团国际销售部
地址：北京市朝阳区新源南路1-3号平安国际金融中心A座15层01-03,05 （100027）
☎ 010- 5933 9211
🖷 010- 5933 9233
MSN：ISGCNmarketing@reedexpo.com.cn
www.reedexport.cn
www.bta-bcn.com

巴塞罗那国际食品、饮料设备及技术展

Bta. Barcelona tecnologías de la alimentación

Bta. Barcelona Food Technology Exhibition

日期：2015/ -
地点：西班牙巴塞罗那
内容：国际食品及饮料加工机械、技术及配料行业展会。一个展览，三个行业子展会，涵盖食品加工行业的所有技术。作为一个重要的国际商贸平台，巴塞罗那国际食品、饮料设备及技术展览会通过其三个子展会——Tecnoalimentaria、Tecnocárnica及Ingretecno——为食品和饮料业的各个领域提供机械及中间食品（调料、添加剂、功能性配料）的技术方案。BTA与HISPACK瞄准同样观众群的两大展会联合同期举办，为顾客带来更高价值，同时为食品和饮料界人士提供满足他们生产需求的从配料到包装所有选择：加工机械、中间食品、容器及包装。
产品及服务：食品和饮料业各领域的机械和技术、中间产品（调料、添加剂、功能性配料等）后勤，冷藏、清洁、安全、销售的技术应用。
周期：三年一届
市场范围：国际性
性质：面向贸易观众
参展费用：光地展位135-145欧元/m^2＋增值税
主办：西班牙Alimentaria
联络：励展博览集团国际销售部
地址：北京市朝阳区新源南路1-3号平安国际金融中心A座15层01-03,05 （100027）
☎ 010- 5933 9211
🖷 010- 5933 9233
MSN：ISGCNmarketing@reedexpo.com.cn
www.reedexport.cn
www.bta-bcn.com

斯里兰卡
Sri Lanka

斯里兰卡国际面料及纱线展

JIFS

日期：2011/05/12 - 14
地点：斯里兰卡
联络：上海比天展览服务有限公司
地址：上海市中山北路900号加禾商务中心3号楼303室(200070)
联系人：刘先生
☎ 021-5655 2843
🖷 021-5655 9981
www.betium.com

2011年斯里兰卡汽车及配件展览会

日期：2011/06/23 - 25
地点：斯里兰卡国际会展中心
内容：整车类：汽车、旅游巴士、轿车、商务车、卡车、客货面包车、轻型货车、摩托车、新能源车、电动车、两轮车、单车、农用车、拖拉机、三轮车；汽车零配件产品：汽配产品发动机、传动系配件、转向系配件、制动系配件、电器仪表件、车身及附件、横向件及其他、轮胎、空调系统、电池等；汽车售后维修及其它：检测设备、维修设备、保养用品及设备、工具、汽车影音娱乐、汽车内外饰用品、汽车安全用品、原材料、全球定位系统、润滑油及加油站、保安系统、4S店维修系统建立成套设备与产品。
市场介绍：商业机会有投资、与当地伙伴参与合资公司、与当地企业进行合作、发展代理商，斯里兰卡往印度、巴基斯坦和欧盟的出口，30%的增值可获取PTA、FTA特惠和自由贸易区协议规定的益处。
周期：每年一届
市场范围：国际性
性质：面向公众
主办：中国贸促会建设行业分会/北京中杰城设国际展览有限公司
地址：北京市海淀区紫竹院路31号华澳中心嘉慧苑1703（100089）
联系人：全静
☎ 010-5979 9850转808,13693550328
🖷 010-5885 7468
✉ quanjing@top-fairs.com.cn
MSN：quanjing@top-fairs.com.cn
QQ：602693071
www.build-ccpit.org
www.btfi.cn

瑞典
Sweden

瑞典斯德哥尔摩国际家具展

日期：2011/02/08 - 12
地点：瑞典斯德哥尔摩
☎ 0411-8378 8831
🖷 0411-8378 8830

2011北欧工程机械展暨瑞典哥德堡建筑机械展

日期：2011/03/08 - 11
地点：瑞典哥德堡
内容：建筑机械和设备和建筑技术、运输机械、挖掘机械、装载机和挖掘机、泵浦、起重机械、脚手架和模板、机床和电动工具、测量和检查仪器、信息技术和通讯设备、清洗的设备和尘土过滤器、安全设备和偷窃预防，开凿机，泵，电梯，脚手架，测量设备，清洗设备，吸尘器，电器设备，管道。
始办年份：1983
周期：两年一届
市场范围：国际性
上届规模 2009：展览面积8,760m^2，参展商300家，参观人数11,274人
主办：Svenska Maumlssan Stiftelse
联络：北京麦田通会国际展览有限公司
联系人：吴珊
☎ 010-8248 4014转801, 5165 9302转8005
🖷 010-5165 9302转8004
✉ xiaoxiangzhishui@yahoo.com.cn
MSN：xiaoxiangzhishui@hotmail.com
www.cornfairs.com

瑞士
Switzerland

瑞士日内瓦国际非织造布展览会（index11）

日期：2011/04/12 - 15
地点：瑞士日内瓦
内容：农业、建筑、防护、医疗卫生、交通运输、家居等产业用纺织品、过滤材料、擦拭布类、非织造布卷材以及相关的设备、纤维原料、复合材料、粘合技术、化学品、测试仪器等
主办：欧洲非织造布协会（EDANA）
联络：中国贸促会纺织行业分会
联系人：郭益理
☎ 010-8522 9478，8522 9074
🖷 010-8522 9295

叙利亚
Syria

叙利亚国际家具及木工机械展

日期：2011/04/25 - 29
地点：叙利亚
☎ 0411-8378 8831
🖷 0411-8378 8830

坦桑尼亚
Tanzania

坦桑尼亚国际贸易展览会

DITF

日期：2011/06 -
地点：坦桑尼亚达累斯萨拉姆
周期：每年一届
市场范围：国际性
主办：中国贸促会机械行业分会
地址：北京市西城区三里河路46号（100823）
联系人：张玉惠,郭旭萍,吕春丽
☎ 010-6859 4811, 6859 4994, 6859 4910
🖷 010-6859 4995
✉ zhangyuhui@ccpitmsc.org
www.chinamachine.org.cn

泰国
Thailand

亚洲金属板材展

SHEET METAL ASIA 2011

日期：2011/05/19-22
地点：泰国曼谷国际贸易展览中心
市场范围：国际性
主办：博闻泰国公司
☎ +66(0)2642 6911
🖷 +66(0)2642 6919-20
✉ info@sheetmetal-asia.com
www.sheetmetal-asia.com

SHEET METAL ASIA 2011 -

15th ASEAN's Intl Sheet Metal Fabrication Technology and Machinery Exhibition

Date：2011/05/19-22
Venue: Bangkok International Trade & Exhibition Center, Thailand
Market Area: International
Organizer: UBM Asia (Thailand) Co Ltd
☎ +66(0)2642 6911
🖷 +66(0)2642 6919-20
✉ info@sheetmetal-asia.com
www.sheetmetal-asia.com

专业运输及材料装卸展

LogisPro Thailand

日期：2011/05/19 - 21
地点：泰国曼谷国际贸易展览中心
主办：博闻泰国公司
☎ +66(0)2642 6911
🖷 +66(0)2642 7433
✉ intermach@intermachshow.com
www.intermachshow.com
www.thai-exhibition.com/intermach

LogisPro Thailand

Date：2011/05/12 - 15
Venue: Bangkok Intl Trade & Exhibition Center, Thailand

Organizer: UBM Asia (Thailand) Co Ltd
☎ +66(0)2642 6911
🖷 +66(0)2642 7433
✉ intermach@intermachshow.com
www.intermachshow.com
www.thai-exhibition.com/intermach

国际汽车生产及配件展览会
Automotive Engineering Asia

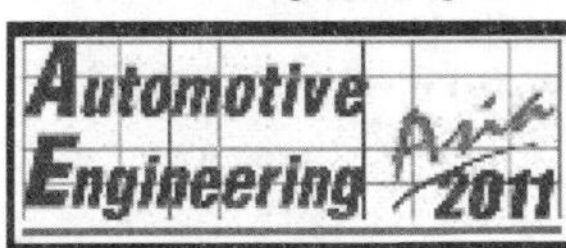

日期：2011/05/19 - 21
地点：泰国曼谷国际贸易展览中心
主办：博闻泰国公司
☎ +66(0)2642 6911
🖷 +66(0)2642 7433
✉ intermach@intermachshow.com
www.intermachshow.com
www.thai-exhibition.com/intermach

Automotive Engineering Asia
Date：2011/05/12 - 15
Venue: Bangkok Intl Trade & Exhibition Center, Thailand
Organizer: UBM Asia (Thailand) Co Ltd
☎ +66(0)2642 6911
🖷 +66(0)2642 7433
✉ intermach@intermachshow.com
www.intermachshow.com
www.thai-exhibition.com/intermach

专业焊接技术及配件工艺贸易展
WeldTech

日期：2011/05/12 - 15
地点：泰国曼谷国际贸易展览中心
主办：博闻泰国公司
☎ +66(0)2642 6911
🖷 +66(0)2642 7433
✉ intermach@intermachshow.com
www.intermachshow.com
www.thai-exhibition.com/intermach

WeldTech
Date：2011/05/12 - 15
Venue: Bangkok Intl Trade & Exhibition Center, Thailand
Organizer: UBM Asia (Thailand) Co Ltd
☎ +66(0)2642 6911
🖷 +66(0)2642 7433
✉ intermach@intermachshow.com
www.intermachshow.com
www.thai-exhibition.com/intermach

机器工具展
工业自动化展
国际专用工具及机械展
MOLDEX IA
Robotics
Machine Tools Thailand

日期：2011/05/12 - 15
地点：泰国曼谷国际贸易展览中心
主办：博闻泰国公司
☎ +66(0)2642 6911
🖷 +66(0)2642 7433
✉ intermach@intermachshow.com
www.intermachshow.com
www.thai-exhibition.com/intermach

MOLDEX IA
Robotics
Machine Tools Thailand
Date：2011/05/12 - 15
Venue: Bangkok Intl Trade & Exhibition Center, Thailand
Organizer: UBM Asia (Thailand) Co Ltd
☎ +66(0)2642 6911
🖷 +66(0)2642 7433
✉ intermach@intermachshow.com
www.intermachshow.com
www.thai-exhibition.com/intermach

国际机器展
Intermach

日期：2011/05/19 - 21
地点：泰国曼谷国际贸易展览中心
主办：博闻泰国公司
☎ +66(0)2642 6911
🖷 +66(0)2642 7433
✉ intermach@intermachshow.com
www.thai-exhibition.com

Intermach
Date：2011/05/19 - 21
Venue: Bangkok International Trade & Exhibition Center, Thailand
Organizer: UBM Asia (Thailand) Co Ltd
☎ +66(0)2642 6911
🖷 +66(0)2642 7433
✉ intermach@intermachshow.com
www.thai-exhibition.com

泰国国际工业转包展
Subcon Thailand

日期：2011/05/19 - 21
地点：泰国曼谷国际贸易展览中心
周期：每年一届
市场范围：国际性
上届规模 2010：展览面积5,000m²
主办：博闻泰国公司
☎ +66(0)2642 6911
🖷 +66(0)2642 6919-20
✉ intermach@intermachshow.com
www.subconthailand.com

Subcon Thailand
Date：2011/05/19 - 21
Venue: Bangkok Intl Trade & Exhibition Center, Thailand
Frequency: Annual
Market Area: International
Statistics 2010: Exhibition Area 5,000m²
Organizer: UBM Asia (Thailand) Co Ltd
☎ +66(0)2642 6911
🖷 +66(0)2642 6919-20
✉ intermach@intermachshow.com
www.subconthailand.com

亚洲世界食品博览会
Thaifex
– World of Food Asia

日期：2011/05/25 - 29
地点：泰国曼谷IMPACT 展览中心
内容：Thaifex亚洲世界食品博览会在泰国成功举办，展会展示了所有食品领域相关的五大块内容，即食品和饮料、食品技术、餐饮、招待、零售和连锁
始办年份：2004
周期：每年一届
市场范围：国际性
性质：面向公众
上届规模 2010：展览面积42,250m², 参展商988家，专业贸易观众21,101人）
主办：科隆展览国际有限公司
地址：北京东三环北路8号亮马河大厦2座1018室（100004）
联系人：潘容
☎ 010-6590 7766 转 715
🖷 010-6590 6139
✉ g.pan@koelnmesse.cn
www.world-of-food.cn

Thaifex
– World of Food Asia
Date：2011/05/25 - 29
Venue: IMPACT, Bangkok, Thailand
Established Year: 2004
Frequency: Annual
Market Area: International
Nature: Open to public
Statistics 2010: Exhibition Area 42,250m², Exhibitors 988，Trade Visitors 21,101
Organizer: KOELNMESSE
Address: Unit 1018, Landmark Tower Ⅱ, No. 8 Dongsanhuan North Rd., Beijing 100004, China
Contact: Grace Pan
☎ 010-6590 7766 ext 715
🖷 010-6590 6139
✉ g.pan@koelnmesse.cn
www.world-of-food.cn

国际环保技术展
Entech Pollutec Asia

日期：2011/06/01 - 04
地点：泰国曼谷国际贸易展览中心
主办：博闻（泰国）公司
☎ +662-642 6911转312
🖷 +662-642 6919-20
✉ Amarin.r@ubm.com
www.entechpollutec-asia.com
www.thai-exhibition.com/intermach

Entech Pollutec Asia

Date：2011/06/01 - 04
Venue: Bangalore Intl Exhibition Center, Thailand
Organizer: UBM Asia (Thailand) Co Ltd
☎ +662 642 6911 ext 312
🖷 +662 642 6919-20
✉ Amarin.r@ubm.com
www.entechpollutec-asia.com
www.thai-exhibition.com/intermach

亚洲再生能源展

Renewable Energy Asia

日期：2011/06/01 - 04
地点：泰国曼谷国际贸易展览中心
主办：博闻（泰国）公司
☎ +662-642 6911转312
🖷 +662-642 6919-20
✉ Amarin.r@ubm.com
www.renewableenergy-asia.com
www.thai-exhibition.com/intermach

Renewable Energy Asia

Date：2011/06/01 - 04
Venue: Bangkok Intl Trade & Exhibition Center, Thailand
Organizer: UBM Asia (Thailand) Co Ltd
☎ +662 642 6911 ext 312
🖷 +662 642 6919-20
✉ Amarin.r@ubm.com
www.renewableenergy-asia.com
www.thai-exhibition.com/intermach

亚洲水泵及阀门展

Pumps & Valves Asia

日期：2011/06/01 - 04
地点：泰国曼谷国际贸易展览中心
市场范围：国际性
主办：博闻（泰国）公司
☎ +662-642 6911转312
🖷 +662-642 6919-20
✉ Amarin.r@ubm.com
www.pumpsandvalves-asia.com
www.thai-exhibition.com/intermach

Pumps & Valves Asia

Date：2011/06/01 - 04
Venue: Bangkok Intl Trade & Exhibition Center, Thailand
Market Area: International
Organizer: UBM Asia (Thailand) Co Ltd
☎ +662 642 6911 ext 312
🖷 +662 642 6919-20
✉ Amarin.r@ubm.com
www.pumpsandvalves-asia.com
www.thai-exhibition.com/intermach

2011年泰国电子展：

国际电子产品制造贸易展及会议

NEPCON Thailand 2011:

The International Electronics Manufacturing Technology Trade Exhibition and Conference

日期：2011/06/23 - 26
地点：泰国曼谷国际贸易展览中心
内容：是国际电子元器件及生产设备展览会(NEPCON)系列展会之一，曾在亚洲8个国家举办。同地举办的展会有泰国国际塑料及橡胶机械展（InterPlas Thailand）即泰国国际塑料和橡胶技术贸易展会及研讨会，泰国国际模具展（InterMold Thailand）即东南亚唯一针对模具生产的机械技术行业展会，泰国国际汽车生产制造展览会（Automotive Manufacturing）即东南亚唯一针对汽车配件制造展会，泰国国际装配技术展（Assembly Technology）即国际自动化制造和装配技术展会
周期：二年一届
市场范围：国际性
性质：面向贸易观众
上届规模 2009：参观人数34,206人
主办：励展泰国公司
联络：励展博览集团国际销售部
地址：北京市朝阳区新源南路1-3号平安国际金融中心A座15层01-03,05（100738）
☎ 010－5933 9206
🖷 010－5933 9233
✉ eric.xue@reedexpo.com.cn
www.reedexport.cn

泰国汽车电子展

Automotive Electronics 2011:

ASEAN's Only Machinery Expo for Automotive Electronics Parts and Components Manufacturing/ Co-located with Automotive Manufacturing 2011

日期：2011/06/23 - 26
地点：泰国曼谷国际会展中心
内容：东南亚地区唯一的汽车电子零部件展会。Automotive Electronics展会同期举办国际装配展（ASSEMBLY）、国际模具展（INTERMOLD）、国际橡胶展（INTERPLAS）、国际汽车展（AUTOMOTIVE）四个主题展会。经过多年精心培育与专业化、国际化运作，目前此展会已成为东南亚规模大、国际性强、影响力大、专业化程度高的知名展会。泰国是东盟成员之一，人口6400万，是东南亚最大的汽车市场，有“东方底特律”之称。汽车巨头均云集于此，投入巨额资金，建立生产线，设立合资厂，使泰国的汽车工业飞速发展。飞速发展的泰国汽车工业，给汽车零配件生产企业及经销商带来了巨大商机，给汽车电子产品的研发与生产 带来勃勃生机。
周期：每年一届
市场范围：国际性
性质：面向贸易观众
参展费用：光地展位280美元/m²，标准展位365美元/m²
主办：励展博览集团国际销售部
地址：北京市朝阳区新源南路1-3号平安国际金融中心A座15层01-03,05（100738）
☎ 010－5933 9206
🖷 010－5933 9233
✉ eric.xue@reedexpo.com.cn
www.reedexport.cn

泰国制造机械展

Manufacturing Expo 2011

ASEAN's #1 Expo on Manufacturing & Processing Technologies

日期：2011/06/23 - 26
地点：泰国曼谷国际贸易展览中心(BITEC)
内容：泰国制造机械展包括InterPlas Thailand、InterMold Thailand、Automotive Manufacturing and Assembly Technology四个部分，分别针对塑料和塑胶、模型和印模、自动化元件、自动化和组装技术等。同时，展会还包括演讲环节、传播业内最新资讯、拓展更多合作机会。
周期：每年一届
市场范围：国际性
性质：面向贸易观众
主办：励展泰国公司（Reed Tradex）
联络：励展博览集团国际销售部
地址：北京市朝阳区新源南路1-3号平安国际金融中心A座15层01-03,05
联系人：薛光
☎ 010-5933 9206
🖷 010-5933 9233
✉ eric.xue@reedexpo.com.cn
www.manufacturing-expo.com

泰国国际模具展

InterMold Thailand 2010

日期：2011/06/23 - 26
地点：泰国曼谷国际贸易展览中心
内容：东南亚唯一针对模具生产的机械技术行业展会。
周期：每年一届
市场范围：国际性
性质：面向贸易观众
主办：励展博览集团国际销售部
地址：北京市朝阳区新源南路1-3号平安国际金融中心A座15层01-03,05（100738）
☎ 010-5933 9206
🖷 010-5933 9233
✉ eric.xue@reedexpo.com.cn
www.reedexport.cn

泰国国际塑料及橡胶机械展

InterPlas Thailand 2011

日期：2011/06/23 - 26
地点：泰国曼谷国际贸易展览中心
内容：泰国国际塑料和橡胶技术贸易展会及研讨会。同期举办泰国国际模具展、泰国国际汽车制造展、泰国国际装配技术展、泰国国际电子产品制造贸易展及会议。
周期：每年一届
市场范围：国际性
性质：面向贸易观众
主办：励展博览集团国际销售部
地址：北京市朝阳区新源南路1-3号平安国际金融中心A座15层01-03,05（100738）
联系人：薛光
☎ 010-5933 9206
🖷 010-5933 9233
✉ eric.xue@reedexpo.com.cn
www.reedexport.cn

泰国国际装配技术展

Assembly Technology 2011:

The Intl Automated Manufacturing & Assembly Technology Exhibition

日期：2011/06/23 - 26
地点：泰国曼谷国际贸易展览中心
内容：泰国国际装配技术展Assembly Technology是泰国唯一的由行业组织的自动化及装配技术展，Assembly Technology是汽车配件和电子配件制造

技术类领域4个国际性展会其中之一。同期展会：泰国国际塑料及橡胶机械展InterPlas Thailand是泰国国际塑料和橡胶技术贸易展会及研讨会，泰国国际模具展InterMold Thailand）是东南亚唯一针对模具生产的机械技术行业展会，泰国国际汽车生产制造展览会Automotive Manufacturing是东南亚唯一针对汽车配件制造技术的展会，及国际工厂自动化技术与设备展览会Factory Automation——国际工厂自动化，电子与电力传输以及物料输送技术展会及研讨会 Fluid Power——国际液压，压缩技术展会及研讨会
周期：每年一届
市场范围：国际性
性质：面向贸易观众
主办：励展泰国公司Tradex
联络：励展博览集团国际销售部
地址：北京市朝阳区新源南路1-3号平安国际金融中心A座15层01-03,05（100738）
☎ 010-5933 9206
🖷 010-5933 9233
✉ eric.xue@reedexpo.com.cn
www.reedexport.cn

泰国国际汽车生产制造展览会

Automotive Manufacturing 2011
- ASEAN's Only Machinery Expo for Automotive Parts Manufacturing

AUTOMOTIVE MANUFACTURING

日期：2011/06/23 - 26
地点：泰国曼谷国际贸易展览中心
内容：是东盟唯一的汽车零部件制造展会，它是在汽车零部件和电子零件制造技术行业中四个国际性展会其中之一。其他展览有泰国国际装配技术展Assembly Technology，致力于展示自动化和组装的前沿技术；泰国国际塑料及橡胶机械展InterPlas Thailand，致力于展示塑料和橡胶前沿生产技术；泰国国际模具展InterMold Thailand，东南亚唯一针对模具生产的机械技术行业展会。
周期：每年一届
市场范围：国际性
性质：面向贸易观众
主办：励展泰国公司
联络：励展博览集团国际销售部
地址：北京市朝阳区新源南路1-3号平安国际金融中心A座15层01-03,05（100738）
☎ 010－5933 9206
🖷 010－5933 9233
✉ eric.xue@reedexpo.com.cn
www.reedexport.cn

亚洲食品加工及包装展

Food Processing and Packaging Asia

日期：2011/09/21 - 23
地点：泰国曼谷Queen Sirikit国家会议中心
主办：亚洲博闻（泰国）公司
☎ +662 642 6911 Ext 313
🖷 +662 642 6919-20
✉ Suchawadee.L@ubm.com
联络：上海博华展览公司
☎ 021-6437 1178转396
🖷 021-6437 0982转396
✉ Flora.in@ubmsioexpo.com
www.fppasia.com

Food Processing and Packaging Asia

Date：2011/09/21 - 23
Venue: Queen Sirikit National Convention Center, , Thailand
Organizer: UBM Asia (Thailand) Co Ltd
☎ +662 642 6911 Ext 313
🖷 +662 642 6919-20
✉ Suchawadee.L@ubm.com
Contact: MS. Flora Ni, Shanghai UBM Sinoexpo Intl Exhibition Co Ltd
☎ +86-21-6437 1178 ext 396
🖷 +86-21-6437 0982 ext 396
✉ Flora.in@ubmsioexpo.com
www.fppasia.com

亚洲国际管材、线材展览会

Tube & Wire Asia

日期：2011/10 -
地点：泰国曼谷
周期：每年两届
主办：中国贸促会机械行业分会
地址：北京市西城区三里河路46号（100823）
联系人：张玉惠, 郭旭萍, 吕春丽
☎ 010-6859 4811, 6859 4994, 6859 4910
🖷 010-68594995
✉ zhangyuhui@ccpitmsc.org
www.chinamachine.org.cn

泰国国际机床和金属加工机械展览会

Thai Metalex

日期：2011/11 -
地点：泰国曼谷
周期：每年一届
主办：中国贸促会
地址：北京市西城区三里河路46号（100823）
联系人：张玉惠, 郭旭萍, 吕春丽
☎ 010-6859 4811, 6859 4994, 6859 4910
🖷 010-6859 4995
✉ zhangyuhui@ccpitmsc.org
www.chinamachine.org.cn

亚洲国际化妆品原料展

in-cosmetics Asia:
The Leading Event in Asia for Personal Care Ingredients

日期：2011/11/02 - 04
地点：泰国曼谷国际会展中心（BITEC）
内容：亚洲国际化妆品原料展是亚洲首个国际性化妆品研发、配方、科技、销售及营销展会。展会涵盖广泛的科技及商业内容，专为配方商和供应商而设计。
产品及服务：磨砂、抗衰老、抗菌、抗脂、去屑、香薰、植物药材、体内/体外临床、润肤剂、乳化剂、去死皮、填料、配方、芳香剂、湿润剂、杂志、生产、营销、微生物学、包装、颜料/色素、防腐剂、肥皂/合成洗涤剂、溶剂、遮光剂、表面活性剂、鞣剂、稠化剂、维他命。
观众来源：研发经理、科学家、配方师、药剂师、销售与营销专家以及来自成品厂商、为成品采购新原料及配料的买家。
参展费用：光地展位320英镑起
上届规模 2010：参展商232家（国外展商31家），参观人数4,691人（国外参观人数1,735 人）
主办：励展英国公司
联络：励展博览集团国际销售部
地址：北京市朝阳区新源南路1-3号平安国际金融中心A座15层01-03,05
联系人：薛光
☎ 010-5933 9206
🖷 010-5933 9233
✉ eric.xue@reedexpo.com.cn
www.reedexport.cn

Furnitech Woodtech 2012

泰国国际木工机械、家具制造机械、零件及相关技术展

日期：2012/06/20 - 23
地点：泰国曼谷国际会展中心
内容：泰国国际木工机械、家具制造机械、零件及相关技术展会及研讨会
周期：三年一届
市场范围：国际性
性质：面向贸易观众
参展费用：光地展位270美元/m², 标准展位340美元/m²
合办：泰国家具工业协会
主办：励展泰国公司
联络：励展博览集团国际销售部
地址：北京市朝阳区新源南路1-3号平安国际金融中心A座15层01-03,05
联系人：薛光
☎ 010－5933 9206
🖷 010－5933 9233
✉ eric.xue@reedexpo.com.cn
www.reedexport.cn
www.furnitechwoodtech.com

GFT 2012

泰国国际服装及纺织品用机械、设备、材料及附件展

Thailand's Intl Presentation of Machinery, Tools & Equipment for Garment & Textile Industries

日期：2012/06/20 - 23
地点：泰国曼谷国际贸易展览中心
内容：泰国国际服装及纺织品用机械、设备、材料及附件展
周期：二年一届
市场范围：面向贸易观众
性质：国际性
主办：励展泰国公司
联络：励展博览集团国际销售部
地址：北京市朝阳区新源南路1-3号平安国际金融中心A座15层01-03,05
联系人：薛光
☎ 010－5933 9206
🖷 010－5933 9233
✉ eric.xue@reedexpo.com.cn
www.reedexport.cn

2013年泰国电子展：

国际电子产品制造贸易展及会议

NEPCON Thailand 2013:
The Intl Electronics Manufacturing Technology Trade Exhibition and Conference

日期：2013/06 -
地点：泰国曼谷国际贸易展览中心
内容：泰国电子展是国际电子元器件及生产设备展览会(NEPCON)系列展会之一，曾在亚洲8个国家举办。同地举办的展会有泰国国际塑料及橡胶机械展InterPlas Thailand，即泰国国际塑料和橡胶技术贸易展会及研讨会，泰国国际模具展InterMold Thailand，即东南亚唯一针对模具生产的机械技术行业展会，泰国国际汽车生产制造展览会Automotive Manufacturing，即东南亚唯一针对汽车配件制造展会，泰国国际装配技术展Assembly Technology，即国际自动化制造和装配技术展会
周期：二年一届

市场范围：国际性
性质：面向贸易观众
主办：励展泰国公司
联络：励展博览集团国际销售部
www.reedexport.cn

土耳其
Turkey

土耳其伊斯坦布尔国际家具展
IMOB2011

日期：2011/02/02 - 06
地点：土耳其伊斯坦布尔
☎ 0411-8378 8831
🖷 0411-8378 8830

土耳其国际工业展览会
WORLD OF INDUSTRY

日期：2011/03/17 - 20
地点：土耳其伊斯坦布尔
周期：每年一届
主办：中国贸促会机械行业分会
地址：北京市西城区三里河路46号（100823）
联系人：张玉惠, 郭旭萍, 吕春丽
☎ 010-6859 4811, 6859 4994, 6859 4910
🖷 010-6859 4995
✉ zhangyuhui@ccpitmsc.org
www.chinamachine.org.cn

土耳其国际汽车制造、销售及维修展览会

日期：2011/04/07 - 11
地点：土耳其伊斯坦布尔
周期：每年两届
主办：中国贸促会
地址：北京市西城区三里河路46号（100823）
联系人：张玉惠, 郭旭萍, 吕春丽
☎ 010-6859 4811, 6859 4994, 6859 4910
🖷 010-6859 4995
✉ zhangyuhui@ccpitmsc.org
www.chinamachine.org.cn

土耳其国际专业纱线展览会
Yarn Fair

日期：2011/05/15 - 18
地点：土耳其
联络：上海比天展览服务有限公司
地址：上海市中山北路900号加禾商务中心3号楼303室(200070)
联系人：刘先生
☎ 021-5655 2843
🖷 021-5655 9981
www.betium.com

土耳其伊斯坦布尔家用纺织品展览会
EVTEKS

日期：2011/05/18 - 22
地点：土耳其伊斯坦布尔CNR会展中心
内容：布艺窗帘、薄纱，窗帘配件，刺绣，装饰纺织品，室内装潢，地毯，毛巾，靠垫，桌布，厨房纺织品，装饰配件，床上用品，卫浴用品，防晒用品，地板、墙面装饰面料、防火材料
始办年份：1985
周期：每年一届
上届规模 2010：展览面积150,000m²，参展商748家（国外展商112家，来自92个国家），参观人数81,300人
主办：德国法兰克福（迪拜）展览公司
地址：浙江省杭州市体育场路229号浙江粮油大厦1202室（310003）
联系人：范传辉 先生
☎ 0571-8577 8500
🖷 571-8577 9709
✉ expo@sinobal.com
http://expo.sinobal.com

联络：上海比天展览服务有限公司
地址：上海市中山北路900号加禾商务中心3号楼303室(200070)
联系人：刘先生
☎ 021-5655 2843
🖷 021-5655 9981
www.betium.com

2011年土耳其家居及厨房用品展览会
AMBIYANS - Household & Kitchenware Fair

日期：2011 /05/18 - 22
地点：土耳其伊斯坦布尔CNR会展中心
内容：家用纺织品：厨房用亚麻制品、厨房用窗帘、厨房用毛巾、围裙、烤箱手套、烹饪用品把手、面包篮、隔热垫、餐桌用亚麻制品；餐桌台布、餐巾、餐桌装饰品；家居、厨房用品类：玻璃制品、塑料制品、有机材料制品、瓷器、陶瓷制品、小型电器、不粘涂层材料制品、银制品、不锈钢制品、铝制品、金属器皿；礼品类：装饰品、纪念品、餐桌附件、餐桌装饰品
周期：每年一届
主办：德国法兰克福（迪拜）展览公司
地址：浙江省杭州市体育场路229号浙江粮油大厦1202室（310003）
联系人：范传辉 先生
☎ 0571-8577 8500
🖷 0571-8577 9709
✉ expo@sinobal.com
http://expo.sinobal.com

中东贸易和伊拉克重建国际工业展览会
EXPO GATEWAY TO MIDDLE EAST

日期：2011/06/02 - 05
地点：土耳其加济安泰普
周期：每年一届
市场范围：国际性
主办：中国贸促会机械行业分会
地址：北京市西城区三里河路46号（100823）
联系人：张玉惠,郭旭萍,吕春丽
☎ 010-6859 4811, 6859 4994, 6859 4910
🖷 010-6859 4995
✉ zhangyuhui@ccpitmsc.org
www.chinamachine.org.cn

土耳其伊斯坦布尔国际服装时尚展览会
Istanbul Fashion Fair

日期：2011/07/29 - 31
地点：土耳其伊斯坦布尔
联络：上海比天展览服务有限公司
地址：上海市中山北路900号加禾商务中心3号楼303室(200070)
联系人：刘先生
☎ 021-5655 2843
🖷 021-5655 9981
www.betium.com

土耳其国际食品包装及食品机械展览会
IPACK

日期：2011/09/22 - 25
地点：土耳其伊斯坦布尔
周期：每年一届
主办：中国贸促会机械行业分会
地址：北京市西城区三里河路46号（100823）
联系人：张玉惠, 郭旭萍, 吕春丽
☎ 010-6859 4811, 6859 4994, 6859 4910
🖷 010-6859 4995
✉ zhangyuhui@ccpitmsc.org
www.chinamachine.org.cn

土耳其伊斯坦布尔国际汽车工业及配件展览会
Otomotive

日期：2011/11/24 - 27
地点：土耳其伊斯坦布尔CNR EXPO
内容：作为土耳其历史最悠久、规模最大的汽车配件展吸引了不少国际品牌汽车和买家。同时该展会已获得UFI国际展会认证。
展品范围：各类车、汽车，配件、组件及零部件GPS导航器、音箱系统和设备、汽车电器，开关、滤清器、汽车修理设备、输油泵，凸轮盘，传动轴，电磁阀等维修保养产品、车轮轮胎、汽车拉索、车内娱乐系统、汽车加工业产品、加油站设备、电池电源、空调制冷系统、汽车装饰产品、电子机械系统、发动机、各种工具、涂料、安全系统等
周期：每年一届
市场范围：国际性
性质：面向公众
上届规模：展览面积45,000m²，参展商857家（国际展商191家），参观人数33,962人
联络：中国贸促会
地址：北京市西城区三里河路46号（100823）
联系人：张玉惠, 郭旭萍, 吕春丽
☎ 010-6859 4811, 6859 4994, 6859 4910
🖷 010-6859 4995
✉ zhangyuhui@ccpitmsc.org
www.chinamachine.org.cn
联络：中国贸促会建设行业分会/北京中杰城设国际展览有限公司
地址：北京市海淀区紫竹院路31号华澳中心嘉慧苑1703室（100089）
联系人：全静
☎ 010-5979 9850转808
🖷 010-5885 7468
✉ quanjing@top-fairs.com.cn
MSN：quanjing@top-fairs.com.cn
QQ：602693071
ww.build-ccpit.org
www.btfi.cn

乌克兰
Ukraine

2011年第19届乌克兰（基辅）国际汽车及零配件展

日期：2011/05/25 - 29
地点：乌克兰展览中心
内容：汽车、摩托整车及摩托配件；运输，配件：汽车零部件、汽车轮胎、汽车通讯、音响电子、安全系统、汽车美容、汽车修理、维护、保养用品等；其它：装饰品、测试测量仪器、维修站设备、喷漆、汽车保险、加油站、技术专业杂志等。

SIA已经成功举办了18届，是乌克兰乃至东欧市场最重要的国际性汽车展，展会规模每年呈现大幅增长态势，SIA2010更是达到供不应求，展览面积达到70000多平方米，全球各大顶级汽车知名厂商均参加了该展，来自中国的奇瑞、长城、GONOW等也亮相该展。有高达60多场的研讨、新车发布会、颁奖会在展会期间举行。

周期：每年一届
市场范围：国际性
性质：面向公众
主办：北京中杰城设国际展览有限公司
地址：北京市海淀区紫竹院路31号华澳中心嘉慧苑1703室（100089）
联系人：全静
☎ 13693550328,010-59799850-808
🖷 01058857468
✉ quanjing@top-fairs.com.cn
MSN：quanjing@top-fairs.com.cn
QQ：602693071
www.build-ccpit.org
www.btfi.cn

乌克兰基辅国际家具展

日期：2011/10 -
地点：乌克兰
☎ 0411-8378 8831
🖷 0411-8378 8830

乌克兰基辅面料纱线展
FTA

日期：2011/10/13 - 16
地点：乌克兰

联络：上海比天展览服务有限公司
地址：上海市中山北路900号加禾商务中心3号楼303室(200070)
联系人：刘先生
☎ 021-5655 2843
🖷 021-5655 9981
www.betium.com

阿联酋
United Arab Emirates

阿布扎比世界未来能源峰会暨新能源与环保展览会
WORLD FUTURE ENERGY SUMMIT

WORLD FUTURE ENERGY SUMMIT

日期：2011/01/17 - 20
地点：阿联酋阿布扎比国家展览中心
ADNEC, United Arab Emirates
内容：ENVIRONMENT 是本地区最重要的展览及会议，关注环保设备、技术和服务部门的综合解决方案。POLLUTEC的主办方、世界最大的环境贸易展会主办机构励展博览集团将依靠其全面的资源拓展ENVIRONMENT展会在未来的规模和展出效率。
始办年份：2001
市场范围：国际性
性质：面向贸易观众
参展费用：光地展位AED 1,100，标准展位AED 1,300/m^2
主办：励展法国公司
联络：励展博览集团国际销售部
地址：北京市朝阳区新源南路1-3号平安国际金融中心A座15层01-03,05
联系人：张志超
☎ 010－5933 9266
🖷 010－5933 9233
✉ ivy.zhang@reedexpo.com.cn
www.reedexport.cn
www.worldfutureenergysummit.com

2011年中东（迪拜）国际秋季商品交易会
2011 IATF

日期：2011/01 -
地点：阿联酋迪拜世界贸易中心
内容：生活用品类、粮油食品类、美容包材类、服装纺织类、五金机电类、皮革鞋帽类、塑料制品类、钟表文具类、礼品玩具类、电子通讯类、石油开采类、五矿化工类、建筑材料类、室内装饰类、汽摩配件类、家电制冷类、医疗保健类、体育用品类等。
周期：每年一届
市场范围：国际性
性质：面向公众
上届规模 2008：展览面积15,750m^2，参展商800家（来自25个国家），参观人数15,000人
主办：Al Fajer展览公司
联络：杭州思诺博会展服务有限公司
地址：杭州市体育场路229号浙江粮油大厦1202室（310003）
☎ 0571-8577 8500
🖷 0571-8577 9709
✉ expo@sinobal.com
www.sinobal.com

阿拉伯管材展览会
Tekno/Tube Arabia

日期：2011/01/08 - 11
地点：阿联酋迪拜
周期：每年两届
主办：中国贸促会机械行业分会
地址：北京市西城区三里河路46号（100823）
联系人：张玉惠，郭旭萍，吕春丽
☎ 010-6859 4811, 6859 4994, 6859 4910
🖷 010-6859 4995
✉ zhangyuhui@ccpitmsc.org
www.chinamachine.org.cn

中东迪拜商业安全及消防器材博览会
2011 Intersec Middle East

日期：2011/01/16 - 18
地点：阿联酋迪拜国际会展中心
内容：商业安全类：门禁设备、警报器、iDVR、闭路电视、监视器、可视出入监控设备、身份识别设备、锁、保险柜、保安服务设备、安防用传感器、声控设备、无线遥控安防用设备；警用装备类：警用交通工具、警用装甲车、警用通讯器材、侦察和排除炸弹设备、警用制服、法庭用设备、生物测定设备、交通控制设备、雷达设备、营救设备、辐射检测和处理设备、武器模拟器、警用路障、毒品侦测设备、X射线检测设备、监控和反监控设备；消防监控类：灭火设备、预警系统、防火系统、疏散设备、灭火器、无线电、瓦斯探测设备、指挥系统、水龙带、急救交通工具、火警用洒水车、环保设备、消防队用设备、火灾演习设备、高压水龙头；工业安全类、空气污染处理设备、废物循环处理设备。

2010年英国、阿联酋、韩国、中国等国家都有组团参展，此次展会共有93家中国企业参展，分布在4个展区内，主要集中在商业安防、消防区内，而劳保及警用产品参展的企业并不多。海湾地区对于全球消防企业来说同样是一个极具挑战的市场，基础设施，建筑和工业部门的投资商们正在不断提高商业和住宅楼宇的消防安全。
周期：每年一届
市场范围：国际性
性质：面向公众
上届规模 2010：参展商710家（来自50个国家），参观人数19,159人
主办：德国法兰克福（迪拜）展览公司
联络：杭州思诺博会展服务有限公司
地址：浙江省杭州市体育场路229号浙江粮油大厦1202室（310003）
联系人：金赛琼小姐
☎ 0571-8577 8500
🖷 0571-8577 9709
✉ expo@sinobal.com

Sweets Middle East

中东（迪拜）国际甜食及休闲食品技术与机械展览会

日期：2012/01/29 – 02/01
地点：阿联酋迪拜
内容：可可，巧克力及巧克力制品，饼干，休闲食品，糖果，零食，烘焙食品，冰激凌及原料
始办年份：2003
周期：每年一届
市场范围：国际性
性质：面向贸易观众
上届规模：展览面积5,000m^2，参展商157家（国外展商184家，来自35个国家），专业贸易观众4,786人
主办：科隆国际展览有限公司
地址：北京市东三环北路8号亮马河大厦2座1018室（100004）
联系人：潘容
☎ 010-6590 7766转ext 715
🖷 010-6590 6139
✉ g.pan@koelnmesse.cn
www.sweetsmiddleeast.com

2011年中东（阿布扎比）国际美容美发博览会
2011 Beauty Vision

日期：2011/02 -
地点：阿联酋阿布扎比国家展览中心
内容：零售：化妆品，香水，美容工具，天然化妆品，护甲、美甲产品，护肤品，美容卫生用品，防晒品，脱毛产品，牙齿美容，时装首饰等；医药：实验室，高级抗老化产品，服务，西药房，药店，营养治疗，美容保养品，保健食品；美发：护发产品，发型装置，美发辅助工具，染发剂，烫发产品，美发沙龙辅助工具，沙龙设计/装置/摆设；原材料：成份，包装，包装材料，标签，装配，原材料，市场推广中介，设计师，咨询师，展示；SPA水疗
周期：每年一届
市场范围：国际性
性质：面向公众
主办：Channels Exhibitions
联络：杭州思诺博会展服务有限公司
地址：杭州市体育场路229号浙江粮油大厦1202室（310003）
☎ 0571-8577 8500
🖷 0571-8577 9709
✉ expo@sinobal.com
www.sinobal.com

2011年中东（迪拜）海湾食品展览会
2011 Gulfood

日期：2011/02 -
地点：阿联酋迪拜国际会展中心
内容：食品及饮料：食品添加剂，罐装食品，食品加工技术，酒精饮品，无酒精饮料，海洋食品，烘焙食品，糖食及糖果加工技术，冷冻食品，冷藏食品，奶制品，咖啡及茶，肉食产品，家禽食品，清真食品，保健食品，方便食品；酒店设备：公共饮食业产品，厨房设备，冷藏设施，酒店设备，酒店供给产品及服务，餐饮服务及产品，餐具及配件，酒店家具；机械设备及技术：食品加工机械及技术，食品包装机械，译码器及度量设备等。
始办年份：1987
周期：每年一届
市场范围：国际性
性质：面向公众
上届规模 2009：展览面积20,494m^2，参展商3000家（来自70个国家），参观人数40,000人
主办：阿联酋迪拜世界贸易中心
联络：杭州思诺博会展服务有限公司
地址：杭州市体育场路229号浙江粮油大厦1202室（310003）
联系人：展览部
☎ 0571-8577 8500
🖷 0571-8577 9709
✉ expo@sinobal.com
www.sinobal.com

2011 年法兰克福中东（迪拜）国际玩具及文具用品展览会
2011 Toy Fair Middle East

日期：2011/03 -
地点：阿联酋迪拜国际会展中心
内容：玩具：自行车，童车，滑板车，电动玩具，填充玩具，木制玩具，益智玩具，模型玩具，动漫产品，玩具乐器，气球，洋娃娃，户外游戏设备，游戏机，糖果和软饮料；文具及学校用品：黑白板，书籍，计算器，教学设备，橡皮，文件夹，胶水，标签，礼品，铅笔，纸，钢笔，尺，剪刀，CD，磁带，书包，校服，便签等；婴幼儿用品。
周期：每年一届
市场范围：国际性
性质：面向公众
上届规模 2009：参展商101家（来自30个国家），参观人数3,234人
主办：德国法兰克福（迪拜）展览公司
联络：杭州思诺博会展服务有限公司
地址：杭州市体育场路229号浙江粮油大厦1202室（310003）
☎ 0571-8577 8500
🖷 0571-8577 9709
✉ expo@sinobal.com
www.sinobal.com

2011年中东国际商用车及零配件展览会
Commercial Vehicle Middle East

日期：2011/03/14 - 16
地点：阿联酋迪拜国际会展中心
内容：是中东及北非地区唯一以巴士，卡车，消防车，警车等商用车及其零配件为主题的专业展会。整个展会将包括各类型的商用车如客车、货车、挂车、摩托车、重型及轻型商用车，以及此行业相关产品、服务、工艺（信息技术处理，燃料，支持维护，金融服务）。此外，座谈会内容涉及到商用车的关键领域如车队管理、绿色交通、商用车维护、人力资源管理、金融以及安全措施等。
周期：每年一届
市场范围：国际性
性质：面向公众
主办：SMG展览公司
联络：杭州思诺博会展服务有限公司
地址：浙江省杭州市体育场路229号浙江粮油大厦1202室（310003）
联系人：金赛琼小姐
☎ 0571-8577 8500
🖷 0571-8577 9709
✉ expo@sinobal.com
www.sinobal.com
主办：北京麦田通会国际展览有限公司
联系人：吴珊
☎ 010-8248 4014转801, 5165 9302转8005
🖷 010-5165 9302转8004
✉ xiaoxiangzhishui@yahoo.com.cn
MSN：xiaoxiangzhishui@hotmail.com
www.cornfairs.com

世界城市可持续发展论坛
The International Forum for Urban Decision-Makers

日期：2011/03/15 - 18
地点：阿联酋阿布扎比酋长国宫殿酒店
Venue: Emirates Palace, Abu Dhabi, United Arab Emirates
内容：会见来自250多个城市的1,000多位重要决策者，从公私合营组织中发掘显著成果，扩展国际城市之间的联系网络，分析适用于国际城市的创新解决方案，对比众多城市的发展战略模式，同行业之间进行经验及方法交流，就城市可持续发展问题发表演讲。
主办：励展中东公司（阿联酋）
联络：励展博览集团国际销售部
联系人：吴祥
☎ 010-5933 9268
🖷 010-5933 9233
✉ ronald.wu@reedexpo.com.cn
www.globalcityforum.com

中东阿布扎比国际家具展

日期：2011/03/28 - 30
地点：阿联酋
☎ 0411-8378 8831
🖷 0411-8378 8830

迪拜纺织服装面辅料展
Motexha

日期：2011/03/29 - 31
地点：阿联酋迪拜
联络：上海比天展览服务有限公司
地址：上海市中山北路900号加禾商务中心3号楼303室(200070)
联系人：刘先生
☎ 021-5655 2843
🖷 021-5655 9981
www.betium.com

2011年中东（迪拜）国际服装、纺织、鞋类及皮革制品博览会
2011 Motexha

日期：2011/04 -
地点：阿联酋迪拜国际会展中心
内容：服装及面料类：男女服装、运动休闲服装、童装、劳保服装、纺织工艺、服装饰品（领带、围巾、胸针等）、各种面料、棉麻织品、针织品、纺织制品、纺织机械、家用纺织品、床上用品、裘皮制品；辅料及配件：拉链、纽扣、衬布及辅料；各类鞋、皮革产品
始办年份：1978
周期：每年一届
市场范围：国际性
性质：面向公众
上届规模 2008：展览面积2,748m²，参展商200家（来自24个国家），参观人数3300人
主办：IIR展览公司
联络：杭州思诺博会展服务有限公司
地址：杭州市体育场路229号浙江粮油大厦1202室（310003）
☎ 0571-8577 8500
🖷 0571-8577 9709
✉ expo@sinobal.com
www.sinobal.com

2011年中东（阿布扎比）国际食品及饮料展览会
2011 Middle East Food

日期：2011/04 -
地点：阿联酋阿布扎比国家展览中心
内容：食品及饮料：特色食品、精美食品、冷冻食品、肉类、伊斯兰食品、乳制品、未加工食品、罐头食品/加工食品、海产品、（非酒精）饮料及咖啡；食品原料：抗氧化剂、生理活性成份、膨松剂、添加剂、补给品、食用油及食用脂肪、草药/香料及原料、乳酸菌、营养物、防腐剂、蛋白质、维他命及矿物；甜食巧克力及糕点；有机健康食品；食品处理、包装及机械；餐饮技术及设备：酒店及餐馆设备、烹饪及厨房设备、冷冻设备、食品照明、售卖设备、专营/零售店设备等。
周期：每年一届
市场范围：国际性
性质：面向公众
主办：Channels Exhibitions
联络：杭州思诺博会展服务有限公司
地址：杭州市体育场路229号浙江粮油大厦1202室（310003）
☎ 0571-8577 8500
🖷 0571-8577 9709
✉ expo@sinobal.com
www.sinobal.com

2011年中东迪拜国际乐器、舞台灯光及舞台音响技术展览会
2011 PALME Middle East

日期：2011/04 -
地点：阿联酋迪拜国际会展中心
内容：小型乐器：弦乐器、铜乐器、口风琴、敲击乐器、木管乐器 大型乐器：钢琴、键盘乐器、教堂管风琴、古典键盘乐器 电子乐器：键盘、合成乐器、数字钢琴、电子鼓、电吉他/贝斯 专业音效及录音设备：舞台工程技术、舞台灯光、激光技术、专业音响、载声设备、功放、卡拉OK系统、麦克风与配件、公共广播系统、录音与重制设备、混音桌与箱架、配件等 乐器配件与乐器用家具 音乐出版品与专业刊物
周期：每年一届
市场范围：国际性
性质：面向公众
上届规模 2009：展览面积5,369m²，参展商162家
主办：英国IIR展览公司
联络：杭州思诺博会展服务有限公司
地址：杭州市体育场路229号浙江粮油大厦1202室（310003）
☎ 0571-8577 8500
🖷 0571-8577 9709
✉ expo@sinobal.com
www.sinobal.com

2011年中东（迪拜）国际地面铺装展览会
2011 DOMOTEX Middle East

日期：2011/05 -
地点：阿联酋迪拜国际会展中心
内容：地板：实木地板、强化复合木地板、实木复合地板、竹地板、集成材地板、软木地板、各种人造板材等；地毯：纯毛地毯、混纺地毯、化纤地毯、塑料地毯及各种地垫、门垫、浴室垫；地砖：釉面砖、通体砖、大理石、花岗岩、毛石、各种复合地材等；塑料地面材料：地板砖、地板革、PVC板材、工程用或特种用塑料地铺；地面材料配件、耗材及铺盖技术：衬垫、模具、安装工具、清洁设备、粘合剂、装饰用品等；地面装饰材料及地毯的加工制造机械设备；地面材料的图案设计及印制。
周期：每年一届
上届规模 2009：展览面积12,000m²，参展商280家（来自26个国家），参观人数6,000人
主办：德国博览会集团公司
联络：杭州思诺博会展服务有限公司
地址：杭州市体育场路229号浙江粮油大厦1202室（310003）
☎ 0571-8577 8500
🖷 0571-8577 9709
✉ expo@sinobal.com
www.sinobal.com

迪拜国际铝工业展
Gateway to the Middle East's Aluminium Industry

日期：2011/05/09 - 11
地点：阿联酋迪拜国际会议展览中心
Dubai Intl Convention and Exhibition Center, Dubai, United Arab Emirates
内容：2011年迪拜中东国际铝工业展览会特别将产品做如下分类：原材料，主要金属产品，半成品，半成品制作，特殊用途铝产品，表面处理，轻金属贸易与回收，铝材生产厂房、机械、零件及设备 提取、加工与提炼，服务与咨询，信息、教育及其它
始办年份：2009
周期：两年一届
性质：面向贸易观众
上届规模 2009：展览面积3,015m²，参展商165家，参观人数3,087人
主办：励展巴西公司Alcantara Machado
联络：励展博览集团国际销售部
联系人：王颖
☎ 010-5933 9208
🖷 010-5933 9233
✉ winnie.wang@reedexpo.com.cn
www.aluminium-dubai.com

2011年法兰克福中东（迪拜）国际五金工具展览会（第12届）
Hardware and Tools Middle East

日期：2011/05/10 - 12
地点：阿联酋迪拜世界贸易中心
内容：工具类：电动工具，手动工具，刀具，测量工具、气动工具和配件，液压工具及配件，焊接工具；五金类：建筑五金（门窗五金，锁具），装修耗材（螺丝钉，粘贴剂，密封剂，油漆涂料），建筑装饰材料（金属材料，楼梯/脚手架，塑料橡胶材料，木材）；机械类：木工机械，机械零配件，切割工具，摸具，钻孔机，所有厂房机械。
简介：中东地区规模最大的五金制品专业展览会。展会旨在为阿拉伯和中东地区五金工业提供一个交流探讨、磋商贸易的平台，促进当地市场的发展。
周期：每年一届
市场范围：国际性
性质：面向公众

上届规模 2010：展览面积8,000m²，参展商320家（来自16个国家），参观人数4,301人
主办：德国法兰克福（迪拜）展览公司
联络：杭州思诺博会展服务有限公司
联系人：汪霞小姐，吴蕾小姐
☎ 0571-8577 8500, 8577 8537
🖷 0571-8577 9709
✉ expo@sinobal.com
http://expo.sinobal.com

法兰克福中东（迪拜）国际园艺及户外休闲用品展览会

Garden and Landscaping Middle East

日期：2011 /05/10 - 2011-05-12
地点：阿联酋迪拜世界贸易中心
内容：户外休闲，运动用品，罐锅等野炊器皿，烧烤架等烧烤用具，园林建筑和灌溉系统游泳池及相关的产品，池塘喷泉，园林工具设备，植物养护设备，肥料等
周期：每年一届
上届规模 2010：参展商162家，参观人数3,500人
主办：德国法兰克福（迪拜）展览公司
地址：浙江省杭州市体育场路229号浙江粮油大厦1202室（310003）
联系人：汪霞
☎ 0571-8577 8500
🖷 0571-8577 9709
✉ expo@sinobal.com
http://expo.sinobal.com

2011年第十一届中东（迪拜）眼镜眼科用品展

Vision-X Dubai

日期：2011/05/24 - 26
地点：阿联酋迪拜世贸中心展览馆
内容：各种光学眼镜、太阳镜、运动用和防护类眼镜产品、眼用消费品和护眼产品、眼镜镜片、框架、配件、人造眼、观景镜头和透镜用织物、镜片镜头切割设备、眼镜器械和设备、眼科外科设备、诊断设备和器械、折光仪器和设备，视轴矫正设备、眼镜展示架等。
简介：中东地区唯一的眼镜眼科类产品行业盛会，同时也是中东地区最大、最具影响力的行业展会之一。参展产品中70%展品为眼镜产品，30%为光学仪器等产品。
周期：每年一届
市场范围：国际性
性质：面向公众
上届规模 2010：展览面积6,000m²，参展商120家（来自20个国家），参观人数3,297人
主办：德国法兰克福（迪拜）展览公司
联络：杭州思诺博会展服务有限公司
地址：浙江省杭州市体育场路229号浙江粮油大厦1202室（310003）
联系人：范传辉，吴蕾小姐
☎ 0571-8577 9914, 8577 8537
🖷 0571-8577 9709
✉ expo@sinobal.com
http://expo.sinobal.com

2011法兰克福中东（迪拜）国际美容展览会

Beautyworld Middle East

日期：2011/05/24 - 26
地点：阿联酋迪拜世界贸易中心
内容：化妆品、护肤品、香水香熏、护发产品、防晒产品；疗养沙龙设备用具、美发沙龙配件设备、美容沙龙用具及设备、美容治疗仪、皮肤护理设备、水治疗设备、植发设备、健身房设备、健身器材、超声波按摩器；美体用品、指甲护理及修脸产品、理发工具、口腔护理品、假发、发饰等有关产品；美容产品包装。
简介：中东地区规模最大、最专业、效果最好的美容展会，在美容产品及专业知识方面的交流是整个中东地区相关美容展会的精华。
始办年份：1996
周期：每年一届
市场范围：国际性
性质：面向公众
上届规模 2010：展览面积24,228m²，参展商709家（来自41个国家），参观人数16,124人
主办：德国法兰克福（迪拜）展览公司
联络：杭州思诺博会展服务有限公司
联系人：汪霞
☎ 0571-8577 8500
🖷 0571-8577 9709
✉ expo@sinobal.com
http://expo.sinobal.com

迪拜机场设备展览会

Airport Show Dubai 2011

日期：2011/05/31 - 02
地点：阿联酋迪拜航空会展中心
内容：中东地区专注于机场建设、发展及运营的重要展会。展示新建及现有机场建造及供应的方方面面，如行李操作、雷达系统、机场内部设施及建筑供应。2008年为促使迪拜机场设备展会的不断壮大，将2007年成功举办的会议项目发展成为独立并相互关联的展示区域：中东航空安全展示、中东地勤服务安全展示及中东交通控制展示。2009年主办方计划增加新的会议项目及垂直展示体系。将维护、修理及操作纳入这一体系将具有非常重要的战略意义，在加燃料、服务、特许权经营方面也具有同等意义。
产品及服务：迪拜机场设备展览会为机场设备制造商及供应商与各领先航空公司提供面对面的交流机会。机场设计与建造—规划、设计与建筑、建造、建筑材料。机场供应—行李运输、客运、内部机场终端 机场运营—维护、管理及服务、航行服务 技术—信息技术/软件、灯光、乘客信息、技术装置及体系 地面支持设备—飞行操作、行李推车（托车、货物装载机、ULD），客梯、多用途车、饮食装备 安全—准入及周界控制、CCTV及监控体系、X-光及探测体系、安全培训及咨询 航空管理及控制体系—ATC塔/移动控制塔、通讯及数据处理系统、控制台及围护结构、着陆体系及航空急救
始办年份：2001
周期：每年一届
市场范围：国际性
性质：面向贸易观众
上届规模 2010：展览面积4,750m²，参展商222家，参观人数4,749人
主办：励展博览集团国际销售部
地址：北京市朝阳区新源南路1-3号平安国际金融中心A座15层01-03,05
联系人：宫卫
☎ 010-5933 9268
🖷 010-5933 9233
✉ david.gong@reedexpo.com.cn
www.reedexport.cn

迪拜国际运输及物流展

SITL Dubai: International Week of Transport & Logistics

日期：2011/06/05 - 07
地点：阿联酋迪拜国际会展中心（Airport Expo）
内容：中东的独特理念 迪拜国际运输及物流展（SITL Dubai），特别针对国际和国内市场的船运、航运和物流服务供应商，为采购，分销和供应市场提供一个平台，展示宣传他们的创新产品和服务。独特的一流展会将在世界上最有活力的新兴市场之一阿联酋举行 为亚洲、欧洲、中东和北非建立的物流和运输市场的业内创新平台 买家计划和SITL商业投资论坛吸引了世界知名专家、决策人和货运公司 全球货运论坛让参展者了解更多市场前景和业内潮流 产品及服务 交通物流服务、物流运输及物流服务、物流基础设施、产业特性、运输&物流技术及信息系统
始办年份：2009
周期：两年一届
参展费用：光地展位1,835 AED，标准展位2,085 AED
主办：励展中东公司（阿联酋）
联络：励展博览集团国际销售公司
地址：北京市朝阳区新源南路1-3号平安国际金融中心A座15层01-03,05
联系人：宫卫
☎ 010-5933 9268
🖷 010-5933 9233
✉ david.gong@reedexpo.com.cn
www.sitldubai.com

2011年中东（迪拜）国际汽车零配件及售后服务展览会

Automechanika Middle East

日期：2011/06/07 - 09
地点：阿联酋迪拜国际会展中心
内容：汽车部件和装置：驱动零配件、底盘、车身、汽车电池、内部装置及元件、汽车动力和电子控制系统；汽车配件和改装车：车辆配件、特殊装备、改装车、性能试验系统、设计改进、赛车部件；汽车维修和保养：车辆服务和维修装置、车体维修、车体彩绘、车库建设和管理；服务站和清洗站、清洗装备。
简介：世界规模最大的汽车零件配件系列展AUTOMECHANIKA全球巡回展之一，每届展会都吸引了大批来自世界各地的汽车配件生产企业的参展商和中东地区的采购商。
周期：每年一届
市场范围：国际性
性质：面向公众
上届规模 2009：参展商1,007家（来自46个国家），参观人数16,058人
主办：德国法兰克福（迪拜）展览公司
联络：杭州思诺博会展服务有限公司
地址：浙江省杭州市体育场路229号浙江粮油大厦1202室（310003）
联系人：金赛琼
☎ 0571-8577 9623
🖷 0571-8577 9709
✉ expo@sinobal.com
http://expo.sinobal.com

2011年迪拜国际地面铺装展览会

DOMOTEX MIDDLE EAST

日期：2011/09/12 - 14
地点：阿联酋迪拜国际会展中心
内容：Domotex系列展会是地毯行业最有影响力的，是MENA（中东北非）地区唯一一个受到国际公认的地面装饰和地毯展。范围有地板：实木地板、强化复合木地板、实木复合地板、竹地板、集成材地板、软木地板、各种人造板材；地毯：纯毛地毯、混纺地毯、化纤地毯、塑料地毯及各种地垫、门垫、浴室垫；地砖：釉面砖、通体砖、大理石、花岗岩、毛石、各种复合地材；塑料地面材料：地板砖、地板革、PVC板材、工程用或特种用塑料地铺；地面材料配件、耗材及铺盖技术、地面装饰材料及地毯的加工制造机械设备、地面材料的图案设计及印制。
始办年份：2005
周期：每年一届
市场范围：国际性
性质：面向公众
上届规模 2010：参展商178家（来自34个国家），参观人数4,864人
主办：德国博览会集团公司
联络：杭州思诺博会展服务有限公司
地址：浙江省杭州市体育场路229号浙江粮油大厦1202室（310003）
联系人：范传辉，汪霞小姐

☎ 0571-8577 8500
🖷 0571-8577 9709
✉ expo@sinobal.com
www.sinobal.com

2011年法兰克福中东（迪拜）国际物流展览会

Materials Handling + Logistics Middle East

日期： 2011 /09/25 - 2011-09-27
地点： 阿联酋迪拜国际会展中心
内容： 多式货运设备、系统、技术和服务，起重机，吊车，传送系统，入库和仓储设备、系统、技术和服务，港口、机场和码头设备、系统、技术和服务，运输和后勤、包装、免税区设备、系统、技术和服务，港口、机场、码头和免税区,货运、货物和快递公司，海运和航线，商业交通工具，免税区，保险，清洁设备，叉车，仓库车，称（量重）设备，存储系统，货垫和货垫系统、安全系统
周期： 每年两届
上届规模 2010：参展商175家（来自27个国家），参观人数6805人
主办： 德国法兰克福（迪拜）展览公司
地址： 浙江省杭州市体育场路229号浙江粮油大厦1202室（310003）
联系人： 范传辉 先生
☎ 0571-8577 8500
🖷 0571-8577 9709
✉ expo@sinobal.com
http://expo.sinobal.com

第21届中东迪拜国际家具展

INDEX2011

日期： 2011/10/20 - 23
地点： 阿联酋迪拜
☎ 0411-8378 8831
🖷 0411-8378 8830

中东（迪拜）国际城市、建筑和商业照明展览会

Light Middle East

日期： 2011/10/31 - 02
地点： 阿联酋迪拜国际会展中心
内容： 建筑照明自动化、便携式及普通荧光灯、装饰灯具、展示技术、景观照明、白炽灯和卤素灯、室内照明、智能化控制、LED、照明电子、照明控制&解决方案、照明器、多房间解决方案、光学、室外照明、剧院灯光、滨水区照明
简介： 此展是法兰克福展览公司最知名的品牌展会之一，同时也是世界建筑灯饰照明行业里规模最大、最具权威的专业展会之一。
周期： 每年一届
市场范围： 国际性
性质： 面向公众
上届规模 2010：展览面积910m²，参展商228家，参观人数15109人
主办： 德国法兰克福（迪拜）展览公司
联络： 杭州思诺博会展服务有限公司
地址： 浙江省杭州市体育场路229号浙江粮油大厦1202室（310003）
联系人： 范传辉先生
☎ 0571-8577 8500
🖷 0571-8577 9709
✉ expo@sinobal.com
http://expo.sinobal.com

2011中东五大行业展览会

BIG 5

日期： 2011/11/21 - 24
地点： 阿联酋迪拜世贸中心
内容： 制冷、暖通，电力，水处理，消防及安全防护，通讯设备，厨房卫浴， 木门及木制品，五金，玻璃，铝塑板，油漆及涂料，门窗，水泵，游泳池设备及配套，建筑设配，基础设施，绿色建材， 大理石及陶瓷区，石材区，综合区
简介： 中东地区最大的建筑、建材及服务类展览会。
始办年份： 1980
周期： 两年一届
市场范围： 国际性
性质： 面向公众
上届规模 2009：展览面积45,198m²，参展商3,143家（来自71个国家）
联络： 杭州思诺博会展服务有限公司
地址： 浙江省杭州市体育场路229号浙江粮油大厦1202室（310003）
联系人： 范传辉
☎ 0571-8577 8500
🖷 0571-8577 9709
✉ expo@sinobal.com
www.sinobal.com

中东国际酒店及餐饮设备展

Equip'Hotel Middle East:

Hotel, Restaurant, Café and Catering Exhibition

EQUIP'HOTEL MIDDLE EAST

日期： 2011/12 -
地点： 阿联酋阿布扎比国家展览中心
内容： 中东国际酒店及餐饮设备展是中东地区唯一展示酒店餐饮业的所有产品、服务、概念及技术的展会。
产品及服务： 150多家展商将展览以下领域的产品：Spa、健身与康乐、浴室，建筑布局及装置，咖啡制作及酒吧设备，食品与饮料，装修与设计，舒适设施，厨房设备及材料，洗衣房、卫生及清洁，织物及职业装 餐馆与酒店概念，声效与灯光，餐具，技术，售货。
观众来源： 展会主要吸引来自阿布扎比、迪拜、其它酋长国及其它海湾国家（科威特、巴林、卡塔尔、阿曼、沙特阿拉伯等国）的关键买家：国际及当地酒店集团，建筑师、室内设计师，工程师、设计及规划部门，分销商、代理商、进口商、批发商，酒店公寓，餐馆及餐饮运营商，当地及国际厨师 当地机构（健康、教育、政府），投资者。
参展费用： 标准展位AED 1,435，光地展位AED 1,250
赞助： 阿布扎比旅游局及阿联酋合德航空公司（Etihad Airways）
主办： 励展中东公司（阿联酋）
联络： 励展博览集团国际销售部
地址： 北京市朝阳区新源南路1-3号平安国际金融中心A座15层01-03,05
联系人： 宫卫
☎ 010-5933 9268
🖷 010-5933 9233
✉ david.gong@reedexpo.com.cn
www.equiphotelme.com

第25届中东（迪拜）国际秋季商品交易会

International Autumn Trade Fair

日期： 2011/12/13 - 15
地点： 阿联酋迪拜世界贸易中心
内容： 生活用品类、粮油食品类、美容包材类、服装纺织类、五金机电类、皮革鞋帽类、塑料制品类、钟表文具类、礼品玩具类、电子通讯类、石油开采类、五矿化工类、建筑材料类、室内装饰类、汽摩配件类、家电制冷类、医疗保健类、体育用品类等。
简介： 海湾地区最有影响力的年度综合展览盛会，通过国际博览会联盟（UFI）认证，随着每年出席人数的稳定增长，迪拜秋交会已经成为一个最富活力的展览贸易交易平台。
始办年份： 1986
周期： 每年一届
市场范围： 国际性
性质： 面向公众
上届规模 2009：展览面积13,000m²，参展商600家（来自20个国家）
主办： Al Fajer展览公司
联系人： 汪霞
☎ 0571-8577 8500
🖷 0571-8577 9709
✉ expo@sinobal.com

阿布扎比国际反恐安全展览会

ISNR (Abu Dhabi) International Security & National Resilience

日期： 2012/03/04 – 06
地点： 阿联酋阿布扎比国家展览中心
内容： 国际反恐安全展览会（ISNR）是独特而及时的一次盛事，展示有效保护国土与对抗国际恐怖主义所需的尖端器械。ISNR是唯一涵盖整个国土安全领域的展会。四天的研讨会及展览将为主要行业商家提供讨论以下相关最新技术方案的独特平台：情报侦察与威胁防范，国界安防及运输安防，反恐，重要基础设施防卫，危机管理，应急准备及救援。
展品范围： 展会是体验国际安保业最新技术的绝好机会。最新安保方法与政策、重要安保课程、最新安保方案与战略
周期： 两年一届
市场范围： 国际性
性质： 面向贸易观众
参展费用： 光地展位355美元/m²，标准展位400美元/m²
主办： 励展中东公司
联络： 励展博览集团国际销售部
地址： 北京市朝阳区新源南路1-3号平安国际金融中心A座15层01-03,05 （100027）
☎ 010-5933 9211
🖷 010-5933 9233
✉ ISGCNmarketing@reedexpo.com.cn
www.reedexport.cn
www.isnrabudhabi.com

阿布扎比国际汽车展览会

Abu Dhabi International Motor Show

日期： 2012/12 -
地点： 阿联酋阿布扎比国家展览中心
内容： 中东地区最大且最全面的汽车展览会。展览场地包括室内和户外，展商在展会上展示豪华车、高性能车、个性特制车、箱式轿车、概念混合动力汽车、运动车、越野车、家庭房车及运动型多用途汽车(SUVs)、摩托车和沙滩车以及商务车型，比如卡车，厢型车和迷你车、豪华客车、豪华轿车、拖车和宿营房车。同时，展会还为您带来汽车配件和自动设备。展会拥有最新车型，中东首发、超级车和概念车。
产品及服务： 汽车类：豪华轿车，高性能名车，个性特制车，高级轿车，概念混合动力汽车，运动车，四驱越野车，家庭房车及运动型多用途汽车(SUVs)，摩托车，沙滩车(quad bikes) 商务用车：敞篷小型载货卡车，货车及中巴车，豪华长途客车，豪华轿车，拖车及宿营房车 其他相关汽车服务：车库及修理公司，保险公司，汽车金融公司，汽车维修公司，维护设备，汽车媒体
周期： 两年一届
市场范围： 国际性
性质： 面向贸易观众
参展费用： 光地展位840迪拉姆/m²，标准展位1,010迪拉姆/m²
主办： 励展中东公司（阿联酋）
联络： 励展博览集团国际销售部
地址： 北京市朝阳区新源南路1-3号平安国际金融中心A座15层01-03,05 （100027）
☎ 010-5933 9211
🖷 010-5933 9233
✉ ISGCNmarketing@reedexpo.com.cn
www.reedexport.cn

2013年迪拜中东国际铝工业展览会

ALUMINIUM Dubai 2013

日期： 2013 -
地点： 阿联酋迪拜国际会议展览中心
内容： 本届展会将引入可以促进本地区铝业发展的新产品、新设备、新技术与新投资。其中包括许多

主流技术，例如：铝材挤压成型技术、铸造与热处理技术，冶炼技术，厂房工程和建筑类技术等。另外还有应用于建筑、交通、机电工程、工厂设备、包装容器生产、设计专用工具等方面的产品。此外，除了吸引了本地区已有的和新兴的铝业企业外，迪拜铝业展还吸引了世界各地杰出的铝业公司前来参展。
周期：两年一届
市场范围：国际性
性质：面向贸易观众
主办：励展中东公司
联络：励展博览集团国际销售部
地址：北京市朝阳区新源南路1-3号平安国际金融中心A座15层01-03,05（100027）
☎ 010-5933 9211
🖷 010-5933 9233
✉ ISGCNmarketing@reedexpo.com.cn
www.reedexport.cn
www.aluminium-dubai.com

英国 United Kingdom

英国伯明翰国际家具、灯具及室内装饰品展

日期：2011/01/23 - 26
地点：英国
☎ 0411-8378 8831
🖷 0411-8378 8830

英国酒店用品展
Hospitality

日期：2011/01/24 - 26
地点：英国伯明翰国家展览中心
National Exhibition Center, United Kingdom
内容：为食品服务商和整个酒店行业提供产品及服务的生产商、供应商和分销商，包括餐饮设备、食品、饮料、内部装修、餐桌、Hostec Marketplace技术
参展费用：光地展位252英镑，标准展位307英镑
上届规模 2007：展览面积6,114m²，参展商321家（国外展商31家），参观人数13,531人
主办：英国Fresh RM
联络：励展博览集团国际销售部
联系人：宫卫
☎ 010-5933 9268
🖷 010-5933 9233
✉ david.gong@reedexpo.com.cn
www.hospitalityshow.co.uk
www.reedexport.cn

英国食品、饮料包装机械、设备展览会
Pro2Pac:
Processing & Packaging Solutions Event, Exclusively for the Food & Drink Industry

日期：2011/03/13 - 16
地点：英国伦敦ExCeL会展中心
ExCeL, London, United Kingdom
内容：唯一一个专为食品和饮料行业提供包装机械、设备的展会，Pro2Pac将与英国最大的食品饮料展IFE——英国国际食品和饮料展同期举办，两个展会将带领大家全方位地透视食品和饮料行业。产品与服务有包装设备，机械，系统，技术，服务及原料。
周期：两年一届
参展费用：光地展位230英镑/m²，标准展位274英镑/m²
上届规模 2009：展览面积1,850m²，参展商111家（国外展商11家），参观人数1598人
主办：励展英国公司
联络：励展博览集团国际销售部
联系人：杜一鸣
☎ 010-5933 9209
🖷 010-5933 9233
✉ martin.du@reedexpo.com.cn
www.reedexport.cn

英国国际食品和饮料展
IFE：International Food & Drink Event

日期：2011/03/13 - 16
地点：英国伦敦ExCel 会展中心
ExCeL, London, United Kingdom
内容：英国国际食品和饮料展（IFE）汇集了全球范围内食品和饮料行业创新产品。本地和国际观众不仅可以率先体验来自1,500家厂商带来的最新产品，还可以了解行业最新动态及未来发展趋势，接触到食品及饮料行业各个层次的客户资源及深入的合作机遇。
产品与服务：烘焙食品和糖果、奶酪和奶制品、饮料、冷冻食品、儿童食品及饮料、方便食品、风俗食品、肉类和家禽类、英国特产和地方食品、有机及天然食品、功能食品、零食/速食等
始办年份：1994
周期：两年一届
参展费用：光地展位261英镑/m²，标准展位313英镑/m²
上届规模 2007：展览面积20,391平方英尺，参展商564家，参观人数24,146人
主办：英国Fresh RM
联络：励展博览集团国际销售部
联系人：杜一鸣
☎ 010-5933 9209
🖷 010-5933 9233
✉ martin.du@reedexpo.com.cn
www.reedexport.cn
www.ife.co.uk

伦敦书展
LBF：
The World's Leading Spring Publishing Event

日期：2011/04/11 - 13
地点：英国伦敦Earls Court展览中心
Earls Court, London, United Kingdom
内容：伦敦书展是出版商进行书籍版权交易、书品贸易及产品服务交流的平台，每年吸引世界各地的业界人士齐聚于此；同时，研讨会及其他活动项目将贯穿整个展会。伦敦书展是全球性的大聚会，已发展成为国际性的出版业中心。它不仅是行业人士进行商务往来、与客户及行业间进行交流、招揽新业务、学习新技术的绝佳平台，来此观展更是一次愉快的经历。
产品与内容：出版包括综合类、学术/科学、技术和医学、儿童书籍、库存书、小批量出版、零售及出版解决方案。
始办年份：1971
周期：每年一届
参展费用：光地展位260英镑/m²，标准展位308英镑/m²
主办：励展英国公司
联络：励展博览集团国际销售部
联系人：王亮
☎ 010-5933 9288
🖷 010-5933 9233
✉ liang.wang@reedexpo.com.cn
www.reedexport.cn
www.londonbookfair.co.uk

2011年英国伯明翰商用汽车及配件展
The Commercial Vehicle Show 2011

日期：2011/04/12-14
地点：英国伯明翰NEC展览中心
内容：是英国最大规模最成功的汽车行业展会。参展范围有物流业运输车辆，汽车及相关服务，轮胎轮毂及相关产品、汽修设备，全系列的汽车配件，各种汽车用品，汽车空调，悬挂件，电池及配件，皮带/管件，车身件，刹车配件，维修工具套间，离合器和变速箱，风扇，发动机及配件，排气系统配件，滤清器，油路配件，密封垫，车灯，车镜，车牌，轮及轴承，座椅及坐垫，车窗玻璃，万向节等。
周期：每年一届
上届规模 2010：展览面积76,650m2，参展商786家
联络：中国汽车工业国际合作总公司
地址：北京市海淀区中关村丹棱街3号A座国机大厦（100080）
☎ 010-8260 6881, 6891, 6893, 6874
🖷 010-8260 6883, 8260 6790
联系人：马蓉，刘岩，娄杰，杨菁
✉ exhibition@cnaico.com.cn
www.autochina.com.cn

欧洲国际计算机信息系统安全展览会
Infosecurity Europe:
Europe's No. 1 Information Security Event

日期：2011/04/19 - 21
地点：英国伦敦Earls Court展览中心
Earls Court, London, United Kingdom
内容：信息安全产品及服务，包括应用安全、反垃圾邮件、杀毒、生物测定、业务延续/灾难恢复、证书管理机构、内容监控、加密/PKI、防火墙、身份管理、IT取证、互联网安全、入侵防卫/探测、立法和标准/BS7799、托管安全服务、网络安全服务、漏洞修补管理、穿透测试/弱点评估、物理安全、远程访问、安全存储、安全策略制订、安全令牌、安全培训/普及/教育、安全网络服务、smart卡、统一威胁管理、VPN与无线/手提安全。
介绍：欧洲涵盖面最广的信息安全专业会展，展会在展出各种创新产品和服务的同时为参会者就当今的战略及技术问题提供无与伦比的教育机会。展会丰富的知识及信息给观众提供如何、何种、为何以及何时定购产品的答案。
始办年份：1995
周期：每年一届
性质：面向贸易观众
参展费用：光地展位490英镑/m²，标准展位540英镑/m²
上届规模：参展商324家，参观人数12,556人
主办：励展德国公司
联络：励展博览集团国际销售部
联系人：杜一鸣
☎ 010-5933 9209
🖷 010-5933 9233
✉ martin.du@reedexpo.com.cn
www.infosec.co.uk

英国国际分包展览会
SUBCON

日期：2011/06/08 - 10
地点：英国伯明翰

周期：每年一届
主办：中国贸促会机械行业分会
地址：北京市西城区三里河路46号（100823）
联系人：张玉惠,郭旭萍,吕春丽
☎ 010-6859 4811, 6859 4994, 6859 4910
℻ 010-6859 4995
✉ zhangyuhui@ccpitmsc.org
www.chinamachine.org.cn

英国曼彻斯特国际家具展
Manchester Furniture Show

日期：2011/07/17 - 20
地点：英国曼彻斯特
☎ 0411-8378 8831
℻ 0411-8378 8830

PPMA Show
第22届英国全套生产线暨加工及包装机械展
UK's annual showcase for Processing & Packaging Machinery

日期：2011/09 -
地点：英国伯明翰国家展览中心
内容：PPMA展会是英国一年一度的加工和包装机械展会。在即将举办的第20届展会上，参展商将获得一个绝佳的机会，向慕名而来的英国买家现场展示自己的机器和技术。产品及服务包括包装及加工机械。观众来源有包装、加工机械及设备的买家及产品规格制定者。
周期：两年一届
上届规模 2009：展览面积6,300m²，参展商300家
主办：励展英国公司；PPMA Ltd（加工与包装机械协会）
联络：励展博览集团国际销售部
地址：北京市朝阳区新源南路1-3号平安国际金融中心A座15层01-03,05 （100027）
☎ 010-5933 9288
℻ 010-5933 9233
✉ liang.wang@reedexpo.com.cn
www.ppmashow.co.uk
www.reedexport.cn

伦敦国际珠宝展
International Jewellery London
The UK 's Only Dedicated Jewellery Trade Event

日期：2011/09/04 - 07
地点：英国伦敦Earls Court2展览中心
内容：伦敦国际珠宝展 (IJL) 已经不知不觉走过了55个年头，在这55年中，伦敦国际珠宝展一直推动着珠宝行业不断向前发展，同时展会也为英国及国际展商呈现出无数场无与伦比的视觉盛宴。展会所展现的是英国最新设计的创新产品，为观众提供舒适的体验环境，从展会中您可以了解到行业发展的最新趋势，与客户建立联系从而达成合作。
产品及服务：精品珠宝首饰、宝石、钻石、手表、钟表、奢华品、包装及陈列品
周期：每年一届
市场范围：国际性
性质：面向贸易观众
参展费用：光地展位265英镑起，标准展位318英镑起
主办：励展英国公司
联络：励展博览集团国际销售部
地址：北京市朝阳区新源南路1-3号平安国际金融中心A座15层01-03,05
联系人：申健
☎ 010-5933 9299
℻ 010-5933 9233
✉ jerry.shen@reedexpo.com.cn
www.jewellerylondon.com

2011 英国石油工业技术展
Offshore Europe 2011:
Oil & Gas Exhibition & Conference

日期：2011/09/06 - 08
地点：英国阿伯丁会展中心
内容：作为东半球最重要的石油勘探及生产工业展会，英国石油工业技术展一直不断发展，全面真实地反映着世界石油工业不断发展的技术要求。
产品及服务：涉及石油勘探与生产各个环节的上游油田技术/服务。
周期：两年一届
市场范围：国际性
性质：面向贸易观众
参展费用：光地展位191～320英磅/m²，标准展位370英磅/m²
上届规模 2010：展览面积22,809m²，参展商1,421家，参观人数30,698人
主办：励展博览集团国际销售部
地址：北京市朝阳区新源南路1-3号平安国际金融中心A座15层01-03,05（100738）
联系人：宫卫
☎ 010-5933 9268
℻ 010-5933 9233
✉ david.gong@reedexpo.com.cn
www.reedexport.cn
www.offshore-europe.co.uk

伦敦信息技术基础架构展览会
360°IT
The IT Infrastructure Event

日期：2011/09/21 - 22
地点：英国伦敦Earls Court1展览中心
内容：英国IT设备展是英国唯一针对数据存储的展会，由于展会中供应商都是行业领先企业，他们带来的都是最为全面的数据存储方案，这为观众们创造了货比多家的难得良机。 英国IT设备展将在一项教育讲座中强调当今一些关键性问题。参加本展会，您日益增长的数据存储需求一定能够得以满足。
产品和服务：英国IT设备展涵盖了行业的各个方面：数据的存储、移动、归档、修复和管理。参展商们在这里展示他们的软、硬件及其他服务。展会中还会涉及战略性风险因素与高技术性问题。以下是展会包含的主要领域：企业永续战略、信息生命周期管理、数据存储、存储归档、存储备份、存储内容管理系统、存储网络、存储服务供应商（SSP）、存储服务（测试及其他服务）、培训、存储软件管理、存储系统（DAS、NAS、SAN等其他系统）、磁带与虚拟化存储。
周期：每年一届
市场范围：国际性
性质：面向贸易观众
主办：励展英国公司
联络：励展博览集团国际销售部
地址：北京市朝阳区新源南路1-3号平安国际金融中心A座15层01-03,05
联系人：张志超
☎ 010-5933 9266
℻ 010-5933 9233
✉ ivy.zhang@reedexpo.com.cn
www.360itevent.com
www.reedexport.cn

第17届100%伦敦室内设计展
100% Design London:
The UK's Leading Contemporary Interior Design Event

日期：2011/09/22 - 25
地点：英国伦敦Earls Court展览中心
内容：100%伦敦室内设计展是英国领先的室内设计和建筑展会，特别针对业内市场，展会吸引了生产商、分销商、代理商、设计师、室内装修产品设计师、室内设计师、建筑师、零售商和其他行业专家。展会分为几个部分，其中100%设计专注于展示最新室内设计发展；100%材料将展示最新装修材料，表面装饰，装饰配件和装饰处理；100%未来将展示新兴设计人才，建筑和室内设计活动。100%设计还包括一系列研讨会，和由高端设计师和建筑师组成的工作室，针对室内设计行业热点问题进行讨论。
产品和服务：配件、建筑玻璃、协会、浴室、地面装饰家居、玻璃器具、厨具、灯具、纺织品、室内装潢、墙面装饰
周期：每年一届
主办：励展英国公司
联络：励展博览集团国际销售部
地址：北京市朝阳区新源南路1-3号平安国际金融中心A座15层01-03,05（100027）
☎ 010-5933 9288
℻ 010-5933 9233
✉ liang.wang@reedexpo.com.cn
www.100percentdesign.co.uk
www.reedexport.cn

英国酒店设备展
Hotelympia

日期：2012/02 -
地点：英国伦敦ExCeL展览馆
内容：英国酒店设备展（Hotelympia）展览范围广泛，包括最新产品和创新科技，为您提供一个与众不同的参展环境和浓郁的展会氛围。参加Hotelympia 2010，您可以挖掘更多业内最新理念和解决方案以及重要商业信息，扩展人际网，与来自业内的朋友和同事们，感受展会现场的热烈气氛和烹饪比赛带来的乐趣。英国酒店设备展分为6个部分，包括食品和饮料、餐饮设备、餐桌、装饰设计、浴室和Spa、建筑设计和设备管理。同时展会将与Hostec-Europe同期举办，期间还会举办酒店职业日活动等。
周期：两年一届
市场范围：国际性
性质：面向贸易观众
主办：英国Fresh RM
参展联络：励展博览集团国际销售部
地址：北京市朝阳区新源南路1-3号平安国际金融中心A座15层01-03,05
联系人：宫卫
☎ 010-5933 9268

📠 010-5933 9233
✉ david.gong@reedexpo.com.cn?
www.reedexport.cn
www.hotelympia.com

英国酒店用品展

Hospitality

日期： 2013/01 -
地点： 英国伯明翰国家展览中心
内容： 机会难得，不容错过，展会将为酒店行业人士提供面对面的交流机会，扩展关系网，建立商务友谊。
周期： 两年一届
市场范围： 国际性
性质： 面向贸易观众
参展费用： 光地展位252欧元，标准展位307欧元
主办： 英国Fresh RM
联络： 励展博览集团国际销售部
地址： 北京市朝阳区新源南路1-3号平安国际金融中心A座15层01-03,05
www.reedexport.cn
www.hospitalityshow.co.uk

英国食品、饮料包装机械、设备展览会

Pro2Pac:

Processing & Packaging Solutions Event, Exclusively for the Food & Drink Industry

日期： 2013/03 -
地点： 英国伦敦ExCeL会展中心
内容： 英国食品、饮料包装机械、设备展览会(Pro2Pac)是唯一一个专为食品和饮料行业提供包装机械、设备的展会，Pro2Pac将与英国最大的食品饮料展IFE英国国际食品和饮料展同期举办，两个展会将带领大家全方位地透视食品和饮料行业。
周期： 两年一届
市场范围： 国际性
性质： 面向贸易观众
参展费用： 光地展位230英镑/m²，标准展位274英镑/m²
主办： 励展英国公司
联络： 励展博览集团国际销售部
地址： 北京市朝阳区新源南路1-3号平安国际金融中心A座15层01-03,05
☎ 010-5933 9268
📠 010-5933 9233
✉ david.gong@reedexpo.com.cn?
www.reedexport.cn
www.hospitalityshow.co.uk

英国国际食品和饮料展

IFE: International Food & Drink Event

日期： 2013/03 -
地点： 英国伦敦ExCel 会展中心
内容： 英国国际食品和饮料展（IFE）汇集了全球范围内食品和饮料行业创新产品。本地和国际观众不仅可以率先体验来自1,500家厂商带来的最新产品，还可以了解行业最新动态及未来发展趋势，接触到食品及饮料行业各个层次的客户资源及深入的合作机遇。
始办年份： 1994
周期： 两年一届
市场范围： 国际性
性质： 面向贸易观众
参展费用： 光地展位261英镑/m²，标准展位313英镑/m²
主办： 英国Fresh RM
联络： 励展博览集团国际销售部
联系人： 杜一鸣
☎ 010-5933 9209
📠 010-5933 9233
✉ martin.du@reedexpo.com.cn
www.reedexport.cn
www.ife.co.uk

英国国际包装新技术展览会

Total Processing & Packaging

日期： 2013/05/21 – 23
地点： 英国伯明翰国家展览中心
内容： 涵盖加工和包装行业各领域，提供完整的生产线方案、行业内情及创新信息。产品及服务：包装原料和容器、加工设备、包装机械、包装设计、其他相关产品及服务。
周期： 三年一届
市场范围： 国际性
性质： 面向贸易观众
协办： 英国加工与包装机械协会（PPMA）；英国材料、矿石和冶金协会
主办： 励展博览集团国际销售部
地址： 北京市朝阳区新源南路1-3号平安国际金融中心A座15层01-03,05
联系人： 宫卫
☎ 010-5933 9268
📠 010-5933 9233
✉ david.gong@reedexpo.com.cn?
www.reedexport.cn
www.totalexhibition.com

美国
USA

美国职业高尔夫球协会高尔夫用品展

PGA Merchandise Show

日期： 2011/01/27 - 29
地点： 美国佛罗里达州奥兰多橙郡会议中心
Orange County Convention Center, USA
内容： 已发展成为世界顶级高尔夫专业展览盛会，在国际高尔夫球市场中起着引领潮流的作用。在上届展会中，博览会纪录的总参观人数达到了45019人，相较前一年增长3%。其中包括PGA的专业人士，主要分销商、零售商、高尔夫俱乐部经理、私人培训学校决策人、高尔夫相关媒体等等。在专业观众方面，博览会每年均保持着14%的人数上的增长。其主办宗旨即是构筑与会参展公司与专业观众的桥梁。作为专业的高尔夫贸易展览，展会同时还举办高尔夫展示日和专家讲座与商务会议，不仅为展商提供良好的贸易洽谈环境，还为买家和观众提供学习和提高高尔夫球技的机会
产品与服务： 高尔夫俱乐部、高尔夫球具、人造草坪、高尔夫球包、高尔夫球帽、高尔夫球服饰、俱乐部产品订制、电脑系统、软件、信用服务；食品、饮料；高尔夫艺术品、工艺品、出版物；模拟练习设备、高尔夫店设备、家俱；培训机构、电子产品和游戏
始办年份： 1954
周期： 每年一届
市场范围： 国际性
性质： 面向贸易观众
参展费用： 光地展位32美元/平方英尺
主办： 励展博览集团国际销售部
地址： 北京市朝阳区新源南路1-3号平安国际金融中心A座15层01-03,05
联系人： 申健
☎ 010－5933 9299
📠 010－5933 9233
✉ jerry.shen@reedexpo.com.cn
www.pgashow.com
www.reedexport.cn

美国TEXWORLD服装面料展

(TEXWORLD USA)

日期： 2011/01/18 - 20
地点： 美国纽约
内容： 各类服装面料及辅料
主办： 法兰克福展览(美国)公司
联络： 中国贸促会纺织行业分会
联系人： 王静
☎ 010-8522 9017转160, 8522 9016
📠 010-8522 9544

美国国际射击展

Firearms, Hunting & Outdoor Products & Law Enforcement Products

日期： 2011/01/18 - 21
地点： 美国拉斯维加斯金沙会展中心
内容： 体育用品，打猎和射击产品：配件，弹药，光学产品，餐具，户外服饰，执法机构和其他打猎相关产品
参展费用： 21.75美元
上届规模： 展览面积689,425平方英尺，参展商25,004家，参观人数31,269人
主办： 励展美国公司
联络： 励展博览集团国际销售部
联系人： 宫卫
☎ 010-5933 9268
📠 010-5933 9233
✉ david.gong@reedexpo.com.cn
www.shotshow.org
www.reedexport.cn

美国拉斯维加斯冬季国际家具展

Lasvegas2011

日期： 2011/01/24 - 28
地点： 美国拉斯维加斯
☎ 0411-8378 8831
📠 0411-8378 8830

美国国际空调、制冷和供暖展览会

AHR

日期： 2011/01/31 - 02
地点： 美国拉斯维加斯
周期： 每年一届
主办： 中国贸促会机械行业分会
地址： 北京市西城区三里河路46号（100823）
联系人： 张玉惠、郭旭萍、吕春丽
☎ 010-6859 4811，6859 4994，6859 4910
📠 010-68594995
✉ zhangyuhui@ccpitmsc.org
www.chinamachine.org.cn

拉斯维加斯国际服装服饰及面料博览会（春）

Magic Show

日期： 2011/02/15 - 18
地点： 美国拉斯维加斯
联络： 上海比天展览服务有限公司
地址： 上海市中山北路900号加禾商务中心3号楼303室(200070)
联系人： 刘先生
☎ 021-5655 2843
📠 021-5655 9981
www.betium.com

美国洛杉机纺织面料展会

GLOBALTEX

日期： 2011/03/02 - 04
地点： 美国
联络： 上海比天展览服务有限公司
地址： 上海市中山北路900号加禾商务中心3号楼303室(200070)

联系人：刘先生
☎ 021-5655 2843
🖷 021-5655 9981
www.betium.com

2011年美国西部天然有机食品博览会

日期：2011/03/11 - 13
地点：美国洛杉矶阿内海姆会展中心
内容：随着经济的逐渐复苏，天然和有机产品市场持续增长。此展会是接触众多客户和同行最经济有效的方式。展会同期举办SUPPLYEXPO和NUTRACON会议，覆盖了保健品行业所有的配料和成品，本展会能让展商接触到最多的天然有机食品的买家和分销商，能找到专业顾客群体，增长销售额和业务。展会将占用阿内海姆所有5个展厅，并根据主题分为有机产品、天然产品、健康产品及相关主题行业。
始办年份：1973
周期：每年一届
市场范围：国际性
上届规模 2010：展览面积20万平方英尺，参展商3,000家（来自28个国家），参观人数36,851人
主办：北京领汇国际展览有限公司
地址：北京市朝阳区农展馆南路13号瑞辰国际中心719（100125）
联系人：刘佳
☎ 010-5129 5359转8505
🖷 010-5129 5379转8505
✉ expo8505@worldfairs.cn
MSN：expo8505@worldfairs.cn

2011美国波士顿国际水产展（第29届）

日期：2011/03/14 - 16
地点：美国波士顿展览中心
内容：展会目前已经是世界渔业领域影响力最大、知名度最高的专业水产贸易展，是世界三大水产品展会中规模最大的一个，是美国发展迅速的前50名展览会之一。该展会展品涵盖了海产品行业中的各个方面：保鲜的、冷冻的、鲜活的、有高附加价值的、品牌的以及私营商标的。展会还是国际买家、供应商、经销商/批发商、进口商、出口商、中间商以及贸易商每年发布或者搜寻新的产品、联系客户、评估行业趋势以及了解最新海产品技术的产品的盛事。
始办年份：1982
周期：每年一届
市场范围：国际性
性质：面向公众
上届规模：展览面积176,845平方英尺，参展商800家（来自500个国家），参观人数11,230人
主办：北京领汇国际展览有限公司
地址：北京市朝阳区农展馆南路13号 瑞辰国际中心719（100125）
联系人：刘佳
☎ 010-5129 5359转8505
🖷 010-5129 5379转8505
✉ expo8505@worldfairs.cn
MSN：expo8505@worldfairs.cn

美国东部国际光学展

International Vision Expo East:

Largest Fashion, Medical, Science & Technology Event in US

日期：2011/03/18 - 20
地点：美国纽约Jacob K Javits会议中心
内容：美国东部领先的眼科保健盛会，聚集所有眼科保健专业人员。
产品及服务：眼镜架、太阳眼镜、眼镜片、隐形眼镜及护理液、眼光学仪器、眼镜相关器材及零部件、眼镜布、眼镜附属产品。
始办年份：1985
周期：每年一届
参展费用：光地展位37美元/平方英尺，角位250美元/平方英尺
主办：励展美国公司
联络：励展博览集团国际销售部
联系人：杜一鸣
☎ 010-5933 9268
🖷 010-5933 9233
✉ martin.du@reedexpo.com.cn
www.visionexpoeast.com

2011年拉斯维加斯工程机械展

Conexpo-Con/Agg

日期：2011/03/22 - 26
地点：美国拉斯维加斯会展中心
内容：此展是世界三大工程机械展之一，与德国Bauma和法国Intermat展齐名，是仅次于Bauma的世界第二大工程机械展。展会迄今有近百年历史，集中了世界知名品牌，是业内展示最新技术、设备和展品的重要平台。展会同期举办国际动力展（IFPE）。拉斯维加斯工程机械展将为中国工程机械行业生产商、贸易商和技术专家提供贸易和技术交流良好契机。
周期：三年一届
市场范围：国际性
主办：美国设备制造商协会；美国预制混凝土协会；美国沙石协会
联络：北京麦田通会国际展览有限公司
联系人：吴珊
☎ 010-5165 9302转ext 8005, 8633 1235, 13426437438
🖷 010-5165 9302
✉ xiaoxiangzhishui@yahoo.com.cn
MSN：xiaoxiangzhishui@hotmail.com
联络：中国贸促会
地址：北京市西城区三里河路46号（100823）
联系人：张玉惠, 郭旭萍, 吕春丽
☎ 010-6859 4811, 6859 4994, 6859 4910
🖷 010-6859 4995
✉ zhangyuhui@ccpitmsc.org
www.chinamachine.org.cn

2011年美国中部卡车展览会

MATS 2011

日期：2011/03/31-04/02
地点：美国路易斯维尔
内容：此展是目前世界上最大的专业卡车展。范围有整车，各类重卡、中卡、轻卡、长头货车、平头货车、自卸车、厢式货车、罐体运输车、冷藏车、全挂车、半挂车、半挂牵引车、集装箱运输车、矿用载重车、起重举升汽车、城市环卫车辆、散装水泥车、工程专用车辆、邮政车、运钞车、军警专用运输车辆、清障车、消防车、解款车及防弹车、邮政、医疗、机场、航天等专用车；配件，卡车用调整臂，转向轴等，柴油发动机，变速箱，轮胎及轮圈，车桥及底盘、座椅，空调，换向/助力器、卡车厢体及集装箱、尾板及装卸平台、各种液压件、ABS 及安全气囊、卡车改装技术及装备、物流运输系统、GPS系统及调度系统等。
周期：每年一届
上届规模 2010：参展商1,144家（来自60个国家），专业观众80,291人（来自109个国家）
联络：中国汽车工业国际合作总公司
地址：北京市海淀区中关村丹棱街3号A座国机大厦（100080）
☎ 010-8260 6881, 6891, 6893, 6874
🖷 010-8260 6883, 8260 6790
联系人：马蓉，刘岩，娄杰，杨菁
✉ exhibition@cnaico.com.cn
www.autochina.com.cn

美国液压、气动、零部件展

IFPE

日期：2011/03/22 - 26
地点：美国拉斯维加斯会展中心
内容：液压、气动、零部件等
周期：三年一届
市场范围：国际性
性质：面向公众
主办：美国设备制造商协会
地址：北京东城区建国门北大街8号华润大厦501室（100005）
联系人：孙红宇
☎ 010-8519 1566
🖷 010-8519 1567
✉ hsun@cm-1.com

美国国际制药工业展览会

Pharmaceutical Manufacturing

日期：2011/03/29 - 31
地点：美国纽约Jacob K Javits会展中心
Jacob K Javits Convention Center, New York, USA
内容：加工设备及供应品、包装设备及材料、实验设备及供应品、研发产品及服务、污染控制、清洁室供应品及服务、进程自动化及控制、原材料、信息技术、外包及承包服务、设施产品及服务、药品交付技术、合成产品。
始办年份：1979
周期：每年一届
上届规模：展览面积207,573平方英尺，参展商773家，参观人数6,774人
主办：励展美国公司
联络：励展博览集团国际销售部
联系人：申健
☎ 010-5933 9268
🖷 010-5933 9233
✉ jerry.shen@reedexpo.com.cn
www.reedexport.cn

纽约楼宇维护技术展

BuildingsNY：

The Largest Buildings Event for the New York Metro Region

Commercial
Residential
Essential
BuildingsNY

日期：2011/03/30 - 31
地点：美国纽约Jacob K Javits会展中心
Jacob K Javits Convention Center, New York, UNITED STATES OF AMERICA, , USA
内容：产品与服务设备 建筑产品及服务 锅炉 楼宇自动化 楼宇监控设备 建筑材料 电器承包商 能源管理 环境管理 地板装饰 绿色产品 屋顶花园建材 保险 内部/外部清洁 厨房与卫浴 照明 修缮与维护 涂料管材 屋顶材料 安保/消防 通讯 公共设施 供水 门窗 其他建材
始办年份：1979
周期：每年一届
主办：励展美国公司
联络：励展博览集团国际销售部
地址：北京市朝阳区新源南路1-3号平安国际金融中心A座15层01-03,05
联系人：宫卫
☎ 010-5933 9268
🖷 010-5933 9233
✉ david.gong@reedexpo.com.cn
www.buildingsny.com
www.reedexport.cn

美国西部国际安防产品博览会

ISC West：

International Security Conference West

日期：2011/04/06 - 08
地点：美国拉斯维加斯会展中心 & 金沙会展中心
Sands Expo & Convention Center, Las Vegas, USA
内容：本届展览会由于增加了许多新的项目和产品，世界级的行业培训、大量的展期和展会网络联络机会，使该展继续成为为安保产品制造商，经销商、安装商、综合商以及最终使用客户参加的主要的行业盛会。
产品及服务：闭路电视、报警设备、监视器、门路控制、无线设备、远程监视器、系统整合、防火和灭火用品和材料等一切与生活相关的安全、安保产品等。
始办年份：1967
周期：每年一届
主办：励展美国公司
联络：励展博览集团国际销售部
地址：北京市朝阳区新源南路1-3号平安国际金融中心A座15层01-03,05
联系人：张志超
☎ 010-5933 9266
🖷 010-5933 9233
✉ ivy.zhang@reedexpo.com.cn
www.reedexport.cn
www.iscwest.com

美国国际模具及机床技术展览会

Amerimold

日期：2011/04/12 - 14
地点：美国芝加哥
周期：每年一届
主办：中国贸促会机械行业分会
地址：北京市西城区三里河路46号（100823）
联系人：张玉惠, 郭旭萍, 吕春丽
☎ 010-6859 4811, 6859 4994, 6859 4910
🖷 010-6859 4995
✉ zhangyuhui@ccpitmsc.org
www.chinamachine.org.cn

美国国际小家电及家居用品展览会

Homewares Show

Homewares Show logo ("where housewares is always at home")

日期：2011/05/10 - 12
地点：美国拉斯维加斯会议中心
内容：针对家用器具产品类零售商需求的日渐强大，美国国际小家电及家居用品展将于09年继续举办。展商来源：小家电、家庭存储与收纳、家庭环境与照明、家用小器具、水处理、清洁用品、小器具、地板、窗户及家装、宠物产品
周期：每年一届
市场范围：国际性
性质：面向贸易观众
主办：励展博览集团国际销售部
地址：北京市朝阳区新源南路1-3号平安国际金融中心A座15层01-03,05
联系人：吴祥
☎ 010－5933 9277
🖷 010－5933 9233
✉ ronald.wu@reedexpo.com.cn
www.reedexport.cn
www.homewaresshow.com

美国国际五金工具及花园用品展览会

Global gathering of newest products for DIY Home Improvement

日期：2011/05/10 - 12
地点：美国拉斯维加斯会议中心
Las Vegas Convention Center, Las Vegas, USA
内容：工具类：手动工具、电动工具、园艺工具、小型加工机械等；五金类：日用五金、建筑五金、装饰五金、紧固件、筛网等；保安器材：锁类、防盗及报警产品、安全器材等；汽车附件：维修工具、泵类及各类配件等；照明器材：灯具及配件、节日灯、圣诞灯、草地灯、各类电工器材和材料等；园艺及庭院产品：园林维护和修剪产品、铁艺产品、庭院休闲产品、烧烤产品等 DIY产品：家庭装饰和装修用品、宠物用品等；厨房及卫浴产品：卫生洁具、浴室设备、厨房设备等 - 国际家居用品展览会；家居清洁产品、储藏、健康及安全、装饰灯具、家装产品、个人用品、礼品
周期：每年一届
参展费用：光地展位24.95美元
上届规模：展览面积535,000平方英尺，参展商2,553家，参观人数30,900人
主办：励展美国公司
联络：励展博览集团国际销售部
地址：北京市朝阳区新源南路1-3号平安国际金融中心A座15层01-03,05 （100027）
☎ 010-5933 9211
🖷 010-5933 9233
✉ ISGCNmarketing@reedexpo.com.cn
www.nationalhardwareshow.com

美国书展－原美国书商协会大会及贸易展

BEA: BookExpo America

日期：2011/05/24 - 26
地点：美国纽约Jacob K Javits会展中心
内容：百年历史缔造书市盛典—美国书展已经有一个多世纪的历史，是全美最大的年度书展，同时也是全球最重要的版权、图书贸易盛会之一。美国书展向与会者提供了一次洞悉美国图书出版市场的全貌，了解全球图书出版行业，接触国际出版商的绝佳机会。在这里，您可以了解未来几年将深刻影响图书出版行业并直接影响您的业务的行业发展趋势、观念以及图书。数字出版激越前进，给出版业带来前所未有的机会。从中可清晰看到，在世界书业越来越倡导绿色阅读、环保阅读的背景下，数字出版被冠以"无冕之王"的桂冠；在数字产品的网络版权保护方面，数字版权管理技术正在推进数字出版健康发展。美国书展期间，来自世界各地的数字出版企业发布新产品、新技术、新服务，并与业界分享它们的全新营销模式。
始办年份：1900
周期：每年一届
市场范围：国际性
性质：面向贸易观众
参展费用：光地展位33美元/平方英尺，标准展位42美元/平方英尺
上届规模 2010：展览面积174,500平方英尺，参展商1,350家（来自116个国家），参观人数21，364人
主办：励展博览集团国际销售部
地址：北京市朝阳区新源南路1-3号平安国际金融中心A座15层01-03,05（100738）
联系人：王亮
☎ 010－5933 9288
🖷 010－5933 9233
✉ liang.wang@reedexpo.com.cn
www.reedexport.cn
www.bookexpoamerica.com

拉斯维加斯国际珠宝展

JCK Las Vegas: The Jewellery Industry's Premiere Trade Event

日期：2011/06/03 - 06
地点：美国内华达州拉斯维加斯曼德勒海湾赌场度假村
Mandalay Bay Resort & Casino
内容：拉斯维加斯国际珠宝展是JCK品牌系列展会之一，它汇集了全国种类最多，品质最好的各式精美珠宝。此次展会为国内及国际珠宝商提供了便捷、全面的优质配套服务。
产品与服务：优质精美珠宝、裸钻、宝石及高档钟表、器材、技术与设备
周期：每年一届
参展费用：光地展位42～44美元/m^2
主办：励展美国公司
地址：北京市朝阳区新源南路1-3号平安国际金融中心A座15层01-03,05
联系人：申健
☎ 010-5933 9299
🖷 010-5933 9233
✉ jerry.shen@reedexpo.com.cn
www.jcklasvegasshow.com

2011美国食品科技展（第68届）

IFT Food EXPO 2011

日期：2011/06/12 - 14
地点：美国新奥尔良Morial会议中心
内容：它是美洲地区规模最大最负盛名的国际食品添加剂、食品配料及科技方面的专业展和行业盛会，及时地反映了食品行业全球科技成果转化为产品的最新情况，反映了食品工业发展的方向和动态，代表了世界食品科技工业发展趋势。
展品：食品添加剂、食品配料、食品包装包装材料和机械、食品加工机械、食品检测技术和设备、各类有机食品、饮料；有关出版物；
周期：每年一届
市场范围：国际性
上届规模：参展商1,000家（来自48个国家）
主办：美国食品技术协会(Institute of Food Technologists)
联络：北京领汇国际展览有限公司
地址：北京市朝阳区农展馆南路13号瑞辰国际中心719（100125）
联系人：刘佳
☎ 010-5129 5359转8505
🖷 010-5129 5379转8505
✉ expo8505@worldfairs.cn
MSN：expo8505@worldfairs.cn

美国TEXWORLD服装面料展

TEXWORLD USA

暨中国纺织品服装贸易展览会(面料)

日期：2011/07/19 - 21
地点：美国纽约
内容：各类服装面料及辅料
主办：中国纺织工业协会；法兰克福展览(美国)公司
联络：中国贸促会纺织行业分会
联系人：王静
☎ 010-8522 9017转160，8522 9016
🖷 010-8522 9544
联络：上海比天展览服务有限公司
地址：上海市中山北路900号加禾商务中心3号楼303室(200070)
联系人：刘先生
☎ 021-5655 2843
🖷 021-5655 9981
www.betium.com

纽约国际服装采购展（APP）暨中国纺织品服装贸易展览会（服装）

日期： 2011/07/19 - 21
地点： 美国纽约
内容： 男装、正装、女装、运动休闲装、童装、内衣、牛仔装、针织服装、睡衣、及饰品
主办： 中国纺织工业协会；法兰克福展览(美国)公司
联络： 中国贸促会纺织行业分会
联系人： 王彤，张涛
☎ 010-8522 9482，8522 9550
🖷 010-8522 9544

纽约国际家纺展（HTFSE）暨中国纺织品服装贸易展览会（家纺）

日期： 2011/07/19 - 21
地点： 美国纽约
内容： 各类家用纺织品面料、辅料及成品
主办： 中国纺织工业协会；法兰克福展览(美国)公司
联络： 中国贸促会纺织行业分会
联系人： 张嘉，龚岩
☎ 010-8522 9376，8522 9145
🖷 010-8522 9544

美国拉斯维加斯国际家具展

Lasvegas2011

日期： 2011/08/01 - 05
地点： 美国
☎ 0411-8378 8831
🖷 0411-8378 8830

拉斯维加斯国际服装服饰及面料博览会（秋）

Magic Show

日期： 2011/08/16 - 19
地点： 美国拉斯维加斯
联络： 上海比天展览服务有限公司
地址： 上海市中山北路900号加禾商务中心3号楼303室(200070)
联系人： 刘先生
☎ 021-5655 2843
🖷 021-5655 9981
www.betium.com

美国职业高尔夫球协会高尔夫用品秋季展

PGA Fall Expo：

Golf's Premier Fall Buying Event for the Golf Industry

日期： 2011/08/22 - 24
地点： 美国内华达州拉斯维加斯百麗宫大酒店（The Venetian Resort Hotel Casino）
内容： 全美最佳的高尔夫服饰、装备、配件秋季购买预定盛会。展会为数以千计的职业高尔夫球协会球员以及高尔夫零售商提供预览春季最热门的高尔夫装备、配件以及服饰的机会。对高尔夫零售商来说是全美最好的秋季交易盛会。
产品及服务： 高尔夫装备、高尔夫产品及服务、高尔夫及度假服饰、旅行、助学用品、球场标志及固定装置、草皮与球场维护、高尔夫推车以及俱乐部管理。
周期： 每年一届
市场范围： 国际性
性质： 面向贸易观众
参展费用： 光地展位17美元
主办： 励展美国公司
联络： 励展博览集团国际销售部
地址： 北京市朝阳区新源南路1-3号平安国际金融中心A座15层01-03,05
联系人： 申健
☎ 010-5933 9299
🖷 010-5933 9233
✉ jerry.shen@reedexpo.com.cn
www.pgaexpo.com

美国西部国际光学展

International Vision Expo West

日期： 2011/09/21 - 24
地点： 美国拉斯维加斯金沙会展中心
内容： 美国西部国际光学展是美洲最大的，拥有时下最新资讯的光学医疗技术盛会。出席世界上最大且最全面的眼部保健盛会，根据展会提供的最新行业流行趋势、最先进的医学技术将有助您扩大业务面、掌握最新技术。
产品及服务： 附件、眼镜盒、展示品、护理液和眼镜布、眼镜架、实验室耗材、镜片加工设备、仪器、镜片、护目镜、人造眼、双筒望远镜和单筒望远镜、隐形眼镜、眼科诊断仪器、分配和检测设备、眼部干燥产品、仪器、视觉教具、护目镜
周期： 每年一届
市场范围： 国际性
性质： 面向贸易观众
主办： 励展美国公司
联络： 励展博览集团国际销售部
地址： 北京市朝阳区新源南路1-3号平安国际金融中心A座15层01-03,05
联系人： 杜一鸣
☎ 010-5933 9209
🖷 010-5933 9233
✉ martin.du@reedexpo.com.cn
www.visionexpowest.com
www.reedexport.cn

美国国际包装机械博览会

Pack Expo

日期： 2011/09/26 - 28
地点： 美国拉斯维加斯
周期： 每年一届
主办： 中国贸促会机械行业分会
地址： 北京市西城区三里河路46号（100823）
联系人： 张玉惠，郭旭萍，吕春丽
☎ 010-6859 4811, 6859 4994, 6859 4910
🖷 010-6859 4995
✉ zhangyuhui@ccpitmsc.org
www.chinamachine.org.cn

第6届纽约国际动漫博览会

New York Comic Con:

The Largest Pop Culture Event on the East Coast

日期： 2011/10/14 - 16
地点： 美国纽约贾维茨会议中心（Jacob K Javits）
内容： 顶级行业出版商、数以千计的追求时尚与新潮大众文化的其他行业人士，以及公众都会参加纽约国际动漫博览会。寻找最具活力、进行最大的交易以及决定将来突破，纽约国际动漫博览会是唯一的选择。它是东部海岸独一无二的展会，带您进入美国最大的大众文化、媒体和版权交易城市。产品及服务：漫画书籍、图画小说、游戏、玩具、日本漫画、动漫、电影/电视、特别来宾、影映、座谈会。观众来源：行业专家，如漫画书籍零售商、购买者、经销商、版权交易者、收藏家、图书馆管理员、教育、媒体、新闻界，以及数以万计的大众文化迷尤其是漫画迷。他们热衷于漫画、动漫、日本漫画、游戏、电影和电视中的新潮流及新突破。
周期： 每年一届
入场券价格： 光地展位20美元/平方英尺
主办： 励展美国公司
联络： 励展博览集团国际销售部
地址： 北京市朝阳区新源南路1-3号平安国际金融中心A座15层01-03,05
联系人： 杜一鸣
☎ 010-5933 9209
🖷 010-5933 9233
✉ martin.du@reedexpo.com.cn
www.nycomiccon.com
www.reedexport.cn

美国国际金属成型及管材展览会

FABTECH International Show

日期： 2011/11 -
地点： 美国芝加哥
周期： 每年一届
主办： 中国贸促会机械行业分会
地址： 北京市西城区三里河路46号（100823）
联系人： 张玉惠,郭旭萍,吕春丽
☎ 010-6859 4811, 6859 4994, 6859 4910
🖷 010-6859 4995
✉ zhangyuhui@ccpitmsc.org
www.chinamachine.org.cn

2011年美国国际齿轮世界展览会

日期： 2011/11/01 - 03
地点： 美国俄亥俄州辛辛那提杜克国际会议中心
内容： 国际上最具影响力的齿轮专业展览会，在展会上可以看到世界齿轮行业最新、最先进的技术和装备。2011年到2015年我国齿轮产品市场将走向成熟。展会范围有齿轮传动，链传动、带传动，传动联结件等。
始办年份： 1986
周期： 两年一届
市场范围： 国际性
主办： 美国齿轮制造商协会AGMA
北京麦田通会国际展览有限公司
联系人： 吴珊
☎ 010-8248 4014转801，5165 9302转8005
🖷 010-5165 9302
✉ xiaoxiangzhishui@yahoo.com.cn
MSN：xiaoxiangzhishui@yahoo.com.cn
www.cornfairs.com

2011年拉斯维加斯改装车零配件展览会

SEMA 2011

日期： 2011/11/02-05
地点： 美国拉斯维加斯
内容： 是世界首屈一指的专业改装车盛会。汇集了业内最先进的技术和最热销的产品。内容包括轮胎及车轮、空调、汽车音响、灯具、防盗、电子设备、安全带、服务设备、汽车保养美容产品、汽车电子和技术、汽车工具设备、维修产品，商业服务，越野车、赛车、卡车、suv、oem制造商。
周期： 每年一届
上届规模 2010：来自100个国家的10万专业买家
联络： 中国汽车工业国际合作总公司
地址： 北京市海淀区中关村丹棱街3号A座国机大厦（100080）
☎ 010-8260 6881, 6891, 6893, 6874
🖷 010-8260 6883, 8260 6790
联系人： 马蓉，刘岩，娄杰，杨菁
✉ exhibition@cnaico.com.cn
www.autochina.com.cn

2011年美国拉斯维加斯国际汽车零配件及售后服务展览会

AAPEX

日期： 2011/11/03 - 05
地点： 美国拉斯维加斯国际展览中心
内容： 全球最大的汽车售后服务市场的专业展览会；该展览会将吸引来自世界各地的汽车采购团前来参观和订购，是比任何其他同类型展会带来

更大利润和销售额的一个非常有实效的展览会。每一年的AAPEX SHOW都云集了来自全球各地零配件及其他市场的高质量的买家和卖家，AAPEX SHOW是中国商家进入北美乃欧洲汽配市场的必经之路。

展品范围汽车售后服务市场产品（AAPEX）、整车区（SEMA）。

始办年份：2010
周期：每年一届
市场范围：国际性
性质：面向公众
上届规模：参展商1,620家，参观者70,000人
主办：中国贸促会
地址：北京市西城区三里河路46号（100823）
联系人：张玉惠，郭旭萍，吕春丽
☎ 010-6859 4811, 6859 4994, 6859 4910
🖷 010-6859 4995
✉ zhangyuhui@ccpitmsc.org
www.chinamachine.org.cn
主办：中国贸促会建设行业分会/北京中杰城设国际展览有限公司
地址：北京市海淀区紫竹院路31号华澳中心嘉慧苑1703室(10089)
联系人：全静
☎ 010-5979 9850转808，13693550328
🖷 010-5885 7468
✉ quanjing@top-fairs.com.cn
MSN：quanjing@top-fairs.com.cn
QQ：602693071
www.build-ccpit.org
www.btfi.cn

美国国际电力展览会

POWER-GEN

日期：2011/12/08 - 10
地点：美国拉斯维加斯
周期：每年一届
主办：中国贸促会机械行业分会
地址：北京市西城区三里河路46号（100823）
联系人：张玉惠,郭旭萍,吕春丽
☎ 010-6859 4811, 6859 4994, 6859 4910
🖷 010-6859 4995
✉ zhangyuhui@ccpitmsc.org
www.chinamachine.org.cn

乌兹别克斯坦 Uzbekistan

2011年中国工业品（乌兹别克）展览会

China Industry Expo—UZBEKISTAN 2011

日期：2011/09 -
地点：乌兹别克塔什干
联络：中国汽车工业国际合作总公司
地址：北京市海淀区中关村丹棱街3号A座国机大厦（100080）
☎ 010-8260 6881, 6891, 6893, 6874
🖷 010-8260 6883, 8260 6790
联系人：马蓉，刘岩，娄杰，杨菁
✉ exhibition@cnaico.com.cn
www.autochina.com.cn

委内瑞拉 Venezuela

中国工业产品（委内瑞拉）展览会

日期：2011/06 -
地点：委内瑞拉加拉加斯
周期：每年一届
主办：中国贸促会机械行业分会
地址：北京市西城区三里河路46号（100823）
联系人：张玉惠,郭旭萍,吕春丽
☎ 010-6859 4811, 6859 4994, 6859 4910
🖷 010-6859 4995
✉ zhangyuhui@ccpitmsc.org
www.chinamachine.org.cn

越南 Vietnam

第6届越南（河内）国际建筑建材装饰材料博览会

VIETBUILD 2011

THE REGISTRATION FORM OF INTERNATIONAL EXHIBITION

日期：2011/03/23 - 27
地点：越南河内讲武国际展览中心
内容：建筑材料类：装饰材料、玻璃与加工玻璃、门窗幕墙、五金件、房屋建筑材料、建筑机械及设备、通风器材及建筑电工、电气、结构建材、建材生产技术及装备、陶瓷、石材、卫浴设施；建筑设计：建筑规划及设计、建筑工程、装饰工程及设计、建筑部品及节能前沿技术、太阳能与建筑一体化、楼宇智能化、建筑施工和安装机械设备、建筑消防设备器材及产品、防耐火材料；房地产类：城市规划、城市形象展示、房地产项目、住宅设施、园林景观、房地产营销策划；家居用品、家用电器、厨房设施、各类灯具、灯饰及配件、电光源产品、照明电器附件配件等。
联络：南宁越中会展商务有限公司
地址：广西南宁是新民路3号永嘉大厦1208室（530012）
☎ 0771-261 7885，261 5157,263 4881转1007
🖷 0771-263 0917
✉ exhibition@china-vn.net
hz.china-vn-con

第21届越南国际贸易博览会

（VIETNAM EXPO）

THE 21th VIETNAM INTL TRADE FAIR IN HA NOI CITY

日期：2011/04/06 - 09
地点：越南河内国际会展中心
联络：南宁越中会展商务有限公司
地址：广西南宁是新民路3号永嘉大厦1208室（530012）
☎ 0771-261 7885，261 5157,263 4881转1007
🖷 0771-263 0917
✉ exhibition@china-vn.net
hz.china-vn-con

2010年中国广告印刷包装造纸技术产品（越南）展览会

日期：2011/04/06 - 09
地点：越南河内国际会展中心
内容：广告技术设备、媒体技术设备、印前印刷、印刷包装、丝网标牌、油墨、造纸、纸业纸制品、柔印凹印等
上届规模 2010：展览面积2,700m²，参展商100家
主办：越南工业贸易部
承办：越南工业贸易部VINEXAD展览广告公司
联络：南宁越中会展商务有限公司
地址：广西南宁是新民路3号永嘉大厦1208室（530012）
☎ 0771-261 7885，261 5157,263 4881转1007
🖷 0771-263 0917
✉ exhibition@china-vn.net
hz.china-vn-con

越南国际纺织展

VTG

日期：2011/04/14 - 17
地点：越南
联络：上海比天展览服务有限公司
地址：上海市中山北路900号加禾商务中心3号楼303室(200070)
联系人：刘先生
☎ 021-5655 2843
🖷 021-5655 9981
www.betium.com

第七届越南河内国际食品暨制药工业展

日期：2011/04/19 - 22
地点：越南河内展览中心
主办：通讯展览公司
地址：香港九龙观塘成业街11号华成工商中心5字楼15室
☎ 852-2763 9011
🖷 852-2341 0379
✉ jenny@paper-con.com.hk
www.paper-com.com.hk

7th Vietnam-Hanoi Intl Food Tech & Pharmaceuticals Industry Exhibition

Date：2011/04/19 - 22
Venue: VEFAC-Vietnam Exhibition Fair Center, , Vietnam
Organizer: Paper Communication Exhibition Service
Address: Rm. 15, 5/F. Wha Shing Center, 11 Shing Ypi St., Kwun Tong, Kowloon, Hong Kong
Contact: Jenny Leung
☎ 852-2763 9011
🖷 852-2341 0379
✉ jenny@paper-con.com.hk
www.paper-com.com.hk

第七届越南河内国际包装及印刷工业展

日期：2011/04/19 - 22
地点：越南河内展览中心
主办：通讯展览公司
地址：香港九龙观塘成业街11号华成工商中心5字楼15室
☎ 852-2763 9011
🖷 852-2341 0379
✉ jenny@paper-con.com.hk
www.paper-com.com.hk

The 7th Vietnam-Hanoi Intl Printing & Packaging Industry Exhibition

Date：2011/04/19 - 22
Venue: VEFAC-Vietnam Exhibition Fair Center, Vietnam
Organizer: Paper Communication Exhibition Service
Address: Rm. 15, 5/F. Wha Shing Center, 11 Shing Ypi St., Kwun Tong, Kowloon, Hong Kong
☎ 852-2763 9011
🖷 852-2341 0379
✉ jenny@paper-con.com.hk
www.paper-com.com.hk

第七届越南-河内国际塑橡胶工业展

日期：2011/04/19 - 22
地点：越南河内展览中心
主办：通讯展览公司
地址：香港九龙观塘成业街11号华成工商中心5字楼15室
☎ 852-2763 9011
🖷 852-2341 0379
✉ jenny@paper-con.com.hk
www.paper-com.com.hk

The 7th Vietnam-Hanoi Intl Plastics & Rubber Industry Exhibition

Date：2011/04/19 - 22
Venue: VEFAC-Vietnam Exhibition Fair Center, , Vietnam
Organizer: Paper Communication Exhibition Service
Address: Rm. 15, 5/F. Wha Shing Center, 11 Shing Ypi St., Kwun Tong, Kowloon, Hong Kong
Contact: Jenny Leung
☎ 852-2763 9011

🖷 852-2341 0379
✉ jenny@paper-con.com.hk
www.paper-com.com.hk

第七届越南–河内国际工具机暨自动化设备展

日期： 2011/04/19 - 22
地点： 越南河内展览中心
主办： 通讯展览公司
地址： 香港九龙观塘成业街11号华成工商中心5字楼15室
☎ 852-2763 9011
🖷 852-2341 0379
✉ jenny@paper-con.com.hk
www.paper-com.com.hk

The 7th Vietnam-Hanoi Intl Machine Tool Automation & Components Exhibition

Date： 2011/04/19 - 22
Venue: VEFAC-Vietnam Exhibition Fair Center, , Vietnam
Organizer: Paper Communication Exhibition Service
Address: Rm. 15, 5/F. Wha Shing Center, 11 Shing Ypi St., Kwun Tong, Kowloon, Hong Kong
Contact: Jenny Leung
☎ 852-2763 9011
🖷 852-2341 0379
✉ jenny@paper-con.com.hk
www.paper-com.com.hk

越南河内国际纺织暨制衣机械展

日期： 2011/04/19 - 22
地点： 越南河内展览中心
主办： 通讯展览公司
地址： 香港九龙观塘成业街11号华成工商中心5字楼15室
☎ 852-2763 9011
🖷 852-2341 0379
✉ jenny@paper-con.com.hk
www.paper-com.com.hk

Vietnam Intl Textile & Garment Industry Exhibition

Date： 2011/04/19 - 22
Venue: VEFAC-Vietnam Exhibition Fair Center, , Vietnam
Organizer: Paper Communication Exhibition Service
Address: Rm. 15, 5/F. Wha Shing Center, 11 Shing Ypi St., Kwun Tong, Kowloon, Hong Kong
Contact: Jenny Leung
☎ 852-2763 9011
🖷 852-2341 0379
✉ jenny@paper-con.com.hk
www.paper-com.com.hk

越南国际制冷、空调、供暖、通风系统展览会

"RAHV 2011" –

International Exhibition on Refrigeration, Air-conditioning, Heating & Ventilation Systems

RAHV VIETNAM

日期： 2011/05/10 - 13
地点： 越南西贡会议展览中心 （SECC）
内容： 制冷、空调、供暖、通风、冷冻设备及技术
市场范围： 国际性
参展费用： 标准展位2,430 美元/9m²
主办： 显辉国际展览有限公司
地址： 香港上环禧利街27号富辉商业中心2403室
联系人： 林先生
☎ 852-2851 8603
🖷 852-2851 8637
✉ topreput@top-repute.com
www.toprepute.com.hk
www.construction-vietnam.com

RAHV 2011 -

International Exhibition on Refrigeration, Air-conditioning, Heating & Ventilation Systems

Date： 2011/05/10 - 13
Venue: Saigon Exhibition & Convention Center (SECC), Vietnam
Profile: Machinery, equipment & technology for refrigeration, air-conditioning、heating & ventilation
Market Area: International
Participated Fee: Standard Booth USD 2,430/9m²
Organizer: Top Repute Co Ltd
Address: Rm. 2403, Fu Fai Commercial Center, 27 Hillier Street, Sheung Wan, Hong Kong
Contact: Mr. Dennis Lam
☎ 852-2851 8603
🖷 852-2851 8637
✉ topreput@top-repute.com
www.toprepute.com.hk
www.construction-vietnam.com

越南国际安防、技防、消防设备和技术展览会

SECURITY & FIRE VIETNAM 2011 –

Vietnam International Security System, Fire Protection Equipment and Technology Exhibition 2011

SECURITY & FIRE VIETNAM

日期： 2011/05/10 - 13
地点： 越南西贡会议展览中心 （SECC）
内容： 安防、技防、消防产品、设备和技术
市场范围： 国际性
参展费用： 标准展位2,430美元/9m²
主办： 显辉国际展览有限公司
地址： 香港上环禧利街27号富辉商业中心2403室
联系人： 林先生
☎ 852-2851 8603
🖷 852-2851 8637
✉ topreput@top-repute.com
✉ dennis@top-repute.com
www.toprepute.com.hk
www.construction-vietnam.com

SECURITY & FIRE VIETNAM 2011

Vietnam International Security System, Fire Protection Equipment and Technology Exhibition 2011

Date： 2011/05/10 - 13
Venue: Saigon Exhibition & Convention Center (SECC), Vietnam
Profile: Machinery, equipment & technology for refrigeration, air-conditioning、heating & ventilation
Market Area: International
Participated Fee: Standard Booth USD 2,430/9m²
Organizer: Top Repute Co Ltd
Address: Rm. 2403, Fu Fai Commercial Center, 27 Hillier Street, Sheung Wan, Hong Kong
Contact: Mr. Dennis Lam
☎ 852-2851 8603
🖷 852-2851 8637
✉ topreput@top-repute.com
✉ dennis@top-repute.com
www.toprepute.com.hk
www.construction-vietnam.com

越南国际建筑展览会

VICB 2011 -

Vietnam International Construction & Building Exhibition 2011

日期： 2011/05/10 - 13
地点： 越南西贡会议展览中心
内容： 建筑/楼宇工程机械、设备、工具、建材及技术
市场范围： 国际性
参展费用： 标准展位2,430美元/9m²
主办： 显辉国际展览有限公司
地址： 香港上环禧利街27号富辉商业中心2403室
联系人： 林先生
☎ 852-2851 8603
🖷 852-2851 8637
✉ topreput@top-repute.com
www.toprepute.com.hk
www.construction-vietnam.com

VICB 2011

- Vietnam International Construction & Building Exhibition 2011

Date： 2011/05/10 - 13
Venue: Saigon Exhibition & Convention Center (SECC), Vietnam
Profile: Machinery, Equipment, Material & technology for construction and building industries
Market Area: International
Participated Fee: Standard Booth USD 2,430/9m²
Organizer: Top Repute Co Ltd
Address: Rm. 2403, Fu Fai Commercial Center, 27 Hillier Street, Sheung Wan, Hong Kong
Contact: Mr. Dennis Lam
☎ 852-2851 8603
🖷 852-2851 8637
邮箱: topreput@top-repute.com
www.toprepute.com.hk
www.construction-vietnam.com

越南国际食品包装机械及技术展览会

Foodpack - Vietnam

日期： 2011/05/10 - 13
地点： 越南胡志明市西贡会议展览中心
内容： 食品包装机械、食品加工机，标签及条码机、称量及封盖机、饮料瓶装机等
始办年份： 1993
周期： 每年一届
市场范围： 国际性
参展费用： 标准展位2,700美元/9m²
上届规模 2010：参展商120家（国外展商10家），参观人数9,000人
主办： 显辉国际展览有限公司
地址： 香港上环禧利街27号富辉商业中心2403室
联系人： 张小姐
☎ 852-2851 8603
🖷 852-2851 8637
✉ topreput@top-repute.com
www.machinery-vietnam.com

Foodpack – Vietnam

Date： 2011/05/10 - 13
Venue: Saigon Exhibition & Convention Center (SECC), Ho Chi Minh City, Vietnam
Profile: Food packaging machine, Food processing, Labeling & bar coding machine, Weighing & Capping Machine, Soft drink bottling
Established Year: 1993
Frequency: Annual

Market Area: International
Participated Fee: Standard Booth USD 2,700/9m^2
Statistics 2010: Exhibitors 120（foreigners 10）, Visitors 9,000
Organizer: Top Repute Co Ltd
Address: Rm. 2403, Fu Fai Commercial Center, 27 Hillier Street, Sheung Wan, Hong Kong
Contact: Ms. Cheung
☎ 852-2851 8603
🖷 852-2851 8637
✉ topreput@top-repute.com
www.machinery-vietnam.com

越南国际印刷、包装机械设备及技术展览会

Print & Pack – Vietnam

PRINT & PACK

日期：2011/05/10 - 13
地点：越南胡志明市西贡会议展览中心
内容：丝刷及移印机、标签机、包装机、膜纸、封口机、制袋机等
始办年份：1993
周期：每年一届
市场范围：国际性
参展费用：标准展位2,700美元/9m^2
上届规模 2010：参展商120家（国外展商10家），参观人数9,000人
主办：显辉国际展览有限公司
地址：香港上环禧利街27号富辉商业中心2403室
联系人：张小姐
☎ 852-2851 8603
🖷 852-2851 8637
✉ topreput@top-repute.com
www.machinery-vietnam.com

Print & Pack – Vietnam

Date：2011/05/10 - 13
Venue: Saigon Exhibition & Convention Center (SECC), Ho Chi Minh City, Vietnam
Profile: Screen & pad printing, Labeling machines, Packaging machines, Film, Sealer machine, Bag making machine, etc.
Established Year: 1993
Frequency: Annual
Market Area: International
Participated Fee: Standard Booth USD 2,700/9m^2
Statistics 2010: Exhibitors 120（foreigners 10）, Visitors 9,000
Organizer: Top Repute Co Ltd
Address: Rm 2403, Fu Fai Commercial Center, 27 Hillier Street, Sheung Wan, Hong Kong
Contact: Ms. Cheung
☎ 852-2851 8603
🖷 852-2851 8637
✉ topreput@top-repute.com
www.machinery-vietnam.com

越南国际自动化展览会

Automation – Vietnam

AUTOMATION

日期：2011/05/10 - 13
地点：越南胡志明市西貢会议展览中心
内容：各类自动化机械
始办年份：1993
周期：每年一届
市场范围：国际性
入场券价格：标准展位2,700美元/9m^2
上届规模 2010：参展商120家（来自10个国家），参观人数9,000人
主办：显辉国际展览有限公司
地址：香港上环禧利街27号富辉商业中心2403室
联系人：张小姐
☎ 852-2851 8603
🖷 852-2851 8637
✉ topreput@top-repute.com
www.machinery-vietnam.com

Automation – Vietnam

Date：2011/05/10 - 13
Venue: Saigon Exhibition & Convention Center (SECC), Ho Chi Minh City, Vietnam
Profile: Industrial automatic machinery
Established Year: 1993
Frequency: Annual
Market Area: International
Participated Fee: Standard Booth USD 2,700/9m^2
Statistics 2010: Exhibitors 120（foreigners 10）, Visitors 9,000
Organizer: Top Repute Co Ltd
Address: Rm 2403, Fu Fai Commercial Center, 27 Hillier Street, Sheung Wan, Hong Kong
Contact: Ms. Cheung
☎ 852-2851 8603
🖷 852-2851 8637
✉ topreput@top-repute.com
www.machinery-vietnam.com

越南国际金属加工设备及技术展览会

Metaltech - Vietnam

METALTECH

日期：2011/05/10 - 13
地点：越南胡志明市西贡会议展览中心
内容：金属加工设备、压缩机、工具及测试仪器、螺杆、切割机及各类金属零件等
始办年份：1993
周期：每年一届
市场范围：国际性
参展费用：标准展位2,700美元/9m^2
上届规模：参展商120家（来自10个国家），参观人数9,000人
主办：显辉国际展览有限公司
地址：香港上环禧利街27号富辉商业中心2403室
联系人：张小姐
☎ 852-2851 8603
🖷 852-2851 8637
✉ topreput@top-repute.com
www.machinery-vietnam.com

Metaltech – Vietnam

Date：2011/05/10 - 13
Venue: Saigon Exhibition & Convention Center (SECC), Ho Chi Minh City, Vietnam
Profile: Metalworking machines, Compressor, Tools and testing equipments, Screws barrel, Cutting tools, and Metal parts, etc.
Established Year: 1993
Frequency: Annual
Market Area: International
Participated Fee: Standard Booth USD 2,700/9m^2
Statistics 2010: Exhibitors 120（foreigners 10）, Visitors 9,000
Organizer: Top Repute Co Ltd
Address: Rm 2403, Fu Fai Commercial Center, 27 Hillier Street, Sheung Wan, Hong Kong
Contact: Ms. Cheung
☎ 852-2851 8603
🖷 852-2851 8637
✉ topreput@top-repute.com
www.machinery-vietnam.com

越南国际塑胶机械及技术展览会

Vietnam Plastic Fair

VIETNAM PLASTICS FAIR

日期：2011/05/10 - 13
地点：越南胡志明市西贡会议展览中心
内容：塑胶机械、产品、塑胶及橡胶原材料、模具、吹模机、注塑机
参展费用：标准展位 2,700美元/9m^2
上届规模：参展商120家，参观人数9,000人
主办：显辉国际展览有限公司
地址：香港上环禧利街27号富辉商业中心2403室
联系人：张小姐
☎ 852-2851 8603
🖷 852-2851 8637
✉ topreput@top-repute.com
www.machinery-vietnam.com

Vietnam Plastic Fair

Date：2011/05/10 - 13
Venue: Saigon Exhibition & Convention Center (SECC), Ho Chi Minh City, Vietnam
Profile: Plastic machinery, Product, Plastic & rubber raw material, Mould, Blow molding, Injection molding, etc.
Participated Fee: Standard Booth USD 2,700/9m^2
Statistics 2010: Exhibitors 120（foreigners 10）, Visitors 9,000
Organizer: Top Repute Co Ltd
Address: Rm 2403, Fu Fai Commercial Center, 27 Hillier Street, Sheung Wan, Hong Kong
Contact: Ms. Cheung
☎ 852-2851 8603
🖷 852-2851 8637
✉ topreput@top-repute.com
www.machinery-vietnam.com

越南制造机械展

Vietnam Manufacturing Expo

VIETNAM MANUFACTURING EXPO

日期：2011/05/19 - 21
地点：越南河内国际展览中心（I.C.E. Hanoi）
内容：越南制造机械展包括"InterPlas Vietnam""InterMold Vietnam""Automotive Manufacturing Vietnam""Automation Vietnam"四个部分，分别针对塑料和塑胶，模型和印模，自动化元件，自动化和组装技术等。同时，展会还包括科技演讲部分，传播业内最新科技。
周期：每年一届
主办：励展巴西公司
联络：励展博览集团国际销售部
地址：北京市朝阳区新源南路1-3号平安国际金融中心A座15层01-03,05
联系人：薛光
☎ 010-5933 9206
🖷 010-5933 9233
✉ eric.xue@reedexpo.com.cn
www.vietnammanufacturingexpo.com

越南电子展

NEPCON Vietnam 2011:

The International Electronics Manufacturing Technology Trade Exhibition and Conference – Vietnam Edition

日期：2011/05/19 - 21
地点：越南河内国际展览中心
内容：越南国际电子生产技术行业展会与研讨会。
产品及服务：表面贴装技术设备及服务、测试及测量设备及服务、电子产品生产服务、电子元器件及移动电话元器件、平板显示模块及应用、汽车部件及元器件生产技术、精密部件及金属部件相关产品、汽车检测与维护仪器及设备相关电子产品、汽车产业相关软件及电子设计、车载电子组件、车载通讯及导航系统、安全与保安系统相关电子设备及设计、发动机控制系统、汽车电器及车载电子系统。
周期：每年一届
市场范围：国际性
主办：励展泰国公司
联络：励展博览集团国际销售部

地址：北京市朝阳区新源南路1-3号平安国际金融中心A座15层01-03,05
联系人：张志超
☎ 010-5933 9266
🖷 010-5933 9233
✉ ivy.zhang@reedexpo.com.cn
www.nepconvietnam.com
www.reedexport.cn

越南国际模具展

InterMold Vietnam 2011:

Vietnam's Only Machinery and Technology Trade Exhibition & Conference for Mould & Die Manufacturing

日期：2011/05/19 - 21
地点：越南河内国际展览中心
内容：是越南唯一针对模具生产的机械及技术行业展会，该展会是越南工业配件制造技术领域四个国际性制造展会其中之一。同期展会：越南国际塑料及橡胶机械展InterPlas Vietnam，越南国际工业自动化、电力传输及材料处理技术展览及研讨会 Automotive Manufacturing Vietnam - 越南唯一针对汽车零部件制造的机械行业展会，越南电子展NEPCON Vietnam。
周期：每年一届
市场范围：国际性
性质：面向贸易观众
主办：励展泰国公司
联络：励展博览集团国际销售部
地址：北京市朝阳区新源南路1-3号平安国际金融中心A座15层01-03,05
联系人：薛光
☎ 010-5933 9206
🖷 010-5933 9233
✉ eric.xue@reedexpo.com.cn
www.reedexport.cn
www.vietnammanufacturingexpo.com

越南国际塑料及橡胶机械展

InterPlas Vietnam: Vietnam's International Plastic and Rubber Technology Trade Exhibition and Conference

日期：2011/05/19 - 21
地点：越南河内国际展览中心
内容：是泰国国际塑料和橡胶技术贸易展会及研讨会，该展会是越南工业配件制造技术领域四个国际性制造展会其中之一。同期展会有Automation Vietnam越南国际工业自动化、电力传输及材料处理技术展览及研讨会，Automotive Manufacturing Vietnam越南唯一针对汽车零部件制造的机械行业展会，越南国际模具展InterMold Vietnam越南唯一针对模具生产的机械及技术行业展会，以及越南电子展NEPCON Vietnam。
周期：每年一届
市场范围：国际性
性质：面向贸易观众
主办：励展泰国公司
联络：励展博览集团国际销售部
地址：北京市朝阳区新源南路1-3号平安国际金融中心A座15层01-03,05
联系人：薛光
☎ 010-5933 9206
🖷 010-5933 9233
✉ eric.xue@reedexpo.com.cn
www.reedexport.cn
www.vietnammanufacturingexpo.com

SAIGON AUTOTECH 2011

第7届越南国际汽车-摩托车工业技术展览会

日期：2011/06/02 - 06
地点：越南西贡国际会展中心
内容：运输工具：各种汽车，客车，巴士；各种货车；建筑车，救护车，医疗车，邮政车，银行车，卫生保健车，军用车等特殊用途汽车；摩托车；自行车；电动车；地铁，海陆运输工具；机车、机摩、自行车、配件类：各种汽车、摩托车，自行车有关专用部件，零配件；各种焊接、浇铸、喷漆、机械加工机器和设备；汽车、摩托车备用零部件的制造模具及机械工艺；燃料及填充设备类；维修及保养：汽车、摩托车维护及保养用品与设备；汽车、摩托车维修服务，各种电动工具；实用运输技术规划、研究、发展
上届规模 2010：展览面积10,000m²，参展商300家，参观人数100,000人
主办：越南工业贸易促进会– VCCI
承办：越南工业贸易部VINEXAD展览广告公司
联络：南宁越中会展商务有限公司
地址：广西南宁是新民路3号永嘉大厦1208室（530012）
☎ 0771-261 7885，261 5157，263 4881转1007
🖷 0771-263 0917
✉ exhibition@china-vn.net
hz.china-vn-con

越南国际鞋类、皮革制成品展览会

International Footwear & Leather Products Exhibition – Vietnam

日期：2011/07/21 - 23
地点：越南西贡会议展览中心
内容：所有鞋类、皮包和箱包、皮革衣服和产品、时尚皮制饰物配件、知名品牌产品
周期：每年一届
市场范围：国际性
主办：显辉国际展览有限公司
地址：香港上环禧利街27号富辉商业中心2403室
联系人：刘小姐
☎ 852-2851 8603
🖷 852-2851 8637
✉ topreput@top-repute.com
www.ifle-vietnam.com

International Footwear & Leather Products Exhibition – Vietnam

Date: 2011/07/21 - 23
Venue: Saigon Exhibition & Convention Center, Vietnam
Profile: All kinds of footwear, Bags & Suitcases, Leather Garments & Leather Product, Fashion Accessories, Brand Name Products
Frequency: Annual
Market Area: International
Organizer: Top Repute Co Ltd
Address: Rm. 2403, Fu Fai Commercial Center, 27 Hillier Street, Sheung Wan, Hong Kong
Contact: Ms. Lau
☎ 852-2851 8603
🖷 852-2851 8637
✉ topreput@top-repute.com
www.ifle-vietnam.com

越南国际鞋类、皮革及工业设备展览会

International Shoes & Leather Exhibition – Vietnam

日期：2011/07/21 - 23
地点：越南西贡会议展览中心
内容：鞋类机械、制革机、皮具机、皮革、原皮料、鞋材、化工、配件/辅料、成品
周期：每年一届
市场范围：国际性
上届规模 2010：参展商110家，参观人数3,700人
主办：显辉国际展览有限公司
地址：香港上环禧利街27号富辉商业中心2403室
联系人：郭小姐
☎ 852-2851 8603
🖷 852-2851 8637
✉ topreput@top-repute.com
www.shoeleather-vietnam.com

International Shoes & Leather Exhibition – Vietnam

Date: 2011/07/21 - 23
Venue: Saigon Exhibition & Convention Center, Vietnam
Profile: Tanning machinery, shoes machinery, raw materials, leather, chemicals, accessories, finished products, etc.
Frequency: Annual
Market Area: International
Statistics 2010: Exhibitors 110，Visitors 3,700
Organizer: Top Repute Co Ltd
Address: Rm. 2403, Fu Fai Commercial Center, 27 Hillier Street, Sheung Wan, Hong Kong
Contact: Ms. Kwok
☎ 852-2851 8603
🖷 852-2851 8637
✉ topreput@top-repute.com
www.shoeleather-vietnam.com

第十届中国机械(越南)展览会

日期：2011/07/27 - 30
地点：越南胡志明市西贡展览会议中心（SECC）
内容：工程建筑机械、矿产机械、冶金机械；机电设备、风机、电机、锅炉、泵类、电子仪表仪器、光电设备；橡塑机械、包装机械、印刷机械、造纸机械；食品生产加工设备；医疗制药设备；金属加工机械、数控设备及机床、锻压设备、锻压及切割设备、激光设备、表面处理设备、模具；纺织、缝制及印染设备；农林养殖机械；其它机械设备。
始办年份：2004
周期：每年一届
市场范围：国际性
性质：面向贸易观众
上届规模 2010：参展商200家
主办：粤召(香港)国际展览有限公司
联络：周文槟 先生
地址：广州市天河区体育东路122号羊城国际商贸中心东塔1108,1208室（510620）
☎ 020-8396 3610转706
🖷 020-3887 1331
✉ cnind99@21cn.com
MSN：gdwenbin@hotmail.com
QQ：406372636

第15届越南国际食品饮料工业博览会

15th session of the Vietnam International Industrial Fair Food and Beverage

日期：2011/08/17 - 21
地点：越南胡志明市新平国际会展中心
内容：食品饮料、食品饮料加工包装机械、食品添加剂及原料、冰淇淋加工技术设备
上届规模：展览面积3,760m²，参展商150家，参观人数15,000人
主办：越南工业贸易部；越南食品标准委员会
联络：南宁越中会展商务有限公司
地址：广西南宁是新民路3号永嘉大厦1208室（530012）
☎ 0771-261 7885，261 5157,263 4881转1007
🖷 0771-263 0917
✉ exhibition@china-vn.net
hz.china-vn-con

越南第11届越南国际医药制药、医疗器材展览会

11th Vietnam Vietnam international medical pharmaceuticals, medical equipment exhibition

日期：2011/08/24 - 27
地点：越南胡志明市新平国际展览中心TBECC
内容：药品类、制药及包装机械、医院装备及用品、保健品、骨科及口腔、医疗康复护理用品用具、医疗器械及实验室用品
上届规模：展览面积5,610m^2，参展商216家，参观人数21,200人
主办：越南卫生部，越南工业贸易部
联络：南宁越中会展商务有限公司
地址：广西南宁是新民路3号永嘉大厦1208室（530012）
☎ 0771-261 7885，261 5157,263 4881转1007
🖷 0771-263 0917
✉ exhibition@china-vn.net
hz.china-vn-con

第13届越南国际建筑建材装饰材料博览会

THE REGISTRATION FORM OF INTERNATIONAL EXHIBITION

VIETBUILD 2011

日期：2011/09/16 - 20
地点：越南胡志明市富寿展览中心
内容：建筑材料类：装饰材料、玻璃与加工玻璃、门窗幕墙、五金件、房屋建筑材料、建筑机械及设备、通风器材及建筑电工、电气、结构建材、建材生产技术及装备、陶瓷、石材、卫浴设施；建筑设计：建筑规划及设计、建筑工程、装饰工程及设计、建筑部品及节能前沿技术、太阳能与建筑一体化、楼宇智能化、建筑施工和安装机械设备、建筑消防设备器材及产品、防耐火材料；房地产类：城市规划、城市形象展示、房地产项目、住宅设施、园林景观、房地产营销策划；家居用品、家用电器、厨房设施、各类灯具、灯饰及配件、电光源产品、照明电器附件配件等。
始办年份：1997
周期：每年一届
市场范围：国际性
上届规模 2010：参展商840家（来自23个国家）
主办：越南国家建设部
联络：南宁越中会展商务有限公司
地址：广西南宁是新民路3号永嘉大厦1208室（530012）
☎ 0771-261 7885，261 5157,263 4881转1007
🖷 0771-263 0917
✉ exhibition@china-vn.net
hz.china-vn-con
联络：北京领汇国际展览有限公司
地址：北京市朝阳区农展馆南路13号瑞辰国际中心719室（100125）
联系人：欧琼芳
☎ 010-5129 5359转8811
🖷 010-5129 5379转8811
✉ qiongfang999@163.com
MSN：expo8811@worldfairs.cn
QQ：479170556
www.lewayfairs.com

第十一届越南国际食品工业展

日期：2011/09/21 - 24
地点：越南胡志明国际展览中心
主办：通讯展览公司
地址：香港九龙观塘成业街11号华成工商中心5字楼15室
☎ 852-2763 9011
🖷 852-2341 0379
✉ jenny@paper-con.com.hk
www.paper-com.com.hk

The 11th Vietnam Food Processing & Pharmaceuticals Industry Exhibition

Date：2011/09/21 - 24
Venue: SECC-Saigon Exhibition & Convention Center, Vietnam
Organizer: Paper Communication Exhibition Service
Address: Rm.15, 5/F. Wha Shing Center, 11 Shing Ypi St. Kwun Tong, Kowloon, Hong Kong
Contact: Jenny Leung
☎ 852-2763 9011
🖷 852-2341 0379
✉ jenny@paper-con.com.hk
www.paper-com.com.hk

第十一届越南胡志明国际技术加工机械展

日期：2011/09/21 - 24
地点：越南胡志明国际展览中心
主办：通讯展览公司
地址：香港九龙观塘成业街11号华成工商中心5字楼15室
☎ 852-2763 9011
🖷 852-2341 0379
✉ jenny@paper-con.com.hk
www.paper-com.com.hk

The 11th Vietnam Intl Metalworking & Accessories Exhibition

Date：2011/09/21 - 24
Venue: SECC-Saigon Exhibition & Convention Center, Vietnam
Organizer: Paper Communication Exhibition Service
Address: Rm.15, 5/F. Wha Shing Center, 11 Shing Ypi St. Kwun Tong, Kowloon, Hong Kong
Contact: Jenny Leung
☎ 852-2763 9011
🖷 852-2341 0379
✉ jenny@paper-con.com.hk
www.paper-com.com.hk

第十一届越南国际印刷工业展

日期：2011/09/21 - 24
地点：越南胡志明国际展览中心
主办：通讯展览公司
地址：香港九龙观塘成业街11号华成工商中心5字楼15室
☎ 852-2763 9011
🖷 852-2341 0379
✉ jenny@paper-con.com.hk
www.paper-com.com.hk

The 11th Vietnam Intl Print & Label Industry Exhibition

Date：2011/09/21 - 24
Venue: SECC-Saigon Exhibition & Convention Center,, Vietnam
Organizer: Paper Communication Exhibition Service
Address: Rm.15, 5/F. Wha Shing Center, 11 Shing Ypi St. Kwun Tong, Kowloon, Hong Kong
Contact: Jenny Leung
☎ 852-2763 9011
🖷 852-2341 0379
✉ jenny@paper-con.com.hk
www.paper-com.com.hk

第十一届越南国际包装工业展

日期：2011/09/21 - 24
地点：越南胡志明国际展览中心
主办：通讯展览公司
地址：香港九龙观塘成业街11号华成工商中心5字楼15室
☎ 852-2763 9011
🖷 852-2341 0379
✉ jenny@paper-con.com.hk
www.paper-com.com.hk

The 11th Vietnam Intl Packaging & Printing Industry Exhibition

Date：2011/09/21 - 24
Venue: SECC-Saigon Exhibition & Convention Center, Vietnam
Organizer: Paper Communication Exhibition Service
Address: Rm.15, 5/F. Wha Shing Center, 11 Shing Ypi St. Kwun Tong, Kowloon, Hong Kong
Contact: Jenny Leung
☎ 852-2763 9011
🖷 852-2341 0379
✉ jenny@paper-con.com.hk
www.paper-com.com.hk

第十一届越南国际塑胶工业展

日期：2011/09/21 - 24
地点：越南胡志明国际展览中心
主办：通讯展览公司
地址：香港九龙观塘成业街11号华成工商中心5字楼15室
☎ 852-2763 9011
🖷 852-2341 0379
✉ jenny@paper-con.com.hk
www.paper-com.com.hk

Vietnam Plas 2011

The 11th Vietnam Intl Plastics, Rubber Industry Exhibition

Date：2011/09/21 - 24
Venue: SECC-Saigon Exhibition & Convention Center,, Vietnam
Organizer: Paper Communication Exhibition Service
Address: Rm.15, 5/F. Wha Shing Center, 11 Shing Ypi St. Kwun Tong, Kowloon, Hong Kong
Contact: Jenny Leung
☎ 852-2763 9011
🖷 852-2341 0379
✉ jenny@paper-con.com.hk
www.paper-com.com.hk

第十一届越南胡志明国际工业自动化设备展

日期：2011/09/21 - 24
地点：越南胡志明国际展览中心
主办：通讯展览公司
地址：香港九龙观塘成业街11号华成工商中心5字楼15室
☎ 852-2763 9011
🖷 852-2341 0379
✉ jenny@paper-con.com.hk
www.paper-com.com.hk

The 11th Vietnam Intl Industrial Automation & Components Exhibition

Date：2011/09/21 - 24
Venue: SECC-Saigon Exhibition & Convention Center, Vietnam
Organizer: Paper Communication Exhibition Service
Address: Rm.15, 5/F. Wha Shing Center, 11 Shing Ypi St. Kwun Tong, Kowloon, Hong Kong
Contact: Jenny Leung
☎ 852-2763 9011
🖷 852-2341 0379
✉ jenny@paper-con.com.hk
www.paper-com.com.hk

第20届越南国际工业产品展览会

日期：2011/10 -
地点：越南讲武国际会展中心
内容：工业自动化技术 工业仪器仪表 工业制冷设备与技术 金属加工技术设备 机床及五金工具 工业模具技术
上届规模：展览面积12,000m^2，参展商500家，参观人数15,000人
主办：越南工业贸易部；越南科学技术部
联络：南宁越中会展商务有限公司
地址：广西南宁是新民路3号永嘉大厦1208室（530012）
☎ 0771-261 7885，261 5157,263 4881转1007
🖷 0771-263 0917
✉ exhibition@china-vn.net
hz.china-vn-con

第5届越南国际机床及金属加工机械贸易展

METALEX Vietnam:

Vietnam's Int'l Machine Tool & Metalworking Technology Expo

日期：2011/10/06 - 08
地点：越南胡志明市西贡展览中心（Saigon Exhibition & Convention Center）
内容：越南国际机床及金属加工机械贸易展是国际顶级的机床及金属加工技术展，隶属于METALEX--东南亚地区最大的机床及金属加工机械专业性展览会。METALEX Vietnam将展出越南买家所需的各种尖端技术，如机床、加工中心、金属板材加工、焊接技术、工厂自动化、模具、控制测量、工具及加工。
展商来源：机械工具和加工中心，金属薄片加工，焊接技术，工厂自动化、泵和阀门，物料传输，模具和铸模，丝、管、缆技术，控制测量，工具和加工技术。
周期：每年一届
上届规模 2010：参展商500家，参观人数11,410人
主办：泰国Reed Tradex
联络：励展博览集团国际销售部
地址：北京市朝阳区新源南路1-3号平安国际金融中心A座15层01-03,05
☎ 010-5933 9288
🖷 010-5933 9233
✉ liang.wang@reedexpo.com.cn
www.metalexvietnam.com
www.reedexport.cn

第九届越南国际木工工业展

日期：2011/10/12 - 15
地点：越南胡志明展览中心
主办：通讯展览公司
地址：香港九龙观塘成业街11号华成工商中心5字楼15室
☎ 852-2763 9011
🖷 852-2341 0379
✉ jenny@paper-con.com.hk
www.paper-com.com.hk

The 9th Vietnam Intl Woodworking Industry Fair

Date：2011/10/12 - 15
Venue: SECC-Saigon Exhibition & Convention Center, Vietnam
Organizer: Paper Communication Exhibition Service
Address: Rm.15, 5/F. Wha Shing Center, 11 Shing Ypi St. Kwun Tong, Kowloon, Hong Kong
Contact: Jenny Leung
☎ 852-2763 9011
🖷 852-2341 0379
✉ jenny@paper-con.com.hk
www.paper-com.com.hk

第十一届越南国际纺织暨制衣机械展

日期：2011/10/19 - 22
地点：越南胡志明国际展览中心
主办：通讯展览公司
地址：香港九龙观塘成业街11号华成工商中心5字楼15室
☎ 852-2763 9011
🖷 852-2341 0379
✉ jenny@paper-con.com.hk
www.paper-com.com.hk

The 11th Vietnam Intl Textile & Garment Industry Exhibition

Date：2011/10/19 - 22
Venue: SECC-Saigon Exhibition & Convention Center, Vietnam
Organizer: Paper Communication Exhibition Service
Address: Rm.15, 5/F. Wha Shing Center, 11 Shing Ypi St. Kwun Tong, Kowloon, Hong Kong
Contact: Jenny Leung
☎ 852-2763 9011
🖷 852-2341 0379
✉ jenny@paper-con.com.hk
www.paper-com.com.hk

2011越南国际鞋机鞋材暨皮革展

日期：2011/10/19 - 22
地点：越南胡志明国际展览中心
主办：通讯展览公司
地址：香港九龙观塘成业街11号华成工商中心5字楼15室
☎ 852-2763 9011
🖷 852-2341 0379
✉ jenny@paper-con.com.hk
www.paper-com.com.hk

2011 Vietnam International Footwear, Leather Machinery & Material Industry Exhibition

Date：2011/10/19 - 22
Venue: SECC-Saigon Exhibition & Convention Center, Vietnam
Organizer: Paper Communication Exhibition Service
Address: Rm.15, 5/F. Wha Shing Center, 11 Shing Ypi St. Kwun Tong, Kowloon, Hong Kong
Contact: Jenny Leung
☎ 852-2763 9011
🖷 852-2341 0379
✉ jenny@paper-con.com.hk
www.paper-com.com.hk

越南国际纺织展

VTG

日期：2011/10/27 - 30
地点：越南
联络：上海比天展览服务有限公司
地址：上海市中山北路900号加禾商务中心3号楼303室(200070)
联系人：刘先生
☎ 021-5655 2843
🖷 021-5655 9981
www.betium.com

2011越南国际农业博览会

Vietnam International Agriculture Fair 2011

日期：2011/11/11 - 14
地点：越南农业展览馆（河内）
内容：农业生产；种子、农药、化肥；农业机械及农产品加工；饲料及畜牧养殖技术；茶叶种植加工技术；农业高新科技术、产品等
上届规模：展览面积10,000m²，参展商300家，参观人数17,000人
主办：越南农业与农村发展部
地址：广西南宁是新民路3号永嘉大厦1208室（）
联络：南宁越中会展商务有限公司
地址：广西南宁是新民路3号永嘉大厦1208室（530012）
☎ 0771-261 7885，261 5157,263 4881转1007
🖷 0771-263 0917

越南通讯展

越南互联网与信息科技展

越南电子展2011

日期：2011/11/16 - 19
地点：越南河内广武展览中心 (VEFAC)
内容：作为越南最大规模及最具影响力的通讯、资讯技术及电子展览会，三展获得海外及本地运营商及知名跨国企业的鼎力支持，展示主题包括优化管理及网络服务、现代企业通讯、光纤通讯、数码内容及娱乐、数码营销、电子商贸、互联网安全、Web 2.0及网上社交网络、消费类电子产品、电子制造、个人数码设备和配件等。
周期：每年一届
市场范围：国际性
性质：面向公众面向贸易观众
入场券价格：免费入场
上届规模 2010：展览面积9,000m²，参观人数18,709人
主办：越南邮政电信集团的新闻及公共关系中心（IPC-VNPT）；越南信息技术协会（VAIP）；雅式展览服务有限公司
联络：雅式展览服务有限公司
地址：香港北角渣华道321号6楼
联系人：曾慧怡小姐，杨雪华小姐
☎ 852-2811 8897
🖷 852-2516 5119
✉ publicity@adsale.com.hk
www.vietnam-comm.com
www.vietnam-internet-it.com
www.vietnamelectronics.com

Vietnam Comm

Vietnam Internet & IT

Vietnam Electronics 2011

Date：2011/11/16 - 19
Venue: Vietnam Exhibition & Fair Center, Hanoi, Vietnam
Profile: Being the largest and most influential ICT and electronics industry events in Vietnam, the trio expos received extensive support from local and overseas giant operators and multi-national renowned corporations. Themed exhibits include managed services, modern enterprise communications, fiber-optic communications, digital content, digital advertising & marketing, e-commerce, information security, Web 2.0 & social networking, consumer electronics, electronics manufacturing, personal digital & accessories.
Frequency: Annual
Market Area: International
Cost to Attend: Free
Statistics 2010: Exhibition Area 9,000m², Exhibitors came from 13 countries，Visitors 18,709
Organizer: Information & Public Relations Center of Vietnam Posts & Telecommunications Group (IPC-VNPT), Vietnam Association for Information Processing (VAIP), Adsale Exhibition Services Ltd
Address: 6th Floor, 321 Java Road, North Point, Hong Kong
Contact: Ms Alice Tsang, Ms Sarah Yeung
☎ 852-2811 8897
🖷 852-2516 5119
✉ publicity@adsale.com.hk
www.vietnam-comm.com
www.vietnam-internet-it.com
www.vietnamelectronics.com

第9届越南（胡志明）国际贸易博览会

（VIETNAM EXPO）

THE 9th VIETNAM INTL TRADE FAIR IN HO CHI MINH CITY

日期：2011/11/30 - 03
地点：越南西贡国际会展中心
内容：投资洽谈、酒店用品、消费电子及小家电产品、体育及休闲用品、玩具及钟表眼镜、文具及办公用品、珠宝首饰、建筑建材，室内外装饰品
始办年份：2000
联络：南宁越中会展商务有限公司
地址：广西南宁是新民路3号永嘉大厦1208室（530012）
☎ 0771-261 7885，261 5157,263 4881转1007
🖷 0771-263 0917
✉ exhibition@china-vn.net
hz.china-vn-con

越南国际工程机械、建材机械、工程车辆及设备博览会

Con-Build

日期：2011/12 -
地点：越南胡志明
周期：每年一届
主办：中国贸促会
地址：北京市西城区三里河路46号（100823）
联系人：张玉惠，郭旭萍，吕春丽
☎ 010-6859 4811, 6859 4994, 6859 4910
🖷 010-6859 4995
✉ zhangyuhui@ccpitmsc.org
www.chinamachine.org.cn

海外展览会议行业分类

Exhibitions Overseas Listed by Industry Category

安全
Safety and Security

中东迪拜商业安全及消防器材博览会
INTERSEC
2011/01/16-18
阿联酋迪拜United Arab Emirates-Dubai

俄罗斯国际安防技术论坛
Intl. Forum & Exhibition on Security and Safety Technologies
2011/02/15-18
俄罗斯莫斯科Russia-Moscow

阿布扎比国际反恐安全展览会
ISNR (Abu Dhabi) International Security & National Resilience
2012/03/04-06
阿联酋阿布扎比United Arab Emirates-Abu Dhabi

美国西部国际安防产品博览会
ISC West:
Intl Security Conference West
2011/04/06-08
美国拉斯维加斯USA-Las Vegas

欧洲国际计算机信息系统安全展览会
Infosecurity Europe:
Europe's No. 1 Information Security Event
2011/04/19-21
英国伦敦United Kingdom-London

巴西国际安防产品博览会
Intl Security Conference & Exposition
2011/04/26-28
巴西圣保罗Brazil-Sao Paulo

越南国际安防、技防、消防设备和技术展览会
SECURITY & FIRE VIETNAM 2011
- Vietnam Intl Security System, Fire Protection Equipment and Technology Exhibition 2011
2011/05/10-13
越南胡志明市Vietnam-Ho Chi Minh City

IFSEC South India
南印度国际安全与消防技术设备展览会
2011/06/01-03
印度班加洛India-Bangalore

日本健康食品原料展
安全及技术展
Health Ingredients Japan
Safety and Technology Japan
2011/10/05-07
日本东京Japan-Tokyo

印度国际安全科技及产品大展
IFSEC India
2011/12/08-12
印度新德里India-New Delhi

法国国际安防展
消防设备展
Expoprotection
Feu: The Exhibition for Risk Management
2012/11-
法国巴黎France-Paris

包装
Packaging

英国食品、饮料包装机械、设备展览会
Processing & Packaging Solutions Event, Exclusively for the Food & Drink Industry
2011/03/13-16
英国伦敦United Kingdom-London

印度尼西亚国际橡塑暨包装展览会
Indoplas 2011
2011/03/30-04/02
印度尼西亚雅加达Indonesia-Jakarta

2010年中国广告印刷包装造纸技术产品（越南）展览会
2011/04/06-09
越南河内-Hanoi

第七届越南-河内国际包装及印刷工业展
7th Vietnam-Hanoi Intl Printing & Packaging Industry Exhibition
2011/04/19-22
越南河内Vietnam-Hanoi

越南国际食品包装机械及技术展览会
Foodpack - Vietnam
2011/05/10-13
越南胡志明市Vietnam-Ho Chi Minh City

越南国际印刷、包装机械设备及技术展览会
Print & Pack - Vietnam
2011/05/10-13
越南胡志明市Vietnam-Ho Chi Minh City

德国国际包装机械、包装及糖果机械展览会
Interpack
2011/05/12-18
德国杜塞尔多夫Germany-Dusseldorf

俄罗斯国际包装工业展览会
Rosupak
2011/06 -
俄罗斯莫斯科Russia-Moscow

巴西国际食品、饮料工业加工技术和包装工业博览会
Fispal Tecnologia
2011/06 -
巴西圣保罗Brazil-Sao Paulo

墨西哥国际包装展览会
Expo Pack
2011/06/23-26
墨西哥墨西哥城Mexico-Mexico City

第22届英国全套生产线暨加工及包装机械展
PPMA Show:
UK's annual showcase for Processing & Packaging Machinery
2011/09-
英国伯明翰United Kingdom-Birmingham

第十一届越南国际包装工业展
11th Vietnam Intl Packaging & Printing Industry Exhibition
2011/09/21-24
越南胡志明市Vietnam-Ho Chi Minh City

亚洲食品加工及包装展
Food Processing and Packaging Asia
2011/09/21-23
泰国曼谷Thailand-Bangkok

土耳其国际食品包装及食品机械展览会
IPACK
2011/09/22-25
土耳其伊斯坦布尔Turkey-Istanbul

美国国际包装机械博览会
Pack Expo
2011/09/26-28
美国拉斯维加斯USA-Las Vegas

世界制药机械、包装设备与材料印度展
P-MEC India
2011/11/30-12/02
印度孟买India-Mumbai

英国国际包装新技术展览会
Total Processing & Packaging
2013/05/21-23
英国伯明翰United Kingdom-Birmingham

承包、转包
Sub-Contracts

国际合同定制服务日本展
ICSE Japan
2011/04/18-20
日本东京Japan-Tokyo

泰国国际工业转包展
Subcon Thailand
2011/05/13-15
泰国曼谷Thailang-Bangkok

英国国际分包展览会
SUBCON
2011/06/08-10
英国伯明翰United Kingdom-Birmingham

印度国际合同服务展
ICSE India
2011/11/30-02
印度孟买India-Mumbai

宠物
Pets

国际观赏鱼及配件展览
Aquarama/Pet Asia 2011
2011/05/26-29
新加坡Singapore

船艇、海事
Boats, Ship Building and Marine

Imabari 海事展
Imabari Maritime Fair
(Bari-Ship)
2011/05/19-21
日本今治Japan-Imabari

挪威国际海事展览会
NOR-Shipping
2011/05/24-27
挪威奥斯陆Norway-Oslo

2011韩国国际游艇展
Korea Intl Boat Show 2011
2011/06/09-13
韩国京畿道South Korea-Gyeonggi

巴西造船、航运及海事展暨学术研讨会
Navalshore –
Shipbuilding and Offshore Industries Expo and Conference
2011/08/03-05
巴西里约热内卢Brazil-Rio de Janeiro

韩国海事展：
韩国国际造船及海事设备展
KORMARINE:
Intl Shipbuilding & Marine Equipment Exhibition
2011/10/26-29
韩国釜山South Korea-Busan

亚洲海上旅游及邮轮展
Cruise Shipping Asia
2011/11/16-18
新加坡Singapore

亚太海事展
Asia Pacific Maritime
2012/03/14-16
新加坡Singapore

灯光照明、灯饰
Lighting

日本国际照明展览会
LED/OLED Lighting Technology Expo
2011/01/19-21
日本东京Japan-Tokyo

英国伯明翰国际家具、灯具及室内装饰品展
2011/01/23-26
英国United Kingdom

2011年沙特国际灯具设备展
The 11th Intl Lighting Equipment Show
2011/05/30-02
沙特阿拉伯Saudi Arabia

中东（迪拜）国际城市、建筑和商业照明展览会
Light Middle East
2011/10/31-02
阿联酋迪拜United Arab Emirates-Dubai

电池、电源
Battery & Power

日本国际二次电池展
Intl Rechargeable Battery Expo
2011/03/02-04
日本东京Japan-Tokyo

电力、电工
Electric Power, Electrical Engineering

东京国际光伏发电展览会
Intl Photovoltaic Power Generation Expo
2011/03/02-04
日本东京Japan-Tokyo

2011年沙特能源电力博览会
14th Intl Electrical Engineering, Power Generation and Distribution Exhibition
2011/05/30-06/02
沙特阿拉伯Saudi Arabia

美国国际电力展览会
POWER-GEN
2011/12/08-10
美国拉斯维加斯USA-Las Vegas

电子
Electronics

日本电子展
Electronics Manufacturing & SMT Exhibition
2011/01/19-21
日本东京Japan-Tokyo

日本汽车电子展
Intl Automotive Electronics Technology Expo
2011/01/19-21
日本东京Japan-Tokyo

巴西国际电子展
Intl Electrical, Energy & Automation Industry Trade Fair
2011/03/28-01
巴西圣保罗Brazil-Sao Paulo

韩国电子展
SMT/PCB & NEPCON KOREA
2011/04/06-08
韩国首尔South Korea-Seoul

中国机械和电子产品展览会
CME
2011/05-
印度尼西亚雅加达Indonesia-Jakarta

2011年第十届沙特（利雅得）国际电子通讯展
The 10th Intl Information & communication Technology Exhibition for Saudi Arabia
2011/05/15-19
沙特阿拉伯Saudi Arabia

越南电子展
NEPCON Vietnam 2011:
Intl Electronics Manufacturing Technology Trade Exhibition and Conference – Vietnam Edition
2011/05/19-21
越南河内Vietnam-Hanoi

马来西亚槟城电子/微电子展览会
NEPCON Malaysia:
Malaysia's Only Event for Electronics Manufacturing Industry
2011/06/14-16
马来西亚槟城Malaysia-Penang

2011年泰国电子展：
国际电子产品制造贸易展及会议
NEPCON Thailand 2011:
Intl Electronics Manufacturing Technology Trade Exhibition and Conference
2011/06/23-26
泰国曼谷Thailand-Bangkok

越南通讯展
越南互联网与信息科技展
越南电子展2011
Vietnam Comm
Vietnam Internet & IT
Vietnam Electronics 2011
2011/11/16-19
越南河内Vietnam-Hanoi

新加坡电子展
Global TRONINCS
2012/09/19-21
新加坡Singapore

2013年泰国电子展：
国际电子产品制造贸易展及会议
NEPCON Thailand 2013:
Intl Electronics Manufacturing Technology Trade Exhibition and Conference
2013/06-
泰国曼谷Thailand-Bangkok

动漫 游戏
Comics and Games

科隆国际游戏展
gamescom
2011/08/17-21
德国科隆Germany-Cologne

第6届纽约国际动漫博览会
New York Comic Con:
The Largest Pop Culture Event on the East Coast
2011/10/14-16
美国纽约USA-New York

防务、警用设备
Defense and Police Equipment

阿布扎比国际反恐安全展览会
ISNR (Abu Dhabi) Intl Security & National Resilience
2012/03/04-06
阿联酋阿布扎比United Arab Emirates-Abu Dhabi

法国国际安防展
消防设备展
Expoprotection
Feu:
The Exhibition for Risk Management
2012/11-
法国巴黎France-Paris

第十三届马来西亚亚洲防务展览会
13th DEFENCE SERVICES ASIA EXHIBITION & CONFERENCE (DSA2012)
2012/04/16-19
马来西亚吉隆坡Malaysia-Kuala Lumpur

房地产
Real Estates

法国国际地产投资交易会
MIPIM featuring MIPIM Horizons:

The World's Property Market
2011/03/08-11
法国戛纳France-Cannes

纺织、服装 服饰及生产机械
Clothing and Textile

2011年法兰克福国际家用及商用纺织品展览会
Heimtextil
2011/01/12-15
德国法兰克福Germany-Frankfurt

美国TEXWORLD服装面料展
TEXWORLD USA
2011/01/18-20
美国纽约USA-New York

墨西哥服装面料展
INTERMODA
2011/01/18-21
墨西哥Mexico

巴黎国际服装、珠宝、银饰及配件展览会
Eclat de Mode
Bijorhca:
Intl Event dedicated to the Fashion Jewellery Universe
2011/01/21-24
法国巴黎France-Paris

哥伦比亚国际纺织服装展
Colombiatex
2011/01/25-27
哥伦比亚Colombia

德国慕尼黑国际面料展览会
MUNICH FABRIC START
2011/02/01-03
德国Germany

孟加拉达卡国际面料展
DIFS
2011/02/02-05
孟加拉Bangladesh

法国国际纺织面料春季博览会
TEXWORLD
2011/02/07-10
法国巴黎France-Paris

意大利米兰国际面料展
INTERTEX MILANO READY TO SHOW
2011/02/08-10
意大利Italy

第一视觉面料博览会（春）
Premiere Vision
2011/02/09-12
法国France

哥本哈根国际服装博览会
CIFF
2011/02/11-14
丹麦Denmark

孟加拉达卡国际纺织展
DTG
2011/02/13-16
孟加拉Bangladesh

拉斯维加斯国际服装服饰及面料博览会（春）
Magic Show
2011/02/15-18
美国USA

俄联邦莫斯科国际轻纺展
Taxtilexpo
2011/02/16-19
俄罗斯Russia

俄罗斯莫斯科服装博览会
CPM
2011/02/21-24
俄罗斯Russia

波兰国际纺织服装展
Tex-Style
2011/03/01-03
波兰Poland

美国洛杉矶纺织面料展会
GLOBALTEX
2011/03/02-04
美国USA

韩国大邱国际纤维展览会
Preview In Daegu
2011/03/10-12
韩国South Korea

迪拜纺织服装面辅料展
Motexha
2011/03/29-31
阿联酋迪拜United Arab Emirates-Dubai

2011年中东（迪拜）国际服装、纺织、鞋类及皮革制品博览会
2011 Motexha
2011/04 -
阿联酋迪拜United Arab Emirates-Dubai

瑞士日内瓦国际非织造布展览会
index11
2011/04/12-15
瑞士日内瓦Switzerland-Geneva

越南国际纺织展
VTG
2011/04/14-17
越南Vietnam

日本国际成衣展（春）
CFF
2011/04/19-21
日本Japan

越南河内国际纺织暨制衣机械展
Vietnam Intl Textile & Garment Industry Exhibition
2011/04/19-22
越南河内Vietnam-Hanoi

新加坡国际缝制设备展览会
Intl Apparel Machinery Trade Show
(JIAM 2011)
2011/05 -
新加坡Singapore

沙特（吉达）国际纺织展览会
The Fashion Arabia Exhibition
2011/05/08-11
沙特阿拉伯Saudi Arabia

阿根廷面料服装展
EMITEX
2011/05/10-12
阿根廷Argentina

斯里兰卡国际面料及纱线展
JIFS
2011/05/12-14
斯里兰卡Sri Lanka

印尼雅加达国际纺织面料及纱线展
JIFS
2011/05/12-14
印度尼西亚Indonesia

土耳其国际专业纱线展览会
Yarn Fair
2011/05/15-18
土耳其Turkey

17th土耳其伊斯坦布尔家用纺织品展览会
EVTEKS
2011/05/18-22
土耳其伊斯坦布尔-Istanbul

2011年法兰克福国际产业用纺织品及非织造布展览会
TECHTEXTIL
2011/05/24-26
德国法兰克福Germany-Frankfurt

印度面辅料展
F&A
2011/06/04-06
印度India

巴西圣保罗国际纺织工业及服装贸易博览会
FENIT
2011/06/17-20
巴西Brazil-

美国TEXWORLD服装面料展
TEXWORLD USA
暨中国纺织品服装贸易展览会(面料)
2011/07/19-21
美国纽约USA-New York

纽约国际服装采购展(APP)暨
中国纺织品服装贸易展览会(服装)
2011/07/19-21
美国纽约USA-New York

纽约国际家纺展（HTFSE）暨
中国纺织品服装贸易展览会(家纺)
2011/07/19-21
美国纽约USA-New York

墨西哥秋季国际服装和面料展
INTERMODA
2011/07/20-23
墨西哥Mexico

第12届孟加拉国际纺织机械展览会
2011/07/20-23
孟加拉达卡Bangladesh-Dhaka

孟加拉达卡国际面料展
DIFS
2011/07/28-31
孟加拉Bangladesh

土耳其伊斯坦布尔国际服装时尚展览会
Istanbul Fashion Fair
2011/07/29-31
土耳其Turkey

丹麦哥本哈根国际服装展览会
CIFF
2011/08/12-15
丹麦Denmark

拉斯维加斯国际服装服饰及面料博览会（秋）
Magic Show
2011/08/16-19
美国USA

捷克布鲁诺国际服装展
Styl&Kabo
2011/08/23-25
捷克Czech Republic

波兰国际纺织服装展
Tex-Style
2011/08/29-31
波兰Poland

2011韩国国际纺织展览会
Preview In Seoul 2011
2011/08/31-02
韩国首尔South Korea-Seoul

中国纺织品服装贸易展览会(巴黎)
CTAF
China Textile and Apparel Trade Fair(Paris)
2011/09 -
法国巴黎France-Paris

法国国际纺织面料秋季博览会
TEXWORLD
2011/09 -
法国巴黎France-Paris

日本国际成衣展（秋）
CFF
2011/09/01-03
日本Japan

意大利米兰国际面料展
INTERTEX MILANO READY TO SHOW
2011/09/08-10
意大利Italy

法国第一视觉面料博览会（秋）
Premiere Vision
2011/09/14-16
法国France

第11届欧洲国际纺织机械展览会
ITMA2011
2011/09/22-29
西班牙巴塞罗那Spain-Barcelona

2011韩国釜山国际纺织、时装展览会
Busan Intl Textile & Fashion Show 2011
2011/10/13-15
韩国釜山Korea-Busan

乌克兰基辅面料纱线展
FTA
2011/10/13-16
乌克兰Ukraine

第十一届越南国际纺织暨制衣机械展
11th Vietnam Intl Textile & Garment Industry Exhibition
2011/10/19-22
越南胡志明市Vietnam-Ho Chi Minh City

法国国际批发商博览会
INTERSELECTION
2011/10/19-21
法国France

法国巴黎服装服饰定牌贸易展览会
FATEX
2011/10/20-22
法国France

秘鲁纺织展
EXPOtextil Peru
2011/10/21-24
秘鲁Peru

越南国际纺织展
VTG
2011/10/27-30
越南Vietnam

埃及国际纺织品交易会
EGYTEX
2011/11/02-04
埃及Egypt

澳大利亚国际采购展
AISF
2011/11/17-19
澳大利亚Australia

澳大利亚中国纺织服装展
CTAF（Australia）
2011/11/17-19
澳大利亚Australia

南非国际纺织品、纺织机械及鞋类展览会
ATF
2011/11/24-26
南非South Africa

泰国国际服装及纺织品用机械、设备、材料及附件展
GFT 2012:
Thailand's 17th Intl Presentation of Machinery, Tools & Equipment for Garment & Textile Industries
2012/06/20-23
泰国曼谷Thailand-Bangkok

巴西纺织机械展
ITMEX Americas:
Intl Textile Machinery Trade Fair
2013 -
巴西圣保罗Brazil-Sao Paulo

工程机械
Construction Machinery

意大利国际工程机械与建材机械展览会
Samoter
2011/03/02-06
意大利维罗纳Italy-Guatemala City

2011北欧工程机械展暨瑞典哥德堡建筑机械展
2011/03/08-11
瑞典哥德堡Sweden-Gothenburg

2011年沙特阿拉伯国际建筑及工程机械展览会
2011/03/13-17
沙特阿拉伯Saudi Arabia

2011年拉斯维加斯工程机械展
Conexpo-Con/Agg
2011/03/22-26
美国拉斯维加斯USA-Las Vegas

2011年印尼国际重型设备及工程机械展览会
2011/03/23-26
印度尼西亚雅加达Indonesia-Jakarta

西班牙国际工程机械与矿山机械展览会
SMOPYC
2011/04/05-09
西班牙萨拉戈萨Spain-Zaragoza

利比亚国际工程建筑机械与建材机械展览会
Libya Build
2011/05 -
利比亚的黎波里Libya-Tripoli

俄罗斯国际建筑及工程机械展览会
CTT
2011/06-
俄罗斯莫斯科Russia-Moscow

南美国际混凝土设备展览会
Concrete Show South America
2011/08 -
巴西圣保罗Brazil-Sao Paulo

巴西国际工程机械零部件及服务展览会
M&T EXPO PARTS AND SERVICES
2011/08/10-13
巴西圣保罗Brazil-Sao Paulo

2011年巴西国际工程机械及矿山机械配件及技术展
2011/08/10-13
巴西圣保罗Brazil-Sao Paulo

哈萨克斯坦国际矿业和工程机械展览会
Mining World
2011/09-
哈萨克斯坦马尼拉Kazakhstan-Manila

沙特国际工程建筑机械与工程车辆展览会
PMV
2011/10 -
沙特阿拉伯利雅得Saudi Arabia-Riyadh

安哥拉国际工程机械与建材机械展览会
CONSTROI ANGOLA
2011/10-
安哥拉罗安达Angola-Luanda

阿尔及利亚国际工程及施工设备展览会
SITP
2011/11 -
阿尔及利亚阿尔及尔Algeria-Algiers

印度国际工程机械与技术展览会
EXCON
2011/11 -
印度班加罗尔India-Bangalore

越南国际工程机械、建材机械、工程车辆及设备博览会
Con-Build
2011/12 -
越南胡志明市Vietnam-Ho Chi Minh City

管道 管材 泵 阀门
Pipeline, Pump and Value

阿拉伯管材展览会
Tekno/Tube Arabia
2011/01/08-11
阿联酋迪拜United Arab Emirates-Dubai

俄罗斯国际管材线材展览会
Tube & Wire Russia
2011/05 -
俄罗斯莫斯科Russia-Moscow

亚洲国际管材、线材展览会
Tube & Wire Asia
2011/10 -
泰国曼谷Thailand-Bangkok

巴西国际管材、配件、管道、阀门及组件展览会
TUBOTECH
2011/10 -
巴西圣保罗Brazil-Sao Paulo

光电
Optp-Electronic

美国东部国际光学展
Intl Vision Expo East:
Largest Vision, Medical, Science & Technology Event in US
2011/03/18-20
美国纽约USA-New York

日本激光光学技术展
An Intl Event representing Asia's Photonics Industry
2011/04/13-15
日本东京Japan-Tokyo

美国西部国际光学展
Intl Vision Expo West
2011/09/21-24
美国拉斯维加斯USA-Las Vegas

广播、电影、电视设备
Broadcasting, Film, Television & Stage Equipment

2011年中东迪拜国际乐器、舞台灯光及舞台音响技术展览会
2011 PALME Middle East
2011/04 -
阿联酋迪拜United Arab Emirates-Dubai

法国戛纳春季电视节
The World's Entertainment Content Market
2011/04/04-08
法国戛纳France-Cannes

柏林国际会展及媒体技术展览会
SHOWTECH:
Intl Show & Conference for Stage Technology, Eqpt. & Event Svs
2011/06/07-09
德国柏林Germany-Berlin

第24届西班牙标识视觉传播及图像设计行业展
Viscom-Sign Espana:
Intl Trade Fair for Visual Communication
2011/10/06-08
西班牙马德里Spain-Madrid

第6届纽约国际动漫博览会
New York Comic Con:
The Largest Pop Culture Event on the East Coast
2011/10/14-16
美国纽约USA-New York

法国戛纳电视节
MIPCOM:
The World's Entertainment Content Market
2011/11/03-06
法国戛纳France-Cannes

意大利国际视觉传播展（第23届）
Viscom Visual Communication Italia:
Intl Trade Fair for Visual Communication
2011/11/03-05
意大利米兰Italy-Milan

世界影像博览会
photokina
2012/09/18-23
德国科隆Germany-Cologne

柏林国际会展技术及媒体技术展览会
SHOWTECH -
Intl Trade Show & Conference for Event Technology & Services
2013/06 -
德国柏林Germany-Berlin

广告 媒介
Advertising & Media

第23届法国巴黎国际视觉广告技术及标识制作展
Viscom Paris:
The Intl Event for Visual Communication
2011/09/27-29
法国巴黎France-Paris

第24届西班牙标识视觉传播及图像设计行业展
Viscom-Sign Espana:
Intl Trade Fair for Visual Communication
2011/10/06-08
西班牙马德里Spain-Madrid

德国国际视觉广告技术与标识制作展
viscom dusseldorf:
Intl Trade Fair for Visual Communication
2011/10/13-15
德国杜塞尔多夫Germany-Dusseldorf

意大利国际视觉传播展（第23届）
Viscom Visual Communication Italia:
Intl Trade Fair for Visual Communication
2011/11/03-05
意大利米兰Italy-Milan

世界影像博览会
photokina
2012/09/18-23
德国科隆Germany-Cologne

焊接
Welding

专业焊接技术及配件工艺贸易展
WeldTech
2011/05/12-15
泰国曼谷Thailand-Bangkok

航空、航天、机场
Aviation, Aerospace & Airport

德国汉堡国际飞机内饰展览会
Aircraft Interiors Expo - Hamburg
2011/04/05-07
德国汉堡Germany-Hamburg

迪拜机场设备展览会
Airport Show Dubai 2009
2011/05/31-02
阿联酋迪拜United Arab Emirates-Dubai

柏林-勃兰登堡国际航空航天展
LIA-Berlin Air Show
2012/06//19-24

环境保护
Environment Protection

阿布扎比环保展
ENVIRONMENT 2011
2011/01/17-20
阿联酋阿布扎比United Arab Emirates-Abu Dhabi

2011韩国太阳能、风能、地能展览会
Solar, Wind & Earth Energy Trade Fair 2011
2011/03/16-18
韩国光州-Gwangju

阿尔及利亚环保及水处理设备展
SIEE - Pollutec 2011:
6th Intl Exhibition of Equipment & Services for Water
2011/05/-
阿尔及利亚阿尔及尔Algeria-Algiers

柏林国际水利技术、污水处理展暨学术会议
WASSER BERLIN INTERNATIONAL
2011/05/02-09
德国柏林Germany-Berlin

国际环保技术展
Entech Pollutec Asia
2011/06/01-04
泰国曼谷Thailand-Bangkok

国际废物处理博览会
ENTECO
2011/06/06-09
德国科隆Germany-Cologne

拉美国际环保及卫生展览会
AmbientalExpo:
Latin America Sanitation & Environmental Solutions Fair
2011/06/28-30
巴西圣保罗Brazil-Sao Paulo

2011韩国国际环境能源产业展
ENVIRONMENT & ENERGY TECH 2011
2011/09/01-04
韩国釜山South Korea-Busan

摩洛哥环保及水处理设备展（第三届）
Pollutec Maroc:
Intl Environmental Equipment, Technologies & Services Event
2011/10/26-29
摩洛哥卡萨布兰卡Morocco-Casablanca

国际环保工业展
POLLUTEC
2011/12 -
法国巴黎France-Paris

奥地利国际汽车生产设备及加油站设备、化学品及环境技术展
Auto Zum:
Intl Trade Fair for the Car & Vehicle Industry
2013/01-
奥地利萨尔茨堡Austria-Salzburg

机械、制造、工业装备、自动化
Machinery, Machine Tools and Technology & Automation

印度国际机床工具展览会
IMTEX&TOOLTECH
2011/01/20-26
印度班加洛India-Bangalore

巴西国际服装制造机械及零部件展
Feimaco:
Intl Garment Industry Machinery & Components Trade Fair
2011/03 -
巴西圣保罗Brazil-Sao Paulo

印度国际机械工业展览会
India Intl Machinery and Equipment Exhibition
2011/03 -
印度孟买India-Mumbai

墨西哥国际机床展览会
TECMA
2011/03/08-11
墨西哥墨西哥城Mexico-Mexico City

土耳其国际工业展览会
WORLD OF INDUSTRY
2011/03/17-20
土耳其伊斯坦布尔Turkey-Istanbul

美国液压、气动、零部件展
IFPE
2011/03/22-26
美国拉斯维加斯USA-Las Vegas

阿根廷国际机床工具展览会
EMAQH
2011/03/25-30
阿根廷布宜诺斯艾利斯Argentina-Buenos Aires

2011年汉诺威国际工业展览会
2011/04/04-08
德国汉诺威Germany-Hanover

美国国际模具及机床技术展览会
Amerimold
2011/04/12-14
美国芝加哥USA-Chicago

日本FPD 制造设备及技术国际展览会
FPD R&D & Manufacturing Technology Expo & Conference
2011/04/13-15
日本东京Japan-Tokyo

第七届越南-河内国际工具机暨自动化设备展
The 7th Vietnam-Hanoi Intl Machine Tool Automation & Components Exhibition
2011/04/19-22
越南河内Vietnam-Hanoi

日本国际模具暨金属加工展览会
NTERMOLD
2011/04/20-23
日本东京Japan-Tokyo

中国机械和电子产品展览会
CME
2011/05 -
印度尼西亚雅加达Indonesia-Jakarta

俄罗斯国际机床展览会
METALLOOBRABOTKA
2011/05 -
俄罗斯莫斯科Russia-Moscow

澳大利亚国际机械制造周
AIEE
2011/05 -
澳大利亚墨尔本Australia-Melbourne

巴西国际机床工具及成套设备展
Intl Machine Tools and Integrated Manufacturing Systems Trade Fair
2011/05 -
巴西圣保罗Brazil-Sao Paulo

巴西农业机械展
Agrishow:
Intl Trade Fair for Agricultural Technology in Action
2011/05/02-06
巴西圣保罗Brazil-Sao Paulo

越南国际自动化展览会
Automation – Vietnam
2011/05/10-13
越南胡志明市Vietnam-Ho Chi Minh City

国际机器展
Intermach
2011/05/19-21
泰国曼谷Thailang-Bangkok

机器工具展/工业自动化展/国际专用工具及机械展
MOLDEX IA Robotics Machine Tools Thailand
2011/05/19-21
泰国曼谷Thailand-Bangkok

越南制造机械展
Vietnam Manufacturing Expo:
Vietnam's Largest Industrial Parts Manufacturing Machinery Event
2011/05/19-21
越南河内Vietnam-Hanoi

越南国际模具展
InterMold Vietnam 2011:
Vietnam's Only Machinery and Technology Trade Exhibition & Conference for Mould & Die Manufacturing
2011/05/19-21
越南河内Vietnam-Hanoi

澳大利亚机械制造周
National Manufacturing Week
2011/05/24-27
澳大利亚悉尼Australia-Sydney

俄罗斯国际模具制造与技术展览会
Rosmould
2011/06 -
俄罗斯莫斯科Russia-Moscow

波兰国际机械与创新技术展览会
MACH-TOOL
2011/06 -
波兰波兹南Poland-Poznan

俄罗斯国际建筑及工程机械展览会
CTT
2011/06 -
俄罗斯莫斯科Russia-Moscow

东京机械零部件及材料技术展
M-Tech:
Mechanical Components & Materials Technology Expo
2011/06/22-24
日本东京Japan-Tokyo

泰国国际装配技术展
Assembly Technology 2011:
The Intl Automated Manufacturing & Assembly Technology Exhibition
2011/06/23-26
泰国曼谷Thailand-Bangkok

泰国制造机械展
ASEAN's #1 Expo on Manufacturing & Processing Technologies
2011/06/23-26
泰国曼谷Thailand-Bangkok

泰国国际模具展
InterMold Thailand 2010
2011/06/23-26
泰国曼谷Thailand-Bangkok

第十届中国机械(越南)展览会
2011/07/27-30
越南胡志明市Vietnam-Ho Chi Minh City

第22届英国全套生产线暨加工及包装机械展
PPMA Show:
UK's annual showcase for Processing & Packaging Machinery
2011/09 -
英国伯明翰United Kingdom-Birmingham

俄罗斯国际动力传动、表面处理及工业自动化展览会
IA Russia
2011/09 -
俄罗斯莫斯科Russia-Moscow

欧洲机床展览会
EMO HANNOVER
2011/09/14-19
德国汉诺威Germany-Hanover

第十一届越南胡志明国际工业自动化设备展
The 11th Vietnam Intl Industrial Automation & Components Exhibition
2011/09/21-24
越南胡志明市Vietnam-Ho Chi Minh City

第十一届越南胡志明国际技术加工机械展
The 11th Vietnam Intl Metalworking & Accessories Exhibition
2011/09/21-24
越南胡志明市Vietnam-Ho Chi Minh City

南非国际模具展览会
Afrimold
2011/09/27-29
南非约翰内斯堡South Africa-Johannesburg

欧洲国际复合材料展
COMPOSITES EUROPE:
European Trade Fair for Composites, Technology & Applications
2011/09/27-29
德国斯图加特Germany-Stuttgart

第20届越南国际工业产品展览会
2011/10-
越南河内Vietnam-Hanoi

安哥拉国际工程机械与建材机械展览会
CONSTROI ANGOLA
2011/10 -
安哥拉罗安达Angola-Luanda

捷克国际机械博览会/
国际机床展览会
MSV & IMT
2011/10/03-07
捷克布尔诺Czech Republic-Brno

德国国际专业电梯设备及配件展览会
Interlift
2011/10/18-21
德国奥格斯堡Germany-Augsburg

泰国国际机床和金属加工机械展览会
Thai Metalex
2011/11 -
泰国曼谷Thailand-Bangkok

埃及国际机床工具展览会
MACTECH
2011/11 -
埃及开罗Egypt-Cairo

2011年美国国际齿轮世界展览会
2011/11/01-03
美国辛辛那提USA-Cincinnati

法国国际工业配件展（第41届）
MIDEST:
The World's Leading Industrial Subcontracting Show
2011/11/15-18
法国巴黎France-Paris

法国国际工业自动化展
SCS
2011/12 -
法国巴黎France-Paris

欧洲模具及机床技术展览会
EuroMold and Turntec
2011/12 -
德国法兰克福Germany-Frankfurt

印度尼西亚国际机床工具展览会
MACHINE TOOL INDONESIA
2011/12 -
印度尼西亚雅加达Indonesia-Jakarta

印度国际工业装备展览会
Industrial Automation INDIA
2011/12 -
印度孟买India-Mumbai

家具、木工机械
Furniture & Woodworking

科隆国际家具展
imm cologne
2011/01/18-23
德国科隆Germany-Cologne

第17届墨西哥国际家具工业展
2011/01/19-22
墨西哥Mexico

法国巴黎国际家具展
Masion&Objet2011
2011/01/21-25
法国France

英国伯明翰国际家具、灯具及室内装饰品展
2011/01/23-26
英国United Kingdom-

美国拉斯维加斯冬季国际家具展
Lasvegas2011
2011/01/24-28
美国USA

澳大利亚悉尼国际家具展
AIFF2011
2011/02/02-04
澳大利亚Australia

土耳其伊斯坦布尔国际家具展
IMOB2011
2011/02/02-06
土耳其Turkey

瑞典斯德哥尔摩国际家具展
2011/02/08-12
瑞典Sweden

马来西亚国际家具展
MIFF2011
2011/03/01-05
马来西亚Malaysia

新加坡国际家具展
IFFS2011
2011/03/09-12
新加坡Singapore

奥地利国际木材加工、处理、装配、木匠用品展
Intl Trade Fair for Woodworking
2011/03/23-26
奥地利萨尔茨堡Austria-Salzburg

中东阿布扎比国际家具展
2011/03/28-30
阿联酋United Arab Emirates

意大利米兰国际家具展
2011/04/12-17
意大利Italy-

叙利亚国际家具及木工机械展
2011/04/25-29
叙利亚Syria

莫斯科国际家具生产、木工及室内装饰展
俄罗斯春季家具展
interzum moscow 2011
EEM
EuroExpoFurniture 2011
2011/05/12-15
俄罗斯莫斯科Russia-Moscow

汉诺威国际林业木工机械展览会
LIGNA
2011/05/14-18
德国汉诺威Germany-Hanover

科隆国际家具生产、木工及室内装饰展
interzum cologne
2011/0525-28
德国科隆Germany-Cologne

埃及开罗国际建材、家具展
INTER BUILD2011
2011/06/23-27
埃及Egypt

东京国际办公家具展览会
Intl Office Furniture Expo
2011/07/06-08
日本东京Japan-Tokyo

英国曼彻斯特国际家具展
Manchester Furniture Show
2011/07/17-20
英国United Kingdom

墨西哥哈里斯科国际家具展
MUEBLE
2011/08 -
墨西哥Mexico

第27届巴西国际家具工业贸易展览会
2011/08 -
巴西Brazil

南非约翰内斯堡家具家居及室内装饰展
DECOREX2011
2011/08/01-05
南非South Africa

美国拉斯维加斯国际家具展
Lasvegas2011
2011/08/01-05
美国USA-

丹麦哥本哈根国际家具展
CODE2010
2011/09/01-04
丹麦Denmark

法国巴黎 Masion&Objet2011
2011/09/09-13
法国France

西班牙瓦伦西亚国际家具展
Ideas&Pasion
2011/09/20-24
西班牙Spain

第22届印度孟买国际家具展
INDEX MUMBAI2011
2011/09/29-02
印度India

阿塞拜疆国际家具展
Caspian Mebel Expo2011
2011/10 -
阿塞拜疆Azerbaijan

乌克兰基辅国际家具展
2011/10 -
乌克兰Ukraine

第19届新西伯利亚国际家具及加工设备、室内装饰展
SIBFURNITURE
2011/10/04-07
俄罗斯新西伯利亚Russia-Novosibirsk

第九届越南国际木工工业展
The 9th Vietnam Intl Woodworking Industry Fair
2011/10/12-15
越南胡志明市Vietnam-Ho Chi Minh City

第21届中东迪拜国际家具展
INDEX2011
2011/10/20-23
阿联酋迪拜United Arab Emirates-Dubai

第23届俄罗斯国际家具、配件及室内装潢展
MEBEL2011
2011/11 -
俄罗斯Russia

第31届日本东京国际家具展
IFFT/ILL2011
2011/11 -
日本Japan

科隆国际家具展
imm cologne
2012/01/17-22
德国科隆Germany-Cologne

泰国国际木工机械、家具制造机械、零件及相关技术展
Furnitech Woodtech 2012
2012/06/20-23
泰国曼谷Thailand-Bangkok

奥地利国际木材加工、处理、装配、木匠用品展
BWS: Intl Trade Fair for Woodworking
2013/04 -
奥地利萨尔茨堡Austria-Salzburg

印度尼西亚家具制造零配件展
iFMAC 2011
Furniture Manufacturing Components Show
2011/03/30-02
印度尼西亚雅加达Indonesia-Jakarta

建筑、建材、装饰及相关机械
Building, Construction, Decoration & Materials

意大利国际工程机械与建材机械展览会
Samoter
2011/03/02-06
意大利维罗纳Italy-Guatemala City

2011北欧工程机械展暨瑞典哥德堡建筑机械展
2011/03/08-11
瑞典哥德堡Sweden-Gothenburg

2011年沙特阿拉伯国际建筑及工程机械展览会
2011/03/13-17
沙特阿拉伯Saudi Arabia-

巴西国际建筑展
ISC Brazil:
Intl Construction Industry Trade Fair
2011/03/15-19
巴西圣保罗Brazil-Sao Paulo

第6届越南（河内）国际建筑建材装饰材料博览会
THE REGISTRATION FORM OF INTL EXHIBITION
VIETBUILD 2011
2011/03/23-27
越南河内-Hanoi

纽约楼宇维护技术展
BuildingsNY:
The Largest Buildings Event for the New York Metro Region
2011/03/30-31
美国纽约USA-New York

2011年俄罗斯莫斯科国际建筑建材展
Mosbuild
2011/04/05-08
俄罗斯莫斯科Russia-Moscow

2011年中东（迪拜）国际地面铺装展览会
2011 DOMOTEX Middle East
2011/05 -
阿联酋迪拜United Arab Emirates-Dubai

越南国际建筑展览会
VICB 2011
- Vietnam Intl Construction & Building Exhibition 2011
2011/05/10-13
越南胡志明市Vietnam-Ho Chi Minh City

莫斯科国际家具生产、木工及室内装饰展/俄罗斯春季家具展
interzum moscow 2011
EEM
EuroExpoFurniture 2011
2011/05/12-15
俄罗斯莫斯科Russia-Moscow

科隆国际家具生产、木工及室内装饰展
interzum cologne
2011/05/25-28
德国科隆Germany-Cologne

南非约翰内斯堡家具家居及室内装饰展
DECOREX2011
2011/08/01-05
南非South Africa-

2011年迪拜国际地面铺装展览会
DOMOTEX MIDDLE EAST
2011/09/12-14
阿联酋迪拜United Arab Emirates-Dubai

2011年迪拜国际地面铺装 展览会
DOMOTEX MIDDLE EAST
2011/09/12-14
阿联酋迪拜-Dubai

亚洲建筑及室内装饰展览会
Build Eco Xpo Asia
（BEX Asia）
2011/09/14-16
新加坡Singapore

第13届越南国际建筑建材装饰材料博览会
THE REGISTRATION FORM OF INTL EXHIBITION VIETBUILD 2011
2011/09/16-20
越南胡志明市-Ho Chi Minh City

2011年越南国际建筑建材展览会
2011/09/16-20
越南胡志明市Vietnam-Ho Chi Minh City

第17届100%伦敦室内设计展
100% Design London:
The UK's Leading Contemporary Interior Design Event
2011/09/22-25
英国伦敦United Kingdom-London

第19届新西伯利亚国际家具及加工设备、室内装饰展
SIBFURNITURE
2011/10/04-07
俄罗斯新西伯利亚Russia-Novosibirsk

国际桑拿及泳池设备展
Aquanale
2011/10/26-29
德国科隆Germany-Cologne

中东（迪拜）国际城市、建筑和商业照明展览会
Light Middle East
2011/10/31-02
阿联酋迪拜United Arab Emirates-Dubai

第28届法国巴黎国际建筑展览会
BATIMAT:
The World's Leading Construction Exhibition
2011/11/10-12
法国巴黎France-Paris

第23届俄罗斯国际家具、配件及室内装潢展
MEBEL2011
2011/11-
俄罗斯Russia

2011中东五大行业展览会
BIG 5
2011/11/21-24
阿联酋迪拜United Arab Emirates-Dubai

柏林国际建筑技术展
bautec
2012/02/21-25
德国柏林Germany-Berlin

米兰国际卫浴展
EXPOBAGNO
2012/03/27-30
意大利米兰Italy-Milan

法国国际建筑门窗展：
汇聚国际领先的门窗、防护和遮阳设备
Intl Windows, Doors, Shutters & Solar Protection Exhibition
2012/11 -
法国巴黎France-Paris

交通 轨道 航运
Transportation

巴西国际交通展览会
Fenatran:
Intl Transport Industry Trade Show
2011/10/24-28
巴西圣保罗Brazil-Sao Paulo

巴西国际铁路工业装备展览会
Business on Rails
2011/11 -
巴西圣保罗Brazil-Sao Paulo

金属加工、冶金、铸造锻造
Metalworking, Metallurgy & Foundry

2011年德国杜塞尔多夫国际铸造展览会
NEWCAST 2011
2011/04/04-08
德国杜塞尔多夫Germany-Dusseldorf

亚洲金属板材展
SHEET METAL ASIA 2011 –
15th ASEAN's Intl Sheet Metal Fabrication Technology and Machinery Exhibition
2011/05/19-21
泰国曼谷Thailand-Bangkok

越南国际金属加工设备及技术展览会
Metaltech - Vietnam
2011/05/10-13
越南胡志明市Vietnam-Ho Chi Minh City

德国国际铸造、铸件展览会
NEWCAST
2011/06/28-02
德国杜塞尔多夫Germany-Dusseldorf

第5届越南国际机床及金属加工机械贸易展
METALEX Vietnam:
Vietnam’s Intl Machine Tool & Metalworking Technology Expo
2011/10/06-08
越南胡志明市Vietnam-Ho Chi Minh City

荷兰国际不锈钢展览会
STAINLESS STEEL WORLD EXHIBITION
2011/11 -
荷兰马斯特里赫Netherlands-Maastricht

美国国际金属成型及管材展览会
FABTECH Intl Show
2011/11 -
美国芝加哥USA-Chicago

泰国国际机床和金属加工机械展览会
Thai Metalex
2011/11-
泰国曼谷Thailand-Bangkok

酒店业
Hotel & Restaurant

英国酒店用品展
Hospitality
2011/01/24-26
英国伯明翰United Kingdom-Birmingham

中东国际酒店及餐饮设备展
Equip'Hotel Middle East:
Hotel, Restaurant, Café and Catering Exhibition
2011/12 -
阿联酋阿布扎比United Arab Emirates-Abu Dhabi

英国酒店设备展
Hotelympia
2012/02 -
英国伦敦United Kingdom-London

法国国际酒店及餐饮设备展
Equip' Hotel:
The World Class Event for the Restaurant, Hotel, Cafes & Catering Industries
2012/11/11-15
法国巴黎France-Paris

英国酒店用品展
Hospitality
2013/01 -
英国伯明翰United Kingdom-Birmingham

消费电子、家用电器
Consumer Electronics & Appliances

美国国际小家电及家居用品展览会
Homewares Show
2011/05/10-12
美国拉斯维加斯USA-Las Vegas

巴西国际影像贸易及消费类电子展
PHOTOIMAGE BRAZIL: Intl Image Trade Fair
2011/08/16-18
巴西圣保罗Brazil-Sao Paulo

国际电子消费品展
IFA
2011年9月2日-7日
德国柏林Germany-Berlin

巴黎国际供暖、制冷、空调、新能源及家用电气展览会
Interclima+elec Home&building
2012/02-
法国巴黎France-Paris

空调、制冷、供暖
Air-conditioning, Heating, Refrigeration & Ventilation

美国国际空调、制冷和供暖展览会
AHR
2011/01/31-02
美国拉斯维加斯USA-Las Vegas

俄罗斯暖通、制冷、空调、卫浴及水池设备展览会
aqua-therm Moscow:
Intl Exhibition for HVAC Sector & Pools
2011/02/8-11
俄罗斯莫斯科Russia-Moscow

2011年西班牙国际制冷、暖通、泵阀及卫浴管件展
2011/03/01-04
西班牙马德里Spain-Madrid

RAHV 2011
越南国际制冷、空调、供暖、通风系统展览会
Intl Exhibition on Refrigeration, Air-conditioning, Heating & Ventilation Systems
2011/05/10-13
越南胡志明市Vietnam-Ho Chi Minh City

2011年沙特国际空调制冷，暖通设备博览会
The 12th Intl Air Conditioning, Ventilation, Heating and Refrigeration Show
2011/05/30-06/02
沙特阿拉伯Saudi Arabia

亚洲水泵及阀门展
Pumps & Valves Asia
2011/06/01-04
泰国曼谷Thailand-Bangkok

巴西国际制冷、空调、通风、供暖和空气处理贸易展
Febrava: Intl Refrigeration, Air-conditioning, Ventilation, Heating and Air Treatment Trade Fair
2011/09/20-23
巴西圣保罗Brazil-Sao Paulo

巴黎国际供暖、制冷、空调、新能源及家用电气展览会
Interclima+elec Home&building
2012/02/-
法国巴黎France-Paris

意大利米兰供暖、空调、制冷、再生能源及太阳能展
Mostra Convegno Expocomfort:
Production & Distribution line for the HVAC & Plumbing Sector
2012/03/27-31
意大利米兰Italy-Milan

矿业 Mining

印度南亚地球勘探科学展览会暨研讨会
The 3rd South Asia Geosciences Conference and Exhibition
(GEO India 2011)
2011/01/12-14
印度新德里India-New Delhi

西班牙国际工程机械与矿山机械展览会
SMOPYC
2011/04/05-09
西班牙萨拉戈萨Spain-Zaragoza

2011年第八届阿根廷国际矿业博览会
2011/05/04-06
阿根廷Argentina

2011年巴西国际工程机械及矿山机械配件及技术展
2011/0810-13
巴西圣保罗Brazil-Sao Paulo

哈萨克斯坦国际矿业和工程机械展览会
Mining World
2011/09 -
哈萨克斯坦马尼拉Kazakhstan-Manila

第30届南美秘鲁国际矿业机械设备展
2011/09 -
秘鲁阿雷基帕Peru-Arequipa

悉尼亚太国际矿业展
AIMEX:
Asia Pacific's Intl Mining Exhibition
2011/09/06-09
澳大利亚悉尼Australia-Sydney

澳大利亚昆士兰采矿机械展
Queensland Mining & Engineering Exhibition
(QME)
2012/07 -
澳大利亚Australia

悉尼亚太国际矿业展
AIMEX:
Asia Pacific's Intl Mining Exhibition
2014 -
澳大利亚悉尼Australia-Sydney

乐器、音乐 Music and Musical Instrument

世界音乐博览会
MIDEM:
The World's Music Market
2011/01/22-26
法国戛纳France-Cannes

2011年中东迪拜国际乐器、舞台灯光及舞台音响技术展览会
2011 PALME Middle East
2011/04 -
阿联酋迪拜United Arab Emirates-Dubai

礼品
Gifts

东京国际礼品采购展
Intl Variety
－ Gift Expo Tokyo
2011/07/06-08
日本东京Japan-Tokyo

旅游 Tourism

柏林国际旅游展
ITB Berlin
2011/03/09-13
德国柏林Germany-Berlin

拉美国际旅游博览会
Fair of the Americas:
Tourism Industry Trade Fair
2011/10/19-21
巴西里约热内卢Brazil-Rio de Janeiro

铝业 Aluminum Industry

迪拜国际铝工业展
Gateway to the Middle East's Aluminum Industry
2011/05/09-11
阿联酋迪拜United Arab Emirates-Dubai

印度国际铝工业展（第三届）
ALUMINIUM INDIA
2011/11/10-12
印度孟买India-Mumbai

2012 年印度国际铝展
Aluminum India 2012
2012 -
印度孟买India-Mumbai

2012 德国国际铝工业展览会
第八届世界铝工业博览会暨学术会议
ALUMINUM 2012
2012/10/09-11
德国杜塞尔多夫Germany-Dusseldorf

2013年迪拜中东国际铝工业展览会
ALUMINIUM Dubai 2013
2013 -
阿联酋迪拜United Arab Emirates-Dubai

美容美发、化妆品 Beauty, Cosmetics, Hairdressing & Spa

2011年中东（阿布扎比）国际美容美发博览会
2011 Beauty Vision
2011/02 -
阿联酋阿布扎比United Arab Emirates-Abu Dhabi

欧洲化妆品原料展
in-cosmetics
2011/03/29-31
意大利米兰Italy-Milan

俄罗斯专业化妆品及美容仪器博览会
Fair for Professional Cosmetics & Equipment for Beauty Salons
2011/04/14-16
俄罗斯莫斯科Russia-Moscow

2011年法兰克福中东（迪拜）国际美容及美发用品展览会
Beautyworld Middle East
2011/05/24-26
阿联酋迪拜United Arab Emirates-Dubai

澳大利亚国际美发展览会
Hair Expo Australia:
Expo, Education, Galas – Australia's Top Hairdressing Event
2011/06 -
澳大利亚悉尼Australia-Sydney

悉尼国际SPA及美容展览会
Sydney Intl Spa & Beauty Expo:
Australia's Premier Spa & Beauty Event
2011/08/13-14
澳大利亚悉尼Australia-Sydney

2011年第九届法国巴黎国际美容展览会
Beyond Beauty Paris
2011/09/12-14
法国巴黎France-Paris

2011年第九届法国巴黎国际美容展览会
Beyond Beauty Paris
2011/09/12-14
法国巴黎France-Paris

日本SPA美容展
Spa Japan
2011/09/26-28
日本东京Japan-Tokyo

纤体及美容展 2011（第十届）
Diet & Beauty Fair (10th)
2011/09/26-28
日本东京Japan-Tokyo

俄罗斯国际化妆品及美容博览会
InterCHARM:
Largest Perfumery & Cosmetics Exhibition in Russia & E. Europe
2011/10/26-29
俄罗斯莫斯科Russia-Moscow

亚洲国际化妆品原料展
in-cosmetics Asia:
The Leading Event in Asia for Personal Care Ingredients
2011/11/02-04
泰国曼谷Thailand-Bangkok

能源、节能 New Energy & Energy-Saving

东京国际光伏发电展览会
Intl Photovoltaic Power Generation Expo
2011/03/02-04
日本东京Japan-Tokyo

2011韩国太阳能、风能、地能展览会
Solar, Wind & Earth Energy Trade Fair 2011
2011/03/16-18
韩国光州South Korea-Gwangju

2011年沙特能源电力博览会
The 14th Intl Electrical Engineering, Power Generation and Distribution Exhibition
2011/05/30-02
沙特阿拉伯Saudi Arabia-

亚洲再生能源展
Renewable Energy Asia
2011/06/01-04
泰国曼谷Thailand-Bangkok

2011韩国国际环境能源产业展
ENVIRONMENT & ENERGY TECH 2011
2011/09/01-04
韩国釜山South Korea-Busan

印度能源展
India Energy
2011/09/29-01
印度孟买India-Mumbai

农业、林业、畜牧业、渔业、花卉 Agriculture, Animal Husbandry, Fishery & Forestry

柏林绿色周-食品工业、农业及园艺博览会
Internationale GrUne Woche Berlin
2011/01/21-29
德国柏林Germany-Berlin

国际果蔬展
FRUIT LOGISTICA
2011/02/09-11
德国柏林Germany-Berlin

法国国际农牧业设备及技术展览会
SIMA
2011/02/20-24
法国巴黎France-Paris

2011美国波士顿国际水产展
2011/03/14-16
美国波士顿USA-Boston

2011年比利时布鲁塞尔水产展
2011/04/27-29
比利时布鲁塞尔Belgium-Brussels

巴西农业机械展
Agrishow:
Intl Trade Fair for Agricultural Technology in Action
2011/05/02-06
巴西圣保罗Brazil-Sao Paulo

汉诺威国际林业木工机械展览会
LIGNA
2011/05/14-18
德国汉诺威Germany-Hanover

2011 越南国际农业博览会
Vietnam Intl Agriculture Fair 2011
2011/11/11-14
越南Vietnam

俄罗斯国际纸浆造纸、林业、生活用纸及纸包装展览会
PAP-FOR Russia: Intl Exhibition and Conference for Russia' s Pulp & Paper, Forestry, Tissue & Converting & Packaging Industries
2012/11-
俄罗斯圣彼得堡Russia-St. Petersburg

汽车、摩托车 Automobiles & Motorcycles

奥地利国际汽车生产设备及加油站设备、化学品及环境技术展
Intl. Trade Fair for Car Workshop & Petrol Station Equipment
2011/01/12-15
奥地利萨尔茨堡Austria-Salzburg

日本EV/MEV驱动系统技术展
EV & HEV Drive System Technology Expo
2011/01/19-21
日本东京Japan-Tokyo

日本汽车电子展
Intl Automotive Electronics Technology Expo
2011/01/19-21
日本东京Japan-Tokyo

南非国际汽车零部件及售后服务展览会
Automechanika South Africa
2011/03/09 - 12
南非约翰内斯堡South Africa-Johannesburg

2011年中东国际商用车及零配件展览会
Commercial Vehicle Middle East
2011/03/14-16
阿联酋迪拜United Arab Emirates-Dubai

2011年日本东京国际汽车零部件及汽保展
2011/03/16-18
日本东京Japan-Tokyo

2011年印尼国际商用车及零配件展
INAPA 2011
2011/03/23-26
印度尼西亚雅加达Indonesia-Jakarta

2011年伊比利亚汽车零部件、设备及售后服务展览会
Motortec Automechanika Ib é rica 2011
2011/03/30-04/02
西班牙马德里Spain-Madrid

2011年美国中部卡车展览会
MATS 2011
2011/03/31-04/02
美国路易斯维尔USA-Louisville

2011年马来西亚国际汽车零配件、设备及服务用品展览会
Automechanika Malaysia 2011
2011/03/31-04/02
马来西亚吉隆坡Malaysia-Kuala Lumpur

2011年巴西国际汽车零部件、维修设备及服务贸易展览会
AUTOMEC 2011
2010/04/05-09
巴西圣保罗巴西圣保罗Brazil-Sao Paulo

土耳其国际汽车制造、销售及维修展览会
2011/04/07-11
土耳其伊斯坦布尔Turkey-Istanbul

巴西国际汽车配件展
Intl Autoparts, Equipment and Services Trade Fair
2011/04/12-16
巴西圣保罗Brazil-Sao Paulo

2011年英国伯明翰商用汽车及配件展
The Commercial Vehicle Show 2011
2011/04/12-14
英国伯明翰United Kingdom-Birmingham

国际汽车生产及配件展览会
Automotive Engineering Asia
2011/05/12-15
泰国曼谷Thailand-Bangkok

澳大利亚汽车配件及售后服务博览会
Australian Auto Aftermarket EXPO
2011/05/12-14
澳大利亚墨尔本Australia-Melbourne

2011年波兰汽车工业及配件展览会
Automotive Technology Fair
2011/05/13-15
波兰波兹南Poland-Poznan

2011年第19届乌克兰（基辅）国际汽车及零配件展
2011/05/25-29
乌克兰基辅Ukraine

2011印度尼西亚国际及零配件展
Indoautomotive 2011
2011/05/25-28
印度尼西亚雅加达Indonesia-Jakarta

泛阿拉伯/非洲地区国际汽车及零配件展览会
AUTOMECH
2011/06 -
埃及开罗Egypt-Cairo

2011年加拿大国际汽车零配件及售后服务展览会
Automechanika Canada 2011
2011/06/01-04
加拿大多伦多Canada-Toronto

第7届越南国际汽车-摩托车工业技术展览会
SAIGON AUTOTECH 2011
2011/06/02-06
越南胡志明市Vietnam-Ho Chi Minh City

2011年捷克布鲁诺国际汽车展
Autosalon Bron 2011
2011/06/03-09
捷克布鲁诺Czech Republic- Bruno

2011年中东（迪拜）国际汽车零配件及售后服务展览会
Automechanika Middle East
2011/06/07-09
阿联酋迪拜United Arab Emirates-Dubai

2011年中东（迪拜）国际汽车零配件及售后服务展
Automechanika Middle East
2011/06/07-09
阿联酋迪拜United Arab Emirates-Dubai

2011年北非（埃及）汽车摩托车整车及零配件展览会
Automech 2011
2011/06/14-18
埃及开罗Egypt-Cairo

2011年斯里兰卡汽车及配件展览会
2011/06/23-25
斯里兰卡Sri Lanka

泰国国际汽车生产制造展览会
Automotive Manufacturing 2011
- ASEAN's Only Machinery Expo for Automotive Parts Manufacturing
2011/06/23-26
泰国曼谷Thailand-Bangkok

泰国汽车电子展
Automotive Electronics 2011:
2011/06/23-26
泰国曼谷Thailand-Bangkok

2011年中美洲国际汽车零配件、原料加工及售后服务贸易展览会
PAACE Automechanika Mexico 2011
2011/07/13-15
墨西哥墨西哥城Mexico-Mexico City

莫斯科国际汽车零配件展览会
Moscow Intl Motor Show
2011/08-
俄罗斯莫斯科Russia-Moscow

2011年莫斯科国际汽车零配件、售后服务及设备展览会
MIMS Automechanika Moscow 2011
2011/08/25-29
俄罗斯莫斯科Russia-Moscow

巴西里约热内卢国际汽车配件展览会
Rioparts
2011/09 -
巴西里约热内卢Brazil-Rio de Janeiro

巴基斯坦国际机械及汽车工业展览会
MTAP
2011/10 -
巴基斯坦卡拉奇Pakistan-Karachi

巴黎国际汽车工业展
EQUIP' AUTO
2011/10/18-23
法国巴黎France-Paris

第11届巴西国际两轮车展览会
Salão Duas Rodas:
Intl Motorcycle, Bicycle, Parts & Equipment Show
2011/10/04-09
巴西圣保罗Brazil-Sao Paulo

2011年拉斯维加斯改装车零配件展览会
SEMA 2011
2011/11/02-05
美国拉斯维加斯USA-Las Vegas

2011年美国拉斯维加斯国际汽车零配件及售后服务展览会
AAPEX
2011/11/03-05
美国拉斯维加斯USA-Las Vegas

印度尼西亚国际汽车制造机械及零配件展览会
2011/12 -
印度尼西亚雅加达Indonesia-Jakarta

越南国际工程机械、建材机械、工程车辆及设备博览会
Con-Build
2011/12 -
越南胡志明市Vietnam-Ho Chi Minh City

沙特国际工程建筑机械与工程车辆展览会
PMV
2011/10-
沙特阿拉伯利雅得Saudi Arabia-Riyadh

交通、车辆、组件-革新产品展
InnoTrans
2012/09/18-21
德国柏林Germany-Berlin

阿布扎比国际汽车展览会
Abu Dhabi Intl Motor Show
2012/12 -
阿联酋阿布扎比United Arab Emirates-Abu Dhabi

科隆国际摩托车、滑板车及自行车展览会
INTERMOT Cologne
2012/10/03-07
德国科隆Germany-Cologne

奥地利国际汽车生产设备及加油站设备、化学品及环境技术展
Auto Zum:
Intl Trade Fair for the Car & Vehicle Industry
2013/01 -
奥地利萨尔茨堡Austria-Salzburg

设计 Design

第17届100%伦敦室内设计展
100% Design London:
The UK's Leading Contemporary Interior Design Event
2011/09/22-25
英国伦敦United Kingdom-London

摄影、影像 Photgraphy & Image

巴西国际影像贸易及消费类电子展
PHOTOIMAGE BRAZIL:
Intl Image Trade Fair
2011/08/16-18
巴西圣保罗Brazil-Sao Paulo

石油、燃气 Petroleum, Gas, Petrochemical

巴西国际海洋石油及天然气工业设备展览会
Brazil Offshore:
Intl Offshore Oil and Gas Industry Trade Show and Conference
2011/06/14-17
巴西马珈耶Brazil-Ma Jiaye

2011 英国石油工业技术展
Offshore Europe 2011: Oil & Gas Exhibition & Conference
2011/09/06-08
英国阿伯丁United Kingdom-Aberdeen

俄罗斯石油和天然气技术展览会
SPE Russian Oil & Gas Technical Conference & Exhibition
2012/10-
俄罗斯Russia

巴西石油化工设备展
Química & Petroquímica:
Intl Trade Fair of Machinery & Equipment for the Chemical & Petrochemical Industry
2012 -
巴西圣保罗Brazil-Sao Paulo

巴西国际海洋石油及天然气工业设备展览会
Brazil Offshore:
Intl Offshore Oil and Gas Industry Trade Show and Conference
2013 -
巴西马珈耶Brazil-Ma Jiaye

食品、酒、饮料及相关机械 Food, Beverage, Spirit & Processing

2011年德国科隆国际糖果及休闲食品展览会
2011 ISM
2011/01-
德国科隆Germany-Cologne

柏林绿色周-食品工业、农业及园艺博览会
Internationale GrUne Woche Berlin
2011/01/21-29
德国柏林Germany-Berlin

科隆国际糖果原料和机械展览会
ProSweets Cologne 2010
2011/01/29-02/01
德国科隆Germany-Cologne

科隆国际糖果及休闲食品展
ISM- Intl Sweets and Biscuits Fair
2011/01/30-02
德国科隆Germany-Cologne

2011年德国柏林国际水果蔬菜博览会
2011 Fruit Logistica
2011/02 -
德国柏林Germany-Berlin

2011年中东（迪拜）海湾食品展览会
2011 Gulfood
2011/02-
阿联酋迪拜United Arab Emirates-Dubai

2011年俄罗斯国际食品展
PRODEXPO 2011
2011/02/07-11
俄罗斯莫斯科Russia-Moscow

奥地利国际食品技术及制造展览会
The Trade Fair for Food Technology & Manufacturing
2011/03 -
奥地利萨尔茨堡Austria-Salzburg

2011年第36届日本国际食品饮料展
2011/03/01-04
日本Japan

2011年美国西部天然有机食品博览会
2011/03/11-13
美国洛杉矶USA-Los Angeles

英国国际食品和饮料展
Intl Food & Drink Event
2011/03/13-16
英国伦敦United Kingdom-London

英国食品、饮料包装机械、设备展览会
Processing & Packaging Solutions Event, Exclusively for the Food & Drink Industry
2011/03/13-16
英国伦敦United Kingdom-London

里斯本国际食品展
Alimentaria&Horexpo Lisboa:
Intl. Exhibition of Food, Food Service & Technology
2011/03/27-30
葡萄牙里斯本Portugal-Lisbon

2011年加拿大蒙特利尔国际食品饮料展览会
2011 SIAL Montreal
2011/04 -
加拿大蒙特利尔Canada-Montreal

2011年中东（阿布扎比）国际食品及饮料展览会
2011 Middle East Food
2011/04-
阿联酋阿布扎比United Arab Emirates-Abu Dhabi

日本美食佳酿暨酒店及餐饮设备展
Wine & Gourmet Japan 2009
2011/04/06-08
日本东京Japan-Tokyo

第七届越南-河内国际食品暨制药工业展
The 7th Vietnam-Hanoi Intl Food Tech & Pharmaceuticals Industry Exhibition
2011/04/19-22
越南河内Vietnam-Hanoi

2011首尔国际食品产业大展
SEOUL FOOD 2011
2011/04/26-29
韩国首尔South Korea-Seoul

2011年比利时布鲁塞尔水产展
2011/04/27-29
比利时布鲁塞尔Belgium-Brussels

越南国际食品包装机械及技术展览会
Foodpack - Vietnam
2011/05/10-13
越南胡志明市Vietnam-Ho Chi Minh City

德国国际包装机械、包装及糖果机械展览会
Interpack
2011/05/12-18
德国杜塞尔多夫Germany-Dusseldorf

2011年第十届埃及食品及食品科技展
Food Fair &Tech
2011/05/23-26
埃及开罗Egypt-Cairo

亚洲世界食品博览会
Thaifex – World of Food Asia
2011/05/25-29
泰国曼谷Thailand-Bangkok

墨西哥国际食品及饮料展
Alimentaria Mexico:
Intl Food & Beverage Exhibition
2011/05/31-02
墨西哥墨西哥城Mexico-Mexico City

巴西国际食品、饮料工业加工技术和包装工业博览会
Fispal Tecnologia
2011/06 -
巴西圣保罗Brazil-Sao Paulo

2011美国食品科技展
IFT Food EXPO 2011
2011/06/12-14
美国新奥尔良USA-New Orleans

菲律宾食品配料展
Food Ingredients Philippines
2011/07/06-08
菲律宾马尼拉Philippines-Manila

第15届越南国际食品饮料工业博览会
15th session of the Vietnam Intl Industrial Fair Food and Beverage
2011/08/17-21
越南胡志明市-Ho Chi Minh City

莫斯科国际食品展览会
World Food Moscow
2011/09/13-16
俄罗斯Russia

亚洲食品加工及包装展
Food Processing and Packaging Asia
2011/09/21-23
泰国曼谷Thailand-Bangkok

第十一届越南国际食品工业展
The 11th Vietnam Food Processing & Pharmaceuticals Industry Exhibition
2011/09/21-24
越南胡志明市Vietnam-Ho Chi Minh City

土耳其国际食品包装及食品机械展览会
IPACK
2011/09/22-25
土耳其伊斯坦布尔Turkey-Istanbul

日本健康食品原料展
安全及技术展
Health Ingredients Japan
Safety and Technology Japan
2011/10/05-07
日本东京Japan-Tokyo

印度食品配料展
Food Ingredients India
2011/10/05-07
印度孟买India-Mumbai

世界食品博览会
Anuga
2011/10/08-12
德国科隆Germany-Cologne

法国国际葡萄酒及果蔬技术展
SITEVI
2011/11 -
法国France

印度食品博览会
Annapoorna - World of Food India
2011/11/16-18
印度孟买Germany-Mumbai

2011欧洲食品及天然配料展
Food ingredients Europe & Natural ingredients
2011/11/29-01
法国巴黎France-Paris

中东（迪拜）国际甜食及休闲食品技术与机械展览会
Sweets Middle East
2012/01/29-02/01
阿联酋迪拜United Arab Emirates-Dubai

2012年西班牙国际食品饮料展览会
Alimentaria 2012:
Intl Food & Beverage Exhibition
2012/03 -
西班牙巴塞罗那Spain-Barcelona

巴塞罗那国际食品、饮料设备及技术展览会
Bta. Barcelona tecnolog í as de la alimentaci ó n:
Bta. Barcelona Food Technology Exhibition
2012/05 -
西班牙巴塞罗那Spain-Barcelona

英国食品、饮料包装机械、设备展览会
Pro2Pac:
Processing & Packaging Solutions Event, Exclusively for the Food & Drink Industry
2013/03 -
英国伦敦United Kingdom-London

里斯本国际食品展
Alimentaria Lisboa:
Intl Food & Beverage Exhibition
2013/04 -
葡萄牙里斯本Portugal-Lisbon

英国国际食品和饮料展
IFE: Intl Food & Drink Event
2013/03 -
英国伦敦United Kingdom-London

巴塞罗那国际食品、饮料设备及技术展览会
Bta. Barcelona tecnolog í as de la alimentaci ó n:
Bta. Barcelona Food Technology Exhibition
2015 -
西班牙巴塞罗那Spain-Barcelona

市场营销 Business & Marketing

网络及手机直销方案展览会
Net & Mobile Direct Marketing Solution Fair
2011/02/24-25
日本东京Japan-Tokyo

Interop 商业科技东京展
Interop Tokyo
2011/06/07-10
日本东京Japan-Tokyo

数码营销博览会
dmexco
2011/09/21-22
德国科隆Germany-Cologne

Interop 商业科技印度展
Interop India
2011/09/28-30
印度孟买India-Mumbai

塑料、橡胶 Plastics & Rubbers

印度尼西亚国际橡塑暨包装展览会
Indoplas 2011
2011/03/30-02
印度尼西亚雅加达Indonesia-Jakarta

第七届越南-河内国际塑橡胶工业展
The 7th Vietnam-Hanoi Intl Plastics & Rubber Industry Exhibition
2011/04/19-22
越南河内Vietnam-Hanoi

巴西国际塑料机械展览会
Brasilplast:
Intl Plastic Industry Trade Fair
2011/05/09-13
巴西圣保罗Brazil-Sao Paulo

越南国际塑胶机械及技术展览会
Vietnam Plastic Fair
2011/05/10-13
越南胡志明市Vietnam-Ho Chi Minh City

越南国际塑料及橡胶机械展
InterPlas Vietnam:
Vietnam’s Intl Plastic and Rubber Technology Trade Exhibition and Conference
2011/05/19-21
越南河内Vietnam-Hanoi

泰国国际塑料及橡胶机械展
InterPlas Thailand 2011
2011/06/23-26
泰国曼谷Thailand-Bangkok

第十一届越南国际像素胶工业展
(Vietnam Plas 2011)
The 11th Vietnam Intl Plastics, Rubber Industry Exhibition
2011/09/21-24
越南胡志明市Vietnam-Ho Chi Minh City

泛阿拉伯/非洲塑料橡胶材料展览会
PLASTEX
2011/11 -
埃及开罗Egypt-Cairo

陶瓷、玻璃 Ceramic and Glass

米兰国际卫浴展
EXPOBAGNO
2012/03/27-30
意大利米兰Italy-Milan

特许经营 连锁加盟 Franchising

巴黎国际特许经营展览会
Intl Franchise Show
2011/03/20-23
法国巴黎France-Paris

体育、休闲 Sports & Leisure

美国国际射击展
Firearms, Hunting & Outdoor Products & Law Enforcement Products
2011/01/18-21
美国拉斯维加斯USA-Las Vegas

美国职业高尔夫球协会高尔夫用品展
PGA Merchandise Show
2011/01/27-29
美国奥兰多USA-Orlando

春季马术用品展
spoga horse(spring)
2011/02/06-08
德国科隆Germany-Cologne

国际健身及休闲运动用品博览会
FIBO - The Leading Intl Trade Show for Fitness, Wellness & Health
2011/04/14-17
德国埃森Germany-Essen

法兰克福中东（迪拜）国际园艺及户外休闲用品展览会
Garden and Landscaping Middle East
2011/05/10-12
阿联酋迪拜United Arab Emirates-Dubai

2011年德国菲德列斯哈芬户外休闲运动博览会
OutDoor
2011/07/14-17
德国菲德列斯-Feder Leeds

2011年德国菲德列斯哈芬户外运动休闲运动博览会
OutDoor
2011/07/14-17
德国菲德列斯Germany-Feder Leeds

美国职业高尔夫球协会高尔夫用品秋季展
PGA Fall Expo:
Golf's Premier Fall Buying Event for the Golf Industry
2011/08/22-24
美国拉斯维加斯USA-Las Vegas

秋季马术用品展
spoga horse (Autumn)
2011/09/04-06
德国科隆Germany-Cologne

国际体育用品、露营设备及园林生活博览会
国际园艺博览会
spoga/gafa
2011/09/04-06
德国科隆Germany-Cologne

第11届巴西国际两轮车展览会
Intl Motorcycle, Bicycle, Parts & Equipment Show
2011/10/04-09
巴西圣保罗Brazil-Sao Paulo

日本东京国际花卉、园艺及户外用品博览会
GARDEX:
Intl Garden & Exterior Expo Tokyo
2011/10/13-15
日本千叶Japan-Chiba

科隆国际休闲、体育设施及泳池设备展2011
FSB2011
2011/10/26-28
德国科隆Germany-Cologne

国际桑拿及泳池设备展
Aquanale
2011/10/26-29
德国科隆Germany-Cologne

秋季马术用品展
spoga horse(Autumn)
2012/09/04-06
德国科隆Germany-Cologne

科隆国际摩托车、滑板车及自行车展览会
INTERMOT Cologne
2012/10/03-07
德国科隆Germany-Cologne

图书
Books

伦敦书展
The World's Leading Spring Publishing Event
2011/04/11-13
英国伦敦United Kingdom-London

美国书展
-原美国书商协会大会及贸易展
BookExpo America
2011/05/24-26
美国纽约USA-New York

东京书展
Tokyo Intl Book Fair
2011/07/07-10
日本东京Japan-Tokyo

玩具、儿童用品
Toys & Children’s Products

2011 年法兰克福中东（迪拜）国际玩具及文具用品展览会
2011 Toy Fair Middle East
2011/03 -
阿联酋迪拜United Arab Emirates-Dubai

东京国际孕婴童用品展
Trade Show Gathering All Kinds of Items for Baby & Kids
2011/07/06-08
日本东京Japan-Tokyo

科隆国际少儿用品展
Kind + Jugend
2011/09/15-18
德国科隆Germany-Cologne

文具、办公用品
Stationery & Office Supplies

2011年法兰克福中东（迪拜）国际玩具及文具用品展览会
2011 Toy Fair Middle East
2011/03 -
阿联酋迪拜United Arab Emirates-Dubai

东京国际办公机械及设备展览会
OFMEX:
Intl Office Machines & Equipment Expo Tokyo
2011/07/06-08
日本东京Japan-Tokyo

日本东京国际文具及办公用品展
Intl Stationery & Office Products Fair Tokyo
2011/07/06-08
日本东京Japan-Tokyo

五金、工具
Hardware & Tools

科隆亚太采购交易会
—五金、家居、家电、园艺产品
Asia Pacific Sourcing
2011/03/09-11
德国科隆Germany-Cologne

西班牙毕尔巴鄂国际五金工具展
Ferroforma 2011
2011/03/23-26
西班牙毕尔巴鄂Spain-Bilbao

美国国际五金工具及花园用品展览会
Global gathering of newest products for DIY Home Improvement
2011/05/10-12
美国拉斯维加斯USA-Las Vegas

2011年法兰克福中东（迪拜）国际五金工具展览会
Hardware and Tools Middle East
2011/05/10-12
阿联酋迪拜United Arab Emirates-Dubai

日本东京国际五金及DIY展览会
Japan DIY Homecenter Show
2011/08 -
日本东京Japan-Tokyo

墨西哥国际五金展览会
Expo National Ferretera
2011/09 -
墨西哥墨西哥城Mexico-Mexico City

casaedecoracaoshow
第2届巴西国际家居用品、室内装饰及五金工具展
Intl. Trade Fair of Products for Refurbishment & Decoration
2011/09/22-25
巴西圣保罗Brazil-Sao Paulo

巴西国际管材、配件、管道、阀门及组件展览会
TUBOTECH
2011/10 -
巴西圣保罗Brazil-Sao Paulo

2011中东五大行业展览会
BIG 5
2011/11/21-24
阿联酋迪拜United Arab Emirates-Dubai

印度国际五金工具展览会
2011/12 -
印度孟买India-Mumbai

科隆国际五金博览会
INTL HARDWARE FAIR COLOGNE
2012/03/04-07
德国科隆Germany-Cologne

物流、仓储、运输
Logistics

巴黎国际实时运输及物流展
Intl Logistics Solutions Show
2011/03/29-31
法国巴黎France-Paris

2011年第四届阿尔及利亚汽配展
2011/04/03-07
阿尔及利亚Algeria

专业运输及材料装卸展
LogisPro Thailand
2011/05/19-21
泰国曼谷Thailand-Bangkok

迪拜国际运输及物流展
SITL Dubai:
Intl Week of Transport & Logistics
2011/06/05-07
阿联酋迪拜United Arab Emirates-Dubai

2011年法兰克福中东（迪拜）国际物流展览会
Materials Handling + Logistics Middle East
2011/09/25-27
阿联酋迪拜United Arab Emirates-Dubai

土耳其伊斯坦布尔国际汽车工业及配件展览会
2011/11/24-27
土耳其伊斯坦布尔Turkey-Istanbul

欧洲国际运输及物流周
SITL Europe:
Intl Event for Transport & Logistics
2012/03 -
法国巴黎France-Paris

巴黎国际实时运输及物流展
SITL Real Time:
Intl Show for Logistics Solutions
2013/03 -
法国巴黎France-Paris

消费品、家居
Consumer Goods

科隆亚太采购交易会—五金、家居、家电、园艺产品
Asia Pacific Sourcing
2011/03/09-11
德国科隆Germany-Cologne

美国国际小家电及家居用品展览会
Homewares Show
2011/05/10-12
美国拉斯维加斯USA-Las Vegas

美国国际五金工具及花园用品展览会
Global gathering of newest products for DIY Home Improvement
2011/05/10-12
美国拉斯维加斯USA-Las Vegas

法兰克福中东（迪拜）国际园艺及户外休闲用品展览会
Garden and Landscaping Middle East
2011/05/10-12
阿联酋迪拜United Arab Emirates-Dubai

2011年土耳其家居及厨房用品展览会
AMBIYANS-Household & Kitchenware Fair
2011/05/18-22
土耳其伊斯坦布尔-Istanbul

第2届巴西国际家居用品、室内装饰及五金工具展
CASA & DECORAçãO SHOW：Intl. Trade Fair of Products for Refurbishment & Decoration
2011/09/22-25
巴西圣保罗Brazil-Sao Paulo

日本东京国际花卉、园艺及户外用品博览会
GARDEX:
Intl Garden & Exterior Expo Tokyo
2011/10/13-15
日本千叶Japan-Chiba

鞋、皮革
Shoes & Leather

巴西国际鞋业、皮革制品及附件展览会
COUROMODA
2010/01/18-21
巴西圣保罗Brazil-Sao Paulo

印度鞋履、原料、制造及技术展览会
Footwear, Materials, Manufacturing and Technology
2011/05/06-08
印度诺伊达India-Noida

越南国际鞋类、皮革及工业设备展览会
Intl Shoes & Leather Exhibition - Vietnam
2011/07/21-23
越南胡志明市Vietnam-Ho Chi Minh City

越南国际鞋类、皮革制成品展览会
Intl Footwear & Leather Products Exhibition - Vietnam
2011/07/21-23
越南胡志明市Vietnam-Ho Chi Minh City

2011越南国际鞋机鞋材暨皮革展
2011 Vietnam Intl Footwear, Leather Machinery & Material Industry Exhibition
2011/10/19-22
越南胡志明市Vietnam-Ho Chi Minh City

信息技术、通信技术
Information Technology & Communication Technology

网络及手机直销方案展览会
Net & Mobile Direct Marketing Solution Fair
2011/02/24-25
日本东京Japan-Tokyo

日本光通信技术展
Fiber Optics Expo
2011/04/13-15
日本东京Japan-Tokyo

欧洲国际计算机信息系统安全展览会
Infosecurity Europe:
Europe’s No. 1 Information Security Event
2011/04/19-21
英国伦敦United Kingdom-London

日本软件开发展览会
SODEC: Software Development Expo
2011/05/11-13
日本东京Japan-Tokyo

2011年第十届沙特（利雅得）国际电子通讯展
The 10th Intl Information & communication Technology Exhibition for Saudi Arabia
2011/05/15-19
沙特阿拉伯Saudi Arabia

Interop 商业科技东京展
Interop Tokyo
2011/06/07-10
日本东京Japan-Tokyo

客户服务中心/客户关系管理展览会及会议大阪展
Call Centre/ CRM Demo & Conference Osaka
2011/06/21-24
日本大阪Japan-Osaka

嵌入式系统会议
Embedded Systems Conference India
2011/07/20-22
印度班加洛India-Bangalore

数码管理解决方案展览会
DMS EXPO
2011/09/20-22
德国科隆Germany-Cologne

数码营销博览会
dmexco
2011/09/21-22
德国科隆Germany-Cologne

伦敦信息技术基础架构展览会
360° IT
2011/09/21-22
英国伦敦United Kingdom-London

Interop 商业科技印度展
Interop India
2011/09/28-30
印度孟买India-Mumbai

国际博物馆及展示技术展览会
EXPONATEC
2011/11/16-18
德国科隆Germany-Cologne

越南通讯展/
越南互联网与信息科技展/
越南电子展2011
Vietnam Comm /
Vietnam Internet & IT /
Vietnam Electronics 2011
2011/11/16-19
越南河内-Hanoi

客户服务中心/客户关系管理展览会及会议
Call Centre/CRM Demo & Conference
2011/11/17-18
日本东京Japan-Tokyo

印度国际安全科技及产品大展
IFSEC India
2011/1208-12
印度新德里India-New Delhi

医药、医疗设备、保健、生物
Medical Equipment, Pharmaceuticals & Health Care

东京健康博览会
Tokyo Health Industry Show
2011/03/16-18
日本东京Japan-Tokyo

科隆国际牙科展
Intl Dental Show 2011
（IDS 2011）
2011/03/22-26
德国科隆Germany-Cologne

美国国际制药工业展览会
Pharmaceutical Manufacturing
2011/03/29-31
美国纽约USA-New York

墨西哥国际制药工业展览会
Expofarma INTERPHEX Mexico
2011/04 -
墨西哥墨西哥城Mexico-Mexico City

第十四届沙特国际医疗及医疗器械展
The 14th Intl Healthcare, Hospital Supplies and Medical Equipment Show
2011/04/10-13
沙特阿拉伯Saudi Arabia-

世界制药机械、设备与材料日本展
P-MEC Japan
2011/04/18-20
日本东京Japan-Tokyo

制药业生物解决方案日本展
BioPh Japan
2011/04/18-20
日本东京Japan-Tokyo

世界制药原料日本展览
CPhI Japan
2011/04/18-20
日本东京Japan-Tokyo

科隆国际牙科展
Intl Dental Show 2011
2011/04/22-26
德国科隆Germany-Cologne

亚洲制药工业展览会
Interphex Asia:
Asia's Dedicated Sourcing Platform for Pharmaceutical Manufacturing
2011/05/30-31
新加坡Singapore

日本国际制药工业展览会
Asia's Largest Pharmaceutical Industry
2011/06/29-01
日本东京Japan-Tokyo

越南第11届越南国际医药制药、医疗器材展览会
11th Vietnam Intl medical pharmaceuticals, medical equipment exhibition
2011/08/24-27
越南胡志明市-Ho Chi Minh City

第8届波多黎各国际制药工业展览会：
生物科技及制药商展览会
INTERPHEX Puerto Rico:
Featuring Medical Device Puerto Rico
2011/10/20-21
波多黎各圣胡安Puerto Rico-San Juan

世界制药原料印度展
CPhI India
2011/11/30-02
印度孟买India-Mumbai

世界制药机械、包装设备与材料印度展
P-MEC India
2011/11/30-02
印度孟买India-Mumbai

艺术
Arts

世界音乐博览会
MIDEM:
The World's Music Market
2011/0122-26
法国戛纳France-Cannes

科隆国际艺术展
ART COLOGNE 2009
2011/04/13-17
德国科隆Germany-Cologne

柏林国际艺术展
art forum berlin
2011/09/29-10/02
德国柏林Germany-Berlin

第38届法国国际当代艺术展览会
FIAC:
Intl Contemporary Art Fair
2011/10/10-23
法国巴黎France-Paris

科隆国际优秀艺术及古董展
Cologne Fine Art and Antiques
2011/11/16-20
德国科隆Germany-Cologne

印刷
Printing

2010年中国广告印刷包装造纸技术产品（越南）展览会
2011/04/06-09
越南河内-Hanoi

第七届越南-河内国际包装及印刷工业展
The 7th Vietnam-Hanoi Intl Printing & Packaging Industry Exhibition
2011/04/19-22
越南河内Vietnam-Hanoi

越南国际印刷、包装机械设备及技术展览会
Print & Pack – Vietnam
2011/0510-13
越南胡志明市Vietnam-Ho Chi Minh City

日本国际印刷展览会
IGAS
2011/09/16-22
日本东京Japan-Tokyo

第十一届越南国际印刷工业展
The 11th Vietnam Intl Print & Label Industry Exhibition
2011/09/21-24
越南胡志明市Vietnam-Ho Chi Minh City

俄罗斯国际印刷设备及技术展览会
POLYGRAPHINTER
2011/10/04-08
俄罗斯莫斯科Russia-Moscow

纸业
Paper

世界卫生纸展览会
Tissue World
2011/03/29-31
法国尼斯France-Nice

俄罗斯国际纸浆造纸、林业、生活用纸及纸包装展览会
PAP-FOR Russia:
Intl Exhibition and Conference for Russia’s Pulp & Paper, Forestry, Tissue & Converting & Packaging Industries
2012/11 -
俄罗斯圣彼得堡Russia-St. Petersburg

眼镜
Optics

美国东部国际光学展
Intl Vision Expo East:
Largest Vision, Medical, Science & Technology Event in US
2011/03/18-20
美国纽约USA-New York

2011年第十一届中东（迪拜）眼镜眼科用品展
Vision-X Dubai
2011/05/24-26
阿联酋迪拜United Arab Emirates-Dubai

眼镜
第24届东京国际眼镜展
IOFT: Intl Optical Fair Tokyo
2011/11/11-13
日本东京Japan-Tokyo

珠宝
Jewelry

巴黎国际服装、珠宝、银饰及配件展览会
Eclat de Mode/ Bijorhca:
Intl Event dedicated to the Fashion Jewellery Universe
2011/01/21-24
法国巴黎France-Paris

东京国际珠宝展
Intl Jewellery Tokyo
2011/01/26-29
日本东京Japan-Tokyo

印度国际宝石及珠宝展览会
Gem & Jewellery India Intl Exhibition
2011/02/26-28
印度钦奈India-Chennai

拉斯维加斯国际珠宝展
JCK Las Vegas: The Jewellery Industry's Premiere Trade Event
2011/06/03-06
美国拉斯维加斯USA-Las Vegas

海德拉巴珠宝珍珠玉石展览会
Hyderabad Jewellery, Pearl & Gem Fair
2011/07/09-11
印度海德拉巴India-Hyderabad

日本珠宝展
Japan Jewellery Fair
2011/09/01-03
日本东京Japan-Tokyo

伦敦国际珠宝展
Intl Jewellery London:
The UK’s Only Dedicated Jewellery Trade Event
2011/09/04-07
英国伦敦United Kingdom-London

孟买珠宝首饰展览会
Mumbai Jewellery & Gem Fair
2011/12 -
印度孟买India-Mumbai

综合博览会
General Fair

2011年中东（迪拜）国际秋季商品交易会
2011 IATF
2011/01 -
阿联酋迪拜United Arab Emirates-Dubai

开罗国际博览会
2011/03 -
埃及开罗Egypt-Cairo

巴西国际洗衣及干洗设备展
Expolav:
Laundry & Dry-cleaning Products & Services Trade Fair
2011/03/-
巴西圣保罗Brazil-Sao Paulo

2011年第四十四届埃及开罗贸易展览会
2011/03/06-10
埃及开罗Egypt-Cairo

2011巴拿马第29届国际博览会
Expocomer 2011
2011/03/23-26
巴拿马Panama

法国国际批发商博览会
INTERSELECTION
2011/04/04-06
法国France

第21届越南国际贸易博览会
VIETNAM EXPO
THE 21th VIETNAM INTL TRADE FAIR IN HA NOI CITY
2011/04/06-09
越南河内-Hanoi

朝鲜国际商品博览会
Intl Fair
2011/05 -
朝鲜平壤North Korea-Pyongyang

2011年澳大利亚全球商品采购交易会
2011 The Global Sourcing & Merchandising Expo
2011/05 -
澳大利亚墨尔本Australia-Melbourne

2011年印尼中国技术设备和商品展
2011 China Technical Equipment & Commodities Exhibition
2011/05/25-28
印度尼西亚雅加达Indonesia-Jakarta

坦桑尼亚国际贸易展览会
DITF
2011/06 -
坦桑尼亚达累斯萨拉姆Tanzania-Dar es Salaam

中国工业产品（委内瑞拉）展览会
2011/06 -
委内瑞拉加拉加斯Venezuela-Caracas

第四十四届北非阿尔及尔国际博览
2011/06/01-06
阿尔及利亚阿尔及尔Algeria-Algiers

中东贸易和伊拉克重建国际工业展览会
EXPO GATEWAY TO MIDDLE EAST
2011/06/02-05
土耳其加济安泰普Turkey-Gaziantep

2011年安哥拉国际贸易博览会
2011/07/14-21
安哥拉罗安达Angola-Luanda

肯尼亚国际贸易博览会
NITF
2011/09 -
肯尼亚内罗毕Kenya-Nairobi

2011年中国工业品（乌兹别克）展览会
China Industry Expo—UZBEKISTAN 2011
2011/09
乌兹别克塔什干Uzbekistan- Tashkent

莫斯科国际食品展览会
World Food Moscow
2011/09/13-16
俄罗斯 Russia

中国贸易展览会
2011/11 -
洪都拉斯圣佩德罗Honduras-San Pedro

中国贸易展览会
2011/11 -
危地马拉危地马拉城Guatemala-Guatemala City

2011年中国工业品（尼日利亚）展览会
Made In China Exhibition 2011
2011/11 -
尼日利亚Nigeria

第9届越南（胡志明）国际贸易博览会
VIETNAM EXPO
THE 9th VIETNAM INTL TRADE FAIR IN HO CHI MINH CITY
2011/11/30-12/03
越南胡志明市Vietnam-Ho Chi Minh City

第25届中东（迪拜）国际秋季商品交易会
Intl Autumn Trade Fair
2011/12/13-15
阿联酋迪拜United Arab Emirates-Dubai

其他
Others

印度南亚地球勘探科学展览会暨研讨会
3rd South Asia Geosciences Conference and Exhibition (GEO India 2011)
2011/01/12-14
印度新德里India-New Delhi

世界城市可持续发展论坛
The Intl Forum for Urban Decision-Makers
2011/03/15-18
阿联酋阿布扎比United Arab Emirates-Abu Dhabi

巴西国际地理信息展览会
GEO Summit Latin America:
Intl Geoinformation Congress & Exhibition
2011/05-
巴西圣保罗Brazil-Sao Paulo

柏林国际建筑物清洁、管理及服务展暨学术会议
CMS-Cleaning.Management.Services
2011/09/20-23
德国柏林Germany-Berlin

2011韩国国际文化创意产业展
Asia Content & Entertainment Industry Fair 2011
2011/09/22-25
韩国光州-Gwangju

德国国际专业电梯设备及配件展览会
Interlift
2011/1018-21
德国奥格斯堡Germany-Augsburg

巴黎国际殡葬展：
殡葬行业供应商与经销商的展会（第13届）
Fun é raire Paris 2011：
The Exhibition for Funeral Suppliers & Distributors
2011/11 -
法国巴黎France-Paris

巴黎国际殡葬展
Fun é raire Paris 2013:
The Exhibition for Funeral Suppliers & Distributors
2013/11 -
法国巴黎France-Paris

行业先锋
展览会议组织与管理

科隆国际展览有限公司

科隆国际展览有限公司 Koelnmesse GmbH 成立于1922年，是世界上最大的展览公司之一。其每年以不同周期定期主办的60多个国际专业博览会和展览会是世界上25个行业的主导博览会。在这些领域，全球90%以上的出口型产品在此展出。科隆展览的核心主题包括：食品行业；居室、园林与休闲；健康与设施；通讯、媒体与时装；家具、室内装饰与纺织品；艺术与文化；技术与环境；IT与数字娱乐。

国内联系方式：
科隆展览中国有限公司
地址：北京市东三环北路8号亮马河大厦2座1018室
邮编：100004
电话：010-6590 7878/7766
传真：010-6590 6139
电邮：info@koelnmesse.cn
网址：www.Koelnmesse.cn

科隆展览中国有限公司 上海办事处
地址：中国上海市淮海中路283号香港广场南楼1202室
邮编：200021
电话：021-6390 6161
传真：021-6390 6858
电邮：info2@koelnmesse.cn

科隆展览中国有限公司 广州办事处
地址：广州市天河区天河北路183号大都会广场3311室
邮编：510620
电话：020-8755 2468
传真：020-8755 2970
电邮：info3@koelnmesse.cn

中国国际贸易中心股份有限公司

中国国际贸易中心股份有限公司展览部是中国国际贸易中心股份有限公司下从事展览组织、管理的专业部门。拥有一支业务娴熟、人员精干的专业队伍，下设展览业务部、市场开发部、现场管理部等，可提供包括展览策划、立项报批、宣传招展、搭建展台、现场管理、展厅设施维护、出租场地设备的全套展览专业服务。凭借丰富的实践经验、外语技能、完善健全的管理制度、同国内外展览业同行的广泛联系以及来自外经贸部等中央国家部委的支持协助，国贸中心展览部参与组织、主办、协办了大量重要展览会，并赢得了国内外同行和展商的普遍好评。

地址：北京建国门外大街一号中国国际贸易中心展览部
邮编：100004
电话：010-6505 2288转80448
传真：010-6505-3260
电邮：cwtced@public3.bta.net.cn
网址：www.ecwtc.com

亚洲博闻

亚洲博闻有限公司隶属于伦敦股票交易所上市的博闻(UBM)。亚洲博闻总部设于香港，子公司遍布亚洲，包括在上海、杭州、广州及北京的博闻中国。集团拥有逾200项产业，涵盖商贸展会、会议、专业杂志、商业对商业或面对消费者的网站及网上虚拟會議及展會。亚洲博闻是亚洲首要的展会主办单位，也是中国和印度两大快速发展的市场之最大的商贸展会主办商。公司举办150个商贸展会、出版34本高质专业杂志，以及营运12个垂直网站，为来自全球逾1,000,000名参展商、买家、会议代表、广告商及读者提供高质素的会面商贸配对、实时市场动向、网上贸易网络、行业信息中心及采购和市场推广平台。亚洲博闻的办事处遍布亚洲，东达日本，西至土耳其，在17个主要城市共有超过800名员工。

公司在中国的主要展览包括：

• 九月香港珠宝首饰展览会 （香港） －全球最大型的珠宝展及香港最大型的展览会

• 中国国际家具展览会(上海) －亚洲最大型的家具展

• 中国国际海事技术学术会议和展览会(上海) －亚洲最大型及最重要的国际海事盛会

• 上海国际儿童、婴儿、孕妇产品博览会(上海) - 亚洲最大型的儿童、婴儿、孕妇产品展会

• 广东国际广告/LED展(广州) - 全球广告行业”奥斯卡”年度盛会及全球最大LED产业盛会

香港总办事处：
香港湾仔港湾道26号华润大厦17楼
电话：+852 2827 6211
传真：+852 3749 7310
电邮：info-hk@ubm.com
网址：www.ubmasia.com

博闻(广州)展览有限公司
中国广州市流花路中国大酒店商业大厦1159-1164室
(邮编：510015)
电话：020-8666 0158
传真：020-8667 7120
电邮：info-china@ubm.com
网站：www.ubmchina.com

博闻中国(上海)
中国上海市中山西路930号云都虹桥大厦1103室
(邮编：200051)
电话：021-6278 7488
传真：021-6219 2209
电邮：marketing-ubmtech@ubm.com

博闻中国(杭州)
浙江省杭州市拱墅区温州路69号南北商务港2-11F
（邮编:310015）
电话：0571-8839 5884
传真：0571-8838 8829

上海博华国际展览有限公司
中国上海市襄阳南路218号现代大厦7-8楼 （邮编：200031）
电话：021-6437 1178
传真：021-6437 0982
电邮：info@ubmsinoexpo.com
网站：www.ubmsinoexpo.com

广州闻信展览服务有限公司
中国广州市天河区林和东路华庭路4号富力天河商务大厦1306室（邮编：510015）
电话：020-3810 6261
传真：020-3810 6200
电邮：info-trust@ubm.com
网站：www.ubmtrust.com

亚洲博闻有限公司-香港总办事处：
香港湾仔港湾道26号华润大厦17楼
电话：852-2827 6211
传真：852-2827 7831
电邮：info@cmpasia.com
网址：www.cmpasia.com

上海博华国际展览有限公司
上海襄阳南路218号现代大厦十楼（邮编：200031）
电话：021-6437 1178
传真：021-6437 0982
电子邮箱：info@cmpsinoexpo.com
网址：www.cmpsinoexpo.com

博闻（广州）展览有限公司
中国广州市流花路中国大酒店商业大厦1151-1153室
邮编：510015
电话：020-8666 0158/ 8666 3388转ext 1151
传真：020-8667 7120
电子邮箱：info@cmpchina.com
网址：www.cmpchina.com

越中会展商务有限公司
VN-CN Convention Exhibition & Business Co Ltd

是一家专业从事策划和运作中国-越南两国之间双向展览会议、商务考察、市场调研、投资咨询、贸易配对、学术交流、商旅等多项服务融为一体的专业商务机构。

本公司与越南各层次政府及商务机构、会展公司、行业协会、企业界有着广泛人脉关系和紧密合作，所开展的商务活动一直得到越南贸易促进局、越南外商投资局、越南工商会、越南驻华大使馆商务处、越南驻南宁总领事馆等官方的大力支持。

由本公司和越南工业贸易部贸易广告博览公司牵头成立的“中越会展联盟”将致力于打造成为中越会展业务开拓先锋，致力于整合中越优势资源联手合作组织承揽中国参展参会商前往越南参加各类展会和合作组织承揽越南参展参会商来华参加各类展会。凭借着联盟的超前合作理念和专业操作平台，现已吸纳了多家中国和越南会展业界有识人士和实体参与联盟合作，目的是将合作操作的项目效果最大化及维护展商、会商利益最大化。

同时，本公司在组织越南商家来华参展参会采购和来华开展各类商务活动等领域也颇有成就，每年均组织和接待近2000名越南商家来华进行各类商务活动。我们曾为广交会、昆交会、、西博会、义乌小商品博览会、中国国际广告节、中国渔博会等国内20多个知名展览会成功邀请越南展商或采购商前来参会，并一直延续着合作关系。另，我司连续多年成为中国-东盟博览会越南参会客商组织接待和越南采购商招商协办机构。

（越南-中国）越中会展商务有限公司
VN-CN Convention Exhibition & Busiess Co Ltd
广西南宁市新民路3号永嘉大厦12楼
电话：0771-261 5157, 263 4998
传真：0771-263 0917
电邮：exhibition@china-vn.com

越南工业贸易部贸易广告博览股份公司（中国南宁办事处）
Vietnam National Trade Fair And Advertising Company
广西南宁市新民路3号永嘉大厦12楼
电话：0771-261 7885, 263 1887
传真：0771-263 1887
电子邮箱：vinexad.xttm@gmail.com

显辉国际展览有限公司

显辉国际展览有限公司成立于1989年，是一家发展迅速、专业从事在中国及东南亚地区筹办各类形专业展览会和会议服务的公司。

自成立以来，本公司便专注于发展展览业务，致力筹办不同的工业展览会，展览题材范围主要包括 ：鞋类、皮革及工业设备；医疗设备及技术；动漫画展；金属加工、塑料、印刷、食品包装的工业机械设备和技术；制冷、空调、供暖、通风及食品冷冻技术；建筑工程及建材设备；酒店、餐饮设备及服务；食品博览会；国际展销会和博览会等。

凭著已累积了20年的展览服务业经验，对亚洲各国和地区的市场动态充分了解、加上高效益的管理与营运，以及广阔的人脉网络，时至今天，我们每年所举办的国际大型展览会都已成为区内的触目盛事，部分的展览会更成为业内翘楚，亦是参展商及供应商推广业务的有效平台。 其中，在广州举办的“国际鞋类、皮革及工业设备展览会”已被誉为国内同类专业展中规模最大及最成功的国际展；还有在越南举办的工业机械展，包括“国际塑胶机械及技术展”；“国际金属加工设备及技术展”；“国际印刷、包装机械设备及技术展”；“国际食品包装机械设备及技术展”均在行内享有相当的美誉和地位。

为配合业务的迅速发展及日益频繁的商业活动需求，我们除了以香港作为总部外，亦早于公司成立之初在上海，广州，越南开设分公司，并在世界各国（包括中国大陆，台湾地区，日本，韩国，新加坡，巴基斯坦，澳大利亚，意大利，西班牙，德国等国家）建立代理服务网络，提供快捷和尽善尽美的服务。

显辉公司力求至臻，凭借广阔的人脉网络极富经验的管理层 ，具专业、富动力的员工团队，我们挚诚为世界各地的客户提供最全面的信息，最完善的服务。

地址：香港上环禧利街27号富辉商业中心2403室
电话：00852-2851 8603
传真：00852-2851 8637
电邮：topreput@hkabc.ne
网址：www.toprepute.com.hk

世界一流的展览及会议活动主办机构—英国励展博览集团早于上世纪80年代就进入中国办展览，现已发展为中国最活跃的国际展览及会议主办机构之一，拥有五家在华成员公司，包括励展中国公司、国药励展展览有限责任公司、励展华博展览(深圳)有限公司、北京励展华群展览有限公司和上海励华国际展览有限公司。励展大中华区现共有员工约450人。未来，励展还将通过持续增长现有展会、开发新项目和建立战略合作合资伙伴关系，为中国相关行业提供更多高品质的展览会，编奏面对面的力量。

励展博览集团在华举办的展览及会议在行业上涵盖了航天与航空，电子制造与组装，机床、金属加工及工业材料，包装，医药医疗及保健，礼品与家居，生活方式、旅游、博彩及地产7个在中国快速增长的专业领域。

2009年，励展各成员公司在华共举办逾40场市场领先展会，将来自海内外的逾2万名供应商和近70万名买家汇聚在一起进行面对面的业务交流和洽谈。

在不断促进相关产业及地区繁荣的同时，励展博览集团还积极履行企业公民责任，通过以下行动促进了中国会展业的可持续发展和回馈社会：

支持并在励展的展会里践行知识产权保护；

拥护展会数据审计及透明化，确保励展展会公布的数据真实有效；

关注环保，带动展会参与者及合作伙伴共同打造绿色展会；

通过“励展中国大学”持续培训中国本地员工；

实施“励展中国奖学金”，推进中国会展教育和人才培养；

捐资扶贫帮困；

举办“励展大中华区高峰会”，与行业领先企业携手推进中国展览业的提升与发展。

欲了解更多励展博览集团大中华区业务，请访问：
www.reedexpo.com.cn

澳门贸易投资促进局
为您提供全方位的商业服务

作为澳门特别行政区促进贸易和投资的机构，我们的使命是：促进本地对外贸易及引进外资，推动澳门与世界各地之间经贸关系的发展，加强相互了解，发展友好合作。

具体来讲，我们提供以下服务：

对投资者的“一站式”服务

对于在澳门的投资计划，我们向投资者提供有专人跟进的“一站式”服务：接受咨询、评估项目、专责公证办理成立公司手续、指引投资程序及所需牌照／准照申請、寻找合作伙伴、跟进有关行政手续及其它协助以便落实投资项目。为了使此项服务更加便捷完善，本局内设“专责公证员”，并且也设立了由九个政府部门主管组成的“投资委员会”。

离岸服务

本局负责非金融离岸业务的审批、技术协助和监管工作，并通过推广活动促进非金融离岸业务在澳之发展。允许在澳门经营的离岸机构分为“离岸商业服务机构”和“离岸辅助服务机构”。政府向离岸商业活动提供多项税务优惠。离岸机构只需向本局繳付一次性的设立费，及每半年一次的运作费。

经贸推广活动

本局每年主办、协办及参与在澳门及全球各地举行的经贸会展和贸易投资合作活动，主要包括：澳门国际贸易投资展览会(MIF)、中国内地及葡语国家的大型经贸洽谈会，以及各地区的投资环境推介会等。同时，本局每年亦曾组织经贸代表团出外考察访问，并接待外地代表到访，促进澳门与海内外企业家的交流与合作。此外，本局对澳门企业参加世界各地的展览会提供多方面支持，包括资助部分的参展及宣传品印刷经费，提供全球多项展览会信息等。

澳门商务促进中心

“中心”的设立是为了让外來投资者在低成本及短时间內了解澳门的营商环境和办理有关行政手续，减低在澳经商的启动成本，并为本地的企业和商会提供一个直接与外地企业和商会交流与合作的服务平台。“中心”向企业提供：

设施设备－包括现代化办公室、洽谈室、产品展示区、电脑设备、无线宽频互联网。另设有收费多功能会议厅、影印及传真等商务设备。

商贸服务—包括“贸促局咨询服务专柜”、“内地商务咨询服务”、秘书服务，以及提供有关本地企业、驻“中心”商会、政府部门行政手续及本地统计资料。另外，尚有与商会合作举办商贸推介及交流活动等。

企业之间及企业与办事处互相交流的平台—“中心”有多间外地商会、团体、机构、组织代表处(统称：办事处)进驻，如“渝澳经济合作促进会澳门秘书处”、“世界华商组织联盟”、“葡中工商协会”、“国际葡语市场企业家商会”、“中国国际贸易促进委员会驻港澳代表处”、“澳门德国商会”、“澳洲商务署澳门办事处”、“欧洲咨询中心”、“澳门葡萄牙商务中心”、“澳门英国商会”及“日资商业服务中心(澳门)有限公司”。企业可向驻“中心”的办事处直接咨询。“中心”为企业及各驻场办事处提供了交流与合作的机会。

中小企服务中心

为加強本澳中小企业之综合竞争力，把握澳门经济发展所带来之商机，并按照澳门政府支持中小企业发展的政策，于澳门贸易投资促进局属下之“澳门商务促进中心”將推出一系列协助本地中小企业之服务，并设立“中小企服务中心”，目的是协助本地中小企开拓海外和本地市场，并结合海外及本地市场需求，促进企业交流合作，引导中小企把握澳门服务业及会展业所带来之商机。

咨询服务

为了推广澳门的经贸环境，向海內外商界提供最新的商贸讯息，本局定期出版“贸易投资快讯”和“澳门经济之窗”，也經常发行“投资者指南”及有关宣传性刊物及光碟。本局的网页是我们向公众提供资讯的。

主要途径：

除了关于澳门和本局的一般资料及主要刊物内容，还有本澳制造商和出口商的资料库以及免费的主商易站等一系列丰富及不断更新的资料，为用户提供在世界各地寻找贸易投资伙伴的机会。

资讯中心

资讯中心也是我们对外提供信息咨询服务的重要窗口之一。公众可以阅读、直接向服务人员或通过电脑查寻资料，并可借阅一些特定刊物。

资讯中心主要有以下的参考资料：

外国及本澳经贸方面的基本情况

本澳经贸政策与规例

本澳及海内外统计数据

本澳及海内外厂商名录

申请居留

在本澳作出有利于澳门特别行政区的重大投资计划或重大投资的权利人、或获本地雇主聘用的、其所具备的学历、专业资格及经验被视为特别有利于本澳的管理人员或具备特别资格的技术人员，均可透过本局的投资居留暨法律处申请本澳的临时居留许可。

地址：澳门友谊大马路918号世界贸易中心一至四楼

电话：853-28 710300

传真：853-28 590309, 710304

电邮：ipim@ipim.gov.mo

网址：www.ipim.gov.mo

24小时电话查询热线 853-28 881212

香港贸易发展局

香港贸易发展局(香港贸发局)成立于1966年，是专责推广香港对外贸易的法定机构，服务对象包括以香港为基地的贸易商、制造商及服务业者。我们在世界各地设有40多个办事处，其中11个在中国内地，为有意开拓海外和内地市场的港商提供服务，同时致力推广香港作为全球企业与中国内地及亚洲经商的平台。

香港贸发局通过不同的服务，包括：贸易展览会、网上的贸易平台及产品杂志，把全世界数以百万计的买家及供货商联系起来。

香港贸发局每年在香港举办超过30个国际贸易展览会，其中10个是亚洲同类型展览中规模最大的，当中3个更是全球之冠。

香港贸发局的网站www.hktdc.com，广受全球商家欢迎，载有来自香港、中国内地及海外近100万名注册买家及12万名供货商的数据。用户可于网站搜寻超过8,000个产品类别，寻找所需的产品或服务，简单快捷。

香港贸发局出版的15本产品杂志及行业专刊，读者超过500万，遍及全球。我们每年又出版150份贸易研究报告、针对个别行业的快讯及商业通讯，提供有关香港、中国内地及海外市场的最新情报。

同时，香港贸发局为中小企业提供商贸配对服务，能为企业物色理想的合作伙伴。

香港贸发局每年举办超过160项研讨会、大型会议、工作坊及论坛，协助港商拓展新市场。此外，我们每年在世界各地举办约600项贸易推广活动，把香港的产品、服务及讯息传达给约10万名来自主要市场的商家，并在香港接待约600个访港贸易代表团。

香港贸发局先后与欧盟、法国、日本、韩国、英国和美国成立双边贸易委员会，以加强香港与这六个国家及地区的经贸联系。同时，香港贸发局亦担任「环球香港商业协会联盟」秘书处，通过遍及全球的香港商业协会，与世界各地建立连系。

有关香港贸发局的最新信息，请浏览：www.hktdc.com

上海里扬展览服务有限公司

2002年1月成立的里扬集团，下属公司分别有：（上海里扬展览服务有限公司、里扬展览（香港）有限公司、上海尼奥建筑装潢有限公司、韩国成都设计（株）。我们紧紧把握时代脉搏，凭借对现代展览、展示形式和内涵的深刻理解，逐渐发展成为具实力和影响力的综合型专业展览公司，是上海市会展行业协会、北京展览馆协会、上海展览展示工程协会、上海韩国商会的会员单位，同时也是韩国釜山国际展览馆上海办事处。公司的主要业务包括：主办、承办、合作举办大型国际展览会；组织出国展览；策划大型商务活动；展台搭建以及品牌产品专柜设计。

目前，公司每年自主举办“上海国际幼儿教育展”、中韩技术转移暨投资洽谈会、产业机器人高峰论坛，专业代理海外28个知名展览会，涉及的行业有建材、电子、教育、食品、IT、化妆品等，并参与400多场展会的特装设计和制作，与SAMSUNG、INTEL、MICROSOFT、GOODYEAR、HYUNDAI、HITACHI、SIEMENS、中国电信等众多国际知名企业建立了良好的合作关系，并吸引了一批韩国和中国优秀的展览技术人才。

上海里扬展览服务有限公司

上海市北京翟路1178号鑫达大厦408-419室

电话：021-5216 4991, 5216 4992

传真：021-5218 9400

上海尼奥建筑装潢有限公司

电话：021-5216 4996, 5216 4997

韩国釜山展览馆上海办事处

021-5216 4993, 5216 4994

里扬展览（香港）有限公司

九龙旺角亚皆街113号2607室

电话；852-2384 2778

传真：852-2384 2778

中国对外贸易广州展览总公司

中国对外贸易广州展览总公司（以下简称中贸展）是著名的中国第一展（广交会）、中国第一展馆（广交会展馆）的组织管理者——中国对外贸易中心（集团）的成员企业，下设若干个专业的展览公司，在展览的各个产业领域全面推进发展。中贸展是目前国内最具实力和影响力的国有展览公司之一。

中贸展以专业诚信、以人为本、追求卓越、专注展览、服务全球为核心理念，赢得了业内的好评。中贸展主要业务包括：主办、承办、合作举办各类大型国际博览会；组织出国展览；策划组织大型商业活动。总公司每年自办、合办、承办各类大型国际专业商贸博览会 20 多个，展览题材涉及家居、家纺、办公、木工、户外、建材、地材、卫陶、汽车、印刷、包装、标签、环保、水处理、自动化、玻璃、自行车等多个方面。在过去的十年里，总公司展览业务不断扩展，国内办展和出国参展面积年均增长率分别为 27.3% 和 15.3%， 2010年总展览面积超过1,220,000平方米。同时，总公司每年组团参加世界各地 20 多个国家和地区的知名展会，展览题材涉及消费品、礼品、玩具、动漫、美容用品、办公用品文具、电子、家电、摄影、广告、印刷、包装、食品、能源、鞋、家纺及服装、安保、家具配件、园林、五金、卫浴建材、灯饰等多个类别，出展面积在全国同行业中名列前茅。

中贸展拥有一支专业办展队伍，重视人才建设，建立起一个系统的围绕展览为核心的专业展览服务团队，包括：展览销售队伍、招商推广队伍、展览服务队伍等，建立了一套规范完整的办展信息化系统（包括自助服务、数据库管理）和办公自动化系统，大大提升了服务的效率。

地址：广州市海珠区新港东路980号广交会展馆C区16号馆A层
邮编：510335
电话：020-8912 8342
传真：020-89128082转803
北京办事处 电话：010-6559 9082
上海办事处 电话：021-6360 5188
邮箱：weijunvikin@163.com
网址：www.fairwindow.com

法国爱博西雅展览（北京）有限公司

爱博集团（EXPOSIUM）是世界最著名的展览公司之一，具有五十年主办展会的经验和专长，得到国际展览界的公认。

爱博集团目前举办115个展览会，其中11个展览会在法国以外的国家举办。爱博集团办展的领域包括：农牧业、工业设备、建筑、印刷、电子、电信、信息、信息技术、食品、食品加工、包装、销售、城市规划与生活环境、旅游等。

爱博集团积极推行国际发展战略，以自己的强势市场为依托，围绕农业，食品工业，公共工程以及物流运输等行业开发市场，并以有潜力的亚洲和拉美地区的新兴国家作为开拓重点。

2004年，爱博集团在北京建立了自己的展览公司（北京爱博西雅展览有限公司），在上海设有代表处。其任务是为在法国举办的展会组织各种宣传促进活动，同时和中国的行业机构或展览公司发展合作关系，积极在华开拓新的展览会业务。

SIAL法国国际食品和饮料展览会创建于1964年，每两年一届，迄今已有40多年的历史，现已成为世界第一品牌的食品专业展会。自2000年SIAL展移植中国以来，SIAL CHINA 中国国际食品和饮料展览会已成功举办了七届。SIAL CHINA展会秉承其母展-SIAL巴黎国际食品展国际性、专业性、贸易性的特点，以客户服务作为展会组织工作的中心，规模不断扩大，现已发展成为中国国际食品第一大展，是国内外食品厂商开拓中国大陆市场、亚洲市场和海外市场的不二选择，是您不容错过的贸易和合作交流平台。

法国爱博西雅展览（北京）有限公司
北京市朝外大街22号泛利大厦1605室
邮编：100020
电话：010-6588 6235, 8879
传真：010-6588 6233
电邮：info@sialchina.cn
网址：www.sialchina.cn

上海国际展览公司

上海市国际展览有限公司成立于1984年是全国首家国营企业专业从事国际来展的展览公司，现由上海世博（集团）有限公司与上海市国际贸易促进委员会共同投资；公司成立以来，已成功举办各类展览会近500个，展览面积近500万平方米；公司现为国际博览联盟（UFI）正式会员，举办的“中国国际模具技术和设备展览会”、“上海国际汽车工业展览会”和“中国国际染料工业暨有机颜料、纺织化学品展会”是国际博览联盟认证的展览会；在2005年会展行业协会首次试评的上海首批8个优质展览会中，本公司举办的5个展览会榜上有名；公司下属的一些投资和合资公司，提供从展览运输、展馆管理、展览搭建、广告业务、展品留购和会议会务等全方位的会展服务产业链。

地址：上海市延安中路841号东方海外大厦8楼
邮编：200040
电话：021-6279 2828
传真：021-6545 5124
网址：www.siec-ccpit.com
电邮：info@siec-ccpit.com

义乌中国小商品城展览有限公司

义乌中国小商品城展览有限公司创办于1998年，注册资金800万元，拥有60多人年轻化、高学历的专业团队，专门从事国内外展览组织业务，是历届中国义乌国际小商品博览会的唯一展务执行机构，也是UFI、IAEE的会员企业。

公司成立多年以来，先后承办过浙江旅交会、浙江农博会、全国百货会、全国化洗会、中国会展财富论坛等国家级、省级会展项目，并自主培育及合作开发了多个品牌展览项目，包括中国义乌文化产品交易博览会、中国国际五金电器博览会、义乌消费品出口交易会、中国国际旅游商品博览会、义乌国际针织及服装机械展、中国水晶及玻璃制品博览会、中国义乌国际森林产品博览会。其中，公司承办的义博会已跻身为广交会、华交会之后的中国第三大出口商品展，成为唯一经国务院批准的日用消费品类国际大型展会。同时，公司还积极走出去，拓展境外展会义乌，组织展商参加法兰克福、拉斯维加斯、伯明翰、马契夫、迪拜等境外知名展会，并取得部分境外知名展览会的出国组展权。

在中国经济新一轮发展的重要时期，我们将继续以“搭建会展平台，促进贸易机会”为宗旨，努力做好工业经济和商业经济的产业纽带。我们愿意在各界朋友的大力支持下，密切同行合作，提升企业服务，打造精英团队，逐步向国际一流的现代展览服务企业迈进。

地址：浙江省义乌市宾王路301号梅湖会展中心三楼
电话：0579-8541 5888
传真：0579-8541 5777
网址：www.yiwufairs.com

宁波雅卓展览服务有限公司
地址：宁波百丈东路650号贵都商务楼7楼
邮编：315040
电话：0574-2771 6625
传真：0574-8784 9306
电邮：younage@younage
网址 ;www.chinamaching.cn

晋江市展务有限公司
地址：福建省晋江市青阳外经贸大厦3楼
邮编：362200
电话：0595-8560 0609, 8530 3030
传真：0595-8567 4572
电邮：jif@cn-jif.com
网址：www.cn-jif.com

中国演艺设备技术协会
地址：北京市东城区安定门东大街28号雍和大厦东楼C座10层
邮编：100007
电话：010-8402 9994,6403 3098转ext201/203
传真：010-8401 0152
电邮：chen@palmexpo.com
网址：www.palmexpo.com

中国哈尔滨国际经济贸易洽谈会
地址：哈尔滨市南岗区美顺街35号
邮编：150090
电话：0451-8234 0100
传真：0451-8234 0226
电邮：chn@ichtf.com
网址：www.ichtf.com

广东玩具文化经济发展研究会
地址：广州市淘金北路正平南街1号2楼
邮编：510095
电话：020-8358 7012, 8358 7037
传真：020-8358 7016
电邮：expo@ctoy.cn
网址：www.chinatoyfair.com

中国贸促会轻工行业分会
地址：北京阜外大街乙22号
邮编：100833
电话：010-6839 6330
传真：010-6839 6422
电邮：ccpitsli@public3.bta.net.cn
网址：www.fi-c.com

中国食品添加剂和配料协会
地址：北京朝外大街甲6号万通中心3座1402
邮编：100020
电话：010-5979 5833
传真：010-5907 1335
电邮：cfaa1990@yahoo.com.cn
网址：www.fi-c.com

中国铸造协会
地址：北京市海淀区紫竹院路甲32号
邮编：100048
电话：010-8851 4541
传真：010-8851 4541
电邮：wangkunyi@foundry.com.cn
网址：www.foundry.com.cn

中国昆明进出口商品交易会办公室
地址：云南省昆明市北京路175号
邮编：650011
电话：0871-316 4305
传真：0871-316 4304
电邮：kmfair@kmfair.org
网址：www.kmsacc.com

大韩贸易投资振兴公社
地址：上海市兴义路8万都中心3110室
邮编：200336
电话：021-5108 8771转ext126
传真：021-6219 6015, 6236 8211
电邮：kotra_exhibition@163.com, kathleen.mxl@hotmail.com
网址：www.entechkorea.net

中国化学与物理电源行业协会
地址：天津市南开区凌庄子道18号
邮编：300381
电话：022-2395 9049, 2395 9268
传真：022-2338 0938
电邮：CIAPS@public.tpt.tj.cn
网址：www.cibf.org.cn

中国机床总公司/北京国机展览中心
地址：北京市朝阳区新源南路1-3号平安国际金融中心A座15层01-03,05
电话：010-5933 9075, 5933 9078
传真：010-5933 9099
电邮：Jenny.chen@reedces.com.cn
网址：www.cimes.net.cn

中国机械工程学会及其焊接分会
地址：北京市海淀区莲花小区2-5-1607
邮编：100036
电话：010-6397 2404, 6398 2928
传真：010-6398 0554
电邮：Whj@cmes.org
网址：essen.cmes.org

行业先锋
展览设计与施工搭建

奥克坦姆集团大中华区
-奥克坦姆系统科技（苏州）有限公司

OCTANORM Vertriebs GmbH在中国投资成立了奥克坦姆系统科技（苏州）有限公司。德国产品素以其出色的品质、信誉和技术水准闻名于世。作为亚洲地区唯一一家工厂，奥克坦姆系统科技（苏州）有限公司秉承OCTANORM全球质量标准和享誉世界的德国技术以及服务理念，所有产品都依照最严格的德 国标准设计生产，以满足在全球化浪潮中日益增长的中国市场需要。

随着中国会展经济的不断高速发展，奥克坦姆在华业务日益扩大，为了进一步发挥奥克坦姆的全方位优势，将展览展示系统行业最优越的技术尽快地转化为中国用户有价值的解决方案，帮助用户更有成效地开展业务，增强竞争优势，降低交易成本，奥克坦姆先后在北京、上海等地设立了分公司及办事处。

奥克坦姆以先进的理念创造出美观环保的铝制系统产品。这些新颖的产品除了可以应用于展览行业外，在室内设计，展示，洁净室等方面也可以广泛使用。并且具有安装快捷、容易拆除，可以重复使用等显著优点，同时也非常方便运输和储存，并提供完善的技术咨询和服务。

奥克坦姆为您化繁为简，以系统实现美。

江苏省苏州工业园区星龙街428号苏春工业坊3A
电话：0512-6283 3338
电话：0512-6283 3332
传真：0512-6283 3330
邮箱：info@octanorm.cn
网址：www.octanorm.cn

上海里扬展览服务有限公司

2002年1月成立的里扬集团，下属公司分别有：（上海里扬展览服务有限公司、里扬展览（香港）有限公司、上海尼奥建筑装潢有限公司、韩国成都设计（株））。我们紧紧把握时代脉搏，凭借对现代展览、展示形式和内涵的深刻理解，逐渐发展成为具实力和影响力的综合型专业展览公司，是上海市会展行业协会、北京展览馆协会、上海展览展示工程协会、上海韩国商会的会员单位，同时也是韩国釜山国际展览馆上海办事处。公司的主要业务包括：主办、承办、合作举办大型国际展览会；组织出国展览；策划大型商务活动；展台搭建以及品牌产品专柜设计。

目前，公司每年自主举办“上海国际幼儿教育展”、中韩技术转移暨投资洽谈会、产业机器人高峰论坛，专业代理海外28个知名展览会，涉及的行业有建材、电子、教育、食品、IT、化妆品等，并参与400多场展会的特装设计和制作，与SAMSUNG、INTEL、MICROSOFT、GOODYEAR、HYUNDAI、HITACHI、SIEMENS、中国电信等众多国际知名企业建立了良好的合作关系，并吸引了一批韩国和中国优秀的展览技术人才。

上海里扬展览服务有限公司
上海市北京翟路1178号鑫达大厦408-419室
电话：021-5216 4991，5216 4992
传真：021-5218 9400

上海尼奥建筑装潢有限公司
电话：021-5216 4996，5216 4997

韩国釜山展览馆上海办事处
021-5216 4993，5216 4994

里扬展览（香港）有限公司
九龙旺角亚皆街113号2607室
电话：852-2384 2778
传真：852-2384 2778

上海新思维传播策划有限公司

上海新思维传播策划有限公司是一家从事与展会相关的综合性展览服务公司：其业务范围包括：展览展示设计制作、商业空间设计制作、会议活动策划布置、室内设计与活动硬件设施的提供；公司业务还包括：企业形象策划、创意与制作、户外媒体发布、电视广告、拍摄、期刊采编，提供影视策划与营销以及商业公关服务等等。

我司在上海浦东新区拥有面积近10000平方米的制作工厂，一支近200人的具有多年展览经验、技艺精湛的制作队伍；公司吸收及培养了一批经验丰富，具有专业素质、实战经验的专业人才；公司也有完善的硬件设施如1000多套用于标准展位的铝合金展架、烤漆房、多台意大利进口三维雕刻机、高精度写真机等。

我司成立于1995年，是上海最早从事展览行业的公司之一。在展览会上成功地完成了意大利馆、韩国馆、新加坡馆、非洲馆等国家馆的展台设计与制作；历年来我们都为全国电子展、玩具展、服装纺织展等知名展览会的主场搭建商，并获得客户的肯定和好评；特殊展台方面，我们已与众多的知名公司成功合作过，如日本马自达、通用、吉利、绿地、农工商、招商地产，顾家工艺、卡森、中国移动等等。

目前我司荣幸的被指定为2010年上海世博会的指定供应商之一，我们将以专业、完善的服务为目标，永远站在高质量不断创新的前列！

地址：上海浦东合庆镇龙江路180号
电话：021-6891 1200
传真：021-6891 1211
电邮：xiaozi1980@126.com

行业先锋
展览会议中心

中国国际展览中心集团公司

中国国际展览中心集团公司（简称“中展集团”）是中国国际贸易促进委员会直属企业，中国展览馆协会理事长单位、国际展览业协会（UFI）成员和国际展览与项目协会（IAEE）成员。中展集团的业务范围涵盖场馆经营管理、国内外组展以及各种展览配套服务。

中国国际展览中心位于北京市朝阳区北三环东路6号，占地面积13.6万平方米，室内展馆面积6万多平方米。每年举办各类展会100多个，展出面积超过100万平方米。

2008年初开业运营的中国国际展览中心（新馆）位于北京顺义天竺空港城商务区，紧邻首都国际机场，第一期工程建筑面积24万平方米、室内展馆面积10万平方米。中国国际展览中心（新馆）是目前北京市规模最大、设施先进、功能完备的展览场馆。

电话：010-8460 0000
网址：www.ciec-expo.com

中国国际贸易中心

中国国际贸易中心展览大厅是中国最大的中外合资商务服务企业——中国国际贸易中心股份有限公司的一个组成部分，于1989年建成并开始投入使用，截止2001年底的十二年间，已经累计举办了各类展览会460多个，成为目前北京知名度最高、展项密度最大、国际展览最多的展览设施之一。

展览大厅地处国贸中心东翼，位于北京最繁华的高级商务区中心地带，内与国贸的商务、办公、会议、饭店、公寓、购物、娱乐等设施连为一体，构成了总面积近50万平方米、服务设施齐全完备的城中这城；总面积达10,000平方米的国贸中心展览大厅由三个展厅及序厅组成，即一号馆（2,000平方米），二号馆（3,500平方米），三号馆（2,100平方米）和可兼作布置并举行展览会开幕式的序厅（2,400平方米）。展览大厅内还设有贵宾室、会议室、咖啡厅等辅助设施，满足接待贵宾、举办专题讲座、召开新闻发布会、展团临时办公、对外联络以及展商、观众休息餐饮等多方面的需要。

展览大厅功能齐全，拥有国内展览场馆中技术最先进的设施，展览现场设立海关办事机构，以协助办理展览物资的报关手续。

地址：北京建国门外大街一号中国国际贸易中心展览部
邮编：100004
电话：010-6505 2288转80448
传真：010-6505 3260
电邮：cwtced@public3.bta.net.cn
网址：www.ecwtc.com

沈阳国际展览中心

沈阳国际展览中心（以下简称：中心）坐落于苏家屯区会展路9号，距市区12公里，距桃仙国际机场13公里。
项目总用地面积95.96万平方米，计划分两期建设。其中一期工程总建筑面积16.6万平方米，室内展览面积10.52万平方米，室外展览面积5万平方米，行政服务区面积2.2万平方米。展馆按照国际专业化水准进行设计和建设。每个展厅既可独立办展，又能通过内部连廊彼此连通，使展区浑然一体。

中心主体结构由8个单层、无柱、大跨度独立展厅组成，每厅面积1.32万平方米，可设625个国际标准展位。室内展馆由东西两侧各4个展厅组成，中间由双层连廊衔接，总体可容纳5000个国际标准展位，东、南、西、北面均设有观众登录厅，可举行各类礼仪活动。中心北广场可举行开幕式、庆典及大型公益活动。

中心设有1间1000人会议厅（内部可灵活分割），1间600人新闻发布厅，5间200人会议厅，6间50人会议室，3间贵宾会议室，4间洽谈室，可承接各种会议、会见、签约等活动，可为国内外客商和旅游人员提供住宿和餐饮服务。

辽宁省沈阳市苏家屯区会展路9号
电话：024-8956 6755
传真：024-8956 6778
邮箱：marketing@shenyang-expo.com
网址：www.shenyang-expo.com

广东现代国际展览中心

广东现代国际展览中心GDE，位于广东省东莞市厚街镇-著名的加工制造产业基地。室内展览面积为10 万平方米，室外广场面积为11万平方米；

引入ISO9000质量管理认证休系；一站式A+服务；
2003,2004年;分别获“会展综合服务最佳场馆、中国会展业最佳场馆”称号；

先后成为香港展览厅会议业协会海外成员、中国展览馆协会会员、2004年加人全球展览业协会(UFI)；

2010年会展信息：
广东（厚街）茶业博览会
第二十三届国际名家具（东莞）展览会
第十一届中国（东莞）国际纺织制衣工业技术展览会
第十一届中国（东莞）国际鞋机鞋材工业技术展览会
励华国际瓦楞展2010中国展/2010励华国际彩盒展
2010中国东莞国际鞋类、皮革制品、配件与生产技术展览会
第十九届华南(东莞)国际电子制造采购博览会
第十届东莞国际印刷造纸胶粘带及广告展览会
广东外商投资企业产品（内销）博览会
第二十四届国际名家具（东莞）展览会
第十五届国际集成电路研讨会暨展览会
2010中国东莞国际鞋类、皮革制品、配件与生产技术展览会
第十二届东莞国际模具展及金属加工展
第十二届东莞国际橡塑胶、包装、压铸和铸造展
2010第十届东莞嘉年华时尚生活用品购物节

地址：广东省东莞市厚街镇家具大道广东现代国际展览中心
邮编：523952
电话：0769-8598 1885
传真：0769-8590 9318
邮箱：Dickson@deexpo.com
网址：www.gdeexpo.com

澳门威尼斯人®酒店-会展中心

澳门威尼斯人®度假村-酒店-会展中心，拥有先进设施，占地100,000平方米之大型会议展览场地，适合举行商务聚会或国际会议。这里，拥有3000间豪华套房、逾300家国际名店、35家寰宇食府，照顾您各式所需。更提供各式精采表演及体育盛事等，都能令您的各项计划，轻松落实。

澳门威尼斯人®-度假村-酒店-会展中心，时刻以商务旅客为本，所有套房均配备传真机、打印机、复印机、安全高速上网系统，及足可容纳手提电脑之保险箱。还有，澳门地理位置优越，是亚洲交通枢纽，邻近各大城市人口更高达世界总人口的一半，提供前所未有的商业契机。

齐备设施于一身：

100,000平方米会议展览场地

3,000间至少70平方米豪华套房，配备传真机、打印机、复印机及专用数据线

6,500平方米无柱宴会厅、108间会议室

35家寰宇食府，1,000雅座之美食坊

逾300家国际品牌名店

15,000座位之威尼斯人综合馆、1,800座位之威尼斯人剧院

拓展无限商机，请即登入 www.venetianmacao.com

电话：853-2882 8800

上海新国际博览中心

上海新国际博览中心(SNIEC)由上海陆家嘴(集团)有限公司、德国汉诺威展览公司、德国杜塞尔多夫展览公司、德国慕尼黑展览有限公司联合投资建造。

自2001年11月2日正式开业以来，上海新国际博览中心(SNIEC)已取得了快速的增长，每年举办约60余场知名展览会，并正吸引着越来越多的展会在此举行。位于上海浦东中国的商业中心，SNIEC凭借其方便的交通地理位置、单层无柱式为特点的展馆设施以及多种多样的现场服务，已博得世界的广泛关注。作为一个多功能的场馆，SNIEC也是举办各种社会、公司活动的理想场地。

目前，SNIEC拥有9个无柱展厅，面积达103,500平方米，室外展览面积100,000平方米。

SNIEC的全面扩建将于2010年完成，届时室内面积将达到200,000平方米，室外面积130,000平方米。SNIEC的扩建将进一步巩固其在中国市场的领导地位，并确保上海作为东亚地区会展中心的领导地位。

地址：上海市浦东新区龙阳路2345号

邮编：201204

电话：021-3876 0488

传真：021-6856 6089

网址：www.sniec.ne

郑州国际会展中心

郑州国际会展中心由郑州市人民政府投资建造，集会议、展览、商务、餐饮、娱乐演出和旅游观光为一体，功能齐备、设施一流的会展场馆，是郑州市的地标性建筑之一。

郑州国际会展中心由国际著名建筑设计大师黑川纪章规划设计，主体建筑由会议中心和展览中心两部分组成。2003年元月20日开工建设，2005年10月21日投入试运营。于2006年6月1日引入国际化管理，由中外合资的专业场地管理公司 — 郑州香港会展管理有限公司专责管理。

郑州国际会展中心占地面积68．6万平方米，建筑面积达22．68万平方米，其设施包括会议中心、展览中心、3．8万平方米的室外展场及4．5万平方米的室外停车场。

会议中心主体建筑共六层，建筑面积6．08万平方米。其中轩辕堂剧院式会议可容纳5000人，课桌式会议可容纳3，160人，10人台圆桌宴会可容纳1，660人；剧院式九鼎厅可容纳1，090人、大河厅、太室厅分别可容纳400人。另外，还有17个大中小型会议室、贵宾接待室和中餐厅、西餐厅、咖啡厅。轩辕堂、九鼎厅拥有8+1路同声传译系统，大河厅、太室厅拥有4+1路同声传译系统。

展览中心主体建筑两层，辅楼六层，建筑面积16．68万平方米。由两个展馆、68个会议室、餐饮间、洽谈间办公室及各类服务商店等组成。室内展览面积6．5万平方米，可设3，394个国际标准展位。一号展馆和二号展馆内均有推拉式活动隔断，可将每个展馆分隔成4个6，000平方米和2个4，500平方米的独立展厅。一号展馆层高14米，地面承重5吨/平方米；二号展馆层高17．6米，地面承重1．5吨/平方米。

地址：郑州市郑东新区商务内环路中央公园1号

网址：www.zzicec.com

亚洲国际博览馆

亚洲国际博览馆位处香港国际机场旁，坐拥完善的海陆空运输网络，交通四通八达，是香港首屈一指的展览及活动场馆，提供超过70，000平方米的可租用面积。

博览馆10个展览馆均采用单层地面无柱式的灵活设计，备有新世代的资讯及通讯科技服务，可独立或打通连接使用，切合不同类型展览活动的需要。自2005年年底开幕以来，已举行众多不同主题的大型国际展览及活动，当中包括：香港有史以来最大型的国际商贸展览暨会议—“国际电信联盟2006世界电信展”、2007年9月更首次举行由新加坡移师至香港的全球最大型民用航天及航空业务及产品展览会暨论增—“亚洲国际航空展览会暨论坛”及每年4月及10月的“环球资源系列采购交易会”，均吸引大量海内外买家及参展商参与，足证博览馆提供一个有效的商贸平台促进中外贸易交流，让内地企业毋须远涉重洋便能有效地开拓全球市场，同时亦是外商进入中国市场的门槛，发挥双向跳板的作用。

除此之外，博览馆拥有香港规模最大的室内多用途场馆，可容纳多达 13，500 位观众，至今已举行了几十个国际级大型演唱会及会议。

地址：香港大屿山香港国际机场

电话：852-3606 8888

传真：852-3606 8889

电邮：info@asiaworld-expo.com

网址：www.asiaworld-expo.com

香港会议展览中心

香港会议展览中心座落于香港金融商业区中心，19年来，一直是无数顶尖国际商贸展会及大型会议的首选场地，先后成功举办多项国际盛事，包括全球和亚洲至具规模的展会、1997香港回归庆典、1997年世界银行/国际货币基金组织理事会年会、世界贸易组织“第六次部长级会议”。

香港会议展览中心总面积达222,000平方米，其中70,000平方米可供租用，备有6个展览厅、2个宽敞雄伟的会议厅、2 个环境高雅的前厅、2个国际级演讲厅、52间可容纳28 至640人不等的会议室及餐厅，提供一系列先进且高质素的技术支持设施及专业服务，适合举办各类型展会、国际会议、商务及文娱活动。自1988年开幕至今，共举行了超过34,000项活动。

香港会议展览中心屡获殊荣，其专业服务水平，蜚声国际，赢尽全球组展商的信心，自然成为举办展览会不作他想的选择。

香港会议展览中心扩建展览厅1、2、3的工程已于2006年7月动工，预算需2009年完成。扩建工程将会为香港会议展览中心增加20,000平方米的实用面积，配合积极现代化及设施提升和翻新工程，继续为用家提供信心的保证。

地址：中国香港湾仔博览道一号
电话：852-2582 8888
传真：852-2802 7384
电邮：info@hkcec.com
网址：www.hkcec.com

行业先锋

酒店

上海新苑宾馆

上海新苑宾馆是锦江集团下属的一家庭院式酒店。座落于外籍人士集聚的古北新区，毗邻世贸商城和国际展览中心。中环和延安路高架近在咫尺，交通便捷。宾馆拥有设施完备的各式客房310间套和1020人大小不等的会议室多个。

步入竹海映衬中的新苑，宛如走进了江南庭院。迟尺之间，移步换景，组合建筑错落有致，假山回廊迂回曲折。推开窗户，没有车水马龙的闹市喧嚣，有的是翠竹幽幽、小桥流水，令人充分领悟到“人与自然的和谐”。

新苑餐饮与其园林景观一样独特，崇尚最好的并非最贵的，将自然、绿色、养生作为菜肴之根本，将中国文化融入其中。以“药膳”闻名的餐饮，带给您的不仅仅是色、香、味的感官体验，更让您感受到触及心灵的愉悦。

地址：中国上海虹桥路1900号
邮编：200336
电话：021-6242 6688
传真：021-6242 3256

行业先锋

展览运输

全球国际货运有限公司

全球国际货运有限公司在全世界约有1500个办事处，55,000名员工。作为世界领先的综合物流服务供应商之一，全球货运能为您提供一系列物流和运输服务，包括：海运，空运和陆运，展览物品运输，移民搬迁运输，特殊项目运输以及为全球体育赛事提供物流服务。全球货运于1979年开始进军中国大陆，目前已在全中国拥有33家办事处和物流中心，4,300多名员工，可为您提供全方位的卓越的物流解决方案。

全球货运有限公司是德国铁路股份公司下属运输和物流子公司。SCHENKER中国被指定为2008年奥运会货运代理和清关服务供应商，并成功地为此世界体育盛事服务。

对于展览会相关的需求，Schenker公司专业的展览队伍会提供给您最适合的私人专属服务。凭借特别的物流平台，专业的解决方案，高等的运作效率，平等的服务态度，我们保证您可以在第一时间以自己的语言得到所需的服务，确保问题永远可以从您的利益角度进行协商解决，协助您在世界各地的展会上马到成功。

我们的优势：

•环球网络：1500个办事处，全球海陆空无缝服务
•现场服务：世界各大主要展览中心驻馆办公，德国15个展会城市均有驻馆
•自有资源：仓库，专业机械设备及特殊工具
•从业人员：经验丰富，高效，专业，灵活，多种语言服务

我们的服务：

•物流方案：私人专属，量身定做，按需出发
•呈送方式：海运，空运，陆运，火车运输，快件服务及海空联运
•货品承揽：展台材料，展览品，展会宣传材料，专业艺术品
•展品清关：与海关及商检部门无间隙沟通，保证展品在正确的时间出现在正确的位置
•展会现场：专业有素的现场督导，展前展中展后全程空箱存储相关服务，包装箱处理
•撤展相关：展览会闭幕后安排货物和设备退返原地，或续往下一个展览地点
•其他服务：展览品运输保险，展会期间安排座谈、会议及舞台所需之设备和物料

华南区－全球国际货运有限公司
香港湾仔港湾道26号华润大厦38楼
电话：852-2585 9688
传真：852-2824 0328
电邮：fairs.hk@schenker.com

华中区－全球国际货运代理（中国）有限公司
上海西藏中路268号来福士广场3802-3806室
邮编：200001
电话：021-6122 5888,2890 6226
传真：021-5292 5194,2890 6223
电邮：fairs.sha@schenker.com

华北区－全球国际货运代理（中国）有限公司北京分公司
北京顺义区天竺空港工业区天纬四街5号
邮编：101312
电话：010-8048 0099
传真：010-8048 0077
电邮：fairs.bjs@schenker.com

泛联展览物流香港有限公司

Agility Fairs & Events(泛联展览物流香港有限公司) 是业内公认的领先企业，可为客户在全球的交易会，博览会和贸易展会运输提供端到端的全方位管理服务。我们敬业的专业人员遍布亚太、中东、欧洲、非洲和美洲等地区各重要展会地点的办事处。我们是一间每年营业收入达60亿美元的上市公司，是业内公认的领先国际性企业，在全球100多个国家和地区内设有超过550家办事处，员工总数超过32,000人。

我们向展览会及项目组织者、推广者和参展商提供一站式的物流解决方案，确保所有展示用品及时、完好地抵达现场。我们的服务包括：

- 展品清关
- 为特殊展品获得政府许可/临时性进口
- 海运/空运/陆运服务
- 仓储和派送
- 展馆物流管理
- 现场派送及开箱
- 展品就位及拼装
- 包装、空箱存储及回运

泛联展览物流香港有限公司
香港湾仔洛克到33号中央广场福利商业中心29楼
电话：852-2866 2505
传真：852-2866 2421
电邮：fairs-china@agilitylogistics.com
网址：www.agilitylogistics.com

泛联展览物流香港有限公司
香港湾仔骆克道33号中央广场福利商业中心29楼
电话：852-2594 9233
联络人：曾浩婷小姐

泛联国际货运代理(上海)有限公司
上海市延安西路2299号上海世贸商城1606室
邮编：200336
电话：13911992219 / 021-6236 6060
联络人：张维聪先生

泛联国际货运代理(上海)有限公司 北京分公司
北京市朝阳区朝外大街22号泛利大厦 1211室
邮编 100020
电话：13911992219 / 010-6588 1961/1962/1963/1964
联络人：张维聪先生

泛联国际货运代理(上海)有限公司 广州分公司
中国广州市东风东路726号704/706室
邮编：510080
电话：020-37655886
联络人：叶岭阳先生

The Industry Leaders

Exhibition Management and Conference Planners

Koelnmesse GmbH

Koelnmessn GmbH was found in 1922. More than 60 international trade fairs and over 2,000 conferences make us the largest organizer of trade fairs on our own exhibition grounds. And Koelnmesse is also the Number 1 trade-fair location for more than 25 economic sectors. For these sectors, Koelnmesse organizes the leading global trade fairs, which present around 90 percent of the export goods produced throughout the world.

Our trade fairs and other events provide crucial momentum in the following sectors:Food/ House, Garden and Leisure/ Health, Lifestyle and Facilities/ Communications, New Media and Fashion/ Furniture,Interior Design and Textiles/ Technology and Enviroment/ Art and Culture/ IT and Digital Entertainment.

Koelnmesse Co Ltd China
Add: Unit 1018 Landmark Tower II, No. 8 Dongsanhuan N.Road, Beijing 100004, PR China
Tel: 010-6590 7766
Fax: 010-6590 6139
E-mail: info@koelnmesse.cn
Web: www.Koelnmesse.cn

Koelnmesse Shanghai Branch
Add: Unit 1202 (South) No283 Huahai (M) Rd.
Shanghai 200021
PR China
Tel: 021-6390 6161
Fax: 021-6390 6858
E-mail: info2@koelnmesse.cn

Koelnmesse Guangzhou Branch
Add: Room3311 Metro Plaza, 183 Tianhe Road (North), Tianhe District, Guangzhou 510620, PR China
Tel: 020-8755 2467
Fax: 020-8755 2970
E-mail: info3@koelnmesse.cn

China World Trade Center Co Ltd

CWTC Exhibition Division under China World Trade Center Co., Ltd. is specially engaged in exhibition organization, who put under several subordinated departments, namely the Marketing Development Management Department. A full range of exhibition services are provided, including planning an exhibition, gaining approvals from governmental authorities concerned, inviting exhibitors and promoting campaign, stand-fitting, on-site management, hall maintenance, and leasing facilities etc. The Exhibition D1ivision has successfully involved itself in hosting, organizing, and co organizing a large number of significant exhibitions, and won favora blecomments from all its counterparts and exhibitors home and abroad, with its experiences, language capabilities, well-established management system, widespread contacts inside and outside the country and also the support from the Ministry of Foreign Trade and Economic Cooperation and other state departments and administrations.

Add: Exhibition Division, China World Trade Center Co Ltd,
1 Jian Guo Men Wai Avenue, Beijing 100004, China
Tel: 010-6505 2288ext 80448
Fax: 010-6505 3260
E-mail: cwtced@public3.bta.net.cn
Web: www.ecwtc.com

UBM Asia Limited

Owned by UBM listed on the London Stock Exchange, UBM Asia operates in 16 market sectors with headquarters in Hong Kong and subsidiary companies across Asia, including UBM China in Shanghai, Hangzhou, Guangzhou and Beijing. We have over 200 products including trade fairs, conferences, trade publications, B2B/B2C portals and virtual event services. As Asia's leading exhibition organiser and the biggest commercial organiser in the two fastest growing markets in Asia: China and India, we stage the leading events of their kind across Asia. Our 150 events, 34 publications and 12 vertical portals serve 1,000,000 plus quality exhibitors, visitors, conference delegates, advertisers and subscribers from all over the world with high value face-to-face business-matching events, quality and instant news on market and industry trends and round-the-clock online trading networks and sourcing platforms. We have over 800 staff in 17 major cities across Asia, stretching from Japan to Turkey. Our leading events in China include:

- September Hong Kong Jewellery & Gem Fair (Hong Kong) – World's largest jewellery fair and the largest ever fair in Hong Kong
- Furniture China (Shanghai) – the largest international furniture exhibition in Asia
- Marintec China (Shanghai) – the largest international maritime event in Asia and the world's second most important maritime event
- Shanghai International Children-Baby-Maternity Products Expo (Shanghai) – the largest children, baby and maternity products fair in Asia
- Sign/LED China (Guangzhou) – China's definitive sign event and the world's largest LED event

Regional Head Office:
17/F China Resources Building
26 Harbour Road, Wanchai, Hong Kong
Tel: +852 2827 6211
Fax: +852 3749 7310
Email: info-hk@ubm.com
Website: www.ubmasia.com

UBM China (Guangzhou) Co Ltd
Room 1159 – 1164, China Hotel Office Tower, Liu Hua Lu
Guangzhou, 510015, P.R. China
Tel: + 86 20 8666 0158
Fax: + 86 20 8667 7120
Email: info-china@ubm.com
Website: www.ubmchina.com

UBM China (Shanghai)
Room 1103, Yundu Tower, No. 930 West Zhongshan Road, Shanghai, 200051 China
Tel: + 86 21 6278 7488
Fax: + 86 21 6219 2209
Email: marketing-ubmtech@ubm.com

UBM China (Hangzhou)
2-11F South West Business Center, No 69 Wenzhou Road, Gong Shu District, Hangzhou 310015, China
Tel: +86 571 8839 5884
Fax: +86 571 8838 8829

Shanghai UBM Sinoexpo International Exhibition Co Ltd
7&8/F, Xian Dai Mansion, 218 Xiang Yang Road (S)
Shanghai 200031, P.R. China
Tel: + 86 21 6437 1178
Fax: + 86 21 6437 0982
Email: info@ubmsinoexpo.com
Website: www.ubmsinoexpo.com

UBM Trust Co Ltd
Room 1306, Fu Li Tian He Business Mansion
No. 4, Hua Ting Road, Lin He Dong Road
Guangzhou 510610, China
Tel: + 86 20 3810 6261
Fax: + 86 20 3810 6200
Email: info-trust@ubm.com
Website: www.ubmtrust.com

Hong Kong Trade Development Council

Established in 1966, the Hong Kong Trade Development Council (HKTDC) is a statutory organisation with a mission to create business opportunities for Hong Kong companies. We are the international marketing arm for Hong Kong-based traders, manufacturers and service providers. With more than 40 global offices, including 11 on the Chinese mainland, the HKTDC promotes Hong Kong as a platform for doing business with China and throughout Asia.

The HKTDC connects millions of international buyers and sellers through a variety of integrated services, namely its trade fairs, online marketplace and product magazines.

One of the world's major trade fair organisers, the HKTDC holds more than 30 international trade fairs annually in Hong Kong. Ten of these are the biggest of their kind in Asia, and three are the largest in the world.

The HKTDC website, www.hktdc.com, features nearly one million registered buyers and 120,000 suppliers from Hong Kong, the Chinese mainland and beyond. Users can browse through nearly 8,000 clearly defined product categories to find products and services quickly and efficiently.

With 15 product magazines and industry supplements and more than five million readers around the world, the HKTDC is a major publisher. The HKTDC also produces about 150 trade reports, sector-specific updates and business newsletters a year, providing timely market intelligence on Hong Kong, the Chinese mainland and international markets.

Supporting these services is HKTDC Business Matching, which helps companies find the right partners.

The HKTDC also produces more than 160 seminars, conferences, workshops and forums a year to help Hong Kong companies develop new markets for their products and services. As well, it organises about 600 Hong Kong promotional events around the world, reaching nearly 100,000 business people in key markets each year, and receives about 600 international business missions a year.

The HKTDC's international reach is reflected in the six bilateral committees it serves. These high-level business forums promote economic ties between Hong Kong and the European Union, France, Japan, Korea, the United Kingdom and the United States. The HKTDC also serves as Secretariat for the Federation of Hong Kong Business Associations Worldwide.

For more information about the HKTDC, visit www.hktdc.com.

Tel: 852-1830 668
Fax: 852-2824 0249
E-mail: hktdc@tdc.org.hk
www.hktdc.com

Top Repute Company Limited

Top Repute Company Limited, established in 1989, is a rapid growing professional exhibition and conference organizer based in Hong Kong. We expertise in organizing international exhibitions, conferences and events in Mainland China and South East Asia.

Our business scope covers Mainland China and South East Asia markets. Every year, we organize numerous of large-scale international exhibitions in Shanghai, Guangzhou, Vietnam and Cambodia such as: "Shoes & Leather", "Medical Equipment & Technology", "Metalworking & Industrial Machinery", "Rubber & Plastics", "Print & Pack","Food Packaging Machinery & Technology", "Construction, Building Industry & Materials", "Refrigeration, Air-conditioning, Heating & Ventilation System", and "International Trade Fair" etc.

With over 20 years of experience and expertise in the exhibition industry, we have maintained good contacts and have a wide consultancy network with the related industry. We have organised numerous leading events each year, such as the largest and most reputable fairs in China, "Shoes & Leather - Guangzhou" and "Medical - Shanghai" as well as the "International Industrial Machinery Exhibition (IIME)" in Vietnam. All our exhibitions have already gained international reputations in their respective fields of industry.

Whether you plan to tap into new markets, expand existing markets, or enhance your corporate communication, Top Repute Company Limited is always your reliable working partner. We and our well-trained energetic staff will, at all times, assure the best services to our worldwide clients.

Add: Room 2403, Fu Fai Commercial Centre, 27 Hillier Street, Sheung Wan, Hong Kong
Tel: 852-2851 8603
Fax: 852-2851 8637
E-mail: topreput@top-repute.com
Web: www.toprepute.com.hk

Shanghai Neon Exhibition Ltd

Neon Group was established in January, 2001, and it has subsidiaries: Shanghai Neon Exhibition Ltd, Neon Exhibition (Hong Kong) Ltd, Shanghai Neon Construction & Decorate Ltd, Korea Chengdu Design Ltd. With our understanding of trends in the industry and modern exhibition forms, we are growing to be a comprehensive and professional exhibition enterprise. We are a member of Shanghai Convention & Exhibition Industries Association,Beijing Exhibition Center. Meanwhile, we are the Shanghai office of Busan Exhibition and Convention Center. Our services include: organizing, undertaking and co-organizing large scale international exhibitions; organizing exhibitors and visitors to participate overseas exhibitions; planning business activities; booth construction and showcase design. At present, we are the organizer of Kids Education Expo Shanghai, the overseas agent of 28 well-known exhibitions, and we take part in the design and construction of special stands for about 400 exhibitions.We establish cooperating relations with many famous international enterprises, such as SAMSUNG, INTEL, MICROSOFT, GOODYEAR, Hyundai Motor, HITACHI, SIEMENS, China Telecommunication and so on. As a result, Neon appeal to many talents from China and Korea.

Tel: 021-5216 4991, 5216 4992
Fax: 021-5218 9400

Reed Exhibitions Greater China

Reed Exhibitions, the world's leading events organiser, first began operating in China in the early 1980s and has since grown into one of the most dynamic events organisers in China. To date, Reed Exhibitions Greater China boasts 5 member companies, namely Reed Exhibitions China, Reed Sinopharm Exhibitions Co Ltd, Reed Huabo Exhibitions (Shenzhen) Co Ltd, Reed Huaqun Exhibitions Co Ltd and Reed Huayin (Shanghai) International Exhibitions Co Ltd. In total, these companies employ 450 staff and have offices in Beijing, Shanghai, Shenzhen and Hong Kong. Reed Exhibitions seeks to attain sustainable development in China through organic growth, new show launches and forging strategic partnerships of joint ventures. By doing so, it aims to deliver even more premium quality events in China.

Reed Exhibitions Greater China serves an array of China's fast growing specialized sectors including Aerospace and aviation, Electronics manufacturing & assembly, Machine Tools, metalworking and industrial Materials, Converting, Pharmaceutical, medical and health care, Gifts and houseware, and Lifestyle, travel, gaming and property via more than 40 market-leading events per year.

In 2009, the Reed Exhibitions Greater China organised over 40 events, bringing together over 20,000 suppliers and about 700,000 visitors for face to face business meetings, exchanges and negotiations.

Apart from continuously expanding its business in China and contributing to the prosperity of related industries and areas, Reed Exhibitions is also committed to its other industrial and social responsibilities in China. It has been promoting the sustainable development of the Chinese conference and exhibition industry and giving back to local community through the following initiatives:

Endorsing and effecting IPR protection at its events;

Advocating exhibition statistics auditing, transparency and verifiable reporting of statistics;

Creating green exhibitions by raising the environmental awareness of the participants and partners and taking green initiatives;

Training its local employees through the Reed Exhibitions China University;

Implementing the scholarship program to promote exhibition education and talent development;

Making donation to those in need of help;

Organising the annual Reed Exhibitions China Summit and joining hands with leading exhibition organizers in China to promote the development of the industry.

For more information on Reed Exhibitions' business in Greater China, please visit www.reedexpo.com.cn

Macao Trade and Investment Promotion Institute

Always at Your Service

As the trade and investment promotion institute in Macau, IPIM's mission is to promote Macau's externaltrade and attract investment, to develop and strengthen economic and trade relationship between Macao and other parts of the world.

One-Stop Service

IPIM provides a personal service "One-Stop Service" for investors, including information enquiries, project assessment, company registration assistance by our notary, guidance on administrative application procedures for licenses, looking for partnership, project follow-up, and assistance in the implementation project. In order to facilitate this service, an independent notary and an investment committee, compose of senior officials from nine different government departments have been established.

Offshore Services

IPIM is responsible for the issuing of licenses, technical assistance and supervision for nonfinancial offshore institutions, and to promote offshore development through various activities. A lot of incentives are offered to offshore businesses, while there is only a set-up fee, and an operating fee every six months.

Economic and Trade Promotional Activities

IPIM annually organized or co-organzized and participated different kinds of local and international trade exhibition and investment cooperation promotional activities, namely: Macao Trade and Investment Fair (MIF), China and Portuguese Speaking Countries Economic Forum and Business Environment Presentation of different parts of the world. Moreover, we organize annually various finding tour for local entrepreneurs and welcome overseas delegation, thus creating a co-operation exchange between Maao and Overseas enterprises.

Besides, for international trade and investment fairs, we actively give subsidies for local enterprises: participation and the printing of promotional materials, to provide international information on Exhibition and Convention Industry.

Macao Business Support Centre

The Centre serves to reduce the initial setup costs for foreign investors, enabling the enterprisesto be familiar with Macao's business environment and the relevant administrative procedures in a relatively short time and to facilitate the implementation of their investment projects, as well as providing a service platform for cooperation exchange between local and overseas enterprises and business association. The center offers the following:Facilities/equipments --- inclue modern offices, meeting rooms, Display Gallery, computers and broad-band Internet services. Apart, there are chargeable fees on multi-functional conference rooms, printing and facsimile services among others business facilities.

Business Service - include "Consultation Service Counter", "Mainland China Business Advisory Service", Secretarial Service and provide administrative procedures and statistical information of local enterprises, business associations stationed in the Centre and Government Services. Moreover, is frequently the organization of Trade and Economic Presentation and Exchange Activities in co-operation with Business Association.

Platform of mutual co-operation between Enterprises and stationed repseresentative offices - several local and overseas business associations/ organizations/ institutions/ representative offices, such as Chongqing-Macao Economic Promotion Association-Macao Office, World Federation of Chinese Entrepreneurs Organization, Portuguese - Chinese Chamber of Commerce and Industry, International Lusophone Markets Business Association, China Council for the Promotion of International Trade Hong Kong and Macau Representative Office, German Macau Business Association, Australian Trade Commission- Austrade, Euro-Info Centre, Macau, Macao-Portuguese Businesse Center, Macau British Business Association and Japan Business Service Centre are stationed at MBSC. Enterprises can either contact these offices directly or through the assistances of MBSC to arrange for various business exchanges or cooperations.

Small and Medium Enterprises Service Centre (SMEC)

In order to enhance the comprehensive competitiveness of local Small and Medium Enterprises (SMEs) and assist them to grasp the opportunities brought about by Macao's economic development and in accordance withto Macao government policies to support SMEs, the Macao Trade and Investment Promotion Institute (IPIM) will launch a series of services to assist local SMEs, which includes the setting-up of the Small and Medium Enterprises Service Centre (SMEC) in the

Macao Business Support Centre (MBSC). SMEC will help local SMEs to develop overseas and local markets and provide exchanges between enterprises and cooperation in accordance with overseas and local market's demands. Thus, it will give Macao's SMEs guidance to grasp the business opportunities brought about by the service, conventions and exhibition industries.

Information Services and Information Centre

In order to promote Macau's business environment and to furnish the business community with the most up-to-date information, we publish "Newsletter", "Macao Image","Investor's Guide"and related promotional CD-Roms or printing materials.The website is our chief means to deliver quality information service. All our major publications have now an on-line version.Not only general information about Macao and our Institute can be found in the site, a business database of all manufacturers and exporterss also open to free access. Moreover, a free "Etrade" service is provided, helping users in their search for suitable trade or investment partners around the globe.

Information Centre

There is an Information Centre located on the 2nd floor of World Trade Center. The Information Centre is one of the means by which we provide information enquiry services. The public can read, search for information by computer or by direct enquiry and borrow some of the materials. Reference materials available at the Information Centre include:

General information on local and worldwide economic and trade situation

Local economic and trade policies and regulations

Local and overseas statistical data, updated information on imports and exports

Local and overseas trade directories

Application for the Right of Residence

Those who have submitted investment projects or made a significant investment; or managerial staff and specialist technicians hired by local employers, who due to their qualifications or professional experience, are considered beneficial to Macao may apply to our Residence Application and Legal Affairs Division for a temporary residency in Macao.

Add: Av. Amizade no 918, Edif. World Trade Centre,
1-4 andares, Macau
Tel: 853-2871 0300
Fax: 853-2859 0309, 2871 0304
E-mail: ipim@ipim.gov.mo
Web: www.ipim.gov.mo
24-hour enquiry hotline 853-28 881212

China Commodities City Exhibition Co Ltd

Yiwu China Commodities City Exhibition Co Ltd (hereinafter referred as "CCC Exhibition" below) is a holding company of Zhejiang China Commodities City Group Co Ltd with registered capital of 8 million Yuan, professional teams composed of over 60 well-educated young people, specially engaging in dometic and overseas exhibition organizing service, as a member of UFI (The Global Association of the Exhibition Industry) & IAEE (International Association of Exhibitions and Events).

As the first exhibition enterprise in Yiwu district, the company was founded in 1998, and was the only execution agency of the past China Yiwu International Commodities Fairs. Dominantly government-guided but specifically hosted by Yiwu China Commodities City Exhibition Co Ltd China Yiwu International Commodities Fair has become the third biggest export commodities exhibition following Caton Fair and East China Fair, and is the sole large international fair for daily consumer goods approved by State Council.

Since the foundation, the company has hosted many national or provincial large convention & exhibition projects, such as National General Merchandise Conference, National Cosmetics & Lavation Conference, China Convention & Exhibition Fortune Forum, Zhejiang Tourism Trade Fair, and Zhejiang Agriculture Fair, Yiwu Sourcing Fair: Consumer Goods, Yiwu International Knitting & garment Machinery Exhibition, China Crystal & Glass industry Fair, China International Woodon Products Fair, and organized the exhibitors' participation in the overseas well-known exhibitions like Frankfurt, LasVegas, Birmingham, Macef, Dubai, achieving the organizing right of part of the overseas well-known exhibitions.

In the newround important economic development of China, we'll continue to function as the bridge between industrial economy and commercial economy, with the aim of "build exhibition platform, and promote trade opportunities". We would like to tighten the cooperation with the company in the same industry, improve the service quality, and build an elite team, gradually close to the international first-class modem exhibition service company, under the support of friends from all walks of life.

Add: 3/F, China Commodities City Exhibition (Meihu)
Centre, Binwang road 301#, Yiwu, Zhejiang.
Tel: 0579-8541 5888
Fax: 0579-8541 5777
www.yiwufairs.com

Shanghai International Exhibition Co Ltd

Shanghai International Exhibition Co Ltd was found in 1984 as the first state enterprise specialized in international exhibitions, which is now jointly invested by Shanghai World Expo (Group) Co., Ltd and CCPIT Shanghai Sub Council. SIEC has held 500 international exhibitions of various themes in China since its founding. SIEC is a full member of Union des Foires International (UFI). Die & Mould China, Auto Shanghai and China Interdye are the approved events of UFI. The five of its show are among the first eight exhibitions awarded as High Quality Trade Show by the Evaluation Committee of Shanghai Convention & Exhibition Industries. The affiliated organizations of SIEC providing a comprehensive solution on exhibition services including Freight Forwarding, Venue Management, Booth Fitting, Advertisement,Trade Liaison and etc.

Add: 8/F, OOCL Plaza, 841 Yan An Zhong Rord,
Shanghai 200040, China
Tel: 021-6279 2828
Fax: 021-6545 5124
E-mail: info@siec-ccpit.com
Web: www.siec-ccpit.com

China Foreign Trade Guangzhou Exhibition Corporation

China Foreign Trade Guangzhou Exhibition General Corporation (hereinafter referred to as CFTE) is a member enterprise under China Foreign Trade Center (hereinafter referred to as CFTC)----the management body of China's No 1 fair (Canton Fair) and China's No 1 fairground (China Import & Export Fair Complex). CFTE comprises several specialized exhibition companies to boost the development of all industries of the exhibition in an all-round way. CFTE is one of the strongest and most influential state-owned exhibition companies in China today.

Based on the core philosophy of specialization & honesty, people-orientation, pursuit of excellence, dedication to exhibition and serving the world, CFTE is well received by the industry. Its main businesses cover: sponsoring, undertaking and co-sponsoring large expos, organizing Chinese enterprises to participate in famous fairs abroad, planning and organizing commercial functions. CFTE sponsors, co-sponsors and undertakes more than 20 large international specialized trade fairs per year. The exhibition themes cover furniture, home textile, office, woodworking, outdoor, building materials, floor materials, sanitary ware, automobile, printing, packaging, label, environmental protection, water treatment, automation, glass and bicycle. In the past 10 years, the company continues to expand exhibition business, and the exhibition area at home and abroad had an average increase of 27.3% and 15.3% respectively per year. The total exhibition area in 2010 was over 1,220,,000 square meters. CFTE also organizes Chinese enterprises to participate in famous international fairs in over 20 countries and regions. The exhibition themes cover consumer goods, gifts, toys, animation & comics, cosmetic products, office supplies & stationery, electronics, household appliances, photography, advertising, printing, packaging, food, energy, shoes, home textile, garment, security, furniture fittings, garden, hardware, sanitary ware & building materials and lighting. The exhibition area tops the industry in China.

CFTE has a professional team specializing in handling exhibitions. It attaches importance to talents growth and establishes a systematic professional exhibition team, including: exhibition sales team, business promotion team and exhibition service team as well as sets up a set of standard & complete exhibition information system (including self-service, database management) and OA system, greatly enhancing service efficiency.

Younage Exhibition Co Ltd

7/F, No. 650 Baizhang East Road Ningbo, China
Tel: 0574-2771 6625, 2771 6618
Fax: 0574-8784 9306, 2771 6616
E-mail: younage@younage.com
Web: www.meonline.com.cn

Jinjiang Exhibition Affairs Co Ltd, Fujian

3F Foreign Economy & Trade Building Qingyang, Jinjiang, Fujian. 362200 China
Tel: 0595-8566 4572, 8567 1572
Fax: 0595-8567 4572, 8560 0610
E-mail: jif@cn-jif.com
Web: www.cn-jif.com

International China Harbin Fair for Trade and Economic Cooperation

35, Meishun Street, Nangang District, Harbin 150090
Tel: 0451-8234 0100
Fax: 0451-8234 0226
E-mail: zhanlanchu@00615.com.cn
E-mail: qying@00615.com.cn
Web: www.00615.com.cn

Guangdong Research Council of Toy Cultural & Economic Development

2/F, 1 Zhengping Street South, Taojin Road North, Guangzhou 510095, China
Tel: 020-8358 7012, 8358 7037
Fax: 020-8358 7016
E-mail: ex@ctoy.com.cn
Web: www.ctoy.com.cn

China Entertainment Technology Association (Formally China Theatrical Equipment Association)

No.1 Xilou Alley,Yonghegong Str., Beijing 100007, China
Tel: 010-8402 9994, 6403 3098 ext 201/ 203
Fax: 010-8401 0152
E-mail: zhao@calmexpo.com.cn
Web: www.calmexpo.com.cn

CCPIT Sub-council of Light Industry

22B, Fuwai Dajie, Beijing 100833 China
Tel: 010-6839 6330
Fax: 010-6839 6422
E-mail: ccpitsli@public3.bta.net.cn
Web: www.fi-c.com

KOTRA

Room 3110, Maxdo Center, No. 8 Xingyi Road, Shanghai, China
Tel: 021-5108 8771 ext 126
Fax: 021-6219 6015
E-mail: kotra_exhibition@163.com
MSN: kathleen.mxl@hotmail.com
Web: www.entechkorea.net

China Food Additives & Ingredients Association

Rm.1402 Tower C Vantone No. 6A Chaowai St., Beijing 100020 China
Tel: 010-5979 5833
Fax: 010-5907 1335
E-mail: cfaa1990@yahoo.com.cn
Web: www.fi-c.com

China Foundry Association

A32 Zizhuyuan Rd, Beijing, China
Tel: 010-8851 4541
Fax: 010-8851 4541
E-mail: wangkunyi@foundry.com.cn
Web: www.foundry.com.cn

China Industrial Association of Power Sources

No.18, Lingzhuangzi Road, Nankai District, Tianjin 300381, China
Tel: 022-2395 9049, 2395 9268
Fax: 022-2338 0938
E-mail: CIAPS@public.tpt.tj.cn
Web: www.cibf.org.cn

Chinese Mechanical Engineering Scociety

2-5-1607 Lianhuaxiaoqu, Haidian District, Beijing 100036, China
Tel: 010-6397 2404, 6398 2928
Fax: 010-6398 0554
E-mail: Whj@cmes.org/ Fanx@cmes.org
Web: essen.cmes.org

China National Machine Tool Corp Capital Exhibition Services

Unit 01-03,05, 15th Floor, Tower A, Ping An International Finance Center, No.1-3, Xinyuan South Road, Chaoyang District, Beijing 100027, China
Tel: 010-5933 9075, 5933 9078
Fax: 010-5933 9099
E-mail: Jenny.chen@reedces.com.cn
Web: www.cimes.net.cn

Exhibit Designers and Producers

OCTANORM® Group Great China - OCTANORM System Technology (Suzhou) Co Ltd

It was in 1968 that a great idea matured into a concept and the concept was transformed into an ingenious product - the OCTANORM® exhibition system. After 40 years development, OCTANORM® has been recognised as the world leader in the manufacture and distribution of aluminium profiles and systems for the exhibition, retail and display industries. Recommended and appreciated by designers to contractors, our range of products has represented the benchmark of quality.

With the years of experience and hard work, OCTANORM® System Technology (Suzhou) Co Ltd (www.octanorm.cn), subsidiary of OCTANORM®-Vertriebs-GmbH, was funded in SIP China in May 2003. We inherit the global standardization of produce and service from Germany. The need to implement exhibit designs more efficiently, more logically and considerably more professionally fired the imagination that eventually resulted in the world of systems.

Boasting over 2,000 product innovations, OCTANORM® is not only the original exhibition system but is also the world market leader in system construction. From the very start OCTANORM® set about identifying and consistently applying the latest developments in both technology and design. Also, from the outset, OCTANORM® pursued a marketing strategy that was based on a partnership concept.

The secret of our success has always been in our innovative ideas, experienced staff, state-of-the-art production methods and meticulous quality control. With the increasing development of exhibition in China, OCTANORM® has got great progress and we have opened the offices in Beijing and Shanghai. We are always focusing on research and development in order to create the most scientific system solutions. Every year, we bring surprising products to the public. Meanwhile, with the support of accumulated experience from thousands experiments and more than 158 OSPI members all over the world, OCTANORM® is providing the most professional exhibition service everywhere.

Add: 3A, 428 Xinglong Street, Suzhou Industrial Park,
Jiangsu, China
Tel: 0512-6283 3338
Fax: 0512-6283 3330
E-mail: info@octanorm.cn
Web: www.octanorm.cn

Shanghai New Trend Medium Co Ltd

Shanghai New Trend Medium Co Ltd, located at the east of Shanghai, is a professional service company with more than 10-year experience of booth design, international exhibitions, conferences, publicizing activities, indoor decoration, and exclusive store image. We have a workshop of about 10000m^2 and over 150 team workers. Further more, there are excellent designers with the ability of combining 3D art and commerce perfectly. They try the best to make every design a masterpiece by their special creativity. With their sensitivity to the market and the understanding to the clients, they turn the original ideas of clients into great works.With the modern management and operation, international standard service, reasonable price, from the original design to the construction of booths, no doubt that we'll provide you effective and high quality service. Therefore, we win the applause and trust from our clients. Our business covers all over China, and our co-operators expand all over the world. With our staff's effort and our unique advantage, Shanghai New Trend Medium is becoming the leader in Shanghai exhibition and show field. we always devote to the customer needs. We want to be their indispensable partner. We are ambitious to create better works than our customers's expectation. We are committed to providing high quality products and loyal services. we are honored to be one of the appointed booth contractors during the 2010 Shanghai Expo.

Tel: 021-6891 1200
Fax: 021-6891 1211
E-mail: xiaozi1980@126.com

Shanghai Neon Exhibition Ltd

Neon Group was established in January, 2001, and it has subsidiaries: Shanghai Neon Exhibition Ltd, Neon Exhibition(Hong Kong) Ltd, Shanghai Neon Construction & Decorate Ltd, Korea Chengdu Design Ltd. With our understanding of trends in the industry and modern exhibition forms, we are growing to be a comprehensive and professional exhibition enterprise. We are a member of Shanghai Convention & Exhibition Industries Association,Beijing Exhibition Center. Meanwhile, we are the Shanghai office of Busan Exhibition and Convention Center. Our services include: organizing, undertaking and co-organizing large scale international exhibitions; organizing exhibitors and visitors to participate overseas exhibitions; planning business activities; booth construction and showcase design.At present, we are the organizer of Kids Education Expo Shanghai,the overseas agent of 28 well-known exhibitions, and we take part in the design and construction of special stands for about 400 exhibitions.We establish cooperating relations with many famous international enterprises, such as SAMSUNG, INTEL, MICROSOFT, GOODYEAR, Hyundai Motor, HITACHI, SIEMENS, China Telecommunication and so on. As a result, Neon appeal to many talents from China and Korea.

Tel: 021-5216 4991, 5216 4992
Fax: 021-5218 9400

Convention and Exhibition Centers

China International Exhibition Center Group Corporation (CIEC)

China international exhibition center group corporation (CIEC) , subordinate to China council for the promotion of international trade (CCPIT) , chairs the China association of exhibition centers (CAEC) and is a member of the global association of the exhibition industry (UFI) and the international association for exhibitors and events (IAEE). CIEC business scope covers venue operation and management, domestic and overseas show organization and various relevant exhibition services.

China international exhibition center, located at 6 east beisanhuan road, Chaoyang District, Beijing, covers an area of 136,000m^2 with over 60,000 m^2 of indoor exhibiting space. More than 100 shows and exhibitions take place in CIEC venue annually with exhibiting space totaling over 1,000,000 m^2 .

New China international exhibition center (NCIEC) , put into operation in early 2008, is located in Tianzhu Airport industrial Zone, Shunyi District, Beijing, close to Beijing capital international Airport. Being the largest exhibition venue with integrated and modern facilities in Beijing, the first phase of NCIEC covers an area of 240,000 m^2 with 100,000 m^2 of indoor exhibiting space.

Tel: 010-8460 0000
Web: www.ciec-expo.com

China World Trade Center Exhibition Hall

The CWTC Exhibition Hall as part of China World Trade Center-China's biggest Sino-foreign joint venture providing business service was finished and came into operation in 1989. Up to the end of 2001, it had hosted more than 460 exhibitions of various kinds during these 12 years, and become one of the most prestigious and the most frequency used fair grounds with the most international exhibitions.

Situated at the east of China World Trade Center, which is at the center of the most flourishing high-class business area, the Exhibition Hall is on the one hand, in conjunction with the CWTC business, office area, conference rooms, hotels, apartment buildings, shopping and recreational facilities etc. thus forming a 500,000 m^2 well-equipment complex called "A city within a city?"

With a gross area of 10, 000 m^2, the CWTC Exhibition Hall is composed of 3 halls and the lobby, namely Hall One (2,000m^2), Hall Two (3,500m^2), Hall Three (2,100m^2) and the Lobby (2,400m^2) which can be used either for exhibiting or for holding opening ceremony. The Exhibition Hall has auxiliary facilities like VIP rooms, meeting rooms, offices, and coffee shop so as to meet the exhibitors and the visitors needs of receiving distinguished guests,holding seminars and press conference, handing office work, maintaining contact with the outside, as well as lounge, food and beverage services etc. This poly-functional exhibition hall is an equipped with most technologically advanced facilities in China. A Chinese Customs office is established right at the exhibition site to facilities clearance of exhibition materials.

Address: Exhibition Division, China World Trade Center Co Ltd
1 Jian Guo Men Wai Avenue, Beijing 100004, China
Tel: 010-6505 2288 ext 80448
Fax: 010-6505 3260
E-mail: cwtced@public3.bta.net.cn
Web: www.ecwtc.com

Shenyang International Exhibition Center

Shenyang International Exhibition Center (SYIEC) is located in No. 9 Huizhan road, Sujiatun district. It is 12 km away from the urban district and 13 km from Taoxian International Airport.

It overall planning 959,600 square meters and it is implemented in two phases, the first one covers 166,000 square meters, including 105,200 square meters indoor and 50,000 square meters outdoor. The comprehensive executive council area occupies 22,000 square meters. It is designed as international standard. Each hall can be used for holding mini-exhibitions separately and they are also connected by corridors. It is propitious to hold large-scale fairs.

It is made up of 8 separated, single-level, column-free and spacious halls. Each hall occupies 13,200 square meters and it can hold 625 international standard booths. They are connected by corridors with 4 landing halls on east, north, west and south. We can supply 5,000 international standard booths. The north square can hold opening ceremony, celebration and public welfare activities.

One meeting room that can hold 1000 people(it can divided as you need), one conference room can hold 600 people, five meeting rooms can hold 200 people, and six meeting rooms can hold 50 people, three VIP meeting rooms and four negotiation rooms of which have advanced conference facilities and quality services. We can provide the high-quality service for the domestic and international customers.

Tel: 024-8956 6755
Fax: 024-8956 6778
E-mail: marketing@shenyang-expo.com

Shanghai New International Expo Center

Shanghai New International Expo Center (SNIEC) is China's leading expo center, boasting state-of-the-art facilities. Situated in Shanghai's Pudong district, the heart of Chinese business, SNIEC has attracted worldwide attention since its opening in November, 2001. Featuring a prime, easily accessible location, a pillar-free, single story structure and a wide array of expert on-site services, SNIEC has been experiencing rapid growth. It now hosts more than 60 world-class exhibitions each year and this number is set to grow in the future.

Currently, SNIEC has 9 exhibition halls with 103500 square meters of indoor exhibition space and 100000 square meters of outdoor exhibition space.

SNIEC plans to complete of all its facilities and reach full exhibition capacity by 2010. By then, the Center will contain 200,000 square meters of indoor floor area and 130,000 square meters of outdoor area. SNIEC's future expansions will cement its market leadership in China and secure Shanghai's position on the forefront of East Asian exhibition destinations.

SNIEC is a multi-functional venue that also caters to a diverse range of both social and corporate events.

Shanghai New International Expo Centre (SNIEC) opened on November 2, 2001, and is jointly owned by Shanghai Lujiazui Development (Group) Co Ltd, Deutsche Messe AG, Messe Duesseldorf GmbH and Messe Muenchen GmbH.

Tel: 021-3876 0488
Fax: 021-6856 6089
Web: www.sniec.net

Guangdong Modern International Exhibition Center (GDE)

Located at the middle of Canton-Hong Kong Golden corridor -HouJie Dong Guan, the acknowledged base of processing and manufacturing.

100,000 m^2 indoor space, 110,000m^2 outdoor.
ISO900 quality management system
"One-stop " services
The Best Exhibition Venue of year 2003 & 2004 in China.
A member of HKECIA, CAEC, UFI

2010 Exhibition Program:
Guangdong (Houjie) Tea Expo
The 23th International Famous Furniture Fair (Dongguan)
The 11th China (Dongguan) Int'l Textile & Clothing Industry fair
The 11th China (Dongguan) Int'l Footwear Machinery &Material Industry
The 10th Dongguan Shoes/ China Shoetes
The 19th (Dongguan) south China Eletronic Fair
The 10th Dongguan International Printing and Packaging and paper advertising, adhesive tape, protective film exhibition
Guangdong Foreign-invested Enterprises Commodities Fair
The 24th International Famous Furniture Fair (Dongguan)
The 15th International IC-China Conference & Exhibition
The 11th Dongguan Shoes/ China Shoetes
The 12th China Dongguan International Mould and Metalworking Exhibition
12th China Dongguan International Plastics Packing Rubber Diecasting & Foundry Exhibition

Hong Kong Convention and Exhibition Centre

As one of the world's freest economies, Hong Kong is renowned for its favourable business environment. Right at the heart of Hong Kong's vibrant and central business district stands the Hong Kong Convention and Exhibition Centre (HKCEC), with a worldwide reputation for service excellence and stringent international standards in management and technology. The HKCEC is highly functional and versatile. Six large exhibition halls, two convention halls, two large foyers, 52 meeting rooms and other function areas offer a total rentable space of 70,000 square metres including the state-of-the-art conference and seminar facilities. The HKCEC plays the leading role in strengthening Hong Kong's position as the Trade Fair Capital of Asia.

Since its opening in 1988, there are more than 34,000 events hosted in HKCEC. The annual attendance of the HKCEC has now reached over five million including exhibitors and delegates along with top buyers and decision makers from more than 150 countries and regions from around the world.

Totally international in outlook and yet fully in tune with Mainland Chinese needs, the HKCEC hosts a wide ranging fair portfolio. This is headed by Asia's largest and world-leading trade fairs for watches and clocks, toys and games, gifts and housewares, jewellery, fashion, textiles, leather, beauty, lighting goods, travel, optical goods, electronics and more. With the expansion of 20,000 square metre exhibition space now underway, and a policy of continues upgrades and modernisation, this is a reputation that is set to endure.

Add: 1 Expo Drive, Wanchai, Hong Kong, China
Tel: 852-2582 8888
Fax: 852-2802 7284
E-mail: info@hkcec.com
Web: www.hkcec.com

AsiaWorld-Expo

AsiaWorld - Expo is Hong Kong's leading exhibition and events venue offering over 70,000 square metres of rentable space. It is fully integrated with the Hong Kong International Airport and located at the centre of an extensive and efficient air, land and marine transport network.

AsiaWorld-Expo has 10 ground-level, column-free, high specification halls. All of the halls are equipped with advanced ICT services, and can be used either separately or in conjunction with each other to provide one continuous space for events. Since its opening in 2005, AsiaWorld-Expo has already staged a lot of large-scale international events, including "ITU TELECOM WORLD 2006" the largest-ever trade exhibition cum forum in Hong Kong; "Asian Aerospace International Expo and Congress" the world's largest dedicated commercial aviation and aerospace event which has moved to AsiaWorld-Expo since September 2007 after 25 years held in Singapore; "China Sourcing Fairs" in April and October each year, which attracted lots of overseas and local exhibitors and visitors; and also act as an excellent platform for Mainland Chinese enterprises to venture into the global marketplace.

In addition, AsiaWorld-Expo includes the Hong Kong's largest indoor seated venue: AsiaWorld-Arena, which accommodates a maximum capacity of 13,500. The venue has already hosted various world-class concerts and conferences.

Tel: 852-3606 8888
Fax: 852-3606 8889
E-mail: info@asiaworld-expo.com
Web: www.asiaworld-expo.com

The Venetian® Macao - Resort-Hotel

The ultimate convention and exhibition destination awaits.

The Venetian® Macao offers world - class entertainment, high - tech meeting facilities, suite accommodations, exquisite shopping and dining all under one roof. The 100,000 square meter state-of-the-art convention and exhibition center can comfortably accommodate an event on any scale, from intimate corporate meetings to international conventions. As a truly integrated resort, The Venetian Macao boasts 3,000 hotel suites, a massive shopping mall featuring over 300 of the world's most exclusive brands and 35 acclaimed restaurants. Other attractions include gondola rides down 3 beautiful Venetian canals, spa facilities beyond compare, plus top international shows and exhibitions from the stars of music, stage and sport.

The Venetian® Macao is built with the business traveler in mind. Luxury and convenience go hand in hand. Every hotel room is a luxury suite 70 square meters or larger, complete with every facility to conduct business, including fax/ printer/ copier, high speed Internet access and a safe large enough for a laptop. Macao's cultivated road, air and sea transportation network also means The Venetian Macao is easily accessible to much of the region. And with more than half of the world's population living within a five hour flight from the enclave, visiting Macao has never been easier for travelers and business executives.

MICE features at a glance:

Over 100,000 square meters of Convention & Exhibition space

3,000 suites over 70 square meters, with fax/copier/printer and dedicated data lines

6,500 square meters of pillarless ballroom and 108 meeting rooms

Over 35 acclaimed restaurants and 1,000 seat food court

Over 300 specialty stores

15,000 seat The Venetian-Arena and 1,800 seat The Venetian-Theater

For further inquiries or to book your next event today, simply visit www.venetianmacao.com or call +853 2882 8800

Zhengzhou International Convention & Exhibition Center

Zhengzhou International Convention & Exhibition Center (ZZICEC) is a fully integrated convention & exhibition facility. It is invested by Zhengzhou Municipal Government, and it integrates convention rooms, exhibition halls, business centres, restaurants, entertainments and performance and tourism facilities all into one. It is one of the signature buildings in Zhengzhou.

Zhengzhou International Convention & Exhibition Centre (ZZICEC) is designed by an internationally acclaimed architect Kisho Kurokawa. The main body of the building is consisted of convention center and exhibition center. ZZICEC has been built since January 20th,2003 and started its operation in October 21st2005 and is managed by Hong Kong - Shanghai Venue Management (Zhengzhou) Limited since June 1st 2006.

ZZICEC covers an area of 686,000 square meters, with a construction area of 226,800 square meters. It consists of a convention centre, an exhibition centre, an outdoor exhibition area of 38,000 square meters and 45,000 square meters of parking space.

The Convention Centre offers 6 levels of multi-purposed function space, with a total construction area of 60,800 square meters. The Grand Hall is an ideal venue for meetings of theatre type up to 5,000 people, meetings of classroom type up to 3,160 people and seated banquets of up to 1,660 guests, the International Theatre can accommodate 1,090 audiences and two theatres seat 400 audiences each. Also included are 17 meeting rooms of varied sizes, VIP reception rooms, a Chinese restaurant, a western restaurant, and a cafe. Simultaneous interpretation can be provided for up to 8 languages plus 1 within the Grand Hall and International Theatre, while the two theatres can provide 4 languages plus 1 simultaneous interpretation.

The Exhibition Centre offers 2 levels multi-purposed function space of the main body and 6 levels of the secondary body. It was built on a construction area of 166,800 square meters. It consists of two exhibition halls and a variety of auxiliary support facilities, including 68 meeting rooms, food concessions, offices and shops.

The inner exhibition space is 65,000 square meters which could set 3,394 international standard booths. Hall 1 and Hall 2 can be divided into 4 6,000 square meters sections and 2 4,500 square meter sections by floor-to-ceiling operable walls, for independent exhibition use. The ceiling height of Hall 1 is 14 meters and floor loading capacity is 5 tons per square meter. The ceiling height of Hall 2 is 17.6 meters and the floor loading capacity is 1.5 tons per square meter.

Exhibition Transportation

Schenker

With a network of around 55,000 people in about 1,500 offices around the world, DB Schenker is one of the world's leading providers of integrated logistics services, offering air, ocean freight and land concepts as well as logistics services for fairs, relocations, projects and global sports events. DB Schenker first entered Mainland China in 1979 and subsequently expanded its presence to nowadays more than 35 locations throughout China with over 4,300 employees working on advanced logistics solutions from one single source.

DB Schenker is part of DB Logistics, the Transportation and Logistics Division of Deutsche Bahn AG.

For all your Fairs & Exhibitions requirements, DB Schenker's dedicated team of specialists will develop the most efficient and suitable solution.

We offer a full range of exhibition services:

•Worldwide coordination of shipments–multimodal transports by air, sea and land

•Consolidated shipments of stand building materials, exhibits and promotional materials

•Expertise in documentation and customs clearance procedures

•Planning and execution of time-defined transports

•On-site handling by experienced and trained staff

•Professional storage at state-of-the-art facilities and handling of "empties"

•Return shipments of complete equipment to the point of origin or to the next fair site

•Arrangements of seminar and conference materials as well as stage equipment

•Professional transport of art material

In 2008 DB Schenker has been appointed as the Official Freight Forwarding & Customs Clearance Exclusive Supplier of the Beijing Olympic Games.

Our contacts:

South China office-Schenker Intl (H.K.) Ltd.
Add: 38/F, China Resources Building No. 26 Harbour RoadWanchai, Hong Kong
Tel: 852-2585 9688
Fax: 852-2827 5363
E-mail: fairs.hk@schenker.com

Central China office-Schenker China Ltd.
Add: Rm.3802-3806, Raffles City (Office Tower) No.268 Xi Zhang Zhong Road, Shanghai 200001, P.R. China
Tel: 021-6122 5888, 2890 6226
Fax: 021-5292 5194, 2890 6223
E-mail: fairs.sha@schenker.com

North China office-Schenker China Ltd., Beijing Branch
5 Tianwei Sijie
Tianzhu Airport Industrial Area A Beijing 101312, P.R. China
Tel: 010-8048 0099
Fax: 010-8048 0077
E-mail: fairs.bjs@schenker.com

Agility

Agility Fairs & Events is the recognized leader in full-service, end-to-end management of global fairs, expositions and trade-show transportation. Our dedicated professionals are in key exhibition venue offices throughout Asia-Pacific, the Middle East, Europe, Africa and the Americas. A publicly traded company, with over US$6 billion in annual revenue, we are part of one of the largest international logistics and freight management companies in the world, with over 550 offices in 100 countries and 32,000 employees.

We provide a one-stop fairs and events logistics service for trade fair organizers, show promoters and exhibitors ensuring that displays arrive on time and in perfect condition. Our services include:

– Customs clearance
– Obtaining Government permits for special cargoes/temporary import
– Sea/air transportation and transhipment
– Storage and delivery
– Venue on-site logistics
– Site handling and unpacking
– Positioning and rigging of exhibits
– Repacking, storage of empties and re-export handling

AGILITY FAIRS & EVENTS LOGISTICS LIMITED
29/F Fook Lee Comm Centre, Town Place,
33 Lockhart Road, Wanchai, Hong Kong
Tel: 852-2594 9233
Contact: Ms Kenly Tsang

AGILITY FAIRS & EVENTS LOGISTICS (SHANGHAI) CO. LTD
Room 1606, Shanghai Mart, No. 2299, Yan'an Road (West),
Shanghai 200336, P. R. China
Tel: 021-6236 6060, 13911992219
Contact: Mr Mitch Zhang

AGILITY FAIRS & EVENTS LOGISTICS (SHANGHAI) CO. LTD
Beijing Branch
Room 1211 Prime Tower, No.22 Chaowai Street,
Chaoyang District, Beijing 100020, PR China
Tel: 010-6588 1961 / 1962 / 1963 / 1964
Mobile: 13911992219
Contact: Mr Mitch Zhang

AGILITY FAIRS & EVENTS LOGISTICS (SHANGHAI) CO. LTD
Guangzhou Branch
Rm.704/706,7F, No 726 Dong Feng Road East,
Guangzhou 510080 PR China
Tel: 020-3765 5886
Contact: Mr Eric Ye